W9-DAZ-221

C. G. Sedlacek, Ph.D.
10506 Burt Circle
Omaha, NE 68114

8-97

MANAGING ATTENTION AND LEARNING DISORDERS IN LATE ADOLESCENCE AND ADULTHOOD

Contributors

Rob Crawford, M.Ed.
Life Development Institute
Phoenix, Arizona

Michael Goldstein, M.D.
Neurology, Learning and Behavior Center
Salt Lake City, Utah

Barbara D. Ingersoll, Ph.D.
Montgomery Child and Family Health Services
Bethesda, Maryland

Patricia H. Latham, J.D.
National Center for Law and Learning Disabilities
Cabin John, Maryland

Peter S. Latham, J.D.
National Center for Law and Learning Disabilities
Cabin John, Maryland

Mary McDonald Richard
Iowa City, Iowa

MANAGING ATTENTION AND LEARNING DISORDERS IN LATE ADOLESCENCE AND ADULTHOOD

A Guide for Practitioners

Sam Goldstein

Contributions by

Rob Crawford
Michael Goldstein
Patricia H. Latham and Peter S. Latham
Mary McDonald Richard

John Wiley & Sons, Inc.
New York • Chichester • Brisbane • Toronto • Singapore

Library of Congress Cataloging-in-Publication Data

Goldstein, Sam, 1952–
    Managing attention and learning disorders in late adolescence and adulthood : a guide for practitioners / by Sam Goldstein : contributions by Rob Crawford . . . [et al.].
        p.   cm.
    Includes bibliographical references and index.
    ISBN 0-471-07662-7 (cloth : alk. paper)
    1. Attention-deficit disorder in adults.   2. Learning disabilities.   3. Attention-deficit disorder in adolescence.
    I.   Title.
RC394.A85G65   1996
616.85'89—dc20
                                                        96-6743
                                                        CIP

For Janet, Allyson, Ryan, and my mother, Sarah

Where he falls short, 'tis nature's fault alone.
Where he succeeds, the merit's all his own.
Charles Churchill

'Tis a lesson you should heed,
try, try again.
If at first you don't succeed,
try, try again.
William Edward Hickson

My goal as a mother was to raise children
who could find joy at the sight of a dandelion.
Brigitte Reid

Foreword

THE PUBLICATION OF this text marks a watershed in our understanding of the impact of childhood learning, attentional, and behavioral problems on adjustment in the adult years. At last, it would seem that we have come to recognize the truth in Wordsworth's axiom "The child is father to the man." At last, as scientists and clinicians, we have come to see that so many problems experienced by our adult patients are an extension of their childhood difficulties, prolonged and repeated in the adult years.

In the past, behavioral scientists and clinicians who addressed children's learning, attentional, and behavioral problems were separated by a vast chasm from those who studied and treated adults with adjustment problems and psychiatric disorders. It is true that analytically oriented therapists have always explored their patients' childhood experiences. Generally, however, this has been with an eye toward understanding the impact of early traumatic experiences on later development: few clinicians have directly addressed the ways in which patients' learning and attentional problems were major factors in an evolving equation of dysfunction.

It is also true that there have been pioneers such as Lee Robins and Paul Wender who attempted to bridge this chasm and remind us that the traits and characteristics that appear in childhood do not simply vanish in the adult years.* For the most part, however, their efforts went unheeded and had little impact on research or clinical practice.

Thus, many clinicians were caught off guard and unprepared to deal with the increasing numbers of adults who asked to be evaluated for ADHD as a result of the recent barrage of media coverage of adult ADHD. And a barrage it has been! Along with the virtually simultaneous publication of several books addressed to lay audiences as well as professionals, there have been numerous television programs and newspaper articles on the topic of ADHD in adults. While not all of this publicity has been positive in nature—indeed, some critics have charged that ADHD is simply the "latest fad"—it has had the undeniably beneficial effect of height-

---

*L. Robins, 1966, *Deviant Children Grown Up: A Sociological and Psychiatric Study of Sociopathic Personalities,* Baltimore: Williams and Wilkins; P.H. Wender, 1987, *The Hyperactive Child, Adolescent, and Adult,* New York: Oxford University Press.

ening public awareness and making treatment available to many who would otherwise have gone without.

It is unfortunate that no such media blitz has highlighted the plight of learning-disabled adults, although it is clear that they, like individuals with ADHD, do not simply outgrow their problems. In terms of scientific inquiry, too, the field of learning disabilities treatment has lagged behind research in ADHD. It is only now that researchers are entering the field and subjecting various treatment approaches to careful scientific scrutiny.

Happily, these efforts have already begun to bear fruit: we know that programs that improve phonological awareness can be of enormous benefit to young children at risk for learning disabilities. There is reason to believe that such programs, as well as those that teach learning-disabled individuals to use compensatory strategies, can also be of help to adults. Happily, too, a great deal of progress has been made in helping young adults with learning and attentional problems gain entry to, and succeed in, postsecondary educational settings. Finally, progress has also been made in safeguarding the rights of these individuals in the labor force.

At present, however, remedial and compensatory approaches are so costly as to be beyond the reach of all but a small minority of learning-disabled adults. Accommodations are often too little and too late to be of real benefit to many adults with ADHD or learning disabilities. Too many individuals are still consigned to a sort of human ash heap, unable to achieve and contribute at a level commensurate with their true potential.

It is clear, then, that there is much work to be done. Yet how should we proceed? As a scientist-practitioner, I am torn when I contemplate the state of our knowledge about adults with learning and attentional problems. As a scientist, I am uncomfortable with the lack of a solid empirical foundation on which to base our interventions. As a clinician, however, I am keenly aware of the urgent need for action now, even in the absence of a more complete database.

In my own work, I will continue to struggle to integrate the results of scientific inquiry with the demands of practical application. In this struggle, I know that I will turn again and again to this comprehensive volume that Dr. Goldstein and his colleagues have so painstakingly compiled. I believe that other professionals who are similarly committed to helping adults with learning and attentional problems will do the same.

Barbara D. Ingersoll
Montgomery Child and Family Health Services
Bethesda, Maryland

Preface

I N THE 1920s, 20% of parents had completed four years of high school or more, with 60% having completed at least eight years of schooling. By the 1980s, the corresponding numbers were 80% and 100%. The shift from farm to urban work over this period meant that greater educational attainment and vocational skill was necessary in order to survive. A large majority of children, nearly 70%, lived in two-parent, farm families in 1830. By 1930 this group had dwindled to a minority of less than 30%. During the same 100 years, the proportion of children living in nonfarm families with breadwinner fathers and homemaker mothers grew from only 15% to a majority of 55%. The move toward urban work reduced children's potential to contribute to the income of their families. This potential was further constricted by the passage of laws restricting child labor and mandating education. Increased specialization in the workplace necessitated increased education. For this reason, people with specific skill weaknesses, such as those related to learning or attention, found themselves at a disadvantage, and rarely able to obtain special educational assistance.

In her life's work, eminent psychologist Emmy Werner (1994) has observed that even in chaotic and impoverished homes, some children develop healthy, stable personalities, function successfully at school and in the community, and progress to vocational success. Werner and others (Fonagy, Steele, Steele, Higgitt & Target, 1994) have repeatedly shown that the ability to learn normally, pay attention, and demonstrate an even temperament in childhood are all positive, protective factors that increase the resilience of children facing adversity and make their future success more likely. By implication, these factors also serve to protect children raised in nonadverse circumstances. As Werner has noted, when protective factors outweigh stressful life events, successful adaptation is possible. However, when protective factors are absent, even minor life stresses can overwhelm some children.

A long history of citations suggests that eminent and extremely influential members of society may have experienced learning disabilities or other related childhood problems. Albert Einstein, Thomas Edison, Woodrow Wilson, Arthur Conan Doyle, Harvey Cushing, Paul Erlich, and Nobel Prize winner Niels Bohr are mentioned time and time again as examples of people who overcame their childhood disabilities. However, the possibility that they did not actually overcome their disabilities but instead adapted to them and dealt with them on a daily basis was not given serious consideration until recently. Moreover, as Weiss and Hechtman (1993) suggest, there are five other outcome possibilities besides growing out of the problem, some of which are not mutually exclusive:

1. The disorder is still present, but resiliency allows the adult to learn to compensate and he or she has no complaints.

2. The disorder in part remits, but some aspects or symptoms remain and are disabling in adulthood.

3. The full syndrome of behaviors similar to childhood continues to be manifested, but in a somewhat altered form compatible with adult status.

4. The childhood disorder predisposes the adult to one or more mental disorders, increasing the risk of developing these into adulthood.

5. The childhood disorder predisposes the adult to display psychiatric symptoms in general but are not indicative of any specific disorder.

In the study of attention deficit hyperactivity disorder (ADHD) and learning disability (LD), the doors to these options have only very recently been opened. In many ways, the fields of ADHD and LD research are in their infancy. Yet, in a very short time great maturity has been required from the educators, physicians, and mental health professionals working with late adolescents and adults suffering from ADHD and LD. For many adult practitioners the concepts are new and often overwhelming. Even the simple idea that ADHD and LD represent different phenomena, a concept accepted in the childhood literature for a number of years, is still questioned in the adult field. It is for this reason that these two topics are presented jointly in this text.

In many ways, the evolution of the concepts, ideas, and understanding of LD and ADHD in adulthood have developed in parallel though overlapping courses. The field of LD in adulthood has been of at least modest interest to a number of researchers since the early 1970s. It was in the 1980s, however, that it began to receive much greater attention. In 1982 the United Nations proclaimed 1983–1992 the decade of disabled persons and made a commitment to the more than 500 million people in the world estimated to be disabled as the result of mental, physical, or sensory impairment. In October 1987, in response to the United Nations proclamation, the First National Congress for Adults with Special Learning Needs was held. This congress became the foundation on which the National Association for Adults with Special Learning Needs was founded in 1989, following the first annual National Conference on Adults with Special Learning Needs. In addition, the National Association for children with Learning Disabilities rededicated itself and the name of its organization to include adults as well.

Along a parallel course, the concept of attention deficit disorder in adults was originally studied by Paul Wender and his colleagues at the University of Utah, as well as by other researchers (Bellak, 1979). In contrast to the adult LD field, however, the adult ADHD field and the concept of the disorder as one of adulthood have recently been embraced by the public. As Racine and Campbell (1995) have noted, there has been an almost evangelical movement to popularize the idea of adult attention deficit, at times leaving limited room for scientific study or debate. Researchers in both fields are concerned that the singleminded pursuit of an ADHD or LD diagnosis will find only these diagnoses—to the person with a hammer, the whole world is a nail.

This text is intended to provide scientist-practitioners in education, medicine, and mental health with a thorough overview of LD and ADHD and a set of practical guidelines to assist the assessment, diagnosis, consultation, and treatment process for late adolescents and adults struggling with LD and ADHD. In a number of other texts (S. Goldstein, 1995; S. Goldstein & Goldstein, 1990; Ingersoll & Goldstein, 1993), I have, with my colleagues, made a conscientious effort to distinguish science from nonscience and to distinguish nonsense from either of these. Well-controlled research, though difficult, is necessary if practitioners are to make diagnostic decisions and offer treatment ethically. Such research, however, especially in the fields of adult ADHD and LD, will require a long and arduous effort. In the meantime, clinicians must be able to distinguish nonsense from nonscience. They must be capable of making diagnostic decisions and offering practical though untested suggestions without unethically recommending nonsense under the rubric "If it can't hurt let's try it." As Jacobson, Mulick, and Schwartz (1995) urge, scientists, practitioners, and others "have an obligation to balance exploratory use of experimental or unproven but seemingly promising techniques with skilled application of treatment methods that conform to accepted community standards and responsible interpretation of evaluation findings" (p. 762). Practitioners, they continue, "must offer both appropriate treatment and protection from inappropriate care" (p. 762).

With more and more children diagnosed with LD and ADHD making the transition to adulthood, this text will serve as a guidepost for those dedicated to helping these individuals.

S.G.
Neurology, Learning and Behavior Center
Salt Lake City, Utah

Acknowledgments

I THANK MY COLLEAGUES and friends Rob Crawford, Michael Goldstein, Patricia and Peter Latham, and Mary McDonald Richard. Their knowledge has made a significant contribution to this work. I also thank Sarah Cheminant for her management and tracking of my research library and for her thorough indices. Finally, Kathleen Gardner's secretarial, editorial, and organizational skills once again allowed me to focus on writing rather than managing a very large clinical volume.

S.G.

Contents

APPENDICES

PART I

Background

CHAPTER 1

Introduction

A SCANT 15 to 20 years ago, learning disabilities (LD) and attention deficit hyperactivity disorder (ADHD) were defined as problems of childhood. Yet approaches to remediating LD and ADHD based on this traditional assumption have generally met with limited success (S. Goldstein, 1995; Poplin, 1988). Therefore, it is not surprising that these two disorders are now recognized as lifetime phenomena. Indeed, researchers now know that LD and ADHD affect people not only of all ages but of all socioeconomic statuses, ethnicities, and levels of intelligence as well (Biederman, Faraone, et al., 1993; Gerber et al., 1990; Hoffman et al., 1987). M. D. Levine (1989) has referred to the growth in adult LD research as "the early adulthood of a maturing concept" (p. 1). Researchers now ask questions about the impact that LD and ADHD have on adult functioning and outcome. The lifelong nature of LD and ADHD are increasingly well recognized; although learning-disabled and inattentive individuals are no longer in school, life continues to be a struggle in many areas. Nevertheless, the implication of these problems in adulthood is still not well understood. Some researchers suggest that individuals with histories of LD and ADHD have difficulty in adulthood making appropriate choices and decisions, using efficient strategies on a daily basis to track their own performance, transferring learning wealth from one activity to another, breaking tasks into smaller parts, and making good life choices (Hill, 1984).

In addition to examining adult impact, researchers have begun to question the validity of using childhood constructs to diagnose, evaluate, and work with adults suffering from LD and ADHD (Patton & Polloway, 1992). Some of the theories, ideas, beliefs, and strategies used with children are thought to be inappropriate in dealing with adults (Lieberman, 1987). Further, although the literature suggests that some people with histories of learning or attention problems may compensate and succeed in adulthood (P. B. Adelman & Vogel, 1990; Polloway, Schewel, & Patton, 1992; G. Weiss & Hechtman, 1993), it is likely that the majority of such people do not fare as well as the normal population (Gerber et al., 1990; Malcolm, Polatajko, & Simons, 1990; Mannuzza, Gittelman-Klein, Bessler, Malloy, & LaPadula, 1993).

Learning-disabled individuals are not intellectually handicapped. They fall on a normal curve of intelligence but may be weak in one or more specific skills necessary for academic achievement. Given their deficits, however, it is not surprising that a common misperception among the public and to some extent among mental health and educational professionals has been that LD and intellectual handicap are variations of the same phenomenon. They are not. Even more perplexing has been the relationship between LD and ADHD (for a review, see S. Goldstein, 1995). Attentional problems were long considered part and parcel of LD. In fact, some researchers suggested that the majority of children with ADHD experienced LD (Safer & Allen, 1976). It is now known, however, that while the groups of individuals experiencing LD and ADHD respectively may overlap by 20%–30%, the majority of each group does not experience the other problem (Barkley, 1990b). However, common sense does dictate that individuals who are inattentive may not perform well and will thus be labeled "learning disabled," while individuals who are learning disabled and unable to perform may be characterized as inattentive. In this text, LD is considered an input problem; skill weaknesses hinder the individual in acquiring certain basic academic and related abilities. ADHD is considered a performance or output problem; in many cases the individual knows what to do, but his or her impulsive qualities prohibit efficient action.

According to the preponderance of the data, outcomes for young adults with histories of learning or attention problems are not good. This group has been characterized as under- or unemployed, not achieving vocationally at a rate commensurate with others, and not achieving at a rate commensurate with their personal or academic potential (J. O. Smith, 1992). In 1982, for example, it was reported that 36% of all juvenile delinquents, a group made up disproportionately of persons from low-income families, suffered from LD (Dunivant, 1982). The educational, employment, personal, and emotional lives of these people show the irreversible effects of their childhood experiences and struggles.

Although P.L. 94–142 in 1975 did not mention adults with LD and ADHD, the increased attention to the rights and needs of children with impaired ability to read, write, spell, communicate, complete mathematical problems, pay attention, and manage their impulses spurred interest in the impact of these problems in adulthood. It is now well documented that LD and ADHD are not limited by any age boundary (Gerber et al., 1990).

Individuals with LD constitute the largest disability group by far (Interagency Committee on Learning Disabilities, 1987; SRI International, 1990), and it is likely that more than half of disabled individuals experience LD, ADHD, or both of these disorders. The focus in dealing with learning-disabled people has been primarily on *transition*—that is, helping learning-disabled and other developmentally impaired people successfully make the move to adulthood. This has led to the development of support services at two- and four-year colleges, vocational services, job training, and employment programs. There has also been attention to mental health issues. Opinion backed by limited scientific data holds that people with ADHD, and to some extent those with LD, are significantly more vulnerable to emotional problems (Biederman, Faraone, et al., 1993) and addictive disorders (Wilens, Biederman, Spencer, & Frances, 1994). In 1984, the Office of Special Education and Rehabilitation Services began to focus on preparing people with LD and other disabilities for successful transition into adulthood. This paralleled a shift in the community during which support groups for children with disabilities began to broaden their scope and even change their names—for example, the National Association for Children with Learning Disabilities changed its name to the Learning Disabilities Association and sought to represent all ages. The concept of lifelong interventions for people with learning and other disabilities was coming to the forefront (Wiederholt, 1982). At the federal level, however, as late as 1978 the Rehabilitation Services Administration refused to acknowledge LD as a mental or physical disorder that might limit employment eligibility; but this appeared to be the last bastion of discrimination against individuals with developmental impairments. In 1983 the federal government organized a conference of professionals to define the needs of adults with LD. Seven basic issues were discussed (Gerber, 1983; Gerber & Mellard, 1985):

1. Understanding, defining, and identifying adults with LD and related disorders
2. Improving the social skills of this population
3. Understanding the vocational needs of this population
4. Developing a system for education and information exchange among professionals studying and treating adult LD
5. Identifying issues critical to this population's successful adjustment to the community
6. Focusing on family issues
7. Identifying and further investigating programs and their fit with this population at a postsecondary educational level

Thus LD and related disorders were coming to be viewed less as educational issues of childhood than as issues with impact across the life span. In the United States both researchers and clinicians began studying countries such as Denmark, in which adults with LD were reported as experiencing less unemployment and better adjustment compared to those in the United States, and even compared to the Danish national average (Gerber, 1984).

The National Joint Commission on Learning Disabilities (1987), an organization made up of eight professional advocacy groups, issued a paper titled "A Call to Action," in which the following conclusions were drawn and recommendations made:

1. LD is both persistent and pervasive in an individual's life. The manifestation of LD can be expected to change during the life span of the individual.
2. At present there is a paucity of appropriate diagnostic procedures for assessing and determining the status and needs of adults with LD. This situation has resulted in the misuse and misinterpretation of tests that have been designed for and standardized on younger people.
3. Older adolescents and adults with LD frequently are denied access to appropriate academic instruction, prevocational preparation, and career counseling necessary for the development of adult abilities and skills.
4. Few professionals have been prepared adequately to work with adults with LD.
5. Employers frequently do not possess awareness, knowledge, or sensitivity to the needs of adults with LD. In general, corporate as well as public and private agencies have been ignorant of this population and therefore have failed to accept their responsibility to develop and implement programs.
6. Adults with LD may experience personal, social, and emotional difficulties that affect their adaptation to life tasks. These difficulties may be an integral aspect of the LD or may have resulted secondarily from past failures.
7. Advocacy efforts on behalf of adults with LD are currently inadequate.
8. Federal, state, and private funding agencies concerned with LD have not supported program development initiatives for adults (p. 172).

On the work front, the Americans with Disabilities Act of 1990 outlawed discrimination in the workplace against people with any type of disability. The President's Committee for the Employment of People with Disabilities recommended an eight-pronged plan for dealing with transition and employment for adults with histories of learning problems. The plan addressed work preparation, vocational entry, job site accommodations, job advancement, attitudes, policy and legislation, social relations, definition, and diagnosis (Gerber & Brown, 1990).

The need to legislate guidelines and programs in the workplace for individuals with LD becomes obvious when the outcome for this population is reviewed. The National Longitudinal Transition Study (Wagner, 1989) showed that 61% of youth with LD graduate from high school, in comparison to 56% of youth with other disabilities but 75% of the general population. It has been reported that 35% of youth with LD drop out of school with minimal educational training and poor vocational preparation. Authors also suggest that few of these dropouts are aware of the extent to which their disabilities will affect them in adulthood, of the dismal vocational and life future potentially ahead of them, or of their legal rights (Aune, 1991; Gerber & Reiff, 1991). Most dropouts assume that their lives will improve once they leave school.

Unemployment rates for dropouts, whether they have learning disabilities or not, are twice as high as for high school graduates (U.S. Department of Labor, Bureau of Labor Statistics, 1987). Studies of nondisabled high school students have suggested that a surprisingly large number drop out. Valdez, Williamson, and Wagner (1990) reported that, of the total student population, 32% drop out, while Malcolm et al. (1990) reported 56%. Again, the dropout rate for the disabled population appears higher. Zigmond and Thornton (1985) give a dropout rate of 53% for high school students with LD. Wagner (1989) reported that just under 17% of individuals with histories of LD were taking any kind of course work in a postsecondary institution: 9% were at vocational or trade schools, 7% at two-year colleges, and 1% at four-year colleges. These figures must be contrasted with the 56% of the general population that goes on to postsecondary education. Sitlington and Frank (1990) found that few learning-disabled students are employed in areas that use technical or vocational training. Thus, even when they graduate from high school, such youth may be ill prepared for the work they are given. Studies have consistently found that these individuals are employed in entry-level positions (Fourquean, Meisgeier, Swank, & Williams, 1991; Sitlington & Frank, 1990).

The available data also suggest that despite their average intelligence, those with LD may derive little benefit from academic remediation provided in childhood (Frauenheim & Heckerl, 1983). However, remedial education in childhood has been found to improve reading ability directly (Naylor, Felton, & Wood, 1990). Fairweather and Shaver (1991) reported a successful outcome for students with disabilities who participated in postsecondary vocational training. In their review, however, an emphasis on occupational training and links with vocational and high school programs appeared to be the best predictors of a better outcome.

Increasingly, individuals with histories of LD and ADHD are enrolling in college after high school. The Higher Education and Adult Training for People with Handicaps (HEATH) Resource Center of the American Council on Education reported that the proportion of first-time, full-time freshmen with disabilities attending college increased threefold between 1978 and 1985, from 2.6% to 7.4% (Astin, Green, Korn, Schalit, & Berz, 1988). Among the 2.6% in 1978, almost 5% reported having LD, compared with over 14% in 1985.

The U.S. Department of Education National Center for Education Statistics began collecting and analyzing data on handicapped full- and part-time college students in 1986. At that time over 10%, or nearly 1.3 million, of 12.5 million students in postsecondary programs reported having one or more disability. Of that number just over 12% (approximately 160,000) reported having a specific LD, 39% a visual handicap, 20% a hearing disability, and just over 17% an orthopedic handicap; ADHD was not among the handicaps evaluated. The accuracy of these data has been questioned by those who argue that at least in the 1980s the sensory and motorically impaired were more likely to report their disabilities than those with learning or attention problems (U.S. Department of Education, 1987). Nevertheless, the dramatic increase in the number of inquiries about college programs for students with LD suggests that the growth in the number of such students will continue (Bogart, Eidelman, & Kujawa, 1988; R. Hartman, 1991). However, the increase in postsecondary college enrollment for individuals with LD and ADHD must be contrasted with data suggesting that these students have difficulty staying in and completing these programs (Sitlington & Frank, 1990). Whether this reflects lack of fit between the student's capabilities and the program or lack of appropriate support is unknown.

The transition to adulthood appears to contain an interim period when all youth adjust to the increasing demands of maturity (Halpern, 1992). Not surprisingly, the more difficult the childhood and adolescent years, the greater the problems during these interim years. Preparation, however, can greatly ease the difficulties experienced during this period, especially for those who are more vulnerable. Some theorists have hypothesized that this is especially true for those with histories of LD and academic performance problems. It may be that adults with histories of LD and ADHD perceive their world very differently than others, as a result of both impairment and experience. Problems that compromise a child's ability to function effectively in the classroom may also compromise an adult's ability to function effectively in life. Schools were originally designed to prepare individuals to be functioning, productive, and successful members of society (S. Goldstein, 1995). It is therefore not surprising that the daily frustrations and failures some children experience at school carry over into their attitudes, beliefs, and behavior as adults. The combination of their disability and their experience may make them pessimistic about their ability to handle change, leading them to resist any kind of change (Lerner, 1985). It has been suggested that "the residual effects of learning disabilities, from frustration about schooling to a lack of satisfaction in one or a number of areas of adulthood, sometimes reverberate in the emotional sphere. For some adults with learning disabilities, a seeming inability to understand why life continues to be a struggle creates a tragic and self-perpetuating cycle of loneliness and despair" (Reiff & Gerber, 1994, p. 72). Thus, helping learning-disabled and inattentive adolescents recognize, understand, and accept their disabilities as a means of preparing them for the many demands of adulthood has become a mainstay of transition programs (Gerber, Ginsberg, & Reiff, 1992).

Although researchers have hypothesized about the impact of LD in the workplace, the scientific data available is limited. Difficulty with social skills, memory, organization, auditory processing, linguistic skills, attention, and impulsivity are all thought to contribute to poor work performance (Clement-Heist, Siegel, & Gaylord-Ross, 1992; Latham & Latham, 1993; R. M. Matthews, Whang, & Fawcett, 1982). The data generated, however, have led some researchers to report multiple problems for workers with LD (Blalock, 1981; Hoffman et al., 1987) and others to report minimal problems (Felton, 1986; Gerber, 1988). Nonetheless, most researchers have found that people with histories of learning and attention problems hold lower-paying jobs and are not promoted (Gittelman, Mannuzza, Shenker, & Bonagura, 1985; Herzog & Falk, 1991; E. S. Shapiro & Lentz, 1991). However, Hughes and Smith reported in 1990 that not a single scientific study had been published that directly evaluated the efficacy of developmental education programs for college students with LD. Most published articles consisted of program descriptions, opinions, surveys, and commentary (Bursuck, Rose, Cowan, & Yahaya, 1989; Fairweather & Shaver, 1991; Nelson, Dodd, & Smith, 1990). As technology advances, the skills required in the workplace are becoming increasingly complex. Higher and higher levels of educational attainment and intellect are needed to compete successfully for jobs with nondisabled workers (D. Brown, 1984). Thus, in addition to their primary work with learning-disabled people, vocational and transitional programs have tried to change employer attitudes toward hiring workers with LD. Minskoff, Sautter, Hoffman, and Hawks (1987) reported that in a population of 326 surveyed employers, only half would hire an individual with LD for a job they supervised. This report was surprising because the question was phrased in a way that made clear that the individual possessed all of the qualifications for the job. Finally, E. S. Shapiro and Lentz (1991) found that many students with LD do not end up in jobs for which they are trained. The implication the authors drew is that general work skills, rather than a specific job skill, should be emphasized in vocational training programs for those with LD, attention deficit, or other developmental impairments. These authors also reported that employers were more willing to make allowances for disabilities they could see than they were for disabilities that are difficult to understand and quantify, such as LD or attention deficit.

Werner (1994) proposes the concept of "balances" in explaining adult outcome for children. A specific risk factor such as LD does not in and of itself guarantee adverse outcome. A variety of other influences may insulate a learning-disabled child. Further, since LD is a lifetime rather than an acute phenomenon that can be repaired, it is not surprising that even early researchers failed to propose a clear relationship between intervention and positive adult outcome (Rogan & Hartman, 1976, 1990). In fact, reports suggest that people with histories of LD or other developmental impairments who receive minimal support and experience other life traumas are often able to make satisfactory progress into adulthood (Gerber et al., 1992; Gerber & Reiff, 1991). In their exceptionally interesting text *Speaking for Themselves: Ethnographic Interviews with Adults with Learning Disabilities,* Gerber and Reiff (1991) described a discovery that researchers in the field of resilience have demonstrated in other populations: A variety of factors within the individual, in the individual's immediate environment, and in the larger community interact in a complex way to shape the individual's life outcome. In fact, these authors suggest that a certain amount of risk in childhood may stimulate resilience.

The concept of resilience—that is, the effect of factors that increase the likelihood that children facing adversity will grow up to be successful—has grown in importance as clinicians and researchers have come to recognize that specific interventions for specific problems may yield symptom relief but themselves be insufficient to insulate the individual for later success. The longitudinal work of Werner (1989), Werner and Smith (1992), and Fonagy et al. (1994) exemplifies this field of study. Their findings reveal a number of consistent trends: First, the impact of reproductive (birth-related) problems diminished with time. Second, the developmental outcome of almost every biological risk condition depended on family variables—that is, it was less the characteristics of the child (e.g., LD or ADHD) and more the characteristics of the family that determined the fate of each child. This phenomenon was even more evident for children with mild biological risks such as ADHD and LD. Thus, rearing conditions were found to be powerful determinants of the outcome of the children studied. Resilient children have been reported to:

- Come from families of higher socioeconomic class
- Have an easy temperament
- Experience no or few cognitive problems
- Be younger at the time of any serious life trauma
- Not experience separation or loss of a parent

- Have a warm relationship with at least one primary care giver
- Have parents who are available
- Develop a network of social relationships
- Succeed at school
- Learn to cope
- Develop an internal locus of control
- Have a sense of self-worth
- Learn to empathize
- Learn to plan
- Have a sense of humor

Werner and Smith (1992) reported that two out of three vulnerable children (exemplified by those born into poverty experiencing a moderate to severe degree of perinatal stress, living in a family environment troubled by chronic discord, parental alcoholism, or mental illness) who encountered four or more risk factors by age 2, developed serious learning or behavior problems by age 10 and mental health problems, delinquency, or teenage pregnancy by age 18. However, one out of three of these high-risk children developed into a functional young adult. For these children it appeared that their internal locus of control, good temperament, good response to parenting, capacity to succeed at school, and ability to develop a good self-concept best predicted their outcome.

Gerber et al. (1992) suggested that certain factors appear to increase resilient outcomes for adults with histories of LD: stamina and persistence, goodness of fit between the person's abilities and the environment, a pattern of support by family members, the person's ability to take control of his or her own life, and creativity. Exactly how much each of these factors contributes to any individual's outcome is not well understood. It is also important to note that by far the majority of adults with histories of LD continue to have multiple life problems, including a higher than average risk of unemployment (Malcolm et al., 1990). Thus, adults with LD "should not be viewed simply as children with disabilities who have grown up" (Bassett, Polloway, & Patton, 1994). If appropriate vocational and educational programs are not provided to individuals with histories of LD and attention deficit as they leave high school, it is likely that they will struggle vocationally and have even greater adjustment difficulties than when they were younger (Minskoff, Sautter, Sheldon, Steidle, & Baker, 1988). The idea that adults continue to develop through their life span has inspired a number of researchers, including state theorists such as Erikson (1950), theorists focusing on age experience (Baltes, Reese, & Lipsitt, 1980) and theorists studying ego and moral development (Gilligan, 1982).

Understanding the personality traits, both good and bad, that learning-disabled and attention-disordered individuals may develop is valuable but does not directly address the practical issues involved in helping this population successfully make the transition into adulthood. Baltes et al. (1980) proposed what has been called an integrative model of life span and development for adults. At any given moment an individual's thoughts, feelings, and behavior are influenced by normative, age-graded events, such as those related to biological and environmental influences correlated with age (e.g., marriage), history-graded events (e.g., economic depression, political change), and events idiosyncratic to a particular individual but not tied to age or immediate cultural experience (e.g., an accident, religious conversion). This model takes into account the effect of previous life experience on present and future functioning. It is called a "pluralistic" model because it encompasses the many forces that shape the adult outcome of children.

In 1976, Bryan suggested that learning-disabled children are not as popular as other children. Research dealing with peer popularity for learning-disabled and attention-disordered children has repeatedly supported this conclusion (Pelham & Milich, 1984; H. Swanson & Trahan, 1986). Studies suggest that children with LD and ADHD are more likely to be rejected and neglected than their nonimpaired peers (Rosenberg & Gaier, 1977; Schumacher & Hazel, 1984; for a review, see S. Goldstein, 1995). The daily social frustrations that learning-disabled and inattentive children face may make a significant contribution to adult outcomes of poor self-concept and social difficulties. Many adults with histories of LD and ADHD are thought to be bitter about their early lives, schooling, sense of self-worth, and life competence (Gerber et al., 1992; Hallowell & Ratey, 1994).

In addition to experience, impairments caused by the developmental impact of LD also are thought to hinder this population in making a successful transition to adulthood socially, emotionally, and interpersonally (Reiff & Gerber, 1989). Adults with LD and ADHD may have difficulty reading social situations (Gerber, 1978; Pelham & Bender, 1982), resulting in poor judgment, impaired social reasoning, and generally inappropriate social skills (Lerner, 1993). Some studies suggest that people with LD and ADHD are less sensitive to the thoughts and feelings of others (Dickstein & Warren, 1980). They may also have difficulty discerning and understanding humor (Pickering, Pickering, & Buchanan, 1987). Twenty years ago, Wiig and Semel (1976) posited that learning-disabled individuals may have social perception deficits that lead to frustration characterized by emotional problems, hostility, insecurity, and even aggression.

Researchers and clinicians worry that the negative feedback people with LD and ADHD receive about themselves, their competencies, and their future becomes a self-fulfilling prophecy, creating a vicious circle of low self-esteem, lower motivation, and repeated failure (Reiff, 1987). Although the relationship between LD and lifetime psychiatric problems is not well established, data demonstrate that the LD population is evaluated more negatively by peers and is at increased risk for juvenile delinquency, school dropout, and possibly psychiatric hospitalization (Roff, Sells, & Golden, 1972). There is also no doubt that the adult ADHD population is at significantly greater risk for the development of antisocial personality, substance abuse, and possibly depression and anxiety-related problems (for a review, see S. Goldstein, 1995; Chapter 5 of this volume).

Although it is accepted that children with LD and ADHD struggle emotionally, it is not clear how much they struggle nor how well these struggles predict their future difficulties. A vast number of variables interact for any individual. Thus, it would be unfair to state that a child with LD or ADHD is more seriously disturbed than a child without these disorders or that an adult with LD or ADHD will always struggle emotionally and interpersonally. However, it is not surprising that adults with histories of LD and ADHD, like those with other life stressors, report anxiety (C. Johnson, 1981), social problems (Meyers & Messer, 1981), and limited social and family relations (W. J. White, 1985). It is possible that the daily struggles of children with LD and ADHD lead to vulnerability as adults in the same way that the struggles of any child with a medical, developmental, or emotional problem may lead to future problems. Gerber et al. (1992) suggested, on the basis of interviews with successful adults with histories of LD, that even these successful people feel anger about their lifetime of struggle.

As noted before, problems in daily life tend to be different from problems in school. But the skills needed for a successful life, for example, for a successful work life, are strikingly similar to skills needed in school. The demands of the workplace vary far more than those of the school setting; however, a comparison between school and a typical "desk job" finds that both require:

- Staying organized
- Planning
- Attending to repetitive, uninteresting information
- Completing tasks not of own choosing
- Meeting deadlines
- Remaining in a sedentary position or in the same place
- Making good choices
- Working independently
- Keeping track of possessions
- Arriving on time
- Listening to and following directions
- Controlling emotions
- Dealing with frustration

Blalock (1982) suggested that the most common difficulties of adults with LD are related to language-based deficits that impair reading and spelling. Overall, however, learning-disabled adults may experience less difficulty with reading, writing, spelling, and arithmetic than they did as children because the daily demands of their lives do not call for these skills. Rather, they and the ADHD population may struggle with tasks of efficient daily functioning, especially vocational activities, organization, planning, language comprehension, impulse control, and social relations. The major sources of referral for adults with LD are not programs promoting adult literacy or vocational training but rather those focused on rehabilitation. Although a discrepancy model may work well in school to identify children with LD or ADHD, it does not work well in the adult world. For adults, the focus of assessment must be on strengths rather than weaknesses, compensation rather than remediation. Further, as the reader has already surmised, assessment of LD and ADHD in adulthood should take into account a person's entire life rather than concentrating on performance in a single setting. Thus, laboratory-based measures are less important, and measures of daily functional impairment are paramount. This approach is well supported by the research literature, which shows that adults with histories of LD and ADHD may function above or below levels suggested by laboratory testing, with much greater variation than found among children (Naugle & Chelune, 1990).

Vocational rehabilitation services have been available to people with LD and ADHD since 1981. Funding constraints, however, are leading some states to cut back on these services. Data from the Rehabilitation Services Administration indicate that in 1988, 5% of all clients in rehabilitation had histories of LD, compared to only 1.3% in 1983 (Rehabilitation Services Administration, 1990). However, the process of assessment traditionally used to qualify clients and plan treatment is less effective for the LD and ADHD populations than for the general population. Differences have been reported not only in tests and in cutoff scores used to indicate significance but alarmingly in the fact that although almost a third of individuals with histories of LD or ADHD applying for benefits are recommended for assessment, only 6% received a neuropsychological evaluation (Sheldon & Prout, 1991).

Thirty million adult Americans are estimated to be illiterate. C. W. Anderson (1994) distinguishes nine groups that constitute the adult illiterate population: 1. the learning disabled, 2. those with intellectual handicaps, 3. those with limited educational opportunities, 4. dropouts, 5. slow learners, 6. those who "fall through the cracks," 7. those from poor-quality schools, 8.

Table 1.1 Other Factors Associated with Increased Risk for Psychiatric Disorder

Reference	Factor	Risk Increased For
J. Anderson, Williams, McGee, & Silva (age 11) (1989)	Lower cognitive abilities	ADD, multiple
	Lower academic self-esteem	Emotional, ADD, multiple
	Lower general self-esteem	Emotional, ADD, multiple
	Poor health	Any
	Poor peer socialization	Multiple
	Family disadvantage	Emotional, ADD
Bird et al. (ages 4–16) (1988)	Lower academic achievement	Behavioral, depressed
	Poor family functioning	Depressed
	High life stress	Behavioral, depressed
Velez, Johnson, & Cohen (ages 9–19) (1989)	Family problems	Behavioral
	Repeated school grade	Any
	High life stress	Behavioral, overanxious
Costello (ages 7–11) (1989)	Urban (vs. suburban)	Behavioral
	Repeated school grade	Behavioral
	High life stress	Any
	No father in home	Oppositional
Offord, Boyle, & Racine (ages 4–16) (1989)	Family dysfunction	Any
	Repeated school grade	Behavioral
	Parental psychiatric problems	Somatization (boys only)
	Parent arrested	Conduct and oppositional
	Chronic mental illness	Any (4–11 only for hyperactivity)

Note. From "Developments in Child Psychiatric Epidemiology [Special section]," by E. J. Costello, 1989, *Journal of the American Academy of Child and Adolescent Psychiatry, 28,* p. 838. Used with permission.

those for whom English is a second language, and 9. unwed mothers. Some researchers believe that the majority of illiterate adults have histories of LD or ADHD. This has yet to be clearly demonstrated, however. Most public schools in the United States serve between 2%–4% of their population as learning disabled, well below the estimated 10%–20% that likely experience some type of learning or attention problem (Baumgaertel, Wolraich, & Dietrich, 1995; Bird et al., 1988; Nichols & Chen, 1981). Thus, it may be the individuals with undetected LD and ADHD in high school who become functionally illiterate adults. However, it is more likely that the majority of those described as illiterate comprise not only people with a history of LD or ADHD but also people with histories of intellectual handicap, those with limited educational opportunities, slow learners, dropouts, even those for whom English is a second language.

The group with limited educational opportunities is interesting because their struggles may result less from lack of ability than from inadequate opportunity. Dunivant (1982) reports that among incarcerated individuals, the level of reading achievement was approximately three years below the grade at which the prisoner dropped out of school. Hogenson (1974) reported that 60% of juvenile delinquents had histories of reading disability. It has also been demonstrated that a significant minority (20%–40%) of individuals with histories of ADHD are at risk for delinquency. An equal number likely experience learning problems as well (for reviews, see

Barkley, 1990b; Barkley, Anastopoulos, Guevremont, & Fletcher, 1991; S. Goldstein, 1995; S. Goldstein & Goldstein, 1990).

Costello (1989) consistently found that educational risk factors were powerful predictors of psychiatric and adjustment problems. In a number of studies reviewed, academic or cognitive problems at school were associated with the development of emotional and learning disabilities. Table 1.1 summarizes these factors and their general risks.

Thus, the data are clear and illustrate Job's law from the Bible: If you have one problem your resistance is lower and you are more likely to develop a second, third, or fourth problem. There appears to be a large group of adolescents burdened with histories of multiple developmental, behavioral, emotional, and temperamental problems as they begin the transition into adulthood. This text begins by providing background information about the childhood and adolescence of people with histories of ADHD and LD. As child is father to man, an understanding of childhood and adolescent problems is essential to understanding the effects of these problems in adulthood. Many readers who work with the adult population may be surprised at the extensive childhood literature available on LD and ADHD, especially in contrast to the minimal adult literature on these subjects. For example, between 1971 and 1994, nearly 3,000 peer-reviewed studies were published on ADHD. Of these, only 80 dealt with adult issues (Resnick & McEvoy, 1995). For this reason, Chapters 2 and 3 provide an overview of the available literature on the history, presentation, definition, comorbidity, evaluation, and treatment of ADHD and LD in childhood. Chapters 4 and 5 then review current knowledge about adult outcome for individuals with histories of these two problems.

Beginning in Chapter 6, new ground is broken. At this time there is no consensus on the best way to evaluate ADHD, LD, and related problems in adulthood. Chapter 6 draws on the author's experience with the Neurology, Learning and Behavior Center model of adult ADHD and LD assessment. This assessment model is based on a neuropsychological functional framework. Clinicians are guided through a process that focuses on evaluating the client and using the resulting assessment to help the client make important life, vocational, and educational decisions. The chapter closes with five complete assessments that show different ways to summarize and present data.

Chapter 7 offers 24 case studies, ranging from examples of individuals with simple, uncomplicated ADHD or LD to those with complex comorbid problems, including obsessive/compulsive disorder, brain injury, bipolar disorder, and borderline personality.

Chapter 8 begins the treatment section. As reviewed, data are sparse not only on the outcome for adults with histories of LD and ADHD but also on medical and nonmedical treatment for these populations. The literature is at its clearest concerning the potential benefits of medications for adults with ADHD. Chapter 9 gives a nonscientific overview of psychosocial treatments suggested for the daily life and family problems of people with histories of ADHD and LD. The reader will discover that many of these suggestions are similar to those offered for the general population (Covey, 1989). This author has chosen to focus on the cognitive model of psychotherapy because adults with ADHD and LD seem to develop many misconceptions that further trouble their lives.

Mary McDonald Richard at the University of Iowa describes the current state of college services for students with ADHD or LD in Chapter 10. The chapter is intended to provide the clinician with an understanding of available services and with essential information for assessment as well as advocacy.

In Chapter 11, Rob Crawford, director of the Life Development Institute, describes the current state of vocational assessment and presents a comprehensive model of postsecondary educational, vocational, and life training for individuals with histories of LD and ADHD.

In Chapter 12, attorneys Peter and Patricia Latham provide an overview of legal rights, focusing on information essential to the clinician when advocating for the legal rights of those with ADHD and LD.

Finally, in Chapter 13, this author and his colleague Michael Goldstein offer an overview of medications affecting learning, attention, and memory. The bulk of this chapter reviews the available data on the use of medications to treat ADHD in childhood and provides guidelines based on the limited data available for adults. The chapter concludes with a review of what is primarily an experimental literature on researchers' efforts to identify drugs that facilitate learning.

CHAPTER 2

Learning Disabilities in Children

MANY TERMS have been applied to the deficient school achievement of some children, including learning disability, school failure, underachievement, learning difficulty, dyslexia, and specific developmental disorder (Hinshaw, 1992). As the concept of adult LD has become more widely accepted, many of these terms continue to be applied to children grown up. Whatever the label, a significant group of children and adults have a history of school failure. A recent survey reported that 23 million people in the American workforce are unable to read or write well enough to compete successfully in the job market (Healy, 1990).

It is not surprising that struggling developmentally with basic academic achievement or other areas of learning increases the likelihood of emotional or behavioral problems. The prevalence of behavior problems assessed using the Child Behavior Checklist among a population of 500 learning-disabled children with an average age of 10 years was 43% (Achenbach, 1975). This study also showed that single-parent upbringing and lower social class increased the risk that learning-disabled students would experience concomitant behavioral problems. Learning-disabled elementary school students are less accepted and less liked by their peers (for a review, see S. Goldstein, 1995). Through their teenage years, learning-disabled adolescents experience not only more behavioral problems than their unaffected peers but also more difficulty with internalizing disorders such as depression and anxiety (Thompson, Lampron, Johnson, & Eckstein, 1990).

Thirty years ago the majority of children with LD were either segregated from the normal population or considered inferior and placed in educational settings affording them even less support and opportunity than their unaffected peers. These children are now middle-aged adults. It is likely that a significant group of them continue to struggle. Formal education is now perceived as crucial to success. Parents and teachers are less willing to accept arguments that learning-impaired children are lazy or unmotivated and should be excluded from programming. Our ability to identify children with learning problems has also increased, as have services for these children. Over the past 20 years, the number of children identified as learning disabled in the public schools has risen from 1% to 5% of the total population. Funds spent on special educational services for learning-disabled children have increased from 5% of funds distributed by the federal Office of Special Education Programs in 1978 to almost 50% in 1990 (Kavanaugh & Truss, 1988). When it was enacted in 1977, just under 800,000 learning-disabled children were served under P.L. 94–142; in 1987, close to 2 million children were served under this category. Although some researchers have asked whether this increase reflects better identification techniques or confusion about the definition criteria, there is no doubt that the past 20 years have seen significant changes in how educators and health professionals view children who struggle to meet expectations at school (Epps, Ysseldyke, & McCue, 1984). Funding for research on LD has increased dramatically. The National Institute of Child Health and Human Development spent $2.9 million in 1980 on projects relating to reading disorders; by 1990 the amount had more than doubled to $7.7 million. Research centers have been structured and funded with the long-term goals of understanding, evaluating, and educating children *and* adults with LD. Thus, the picture of today's adults with learning problems is unlikely to reflect what the future holds for today's learning-disabled children.

Definition

Confusion about LD stems in part from the way these disabilities are identified. It has been suggested that LD is a definition rather than a diagnosis (McCue, 1994). Within school settings, the term "learning disabled" has traditionally been reserved for children failing to learn despite an apparently normal capacity for learning (Ingersoll & Goldstein, 1993). Therefore, not all children performing poorly in school are learning disabled. Federal guidelines have taken a very product-oriented approach to defining LD. Thus, within the public school setting LD is defined on the basis of inclusionary or exclusionary criteria. Despite valid criticism, a discrepancy model is often used, requiring a specific gap between expected and actual performance (Mather & Healey, 1990). Thus, children with process-related problems such as inattentiveness or memory difficulty may be unable to qualify as learning disabled in the public schools unless they struggle to perform in a basic area of competence, such as oral expression, listening comprehension, written expression, basic reading, reading comprehension, mathematical calculation, or mathematical problem solving. Children who have neuropsychological deficits that affect their daily performance in the classroom, such as speed of information processing, concept formation, or social relations, but who are not necessarily delayed according to standardized achievement tests usually do not qualify for special educational services despite the fact that they are clearly handicapped relative to their nonimpaired peers (S. Goldstein & Goldstein, 1990).

Definitions of LD arose fairly independently in the fields of neurology, psychology, and education (A. A. Silver & Hagin, 1990). The term "word blindness" was first applied in 1877 to individuals with aphasia and the loss of the ability to read (Kussmaul, 1877). In 1896, Morgan described a case of reading difficulty that he referred to as "congenital word blindness." The term "dyslexia" first appeared in a German monograph in 1877 (Critchley, 1964). In 1922, Hohman described a group of children with behavioral problems, hyperactivity, and learning difficulty resulting from encephalitis. These symptoms were considered postencephalitic in presentation. Subsequent research and labels for this population of learning- and attention-impaired children reflected the belief that these disabilities were the result of some brain-based dysfunction. The term "minimal brain damage" was introduced in the 1940s by Strauss and Lehtinen (1947). Broca (1861) studied individuals with aphasia. He was the first to identify a

Table 2.1   Historical Definitions of Learning Disorders

Year	Definition
1887	Dyslexia (Berlin)
1895–1917	Congenital word blindness (Hinshelwood; Kerr; Morgan)
1922–25	Postinfluenzal behavioral syndrome (Ebaugh; Hohman; Stryker)
1928	Strephosymbolia (Orton)
1929	Congenital auditory imperception (Worcester-Drought & Allen)
1934	Organic driveness (Kahn & Cohen)
1941	Developmental lag (L. A. Bender & Yarnell)
1943–47	Brain-injured or damaged child (Strauss & Lehtinen; Strauss & Werner)
1947	Minimally brain-damaged child (Gesell & Amatruda)
1960	Psychoneurological learning disorders (Mykelbust & Boshes)
1962	Learning disabilities (Kirk)
1962–63	Minimal brain dysfunction (MBD) (Bax & MacKeith)
1964	Developmental dyslexia (Critchley)
1967–68	Specific learning disabilities (National Advisory Committee on Handicapped Children, U.S. Office of Education)
1969	Specific learning disabilities (P.L. 91-230)
1971	Psycholinguistic learning disabilities (Kirk & Kirk)
1977	Learning disabilities (P.L. 94-142)
1980	Specific developmental disorders (*Diagnostic and Statistical Manual of Mental Disorders,* Third Edition)
1987	Specific developmental disorders (*Diagnostic and Statistical Manual of Mental Disorders,* Third Edition–Revised)

Note. From *Disorders of Learning in Childhood,* by A. A. Silver and R. A. Hagin, 1990, New York: Wiley. Copyright 1990 by John Wiley and Sons, Inc. Used with permission.

neurological origin for learning problems. A variety of other terms have also been used to describe this population of children (see Table 2.1).

Sam Kirk in 1962 initiated the movement away from labels for children's learning problems that reflected cause toward labels that reflected measured behavior. The term "learning disability" was intended to mean impaired learning capacity. Kirk (1962) described LD as

> retardation, disorder or delayed development in one or more of the processes of speech language, reading, spelling, writing or arithmetic resulting from possible cerebral dysfunction and/or emotional or behavioral disturbance and not from mental retardation, sensory deprivation or cultural or instructional factors. (p. 261)

Kirk's concepts greatly contributed to the definition of LD presented to Congress by the National Advisory Committee on Handicapped Children (1968). The committee defined children with specific LD as

> those children who have a disorder in one or more of the basic psychological process involved in understanding or using language, spoken or written, which disorder may manifest itself in

imperfect ability to listen, think, speak, read, write, spell or do mathematical calculations. Such disorders include such conditions as perceptual handicaps, brain injury, minimal brain dysfunction, dyslexia and developmental aphasia. This term does not include learning problems which are primarily the result of visual, hearing or motor handicaps of mental retardation, of emotional disturbance or of environmental, cultural or economic disadvantage. (p. 82)

In 1975, this basic definition was incorporated into P.L. 94–142, which guaranteed specialized services for children with a variety of problems, including LD. This federal law mandated education for all handicapped children, but it also went further and disqualified emotional and behavioral factors as causative for LD. In such cases, children were to be referred to as behaviorally rather than learning impaired.

In 1981, six professional organizations—the American Speech and Hearing Association, Association for Children and Adults with Learning Disabilities, Council for Learning Disabilities–Division for Children with Communication Disorders, Council for Exceptional Children, International Reading Association, and Orton Dyslexia Society—met and reached a consensus definition for LD. This definition refined the original concept of LD as a general description of children failing to learn despite apparently adequate capacity:

Learning disabilities is a generic term that refers to a heterogenous group of disorders manifested by significant difficulties in the acquisition and use of listening, speaking, writing, reasoning or mathematical abilities. These disorders are intrinsic to the individual and presumed to be due to central nervous system dysfunction. Even though a learning disability may occur concomitantly with other handicapping conditions (i.e., sensory impairment, mental retardation), social and emotional disturbances or environmental influences (i.e., cultural differences, insufficient/inappropriate instruction, psychogenetic factors), it is not the direct result of those conditions or influences. (Hammill, Leigh, McNutt, & Larsen, 1981)

In 1987, the Interagency Committee on Learning Disabilities maintained this basic definition but added deficits in social skills as potentially stemming from LD. Despite the lack of consensus on all issues, clearly the term "learning disability" now implies performance rather than etiology. The term now reflects the perception that the learning-disabled child or adult is unable to accomplish academic or interpersonal tasks that others can accomplish and, further, that this lack of accomplishment is the result not of poor teaching, environmental deprivation, or limited experience but of a biological process (Kavanaugh, 1988).

Despite continuing efforts at clarification, means of determining who should be called learning disabled still vary within academic, community, and vocational settings. Rutter, in 1978, concluded that the term "learning disability" will never allow a precise and clear working definition. As J. M. Fletcher and Satz (1985) point out, there are two significant sources of variability in studies of learning-disabled children. First is construct validity of the dependent variables, that is, how one goes about defining and measuring the data. Second is the heterogeneity of most learning-disabled populations studied. This was a significant factor in the Florida longitudinal project, for example (J. M. Fletcher, Satz, & Morris, 1984). In this project, when the authors attempted to define dyslexia as a function of minimal brain dysfunction, they discovered that the defining attributes for these disorders could not be adequately differentiated for other disabled learners with poor intelligence, cultural deprivation, or other problems (Satz & Fletcher, 1980).

The difficulty of developing a qualitative definition for LD and the need to make funding decisions have prompted school districts to look toward statistical methods of identifying this group of children (A. A. Silver & Hagin, 1990). This approach has traditionally used a discrepancy score, the difference between basic achievement and the achievement expected on the basis of the student's age, grade, placement, academic history, or intelligence. Each type of comparison has advantages and disadvantages (C. R. Reynolds, 1983). The inclusionary criteria of IQ-achievement disparity, for example, may restrict sampling of achievement problems and neglect the importance of motivational, social, and experiential factors as they relate to poor academic performance (H. G. Taylor, 1989). Nonetheless, at this time in public school and vocational settings, the most widely accepted definition of LD calls for a difference of at least 20 scale score points or 1.5 standard deviations between intelligence and achievement test scores. Based on this definition, it is estimated that LD occurs in approximately 10% of the child and adult populations. Males and females appear to be equally affected, but males appear to be referred for help more often (Ingersoll & Goldstein, 1993; Shaywitz, Shaywitz, Fletcher, & Escobar, 1990). Shaywitz et al. (1990) note that the difference in referrals to learning-disabled programs may result from gender-related differences in accompanying behavior problems rather than in the absolute level of student underachievement.

Some authors believe that the classification of LD should be based on four considerations:

1. Multidimensional factors
2. Multidisciplinary data provision for variation within age group and sample
3. Provision for variation in measurement used by different investigators
4. Taxonomy of clinical and research usefulness for these definitions (A. A. Silver & Hagin, 1990)

These authors suggest that a diagnosis of LD should apply to "all children whose academic achievement is below that expected from their age and intelligence" (A. A. Silver & Hagin, 1990, p. 25). Although these and other authors have suggested that LD is a broad nonspecific symptom for which a cause must be identified, it has yet to be demonstrated that different causes lead to different types of LD or require different treatments.

The work of Boder (1973) and Bakker (1979) exemplifies efforts to classify and identify LD on the basis of educational criteria. Boder described three subtypes of children with LD: 1. a dysphonetic group lacking word analysis skills and having difficulty with phonetics; 2. a dyseidetic group experiencing impairment in visual memory and discrimination; and 3. a mixed dysphonetic, dyseidetic group. According to Boder's research, the dyseidetic group included 67% of those identified as learning disabled, and the mixed group 23%. Thus children with visual learning problems constituted a very small group of the learning-disabled population. Bakker's work described the L- and P-type dyslexias. Children with L-type dyslexia read quickly but made errors of omission, additions, and word mutilation. The P-type group tended to work slowly and make time-consuming errors involving fragmentations and repetitions.

Among the more interesting and promising attempts to define LD are those studies involving multivariate analysis. Efforts to subgroup LD using such analysis suggest that differences between good and poor readers may reflect impairment in minor skills, such as oral word rhyming, vocabulary, discrimination of reversed figures, speed of perception for visual forms, and sequential processing (Doehring, 1968). In 1979, Petrauskas and Rourke used a factor-analytic method to describe the difficulties of a group of deficient readers as falling into four subtypes: 1. primarily verbal problems, 2. primarily visual problems, 3. difficulty with conceptual flexibility and linguistic skills, and 4. no specific weaknesses.

Mattis, French, and Rapin (1975) identified three distinct syndromes of LD: 1. children struggling to read as a result of language problems, 2. children with articulation and graphomotor problems affecting academic achievement, and 3. children with a visual spatial perceptual disorder. The third group displayed better verbal than nonverbal intellectual abilities. Almost 80% of the impaired children fell in the first two groups. Denckla (1972, 1977) found similar statistics, noting that approximately 16% of learning-disabled children experience some type of visual spatial or perceptual motor problem.

Factor-analytic studies of LD consistently yield a very large group of problems related to verbal weaknesses and a smaller but significant group related to perceptual weaknesses. Joschko and Rourke (1985), based on analysis of the Wechsler Intelligence Scale for Children (WISC), found a clear distinction between children with learning problems stemming from verbal weaknesses and those whose problems stemmed from nonverbal weaknesses.

Satz and Morris (1981) found five distinct groups of reading-disabled children, again along the verbal-nonverbal continuum: 1. those with language impairment, 2. those with specific language problems related to naming, 3. those with mixed global language and perceptual problems, 4. those with perceptual-motor impairments only, and 5. an unexpected group in which no significant impairments were identified. The last group often is found in LD studies and presents a thorny problem for etiological theorists. Some researchers hypothesize that this group of children simply has not had adequate educational experience or models. Others suggest that children in this last group have greater emotional problems, which interfere with their capacity to learn. Using cluster analysis of a neuropsychological battery, Phillips (1983) identified a fairly similar profile of five LD subtypes, including individuals with normal test scores, auditory processing problems, difficulty with receptive and expressive language, spatial weaknesses, and a global pattern of low test scores.

Rourke (1978) concluded that cluster-analytic studies have identified some association between learning delay and a wide variety of perceptual, linguistic, sequential, and cognitive skills. This finding has been reinforced in the work of others (Benton, 1975). According to Swartz (1974), a pattern consisting of depressed scores on four Wechsler subtests, *the ACID pattern* (an acronym for Arithmetic, Coding, Information, and Digit Span subtests), characterizes the weaknesses of most learning-disabled children. Although this view is held by many others, not all learning-disabled children display the ACID pattern. Children who do, however, are thought to have a particularly poor prognosis for academic performance in reading, spelling, and arithmetic (Ackerman, Dykman, & Peters, 1977). Some researchers have suggested that in a population of learning-disabled children demonstrating the ACID pattern, one subgroup experiences particularly poor auditory-verbal memory and sequencing, while a second group experiences poor visual spatial abilities. This distinction is similar to that described by Joschko and Rourke (1985). However, these authors reported a further distinction in ACID pattern by age between a younger group 5–8 years old and an older group 9–15 years old. On the basis of an extensive neurological battery, they found a distinct pattern of differences resulting in four subtypes (see Table 2.2). Joschko and Rourke (1985) noted that "although the ACID subtypes generated in this research do not differ significantly in terms of *level* of academic performance, the plots of the factor-score profiles for each of the reliable subtests indicate that they have *qualitatively different ability profiles which may have practical applications*" (p. 77). These authors also concluded that the best type of remediation has not been demonstrated to be based on this pattern of weaknesses but rather on each child's strengths and weaknesses. Thus, one cannot determine treatment solely by inferences drawn from group data.

The inclusion of LD among the disorders evaluated and diagnosed by the medical and mental health community has traditionally been considered an adjunct to more formal psychiatric

Table 2.2   Performance Characteristics of Reliable ACID Subtypes

Neuropsychological Measures	ACID Subtypes			
	Younger Subtype 2	Younger Subtype 4	Older Subtype 1	Older Subtype 3
Tactile perceptual	Poor	Average	Average	Poor
Visual perceptual	Poor	Average	Average	Average
Auditory perceptual and language related	Poor	Poor	Poor	Poor
Sequencing	Average	Poor	Poor	Average
Concept formation and reasoning	Average	Average	Average	Average
Motor	Poor	Average	Average	Poor
Academic	Poor	Poor	Poor	Poor

Note. "Poor" indicates a tendency for poorer test performances in comparison to the norms for the test. "Average" indicates test performance generally within one standard deviation of the normative mean. From *Neuropsychology of Learning Disabilities,* by B. P. Rourke, 1985, New York: Guilford. Used with permission.

or psychological evaluation. However, as it has been recognized that learning-disabled individuals appear more likely than others to develop psychiatric problems, efforts have been made to refine the clinical diagnosis of learning impairments. The *Diagnostic and Statistical Manual of Mental Disorders, 4th Edition (DSM-IV)* lists four academic skill disorders (American Psychiatric Association [APA], 1994): reading disorder, mathematics disorder, disorder of written expression, and learning disorder not otherwise specified. All four are qualified as reflecting the collection of standardized test data indicating performance substantially below what would be expected based upon the individual's age, intelligence, and educational experience. According to these definitive criteria, the problem must interfere with the individual's academic performance or activities of daily living. The "not otherwise specified" category reflects LD such as an isolated spelling weakness independent of other written language difficulties. The *DSM-IV* also contains a developmental coordination disorder diagnosis, reflecting weak large or fine motor skills that may interfere with academic achievement or daily living and are not due to a specific medical condition.

From the clinician's perspective, a practical or functional conceptualization of LD is critical and likely of greatest importance. It is the clinician's job not only to evaluate but to transmit information to educators, vocational counselors, family members, and the affected person in a way that will facilitate practical understanding, increase motivation, and define intervention. Table 2.3 lists basic skills necessary for successful academic achievement, beginning with the simplest and building to the more complex. These skills are hypothetically conceived as essential to the development of basic reading, spelling, writing, and mathematical abilities. This conceptualization is adapted from and based on the work of developmental pediatrician Mel Levine (1990).

The consensus in current factor-analytic research is that there are two broad groups of skills necessary for efficient learning:

1. *Auditory-verbal processes.* Weaknesses in these areas result in reading disorders and other language-based learning problems.
2. *Visual, perceptual, and motor (nonverbal) processes.* Weaknesses in these areas may result

Table 2.3   Basic Skills Necessary for Successful Academic Achievement

Reading problems

Appreciating language sounds	Language sounds don't seem very clear.
Remembering sound-symbol association	The sounds of combinations of letters are difficult to remember.
Holding together the sounds in a word	The sounds of letters are known, but it's difficult to put together the sounds in the right order to make the words during reading.
Reading fast enough	It takes too long to pronounce or understand each word.
Understanding sentences	The vocabulary or grammar is too difficult.
Understanding paragraphs or passages	It's difficult to find the main ideas and the important details, or it's difficult to understand the concepts, ideas, or facts.
Remembering while reading	Ideas don't stay in memory during reading.
Summarizing what was read	It's too difficult to decide and remember what's important and to organize important ideas in your own words and sentences.
Applying what was read	It's difficult to use what you've read.
Enjoying reading	Reading is too much work; it's not automatic.

Spelling problems

Remembering letters and sounds	It's difficult to remember that a certain combination of letters stands for a certain language sound. It's difficult to understand how sounds are different from each other.
Picturing words	It's difficult to remember how words look.
Spelling longer words	It's difficult to recall and sequence the sounds of multisyllable words.
Understanding spelling rules	It's difficult to understand what combination of letters is allowed. It is also difficult to understand the vowel rules.
Using inconsistent spelling	It's difficult to concentrate on little details.
Writing and spelling at the same time	It's difficult to write and spell at the same time. It's difficult to remember how to spell when writing words in sentences or paragraphs.
Making mixed spelling errors	It's difficult to distinguish word sounds, remember the rules, and picture words.

Writing problems

Fine motor problems	It's difficult to keep track of just where the pencil is while writing.
	It's difficult getting the right muscles to work together quickly and easily.
	It's difficult getting finger muscles in touch with memory through many different nerve connections between the hand and the brain.
	It's difficult getting eyes and fingers to work together.

Table 2.3 *(Continued)*

Remembering and writing at the same time (mechanics)	It's difficult to remember punctuation, spelling, capitalization, grammar, vocabulary, letter formation, and ideas all at the same time.
Thinking about ideas and writing at the same time	It's difficult to think fast about ideas at the same time you are writing.
Planning and organizing	It's difficult thinking up something to write about or understanding what the teacher expects; deciding who will read the writing; thinking up many good ideas and writing them down; taking all the ideas and putting together the ones that belong together; knowing what ideas to put first and what ones to put second; getting rid of ideas that don't fit; making sure that things make sense; and reorganizing what has been written.
Knowing how to translate ideas into language on paper	It's difficult to get ideas into good language when writing.
Math problems	
Grasping the concepts	It's difficult to understand concepts that include things such as number, place value, percentage, decimals, and equations.
Remembering mathematics	Mathematics is a big memory strain. Mathematical facts need to be remembered very quickly or you may forget something you need to do. When you finish doing one part of a math problem, you need to remember what it was that you were going to do next.
Understanding the language of mathematics	There is a lot of language (e.g., labels) in a math class, which makes it difficult keeping up with what the teacher is saying and understanding certain assignments.
Using problem-solving skills	It's difficult to think up the best way (or ways) to come up with a correct answer. It's difficult to take time to think about a solution.
Visualizing	It's difficult to see what you are able to describe in words. It's tricky to understand some concepts unless you can see clear pictures or images of them in your brain.
Remembering things in the right order	It's difficult to put things, do things, or keep things in the correct order. It's difficult to do the right steps in the right order to get the right answer.
Paying attention to detail	It's difficult to be alert and tuned in to the many little details in mathematics.
Recognizing or admitting a lack of understanding	It's difficult to recognize or admit that you do not understand or remember basic concepts in order to understand the new ones.

Note. Adapted from *Keeping a Head in School,* by M. Levine, 1990, Boston: Educators Publishing Service. Copyright 1990 by Educators Publishing Service, Inc. Used with permission.

in reading problems but more likely affect handwriting, mathematics, and certain social skills. Tables 2.4 and 2.5 present a model for conceptualizing these skills and examples of these skills in a 2 × 2 grid. The model conceptualizes learning skills on rote/automatic and conceptual levels, auditorily and visually.

READING DISORDERS AND OTHER LANGUAGE-BASED LEARNING DISABILITIES

Reading disorders continue to be referred to collectively as "dyslexia." They account for the vast majority of all referrals among children and adults for LD diagnosis and remediation. Lerner (1985) estimates that 80% of all learning-disabled children experience problems with reading when they are school-aged. In contrast, poor handwriting, weak mathematical skills, and poor coordination may not lead to significant problems at school and often cause only mild nuisances in daily life in the adult years. It is not uncommon to meet many competent and successful people who struggle with athletic activities or to balance their checkbooks. Poor reading skills, however, cause significant life problems in adulthood.

Reading disorders have been explained many ways, by faulty eye movements, problems with visual perception or with coordination between visual-motor functions, failure of the eyes to work cooperatively, and a list of other physical problems and language deficits. It is not difficult to understand how the myth that reading disability is exclusively a function of visual spatial weakness developed. The connection between the eyes and reading is obvious. Good and poor readers clearly demonstrate differing patterns in eye movements during reading. Poor readers often struggle with reversals of letters and words. They may transpose words when reading and often demonstrate a shorter visual span. Whether these problems are cause or consequence of their reading disability is unclear. Although visual processes are no doubt important to reading, the preponderance of data suggests that they are not primarily responsible for reading disorders in most people. The evidence instead suggests that most reading-disabled individuals suffer from impaired language skills, especially those related to phonological processes. As Pennington (1991) writes, based on his extensive research:

> Over and over again when we read, we must translate printed letter strings into word pronunciations. To do this we must understand that the alphabet is a code for phonemes, the individual speech sounds in a language, and we must be able to use that code quickly and automatically so that we can concentrate on the meaning of what we read. The difficulty that dyslexics have with *phonetics,* the ability to sound out words, makes reading much slower and less automatic and detracts considerably from comprehension. (p. 59)

For many children with reading disorders, poor comprehension results from poor rote skills, such as an inability to distinguish similar sounds, which then leads to poor auditory discrimination and weak phonetics. Problems with verbal short-term memory are also common among reading-impaired individuals. Memory requires phonological skill. Poor readers may experience problems recalling letters, digits, words, or phrases in exact sequence. Some children struggle to master basic foundational academic skills because of auditory, visual, or rote/automatic problems. Most learning difficulty by far stems from the linguistic problems these children experience. Other children are capable of learning to read, but when the curriculum begins to accelerate in second grade and they must read to learn, they struggle as a result of weak conceptual skills.

It is also not surprising that related skills, such as spelling and writing, are impaired in

Table 2.4 Categories of Academic Skills

	Auditory-Verbal	Visual-Motor
Conceptual	Verbal-conceptual	Visual nonverbal–conceptual
Rote/Automatic	Auditory-motor Auditory perceptual	Letter perception Spatial organization and nonverbal integration
	Rote auditory-sequential memory	Rote visual-sequential memory and retrieval
	Rote and association memory and retrieval	Motor sequencing and fine motor control

Note. Adapted from table prepared by Sally I. Ingalls. Copyright 1991 by Neurology, Learning and Behavior Center, Salt Lake City, UT. Adapted with permission.

reading-disabled children. For many, spelling is even more impaired than reading (Snowling & Hulme, 1991). Weak auditory-verbal abilities may also impair written production because the same coding processes are used for reading and writing. But writing requires additional skills involving automatic and conceptual ability. The writer must not only remember a phonological code but must think of the words to express meaning, organize those words according to the rules of grammar and syntax, and mechanically place them on the paper, all the while paying close attention to size, shape, spacing of letters, and punctuation. Similarly, children with verbal-based LD may be capable of mastering basic mathematical processes but then struggle with more complex mathematics because of difficulty with concept formation, memorization, and the ability to remember essential, sequential steps.

VISUAL-MOTOR LEARNING DISABILITIES (NONVERBAL LEARNING DISABILITY)

Visual-motor LD tends to cause problems with arithmetic and handwriting, often independent of associated reading disability. Included in this category by most neuropsychology researchers are disabilities and skills involving social awareness and judgment. These problems do not appear to be primarily language based and have been referred to collectively in the neuropsychology literature as "nonverbal learning disabilities" (Pennington, 1991; Rourke, 1989). Strang and Rourke (1985) suggest that children with such disabilities experience seven areas of difficulty: problems with spatial organization; problems paying attention to visual detail; procedural errors in mathematics; failure to shift psychological set—for example, when two or more operations of one kind (e.g., addition) are followed by an operation of another kind (e.g., subtraction); graphomotor weaknesses; poor factual memory; and poor judgment and reasoning. These authors contend that nonverbal LD is much less common than language-based disabilities, occurring in approximately 1%–10% of children referred for learning problems.

Harnadek and Rourke (1994) suggest that individuals with nonverbal LD experience the greatest deficits in visual, perceptual, organizational, psychomotor coordination and complex tactile perceptual skills. This area of LD is sometimes characterized as reflecting right-hemisphere deficit. However, because the connections between the right and left hemispheres of the brain are highly complex, it is an oversimplification to speak of one hemisphere as if it

Table 2.5 Levels of Processing Related to LD and Disability Characteristics

	Auditory-Verbal	Visual-Motor
Conceptual	Language semantics: word meaning, definition, vocabulary Listening comprehension: understanding and memory of overall ideas Reading comprehension: understanding and memory of overall ideas Specificity and variety of verbal concepts for oral or written expression Verbal reasoning and logic	Social insight and reasoning: understand strategies of games, jokes, motives of others, social conventions, tact Mathematical concepts: use of 0 in $+$, $-$, $\times$; place value; money equivalences; missing elements, etc. Inferential reading comprehension; draw conclusions Understand relationship of historical events across time; understand scientific concepts Structure ideas hierarchically; outlining skills Generalization abilities Integrate material into a well-organized report
Rote/Automatic	Early speech: naming objects Auditory processing: clear enunciation of speech; pronouncing sounds or syllables in correct order Name colors Recall birthdate, phone number, address, etc. Say alphabet and other lists (days, months) in order Easily select and sequence words with proper grammatical structure for oral or written expression	Assemble puzzles and build with construction toys Social perception and awareness of environment Time sense: doesn't ask, "Is this the last recess?" Remember and execute correct sequence for tying shoes Easily negotiate stairs; climb on play equipment; learn athletic skills; ride bike Execute daily living skills such as pouring without spilling, spreading a sandwich, dressing self correctly

Auditory "dyslexia": discriminate sounds, esp. vowels, auditorily; blend sounds to words; distinguish words that sound alike, e.g., mine/mind

Labeling and retrieval reading disorder: auditory and visual perception okay but continually mislabels letters, sounds, common syllables, sight words (b/d, her/here)

Poor phonic spelling

Poor listening and reading comprehension due to poor short-term memory, especially for rote facts

Labeling and retrieval math disorder: trouble counting sequentially; mislabels numbers (e.g., 16/60); poor memory for facts about numbers and sequences of steps for computation (e.g., long division)

Recall names, dates, and historical facts

Learn and retain new scientific terminology

Use the correct sequence of strokes to form manuscript or cursive letters

Eye-hand coordination for drawing, assembling art projects, and handwriting

Directional stability for top/bottom and left/right tracking

Copy from board accurately

Visual "dyslexia": confused when viewing visual symbols; poor visual discrimination; reversals/inversions/transpositions due to poor directionality; may not recognize the shape or form of a word that has been seen many times before, i.e., "word-blind"

Spelling: poor visual memory for the nonphonetic elements of words

Note. Adapted from table prepared by Sally Ingalls. Copyright 1991 by Neurology, Learning and Behavior Center, Salt Lake City, UT. Adapted with permission.

existed in isolation from the other. Nonetheless, the organization of the brain does appear such that the left hemisphere processes language and the right hemisphere processes nonverbal information, including spatial awareness, recognition, organization of visual patterns, and co-ordination of visual-motor information. Children with nonverbal LD, not surprisingly, are often described as poorly coordinated in their fine and large motor skills. As adults, they may be extremely awkward in athletic activities and extremely disorganized in tracking their possessions. They frequently experience great difficulty adapting to new or complex vocational, personal, or social situations. They frequently struggle with handwriting, mathematics, social cues, and emotional health (Weintraub & Mesulam, 1983). They also struggle with interpersonal relations—not surprising, given estimates that 65% of communication is nonverbal. Nonverbal behavior appears especially important in communicating feelings, emotions, and preferences. Voice cues, such as pitch and volume, as well as facial expression and eye contact, play a significant role in daily communication (Mehrabian & Ferris, 1967).

It is also suspected that children and adults with nonverbal LD experience greater internalizing problems related to depression and anxiety than those with language-based LD. It is unclear whether this pattern contributes to the disability or is a consequence of the disability. Rourke (1989) suggests that the evidence is strongest for a disturbance in the right hemisphere that underlies all these learning, interpersonal, and emotional problems. Finally, many of these individuals are reported to experience attention problems without significant hyperactive or impulsive difficulty.

Epidemiology

Given the wide variation in definitions and in populations studied, it is not surprising that the reported prevalence of LD among children and adults varies. Definition is often driven by available resources and referral practices. Within the school setting, for example, the number of children qualifying for special educational services as learning disabled can be manipulated easily by adjusting the discrepancy criteria. In addition, evaluation instruments and methodologies are rarely comparable.

Flynn and Rahbar (1994) found that when teachers were asked to identify students with LD, the number of boys they chose exceeded the number of girls by a 2:1 ratio in a group of first- and third-graders. Test-identified ratios, however, did not demonstrate this discrepancy. Nor did identification for Chapter One services (reading assistance) demonstrate this gender difference.

With these factors in mind, it is fair to say that available research supports LD prevalence rates among children, and likely adults, ranging from 2% to 20% in the United States (A. A. Silver & Hagin, 1990). In 1987, the Interagency Committee on Learning Disabilities concluded that lacking good prevalence data, it could only be estimated that somewhere between 5% and 10% of the population of children and adults is affected by LD. Prevalence was reported as being higher among socioeconomically disadvantaged populations and higher among males than among females. The Collaborative Perinatal Project (Nichols & Chen, 1981) reported an incidence of 6.5% experiencing LD in a population of almost 30,000 children. Rutter, Tizard, and Whitmore (1970) in their Isle of Wight study reported a prevalence of just under 8% experiencing LD in a sample of 2,300 nine- and ten-year-olds. Fifteen percent of a population of 2,800 third- and fourth-graders was reported as underachieving by Myklebust and Boshes (1969). In 1987 almost 5% of all elementary school children were receiving special education services for LD (Kavanaugh & Truss, 1988). In 1966, Eisenberg reported that 28% of a population of 12,000 metropolitan-area children were reading two or more grade levels below expectation. In this study, the inner-city children were four times more likely to be behind than those being raised in the suburbs. Prevalence estimates for LD also varied depending on definition and population measured. Table 2.6 summarizes some of these and other estimated prevalence figures.

Cause

Heredity accounts for the majority of LD by affecting proficiency in certain skills essential for mastering basic academic and interpersonal activities. Thirty-five to 40% of close relatives of children with LD report experiencing similar problems. Genetic research involving twins has identified heritable, familial factors in 25%–50% of those with reading disability (DeFries, 1985; DeFries & Fulker, 1985, 1988; S. D. Smith, Kimberling, Pennington, & Lubs, 1983). In some families, dyslexia has been linked to a genetic marker on chromosome 15 (S. D. Smith et al., 1983); in others, chromosome 6 (DeFries & Decker, 1982) has been implicated. Environmental factors such as toxins, drug use, or low socioeconomic status may also play a role in a child's failure to develop basic academic skills at a critical period. This failure may then lead to chronic learning problems. For example, there is a reported relationship between reading disorders, family size, low educational level of mother, later-born status in family, and low socioeconomic status (Melekian, 1990). These extrinsic factors likely contribute over time to poor academic achievement (Badian, 1984).

In 1981, Nichols and Chen, after an extensive study of nearly 30,000 children reported that LD is associated with demographic and maternal variables (large family size, frequent changes in residence, low socioeconomic status, intellectually handicapped younger siblings, and receipt of public assistance), pregnancy and delivery variables (lack of prenatal visits during pregnancy and hospitalizations during pregnancy), and childhood variables (small head circumference, low intellect, and right-left discrimination problems).

Among school-aged children, speech and language problems, clumsiness, incoordination, right-left confusion, and mixed or inconsistent cerebral dominance has been associated with impaired reading ability (Benton & Pearl, 1978). Identification as dyslexic has been reported to correlate with large family size (Varlaam, 1970), antisocial behavior (Rutter, Graham, & Birch, 1970), autoimmune disorders (Pennington et al., 1987), and perinatal complications (Rutter, 1978).

Although a variety of sites in the brain have been proposed as related to LD, at this time no single set of data suggests that a specific brain site is primarily responsible for LD in a functional way (Ingersoll & Goldstein, 1993). As with ADHD, the cause of LD was long presumed to be based in central nervous system dysfunction interacting with a variety of environmental variables. Researchers now agree that the nervous system dysfunction for LD and ADHD may represent a specific physical difference but more likely represents a difference in the operation of the brain (Galaburda, 1985, 1989, 1991). Galaburda reports the presence of microscopic changes in the cortex of the brain, involving poor organization of brain cells, focal cortical dysgenesis (misplaced nests of cells in the outermost layer of the cortex), and the presence of polymicrogyra (deeper folds in the cortex). Anatomic asymmetries and symmetries differing from normals have also been found in the brains of adults with LD and ADHD (Galaburda, 1985, 1989, 1991; Hynd, Hern, Voeller, & Marshall, 1991). Specifically, differences in the planum temporale reflecting symmetry for both sides were found in 100% of the people with LD

Table 2.6 Prevalence of Learning Disabilities

Source	Year	Sample	Estimates (%)	Definition Used
Rutter et al.	1964	2,199 children	3.9 (refers to reading problems only)	Reading ability greater than 28 months below predicted level based on age and WISC IQ
Meier	1967	30 second-grade classes (about 900 children)	11	Classroom Screening Instrument (measure developed for this study)
Meier	1968	80 second-grade classes (about 2,400 children)	4–40 per class (about 15 total)	Same as above
National Institute for Juvenile Justice and Delinquency Prevention	1976	Illiterate prisoners and juvenile delinquents	50 (illiterate prisoners) 30 (juvenile delinquents)	
Nichols & Chen	1981	29,889 first- and second-grade students	8.36	Performance on compilation of cognitive, perceptual-motor, academic, neurological, and behavioral tests and evaluations

Source	Year	Sample	Percentage	Definition/Notes
Interagency Committee on Learning Disabilities	1987		5–10	Informal meta-analysis of available LD research
Shaywitz et al.	1987	First-grade students	11	Discrepancy between ability and achievement
Shaywitz et al.	1988	Same sample as 1987 study	12.6	Discrepancy between ability and achievement
U.S. Department of Education	1976–77	K–12 public school students served in special education programs	1.80	P.L. 94-142[a]
	1977–78		2.21	
	1978–79		2.66	
	1979–80		3.06	
	1980–81		3.57	
	1981–82		4.04	
	1982–83		4.39	
	1983–84		4.59	
	1984–85		4.66	
	1985–86		4.71	
	1986–87		4.80	
	1987–88		4.82	

[a]U.S. Department of Education numbers refer to percentage of students receiving special education services for learning disabilities; they are not estimates of the prevalence of LD.

in 25% or less of the nonaffected individuals (Larsen, Høien, Lundberg, & Ødegaard, 1990).

Without a doubt, however, sensory information passes through a number of key brain locations during academic processes (Conners, 1992). For example, an auditory signal, after being processed by the hearing mechanism, arrives at the medial geniculate of the thalamus. From that point three separate circuits leave the thalamus simultaneously, one to the hippocampus to evaluate the familiarity or unfamiliarity of the sound, one to the amygdala to prepare for motor and automatic reactions, and one to the sensory cortex to perform a detailed analysis of the sound (LaDoux, 1986).

Comorbidity

Among populations of children referred primarily for psychiatric disorders, language impairments are found with prevalence estimates ranging from 25% to 97% (N. J. Cohen & Lipsett, 1991; T. Gualitieri, Koriath, Van Bourgondien, & Saleeby, 1983). As previously noted, problems related to language disability have been repeatedly found to affect not only learning but behavior as well. It is difficult to transmit this information to practical use, however. In 1989, Gibbs and Cooper found that 96% of a population of nearly 250 learning-disabled children experienced speech, language, or hearing problems. Unfortunately, only 6% of the children were receiving any type of service by a speech language pathologist. Since language is essential for social relations, thinking, feeling, behaving, and learning, it is, as Beitchman and Inglis (1991) note, a "window into the mind." Language disorders are reported to occur in 3%–15% of all children (Stark, Bernstein, & Condino, 1984).

N. J. Cohen, Davine, Horodezky, Lipsett, and Isaacson (1993), in a study of nearly 300 children referred for psychiatric problems, found that nearly one-third suffered from a previously undiagnosed language impairment detected only when a routine systematic assessment was completed. A significant group of these children also experienced ADHD. In such cases, failure to identify linguistic disability may exacerbate dysfunctional child-adult interactions and lack of compliance (Goldstein & Hinerman, 1988; Howlin & Rutter, 1987).

Although it has been suggested that comorbidity of disruptive externalizing disorders with specific LD is less frequent than commonly reported, there is no doubt that a significant group of learning-disabled children experience disruptive behavioral problems (Dunivant, 1982; Hinshaw, 1992). The overlap between externalizing behavioral syndromes and underachievement occurs at levels well beyond chance, with estimates ranging from less than 10% to more than 50%. It has been well demonstrated, however, that parental substance abuse, socioeconomic status, and oppositional behavior over a six-year period are the best predictors of the development of conduct disorder in preadolescent males. LD is not (Loeber, Green, Keenan, & Lahey, 1995). Among carefully evaluated learning-disabled children the most frequent pattern of accompanying behavioral problems appears to be internalizing difficulties related to anxiety or depression (Fuerst, Fisk, & Rourke, 1989). Nevertheless, learning-impaired children are not completely free of disruptive disorders. The incidence of ADHD among learning-impaired children is well beyond a chance level, often estimated at 20%–30% (for a review, see S. Goldstein & Goldstein, 1990).

Although the data strongly suggest that speech and language impairment is associated with a variety of childhood disruptive behavioral and nondisruptive emotional and learning problems, the relationship between these disorders and the extent to which they follow similar paths or share a common pathway is unknown (Beitchman, Nair, Clegg, Ferguson, & Patel, 1986;

Cantwell & Baker, 1987a). The direction of the relationship is also unknown. For example, it is yet to be demonstrated whether language disability leads to symptoms of ADHD and other disruptive problems or whether disruptive problems lead to delay in the development of competent linguistic skills. Whatever the relationship, LD and other disorders frequently occur, and obviously, the more stones around one's neck, the quicker one sinks. Thus, it is not surprising that as the number of comorbid problems a learning-disabled child experiences increases, the potential for positive outcome decreases.

Rourke and Fuerst (1991) reviewed nearly 700 articles published in the previous two decades dealing with the psychosocial and emotional functioning of children with LD. Many of these articles suggested a causal link between LD and emotional function—specifically, that LD produced emotional or behavioral problems. Rourke and Fuerst (1991) concluded, however, that most of the research supporting these claims was confused, contradictory, poorly done, and generally unreplicable. As a response, Fuerst and Rourke (1995) evaluated the psychosocial functioning over three different age ranges of more than 700 children with LD. These authors reported that the psychosocial functioning of children with LD was stable between the ages of 7 and 13 years. There was no evidence that these children manifested increased psychopathology with increasing age. While the cumulative negative experiences resulting from LD do affect some children, the results of this study, and of others as well (Jorm, Share, Matthews, & MacLean, 1986; Strang, 1981), contradict the idea that most learning-disabled children experience significantly more symptoms of psychiatric disturbance, especially emotional distress, than others. The development of pathological patterns of functioning in these studies did not appear to increase with age, which indicates that factors other than increased age and cumulative negative school experiences secondary to LD should be considered if learning-disabled children are hypothesized to be predisposed to greater emotional problems. However, it is also important to note that internalizing or externalizing problems found in young learning-disabled children tend to continue as the children mature (Fuerst & Rourke, 1993). Thus, as with all children, those children with LD demonstrating emotional or behavioral problems at young ages, independent of other factors, are more likely to demonstrate those problems at later ages.

Finally, data suggest that the lives of nonimpaired siblings of children with LD and ADHD are also affected by these disorders. Although there is no simple linear relationship between the adjustment of siblings and the severity of LD, it is clear that the effect is mediated by the relative birth order of siblings within the family, sex of the nonimpaired sibling, and nearness in age of the sibling to the disabled child (Coleby, 1995). The additional time parents must spend with their affected child may limit their availability and therefore affect their relationships with their other children. This phenomenon may become even more powerful as the disruptive problems the affected child experiences become more severe.

Finally, Nabuzoka and Smith (1993) reported that, at least among 8–12-year-olds, more learning-disabled than non-learning-disabled children are rejected by their peers and fewer are popular. In this study, learning-disabled children were described as shy by other children, sought help, and were victims of bullying significantly more often than non-learning-disabled children. Reports of aggressive behavior did not distinguish between the affected and non-affected groups, however.

CHAPTER 3

Attention Deficit Hyperactivity Disorder in Children

O VER 20 YEARS AGO, problems related to inattentiveness and hyperactivity were the most commonly reported among children and the largest single source of referrals for childhood problems (Barkley, 1981a). Researchers have come to recognize that complaints of inattention, difficulty with impulse control, hyperactivity, and difficulty responding consistently to consequences characterize a syndrome that appears to occur in the current group of children and adults beyond a chance level. However, it has also been recognized that these same complaints are among the most common and may occur individually as a result of other childhood and adult disorders (S. Goldstein, 1995).

Evaluation of these symptomatic problems is complicated. There is no litmus test for ADHD. There appear to be few exclusionary developmental criteria and no unequivocal positive developmental markers (Conners, 1975b). Ross and Ross (1982) describe attention deficit as differing from other disorders in intensity, persistence, and clustering of symptoms rather than in the absolute presence or absence of diagnostic symptoms. That is, problems related to inattentiveness, hyperactivity, and impulsivity fall along a continuum. All children and adults exhibit some of these problems on occasion. It is when they are more severe and more frequent than average that they take on diagnostic significance.

In the past 100 years, the labels for this cluster of problems have changed dramatically, from labels describing behavior (the fidgeties), progressing through labels describing cause (minimal brain dysfunction and postencephalitic disorder), to a set of labels describing what is believed to be the core problem of the disorder (hyperactivity and attention deficit). In the past 20 years, attention deficit has also come to be viewed as a lifetime rather than just a childhood set of problems. The term "attention deficit disorder" or "attention deficit hyperactivity disorder" is now the one most familiar to medical and mental health professionals, as well as to educators and the lay public. There continues to be disagreement about what drives this set of problems as well as the best diagnostic label. Researchers have variously argued that attention deficit might best be referred to as a reward system dysfunction (Haenlein & Caul, 1987), a learning disability (McGee & Share, 1988), or a self-regulatory disorder (Kirby & Grimley, 1986). Barkley (1994) argues that ADHD is a disorder of response inhibition and executive dysfunction leading to deficits in self-regulation, impairment in the ability to organize behavior toward present and future goals, and difficulty adapting socially and behaviorally to environmental demands.

Definition

ADHD is classified as a disruptive disorder because of the impact suffering individuals have on those around them. In contrast to the other two disruptive childhood disorders—oppositional defiant disorder and conduct disorder—ADHD is thought to reflect limited behavior as the result of incompetent and developmental impairments rather than purposeful noncompliance. Thus, ADHD is a behavioral diagnosis (Schaughency & Rothlind, 1991). It was originally described in the second edition of the *Diagnostic and Statistical Manual of Psychiatric Disorders* as "hyperkinetic reaction of childhood" (APA, 1968). The third edition of this manual, published in 1980, expanded the definition and retitled the syndrome "attention deficit disorder" (ADD). Two separate diagnostic criteria were offered: attention deficit with and without hyperactivity (ADD-H and ADD-R). A residual category, primarily for adults presenting some symptoms with a history manifesting a period when the full disorder was exhibited, was also described.

However, researchers argued that there was minimal support for an independent syndrome of ADD without hyperactivity (August & Garfinkel, 1989). This line of research affected the development of the *DSM-III-R,* in which the symptomatic descriptions of impulsivity, hyperactivity, and inattention were collapsed into a list of 14 descriptive behaviors. A single diagnostic entity was provided, attention-deficit hyperactivity disorder. The rationale for this decision was that the diagnosis of attention deficit without hyperactivity "is hardly ever made" (APA, 1987, p. 411).

However, there continues to be a strong clinical and research basis for distinguishing symptomatically, behaviorally, and in adult outcome between attention deficit with and without hyperactivity (Lahey, Schaughency, Hynd, Carlson, & Nieves, 1987). The *DSM-III-R,* published in 1987, described the collapse of the diagnostic criteria as resulting from a set of field studies. These field studies have been criticized as incomplete and unsound, however (Barkley, 1990c). Cantwell and Baker (1988) criticized the field studies as not meeting the standards of "solid scientific study" (p. 527). Moreover, Rutter (1988) reported that results of the field study data were not available for review before the *DSM-III-R* was published. Werry (1988) called the *DSM-III-R* ADHD criteria "hastily-derived" and "largely untested" (p. 139). Epidemiological studies did not support the conclusion that these were identical disorders (Cantwell & Baker, 1985). Finally, Shaywitz and Shaywitz (1988a) stated that there was no evidence that the revised 1987 criteria for ADHD were superior to the *DSM-III* criteria for ADD with and without hyperactivity. In reviewing the available literature, Driscoll and Zecker (1991) found substantial data supporting a difference between attention deficit with and without hyperactive-impulsive problems. These authors reported that inattentive children demonstrating hyperactive-impulsive problems experienced significantly more conduct difficulty and more incidents of mild depression. Children with attention deficit without hyperactivity were described as shy, withdrawn, sluggish, were reported as experiencing greater problems with depressive symptoms, and were more likely to repeat a grade. According to the available literature, the two groups experienced similar problems with inattentiveness, weak school performance, low academic motivation, weak self-concept, and difficulty with peers. Clearly, the two disorders are not completely independent, but certainly, they are not one and the same.

In 1989, Newcorn and colleagues suggested that *DSM-III* ADD-H and *DSM-III-R* ADHD were not operationally identical diagnoses. Thus, caution must be used when generalizing from research based on one diagnostic group to the other. In Newcorn et al.'s study, a group of children with ADD who did not meet criteria for ADD-H did meet the criteria for ADHD. These children were hyperactive and impulsive but were not reported as significantly inattentive. This distinction is consistent with new *DSM-IV* diagnostic criteria. The *DSM-III-R* revised criteria also included a diagnosis of undifferentiated attention deficit disorder described as a diagnosis "for disturbances in which the predominant feature is the persistence of developmentally inappropriate and marked inattention that is not a symptom of another disorder such as retardation or a disorganized, chaotic environment" (APA, 1987, p. 96).

In reviewing the literature concerning attention deficit with and without hyperactivity, Cantwell and Baker (1992b) identified differences not only in core symptoms but also in associated conduct and emotional symptoms, social relations, family history, clinical course, and outcome. In this study as in others, children with ADD-H demonstrated increased rates of impulsivity, distractibility, greater aggression, antisocial behavior, and conduct problems than children with just ADD. However, the children with ADD also did not experience greater problems with depression and anxiety, findings somewhat contradicting the reports of others (Ben-Amos, 1992; Pliszka, 1992). Nonetheless, Cantwell and Baker (1992b) suggested that children referred for learning or internalizing problems should be evaluated for ADD. They also suggested that since ADD is a nondisruptive disorder, these children will likely be referred later in their school careers when faced with increasing academic failure and social problems. Interestingly, children with ADD-H have been reported as experiencing more soft neurological signs than normal children (e.g., problems standing on one foot and sequential motor movements) at all ages and more difficulty than children with ADD above 96 months of age (Hern & Hynd, 1992). Thus, children with ADD do not demonstrate more motor and sensory deficits than children with ADD-H, in contrast to previous reports.

The new *DSM-IV* criteria, when used in isolation, require great expertise and understanding of normal development. Even when data meeting APA criteria for ADHD are gathered from many sources, including parents, teachers, and child interviews, there is a significant risk of overincluding children and adults with any of a wide variety of other etiological problems. For example, in a study screening six-to-nine-year-old boys in the general population, 24% met the *DSM-III* ADD criteria (Satin, Winsberg, Monetti, Sverd, & Ross, 1985). These data were reanalyzed by Ostrom and Jenson (1988), who found that 16% of that population would have met the *DSM-III-R* ADHD criteria as well. August, Ostrander, and Bloomquist (1992) evaluated a population of almost 1,500 elementary school students and found that those children meeting the ADHD *DSM-III-R* criteria were more impaired on adjustment measures and more likely to experience coexisting disruptive behavioral problems than those meeting the previous *DSM-III* ADD criteria.

Baumgaertel et al. (1995) compared *DSM-III-R, DSM-III,* and *DSM-IV* criteria within a population of 1,000 elementary school students in five rural and five urban public schools in Germany. Overall, they found the prevalence of ADHD to have increased from 9.6% using *DSM-III* diagnostic procedures to 17.8% using *DSM-IV.* The new cases were identified as the inattentive type and to a lesser degree the hyperactive-impulsive type. The inattentive type was associated with academic problems; the hyperactive type was associated with significant behavioral problems. The combined type showed significant behavioral and academic problems. These authors concluded that application of the *DSM-IV* criteria increased the diagnosis of ADHD by 64% and identified the majority of children with academic or behavioral problems within the school setting. It is important to note that subjects were identified using only a teacher report questionnaire. Not surprisingly, there may be a large number of children in this group experiencing ADHD-like symptoms secondary to other unidentified problems. Finally, these researchers found the following striking phenomena: Two-thirds of urban children were reported to display symptoms of the inattentive type of ADHD. Two-thirds of the rural ADHD group were identified as experiencing oppositional defiant disorder as well. In general, both of these statistics are much higher than the epidemiological statistics cited by others.

The *DSM-IV* diagnostic criteria (APA, 1994) represent a much sounder set of field studies than did the *DSM-III-R* criteria (Barkley, 1994). The *DSM-IV* criteria reflect three diagnostic categories: predominantly inattentive type (ADHD-I), hyperactive-impulsive type (ADHD-HI), and combined type (ADHD-C). To be diagnosed with ADHD, the child must have one, the other, or both sets of symptomatic problems (see Table 3.1). The first set relates to inattention. A child or adult must demonstrate six of nine symptomatic problems over a period of at least six months, resulting in maladaptive and inconsistent behavior. The second set of symptomatic problems relates to hyperactive and impulsive behavior. As Lahey has noted, these symptoms co-occur so often that they should likely be considered one factor. Children or adults meeting both sets of criteria are considered to demonstrate ADHD-C. The onset of these symptoms must be no later than seven years of age, present in two or more situations, and not the result exclusively of pervasive developmental disorders, schizophrenia, or psychotic disorders. These symptoms should also not be better accounted for by a diagnosis of mood, anxiety, or personality disorder. Concerns about the misdiagnosis of these symptoms as ADHD when they may in fact reflect other disorders should not be taken lightly. Cotugno (1993) found that in a group of children previously diagnosed with ADHD, a comprehensive reassessment yielded only 22% with a primary diagnosis of ADHD and 37% with a secondary diagnosis. Many of the children were instead diagnosed with previously unrecognized problems related to primary anxiety and mood disorders. The possibility that bipolar disorder and borderline personality disorder symptoms mimic ADHD is clearly pertinent when making the ADHD diagnosis in adults. This problem is not addressed in *DSM-IV*, however.

Lahey et al. (in press) completed the *DSM-IV* ADHD field study of 380 children referred to clinics, finding 152 (55%) diagnosed with ADHD-C, 74 (27%) with ADHD-I, and 50 (18%) with ADHD-HI. The field trials found that:

1. Less than half of the *DSM-IV* ADHD-HI group (44%) would have received a *DSM-III* ADD-H diagnosis.
2. The ADHD-HI group demonstrated fewer symptoms of inattention and had fewer symptoms of hyperactive-impulsive problems even in comparison to young children in a narrow age range (four to six years). This suggests that ADHD-HI may be less severe than ADHD-C.
3. The majority of children receiving an ADHD-HI diagnosis were rated by clinicians as meriting the full ADHD-C diagnosis, even though they did not meet all of the criteria.
4. The ADHD-HI group was 20% female, midway between the 12% female ADHD-C group and the 27% female ADHD-I group.
5. The ADHD-HI group was younger, with three-quarters between the ages of four and six years. The average age of children referred was five and a half years for the ADHD-HI

Table 3.1   *DSM-IV* Criteria for Attention Deficit Hyperactivity Disorder

Criteria

A. Either 1 or 2:

  1. Six or more of the following symptoms of *inattention* have persisted for at least six months to a degree that is maladaptive and inconsistent with developmental level:

    a. Often fails to give close attention to details or makes careless mistakes in schoolwork, work, or other activities

    b. Often has difficulty sustaining attention in tasks or play activities

    c. Often does not seem to listen when spoken to directly

    d. Often does not follow through on instructions and fails to finish schoolwork, chores, or duties in the workplace (not due to oppositional behavior or failure to understand instructions)

    e. Often has difficulties organizing tasks and activities

    f. Often avoids, dislikes, or is reluctant to engage in tasks that require sustained mental effort (such as schoolwork or homework)

    g. Often loses things necessary for tasks or activities (e.g., toys, school assignments, pencils, books or tools)

    h. Often easily distracted by extraneous stimuli

    i. Often forgetful in daily activities

  2. Six (or more) of the following symptoms of *hyperactivity-impulsivity* have persisted for at least six months to a degree that is maladaptive and inconsistent with developmental level:

  Hyperactivity

    a. Often fidgets with hands or feet or squirms in seat

    b. Often leaves seat in classroom or in other situations in which remaining seated is expected

    c. Often runs about or climbs excessively in situations in which it is inappropriate (in adolescents or adults, may be limited to subjective feelings of restlessness)

    d. Often has difficulty playing or engaging in leisure activities quietly

    e. Often "on the go" or often acts as if "driven by a motor"

    f. Often talks excessively

  Impulsivity

    g. Often blurts out answers before questions have been completed

    h. Often has difficulty awaiting turn

    i. Often interrupts or intrudes on others (e.g., butts into conversations or games)

B. Some hyperactive-impulsive or inattentive symptoms that caused impairment were present before age seven years.

C. Some impairment from the symptoms is present in two or more settings (e.g., at school [or work] and at home).

D. There must be clear evidence of clinically significant impairment in social, academic, or occupational functioning.

Table 3.1   (*Continued*)

Criteria

E. The symptoms do not occur exclusively during the course of a pervasive developmental disorder, schizophrenia, or other psychotic disorder and are not better accounted for by another mental disorder (e.g., mood disorder, anxiety disorder, dissociative disorder, or a personality disorder).

Types

Attention deficit hyperactivity disorder, combined type (ADHD-C): if both criteria A1 and A2 are met for the past six months

Attention deficit hyperactivity disorder, predominantly inattentive type (ADHD-I): if criterion A1 is met but criterion A2 is not met for the past six months

Attention deficit hyperactivity disorder, predominantly hyperactive-impulsive type (ADHD-HI): if criterion A2 is met but criterion A1 is not met for the past six months

Coding note: For individuals (especially adolescents and adults) who currently have symptoms that no longer meet full criteria, "in partial remission" should be specified.

Attention deficit hyperactivity disorder not otherwise specified: This category is for disorders with prominent symptoms of inattention or hyperactivity-impulsivity that do not meet criteria for ADHD.

Note. Adapted from *Diagnostic and Statistical Manual of Psychiatric Disorders* (4th ed.), by American Psychiatric Association, 1994, Washington, DC: Author.

diagnosis, but eight and a half years for the ADHD-C diagnosis and almost ten years for the inattentive type ADHD-I diagnosis.

6. Surprisingly, the ADHD-HI group demonstrated fewer symptoms of oppositional defiant disorder and conduct disorder than the ADHD-C group but did not differ from the ADHD-I group even after controlling for age differences.
7. The ADHD-HI group demonstrated the same level of academic difficulty as the control group, a lower level of difficulty than for the other two types of ADHD, even after controlling for age and comorbid behavior problems.
8. The ADHD-HI group demonstrated the same type of peer functioning problems as the ADHD-I group but was less impaired than the ADHD-C group, again after controlling for age and comorbid problems.
9. The ADHD-HI and ADHD-C groups demonstrated the same frequency of accidental injury, which was higher than the rate obtained for the control children.

Lahay et al. (1994) and Frick et al. (1994) concluded that many of the children qualifying for ADHD-HI are young and essentially have ADHD-C but because they are not in school are not able to demonstrate that they also meet the inattentive criteria.

DSM-IV criteria have also continued the ADHD not otherwise specified category. This is provided when the predominant symptoms of attention deficit or hyperactive-impulsive difficulties are present but the full criteria are not met for any of the three diagnostic categories.

In a critical analysis of the current *DSM-IV* ADHD criteria, Barkley (1995b) notes that although these criteria are a significant advance in the field, questions remain about the appropriateness of the item set for different ages and developmental periods. As noted, there is a high probability that the ADHD-HI type, given its early mean age of onset, actually represents the early onset of ADHD-C. Whether significant inattention is necessary to diagnose ADHD can also be questioned. It is clearly the hyperactive-impulsive symptoms that best predict future outcome. Barkley also notes the failure of the *DSM-IV* criteria to provide a lower boundary age for making the diagnosis and the confusion between environment and reporter concerning symptoms of ADHD. The latter issue is critical because the degree of agreement between parents and teachers, for instance, concerning behavioral symptoms, is only modest, ranging from 0.3 to 0.5, depending on the behavioral dimension being rated (Achenbach, McConaughy, & Howell, 1987). Thus, disagreement between raters may reflect differences in a child's behavior as a function of differential setting demands. However, such disagreements also likely reflect differences between raters in attitude, judgment, opinion, tolerance, and so forth.

COMMONSENSE DEFINITION

To facilitate a practical understanding of how people with ADHD interact with their environment, S. Goldstein and Goldstein (1990) offer a commonsense definition of ADHD based on hypotheses of Douglas and Peters (1979) and Douglas (1985). These authors suggest that inattentive individuals "experience a constitutional predisposition to experience problems with attention, effort and inhibitory control; poorly modulated arousal; and a need to seek stimulation" (S. Goldstein & Goldstein, 1990, p. 8). This commonsense definition may also help others interacting with individuals with ADHD change their view of these individuals from being noncompliant, odd, or dysfunctional to operating under the same rules as others but requiring different parameters (e.g., greater rewards or more consistent management).

The definition has four components:

1. *Inattention.* It has long been reported that people with ADHD experience greater difficulty than their counterparts without ADHD in remaining on task, especially for boring, repetitive, or especially challenging activities. This population of children and adults struggles to maintain extended effort (Barkley, 1990b). Although distractibility was once considered the core problem of ADHD (Strauss & Kephart, 1955), it is now recognized that the individual's inability to invest in the task, rather than the presence of distractors, is the primary problem. It is also important to acknowledge that in laboratory settings, inattentiveness is not consistently demonstrated for this population. When tasks are repetitive, uninteresting, require effort, and not of the individual's choosing, the individual with ADHD appears to experience the greatest problems. As those variables modulate, fewer problems with attention are noted. Thus, it is less that these individuals are inattentive than that they are inconsistent in applying their attentional skills under certain circumstances.

2. *Overarousal.* People with ADHD have been consistently described as excessively restless, overactive, and easily aroused emotionally. The earliest description of the adult with ADHD noted problems with stress intolerance (P. H. Wender, 1975). It is important to realize that the symptomatic descriptor of hyperactivity best discriminates the person with ADHD from those with other disorders (Halperin, Matier, Bedi, Vandsheep, & Newcorn, 1992). The individual's difficulty controlling body movements is apparent when he or she

must remain in one place for a long time. As younger children, most are overactive, although some are simply restless and fidgety. Problems with hyperactivity appear to diminish in overt severity as individuals mature into adolescence and later adulthood. However, adults with ADHD are often described by others and describe themselves as restless. These individuals also become emotionally aroused more quickly. Their extremes of emotion are much more intense as well. They also appear to have a lower threshold of emotional responsiveness to environmental stress.

3. *Impulsivity.* People with ADHD have consistently been reported to experience difficulty before they act. They appear not to weigh consequences effectively, nor do these consequences influence their future behavior. They have difficulty following rule-governed patterns of behavior (Barkley, 1981a). For these people, the problem is less not knowing what to do than stopping long enough for that knowledge to influence their behavior. Thus, they do not always do what they know. As a result, others tend to view them as impetuous, unthinking, and unable to benefit from experience. This group is often described as repeat offenders. Because of their poor ability to use knowledge gained from repeated experience, they require close supervision and are extremely frustrating to everyone they deal with on a daily basis. Often this pattern of behavior is perceived as purposeful, noncaring, and oppositional when in reality it reflects the individual's immediate need for gratification and inability to stop and think. This misunderstanding creates repetitive problems. The solution may lie in management and education to improve incompetent behavior rather than in punishment to deter noncompliance (S. Goldstein, 1995).

4. *Difficulty with gratification.* Children, and adults for that matter, with ADHD do not appear to work well for long-term rewards. They appear to need brief, repeated payoffs instead of a single, delayed reward. The frequency, predictability, saliency, and immediacy of reinforcers appear to operate differently for this population. In addition, researchers have suggested that this population may not respond to rewards in the same manner as others (Haenlein & Caul, 1987). Methylphenidate treatment has also been found to increase sustained effort for reinforcement on difficult tasks (P. C. Wilkinson, Kercher, McMahon, & Sloane, 1995). Reward mechanisms may underlie the therapeutic effects of stimulants observed across a wide range of tasks and settings. Reinforcers do not appear to change the ADHD individual's behavior in the long term. Once the reward and the accompanying structure of the behavior change program is extinguished, the ADHD individual often quickly regresses to preintervention behavioral or performance problems. S. Goldstein and Goldstein (1990) hypothesize that because this population receives a higher rate of repeated negative reinforcement than others, they learn to respond to demands when an aversive stimulus is removed contingent upon performance rather than when a future reward is promised. The operation of this model in adulthood results in individuals passively waiting for aversive consequences to motivate them to complete important tasks (e.g., school assignments, work duties, and tax payments). Even spouses fall prey to this model of negative reinforcement. The high rate of negative reinforcement this group of ADHD individuals receives is not only very time consuming but also seductively attractive. When applied by a parent, spouse, educator, or employer, it appears to be effective. With each use, however, the probability increases that the next day a similar level of negative attention will be necessary to stimulate the individual's response. Very clearly, as S. Goldstein (1995) notes, "negative reinforcement does not build responsibility and independence, two characteristics that this ADHD population . . . very much need[s] to

develop" (p. 61). Thus, for people with ADHD, behavioral interventions may manage behavior but they do not seem to produce long-term modification consistently or efficiently when consequences are withdrawn.

Developmental Course and Comorbidity

Although children with ADHD experience many of the same problems, each child manifests symptoms and associated comorbid problems in a unique way (S. Goldstein & Goldstein, 1990). As children mature, behavior that is easily overlooked at one age may not be tolerated at another. A brief introduction will be provided about infant and toddler behavior related to early symptoms of ADHD. A more in-depth analysis will then discuss issues involving school-aged children.

It has been suggested that approximately 10% of infants and toddlers have a history of difficult childhood temperament (Carey, 1970; Chess & Thomas, 1986; A. Thomas & Chess, 1977). As infants, these children may withdraw in a negative manner from new stimulation. They often do not deal well with changes in routine. They have been reported to demonstrate negative mood significantly more often than positive mood on a daily basis. They are often described as rather intense in responding to events in their environment. Follow-up of a population of three-year-olds defined by the criteria of negative mood and intense reaction demonstrated that by school age, all the children experienced school-related problems (Terestman, 1980). It is suggested that as many as 70% of this difficult infant population developed school problems detected in follow-up studies. Infants with difficult temperament are reported to be extremely active, to cry at a very high pitch, to be difficult to comfort, and to be inconsistent in sleep and appetite patterns; they are often described by parents as obstinate and obstructive (Ross & Ross, 1982). There is also an unexplained higher incidence of formula allergy in this group. Longitudinal studies have suggested that early difficult temperament may interact with a number of family and environmental variables, including socioeconomic status, to contribute to a wide range of childhood behavioral problems (Werner, 1994; Werner & Smith, 1977).

It has been hypothesized that the pattern of difficult temperament exhibited by some infants has a significant effect on the relationship and bond between parents and child. Difficult infants challenge even the best and most competent parents. An impaired parent-child relationship is often the result, which then affects the child's future development and likely adult status. Thus a theme repeated throughout this text must be emphasized here: The childhood experiences of individuals with ADHD or LD significantly shape the future life outcomes of these individuals. Battle and Lacey (1972) report that disharmonious early mother-child relationships were frequently experienced by children later diagnosed as having behavioral problems consistent with ADD. Although mothers in general have been found to be accurate reporters of their children's behavior (Faraone, Biederman, & Milberger, 1995), mothers of difficult infants subjectively report experiencing higher levels of parenting stress and lower levels of self-esteem (Mash & Johnston, 1983). Mash and Johnston reported that the greater the intensity of these two variables, the more inaccurate the mother's perception of her child's problems. This inaccuracy further fueled a lack of fit between parent and child and subsequent escalating behavioral problems. As has been well recognized, this pattern of misbehavior for higher risk individuals, such as those with ADHD, persists into adulthood for the majority.

The erratic nature and variability of ADHD symptoms are sometimes a function of situation, making identification of at-risk preschoolers difficult (Whalen & Henker, 1980). S. B. Campbell

(1985) describes the inconsistencies often observed in young children's behavior as a function of setting. Some children may do well in structured situations but be out of control when there is less structure. Although some researchers and clinicians choose to see these early symptoms of ADHD as transient problems of young children, research data suggest that ignoring these signs results in the loss of valuable treatment time. At least 60%–70% of children later diagnosed with ADHD could have been identified by their symptoms during the preschool years (Barkley, 1981b; N. J. Cohen, Sullivan, Minde, Novak, & Helwig, 1981). It has also been suggested that the earlier children with ADHD symptoms are identified, the worse their life course outcome (McGee, Williams, & Feehan, 1992). Thus, our ability to identify at-risk children early does not appear to insulate them from future life problems.

It has also been reported that young children manifesting ADHD symptoms present with greater than chance speech and language problems (Baker & Cantwell, 1987; Beitchman, 1987). They are often reported to develop a wide range of behavior problems (Cantwell & Baker, 1977; Cantwell, Baker, & Mattison, 1981; N. J. Cohen, Davine, & Meloche-Kelly, 1989). In a study of behavior problems in 116 preschoolers, Love and Thompson (1988) reported that 65% manifested a diagnosable language disorder. Of this group, almost three-quarters also met the diagnostic criteria for ADD. Beitchman, Hood, Rochon, and Peterson (1989) reported that risk of a psychiatric disorder, particularly ADHD, is greatest among children with general linguistic impairment as opposed to those experiencing specific problems with receptive or expressive language. Language-impaired children often have difficulty advancing from a tactile to a visual-linguistic means of dealing with their environment (Funk & Ruppert, 1984). Thus, preschoolers with ADHD and linguistic impairments need to touch and feel objects and people as a means of gaining sensory input from their environment. Unfortunately, they do so in an impulsive, disorganized manner. It has also been suggested that the combination of boundless energy, poor judgment, and limited reflective skill results in increased accidental poisonings, injuries, and trips to the emergency room for this population (Ross & Ross, 1982; Stewart, Thatch, & Freidin, 1970). It is important to note, however, that more recent data suggest that it is the presentation of conduct disorder that more powerfully mediates these types of problems (Davidson, Taylor, Sandberg, & Thorley, 1992). This combination of issues contributes to the increased incidence of social problems among young ADHD children. This pattern presents well beyond the 20% of the normal population reported to experience social difficulty (S. B. Campbell & Cluss, 1982). Campbell and Cluss reported that preschoolers with ADHD demonstrated a disproportionate rate of aggressive interactions with their peers, a pattern of behavior likely signaling risk for later onset of other disruptive disorders. This group of children has been reported to engage in more transitional behavior, to be less competent with peers, and to be less cooperative in group settings (Alessandri, 1992).

Thus, before the young child demonstrating early risk signs of ADHD or already carrying a diagnosis of ADHD enters an organized school setting, "his or her temperament exerts a significant influence on life experience and interaction with the environment, family and peers" (S. Goldstein, 1995, p. 63). In an escalating cycle, adult and peer responses to this pattern of behavior further shape the dysfunctionality and lack of fit between this group of children and their environment. This pattern also significantly affects self-esteem and general personality. Children manifesting early signs of ADHD enter school with a number of misperceptions about themselves and their environment. From the very beginning within school settings, they appear to be victims of a temperament that makes it difficult for them to persist with repetitive, effortful, uninteresting activities and of a learning history that accustoms them to beginning but not completing tasks.

Some researchers have suggested that children with ADHD are intellectually less competent than their same-age peers (Palkes & Stewart, 1972). It is more likely, however, that their weak performance on intellectual tasks results from the impact of impulsivity and inattention on test-taking behavior rather than from an innate lack of intelligence (Ross & Ross, 1982). A number of researchers have reported that the range of intellectual skill among children and adolescents with ADHD is similar to that found in the normal population (Loney, 1974; Prinz & Loney, 1974). Thus, 2% of the ADHD population demonstrate subborderline intellectual skills, and 2% demonstrate gifted intelligence.

The connection between intellect and ADHD may be rooted in the relationship between inhibition and executive functions involving working memory, internal speech, self-regulation of affect, and analysis and synthesis of daily life experiences (Barkley, 1994). Specifically, ADHD may affect intelligence in two ways: it may affect, to a small degree, the acquisition of abilities and, to a larger degree, the application of abilities. Empirical research suggests that IQ and ADHD are linked, both among otherwise normal individuals (Hinshaw, Morrison, Carte, & Cornsweet, 1987) and among those with disruptive behavioral problems (Sonuga-Barke, Lamparelli, Stevenson, Thompson, & Henry, 1994). Sonuga-Barke et al. and others find a significant negative association between degree of rated hyperactive-impulsive behavior and measures of intelligence. In contrast, associations between ratings of conduct problems and intelligence are much smaller or even nonsignificant, particularly when hyperactive-impulsive problems are partialed out (Lynam, Moffitt, & Stouthamer-Loeber, 1993; Sonuga-Barke et al., 1994). This line of research suggests that the relationship of verbal IQ and achievement to disruptive behavior may be specific to the hyperactive-impulsive element of the disruptive problems (Hinshaw, 1992).

Many studies have found that when children are selected for study without equating groups for intellect, ADHD groups differ significantly from control groups, especially in verbal intelligence (Barkley & Cunningham, 1979; Barkley, Karlsson, & Pollard, 1985; Mariani & Barkley, 1995; McGee et al., 1992). These differences have also been found between hyperactive boys and their normal siblings (Barkley et al., 1985; Halperin & Gittelman, 1982). These findings suggest that deficits in intellectual ability may be an inherent part of ADHD. Thus, matching individuals with ADHD to control individuals based on IQ, or controlling for IQ differences statistically, may reduce or eliminate the effects of the independent variable (ADHD) one is attempting to study. As Werry, Elkind, and Reeves (1987) noted, group differences in verbal IQ should not be viewed as an artifact of group selection or as a source of error to be removed. Such error may in fact account for only 6%–10% of the variance in verbal IQ (Barkley, 1995a). Primarily, however, ADHD affects the ability to perform and to use one's intelligence effectively; it may directly affect intellectual development only to a minor degree. Further, Zentall, Smith, Lee, and Wieczorek (1994) have demonstrated that boys with ADHD earn significantly lower problem-solving scores on tests of mathematical concepts and show slower computational performance.

Clinicians often observe that more intelligent individuals with ADHD manage to survive through much of their school career. They may not be referred for problems related to academics until the later high school grades, when performance and organizational demands exceed even their abilities to compensate intellectually.

Early research shows that children with ADHD underachieve academically in elementary school relative to their same-age peers (Cantwell & Satterfield, 1978; Minde et al., 1971). Such children have been reported to experience a higher incidence of LD (Lambert & Sandoval, 1980; L. B. Silver, 1981). However, much of this research struggled to control potentially intervening variables. In 1976, based only on grade scores, Safer and Allen reported that 80% of children with LD experienced hyperactivity. Holborow and Berry (1986b) reported that 41% of a learning-disabled population exhibited symptoms of ADD. Reading and mathematics problems have been reported to occur at beyond a chance level for those with ADHD (Pennington, Grossier, & Welsh, 1993; Zentall & Terkis, 1993). The group with ADHD-I appears to experience the greatest problems (Lamminmaki et al., 1995). In contrast, Halperin, Gittelman, Klein, and Rudel (1984) reported that only 9% of a sample of 241 elementary school children with ADHD suffered from reading disability. It is now reasonable to conclude that, as in Shaywitz (1986), the majority of children with ADHD achieve as well as the normal population in elementary school. However, in this particular study, one-third of the learning-disabled children also met diagnostic criteria for ADD. Thus, although most children with ADD do not experience specific LD in elementary school, children with ADD constitute a significant group within the learning-disabled population. Shaywitz and Shaywitz (1988b) concluded that although the overlap between LD and ADD is real, "it is not reasonable to believe that all or even a majority of ADHD children have LD" (p. 457).

The causal relationship between LD and ADHD is unclear. A recent series of studies concluded that approximately 20%–30% of children with ADHD experience concomitant LD (Barkley, 1990b). Nussbaum, Grant, Roman, Poole, and Bigler (1990) found that older children with ADHD were more likely than younger children with the disorder to experience academic and social-emotional problems. It has been suggested that by adolescence the ADHD group will fall behind in academic skills requiring practice (e.g., spelling, punctuation, and mathematical facts).

De Sonneville, Nijokiktjien, and Vos (1994) found a very clear pattern of differences in information processing between ADHD and control groups, but also between medication responders and nonresponders. The ADHD group was slower, less accurate, and more variable in their responses to a variety of measures. Problems were reported in encoding, memory search, and decision, as well as in focus and sustained attention and vigilance. Discriminant analyses reported a specific deficit profile, with the ADHD group demonstrating a notably slow and inefficient memory search process, an inability to handle complex information, and reduced sustained attention. Differences between medication responders and nonresponders appeared to be associated with an increase in the severity of those deficits, as well as with the failure to ignore irrelevant information and to control impulsivity. Interestingly, the latter characteristic was not found to discriminate between controls and medication nonresponders.

In a study of 5,000 students, aged 5–14 years, Rowe and Rowe (1992) found that regardless of family socioeconomic status, age, and gender, students' inattentiveness had a strong negative effect on achievement, attitude toward reading, and reading activities at home. Symptoms of ADHD, therefore, may exert a much more powerful influence on academic drive and related behaviors than do socioeconomic variables. Inattentive behavior appeared to lead to reduced achievement and less reading activity at home, which then led to increased reports of inattentiveness in class.

Some researchers have suggested that the achievement needs of children with ADHD and LD can be conceptualized as reflecting a single causative factor, namely, language deficit (Cherkes-Julkowski & Stolzenberg, 1983). The preponderance of the literature, however, does not support a single-factor explanation (Barkley, 1990b; S. Goldstein & Goldstein, 1990). It is clear that youngsters with ADHD or LD require special programming. However, the performance and achievement problems of each group are generated by qualitatively different sets of factors and disabilities. Although ADHD may prevent a child from achieving his or her academic potential (Stott, 1981), it is well recognized that LD often makes a child look more inattentive than others (McGee & Share, 1988). It is also clear that ADHD coexists with LD at levels beyond chance, possibly due to an underlying set of similar cognitive, language-related deficits. In a study of 123 children followed over an eight-year period into adolescence, Fischer, Barkley, Fletcher, and Smallish (1993) concluded that adolescent academic skills were related to childhood cognitive and academic competence. School conduct was predicted by other variables, including family stress. Childhood impulsivity, hyperactivity, and paternal antisocial acts were associated with later development of oppositional defiant behavior. Interestingly, these authors concluded that promoting family and parental competence, as well as assessing and treating defiant and aggressive behavior early on, may improve the outcome for individuals with ADHD.

It would appear reasonable to conclude then that, although the incidence of LD among children with ADHD is higher than in the normal population, the majority of inattentive children do not present with learning problems (Cantwell & Satterfield, 1978; S. Goldstein & Goldstein, 1990; for a review, see S. Goldstein, 1995) and that, conversely, the majority of learning-disabled children do not have ADHD. The data, however, are fairly powerful in suggesting that by the later school years the cumulative effect of ADHD on a student's ability to complete tasks hurts academic achievement (Loney, Kramer, & Milich, 1981). Meichenbaum and Goodman (1969) believe that this pattern may begin in the first years of life. They report, for example, that impulsive kindergartners perform worse than reflective kindergartners on a range of basic cognitive skills. Children with ADHD may perform poorly at school because of their inability to develop effective reasoning skills, leading to a slow but steady decrease in intellectual development and achievement (Achenbach, 1975). Reader, Harris, Schuerholz, and Denckla (1994) found executive function weaknesses (self-regulation, response inhibition, cognitive flexibility, etc.) in a group of children with ADHD. However, a consistent relationship has not always been reported (Lorys, Hynd, & Lahey, 1990; Pennington et al., 1993). Reader et al. (1994) evaluated a sample of 48 children on a battery of standardized tests sensitive to executive dysfunction. Below average performance was found on the Wisconsin Card Sorting Test and on a continuous performance test (Tests of Variables of Attention) but on no other measures. Unlike Pennington et al.'s (1993) report on ADHD and its relationship to LD, no significant differences between the ADHD reading-disordered and non-reading-disordered groups were found on any of the executive function measures. Reader et al. (1994) concluded that children with ADHD may be at risk for executive function problems but that this finding may not be consistent and that executive functioning may be only moderately correlated with intelligence scores.

In classroom settings throughout elementary and secondary school, the ADHD population is described as daydreaming and as disinterested in tasks the teacher may be emphasizing (Douglas, 1972). These tendencies lead to significantly more nonproductive activity, a pattern that often continues into adulthood and at the workplace. Students with ADHD often demonstrate an uneven and unpredictable pattern of behavior, distressing teachers and often leading them to conclude that the student is noncompliant rather than incompetent. Not surprisingly, the overall rate of negative teacher-child interactions differs between normal students and students with ADHD. For example, teachers have been reported to be more intense and controlling when interacting with boys with ADHD than with other male students (Whalen, Henker, & Dotemoto, 1981).

Individuals with ADHD may affect their environment as well. Greater rates of negative teacher-child interactions involving normal students have been reported in classrooms containing children with reported attention problems (S. B. Campbell, Endman, & Bernfeld, 1977). Sociometric and play studies suggest that children with ADHD are less often chosen by peers as best friends, partners in activities, or seatmates (Pelham & Milich, 1984). Moreover, this group is reported to be aware of their difficulties, which likely precipitates lower self-esteem, feeding on itself into adulthood (Glow & Glow, 1980). It is important to recognize that the ability to develop and maintain appropriate peer relationships has been repeatedly found to be an important predictor of positive adult adjustment and behavior (Cowen, Pederson, Babigan, Izzo, & Trost, 1973). Pelham and Bender (1982) report that problems with peer interactions are an efficient way of distinguishing children with ADHD from normal children. Diagnostically, social problems experienced by the ADHD group are as powerful as symptoms of inattention, impulsivity, and hyperactivity. Teacher observations of the social interaction of children with ADHD frequently describe fighting, interrupting, and being disliked or neglected (Pelham & Bender, 1982). Mothers of hyperactive children frequently report that their children have social problems (S. B. Campbell & Paulauskas, 1979). Barkley (1981b) reported that, according to ratings they provided, 80% of parents of hyperactive children believe that their children experience serious social problems. Waddell (1984) suggested that the social problems of children with ADHD, especially those with hyperactive-impulsive problems, increase rather than decrease as they grow older. "Behavioral excesses leading to rejection and social skill deficits leading to low acceptance" (p. 560) clearly set children with ADHD apart from others at fairly young ages (Pelham & Milich, 1984).

Researchers have also asked whether, in addition to the severity of ADHD, the age at which a child is identified as experiencing ADHD may affect outcome. McGee et al. (1992) studied three groups of children identified with ADHD at age 11 years. Onset of the disorder for one group occurred during the preschool years. For the second group, symptoms were noted immediately on entering school or during the first year of school. For the third group, symptoms were not observed or reported until the end of the second year of school. Onset appeared to be strongly related to informant source at age 11. Three-quarters of the children with onset of problems before age six were experiencing one or more *DSM-III* disorder. Keeping in mind that the female population in this study was small, none of the females demonstrated the late-onset type of ADHD. The two early-onset groups for both males and females displayed what appeared to be a pervasive pattern of attention deficit associated with teacher and self-identified problems. McGee et al. suggested that when attention deficit behavior is first observed later in one's school career, it may occur secondary to reading failure and may not reflect a long-term disorder of impulse and inattention. This conclusion fits the hypotheses of others (Barkley, 1981a). As noted earlier, the data suggest that early onset ADHD has a poor course and increased risk of comorbid problems. Thus, it likely has increased risk for long-lasting impact into adulthood.

Data clearly support the conclusion that all types of disruptive behavior lead to teacher dislike and increase risk for social rejection by peers (Wentzel & Asher, 1995). In elementary school classrooms, children with ADHD exhibit more frequent negative verbalizations and acts of physical aggression than their peers (Abikoff, Gittelman-Klein, & Klein, 1977; Whalen, Henker, Collins, Fink, & Dotemoto, 1979). In play situations, these children exhibit 10 times as many negative verbalizations directed at others and three times as many acts of physical aggression (Pelham & Bender, 1982). It is in fact the absolute number of negative interactions, and not the total number of social interactions or the frequency of positive interactions, that distinguishes children with ADHD from nonaffected children (Pelham & Bender, 1982; Riddle & Rapoport, 1976).

The seeds of the interpersonal difficulty many adults with ADHD experience appear to be planted in childhood. Children with ADHD are reported to experience social difficulties involving attending to the conversation of others, engaging in disturbing behavior, being aggressive and immature, and struggling with basic communication. Those with ADHD have also been reported to have difficulty adapting their behavior to different situational demands (Whalen, Henker, Collins, McAuliffe, & Vaux, 1979). Aggressive behavior has also been found to be a negative predictor for positive treatment outcome for ADHD children (Loney & Milich, 1981). Pelham and Bender (1982) suggest that impulsivity is more highly correlated with peer problems than is hyperactivity. Thus the child with ADHD whose behavior is highly impulsive and aggressive appears to be at greatest risk of progressing to more serious adult problems.

In a study of 249 elementary school children with histories of low achievement, LD, and ADHD, Flicek (1992) reported that serious problems with peer rejection, peer popularity, and social behavior were most strongly related to the combination of ADHD and LD. The natural setting appears to best discriminate ADHD problems. Platzman et al. (1992), after reviewing 39 studies, concluded that classroom behavior distinguished ADHD children from nonaffected children better than laboratory studies. The behaviors that most consistently distinguished the ADHD group from comparison groups included measures of attention, activity, and vocalization. Off-task behavior, excessive large motor activity, and negative vocalization (speaking when you are not supposed to) all demonstrated differential diagnostic validity for the ADHD group.

Competent social skills are essential for life success. Children with ADHD are often described qualitatively as immature and incompetent socially. Some may lack basic social skills. Their deficits result from a pattern of high-incidence, low-impact behaviors. They struggle to join an ongoing activity or conversation. They do not know how to take turns. They appear to lack the basic social graces. These are not terribly aversive behaviors, but they result in this group of children's being less socially popular. Other children with ADHD, especially those with greater hyperactive-impulsive problems, demonstrate a pattern of low-incidence, high-impact behaviors. These aggressive acts, although they occur infrequently, result in the child's or adolescent's being rejected and disliked (Pelham & Milich, 1984).

It has been suggested that ADHD, oppositional defiant disorder, and conduct disorder fall along the continuum of increasing levels of familial and etiological factors as well as correspondingly severe disability (Biederman, Faraone, Keenan, & Tsuang, 1991). Thus ADHD may be more powerfully mediated by genetic and biological factors, while conduct disorder may be more significantly affected by experiential factors. Cummings (1995), in fact, goes so far as to suggest that oppositional defiant disorder and conduct disorder may be genetically linked to ADHD. Further, the development of childhood ADHD in and of itself has been posited as a significant risk factor for the later development of conduct disorder (Gittelman et al., 1985; Loeber, Stouthamer-Loeber, Van Kammen, & Farrington, 1991; Mannuzza et al., 1991). The key factor for conduct disorder in adolescents is thought by some to be the persistence of childhood ADHD (Mannuzza et al., 1991). Mannuzza et al. (1993) report this connection in adulthood as well. These authors suggest that the persistence rather than the presence of ADHD is critical in determining the risk for developing conduct disorder and later adult problems.

Studying 177 clinic-referred preadolescent boys followed for six years, Loeber et al. (1995) attempted to identify the boys who appeared at greatest risk to develop conduct disorder and the factors that appeared to contribute most. Of all conduct disorder symptoms, physical fighting best predicted the onset of conduct disorder. ADHD predicted an increased risk for early-onset conduct disorder. However, parental substance abuse, low socioeconomic status, and oppositional behavior appeared to be the primary factors in contributing to a boy's progression to conduct disorder. Based on these data, ADHD was implicated in early-onset conduct disorder (prior to age 10) but not in late-onset conduct disorder. These authors suggested, however, that the group of boys with early-onset conduct disorder fared far worse in adolescence than those with the late-onset disorder. There is no doubt that impulsivity in and of itself is a risk factor contributing to the development of disruptive and, later antisocial, behavior problems (J. L. White et al., 1994). However, it is also very clear that other factors influence the development of antisocial behavior, including, as noted, parental psychopathology, negative child-rearing practices, and academic failure (Hinshaw, Lahey, & Hart, 1993; J. G. Parker & Asher, 1987; Patterson, DeBaryshe, & Ramsey, 1989).

Further, Loney et al. (1981) reported that aggression in children with ADHD predicted high risk for the development of conduct disorder but not necessarily hyperactivity. In contrast, Mannuzza et al. (1991) found that children with ADHD who did not display conduct disorder at a young age were in fact still at risk for an antisocial disorder in adolescence. Differences are likely the result of variations in data collection methods. Abikoff and Klein (1992) suggested that the manner in which aggression is defined and evaluated may be critical in determining comorbidity. Aggression may not be a permanent trait. Some children with ADHD who are not aggressive may eventually develop aggressive behavior, putting them at risk for conduct disorder. These authors suggested that conduct disorder and ADHD share a common dysfunction, one that maximizes interpersonal conflict and then precipitates the development of aggressive behavior. Aggressive behavior in and of itself may be insufficient for a diagnosis of conduct disorder, but it is a key symptomatic problem. The co-occurrence of ADHD and other family adversity (e.g., depressed mother or alcoholic father) likely increases the risk of the development of conduct disorder (S. Goldstein & Goldstein, 1992).

Schachar and Tannock (1995) evaluated the relationship between ADHD and conduct disorder. In a study of males 7–11 years of age with a combination of ADHD and conduct disorder, these authors concluded that ADHD and conduct disorder reflected a distinct set of symptomatic problems. The comorbid condition of ADHD and conduct disorder appeared to be a hybrid of pure ADHD and pure conduct disorder. Therefore, it was unclear whether either of these two disorders caused the other. The hybrid theory suggests that one set of risk factors increases the likelihood of the other. The environmental adversity of conduct disorder might lead to cognitive deficits and developmental delay. The impulsive, poorly regulated behavior of children with ADHD would likely lead to conduct-disordered behavior. These authors concluded that psychosocial adversity is central to the development of both conduct disorder and ADHD combined with conduct disorder.

Based on a continuing series of studies, Schachar and Tannock (1995) reported that a group of children with ADHD demonstrated a specific pattern of weak inhibitory control and response alteration as well as delayed reading development. A comparison group with conduct disorder had a history of greater environmental adversity and weak mathematical skills. Finally, the group experiencing ADHD and conduct disorder demonstrated both sets of problems.

Other authors have suggested that the group with comorbid ADHD and conduct disorder is more severely affected (McGee, Williams, & Silva, 1984). Still others have suggested that social cognition deficits may be responsible for the combined disorder (Milich & Dodge, 1984). The combined group has been reported to experience more developmental delay than the pure ADHD group and more psychosocial adversity than the pure conduct-disordered group (Szatmari, Boyle, & Offord, 1989). Szatmari et al. cautiously concluded that treatment for ADHD "might reduce the risk of developing conduct disorder." Their findings provide additional evidence that cognitive factors, especially poor inhibitory control and difficulty with cognitive flexibility, play a role in the development of ADHD.

The impact of one symptomatic problem on another has not been well studied or understood. Abikoff, Courtney, Pelham, and Koplewicz (1993) asked teachers to rate classroom videotapes of child actors following prepared scripts characteristic of pure ADHD, pure oppositional defiant disorder, or normal behavior. Teacher ratings of hyperactivity were accurate for the ADHD group but were spuriously high for conduct problems associated with oppositional defiant disorder. In contrast, teacher ratings of oppositional, conduct problem behaviors were accurate whether or not hyperactivity was included. These data raise the possibility that the reported comorbidity patterns among ADHD and oppositional or conduct problems may be a function of negative halo effect. A similar unidirectional halo effect was reported by Schachar, Sandberg, and Rutter (1986). This issue may explain the asymmetrical overlap of teachers' ratings of hyperactivity and oppositional behavior in school-aged children (Pelham, Gnagy, Greenslade, & Milich, 1992). Very clearly, a child's noncompliant behavior exerts a negative halo effect on ratings by adults with whom the child interacts (Bauermeister, 1992).

In clinical samples, the influence of conduct problems on the diagnosis of ADHD is not straightforward. Often ADHD symptoms precede the development of conduct disorder. This pattern has been reported in retrospective and prospective studies (Mannuzza et al., 1991). It is important to note, however, that a small subgroup of children with ADHD do not in fact receive comorbid diagnoses. Further, this group of children can be clearly distinguished from children with pure anxiety or other disruptive disorders (Halperin et al., 1993).

Compared directly to children with conduct disorder, those with ADHD appear to have lower IQ and academic performance, as well as substantially lower rates of parental psychopathology (Lahey et al., 1988; Schachar, 1991). Maternal rejection and poor parental supervision, on the other hand, as well as parental alcohol abuse, appear more strongly associated with conduct disorder than with ADHD (Loeber, Brinthaupt, & Green, 1990; Reeves, Werry, Elkind, & Zametkin, 1987).

In an interesting analysis, Halperin et al. (1990) suggested that impulsivity rather than inattention may be differentially associated with comorbid problems. Children experiencing comorbid disruptive disorders with their ADHD made more impulsive errors on a continuous performance task than those who had ADHD but were not hyperactive and aggressive. Children with comorbid ADHD and conduct disorder have been reported to experience greater severity of a wide range of symptoms (J. L. Walker, Lahey, Hynd, & Frame, 1987), increased risk for later antisocial disorders (Farrington, Loeber, & Van Kammen, 1990), greater levels of parental psychopathology and psychosocial adversity (Lahey et al., 1988; Schachar & Wachsmuth, 1990), and greater peer rejection (Johnston & Pelham, 1986) than individuals with either disorder alone. As Barkley has hypothesized, the link between ADHD and other disruptive disorders may in fact relate to impulsive problems. Further, parents of children with comorbid ADHD and conduct disorder present with higher rates of psychopathology, weaker parenting skills, and greater marital discord than parents of children with either disorder alone (Lahey et al., 1988; Schachar & Wachsmuth, 1990).

In the Ontario Child Health Study, a population of almost 2,700 children aged 4–16 years, ADHD and conduct disorder occurred more often than by chance, especially among females (Szatmari et al., 1989). Children with ADHD in this population were younger and had experienced more developmental delays and less psychosocial disadvantage than children with just conduct disorder. No differences were found for other impairments. Children with both disorders represented what Szatmari et al. (1989) described as a "true hybrid" disorder rather than one diagnosis or the other. These authors concluded that conduct disorder reflects "a disorder related to psychosocial disadvantage" whereas ADHD appears to be a "developmental disorder correlated with other maturational impairments" (p. 871).

It has been suggested that many of the primary symptoms of ADHD diminish by adolescence (G. Weiss & Hechtman, 1986). However, a review of related research shows clearly that inattentive adolescents continue to experience significant problems (Milich & Loney, 1979; for a review, see E. H. Wender, 1995). In their sample of hyperactive children followed into adolescence, Barkley, Fischer, Edelbrock, and Smallish (1990) found that at least 80% continued to manifest symptoms consistent with ADHD while 60% demonstrated a second disruptive disorder. Conduct disorder appeared to best account for most but not all of the additional problems in this population. From 20% to 60% of adolescents with ADHD have been reported to be involved in antisocial behavior; normal occurrence is suggested to be 3%–4% (Sassone, Lambert, & Sandoval, 1982; Satterfield, Hoppe, & Schell, 1982). More recently, however, it has been demonstrated that the high prevalence of antisocial problems in the ADHD population likely reflects the comorbidity of ADHD with other disruptive disorders (principally conduct disorder; Barkley, Fischer, et al., 1990; Loney, 1986). As will be discussed in the adult outcome chapter, the development of more serious disruptive problems appears to be a critical predictor variable in determining the adult outcome of an individual with ADHD. Other studies have reported that as many as one-third of adolescents with ADHD have been suspended from school at least once (Ackerman et al., 1977), with up to 80% falling behind one or more years in at least one basic academic subject (Cantwell & Satterfield, 1978; Loney et al., 1981). Again, although these older studies may be describing a population somewhat different from the current ADHD population, the implication is clear. The secondary problems of ADHD appear to persist, intensify, and become increasingly complex in affected adolescents.

Adolescents with ADHD, compared to a normal control group, have been reported by parents and teachers to experience significantly more problems (Barkley, Anastopoulos, et al., 1991). In this population, 68% received a diagnosis of oppositional defiance, with 39% progressing to conduct disorder. Reported problems included impairment in social competence, behavioral and emotional adjustment difficulty, and poor school performance. Interestingly, these youths rated themselves as better adjusted than their parents and teachers did. This lack of insight appears to persist into adulthood. This group also demonstrated poor performance when compared with controls on tasks of verbal learning, vigilance, and mathematics. The adolescents with ADHD in this study most commonly experienced problems with theft (30%), followed by assault (27%), vandalism (21%), and disorderly conduct (12%). All of these occurrence rates were significantly higher than in the control group. Once again, it is demonstrated that the progression to more serious conduct and aggressive problems predicts dire outcome for individuals with ADHD.

Martin, Earleywine, Blackson, and Vanyukov (1994) found that the three core symptoms of ADHD—inattention, impulsivity, and hyperactivity—when combined with aggression in male preadolescents strongly predicted later risk for substance abuse. These authors suggested that the four behaviors may represent a single superordinate factor reflecting risk for later substance abuse. Adolescents hospitalized for substance use disorders appear to experience ADHD at a rate approximately equivalent to adolescents hospitalized for other psychiatric problems (approximately one-third with ADHD; Grilo et al., 1995). Thus, ADHD has not been found to be significantly comorbid with substance abuse when the presence of other psychiatric disorders is controlled for. However, when disruptive behavioral disorders were collapsed (conduct disorder, oppositional defiance, and ADHD), there were significantly more disruptive disorders in the substance-abusing group. This finding was principally contributed to by those with conduct disorder (75% conduct disorder vs. 34% other disruptive problems).

Barkley, Anastopoulos, et al. (1991) found that there appear to be differences in mother-adolescent interactions between adolescents with ADHD alone and those with oppositional defiant disorder and ADHD. Both groups experienced greater conflicts with their mothers and more angry conflicts at home than controls. However, the oppositional defiant ADHD adolescents reported more conflicts, endorsed more extreme and unreasonable beliefs about their parental relationships, and demonstrated more negative interactions during what were described as neutral discussions. In addition, their mothers displayed more negative interactions during discussion, more extreme and unreasonable beliefs about their teens, greater personal distress, and less satisfaction in their marriages. Although causality is uncertain, it is likely to be bidirectional. The adolescent with ADHD affects the family, and the family's dysfunction affects the development of additional disruptive problems.

Although it is accepted that depression and ADHD have very different symptoms and life course, differential diagnostic questions addressing mania, manic depressive disorder, or bipolar disorder still remain. Wozniak and Biederman (1994) found that 16% of referred children in their sample met the diagnostic criteria for mania. All but one of the children who met those criteria also met the criteria for ADHD. In an excellent brief overview of differential diagnosis for ADHD and bipolar disorder, Glasser (1995) concludes that children seen for ADHD symptoms who have family histories of bipolar disorder and are demonstrating extreme, irritable, or aggressive behavior or hypomania in response to stimulant treatment may in fact be demonstrating the prodromal signs of bipolar disorder. G. A. Carlson (1993) reported that crying and irritability were characteristic of depressed children and that children receiving diagnoses of ADHD seldom demonstrated evidence of grandiosity, paranoia, hallucinations, or excessively euphoric mood. Neither the depressed nor the manic groups demonstrated the hyperactive-impulsive patterns characteristic of ADHD.

Although one step removed from this text, it is important to note that the consensus of studies on anxiety disorder is that disruptive and anxiety disorders co-occur far more than expected by chance in childhood, adolescence, and adulthood. Females with conduct disorder and an antisocial adult outcome are also reported to develop depressive or anxiety disorders by early adulthood. For both sexes, more severe antisocial behavior in adolescence appears to be associated with increased risk of an emotional disorder. There is strong evidence that depression occurs much more commonly than expected in children and adolescents with conduct disorder (Costello, 1989). The evidence is weaker but still significant for anxiety disorders. No clear-cut etiological explanation can be found for this greater than chance occurrence. It has been suggested that shared risk for both disorders, one disorder's representing the early manifestation of the other, one disorder's being a part of the other, or an artifact of comorbidity related to referral and screening bias may explain this relationship. However, because a significant minority (in some studies nearly 50%) of children with ADHD develop conduct disorder in adolescence, the combined group is undoubtedly at greater risk for developing internalizing disorders, perhaps directly due to these disorders. Milich and Okazaki (1991) suggested that children receiving a diagnosis of ADHD demonstrate greater learned helplessness than their counterparts without ADHD. Such behavior is thought to play an integral role in the development of depressive disorders (Seligman et al., 1984).

In a recent study of a large sample of children and adolescents hospitalized for serious psychiatric problems, Biederman, Faraone, Mick, and Lelon (1995) reported the comorbidity of ADHD and major depression to be 74% in those with severe depression and 77% in those with mild depression. This rate of ADHD represented the greatest comorbidity for these depressed youth. Oppositional defiant disorder was second, and surprisingly, specific anxiety disorders were third. It should be noted that, as found in other studies, when the anxiety disorders were collapsed into one category they moved up to the highest comorbidity with depression.

Steingard, Biederman, Doyle, and Sprich-Buckminster (1992) found that children with ADHD received significantly worse scores on both internalizing and externalizing scales of the Child Behavior Checklist compared with normal controls. The findings, however, appeared to be accounted for by the subgroup of children experiencing attention deficit with hyperactivity. The increased risk for the development of anxiety and depressive problems among the ADHD population, although not a consistent finding by all researchers, appears intuitively valid. Those with ADHD have long been reported to lack confidence and experience greater feelings of helplessness (Battle & Lacey, 1972) and to struggle to maintain social contact (Waddell, 1984).

Pliszka (1992) reported that anxiety problems occurred in one out of four children with a diagnosis of ADHD. Further, children with ADHD and comorbid anxiety problems demonstrated less impulsiveness on laboratory measures and experienced longer, sluggish reaction times on a memory-scanning test than those with ADHD without anxiety (Pliszka, 1989). Biological differences between the ADHD and the ADHD with anxiety groups have also been reported (Pliszka, 1992). The ADHD with anxiety group demonstrated a significantly poorer response to stimulants than those without anxiety, whereas the comorbid oppositional defiant or conduct group with ADHD did not. Pliszka suggested that the ADHD with anxiety group may represent children with a primary anxiety disorder developing inattentiveness. This finding is supported by others (Tannock, Ickowicz, & Schachar, 1995). This group may represent a subtype similar to the ADHD-I type. This ADHD with anxiety group has also demonstrated a response to stimulants at a rate not significantly better than placebo. The incidence of ADHD among children with separation and overanxious disorders is approximately 15%–20% (Pliszka, 1989).

When LD is added to the mix of disruptive and nondisruptive disorders, understanding the complex relationship between each disorder becomes even more complicated. Frick et al. (1991) found in a clinic-referred sample of 177 boys with ADHD or conduct disorder that academic underefficiency was associated equally with both disorders. However, the relation between conduct disorder and academic underefficiency was found to be primarily due to the comorbidity with ADHD. Further, when boys with ADHD were divided into two groups (those with attention problems only and those with co-occurring hyperactivity), no difference was found in the association of learning problems.

A later chapter will review the complex adult outcome for individuals with ADHD. Briefly, Mannuzza et al. (1991) suggested that when hyperactive and inattentive children grow up they do not appear to be at significantly greater risk for developing any disorder other than antisocial problems and substance abuse. This, however, is in contrast to the growing body of findings of others suggesting increased risk of depressive and anxiety disorders as well (Biederman, Munir, & Knee, 1987). Mannuzza et al. (1991) found that in a young adult population with a history of ADHD, 43% still manifested a full syndrome of ADHD symptoms, 32% met the diagnostic criteria for an antisocial disorder, and 10% suffered from drug abuse. Although it was initially suggested that the majority of children with ADHD outgrow core symptoms and are not afflicted as adults, the preponderance of the data suggests that ADHD is a lifetime impairment. The extent of disability into adulthood appears to be a function of many other variables interacting with the ADHD.

Epidemiology

The issue of epidemiology for ADHD in childhood and adolescence is critical to understanding and assessing risk for the lifetime implications of this disorder. Initial efforts to identify hyperactive or inattentive children almost 40 years ago suggested that half the boys and almost half the girls in elementary school settings suffered from these problems (LaPouse & Monk, 1958). Somewhat later studies cited incidence rates as high as 20% (Yanow, 1973). Incidence of a behavioral disorder is based on a number of issues, however. Most important are the diagnostic criteria, the manner in which data are collected (observation, direct assessment, questionnaires, etc.), and the cutoff scores used to differentiate the effective from the uneffective group. Such scores are often determined arbitrarily.

August and Garfinkel (1989) suggest that attention deficit symptoms are reported in approximately 9% of nonreferred elementary school children. These authors described cognitive and behavioral forms of ADHD. The behavioral type included approximately 80% of the identified population. These children appeared to meet the combined *DSM-IV* criteria, reflecting inattentive, impulsive, and hyperactive problems. Of those demonstrating more severe difficulties, conduct disorder was a second diagnosis. The cognitive, less prevalent type of ADHD constituted the remainder of the identified population. This group included children with severe academic underachievement and reported inattention, mild impulsivity, and overactivity. This group of children was also described as experiencing problems with information processing involving inadequate coding and retrieval of linguistic information characteristic of reading disability as measured by neuropsychological tests. Children with the behavioral type of ADHD did not exhibit these test-based deficits.

When a consistent set of diagnostic criteria is applied across situations, using ecologically valid means of assessment, the incidence rate for ADHD drops to a reasonable 1%–6% (Lambert, Sandoval, & Sassone, 1978). Recent authors estimate ADHD prevalence among children and adolescents to be in the range of 3%–5% (Barkley, 1990b; S. Goldstein & Goldstein, 1990). Prevalence estimates depend on a number of variables, including assessment criteria, sampling procedures, and population studied (epidemiological vs. clinical). A higher incidence of ADHD as well as other adjustment and developmental problems in children is reported in lower socioeconomic areas. This higher prevalence may result from environmental or family variables as well as from the likelihood that a percentage of children with ADHD become adults with the same affliction. In adulthood, they may not succeed, they fall to a low socioeconomic stratum, and their children cluster in certain neighborhood schools.

ADHD is estimated to be five to nine times more prevalent in males than females (for a review, see S. Goldstein & Goldstein, 1990; Ross & Ross, 1982). The majority of the studies cited are based on clinic-referred samples, however. In epidemiological studies, the ratio of males to females is closer to 3:1 (for a review, see S. Goldstein & Goldstein, 1990). Lahey et al. (1994), as previously noted, report a 4:1 ratio for ADHD-I and an 8:1 ratio for ADHD-C. It is important to note that the incidence of conduct disorder in 3%–7% of children appears to occur at a male-to-female ratio of 2:1 or 3:1 (Robins, 1991). Definitive figures for oppositional defiant disorder are still unavailable (Hinshaw, 1992). Thus, the comorbidity of these other disruptive disorders as well as other family and psychiatric variables could influence the gender ratio observed for ADHD. It is also well recognized that symptomatic problems among four- and five-year-olds are more frequently found in males than in females and reflect a general externalizing behavioral disability. Among this population, boys are often described as having more trouble concentrating and being more restless and difficult to control than girls (B. H.

Thomas, Byrne, Offord, & Boyle, 1991). Gender has not demonstrated a consistent predictive trend, however. In a long-term follow-up of individuals with ADHD, Klein and Mannuzza (1991) reported that adult dysfunction related to the development of antisocial personality and nonalcohol substance abuse was also associated with criminality. These authors reported that past attempts to identify children with ADHD at greatest risk for poor adult outcome had been unsuccessful in general. Gender was cited as a variable that did not predict outcome.

McGee, Williams, and Silva (1987) suggested that when males and females are compared with same-sex normative groups and controls are present for symptoms of hyperactivity and antisocial behavior, there may be an equal occurrence of attention problems in both sexes. Breen and Altepeter (1990) found a lack of uniform gender differences in parental reports of behavior problems within the home. Males and females with ADHD appeared to present care givers with similar degrees of behavior management problems and situations that precipitated parent-child conflict.

Some researchers have suggested that females with attention deficit may experience more mood, affect, and emotional problems (Kashani, Chapel, & Ellis, 1979). Ackerman, Dykman, and Oglesby (1983) and others have suggested that girls with ADHD experience greater cognitive and language impairments (Berry, Shaywitz, & Shaywitz, 1985). According to the preponderance of the data, however, in clinic-referred samples males and females with ADHD generally have similar problems. Observed differences are more likely to be the result of societal beliefs, attributions, and disparate treatment of males and females than a reflection of actual differences caused by the disorder.

Finally, it is important to recognize in that in clinic-referred samples, the ADHD-C type constituted approximately 70%–80% of the population. This group often presented as more aggressive, unpopular, and seemingly guiltless and with greater conduct difficulties than the ADHD-I type (King & Young, 1982; Pelham, Atkins, Murphy, & White, 1981). The ADHD-I group has been described as shy, socially withdrawn, moderately unpopular, and poor at sports (Lahey, Schaughency, Frame, & Strauss, 1985; Lahey, Schaughency, Strauss, & Frame, 1984). Intelligence testing associates significantly lower full-scale IQ scores and lower verbal IQ scores to ADHD-C than to ADHD-I (C. L. Carlson, Lahey, & Neeper, 1986). Both groups have a higher incidence of depressive behavior, poorer school performance, and lower self-concept than their same-age peers (Lahey et al., 1984).

Cause

Diagnosing ADHD does not require any understanding or reporting of cause, but the issue of cause and its relationship to intervention is of great interest to researchers and clinicians alike.

The cause of ADHD can be viewed environmentally and biologically (S. Goldstein & Goldstein, 1990). Accumulating evidence from genetic, biochemical, neurobehavioral, and neuroimaging studies strongly supports a neurological etiology in most children with ADHD (Hynd et al., 1991). Hynd et al. cautioned, however, that "it cannot be concluded that *all* children with ADHD have symptoms that reflect neurological dysfunction" (p. 182). In addition to heredity, environmental factors can cause ADHD behaviors (Cantwell, 1972; Morrison & Stewart, 1973). A number of commonly suspected environmental causes (e.g., fluorescent lights and diet) have been disproved in general (for a review, see S. Goldstein & Goldstein, 1990; Ingersoll & Goldstein, 1993). Some of these are briefly reviewed below.

Despite intense efforts to demonstrate the effect of sugar on behavior, controlled studies have consistently failed to show that dietary sugar is a significant cause of ADHD (H. K. Kaplan, Wamboldt, & Barnhardt, 1986; Milich & Pelham, 1986). The Feingold hypothesis that food additives and natural salicylates cause ADHD has also been subjected to scientific study. These substances, considered environmental toxins by some, have generally not been demonstrated to have a significant effect on the behavior of the majority of children with ADHD (E. H. Wender, 1986). Nonetheless, a small group of extremely hyperactive preschool boys with histories of significant allergy may in fact respond to dietary manipulation (H. K. Kaplan et al., 1986).

Pregnancy and delivery complications, as reflected by Apgar scores and other birth experiences, do not appear to consistently correlate with the development of ADHD. However, in some studies, mothers of children with ADHD have been reported to have experienced a higher incidence of poor maternal health during pregnancy or eclampsia, postmaturity, and long labor (Hartsough & Lambert, 1985). Other studies find contradictory results, with no difference between mothers' or infants' experiences prior to, during, or immediately following birth (McGee et al., 1984). It has been suggested that the increased risk for pregnancy, delivery, and infancy complications in children with nonfamilial ADHD and the lack of evidence for increased risk among children with familial ADHD imply that these events may be part of a nongenetic, etiological mechanism in a small group of children with ADHD, especially those experiencing ADHD with comorbid disorders (Sprich-Buckminster, Biederman, Milberger, Faraone, & Lehman, 1993). These authors suggest that pregnancy, delivery, and infant complications place children at risk for a wide range of emotional, behavioral, and educational disorders.

In isolated cases, medical factors such as iron deficiency and anemia may contribute to ADHD symptoms. Evidence exists that children with ADHD are also more likely to have suffered frequent ear infections (otitis media) in infancy (Hagerman & Falkstein, 1987). Otitis media is a common childhood infection reaching peak prevalence between 6 and 36 months of age (Bluestone, 1989). By three years of age, 70% of children have experienced at least one bout and slightly over 30% have had three or more bouts (Teele, Klein, & Rosner, 1980). The earlier the onset of the first infection, the greater the risk of subsequent infections (Klein, 1987). The relationship between recurrent bouts of otitis media and subsequent language and cognitive development has been debated (Black & Sonnenshein, 1993). Black and Sonnenshein contend that otitis is not necessarily an additional risk factor for children of low socioeconomic status because other life variables already compromise this group's language and developmental scores. This assumption is consistent with a threshold risk model and suggests that otitis media represents a risk factor in middle- and upper-class populations of children (Teele, Klein, & Chase, 1990). Although debated, the exact relationship between otitis and inattentive symptoms remains unclear. Contrary to the report of a strong association between otitis and attention by Paradise (1981), Arcia and Roberts (1993) found no association during the first few years of life between otitis and two laboratory measures of attention. These authors suggest that a relationship might exist between inattention and otitis but that it may be best observed in a classroom or home situation rather than on a structured, laboratory task.

Medications such as phenobarbital or other anticonvulsants used to treat medical illness may precipitate symptoms of ADHD (for a review, see S. Goldstein & Goldstein, 1990). Antihistamines have also been implicated as precipitating ADHD symptoms.

Recently, researchers at the National Institutes of Health demonstrated a relationship between generalized resistance to thyroid hormone (GRTH) and ADHD. Thyroid hormone regulates a number of functions in the body. Too little of the hormone can cause feelings of fatigue, depression, and other symptoms that may slow growth in children. Some individuals possess sufficient thyroid hormone but cannot use it because a genetic defect in the thyroid receptor cells keeps the hormone from binding with the cells. Such individuals have high levels of thyroid hormone in the blood but symptoms similar to someone with too little hormone. This is a rare genetic condition that appears to present repeatedly in certain families. Hauser et al. (1993) found that persons with GRTH are much more likely to demonstrate ADHD symptoms than persons without GRTH within the same family. Although a person with GRTH may frequently have ADHD symptoms, the reverse is usually not true. This genetic linkage study suggests that the gene or genes responsible for GRTH may reside close to those responsible for ADHD symptoms. It does not imply that GRTH or thyroid dysfunction is responsible for the majority of cases of ADHD.

In a preliminary study of twenty-three 4–17-year-olds, most of them male, with ADHD and their families, Warren et al. (1995) reported that levels of a blood protein important in defending against viral and bacterial infections (C4B) were lower in the ADHD subjects and their mothers than in controls. The lower levels were not found in fathers. If this result can be replicated, C4B levels may be an important marker of ADHD or a subgroup. These authors suggested that C4B levels may represent an etiological factor for ADHD because this protein has been associated with increased bacterial and viral infections. Thus, deficient C4B levels in mothers may allow a virus or some other pathogen to persist and spread, affecting the developing fetus in ways that lead to symptoms of ADHD after birth.

Finally, low levels of lead ingestion (Needleman et al., 1979), fragile X syndrome (Hagerman, Kemper, & Hudson, 1985), and other genetic abnormalities have been proposed as the cause of ADHD in some individuals. In a very small group of children with ADHD, a demonstrable history of brain injury appears to be the precipitating factor for the development of the ADHD symptoms (Routh, 1978; Stewart & Olds, 1973).

Research has also consistently demonstrated that heredity is a significant risk component for developing ADHD. The heritability for ADHD has been estimated at approximately 40%. This represents a significant correlation. Although a gene has not been identified, twin studies suggest a clear genetic relationship, with identical twins demonstrating a much higher concordance rate than nonidentical twins or siblings (Willerman, 1973). A genetic study underway is attempting to locate the gene or genes most likely responsible for ADHD (M. Stein, personal communication, October 1993).

From a biological perspective, ADHD can be viewed as the result of brain dysfunction. Neurotransmitters involving dopamine, serotonin, and norepinephrine have all been implicated as essential building blocks for effective attention and impulse control. Other research studies point to the right hemisphere, frontal lobe, or other areas of the brain as the "location" of this dysfunction (Hauser et al., 1993; Zametkin & Rapoport, 1987).

Evaluation

Although evaluation of childhood and early adolescent ADHD is not the focus of this text, the reader must recognize that the process recommended for evaluation in adults has been developed using primarily the childhood model. Because ADHD is biopsychosocial in nature a comprehensive evaluation of behavior in the home, community, workplace, and school is essential. Data on academic and intellectual achievement, medical status, and emotional development must be obtained. Observation has been found to be the most ecologically valid means of identifying the ADHD population (Barkley, 1991). A thorough history as well as completion of well-standardized, factor-analyzed questionnaires is a useful alternative.

Although children with ADHD have been reported to experience impaired performance on laboratory frontal lobe measures related to achievement, cognitive ability, capacity to inhibit impulsive responding, and sustained attention (for a review, see DuPaul, Guevremont, & Barkley, 1992; S. Goldstein & Goldstein, 1990), there continues to be debate as to whether these measures are essential to a clinical diagnosis. From the *DSM-IV* diagnostic perspective they clearly are not. Nevertheless, they may help a clinician understand the specific problems a child, or an adult for that matter, with ADHD is facing. It is important to remember, however, that there is disagreement in the field. Although some researchers suggest that ADHD represents a frontal lobe disorder, other studies have not supported the hypothesis that a disturbance in frontal lobe function is responsible for ADHD behavior (Lorys et al., 1990).

Intervention

Again, although the scope of this book is the treatment of late adolescents and adults with ADHD, much of what is known, hypothesized, and used with adults is rooted in the extensive childhood literature. There is a consensus that treatment for ADHD in the child and adolescent years should be multidisciplinary, multimodal, and of long duration (Barkley, 1991; S. Goldstein & Goldstein, 1990, 1992). By far the most effective interventions for children and adolescents with ADHD use behavioral techniques and medication. The cognitive-behavioral interventions that have been successful with a variety of other childhood and adult populations have not yielded consistent benefits for children with ADHD. More recent studies show that medication is the most powerful treatment for ADHD by far, with slight but in many cases nonsignificant benefits obtained when other interventions such as behavior management or educational support are provided (Abikoff, 1991). It is important to note that these authors are not making any argument about the benefits of these treatments for non-ADHD symptoms (e.g., LD) but are asserting that these treatments do not directly affect ADHD symptoms.

Finally, a significant literature attests to the benefits of methylphenidate (Ritalin) in reducing key symptoms of ADHD, including inattentiveness, motor overactivity, and impulsiveness (Klein, 1987; for a thorough review, see Greenhill & Osman, 1991). This literature will be reviewed in Chapter 13. Ongoing, multimodal treatment programs for children with ADHD and comorbid problems related to disruptive or nondisruptive behavior will likely yield better information about comorbidity of symptoms, the development of these problems, and most important, long-term outcome (Abikoff, 1991; Hinshaw & Erhardt, 1991; Richters et al., 1995).

CHAPTER 4

Children with Learning Disabilities Grown Up

T HE DAILY DEMANDS and forces that affect adults are different from those affecting children. Certain skill weaknesses or temperamental traits may be liabilities in childhood but through planning or luck become assets in adulthood. Nevertheless, it is fair to begin with the generalization that learning-disabled children grown up are for the most part learning-disabled adults. The questions to be asked then are related to the types of academic, vocational, interpersonal, and emotional difficulties they experience. In 1989, Minskoff, Hawks, Steidle, and Hoffmann proposed that intelligence, cognitive-processing deficits, language deficits, academic achievement level, psychological adjustment, and vocational-employability factors were the six most important variables in determining the severity of adult LD. In this system, individuals with mild LD were described as having above average intellect, limited processing and language deficits, high academic achievement, adequate psychological adjustment, and at least some skills necessary for successful employment. Those with moderate deficits were described as having average intelligence, some cognitive and language problems, one or more academic disability, some psychological adjustment problems, and weak vocational skills. Finally, those at the severe end of the continuum suffered from below average intellect, significant cognitive-processing or language deficits, low academic achievement, poor psychological adjustment, and very weak vocational abilities. As individuals move to the more severe end of the continuum they require greater and more diverse services, including basic life skills training (Schloss & Smith, 1990).

A rough correspondence between child and adult subtypes of LD has been reported (Spreen, 1987; Spreen & Haaf, 1986). However, the language-based LD frequently described as most common in children (Mattis et al., 1975) is not as easily identified in adults. Spreen (1987) argues that linguistically weak children evolve into more globally impaired adults with general learning and life skill disabilities.

It is has been suggested that there is little empirical evidence to distinguish children with LD from the larger unclassified school-aged population of nonhandicapped low achievers (Jenkins, Pious, & Peterson, 1988). As noted in Chapter 2, however, the great majority of the data indicates that learning-disabled children can be distinguished from those with weak intellect or cognitive deficits by a broad variety of achievement and performance factors. Similarly, Mangrum and Strichart (1988) propose a wide range of problems that presumably differentiate learning-disabled college students and adults from others who are academically unprepared to attend college or participate in vocational training. These authors suggest that learning-disabled college students and adults are differentiated from other low achievers by

1. Decoding rate and comprehension problems in reading
2. Legibility, capitalization, spelling, punctuation, and syntax errors in writing
3. Computational arithmetic reasoning and verbal problem solving difficulties in mathematics
4. Auditory comprehension, memory, and oral expression problems
5. Low self-esteem, poor social reasoning, and inadequate personal relations
6. Poor executive skills, including difficulty with organization, note taking, outlining, studying, and test taking

As discussed in Chapter 2, there has never been, and in the near future is unlikely to be, a consensus definition of LD in childhood. As noted, in some settings LD is defined as a discrepancy, in others as a neurological deficit, and in others as a specific weakness. Not surprisingly then, the problem of definition exists in the adult field as well. The most concise definition of adult LD has been proposed by Reiff, Gerber, and Ginsberg (1993):

> Learning disabilities in adulthood affect each individual uniquely. For some, difficulties lie in only one specific functional area; for others, problems are more global in nature, including social and emotional problems. For many, certain functional areas of adult life are limited compared to other areas. Adults with learning disabilities are of average or above average intelligence, but intelligence often times has no relation to the degree of disability. Learning disabilities persist throughout the life span, with some areas improving and others worsening. Although specific deficits associated with learning disabilities are real and persistent, such deficits do not necessarily preclude achievement and, in some cases, may have a positive relationship with achievement. In almost all cases, learning disabilities necessitate alternative approaches to achieve vocational and personal success. (pp. 19–20)

Bruck (1993) found that college students with childhood diagnoses of dyslexia continued to have problems acquiring knowledge of the mappings between spelling and sounds of English. This group's use and knowledge of morphological information and visual information for spelling was predictable from their reading problems. This finding is reported by others (Pennington et al., 1986; Scarborough, 1984). Bruck reports that misspelling by dyslexics indicates that although they preserve the phonological structure of words, their spelling is less phonologically accurate.

People with histories of reading disability as children appear to experience similar patterns of problems as adults (Bruck, 1990, 1992). These adults have word recognition difficulties associated with poor knowledge of spelling, difficulty with sound correspondence, and poor levels of phonological awareness. Bruck suggests that in addition most of these adults are able to overcome earlier deficits in skills involving knowledge of sound-spelling correspondence. As adults, this group's spelling difficulties reflect problems with more complex spelling patterns involving the use and knowledge of morphological and orthographic information. For many of these individuals, deficits in sound-spelling knowledge persist, but more complex linguistically based and possibly visually based compensatory skills develop. Stanovich and West (1989) found that the ability to spell morphologically appearing words was related to measures of print exposure. Scarborough (1984) found that adults who are poor readers and who have reported childhood histories of LD performed worse than normal adults on a nonword spelling task.

In 1985, Bruck found that subjects with histories of LD who were in college at the time of testing obtained higher scores than subjects with the same educational level, intelligence, and socioeconomic status who were not in college. If adults with childhood histories of reading disabilities were not in educational environments, they rarely engaged in literary activities. In 1993, Bruck found further that adults with childhood histories of LD had persisting difficulties in a wide general array of component, reading, and spelling skills.

Despite attempts at more sophisticated and scientific diagnostic classification and remediation in childhood, LD generally remains a heterogenous category of low achievement that persists into adulthood (Algozzine & Ysseldyke, 1983). In fact, it has been suggested that those with LD are simply people at the lower end of the learning spectrum who do not possess specific deficits (Shaywitz et al., 1990). Thus, as Yanok (1992) has noted, this "classification conundrum" has resulted in underprepared and possibly unintelligent students managing to enter higher educational settings and ultimately being misdiagnosed as learning disabled. In 1987, Vogel (1987a) reported that the initial statewide administration of the California assessment system for adults with LD resulted in the disqualification of approximately 40% of individuals who had been previously classified as learning disabled as children. Programs such as those at the University of Connecticut and at Adelphi have had to come to grips with the fact that structured postsecondary special educational programs differ very little from the more common campus developmental learning centers that assist all low-functioning students (Shaw, Norlander, & McGuire, 1987). All of these programs aim ultimately to provide supplemental instruction that allows academically underprepared students to succeed in the educational mainstream.

Efforts have been made, principally over the past 15 years, to subtype patterns of LD in adult populations. McCue, Shelly, Goldstein, and Katz-Garris (1984) replicated with adults Rourke's (1982) work with children, identifying adults who performed well on the Wide Range Achievement Test (WRAT) Reading subtest relative to the Arithmetic subtest as having deficits in visual spatial skills, nonverbal problem solving, and complex psychomotor abilities. Those with relatively good arithmetic and poor reading scores had higher ability levels but relatively poor linguistic skills. This pattern was also reported by Harvey and Wells (1989) in research with the Wechsler Adult Intelligence Scale (WAIS) and the Luria-Nebraska Neurophysiological Battery. Differences in level of performance were found among intellectual, academic, and neuropsychological measures.

In 1985, Joschko and Rourke suggested that the ACID profile found among learning-disabled children also characterized adults. This result was replicated by Katz and Goldstein (1993). It is important to note, however, that this pattern is not associated with a particular subtype of LD and may reflect general information-processing deficits.

G. Goldstein, Katz, Slomka, and Kelly (1993) evaluated 102 adults with LD using two methods: a cognitive profile and a rule-based empirical classification. They focused on levels of reading and arithmetic to generate subtypes of LD. Both methods indicated that a specific reading disability was associated with the most impaired cognitive profiles of the three subtypes identified. Both methods discriminated among subtypes more by pattern than by level of performance. The Rourke subtypes are based entirely on pattern. As long as the pattern is present, the subtype can be identified across a wide continuum of performance levels. In this study, cluster analysis for the WAIS found a globally disabled subgroup, a poor-arithmetic subgroup characterized by poor performance on the Information, Digit Span, Vocabulary, Arithmetic, and Digit Symbol subtests, and a poor-reader subgroup with a similar pattern but a lower level of performance. Neither classification method, however, produced a remarkable profile of pattern differences among the subtypes. Level rather than pattern of performance was the major influence between groups.

In 1987, L. W. Walters studied 104 college students in need of academic assistance. The Rourke type-1 deficit (all achievement scores below a standard score of 85) and type-2 deficit (reading difficulty with relatively good arithmetic) were not identified. However, 30 cases of the Rourke type-3 deficit (arithmetic deficit with relatively good reading) were found.

Katz and Goldstein (1993) found that the WAIS (Wechsler, 1981) and the Luria-Nebraska Neuropsychological Battery (C. J. Golden, Hammeke, & Purisch, 1980) are capable of distinguishing between adults with and without LD. However, classification of individual cases was subject to high error rates for both instruments. It has repeatedly been suggested, as noted before, that these instruments are sensitive to LD because they reflect general information-processing problems. Efforts at identifying specific patterns of cognitive function, as related to specific LD, have had limited success (Gaddes, 1985; Rourke, 1985). However, some positive findings have been reported. Sequencing and reversal problems, for example, have been associated with mathematical calculation deficits. Language, memory, and conceptual deficits have been reported to be related to poor reading comprehension.

Shafir and Siegel (1994) evaluated 331 individuals 16–72 years of age in an effort to subtype adult LD. Individuals with an arithmetic disability, a reading disability, or combined disabilities were evaluated on a variety of cognitive and achievement measures and compared with a normally achieving group. The reading-disabled and combined groups demonstrated deficits in phonetic knowledge and phonological processing, vocabulary, spelling, and short-term memory. The arithmetic disability group performed similar to the normal group on reading and phonological processing but performed worse than the normal group on word reading and vocabulary.

Minimal differences in subtest Wechsler scores between reading-impaired subjects and controls was reported by E. Feldman et al. (1993). These authors reported a difference in Block Design performance, with better Block Design subtest performance among dyslexic subjects. This pattern has also been reported by Rugel (1974). In the Feldman et al. study, reading-disabled individuals tended to continue their education beyond high school to the same extent as familial control subjects. It is important to note that the mean IQ of both the reading-disabled and control groups in this study was 110, almost two-thirds of a standard deviation above the average. These authors also did not find a higher proportion of males in their reading-impaired sample. This supports the suggestion by other authors that the disproportionate number of males with reading problems may be due to reporter bias rather than a true sex difference in the incidence of the disorder (Shaywitz et al., 1990). The Feldman et al. study also found that left-handers were not disproportionately represented among persons with reading disability, a phenomenon reported by others (Hugdahl, Synnevag, & Satz, 1990; Pennington et al., 1987). Further, Sulzbacher, Thompson, Farwell, Temkin, and Holubkov (1994) report that over a six-year period during childhood, no relationship was found between cross-laterality, intelligence, or achievement. Based on available data, it is reasonable to conclude that adults with LD demonstrate a similar pattern of linguistic-perceptual and rote-conceptual strengths and weaknesses as children.

Oestreicher and O'Donnell (1995) used the Halstead-Reitan Neuropsychological Test Battery (Reitan & Wolfson, 1988) to show that the General Neuropsychological Deficit Scale (GNDS) could discriminate learning-disabled from normal and brain-injured individuals, placing the LD group somewhere between the normal and brain-injured populations. This finding confirmed the results of past research with learning-disabled adults (O'Donnell, Kurtz, & Ramanaiah, 1983). It is important to note, however, that although the scale could distinguish the learning-disabled group from these other populations, it did not identify subtypes of LD.

Much less is known about the psychiatric outcome for adults with histories of LD. Although many authors hypothesize that these individuals have greater problems with self-esteem, life satisfaction, and general emotional functioning, current findings are inconsistent. Balow and Bloomquist (1965) and Dyckman, Peters, and Ackerman (1973) reported a greater frequency of psychiatric problems among reading-disabled adults. However, other authors (E. Feldman et al., 1993) have not consistently replicated this finding.

The scope of questions concerning adult outcome for learning-disabled individuals extends beyond their skill deficits into vocational, personal, and life outcome issues. E. Feldman et al. (1993) investigated the developmental, demographic, educational, and psychosocial outcomes of 36 adults with third-generation familial dyslexia. Compared with control subjects, those with familial dyslexia had a similar incidence of perinatal complications, left-handedness, and right-left confusion but experienced more early speech language problems. Those with weaker academic skills demonstrated greater symptoms of depression and anxiety, were more likely to suffer from ADHD (15% vs. 2%), and demonstrated similar marital history, stability, and mean income.

In a review of the available literature in 1968, Rawson reported favorable vocational and educational outcomes for a sample of reading-disabled boys coming from higher income families and attending a private school for children with learning disabilities. Naylor et al. (1990) found that reading-impaired adults managed to complete high school and obtain gainful employment when other variables were held constant. Thus, the inconsistent outcome across studies may be attributed to related but indirect factors, such as socioeconomic status and intelligence, but not necessarily LD. Socioeconomic status and intelligence have clearly been found to influence outcome in adulthood for reading-disabled children (Bruck, 1989; Schonhaut & Satz, 1983).

Other researchers have criticized methodological practices involving subject selection, measures used to assess outcome, and other variables as contributing to the inconsistent results found across adult outcome studies for LD (W. Horn, O'Donnell, & Vitulano, 1983). Horn et al. note that in many studies, subjects were not screened for other neurological problems, psychiatric disturbance, or the presence of generally lower cognitive skills. The contribution of these phenomena would produce a heterogenous sample of reading-impaired children whose deficits are the result of numerous contributing factors beyond specific skill weakness related to LD.

Spreen (1981, 1982, 1984) evaluated the psychosocial and vocational outcomes of children with reading disability into adulthood. This group was reported to be more likely than others to drop out of school and to have lower occupational achievement. In contrast, other researchers have found no differences in educational or occupational achievement between disabled and normal readers (Bruck, 1985, 1986; Finucci, Gottfredson, & Childs, 1985).

Frauenheim and Heckerl (1983) followed a small sample of learning-disabled children into adulthood. This group, despite average intelligence, did not benefit from the academic remediation they were provided in childhood. Thus, as adults they continued to struggle academically.

This finding is in contrast to the work of Naylor et al. (1990), who reported that adults with histories of LD who received remedial education in childhood demonstrated improved reading abilities.

The consensus has been that individuals with LD grow up and fail to achieve vocational and social competence at levels commensurate with others, despite receiving special services (Haring, Lovett, & Smith, 1990; Zigmond & Thornton, 1985). Nonetheless, individually, learning-disabled people may progress to advanced academic placement. J. A. Walters and Croen (1993) reported that learning-disabled adults have been present in medical school settings but until recently were not identified or provided with special assistance. These authors describe the cognitive skills program developed in 1989 at the Albert Einstein College of Medicine. Approximately 1%–2% of each medical school class is referred for evaluation because of suspected LD. Often these are intellectually gifted students possessing well-developed compensatory strategies that begin to be taxed by the demanding medical school curriculum.

The literature on postsecondary education for persons with LD is small, and it is not based on sound research in general (Yanok & Broderick, 1988). In 1990 Hughes and Smith reported that there was not a single scientific study published that directly evaluated the efficacy of developmental education programs for college students with LD. Recent relevant articles published in authoritative journals consist for the most part of program descriptions, opinions, survey reports, and general commentary (Bursuck et al., 1989; Fairweather & Shaver, 1991; Nelson et al., 1990).

Fifteen years ago, students with LD were not a recognized population at the college level (Hoy & Gregg, 1986). However, this situation has clearly changed. In 1986, approximately 230,000 entering college freshmen identified themselves as suffering from LD (Fishlock, 1987), and there is no doubt that the number of college students with LD will increase in the future (Bogart et al., 1988). Further, in 1987, Hoffman et al. reported that 29% of learning-disabled students surveyed had enrolled in technical, vocational, or trade school after high school.

Fifty thousand recipients of high school diplomas and 161,000 students enrolled in postsecondary educational institutions during 1988 were identified as learning disabled ("Illinois Program Helps," 1990). A report released by the HEATH Resource Center of the American Council on Education stated that more than 40% of recent inquiries received by this national information clearinghouse concerned college programs for students with LD (R. Hartman, 1991).

These data suggest that persons with LD will continue to seek access to higher education in substantial numbers. Moreover, these adults will arrive in advanced training settings with the expectation of receiving assistance. Although the provisions of Section 504 of the Rehabilitation Act of 1973 (P.L. 93–112) and the Americans with Disabilities Act (1990) require publicly supported institutions of higher learning to afford equal educational opportunity to persons with disabilities, private colleges and universities are not obligated to provide postsecondary special educational services (Yanok, 1985).

Dexter (1982) noted that on most college campuses, special classes, resource rooms, and other services common in elementary and secondary schools are not available. A 1983 nationwide survey of 300 campuses by Gruenberg found that 80% of the responding colleges and universities had established learning centers on their campuses. The general goals of these centers were to provide support for those students in need and to reduce the number of course failures and academic dismissals.

The National Longitudinal Transition Study (Wagner, 1989) reported that only 9% of adults with LD were enrolled in a two- or four-year college program. Fourquean et al. (1991) reported that 26% of learning-disabled students attended a college, vocational, or technical program while another 35% completed other educational programs in on-the-job training or military service. Succimarra and Speece (1990) reported that 17% of learning-disabled individuals entered job training, 8% went to private training, 6% were in community college, and 5% were in apprenticeship programs. The highest percentage of postsecondary participation was reported in a statewide study by Sitlington and Frank (1990). In this study of learning-disabled adults, 44% of the employed respondents and 50% of the unemployed respondents had received some training since high school.

The Office of Special Education and Rehabilitation Services (1986) reported that over 1.9 million students with LD were served by special educational, elementary, and secondary programs in 1985. As increasing numbers of youth with LD complete high school, they are faced with more postsecondary opportunities. College is now a viable option given the special services available (Decker, Polloway, & Decker, 1985; Levinson, 1986; R. Stone, 1985). For example, in 1982 the California Community College System was directed by the state legislature to establish an LD eligibility model for the state's 106 community colleges. Until then, individual colleges had followed their own eligibility models, deciding which students qualified for services (Ostertag, Baker, Howard, & Best, 1982). The California Community College System is reported to serve approximately 1% of its students as learning disabled. This percentage represents approximately one-third of all students with disabilities, clearly making LD the largest category of disability in the system (California Community College Chancellor's Office, 1992).

Fairweather and Shaver (1991) report that learning-disabled students constitute the single largest category of disabled students participating in postsecondary education. Limited data are available, however, for understanding the needs of this population and creating effective programs for them (Wilczenski & Gillespie-Silver, 1992). As Vogel (1990a) notes, only a longitudinal prospective study can provide a valid assessment of the academic performance of learning-disabled students. No such study has yet been undertaken.

Wilczenski (1991) reports that all academic performance indicators, including graduation rate and timing of dropout, are lower for learning-disabled than non-learning-disabled students. Although withdrawal rates do not differ significantly between the two groups, non-learning-disabled students tend to drop out of college early in their careers, whereas learning-disabled students appear to drop out later in their careers. This is a troubling finding and suggests that students with LD may be unable to cope with the increasing demands of course work ultimately required for graduation.

Increasingly, researchers are asking what percentage of the adult population is illiterate because of experience and what percentage is actually learning disabled. Clearly, as adults learning-disabled individuals are harder to distinguish from illiterates than they were as children. More and more, the term "functional literacy" is used interchangeably with the term "literacy." Although adults who are not functionally literate certainly deserve services, the method, duration, and type of services they need may be very different from those required by the adult LD population. Therefore, presenting a distinction between these groups is in order, beginning with a review of the literacy literature.

Literacy has traditionally been regarded as the ability to read, even on a simple level, while functional literacy refers to the ability to read, write, and perform mathematics with the functional competence required in adult daily living. But the term "literacy" is now being defined more and more functionally. Congressional legislation proposed in the House and Senate has required literacy to be defined in terms of skills needed to function in society and the economy (National Literacy Act of 1989, S.1310; Literacy for All Americans Act of 1990, H.R. 5115).

Four basic concepts of literacy have been used to define the term and then estimate the population:

1. Ability to read and write
2. Level of educational attainment
3. Grade level equivalent of reading or mathematical skills
4. Level of English-language comprehension

It is important to recognize that the level of competency that is equated with literacy has also increased. In the 1960s an individual reading at a fourth- or fifth-grade level was considered literate. Since the mid-1970s a sixth- to eighth-grade level has more often been the standard (Marsh & Price, 1980). In 1990, the U.S. Department of Health and Human Services defined the basic skills competency or literacy needed to function in society as the ability to read at the late eighth-grade level.

Not surprisingly, issues related to literacy are as hotly debated as those related to LD. Functional literacy has been defined along different dimensions involving basic daily communication, problem solving, consumer economics, reading, and document utilization. Table 4.1 contains an overview of studies and estimates of the percentages of literate and functionally literate individuals in our society.

Excluding the high and low extremes, the estimates of functional illiteracy in the adult population range from 4% to 19%. The rate of illiteracy appears to be higher for minorities than for the economically disadvantaged. Some of these estimates may be overstated, however, as the result of possible cultural biases in traditional testing methods. Regardless of the reason (e.g., cultural bias, testing methods, lack of equal educational opportunity, or socioeconomic disadvantage), the majority of formal research demonstrates higher rates of illiteracy for minorities and economically disadvantaged persons. The rate of LD among these populations, however, remains unknown.

There is some evidence of a high incidence of LD and functional illiteracy among the economically disadvantaged. Depending on which of several definitions is used, 20%–30% of economically disadvantaged adults may be functionally illiterate. Even controlling for lower cognitive abilities and opportunity among this population, this proportion is excessive. Programs for adult basic education are the only major source of population data about learning-disabled individuals. These uncontrolled studies suggest that 50%–80% of adult basic education students are learning disabled. It has been estimated that 15%–23% of all Job Training Partnership Act (JTPA Title IIA) participants may be learning disabled, with the majority reading below a seventh-grade level. It is also estimated that 25%–40% of all adults receiving Aid to Families with Dependent Children (AFDC) and participating in the Job Opportunities and Basic Skills (JOBS) program may also be learning disabled. Figure 4.1 presents a schematic representation of the population overlap among the illiterate, economically disadvantaged, and learning-disabled populations.

On the vocational front, it is common for individuals with histories of LD to hold low-paying jobs (Herzog & Falk, 1991; E. S. Shapiro & Lentz, 1991). Further, E. S. Shapiro and Lentz (1991) report that even two years after graduation students with LD held jobs paying near-minimal-level wages. These authors observe that many students with LD end up in jobs other than the ones for which they are trained. For this reason, these authors suggest that learning-disabled individuals be offered general work skills training rather than vocational training in high school for a specific occupation.

Researchers have hypothesized about the impact of LD in the workplace, naming problems such as difficulty with social skills; poor memory, organization, and auditory processing; linguistic weakness; and general weak academic ability as likely to contribute to poor work performance of the LD population (Clement-Heist et al., 1992; R. M. Matthews et al., 1982). There continues to be a paucity of scientific data, however. Even the contention that underemployment is a specific problem for learning-disabled adults has been difficult to consistently demonstrate. It is fair to conclude that while learning-disabled individuals may have difficulty obtaining, maintaining, and succeeding in a job, the extent or exact nature of their problems is unclear. Some researchers report a broad range of problems (Blalock, 1981; Hoffman et al., 1987); others report problems no different from the norm (Felton, 1986; Gerber, 1988). Some authors suggest considerable unemployment among adults with LD (Blalock, 1981; Haring et al., 1990), while others report equal levels of employment (Bruck, 1985; E. S. Shapiro & Lentz, 1991). Even if the absolute percentage of employed individuals with LD does not differ significantly from the normal population, their level of vocational attainment may in fact be very different. In addition, other, confounding factors, such as geographical location and socioeconomic background, may influence employment outcome for learning-disabled individuals more than the LD itself. Even gender has been proposed as an outcome variable, with females suffering from LD reported to be unemployed at a much higher rate than their male counterparts

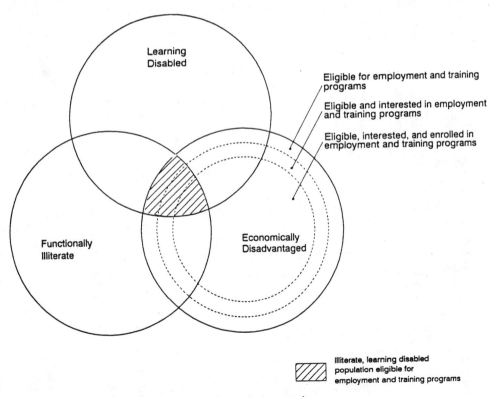

Figure 4.1   Schematic representation of population overlap.
Note. From *The Learning Disabled in Employment and Training Programs,* 1991, Washington, DC: U.S. Department of Labor, Employment and Training Administration. Used with permission.

Table 4.1 Estimates of Literacy and Functional Literacy

Definition	Study (Source)	Estimates	Comments
1. Ability to read and write	CPS sample of persons 14 years old and older (U.S. Department of Commerce, 1979)	0.6 % of all are unable to read and write; 0.44% of whites and 1.6% of blacks	Incidence is based on self-report
2. Level of educational attainment	CPS sample of persons 25 years old and older (U.S. Department of Commerce, 1989)	24% of all completed less than four years of high school; 23% of whites, 37% of blacks, and 49% of Hispanics	
3. Grade level equivalent of reading skills	Profile of American Youth, 18–23 years old using Armed Forces Qualifying Test (Office of Assistant Secretary of Defense, 1982)	7% of all 1,980 young adults did not qualify for military service; 8% of males, 7% of females, 26% of blacks, 20% of Hispanics, and 3% of whites	Median grade level for reading 9.6; for blacks 6.8 and for Hispanics 7.5
	Nationally representative sample of WIN registrants (Goodison, 1982)	50% reading below the 8–9th-grade level	WIN mandatory population: AFDC recipients with youngest child under 6 years old
	(U.S. Department of Labor, 1990)	29% of Title IIA terminees reading below the 7th-grade level	
4. Level of English-language comprehension	Survey of 3,400 adults using the Measure of English Language Proficiency Test (26 written questions; U.S. Department of Education, 1982)	13% of adults are illiterate	Illiterate adults are more likely to live in major cities, and most were 50 years old or under 70% of the native English speakers classified as illiterate did not finish high school 37% of the illiterate adults speak a non-English language at home

	Survey	Findings	Notes
5. Requirements for adult living	Survey of 1,985 persons over age 15 (Harris, 1970)	13% of persons have marginal functional skills	Skills include writing, speaking, and listening
	Survey of 7,500 persons over age 18 (Lyle, 1977)	19% of adults function with difficulty	Skills include communication, computation, problem solving, occupational knowledge, law, community resources, government, and health
6. Ability to use printed materials	Survey of 3,600 persons 21–25 years old (Kirsch & Jungeblut, 1985)	Prose illiterate: 4% of all, 2% of whites, 14% of blacks, and 6% of Hispanics Document illiterate: 0.3% of all, 0.1% of whites, 1% of blacks, Quantitative illiterate: 8% of all, 5% of whites, 25% of blacks, and 13% of Hispanics	Percentages are those meeting minimum NAEP competency levels Prose: Understanding and using text information Document: locating and using information on forms and tables Quantitative: applying arithmetic methods
	Survey using NAEP, 607 persons 18 years old and older (Philadelphia Literacy Survey, 1988)	11.4% classified as lower level illiterate	
	Workplace Literacy Survey (U.S. Department of Labor, 1990)	N/A	Ongoing study will assess literacy of JTPA, ES, and UI populations
	Survey of 13,000 persons 13–64 years old (National Center for Education Statistics, 1990)	N/A	Results expected in 1992

Note. Adapted from *The Learning Disabled in Employment and Training Programs*, 1991, Washington, DC: U.S. Department of Labor, Employment and Training Administration. Used with permission.

(Buchanan & Wolf, 1986). Although estimates may be based on empirically weak statistics, in general they suggest a high incidence of LD (a developmental reason for delayed achievement) among adults in job training, remedial education, and welfare programs.

It can be said with some confidence that unemployment rates for dropouts, whether they have LD or not, are twice as high as for high school graduates (U.S. Department of Labor, Bureau of Labor Statistics, 1987). Although data are scarce, the obvious conclusion is difficult to deny: If appropriate vocational and educational programs are not provided to individuals with LD leaving school, they will struggle vocationally and experience great adjustment difficulties in adulthood (Minskoff et al., 1988).

In 1987, Hoffman et al. reported that 29% of learning-disabled students surveyed had enrolled in technical, vocational, or trade school after high school. Hoffman et al. (1987) and Succimarra and Speece (1990) report strong evidence that high school vocational training programs are either unavailable or ineffective for individuals with LD. Taymans (1982) surveyed former students with LD who had successfully completed vocational and technical programs between 1986 and 1988. Sixty-one percent reported that they were not qualified for the jobs in the vocational area in which they were trained. Approximately 40% had received career guidance, and 22% had selected vocational courses as the result of a counselor's recommendation. The rest chose these courses for personal reasons or because of parent recommendations. E. S. Shapiro and Lentz (1991) completed a two-year follow-up of students with LD who had attended vocation-technical programs. Fifty percent of the students with LD felt that they had not received the training nor been taught the academic job-related skills they desired. Furthermore, 50% held a job for which they had not been trained.

The National Longitudinal Transition Study (D'Amico, 1991) identified a national sample of more than 8,000 youth between the ages of 13 and 23 years who were in special educational programs during the 1985–86 school year. In a description of the sample, Butler-Nalin and Wagner (1991) reported that the subjects included youth with disabilities who were receiving special educational services in public secondary schools or state-operated special schools. Sixty-two percent of the students who had worked during high school held jobs after graduation, compared with only 45% of the students who had not worked. Sixty-three percent of the students who had taken at least one vocational course during high school held jobs, compared to 48% of the students who had taken no vocational courses. Sixty-four percent of students with LD who graduated from high school were employed, compared to 47% among students with LD who had either dropped out or been expelled. DeBettencourt, Zigmond, and Thornton (1989) found that in rural areas dropping out of high school did not affect employment. Zigmond and Thornton (1985) found that in urban areas students with LD who did not finish high school experienced greater difficulty finding employment than those who had graduated. Butler-Nalin and Wagner (1991) found that 23% of learning-disabled students enrolled in postsecondary education. This is much lower than the 56% reported in the general population. Twelve percent of these learning-disabled students were in college programs, and the remainder in vocational trade schools. As Vogel and Adelman (1993) noted, and as is still true today, there are no data available on the effect of attending or completing a vocational program or graduating from college on the career attainment of students with LD.

Schonhaut and Satz (1983) reviewed 18 follow-up studies, concluding that socioeconomic factors were powerful variables related to the probability of developing learning problems and to academic prognosis. Further, age at identification has also been found to be an indication of poorer prognosis, with children identified at younger ages faring worse than those identified later (Kavale, 1988; McGee et al., 1992). It is also important to repeat that when progression to conduct disorder is the dependent variable, LD is not predictive, while substance abuse, socioeconomic status, and the exhibition of oppositional behavior are (Loeber et al., 1995).

Finucci and Childs (1981) note that many LD research samples consist of males. The tendency has been to assume that findings for males generalize to females. Limited information is available concerning females. Vogel (1990b) found that in order to be identified in the schools, females with LD had to be significantly lower in intelligence, be more severely impaired in language and academic achievement, and have a greater aptitude-achievement discrepancy than their male counterparts.

Finally, in a thorough summary, P. B. Adelman and Vogel (1993) cite numerous methodological shortcomings in studies of adult LD. Problems with choice of outcome, selection criteria, severity of populations studied, sample size, subject attrition, intellectual level, demographics, educational opportunity, interventions offered, comparison groups, and instrumentation used to assess change are all factors that can be responsible for the varying outcomes reported for adults with LD. As Herjanic and Penick pointed out in 1972, most studies up to that point ignored the possibility that intervening, situational variables, behavioral and personality characteristics, and family variables contributed to variability in outcome. Since that time, little has changed. A. A. Silver and Hagin (1985) emphasized differences in severity of LD as contributing to outcome. Rawson (1968) and Rogan and Hartman (1990) very clearly demonstrated that intellectual level was a significant variable predicting success for learning-disabled individuals. In the latter study, mean full-scale IQ scores differed significantly, with a group of learning-disabled college graduates obtaining an IQ almost 1 full standard deviation above the average, high school graduates with LD obtaining an average IQ, and students in self-contained special educational classrooms for the more severely impaired obtaining an IQ over 1 standard deviation below the average.

CHAPTER 5

Children with Attention Deficit Hyperactivity Disorder Grown Up

B Y THE MID-1950s the seamless relationship between a variety of childhood emotional and behavioral problems and adult psychiatric status was recognized (O'Neal & Robins, 1958). By the mid-1960s, long-term follow-up studies of children more narrowly defined as hyperkinetic or experiencing minimal brain damage demonstrated that these children had outgrown few of their symptomatic problems (Hartocollis, 1968; Menkes, Rowek, & Menkes, 1967). By the late 1970s, a number of studies evaluating parents of children receiving diagnoses of hyperactivity demonstrated that these children continued to present similar symptoms into adulthood (Cantwell, 1972; Morrison, 1979, 1980). The concept of ADHD as an adult entity has been given serious consideration in the medical and mental health communities since the early 1980s. Initial discussions of adult hyperactivity centered on the concept of minimal brain dysfunction as a disorder extending into adulthood (P. H. Wender, 1975). Researchers recognized that the symptom course in childhood related to ADD could be carried over into adulthood (Amado & Lustman, 1982). It was initially suspected that when children referred to as hyperkinetic grew up, they became less impulsive and hyperactive but remained more distractible, restless, emotionally immature, and aggressive than others (Minde, Weiss, & Mendelson, 1972). By the mid-1980s over 30 prospective and retrospective studies had been published addressing the persistence of attention deficit disorder into adulthood. As reviewed in Chapter 3, it is now clear that the majority of children with ADHD grow up to be adults experiencing some, if not all, of the symptoms consistent with ADHD. Surprisingly, G. Weiss and Hechtman (1993), based on their review of the available literature and longitudinal research, suggest that deficient social skills appear to be the most lasting and disabling comorbid aspect of adult ADHD.

Although some researchers suggest that the persistence of ADHD characteristics into adulthood might reflect learned behavior, the concept of a fundamental disturbance in the central nervous system has been well documented (Lou, Henriksen, & Bruhn, 1984; Zametkin et al., 1990). Even in 1982, it was the conclusion of Amado and Lustman that "psychiatrists stand to benefit from familiarity with the ADDs" (p. 312).

Parallel to the mental health community's interest in adult ADHD has been interest in

ADHD as a vocational disability. More disability evaluators now recognize the concept of ADHD and the impact adult ADHD symptoms may have on vocational choice and success. The Social Security Act provides in Titles II and XVI for the payment of a supplemental security income to disabled persons. The disabilities presently covered in the United States include ADHD. The disorder is defined in the act as being manifested by developmentally inappropriate degrees of inattention, impulsiveness, and hyperactivity. The disorder can affect adults as well as children. The regulations state that when medication controls the primary symptoms of the disorder, the functional limitations that persist despite treatment must also be taken into account. In *Aviles v. Bown* (1989) the court held that ADHD was a functional, nonpsychotic disorder with co-occurring anxiety, depression, and oppositional behavior under the social security regulations as they then stood and that a person with ADHD is entitled to social security payments. Further, the courts have held that the Individuals with Disabilities Education Act of 1975, the Rehabilitation Act of 1973, and the Americans with Disabilities Act of 1990 all provide protection for children and adults with ADHD.

In 1992, law school graduates sued for the right to take the bar exam with special accommodations for ADHD. The matter was settled out of court but in the plaintiffs' favor (P. Jaffe, 1993b). A major league pitcher was reinstated after it was ruled by the baseball commissioner that his expulsion for attempting to purchase cocaine had failed to consider the implications of his ADHD diagnosis (P. Jaffe, 1993a). In general, however, the courts have not heard many such arguments, nor have they been receptive to the concept of ADHD either as a mitigating factor in criminal behavior or as a serious factor to consider in sentencing. Nevertheless, the legal aspects of ADHD are becoming more significant; they will be reviewed in Chapter 12.

As Hechtman reported in 1989 and as continues to be the case today, the picture of ADHD in adulthood "can be extremely varied" (p. 602). Hechtman hypothesized that adults with histories of ADHD fall into three categories: those who experienced childhood ADHD but seem to function fairly normally as adults; those who continue to have significant problems with ADHD as well as life difficulty involving work, interpersonal relations, self-esteem, anxiety, and emotional lability; and the small group of those who develop significant psychiatric or antisocial personality, including serious depression, substance abuse, or criminality. The second group appears to be by far the largest. A particular outcome does not seem to be associated with a particular initial variable but with the additive interaction of personality characteristics and social and family parameters. The mental health of family members, intelligence, and socioeconomic status appear to best predict outcome. The severity of ADHD symptoms continuing into adolescence and then adulthood also appears to correlate positively with problems related to aggression, conduct, and oppositional disorders. Thus, as noted in other studies (Werner, 1994), the most powerful factors associated with positive or negative outcome for children with ADHD are not symptoms of ADHD. Adult outcome of individuals with ADHD has not been proved to be solely tied to particular ADHD variables or treatment but likely interacts with a variety of life factors, with family issues paramount.

Studies of adult outcome for children with ADHD have focused on four areas. Some studies have prospectively followed a group of individuals in comparison to a control group. Others have studied an adult population retrospectively. Still others have focused specifically on the adult ADHD syndrome without longitudinal, retrospective analyses. Finally, studies have focused on the parents and relatives of children diagnosed with ADHD.

Family studies of children with ADHD have reported a higher prevalence of sociopathy, hysteria, and alcoholism among their parents (Morrison & Stewart, 1971), as well as more instances of parents perceiving themselves to have been hyperactive as children (Cantwell,

1972). Increased pathology, however, is not reported in adoptive parents of children with hyperactivity (Morrison & Stewart, 1973).

Early family studies (Hechtman, 1981; Morrison, 1980; Stewart, 1980) did not adequately distinguish between children with ADHD and children who experienced more serious comorbid problems, including those involving disruptive behavior. Better designed studies, including the series by Biederman and colleagues, which will be reviewed, have controlled for these issues and collected data on first-degree relatives of children with ADHD. In general, relatives of this group have higher rates of antisocial problems, oppositional disorder, nonbipolar depression, overanxious disorder, and, not surprisingly, ADHD.

Retrospective studies find that in comparison to their sibling controls, adults with ADHD have lower educational achievement, worse self-esteem, and more problems with drug and alcohol abuse (S. Feldman, Denhoff, & Denhoff, 1979). Adults with childhood histories of ADHD have been reported to have higher rates of adult anxiety and depression (Eyestone & Howell, 1994; C. T. Gualitieri, Ondrusek, & Finley, 1985). Interestingly, although P. H. Wender, Reimherr, and Wood (1981) reported that retrospective parent ratings of childhood ADHD symptoms are the best predictors of stimulant responsiveness in adults, Mattes, Boswell, and Oliver (1984) found that the presence or absence of childhood ADHD did not predict adult drug responsiveness. In a group of adults fitting a set of criteria for ADHD, including symptoms involving restlessness, excitability, impulsivity, and irritability, just under half had childhood histories of ADHD. Subjects with childhood histories of ADHD had a somewhat worse adult picture than those without. Subjects in both groups had a high incidence of what were referred to as neuroses and personality disorder diagnoses. Thus, the complexities of adult outcome and symptoms remain. Some adults may fit the criteria for adult ADHD without a confirmed childhood history (C. T. Gualitieri et al., 1985). Do these individuals have ADHD or a related problem? If in fact ADHD is a behavioral diagnosis, one that does not require proof of etiology, should adults who meet the criteria but who either did not or cannot demonstrate that they met the criteria as children be given a diagnosis of ADHD? This thorny issue will be discussed in Chapter 6.

It is well documented that ADHD is comorbid with more disorders than any other single disorder (for a review, see S. Goldstein & Goldstein, 1990). The increased risk of comorbidity is likely the impact of primary symptoms of ADHD on everyday functioning, although a variety of mechanisms (e.g., biological, genetic, and modeling) certainly play a role. Thus, the differential diagnosis of ADHD in adulthood poses very similar problems to diagnosis in childhood. That is, understanding the relationship of comorbid disorders and the forces that affect adult functioning is critical. There is no doubt that individuals with ADHD, when compared to the normal population, are at higher risk for developing affective disorders, substance abuse, and personality disorders, including those related to antisocial and possibly borderline personality (Biederman, Munir, & Knee, 1987; Gomez, Janowsky, Zetin, Huey, & Clopton, 1981; Morrison & Minskoff, 1975; Tarter, McBride, Buonpane, & Schneider, 1977). It is important to recognize that symptoms of inattentiveness and impulsiveness in and of themselves occur across the range of childhood and adult disorders, from those involving personality, depression, and anxiety and to those related to medical problems, especially problems resulting from head trauma and chronic substance abuse.

Ratey (1991), based on clinical experience, suggested that adults with ADHD not identified in childhood tend to have milder problems and less obvious areas of dysfunction. He hypothesized that higher intelligence or socioeconomic advantage may have prevented a childhood diagnosis. Ratey reported on a clinical sample of 70 adults. Forty percent presented with disorders of mood such as depression, dysthymia, or bipolar disorder, along with ADHD; a very small percentage presented with antisocial personality disorder. Ratey reported that the majority of this sample had adapted adequately, "harnessing their talents while compensating for their deficits" (p. 13). However, the majority had interpersonal problems and difficulties with academic underachievement. The personality feature described for all members of this group was their "feeling of drivenness" (p. 13). Clinically, Ratey described these individuals as "immature"—full of fleeting passions, childlike enthusiasm and a tendency to lag behind others in achieving life steps" (p. 13).

Further, Ratey (1991) reported that as a "major internal goal" these individuals strive "to reach a state of calmness and equilibrium which paradoxically they find when they are living on the edge immersed in mental or emotional struggles or responding to a physical challenge" (p. 13). While these descriptions may make clinicians more sensitive, they may also unfairly bias clinicians because states of calmness and equilibrium are difficult to operationally define and are not characteristic criteria for the disorder.

Ratey, Greenberg, Bemporad, and Lindem (1992) followed 60 adults who had childhood and adult symptoms of ADHD but whose ADHD had not been recognized until adulthood. This study generated objective findings. These subjects shared characteristics of physical and mental restlessness, impulsivity, distractibility, low self-esteem, and a sense of underachievement. Learning and behavior problems often presented. Ratey et al. suggested that a diagnosis of ADHD was missed because the subjects presented with atypical symptoms or had found ways to compensate. Many of these people had sought treatment for other problems with unsuccessful outcome. Most had been treated for mood or anxiety problems. Interestingly, 61% of this population was reported as responding well to low doses of desipramine.

A brief overview of longitudinal research in regard to childhood emotional and behavioral problems sets the stage for understanding the outcome for children with ADHD. Achenbach, Howell, McConaughy, and Stanger (1995) assessed a national sample of youth aged 13–16 years and 16–19 years. These two groups were then reassessed at 19–22 years. These authors reported that a syndrome designated as irresponsible behavior in young adulthood was predicted by symptoms of ADHD in adolescence. They went so far as to claim that this irresponsible pattern of behavior in young adulthood may reflect adult ADHD. Further, a syndrome described by patterns of aggressive behavior and showing off in adulthood was predicted by adolescent aggressive behavior problems. These authors found that some adolescents developed overt aggression in adulthood while others developed annoying but not physically aggressive problems. Achenbach et al. concluded that there was a developmental transition away from overt aggression for some but not for others. Overall, there appeared to be a very strong predictive relation between adolescent and adult disruptive behavior.

A group of 364 individuals, between 15 and 18 years of age were followed for four years by Ferdinand, Verhulst, and Wiznitzer (1995). Nearly 40% of the group classified as experiencing problems initially were still deviant four years later. There was no significant difference in continuity between internalizing emotional and externalizing disruptive problems. All problems appeared to persist to a similar degree. This included problems with ADHD. It is also important to note that Ferdinand and Verhulst (1994), based on a sample of young adults from the general population, found that attention problems predicted the need for help without actually receiving help across a two-year time span independent of other problems. These authors concluded that intervention research should be generated to determine whether therapeutic intervention for ADHD problems can lead to symptomatic relief, as well as long-term benefits. This question continues to be discussed in the scientific and clinical communities.

Lack of specificity about childhood diagnoses of ADHD and comorbidity is a major problem with longitudinal studies of ADHD in adulthood. It is quite likely that in a population of children evaluated and initially diagnosed 15 years ago, the forces in their lives and the behaviors assessed and reported were different from those encountered in groups of children identified with ADHD today.

In a 15-year follow-up of a group of adults with histories of ADHD, 66% still reported at least one symptom of ADHD (G. Weiss, Hechtman, Milroy, & Perlman, 1985), and one-fifth reported having antisocial problems (G. Weiss & Hechtman, 1986) and more frequent than normal suicide attempts. Individuals with hyperactivity in this population had by young adulthood moved more often, been in significantly more car accidents, shown lower academic achievement, and failed more grades than adults in the control sample (Hechtman, Weiss, Perlman, Hopkins, & Wener, 1979). By the 15th year of follow-up, this group was not achieving as well vocationally either (G. Weiss, Hechtman, & Perlman, 1978). Compared to the control sample, they had more court referrals, had tried more nonmedical drugs, and showed a pattern of more impulsive, immature personality traits, as well as retrospectively rating their childhoods more negatively (G. Weiss, Hechtman, Perlman, Hopkins, & Wener, 1979).

In describing her years of longitudinal study with hyperactives, Hechtman (1989) reported data collection problems involving attrition rates, small samples, lack of controls, assessment procedures, age, and length of follow-up. Length of follow-up is a critical issue because some studies have followed children for as little as 2 years (Riddle & Rapoport, 1976), while others may follow children for as long as 25 years (Borland & Hechtman, 1976). Other longitudinal studies fall between these extremes. Further, differing theoretical views of ADHD continue to affect research design, with some theorists regarding ADHD as a developmental lag that children outgrow and others regarding it as a syndrome that progresses into adulthood. The latter group is growing, of course, as a result of the emerging data. Still others, however, suggest that the syndrome of ADHD is the precursor of more serious adult pathology and that ADHD may be an early pathway for other psychiatric disorders (Cantwell, 1985).

A review of the well-controlled prospective studies of children with ADHD shows that at least 70% progress through adolescence with ADHD (Ackerman et al., 1977; Gittelman et al., 1985; Sassone et al., 1982; Satterfield et al., 1982; Satterfield, Satterfield, & Cantwell, 1981; G. Weiss, Minde, Werry, & Douglas, 1971). Findings include issues for this population with low self-esteem and academic problems (G. Weiss et al., 1971), oppositional and delinquent behavior (Ackerman et al., 1977), felonies and a lack of stimulant treatment predicting outcome (Satterfield et al., 1982), increased school suspension (14% vs. 2%), problems with law enforcement agencies (19% vs. 3%), and admission to juvenile facilities (5% vs. 0%; Sassone et al., 1982). It has also been suggested that nearly 70% of adults with ADHD have histories of dysthymia (P. H. Wender, Reimherr, & Wood, 1985). It is therefore natural to ask whether chronic low mood is the result of chronic life failure or whether it presents comorbidly with ADHD as a depressive manifestation.

Mannuzza et al. (1993) followed 91 men with ADHD and 95 controls into their mid-20s. Outcome measures included educational achievement, occupational rank, psychiatric status, and persistence of ADHD symptoms into adulthood. The subjects with ADHD had completed less formal schooling than the controls, but 90% were gainfully employed. Their jobs, however, were of lower occupational ranking. The ADHD group was seven times more likely than the controls to have developed an antisocial personality disorder or a drug abuse problem in adulthood.

Individuals with self-reported attention deficit symptoms, from 15–18 years of age, were evaluated as part of the New Zealand longitudinal study in Dunedin (Schaughency, McGee, Nadaraja, Fehen, & Silva, 1994). Symptoms of ADHD were estimated at age 15 and then followed. Self-reported attentional difficulties at 15 years of age were associated with continued symptoms at 18 years of age. Interestingly, no gender differences were found. At age 15, adolescents who reported ADHD symptoms without other behavioral problems were identified. No differences were found between this subgroup and the larger group of individuals with ADHD in self-reported inattention or impulsivity. The larger group was in general more likely to experience adjustment difficulties at age 15 and continued to experience ADHD symptoms, adjustment problems, and social disadvantage at age 18. Most powerfully, the findings suggest that adolescent self-report should be considered in the assessment and diagnostic decision-making process for ADHD. It appears that adolescents, like adults, can when motivated be accurate reporters of their behavior. As Dulcan (1986) suggests, adolescents who report attentional difficulties are likely to reflect symptoms of clinical significance.

In a three-to-five-year follow-up of 35 subjects between 16 and 22 years of age, those with ADHD were found to have less sound driving habits (Barkley, Guevremont, Anastopoulos, DuPaul, & Shelton, 1993). They were reported to have experienced more driving-related negative outcomes in all categories surveyed. They were more likely to have been in auto accidents, were in more accidents, had more bodily injuries associated with accidents, and were more often at fault for accidents than controls. They were also more likely to have received traffic citations and had more citations than controls, particularly for speeding. The subgroup of ADHD sufferers with greater comorbid disruptive problems appears to be at highest risk for deficient driving skills and habits and negative driving-related outcomes. Even before receiving a driver's license, the ADHD group was three times more likely to have driven a vehicle without a valid license and to have done so nine times more often than the control group of normal peers. Further, the ADHD group was more likely to have had their licenses suspended or revoked.

This research by Barkley and colleagues parallels the findings of G. Weiss and Hechtman (1986) and S. Feldman et al. (1979). S. Feldman et al. (1979) reported that when hyperactive children grow up they experience lower educational achievement, poorer self-esteem, and more frequent substance abuse. G. Weiss and Hechtman (1986) reported that adults with histories of hyperactivity as children are in significantly more accidents than matched controls and make more geographical moves. G. Weiss et al. (1979) reported that the academic histories of children with hyperactivity are characterized by completing fewer years of education, failing more grades, and obtaining lower marks than controls. In a 15-year follow-up, 66% of the sample demonstrated at least one symptom consistent with ADD (G. Weiss et al., 1985). In this population, 23% were diagnosed with an antisocial personality disorder (G. Weiss & Hechtman, 1986). Vocational histories for this group were also more problematic than those for the controls (G. Weiss et al., 1985).

Gittelman et al. (1985) followed 101 male adolescents with histories of hyperactivity compared to a control group of 100 normal children. These authors found that at least one-third of the ADHD group continued to manifest the full diagnostic profile into adulthood. In this one-third there was also a significant presentation of conduct disorder and substance abuse. The ADHD group demonstrated a very consistent profile of life problems into adulthood, reporting difficulty with work, involvement in theft, and additional symptoms of antisocial personality disorder (Mannuzza, Klein, Bonagura, Konig, & Shenker, 1988). It is also interesting to note that hyperactive children and their male siblings differ significantly in outcome, with continued symptoms of hyperactivity noted in the identified population but not in siblings

(Borland & Hechtman, 1976). However, as Moffitt (1993) demonstrates, there are at least two paths to juvenile delinquency and negative adult outcome. In the first, deviant behavior appears in the preschool years and remains relatively stable into adulthood. In the second, deviant behavior appears and disappears during adolescence. Individuals with ADHD with early onset behavioral problems appear to be in the former group, possibly because of their other problems but not necessarily because of their ADHD.

Kramer (1987) reports two cases of males with histories of ADHD. These cases exemplify the work that Loney and colleagues (Loney et al., 1980) have done to demonstrate that symptoms of ADHD at referral do not correlate with later antisocial behavior. Instead, it is aggression at referral, such as fighting or destruction of property, that best predicts antisocial problems later in life.

There is a growing body of longitudinal data, however, suggesting that the combination of aggression, hyperactivity, and oppositional behavior presenting in kindergarten continues to be observed by the end of the elementary school years (ages 10–12). These factors later lead to substance abuse, defined as having been drunk or having used other drugs prior to 14 years of age (Dopkin, Tremblay, Masse, & Vitaro, 1995). Dopkin et al. propose that it is individual characteristics rather than friends' characteristics that are central to the development of substance abuse. This finding is consistent with the work of others (Baumrand, 1991; Jessor, 1992). Thus, ADHD—principally the hyperactive-impulsive symptoms—may be catalytic, combining with other problems of disruptiveness and leading to risk of substance abuse.

There have been few attempts to provide quantifiable laboratory measures of ADHD symptoms in adults. Klee, Garfinkel, & Beauchesne (1986) described a study of 12 males with a history of ADD being treated in an outpatient psychiatric facility. These individuals demonstrated problems related to non-goal-directed motor activity, impulsivity, aggression, and poor attention. All were treated with stimulant medication for a minimum of one year. They also received psychiatric treatment, including psychotherapy and remedial education. This group of individuals demonstrated weak performance on psychometric measures, including a task of continuous performance and tasks thought be sensitive to sustained attention and impulsivity. They rated themselves as having been more active, restless, nervous, and impulsive and as having had more concentration problems and frustration tolerance difficulty than non-ADD controls. Interestingly, behavioral differences were not reported when their current behavior was compared to that of non-ADD controls. The authors concluded that many childhood behavioral deficits associated with ADD may diminish in adulthood or may develop into sociopathy, depression, or alcoholism. This finding is also reported by others (Wood, Reimherr, Wender, & Johnson, 1976). It is also important to note that despite the reduction in symptomatic complaints, the group with ADD as adults still scored worse than the non-ADD controls on several laboratory psychometric measures.

Interestingly, a screening of 400 college males on a computerized continuous performance test found that there were some who did not present with a history of childhood hyperactivity, neurological disease, or psychiatric disorder but who nevertheless appeared to have difficulty paying attention to this task (Buchsbaum et al., 1985). This group demonstrated problems with short-term memory and reaction time. It was hypothesized that this group of individuals had experienced ADD without hyperactivity, which went undiagnosed in childhood. These data suggest that both the inattentive and hyperactive subtypes of attention deficit persist into adulthood.

It has been reported that boys with ADHD often grow up to have problems with alcohol and other substance abuse in adolescence and adulthood (Baker, Knight, & Simpson, 1995; Pelham, 1991). The issue of the exact substances they abuse, alcohol as opposed to others, has also been debated (Gittelman et al., 1985). Pelham reports that fathers of boys with ADHD demonstrate greater problems with alcohol than do fathers in society at large. Adults with alcohol problems often have symptoms characteristic of ADHD. The offspring of alcoholics, a group of individuals at risk for alcohol problems themselves, often exhibit difficulties with attention, impulse control, and other ADHD characteristics. It has been estimated that 30%–50% of fathers of boys with ADHD, especially those with conduct problems themselves, have had problems with alcohol. This tendency is not apparent among mothers, however. Some researchers have argued that adults with symptoms of ADHD and alcohol problems represent a distinct subgroup of the disorder. After consuming alcohol, parents of children with ADHD pay less attention to the children, give more commands, engage in more irrelevant talk, and generally increase the amount of physical contact. The effects appear to be larger among fathers than among mothers. However, for some effects the results are inconsistent. Mothers receiving alcohol appeared to increase contact with their children, and fathers to decrease contact. In general, both mothers and fathers when intoxicated give less appropriate attention to children. In combination with the fact that intoxicated fathers rated the children with whom they interacted with as behaving better and as less problematic than did fathers not given alcohol, it appears that fathers who drink see their children as well behaved and decrease attempts to control their behavior. In contrast, alcohol may not influence how mothers perceive their children's behavior, but mothers appear to increase their attempts to control their children's behavior when intoxicated. Pelham (1991) suggests that a child's behavior may serve as a stressor, which some fathers turn to alcohol to cope with. In contrast, mothers do not necessarily increase their drinking in response to a child's misbehavior but rather exert greater efforts to control the child. This can lead to arguments between parents about how to discipline the child and to an inconsistent style of discipline. Pelham states that "child behavior can certainly produce stress in parents and stress can mediate a dysfunctional coping style that leads to alcohol abuse" (p. 3).

Shekim (1990) points to the difficulty of distinguishing adult ADHD from other psychiatric disorders due to the frequent co-occurrence of anxiety and depression. In his clinical work and research (Shekim, Antun, Hanna, McCracken, & Hess, 1990), the diagnosis of ADHD rarely occurs alone; over 50% of his clients with ADHD also experience minor chronic depression, alcohol, or drug abuse. Winokur, Coryell, Endicott, and Akiskal (1993) found that the proportion of adults who reported having at least two symptoms of ADHD as children was greater among bipolar patients (21%) than among patients with unipolar depression. Strober and Carlson (1982) reported that nearly one-quarter of their adolescent patients with type-1 bipolar disorder had a history of childhood ADHD.

ADHD has also been implicated as playing an etiological role in cocaine abuse—the contention being that abuse of cocaine results from an effort to self-medicate for a dopamine-deficient state (Cocores, Davies, Mueller, & Gold, 1986). These authors reported on four individuals suffering from cocaine abuse who had histories of ADHD. Treatment with a dopamine agonist bromocriptine (Parlodel) was reported to be effective in reducing ADHD symptoms in these four individuals and in promoting cocaine abstinence.

Adult outcome studies of individuals with ADHD find no abnormalities in most physiological measures. No differences in height, weight, blood pressure, or pulse (Hechtman, Weiss, & Perlman, 1978) or EEG (Hechtman, Weiss, & Metrakos, 1978) have been reported. Abnormal EEG findings reported in some studies of younger children with ADHD tend to normalize in adolescence (Hechtman, Weiss, & Metrakos, 1978). The growing interest in beta/theta brain-wave differences reported in some children with ADHD (Lubar, 1992) has yet to generate data describing the natural course of these differences as individuals with ADHD mature.

L. Weiss (1992) notes that 20%–30% of individuals with histories of ADHD develop problems with substance abuse. This group is more likely to experience the continuation of ADHD symptoms and conduct disorder. As Cantwell (1972) reported, the link between hyperactivity and substance abuse has been found to run in families experiencing elevated rates of substance abuse and antisocial problems. Once again the data show that children with attention deficit alone are at only slightly greater risk for substance abuse than their normal peers. Those with ADHD that persists and grows in severity as they mature and those in certain family settings are much more likely to develop substance abuse problems.

Wilens et al. (1994) emphasize the overlap of ADHD and addictive disorder. These authors note that ADHD in early childhood affects 6%–9% of juveniles and approximately 2%–3% of adults. Substance disorders appear to start in adolescence and early adulthood and may affect 10%–20% of adults. The two disorders share several important characteristics: male predominance, family contributions, and genetic influences. Higher rates of other psychiatric disorders, such as antisocial, conduct, and mood disorders, occur with both (Biederman, Newcorn, & Sprich, 1991). Elevated rates of substance abuse are reported in adults with ADHD, compared to the general population (Biederman, Faraone, et al., 1993). Biederman et al. report that in a group of adults with ADHD, approximately one-third will have a history of alcohol abuse or dependence and approximately one-fifth will have a history of drug abuse or dependence. The impact of comorbid conduct problems on these data is unclear. These authors further suggest that most adults with ADHD and substance abuse disorder also have mood, anxiety, or antisocial problems.

Despite some unsubstantiated claims (Hallowell & Ratey, 1995), it is not clear whether ADHD leads to substance abuse. As Wilens and Lineham (1995) note, "There is a robust literature supporting a relationship between ADHD and substance abuse. There appear to be family-genetic, environmental and other psychiatric conditions relating ADHD to substance abuse. Complex genetic, behavioral and self-medication influences contribute to the development and persistence of substance abuse in those with ADD" (p. 30).

From the other perspective, Tarter et al. (1977) reported elevated rates of ADHD symptoms in alcohol-dependent individuals. Those with more severe drinking habits had more severe ADHD symptoms. Cocaine and opiate abusers have also demonstrated a much higher incidence of ADHD symptoms; in some studies nearly 40% would have met the ADHD criteria as children (Wilens et al., 1994). In the majority of these studies, adolescents and adults with ADHD were younger at presentation, had an earlier onset, had more severe substance-abusing habits, and had higher rates of antisocial disorders than non-ADHD substance abusers.

The work of Biederman, Faraone, et al. (1993) reflects the recent set of well-controlled studies delineating the emotional, cognitive, and psychiatric characteristics of adults with histories of ADHD. These authors studied 84 adults of mixed gender referred for treatment of ADHD. Each adult presented a clear childhood onset of ADHD symptoms. Findings were compared with a preexisting study group of 140 referred children with ADHD, their nonreferred adult relatives with ADHD, and adult relatives of normal comparison children who did not have ADHD (Biederman et al., 1992). In the 1992 study, 42 adult relatives of the 140 children diagnosed with ADHD were also reported to exhibit symptoms consistent with ADHD. Six of these relatives subsequently sought treatment. These six were included in the referred group.

The assessment consisted of an initial structured clinical interview for *DSM-III-R* (SCID; Spitzer, Williams, Gibbon, & First, 1990). To be diagnosed with adult ADHD, individuals had to meet the *DSM-III-R* criteria for the diagnosis by age seven, have at least five *DSM-III-R* symptoms of the disorder at the time of assessment, and describe a chronic course of symptoms of the disorder from childhood into adulthood.

Academic achievement was then evaluated with the Arithmetic subtest of the WRAT-R (G. S. Wilkinson, 1993) and the Gilmore Oral Reading Test (Gilmore & Gilmore, 1968). Cognitive functioning was evaluated with subtests from the WAIS-R (Wechsler, 1981). In this population, LD was determined by using a discrepancy criteria suggested by C. R. Reynolds (1985). Psychosocial functioning was assessed with the Global Assessment of Functioning Scale of the *DSM-III-R*. Socioeconomic status was measured with the Hollingshead Four-Factor Index of Social Status (Hollingshead, 1975).

Using these data, Biederman, Faraone, et al. (1993) demonstrated that referred and nonreferred adults with ADHD were similar to one another but significantly more impaired than individuals without ADHD. The pattern of psychological problems, cognitive difficulty, and daily life struggles among adults with ADHD was similar to the pattern found among children with the disorder. It is important to note that compared with the adult subjects without ADHD, a significantly greater percentage of the two adult groups with ADHD were male, divorced or separated, and of lower socioeconomic status. This finding is reported by others (Gittelman et al., 1985). The two adult groups with ADHD did not differ significantly from each other in regard to psychiatric problems. The two groups demonstrated higher rates of antisocial personality disorder, conduct disorder, oppositional defiant disorder, substance use, anxiety disorders, enuresis, stuttering, and speech and language disorders throughout their life span. Even after gender was statistically controlled, these differences remained. When the child and adult ADHD groups were compared, the children demonstrated higher rates of oppositional defiant disorder and conduct problems, and the adults higher rates of substance use, anxiety, and stuttering. Further, compared to adults without the disorder, the adults with ADHD had academic histories with significantly higher rates of grade repetition, need for tutoring, placement in special classes, and reading disability. Compared to adults without ADHD, the adults with ADHD had significantly lower estimated Full Scale and Freedom from Distractibility Wechsler factor scores. They also had lower Vocabulary, Block Design, and Digit Symbol subtest scores on the WAIS-R and lower Arithmetic and Reading scores on the WRAT-R.

Twenty-eight percent of the referred and nonreferred adults with ADHD demonstrated no psychiatric problems. They appeared to experience an uncomplicated pattern of ADHD similar to a group observed in childhood. The majority demonstrated symptoms consistent with attention deficit without hyperactivity.

Two-thirds of the adults with ADHD were men. The similarity between referred and nonreferred adults with ADHD further suggests that nonreferred cases of the disorder observed in family-genetic studies are not due to biases in those studies or to the influence of having a child with ADHD. As Biederman et al. note, this supports the idea that adults share with their children a biological substrate that leads to familial transmission and ultimately diagnosis. It is important to note that family-genetic studies have consistently found only a small percentage of parents in the general population who endorse symptoms of ADHD (Biederman et al., 1992; Biederman, Faraone, Keenan, Knee, & Tsuang, 1990).

This study also showed that—contrary to some assertions (Loeber, Green, Lahey, & Stouthamer-Loeber, 1989)—adults with histories of ADHD can accurately report their symptoms. Nonetheless, it is important to note that this study used a group of individuals who were referred because of distress over their symptoms or who were seeking help for their children. As of yet, there is no clear picture of the differences between those who seek help for ADHD and those in the general population who do not seek help but still struggle with the disorder. In clinical settings it has become increasingly apparent that adults with ADHD are referred for many reasons. For example, many clinics are reporting males sent in for evaluation after pressure from their spouses to do something about their lives "or else." Such men may under-report symptoms because they are not seeking help of their own accord.

Biederman, Faraone, et al. (1993) conclude, "Our studies suggest that both referred and nonreferred adults with ADHD may have a pattern of demographic, psychosocial, psychiatric and cognitive features that mirrors well-documented findings among children with ADHD" (p. 1797).

Until many more studies like these completed by Biederman and his colleagues at the University of Massachusetts are generated, predictions of adult outcome for individuals with histories of ADHD are like strands of DNA with key components missing. A general portrait exists of the adult outcome of individuals with ADHD, but many specific questions remain unanswered.

Definition

Paul Wender (1979) and colleagues at the University of Utah were the first to describe the constellation of adult ADHD symptoms that bears closest similarity to today's criteria. Wender described adult ADHD, then called "minimal brain dysfunction," as consisting of restlessness, distractibility, mood swings, disorganization, hot temper, impulsivity, and low tolerance for stress. In this model, adults with ADHD had to meet the first two traits and at least two of the others. The Utah criteria for the diagnosis of ADD, residual type, as they became known, were a first step toward defining the disorder in adulthood. The criteria also stipulated that, as a child, the individual must have demonstrated problems with hyperactivity and attention deficit, and at least one difficulty with behavior at school—impulsivity, overexcitability, or temper outbursts. In addition, the criteria stated that a report from the parent was necessary to corroborate the history. Further, individuals experiencing antisocial personality, major affective disorder, schizophrenia, schizoaffective disorder, and schizotypal or borderline personality disorders were excluded from the diagnosis of ADHD.

The Utah criteria were not based on extensive, empirically validated field studies. They are therefore a good initial step that certainly will continue to be adjusted. One of the first questions current researchers ask in regard to these criteria is, How deviant must an individual's behavior be to fulfill a cutoff? Further, symptoms related to temper outbursts, hostility, and stress intolerance appear to confound the diagnosis of ADHD with other disruptive disorders.

In defining adult ADHD, Barkley (1990b) noted the need for evidence of the problem in childhood based on current diagnostic criteria. Barkley suggested that disorders previously mentioned, except for antisocial personality disorder, be considered to exclude a diagnosis of ADHD. Personality disorder has clearly been implicated as related to ADHD but not necessarily caused by ADHD (Gittelman et al., 1985; G. Weiss & Hechtman, 1986).

A. L. Robin (1992) suggests that the core symptoms of ADHD in adults include poor persistence of effort, impulsivity, hyperactivity, diminished rule-governed behavior, and increased work task variability. T. E. Brown (1995) reports that, while most descriptive symptoms of ADHD focus on overt behaviors, the most problematic symptoms are internal, influencing cognition and affect. In response he developed the Brown Attention Activation Disorder Scale (BAADS; T. E. Brown, 1995). This self-report measure groups ADHD symptoms into five clusters:

1. Activating and organizing work (starting work tasks, staying organized, completing essential daily activities)

2. Sustaining attention and concentration (distractibility, daydreaming, etc.)
3. Sustaining energy and effort (daytime drowsiness, slow processing of information and adequate task completion, etc.)
4. Low emotional threshold (irritability, depressed mood, chronic discouragement, apparent lack of motivation, sensitivity to criticism, etc.)
5. Poor working memory (excessive forgetfulness, difficulty memorizing, etc.)

It has also been suggested that the complaints of adults requesting assessment for ADHD might well define the disorder. Barkley (1990b) listed the major complaints of adults seeking assessment for ADHD:

- Difficulty locating and maintaining vocation
- Performing below level of competence vocationally
- Inability to perform up to capability at school
- Difficulty concentrating
- Lack of organization
- Difficulty establishing and maintaining rules
- Poor self-discipline
- Low self-esteem
- Feelings of depression
- Forgetfulness
- Feelings of poor memory
- Perceptions of confusion or reports of difficulty thinking clearly

Hallowell and Ratey (1994) propose a similar list of 20 hypothesized symptoms of adult ADHD, including those related to difficulty sustaining attention, low frustration threshold, impulsiveness, and restlessness. However, these authors have further hypothesized that adults with ADHD also have strong feelings of underachievement, crave stimulation, may be intolerant of boredom, can be creative and unconventional, have low self-esteem, and worry excessively. Because of the popularity of these authors' text, this symptom list has, in the absence of empirical research, become the "gold standard of symptoms" in the public arena. Efforts are underway to empirically test this symptomatic profile (see Chapter 6).

The *DSM-III* (APA, 1980) provided for a diagnosis of ADD, residual type: "Signs of hyperactivity are no longer present, but other signs of the illness have persisted into the present without periods of remission as evidenced by signs of attention deficits and impulsivity" (p. 45). These symptoms were required to impair social and occupational functioning on a daily basis.

Despite a range of hypothetical and in some cases tested symptom profiles for adult ADHD, at this time the clinical standard is to apply the *DSM-IV* criteria to the adult population. As Murphy and Barkley (1995a) have noted on the basis of preliminary data, however, cutoff scores of four out of nine symptoms for the inattentive factor and five out of nine for the hyperactive-impulsive factor may be sufficient to cross the threshold of clinical significance in adults below 50 years of age. The sample population of people over 50 years old is too small at this time to allow general conclusions. Further, these authors report no differences between males and females in regard to ADHD symptom presentation.

Evaluation

Basic guidelines for the evaluation of ADHD in adults are gradually being developed. There is an initial consensus that the diagnosis of ADHD in adulthood should include

1. A childhood history with evidence that the child met the *DSM-III-R* or *International Classification of Diseases—9th Edition* (*ICD-9*) diagnostic criteria for ADHD
2. Current ADHD symptoms with at least six of the present *DSM-IV* inattentive or hyperactive-impulsive criteria
3. Symptoms producing impairment in many areas, including some but not necessarily all of the following: job, school, social acceptance, daily responsibilities, relationships, marriage, and emotional adjustment
4. Assessment conducted by someone trained in this field
5. Other comorbid problems understood and delineated (S. Goldstein, 1994; Murphy & Barkley, 1995a)

Some clinics devoted to the treatment of adult ADHD also routinely emphasize and screen for alcohol and related substance abuse problems.

As with children, efforts have been made to identify laboratory measures that might correlate well with a diagnosis of ADHD in adults. However, as with children, laboratory measures may yield questionable results involving negative predictive power. Wood et al. (1976), in studying 15 adults with histories of attentional problems, found marked difficulty in mathematics performance on the WRAT despite above average intellect in these individuals. P. H. Wender et al. (1981) replicated this study, finding normal IQ but problems with academic achievement. As noted, Klee et al. (1986) in their study of 12 adults with histories of ADHD found selected difficulties, such as accuracy of performance on the Digit Symbol subtest of the Wechsler and omission errors on a continuous performance task. At this time no single battery of tests has demonstrated reliability and validity in identifying adult ADHD in a laboratory setting beyond the accuracy of diagnosis obtained by careful history. This author (S. Goldstein & Goldstein, 1990) and others (Barkley, 1990b) have routinely recommended laboratory measures as a means of providing confirmatory evidence of the diagnosis of ADHD in children. However, recent research has suggested that laboratory data may not yield much in the way of increased accuracy. Psychometric and emotional evaluation, however, is essential in order to assess the myriad comorbid psychiatric and developmental disorders children and adults with histories of ADHD demonstrate.

It is likely that the pattern demonstrated over the past 20 years in efforts to identify laboratory measures to accurately assess childhood ADHD will be played out in the adult field as well. A number of theorists have hypothesized and tested factoral models of attention. Based on these theories, a laboratory or clinical test battery has been suggested (Barkley, 1990b). Barkley's battery is based on the work of Mirsky (1987, 1989), which outlines a four-factor model of attention, including

1. The capacity to focus on and execute tasks over a short time span
2. The capacity to encode and mentally manipulate information
3. The capacity to sustain attention over a longer period of time
4. The capacity to shift attentional focus flexibly

Barkley (1990b) recommends the Trail Making tests, Parts A and B, and the WAIS-R Digit Symbol subtest to measure focused attention, the WAIS-R Digit Span and Arithmetic subtests to measure encoding, a continuous performance task to measure sustained attention, and the Wisconsin Card Sorting Test (Heaton, 1981) to measure flexibility. However, it must be emphasized that even these instruments have not been consistently found to discriminate people with ADHD accurately on an individual, clinical basis from normal people or those with other disorders. Other novel measures of attention, such as the Paced Auditory Serial Addition Test (PASAT; Gronwall & Wrightson, 1981) and the Stroop test (Grodzinsky, 1990), have also been recommended as possibly beneficial for the laboratory evaluation of attention symptoms. These assessment tools will be discussed in greater depth in Chapter 6.

Similar models have been offered based on research with individuals experiencing traumatic brain injury (Levin, Benton, & Grossman, 1982). S. Goldstein and Goldstein (1990) discussed the value of obtaining laboratory measures of sustained and divided attention, planning and reflection, and vigilance.

Of all the clinical laboratory measures, the continuous performance tasks are by far the most popular and appear to hold the most potential benefit in regard to their positive predictive power. Single case studies have demonstrated that the Delay, Vigilance, and Distractibility tasks from the Gordon Diagnostic System, for example, appear to be sensitive in identifying individuals complaining of ADHD symptoms (Roman, Nussbaum, & Bigler, 1988). Although this instrument may have good positive predictive power, it may have much weaker negative predictive power. Individuals failing the instrument may have ADHD, but those passing may or may not suffer from ADHD. Saykin (1989) reports that on the Gordon system, both young and elderly normal subjects demonstrate a ceiling effect. This is especially true on the Vigilance task, which may thus have limited sensitivity to an adult population. The Distractibility task, on the other hand, demonstrates a range of performance across both age groups. This suggests that it may be more sensitive and have lower specificity, leading to occasional false positives. Neither race nor IQ affect commission or correct scores on the Vigilance task of the Gordon (Hamsher, 1987).

A number of questionnaires, including the BAADS, the Wender adult questionnaire, and the Conners adult questionnaire, have been developed and are being studied to aid the diagnosis of adult ADHD. These questionnaires will be reviewed in Chapter 6. Preliminary data suggest that they may have clinical, diagnostic utility. In a study of 50 consecutive adults referred to a private outpatient practice, the adult version of the BAADS discriminated between subjects diagnosed clinically with ADHD and nonclinical controls. There was a difference of over 40 points between the two groups (group mean for normals 32.6, group mean for ADHD 76.5). The BAADS-1 assesses problems that appear to factor into five clusters related to ADHD, primarily without hyperactivity (Brown, 1995). As noted, these clusters include activating and organizing work, sustaining attention and concentration, sustaining energy and effort, low emotional threshold, and poor working memory.

In Chapter 6 we will offer a comprehensive model for the evaluation of ADHD and related problems based on currently available research and the concept of functional assessment.

Treatment

A number of authors have suggested a variety of cognitive, behavioral, and medical treatments for ADHD (Hallowell & Ratey, 1994; Murphy & Vervock, 1995; Nadeau, 1995). Among the nonmedical or psychosocial treatments thought to be beneficial for ADHD are psychoeducation, structuring the environment and psychotherapy (Ratey et al., 1992), behavioral therapies, parenting and marital support (G. Weiss & Hechtman, 1986), long-term therapy (Ratey, Hallowell, & Miller, 1995), and group therapy (Hallowell & Ratey, 1994). At this time, however, the available research literature is extremely limited in demonstrating the efficacy of all but treatment by medication. Over 20 years ago, Wood et al. (1976) reported positive findings on double-blind trials of methylphenidate in adults with attention deficit. This study also reported positive effects of pemoline and a number of tricyclic antidepressants; it is important to note, however, this was an open, nonblinded study. P. H. Wender et al. (1981) found pemoline beneficial for adult ADHD symptoms. P. H. Wender, Wood, and Reimherr (1985) reported that 60% of adults with ADHD responded to treatment beginning with methylphenidate or d-amphetamine. It is important to note that neither methylphenidate nor tricyclic antidepressants have received FDA approval for treatment of ADHD in adults.

Dopamine agonists have also been studied in the treatment of posttraumatic ADHD. C. T. Gualitieri and Evans (1988) studied medications, including bromocriptine, mantadine, and deprenyl. The last is known to increase the amount of available dopamine in the brain. Deprenyl has also been demonstrated to improve symptoms of ADHD in adults (P. H. Wender, Wood, & Reimherr 1985). Further, Reimherr, Wood, and Wender (1980) treated three adults in an open trial with L-dopa and carbidopa for ADHD symptoms. Although the benefits were less robust than those of stimulants, there were clear, positive effects for all three individuals. In one adult, these drugs appeared to potentiate the benefits of the stimulants. P. H. Wender and Reimherr (1990) treated 19 adults with ADHD in an open trial with buproprion. These individuals had been receiving either stimulant or alternative medication for almost four years. Fourteen of the 19 experienced moderate to marked benefits from the buproprion. Ten chose to continue this medicine rather than return to their former medication. These authors hypothesized that buproprion was beneficial because of its dopamenergic activity. Chapter 13 will review these studies in depth.

CHAPTER 6

Evaluating Adults

I T IS CRITICAL that clinicians understand the broad symptoms and heterogeneity of problems among people with LD or ADHD (Ackerman, McGrew, & Dykman, 1987). A narrow focus reveals only that individuals with LD have problems with reading, writing, and spelling while those with ADHD have problems with impulsivity, organization, task initiation, and attention. These difficulties are likely the tip of the iceberg. Follow-up studies show that people with ADHD or LD struggle more than their unimpaired peers with a broad range of school, vocational, and life issues. Some of these struggles may be related to their disorder, but others are related to various coexisting problems (Rogan & Hartman, 1990). For example, no fewer than 134 problem characteristics of postsecondary students with LD have been identified in the research literature (Mangrum & Strichart, 1984). Categories include difficulties with thinking, spoken and written language, academic achievement, perceptual-motor skills, note taking, study and test-taking habits, and social and affective behaviors. For adults with ADHD, the list of problems that have been reported and empirically studied is just as long (Barkley, 1990b; S. Goldstein & Goldstein, 1995; Hallowell & Ratey, 1994; Nadeau, 1995).

In the realm of skill deficiency, commonly reported areas of adult LD difficulty include practical mathematics, specifically the use of time, money, and measurement (D. J. Johnson & Blalock, 1987). A. C. Stone (1987) reported that many adults with LD experience problems with concept formation and abstract reasoning. On reviewing 18 follow-up studies, Schonhaut and Satz (1983) found that even educationally and occupationally successful learning-disabled adults continue to experience significant problems with spelling, leading these researchers to conclude that this is the major residual deficit of adults with LD. Vogel and Moran (1982), however, report frequent problems with written language skills as well in this population.

In a later publication, Vogel (1993b) suggests that the most common deficits among adults with LD are in reading rates, spelling, and the mechanics of writing. Others believe that individuals with ADHD or LD are often equally troubled by problems related to organization, time management, and self-esteem (S. Goldstein & Goldstein, 1995). Adults with LD have been described as commonly reporting auditory or visual perceptual problems and difficulty with memory (Houck, Englehard, & Geller, 1989; D. J. Johnson & Blalock, 1987). Further, many clinicians have observed that adults with histories of ADHD show long-standing patterns of struggling with academic tasks requiring practice and repetition, such as nonphonetic spelling, the mechanics of written language, and mathematical facts (S. Goldstein, 1995).

Cognitive, experiential, and academic variables have been used to predict academic and vocational success. It has been suggested, for example, that parental encouragement and support influences students' success (Bruck, 1989; Haring et al., 1990). Family variables have been found to very powerfully predict high school academic success, even among the unimpaired population (Christensen, Rounds, & Gorney, 1992). Further, the interest of parents in their children's education has been found to stimulate career exploration (Dowdy, Carter, & Smith, 1990). Interestingly, students participating in extracurricular activities in high school are more likely to seek postsecondary education (R. J. Miller, Snider, & Rzonca, 1990).

Verbal strengths have been found to predict job success for learning-disabled individuals. Faas and D'Alonzo (1990) found that the WAIS Comprehension, Information, and Similarities subtests were powerfully predictive of successful employment for this population. F. C. Leonard (1991) reported that global scores on the WAIS did not predict college success for students with LD. However, as other authors have noted, the Comprehension and Similarities subtests were positively correlated with grade point average. Litowitz (1987) found that many adults with histories of LD possessed good verbal intelligence and knowledge, as indicated by the WAIS, but that these gross measures did not reveal the subtle oral language, semantic, and pragmatic difficulties that these individuals experienced. However, the better their subtest scores, the more likely it was that they were successful in employment settings. These authors also reported that a general verbal IQ measure was just as powerful in predicting job success. The issue of IQ and its relationship as a predictor variable to life success has been hotly debated (Fraser, 1995; Herrnstein & Murray, 1994). Yet intelligence has been found to be a predictor of the types of educational programs that learning-disabled individuals enter. Minskoff et al. (1989) reported that learning-disabled adults in vocational rehabilitation programs often have full-scale Wechsler IQ scores in the low average range (80–90) whereas those in two- or four-year college programs possess normal or better intelligence.

Some authors have suggested that a high verbal Comprehension score paired with a low Freedom from Distractibility index on the WISC-III or low Digit Span and Arithmetic subtest scores on the WAIS indicate the presence of auditory-processing or memory problems. The pairing of high Arithmetic and lower Digit Span scores is thought to reflect better language ability with limited auditory memory, while the opposite is thought to reflect language-processing deficits with stronger rote auditory sequential memory skills (Malter & Frank, 1995). As explained in an earlier chapter, the clinician must remember that the ability of a pattern of IQ subtest scores to predict LD or more specifically ADHD, or for that matter to help in clinical diagnosis, has not been borne out by well-controlled research (Anastopoulos, Spisto, & Maher, 1994; Barkley, 1990b).

Recently published research has reflected efforts to generate cognitive profiles for those college students with LD who are most likely to succeed (Cordoni & Goh, 1989). Although it is difficult not to argue that the higher an individual's overall level of intellectual function, the greater his or her likelihood of success, intelligence is not the only predictor of success for the LD and ADHD populations.

Among the population of learning-disabled students with the basic skills to attend college, many lack the academic preparation necessary to succeed (Dalke & Franzene, 1988): Some have not completed basic, required course work (McGuire, Norlander, & Shaw, 1990); some need counseling about postsecondary options (Seidenberg, 1986b); some have inadequate organizational and study skills (Dexter, 1982); some have inadequate learning and study strategies (Deshler & Schumacher, 1986).

Other research has suggested that learning-disabled students are simply not exposed to the same range of academic and vocational career options as their unimpaired peers are (Viller, 1985). Researchers have asked whether students with LD are mature enough to function independently in college (Manganello, 1990)—in particular, whether these students possess the skills necessary to adjust to living away from home (Barbaro, Christman, Holzinger, & Rosenberg, 1985), as well as personal independent skills (Price, 1988). It is increasingly evident that adults with LD or ADHD should obtain an evaluation that systematically considers all of these skills and issues, incorporating them into a logical framework, before making school or vocational decisions (Aune, 1991; Vogel & Adelman, 1990a). It is not surprising, however, that the primary conclusion of a review of available evaluative models and programs is that comprehensive assessments of this nature are rarely available (Dowdy et al., 1990).

D. J. Johnson (1993) eloquently described the complex interaction of skill and skill-related problems that people with LD may experience:

> For example, students with problems in conceptualization or concept formation often have difficulty with higher level listening, reading comprehension, math reasoning and certain social skills. Similarly, listening comprehension problems typically interfere with oral expression and reading comprehension. Most dyslexics have spelling and written language difficulty; many also have other verbal deficits as indicated by the research on subtypes. (p. 117)

A similar statement about attention and impulse problems can be made for ADHD.

It is critical that clinicians asked to evaluate individuals with LD or ADHD understand these issues, as well as the setting in which a particular person will need to function. More clinicians are beginning to recognize that, although laboratory-generated skill measures such as IQ scores may be valuable, without an understanding of the functional setting in which those skills are to be used functioning will be extremely difficult to assess and predict accurately. For example, the demands of college are different from those of high school. College programs are characterized by significantly less teacher-student contact, more academic competition, and less available support than in high school (Dalke & Schmitt, 1987).

College course work also requires more advanced academic, note-taking, studying, and test-taking skills (Houck et al., 1989). It has been shown repeatedly that the college-aged LD and ADHD populations lack competence in the basic executive skills necessary for success, including problem solving (A. C. Stone, 1987), time management (Vogel, 1985, 1987b), note taking (Rose & Sloan, 1990), test taking (Mangrum & Strichart, 1988), textbook reading (Vogel, 1985, 1987b), and organizing written material (D. J. Johnson, 1987b). Not surprisingly, persistence is also thought crucial to collegiate and vocational success. Unfortunately, young adults with ADHD or LD have been reported to have difficulty with persistence and goal setting (Mangrum & Strichart, 1988). The ADHD population especially has a long history of lacking academic persistence. Thus, clinicians must focus on providing a functional assessment that integrates skills and the settings in which they must be used. Teaching independent study skills, for example, has become a critical component of services for these populations (Bursuck & Jayanthi, 1993). Chapter 10 will describe strategies used to teach and facilitate generalization in the use of independent study skills.

A Framework for Assessment

Although some college and vocational programs have established standard test batteries and entrance criteria (Mellard, 1990), the majority have not specified the tests or the cutoff scores required on tests to qualify for special programming. It is critical, however, that a clinician evaluating someone who may apply to a vocational or postsecondary program ensure that data generated in the assessment are useful in any review of the individual's skills and qualifications.

Before focusing on a specific battery of tests for assessment, a clinician must have a framework for the assessment process. In general, when making an assessment, a clinician tries to integrate history, current functioning, skills, achievement, emotional status, and personality so as to see the world through the eyes of the person being evaluated. The most important use for these data is in generating interventions. However, clinicians must also make certain that referral sources provide an operational, specific list of questions that they would like the assessment to address. Ideally, referral for assessment will include as much background information as possible. In most cases, however, referrals are made because limited information is available to make important decisions.

The assessment of skills focuses on a number of domains, including memory, reasoning, problem solving, language skills, literacy, perceptual-motor skills, personality, psychiatric status, and attentional capabilities. This list suggests that assessment for LD and ADHD is very much based on neuropsychology. That is, assessment focuses on identifying strengths and weaknesses that contribute to an individual's daily life functioning. Viewed more globally, a comprehensive assessment of someone suspected of having LD or ADHD should generate data addressing 10 areas, including intelligence, personality, processing skills, language, reading, written language and spelling, mathematics, adaptive behavior, self-esteem, and the ability to integrate and make efficient daily use of skills. Vogel and Adelman (1993) structure the skill profile differently, breaking the skills down into educational, social, and psychological attributes:

Educational attributes
- Study skills
- Organization
- Reading
- Writing
- Speaking

Social attributes
- Relating to others
- Perception of self in social settings
- Age-appropriate behavior
- Group interaction
- Authority figure interaction

Psychological attributes
- Problem solving (school, self, career)
- Self-concept
- Attitude toward school

- Academic stress
- Dependence on others*

For each attribute, the clinician assesses the student's self-awareness as it relates to that attribute. For example, the following questions are asked about study skills: "Can the student identify areas of specific strengths and weaknesses in study habits? Examples? . . . Can the students identify specific strategies that they use? Examples? Can they discuss how and when to change strategies as they study?"

Newill, Goyette, and Fogarty (1984) outline a comprehensive process by which data concerning skills may be gathered:

I. Preliminary assessment
   A. Client history: Examples of areas that should be reviewed within sections are provided
     1. Family background and dynamics
      History of learning disabilities in family
      Current family composition
      Relationship between parents and client
     2. Medical information
      Under care of physician or taking medication
      Unusual illnesses, accidents, surgeries
      Difficulties with alcohol or drugs
     3. Interpersonal functioning
      Friendship patterns
      Interactions with opposite sex
      Ease of making friends
     4. Psychological functioning
      Treatment for psychological problems
      Feelings of inferiority
      Antisocial behaviors
     5. Educational background
      Levels and type of education (special education or regular education)
      Repeated grades
      Attitudes toward school
     6. Vocational history
      Current employment status
      History of frequent job changes
      Relationship between handicap and vocational success
   B. Behavioral observations: A conscious effort to attend to the client will reveal valuable information relative to the client's:
     1. Communication abilities
     2. Interpersonal style
     3. Levels of attention
     4. Cognitive abilities

*Adapted from *Success for College Students with Learning Disabilities* (pp. 233–234), by S. A. Vogel and P. B. Adelman, 1993, New York: Springer. Used with permission.

   5. Emotional maturity

   6. Problem-solving style

C. School records: The vocational rehabilitation counselor should request:

   1. A complete transcript

   2. Results of formal testing

   3. Description of any special education services received

   4. Incidence of behavior problems

Once this information is obtained, the counselor should look for the following patterns:

   1. Lower performance on achievement tests than expected from IQ scores

   2. History of specific learning problems dating from the primary grades

   3. Placement in special education classes (any information available)

   4. Behavioral notes indicating peer interaction problems (either aggressiveness or passivity)

II. Formal diagnostic procedures

  A. Medical assessment: The medical assessment is viewed as an essential component of the diagnostic package as it serves to both: 1. identify any physical condition that may be contributing to, or causing, the learning problem and 2. identify any physical problem that may exist concurrently with the LD. The medical assessment should include the following two components:

   1. Medical history

   2. Comprehensive medical examination

  B. Psychological/evaluation examination: At minimum, the psychologist should administer the following tests to make an appropriate diagnosis:

   1. Individual intelligence test (WAIS-R is recommended). The test should provide the following information:

   Full-scale IQ

   Verbal and performance IQ's

   Subscale scores for each verbal and performance measure

   Interpretation of test profile

   2. Individual achievement tests

   Word recognition (decoding)

   Reading comprehension

   Mathematics

   Spelling

Each test should provide the following information:

   Grade level

   Standard score (when available)

   Discussion of discrepancy (if any) between achievement results and aptitude

   3. Measure of personality functioning: The test should provide the following information:

   Presence/absence of emotional dysfunction

   Significance of emotional problems (psychotic/neurotic)

   Relationship between emotional problems and specific LD

  C. Vocational assessment: The vocational assessment should consist of four components:

   1. Informal ascertainment of client's vocational goals

   2. Preliminary deterioration of client's vocational aptitudes and strengths

   3. Formal vocational aptitude and vocational interest testing

4. Diagnostic vocational evaluation (assessments which provide client with "hands-on" experiences in a variety of job simulations)*

Still another assessment outline is suggested by the Office of Student Disability Services at the University of Iowa (Richard 1995a):

I. Intellectual functioning
    WAIS-R (including subtest scores) is an absolute requirement.

II. Psychological-cognitive processes (as indicated by WAIS-R subtest scores)
    (The following tests are examples of instruments that are appropriate for adults.)
    Auditory memory (e.g., Rey Auditory Verbal Learning Test; sentence repetition; Wechsler Memory scale; word fluency)
    Visual memory (e.g., Benton Visual Retention Test; Wechsler Memory scale)
    Abstract/conceptual reasoning (e.g., Woodcock-Johnson Analysis, Concept Formation; Stanford-Binet Proverbs, Analogies, and Essential Differences)

III. Academic
     Reading (e.g., WRAT; Nelson-Denny; Advanced Reading Inventory; California or Stanford achievement tests)
     Math (e.g., WRAT; Woodcock-Johnson; California or Stanford achievement tests; writing sample)
     WRAT alone is not an adequate achievement measure.

IV. Modern Language Aptitude Test (MLAT)
    If a student is having difficulty with acquiring a second language and has requested foreign language substitution courses, this test can be used in addition to the other tests; however, it is not required.
    [Scores for any test instruments used should be included in this report.]

V. Specific academic recommendations
    Recommendations should be made as part of the final report concerning academic compensatory strategies, e.g., foreign language requirement substituted with courses in foreign culture, mathematics requirement substituted with courses that emphasize logic and/or quantitative reasoning.†

Some evaluators will feel the need to assign a marker or grade of severity (e.g., an Impairment Rating) to problems the evaluated individual is experiencing. While this is sometimes helpful, it does facilitate the kind of functional assessment needed to determine whether the evaluated individual has the skills necessary for a particular program or what types of remedial or compensatory support the individual may require. Minskoff (1994) suggests that the severity of LD be judged on the basis of several variables, including 1. level of intelligence, 2. special skills the individual possesses, 3. psychological processing abilities (attention, reasoning, perception, and memory), 4. language skills, 5. academic achievement, 6. emotional and social adjustment, and 7. vocational-employability skills.

*Adapted from "Diagnosis and Assessment of the Adult with Specific Learning Disabilities," by B. H. Newill, C. H. Goyette, and T. W. Fogarty, 1984, *Journal of Rehabilitation, 8,* pp. 188–189.
†Adapted from "Recommended Assessment Instruments for Cognitive Processing Evaluation," by M. Richard, 1995, Iowa City: University of Iowa, Office of Disability Services. Used with permission.

Clinical assessment should be structured toward meeting the goal of the referral. If the purpose of the referral is to qualify someone for a specific program, it is important that the clinician understand the qualification requirements before beginning the assessment. Similarly, if the assessment is to be used to identify a student's strengths and weaknesses in order to help that student choose classes in a college program, knowledge of the program and classes available is essential. It is important that referral sources list very clearly the questions they would like answered or addressed in the assessment.

Assessment must also focus on the relationship between laboratory test data and functional impairment. LD is more difficult to quantify functionally than physical injuries (the latter uses a standard measure, the Guides to Permanent Impairment). An assessment for LD must yield data that are useful for understanding the functional limitations the individual has in daily life and what can be done about them.

Halpern and Fuhrer (1984) define functional assessment as the analysis and measurement of specific behaviors that occur in real environments and are relevant to life or vocational goals. For ADHD or LD, functional assessment is essential in order to determine the impact of the disability on daily functioning. Functional assessment entails understanding not only what a person can and cannot do but also what demands a particular setting will place on the person. Thus, an assessment of an adult with LD or ADHD focuses on skills, abilities, and their impact on daily functioning.

The California Community College Assessment System for Adults with Learning Disabilities (CCC; Mellard, 1990) was developed over several years, culminating with implementation in 1987, through the cooperation of the California Community College System and the University of Kansas Institute for Research in Learning Disabilities. It was designed as a data-based eligibility model and is intended to provide guidelines for the diagnosis of LD in college-aged individuals for the purpose of minimizing inequities and biases. It continues to represent one of the few well-coordinated efforts to offer a set of guidelines for qualification to receive student disability services and accommodations on the basis of disability as defined in Section 504 of the Rehabilitation Act (1973; see Chapter 12). Using a variety of specific test procedures, normative data were collected on a random stratified sample of 900 nonhandicapped California Community College students and 900 students previously diagnosed with LD. The sample provided baseline data and allowed for the development of eligibility criteria. Local norms were generated from these data, and cutoff scores were selected.

The CCC model relies on formal and informal evaluation procedures, providing information on present problems; history, including educational and vocational experience; language, academic, and vocational skills; and expected achievement level.

The seven components of the CCC eligibility model are based on structured assessment and, most important, clinical judgment:

1. *Intake screening.* An in-depth history is taken. Self-report measures are gathered. Prior testing, academic, and vocational records are reviewed.

2. *Measured achievement.* Efforts are made by the evaluator to review available records and make an initial determination as to whether there are indications in the individual's history or academic or vocational performance to suggest that he or she is learning disabled as opposed to low achieving or intellectually deficient. Measured achievement is demonstrated by formal testing such as college entrance or placement exams, academic success in high school or college, and employment experience.

3. *Adaptive behavior.* Through self-report and interview measures, an assessment is made of the individual's daily living skills involving independent care, personal skills, money management, social relations, and so forth.

4. *Ability level.* This component consists of structured assessment using instruments to provide an overview of the individual's language, cognitive, and academic achievement.

5. *Processing deficits.* Strengths and weaknesses are evaluated using factor and related methods. The test data is used to provide a profile of the individual's ability to integrate, store, retrieve, and express information. Discrepancies among these skills are used to justify the diagnosis of LD.

6. *Aptitude-achievement discrepancy.* This component is similar to that employed in the special education Individuals with Disabilities Education Act model for school-aged children. A significant discrepancy must be noted between potential aptitude and academic achievement.

7. *Eligibility recommendation.* At the completion of each of the first six steps, the evaluator must determine whether there is enough data to make an accurate determination. If not, the evaluator has the option of deciding that valid and accurate data were not collected and attempting alternative means of collecting the data. The model implemented, however, requires that evaluators not use alternative assessment methods for more than 1 out of every 100 individuals they evaluate; the college chancellor's office must be notified of exceptions. Based on the assessment of the first six steps, the evaluator may determine whether criteria have been met, integrate quantitative and qualitative data as well as clinical judgment, and make a final determination and set of recommendations.

Kanter, Halliday, Mellard, and Howard (1987; cited in Mellard 1990) reported that 34% of the 900 randomly selected clinically diagnosed students with LD in the CCC standardization fell below an IQ of 78. Further, Mellard (1987) reported that among the random control sample of 900, 32% met the discrepancy criteria, suggesting that one in three students not identified as learning disabled have an aptitude-achievement discrepancy. However, the aptitude-achievement discrepancy method was very accurate in identifying all of the learning-disabled students. It was concluded that if the achievement discrepancy formulation was the only method used to identify learning-disabled students, many non-learning-disabled students would be identified as learning disabled (C. R. Reynolds, 1985).

Neuropsychological batteries such as the Halstead-Reitan (Reitan & Wolfson, 1985) and the Luria-Nebraska Neuropsychological Battery (C. J. Golden et al., 1980) offer broad screening of a number of neuropsychological constructs. Research studies with adults have developed a variety of profiles on these instruments consistent with LD (Harvey & Wells, 1989; R. D. Lewis & Lorion, 1988; McCue, Shelly, & Goldstein, 1986). A recent study by Oestreicher and O'Donnell (1995) using the Halstead-Reitan Neuropsychological Test Battery exemplifies the work with learning-disabled individuals in this area. The battery was used to determine whether the GNDS could discriminate learning-disabled from normal and brain-injured individuals. Twenty-two female and 38 male young adults participating in a LD college support program were evaluated along with a sample of head-injured and nondisabled individuals. The Halstead-Reitan differentiated the LD group successfully, placing them somewhere between the normal and brain-injured populations. This finding confirmed the results of past research with learning-disabled adults (O'Donnell et al., 1983), suggesting that the use of this battery, and specifically of the GNDS, is appropriate with learning-disabled individuals and is sensitive to the mild neurobehavioral deficits hypothesized as characterizing this population (Duane, 1991). It is important to note, however, that this scale was not found to be capable of differentiating subtypes of LD. Nevertheless, for each individual certain patterns of underlying skills, strengths, and weaknesses were generated. Theoretically, these could be helpful in leading to functional treatment intervention. The inability of neuropsychological test batteries to consistently differentiate subtypes of LD (Rourke, 1985) or ADHD (Goodyear & Hynd, 1992) should not be taken as evidence that these populations are homogeneous.

Arcia and Gualitieri (1994) evaluated neurobehavioral performance in adults with closed head injury, adults with ADHD, and controls. These authors found that the groups with closed head injury and ADHD had greater difficulty than controls with sustained attentional tasks. The head-injured group had problems with these tasks because of general slowness and longer response times. The attention-disordered group, in contrast, had problems characterized by impulsivity and inability to regulate attention and inhibit impulsive tendencies to respond.

Barkley (1990b) suggests a neuropsychological approach to the assessment of adult ADHD, following Mirsky's (1989) four-factor model of attentional processes (focused attention, encoding and manipulating, sustained attention, and flexibility). Tests such as the Trail Making and Digit Symbol subtests from the Wechsler are suggested to evaluate focused attention, the Wechsler Digit Span and Arithmetic subtests to evaluate encoding/manipulation, the Wisconsin Card Sort to evaluate flexibility, and finally a variety of problem-solving tasks to evaluate sustained attention. As reviewed, however, the neuropsychological approaches to the measurement of ADHD symptoms have had mixed success despite their continued popularity.

As Barkley and Grodzinsky (1994) report, neuropsychological tests generally display low levels of sensitivity for individuals with attention deficit disorders. Positive predictive power for the diagnosis of ADD with hyperactivity in this study was poor for eight of nine tests examined, reaching levels exceeding 50% only for a CPT commission score. Combining the two groups having attention deficit with and without hyperactivity provided positive predictive power reaching acceptable levels only for the CPT and a version of controlled oral word association.

As Racine and Campbell (1995) note, "It is perhaps also a questionable assumption that the types of problems in attention described by patients are the same as those measured on discrete neuropsychological tests" (p. 8). This observation is likely to be true of LD as well. It is not surprising that at this time there is no universally agreed upon battery of assessment instruments for adults with LD or ADHD. In the field of LD research, it is generally agreed that assessment must provide an overview of the client's skills as well as his or her levels of achievement. In contrast, there has been little empirical research suggesting that any type of laboratory or structured test is consistently able to support, confirm, or disconfirm the diagnosis of ADHD on a clinical basis (Hechtman, 1989; Klee et al., 1986). Some writers suggest that, because only limited data are available to guide the clinician in making assessment decisions (principally in regard to symptom significance) for adult ADHD, these decisions should be made based on what is known about children and using general clinical observation (Biggs, 1995). This writer cannot agree with this logic. Stating that something does not exist is insufficient justification for then making decisions about what should be done. At this time, the diagnosis of ADHD in adults, as in children, is made primarily through the compilation and analysis of a very well defined history. The history sets the critical stage for diagnosing ADHD. Additional support is provided by self-report and observer report instruments. Limited data are available suggesting that certain laboratory measures (e.g., computerized tasks) may someday be useful. However, in regard to adult LD, laboratory assessment is essential to understanding skills and achievement. Thus, the assessment process for ADHD emphasizes the initial history and interview stages, whereas the assessment process for LD emphasizes the testing stages. In fact, testing in an ADHD evaluation is not necessarily undertaken to make the diagnosis of ADHD but rather to understand and diagnose potential comorbid conditions and to evaluate academic and cognitive functioning and personality.

Finally, clinicians may be asked to assess individuals receiving a number of different psychotropic or related medications. Of relevance is the potential for these medications to either positively or adversely affect symptom report and test data. At this time there is no reason to assume that any of the medications administered for psychiatric or behavioral problems will have a positive impact on basic academic achievement test performance; some medicines, such as anticonvulsants, may impair test performance (these issues will be reviewed in Chapter 13). Nevertheless, clinicians must be aware of any medicines taken and consider their possible effect on test performance. As reviewed in Chapter 13, stimulants are likely to improve the behavior and, in some cases, test performance of children with ADHD. For example, Douglas, Barr, Desilets, and Sherman (1995) evaluated the effect of three dosage levels of Ritalin (0.3, 0.6, and 0.9 mg/kg) on a group of 17 boys with ADHD by setting five tasks assessing divergent and convergent thinking, perseveration, ability to shift mental set, problem solving, and speed and accuracy of processing. As dosage increased, measures of mental flexibility and other cognitive processes improved. Perseveration was not observed. Methylphenidate was demonstrated to improve persistence. These authors interpreted the observed changes as support for the hypothesis that methylphenidate acts on central self-regulatory processes. Data that suggest how much improvement a clinician might expect are not available. Nor is it known whether administering some instruments twice, with and without medication, yields clinically relevant data.

Neurology, Learning and Behavior Center LD and ADHD Adult Evaluative Model

The Neurology, Learning and Behavior Center (NLBC) assessment model begins with a thorough history. The clinician should provide the client in advance with a history form and self-report measures. The completed history form can be used as a framework for the initial, history-taking session. It is strongly recommended that a 10-minute telephone triage be conducted before an intake visit is scheduled and forms are provided to the client. During this phone contact, the clinician can tell the client what to expect. As part of this contact, the clinician should clarify the purpose of the referral, confirm the specific referral questions to be addressed, and most important, obtain a brief history of the client's previous treatment and academic and vocational activities. The clinician can then direct the client to obtain copies of relevant records and sign releases of information that will allow the clinician to begin gathering records. These records will thus be available at the time of the history-taking session.

The history should begin with an overview of the client's perceived problems. In fact, the clinician should consider listing these and summarizing them briefly once they are obtained. The history taking can then continue with a discussion of early development; health, school, emotional, and social histories during childhood; marital and family information; vocational history; and substance abuse history, if any. There should also be a discussion about what the client hopes to achieve once the assessment is completed. In the case of adolescents, it is strongly recommended that a parent complete a history form specifically designed for children and adolescents (S. Goldstein & Goldstein, 1994). It is also suggested that the history-taking session continue with parents while the adolescent is completing self-report instruments. This will give parents the opportunity to voice their concerns freely. The clinician can then interview the adolescent alone, reviewing the basic history obtained and soliciting the adolescent's comments, observations, and perceptions. The adult questionnaire used at the NLBC asks detailed questions about the client's clinical, developmental, health, employment, marital, family, and social histories (for the full form, see Appendix C).

Hoy and Gregg (1985) offer the following guidelines and sample questions for clinicians to use when interviewing people with LD:

Interview Behavior

The following guidelines are suggested for structuring the interview environment.

1. Become an active listener. The learning disabled adult is often telling you the diagnosis. Exhibit a keen interest in what is said. Be accepting and let the individual tell his or her own story. It is important to find out what the adult considers to be important. Do not interrupt; however, do not encourage rambling and keep the adult on track.

2. Ask questions and elicit information in a warm, nonthreatening, nonjudgmental way.

3. Remain sensitive to "touchy" areas. Communicate that you realize certain things are hard to discuss.

4. Remember the information you read in the file. Remember means you care.

5. Respond to the adult's feelings as facts.

6. Be truthful and honest.

7. Respect confidentiality.

8. Keep in mind the purpose of the interview and integrate the formation as you go. You are not looking for isolated information but patterns of how the individual has been functioning.

9. Refrain from making decisions for the adult.

10. Do not cut the adult off because he or she is not following your order of chosen questions.

11. Do not make a guarantee you cannot keep, i.e., "I'm sure that everything will be fine." (Can you be sure of that?)

12. Refrain from utilizing educational jargon.

13. Refrain from asking questions that you could not give an explanation for asking.

14. Refrain from playing "junior shrink." Counseling is not your purpose.

15. Refrain from appearing shocked by anything.

16. Refrain from blaming, condemning, or jumping to conclusions.

17. Refrain from appearing authoritative.

18. Refrain from becoming impatient.

19. Refrain from comparing your personal experiences to what the adult is saying. His or her problem is unique.

20. Appear well organized and handle all forms or papers inconspicuously.

Sample Questions

Listed below are some suggested questions for use in interviewing an adult who may be learning disabled.

1. Why don't you explain in your own words some of the ways learning has been difficult for you?

2. Do these learning problems affect areas other than academic learning. For instance, how does this problem affect you on your job?

3. What are some things you have done to get around some of these problems?

4. When teachers gave you difficult tasks in school, how did you handle the situation?

5. Do you feel the learning problem interferes in your making stable relationships (i.e., work, intimate, friend)? How?

6. Describe your family's response to your learning problems.

7. Describe what you think are your strengths.

8. Where do you see yourself ten years from now?

9. What do you think would help you reach your goals?

10. Describe someone who has been a support in your life.*

Self-report and observer report measures in regard to ADHD are still in their infancy. For that reason, many of them have very limited normative databases from which to draw conclusions about the significance of a specific individual's characteristics. Nonetheless, they often provide qualitative information that can be useful in the history-taking session. When a client is a married adult, it is suggested that the spouse accompany the client and participate during the history-taking session. Figure 6.1 presents the spousal checklist used at the NLBC.

Keith Conners, the developer of the Conners Parent and Teacher Questionnaires, and colleagues recently developed and standardized two new questionnaires, the Conners Adult ADHD Rating Scale—Self and the Conners Adult ADHD Rating Scale—Observer (Conners, Erhardt, & Sparrow, 1995). Each form consists of 93 items similar to those on the original Conners Parent Questionnaire (Conners, 1972). Figures 6.2 and 6.3 contain sample items from these two questionnaires. As with Conners's earlier questionnaires, the goal is to generate scores allowing for cutoffs of clinical significance for a number of scales, including hyperkinesis and inattention.

In regard to adolescents, the Revised Conners Parent Questionnaire (Conners, 1989) and the Child Behavior Checklist (Achenbach & Edelbrock, 1991) are recommended (see Figures 6.4

*From "Appraisal and Assessment of Learning Disabilities, Including a Special Bibliography," in *Academic Assessment and Remediation of Adults with Learning Disabilities: A Resource Series for Adult Basic Education Teachers,* by C. A. Hoy and K. N. Gregg, 1985, sponsored by the Georgia State Department of Education, Adult and Community Education Unit, Atlanta, GA.

Patient Name _____

Name of Spouse _____ Date _____

Below is a list of problems and behaviors that some people have. Beside each item indicate how much of a problem each one is for the person you have been asked to rate in *your* opinion.

5   very significant problem
4   this is a significant problem
3   this is a problem that occurs on a regular basis
2   this problem rarely occurs
1   this problem does not occur at all

____   1.   Often fails to give close attention to details or makes careless mistakes.
____   2.   Has difficulty sustaining attention for tasks that must be completed.
____   3.   Doesn't appear to listen when spoken to directly.
____   4.   Doesn't follow through consistently with instructions or with duties in the work place.
____   5.   Has difficulty organizing tasks and activities.
____   6.   Avoids, dislikes or is reluctant to engage in tasks that require sustained mental effort.
____   7.   Often loses things that are necessary for tasks or activities.
____   8.   Is easily distracted by extraneous events.
____   9.   Is forgetful in daily activities.
____   10.   Fidgets with hands, feet or squirms in seat.
____   11.   Has difficulty remaining seated, often gets up.
____   12.   Reports feeling restless.
____   13.   Difficulty engaging in leisure activities quietly.
____   14.   Acts as if driven by a motor.
____   15.   Often talks excessively.
____   16.   May blurt out or interrupt others in conversation.
____   17.   Difficulty waiting turn.
____   18.   Often blurts out answers before questions have been completed.

How long have these behaviors been present?

Figure 6.1   Spousal checklist

Note. Copyright 1994 by S. Goldstein, Neurology, Learning and Behavior Center, Salt Lake City, UT. Used with permission.

and 6.5). These are well-standardized instruments with good reliability and validity. Teacher versions of these instruments are also available. It is urged that data from teachers be obtained when possible. A thorough review of these adolescent instruments can be found in S. Goldstein (1995).

Murphy and Barkley (1995a) offer the ADHD Behavior Checklist for Adults. This checklist parallels the *DSM-IV* diagnostic criteria for ADHD (see Figure 6.6). Based on their ongoing research with adults, Murphy and Barkley (1995b) offer mean and standard deviation symptom scores as well as the number of positively endorsed items for each subscale and total item list (see Tables 6.1 and 6.2). Like the *DSM-IV* diagnostic criteria, this questionnaire generates three factors (inattentive, hyperactive-impulsive, and combined). The endorsed items are totaled for each factor (odd items for inattentive symptoms and even items for hyperactive-impulsive symptoms). These two subscores are totaled for a combined score. The clinician can then com-

Name: _____ Age: _____ Birthdate: _____

Sex: ☐ Male ☐ Female Date _____

INSTRUCTIONS: Listed below are items concerning behaviors or problems sometimes experienced by adults with ADHD. Read each item carefully and decide how much or how frequently each item describes you recently

- Not at all, or never
- Just a little, or once in a while
- Pretty much, or often
- Very much, or very frequently

Indicate your choice by circling the number in the appropriate column to the right of each item.

PLEASE ANSWER ALL ITEMS!	Not at all; never	Just a little; once in a while	Pretty much;	Very much; very frequently
1. I make careless errors because I don't pay attention to details.	0	1	2	3
2. I just can't get my act together.	0	1	2	3
3. I don't read other people well.	0	1	2	3
4. I tend to squirm or fidget.	0	1	2	3
5. I'm disorganized.	0	1	2	3
6. I can't stick with things for more than a few minutes.	0	1	2	3

Figure 6.2   Sample items from the Conners Adult ADHD Rating Scale—Self

Note. Copyright 1995 by Multi-Health Systems, Inc. All rights reserved. In the United States, 908 Niagara Falls Blvd., North Tonawanda, NY 14120-2060, 800-456-3003; in Canada, 65 Overlea Blvd., Suite 210, Toronto, ON M4H 1P1, 800-268-6011, 416-424-1700. Used with permission.

pare these three scores to the 1.5 standard deviation cutoff listed in Table 6.1. It is important to caution the reader that the data generated thus far include information on a limited number of people over 50 years of age, making statistical conclusions about this group speculative.

Figures 6.7 and 6.8 present rating scales to be completed by the parents of an adult client. As noted, clinicians considering an adult diagnosis of ADHD must generate a very clear, convincing, and consistent history showing that the individual being evaluated experienced ADHD problems as a child. The clinician must keep in mind that the current *DSM-IV* diagnostic guidelines require symptoms to have been observed or reported before age seven.

Self-assessment scales, although not well standardized for adults with histories of LD or ADHD, have demonstrated their value in providing qualitative and some quantitative data about daily functioning. For example, Houck et al. (1989) found that learning-disabled college students perceive themselves as having greater problems in reading, written expression, visual processing, and short-term memory, specifically, than their nondisabled peers.

As discussed in Chapter 5, the BAADS (T. E. Brown, 1995) is a self-report instrument generating five clusters of symptoms hypothesized to be characteristic of adults with histories of ADHD. This questionnaire generates five subscale scores and an overall score, with a score of 50 or above considered indicative of adult ADHD symptoms. Figure 6.9 contains a sample of the Brown questionnaire.

Name: _____ Age: _____ Birthdate: _____
Sex: ☐ Male ☐ Female   Date _____

INSTRUCTIONS: Listed below are items concerning behaviors or problems sometimes experienced by adults with ADHD. Read each item carefully and decide how much or how frequently each item describes you recently --

- Not at all, or never
- Just a little, or once in a while
- Pretty much, or often
- Very much, or very frequently

Indicate your choice by circling the number in the appropriate column to the right of each item.

PLEASE ANSWER ALL ITEMS!	Not at all; never	Just a little; once in a while	Pretty much	Very much; very frequently
1. Makes careless errors because s/he doesn't pay attention to details.	0	1	2	3
2. Just can't get his or her act together.	0	1	2	3
3. Doesn't read other people well.	0	1	2	3
4. Tends to squirm or fidget.	0	1	2	3
5. Is disorganized.	0	1	2	3
6. Can't stick with things for more than a few minutes.	0	1	2	3

Figure 6.3   Sample items from the Conners Adult ADHD Rating Scale—Observer

Note. Copyright 1995 by Multi-Health Systems, Inc. All rights reserved. In the United States, 908 Niagara Falls Blvd., North Tonawanda, NY 14120-2060, 800-456-3003; in Canada, 65 Overlea Blvd., Suite 210, Toronto, ON M4H 1P1, 800-268-6011, 416-424-1700. Used with permission.

Child's Name: _____ Child's Age: _____ Child's Sex: ____
Parent's Name: _____

Instructions: Read each item below carefully, and decide how much you think your child has been bothered by this problem during the past month.

Not at All	Just a Little	Pretty Much	Very Much	CPRS-48
0	1	2	3	1. Picks at things (nails, fingers, hair, clothing)
0	1	2	3	2. Sassy to grown-ups.
0	1	2	3	3. Problems with making or keeping friends.
0	1	2	3	4. Excitable, impulsive.
0	1	2	3	5. Wants to run things.

Figure 6.4   Sample items from the Revised Conners Parent Questionnaire

Note. From Conners Parent Questionnaire, by C. K. Conners. Copyright 1988 by Multi-Health Systems, Inc. All rights reserved. In the United States, 908 Niagara Falls Blvd., North Tonawanda, NY 14120-2060, 800-456-3003; in Canada, 65 Overlea Blvd., Suite 210, Toronto, ON M4H 1P1, 800-268-6011, 416-424-1700. Used with permission.

Name _____ Date of Birth _____

Below is a list of items that describe children. For each item that describes your child now or within the past 6 months, please circle the 2 if the item is very true or often true of your child. Circle the 1 if the item is somewhat or sometimes true of your child. If the item is not true of your child, circle the 0. Please answer all items as well as you can, even if some do not seem to apply to your child.

0 = Not True (as far as you know)
1 = Somewhat or Sometimes True
2 = Very True or Often True

0	1	2	1.	Acts too young for his/her age.
0	1	2	2.	Allergy (describe):_____
0	1	2	3.	Argues a lot.
0	1	2	4.	Asthma.
0	1	2	5.	Behaves like opposite sex
0	1	2	31.	Fears he/she might think or do something bad.
0	1	2	32.	Feels he/she has to be perfect.
0	1	2	33.	Feels or complains that no one loves him/her.
0	1	2	34.	Feels others are out to get him/her.
0	1	2	35.	Feels worthless or inferior.

Figure 6.5   Sample items from the Child Behavior Checklist—Parent Form
Note. From Child Behavior Checklist for Ages 4–12—Parent Form, by T. M. Achenbach. Copyright 1990 by T. M. Achenbach. Used with permission.

Figure 6.10 presents a sample from a feedback form that clinicians can use to obtain data from parents and high school and college-level faculty about the client's academic and behavioral functioning in the classroom.

The first rating scale developed for adults, the Wender Utah Rating Scale (WURS), has been studied by a number of researchers. Ward, Wender, and Reimherr (1993), based on a factor analysis of 25 of the 61 items on the questionnaire, identified a cutoff score of 46 or above as indicative of adult ADHD problems consistent with the Utah diagnosis of adult ADHD. A sample of the WURS appears in Figure 6.11, along with the scoring key and item numbers composing the inattentive factor.

Based on a factor analysis of males and females, M. A. Stein et al. (in press) generated an attention problems factor consisting of seven items for males and an inattentive/oppositional factor consisting of eight items for females. They also suggested clinical cutoffs for each of these two factors (see Table 6.3).

Finally, Figure 6.12 presents the Life Issues Questionnaire developed by S. Goldstein (1995) in an effort to generate factor-analytic results about the 20 diagnostic and descriptive items offered by Hallowell and Ratey (1994). These authors suggest that 15 of the 20 symptoms of even mild severity might be sufficient for a diagnosis of adult ADHD. These 20 items have not been factor analyzed, however. At this juncture it is uncertain whether these items will form a unitary factor or a number of distinctive factors related to ADHD.

A number of additional self-report measures that have been developed and tested include the Patient's Assessment of Own Functioning Inventory (Heaton & Pendleton, 1981) and the Patient Competency Rating Scale (Fordyce, 1983). Parallel forms of both of these question-

Your Name _____

Circle the number that *best describes* your behavior over the past 6 months:

		Never or rarely	Sometimes	Often	Very Often
1.	Fail to give close attention to details or make careless mistakes in my work.	0	1	2	3
2.	Fidgets with hands or feet or squirm in my seat.	0	1	2	3
3.	Difficulty sustaining my attention in tasks or fun activities.	0	1	2	3
4.	Leave my seat in classroom or in other situations in which seating is expected.	0	1	2	3
5.	Don't listen when spoken to directly.	0	1	2	3
6.	Feel restless.	0	1	2	3
7.	Don't follow through on instructions and fail to finish work.	0	1	2	3
8.	Have difficulty engaging in leisure activities or doing fun things quietly.	0	1	2	3
9.	Having difficulty organizing tasks and activities.	0	1	2	3
10.	Feel "on the go" or "driven by a motor."	0	1	2	3
11.	Avoid, dislike, or reluctant to engage in work that requires sustained mental effort.	0	1	2	3
12.	Talks excessively.	0	1	2	3
13.	Lose things necessary for tasks or activities.	0	1	2	3
14.	Blurt out answers before questions have been completed.	0	1	2	3
15.	Easily distracted.	0	1	2	3
16.	Having difficulty awaiting turn.	0	1	2	3
17.	Forgetful in daily activities.	0	1	2	3
18.	Interrupt or intrude on others.	0	1	2	3

Figure 6.6   Attention Behavior Checklist for Adults

Note. Items adapted from the *Diagnostic and Statistical Manual of Psychiatric Disorders* (4th ed.), by American Psychiatric Association, 1994, Washington, DC: Author.

naires, to be completed by spouses or family members, are also available. Dowdy (1990) developed an observer checklist, the Learning Disabilities Characteristic Checklist, to be consistent with the U.S. Department of Education Rehabilitation Services Administration's 1985 definition of specific LD. In addition, an increasing number of adult ADHD skill measures are entering the marketplace. Trillo (1995), for example, offers a 54-item questionnaire containing multiple subscales related to, for example, attention, interpersonal behavior, academic achievement, emotional development, and social relations. The questionnaire uses a 5-point Likert scale. The manual for scoring gives multiple guidelines for interpretation as well (Trillo & Murphy, 1995).

The CITE Learning Styles Inventory (CITE Inventory, 1995) is a qualitative self-report measure that allows the clinician to discover how clients think that they learn best. The CITE Learning Styles Inventory and scoring sheet appear in Figures 6.13 and 6.14, respectively.

TABLE 6.1   Subscale and Total Scores

Score	Age	Mean	SD	+1.5 SD Cutoff	N
Inattention	17–29	6.3	4.7	13.4	193
Inattention	30–49	5.7	4.6	12.3	212
Inattention	50+	4.6	3.7	10.2	42
Hyper-Impulsive	17–29	8.4	4.8	15.6	193
Hyper-Impulsive	30–49	6.8	4.5	13.5	209
Hyper-Impulsive	50+	5.0	3.6	10.5	41
Total score	17–29	14.7	8.9	28.0	186
Total score	30–49	12.2	8.1	24.4	200
Total score	50+	9.6	6.5	19.4	39

Note. From "ADHD Preliminary Normative Data on *DSM-IV* Criteria for Adults," by K. Murphy and R. A. Barkley, 1995, *The ADHD Report, 3*(3), 6–7. Used with permission.

TABLE 6.2   Number of Positively Endorsed Items (score of 2 or 3) for Each Subscale and Total Item List

Score	Age	Mean	SD	+1.5 SD Cutoff	N
Inattention	17–29	1.2	1.8	4.0	193
Inattention	30–49	1.0	1.7	3.5	212
Inattention	50+	0.5	1.2	2.3	42
Hyper-Impulsive	17–29	2.0	2.0	5.0	193
Hyper-Impulsive	30–49	1.5	1.8	4.2	209
Hyper-Impulsive	50+	0.7	1.4	2.8	41
Total score	17–29	3.2	3.5	8.5	186
Total score	30–49	2.4	3.1	7.0	200
Total score	50+	1.2	2.4	4.8	39

Note. From "ADHD Preliminary Normative Data on *DSM-IV* Criteria for Adults," by K. Murphy and R. A. Barkley, 1995, *The ADHD Report, 3*(3), pp. 6–7. Used with permission.

Finally, two other questionnaires are suggested. The Test-Taking Skills Self-Assessment Form may be useful in providing the clinician with specific data about the client's self-perceived test-taking skills (see Figure 6.15). The Student Interest Survey provides a very brief overview of vocational interests (see Figure 6.16).

Many questionnaires have been presented here, but the list is certainly not exhaustive. It is understood that some clinicians prefer one questionnaire over another. However, clinicians should be sensitive to the fact that the majority of the questionnaires presently used to tap for symptoms of ADHD and LD in adults, by either self-report or observer report, are still speculative in terms of allowing the clinician to draw conclusions based on a quantitative analysis of the individual's responses. Nonetheless, questionnaires for ADHD such as those of Murphy and Barkley (1995b), T. E. Brown (1995), and Conners (1994b) will likely generate a large base

Patient's Name _____

Parent's Name _____

Circle the number in the one column which best describes your son/daughter as a child (ages 5 to 12)

		Not at all	Just a little	Pretty much	Very much
1.	Was often fidgety or squirming in seat.	0	1	2	3
2.	Had difficulty remaining seated.	0	1	2	3
3.	Was easily distracted.	0	1	2	3
4.	Had difficulty awaiting turn in groups.	0	1	2	3
5.	Often blurted out answers to questions.	0	1	2	3
6.	Had difficulty following instructions.	0	1	2	3
7.	Had difficulty sustaining attention to tasks.	0	1	2	3
8.	Often shifted from one uncompleted activity to another.	0	1	2	3
9.	Had difficulty playing quietly.	0	1	2	3
10.	Often talked excessively.	0	1	2	3
11.	Often interrupted or intruded on others.	0	1	2	3
12.	Often did not seem to listen.	0	1	2	3
13.	Often lost things necessary for tasks.	0	1	2	3
14.	Often engaged in physically dangerous activities without considering consequences	0	1	2	3

Figure 6.7   Childhood ADHD Rating Scale (Parent)

Note. Copyright 1992 by K. R. Murphy, University of Massachusetts Medical Center, Worchester, MA. Used with permission.

of normative data that will, in the coming years, allow clinical conclusions to be drawn with greater certainty. Even within the NLBC, clinicians vary in their choice of questionnaires. In general, however, the standard history form is used, usually combined with a limited number of self-report and other report measures for ADHD. For adolescents, the Conners and Child Behavior Checklists are standard. For adults, the Brown, Conners, and Attention Behavior Checklists are used increasingly.

At the conclusion of the history-taking session, the clinician should have enough information to be able to provide the client with initial impressions and hypotheses—for example, "Your history appears to fit ADHD. Given your poor academic performance, however, further assessment may be worthwhile." The NLBC assessment model is a multistage process, with second-stage assessment recommended based on the history obtained. If, as judged according to the history, the individual's intellectual, academic, and emotional functioning are not issues, the only additional first-stage assessment procedure completed would be a measure of personality functioning (e.g., Millon Adolescent Personality Inventory or Minnesota Multiphasic Personality Inventory). If questions are raised about a history of emotional problems, however, a number of additional interview sessions are scheduled to allow the clinician to better understand the individual's history and current functioning. If questions are raised about LD or vocational skills, in-depth cognitive and academic assessment is recommended. As in Lezak's (1995) model, the structure and complexity of assessment is determined by the number and complexity of the diagnostic questions being asked.

Patient's Name _____

Filled out by: Mother _____ Father _____ Other _____

Directions: For each item that describes your son/daughter during the ages of 5 through 12, check whether the item was Not True, Somewhat or Sometimes True, or Very or Often True. Please check all items as well as you can, even if some do not seem to apply to your son/daughter.

1. Failed to finish things he/she started.	[ ]	[ ]	[ ]
2. Couldn't concentrate, couldn't pay attention for long.	[ ]	[ ]	[ ]
3. Couldn't sit still, restless, or hyperactive.	[ ]	[ ]	[ ]
4. Fidgeted.	[ ]	[ ]	[ ]
5. Daydreamed or got lost in his/her thoughts.	[ ]	[ ]	[ ]
6. Impulsive or acted without thinking.	[ ]	[ ]	[ ]
7. Difficulty following directions.	[ ]	[ ]	[ ]
8. Talked out of turn.	[ ]	[ ]	[ ]
9. Messy work.	[ ]	[ ]	[ ]
10. Was inattentive, easily distracted.	[ ]	[ ]	[ ]
11. Talked too much.	[ ]	[ ]	[ ]
12. Failed to carry out assigned tasks.	[ ]	[ ]	[ ]

Please feel free to write any comments about your son's or daughter's past or present behavior that you think would be helpful.

Figure 6.8   Retrospective Attention Profile

Note. Copyright 1992 by K. R. Murphy, University of Massachusetts Medical Center, Worchester, MA. Used with permission.

As S. Goldstein and Goldstein (1990) explain, the purpose of assessment is to provide structured data about behavior, emotional functioning, and achievement, as well as the situational impact that these levels of functioning have on the individual's daily activities. The issue of differential diagnosis is paramount. Shaffer and Schonfeld (1984) note, for example, that problems with attention are often inferred from inadequate work product. In fact, the inadequacy could also be caused by lack of interest, inappropriate reinforcement, or cognitive or learning impairments.

OBSERVATION DURING ASSESSMENT

A client's attitude, motivation, and behavior during assessment is a critical variable, allowing the clinician to draw conclusions about the reliability and accuracy of test performance. Further, observations made during the assessment often provide valuable qualitative data about the client's general emotional state, language skills, physical manifestations and behavior, even thought processes. The growing recognition of the importance of behavior observed during testing is illustrated by the WISC, which has expanded from previous editions the amount of space offered for observations.

The psychometric assessment may last anywhere from one to five hours and may be completed in one or two sessions. The clinician should qualitatively evaluate the client's behavior from the moment of meeting until the close of the evaluation. A number of published forms designed to organize the clinician's observations during assessment are available. S. Goldstein (1989) developed a simple one-page form to meet this need. It appears in Figure 6.17.

Name _____ Date Completed _____
Highest School Grade Completed _____ Age _____ Evaluator _____

Instructions: Using the codes below, mark each item to show how much that feeling or behavior has been a problem within the past month.

    0   not at all a problem; never occurs
    1   just a little problem; occurs rarely
    2   pretty much a problem, occurs a few times in a week
    3   very much a problem; occurs almost every day

Score:

_____   1. When trying to pay attention to someone, e.g., class, conversation, mind drifts off and briefly loses focus so you miss information you want to get.

_____   2. Excessive difficulty getting started on tasks, e.g., homework.

_____   3. Feels excessively stressed or overwhelmed, e.g., "no way I can do this now", by tasks which should be manageable.

_____   4. Involuntary "spacing out" occurs intermittently when reading.

_____   5. Easily "sidetracked", disrupts a task in progress and switches to doing something else which is less important.

_____   6. When reading, loses track of what has just been read so needs to read it again.

_____   7. Information learned cannot be remembered easily when it is wanted, e.g., knows it will the night before a test, but cannot recall it adequately for est the next day.

_____   8. Easily loses track of the main point in reading books, magazines or newspapers.

_____   9. Easily frustrated; excessively impatient.

_____ 10. When presented with many things to do, has difficulty deciding what to do first and then getting started.

Figure 6.9   Sample items from the Brown Attention Activation Disorder Scale
Note. Copyright 1995 by T. E. Brown, Psychological Corporation, New York. Used with permission.

The clinician should observe the client's initial response during the history-taking session, as well as during later psychometric assessment. Observations of eye contact, the ability to initiate and maintain conversation, general language skills, including voice quality (pitch, rhythm, and tone), syntax, articulation, and pragmatics, are also important.

Clinicians may also wish to make a distinction between being alert (remaining awake), paying attention for short periods of time sufficient to follow task instructions, and sustaining attention enough to complete required tasks.

The clinician should also observe the client's level of muscular tension, habitual mannerisms, and general activity level. At times it may be difficult to distinguish between psychiatric symptoms consistent with anxiety and symptoms related to restlessness secondary to ADHD. The client's level of self-confidence in regard to task completion and his or her frustration level should also be observed.

ASSESSMENT BATTERY

As described, the NLBC model for LD and ADHD assessment has two stages. The initial stage focuses on history, self-report and observer report data, and the assessment of personality and

Name _____ Date _____

Completed by _____ Relationship to Individual _____

Directions: This checklist should be completed during an interview or given to parents, teachers or other professionals to complete. Informants should rate each item according to the frequency of the behavior. Specific examples or comments should be provided when possible. Any item rated 1 <u>may be</u> considered an ability or strength. Items rated 2 or 3 may pose functional limitations in an academic or vocational setting.

1	Seldom or Never	3	Very Often
2	Often	4	No opportunity observe

Specific examples or comments should be provided whenever possible.

I.   *ATTENTION/CONCENTRATION

___   1.   Excessive non-purposeful movement (can't sit still/stay in seat).
___   2.   Easily distracted by auditory and/or visual stimuli.
___   3.   Does ont respond appropriately to questions or directions, as if not listening.
___   4.   Does not stay on task for appropriate periods of time.
___   5.   Difficulty completing assignments.
___   6.   Verbally or physically interrupts others.
___   7.   Loses place when reading orally.
___   8.   Sits and does nothing (day dreams).
___   9.   Rushes through with work with little regard for detail.
___   10. Does not pay attention to most important stimuli.

COMMENTS/Other Attention/Concentration Deficits: _____

*Section adapted from the *Diagnostic and Statistical Manual of Mental Disorders* (4th ed.), by American Psychiatric Association, 1994, Washington, DC: Author.

Figure 6.10   Sample items from the Rating Scale of Functional Limitations

Note. In addition to questions about attention, the form has sections on reasoning and processing, memory, interpersonal skills and emotional maturity, coordination and motor function, communication, reading, writing and spelling, and math. Adapted from Attention Deficit Rating Scale, by C. A. Dowdy, in *Attention-Deficit/Hyperactivity Disorder in the Classroom,* by C. A. Dowdy, J. R. Patton, T. E. C. Smith, and E. A. Polloway, 1995, Austin, TX: Pro-Ed.

emotional status. The second stage is intended to address questions about cognitive and related functioning and its impact on academic achievement. It is important for the reader to keep in mind that there has been limited empirical research on laboratory testing as a means of supporting or confirming the diagnosis of ADHD (Hechtman, 1989; Klee et al., 1986). Further, as reviewed in Chapter 2, although neuropsychological data exist that suggest a variety of subtypes of LD that can be distinguished on the basis of test performance, most individuals in these subtype groups have equally poor academic skills. It is hoped that future research will determine which specific types of academic interventions are particularly suited to specific subtypes of LD. Referral sources, other professionals, educators, and the client should understand that the purpose of cognitive and related assessment is to better understand the client's skills and abilities in order not only to assist in making placement and intervention recommendations but to guide intervention.

The NLBC assessment battery is presented below, organized by skill, ability, or functional

Patient's Name _____ Date _____

As a child, I was (or had):	Not at all or very slightly	Mildly	Moderately	Quite a bit	Very much
1. Active, restless, always on the go.					
2. Afraid of things.					
3. Concentration problems, easily distracted.					
4. Anxious, worrying.					
5. Nervous, fidgety.					
6. Inattentive, daydreaming.					

Figure 6.11   Sample items from the Wender Utah Rating Scale

Note. Score all items as: 0 = not at all; 1 = mildly; 2 = moderately; 3 = quite a bit; 4 = very much. To obtain the inattentive factor, score the following 25 items: 3, 4, 5, 6, 7, 9, 10, 11, 12, 15, 16, 17, 20, 21, 24, 25, 26, 27, 28, 29, 40, 41, 51, 56, 59, and total. A Cutoff score of 46 or above is indicative of adult ADHD. Questionnaire from "Wender Utah Rating Scale (WURS): Reliability and Factor Structure for Men and Women," by M. A. Stein, R. Sandoval, E. Szumowski, N. Roizen, M. A. Reinecke, T. A. Blondis, and Z. Klein, in press, *Psychopharmacology Bulletin.* Scoring key from "The Wender Utah Rating Scale: An Aid in the Retrospective Diagnosis of Childhood Attention Deficit Hyperactivity Disorder," by F. F. Ward, P. H. Wender, and F. W. Reimherr, 1993, *American Journal of Psychiatry, 150,* pp. 885–889. Used with permission.

area. The specific structure, reliability, validity, and related information for each of these test instruments will not be presented. It is assumed that clinicians are familiar with the majority of the instruments. Interested readers are referred to the specific instruments and their manuals.

Cognitive

The Wechsler Adult Intelligence Scale—Revised (WAIS-R) continues to be the standard cognitive measure of intellectual functioning in adulthood. Data collection for the third edition of this instrument is underway. However, publication is not expected until sometime in 1997 or 1998 (Psychological Corporation, November 1995, personal communication). The Wechsler provides a general measure of intellect as well as verbal and nonverbal summary scores (Wechsler, 1981).

Memory and Learning

The Denman Neuropsychological Memory Scale (Denman, 1984) provides verbal, nonverbal, and full-scale memory scores. The instrument assesses immediate and long-term memory and contains a single measure for the assessment of verbal learning. The Denman contains normative data for 10 years of age through adulthood.

The Wide Range Assessment of Memory and Learning (Adams & Sheslow, 1990) offers nine subtests assessing verbal and visual memory, as well as verbal, visual, and verbal-visual learning

TABLE 6.3   Wender Utah Rating Scale ADHD-Related Factors and Cutoff Scores

Item Number	Item Content
For Males, the *Attention Problems* Factor Consists of:[a]	
3	Concentration problems, easily distracted
6	Inattention, daydreaming
10	Trouble with stick-to-itiveness
19	Sloppy, disorganized
23	Well-organized, tidy, neat
25	Tend to be immature
For Females, the *Inattentive/Oppositional* Factor Consists of:[b]	
3	Concentration problems, easily distracted
6	Inattention, daydreaming
10	Trouble with stick-to-itiveness
19	Sloppy, disorganized
23	Well-organized, tidy, neat
41	Trouble with authorities
59	Not achieving to potential
61	Suspended or expelled

Note. Score 0 for *not at all* and 4 for *very much*. Reverse score for item 23 by subtracting subject's score from 4. Adapted from "Wender Utah Rating Scale (WURS): Reliability and Factor Structure for Men and Women," by M. A. Stein, R. Sandoval, E. Szumowski, N. Roizen, M. A. Reinecke, T. A. Blondis, and Z. Klein, in press, *Psychopharmacology Bulletin;* "The Wender Utah Rating Scale: An Aid in the Retrospective Diagnosis of Childhood Attention Deficit Hyperactivity Disorder," by F. F. Ward, P. H. Wender, and F. W. Reimherr, 1993, *American Journal of Psychiatry, 150,* pp. 885–889; *How to Operate an ADHD Clinic or Subspecialty Practice,* by Michael Gordon, 1995, DeWitt, NY: GSI Publications. Copyright 1995 by GSI Publications. Used with permission.
[a]The recommended cutoff is 16.
[b]The recommended cutoff is 10.

over four trials. The instrument provides normative data for childhood through 16 years of age. Analysis of subtest performance often offers data consistent with the verbal-visual/rote-conceptual analysis of underlying skills necessary for efficient learning.

The Wechsler Memory Scale—Revised (Wechsler, 1987) is by far the most popular assessment of memory skills in adulthood. In addition to offering a summary score, the instrument assesses verbal and visual memory, learning, and attention. Unfortunately, the attention measure has not been demonstrated to correlate with the diagnosis of ADHD.

The Learning and Memory Assessment Battery (LAMB; J. P. Schmidt & Tombaugh, 1995) is normed for ages 18 years and above. This instrument represents the new generation of memory tests in comparison with other batteries, including those not reviewed in this section (the California Verbal Learning Scale and the Memory Assessment Scale). It offers normative data with groups equated to population for gender, intelligence, and education. The normative group sizes are age stratified. This instrument provides evaluation of learning and retention, including comparisons of initial versus repeated trial learning, immediate versus delayed recall, and free versus cued versus recognition recall for verbal, visual, and numerical learning and

Protocol No. _____   ___ Male ___ Female

Have you ever received a diagnosis for inattentive or hyperactive
    problems as a child or adult?   ___ Yes ___ No
Have you ever received a diagnosis for any type of depressive
    problem as a child or adult?   ___ Yes ___ No
Did you struggle in school?   ___ Yes ___ No
Did you receive special services in school for learning disabilities? ___ Yes ___ No

Please rate the following about yourself:

		Not True	Somewhat True		Very True
1.	I experience a strong feeling of under-achievement in not meeting my life goals (I just can't get my act together).	1	2	3	4	5
2.	I have a significant problem getting and staying organized.	1	2	3	4	5
3.	I procrastinate and have difficulty starting tasks that must be completed.	1	2	3	4	5
4.	I start too many tasks and then have trouble following through with all of them.	1	2	3	4	5
5.	I say what is on my mind, sometimes without thinking about what I am saying.	1	2	3	4	5
6.	I crave high stimulation.	1	2	3	4	5
7.	I am intolerant of boredom.	1	2	3	4	5
8.	I find myself easily distracted on routine, repetitive tasks that must be completed.	1	2	3	4	5
9.	I consider myself creative.	1	2	3	4	5
10.	I often resolve problems in unconventional ways. I don't follow established channels.	1	2	3	4	5
11.	I am impatient and frustrate easily.	1	2	3	4	5
12.	I often act impulsively (e.g., spend money that I shouldn't).	1	2	3	4	5
13.	I worry excessively and often needlessly.	1	2	3	4	5
14.	I often feel insecure. No matter how well things are going, I worry they may fall apart.	1	2	3	4	5
15.	My moods change easily.	1	2	3	4	5
16.	I am restless.	1	2	3	4	5
17.	I have a tendency to engage in activities to excess (e.g., alcohol, shopping, working, etc.).	1	2	3	4	5
18.	No matter how much I accomplish, my self-esteem is low.	1	2	3	4	5
19.	Other people view me differently than I view myself.	1	2	3	4	5
20.	I have a family history of attention deficit disorder, depression or substance abuse.	1	2	3	4	5

Figure 6.12   Life Issues Questionnaire

Note. Copyright 1995 by S. Goldstein, Neurology, Learning and Behavior Center, Salt Lake City, UT. Used
with permission.

Name _____ DOB _____ Date _____
Age _____ School _____ Grade _____

	Learning Style	Most Like Me		Least Like Me	
1.	When I make things for my studies, I remember what I have learned better.	4	3	2	1
2.	Written assignments are easy for me to do.	4	3	2	1
3.	I learn better if someone reads a book to me than if I read silently to myself.	4	3	2	1
4.	I learn best when I study alone.	4	3	2	1
5.	Having assignment directions written on the board makes them easier to understand.	4	3	2	1
6.	It is harder for me to do a written assignment than an oral one.	4	3	2	1
7.	When I do math problems in my head, I say the numbers to myself.	4	3	2	1
8.	If I need help in the subject, I will ask a classmate for help.	4	3	2	1
9.	I understand a math problem that is written down better than one I hear.	4	3	2	1
10.	I do not mind doing written assignments.	4	3	2	1
11.	I remember things I hear better than I read.	4	3	2	1
12.	I remember more of what I learn if I learn alone.	4	3	2	1
13.	I would rather read a story than listen to it read.	4	3	2	1
14.	I feel that I talk smarter than I write.	4	3	2	1
15.	If someone tells me three numbers to add, I can usually get the right answer without writing them down.	4	3	2	1
16.	I like to work in a group because I learn from the others in the group.	4	3	2	1
17.	Written math problems are easier for me to do than oral ones.	4	3	2	1
18.	Writing a spelling word several times helps me remember it better.	4	3	2	1
19.	I find it easier to remember what I have heard than what I have read.	4	3	2	1
20.	It is more fun to learn with classmates at first, but it is hard to study with them.	4	3	2	1
21.	I like written directions better than spoken ones.	4	3	2	1
22.	If homework were spoken, I would it all.	4	3	2	1
23.	When I hear a phone number, I can remember it without writing it down.	4	3	2	1
24.	I get more work done if I work with someone.	4	3	2	1

Figure 6.13   CITE Learning Styles Inventory

Note. From CITE Inventory, in *Transition: School to Work,* edited by F. J. Krieg, P. Brown, and J. Ballard, 1995, Washington, DC: National Association of School Psychologists. Used with permission.

	Learning Style	Most Like Me		Least Like Me	
25.	Seeing a number makes more sense to me than hearing a number.	4	3	2	1
26.	I like to do things like simple repairs or crafts with my hands.	4	3	2	1
27.	The things that I write on paper sound better than when I say them.	4	3	2	1
28.	I study best when no one is around to talk or listen to.	4	3	2	1
29.	I would rather read things in a book than have the teacher tell me about them.	4	3	2	1
30.	Speaking is a better way than writing if you want someone to understand it better.	4	3	2	1
31.	When I have a written math problem to do, I say it to myself to understand it better.	4	3	2	1
32.	I can learn more about a subject if I am with a small group of students.	4	3	2	1
33.	Seeing the price of something written down is easier for me to understand than having someone telling me the price.	4	3	2	1
34.	I like to make things with my hands.	4	3	2	1
35.	I like tests that call for sentence completion or written answers.	4	3	2	1
36.	I understand more from a class discussion than from reading about a subject.	4	3	2	1
37.	I remember the spelling of a word better if I see it written down than if someone spells it out loud.	4	3	2	1
38.	Spelling and grammar rules make it hard for me to say what I want to do in writing.	4	3	2	1
39.	It makes it easier when I say the numbers of a problem to myself as I work it out.	4	3	2	1
40.	I like to study with other people.	4	3	2	1
41.	When the teachers say a number, I really do not understand it until I see it written down.	4	3	2	1
42.	I understand what I have learned better when I am involved in making something for the subject.	4	3	2	1
43.	Sometimes I say dumb things, but writing gives me time to correct myself.	4	3	2	1
44.	I do well on tests if they are about things I hear in class.	4	3	2	1
45.	I cannot think as well when I work with someone else as when I work alone.	4	3	2	1

Figure 6.13   *(Continued)*

Name _____ DOB _____ Date _____

Age _____ School _____ Grade _____

Visual Language
5 _____
13 _____
21 _____
29 _____
37 _____
Total _____ x 2 = _____ (Score)

Individual
4 _____
12 _____
20 _____
28 _____
45 _____
Total _____ x 2 = _____ (Score)

Visual Numerical
9 _____
17 _____
25 _____
33 _____
41 _____
Total _____ x 2 = _____ (Score)

Social-Group
8 _____
16 _____
24 _____
32 _____
40 _____
Total _____ x 2 = _____ (Score)

Auditory Language
3 _____
11 _____
19 _____
36 _____
44 _____
Total _____ x 2 = _____ (Score)

Expressiveness-Oral
6 _____
14 _____
22 _____
30 _____
38 _____
Total _____ x 2 = _____ (Score)

Auditory Numerical
7 _____
15 _____
23 _____
31 _____
39 _____
Total _____ x 2 = _____ (Score)

Expressiveness-Written
2 _____
10 _____
27 _____
35 _____
43 _____
Total _____ x 2 = _____ (Score)

Tactile-Kinesthetic
1 _____
18 _____
26 _____
34 _____
42 _____
Total _____ x 2 = _____ (Score)

SCORE
34-40 = Major Learning Style
20-32 = Minor Learning Style
10-18 = Negligible Use

Figure 6.14   CITE Inventory Control Sheet

Note. MAJOR: The student prefers this mode of learning, feels comfortable with it, and uses it for important (to the student) learning; a student does not necessarily have one and only one preferred style. MINOR: The student uses this mode but usually as a second choice or in conjunction with other learning styles. NEGLIGIBLE: The student prefers not to use this mode if other choices are available; the student does not feel comfortable with this style. From CITE Inventory, in *Transition: School to Work,* edited by F. J. Krieg, P. Brown, and J. Ballard, 1995, Washington, DC: National Association of School Psychologists. Used with permission.

Student's Name _____   Date _____

Teacher's Name _____   Date _____

Directions: Please read each statement and circle YES or NO according to your own test-taking behaviors. Be sure to mark every item.

1.	I am aware of how much time I have to take tests.	Y	N
2.	I answer questions that I know first.	Y	N
3.	I go back to more difficult, time-consuming questions.	Y	N
4.	I check my answers after I finish my test to avoid careless mistakes.	Y	N
5.	I know what type of question to answer.	Y	N
6.	I look for clue words to determine what information is given and what information I need to answer myself.	Y	N
7.	I spend less time on questions I know, saving my time for those that I am unsure of.	Y	N
8.	I read all the directions before beginning the test.	Y	N
9.	When I don't understand directions, I ask for help.	Y	N
10.	I read the entire questions and answers when they're given.	Y	N
11.	I read over my answers.	Y	N
12.	I ask myself if my answers make sense.	Y	N
13.	I guess only after honestly attempting to answer.	Y	N
14.	I use information given to help estimate my answer.	Y	N
15.	I check over my answers before handing in my tests.	Y	N
16.	My work is neat and legible on tests.	Y	N
17.	I check to make sure all questions are answered before handing in my tests.	Y	N
18.	I always make sure my name is on my test.	Y	N

Figure 6.15   Test-Taking Skills Self-Assessment Form

Note. Adapted from *A Test-Taking Strategy Assessment Tool for Students with Learning Disabilities,* by B. Beausoleil, L. Galen, C. Himmel, W. Holly, and K. Myszka, 1989, unpublished manuscript, Northern Illinois University, Faculty of Special Education. Used with permission.

retention. The administration manual also gives an excellent overview of the process of qualitative data analysis. The reader will not find the LAMB used in any of the sample assessments or case studies presented in the following chapters because the publication of this instrument coincides with the publication of this text. However, as the authors note, "the uniqueness of the LAMB does not lie in developing entirely new memory assessment methodologies, rather its uniqueness lies in applying existing methods in a standardized manner with adequate norms to enhance more systematic interscale comparison and clarity of interpretation" (J. P. Schmidt & Tombaugh, 1995, p. 18). The ability to provide in-depth analysis of learning curves is a significant advantage over other memory batteries.

Executive Functioning and Reasoning

Measures of executive function have long been touted as possibly beneficial in the differential diagnosis of ADHD (for a review, see S. Goldstein & Goldstein, 1990). However, tasks such as the Halstead Category Test (Halstead, 1947), the Wisconsin Card Sorting Test (Grant & Berg,

Name _____ Grade _____ Age at time of High School Graduation _____ Date of Birth _____

1. Have you earned money for doing workin the last six months?

   ☐ Yes   ☐ No

   If yes, describe job and estimate how much you earned

   _____

2. What kind of work would you like to do when you graduate from high school?

   _____

   What kind of training or education will you need to prepare for this job?

   _____

3. Name two careers that you would like to know more about.

   1. _____
   2. _____

4. Read the list of activities listed below and check each one in which you would like to participate:

   ☐ Job Shadow: Visit a business that interests you and follow a worker to learn more about the job.

   ☐ Interview: Conduct an interview with a worker who has a job you think you would like to do when you graduate.

   ☐ In-School Work Experience: Learn to do different jobs in the school setting.

   ☐ Tour Vocational School: Spend a day at the vocational school to learn about the programs.

   ☐ Paid Work Experience: Get paid to do a job and attend school at the same time.

   ☐ Community College: Learn what it takes to get into college and see if college will help prepare you for a career.

   ☐ University/College: Learn what it takes to get into college and see if college will help prepare you for a career.

   ☐ Career Exploration: Learn more about careers so you can choose one you like.

   ☐ Career Planning: Match career choices to needed training and preparation.

   ☐ Vocational Assessment: Take a test to mach personal interests and strengths to different types of jobs.

   ☐ Transition Planning: Be involved in a plan to target outcomes to achieve after high school and help develop strategies to achieve those outcomes.

   ☐ Portfolio Development: Create a record of skills and training to show to a prospective employer, training agency, or college.

Figure 6.16 Student Interest Survey

5. Read the list of programs and services listed below and check each one that you think should be included in your high school program.

☐ Vocational Education
☐ College Preparation Courses
☐ Personal Finance Coursework (Budgeting, money management)
☐ Daily Living Skills
☐ Driver Education
☐ College Entrance Exams (Preparation, practice)
☐ Learning Styles Assessment

☐ Business Courses (Typing, Accounting)
☐ Career Counseling
☐ Job Skills Training
☐ Computer Courses
☐ Art and Design
☐ Social Skills Training (Social skills needed for employment)

6. Below is a list of community agencies. Please read the list and check the ones that you would like to know more about:

☐ Bureau of Motor Vehicles
☐ Social Security and SSI
☐ Housing Agencies
☐ Youth Services
☐ Job Training Partnership (JTPA)
☐ Vocation Rehabilitation
☐ Mental Health/Counseling Agencies
☐ Public Health Agency
☐ Family and Children's Services
☐ Bureau of Employment Services (Job Service)

7. Read the list of Daily Living Skills listed below. Check each one that you think you need to know more about:

☐ Household Management: Finding a place to live and managing household responsibilities.
☐ Money Management: Developing personal budget, opening bank account, paying bills, establishing good credit.
☐ Getting Along with Others: Developing and maintaining relationships at school, at work, at home.
☐ Health and Exercise. Making healthy lifestyle choices.
☐ Homemaking Skills: Laundry, housecleaning, meal planning.
☐ Emergencies, First Aid: Handling emergencies.
☐ Family and Marriage Planning: Applying decision-making skills to major life decision - parenting, birth control
☐ How to Get Medical Services: Assess personal and medical needs and know how to obtain needed services.
☐ Responsible Citizenship: Voting, taxes, driver's license, car insurance, legal assistance.

8. As an adult you will have leisure time to participate in activities in the community. Please check the type of activities you would like to do as an adult:

☐ Memberships in clubs
☐ Adult Recreational Leagues (Sports)
☐ Continuing Education
☐ Church groups
☐ Volunteer
☐ Family Activities
☐ Other Activities (describe) _____

Figure 6.16 (Continued)

Name_____ Age_____
Date_____

Size _____	Habitual mannerisms: Tics _____
Appearance _____	Rocking _____
Separation and waiting room _____	Twisting hair _____
Eye contact _____	Facial mannerisms _____
Speech and Language: Receptive _____	Sucking _____
Expressive syntax _____	Flapping arms _____
Expressive articulation _____	Activity: Underactive, little spontaneous
Maintains conversation _____	movement _____
Initiates conversation _____	Normal _____
Expression: Anxious _____ Sad _____	Tendency to increased activity _____
Miserable _____ Unhappy _____	Markedly overactive relative
Calm _____	to situations _____
Concerned about performance _____	Extremely overactive, tempo of
Lack of Affect _____ Labile _____	activity increases _____
Other _____	Fidgetiness: Normal _____
Emotional Stability _____	Occasional squirming or wriggling _____
Tearfulness _____	Marked fidgetiness _____
Alert _____	Distractibility: Not distracted _____
Attention _____	Occasionally distracted _____
Concentration _____	Easily distracted _____
Cooperation _____	Seeks distraction _____
Attempt _____	Orientation to purpose of testing _____
Motivation _____	Self-Confidence: Extremely confident _____
Maturity _____	Overly confident _____
Persistence: Normal _____	Moderately confident _____
Needs occasional prompting _____	Inclined to distrust abilities _____
Needs continuous examiner praise and	Very insecure _____
encouragement _____	Comprehension _____
Inconsistent effort _____	Orientation to testing _____
Preoccupation with topics of:	Relationship with examiner _____
Anxiety _____	Emotional responsiveness to examiner _____
Depressive _____	Smiling: Smiles appropriately _____
Aggressive _____	Smiles only occasionally _____
Muscular tension: Clinching jaw _____	No, or very little smiling _____
Sitting stiffly in chair _____	Final adjustment _____
Gripping table or chair _____	Thought processes: Logical _____
Gripping hands together _____	Focused _____
Other _____	Relevant _____

Figure 6.17   Goldstein Behavioral Observation Checklist

Note. Copyright 1989 by Neurology, Learning and Behavior Center, Salt Lake City, UT. Used with permission.

1984), and the Porteus Maze Test (Porteus, 1950) have not been consistently shown to contribute much to the differential diagnosis of ADHD. These instruments, and others such as the Test of Nonverbal Intelligence—Revised (L. Brown, Sherbenou, & Johnsen, 1990), may allow qualitative observation of the individual's ability to sustain attention and inhibit impulsive responding under increasingly difficult task demands, and give measures of the reasoning deficits suspected for some individuals with LD.

Verbal Ability

The research literature has consistently shown that a significant majority of people with LD have long-standing language-based deficits (Cantwell & Baker, 1987a). Further, childhood data suggest that a significant minority of children with ADHD have specific language deficits (Cantwell & Satterfield, 1978).

Although verbal subtests from the WAIS, and other simple measures of verbal ability such as the Peabody Picture Vocabulary Test—Revised (Dunn & Dunn, 1981), may offer the clinician estimates of the individual's verbal skills, only an organized speech language battery can give a true picture of verbal linguistic functioning. If the assessment gives reason to suspect verbal weaknesses, especially those related to semantics, a referral to a speech language pathologist for further language assessment should be considered mandatory.

Academic

The Woodcock-Johnson Psycho-Educational Battery—Revised (Woodcock & Johnson, 1989) offers by far the most thorough, well-developed assessment of academic skills. Normative data are available from childhood through adulthood. Subtest analysis often reveals patterns consistent with verbal or visual, rote or conceptual, weaknesses. Achievement tests such as the Woodcock Reading Mastery Tests—Revised (Woodcock, 1987) offer a shorter skill-based reading assessment. If applicable, a review of school-age or college entrance Scholastic Achievement Tests, Iowa Tests of Basic Skills, or college entrance American College Tests (ACTs) can also provide a thorough quantitative overview of general academic achievement and basic achievement abilities. However, instruments that may generate more qualitative data about academic functioning can also be of great assistance. The NLBC model uses the Wide Range Achievement Test—3 (WRAT-3; G. S. Wilkinson, 1993) to generate observations of conceptual versus rote sequential mathematical abilities, phonetic versus visual memory deficits in spelling, and phonetic versus visual memory aspects of single-word reading. The Story Writing subtest from the Test of Written Language—3 (Hammill & Larsen, 1996) is used to observe differences in written thematic maturity, vocabulary, capacity to organize ideas, grammar, punctuation, and general execution.

Oral reading subtests from the Gilmore (Gilmore & Gilmore, 1968), the Gray Oral Reading Tests—Third Edition (Wiederholt & Bryant, 1992), or the Test of Reading Comprehension—Third Edition (V. L. Brown, Hammill, & Wiederholt, 1995) allow the clinician to assess oral reading capacity, specifically ability to read in context, rate of reading, and simple comprehension. Overall, administration of academic instruments should allow the clinician to draw conclusions not only about the client's quantitative skills (e.g., grade levels) but about distinctions in reading, writing, and mathematical abilities as described.

Attentional Skills

A number of paper-and-pencil and auditory tasks, including the Trail Making tests, Parts A and B, of the Halstead-Reitan Neuropsychological Test Battery (Reitan, 1986), the Paced Auditory Serial Addition Test (Gronwall, 1977), and the Stroop Color and Word Test (Rudel, Holmes, & Pardes, 1988), have been effective in tapping ADHD behaviors in a laboratory setting. However, none of these have consistently yielded data that imply their usefulness in making clinical diagnostic decisions about ADHD. Researchers have increasingly worked toward measures that provide better control of the assessment process and thereby allow interpretations of attentional problems to be made with greater confidence. Computerized measures of sustained attention represent this next generation of assessment tools.

Computerized measures of sustained attention and the ability to inhibit impulsive responding (continuous performance tests [CPTs]) were first introduced as mechanical measures by Rosevald, Mirsky, Sarason, Branson, and Beck (1956). These researchers evaluated inattention secondary to petit mal epilepsy. Variations of the CPT have been used with a variety of populations. The introduction of computer technology has allowed a myriad of CPTs to be developed. Newer tasks require response inhibition rather than initiation.

In 1957 Mackworth first used the CPT specifically to study sustained attention. It has also been used with other populations (for a review, see Pasuraman, 1994). It is beyond the scope of this text to review the CPT literature in depth. The interested reader is referred to a concise outline by Conners (1994a) and an ongoing database compiled by Gordon (1994).

Approximately one-third of children with a *DSM-III-R* diagnosis of ADHD are not detected by presently available CPT measures. Children with ADHD classified as abnormal on the CPT, however, have also been found to score below those classified as normal on other measures, such as abstract reasoning, logical problem solving, simple verbal reasoning, nonverbal problem solving, and simple arithmetic skills (for a review, see Conners, 1994a). The CPT, therefore, may offer a measure of more than just the capacity to inhibit impulsive responding and sustained attention. It can, therefore, provide false negatives or positives. In fact, many of the initiation CPTs (in which one must inhibit responding the majority of the time and respond only when the target appears) may have good positive predictive power in identifying people with ADHD symptoms. It is problems with their negative predictive power, however, that make these tasks inefficient in general: If one passes the test, no conclusions can be drawn. The Conners CPT, which will be reviewed below, requires response inhibition; that is, one must respond continuously and inhibit responding when the target appears. This may make it a more efficient measure by avoiding problems related to negative predictive power.

The CPT has been effective in identifying children described as impulsive and inattentive and is sensitive to improvements observed with drug treatment (Conners, Eisenberg, & Barcai, 1967). Although CPTs are designed to measure sustained attention, some studies have not found a consistent decline in performance over time (Schachar, Logan, Wachsmuth, & Chajczyk, 1988). As H. L. Swanson (1993) reported, the performance decline for some children with ADHD may not result from changes in target detection but may indicate that, while completing a boring task, some children become less efficient as they become less strict in deciding whether a signal is a target. However, their *ability* to detect the target, that is, their ability to sustain attention, does not deteriorate.

Coons et al. (1981) found that 20 mg of methylphenidate elevated heart rates in young adults but did not affect performance on a CPT. A second study using a more complex CPT, however, demonstrated improvement with methylphenidate in these normal individuals.

In a study of 10 females and 54 males, aged 5–15 years, referred for ADHD evaluation, Kirby, VandenBerg, and Sullins (1993) administered a CPT with and without methylphenidate. Reactions were faster while receiving the methylphenidate, standard errors were smaller, and the percentage of correct responses was significantly higher.

J. W. Campbell, D'Amato, Roggio, and Stephens (1991) found that, in a group of 5–15-year-olds, an academic achievement factor loaded closely with CPT performance. In general, more and more work is being done to understand the relationship among the ability to pay attention, educational achievement, and intelligence (Barkley, 1995a). The consensus of data suggests that ADHD has only a minimal direct impact on intelligence and the acquisition of intellectual skills. It likely has more impact on the efficient use of those skills, principally through the effect of impulsive behavior on test performance and daily activities.

Conners Continuous Performance Test (CPT). The Conners CPT, Version 3.0, measures omission and commission errors as well as reaction time. The task requires the child, adolescent, or adult to respond continuously for 14 minutes as single letters are exposed to the screen for brief periods of time with varying intervals between them. The individual must inhibit responding when the target (an X) appears. A person with ADHD may respond slowly to a target, which produces an omission error, followed by a commission error (Conners & Rothchild, 1968). This instrument allows for multiple variations, making it extremely attractive to researchers. Ultimately, this form of CPT—requiring inhibition of response as a measure of the ability to manage impulsivity—may prove to be effective in operationally defining impulsivity—the central quality of those with ADHD.

Tests of Variables of Attention (TOVA). The TOVA is a 25-minute CPT (L. M. Greenberg & Crosby, 1992). It is non–language based and sets a repetitive task in which individuals are asked to watch for a designated target and ignore nontargets. The individual is to respond when a small square appears inside of a larger square. The TOVA, like the Conners, offers normative data through adulthood (L. M. Greenberg & Crosby, 1992). The TOVA measures omissions, commissions, correct response time, and anticipatory errors. The length of the task is thought to make it more sensitive to ADHD-related problems in adults. The TOVA has also been suggested as an effective way to monitor response to methylphenidate (L. M. Greenberg & Waldman, 1991).

Gordon Diagnostic System (GDS). The GDS is a portable electronic device designed to assess deficits in impulse control and inattention (Gordon, 1988). The instrument was developed for use in the diagnosis of ADHD and has been increasingly employed as a neuropsychological assessment tool as well. Three types of tasks are administered, the Delay, Vigilance, and Distractibility tasks. The first measures the ability to refrain from responding in a self-paced setting. The individual must time responses so as to earn a maximum number of points. A premature response does not earn a point. The second set of tasks assesses how well an individual maintains self-control in situations requiring sustained attention. This is a standard CPT in which the individual must respond whenever the target (the number 9) immediately follows the cue (the number 1). The third set of tasks (Distractibility) is similar to the second but includes distraction. Single-digit numbers flash alternately on either side of the spot the individual must observe and respond to. Although normative data were available initially only through 16 years of age, a number of researchers have now generated limited normative data for younger adults and the elderly. The GDS has been reported to differentiate accurately between children experiencing ADHD and those classified in the school setting as reading disabled, overanxious, or unimpaired (Gordon & McClure, 1983). However, the CPT has also been reported to be unrelated to academic functioning (Lassiter, D'Amato, Riggio, Whitten, & Bardos, 1994). Lassiter et al. did report, however, that commission errors on the CPT correlated with behavioral measures. Specifically, commission errors were related to oppositional behavior as reported on the Conners hyperactivity index.

Intermediate Test of Auditory and Visual Attention. Sanford (1994) has developed an integrated 13-minute auditory and visual performance test designed to combine visual and auditory measures of attention and impulse control. Normative data are provided for 5–55 years of age. The computerized printout offers a fairly complex analysis evaluating aspects of sustained attention and impulse control.

Personality and Emotion

Self-report measures such as the Minnesota Multiphasic Personality Inventory—II (Hathaway & McKinley, 1989) and the Millon Clinical Multiaxial Personality Inventory—II (Millon, 1987) offer very comprehensive, actuarially based overviews of acute psychiatric status and personality function. These instruments are often extremely valuable during the differential diagnostic process. For adolescents, the Millon Adolescent Personality Inventory (Millon, Green, & Meagher, 1982) is an excellent tool for assessing emerging personality qualities. As of this date, no subtypes for these instruments have been found to be specifically indicative of ADHD or LD. However, the Millon does address the issue of whether a profile reflects an individual prone to impulsive or reflective behavior.

The Beck Depression Scale (Beck, 1978) is the most widely used adolescent and adult depression instrument. It offers well-validated qualitative scores reflecting the degree of depressive thinking, feelings, and behavior the individual self-reports. The Epidemiologic Studies Depression Scale (Ridloff, 1977) and the Interviewer Rated Hamilton Depression Rating Scale are other instruments that may be used clinically. For an overview of the experimental use of these instruments, the reader is referred to Lewison, Gottleib, and Seeley (1995).

For adolescents, the Revised Children's Manifest Anxiety Scale (C. R. Reynolds & Richmond, 1985) and the Reynolds Adolescent Depression Scale (W. M. Reynolds, 1986) also offer excellent overviews of self-reported emotionally distressing thoughts, feelings, and behaviors.

INTEGRATING THE DATA

Data integration and the consideration of differential diagnosis are not simple matters. This chapter concludes with five sample assessments and Chapter 7 presents 24 case studies because studying complete specific examples is the best way for the clinician to become sensitive to these processes.

The data should make sense. The client's history, level of vocational or academic achievement, and behavioral or emotional functioning should blend seamlessly with assessment data collected. This is not always easy or possible, and experienced clinicians recognize that assessment is a complex process. When care and time are taken to collect enough data, however, the data will often make sense and lead intuitively to the consideration of differential diagnostic issues and recommendations.

DIFFERENTIAL DIAGNOSIS

In regard to LD, the basic differential diagnostic task facing clinicians is to determine whether the client's level of achievement actually reflects his or her overall level of functioning or in fact represents a discrepancy between actual and expected functioning due to specific skill weaknesses. It is strongly recommended that clinicians consider the verbal-visual/rote-conceptual model presented in Chapter 2 when attempting to address this basic question. The sample reports and case studies provide ample illustrations of this process.

In regard to ADHD, differential diagnostic questions may be more complicated. While laboratory tests will not add much to the ADHD diagnostic process, history certainly will. Clinicians must use care, however, for a number of other factors may be responsible for a history of ADHD-like symptoms. These factors include:

1. *Learning disabilities.* LD leads to symptoms of ADHD primarily as the result of long-term frustration. As Cantwell and Baker (1985) have reported, individuals with histories of language-based difficulties, for example, demonstrate increasing symptoms of ADHD as they progress through the greater demands of higher school grades. When LD and ADHD coexist, the clinician must gather history very carefully to ascertain that symptoms of ADHD were in fact demonstrated before the academic demands of school overwhelmed the client. For children with histories of early severe language delays, however, this differential diagnostic question may never be answered.

2. *Normal variations in attention, impulse control, and activity level.* These factors may in some circumstances appear symptomatic of ADHD but overall do not impair daily life functioning. It is important for clinicians to recall that a key premise in the diagnosis of adult ADHD is the demonstration of inattentive symptoms in childhood before age seven.

3. *Depression.* Although symptoms of depression such as problems with concentration and physical agitation may overlap with ADHD, in general individuals suffering from major depression as a primary disorder do not demonstrate sufficient symptoms or history to warrant a diagnosis of ADHD. It is certainly possible, however, that an adult will be evaluated during the course of a major depressive episode and will in fact also have a history of ADHD. Differential diagnosis may allow for the conclusion that both disorders are present. However, firm decisions about the severity of the ADHD must usually be reserved until the depression lifts. One rule of thumb is to treat the more severe symptoms first. These are usually the symptoms related to depression.

Adult hypomanic symptoms, however, including irritability, pressured speech, disorganized thinking, sleep disturbances, and restlessness, may at times masquerade as ADHD. In fact, a manic depressive disorder was identified as a characteristic problem for a group of people with ADHD (Weinberg & Brumback, 1976). For clinicians, among the key differential diagnostic issues is a history of repeated depressive episodes. Further, hypomanic individuals experience ongoing euphoria and cheerfulness despite their symptoms, while many adults with ADHD are bothered by their troubles. The hypomanic may not report symptoms that are ego dystonic. The adult with ADHD usually will.

4. *Personality disorders* (e.g., borderline personality, histrionic personality, and intermittent explosive personality). The *DSM-IV* lists a number of personality disorders in the main section in addition to those under consideration, listed in that work's Appendix. The interested reader will note apparent symptoms of ADHD present in many of these personality disorders. The clinician should also recall that a significant minority of adults with ADHD demonstrate antisocial personality disorder. History suggests, however, that this disorder develops secondary to other non-ADHD experiences.

Among the most perplexing differential diagnostic issues are those involving borderline personality. Borderline personality characteristics include impulsivity and impaired social relationships. However, borderline individuals also experience intense relations and may engage in impulsive suicidal acts, characteristics that are not usually observed for adults with ADHD. The issue of personality styles and disorders and their relationship to ADHD requires significantly more study.

5. *Anxiety disorders.* These disorders may produce restlessness, sleep problems, impatience, and an inability to relax. These symptoms are the subject of characteristic questions asked on many adult ADHD questionnaires. Individuals with anxiety disorder, however, also

worry a lot about themselves and their future, tend to ruminate, and have long-lasting feelings of anxiety. The last group of symptoms has also been described as a by-product of adult ADHD (Hallowell & Ratey, 1995). It has been suggested that a key diagnostic point in differentiating between anxiety and ADHD may be the fact that when these symptoms stem from anxiety, they are often accompanied by autonomic nervous system overactivity (e.g., reports of fast heart rate, dizziness, and somatic complaints), a phenomenon not reported in adults with ADHD (G. Weiss & Hechtman, 1993).

6. *Compulsive behavior.* Clinicians must be able to distinguish between impulsive and compulsive behavior. During the history-taking session, clients may describe their gambling or alcohol use as compulsive. In fact, these are often impulsive behaviors and not accompanied by extreme anxiety. It is rare, however, for obsessive/compulsive disorder to be confused with ADHD.

7. *Substance abuse.* Individuals suffering from substance abuse may report ADHD-like symptoms. It has been suggested, for example, that signs of cocaine abuse mimic those of ADHD because they include overactivity and acute symptoms of increased alertness, higher energy level, and excessive talking (Werner, 1993). When substance abuse is suspected or in fact occurs, clinicians are advised to defer final diagnostic decisions about problems such as ADHD until the substance abuse problems are better understood and at least until treatment for them has begun.

8. *Symptoms or co-occurring problems of adult medical disorders.* Some adult medical disorders can cause problems characteristic of ADHD. The case studies include a number of such examples. As when medications are involved, clinicians are advised to evaluate and understand the individual's medical history very carefully. Every clinician should have some knowledge of medical disorders and their related cognitive, emotional, and attentional effects. The interested reader is referred to Tarter, Van Thiel, and Edwards (1988).

Barkley and Murphy (1993b) have contended that ADHD has the earliest onset of any disorder and that it is therefore foolish to assume that other adult disorders precede ADHD. Among the most common comorbid disorders presenting in a small group of individuals with ADHD were substance abuse, dysthymia, and personality disorders, including narcissism and dependent and antisocial personality disorders. These authors argued that diagnosis of ADHD can be made when these other disorders are present because the ADHD likely preceded these in onset. However, bipolar disorder, borderline personality, or schizophrenia may represent a lifetime pattern of dealing with the environment beginning in early childhood. Barkley and Murphy (1993b) concluded that ADHD and bipolar disorder do not appear to be related "in any significant way developmentally, etiologically, conceptually or otherwise" (p. 3). They argued that when dealing with these two disorders, even if a childhood diagnosis of ADHD is present, the bipolarity needs to take priority and be treated first before firm conclusions about ADHD in adulthood can be made. This author agrees with their opinion and suggests that, while it is likely that borderline personality or bipolar disorder can coexist with ADHD, when these disorders are observed in adulthood they must represent the primary diagnostic formulation and be the initial focus of treatment.

As noted in Chapter 5, much research is needed before the relationship of adult psychiatric disorders and ADHD will be thoroughly understood. For the time being, clinicians must use a reasoned and reasonable approach when attempting to assign cause and meaning to impulsive, inattentive symptoms.

GENERAL RECOMMENDATIONS

The sample assessments give an overview of the general recommendations made at the conclusion of LD and ADHD assessments. These recommendations fall into general areas, including those related to referral for additional consultation, such as psychiatric consideration of medication, vocational assessment, or speech language evaluation; those related to life issues and placement, such as vocational and educational programs; and those related to additional treatment, such as assistance with socialization, family, individual, and marital counseling, and parent training.

The treatment chapters, Chapters 8–13, offer a thorough overview of these recommendations. A number of related issues will be briefly addressed in this section.

As one of their key services, more and more evaluators will be asked to contribute to or actually structure a transition profile to guide the process of transition from high school or college into vocational and adult life. Appendix D contains an in-depth transition profile that provides a structured, systematic way of organizing all of the data collected about a client into a multiyear plan for the client's future. Although cumbersome on first observation, this plan is by far the most comprehensive of those currently available.

To facilitate the transition-planning process, McCarney (1989) offers a Transition Behavior Scale. This scale was developed to assist in the screening process. It provides a profile of strengths and weaknesses and of behaviors recognized as the best predictors of employment and independent living success. While some clinicians may wish to use this questionnaire as part of the assessment process, others may choose to wait until the assessment is completed. The profile consists of 62 items associated with characteristics related to work, interpersonal relations, and adherence to rules. The questionnaire is generally applicable to people exiting high school. It generates three subscale scores and an overall rank in comparison to the same-sex and overall populations. Each item on this scale is rated on a 3-point Likert system describing the behavior as nonexistent, inconsistent, or consistently demonstrated. A sample of this questionnaire appears in Figure 6.18.

McCarney (1989) offers a cookbook of practical suggestions for dealing with the work-related, interpersonal, and social and community problems identified by his Transition Behavior Scale. The intervention manual also includes a system for structuring an Individualized Education Plan (IEP) with transition goals. For example, for Behavior 41, McCarney (1989) outlines the following interventions, among others:

1. Reinforce the student for appropriate care of personal property:

    (a) Give the student a tangible reward (e.g., classroom privileges, line leading, passing out materials, five minute free time, etc.) when he/she appropriately cares for personal property, or

    (b) Give the student an intangible reward (e.g., praise, handshake, smile, etc.) when he/she appropriately cares for personal property.

2. Speak with the student to explain: (a) what he/she is doing wrong (e.g., failing to maintain organization or use materials appropriately) and (b) what he/she should be doing (e.g., keeping inside of desk organized, organizing materials on top of desk, using materials as instructed, etc.).

TO RATER: Rate the student using the quantifiers (0 to 2) provided. Every item must be rated. *Do not leave any items blank.*

DOES NOT PERFORM THE BEHAVIOR	PERFORMS THE BEHAVIOR INCONSISTENTLY	PERFORMS THE BEHAVIOR CONSISTENTLY
0	1	2

WORK RELATED

☐ 1.   Attempts new assignments
☐ 2.   Begins assignments after receiving directions.
☐ 3.   Completes assignments within a specified time period.

INTERPERSONAL RELATIONS

☐ 26.   Responds appropriately to typical exchanges with peers (being bumped, touched, brushed against, etc.)
☐ 27.   Responds appropriately to friendly teasing (e.g., joking, name calling, sarcastic remarks, etc.)
☐ 28.   Cares for personal appearance (e.g., grooming, clothing, etc.)

SOCIAL/COMMUNITY EXPECTATIONS

☐ 41.   Is responsible for appropriate care of personal property.
☐ 42.   Responds appropriately to environmental cues (e.g., bells, signs, etc.)
☐ 43.   Stays in an assigned area for the specified time period (e.g., classroom, building, school grounds, etc.)

Figure 6.18   Sample items from the Transition Behavior Scale
Note. From Transition Behavior Scale, by S. B. McCarney. Copyright 1989 by Hawthorne Educational Services, Columbia, MO. Used with permission.

3. Establish classroom rules (e.g., work on task, work quietly, remain in your seat, finish task, meet task expectations, etc.). Reiterate rules often and reinforce students for following rules.

4. Reinforce the student for appropriate care of personal property based on the length of time the student can be successful. Gradually increase the length of time required for reinforcement as the student becomes more successful.

5. Write a contract with the student specifying what behavior is expected (e.g., organization and appropriate use of materials) and what reinforcement will be made available when the terms of the contract have been met.

6. Communicate with the parents (e.g., notes home, phone calls, etc.) in order to share information concerning the student's progress and so that they may reinforce the student at home for organization and appropriate use of materials at school.

7. Evaluate the appropriateness of tasks to determine if: (a) the task is too easy, (b) the task is too difficult, and (c) the length of time scheduled for the task is appropriate.

8. Assign a peer to work directly with the student to serve as a model for appropriate use of materials and organization.

9. Provide time at the beginning of each day for the student to organize his/her materials.*

Clinicians may also want to include more generic suggestions at the conclusion of their assessment. Nancy Payne has compiled a list of such general recommendations and accommodations for the learning-disabled individual seeking education, training, or employment, based on the work of Abbott (1978), D. Brown (1980), and Closer Look (1981):

Work is for everyone, disabled or not. Because of federal and state laws regulating the education and employment of the handicapped, more and more individuals with learning disabilities are accessing post-secondary education, training, and/or employment opportunities. In helping these individuals obtain appropriate skills and secure employment, we are faced with a need to provide reasonable accommodations, thus allowing for maximum opportunities within education, training, and/or employment environments. The following is a basic list of suggestions that will help in counseling and working with the learning disabled individual in education, training and/or employment settings.

Ensure that the individual understands the types of learning disabilities that have been diagnosed and can explain them in a clear, reasonable manner.

Educate the individual as to opportunities available under the laws of the state and federal government.

Be aware, and make sure the individual is aware, of his/her best learning modality and that he/she can identify and utilize reasonable accommodations related to the learning disability.

Encourage the individual to speak about the disability with school counselors, special student services personnel, employers, immediate supervisors, and coworkers when appropriate.

Alert the individual of techniques of handling negative responses; make him/her aware of available faculty and/or personnel who might be more sensitive to his/her needs.

If permissible, alert faculty and/or employers to strategies which might be helpful to the individual in accommodating for learning difficulties.

---

*From *The Transition Behavior Scale IEP and Intervention Manual,* by S. B. McCarney, 1989, Columbia, MO: Hawthorne Educational Services. Copyright 1989 by Hawthorne Educational Services. Used with permission.

When in a training or classroom situation, recommend that the individual carry a reduced load (part-time is ideal for beginning learning disabled students).

Identify and train in areas of previous success or knowledge; take a specific weak or difficult area, start at a lower level so the individual is comfortable, then overtrain, advancing slowly to ensure competence and success.

Use materials that relate to experiences; design or use special workshops/activities that help break down subject matter; help individual communicate acquired knowledge through other medical methods (i.e., oral, taped, or recorded responses, or experimental demonstrations).

Break tasks into small, sequential steps; show how first, then teach steps and application; keep schedules similar throughout the day or week, and encourage the individual to set daily/weekly schedules, identifying tasks for completion.

Suggest tutoring, study groups and/or mentoring during a learning process; reduce long written and/or reading assignments; keep oral discussion on target; speak directly to the individual, taking time to see if there is understanding; decrease the amount of oral or written directions given at a time.

Encourage the use of aids and tools—calculators, highlighter pens, extra worksheets, computerized learning, records, tape records, films, demonstrations, maps, charts, experiences, fingers, rulers, etc.; use visual aids whenever possible, helping to create a picture in the "mind's eye."

Examinations for employment, college entrance, subject competency and the like should be administered with the appropriate accommodations for the type of disability; shorter, untimed tests should be utilized which test only the subject at hand, not extras such as grammar or spelling.

When trying to locate information, especially in the newspaper or phone book, the individual may have difficulty reading the small print or may reverse when trying to copy.

Individuals with learning disabilities sometimes have difficulty making first impressions, an important item when interviewing or meeting someone for the first time, however, not particularly an important skill to maintain a job or a friendship.

Show by example; help the individual prepare sample application forms, resumes, cover letters, letters of inquiry, and in general sample written copy which allows for a more independent level of functioning.

Provide information that allows the individual to assess skill levels, choose appropriate education or training facilities, and access the job market competently.

Remember, do not embarrass, insinuate laziness, or discourage publicly or privately; behavioral and emotional problems are the result of the disability, not the cause; do not excuse from normal responsibility or normal tasks; accommodations in how to perform the tasks should be implemented; be aware that careless errors may be the result of the learning disability.

Finally, be sensitive to the individual and help provide the necessary support by identifying the strongest learning modality and providing appropriate accommodations for the weaker modalities. By creating an atmosphere in which the individual will feel positive about learning, whether it be academic or job related, many successes will be realized.

As S. Goldstein (1995) reported based on a review of the available literature, teacher personality styles and classroom operations vary greatly. Often generic or even specific suggestions that are usually beneficial do not fit with a teacher's style or classroom structure. The Accommodations for Students with Learning Disabilities questionnaire allows the clinician or advocate to assess the types of interventions an educator would be willing to consider if a learning-disabled student or, for that matter, a student with ADHD presented in their classroom (see Figure 6.19).

Hand-held spell checkers, dictionaries, and thesauri, as well as a myriad of new computer software containing spelling and grammar checkers, offer great assistance and accommodation to those with LD or ADHD. Clinicians should not be reserved in recommending these because they are not intrusive and are tools often used outside of the classroom.

Strichert and Mangrum (1985) and Michaels (1987) noted that when clinicians consider college placement as a recommendation for the learning-disabled individual, the following issues must be considered:

1. Availability of supportive aids, such as computers
2. Academic advisors knowledgeable about LD
3. Tutorial assistance
4. Peer group support
5. Available diagnostic testing
6. Counseling and student disability services
7. Campus orientation programs

It is quite likely that these same support services are also beneficial for students with ADHD.

R. C. Hartman and Krulwich (1983) reported that the ACT and SAT can be altered to accommodate students with LD or ADHD by extending the time allotted to complete these tests and allowing the use of readers, the use of larger type, and assistance with marking. Centra (1986) found that extending the time limit on the SAT resulted in an average gain of 30–38 points for persons with LD. Clinicians should not hesitate to recommend extended time or other accommodations on college entrance examinations for those with LD or ADHD.

Finally, most authors offer generic lists of practical, though largely untested, approaches to the learning, memory, test-taking, organizational, attentional, and self-confidence problems that people with LD or ADHD experience in daily life, at school, and in the workplace. Vogel (1995) and Latham and Latham (1992, 1994, 1995) are representative of this approach. For example, in regard to memory problems, Vogel (1995) suggests repetition, color coding, highlighting, reading out loud, and frequent review; he suggests taking practice exams, reading test instructions carefully, answering the easiest questions first, self-pacing, and seeking clarification as helpful test-taking strategies. One of the most useful resources clinicians can provide is a list of these types of publications. A number of these appear in Appendix A.

This questionnaire is an attempt to ascertain how the faculty feel about making accommodations in their classes for students with learning disabilities. Consider how you would respond to a student in your class with a documented learning disability, if he/she requested any of the following. Please check (x) the first column if you *would* make the accommodation, the second column if you *would not*, and the third column if you *do not know* if you would make the accommodation.

	Would	Would Not	Do Not Know
1. Extend deadlines for completion of class projects, papers, etc.	_____	_____	_____
2. Analyze the process as well as the final solution. (For example, give the student partial credit if the correct mathematical computation was used even though the final answer was wrong).	_____	_____	_____
3. Allow the student to complete alternative assignments.	_____	_____	_____
4. Allow the student to do an extra credit assignment when this option is not available to other students.	_____	_____	_____
5. Allow the student to give oral presentations or tape-recorded assignments rather than produce written projects.	_____	_____	_____
6. Allow the use of proofreaders to assist in the correction of spelling, grammar, and punctuation.	_____	_____	_____
7. Allow the use of proofreaders to assist in the reconstruction of the student's first draft of a written assignment.	_____	_____	_____
8. Allow the use of a proofreader to assist the student in the substitution of a higher level vocabulary for the original wording.	_____	_____	_____
9. Allow the student to take an alternative form of your exams. (For example, some students with learning disabilities have trouble taking tests using computer-scored answer sheets. Others might do better on multiple-choice tests than essay tests.)	_____	_____	_____

Figure 6.19   Accommodations for students with learning disabilities

Note. Adapted from "Faculty Attitudes toward Accommodations for College Students with Learning Disabilities," by P. R. Matthews, D. W. Anderson, and B. D. Skolnick, 1987, *Learning Disabilities Focus, 3,* pp. 46–52. Used with permission.

	Would	Would Not	Do Not Know
10. Allow a proctor to rephrase test questions that are not clear to the student. (For example, a double negative may need to be clarified.).	____	____	____
11. Allow the student extra time to complete tests.	____	____	____
12. Allow the student to dictate answers a proctor.	____	____	____
13. Allow the student to respond orally to essay questions.	____	____	____
14. Allow exams to be proctored in a separate room to reduce distractions.	____	____	____
15. Allow the student to use calculators during tests and in-class assignments.	____	____	____
16. Allow misspellings, incorrect punctuation, and poor grammar without penalizing the student.	____	____	____
17. Allow the student to substitute a course for a required course. (For example, substitute for a foreign language requirement.)	____	____	____
18. Provide the student with an early syllabus to give ample time to complete reading and writing assignments.	____	____	____
19. Allow the student to tape record classroom lectures.	____	____	____
20. Provide the student with copies of instructor's lecture notes after he/she attends the lecture.	____	____	____
21. Allow the student to withdraw from a course after the usual cutoff date.	____	____	____
22. Allow the student to take advantage of priority registration. (For example, be among the first to register.)	____	____	____
23. Protect the student against undue anxiety by relaxing academic probation and suspension procedures.	____	____	____

Comments: _____

Figure 6.19   *(Continued)*

Sample Assessments

The remainder of this chapter presents five sample assessments that illustrate a number of different styles and formats for summarizing and presenting data, drawing conclusions, making diagnoses, and, most important, offering recommendations. Each clinician must tailor the format, length, and structure of the written report to his or her style and needs. Some clinicians find brief reports summarizing test data and impressions and making recommendations sufficient. Others feel strongly that lengthy, in-depth assessments are necessary in order to very carefully review, present, and evaluate data as well as to offer a rationale for opinions and recommendations. The first assessment, completed by clinical and school psychologist Terrance G. Lichtenwald, offers a well-structured, comprehensive means for presenting assessment data, as well as comparing and contrasting strengths and weaknesses. The second assessment, completed by school psychologist James R. Denning, offers a model often used by school psychologists for data presentation and summary. It leaves recommendations to the discretion of the counseling staff working directly with the student being evaluated. Although this model has not been highly recommended in this text, in some circumstances refraining from making recommendations, especially when the client is already involved in a treatment program, may be the appropriate course. This is especially so if the primary reason for the referral was to provide diagnostic impressions.

The third, fourth, and fifth assessments were completed by this author at the NLBC. The third is included because it covers ADHD and its relationship to nonverbal LD. The fourth offers a framework for dealing with ADHD symptoms when LD and emotional problems are comorbid and create a diagnostic conundrum. Finally, the fifth covers ADHD and LD in a college-bound high school senior with great athletic potential. These assessments represent actual cases. Names and relevant circumstances have been modified.

SAMPLE ASSESSMENT 1

NAME:	William Smith
GENDER:	Male
AGE:	16 years, 2 months
BIRTHDATE:	06/15/77
GRADE:	Eleventh

REASON FOR EVALUATION

William was referred for a complete psychoeducational evaluation by his attending psychiatrist. He requested the evaluation to address possible learning disabilities and attention deficit disorder with or without hyperactivity issues. A second purpose in this examination was that if William was found to exhibit academic deficits, then the evaluation could be used to assist him in completing the college entrance exam test. In addition, if William was in the position that he was interested in attending college, a copy of this evaluation would be beneficial in that it could be sent to universities that had learning differences programs.

Sources of information for this evaluation include the review of medical records, discussion with William's mother, and discussion with William's physician.

William has had no previous evaluations for academic problems, attention problems, contact problems, emotional problems, possible learning disabilities, or developmental delays. Although William has not had formal evaluations conducted, he has received the assistance of a tutor through much of his educational history.

PSYCHOLOGICAL TEST(S) ADMINISTERED AND INTERVIEW(S) CONDUCTED

Wechsler Intelligence Scale for Children—III
Wide Range Achievement Test—Revised
Woodcock-Johnson Test of Achievement—Revised
Stroop Color and Word Test
Benton Visual Retention Test
Symbol Digit Modality Test
Personal History Checklist
Conners Parent Rating Scale—48 (CPRS-48)

DEVELOPMENTAL HISTORY

At the time of his birth William's father and mother were in their 20s. William had a normal delivery without complications. He was a healthy newborn. During infancy, motor milestones were reached at an average rate. He started to walk before his first birthday and started to talk between one and one and a half years. Motor development between the ages of two and five was described as average in comparison to other children of his age. Early language formation was also rated as average. William's social skills were average in comparison to his peers. Mental development was slow in comparison to other children. He had difficulty learning the alphabet.

William received regular medical check-ups, hearing tests, and dental check-ups. He experienced chicken pox. He did not undergo any surgical procedures. He is not currently being treated for any medical or psychological disorder.

William reported that during his preteen years he had few close friends. He felt that he was always getting into trouble. In reflecting upon his preteen years he described himself as being active, happy, and unhappy. Family dynamics during this developmental period were described as being warm and close. William recalled being treated with strict discipline during his childhood.

William denied any significant medical injuries or illnesses during his adolescent years. William denied having any blows to the head, or accidents which would cause blackouts. William denied any untreated physical problems which he felt should receive medical attention.

William reported that he is a nonsmoker. He had no prior history of cigarette smoking.

The use of alcohol was denied. William denied any past use of alcohol. William denied any alcohol-related problems such as impaired school or work performance, tremors, blackouts, memory loss, hallucinations, or effects on relationships. The use of illegal drugs was denied.

ANALYSIS OF EDUCATIONAL HISTORY

William reported that he attended preschool. He was six years old when he began first grade. Since starting school he has attended only public schools and a private school. On starting school he reported that he was frequently sick and missed classes. His academic performance in elementary school was described as generally poor. In retrospect William recalled disliking school during these early years. William reported that he usually got along poorly with his teachers and had to be disciplined in school frequently. He reported that the school did not conduct any assessments to determine why he was experiencing behavioral difficulties as well as academic failure during these early years.

William reported that he began his secondary school education (ninth grade) at the age of 14. When he began high school he anticipated that he would not fit in socially. In high school, he reported that he has earned poor grades. William reported that he gets along poorly with his teachers and dislikes school.

At school William reported that he participates in team sports. He reported that his skill weaknesses are in taking tests, reading speed, reading comprehension, and spelling. He reported that he plans on returning to high school this fall to complete his course work.

ANALYSIS OF FAMILY STRUCTURE AND DYNAMICS

William has been raised by his natural parents. In respect to family structure, there are two other children in the family, and William is the youngest. William's father is a high school graduate and runs both a small family business and works for a large corporation. William's mother is a high school graduate and has worked primarily as a business manager.

The marriage is the first one for both William's mother and father.

William reported that he does not have any responsibilities or chores at home such as yard work, baby sitting, taking out the garbage, doing the laundry, etc. However, he has worked in the family business (car washes). William reported that he is allowed to drive the car alone, both during the day and at night. He is allowed to use the telephone when he wants to, stay home when his parents are away, buy his own clothes, choose his own hairstyle, and spend his own money. William reported that he is allowed to spend the night at a friend's house, go only to chaperoned parties, and go to concerts with friends.

William reported conflict with his parents over driving, bad language, and his curfew. He reported that when he breaks a rule or misbehaves, his parents usually employ yelling, privilege withdrawal, and grounding to enforce discipline. In respect to discipline William reported that in his view his parents are average.

William reported a positive relationship with his parents. He reported a very positive relationship with his siblings. In his view, his parents are concerned about financial matters. The family system was described as being marked by frequent arguments. William reported that he views himself as an important member of the family and reported no parental abuse of any kind.

ANALYSIS OF BEHAVIOR EXHIBITED DURING TESTING

There was a slight difference in William's behavior during the testing sessions. During the tests which were administered by this examiner (Dr. Lichtenwald) William demonstrated behaviors on specific WISC-III subtests which were judged to be very impulsive and reflective of an individual with low self-esteem, in respect to academic tasks. When William reached the arithmetic subsection test on the WISC-III test, he demonstrated significant difficulty with reading and math problems. Specifically, this examiner noted that on two occasions William did not read the math problem correctly. Specifically, in reading the story problem William did not get the original numbers to work with correct and thus, although he did the correct mathematical computation, his answer was wrong. In addition, during the math section William challenged the examiner, asserting that the examiner may not be adminstering the test correctly. The examiner stopped the testing session and asked William if this is what he does in the classroom. William reported that he hates working with math and fractions and that he was *"Just screwing around with you."*

During the administration of the achievement test William's behavior was ranked as cooperative and friendly. Rapport was easy to establish and maintain. William appeared more relaxed and comfortable. He required repetition of instructions because of problems in attention.

William's responses during the achievement testing were judged as inconsistent, varying between careful and careless responses. He adapted readily and easily to new tasks as the testing progressed. In response to difficult tasks, he reacted inconsistently. At times William adapted readily and easily to new tasks. At other times William showed confusion in the face of new tasks.

During the achievement testing, William was judged as displaying an average level of gross motor activity for his age. He was calm and controlled during the achievement testing. However, his responses varied in manner, sometimes reflecting care and deliberation while at other times indicating haste and impulsivity. William's attention and concentration skills fluctuated significantly during the evaluation. Emotional factors appeared to have a mild negative affect on his performance.

Despite the element of distractibility, the results of the evaluation are believed to reflect an acceptable estimate of William's current level of functioning. The following are the academic and extended behavior observations derived during this examination.

READING STRENGTHS:
    Recites letter names
    Pronounces blends
    Pronounces consonant sounds
    Determines main idea
    Identifies specific details
    Follows written directions

READING WEAKNESSES:
    Confuses similar words
    Disregards punctuation
    Guesses words
    Hesitates
    Loses place
    Mispronounces words
    Omits words
    Omits suffixes
    Omits prefixes
    Poor phrasing
    Substitutes words
    Fails to syllabicate words
    Poor use of word attack
    Reads word by word
    Reads without expression
    Reads too slowly

SPELLING STRENGTHS:
    Writes letters
    Writes names

SPELLING WEAKNESSES:
    Fails to capitalize
    Inserts extra letters
    Makes poor phonetic attempts
    Omits letters
    Uses double consonants incorrectly
    Uses long vowels incorrectly
    Uses prefixes incorrectly
    Uses short vowels incorrectly
    Uses vowel digraphs incorrectly

PENMANSHIP STRENGTHS:
    Grips pencil correctly
    Plans page usage
    Uses adequate pencil pressure on paper
    Uses good spacing of letters
    Writes neatly

PENMANSHIP WEAKNESSES:
    Gets fatigued
    Gets frustrated
    Spreads words far apart

WRITTEN LANGUAGE WEAKNESSES:
Fails to make subject and verb agree
Fails to use any punctuation
Fails to use correct punctuation
Uses incorrect punctuation
Uses incorrect verb tenses
Uses poor sequence and organization
Writes incomplete paragraphs
Writes incomplete sentences

VISUAL-MOTOR STRENGTHS:
Coordinates gross motor smoothly
Draws from memory
Imitates motor movements
Knows right and left
Prefers one hand consistently
Shows greater ease on nonverbal tasks

SPEECH AND LANGUAGE
STRENGTHS:
Articulates well
Converses well
Expresses ideas well
Follows multiple-step instructions
Follows one-step instructions
Responds to questions well
Talks about variety of subjects
Understands abstract words
Understands simple vocabulary
Uses concrete examples
Uses good grammar and syntax
Uses good sequence and logic

ATTENTION AND CONCENTRATION
STRENGTHS:
Completes tasks independently
Ignores distractions
Maintains attention on one task
Stays seated quietly
Waits for instructions
Waits turn
Works quietly

VISUAL-MOTOR WEAKNESSES:
Moves very quickly

BEHAVIORAL AND EMOTIONAL
STRENGTHS:
Acts happy and content
Asks for clarification
Eager to work
Is objective about performance
Parts readily from parent
Remains calm in face of difficulty
Respectful of authority
Shows humor when appropriate
Takes care of materials

BEHAVIORAL AND EMOTIONAL
WEAKNESSES:
Becomes disappointed after failure
Becomes tense on academic tasks
Becomes tense when timed
Voices self-criticism
Works less effectively after failure

ANALYSIS OF WECHSLER INTELLIGENCE SCALE FOR CHILDREN—III

The Wechsler Intelligence Scale for Children—III (WISC-III) consists of a battery of tests that evaluate an individual's intellectual abilities. The WISC-III consists of two scales: the verbal scale and the performance scale. Each of the verbal performance scales have several subtests (See Table 1).

TABLE 1   WISC-III Subtest Scores

Subtest	Scaled Score	Difference from Mean	Percentile Rank	Strength or Weakness
Verbal subtests				
Information	10	−1.2	50	−
Similarities	11	−0.2	63	−
Arithmetic	8	−3.2	25	Weakness
Vocabulary	12	0.8	75	−
Comprehension	16	4.8	98	Strength
Digit span	10	−1.2	50	−
Performance subtests				
Picture Completion	14	3.7	91	Strength
Coding	7	−3.3	16	Weakness
Picture Arrangement	14	3.7	91	Strength
Block Design	9	−1.3	37	−
Object Assembly	8	−2.3	25	−
Symbol Search	8	−2.3	25	−
Mazes	12	1.7	75	−

The verbal scale was designed to measure an individual's language expression, comprehension, listening, and the ability to apply these skills to solving problems. During the administration of the tests on the verbal scale, the examiner presented the questions orally and William gave a spoken response. The performance scale assesses nonverbal problem solving, perceptual organization, speed, and visual-motor proficiency. Tasks on the performance scale include such things as puzzles, analysis of pictures, imitating designs with blocks, and copying.

Several scores are from the WISC-III (see Table 2). Scale scores are converted to verbal and performance intelligence quotient scores. The full-scale IQ is in the index of general intellectual functioning. Factor scores and subtest combinations (see Table 4) address cognitive ability. These scores provide additional hypotheses about William's learning style and factors underlying his score on the WISC-III. Scale, factor, and subtest scores show strengths and weaknesses when compared to others of William's age or William's own pattern of development.

TABLE 2   WISC-III Composite Scales

Composite Scales	IQ Scale Score	Percentile Rank	Confidence Interval	Classification
Verbal IQ (VI)	108	70	102–114	Average
Performance IQ (PDQ)	103	58	96–110	Average
Full-scale IQ (FSIQ)	106	66	101–111	Average

TABLE 3   WISC-III Percentile Ranks

		0 25 50 75 99
Scales and Subtests		+----+----+----+----+----+----+----+----+
WISC-III Composite Scales		
Verbal IQ	70	***********************
Performance IQ	58	*********************
Full-scale IQ	66	**********************
Verbal subtests		
Information	50	*****************
Similarities	63	**********************
Arithmetic	25	*********
Vocabulary	75	**************************
Comprehension	98	**********************************
Digit Span	50	*****************
Performance subtests		
Picture Completion	91	*******************************
Coding	16	******
Picture Arrangement	91	*******************************
Block Design	37	*************
Object Assembly	25	*********
Symbol Search	25	*********
Mazes	75	**************************

TABLE 4   Factor-based Index Summary

Subtests	Index Score	Percentile Rank	True Score (68% Level)	Retest Score (68% Level)
Verbal Comprehension	113	81	108.8–115.7	107.1–117.3
Perceptual Organization	109	73	103.8–112.4	101.6–114.6
Freedom from Distractibility	96	39	92.1–100.7	89.8–102.9
Processing Speed	88	21	85.0– 93.2	82.9– 95.3

William obtained a WISC-III full-scale IQ score of 106, which placed him in the average range of intelligence. Because the full-scale IQ score is subject to a small degree of error, the true intelligence score is usually reported in a range. The probability is 90 out of 100 that William's true full-scale IQ falls between 101 and 111.

William's verbal IQ and performance IQ scores did not differ significantly. This is an indication that William's ability in his verbal and visual motor skills are similar.

The detailed analysis of William's performance on the WISC-III can be obtained by examining his performance on each subtest in the verbal and performance scales (see Table 1). Subtest scores can be compared to those of other individuals in the same age group and provide an indication of William's strengths and weaknesses compared to his age peers (see Table 3). In addition William's profile of subtest scores can be examined to determine his personal strengths and weaknesses.

In essence, there are two ways to clarify the meaning of high and low scores. First, the scores may differ from one's own average scores (ipsilateral analysis). Second, a score can be compared to those of one's same age. The score could be substantially higher or lower than age peers. If significant, this is a personal strength or weakness. Note that a score might not be a personal strength or weakness but differ from age peers, or could be a personal strength or weakness without differing from those in the age group.

William's score on the Arithmetic subtest (Table 1) shows a weakness in mental computation and concentration on orally presented mathematical problems. As noted in a prior section William's reading ability interfered with his correctly solving two math problems. The arithmetic questions on the subtest range from simple operations to complex word problems, with the computation performed mentally and the answer spoken. William's ability on this subtest was not significantly poorer than that of his age peers, but it was a personal weakness.

William's Comprehension subtest score (see Table 1) shows better knowledge of social standards of behavior, practical judgment, and commonsense reasoning skill. Answering the comprehension questions required applied knowledge to common situations, a developed sense of morality, and exposure to a wide range of experiences in people. On this subtest William's performance was significantly better than that of his age peers and was also a personal strength.

William's performance on the Picture Completion subtest (see Table 1) suggests a strength in his differentiation of essential from nonessential details or good visual alertness in judgment. The goal on this subtest was to find the missing part in a picture. Concentration, persistence, and visual skill are needed to succeed on this task. On this subtest, William's performance was significantly better than that of his age peers (see Table 3) and also a personal strength.

On the Coding subtest the derived score pointed to William's poor speed of eye-hand coordination, poor visual short-term memory, or lower motivation to do this rote learning task. This subtest required filling in designs on paper within a specific time limit. William's performance on this subtest was significantly poorer than that of his age peers and was also a personal weakness (Table 1, Table 3).

The high Picture Arrangement subtest score suggests good planning ability and understanding of the sequence and pattern of social situations. The Picture Arrangement subtest required that William put pictures which tell a story in a correct order. Knowledge of behavior, understanding temporal sequences, and the ability to comprehend a situation are conducive to success on this subtest. On this subtest William's performance was significantly better than that of his age peers and was also a personal strength.

The factor analysis of William's protocol indicated that the Arithmetic and Digit Span subtests indicate a consistently lower pattern of scores on tests that require freedom from distraction. This finding suggested that the obtained WISC-III may an underestimate of William's ability, due to behavioral interference and poor attention.

In relation to the individual skills that are polled on the specific subtests William's performance indicated that on tasks that entail people or concrete things he was superior as opposed to his ability on subtests which involved abstract symbols or designs. It is theorized that William's ability to manipulate abstract stimuli is important in learning mathematics, developing reading skills, and acquiring new concepts.

William's accomplishment on problems of visual organization was superior to that of problems of perceptual-motor coordination. Thus, William's performance on nonverbal tasks may be influenced by a relative weakness in fine motor skill rather than visual perceptual difficulties.

William did better on problems that require greater verbal expression or spontaneous and varied answers than on those that required limited expressive ability.

ANALYSIS OF STROOP TEST

The Stroop Color and Word Test is used to diagnose lateralized and frontal cerebral dysfunction, as well as some learning and reading disorders. William's average word, and color scores, combined with a low color word score, was similar to the pattern which is produced by individuals who may suffer from an isolated prefrontal injury. Research on individuals who perform similar to William indicated that this function may be bilateral or the left hemisphere. This pattern of scores is also sensitive to early forms of atrophy or similar conditions secondary to chronic drug abuse. Given the findings of this examiner (i.e., absence of chronic drug abuse, no evidence of atrophy), the clinical evidence supports the presence of a significant learning and reading disorder.

ANALYSIS OF BENTON VISUAL RETENTION TEST

The Benton Visual Retention Test is used to assess visual constructive ability, visual memory, and visual perception. William's expected number correct and obtained number correct fell within the range that indicated his performance was average.

ANALYSIS OF SYMBOL DIGIT MODALITIES TEST

The Symbol Digit Modalities Test is similar to that of the Wechsler coding or digit symbol subtest. The Symbol Digit Modalities Test requires fine motor dexterity and speed, as well as rote learning and memorization of visual associations. William's performance on this test fell within the average range for his age.

ANALYSIS OF WIDE RANGE ACHIEVEMENT TEST—REVISED

The Wide Range Achievement Text—Revised (WRAT-R) is a brief individually administered achievement test which contains three subsections. The first subsection is reading, the second is spelling, and third is arithmetic. The Reading subtest assessed William's ability to recognize the name letters and pronounce words. The Spelling subtest measured William's ability to copy marks and write single words from dictation. The Arithmetic subtest measured William's skills at recognizing numbers and performing mathematical computations.

It is widely recognized that an individual administered achievement test can produce results that are different from a group achievement test (e.g., scholastic achievement test). Various factors can cause a disparity such as the fact that the individual maintained consistent attention and effort in a structured testing setting or the fact that each test measured distinct skills.

Table 5 below is William's performance on the WRAT-R. Interpretation of Table 5 is based on the standard deviation of 15. It is important for the reader of this report to recognize, and it is well documented in the WRAT-R manual, that grade-equivalent scores can be misleading. On this test, which can also be administered in a group setting, it is perhaps more important to note William's percentile ranking. That is, in spelling and arithmetic William's performance fell in less than the first percentile for individuals his age. His reading ability fell within the lower 2% of individuals his age (see Table 6).

TABLE 5 WRAT-R Subtest Scales

Subtest	Raw Score	Standard Score	Percentile Rank	Band of Error	Grade Equivalent
Spelling	8	55	<1	53–57	3
Reading	38	70	2	68–72	4E
Arithmetic	18	57	<1	55–59	4B

TABLE 6   WRAT-R Percentile Ranks

Subtest		0 25 50 75 99
		+----+----+----+----+----+----+----+----+
Spelling	<1	*
Reading	2	*
Arithmetic	<1	*

ANALYSIS OF WOODCOCK-JOHNSON TEST OF ACHIEVEMENT

The Woodcock-Johnson Psychoeducational Battery—Revised is an individually administered battery of tests designed to measure an individual's academic achievement and knowledge. The Woodcock-Johnson consists of four test clusters (reading, mathematics, written language, knowledge). Each test cluster contains several subtests (see Table 7). The reading and mathematics test clusters contain subtests which measure basic reading and mathematics skills, respectively. The written language test cluster consists of subtests which assess spelling, punctuation, capitalization, and word use. The knowledge test cluster consists of subtests which measure knowledge across major areas of the school curriculum, such as science and social studies.

TABLE 7   Woodcock-Johnson–R Subtest and Composite Scores

Cluster/Subtest	Raw Score	Standard Score	Percentile Rank	Band of Error	Grade Equivalent
Reading tests					
Letter/Word					
Identification	22	89	23	84–94	7.1
Passage Comprehension	31	102	55	97–107	11.0
Word Attack	19	91	27	87–95	4.9
Reading Vocabulary	40	97	42	93–101	9.8
Broad Reading	77	94	37	90–98	8.6
Mathematics tests					
Calculations	34	98	45	93–103	9.4
Applied Problems	43	100	50	95–105	10.8
Quantitative Concepts	36	92	30	85–99	7.6
Broad Mathematics	77	99	47	95–103	10.2
Written language tests					
Dictation	33	72	3	67–77	4.3
Knowledge tests					
Science	30	97	42	91–103	9.2
Social Studies	30	96	39	91–101	9.1
Humanities	32	93	32	85–98	8.2
Broad Knowledge	62	95	37	92–98	9.5

The Woodcock-Johnson allows for several scores to be obtained. Standard scores for tests provide general measures of achievement areas. The subtest scores provide measures of specific achievement areas.

William's performance on each of the subtests with cluster scores is presented in Table 8.

TABLE 8   Woodcock-Johnson–R Percentile Ranks

Cluster/Subtest		0 25 50 75 99 +----+----+----+----+----+----+----+----+
Reading tests	23	*******
Letter/Word Identification		
Passage Comprehension	55	********************
Word Attack	27	*********
Reading Vocabulary	42	***************
Broad Reading	34	*************
Mathematics tests		
Calculation	45	****************
Applied Problems	50	******************
Quantitative Concepts	30	**********
Broad Mathematics	47	*****************
Written language tests		
Dictation	3	**
Knowledge tests	42	***************
Science		
Social Studies	39	**************
Humanities	32	***********
Broad Knowledge	37	**************

Below are listed William's Woodcock-Johnson–R cluster and subtests analyses for both strengths and weaknesses.

CLUSTER STRENGTHS:
   No strengths were revealed

CLUSTER WEAKNESSES:
   Broad Reading
   Broad Mathematics
   Broad Written Language
   Broad Knowledge

SUBTEST STRENGTHS:
   No strengths were revealed

SUBTEST WEAKNESSES:
   Letter/Word Identification
   Word Attack
   Reading Vocabulary
   Calculation
   Applied Problems
   Quantitative Concepts
   Dictation
   Writing Samples
   Proofing
   Writing Fluency

Punctuation and Capitalization
Spelling
Usage
Science
Social Studies
Humanities

ANALYSIS OF CONNERS PARENT RATING SCALE

During this evaluation both of William's parents were offered an opportunity to complete the Conners Parent Rating Scale. They were instructed to complete the inventory without consulting the other individual. The results from the Conners Parent Rating Scale are presented in Table 9. Table 9 is a T-score representation of each parent's perception of William's behavior while at home. T-scores over 70 are considered significant. The analysis of Table 9 indicates an overlap between the hyperactivity index which was judged as significant by the mother, and the anxiety index which was judged as significant by the biological father. In addition, the biological father also indicated that learning problems were significant. The biological father's responses indicated that the hyperactivity index was elevated close to the point of being statistically significant.

TABLE 9   Conners Parent Rating Scale: T-Score

Index	Mother	Father
Conduct problem	48	48
Learning problem	66	80
Psychosomatic	55	55
Impulsive-hyperactive	61	46
Anxiety	57	74
Hyperactivity	72	64

SUMMARY

William was referred for a psychoeducational evaluation by his attending physician. He requested that the evaluation assess the presence of a learning disability, attention deficit disorder with or without hyperactivity. In addition, he was concerned in respect to William's neurological functioning.

Given that examinations of this type are lengthy endeavors, it was also suggested that the report be written in a fashion that would be of benefit to the Smiths were William to apply for college. This report has been written so that it will not only address the requirements of the attending physician, but the requirements for the consideration of special testing for college entrance exams and also the requirements for consideration of enrollment in universities and colleges which have a specialized track for learning disabled college students.

The analysis of the Wechsler scale indicated that William's intellectual potential falls within the average range. The in-depth analysis of the protocol did raise the issue that William's overall cognitive ability may be somewhat lower than presented in this examination due to his difficulties with attending and concentration. Nevertheless, this evaluation found William's intellectual functioning to fall within the average range and exceed that of 66% of the individuals in the standardized group, which was roughly representative of the United States population.

An in-depth analysis of the WISC-III yielded numerous insights into William's area of weakness, as well as several strengths. William demonstrated a weakness in mental computation and concentration. The clinical observation was that on several occasions William's score in the mathematical subsection was lowered because he did not read and understand the mathematical problem correctly before he engaged in the mathematical computations. William may have difficulty with manipulating abstract stimuli. William's performance on nonverbal tasks may be influenced by a relative weakness in fine motor skill rather than visual-perceptual difficulties.

A finding of strength in William's protocol was that of his ability to differentiate essential from nonessential details and his common sense and judgment. William shows a better knowledge of social standards of behavior, practical judgment and common sense reasoning skills.

The analysis of the neurological tests administered during this examination indicated (Stroop Color and Word Test) that William is most likely suffering from a significant difficulty in reading.

The analysis of the achievement test indicated that William's performance across a wide range of academic domains was below that which would be expected. Specifically, William experienced significant difficulty across all three achievement domains on the WRAT-R. On the Woodcock-Johnson William experienced significant difficulty in Letter/Word Identification, Word Attack, and Broad Reading. He also experienced significant difficulty in mathematical tests, specifically quantitative concepts. An area of significant weakness was that of Dictation.

The analysis of the grade equivalence on the Woodcock-Johnson–R indicated significant discrepancies in reading (Word Attack) and written language (Dictation).

The finding of the discrepancy test based on a Bond-Tanker formula indicated that William's performance fell below expected level in the domains listed above.

The anaysis of the Conners Parent Rating Scale confirmed the findings of this examination. Specifically, William is a young man experiencing significant hyperactivity behavior and at times anxiety. There were indications, at least through the father's perception, that William is experiencing significant learning problems.

EDUCATIONAL RECOMMENDATIONS

Based on his level of intelligence William should be in the average range in most academic areas. This assumption is based on the theory that there are no learning or behavioral problems contributing to William's difficulty in school.

William produced lower scores on subtests that require freedom from distractibility and this suggests that classroom management techniques may be needed to control behaviors that interfere with William's school performance. Efforts should be made to establish consistent explicit rules and consequences so that William can learn good work habits, maintain his attention, and complete assignments. Failure to do so may lead to poor academic performance for William. The poor academic performance for William may fulfill a significant discrepancy between level of expected achievement and actual achievement.

Behavioral observations presented during this examination confirm that William needs to have limits set.

A significant finding in this examination was that there was a substantial discrepancy between William's expected ability in terms of his overall intelligence score and his mathematical achievement. This indicates a need for academic remediation in the domain of mathematics. There are a wide variety of specific remediation techniques that could be used to assist William in his difficulty with mathematics. For example, William should be encouraged to read the math problems out loud. William should be encouraged to paraphrase the problem out loud. He should utilize visualization techniques. He should learn to state the problem and underline the most information in the problem and then complete the problem. William should learn to do an estimate of the answer he will get, and utilize a calculator. William should be encouraged to use techniques such as self-check.

Compared to William's expected ability in terms of his overall intellectual test score, he should be reading at a much higher level. This examination found a significant discrepancy between William's ability to read and his actual reading level. This indicates a reading deficit and a need for remedial instructions. William may qualify for receiving his books on tape. Given that William's passage comprehension is one of his strengths, this would allow him to learn the material. In addition, William may benefit from receiving a study guide or a clause passage to complete as he listens to the text. He should use the pause button or turn off the tape recorder whenever he needs to write information. William may benefit from tape recording all lectures in classes. Before William reads a textbook he should color code the book with a yellow high-lighter to indicate those sections that are most important for him to read. Based on William's present level of reading achievement, he would benefit from individual or small group instruction from a qualified tutor, reading specialist, or learning disabilities specialist.

There was a significant discrepancy between William's expected ability to perform on spelling and his actual level of spelling performance. His spelling achievement was well below expected ability when compared to his intelligence test scores. Remediation of this academic deficit is in order. For example, William may benefit from receiving a poor speller's dictionary. This is a book with words listed according to many of their possible misspellings, with a correct spelling after each listing. William may benefit from using a pocket-sized computerized spell checker. William would benefit from learning to use a computer system which has a word-processing program that would assist in checking both his spelling and grammar. William may benefit from learning keyboarding so that he could type all of his reports. However, William may also benefit from using a dictation system and hiring a typist.

Clearly, the issue of attention deficit disorder needs to be addressed. William is a likely candidate for a trial of medication to address the attending deficit. It is suggested that the parents use the Conners Behavior Rating Scale in conjunction with the medication received from his physician. The teachers in William's school should be encouraged to rate this behavior prior to the administration of the medication and following the administration of the medication.

SAMPLE ASSESSMENT 2

NAME:	Daniel Brown
SEX:	Male
DATE OF BIRTH:	June 3, 1963
GRADE:	17
CHRONOLOGICAL AGE:	31 years

ASSESSMENT TECHNIQUES USED

Wechsler Intelligence Scale for Adults—Revised
Woodcock-Johnson Tests of Achievement—Revised
Bender Gestalt Visual Motor Test
Examiner Interviews
Curriculum-Based Assessment

REASON FOR REFERRAL

To determine if any significant changes have occurred in Daniel's academic performance since his last evaluation, 3/29/82.

BACKGROUND INFORMATION

Daniel is currently 31 years old and is a graduate student in the psychology rehabilitation program at Utah State University. Daniel is married and has no children. He currently lives with his wife Judy. He has a brother Mark, age 28, who is learning disabled.

Daniel's speech was delayed. Before one year of age he had his tongue surgically clipped to separate it from the floor of his mouth. Subsequently, he had speech problems in preschool through first grade and received remedial services at a speech and hearing clinic. Daniel currently shows no evidence in speech difficulties. All other developmental milestones were reached at an appropriate age. Daniel suffers from chronic allergies. He presently takes Rynatan to help relieve the symptoms. In the past, Daniel had problems with periodic stomach ulcers. Currently, he shows no evidence of having ulcers. Daniel wears contact lenses. He has normal hearing and is right-handed.

In Daniel's leisure time, he enjoys walking in the woods, fishing, karate, and has in the past participated in the Renaissance fairs as a storyteller. Daniel enjoys folklore and knows many folktales by memory. He enjoys research and working with computers. Daniel also is active in a hospice program and currently does volunteer work in the program.

EDUCATIONAL HISTORY

Daniel received tutoring in school from the fourth grade on. This was not a placement in special education classes as an LD student. Daniel was first evaluated and labeled LD in the fifth grade. In the sixth grade, he attended a "special school," providing him with remediation services. Daniel experienced his greatest difficulties in grammar and spelling. He also acknowledges difficulties with math and reading. Specifically, Daniel would make both letter and number reversals. In addition, he has experienced difficulties with reading comprehension. In general, Daniel has a hard time sustaining attention to a task. He has a history of being highly distractible.

Throughout the first and secondary grades, Daniel typically was a poor student, although he failed no grades. He often felt discouraged and different from the other children. Throughout school his parents have typically been supportive and have tried to provide him with the special help he needed.

Daniel decided to go on to college. He found it very difficult and discouraging finding a college that was willing to work with and meet his special needs. He attended the University of Utah prior to attending Utah State. He typically experienced failure and states that at one point he was told he had no business attending the university, that he was taking up another student's place. When Daniel came to Utah State University, he was evaluated and diagnosed as learning disabled. He then received help from the learning disability program.

Daniel received tutoring services in math and help with his grammar. He used a tape recorder to record lectures. Daniel would occasionally experience difficulties taking multiple choice tests; subsequently, he developed a strategy he now applies when taking multiple choice tests. When doing written work, Daniel only prints. He experienced such difficulties learning cursive that he stopped using it long ago and has since forgotten the letters. Daniel has also found books on tape to be very helpful with his studies.

Daniel typically did well once he began to participate in the learning disability program. Although he has dropped out of school on several occasions, he has always returned. Daniel currently is a graduate student in the psychology department at Utah State. He has an assistantship doing research-related work. He will be starting an internship in December 1990. Daniel's persistence, positive attitude, and intellectual abilities have enabled him to adjust well, learning to effectively compensate and deal with his learning difficulties.

GENERAL BEHAVIORAL OBSERVATIONS

Throughout testing, Daniel was highly motivated and cooperative. He maintained optimal eye contact. Daniel was very open, spontaneously conversing with the examiner throughout testing. Daniel was generally eager in his approach to tasks, although on occasion he displayed some anxiety when he found a task to be difficult. Daniel exhibited good attention to all tasks. His persistence varied across subtests.

Daniel is very verbal and appeared confident when working with the verbal subtests such as Vocabulary, Information, and Similarities. He exhibited above average to superior verbal reasoning and evaluation skills. Daniel tended to respond more impulsively on the math subtest, when he had to do calculations in his head. Occasionally, Daniel exhibited retrieval problems. When this occurred, he compensated by using a simpler word. Generally, he verbally expressed himself well and with ease.

On the performance scale, Daniel worked with relative ease, speed, and accuracy. He exhibited above average visual perception and organizational skills, obtaining near perfect scores on the Picture Arrangement and Object Assembly subtests. On Block Design, Daniel worked methodically but exhibited some anxiety when he could not quickly replicate the design. Daniel worked carefully and attended well to the coding subtest.

TEST RESULTS

Intelligence: WAIS-R

Verbal Scale	Scaled Score	Performance Scale	Scaled Score
Information	10	Picture Completion	11
Digit Span	10	Picture Arrangement	13
Vocabulary	13	Block Design	12
Arithmetic	7	Object Assembly	14
Comprehension	15	Digit Symbol	10
Similarities	13		
$\overline{X}$.V.S. = 11.3		$\overline{X}$.P.S. = 12	

Verbal IQ = 105 (average)
Performance IQ = 114 (high average)
Full-scale IQ = 109 (average)

The results of Daniel's cognitive evaluation indicate a verbal IQ of 105, a performance IQ of 114, and a full-scale IQ of 109± 4 at the 95% confidence level. His full-scale IQ ranks him at the 73rd percentile rank which means that he performed better than 73 out of 100 people his age who took the test. Currently, he is functioning in the average range. The chances that the range of scores from 105 to 113 includes his true IQ are approximately 95 out of 100.

A 4-point discrepancy exists between Daniel's verbal and performance IQ's. Such a discrepancy is not significant and indicates that Daniel's verbal abilities and performance abilities are fairly equally developed.

A moderate amount of variability was observed in Daniel's ability on the verbal subtest. He had a mean verbal score of 11.3 as compared to a normative mean of 10. Daniel's mean verbal performance is within the average range. All of Daniel's verbal subtest scaled scores were within the superior to average range except for one (Arithmetic), where performance was in the significantly below average range.

Daniel's verbal subtest profile indicates a number of strengths and weaknesses. His relative verbal strengths were on the Vocabulary, Comprehension, and Similarities subtests (his standard score of 15 on the Comprehension subtest places him in the superior range, respectively being his greatest strength). This indicates that Daniel has highly developed skills of practical judgment and common sense as well as having superior awareness of social norms. On the Similarities subtest Daniel was presented pairs of words; he then had to explain the similarities between the two words in each pair. On the subtest he demonstrated above average abstract and concrete verbal reasoning skills. He exhibited the ability to generalize and discriminate between objects and ideas. The Vocabulary subtest is the best measure of verbal intelligence; however, it does reflect cultural background. Here Daniel's results indicate that his verbal expressive abilities are in the high average range. His general thought processes reflect a richness of ideas. Daniel performed within the average range on the Digit Span and Information subtests. The Digit Span subtest is a measure of Daniel's attention span, organizational strategies, short-term memory, and ability to concentrate. The Information subtest is a measure of Daniel's range of knowledge, long-term memory, and verbal comprehension skills.

Daniel's only weakness on the verbal scale (SS-7) was on the Arithmetic subtest. He demonstrated low average mathematical reasoning and concentration abilities. Daniel often answered in an impulsive manner, appearing to give little thought to the more difficult test questions. His answer to many items was a good estimation, indicating he knew the general computative process needed to work through a problem. His impulsive approach with more difficult items may reflect poor concentration, distractibility, and anxiety.

On the performance scale, Daniel worked with speed and accuracy. When he experienced difficulties he sometimes appeared rather anxious. Daniel's results indicate some variability across subtests. His mean performance score was 12. Daniel exhibited a superior ability to deal with part-whole relationships, persistence, and the ability to anticipate an outcome, as he had a near perfect score on the Object Assembly subtest. This subtest required Daniel to fit together jigsaw pieces to form a common object. On the Picture Arrangement subtest Daniel was required to place a series of individual pictures into a logical sequence. Here he demonstrated a high average ability to comprehend and sequence a number of social interactions as well as the ability to pick out and perceive details. Daniel's performance on the Picture Completion, Block Design, and Digit Symbol subtests were all within the average range. Block Design and Picture Completion both measure perceptual organization, although Block Design does so on a more abstract level. Picture Completion is also a measure of one's attention to detail in pictures of common objects. Digit Symbol is a measure of visual-motor coordination and speed.

Daniel's overall performance indicates that his verbal and performance skills are fairly equally developed. Daniel's expressive language is very good, as his high average to superior performance on the Vocabulary, Comprehension, and Similarities subtests indicates. He has very good abstract verbal reasoning, while his mathematical reasoning ability is in the low average range. Daniel performed significantly lower on the Arithmetic subtest when compared to all other verbal subtests. His impulsive approach to more difficult items may be reflective of anxiety, which further impedes his ability to concentrate. Daniel's results indicate no weaknesses on the performance subtests. He showed strengths in the areas of perceptual organization and attention to detail. Daniel's short-term memory skills are average, and his long-term memory skills are adequately developed.

ACHIEVEMENT

Woodcock-Johnson—Revised

Subtest	Standard Score	Percentile Rank
Letter/Word Identification	109	72
Passage Comprehension	102	54
Calculation	109	74
Applied Problems	93	32
Dictation	78	7
Writing Samples	107	68

Cluster Scores

Cluster	Standard Score	Percentile Rank	Discrepancy
Broad Reading	106	65	3
Broad Mathematics	99	48	10
Broad Written Language	86	18	23
(Skills)	92	30	17

Daniel's achievement performance as indicated by his standard scores and percentile rank reveals varied strengths and weaknesses. In general, his reading achievement is above average. Daniel did as well or better than 65% of other students his age. Daniel shows a strength in the area of letter/word identification, whereas his comprehension score is average. In mathematics, Daniel performed as well or better than 48% of other students his age. Calculation is a relative strength for Daniel, whereas mathematical application is a weakness. Daniel evidences particular difficulties with grammatical writing skills (Dictation). Daniel showed difficulties spelling words with double consonants and mixing up the vowels *a* and *e*. He exhibited difficulties with writing the plural form of words such as *oxen* and *crises*. Daniel also omits notation marks such as hyphens and commas. Although Daniel makes many grammatical errors, his writing content is good. Daniel is able to write complete thoughts (beyond simple sentences) and uses descriptive words effectively.

CURRICULUM-BASED ASSESSMENT

WRITTEN EXPRESSION

Daniel was asked by the examiner to write a short story. His story revealed an array of grammatical errors. Specifically, he made the following errors (typical examples are included):

1. Omits word ending *ed*—pleaed for pleaded
2. Adds word ending *ed* inappropriately—agreeed for agreed
3. Interchanges short vowels *a* for *i*—anamals for animals
4. Omits vowel *e* from word ending—surley for surely
5. Interchanges vowels *ei* to *ie*—thier for their
6. Omits last letter of words—the for then and brid for bribe
7. Writes words out of sequence—frist for first
8. Omits commas when needed

In addition, Daniel will sometimes forget to write the last word of a sentence. Aside from the grammatical errors, Daniel's story content is very good. Daniel generally writes with good thought continuity. His sentence structure is adequate. Daniel also uses descriptive words and quotes well.

READING

Daniel was asked to read a passage from one of his textbooks, first aloud and then silently. The examiner timed Daniel while he read. It took Daniel 3 minutes and 17 seconds to read the passage aloud, while it took him 1 minute and 30 seconds to read the same passage silently. While Daniel read aloud, the examiner followed along and made note of his errors. The most common error he made was to omit whole words, particularly connectors such as *and, to,* and *the.* He would occasionally omit other words, subsequently affecting the meaning of the sentence. Daniel would also drop word endings or add a word prefix where it did not belong. In addition, occasionally he would add an extra word or words to a sentence. Daniel read fairly slowly. When he did start to pick up speed, he would make more mistakes, often omitting words.

The examiner tested Daniel to see if he comprehended what he had read. The questions reflected both rote memory and inferential abilities. Daniel appeared to have more difficulties answering inferential-type questions.

VISUAL MOTOR

BENDER GESTALT VISUAL MOTOR TEST

The Bender was used to measure perceptual-motor functioning. Daniel's overall rate of performance was average as it took him 5 minutes and 32 seconds to draw all nine designs. Daniel worked from a right-to-left sequence rather than from a left-to-right sequence. He was right-handed on all tasks. Daniel made no errors, which is consistent with the error index that one his age should obtain on the Bender. All nine designs were drawn very neatly. According to Koppitz's scoring system, Daniel's visual-motor and perceptual integration skills are adequately developed and are within the average range.

SUMMARY

The results of the evaluation indicate that Daniel is functioning globally in the average to high average range. Daniel's verbal abilities are in the average range, while his nonverbal abilities are in the high average range. Reading and math achievement are both within the average range although Daniel shows a weakness in math application and a strength in math calculation. Daniel's most significant difficulties are in written language, where Daniel functions well below average as demonstrated by his curriculum-based assessment, Daniel also exhibits difficulties with reading. He appears to comprehend some of what he reads, but he does not exhibit a thorough understanding of all that he reads. While reading, the word omissions and grammatical errors he makes contribute to a lack of fluent understanding of what he is reading.

Although Daniel continues to exhibit characteristics common to learning disabled students, he has in the past, and continues to, compensate effectively with his learning deficits. Daniel's grades and achievement indicate just how well he has been able to develop alternate learning strategies. Daniel's high motivation, persistence, and generally positive attitude suggest that he will continue to develop his academic skills and reach his educational goals.

SAMPLE ASSESSMENT 3

NAME:	John Franklin
DOB:	January 8, 1976
DATES OF EVALUATION:	December 29, 1994
CA:	18 years 11 months
HIGHEST GRADE COMPLETED:	Twelve
CURRENT OCCUPATION:	Clerk

REASON FOR EVALUATION

John has a history of social isolation and difficulty with school achievement. Concerns have been raised about John's ability to set goals for his future. Consultation was requested in an effort to better understand and define relevant issues as well as assist with treatment recommendations.

BACKGROUND INFORMATION

John and his parents were seen, to review John's social and developmental history. John is a nonidentical twin. His 18-year-old sister Rachel may have experienced attention deficit but has functioned quite well in life. John also has a four-year-old sister Ariel. Ms. Franklin completed a Bachelor of Science in elementary education and has been employed in the past as a teacher. She recalled that perhaps she had a learning problem as a child but compensated quite well. She has struggled with mild depression since age seventeen and postpartum depression during the past two and a half years. Ms. Franklin is adopted and has limited information about her biological family. Mr. Franklin completed a Bachelor of Science in chemical engineering and is employed as a supervisor of planning. He noted that his mother has a history of depression.

John was the six-pound product of an uncomplicated pregnancy. However, at birth John appeared four to five weeks premature, raising the possibility that he and his sister were conceived a numbers of weeks apart.

As a newborn John did not suck well and lost quite a bit of weight. He presented as a normal infant otherwise. As a toddler he was often content to sit and play quietly. He didn't experience problems with attention during that period of time. He didn't adapt well to new situations. He was slow to make transitions. He has always been rather demonstrative with his emotions. His moods as a toddler were generally good.

John received pressure equalization tubes at three or four years of age. He fell out of a high chair at six to nine months of age and in the bathroom at six to seven years of age without complications. He has had a number of allergies.

John settles down to sleep and is able to sleep through the night without disruption. He was a bedwetter consistently up through seven years of age. He sleeps deeply. His appetite is average. He is not presently taking any medications on an ongoing basis. A brief trial of Paxil was attempted in 1990 and again in 1994.

Early developmental milestones were reached somewhat late. John experienced diurnal and nocturnal enuresis. He did not ride a bicycle without training wheels until 12 years of age. John's large and fine motor skills generally appear poor. His handwriting is poor. His peripheral vision is limited, and this may, in part, be responsible for his multiple minor accidents.

John may not always understand instructions and directions as well as others. He frequently misinterprets. Intellectually he appears above average. His reading and spelling skills have excelled. His math skills have always lagged behind. Over a period of time he received monitoring and support from the Resource program. School history is noted by struggles with independent work, difficulty with math concepts, poor organization, difficulty prioritizing work, and test taking skills. In contrast, his school experiences in relation to behavior were generally good.

John's school history is noted by receiving services for speech therapy as well as academic support. He struggled to a much greater extent when he entered junior high school. In ninth grade he participated half-time each day in the special education program. He continued to require support in high school, tested poorly, and struggled somewhat socially.

John is kind and tenderhearted. He seeks out peers for friendship but is not as often sought out. He has always befriended younger children, primarily females. He doesn't read or interpret body language well.

John is easily distracted and doesn't follow through with instructions. He shifts from one uncompleted activity to another and may often talk excessively. He loses things that are necessary for tasks or activities at home. His judgment is poor. He frustrates easily. John has experienced an excessive number of accidents and doesn't seem to learn well from his experiences. He works well for short-term rewards but not well for long-term rewards. Much of his problems occur nonpurposely.

John may escape to Nintendo or reading fantasy texts. He had a very positive experience this summer working in Jackson Hole, Wyoming, and participating in a special church ranching program. John also enjoys computer activities. The Franklins noted they have a very positive relationship with John, describing him as sensitive, tender, and kindhearted.

The Franklins expressed concern as to how to best interact wth John. In the past a school psychologist concluded that John felt small and threatened by others and withdrew for this reason.

John and his parents appeared motivated and interested to both understand and effectively formulate a plan for John's future.

ASSESSMENT PROCEDURES

Child Behavior Checklist
Revised Conners Parent Questionnaire
Home Situations Questionnaire
Social Skills Assessment
Brown Attention Activation Disorder Scale
Review of Academic File
Clinical Interview
Millon Adolescent Personality Inventory
Conners Continuous Performance Test

ADAPTIVE FUNCTIONING

On the basis of the Franklins' responses to the Child Behavior Checklist, John presents at above the 98th percentile in comparison to adolescents of his chronological age for the scales of social and attention problems (50th percentile is average; high score indicates problem). John acts immaturely, has difficulty concentrating, and daydreams. He may be teased and disliked by others. The internalizing scales, though slightly elevated, were still within the normal range. The anxious/depressed scale was elevated at the 95th percentile due to John's loneliness, feelings of worthlessness, and at times, sad or worrisome behavior.

On the basis of the Franklins' responses to the Conners questionnaire, John, in comparison to boys of his chronological age within the home setting, presents at the 98th percentile on the hyperkinesis index (50th percentile is average; high score indicates problem). Severe problems are noted with distractibility, inattention, being easily frustrated in his efforts, and failing to finish things. Moderate problems are noted with being more emotionally sensitive. No problems are noted with excitable, impulsive, or hyperactive behavior.

On the basis of the Franklins' responses to the Home Situations Questionnaire, John demonstrates severe problems being socially isolated, with routine care such as washing and bathing, daydreaming, not self-monitoring during chores, and struggling to work independently. Moderate problems are noted daydreaming in public places. Mild problems are observed in other situations. For the most part all of these problems are nondisruptive.

Socially, John appears isolated. He appears to have fewer friends than others. He can strike back with angry or argumentative behavior. He can respond and initiate conversation, will engage in long conversation and will share laughter with friends. John will also contribute to a family discussion. John in the past, has been manipulated by peers. He has two good friends with whom he has a close relationship.

The Franklins' responses to the Brown questionnaire yielded a score of 65, above the cutoff of 50 indicative of adult inattentive problems.

REVIEW OF PREVIOUS EVALUATION

An educational consultation evaluation was completed in April 1990. On this assessment John obtained a verbal IQ of 114, performance IQ of 98, and full-scale IQ of 107. John's verbal skills including information, reasoning, and vocabulary were well above average. His perceptually related, nonverbal skills were average to below. On the Woodcock-Johnson Psycho-Educational Battery his verbal abilities score was at the 99th percentile while his visual perceptual scores were at or below the 20th percentile. John was at the 99th percentile for reading but only the 74th percentile for mathematics. John performed a year lower than his chronological age on the Developmental Test of Visual-Motor Integration and poorly on a task requiring oral directions. It was concluded that John demonstrated a learning disability related to organization and visual-motor skills. In addition to special placement, accommodations were recommended involving note taking, studying, organization, and making an effort to capitalize on John's exceptional verbal abilities.

In May of 1993 John's specialist teacher noted that efforts had been made to improve John's organizational and responsibility skills. With supervision John was noted as following through quite well. John was noted as having trouble budgeting his time and continuing to struggle with organization.

Copies of John's Stanford Achievement Tests were reviewed beginning in seventh grade. Only selective comparison scores are presented (in percentiles):

	Grade			
Test	7th	9th	10th	11th
Total reading	75th	73rd	72nd	77th
Total mathematics	32nd	42nd	35th	21st
Basic battery	63rd	60th	53rd	61st

John completed the ACT in June 1993. He performed at the following percentiles for college-bound students:

Test	Percentile
English	60th
Mathematics	10th
Reading	73rd
Science Reasoning	53rd
Composite	53rd

BEHAVIORAL OBSERVATION

John, a young adult of average size and appearance, was neatly dressed and presented with adequate care during both assessment sessions. Eye contact was appropriate. John maintained and initiated conversation.

John was alert and attentive, manifesting adequate concentration. He was cooperative and attempted all tasks requested.

No muscular tension nor habitual mannerisms were noted. John presented with a normal activity level. He was not fidgety. He was also not distracted. John was responsive to the examiner. He smiled appropriately. His thoughts appeared logical, focused, and relevant. Overall, it was not significantly difficult to establish a working relationship with this pleasant individual.

ASSESSMENT RESULTS AND INTERPRETATION

Due to historical reports of inattentiveness, the Conners Continuous Performance Task was administered. John's overall response pattern did not appear to strongly suggest difficulty with attention. However, John made a large number of commission errors indicating some difficulty inhibiting responses and a large number of omission errors indicating poor attention to the task. Overall, this pattern appeared to reflect poor perceptual sensitivity consistent with his history of reported perceptual weaknesses. John appeared to experience difficulty quickly and efficiently, discriminating the perceptual features of the letters presented and responding accordingly.

John's responses to the Brown questionnaire yielded a score of 54, just above the cutoff indicative of adult complaints for inattentive problems.

During the clinical interview John was quite open and responsive to the examiner. When asked what he would like to change about himself he responded, "Be more coordinated." John described his favorite actvities as reading and playing strategy games. He felt he wasn't as happy as others because "I don't have as many friends and not much of a social life." John reported having a best friend. He noted he has attempted to date but "I've not had much luck with girls [laughs]."

John noted that he was enjoying his job but wished he could find a job that was more fulfilling. He felt he was as smart as others but recalled struggling in school, especially with mathematics. John noted that this past semester in college was difficult. He found it hard to follow through with tasks and often daydreamed. John was uncertain if he was depressed. He reported occasionally feeling sad but not finding difficulty locating enjoyable activities. He reported feeling somewhat guilty about his present life situation.

John felt that he was confident in most areas of his life. Nonetheless, he denied he was satisfied with his life, noting he wished he had a girlfriend and could "do better in just about everything." John described acting in several plays and being an extra in a movie as something he was quite proud of doing. He described the most difficult part of growing up as associating with people when his family lived in Illinois. John described recalling being made fun of, ignored, and shunned. He noted he was mad but couldn't do anything about it.

John's goals for the future include "getting a decent job, maybe getting married, and hopefully going on through college."

John noted that this past year his relationship with his parents has been somewhat strained because he has wanted more freedom. Overall, he felt his parents treated him fairly at home. He described difficulty falling asleep primarily due to his sister waking frequently during the night. John reported a history of headaches the past two to three weeks but no other significant somatic complaints.

On the basis of his history and presentation John appears to be rather self-critical and self-deprecating. What is most characteristic about his overall personality style is his apprehensiveness and fearfulness, lack of a clear sense of identity, marked deprecation of self-worth, a general degree of social oversensitivity and awkwardness, shyness and hesitation with peers, and discomfort concerning family relations. John clearly desires closeness and affection but may self-protectively deny or restrain himself. He is likely often sad, feeling friendless and experiencing recurrent anxieties about school and work. It is likely that he feels a pervasive disharmony of mood much of the time. Rarely does John act out or become overly resentful. Rather he is overconcerned with social rebuff, a worry that is often intensified by his tendency to anticipate and at times elicit rejection, particularly from peers.

Characteristic traits for John at this time include a general lack of initiative and competitiveness and a general avoidance of autonomous behavior. Despite John's strong need to depend on others he has often felt it best to deny these needs and maintain a safe measure of interpersonal distance. John will typically assume a passive role in which he willingly submits to the demands of others in order to fill his dependency needs.

On the Millon the lack of a clear self-image and his view of himself as weak, fragile, and ineffective is clearly evident. John appears to be frequently self-absorbed and lost in daydreams.

At times it is likely that he is distracted by inner thoughts that intrude upon his daily activities. To counteract the pain these ideas and preoccupations engender John may avoid emotional experiences that stir these disturbing feelings. His self-protective efforts only add to his lack of a socially rewarding lifestyle. As a consequence John appears to have begun to drift into an increasingly detached, socially anxious, and passive lifestyle.

On the Millon, in comparison to adolescents of his age, John reports feeling confused and uncertain about his life directions. He feels that others have a much clearer sense of who they are and their identity and goals. Moreover, John appears to be upset by his incapacity to achieve greater clarity in this regard.

John also reports wanting to belong socially and often being unwanted and isolated. Social interactions are experienced as painful.

On the positive side, John is gentle and compassionate toward others. He is freely accepting of them regardless of their frailties and vulnerabilities. He is willing to provide help and support where needed. He views his family as a support and resource.

DIAGNOSTIC IMPRESSION

John, an adolescent with past assessment data reflecting exceptional cognitive abilities, demonstrates a long-standing pattern of academic, social, and emotional issues consistent with a pattern of right-hemisphere dysfunction. His problems, at this time, appear chronic and of mild to moderate severity.

Problems with right-hemisphere skills often manifest themselves as difficulty with social interactions in a nondisruptive way, struggles to read and interpret social cues effectively, a passive pattern of inattentive disorganized behavior, a tendency toward emotional distressing rather than disruptive behavioral symptoms, visual perceptual weaknesses and relative struggles with mathematics. From the data provided as well as John's current presentation he appears to very clearly fit this pattern.

From a diagnostic perspective John's pattern of difficulty with sustained attention appears more characteristic of this right-hemisphere pattern than attention deficit hyperactivity disorder. Nonetheless, by his report and the current data he does fit the criteria for the inattentive type of attention deficit.

What is most characteristic of John at this time is his apprehensiveness and fearfulness, a lack of a sense of identity, a marked deprecation of his self-worth, a degree of oversensitivity and awkwardness socially, and a rather pervasive disharmony of mood. John lacks initiative and competitiveness and generally avoids autonomous behavior.

RECOMMENDATIONS

The texts by Gerald Patterson and Marion Forgatch, *Parent and Adolescent Living Together. Part 1: The Basics* and *Parent and Adolescent Living Together. Part 2: Family Problem Solving* (Castalia Publishing Co.), are recommended to John's parents as resources to assist them in interacting with John and his siblings.

An overview of suggestions for individuals with histories of right-hemisphere difficulties is included with this evaluation.

John is likely to resist or deny the need for counseling since he is inclined to be both embarrassed by and fearful of the implications of emotional problems. He is liable to be hesitant about making what is considered to be a fuss over his problems and fear that a counselor will be angry or rejecting if he complains too bitterly. Similarly, he may distort symptoms to match what he believes the therapist wants to hear. Lacking in confidence and initiative, John may become passive, if not immobile, in counseling. Helpless or incompetent appeals should be listened to sympathetically. Counseling for John must first be focused on helping him understand his pattern of skills and abilities and slowly teaching him how to interact differently with his world. Counseling will require a long-term commitment.

There is a possibility that a psychotropic medication may be of benefit to John. If he is sufficiently motivated, a psychiatry consult is recommended.

In regard to school John very clearly possesses the cognitive abilities to succeed in college. Nonetheless, he is going to require supportive services. This examiner is prepared to assist John in the process of selecting and applying to a new college or life development program if he so desires as well as qualifying for supportive learning disabled college programs.

SAMPLE ASSESSMENT 4

NAME: Roberta Fisher
DOB: January 24, 1976
DATE OF EVALUATION: March 1, 1994
CA: 18 years 1 month
GRADE: Twelve

REASON FOR EVALUATION

Roberta was referred by her educational specialist at St. John's Academy. Since coming to St. John's, Roberta has experienced difficulty remaining on task. She has reported diffuse feelings of anger. Roberta also has a history of depression. An evaluation of Roberta's skills, adjustment, and development was recommended in an effort to better understand her current difficulties and assist with long-term educational and life planning.

BACKGROUND INFORMATION

Background data was provided by correspondence from Roberta's father and stepmother. Roberta's father is a school principal. He completed a master's in education. Roberta's mother was an educator. She committed suicide when Roberta was seven years of age. Roberta has one stepbrother, Ryan, five years of age.

Roberta was the full-term product of a preganancy noted by threatened miscarriage; labor and delivery were normal. Roberta presented as a normal infant. As a toddler she did not deal with transition and change well. Nonetheless, she demonstrated a normal intensity of reaction and approach to new situations. She was generally stable in her moods and predictable in fitting routines.

Roberta's medical history has been unremarkable. She has had her tonsils removed. She was hospitalized at two years of age for dehydration. She wears corrective lenses and has a number of allergies. She has a history of sleep difficulty. Her appetite is average.

Roberta's developmental milestones were reached within normal limits. Her coordination appears good.

Roberta appears to experience difficulty remaining on task. Intellectually compared to others she appears average.

Mr. Fisher recalled he was not concerned about Roberta before she entered kindergarten. Her school experiences in relation to academic learning have been good. Her difficulties at school have included problems remaining on task and maintaining a positive attitude toward school.

Roberta was in gifted education in kindergarten and first grade. Her mother passed away during her first-grade year. Her performance for the remainder of her elementary school years appeared adequate. In seventh and eighth grade her school performance began to decline. There were increasing complaints of off task behavior. As a freshman in high school, Roberta struggled. She gave up in difficult classes. She became more rebellious at home. As a sophomore she continued to struggle academically and became increasingly more rebellious. She spoke about running away from home. She spent nine months in a adolescent treatment center. Upon returning from the program she had a very successful last nine weeks of school. As a junior her first semester was adequate. Her second semester was "a disaster" when a friend moved back from Georgia. Roberta moved out of her home for two weeks and then moved out again from April until August. She did very poorly while living by herself. Due to her struggles Roberta was registered at St. John's Academy. She has done much better at St. John's. Her grades, nonetheless, have suffered due to her inability to perform successfully on major tests.

Roberta seeks out and is sought out by peers for friendship. She has been influenced "a great deal by negative peers." She appears to reject peers who attempt to be more supportive.

While living at home, Roberta would fidget and was easily distracted. She did not follow through with instructions well. She would shift from one uncompleted activity to another and was very impulsive. She often talked excessively. She often did not listen to what was being said. She lost things that were necessary for tasks or activities at home. Roberta demonstrated poor judgment and poor self-control. She frustrated easily. She did not appear to learn well from her experiences.

Roberta has not worked well for short-term reward and even less so for long-term reward. Mr. Fisher reported that they have tried a variety of interventions in an effort to assist Roberta before placing her at St. John's.

Roberta enjoys music, sports, and parties. At one time she was quite accomplished at sports. She dislikes taking orders and doing "what would be considered normal." While Mr. Fisher noted that at this point he and Roberta may not have a very good relationship, he described her as "really a good person at heart."

ASSESSMENT PROCEDURES

Child Behavior Checklist
Revised Conners Parent Hyperkinesis Questionnaire
Home Situations Questionnaire
Social Skills Assessment
Review of Psychiatric File
Comprehensive Teacher's Rating Scale
Wechsler Adult Intelligence Scale—Revised
Peabody Picture Vocabulary Test—Revised (Form L)
Test of Nonverbal Intelligence—Revised (Form B)
Wide Range Assessment of Memory and Learning
Rey Complex Figure Drawing
Gordon Diagnostic System
Wide Range Achievement Test—3
Gilmore Oral Reading Test
Adult Reading Sample
Test of Written Language—Story Writing Test
Brown Attention Activation Disorders Scale
Revised Children's Manifest Anxiety Scale
Reynolds Adolescent Depression Scale
Clinical Interview
Millon Adolescent Personality Inventory

ADAPTIVE FUNCTIONING

On the basis of Mr. Fisher's responses to the Child Behavior Checklist, when Roberta last lived at home in comparison to females of her chronological age, she presented at above the 98th percentile for the scales of withdrawn, somatic complaints, attention problems, and delinquent behavior (50th percentile is average; high score indicates problem). Roberta was secretive and would sulk and be sad. She complained of fatigue and headache. She had difficulty concentrating and was impulsive. She appeared to lack guilt and had experimented with marijuana and alcohol.

On the basis of Mr. Fisher's responses to the Conners questionnaire, Roberta within the home setting presented at above the 98th percentile on the hyperkinesis index in comparison to females of her chronological age (50th percentile is average; high score indicates problem). Severe problems were noted with excitability, impulsivity, failing to finish things, distractibility, and inattention. Moderate problems were noted with being easily frustrated in her efforts and restlessness.

On the basis of Mr. Fisher's responses to the Home Situations Questionnaire, despite her disruptive behavior, Roberta presented with problems only doing chores and homework. No problems were noted in other situations.

PREVIOUS EVALUATION

This examiner reviewed assessment reports completed at Fairview Hospital in December 1991. Roberta was admitted to this facility due to her resistance to treatment and her increasing self-destructive behavior. There were concerns of suicidal thought. Concerns were raised that whatever caused Roberta's mother to commit suicide suddenly may be presenting in Roberta. Roberta admitted to having severe mood swings, irritability, and sleep disturbance. Justification for hospitalization included self-destructive behavior, suicidal concerns, and attempts to run away. Past psychiatric history included four outpatient treatment sessions in which she was noncompliant, oppositional, depressed, and negative. The diagnostic impression by the psychiatrist included provisional diagnoses of a single episode of major depression, cyclothymia, and a mixed personality disorder with avoidant and narcissistic features.

A psychosocial assessment completed at this time as well noted that Roberta's mother's suicide occurred the day before she and her husband were to go to marital therapy. In this assessment Roberta's stepmother noted that in the five years she had known her, Roberta had always been difficult and had been quite manipulative. She experienced difficulty separating from her mothers as an infant and toddler. This history also noted that Roberta was "an excellent student in first and second grade." In third, fourth, and fifth grades she received Bs and Cs. She was on the honor roll in sixth grade and was reported as doing well in seventh grade. This report also notes that Roberta had one close friend whom she did not want to share and had difficulty maintaining long-term friendships.

A psychological evaluation was completed during this hospitalization. Roberta's performance yielded the following test results:

Wechsler Adult Intelligence Scale—Revised

Full scale IQ = 104
Verbal IQ = 96
Performance IQ = 114

Verbal Subtests	Scaled Score (mean = 10; SD = 3)
Information	6
Similarities	12

Verbal Subtests	Scaled Score (mean = 10; SD = 3)
Arithmetic	9
Vocabulary	8
Comprehension	12

Performance Subtests	Scaled Score (mean = 10; SD = 3)
Picture Completion	9
Coding	12
Picture Arrangement	14
Block Design	13
Object Assembly	12

Neurocognitive screening yielded negative results. There were no indications of "information processing deficiencies that would result in reading, spelling or arithmetic disorders." He also noted no indications of psychotic thinking and the fact that Roberta denied major affective symptoms. She was described as being inclined to believe that others did not appreciate her, understand her needs, feelings, or wishes. Although standardized depression and anxiety questionnaires were administered to Roberta, this assessment did not report specific results other than to mention Roberta's denial. It was the evaluator's impression that Roberta appeared depressed. There are no indications of any other type of cognitive or developmental impairment.

SCHOOL FUNCTIONING

This examiner reviewed a copy of Roberta's high school transcript. Her pre-ACT scores appear below:

Test	Percentile
English	31st
Math	27th
Reading	32nd
Science	32nd

Although Roberta's GPA generally hovered in the B to C range, her total GPA at the end of her junior year was a 2.5. Her grades were consistently weak with the only As during the three-year period occurring in physical eduation. The majority of her grades were in the C and D range. Although this seems to not fit her general GPA, this examiner is unclear exactly how Roberta's semester GPA was generated. For example one semester in her sophomore year she earned two Ds and three Cs, yet she was reported as having a semester grade point average of 2.6.

The examiner reviewed Roberta's past academic records. On SRI achievement tests in first grade, she appeared at the 99th percentile for reading and the 94th percentile for mathematics. In second grade, her reading score was at the 86th percentile while mathematics was at the 95th percentile. Finally, in third grade Roberta's composite was at the 78th percentile. This was composed of 74th percentile reading, 63rd percentile mathematics, and 61st percentile language arts scores.

A number of Roberta's present teachers completed the Comprehensive Teacher's Rating Scale. Their scores appear below in comparison to a secondary school female population (50th percentile is average; low score indicates problem):

Teacher	Attention Span	Hyperactivity	Social Skills	Oppositional Behavior
Beeslay	20	−5	40	10
Strippoli	35	40	50	50
Rhodes	12	−5	20	20
Jonotone	10	−5	15	10
Allen	50	60	50	50
Granger	50	60	50	50

Roberta's ratings were quite variable. While a number of teachers described her difficulty working independently and persisting on task, an equal number note that she functions well, follows instructions and works well independently. It is likely that differences are a function of the academic demands of the classes in which she is in. Again some teachers describe her as quite overactive, impulsive, restless and fidgety while others note minimal restless, overactive problems. Only one teacher reports any kind of oppositional problems with all the others reporting reasonably good interpersonal and social skills. Teachers note that Roberta is accepted but not as often in demand for activities. All teachers rate her as requiring a moderate amount of assistance in the classroom.

BEHAVIORAL OBSERVATION

Roberta, a casually dressed adolescent of normal appearance, presented with adequate self-care. She wore no makeup or jewelry. Her dress appeared to reflect minimal interest in her appearance. Roberta was seen for two assessment sessions with a lunchtime break. Her behavior during both sessions was similar. She completed a number of additional instruments during the afternoon session.

Eye contact was appropriate. Roberta maintained but rarely spontaneously initiated conversation. Receptive and expressive language skills appeared adequate though Roberta rarely extended herself verbally.

At times Roberta appeared mildly anxious. Primarily, however, her affect was rather flat. She was not labile. Roberta was emotionally stable.

Roberta was alert and attentive, manifesting reasonably good concentration. She was cooperative and despite her tendency to distrust her abilities, willing to attempt all tasks presented. Her persistence with occasional prompting was good. No muscular tension nor habitual mannerisms were noted. Roberta presented as mildly underactive relative to this setting. Little spontaneous movement was noted. She was not fidgety nor distractible. With explanation Roberta appeared adequately oriented as to the purpose of the present evaluation.

Roberta would smile occasionally. By the close of the morning assessment she was reasonably responsive to the examiner and willing to engage in a discussion concerning her goals and future.

Roberta's thoughts were logical, focused and relevant. Overall it was not significantly difficult to establish a working relationship with this pleasant adolescent.

ASSESSMENT RESULTS AND INTERPRETATION

Roberta's performance on the Wechsler Adult Intelligence Scale appears below in comparison to a sample of her chronological age (50th percentile is average; low score indicates problem). Age-corrected scores are also offered.

Verbal Subtests	Scaled Score	(mean = 10; SD = 3)	Age-Corrected Score
Information	4		5
Digit Span	9		10
Vocabulary	6		8
Arithmetic	6		6
Comprehension	9		10
Similarities	8		9

Performance Subtests	Scaled Score	(mean = 10; SD = 3)	Age-Corrected Score
Picture Completion	9		9
Picture Arrangement	9		10
Block Design	13		14
Object Assembly	10		11
Digit Symbol	14		14

Verbal IQ = 86
Performance IQ = 110
Full-scale IQ = 96 (40th percentile)
  (mean = 100; SD = 15)

As observed a number of years ago during assessment, Roberta's verbal skills appear markedly weaker than her nonverbal ablities. Also as observed previously, her fund of information continues to be quite weak. In contrast, her visual perceptual skills are exceptionally good. Some degree of intratest scatter on the verbal tasks speaks to potentially better intellectual potential. For example, on the Information subtest, although Roberta reached a ceiling, the examiner continued asking questions. She was then able to almost double her score. Nonetheless, it is clear that her fund of information is poor (e.g., she did not know in which direction the sun set, nor who was president presently). Yet there were also indications that when pressed her capacity to reason and problem solve could be good. For example, when asked what the saying "One swallow doesn't make a summer" means, although Roberta misunderstood the statement and interpreted swallow as "what you do when you eat" she was able to problem solve and explained that to do things it will take more than one time. The 24-point difference between her verbal and nonverbal skills represents a significant discrepancy in light of her history and family socioeconomic status.

The Peabody Picture Vocabulary Test was administered as a one-word measure of receptive vocabulary. On this task, Roberta obtained a standard score of 116, equivalent to the 86th percentile. This is well above expectation based upon her verbal intellectual skills. In part, she was quite lucky and reasoned through quite well even for items which she did not know. In part also this score again reflects her better intellectual potential.

The Test of Nonverbal Intelligence was administered as a simple measure of reasoning, judgment, and concept formation. Roberta completed this task with a standard score of 86, equivalent to the 18th percentile. Roberta's performance on the Wide Range Assessment of Memory and Learning appears below. Her scores were compared to a 17-year-old sample, the eldest available for this instrument.

Subtests	Scaled Score (mean = 10; SD = 3)
Story Memory	12
Sentence Memory	13
Number/Letter	9
Picture Memory	12
Design Memory	8
Finger Windows	9
Verbal Learning	13
Sound Symbol	10
Visual Learning	10

Index	Index (mean = 100; SD = 15)	Percentile
Verbal memory	109	73
Visual memory	98	45
Learning	107	68
General memory	106	66

Roberta's relatively good verbal memory for complex information was surprising in light of her verbal weaknesses. Her average to above learning scores again speak to better intellectual potential.

Roberta held a pencil in her right hand with an appropriate pincer grip. Casual observation indicated no large motor abnormalities. Roberta's reproduction of the Rey Complex Figure yielded a score at the 63rd percentile, reflecting average visual perceptual and pencil control skills.

The Vigilance and Distractibility tasks from the Gordon Diagnostic System were administered as simple measures of Roberta's ability to sustain attention and inhibit impulsive responding. On the Vigilance tasks, Roberta's error and commission rates were in the low average range. Yet on the more complex Distractibility tasks, her performance was above average. The data appear to suggest that Roberta may not exert sufficient effort to meet task demands or may underestimate the demands of particular tasks. As the tasks become more difficult she is capable of mustering better capacity.

Roberta's academic skills were screened utilizing a number of instruments. Her performance on the Wide Range Achievement Test appears below:

Subtest	Standard Score	Percentile	Grade Equivalent
Word Reading	93	32	High school
Spelling	110	75	Post–high school
Arithmetic	82	12	Sixth

Roberta read for accuracy, comprehension, and rate at well above a 10th-grade level (ceiling) for the Gilmore Oral Reading Test. Her decoding skills are excellent until words move above her range of experience. Her comprehension, however, is inadequate at higher levels. On the

Adult Reading Comprehension sample, when reading silently she misses almost all information. When rereading aloud her performance improves somewhat. However, she becomes confused, misses the point, and then simply reads to complete the task rather than to comprehend.

Roberta worked very diligently on the Story Writing Test. Her performance yielded a score at the 85th percentile, while for thematic maturity her score was at only the 23rd percentile. Her language usage is reasonably good. Her mechanics, sentences, capitalization, periods, and punctuation are good. At times she does not always realize where a sentence begins and ends. She does not use apostrophes. As with other instruments, her higher vocabulary score reflects her effort and rote knowledge, while her thematic maturity score reflects conceptual issues. She simply is not effective in organizing and putting her ideas on paper.

The preponderance of the data suggests that Roberta's rote skills are not significantly weak. She misses rote information (e.g., general information) as the result of a lack of an overall conceptual grasp. This leads to not realizing when and how a basic skill should be used. She does, however, miss rote facts in mathematics but again this appears more a conceptually related problem. Her multiple errors with fractions clearly reflect her weak conceptual grasp in mathematics. She doesn't get the "big picture." Roberta's slow and steady decline on academic achievement instruments, at least through the first three grades, appears to be consistent with this type of problem.

The preponderance of the data suggests that Roberta experiences higher level language processing difficulty. She struggles to integrate information into concepts, hierarchies, etc. Reading comprehension problems and the types of writing errors she makes clearly reflect her verbal linguistic concept limitations.

Although Roberta can repeat short stories adequately and directly retrieve from short-term memory quite well, she struggles when tasks become more verbally complex and abstract. It may be this pattern that resulted in her at a young age being perceived as quite intelligent and gifted but as the demands of academics have increased she has appeared less and less advanced. Her learning curve suggests she has good initial retention but then has trouble organizing and consolidating information to retain it long term. Thus, assistance in studying for Roberta will require not so much focusing on short-term retention but helping her develop strategies and solidify information so that it is organized and retained long term. It is likely as the result of this disability that Roberta struggles to know what to study for. She likely is confused concerning what is important and how to study information. She likely often relies on her rote memory skills, which are adequate in some settings but fail her in more complex academic settings.

It is interesting that Roberta spells quite a bit better than she reads. She is quite good nonverbally, spatially, and sequentially, which likely reflects part of her spelling strengths.

On the Brown Attention Disorders self-report, Roberta's score of 82 was significantly above the 50-point cutoff considered to reflect symptoms of attention deficit. It is important to note, however, that a score at this elevation is also consistent with other comorbid emotional problems. Roberta reports that she frequently struggles to pay attention, daydreams, is easily sidetracked, loses track of what she is reading when she reads, struggles to remember information, has trouble knowing what to do first, forgets what needs to be done, and has difficulty memorizing. Again from the analysis of the data generated, it is clear that the majority of these problems are more likely related to cognitive weaknesses and emotional status than attention deficit hyperactivity disorder.

Roberta's responses to the Adolescent Depression Scale yielded a score at the 51st percentile (50th percentile is average; high score indicates problem). This score suggests Roberta does not experience significantly more depressed or helpless ideation than others of her age. It is interesting to note that on this questionnaire she reported that most of the time she worries about school.

Roberta's responses to the Manifest Anxiety Scale yielded average scores. Roberta does not appear significantly more anxious or worried than others of her age. She comments, however, that she gets nervous when things do not go the right way for her, worries what her parents and teachers may think or say about her, has her feelings hurt easily, and finds it difficult to keep her mind on school work.

During the clinical interview, Roberta was quite responsive to the examiner. When asked for three wishes she wished to be 25 years old, have plenty of money, and become a famous photographer. When asked what she would like to change about herself, she responded "be better at school."

Roberta described her favorite activity as hanging out with friends. She felt she was best at listening to people. She reported being as happy as other people at school because "no one is really happy at school." She felt that at times she may be more sad than others but never more angry.

Roberta spoke about a group of friends and a number of social activities. She described herself as "I like to have fun." She noted she disliked the fact that she had "mood swings." Roberta described these mood swings as occurring daily, for no particular reason. She noted that going with friends or keeping busy is helpful.

Roberta described meeting people as her favorite part of school this year and homework as her least favorite part. She felt at times she was as smart as others but at times not so. She described difficulty learning, especially mathematics. Roberta noted that when she was younger school was easier. She described difficulty concentrating but also noted that if she likes the work and enjoys it she does not experience difficulty sticking with it. She described difficulty finishing work at school, listening to the teacher for long periods of time, staying organized, waiting her turn, and remaining seated.

Roberta described the most difficult part of growing up as "when people don't understand." She denied excessive anxiety and reported being average in her confidence. She felt she was not particularly satisfied with her life presently, noting that she would like to change some of the things that have happened in her past.

On a structured depression symptom interview, Roberta denied excessive feelings of sadness or inability to derive pleasure. She did acknowledge difficulty sleeping over the past few weeks, noting difficulty falling asleep. However, when asked to explain further she reported that she had been in trouble for smoking marijuana at school, a problem that was discovered with a urinalysis for a number of students. One of her best friends was caught for a second time and discharged from school. Roberta felt this was part of the reason she was experiencing difficulty sleeping. She denied any excessive problems with nightmares.

Roberta spoke openly about her dreams and desires in her life. She reported that she would like to become a photographer. She noted she was most proud of bringing her grades up and taking a chance going to a boarding school. She described the most difficult part of growing up as "when people don't understand."

On a scale of 1 to 10 with 10 being the best, Roberta described her life presently as a 5, friends as a 10, her mood as a 5, and family as a 3. Roberta explained that her last visit home was frustrating and she and her parents fought frequently. Since family issues were not the focus of this assessment, this examiner did not pursue further data concerning Roberta's current relations with her father and stepmother.

Roberta denied that the death of her mother presently contributed to her problems noting, "I don't think it has a lot to do with it, people think it does." She denied remembering very much during the period after her mother's death but did recall discovering her mother's body. She also noted that her father "was really weird" after her mother's death and that she and her stepmother, whom her father knew at the time of her mother's death, have never gotten along very well.

On the basis of her history and presentation, Roberta presents as an adolescent with adequate reality testing and generally age-appropriate thought processes. Her behavior appears best characterized by a submissive dependency on others for affection, attention and security. Her fear of abandonment may lead her to seek nurturance by acting in a compliant and obliging way with peers. She appears more naive in her attitudes concerning social and interpersonal problems. Though faced in the past and to some extent presently with personal and family tensions, Roberta makes an effort to maintain an air of buoyancy, denying disturbing emotions and concealing her likely inner discomforts. Roberta's Millon profile suggests that she is somewhat preoccupied with pleasing others and gaining their approval. In response, she may have denied herself opportunities to gain a sense of identity. Thus, she does not appear to value herself in terms of her own traits but in terms of the friends to whom she feels most attached. By allying herself with the attributes and attractiveness of others, she creates an illusion of having shared their competence. Morever, she is likely to find solace in the belief that her bonds with them are thereby unshakable.

Roberta's personality profile suggests that she has learned to be alert to signs of potential hostility and rejection from others. However, by paying close attention to subtle signs that others convey, she is able to reshape her behavior to conform to their desires.

On the Millon, Roberta reports being significantly unhappy with both her body maturation and her attractiveness. She describes this area as a significant focus of her present stress. Her pervasive sense of inadequacy in this sphere causes her to retreat and thereby avoid the rejection she anticipates from others. She appears somewhat confused and upset in relation to her sexual impulses.

Complicating her other difficulties, Roberta on the Millon described serious problems in her family setting. Tension and a lack of support appear typical from her perception.

Despite these difficulties, Roberta appears to have an increasingly clear sense of her values. She finds social relationships to be satisfactory and possesses a sense of belonging.

It may well be that Roberta's cognitive weaknesses further contribute to her personality style. Her inability to "see the big picture" may compound her inability to deal efficiently with her feelings and experiences.

DIAGNOSTIC IMPRESSION

Roberta, an adolescent functioning in the average range of intellectual skill, with a long-standing history of nonverbal strength and verbal weakness, presents a somewhat perplexing pattern of behavior, adjustment, and developmental difficulties. These appear chronic and of mild to moderate severity.

Although there are indices suggesting that Roberta's intellectual potential is better, the preponderance of the data suggests that she experiences higher level language processing difficulty. She struggles to integrate information into concepts and hierarchies. Her reading comprehension problems and the types of writing errors she makes clearly reflect her verbal linguistic conceptual limitations. Although at a very young age she tested exceptionally well, this appeared to be a function of her rote strengths. Thus during the first few grades while learning to read, Roberta did well. As school became more complex and the need to read to learn increased, Roberta's struggles increased.

The question of attention deficit is complex. The preponderance of the data does not consistently reflect long-standing problems with attention deficit symptoms. Even now while some teachers describe Roberta as inattentive and restless, others do not. It also must be noted that while Roberta reports significant symptoms consistent with attention deficit, her excessive complaints are often characteristic of individuals experiencing problems related to emotional distress. Although Roberta denies these problems, her personality style is very clearly consistent with someone who would in fact deny. This is a pattern that has been reported and observed by other evaluators in the past as well. Until Roberta is followed more closely in a counseling relationship, firm diagnostic conclusion concerning attention deficit must be reserved.

Roberta appears to possess strong dependency needs and is somewhat preoccupied with pleasing others and gaining their approval to the extent that she may deny herself the opportunity to develop a clear sense of identity. She does not appear to value herself in terms of her own traits.

An assessment of this brevity cannot fully appreciate the depth of Roberta's history and experiences. There is every reason to suggest, given the sudden, unexpected death of her mother and her discovery of her mother's body, that Roberta would in fact be at risk to experience symptoms consistent with post-traumatic stress and potentially long-standing mood problems. Her personality style appears to have further contributed to her history of cognitive weakness.

RECOMMENDATIONS

Roberta's goal to become a photographer certainly fits her cognitive skills. It is suggested, however, that she consider a two-year technical rather than a four-year academic college program. A part-time job during this period to build self-esteem and status from earning money would be helpful.

Roberta should attempt to learn to enjoy reading on her own. Novels, etc., will help build her skills and comprehension.

While studying, efforts need to be made to help Roberta organize information, rehearse, and solidify information for retention. It is likely that immediately after studying, Roberta will retain quite a bit more than she will remember even after a short period of time. She will need to overlearn information. Efforts also need to be made to help her see the "big picture" as she studies.

Roberta would benefit from instruction and practice in study skills, particularly those involved in note taking and efficient gathering of information for tests. She may find it helpful to tape record class lectures or obtain copies of class notes from others. A study group or sharing of study materials would be helpful.

Roberta works best at a concrete level, seeing and dealing with what is directly in her view. She learns best from diagrams, models, and examples along with repeated verbal explanation. She will require very carefully sequenced instructions, moving slowly from one step to the next. In learning situations she would benefit from an advanced organizer, someone who can explain to her the big picture and show her how supporting details relate to overall ideas.

Roberta needs to develop the ability to stop after reading a short amount and restate to herself what she has just read. She needs to learn how to preview chapters before reading them and develop a system for tracking through headings, subheadings, and end of chapter questions.

Roberta will require more support than average when completing a project or research paper. Research which involves integrating information from many sources will likely be problematic and require guidance.

Roberta requires support from all those involved with her in regard to her school performance. Warm regard, praise for partial achievements, and grades which reflect assignment completion, as well as subject mastery will be very important for Roberta.

It is suggested that in 6–12 months Roberta and her counselors review her progress and once again consider the issue of attention deficit hyperactivity disorder. However, it is this examiner's impression that until Roberta's cognitive weaknesses are better understood and supported and her emotional status is better understood, firm conclusions concerning attention deficit hyperactivity disorder cannot be made.

It would be helpful for Roberta to consider counseling. Efforts will need to be made to help her identify life goals and better understand how life experiences have shaped her present behavior and personality. She has a desire to be seen as good, cooperative, and pleasant. She is likely to judge a counselor as helpful and supportive. The negative side of this pleasant outlook is that Roberta may become too dependent and attached to the counselor. Roberta is likely to be a good counseling candidate once she understands the process of counseling and goals.

SAMPLE ASSESSMENT 5

NAME:	Douglas Dillon
DOB:	February 12, 1978
DATES OF EVALUATION:	August 7, 19, 1995
CA:	17 years 6 months
GRADE:	Entering Grade Twelve

REASON FOR EVALUATION

Douglas has a history of school performance problems related to inattentiveness and possible learning disability. Evaluation was recommended in an effort to better understand and define Douglas's current functioning and assist with treatment planning and college application.

BACKGROUND INFORMATION

Douglas and his mother were seen, to review his social and developmental history. Douglas is the eldest of three adopted children. He has a nine-year-old sister, Nicole—she has a history of mood swings—and a three-month-old sister, Kristina. No information is available concerning Douglas's biological parents. Mrs. Dillon is employed as a reservationist. She completed two years of college. Mr. Dillon is employed in advertising. He also completed two years of college.

Douglas was adopted at three years of age. No information is available concerning his early history. His medical history has been unremarkable. He was given three sets of pressure equalization tubes due to recurrent ear infections. He suffers from hay fever. Douglas settles down to sleep and is able to sleep through the night without disruption. His appetite is very good.

Douglas presently receives Desoxyn for attention deficit symptoms. A trial of Ritalin was not particularly beneficial. He has been taking 10 mg of Desoxyn each morning for the past two years. Douglas received tutorial assistance in 3rd through 10th grades. He is receiving tutoring this summer for the ACT because his ACT scores were below the cutoff necessary to qualify for an NCAA college athletic scholarship.

For in-depth developmental data the reader is referred to a neuropsychological evaluation completed in January 1987. Douglas was referred at that time due to poor school performance and inattentiveness. He was described as outgoing and athletic. He was receiving Resource assistance evidently for behavioral problems. These test results and conclusions will be described further in the section titled "Previous Evaluation." Douglas continues to have a history of difficulty sitting still in class, waiting his turn, and paying attention. He has succeeded in high school due to his athletic abilities. He holds two state records in track and is a football tailback. He recently won an MVP award at a university football camp. He has been recruited and received letters of interest from a number of national colleges.

Douglas does well socially. He is dating. He has no history of substance abuse problems.

Douglas has trouble at home fidgeting and is easily distracted. He doesn't wait his turn well. He has problems following through with instructions and paying attention. He tends to shift from one uncompleted activity to another. Douglas interrupts and doesn't appear to listen to what is being said often. He loses things that are necessary for tasks or activities at home. Douglas demonstrates boundless energy and poor judgment. He is impulsive. Douglas has difficulty with repetitive activities. He wears out shoes more frequently than his siblings. He doesn't appear to learn from his experience. Douglas has never worked well for short-term or long-term rewards. Nonetheless, he has never created significant problems at home. No particular form of discipline has been effective in motivating him toward school.

Douglas has worked for the past three summers as a mover. He noted that this type of manual labor has convinced him that he wants to attend college. He has been pulled over 11 times for driving but never received a ticket. Most have been for driving over the speed limit or not completing stopping at a stop sign. Douglas's mother reported that he is "hard on cars."

Douglas is kind to everyone and well liked. He most enjoys sports. Douglas and his mother appeared motivated and interested to both understand and effectively work with Douglas's problems.

PREVIOUS EVALUATION

A number of assessment instruments were completed with Douglas in 1987. Douglas's performance on the Revised Wechsler Intelligence Scale appears below:

Verbal Subtests	Scaled Score (mean = 10; SD = 3)
Information	6
Similarities	10
Arithmetic	10
Vocabulary	9
Comprehension	10
Digit Span	6

Performance Subtests	Scaled Score (mean = 10; SD = 3)
Picture Comprehension	12
Picture Arrangement	12
Block Design	11
Object Assembly	15
Coding	12
Mazes	5

Verbal IQ = 94
Performance IQ = 117
Full-scale IQ = 104
     (mean = 100; SD = 15)

It was noted that Douglas was quite accomplished in visual perceptual abilities but markedly weaker in his verbal skills. Mild problems on other tasks with reasoning and cognitive flexibility were noted. Academically, Douglas performed in the average range or a Vocabulary task and low average (approximately 30th percentile) on the Reading, Spelling, and Arithmetic subtests of the Wide Range Achievement Test.

It was concluded that Douglas appeared somewhat developmentally delayed, demonstrating symptoms of attention deficit disorder and difficulty processing visual symbols. A compounding problem, the result of weakness of language conceptual skills was also reported. A trial of psychostimulant medication and academic support were recommended.

ASSESSMENT PROCEDURES

Child Behavior Checklist
Revised Conners Parent Questionnaires
Home Situations Questionnaire
Social Skills Assessment
Brown Attention Activation Disorder Scale
Review of Academic File
Peabody Picture Vocabulary Test—Revised
Test of Nonverbal Intelligence—Revised (Form B)
Stanford-Binet Verbal Absurdities Task
Wide Range Assessment of Memory and Learning
Rey Complex Figure Drawing
Wide Range Achievement Test—3
Gilmore Oral Reading Test
Test of Written Language—Story Writing Test
Revised Children's Manifest Anxiety Scale
Reynolds Adolescent Depression Scale
Millon Adolescent Personality Inventory
Clinical Interview

ADAPTIVE FUNCTIONING

On the basis of Mrs. Dillon's responses to the Child Behavior Checklist, Douglas presents behavior within the normal range in comparison to adolescents of his chronological age within the home setting. Highest scale elevations were on the scales of attention problems and delinquent behavior (50th percentile is average; high score indicates problem). Douglas scored at approximately the 85th percentile on both of these scales. These elevated scores were the result of his appearing to lack guilt, willingness to lie, problems with concentration, restlessness, poor school performance, and impulsivity.

Mrs. Dillon's responses to the Conners questionnaire compared Douglas with and without stimulant medication. Although marked improvements have been noted with a stimulant, even with the medication, based on Mrs. Dillon's observations Douglas still presents at above the 98th percentile on the hyperkinesis index (50th percentile is average; high score indicates problem). Without medication significant problems are noted with excitable, impulsive, restless, destructive, inattentive, distractible, and disturbing behavior and failing to finish things. With medication, the majority of these problems, except for restlessness fall to the mild to moderate range.

On the basis of Mrs. Dillon's responses to the Home Situations Questionnaire, Douglas bores easily in public places such as restaurants and has a difficult time getting started with homework. No problems have been noted in other home situations or with public behavior.

On the basis of Mrs. Dillon's responses to the Social Skills Assessment, Douglas can be some-what argumentative with his parents but relates well to others. He responds and initiates con-versation, can engage in long conversation, and shares laughter. Douglas's greatest problems socially result when he has to sit "and listen to a speaker for any length of time."

Mrs. Dillon's responses to the Brown questionnaire yielded a score of 61, above the cutoff of 50 indicative of late adolescent and adult inattentive problems. Douglas was described as hav-ing marked problems with procrastination, paying attention, sticking to activities, misunder-standing directions, and completing academic tasks successfully.

SCHOOL FUNCTIONING

This examiner reviewed selected parts of Douglas's academic record. His 11th grade report card yielded a cumulative grade point average of 2.94 (B). Douglas's behavior generally was rated as satisfactory, although in a number of classes he was noted as needing improvement. His lowest scores were in solid academic subjects.

Douglas's sophomore pre-ACT scores follow:

Test	Percentiles (national college-bound tenth-graders)
English	13th
Usage/Mechanics	9th
Rhetorical Skills	19th
Mathematics	9th
Pre-Algebra	38th
Geometry	2nd
Reading	28th
Science Reasoning	57th
Composite	17th

This overall ACT yielded a standard score of 13.

Results of Douglas's Sylvan Learning Center testing completed in June 1995 noted a Peabody Picture Vocabulary Test score at the 16th percentile with marked weaknesses in a variety of mathematics and comprehension skills.

BEHAVIORAL OBSERVATION

Douglas, a well-groomed young man of average size and appearance, had no apprehension during either assessment session. During the initial session he joined his mother while the his-tory and self-report measures were completed. During the second session structured assessment data was collected. Douglas's behavior during both sessions was similar.

Douglas maintained and initiated conversation. Eye contact appeared appropriate. Douglas worked very hard and was quite motivated. He was alert and attentive and concentrated reason-ably well. Douglas received his stimulant medication on the morning of structured assessment.

No muscular tension or habitual mannerisms were noted. Douglas presented with a normal activity level. He was not fidgety. He was also not distracted.

Overall, it was not significantly difficult to establish a working relationship with this pleasant, motivated adolescent.

ASSESSMENT RESULTS AND INTERPRETATION

Douglas's performance on the Peabody Picture Vocabulary Test yielded a standard score of 82, equivalent to the 12th percentile. This score represents an approximately four-year delay in his receptive vocabulary skills. His performance on this instrument is somewhat lower than expected based on his 58th percentile performance a number of years ago but similar to that obtained recently at Sylvan.

The Test of Nonverbal Intelligence was administered as a reasoning task with figures. Not surprisingly, Douglas completed this task with a standard score of 116, equivalent to the 86th percentile for his chronological age (50th percentile is average; high score indicates problem). As noted in earlier years Douglas's nonverbal abilities, both rote and conceptual, appear markedly better than his verbal skills.

Not surprisingly, Douglas struggled on the Standard Binet Absurdities Task, passing items only through an 11-year-old level.

Due to concerns of memory and learning, the Wide Range Assessment of Memory and Learning was administered. Douglas's age-equivalent scores appear below:

Subtest	Scaled Score (mean = 10; SD = 3)
Story Memory	11
Sentence Memory	8
Number/Letter	8
Picture Memory	8
Design Memory	9
Finger Windows	13
Verbal Learning	15
Sound/Symbol	8
Visual Learning	7

Index	Index (mean = 100; SD = 15)	Percentile
Verbal memory	94	34th
Visual memory	100	50th
Learning	100	50th
General memory	97	42nd

Verbally, Douglas appears to recall meaningful information quite a bit better than rote non-meaningful information. His Story Memory recognition score was in the bright average range. Visually, his performance was just the opposite. He performs rote visual tasks better than conceptual or meaningful tasks. His learning profile was interesting in that despite his good visual perceptual abilities he struggled on the Visual Learning task, yet he performed exceptionally well on the Verbal Learning task. His below average Sound/Symbol performance likely reflects weak phonetic abilities.

Douglas's reproduction of the Ray Complex Figure was approached from a configural basis. The figure was exceptionally well drawn and almost appeared as if it had been constructed with a ruler. The performance yielded a score at or above the 90th percentile for visual perceptual ability for Douglas's chronological age.

Douglas's academic skills were screened utilizing the Wide Range Achievement Test. His scores appear below:

Subtest	Standard Score	Percentile
Word Reading	86	18th
Spelling	87	19th
Arithmetic	84	14th

On the Gilmore, Douglas read at the ceiling for this test (10th grade) for accuracy and comprehension. His rate of reading up through approximately an eighth-grade level is fairly adequate. He reads carefully and uses context as he reads. His visual processing is adequate. He makes a few small errors on word endings, but his errors generally occur on longer words that he doesn't recognize or can't sound out well. His comprehension is approximately equivalent to his decoding skills. Douglas becomes confused as the complexity of language increases. Lengthier words and more complex sentence structure are clearly more difficult for him to process. Douglas was not able to successfully read a more complex adult reading sample consisting of material from a 12th-grade biology text.

Douglas worked very hard on his written story. The story contained 162 words. There were only 11 misspellings. There were nine approximate sentences. One was incomplete. Most were rather disorganized or strung out. Punctuation was adequate for his age. Douglas's story yielded a score at the 15th percentile for vocabulary and structure but at the 63rd percentile for thematic maturity.

The preponderance of the past and current data very clearly reflects Douglas's history of inattentiveness and an overall semantic language weakness. The latter problem appears compounded by difficulty with auditory processing for both sounds and meaning as well as a rote verbal memory deficit. These weaknesses are reflected in Douglas's performance and likely daily activities. He works very hard to process verbal information. He understands concepts but has trouble processing long sentences for meaning the first time around. He often asks to have longer questions or statements repeated. He has been taught to use memorization strategies which he tries to utilize to compensate for weak memory. His visual spatial perception is especially good for visual-motor activities such as drawing and nonverbal reasoning.

Douglas's overall reading skills are approximately two years below his grade placement for reading. His instant sight recognition is low. He has to sound out many words. This slows him down. He doesn't sound out effectively and misses essential bits in longer words. His vocabulary is diminished so that when he becomes close to sounding out a word he doesn't recognize it by context. He comprehends adequately up to his level of decoding and language ability. As with his listening comprehension, his ability to understand fails when sentences become longer or structurally complex. His reading style is adequate for his abilities. Very clearly, Douglas's reading shows signs of prior remediation. He reads in context better than single words.

In regard to spelling Douglas's skills again are low overall. He struggles with auditory discrimination and the visual memory aspects of spelling. He attempts to use phonic sounding out as he has been trained to and does so as best he can, but he still may not always hear the sounds in longer words.

Douglas's writing demonstrates weaknesses in language skills. His vocabulary is simple; structure is adequate; his ideas are good.

Finally, Douglas's math skills are adequate to a point and then quite poor. He doesn't understand fraction or decimal concepts. He has been taught algebra but still cannot complete basic algebra activities.

Douglas's responses to the Brown questionnaire yielded a score of 61, similar to his mother's observations of difficulties and inattentiveness. Douglas noted his difficulty attempting to pay attention, daydreaming, become easily sidetracked, being unable to complete assignments, procrastinating, misunderstanding, and being easily distracted.

Douglas's responses to the Depression Scale yielded a score at the 77th percentile (50th percentile is average; high score indicates problem). This score is still within the normal range. The slight elevation appeared to be the result of Douglas's acknowledging that at times he worries about school, feels lonely, that life is unfair, that he may be bad, and that at times nothing he does helps anymore.

Douglas's responses to the Manifest Anxiety Scale yielded the following results in comparison to males at his grade level (50th percentile is average; high score indicates problem):

Scale	Percentile
Total anxiety	42nd
Physiological	68th
Worry/oversensitivity	39th
Social/concentration	49th
Lie	73rd

Once again despite average scores, Douglas noted that at times he worries and finds it difficult to keep his mind on his school work.

On the basis of his history and responses to the Millon questionnaire, Douglas presents as an adolescent with adequate reality testing and age-appropriate thought processes. His Millon profile suggests that he works very hard to portray a public front of social propriety and friendliness. Nonetheless, Douglas may at times feel that life is unfair and anticipates disapproval due to an inability to perform successfully. It is clear that this pattern does not present athletically but rather academically. Douglas's Millon profile suggests that at times he may feel some degree of dissatisfaction with himself due to his academic struggles. The profile is similar to adolescents who may believe that others feel equally negative about them.

On the positive side, Douglas appears to be reasonably satisfied with his maturation. He perceives social relationships as satisfactory and is a gentle and kind individual. He appears to be someone fairly accepting of others regardless of their frailties and willing to provide help and support when needed.

Most glaring in Douglas's Millon profile are his feelings of dismay when evaluating his academic performance in comparison to others. Although Douglas is very clearly hooked into high school athletics, his Millon profile was similar to adolescents who find little relevance in either course work or extracurricular activities.

DIAGNOSTIC IMPRESSION

Douglas, an adolescent functioning in the average range of intellectual skill, demonstrates a history of developmental and temperamental problems. These appear chronic and of mild severity.

Despite average intellectual abilities, past and present data very clearly reflect Douglas's well above average rote and conceptual nonverbal abilities but below average rote and conceptual verbal skills. Overall, Douglas demonstrates a consistent semantic language weakness. This problem is compounded by poor auditory processing for sounds and meaning as well as weaknesses in rote verbal memory. This profile was identified early in Douglas's academic career and not surprisingly has persisted. It is to Douglas's credit, and those who have worked with him, that he has progressed as consistently in school as the current data reflect. Overall, his basic reading and writing skills appear approximately two grades below his present educational placement.

By history and current symptoms Douglas demonstrates problems consistent with a diagnosis of attention deficit hyperactivity disorder—primarily the inattentive type. At a younger age Douglas experienced greater problems with restless, hyperactive, and impulsive behavior. At the present time his problems appear primarily characterized as difficulty attending to repetitive, effortful, uninteresting activities. It is positive to note that a low dose of stimulant medication has resulted in marked improvement, though problems continued in this area.

It does not apear that Douglas experiences any specific type of emotional problems. He has been able to use his athletic gifts to compensate for academic weaknesses. Current assessment data, however, suggest that Douglas's academic self-esteem not surprisingly is somewhat weak.

RECOMMENDATIONS

It is strongly recommended that Douglas's physician review the current assessment and continue the stimulant medication. Previous trials of Ritalin were unsuccessful. It is suggested that this fall, data be obtained from Douglas's classroom teachers. Should complaints of inattentiveness be reported and partialled out from poor performance as the result of academic weakness a retitration of stimulant medication may be warranted. Should a retitration be undertaken, this examiner is prepared to assist in the collection of behavioral data within the school setting.

It is strongly recommended that Douglas continue to receive academic support. Once the Sylvan course is completed, this examiner is prepared to make a referral for intensive one-on-one ACT preparation. Douglas needs preparation specifically in:

1. Vocabulary building
2. Building and strengthening reading skills, including sight words, phonic decoding, and comprehension strategies
3. Reviewing and relearning math skills, including relating fractions, decimals, and percentages, and strengthening Douglas's algebra knowledge

Given Douglas's history of learning problems and diagnosis of attention deficit hyperactivity disorder it is this examiner's recommendation that he be allowed to complete his ACT exams and any other college entrance testing untimed.

The texts by Mel Levine, *All Kinds of Minds,* and Ned Hallowell and J. Ratey, *Driven to Distraction,* are recommended as helpful resources for Douglas. It will be important for him to understand his weaknesses and how they affect him as well as be able to focus on his above average intellectual strength and academic prowess.

Douglas may also wish to work with a cognitive rehabilitation specialist in an effort to develop more effective memorization strategies. In addition, Douglas should be taught strategies to improve his ability to comprehend either through remediation or compensation (e.g., reading slower or rereading).

It is likely that academically, college is going to be difficult for Douglas. It is strongly recommended that he seek student disability services support including assistance with study skills development, note taking, allowances for taking tests untimed, a focus on classes allowing him to utilize his exceptional visual perceptive and nonverbal skills, and reduced course. Douglas has indicated an interest in majoring in physical education, an area that will allow him to make the most of his athletic and intellectual strengths.

Periodic reevaluation.

CHAPTER 7

Case Studies

THE GREATEST RISK a practitioner can take is to make a diagnosis of ADHD or LD based on a narrow scope of evaluation; limited historical, behavioral, or assessment data; and the presumption that no other disorders contribute to symptom presentation. The risk of false diagnosis can be minimized by using a systematic approach, however. Such an approach will help the practitioner face the two greatest problems involved in making diagnoses of ADHD and LD: alternative etiologies that are difficult to rule out and objective data that do not provide a consistent profile. Because symptoms of poor academic achievement, impulsiveness, and inattentiveness are common complaints in adulthood, the practitioner is unlikely to encounter "clean cases" in which symptoms are very easily tied to ADHD or LD.

This chapter contains 24 brief case studies. Together, these cases provide a descriptive overview beginning with individuals presenting with generally uncomplicated ADHD or LD, progressing to those with multiple comorbid problems, and ending with those whose apparent symptoms of LD or ADHD are in fact caused by other disorders.

Case 1: ADHD

R.B., a 48-year-old male, was self-referred at the insistence of his spouse. R.B. reported a normal childhood. However, his mother died when he was three years of age, and he was raised by a grandmother and great-aunt until he was six, at which time his father remarried. He denied any significant behavioral, cognitive, or emotional problems in childhood but noted that he should have been retained in third grade because of poor reading skills. Nonetheless, R.B. progressed through high school and graduated with a four-year college degree and a B average.

R.B. was employed in sales full time. He had worked for the same company for nine years but expressed concern that he had missed promotions because he was disorganized and had difficulty getting along with supervisors.

R.B. and his first wife were married for 20 years. They have four children. Their youngest, an 11-year-old boy, was diagnosed with ADHD, which in part prompted R.B. to consider assessment for himself.

R.B. described chronically feeling tense, unable to relax, and fatigued and having difficulty with concentration and memory. R.B. noted that at times he feels stupid and that his moods will change frequently or unpredictably. He reported numerous citations for speeding violations but only one automobile accident.

R.B.'s self-report on the Wender and Brown questionnaires crossed the clinical cutoffs. R.B.'s father reported that as a child R.B. was easily distracted and fidgety, had difficulty sustaining attention, and often seemed not to listen. R.B.'s wife's observations on the Brown questionnaire crossed the clinically significant threshold. Eleven out of 14 *DSM-III-R* symptoms of ADHD were also acknowledged by R.B.'s wife.

R.B.'s presentation was unremarkable. On demanding tasks, however, he frequently became frustrated and less efficient. His mannerisms were appropriate. Brief structured assessment detected average verbal and nonverbal intellectual skills. R.B. demonstrated difficulty sustaining attention on a computerized measure of continuous performance.

Data generated from the Beck and Millon did not reflect significant symptoms of depression; however, personality characteristics suggested that R.B.'s veneer of confidence covered strong feelings of inadequacy, impulsive acts resulting from minimal deliberation, poor judgment, and difficulty admitting responsibility. Rationalization and projection were identified as primary psychological defenses.

The preponderance of the data most powerfully reflected R.B.'s lifetime patterns of ADHD symptoms. Given his intelligence and lack of learning problems, R.B. had developed numerous strategies to manage problems and allow him to function adequately on a daily basis.

Recommendations included a trial of medication, video resources relevant to ADHD, and psychosocial interventions, as well as further consultation concerning R.B.'s current problems at work.

Case 2: ADHD

M.B., an almost 16-year-old female, demonstrated a history of disruptive behavior consistent with ADHD from preschool. Family history was positive for ADHD in a number of immediate and extended family members. M.B.'s treatment history included preschool play therapy at four years of age and intermittent counseling with a number of mental health professionals throughout childhood and early adolescence. More recently, counselors reported M.B.'s reluctance to discuss her feelings and life problems and her general tendency to deny the need for treatment. M.B.'s medical treatment history included the therapeutic use of a number of stimulants, including Ritalin and Dexedrine; Imipramine begun in midadolescence due to concerns about mood fluctuations; and more recently, a trial of Zoloft due to parental complaints of disruptive behavior at home.

M.B.'s parents described the home situation as her primary area of difficulty. M.B.'s mother reported an ongoing and fairly severe pattern of conflict between herself and her daughter. M.B.'s father was often placed in the role of mediator. Approaching late adolescence, M.B. had become more independent, challenging her parent's authority, their post–high school goals for her, and what she perceived as their unequal treatment of her and her older sister. Current referral resulted from a particularly nasty family battle coinciding with a poor report card.

Despite behavioral difficulties, M.B.'s academic records reflected average grades in general.

A number of M.B.'s teachers reported that she appeared to be capable of better work. She had become more passive in some classes and was actively missing other classes.

Questionnaires completed by M.B.'s parents reflected scale elevations on the Child Behavior Checklist, including aggressive and withdrawn behavior, as well as inattentiveness. On a Conners questionnaire, M.B. presented at above the 98th percentile without stimulant medication. Problems were noted with distractibility, inattention, failing to finish things, wide or drastic mood changes, excitability, and impulsivity. With the present regime of Dexedrine and Zoloft, M.B.'s parents reported a marked decline in these problems. Nonetheless, continued situational problems, primarily with noncompliance, were reported at home.

M.B. was an attractive adolescent. She was pleasant and cooperative during the assessment process. No overt signs of depression or anxiety were noted. M.B. related well to the examiner.

Brief structured assessment reflected M.B.'s average to high average verbal and nonverbal skills. Her approach to test tasks tended to become more hesitant and reticent as task complexity increased. When prompted by the examiner, it was clear that M.B.'s intellectual skills were likely even better than these average measures reflected.

M.B.'s responses to self-report measures did not yield symptoms related to anxiety or depression. Her personality was typified by a confident social style, the enjoyment of seeking attention, and a tendency to seek praise and approval from others through immature or histrionic means. M.B.'s personality reflected an adolescent easily excited and then quickly bored. This pattern did not appear to result from hostile or malicious tendencies but rather from M.B.'s somewhat self-centered narcissism. Nonetheless, she presented with a fairly clear self-concept and a general measure of comfort when describing herself and her current life. M.B.'s primary focus of problems was on the unfair means by which her parents had related and continued to relate to her. She reported her family as the primary source of tension and conflict.

By history and presentation, M.B. met symptomatic qualifications for ADHD. Although M.B.'s parents reported improvements in her behavior at home with the introduction of the Zoloft, an anecdotal log over a period of weeks did not clearly support their perceptions. Both M.B. and her parents, however, reported that the Dexedrine appeared to be beneficial when M.B. chose to participate and complete schoolwork.

Further psychiatric consultation was recommended in an effort to provide clear target symptoms to evaluate the potential need for and benefits from the antidepressant medication. M.B. decided to continue with the Dexedrine and to make an effort to participate more actively in school so as not to jeopardize her upcoming graduation. M.B. was also provided with additional information about ADHD in adolescence and adulthood. Finally, after communicating with a number of other professionals who had failed to improve family relations, the examiner decided to recommend individual counseling for M.B. in an effort to provide her with some additional support and guidance as she began planning her future life. M.B.'s parents were given additional information concerning ADHD and urged to allow M.B. to take a more active and independent role in her life.

Case 3: ADHD and Gifted Intellect

D.O., a 17 and a half year old 11th-grade male, was referred because of a history of poor academic motivation, symptoms suggestive of ADHD, and the recent reports of increasingly low self-esteem. D.O.'s family history was significant for obsessive/compulsive disorder, ADHD, alcoholism, and depression.

D.O.'s history was positive for a fall at two years of age, which resulted in a concussion followed by a convulsion. For several years afterward when D.O. fell or got hurt, he would either black out or experience a convulsion. No clear etiologies for these problems were identified.

During his fifth-grade year, D.O. was diagnosed by a family physician with ADHD. A trial of Cylert was initially beneficial, but then benefits seemed to wane. In 10th-grade, because of continued problems with inattentiveness, a brief trial of Ritalin was attempted, with equivocal results.

D.O.'s parents recalled being concerned about him before he entered kindergarten because of his late summer birthday and tendency to bore easily. D.O. was placed in a gifted educational program in fourth and fifth grades but did not perform well and was moved back into a regular educational setting.

In 11th-grade, D.O. was described as disorganized, not completing assignments, inattentive, and scoring poorly academically. D.O. had a group of friends and was not involved in antisocial or substance abuse problems.

D.O.'s parents reported that he had become more withdrawn, less involved with friends, and more resistant at home. School was described as a major area of conflict between D.O. and his parents. Nonetheless, D.O. was described by his parents as loving and kind.

Psychiatric evaluation completed in 1988 yielded a diagnosis of ADHD. A second evaluation completed in 1992 noted ADHD as well as depressive symptoms, including sadness, decreased appetite, loss of interest in pleasurable activities, fatigue, and poor concentration.

Complicating D.O.'s problems was a 15-year-old brother physically bigger and much more accomplished at school than D.O. This brother frequently tormented and intimidated D.O.

Parent responses to the Child Behavior Checklist were consistent with significant problems on the withdrawn, attention problems, and delinquent behavior scales. The Conners Parent hyperkinesis index was above the 98th percentile, reflecting marked problems with failing to finish things, being inattentive, and being easily frustrated in his efforts. Interestingly, D.O. was described as only mildly impulsive and not particularly restless.

Reports from D.O.'s teachers noted mild difficulty with inattentive behavior. However, only one teacher felt that this problem was excessive. Teachers described D.O. as not a behavior problem and frequently overlooked because he did not misbehave or contribute in class.

D.O. was an adolescent of average size and appearance. He drove himself to the evaluation, meeting his parents for the intake session. His affect appeared a bit flat. He did not smile very often. Nonetheless, he was cooperative and completed all tasks presented.

Intellectual assessment placed D.O. in the gifted range, at the 98th percentile. D.O.'s performance on a computerized measure of sustained attention demonstrated a tendency to become more inconsistent as time passed. Numerous indices of impulsive responding were noted. D.O.'s academic skills appeared advanced, although his nonphonetic spelling, rote mathematical knowledge, and written language skills (grammar, punctuation, etc.) appeared in the average range at best. From a personality perspective, D.O. seemed to perceive himself as fairly well functioning. His personality style was consistent with someone who may act impulsively but who is not experiencing any specific emotional problems. Nonetheless, D.O. acknowledged that he was beginning to feel less confident that he could succeed at school and progress successfully to college.

D.O.'s history and current presentation were consistent with a diagnosis of ADHD. Although the assessment was completed during the time of the *DSM-III-R*, retrospective analysis suggests that D.O.'s problems were primarily consistent with the inattentive type of this disorder.

As he matured, D.O. demonstrated significantly fewer problems with overt hyperactivity and impulsivity. It was clear that from an early age, D.O. was often able to use his gifted intellect to compensate in many situations. At the time of assessment, D.O. did not demonstrate enough symptoms for a diagnosis of depression or anxiety. Concern existed, however, about D.O.'s lowered academic self-esteem as well as D.O.'s perception of his family, specifically his relationship with his younger brother, as a source and focus of tension.

D.O.'s parents were given additional information about ADHD in adolescents. They were also referred to a number of resources about facilitating parent and adolescent communication. It was recommended that D.O.'s physician once again consider the use of stimulant medication if D.O. expressed an interest in participating in this form of treatment. An effort was made to ensure that D.O. understood his assets as well as his liabilities. The use of a word processor, calculator, and possibly an academic coach to assist with complex assignments and school problems was recommended. Finally, it was recommended that D.O. participate in short-term counseling, picking specific goals, such as improving his performance in a specific class or his relationships with siblings. D.O.'s personality style was such that he was unlikely to be interested in or willing to participate in long-term counseling, given his perception that if left alone he was capable of working out his own problems without support.

Case 4: ADHD, LD, and Low Self-Esteem

J.N., a 16-year-old 10th-grade male, was referred because of a history of inattention and poor school performance and increasing concerns about social relations and self-esteem. J.N. was the third of his parents' five children. Sibling history was significant for learning and language problems. Family history was significant for ADHD.

J.N.'s medical and developmental history noted recurrent ear infections and placement of pressure equalization tubes. J.N. had a history of lazy eye and suffered from hay fever. J.N. received surgery in second grade to correct his visual problem. For this reason he repeated the second grade. From an early age, J.N. was described as not taking enough time to complete tasks appropriately, struggling with instructions, and showing poor early academic achievement.

J.N. had never received special education assistance despite his struggles with school, and his parents reported he was at least two grade levels behind in basic academic subjects. J.N. had also never received counseling or any kind of medication for attention or emotional problems.

Within the home setting, J.N. was described as being in frequent and escalating conflict with siblings. Socially, he appeared rather isolated, and he had never had a best friend. He spent the majority of his time at home watching television or playing Nintendo. He worked well for short-term but not for long-term rewards. He passed his driver's license examination after a number of failures.

The one shining light in J.N.'s life was his exceptional soccer playing. He played on a competitive team. His coach noted, however, that at times J.N. was inattentive. J.N. had also earned his Eagle Scout badge.

J.N.'s parents noted that he was increasingly hesitant to try new activities that he felt he could not succeed at. He complained of boredom and difficulty finding pleasurable activities. Nonetheless, J.N.'s parents felt they had a positive relationship with him.

Parental questionnaires revealed significant scores on the Child Behavior Checklist for attention, withdrawn, and delinquent problems. On the Conners questionnaire, the hyperkinesis index was above the 98th percentile as a result of J.N.'s restlessness, distractibility, inattention, and inability to finish tasks. Moderate problems were described with excitability and impulsivity.

Assessment at school was completed when J.N. was in eighth grade and failing. Intellectual assessment detected borderline verbal skills but average nonverbal abilities. Educational assessment noted well below average reading, math, and written language skills. Teacher reports at that time consistently described inattentiveness and difficulty completing schoolwork. Nonetheless, no steps were taken at school to provide remedial or compensatory activities.

J.N.'s 10th-grade report card listed a C− average. J.N. was failing one class and receiving D grades in three others. Teacher reports on standardized questionnaires described moderate problems with academic performance, primarily reflecting difficulty in working independently and persisting on and completing tasks and an increased need for the teacher's attention and time. J.N. was not described as significantly disruptive but was noted to be somewhat isolated socially.

J.N. was an adolescent of average appearance. He was seen at two assessment sessions. As the assessment progressed, J.N. appeared to become more fatigued, stressed, and apathetic about what he perceived to be his failure. He was rather distant with the examiner, rarely initiating conversation. His approach to the test tasks was mildly impulsive.

Structured assessment yielded a Wechsler verbal IQ of 76, a performance IQ of 91, and a full-scale IQ of 83. J.N.'s pattern of weak verbal and stronger nonverbal skills was consistent with previous assessment. Verbally, J.N. performed best on tasks requiring rote memory and much weaker on tasks requiring reasoning and judgment. Further assessment of J.N.'s memory, however, reflected very poor rote recall. His performance on a computerized measure of attention and the ability to inhibit impulsive responding was consistent for individuals struggling with attentional skills.

Academic screening noted well below average spelling abilities and reading skills at an early seventh-grade level at best. J.N.'s written language skills were also quite poor.

A qualitative description of J.N.'s academic performance noted retrieval problems and label difficulty (e.g., a/the). These problems were not serious but did affect his accuracy in reading. They did not appear to affect his comprehension as much. He was somewhat better at reading in context than at reading words in isolation. J.N. also tended to juxtapose words as he read, reflecting rote sequential weakness. His visual processing for reading appeared adequate, but J.N. was not an efficient reader. He tended to omit or insert words as well as to miss word endings. He recognized words that he saw but occasionally made errors because of his tendency to predict by context. He did not always fully comprehend what he read, likely due to the effort he needed to expend to decode the material. His visual memory for spelling was weak. His phonic spelling for short words was adequate but for longer words was poor. J.N. struggled to sequence the sounds of multisyllable words. Finally, J.N.'s conceptual knowledge of mathematics was good. Surprisingly, his rote knowledge of number facts was also good.

J.N.'s cognitive and academic test data and history were somewhat difficult to integrate. On measures of intellectual skills, J.N. scored poorest on tasks requiring semantic knowledge and concept formation and performed better on rote tasks such as general information. On the memory battery he scored better on ability to recall meaningful information but worse on rote recall. The overall pattern reflected some type of auditory processing, rote memory, or sequential language disability. Further consultation with a speech language pathologist yielded data consistent with this hypothesis. J.N.'s problems appeared to be exacerbated by a history of inattentive, impulsive behavior.

Although J.N. denied excessive feelings of depression or anxiety, he acknowledged perceiving that other students were able to do things more easily than he could and that other people were happier in their lives. J.N. was rather limited in his responses during the clinical interview. His personality style was that of an adolescent who often felt misunderstood and unappreciated. J.N. seemed to expect criticism and feared condemnation by others. In response, he appeared to be acting more and more defensively and precipitating the reaction he feared and anticipated. J.N. seemed increasingly to expect that things would not work out well for him. He appeared to lack confidence in himself and others. Overall, J.N. was having a more painful early adolescence than others.

Despite the lack of early identification, J.N.'s history and functioning was consistent with a diagnosis of ADHD. Retrospectively, J.N.'s presentation at the time appeared consistent with a *DSM-IV* diagnosis of ADHD-I, although a history of impulsive and at times restless behavior had been reported. Structured testing reflected J.N.'s language-based LD, which affected auditory processing, rote memory, and sequential linguistic skills. These weaknesses resulted in a pattern of poor reading, spelling, and written language abilities. In addition, although J.N.'s presentation and history did not meet the symptomatic cutoff for a mood or anxiety disorder, it was clear that he was struggling to adjust emotionally to the demands of adolescence.

Short-term counseling was recommended as a way to help J.N. begin focusing on his strengths and develop a clear sense of his identity and future goals. Concerns were raised that J.N.'s fragile trust might be easily shaken, resulting in a reluctance to invest in counseling. The importance of building a trusting relationship between J.N. and a counselor was strongly emphasized. It was also recommended that J.N. and his family review with their physician the risks and benefits of a trial of stimulant medication as part of J.N.'s treatment plan. Private academic tutoring was recommended to teach J.N. basic school success skills (e.g., note taking, organization, etc.), as well as to improve his reading decoding accuracy, comprehension, and written language skills. J.N. was urged to use a word processor to complete assignments as often as possible. Additional information about ADHD was given to J.N. and his parents. It was also strongly recommended that J.N. continue playing soccer as this activity was a significant builder of self-esteem. Finally, given J.N.'s history and pattern of test data, careful transition planning was recommended to help J.N. to begin examining future vocational opportunities.

Case 5: ADHD and LD

A.G., a 15-year-old ninth-grade female, demonstrated a history of immature social behavior, developmental delay, poor academic achievement, and complaints of inattentive behavior. Limited information was available concerning A.G.'s biological father. He had never met A.G., but he was reportedly a good student and subsequently became a physician. A.G.'s mother married just after A.G. was born. The marriage lasted eight years. Concerns were raised about A.G.'s having been sexually abused by her stepfather. A.G.'s present adoptive father and mother were married for seven years. Maternal family history was positive for ADHD, anxiety, and LD.

A.G. was reported to have been cyanotic at birth and requiring incubator care. During her first two years of life she experienced multiple medical complications and was frequently hospitalized. A.G.'s pituitary and thyroid glands were reported to be underdeveloped, for which A.G. was receiving a number of medications.

A.G.'s achievement of developmental milestones was always slow. She was retained in kindergarten and received special education services throughout her academic career. In contrast to her slow development, there were no complaints about disruptive behavior. A.G. was reported to relate well to adults but to be extremely immature and to lack insight in interactions with peers, resulting in increased social isolation.

Within the home setting, A.G. was described as impulsive, inattentive, and restless. She did not work well for long-term rewards. Responses to parental questionnaires yielded elevations on the Child Behavior Checklist for the scales of somatic complaints, anxious/depressed, social, thought, and attention problems. A.G.'s Conners Parent hyperkinesis index was above the 98th percentile. Situational problems were noted within both the home and public settings.

A.G. was an attractive, neatly groomed adolescent. A.G.'s conversational skills were limited. She was calm, attentive, and responsive. She appeared to distrust her abilities. Nonetheless, with prompting she was willing to attempt all tasks presented.

Standardized assessment detected weaker nonverbal than verbal abilities and an overall level of intellectual skill in the mildly handicapped range. Nonetheless, A.G. performed within the average range on tasks of verbal reasoning and vocabulary, struggling with comprehension. A review of past records revealed intellectual scores in the borderline range. Academic data placed A.G. in the low average range for rote skills such as word reading but below the 2nd percentile for comprehension and written language. Responses to teachers' questionnaires noted fairly consistent work completion problems in more academically demanding classes, as well as inattentive behavior and social isolation.

Measures of memory skills detected borderline abilities, with near average ability to recall meaningful information but great difficulty in recalling rote, repetitive information. Performance on a computerized measure, even when compared to a lower developmental level, reflected marked problems in sustaining attention and inhibiting impulsive responding.

A.G.'s history and data reflected significant weaknesses in verbal and nonverbal conceptual abilities. A.G. solved problems very inefficiently. She did not appear to learn well across trials or to initiate or develop strategies. She appeared to lack an internal framework to consistently guide her behavior. Conceptual problems revealed her very poor understanding of mathematics. A.G. attempted rote solutions in math when she could recall them but used them without any conceptual insight. Her interpretive comprehension was very poor. She struggled to identify the main point, draw conclusions, and generalize when reading. She did not appear to connect ideas or to put information into hierarchies well.

A.G.'s responses to self-report measures did not suggest marked problems with hopelessness, unhappiness, or helplessness. In contrast, she reported significant feelings of anxiety, including difficulty making up her mind, worrying about herself and others, and believing that she was a nervous person.

A.G.'s personality appeared, not surprisingly, to be marked by strong dependency needs and anxious seeking of attention and reassurance from others, as well as intense fear of separation from those providing support. A.G.'s behavior could be unpredictable, irritable, and pessimistic. Her interpersonal insight appeared limited. This problem resulted in A.G.'s being taken advantage of by a number of friends, as well as potential boyfriends.

A.G.'s overall profile was consistent with some unknown organic etiology for her problems. Oxygen deprivation at birth appeared to be the most plausible explanation, combined with A.G.'s early complicated medical history. From a developmental perspective, A.G. demonstrated at best borderline intellectual skills with fairly significant verbal and nonverbal conceptual weaknesses. As life had become more complex, A.G. appeared to struggle more. The pattern of conceptual weakness with significant visual perceptual difficulties resulted in significant mathematical problems. In contrast, A.G.'s rote reading skills seemed adequate, though her comprehension was limited. Finally, A.G.'s history presented symptoms of inattentiveness, impulsivity, and hyperactivity consistent enough to meet the *DSM-III-R* diagnostic criteria for ADHD.

A trial of stimulant medication resulted in parent and teacher reports of improved behavior. A.G. also began working with a counselor on a regular basis in an effort to gain support and improve her insight. Continued academic support was recommended in order to help A.G. consider a variety of vocations in planning for post–high school training. Finally, A.G.'s parents were given additional insight into her daily functioning and suggestions for communicating, disciplining, and interacting with A.G. effectively.

Case 6: LD and ADHD

S.K., a 27-year-old male, was self-referred because of a reported history of learning and attention problems. S.K. reported having had lifetime difficulty with reading, listening, focusing, following through, and being impulsive. It was his impression that he had developed compensatory strategies and had a stimulating lifestyle. S.K. reported participating in competitive mogul skiing and motorcycle racing. He described numerous head injuries without loss of consciousness or serious repercussions. He felt, however, that he had problems with memory and financial difficulties that were secondary to his attentional problems. S.K. reported five speeding violations over the past three years and two automobile accidents over eight years.

S.K. was currently employed as a sales representative and skiing coach. He graduated from high school with a C average and reported receiving special education services. S.K. denied a family history of psychiatric problems but reported that his grandfather had had ADHD.

S.K.'s responses to adult self-report ADHD questionnaires yielded scores beyond the clinical cutoff. S.K.'s parents completed a number of retrospective questionnaires and described S.K. as a child and adolescent as unable to finish tasks, hyperactive, fidgety, and inattentive. S.K. was also described as having social problems and LD. S.K.'s mother described his childhood learning problems as related to memory and labeling difficulty. As a young child, S.K. was in "perpetual motion" and struggled with early academic achievement. A speech pathologist and family friend described S.K. as a child as presenting with severe word-finding problems, difficulty following multiple commands, problems with reading comprehension, impulsivity, hyperactivity, and inattention. Nonetheless, S.K. had never been treated for ADHD in childhood.

Structured assessment yielded a Wechsler full-scale IQ of 91 (verbal IQ = 83; performance IQ = 106). When compared to individuals of his age and academic history, S.K.'s nonverbal abilities were rated above average and his verbal abilities nearly 1.5 standard deviations below average. This pattern was amplified on the memory battery on which S.K. performed below the 1st percentile verbally but at the 60th percentile nonverbally. Further, S.K.'s fund of verbal and nonverbal information was poor, not surprising given his academic struggles. Neuropsychological screening also revealed problems with reasoning, judgment, and concept formation. Academic assessment reflected low average basic academic skills, with spelling at well below 1st-percentile ability.

The pattern of S.K.'s errors when reading and spelling reflected basic weaknesses in perceiving and recognizing phonemic sounds of language. S.K. spelled *enter* as *intire*, *material* as *miteral*, and *recognize* as *recagnise*. When reading, he used a sight word approach. Analysis of mathematical errors revealed that S.K. did not know basic mathematical facts.

From a personality perspective, S.K. had an easygoing and nonconforming style. He appeared to seek challenges and risks with a tendency toward exhibitionist and contentious behavior. S.K. seemed to be an individual seeking praise and attention and easily bored. Underlying S.K.'s basic personality appeared to be a very strong, competitive, and power-oriented attitude, an air of self-assurance, and a sometimes careless indifference to the feelings of others.

S.K.'s history and presentation met the diagnostic profile for ADHD-I. Although somewhat impulsive, S.K.'s presentation did not meet six of the nine criteria necessary for the hyperactive-impulsive component of this diagnosis. S.K.'s history also reflected a lifetime pattern of developmental impairments comprising of weak verbal abilities and above average nonverbal skills. The data were consistent with severe verbal memory problems and rote verbal LD.

It was recommended that a psychiatric consultation be considered to evaluate the potential risks and benefits of psychotropic medication as part of S.K.'s treatment plan. S.K. was given additional resources about ADHD in adulthood. Although S.K. might have benefited from short-term counseling, he made it very clear during the assessment that he was interested in diagnosis but not necessarily in treatment.

Case 7: ADHD and LD

J.H., a 43-year-old male, was self-referred because of complaints of short-term memory problems and inattention. J.H. denied significant childhood problems but reported that his academic performance at school had been unacceptable. He recalled being left back one year in elementary school. He also described being picked on by others.

J.H. had never married. Immediate family history was positive for ADHD in a sibling and in his father. J.H. had completed a four-year college degree. He recalled being bored at school. He graduated with a B− grade point average. He was employed in sales for a number of years, then as a bus driver, and at the time of assessment in telephone mutual-fund sales.

J.H. denied a history of substance abuse or previous psychiatric treatment. He reported receiving four or five traffic citations for moving violations over the past 10 years. He also reported five automobile accidents.

J.H.'s responses to the Brown questionnaire yielded a score above the clinical cutoff. J.H. acknowledged problems with paying attention, initiating activities, tracking when reading, remembering certain kinds of information easily, procrastinating, and being easily distracted. In contrast, J.H.'s responses to the Wender questionnaire yielded a score below the clinical cutoff because J.H. denied problems with restlessness, irritability, or stress. J.H.'s parents reported that as a child J.H. was easily distracted, did not follow instructions, and had difficulty sustaining attention. Their responses were very consistent with the *DSM-III-R* description of ADHD.

J.H. was an adult of average size and appearance. During the interview he was very pleasant. During structured testing he showed signs of increasing stress and anxiety. His thoughts appeared logical, focused, and relevant.

Assessment yielded average intellectual scores for a college graduate male of J.H.'s age. Nonetheless, a significant degree of subtest scatter was noted; J.H. experienced marked problems on simple rote measures requiring sustained attention but performed well above average on measures of general information, vocabulary, verbal reasoning, and comprehension. Administration of a memory battery detected 7th-percentile verbal memory skills but 66th-percentile nonverbal memory skills. Despite an exceptionally good fund of verbal information and knowledge, J.H. struggled to process, recall, and, over the short term, retain meaningful and non-meaningful verbal information. These test data appeared to confirm J.H.'s lifetime complaints of short-term memory difficulty. Brief academic screening yielded above average reading but below average spelling and arithmetic performance, primarily due to rote rather than conceptual errors.

J.H. had no significant complaints of depression or anxiety. His personality was that of someone concerned with public appearance, wanting to be seen by others as composed, virtuous, and conventional. Such individuals often downplay distressing problems in their lives.

Although requested, J.H.'s school transcripts were never provided. J.H. also declined to participate in further assessment. Based on the data generated, J.H. appeared to have struggled from an early age with a rote LD that continued to plague him through college and in vocational endeavors. Further discussion with J.H. revealed that he had moved from sales to bus driving because of missed promotions resulting from his poor memory. J.H. seemed to have been able to use his good intellectual skills to compensate for his rote memory problems, but he continued to be painfully aware of his difficulties. Further, J.H.'s history and current presentation appeared consistent with the *DSM-IV* categorization of ADHD-I.

J.H. reported that a brief trial of stimulant medication produced improved memory and attention at work. A number of texts about ADHD, as well as texts to assist with organization and memory, were recommended. Finally, as J.H. was preparing to take a number of examinations to progress in his current vocation, short-term consultation with an educational therapist was recommended in order to provide J.H. with additional study skills and memory strategies.

Case 8: ADHD and LD

S.C., an almost 17-year-old male 11th-grader, had a history of inattentiveness, poor school performance, and a reported period of depression. S.C. was adopted by his physician father and mother. No information was available about his biological family. S.C.'s older adopted sister had struggled with chronic depression.

From an early age, S.C. was hyperactive and inattentive. He had a childhood history of chronic headaches of unknown etiology. Stimulant medication was initiated in first grade with reported benefits but also side effects, including increased headache. Stimulants had been attempted intermittently throughout S.C.'s child and adolescent years.

S.C.'s parents reported that as he reached adolescence he became markedly less hyperactive and impulsive but was still inattentive. Despite his performance problems at school he was described as an average student. In junior high school he struggled socially and was ostracized by a small group of disruptive males. S.C.'s parents felt that he had never recovered socially or emotionally from that experience, and in high school he continued to be extremely isolated socially. S.C.'s parents noted during the previous six months an increase in withdrawn, apathetic, and seemingly unhappy behavior.

A year prior to the assessment, S.C. was diagnosed with depression by a local psychologist. Short-term therapy appeared to yield some immediate benefits, but S.C. was not interested in continuing counseling. During this series of counseling sessions, S.C. raised concerns about possible homosexuality but decided that this was something he feared rather than something he felt.

Questionnaires completed by S.C.'s parents noted significant scale elevations on the Child

Behavior Checklist for somatic complaints, social problems, anxious/depressed, and attention problems. On the hyperkinesis index of the Conners, S.C. was above the 98th percentile. He was described as at times argumentative with family members but in general socially isolated. Responses by S.C., as well as by his parents, to the Brown questionnaire yielded scores above the clinical cutoff suggestive of problems with inattention.

Standardized questionnaires completed by S.C.'s teachers noted his social isolation and difficulty completing schoolwork but no other disruptive or withdrawn complaints. Teachers noted that S.C. appeared polite and insightful and that he was not a discipline problem. A review of past group achievement tests noted S.C.'s very weak spelling and math computation scores together with above average vocabulary, listening comprehension, and language scores.

S.C. was a slightly overweight adolescent wearing loose-fitting clothing. He was pleasant, and he warmed up quickly during the two evaluative sessions. He appeared to distrust his abilities while working and made frequent negative self-statements.

Intellectually, S.C. performed on the Wechsler with a verbal IQ of 95, a performance IQ of 125, and a full-scale IQ of 106. S.C.'s nonverbal skills were markedly better than his verbal abilities. He struggled on tasks that required sustained and divided attention. A brief memory battery detected very good logical memory skills and weaker rote memory skills. S.C.'s reproduction and spontaneous recall of a complex figure was in the 95th percentile, reflecting his exceptional perceptual abilities. Performance on a computerized battery did not reflect problems in sustaining attention or managing impulses.

S.C.'s self-report did not reflect significant complaints of anxiety or depression. S.C. noted, however, that he felt other people were happier than he was. He was open and introspective during the clinical interview. His personality was that of an adolescent who tended to be too self-critical and self-deprecating. S.C. appeared to have a long history of social awkwardness and hesitation in dealing with others. Further interviews reflected S.C.'s somewhat obsessive worries about his social deficits and academic failures. His personality style was such that he rarely acted out or displayed resentment. He had adopted a strategy of fading into the social background, assuming a passive role. As a consequence, S.C. had become more and more peripheral in social interactions, drifting further into a detached, ineffective life pattern. On a positive note, although S.C. described social interactions as painful, he clearly reported a desire to improve his social life, and he appeared to be a sensitive empathetic person willing to help others in need.

S.C.'s early history and current symptoms appeared consistent with the *DSM-III-R* diagnosis of ADHD. The constellation of symptoms was consistent with the *DSM-IV* categorization ADHD-I. From a cognitive perspective, S.C. demonstrated exceptional nonverbal, or right-hemisphere, skills and average verbal abilities. The overall pattern appeared to reflect mild rote LD with academic achievement further impaired by S.C.'s inattentiveness and declining effort and participation in school. S.C.'s emotional history and current data revealed problems on the depression dimension, with a categorical *DSM-III-R* diagnosis consistent with mild dysthymia and increasing social avoidance.

A course of psychotherapy was initiated with S.C., initially providing a high level of sympathy and understanding and patiently working to develop a trusting relationship. With support, S.C.'s attitude and affect improved. His willingness to take social risks increased, and he slowly developed a social network. His participation in school improved as well. By his choice, S.C. decided to delay the initiation of any type of psychotropic medication. S.C., with his therapist, began exploring post–high school vocational and academic options.

Case 9: ADHD and Right-Hemisphere Disorder

S.F., an almost 19-year-old high school graduate male, had a history of inconsistent school performance and social isolation. S.F.'s fraternal twin had a history of ADHD but was academically competent. S.F.'s family history was positive for LD and depression. S.F.'s medical history was unremarkable, although he had received pressure equalization tubes twice at a young age and had suffered from a number of allergies. He had been nocturnally enuretic through seven years of age. At 13 and 17 years of age, brief trials of antidepressants were attempted with little reported benefit.

S.F. had a history of awkward fine and large motor skills, delayed motor skill development, and poor handwriting. S.F. was reported to have achieved well in reading and spelling but to have struggled with mathematical skills from a young age. He received special education services periodically throughout his academic career. He required support through high school but was able to graduate. He earned marginal grades during one semester in a community college. S.F. decided to join the workforce full time temporarily and was employed as a checker at a large department store.

S.F.'s parents described him as having poor judgment and not working well for rewards. Nonetheless, he was not described as having behavior or disruptive problems growing up. S.F.'s parents noted that he had always been somewhat isolated socially. Their responses to the Child Behavior Checklist yielded scores in the clinically significant range for social, attention, and anxious/depression scales. On the Conners questionnaire, S.F. obtained a hyperkinesis index above the 98th percentile. He was reported as able to initiate social interaction but as rather isolated in general. He had two childhood friends with whom he had maintained a reasonably close relationship. S.F.'s and his parents' responses to the Brown questionnaire yielded scores above the clinical cutoff range suggestive of inattentiveness.

At age 14, an in-depth psychoeducational evaluation had been completed. S.F. obtained a Wechsler verbal IQ of 114, a performance IQ of 98, and a full-scale IQ of 107. S.F.'s verbal skills, including fund of information, reasoning, and vocabulary, appeared well above average. On the Woodcock-Johnson Psycho-Educational Battery, cognitive cluster, S.F.'s verbal abilities were scored at the 99th percentile with visual perceptual scores below the 20th percentile. Academically, S.F. at the time scored at the 99th percentile for reading but at the 54th percentile for mathematics. A diagnosis of LD related to organizational and visual-motor skills was made.

A review of S.F.'s academic file noted group achievement test scores consistently above average in reading but below average in mathematics. ACT testing (college entrance), completed two years before, measured 73rd-percentile reading skills, 60th-percentile English skills, and 10th-percentile mathematical skills in comparison to college-bound high school students.

S.F. was a soft-spoken young adult of average size and appearance. He related well to the examiner and was cooperative and responsive. Brief neuropsychological screening with S.F. indicated clear and consistent right-hemisphere problems related to rote and conceptual nonverbal skills. S.F.'s performance on a computerized attention battery revealed difficulty with perceptual sensitivity, mild impulsiveness, and difficulty in sustaining attention.

During the interview S.F. was quite open and responsive with the examiner. He described his limited social life and while discussing dating noted that it was often difficult for him to understand "what girls like." He spoke fairly introspectively and was clearly frustrated by his academic and social problems. He reported enjoying his current job but felt that it was not something he could make into a career.

S.F.'s personality appeared characteristic of individuals with right-hemisphere weakness. He was self-critical and self-deprecating. S.F. was rather apprehensive, socially oversensitive, awkward, shy, hesitant, and uncomfortable when interacting with others. S.F. appeared to be rather sad and reported recurrent anxieties about school and work. A pervasive disharmony of mood appeared increasingly to characterize his daily functioning. Concerned with social rebuff, S.F. was unlikely to act out or become openly resentful. He appeared to lack initiative and competitiveness and struggled to achieve the level of autonomous behavior required for adolescents entering adulthood. He perceived himself as rather weak, fragile, and ineffective. Not surprisingly, given his excellent verbal intellect, S.F. reported feeling confused and uncertain about his life direction, believing that others had a much clearer sense of their identity and goals. On the positive side, S.F. presented as gentle and compassionate, accepting others regardless of their frailties or vulnerabilities and willing to provide help and support when needed. He viewed his family as a support and a resource.

S.F.'s cognitive, academic, and emotional presentation was consistent with right-hemisphere weakness. Individuals with this condition struggle with social interaction in nondisruptive ways and end up being neglected. They struggle to read and interpret social cues effectively, demonstrate a passive pattern of inattentive, disorganized behavior, and are prone to emotionally distressing rather than disruptive behavioral symptoms. S.F. also demonstrated the visual perceptual and relative mathematical weakness consistent with nonverbal, or right-hemisphere, LD.

From a categorical perspective, S.F.'s history was consistent with the *DSM-IV* diagnosis of ADHD-I. In addition, his emotional functioning was consistent with a diagnosis of dysthymia and increasing adjustment problems reflecting mixed emotional features. The *DSM-III-R* categorization of identity disorder in adolescence also appeared to fit S.F.'s current life situation.

S.F. and his parents were given additional insight into and information about S.F.'s disabilities and how the disabilities had affected his past history and current life functioning. Psychotherapy was initiated in an effort to help S.F. begin to focus on his assets and thus develop a more effective set of coping skills. Because S.F. hesitated to make what might be considered a fuss over his problems, fearing that a therapist might be angry or rejecting if he complained too bitterly, initial progress in therapy was slow though clearly positive. S.F. was also referred for a psychiatric consultation because he had decided to consider the potential benefits of medication as part of a treatment plan. S.F. planned to continue working for the present and considered applying for supportive services for learning-disabled students as he prepared to reenter college.

Case 10: ADHD, Multiple Sclerosis, and Generalized Anxiety

R.B., a 46-year-old male college graduate, was self-referred because of growing difficulty with memory, attention, and stress. At age 34 R.B. had been diagnosed with multiple sclerosis. He expressed concern that over the past few years he had been having worsening problems with memory, resulting in a demotion at work from supervisor to computer data entry technician.

R.B. recalled a childhood history suggestive of ADHD. He described engaging in high-risk behavior, being in multiple accidents, and displaying inattentiveness. He recalled obtaining B grades in high school, nonetheless, completing an associate's degree and finally a four-year degree with a B average. His recent agreed-upon demotion at work resulted from his inability to master the skills necessary to supervise others on a new computer system.

R.B. recalled multiple accidents as a child, including being buried in a cave-in at 11 years of age and nearly dying from lack of oxygen. He reported being legally blind in his left eye and having a history of mild hearing loss secondary to the multiple sclerosis. R.B. denied an extended family history of psychiatric problems but noted that an uncle committed suicide for unknown reasons.

R.B. and his first wife were married for 23 years. Their five children had all done fairly well at school. He noted that one child had possibly had a history of ADHD.

Symptomatically, R.B. described having occasional migraines, ringing in his ears, and difficulty with short-term and immediate memory. These symptoms caused him many daily problems at work and at home. Responses to the Brown questionnaire by R.B. and his wife yielded scores above the clinical cutoff, suggestive of problems with inattentiveness in adulthood. R.B. and his wife noted his difficulty in sustaining activities, tendency to leave things unfinished, and increasing difficulty in initiating activities. It must be noted, however, that on this questionnaire both R.B. and his wife's scores were extremely high, strongly suggesting compounding psychiatric problems contributing to R.B.'s attention difficulties. On retrospective questionnaires, R.B.'s mother recalled that as a child he was impulsive, inattentive, and rather hyperactive.

R.B. was a moderately obese individual of otherwise normal appearance. He appeared to be mildly dysnomic and had difficulty following instructions during structured testing. During testing he demonstrated a moderate degree of performance anxiety, at one point reporting that he felt overwhelmed. He appeared to distrust his abilities. It was clear that he struggled to sequence, detail, and reason.

Extended neuropsychological assessment yielded intellectual scores in the low average range for individuals of R.B.'s demographic background. His greatest problems involved more complex abstract tasks such as the Comprehension and Similarities subtests of the Wechsler. Intratest scatter on all tasks appeared to reflect potentially better or previously better functioning. R.B. performed best on simple rote tasks. His nonverbal memory skills appeared to be stronger than his verbal memory skills overall. R.B. obtained a standard score equivalent to the 87th percentile on the Peabody Picture Vocabulary Test, strongly suggestive of better intellectual functioning in the past. General academic assessment reflected above average academic skills, with mathematical skills at the 84th percentile and word reading skills at the 77th percentile. R.B.'s self-report on the Beck was consistent with mild depression. He appeared to be experiencing a prolonged period of futility and dejection.

R.B.'s personality appeared to be characterized by anxious dependency, the persistent seeking of reassurance from others, and the expectation that things were likely to get worse. R.B. appeared to be an individual using guilt and self-condemnation as means of coping with stress. His sense of helplessness appeared to be strong. Increasingly, however, R.B. appeared to be turning to anger and resentment about his life situation as ways of dealing with his emotional distress.

R.B.'s history and presentation produced enough data to be consistent with the *DSM-III-R* diagnosis of ADHD. However, R.B.'s problems with inattentiveness appeared to be compounded by emotional and cognitive difficulties. R.B. demonstrated difficulty simultaneously processing multiple sources of information, a slow speed of information processing, and intermittent problems with reasoning. These problems appeared to be exacerbated in part by R.B.'s anxious, hesitant response. These types of frontal lobe cognitive weaknesses were uncharacteristic, given R.B.'s history. R.B.'s difficulty tracking the ebb and flow of changing environmental or nonverbal stimuli, his difficulty tracking efficiently through instructions, and his previously mentioned difficulties appeared consistent with a small population of multiple sclerosis patients. In the majority of multiple sclerosis cases, physical symptoms manifest themselves long before cognitive or behavioral symptoms. However, when cognitive symptoms are manifested they often present as low cognitive efficiency and difficulty with frontal lobe functions, including abstraction, concept formation, judgment, mental speed, and, for some individuals, concentration.

Finally, from an emotional perspective it was not surprising that R.B. was experiencing increasing unhappiness and stress, given his disease, current life situation, and forced vocational change.

Based on the assessment data, R.B.'s physician initiated a trial of stimulant medication. R.B. reported marked benefits at work. R.B. and his wife noted marked improvements in his daily functioning at home as well. R.B. was referred for short-term counseling so that he could learn stress management skills. Based on what he perceived as a discriminatory change in his vocational status due to his disease, R.B. also initiated arbitration with his employer.

Case 11: ADHD, Anxiety, and Dysthymia

G.H., a 47-year-old male, was self-referred because of concerns about ADHD. G.H. reported childhood symptoms of inattentiveness and difficulty with concentration. He noted that he had difficulty learning, forgot things, and had problems with organization and setting priorities.

G.H. graduated from high school with a C average and received a bachelor's degree in botany with a C+ average. G.H. recalled school as being very difficult. G.H. had worked for a number of years as a civilian employee of the air force.

G.H. denied a family history of psychiatric problems. He noted, however, that as a child he angered easily and had engaged in antisocial behavior, including shooting out streetlights. G.H. recalled adolescence as particularly painful.

He reported a history of frequent motor accidents, including a spinal injury at age 35 that required two surgeries. G.H. also noted head injuries from previous motorcycle accidents, falls from trees as a child, and parachute jumping in the military. G.H. reported receiving approximately 10 traffic citations for moving violations and having been in three automobile accidents.

G.H.'s psychiatric history revealed a diagnosis of depression a number of years earlier and a trial of Prozac. He reported that the medication had seemed to be beneficial, but for reasons that were unclear he did not follow through with medication treatment.

G.H. and his first wife had been married for seven years. They had two children. The eldest, four years of age, had been recently diagnosed with ADHD. G.H. noted that interacting daily with the children was extremely stressful.

G.H.'s responses to self-report instruments were much higher than the clinical cutoff suggestive of ADHD. The overall pattern appeared to indicate symptoms of inattentiveness, compounded with problems with stress, anxiety, and depression. G.H.'s wife described her husband as being forgetful in daily activities and as having problems with organization, following instructions, and being inattentive. Nonetheless, she described these problems as being much less severe than her husband did. G.H.'s mother on retrospective questionnaires noted that G.H. had had difficulty concentrating and was impulsive and hyperactive as a child. Although G.H. reported symptoms of unhappiness, his responses to the Beck Depression Inventory did not cross into the clinically significant range.

Brief cognitive screening placed G.H. in the average range intellectually. Basic academic skills also appeared in the average range. There were no indices of specific LD.

By history and symptom presentation, G.H. clearly met the criteria for a diagnosis of ADHD. Further interviews with G.H. revealed fairly strong feelings of inadequacy, hypersensitivity to criticism, and a pattern of social inhibition. G.H.'s wife later noted that he had become more isolated from family members, choosing to not participate in family activities. G.H.'s presentation and profile, as well as his responses to personality instruments, revealed symptoms consistent with long-standing dysthymia, anxiety, and possibly the entrance into a major depressive episode.

G.H.'s physician reinitiated a trial of Prozac, which G.H. found beneficial. Supportive psychotherapy was strongly recommended and undertaken. G.H. and his wife were given additional information about ADHD.

Case 12: ADHD, LD, and Anxiety

S.T., a 15-year-old ninth-grader, was referred because of a history of inattentiveness, impulsive behavior, and poor school performance. S.T. was the youngest of his family's five children. An older sibling had experienced LD. Otherwise, there did not appear to be any extended family history of emotional or disruptive behavioral problems. S.T.'s parents were both college graduates.

S.T. had appeared to be cyanotic at birth. He was jaundiced and a number of congenital heart defects were diagnosed. These were corrected at 25 months of age. S.T.'s developmental history was unremarkable. His medical history revealed unilateral migraine occurring in clusters every few months. S.T. was also reported to be somewhat anxious and overconcerned about his health, especially his heart.

S.T.'s coordination was described as average; however, he was described as poor in athletics. His handwriting was also described as poor. S.T.'s parents recalled a pattern of his beginning each school year adequately but slowly and steadily falling behind. In 10th-grade S.T. was struggling consistently to complete schoolwork.

Socially, S.T. was somewhat isolated, without a best friend or a consistent group of friends. Within the home setting he was described as fidgety, easily distracted, inattentive, easily frustrated, and experiencing difficulty with self-control. S.T. was described as somewhat oppositional and strong-willed. He boasted, lied, and embellished, which alienated others.

Parental questionnaires noted S.T.'s problems on the Child Behavior Checklist, including those related to anxiety, depression, social difficulty, inattentiveness, and disruptive behavior. S.T. had experimented with tobacco and alcohol. He had run away from home once. He enjoyed making small fires with a lighter. Parent responses to the Conners questionnaire placed S.T. above the 98th percentile on the hyperkinesis index. A variety of situational problems were described.

In general, S.T.'s teachers described him as inattentive, impulsive, and hyperactive. He was noted as having difficulty following instructions and persisting on task. Teacher responses to the Comprehensive Teacher's Rating Scale placed S.T. below the 10th percentile in almost all classes for attention span and hyperactivity. Nonetheless, none of the teachers described S.T. as purposely disruptive. All noted his difficulty completing schoolwork.

A review of S.T.'s group academic testing revealed 80th-percentile overall academic skills in ninth grade, with 88th-percentile reading, 42nd-percentile spelling, and 39th-percentile mathematical skills. S.T.'s social studies score was at the 82nd percentile, and his science score at the 92nd percentile.

Individual academic testing completed with S.T. the same year detected above average reading comprehension, average mathematical skills, and slightly below average spelling and written language skills. A WISC-R was completed when S.T. was 14 and a half years of age and yielded a verbal IQ of 123, a performance IQ of 106, and a full-scale IQ of 116.

In general, S.T. was calm and pleasant during the assessment. His thoughts appeared logical and focused. He related well to the examiner. No odd mannerisms were noted.

A readministration of the Wechsler yielded a full-scale IQ of 113. The quality of S.T.'s responses suggested even better intellectual potential. Further, S.T. performed at the 96th percentile on the Peabody Picture Vocabulary Test. Measures of verbal memory detected excellent conceptual and general memory and weaker rote memory skills.

A screening of S.T.'s academic abilities measured average spelling and mathematical skills and above average word reading and comprehension skills. S.T.'s written story was characterized by good themes and ideas but poor organization.

The preponderance of the data reflected S.T.'s exceptionally good conceptual verbal and nonverbal abilities. His mathematical achievement appeared to be impaired by his weakness in abstract nonverbal reasoning, compounded with his impulsive lack of attention to detail. In combination with spelling and written language weaknesses, the data appeared to reflect a mild rote memory difficulty exacerbated by S.T.'s inattentiveness.

S.T.'s responses to self-report measures placed him at the 87th percentile on the Reynolds Adolescent Depression Scale and the 83rd percentile on the Revised Children's Manifest Anxiety Scale. S.T. reported having more helpless, unhappy, and anxious thoughts than others. His personality appeared to reflect an adolescent excessively self-deprecating, vulnerable, and defenseless. During the interview, S.T. reported feeling misunderstood, unappreciated, and demeaned by others. He had learned to be on guard against ridicule. He seemed to find within himself few of the attributes that he admired in others. When compared to the standardization sample, his responses to the Millon Adolescent Personality Inventory reflected his strong feelings of confusion and identity difficulty. He described his family as a source of tension and conflict.

Diagnostically, S.T. demonstrated a history of high average to likely superior intellectual skills. His history and current functioning were consistent with a diagnosis of ADHD-C. Further, despite being exceptionally bright, S.T. demonstrated slight conceptual weaknesses with abstract nonverbal reasoning and rote memory that appeared to affect his spelling, mathematical, and written language skills. From an emotional perspective, S.T. demonstrated symptoms consistent with anxiety and the possible onset of a major depressive disorder.

S.T. was referred for psychiatric consultation in order to evaluate the potential benefits of psychotropic medication as part of his treatment plan. Short-term counseling was recommended as a way to help S.T. focus on his positive traits and deal in a more effective way with his anxious, helpless thoughts. S.T. and his family were given additional information about ADHD and LD and were taught strategies to improve communication and problem solving at home. Finally, it was recommended that S.T. work with an academic coach to improve his study and organizational skills. S.T.'s school counselor was also apprised of his intellectual strengths and mild learning problems so that the counselor could better help S.T. over the coming years in planning for post–high school education or vocational experiences.

Case 13: ADHD, LD, and Adjustment Problems

S.J., a nearly 18-year-old male, was referred because of a history of disruptive behavior and poor school performance. S.J. dropped out of school in 10th grade but was currently completing a general equivalency degree (GED).

He was the eldest of his parents' two children. His younger, 14-year-old brother did not have a history of behavioral or developmental problems. S.J.'s parents were college graduates. There was a family history of alcoholism, ADHD, and the suicide of a grandparent.

S.J.'s developmental milestones were reached without difficulty. His medical history was unremarkable. School problems were first observed in second grade when S.J. appeared to begin struggling. He began receiving special education services. By 10th grade, S.J. was skipping school and flunking classes.

S.J. had a small group of friends and was dating. His parents noted a long history of inattentive, impulsive behavior. S.J. was charged at age 16 as a minor in possession of alcohol and, on turning age 17, with forging his parents' checks. He was later placed in a detention center for 14 days for probation violation. His treatment history also included residential rehabilitation in an alcohol and drug abuse facility. S.J.'s accomplishments included being an all-star baseball player for four years and hunting with his father on a regular basis.

Parental responses to standardized questionnaires reflected problems with anxiety, depression, inattention, and delinquent behavior. The Conners Parent hyperkinesis index placed S.J. at above the 98th percentile. Although S.J.'s parents described him as sensitive, they also noted that he could be quite manipulative.

Group achievement tests completed when S.J. was in 10th grade measured 21st-percentile reading skills, 32nd-percentile language skills, 19th-percentile mathematical skills, and a total battery at the 23rd percentile.

S.J. was a casually dressed, handsome adolescent. He was passively cooperative but did not appear particularly motivated during structured testing.

S.J. obtained a full-scale IQ of 86, a performance IQ of 87, and a verbal IQ of 86 on the Wechsler. Within verbal areas, S.J.'s pattern of scores was consistent with complex language processing problems. Weaknesses were noted with conceptual reasoning, verbal comprehension, and factual information. Relative strengths were noted in rote skills. S.J. performed at the 32nd percentile on the Peabody Picture Vocabulary Test and the 27th percentile on the Test of Nonverbal Intelligence. On the memory battery, he performed at the 4th percentile overall, with low average nonverbal memory skills and below 1st-percentile verbal memory. S.J. struggled to learn and recall both simple and complex verbal information.

Academic screening placed S.J. in the average range, with slightly weaker spelling skills. His reading for accuracy was quite good, but his comprehension was barely at the fifth-grade level. The preponderance of the data indicated that S.J. had problems processing and dealing with conceptual and abstract information. It was not surprising that his academic problems grew as the demands of high school increased.

S.J.'s responses to self-report attention measures yielded a score above the clinically significant cutoff for the Brown questionnaire but below the cutoff for the Wender questionnaire. Although S.J. acknowledged symptoms of inattention and difficulty initiating activities, he denied stress-related problems. S.J.'s responses to the anxiety and depression questionnaires yielded scores above the 90th percentile. S.J. reported becoming anxious easily, worrying, and perceiving that life was unfair.

The data and personality measures reflected a late adolescent with an immediate history of moody, impulsive, and unpredictable behavior. S.J. appeared to feel misunderstood and unappreciated. Thus, he was easily offended by minor trifles and quickly provoked into angry, resentful outbursts. S.J. appeared to lack confidence in others and reported being disappointed in the responses he received. His view of himself suggested a rather aimless, undirected existence. His family was described as a source of tension and conflict. S.J.'s responses to the Millon were consistent with those of adolescents with repeated problems as the result of impulsive behavior.

Although there was no doubt that S.J. demonstrated symptoms related to ADHD, his overall profile appeared to be compounded by a long-standing pattern of language-based LD that affected his reasoning and concept formation. Although S.J.'s rote academic skills (e.g., word reading) appeared adequate, his reading comprehension was quite limited. His overall behavioral profile at the time of assessment was consistent with a *DSM-IV* diagnosis of a chronic adjustment disorder with mixed disturbance of emotions and conduct. There was also not doubt that S.J. demonstrated symptoms of oppositional defiance and at least two symptoms in the past year consistent with conduct disorder.

S.J. was directed to the vocational rehabilitation program in his community. Further language assessment was recommended as part of the overall vocational evaluation. S.J. and his parents were given additional information about ADHD and LD in late adolescence and adulthood. S.J. was also urged to consider counseling to help him learn strategies to manage his anger, impulsivity, and frustration. Finally, given S.J.'s endorsement of ADHD, anxious, and depressive symptoms, psychiatric consultation was suggested in order to obtain further diagnostic opinion about the potential benefits of medication treatment.

Case 14: ADHD, Past Substance Abuse, and Obsessive/Compulsive Personality

R.J., a 43-year-old male with two years of college experience, was referred by his neurologist. R.J. was employed as a silver refinery operator. R.J. sought a medical consultation because of what he described as dissociative-like experiences beginning at age 11. R.J. described these as "the unusual sensation that he is watching a movie and that his life is not real."

R.J. reported a childhood history of inattention, overactivity, and LD. R.J.'s father committed suicide after learning he had cancer. His mother died as the result of AIDS contracted from a blood transfusion. R.J.'s four siblings had not experienced similar developmental or emotional problems.

R.J.'s life history was complex. At the time of assessment he had been divorced for seven and a half years; his wife had declared her lesbianism and gone to live with a girlfriend. R.J.'s two daughters were in their late teens. Both had dropped out of school and were working. Neither had experienced behavioral or developmental problems.

R.J. had to consciously think about every action no matter how trivial. He related this to a machine in which every movement has to be directed and controlled. He noted that he could cover up his problems well and that most people were not aware of how hard he had to think before acting. He reported mild obsessive behaviors involving repeated checking, explaining "I have to be sure." He also reported experiencing no emotions.

R.J. had immigrated to the United States 15 years before the assessment. He worked for a number of companies producing metal products throughout his vocational history. He had never been reprimanded or discharged from work.

R.J. reported that his alcohol problems started because of his attempts to treat his feelings of disassociation. R.J. reported he had not drank in the past five years.

Symptomatically, R.J. described a wide range of difficulties involving numbness in his limbs; problems with memory, dizziness, and ringing in his ears; difficulty with attention and concentration; and, at times, problems completing daily activities. R.J.'s responses to self-report attention questionnaires yielded scores well above the clinical cutoff, reflecting not only problems with inattentiveness but also problems with stress and general inefficiency in daily living. R.J.'s responses to the Beck Depression Inventory yielded a score below the clinical cutoff for mild depression.

R.J. was an average-appearing adult. He was soft spoken and mildly dysnomic. No excessive signs of anxiety were observed. Although English was R.J.'s second language he reported speaking fluent English since childhood.

R.J. completed the Wechsler with average scores. His fund of information and rote verbal memory tested weakest; on measures of higher order thinking (Similarities subtest) he scored well above average. R.J.'s performance on the memory battery was also average. Screening of R.J.'s academic skills revealed above average word reading and comprehension but low average spelling and arithmetic. His performance on arithmetic problems reflected lack of conceptual knowledge and errors in attention to detail.

R.J.'s responses to personality measures reflected an individual with a well-established need for social approval, self-condemnation, and a general naïveté about psychological matters, including deficits in insight. R.J.'s personality style was that of someone inclined to blame himself, to deny strong feelings, and to fear that expressing emotion might lead to a loss of emotional control. The overall profile, however, did not appear consistent with that of an individual struggling with true dissociative problems.

R.J.'s history and current symptomatic complaints met the diagnostic criteria for ADHD. Questions existed, however, about the complication of these symptoms as the result of what appeared to be a long-standing pattern of dysthymia and generalized anxiety. Further, R.J.'s behavior appeared consistent with an obsessive/compulsive personality.

During a brief trial of low-dose stimulant medication R.J. reported feeling better and his complaints of disassociation lessened. R.J. was provided with reading materials about adult ADHD and was taught strategies to manage anxiety. Although counseling was strongly recommended, R.J. chose to not participate further.

Case 15: LD, Borderline IQ, Somatization, Borderline Personality, and ADHD

C.B., a 26-year-old unemployed male, was self-referred because of long-standing complaints of LD, temper outbursts, and attention problems. C.B. was currently unemployed.

By correspondence, C.B.'s mother recalled that C.B. was developmentally delayed from a very early age. It was suspected that C.B. may have experienced brain damage due to birth trauma. C.B. received special education services throughout his school career. He was teased and socially isolated. C.B.'s mother recalled that he was inattentive, impulsive, and hyperactive as a child.

On graduating from high school, C.B. was employed in a number of positions part time and attempted to attend college. He was frequently fired from jobs because of his absence or tardiness. He tried and failed four different courses of study.

C.B.'s physician reported that over the past 10 years C.B. had made frequent visits as the result of diffuse, undefinable physical complaints. These included difficulty with various aches and pains, dizziness, sexual problems, and rectal bleeding.

C.B. was married to his first wife for approximately one year. Their marriage appeared to have been extremely stressful and conflicted. They had separated for a number of weeks and recently reconciled. One reason for their separation was C.B.'s use of a phone sex line several times each day over the past five to six months, resulting in phone bills of $400–$500 per month. Further, C.B. had recently met another woman at a multiple marketing conference. They had started speaking by phone every day.

C.B. reported five speeding tickets and several car accidents. He denied any history of substance abuse.

C.B.'s responses to self-report attention measures yielded a score just above the clinical cutoff on the Brown questionnaire due to complaints of procrastination, inattentiveness, and difficulty with memory and organization. On the Wender, C.B.'s scores were low because his complaints of irritability, restlessness, or stress intolerance were minimal.

Questionnaires completed by C.B.'s parents described a childhood characterized by hyperactivity, inattention, and impulsivity. The spousal checklist described C.B.'s problems with tasks requiring sustained mental effort and his distractibility, restlessness, and impulsive behavior.

C.B. was an average, neatly groomed young adult. All of the conversations he initiated during his two assessment sessions focused on illnesses. He appeared overconfident but rather disorganized in his approach to the test tasks.

C.B.'s Wechsler measured a verbal IQ of 74, a performance IQ of 81, and a full-scale IQ of 76. Compared to a demographically corrected population, C.B.'s overall IQ was nearly 2 standard deviations below expectation. In general, C.B.'s intellectual skills were in the borderline range. He completed the Peabody Picture Vocabulary Test with a performance at the 5th percentile and the Test of Nonverbal Intelligence with a performance at the 14th percentile. A memory battery measured below 1st-percentile memory skills. C.B. demonstrated low average rote skills but struggled to recall any type of complex information. A brief screening of C.B.'s academic abilities detected low average word reading skills but very poor comprehension. Spelling and arithmetic skills appeared to be at a late elementary school level.

C.B.'s history and current assessment data reflected a disturbed individual. Although C.B.'s behavior reflected a style of friendliness and sociability, it appeared to hide an abrasive hypersensitivity to criticism and a marked tendency to project blame onto others. C.B.'s behavior was unpredictable, impulsive, resentful, and moody. Relationships were shallow and fleeting. They were often characterized by manipulative deceptions and were frequently disrupted by C.B.'s caustic comments and hostile outbursts. C.B. appeared to be unable to delay gratification, acting on impulses with insufficient deliberation and poor judgment. As a result, others perceived C.B. as irresponsible and undependable. C.B.'s history and Millon profile suggested that he was prone to manic episodes of an expansive and hostile nature. During these periods he was talkative, restless, distractible, hostile, excitable, and interpersonally disruptive. During at least two of these periods he had frightened his wife enough that she had moved out of the house. At one time he nearly strangled her. If provoked during these outbursts, it was clear that C.B. could explode into uncontrollable rage.

Diagnostically, C.B. appeared to be functioning in the borderline range of intellectual skill. Not surprisingly, therefore, his learning abilities were quite poor as a result of what appeared to be complex memory problems and poor conceptual abilities. C.B. demonstrated symptoms of ADHD. However, these appeared to be one part of C.B.'s more global personality, intellectual, and memory problems. C.B.'s symptom presentation was consistent with diagnoses of somatization and borderline personality disorder. C.B. presented with affective instability, chronic feelings of emptiness, inappropriate intense anger, and self-damaging impulsivity.

C.B. was referred to a day treatment program for further observation and treatment planning.

Case 16: Acquired ADHD and Related Cognitive Problems Secondary to Head Injury

M.M., a 23-year-old college student, was referred by his neurosurgeon. Two years prior to the evaluation, while at work M.M. was struck by a falling piece of pipe and seriously injured. Assessment was requested because of ongoing problems related to this injury. M.M. described difficulty with blurred vision, muscle weakness, immediate and short-term memory, concentration, reasoning, and dysnomia.

At the time of the accident M.M. had been employed as a welder. He had been attending school part time. At the time of the evaluation, he had returned to school full time with worker's compensation support.

M.M. denied a preaccident history of psychiatric problems or substance abuse. He acknowledged, however, that there was a history of alcoholism in his family. M.M. reported a B+ average in high school and a summary ACT score of 24.

A review of M.M.'s medical records revealed multiple physical problems, concussion, and post-traumatic amnesia as the result of the work-related accident. A 12% permanent impairment in cognitive functioning had been assigned. A review of cognitive and related testing completed during M.M.'s recovery indicated that he had recovered to low average cognitive, memory, and academic skills.

M.M. was a casually dressed, well-groomed, tall adult. Although slightly anxious, his behavior and interaction with the examiner was appropriate.

On the Wechsler, M.M. obtained a verbal IQ of 111, a performance IQ of 98, and a full-scale IQ of 106. Corrected demographic scores placed M.M. well in the average range. M.M.'s performance on the memory battery, in contrast, placed him at the 4th percentile for verbal skills and the 66th percentile for nonverbal skills. M.M. struggled to recall, immediately and over the short term, both simple and complex verbal information. In contrast, he performed much better when recalling nonverbal information.

M.M. achieved a performance at the 66th percentile on the Peabody Picture Vocabulary Test, a performance at the 77th percentile on the Test of Nonverbal Intelligence, and an average performance on the Halstead Category Test. M.M.'s performance on related neuropsychological measures placed him in the low average range. He performed at the 15th percentile for completion time on the Tactual Performance Test and struggled somewhat to divide his attention efficiently on Trails B.

Academic screening revealed M.M.'s above average basic academic skills. His reading comprehension, however, was just average, in contrast to his higher rote skills such as independent word reading and spelling.

M.M.'s performance on a computerized attention battery reflected his problems in sustaining attention and inhibiting impulsive responding. M.M.'s self-reports placed him at the cutoff on the Brown questionnaire indicative of concentration difficulty.

M.M.'s personality was that of a somewhat egocentric individual, self-reliant and competitive. M.M.'s self-reports did not reveal strong indices of symptoms of depression or anxiety. However, M.M. described a period of depression immediately following his accident. Overall, there did not appear to be any major post-traumatic change in M.M.'s personality.

The preponderance of the data suggested that M.M. functioned fairly well before his accident. Since that time, although he appeared to make a good recovery, residual, and likely permanent, problems were noted in M.M.'s ability to concentrate efficiently, in his speed and efficiency in processing information, and in his short-term and immediate verbal memory.

It was the examiner's impression that M.M.'s solid premorbid skills, combined with his personality, had helped him make a fairly good recovery from a very serious head injury.

M.M. was started by his physician on a low-dose trial of stimulant medication. He subjectively reported benefits at school and during daily activities. Further ophthalmologic consultation for visual problems was recommended. M.M. was also asked to consider working with a cognitive rehabilitation specialist as he completed school and reentered the workforce.

Case 17: Memory Problems, Acquired ADHD, and Depression Secondary to Brain Injury

A.L., a 40-year-old female stained-glass artist, collided head on with another bicyclist while bicycling on a steep hillside. Although she was wearing a helmet, A.L. lost consciousness for a brief period of time. She suffered numerous physical injuries and was reported to have experienced a convulsion at the site of the accident. A.L. reported pre-traumatic amnesia of a few moments and post-traumatic amnesia of nearly 12 hours. She was referred for assessment six months after the accident because of her continued complaints of cognitive difficulty.

A.L.'s history appeared unremarkable. She completed two years of college and had been self-employed over the previous 10 years as a very successful stained-glass artist. At the time of the accident she had been separated from her second husband of nine years and was engaged in a custody battle for their three daughters.

A.L. recalled always being quite active as a child and adolescent but denied any behavioral, emotional, or academic problems. A.L. graduated from high school with a B+ average.

At the time of assessment, A.L. continued to receive physical therapy three times per week. Symptoms included neck, arm, back, and head pain; sleep problems; obsessive worrying; feelings of hopelessness; difficulty with short-term memory; problems with concentration; and feelings of apathy. These core difficulties resulted in a diffuse set of problems affecting A.L. throughout each day.

A.L. was an attractive, well-groomed adult. Her behavior during assessment was appropriate. Her work style, however, was characterized by a tendency to make minor errors of detail and to attempt to work very slowly in an effort to compensate. A.L. was motivated to perform and appeared to make her best effort.

On the Wechsler, A.L. obtained a verbal IQ of 114, a performance IQ of 97, and a full-scale IQ of 106. Demographically, this placed A.L. in the average range with a significant discrepancy between her verbal and nonverbal skills. Interestingly, A.L.'s weakest performance was on the Block Design and Object Assembly subtests. These two tasks measure skills in which, given A.L.'s vocational history, she would be expected to be quite strong.

A.L. completed the Peabody Picture Vocabulary Test with a score at the 66th percentile and the Test of Nonverbal Intelligence with a score at the 70th percentile. On the neuropsychological battery, A.L. completed the Halstead Category Test with a score at the 99th percentile for individuals of her demographic background. A.L. did not have problems on the Halstead; she could form an idea and track that idea consistently. On the Test of Nonverbal Intelligence, however, A.L. appeared to experience some difficulty switching from idea to idea as she attempted to complete the task.

A.L. completed the memory battery with average scores. However, she appeared to have greatest problems recalling complex verbal information. Her performance on measures of distractibility, divided attention, and impulsiveness yielded scores in the low average range. Academic screening also placed A.L.'s skills in the average range.

A.L.'s self-reports yielded a score beyond the clinical cutoff on the Brown questionnaire due to current complaints of inattention and difficulty initiating activities. On the Beck she scored 26, indicative of moderate depressive thinking.

A.L.'s personality style suggested someone who had difficulty admitting responsibility for problems or was prone to rationalize or project problems. She appeared to be someone who when upbeat could be high spirited and animated but could quickly revert to anger to control others. However, the majority of her history suggested that prior to the accident in question, A.L. had not experienced any symptoms related to mood or anxiety. Her profile at the time of assessment strongly suggested a major depressive episode and generalized anxiety.

Diagnostically, A.L. demonstrated a diffuse pattern of emotional, cognitive, and behavioral difficulty secondary to a traumatic brain injury. Cognitively, A.L. experienced problems processing information quickly as a result of her difficulty with attention to detail, poor visual perception, and limited concentration. Symptoms consistent with acquired ADHD were reported by A.L. as well as other family members. From an emotional perspective, A.L. appeared to have entered a major depressive episode. Her functioning reflected problems related to anxiety and post-traumatic stress as well. At the time of assessment she appeared to be on a downward spiral in terms of her efficiency at daily living.

A.L.'s physician initiated trials of antidepressant and stimulant medications. A serotonin-based antidepressant improved A.L.'s general mood and reduced her obsessive worrying within a few weeks. The initiation of the stimulant resulted in A.L.'s reporting increased daily efficiency and, for the first time in six months, the ability to begin stained-glass work. Cognitive rehabilitation on a weekly outpatient basis was initiated to provide A.L. with additional compensatory strategies to improve her efficiency at everyday activities. Supportive psychotherapy was also initiated to help A.L. understand her experiences in the previous six months and to reverse the downward spiral of her emotional problems.

Case 18: Organic Personality, LD, and ADHD Symptoms Secondary to Traumatic Brain Injury

A.R., a 48-year-old female, was referred by her rehabilitation specialist because of increasing disruptive and emotional symptoms. Although A.R. had a long history of developmental impairments as the result of severe anoxia at birth, over the previous six years symptoms of depression, anxiety, obsessiveness, and anorexia had escalated steadily and significantly.

A.R. was the only survivor of a set of triplets. Both of her siblings died during their first three months of life. Despite being slow in development, A.R., with special education support, was able to graduate from high school. She had been employed in the family jewelry business since that time. She continued to live at home with her parents. Now in their late 70s, A.R.'s parents were having increasing difficulty supporting and managing her. A.R. was described as increasingly rigid, aggressive, and obsessive.

A.R. described her current symptomatic complaints, including crying; having suicidal thoughts; feeling lonely, apathetic, and sad; lacking appetite; and angering easily.

On retrospective measures, A.R.'s parents recalled that as a child she was inattentive, impulsive, and rather restless. She was never diagnosed or treated for hyperactivity or attention deficit.

A.R.'s medical records revealed diagnoses of minimal brain dysfunction and at 30 years of age initiation of treatment with antidepressant and antipsychotic medications. Cognitive testing completed when A.R. was 40 years of age yielded a verbal IQ of 74, a performance IQ of 66, and a full-scale IQ of 69. Discharge diagnoses from a psychiatric hospitalization at age 40 included major depression, an organic personality disorder, an obsessive/compulsive personality disorder, and mild mental retardation.

Neurology consultation at the time of the present evaluation yielded impressions of symptoms of anxiety and depression, possibly the result of progressive neurological problems.

A.R. was a neatly groomed, middle-aged female. She was anxious during both assessment sessions and cried frequently. Her conversation was often self-centered. She was easily redirected, however. With support, A.R.'s concentration was good. She quickly became apologetic as tasks became more difficult. Her thoughts appeared logical though mildly unfocused and irrelevant.

Cognitive assessment on the Wechsler yielded a verbal IQ of 76, a performance IQ of 70, and a full-scale IQ of 73. A.R.'s skills appeared evenly balanced, with slightly stronger verbal than nonverbal abilities. A memory battery, however, measured below 1st-percentile memory skills, again with slightly better verbal than visual memory. A.R. was unable to complete either the Test of Nonverbal Intelligence or the Halstead Category Test. Computerized measures revealed her difficulty in sustaining attention and her tendency to respond impulsively. A.R. appeared to be extremely slow in processing information on a number of neuropsychological tests. Academically, she performed in the low average range for reading and spelling. Her handwriting was quite fast, efficient, and well integrated. Her arithmetic skills, in contrast, were at the 2nd percentile for her age.

On self-report measures, A.R. described depressive symptoms in the severe range. From a personality perspective, it appeared that much of A.R.'s behavior was intended to gain the attention and favor of others, not only by appearing in an attractive or positive light but also by exposing her troubled state. A.R. demonstrated a very clear tendency toward self-defeating cycles. Her markedly deflated self-worth and her expectations of failure and humiliation appeared to constrain her efforts to function more efficiently and autonomously. A.R. appeared to feel that others had either depreciated or disapproved of her occasional attempts at autonomy. She seemed to perceive no alternative but to depend on supporting persons and groups. She deeply resented this restriction, however, and was impelled to act in a petulant, unpredictable, and often aggressive manner. It was clear that over the past 20 years, A.R.'s discontent, impulsive outbursts, and chronic moodiness had tended to evoke rejection and humiliating reactions from others. This in turn reinforced her self-protective social withdrawal and retreat into increasing isolation.

Diagnostically, A.R.'s fretful and anxious feelings were interwoven with clear signs of a major depressive disorder overlying a characterologic mix of dysthymic features. A.R.'s thinking at times appeared to be somewhat fragmented. Irritable and fretful at the time of assessment, A.R.

appeared to be experiencing a significant level of dysphoria, sufficient to justify a diagnosis of generalized anxiety as well. Her symptoms and preoccupations were consistent with a somatoform disorder that appeared to be contributing to her gastrointestinal discomfort, pain, hypochondriasis, and anorexia.

A.R.'s cognitive strengths and weaknesses, as well as her concentration difficulty, reflected a long-standing history of organically based problems. Her symptomatic difficulties were not consistent with a typical pattern of developmental or intellectual handicap but appeared to reflect the checkerboard pattern of loss as the result of neurologic insult.

A.R. did not read or follow nonverbal routines or expectations very well. She missed the usual signals about when to start or stop tasks. She did not realize what tasks were required to do well. As a result, this difficulty combined with her anxiety and resulted in very poor problem solving, judgment, and comprehension. It appeared that most of the time A.R. did not have a good grasp of what was going on around her. This pattern of organic problems appeared to be responsible for her anxiety difficulties. Further, A.R. demonstrated very few coping abilities, even for someone of her intellectual capability. She did not appear to see, do, or understand as an adult, so she was unable to act like one. She appeared to have major right-hemisphere problems, a difficulty she had experienced since birth. She struggled with visual-motor and perceptual skills. Her mathematical skills reflected her weakest area of academics. Individuals with this pattern often struggle with emotionally distressing symptoms related to anxiety and depression. Despite her perceptual difficulties, however, A.R.'s handwriting and spelling skills were spared.

The examiner raised the possibility that A.R.'s skills were declining. This was not thought to be inconsistent for someone with her history reaching middle age. Additional evidence of a slow decline included increased problems reading, some slurring in her speech, increased motor tremors, and an escalation in psychiatric symptoms.

Very clearly, A.R.'s parents were no longer capable of caring for her or providing the structure she needed on a daily basis. A.R. was referred to a state rehabilitation team in an effort to begin making plans for her transition into a group home setting. Continued psychological and psychiatric support was strongly recommended. A.R. was referred to a day treatment psychiatric program in an effort to obtain additional observations of her behavior and to make decisions concerning the potential benefits of psychotropic medications.

Case 19: LD, Oppositional Problems, and Possible ADHD

J.M., a 15-year-old ninth-grader, was referred because of disruptive behavior, increasing reports of emotional distress, and LD. J.M.'s family history was extremely complex. J.M.'s mother was married to her fourth husband and had a history of depression and previous psychiatric hospitalization. J.M. did not get along with his stepfather. In addition, J.M.'s relationship with his biological father was inconsistent. His father had molested stepdaughters and had been charged with incest, convicted, and imprisoned. J.M.'s half-brother had had a history of criminal behavior and had been murdered in prison.

J.M.'s early developmental milestones were unremarkable, although J.M.'s mother recalled that he had received speech language therapy. J.M. struggled in school, was retained, and then evidently moved a year ahead. He began receiving special education services in the second grade. J.M.'s mother married her fourth husband five years before the assessment. At that time J.M. developed severe psychiatric symptoms and was placed in a residential psychiatric program. At the time of assessment, J.M. was participating in outpatient group therapy for adolescents with histories of alcohol abuse. J.M.'s criminal history included being charged and convicted of stealing the family car, stealing his stepfather's work products, and possession of marijuana. J.M. was described as socially isolated. He tended to interact with older adolescents, most of whom had been involved with repeated juvenile offenses.

Within the home setting, J.M.'s mother noted that he had a long history of inattentiveness, impulsivity, and disorganization. J.M. was described as having had temper tantrums from a young age. He was aggressive with minimal provocation. J.M.'s mother indicated that at the time of assessment she had a very poor relationship with him.

Psychiatric records from the previous year revealed diagnoses of mixed substance abuse, dysthymia, LD, and oppositional defiant disorder. Not surprisingly, J.M.'s mother's responses to the Child Behavior Checklist indicated significant complaints of disruptive and nondisruptive problems, well above the 98th percentile. J.M. also scored above the 98th percentile on the hyperkinesis index of the parent Conners.

A review of J.M.'s school records showed average academic skills with weak spelling in first grade. This pattern continued through fourth grade. By eighth grade, J.M.'s group achievement tests measured his reading at the 6th percentile, math at the 21st percentile, language at the 3rd percentile, spelling at the 2nd percentile, and an overall battery at the 4th percentile. A review of report cards did not indicate problems with attention, work completion, or behavior in kindergarten through second grade. By third grade, complaints were noted about delayed spelling and handwriting as well as marginal mathematical skills. Problems by fourth grade also included difficulty with reading achievement. Fifth-grade notes reflected the first complaints about J.M.'s disruptive behavior, at a time that coincided with his mother's fourth marriage. In sixth grade, J.M. was out of school 51 days.

Assessment at school two years prior to the evaluation yielded an average Wechsler IQ but a verbal IQ of 90 and a nonverbal IQ of 111. The evaluator described J.M. as guilty, anxious, and hostile.

J.M. was a tall, mature-appearing adolescent. His face was marred by severe acne. His nails were mildly bitten. He wore a baseball cap and kept his coat on during the assessment. J.M.'s affect was somewhat flat, but he was not particularly resistant. In fact, once he warmed up during the assessment process, he became rather pleasant.

J.M. obtained a full-scale Wechsler IQ of 90, a verbal IQ of 87, and a performance IQ of 96. Intratest scatter suggested that J.M.'s potential IQ was likely better than this measure reflected. Memory assessment yielded 63rd-percentile visual memory skills but only 10th-percentile verbal memory skills. J.M. demonstrated significant problems with rote sequential memory. He performed at the 11th percentile on the Peabody Picture Vocabulary Test and at the 34th percentile on the Test of Nonverbal Intelligence. No signs of difficulty in sustaining attention or inhibiting impulses were noted on a computerized attention battery. Academically, J.M. appeared to be at the mid-fifth-grade level for word reading, comprehension, and spelling. He appeared to be at the seventh-grade level for arithmetic. The data seemed to indicate that J.M.'s verbal and nonverbal conceptual abilities were average but somewhat underdeveloped as a result of his educational history and poor school motivation. His LD appeared to reflect problems with rote verbal memory, causing difficulty with number facts, spelling, following instructions, vocabulary, and comprehension.

J.M.'s self-reports did not reflect any complaints of anxiety or unhappiness. During the interview, J.M. noted he would like to have more control over his life and the lives of others. When asked whom he would like to be for a day, he responded, "God." J.M. also acknowledged frequent and repeated drug use beginning at age 13, including marijuana, alcohol, and hallucinogenics.

J.M.'s behavior was typified by unpredictable and pessimistic moods, an edgy irritability, and a tendency to engage in self-defeating behaviors. J.M.'s responses to the Millon reflected his feelings of being misunderstood and unappreciated. J.M. expressed momentary thoughts and feelings impulsively and was easily provoked by outside stimuli into sudden and unpredictable reactions. He appeared to anticipate being disillusioned by others and for this reason would behave obstructively. Parent family relationships were fraught with wrangles and antagonism, provoked by J.M.'s characteristic carelessness and complaining passive/aggressive attitude. His behavior induced others to react in a negative manner. As a consequence, J.M. felt all the more misunderstood and unappreciated. Further, he appeared to be rather self-critical, oversensitive, and defensive. He lacked empathy and viewed the problems of others rather harshly. Family difficulties were reported to be a central focus of J.M.'s expressed problems.

Diagnostically, J.M. demonstrated a long-standing pattern of language-based LD. As a result of these weaknesses, J.M.'s verbal memory skills appeared quite poor. Further, it appeared that J.M.'s family and life history had slowly and consistently impaired his overall adjustment and behavior. J.M. demonstrated symptoms consistent with diagnoses of oppositional defiance, conduct disorder, and mixed substance abuse. Although J.M. denied significant complaints of anxiety or depression, his overall behavior and reports of his comments to his parents suggested dysthymia somewhat. J.M.'s overall pattern and presentation, however, also appeared to demonstrate early risks of an emerging borderline personality disorder. Finally, although symptoms of ADHD were present, the history and current presentation strongly argued that these behaviors were etiologically related to other developmental and emotional problems. Moreover, at the time of assessment, J.M. did not meet the full criteria necessary for a diagnosis of ADHD.

Given the history and increasing conflict between J.M. and his parents, it was strongly recommended that a residential treatment program for disruptive, substance-abusing adolescents be considered. Academic support and consideration of vocational training with an academic mentor, someone whom J.M. was willing to trust, were strongly recommended. Finally, although medications might have been beneficial for J.M., it was suggested that until he was in a consistent environment, medication treatments be withheld, especially in light of his history of substance abuse.

Case 20: LD, Dysthymia, and Possible ADHD

J.S., an 18-year-old 12th-grader, was referred by her educational team at a private, residential school for adolescents. Concerns were raised about J.S.'s difficulty remaining on task and about possible LD.

J.S.'s mother committed suicide when J.S. was seven years of age. Her father later remarried. J.S. had not gotten along with her stepmother, and in part this was responsible for her out-of-home school placement.

J.S.'s early developmental history was unremarkable. J.S. participated in gifted educational programming during her first few years of elementary school. By junior high school there appeared to be increasing complaints of off-task behavior. J.S. became rebellious as a freshman in high school and struggled academically. By her sophomore year she had run away from home a number of times and was later placed in an adolescent psychiatric treatment center for nine months.

J.S.'s father described her as from an early age being rather inattentive, shifting from one uncompleted activity to another, acting impulsively, and demonstrating poor self-control. Residential staff at J.S.'s school described symptoms related to social isolation, frequent somatic complaints, inattentiveness, and mild disruptive behavior.

A review of J.S.'s records revealed diagnoses of major depression, cyclothymia, and a mixed personality disorder with avoidant and narcissistic features. Intellectual assessment when J.S. was 15 years of age measured a Wechsler verbal IQ of 96, a performance IQ of 114, and a full-scale IQ of 104. "Information processing deficiencies" were hypothesized to be responsible for J.S.'s weak fund of information and vocabulary.

J.S.'s teachers noted marked variability in her attentional skills, with some teachers reporting good attention and others poor attention. In addition, some teachers described J.S. as overactive, impulsive, restless, and fidgety, while others noted minimal difficulties in these areas.

J.S. was a casually dressed, neatly groomed adolescent. She appeared mildly anxious, although her affect was generally flat. She was inclined to distrust her abilities but willing to persist with support. Her thoughts appeared logical, focused, and relevant.

Intellectual assessment measured a verbal IQ of 86, a performance IQ of 110, and a full-scale IQ of 96. In agreement with the previous assessment, this pattern reflected a fairly consistent trend of weak verbal and stronger nonverbal abilities. J.S. performed at the 86th percentile on the Peabody Picture Vocabulary Test but at only the 18th percentile on the Test of Nonverbal Intelligence. Her performance on the memory battery revealed above average verbal and nonverbal memory for meaningful information but poor sequential memory. Performance on a computerized attention measure indicated difficulty in sustaining attention and inhibiting impulsive responding. Academic assessment reflected difficulty with comprehension and poor written language skills. J.S.'s rote skills did not appear to be particularly weak. Most of her problems appeared to be the result of an overall conceptual weakness. Her slow and steady decline on academic achievement measures during her career, starting from an initial good performance at school, appeared consistent with an individual suffering from conceptual rather than rote LD. Higher level language processing problems were subsequently identified following a speech and language assessment. In general, J.S. struggled when tasks became more verbally complex and abstract.

J.S.'s self-report measures did not reflect symptoms of depression or anxiety. However, J.S. scored above the clinical cutoff on the Brown questionnaire, describing symptoms consistent with inattention, disorganization, and mild restlessness.

The clinical interview revealed J.S.'s apparent amnesia for the period of time immediately preceding and following her mother's suicide, despite the fact that J.S. discovered her mother's body. Although J.S. denied that the loss of her mother contributed to the increase in her behavioral problems a number of years ago, she was willing to acknowledge that her problems apparently began at that time. J.S. chose to focus the majority of her complaints on her relationship with her stepmother. J.S. also recalled that her father "was really weird" after her mother's death and that her father and stepmother evidently had had some kind of relationship prior to her mother's death.

J.S.'s behavior was characterized by submissive dependency and fears of abandonment, leading her to be compliant and obliging with anyone willing to pay attention to her. J.S. did not appear to value herself in terms of her own traits but in terms of the traits of those to whom she felt most attached. By allying herself with the attributes and attractiveness of others, J.S. created an illusion of sharing their competence. On the Millon, J.S. reported being unhappy with her body maturation and attractiveness. She described serious problems in her family setting. It appeared that her inability to function on a more complex cognitive level was in part responsible for the development of these personality traits.

The question of ADHD was complex for J.S. The preponderance of the data did not reflect consistent long-standing problems with ADHD symptoms. The more serious onset of these symptoms appeared to follow the loss of J.S.'s mother. Even at the time of assessment, complaints of inattentiveness were inconsistent from one classroom to the next. A diagnosis of ADHD was deferred until J.S. could be worked with more closely.

The data, however, very clearly reflected J.S.'s higher level language processing difficulty. She struggled to integrate information into concepts and hierarchies. Her reading comprehension problems and the types of writing errors that she made clearly reflected her verbal linguistic conceptual limitations. At a very young age she functioned exceptionally well because of her rote strengths. Thus, during the first few grades while learning to read, J.S. did well. As school became more complex and her life was complicated by emotional stress and as the need to read to learn increased, J.S.'s struggles increased.

The examiner raised questions about the possible contribution of post-traumatic stress disorder leading to a general dysthymic adjustment to life following the death of J.S.'s mother.

J.S.'s educational team was directed to begin guiding her toward post–high school vocational options. J.S. was interested in photography and efforts were undertaken to help her apply to two-year colleges offering photography course work. Suggestions were also made to assist J.S. in regard to academic tasks. A strong focus was placed on helping J.S. organize information and work at a concrete level, seeing and dealing with what was directly in front of her. The use of carefully sequenced instructions and working slowly from one step to the next, especially in more complex academic classes, were also emphasized.

J.S. was provided with additional information about LD in adolescence and adulthood. J.S. was referred to counseling in an effort to help her identify life goals and possibly make some modifications in her personality style. It was recommended that J.S. participate in consultation in 6–12 months to once again address the issue of ADHD and the possible risks and benefits of medication treatment.

Case 21: Apparent ADHD Symptoms Secondary to Personality

R.Z., a 21-year-old female college junior, was referred because of reports of increasing difficulty with academic achievement. After viewing a television program dealing with adult ADHD, R.Z. hypothesized that her growing problems at school might be related to attention deficit.

R.Z.'s childhood and developmental history were unremarkable. She denied that as a child she experienced problems with inattention, impulsivity, or hyperactivity. She reported, however, being somewhat unmotivated, but she graduated from high school with a B+ average. In college R.Z. received Cs and Ds and failed calculus, linear algebra, chemical principles, and differential equations. R.Z. noted that she could "charm her way through high school but can't anymore." R.Z. acknowledged, however, that she did not spend much time studying in college.

R.Z. had been employed for three and a half years as a grocery store checker. She lived at home with her parents while attending college. Her brother was diagnosed with ADHD as a child. Other siblings had not experienced attention or developmental problems. There was no extended family history of psychiatric or behavioral difficulties.

R.Z. received two speeding tickets but had not had any other legal problems. She described herself as lacking the willpower to start tasks and to put off enjoyable activities. She reported dating on a casual basis.

R.Z.'s mother noted that as a child R.Z. experienced very mild problems with attention but that these did not cause her any difficulty in daily functioning. R.Z. evidently excelled in elementary school but when placed in a gifted junior high school program struggled somewhat. Responses by R.Z. and her mother to the Brown questionnaire yielded scores just below the clinically significant cutoff. R.Z. was described as being easily sidetracked, procrastinating, and inconsistent.

R.Z. was an attractive, well-groomed female. It was not difficult to establish a working relationship with her.

Cognitive screening revealed an individual with average intellectual skills. Consistent with her responses and interaction during the clinical interview, R.Z.'s Millon profile indicated an individual working very hard to present a socially acceptable front but also resistant to admitting personal shortcomings. R.Z.'s behavior was typified by an easygoing and nonconforming social style, the seeking of attention as a means of excitement, and self-dramatizing behavior. R.Z. appeared to be easily excited and quickly bored. A general intolerance of inactivity was reflected in her impulsiveness, her attraction to, at times, dangerous behavior, and a seeming disregard for consequences.

Although R.Z. demonstrated some symptoms consistent with ADHD, she did not present with enough symptoms or severe enough symptoms to warrant a diagnosis of ADHD. In addition, her school performance and academic history revealed problems in some courses that required substantial effort and thus more study time but not in others. A review of R.Z.'s high school transcript noted As in honors classes such as chemistry, geography, advanced algebra, physics, and trigonometry. Her struggles in college appeared to be a function of her personality and her lack of investment in preparing assignments and studying for tests.

Just as R.Z. withdrew when she was not the best in her early school years, she found it increasingly difficult to complete tasks requiring effort that might not result in the highest score. Finally, R.Z.'s self-report suggested no symptoms of anxiety, depression, or other psychiatric disturbance.

R.Z. was referred for a series of supportive counseling sessions in an effort to help her better understand the ways in which her personality style affected her daily functioning and to help her make academic and vocational decisions. Given R.Z.'s belief that her problems stemmed from ADHD, it was recommended that the issue of ADHD as a contributing factor be reconsidered after R.Z. had participated in supportive counseling and made some changes in her approach to academic tasks.

Case 22: LD, Mild Anxiety, and Apparent ADHD

J.J., a 16-year-old 10th-grade female, was referred because of poor schoolwork, questions about anxiety, and inattentive behavior. J.J. was the eldest of three siblings. One of the younger siblings had a history of LD and ADHD. The family history was positive for ADHD and LD.

J.J. had been a normal infant, toddler, and preschooler. Developmental milestones were reached within normal limits. An atypical period of repetitive hand washing was noted at 10 years of age when one of J.J.'s younger siblings was born. This behavior remitted spontaneously.

The year prior to assessment, J.J. became increasingly noncompliant in completing schoolwork. Her parents noted that her life appeared to be "directed by her emotions." In general, they reported a positive relationship with her.

J.J. had been evaluated at 10 years of age when referred because of learning and possible emotional problems. A Wechsler completed at the time measured a verbal IQ of 96, a performance IQ of 86, and a full-scale IQ of 90. Academic screening at that time indicated low average written language and reading skills and average mathematical skills. Questionnaires completed by parents and teachers reflected shy but not inattentive behavior. Diagnoses at the time included overanxious disorder and a specific LD.

Parental responses to the Child Behavior Checklist noted problems with attention, anxiety, depression, and social withdrawal. J.J. presented at above the 98th percentile on the hyperkinesis index. She was described as somewhat argumentative with family members. She appeared to have a reasonably good peer network.

Teacher responses to the Conners questionnaire indicated problems in one class with completing tasks but no significant complaints in other classes. A review of J.J.'s report cards noted a comment of "excellent seat work habits" in first grade. Nonetheless, by second grade J.J. was described as struggling with reading and spelling. In third grade she was described as pleasant, cooperative, and a good worker. Her fifth-grade teacher also noted her effort despite academic struggles. Junior high school began with A and B grades, but by eighth grade J.J. was having much more difficulty.

A review of group achievement tests revealed average to low average achievement throughout elementary school. In ninth grade J.J. achieved at the 81st percentile for reading, 37th percentile for mathematics, 58th percentile for language skills, 17th percentile for spelling, and obtained a basic total battery at the 45th percentile.

J.J. was an attractive, well-groomed adolescent. She was alert and attentive. Her concentration was good. She appeared inclined to distrust her abilities. Overall, she related well to the examiner.

J.J. obtained a verbal IQ of 97, a performance IQ of 87, and a full-scale IQ of 92 on the Wechsler. These scores, however, appeared to underestimate J.J.'s abilities. The quality of her verbal responses and insight suggested better potential. Her pattern was often to correctly respond to more difficult task items while failing easier items. She performed at the 78th percentile on the Peabody Picture Vocabulary Test. Memory screening detected average to above average verbal memory for complex information but low average rote memory. J.J.'s performance on a computerized battery did not reflect problems in sustaining attention or any difficulty with impulsivity. Nonetheless, J.J. experienced some difficulty initially grasping the nature of the task.

Academic screening placed J.J. in the average range. She presented as a quick, accurate visual processor when reading. She had difficulty summarizing and comprehending, however. Her written story was well done with respect to vocabulary and theme.

J.J.'s test data and history reflected something of an enigma. She appeared to possess excellent capacity for awareness, insight, and depth, but these skills were not often triggered unless J.J. was carefully directed. She appeared to go through the world usually perceiving, organizing, and understanding on a superficial, disorganized, discrete, rather concrete level. Her basic problem appeared to be one of immediate abstraction and insight. J.J. appeared to have difficulty grasping and organizing new tasks as they were presented, but typically, with added experience she was able to sort out, see what was required to perform well, understand the nature and demands of tasks, and then perform them with accuracy and efficiency. Her basic academic skills appeared good. In problem-solving situations when concept, insight, or generalization processes were not triggered, J.J. appeared weaker. Her mathematical skills indicated mild conceptual weakness. Her spelling weaknesses reflected a lack of rule generation and generalization as opposed to poor phonics or weak visual memory.

Her parents' and J.J.'s responses to the Brown questionnaire placed her above the clinical cutoff for inattentive problems. J.J.'s responses to a depression questionnaire placed her in the nonsignificant range. However, on a questionnaire screening anxiety, J.J. described herself as worrying excessively, having her feelings hurt easily, and experiencing difficulty making up her mind.

J.J.'s history and her responses to the Millon profile suggested that underneath her calm facade, she experienced a high degree of emotional lability and irritable hypersensitivity to criticism. J.J. appeared to struggle to express attitudes that were contrary to her actual feelings and thus would display short-lived dramatic or superficial emotions. J.J. appeared to be easily excited and quickly bored.

J.J. also demonstrated a history of mild anxiety. Although she and her parents reported some degree of inattentive symptoms, the history, combined with an insufficient number of symptoms presenting, precluded a diagnosis of ADHD.

A psychiatry consultation was recommended to determine whether a psychotropic medication might ease J.J.'s anxiety difficulties. J.J. was also directed to work with an academic coach in an effort to help her function more efficiently on an independent basis. Short-term counseling was also recommended to help J.J. better understand her rather complex pattern of difficulties and the manner in which she functioned.

Case 23: Bipolar and Borderline Personality Disorder

M.T., a 45-year-old female with a master's degree in education, was self-referred, having read a book on ADHD. Despite her advanced degree, M.T. had only taught as a substitute teacher.

M.T. reported having been anxious since childhood but having her symptoms become exaggerated "since my kids have been teenagers." She described her current problems as disorganization, anxiety, unstable emotions, worry, impatience, impulsivity, and a negative attitude. M.T. described a history of frequent, abrupt, and unpredictable mood changes. Nonetheless, she denied a significant history of a major depressive episode.

M.T. denied a childhood history of developmental or behavioral problems. M.T. had been married to her first husband for 25 years. She described her marriage positively. M.T. had two adopted children, one in college, the other completing high school. The younger had a history of ADHD and LD. M.T. reported frequent and chronic conflicts with her children, noting that they thought she wanted to run their lives. She denied a close history with her parents, describing her mother as "a witch to live with." Her relationships with five siblings were also described as negative. M.T. had something derogatory to say about each.

M.T.'s responses to self-report attention measures yielded scores well above the clinical cutoff. M.T. described excessive problems with inattention, procrastination, stress intolerance, impulsivity, distractibility, anger control, and fatigue. Her husband described his wife's difficulty with organization and consistency. He noted that she failed to follow through with attention to detail and was easily distracted. These behaviors had been present throughout their marriage.

M.T. was an attractive woman, neatly groomed, and of average appearance. She maintained and initiated conversation. Her conversational style was often animated and rapid. She would start one conversation and then almost tangentially switch to others. She was quite active during the clinical interview, leaning forward and back in her chair and slapping at the table for emphasis.

Given M.T.'s academic history, cognitive and academic assessment was not completed. M.T.'s responses to the Beck Depression Inventory yielded a score well below the clinical cutoff. Her responses to the Millon, however, were much more revealing.

M.T.'s behavior appeared to reflect her inflated sense of self-worth, a superficially charming style, and the persistent seeking of attention and stimulation. This pattern was repeatedly evident in her immature exhibitionistic and self-dramatizing behavior. M.T.'s relationships appeared characteristically shallow, self-indulgent, and fleeting. She appeared only minimally aware that her undependability and exploitation were seen by others as inconsistent and presumptuous. Over the years, one by one, she had relegated friends and family members to positions of antagonism with her caustic comments. Her behavior did not appear to reflect hostile or malicious tendencies but was derived from feelings of omnipotence and the arrogant assumption that she did not have to follow everyone else's rules. M.T.'s history revealed her pattern of, at times, manic hyperactivity and excitement. Her history also reflected repetitive periods of euphoria and hostility marked by pressured speech, less need for sleep, hyperdistractibility, and general restlessness. Periods of buoyant cheerfulness appeared to be manifested for brief spans of time only to be suddenly and unpredictably replaced by temper outbursts, belligerence, and explosive anger.

Diagnostically, M.T. presented as an individual with likely above average intellectual skills and academic achievement. Despite her advanced degree she had never entered the workforce. Although her self-reports and those of her husband reflected symptoms consistent with ADHD, the overall profile suggested that these symptoms were more likely secondary to borderline personality disorder and possibly bipolar disorder. At the time of assessment M.T.'s endorsed symptomatology was consistent with a manic episode. She demonstrated inflated self-esteem, wide and rapid mood changes, irritability, pressured speech, and distractibility. M.T.'s borderline personality qualities included affective instability, frequently in response to anxiety or provoking situations.

M.T. was carefully counseled that the source of her inattentive problems appeared to be emotional and not developmental. She was referred for further psychiatric consultation. A recommendation was also made for supportive psychotherapy given the examiner's concern that M.T.'s outbursts over the years were becoming more severe in their presentation.

Case 24: Bipolar Disorder, Borderline Personality Disorder, and Borderline IQ

W.K., a 24-year-old female high school graduate, was referred after her friend suggested that her problems might be the result of ADHD. W.K. reported a childhood history of learning difficulty, inferior feelings, depression, and possibly inattention. She described peers as particularly abusive and aggressive. She reported a history of LD. She had received special education services throughout her high school career. She attended a two-year college for one semester but later dropped out. At the time of the assessment, W.K. was recently divorced and unemployed.

W.K. described physical symptoms, including headache and aches and pains, feelings of tension and depression, thoughts of suicide, feelings of inferiority, difficulty with concentration, mood swings, and sexual problems. She also noted that "I don't think I have ever rested for a long time, I never really sleep." W.K. noted that one of the more significant problems in her marriage was her dislike of sexual activities, explaining that she did not like being nude.

The symptomatic problems that W.K. described were egodystonic. She noted that they were quite troublesome; she would like to "function like a normal person." W.K. described a long history of getting mad easily, losing her temper, and acting aggressively toward persons or objects; of frequent, abrupt, and unpredictable mood changes; and of impulsive behavior as well. She had received two moving violations and had been in two automobile accidents.

W.K. was an only child. Her family history was positive for ADHD and LD.

On self-report measures related to attention, W.K.'s scores were far beyond the clinical cutoff. W.K. endorsed nearly all items on these questionnaires to the extreme. On the Retrospective Attention Profile, her mother reported that as a child W.K. was extremely hyperactive and fidgety, daydreamed, did not follow directions, and acted impulsively. Nonetheless, her mother described W.K. as usually happy as a child.

W.K. was a well-groomed, attractive woman. She worked hard throughout the structured assessment. She was alert and attentive, manifesting good concentration. Her approach to test tasks was methodical.

On the Wechsler, W.K. obtained a verbal IQ of 74, a performance IQ of 83, and a full-scale IQ of 76. The overall profile reflected generally weak intellectual skills. Her performance on the memory battery indicated a similar relative verbal weakness, with W.K. performing at the 2nd percentile for verbal memory, 17th percentile for nonverbal memory, and 4th percentile for overall memory skills. W.K. experienced greatest problems, not surprisingly given her intellectual weaknesses, on tasks requiring complex memory.

W.K. completed the Peabody Picture Vocabulary Test with a score at the 4th percentile and the Test of Nonverbal Intelligence with a score at the 7th percentile. Academic screening placed W.K.'s academic skills at or below the 5th percentile. Reading comprehension skills were measured at a sixth-grade level.

W.K.'s responses to the Beck yielded a score suggesting a moderate level of reported depressive symptoms. Her moods appeared highly labile, with impulsive, angry outbursts alternating with recurrent depressive complaints and sulking.

W.K.'s responses to the Millon reflected an irritable hypersensitivity to criticism, low frustration tolerance, short-sighted hedonism, immature behavior, and an erratic search for momentary excitement and stimulation. Impulsive and unmoderated emotions surged readily to the surface for W.K., making her behavior capricious, distractible, and egocentric. Unpredictable, contrary, manipulative, and volatile, W.K. frequently elicited rejection rather than the support she sought from others. Her moods appeared brittle and variable. She appeared to be an individual capable of displaying short-lived, dramatic but superficial emotions. Her moods appeared to be highly reactive to external stimuli. Feeling misunderstood and disappointed with life, W.K. had begun behaving in an irrational, negativistic, critical, and envious manner, begrudging others their good fortune.

Diagnostically, W.K. demonstrated a long-standing history of borderline intellectual skills of uncertain etiology. Although she was strong at simple, rote types of tasks, her abstract and conceptual reasoning skills presented at well below the 2nd percentile. Her arithmetic skills were at a late elementary school level. Further, W.K.'s memory for complex verbal and nonverbal information was extremely weak.

W.K. endorsed symptoms of rapidly alternating moods accompanied by manic and depressive episodes. Symptoms include agitation, insomnia, and suicidal thoughts. Her pervasive pattern of instability in interpersonal relationships, her instability, and her impulsivity were consistent with a diagnosis of borderline personality disorder. Although symptoms of ADHD were reported, the overall profile did not warrant a diagnosis of ADHD at the time.

W.K. was referred for psychiatric consultation to evaluate the potential benefits of psychotropic medication as part of her treatment plan. W.K. was also urged to participate in supportive psychotherapy and to consider evaluation with her local vocational rehabilitation office. With her approval, the results of the assessment were explained to W.K.'s parents in an effort to help them advocate for their daughter.

PART II

Treatment

CHAPTER 8

Introduction

O NCE ADOLESCENTS and adults with ADHD or LD are appropriately identified and evaluated, many interventions are available. For those in late adolescence or young adulthood, intervention usually focuses heavily on transition. Transition is a process rather than a product; it takes place over a period of time. It is usually tailored to the needs of each person (Evelo & Price, 1991; Getzel, 1990). Often formal transition teams are established, composed of secondary school personnel, parents, and the person with ADHD or LD (Haring et al., 1990). It is now recognized that the ultimate success of adolescents and adults with ADHD or LD depends greatly on the understanding and acceptance that they receive from others. In addition to educating the affected individual about his or her disorder, the practitioner should strive to give family members, spouses, educators, and employers a reasonable understanding of the strengths and weaknesses of this individual. For example, Table 8.1 lists problems reportedly experienced by people with LD or ADHD. Although this list is clearly unscientific, such an outline may be effective in educating unaffected individuals. As Ginsberg and Gerber (1990) note, understanding, acceptance, and action are key words for success with adults experiencing LD and ADHD.

The guidance, intervention, and transition process may focus on the remediation of basic academic skills, the development of vocational skills, or the development of compensatory strategies necessary for successful adult living. The third approach has been gaining popularity. Its goal is to help individuals learn and apply compensatory strategies in order to cope with their disabilities at school, in the community, or in the workplace. For learning-disabled and attention-disordered adults, this focus has emphasized the development of efficient problem solving and daily life strategies rather than the teaching of specific skills that may be difficult to generalize (Deshler, Schumacher, Lenz, & Ellis, 1983).

The treatment chapters in the remainder of this book offer a comprehensive overview of available scientific knowledge and practical clinical guidelines. As Lipsey and Wilson (1993) report in a concise, analytic review of the efficacy of psychological, educational, and behavioral treatments targeting the specific problems of people with learning and attention problems, well-developed programs are effective. A summary of some relevant articles appears in Table 8.2.

Table 8.1   Symptoms of a Learning Disability
and Attention Problems

Any student who evidences a large number of these symptoms may
well be experiencing a specific LD.

Reading
 1. Reads very slowly
 2. Never reads for pleasure; reading is not pleasant
 3. Can't remember what was just read
 4. Skips words or lines
 5. Reads out of sequence
 6. Reads literally
 7. Has trouble with metaphors
 8. Cannot tell main idea from supporting details
 9. Has trouble associating letters and their sounds
10. Mistakes one word for another
11. Becomes tired, sleepy, or develops headaches when reading
12. Sometimes judges difficulty by thickness of material

Writing
 1. Has trouble organizing thoughts
 2. Freezes and blocks when trying to write
 3. Has trouble formulating the overall thesis
 4. Has difficulty visualizing the topic
 5. Has difficulty sequencing ideas
 6. Great ideas vanish before reaching paper
 7. Cannot proofread effectively
 8. Ideas are great but mechanics and structure are weak
 9. Handwriting is poor and barely legible

Spelling
 1. Spelling of words varies from one time to the next
 2. Rotates letters: *b* for *q, d* for *p, m* for *w*
 3. Reversals: *was* for *saw, gril* for *girl*
 4. Drops or adds letters or parts of words
 5. Cannot spell common words as well as hard ones
 6. Letters often out of sequence
 7. Cannot sound out unfamiliar words
 8. Writes only with words he or she is sure of

Mathematics
 1. Reverses numbers
 2. Has difficulty with mathematical concepts
 3. Has problems with basic calculations
 4. Makes careless errors and oversights
 5. Has trouble with geometry but not algebra, or vice versa
 6. Has difficulty memorizing formulas
 7. Has trouble with word problems
 8. Has difficulty with proper sequencing

Table 8.1 *(Continued)*

Science
1. Has trouble with written material but not math
2. Does better in one science than in another
3. Has trouble with concepts
4. Has trouble with graphs and drawings
5. Has trouble memorizing formulas
6. Cannot read periodic charts
7. Has difficulty with long scientific names

Foreign language
1. Has difficulty with vocabulary and grammar
2. Has difficulty understanding spoken words
3. Shows word retrieval difficulties
4. Is able to translate written, but not oral, information

Speaking
1. Has trouble pronouncing unfamiliar words
2. Cannot get a point across orally
3. Has difficulty reading aloud
4. Evidences hesitancy in speech or stutters
5. Has difficulty understanding spoken language
6. Has trouble with variant word meanings or figurative language

Word assocation
1. Has trouble translating oral and written words
2. Cannot take notes and listen at the same time
3. Spoken words mean one thing, written another
4. Words are heard, yet not comprehended

Coordination
1. Cannot tell right from left automatically
2. Has trouble with local geography
3. Has problems following directions
4. Often feels lost in familiar settings
5. May become confused when going up or down stairs
6. Has difficulty with simple mechanical tasks
7. Cannot get organized
8. Is hyperactive or compulsive in order to compensate

Memory
1. Has problems with common names, places, and dates
2. Evidences word retrieval difficulties
3. Cannot copy accurately from chalkboards or readings
4. Frequently uses less precise words
5. Has trouble memorizing strings of letters or numbers
6. Often misplaces, loses, or forgets things
7. Lives by lists and even lists of lists.

Table 8.1   *(Continued)*

Concentration and impulsivity
   1. Cannot concentrate with background noise
   2. Thoughts wander or are incomplete
   3. Is distractible; has trouble focusing attention
   4. Becomes overloaded and tires easily
   5. Cannot do two things at once
   6. Has trouble meeting deadlines
   7. Has to be compulsive to get anything done
   8. Often acts without thinking

Tests
   1. Blanks out on exams
   2. Class work is an A; tests are a D
   3. Has trouble with multiple choice questions
   4. Has trouble getting to the point on essays
   5. Is unable to complete exams in the time allotted
   6. Misinterprets questions
   7. Has trouble organizing time or pacing self
   8. Anxiety is always present at testing time

Psychological issues
   1. Is moody, quick tempered, or easily frustrated
   2. Misunderstands facial expressions or gestures
   3. Makes literal interpretations of what is said
   4. Finds it difficult to sit down to read or write
   5. Takes too long to organize thoughts
   6. Feels lazy, stupid, or humiliated by problems
   7. Is constantly behind despite enormous effort
   8. Sees own work as crude or infantile
   9. Is afraid to let others know of trouble
   10. Is frustrated by unsuccessful efforts to read, write, and speak
   11. Feels that even good grades do not equal success
   12. Is afraid of deadlines
   13. Is afraid of filling out applications
   14. Is fearful of being misunderstood
   15. Is tongue-tied in a crowd
   16. Appears shy and isolated; has only a few friends
   17. Is self-conscious
   18. Blames self for failure, attributes success to luck

Note. Adapted from *Understanding and Teaching the Student with Learning Differences at Proctor Academy,* Project coordinator, E. B. Miller, revised May 1994. Used with permission.

Table 8.2   Meta-analysis Studies

Treatment Area and Reference	Meta-analysis Effect Size	N
Education		
Computer-based instruction; effects on achievement (Gillingham & Guthrie, 1987)	1.05	13
Computer-based instruction; K-12; effects on achievement (J. A. Kulik & Kulik, 1987)	0.31	199
Computer-based instruction with elementary school students; all outcomes (Niemiec, 1985; Niemiec, Sampson, Weinstein, & Walberg, 1987)[a]	0.45	48
Computer-assisted instructed with elementary school students; effects on achievement (Ryan, 1991)[a]	0.31	40
Computer-assisted vs. conventional instruction for elementary students; effects on achievement (C. C. Kulik, Kulik, & Bangert-Drowns, 1984)	0.48	25
Computer-aided instruction vs. conventional methods in secondary school classrooms; effects on achievement (J. A. Kulik, Bangert, & Williams, 1983)[a]	0.32	51
Computer-based education for junior and senior high school students; effect on achievement (Bangert-Drowns, Kulik, & Kulik, 1985)	0.26	42
Computer-aided instruction vs. conventional methods for college instruction; effects on achievement (C. C. Kulik, Kulik, & Cohen, 1980)[a]	0.25	59
Computer-assisted instruction for exceptional (special education) students, elementary through high school; effects on achievement (M. Schmidt, Weinstein, Niemiec, & Walberg, 1986)[a]	0.66	18
Computer-aided instruction with learning-disabled and educable mentally retarded students; effects on achievement (McDermid, 1990)	0.57	15
Computer-assisted mathematics instruction vs. traditional instruction, elementary and secondary students; effects on math achievement (Burns, 1982)	0.35	40
Computer-assisted mathematics instruction and computer programming, elementary and secondary students; effects on math achievement (Lee, 1990)[a]	0.38	72

Table 8.2   *(Continued)*

Treatment Area and Reference	Meta-analysis Effect Size	N
Programmed or individual instruction		
Individualized instruction; effects on achievement (Hood, 1991)[a]	0.17	70
Individualized systems of instruction for 6–12th-grade students; effects on achievement (Bangert, Kulik, & Kulik, 1983)	0.10	51
Individualized instruction in science courses vs. traditional lecture methods, secondary school students; effects on achievement (Aiello, 1981; Aiello & Wolfle, 1980)[a]	0.35	115
Individualized mathematics instruction for elementary and secondary students; effects on math achievement (Hartley, 1977)[a]	0.29	153
Self-paced modularized individualized mathematics instruction vs. traditional instructions for elementary and secondary students; effects on achievement (Horak, 1981)	−0.07	41
Programmed instruction vs. conventional instruction with secondary school students; effects on achievement (C. C. Kulik, Schwalb, & Kulik, 1982)[a]	0.08	48
Programmed instruction vs. conventional instruction for college teaching; effect on achievement (J. A. Kulik, Cohen, & Ebeling, 1980)[a]	0.28	56
Keller's personalized system of instruction (PSI) vs. traditional lecture methods for college teaching; effects on achievement (J. A. Kulik, Kulik, & Cohen, 1979)[a]	0.49	72
Mastery learning with Keller's PSI and Bloom's Learning for Mastery with college students; all outcomes (C. C. Kulik, Kulik, & Bangert-Drowns, 1990)[a]	0.52	103
Feedback about correct answers in computerized and programmed instruction with adult learners; effects on learning (Schimmel, 1983)[a]	0.47	15
Audio- and visual-based instruction		
Visual-based instruction (film, TV, etc.) vs. conventional teaching for college students; effects on achievement (P. A. Cohen, Ebeling, & Kulik, 1981)[a]	0.15	65

Table 8.2 *(Continued)*

Treatment Area and Reference	Meta-analysis Effect Size	N
Postlethwait's audio-tutorial method of instruction vs. traditional lecture methods in college teaching; effects on achievement (J. A. Kulik, Kulik, & Cohen, 1979)[a]	0.20	47
Visual media instruction for students in nursing education; effects on attitude change (Schermer, 1984)[a]	0.68	12
Interactive video instruction; effects on achievement (McNeil & Nelson, 1990)[a]	0.50	63
Interactive video instruction in defense training, industrial training and higher education; effects on knowledge, performance, retention and instruction completion time (J. D. Fletcher, 1990)	0.50	28
Cooperative task structures		
Cooperative vs. uncooperative task structures; effects on achievement and productivity (D. W. Johnson, Maruyama, Johnson, Nelson, & Skon, 1981)[a]	0.72	122
Cooperative learning with K–12 students; all outcomes (Hall, 1989)	0.30	137
Cooperative vs. competitive and individualistic instructional approaches in adult education; effects on achievement (D. W. Johnson & Johnson, 1987)[a]	0.62	133
Cooperative learning with students with mild disabilities; effects on achievement (Stevens & Slavin, 1991)	0.31	11
Cooperative learning methods with handicapped K–12 students in mainstreamed classrooms; effects on achievement (G. A. Carlson, 1987)	0.16	13
Cooperative vs. noncooperative task arrangements for handicapped-nonhandicapped and ethnically different groups; all outcomes (D. W. Johnson, Johnson, & Maruyama, 1983)[a]	0.75	98
Student tutoring		
Student tutoring of elementary and secondary students (tutor's experience); effects on achievement (P. A. Cohen, Kulik, & Kulik, 1982)[a]	0.33	38
Student tutoring of elementary and secondary students; effects on achievement (P. A. Cohen et al., 1982)[a]	0.40	52

Table 8.2   *(Continued)*

Treatment Area and Reference	Meta-analysis Effect Size	N
Tutoring of special education students by other special education students (tutor's experience); effects on achievement (Cook, Scruggs, Mastropieri, & Casto, 1986)[a]	0.65	19
Tutoring of special education students by other special education students; effects on achievement (Cook et al., 1986)[a]	0.59	19
Tutorial methods of training the conservation concept in preoperational children; effects on mastery (Phillips, 1983)[a]	0.98	302
Behavioral objectives, reinforcement, cues, feedback, etc.		
Behavioral objectives for instruction with elementary through adult students; effects on achievement (Asencio, 1984)[a]	0.12	111
Positive reinforcement in the classroom; effects on learning (Lysakowski & Walberg, 1980, 1981)[a]	1.17	39
Instructional cues, student participation, and corrective feedback in the classroom; effects on learning (Lysakowski & Walberg, 1982)	0.97	54
Other general education		
Mastery learning, group-based, grades 1–12 and college; all outcomes (Guskey & Pigott, 1988)[a]	0.61	43
Mastery learning, group-based, primary and secondary students; effects on achievement (Slavin, 1987)	0.25	17
Home instruction supported by school-based programs for elementary school children; effects on achievement (Grane, Weinstein, & Walberg, 1983)[a]	0.68	29
Assignment of homework to elementary and secondary students; effects on achievement (Paschal, Weinstein, & Walberg, 1984)[a]	0.30	15
Modality-based instruction; effects on achievement (Kavale & Forness, 1987)[a]	0.14	39
Technology-based instructional approach with American and Japanese students; effects on achievement (Schwalb, 1987)[a]	0.41	116
Use of simulation games in instruction; effect on achievement (Dekkers & Donatti, 1981)[a]	0.28	93
Instructional simulation games vs. conventional instruction; effects on cognitive learning (Szczurek, 1982)	0.33	33

Table 8.2 *(Continued)*

Treatment Area and Reference	Meta-analysis Effect Size	N
Enrichment programs for gifted students; cognitive, creativity and affective outcomes (Wallace, 1990)[a]	0.55	20
Psychological and affective interventions for underprepared learners; grade point average and persistence outcomes (W. L. Collins, 1987)[a]	0.36	14
Test taking		
Coaching programs for achievement test performance, elementary through college; effects on test scores (Bangert-Drowns, Kulik, & Kulik, 1983)[a]	0.25	30
Coaching programs on SAT for college students; effects on test scores (DerSimonian & Laird, 1983)	0.19	22
Coaching programs for SAT and other aptitude tests, elementary through college; effects on test scores (J. A. Kulik, Bangert-Drowns, & Kulik, 1984)[a]	0.33	35
Coaching for the SAT; effects on test scores (Messick & Jungeblut, 1981)	0.15	12
Becker, 1990	0.30	23
Training in test-taking skills for elementary and secondary students; effects on achievement test scores (Samson, 1985)[a]	0.33	24
Training in test-taking skills on standardized achievement tests for elementary students; effects on test scores (Scruggs, Bennion, & White, 1984)	0.21	24
Practice test taking on aptitude and achievement tests, elementary through college; effects on test scores (J. A. Kulik, Kulik, & Bangert, 1984)	0.32	40
Test anxiety		
Therapy for test anxiety; effects on performance (O'Bryan, 1985)	0.36	119
Therapy for test anxiety; effects on anxiety (O'Bryan, 1985)	1.07	119
Therapy for test anxiety; all outcomes (Hembree, 1988)	0.63	125
Thompson, 1987[a]	0.57	195
Therapy for text anxiety (college students); all outcomes (Dole, Rockey, & DiTomasso, 1983)	0.80	46
Therapy for test anxiety (college students); effects on anxiety and performance (M. M. Harris, 1988)	0.58	70

Table 8.2   *(Continued)*

Treatment Area and Reference	Meta-analysis Effect Size	N
Early intervention for disadvantaged or handicapped children		
Headstart early childhood education programs; cognitive outcomes (Administration for Children, Youth, and Families, 1983)[a]	0.34	71
R. C. Collins, 1984	0.33	49
Preschool intervention programs for culturally disadvantaged children; 5–14-year follow-up effects on achievement and cognitive outcomes (Goldring & Presbrey, 1986)[a]	0.24	8
Early intervention programs for environmentally at-risk (disadvantaged) infants; effects on IQ and other variables (Casto & White, 1984; Utah State University Exceptional Child Center, 1983)[a]	0.43	26
Intervention programs for kindergarten children; all outcomes (R. J. Lewis & Vosburgh, 1988)	0.41	65
Special education programs or classrooms		
Special education classroom placement vs. regular class placement for exceptional children; effects on achievement (Carlberg & Kavale, 1980)	−0.15	50
Early childhood special education; all outcomes (Snyder & Sheehan, 1983)	0.48	8
Mainstreaming vs. segregated special education for disabled K–9 students; effects on achievement (Wang & Baker, 1986)	0.44	11
Direct instruction in special education; effects on achievement, intellectual ability, readiness skills, on-task behavior, and affect (W. A. T. White, 1987)[a]	0.84	25
Educational interventions for at-risk populations (students in danger of failing to complete their education), K–12; effects on achievement (Slavin & Madden, 1989)[a]	0.63	28
Computer-assisted instruction for exceptional (special education) students, K–12; effects on achievement (M. Schmidt et al., 1986)[a]	0.66	18
Computer-aided instruction with learning-disabled and educable mentally retarded students; effects on achievement (McDermid, 1990)	0.57	17
Cooperative learning with students with mild disabilities; effects on achievement (Stevens & Slavin, 1991)	0.31	11

Table 8.2 *(Continued)*

Treatment Area and Reference	Meta-analysis Effect Size	N
Cooperative learning methods with handicapped K–12 students in mainstreamed classrooms; effects on achievement (G. A. Carlson, 1987)	0.16	13
Cooperative vs. noncooperative task arrangements for handicapped-nonhandicapped and ethnically different groups; all outcomes (D. W. Johnson et al., 1983)[a]	0.75	98
Perceptual-motor and sensory stimulation treatment for developmental disabilities		
Perceptual-motor training for learning-disabled and disadvantaged children; effects on academic, cognitive, and perceptual-motor outcomes (Kavale & Mattson, 1983)	0.08	180
Frostig training for development of visual perception in children with learning problems; effects on perceptual skills and academic achievement (Kavale, 1984)[a]	0.09	59
Sensory integration therapy for patients with developmental disabilities or learning disabilities; effects on academic achievement, motor performance, and language function (Ottenbacher, 1982)	0.79	8
Clinically applied vestibular stimulation as a sensory enrichment therapy for infants at risk and children with developmental delay; effects on cognitive, language, motor, alertness, and physiological outcomes (Ottenbacher & Petersen, 1984)[a]	0.71	14
Tactile stimulation of developmentally delayed and at-risk infants; all outcomes (Ottenbacher et al., 1987)	0.58	19

Note. From "The Efficacy of Psychological, Educational and Behavioral Treatment," by M. W. Lipsey and D. B. Wilson, 1993, *American Psychologist, 48,* pp. 1181–1209. Used with permission.
[a]Studies included in refined distribution.

Nearly 2 million students with LD were served in elementary and secondary school settings in 1985 (Office of Special Education and Rehabilitation Services, 1986). Nevertheless, as of this writing there continues to be a dearth of systematic, scientific research identifying the college or vocational programs that are the most effective in the long term for students with LD or ADHD (McGuire et al., 1990; Vogel & Adelman, 1990b). The heterogeneity of these populations suggests that such research will be detailed, lengthy, and difficult to complete. In the meantime, clinicians must prepare students with LD or ADHD for college programs and must educate the professional community at large about these programs and about the types of information college counselors and special educators will need to work effectively with the LD and ADHD student populations. Rothstein (1986) notes that it is also the responsibility of clinicians to teach learning-disabled people to be assertive and not embarrassed about their disabilities. The responsibility of obtaining services falls on the shoulders of the person with LD or ADHD, the responsibility of generating data so that appropriate services can be implemented falls on the clinician, and the responsibility of developing and implementing appropriate programs falls on the college or university.

Which individuals with LD or ADHD should be counseled into college programs? Researchers find that those accepted into four-year colleges often have less severe academic achievement problems and are more likely to come from enriched home environments and educational experiences (Gajar, Salvia, Gajria, & Salvia, 1989; Shaywitz & Shaw, 1988; Vogel, 1986). Hoy and Gregg (1986) list seven characteristics that when present increase the likelihood that a learning-disabled student will succeed in college:

1. High motivation
2. Willingness to experiment with new ideas
3. Verbal intellectual skills at a standard score of 90 or above (23rd percentile or better)
4. Ability to comprehend abstract language
5. Emotional maturity
6. Socially appropriate behavior
7. Career goals congruent with ability

Many clinicians, including school counselors, either know too little about LD and ADHD support services available at the college level or, because their experience is limited, do not view students with LD or ADHD as college material (National Joint Commission on Learning Disabilities, 1983). Such clinicians cannot adequately serve the transitional needs of students with LD or ADHD (Shaw, Byron, Norlander, McGuire, & Anderson, 1987). It is now recommended that public schools become more involved in preparing students with LD or ADHD capable of entering college to do so (Seidenberg, 1986a; Wooten & Wooten, 1987). Even with support, however, the choice is not easy, and a risk-benefit analysis is essential. Community colleges, for example, offer accessibility, less stringent admission requirements (if any), a wide variety of course work, basic educational courses, transition services, and often special education support. They are not expensive because they are community based. Money that might otherwise have been spent on housing or campuses can be used to provide other special services.

Rose (1991) suggests three kinds of support for individuals with LD in college programs:

1. Appropriate accommodations under Section 504 or related law
2. Remedial services
3. Special support services

A remedial model of intervention for LD and ADHD focuses on improving basic academic skills such as reading, mathematics, writing, and spelling and basic executive skills such as attention, planning, and organization. Remedial programs have a long and honorable history in the elementary and secondary education and clinical literature. However, the benefits of these programs are difficult to measure, and they may not yield as much long-term advantage as programs that focus on strengths and compensation. Further, the short- and long-term results of cognitively based remedial programs for children and adolescents with ADHD have been dismal (Abikoff, 1991). As noted earlier, it is not that these students cannot learn how to plan, think, or solve problems, but that they do not do these things consistently in their daily lives.

Remediation has traditionally focused on organized, repetitive practice as a way to improve skills. In the LD area, most advocates of remedial approaches emphasize the understanding of learning styles and multisensory teaching techniques as ways to facilitate the acquisition of educational material. In fact, some educators suggest that without knowledge of an individual's learning style, intervention will be compromised (Bingham, 1989). Proponents of the learning styles model characterize styles according to the following four types:

- *Visual.* The visual learner is comfortable with books and graphs.
- *Auditory.* The auditory learner tends to talk, memorize easily, perform poorly on group tests, and have poor perception of time and space.
- *Kinesthetic.* The kinesthetic learner functions best by moving and touching.
- *Tactile.* The tactile learner has trouble with one-to-one correspondence, rote computing, and sequencing at any level. This student requires concrete objects for learning and has difficulty learning abstract symbols. Diagrams and other illustrations are essential (Marsh & Price, 1980).

As noted in Chapters 2 and 6, an alternative way of looking at learning is to focus on the rote, conceptual, visual, or verbal skills necessary to perform a particular academic task. This model dovetails nicely with the learning styles approach. However, the clinician must keep in mind that much of the work in this area is based on theory and clinical practice rather than on firm scientific evidence.

Once an individual's learning style has been identified, the remedial approach concentrates on improving the skills necessary to perform the academic task being remediated more competently. The four traditional approaches used for educational remediation are

1. Traditional phonics
2. A sight word approach
3. A word pattern approach (this primarily teaches decoding and relies on the ability to rhyme ending sounds)
4. A language experience or whole language approach

Again, despite the popularity of this model, limited research data exist to suggest that it is a better intervention or offers greater understanding of individuals with LD or ADHD than other available models. This model simply appears to make the most sense. Caution is needed not so much because these interventions are ineffective as because they are untested.

Many university administrators are not fully responsive to the needs of the handicapped, especially the learning disabled and those with ADHD, and graduate school administrators are even less responsive (Parks, Antonoff, Drake, Skiba, & Soberman, 1987). Often at the administrative level, modifications are made based on funding availability and legal requirements rather than on the actual needs of the student population. These issues will be addressed in depth in Chapter 12.

Increasingly with university faculty, the emphasis has been on identifying the specific needs of students with LD or ADHD and providing them with accommodations. For example, the following set of teaching accommodations has been suggested for college students with LD or

ADHD. As with other strategies, these interventions may not reflect the culmination of science, but they are certainly practical. In fact, many of these suggestions are beneficial for all students and simply constitute good teaching. Instructors should consider

- Making the syllabus available four to six weeks before the beginning of the class and, when possible, being available to discuss it with students considering taking the course
- Beginning lectures with a review of the previous lecture and an overview of topics to be covered that day or an outline of the lecture
- Using a chalkboard or overhead projector to outline and summarize lecture material, being mindful of legibility and the need to read aloud what is written
- Explaining technical language, specific terminology, or foreign words
- Emphasizing important points, main ideas, and key concepts orally in lecture or high-lighting them with colored pens on an overhead projector
- Speaking distinctly and at a relaxed pace, pausing occasionally to respond to questions, offering students a chance to catch up in their note taking
- Noticing and responding to nonverbal signs of confusion or frustration in students
- Trying to diminish, if not eliminate, auditory and visual classroom distractions such as hallway noise or flickering fluorescent lights
- Leaving time for a question-and-answer period and/or discussion periodically and at the end of each lecture
- Trying to determine whether students understand the material by asking volunteers to offer an example, summarize, or respond to a question
- Providing periodic summaries during lectures emphasizing key concepts
- Offering assignments in writing as well as orally and being available for clarification
- Providing a suggested time line when making long-range assignments and suggesting appropriate checkpoints
- Being available during office hours for clarification of lecture material, assignments, and reading
- Selecting a textbook with a study guide, if available, offering questions and answers to review and quiz sections
- Helping students find study partners and organizing study groups
- Providing study questions for exams that demonstrate the format to be used as well as the content
- Asking the student how the instructor can facilitate his or her learning
- Discussing in private with a student suspected of LD, describing what was observed, and, if appropriate, referring the student for available support services

It has also been suggested that technology has become more valuable in assisting individuals with LD or ADHD (P. Green & Brightman, 1990; Raskin, 1993). As defined by the Technology-Related Assistance for Individuals with Disabilities Act of 1988, an "assistive technology device" is "any item, piece of equipment or product system, whether acquired commercially off the shelf, modified or customized, that is used to increase, maintain or improve functional capabilities of individuals with disabilities." This technology is not intended to teach or instruct but is used to increase access to instruction. Assistive technology has demonstrated the potential, though research has been limited, to help adults with LD or ADHD compensate for their problems (T. Collins, 1990). Assistive technology includes word-processing software (with its spelling and grammar checkers), personal data managers, laptop computers, talking calculators, listening aids, and the like. A review of the available research suggests that very little debate has occurred in the LD and ADHD fields concerning these devices (T. Collins, 1990; Primus, 1990). Yet, as will be discussed in Chapter 10, the use of everything from personal tape recorders, to day planners, to computers is being suggested as helpful to the LD and ADHD populations.

It is common for individuals with LD to receive lower paying jobs than their nondisabled peers (Herzog & Falk, 1991; E. S. Shapiro & Lentz, 1991). Further, E. S. Shapiro and Lentz (1991) report that learning-disabled students, even two years after graduation, hold near minimal wage jobs. Unemployment rates for dropouts, whether they have LD or not, are twice as high as for high school graduates (U.S. Department of Labor, Bureau of Labor Statistics, 1987). Although data are scarce, the logic is difficult to deny: If appropriate vocational and educational programs are not provided to students with LD and ADHD who leave school, it is likely that they will struggle vocationally and experience great adjustment difficulties as they enter adulthood (Minskoff et al., 1988). Though researchers have hypothesized what the negative impact in the workplace might be, limited scientific data are available. Problems such as difficulty with social skills; problems with memory, organization, and auditory processing; and linguistic weaknesses are all thought to contribute to poor work performance (Clement-Heist et al., 1992; R. M. Matthews et al., 1982). Nonetheless, the data are inconsistent. Some researchers report problems (Blalock, 1981; Hoffman et al., 1987), while others assert that the LD and ADHD populations experience no problems different from the norm in the workplace (Felton, 1986; Gerber, 1988).

A number of variables appear critical in predicting successful vocational outcome for adults with LD or ADHD. In their review of the literature, Vogel and Adelman (1993) identified 10 employment issues for adults with LD:

1. Transitions into the workplace
2. Obtaining employment
3. Type of employment
4. Rate of employment
5. Wages
6. Job satisfaction
7. Job success
8. Effect of LD on vocational performance
9. Development of compensatory strategies
10. Employer perceptions of disability

These authors concluded that despite "considerable evidence that some adults with LDs achieve success in the workplace, they still experience a disproportion of unemployment and underemployment" (Vogel & Adelman, 1993, p. 230). In particular, it appears that females with histories of LD or ADHD are underrepresented in the workforce. Furthermore, individuals with LD or ADHD, even after several years of employment, are found overwhelmingly in entry-level positions, earning near minimum wage salaries, and experiencing greater levels of unemployment (Mannuzza et al., 1993). How much of these two groups are composed of individuals with lower cognitive skills rather than those with true LD or ADHD has yet to be determined (Herrnstein & Murray, 1994). Adelman and Vogel reported that a major factor differentiating successful from unsuccessful individuals is a match between career and ability.

Finally, limited data are available concerning the difference in vocational outcome for adults with LD or ADHD when those completing college programs are compared with those who simply enter job training. In fact, there are also limited data to suggest that learning-disabled students who graduate from college enter the white-collar workforce (P. B. Adelman & Vogel, 1990).

There is a small but growing body of research about programs that are successful at providing occupational skills training to learning-disabled individuals. These programs fall into two broad categories, those that help the individual to understand and develop compensatory strategies and those that attempt direct remediation.

It has often been reported that the family-friend network is the primary and perhaps most successful way for people with LD or ADHD to find employment (Haring et al., 1990; E. S. Shapiro & Lentz, 1991; Taymans, 1982). Further, D'Amico (1991) found that certain demographic factors, including low socioeconomic status and urban residence, place learning-disabled individuals at risk for greater employment problems.

Minskoff and DeMoss (1993) proposed a structured model for the skills needed for success in the workplace. These authors developed the TRACT model to assess and develop the basic academic skills necessary for 26 vocational education programs. The model was designed to be used by special education teachers in conjunction with vocational educators. It was intended to provide a positive first experience for students with LD in the transition to adult vocation.

Another model was developed as part of a LD training project (Dowdy, 1990). It focuses on compensation, accommodations, modifications, and strategies (CAMS) for the LD population entering the workforce. Table 8.3 shows an example of this model.

In 1991 in response to the increasing volume of information about vocational training for the learning disabled, the U.S. Department of Labor recommended the following:

- *Incorporate appropriate instructional strategies into job search training and preemployment components.* Since a large proportion of JTPA adults who are reading below the seventh-grade level may be learning disabled, even if a program does not routinely screen for LD, it makes sense to integrate into group components some of the simpler instructional techniques (e.g., small groups, video and verbal material rather than just written manuals, verbal and untimed tests) that work well for persons with LD and ADHD.

- *Combine basic skills instruction with functional occupational skills instruction.* Learning-disabled persons benefit from a training program integrating basic education with applied functional skill development. Such training can be done in a traditional classroom, in a vocational training setting, or in the workplace on the job.

- *Avoid arbitrary referral of persons with low reading skills to possibly inappropriate remediation programs.* Many JTPA and JOBS programs refer persons with low reading levels to adult education programs. However, one reason for the high dropout rate from traditional, education, or remedial programs may be that the classes are not designed to accommodate the learning disabled or those with attention deficit. Some screening system needs to be developed to identify those at risk due to LD or ADHD and to refer them for appropriate assessment and service.

At the national level:

- *An interagency work group on adult LD should be established.* This group should include representatives from JTPA, vocational rehabilitation, adult education, jobs, and vocational

Table 8.3 Learning Disabilities: Characteristics, Vocational Impact, and CAMS

LD Characteristics	Vocational Impact	CAMS
Attention: Diagnostic Statistical Manual—III-R (1987) Criteria		
1. Fidgets—feels restless	Difficulty with jobs that are primarily sedentary (clerical, benchwork) Difficulty concentrating on tasks Agitates coworkers or supervisors Increases risk for accidents Low stress tolerance	Build movement into activity Let client work standing up Chart or time productivity or work rate
2. Has difficulty remaining seated when required to do so	Inability to work in sedentary job Difficulty concentrating on and completing a task Low stress tolerance	Build movement into activity Let client work standing up Chart or time productivity or work rate
3. Easily distracted	Difficulty working in clerical pool or group setting Problems around machinery, breakroom, high traffic areas in office Cannot work with Muzak or by window Increased risk for accidents, mistakes, and misunderstanding of instructions, etc. Reduces rate of job performance and production Reduces or interferes with concentration to task Produces job fatigue or emotional stress	Highlight significant characteristics of the activity Minimize distractions Isolate client to worksite Use earphones or plugs Provide step-by-step checklist; ask client to record own behavior

Note. The table lists specific behaviors characteristic of LD, examples of the possible vocational impact of each, and possible compensations, accommodations, modifications, and strategies (CAMS). The vocational impact may be used to assist in career counseling; implementation of the CAMS will maximize success in the environment. Adapted from model by C. A. Dowdy, Education Building, Room 125, University of Alabama in Birmingham, University Station, AL 35294. Copyright 1990 by UAB 1990 LD Training Project. Used with permission.

education. The purpose of the group would be to improve the quality of services to the adult LD and even ADHD population. A coordinated federal agency effort at sharing knowledge and experience could encourage the development of integrated policy guidelines for various programs, joint research, and technical assistance.

- *The Department of Labor should review the need for a department research and technical assistance agenda to examine the LD population and current practices for serving them.* This should include:

1. Research on the size and characteristics of the LD and ADHD populations
2. Studies to examine different employment-related problems and service needs for subgroups within these populations (e.g., older adults vs. teenagers and young adults)
3. A review of various assessment tools and the development of a technical assistance package for use by program operators
4. Research on the current practices and extent of services for LD and ADHD adults by JTPA jobs, vocational rehabilitation, community colleges, and other entities. Once more knowledge has been accumulated, it will be useful to conduct studies to identify and document exemplary service models and establish pilot and demonstration projects.

Although educational training and vocational development have been the traditional foci of transition planning for those with LD and ADHD (Will, 1984), emphasis has shifted to the development of general life skills, interpersonal relations, and stress and even money management. G. Weiss and Hechtman (1993) report that "it is our clinical belief that adult patients with ADHD can be helped by . . . behavioral therapies and psychoeducation. When the patients are married or living in couple relationships, marital therapy is likely to be needed. If they are parents they will also require help in the parenting role" (p. 406). However, of all of the areas of remediation and compensation, these are the least researched or understood in terms of their potential benefits to the LD and ADHD populations. Nonetheless, as Halpern (1993) notes, these may be the very issues upon which vocational or academic success hinges. Barton and Fuhrman (1994) suggest that the effects of LD or ADHD in adult adjustment fall into four categories:

1. Stress and anxiety resulting from being overwhelmed by the complexity of life's demands
2. Low self-esteem and feelings of incompetence
3. Unresolved grief
4. Helplessness resulting from limited understanding of abilities and disabilities

When they experience emotional difficulty, adults with histories of LD or ADHD may bring a unique set of needs and problems to the therapy setting. Regardless of theoretical perspective, it is critical for therapists to understand that individuals with LD or ADHD, although they share many life experiences with others, also have a unique set of experiences that sets them apart. The learning-disabled individual's linguistically based problems may make insight and problem solving difficult in therapy. For someone with ADHD, a history of impulsivity and lack of reflection may create unique problems in therapy.

The science of medicines to help adults with ADHD or LD is still in its infancy. Much of the available literature concerns the use of stimulant medications for the treatment of childhood ADHD. In regard to late adolescent and adult ADHD, though certainly much less research is available than for young children, the data are clear: medications offer an important component of treatment for this population. In regard to medications that might facilitate learning, the literature is less clear. A generally scientific presentation of the current situation will be offered in Chapter 13. As the reader will learn, there are a number of very promising medications that may in the future become standard as part of the treatment for LD.

CHAPTER 9

Psychosocial Treatments

ADULTS WITH HISTORIES of LD or ADHD usually seek assistance for life problems related to emotional discomfort and marital or family issues for the same reasons as everyone else in our society. As Gordon and McClure (1983) report, "The best non-medical interventions (for ADHD) are practical, commonsense adjustments to an impulsive and disorganized style" (p. 95). Unfortunately, common sense suggests that people with ADHD or LD will be more frustrated, apathetic, and pessimistic than others about psychosocial treatments, decreasing the probability of treatment success. Nevertheless, there is very little research that describes accurately, even in a general way, the unique emotional, cognitive, and behavioral difficulties these people experience, or the benefits they may derive from psychosocial treatments. There are, instead, a number of untested hypotheses about the specific life problems of the adult LD and ADHD populations. Barton and Fuhrman (1994) suggest that individuals with histories of LD or ADHD bring four problems when they seek counseling:

1. Stress and anxiety resulting from struggles to meet life's demands
2. Low self-esteem and feelings of incompetence
3. Grief over lack of accomplishments
4. Helplessness

Yet these same issues likely also affect adults without ADHD or LD.

People with histories of LD or ADHD are reported to have a lower self-concept and to be less motivated to succeed academically than their nonimpaired peers (Deshler, 1978). However, well-controlled studies have not found that it is specifically the LD or ADHD symptoms that place individuals at risk for these difficulties. As discussed in an earlier chapter, Rourke and Fuerst (1991) reviewed nearly 700 articles published beginning in 1970 dealing with the psychosocial functioning of children with LD. Although a causal link between LD and emotional functioning, in which the first contributes to the second, has been claimed repeatedly, most of the research purportedly supporting these claims is inconsistent. A recent study of the psychosocial functioning over three age ranges of more than 700 children with histories of LD found that their functioning was stable between the ages of 7 and 13 years (Rourke, 1985). Furthermore, there was no demonstration in this large population that children with LD manifested increasing psychopathology with increasing age. As reviewed in Chapter 2, it appears that the majority of children with LD do not experience many more symptoms of psychiatric disturbance—in particular, of emotional distress—than others. The development of pathological patterns of functioning in this group does not appear to increase with age. Factors other than increased age and cumulative exposure to negative school experiences secondary to LD appear to account for increased risk for emotional problems (Jorm, Share, Matthews, & MacLean, 1986). Loeber et al. (1995) studied a population of almost 200 clinic-referred preadolescent boys over a six-year period. They found that parental substance abuse, socioeconomic status, and oppositional behavior appeared to be the key factors in predicting which boys would progress to more serious psychiatric disorders, including conduct disorder. LD was not found to be a predictor in this study.

Nonetheless, common sense and clinical observation suggest that as the ADHD and LD populations move into adulthood, they struggle emotionally and must work to overcome problems such as denial and underconfidence (Ness & Price, 1990). An important first step in treating adults with ADHD or LD is helping them to become active participants in their treatment. They must learn to understand their disability and the impact it has on their daily lives and must begin to focus on their strengths (S. Goldstein & Goldstein, 1990; Ness & Price, 1990). It is critical that adults with ADHD or LD come to understand the effect their disability has on learning, working, and daily life, and that they do so in a way that is practical and avoids assigning blame.

This chapter begins with an overview of research on psychosocial treatments for the ADHD and LD populations. These treatments have focused on either alleviating the symptoms of ADHD or LD (e.g., increasing attention) or resolving emotional problems secondary to these or comorbid disorders. Treatments for children are discussed briefly because of the extensive literature on this subject. As of this writing, there is almost no literature on similar interventions for the adult population. For example, no multitreatment study or, for that matter, treatment study specifically focusing on a psychosocial treatment for adult ADHD has been published. Because there is no specific literature in this area, a commonsense, clinical rationale will be offered, suggesting the potential benefits of psychosocial interventions and discussing them in light of the overlapping and separate issues related to ADHD and LD. The counseling, marital, parenting, and related psychosocial treatments offered to people with LD are similar to the treatments offered to people with ADHD (Gerber & Reiff, 1994; Hallowell & Ratey, 1994).

The suggestions in this chapter are just that, suggestions. They may hold clinical benefit, but they have not yet been scientifically validated. Further, it is important to recognize that these interventions, taken generically, may operate differently for different individuals, even within a specific LD or ADHD population. Thus, for example, the qualities of impulsiveness that affect some people with ADHD and not others may result in different treatment outcomes. Similarly, people with conceptually based adult LD may have difficulty with a cognitively based treatment, while those with rote learning problems and fairly intact reasoning skills may greatly benefit.

The chapter continues with a review of marital issues; an extensive set of suggestions for families in which a child, parent, or both experiences ADHD or LD; and a review of models suggested for counseling, with emphasis on cognitive treatment. The chapter concludes with troubleshooting tips and general suggestions for clinicians who work with the adult ADHD and LD populations.

Review of Psychosocial Treatments for Children with ADHD or LD

The cognitive mediational strategies used with developmentally impaired children, including those with ADHD or LD, represent one of the major therapy foci for these populations. This work is rooted in the research and writings of Luria (1959, 1961) and Vygotsky (1962). These Russian psychologists hypothesized that behavioral self-control is developed in three stages. In the initial stage, children's behavior is controlled and mediated from the outside by others. In the second stage, children learn to control their own behavior but require self-generated external direction (talking to themselves) as a means of initiating and following through with tasks. By the third stage, children develop the ability to internalize mediational strategies. Thus, behavior is controlled by the individual through a covert, unobserved process. Because this theory appeared to best explain the self-control inadequacies observed in inattentive, impulsive, and some learning-disabled children, it was embraced by a number of researchers starting in the early 1960s. The 1960s and 1970s witnessed an increase in applied research into ways to help impulsive and inattentive children to develop skills and successfully pass through these three stages. As Keough and Barkett (1980) noted, cognitive-behavioral training promised to reduce impulsive behavior and promote more effective problem-solving strategies with good potential for generalization.

Early research studies using these strategies with impaired children were innovative and appeared to yield positive results (Palkes, Stewart, & Freedman, 1971; Palkes, Stewart, & Kahana, 1968). This theoretical model was eventually integrated with behavior modification technology. The resulting school of psychology has come to be known as "cognitive behavior modification" (Meichenbaum, 1975a, 1977; Meichenbaum & Goodman, 1971). This area of psychology has gained widespread attention. Techniques developed by these and other researchers have been used with populations of developmentally impaired children, including those with LD (Hallahan & Sapona, 1983), behavioral problems (Rhode, Morgan, & Young, 1983), brain injury (Gajar, Schloss, Schloss, & Thompson, 1984), and ADHD (for a review, see Braswell & Bloomquist, 1991). Positive effects for children with ADHD have been observed in special education settings (Hallahan, Marshall, & Lloyd, 1981), as well as in regular classrooms (Rooney, Hallahan, & Lloyd, 1984).

As reviewed by S. Goldstein and Goldstein (1990), these cognitive-behavioral techniques attempt to alter thinking skills in order to improve social and related behavior, including on-task performance (K. R. Harris, 1986), behavioral compliance (Christie, Hiss, & Lozanoff, 1984), positive attribution (Licht, Kistner, Ozkaragoz, Shapiro, & Clausen, 1985), and social interaction (Kirby & Grimley, 1986). The idea that children can change their behavior by changing their thinking has been a popular one. It has been hypothesized that, through improved patterns of thinking, children can gain self-control, which increases their chances of managing their behavior effectively as they interact with the environment.

In regard to cognitive strategy research, techniques studied over the past 20 years with children have included self-recording (Broden, Hall, & Mitts, 1971), self-evaluation (Kanfer, 1970), self-reinforcement (Lovitt & Curtiss, 1969), self-punishment (Kaufman & O'Leary, 1972), self-instruction (Meichenbaum, 1975b), external cuing (Blick & Test, 1987), and attribution training (M. K. Reid & Borkowski, 1987). Although these techniques hold intuitive appeal as ways to help people with ADHD or LD, a scientific, well-controlled literature documenting the short- and long-term benefits of these interventions for children has not been forthcoming. Abikoff (1985, 1987) and Abikoff et al. (1988) have argued on the basis of their review of the literature that, whereas some of these interventions may be helpful for normal or even learning-disabled children, they are clearly not of benefit to those with ADHD or with a combination of ADHD and LD. However, even these critics have acknowledged that within-group comparisons demonstrate some benefits from these interventions, based on teacher-reported behavior (Abikoff et al., 1988). Even though it is unlikely that children with ADHD or LD will greatly benefit from these treatments (Abikoff, 1991), the treatments continue to be extremely popular with clinicians and school counselors (DuPaul & Stoner, 1994; Polirstok, 1987).

For an in-depth review of the research on cognitive and cognitive-behavioral strategies and their use with children with ADHD or LD, the interested reader is referred to S. Goldstein and Goldstein (1990), S. Goldstein (1995), and Braswell and Bloomquist (1991). Finally, it is essential to note that in general these strategies remain untested in regard to problems related to adult ADHD and LD. It is unclear whether these strategies can be extended upward into the adult affected population. The success of these interventions with adults experiencing other problems that often co-occur with ADHD and LD, such as depression or anxiety, however, gives reason for optimism (Beck, 1976).

As this text goes to press, there does not appear to be even a small definitive literature critically examining the potential benefits for adults with ADHD or LD of psychosocial treatments—neither treatments targeting problems unique to these two populations nor, for that matter, those targeting the general life problems that all people experience. For this reason, in the absence of sound research on these populations, this chapter will focus on the practical suggestions offered in the clinical literature. A cognitive focus will be emphasized because related research with other populations implies that cognitive treatments may also benefit people with ADHD or LD. It is also important to mention that with the explosion of interest in adult ADHD, most resources available to clinicians offering these types of interventions are directed at ADHD rather than LD.

Overview of Psychosocial Treatment

Psychosocial treatment for ADHD or LD begins with the diagnosis. Many people report to clinicians that finally understanding the source of their problems and the relationship of one problem to another is very helpful. For example, Murphy and LeVert (1995) outlined six stages through which adults pass when coping with a diagnosis of ADHD. These stages are initial relief and optimism followed for some by denial, anger and resentment, grief, immobilization, and accommodation.

Ratey et al. (1992) argued that the treatment of adult ADHD has five aspects, four of them psychosocial. In addition to medication, these authors noted diagnosis and identification, structuring of the environment, psychoeducation, and "character assault." Psychoeducation appears to address the rippling effects that ADHD symptoms have on related problems with mood, lability, daily activities, and so forth. Character assault is described as psychotherapy to help individuals with ADHD understand their maladaptive characteristics and modify them. In fact, without any empirical foundation, Ratey et al. (1995) write, "Long term therapy usually is indicated for the ADHD individual" (p. 231).

Murphy and LeVert (1995) suggest that

therapy for ADD really begins at the moment of diagnosis, when you learn the name of the condition with which you have suffered so long. In fact, the primary aim of therapy is to help patients fully understand the disorder and how it manifests itself in their lives. From this knowledge stems all other benefits and goals of treatment. (p. 104)

Thus, the axiom "Knowledge *must be* power" has been embraced almost evangelically in the primarily popular literature about the psychosocial treatment of adult ADHD. The literature on the treatment of adult LD is minimal, but it is similar. These popular texts are short on science, long on nonscience, and possibly even longer on nonsense. Some authors clearly state that they make no claims about the benefits of certain interventions, such as diet, exercise, and stress management for ADHD or confidence building for LD, and then proceed to enthusiastically and often without reservation recommend these interventions (K. Kelly & Ramundo, 1993; Murphy & LeVert, 1995; G. Weiss, 1992).

Marital Issues

It has been suggested, on the basis of clinical experience, that adults with histories of ADHD, and possibly those with histories of LD, have greater and more varied marital problems than unaffected individuals (Gerber & Reiff, 1994; Hallowell & Ratey, 1994; K. Kelly & Ramundo, 1993). From their clinical work, Hallowell and Ratey (1994) derive 25 tips to help couples with marital issues when one partner suffers from ADHD. Many of these suggestions would probably also be helpful for adults affected with LD or any other debilitating condition. These suggestions offer a fairly comprehensive practical framework that can be incorporated into any model of marital counseling.

1. Obtain an accurate diagnosis. Although obtaining a diagnosis will not solve problems, and in some cases even in the face of diagnostic data the unaffected partner will continue to attribute problems incorrectly to another cause, the diagnosis offers marital partners the opportunity to evaluate their problems without assigning blame or making threats. When working with a couple in which one partner or both experiences ADHD or LD, it is critical to understand the impact these disorders may have on the couple's everyday life. It is also critical that these data be used to set realistic goals. Couples in which a partner experiences ADHD, for example, will not operate like other couples, no matter how much treatment is provided.

2. Maintain a sense of humor. As Emmy Werner has found in her longitudinal research (Werner, 1994), humor is a resilience factor. That is, people able to laugh at themselves and maintain a good sense of humor in the face of adversity appear to fare better than those who cannot.

3. Declare a truce once an accurate diagnosis is made. Once again, the goal is to use accurate information as a way to begin the cooperative endeavor of improving the marriage. Without a truce, even in couples in which neither partner experiences a specific disability, conflicts continue.

4. Keep the lines of communication open. Coming to counseling implies a willingness to work to make things better. Information must be passed along without judgments, threats, or anger.

5. Honestly relate to each other. This is important in any good relationship.

6. Maintain a list of issues, good and bad, to discuss.

7. Set up a treatment plan. It is critical to set goals, determine their priority, and develop a plan to evaluate success in reaching those goals.
8. Follow through with the plan.
9. Make lists. If things are written down, issues do not have to be dealt with the moment they occur.
10. Use bulletin boards and other ways to communicate besides talking.
11. Keep note pads available.
12. Help the family function effectively by maintaining a master appointment schedule.
13. Deal with intimacy problems.
14. Avoid codependence and enabling when possible.
15. Avoid the pattern of victim and victimizer.
16. Avoid the pattern of master and slave.
17. Speak of one's feelings about the problem, not about the person.
18. Develop more effective ways of communicating. For example, avoid pestering.
19. Beware of battles for control.
20. Praise rather than criticize.
21. Be optimistic rather than pessimistic.
22. Deal with mood issues if they affect the relationship.
23. Allow the better organized partner to assume responsibility for organization.
24. Make time for each other.
25. Do not use ADHD, LD, or other problems as an excuse. This completes a circle back to the initial suggestion, which recommends using an accurate diagnosis as a way to begin a new path toward change.

Family Issues

Hallowell and Ratey (1994) also have 25 tips to help families function more effectively when a family member, child or adult, is struggling with ADHD. Once again, many of these tips are likely to help families dealing with LD or other debilitating problems as well.

1. Obtain an accurate diagnosis.
2. Educate all family members about the problem. Tell the truth.
3. Work to help the affected individual change his or her identity as the family problem. When a child experiences ADHD or LD and his or her behavior affects family functioning, siblings very quickly perceive that this child is the family problem (S. Goldstein & Goldstein, 1992). When things go wrong, this child often takes the blame. In families in which one or the other adult experiences ADHD, the same phenomenon occurs, with a pattern of cross-generational alliance often resulting when one parent and the children side against the affected parent (A. L. Robin & Foster, 1989).
4. Present problems in a way that avoids assigning blame.
5. Make certain that everyone understands that this is a family, not just an individual, set of problems.
6. Keep a balance of attention toward all family members, not just the affected member. In the case of children, if siblings complain that the child with ADHD is receiving special consideration, a parent's initial response can be to ask whether they would like to be the

affected child. Often the response is no. At that point, the parent can focus on the un-affected children's needs rather than on a comparison that results in a pattern of one-upmanship.

7. Avoid major power struggles.
8. Negotiate a family plan.
9. Seek professional help when needed.
10. Role play as a way to solve problems.
11. Develop strategies to avoid power struggles.
12. Give everyone in the family a chance to be heard during family meetings.
13. Develop new strategies for dealing with family problems.
14. Assign responsibility clearly.
15. Separate the person from the problem.
16. Be consistent. Follow through with what has been agreed upon.
17. Do not keep the problem a secret from extended family members.
18. Target high-priority problem areas first.
19. Hold family brainstorming sessions.
20. Seek and accept feedback from people outside of the family.
21. Accept the problem. ADHD is a problem that must be managed. It will not be cured.
22. Recognize that ADHD can drain a family emotionally. As J. Taylor (1990) observed, children with ADHD, and likely adults with ADHD as well, can emotionally bankrupt a family.
23. Develop an extended support system outside of the family.
24. Respect peoples' boundaries.
25. Maintain a sense of hope and dignity.

Other clinicians have offered very similar sets of suggestions to help families in which an adult or child is affected with ADHD operate more effectively. For example, K. Kelly and Ramundo (1993), based on their clinical work, make the following 15 recommendations:

1. Make sure everyone has enough space.
2. Teach respect for boundaries.
3. Have rest and relaxation zones.
4. Designate quiet zones within the house.
5. Develop rules for communication.
6. Have specific time periods for quiet.
7. Observe periods of silence.
8. Ask permission to interrupt others.
9. Stop, look, listen, and speak as a model of communication.
10. Determine what constitutes an emergency.
11. Prohibit yelling among family members.
12. Prohibit conversations on the run among family members.
13. Enforce the rules to prohibit unwanted teasing or joking among family members.
14. Set up a message center.
15. Monitor the family's emotional temperature. That is, when things begin to get out of hand emotionally, take action.

Murphy and LeVert (1995) suggest 10 steps to improve family functioning. These include educating everyone in the family about ADHD, wiping the slate clean and starting over in relationships, accentuating the positive, keeping communication lines open, setting priorities among problems and goals, clarifying expectations, attempting to be consistent, respecting people's boundaries, minimizing stress as much as possible, and finding acceptance and support.

The remainder of this section will focus on issues involved in parenting children with ADHD, as well as on guidelines for communication and parenting strategies. Once again, the literature offers little information about the types of interventions that are effective for families in which an adult has ADHD or LD. It is unclear whether comprehensive parenting programs such as Megaskills (Rich, 1992), Active Parenting (Popkin, 1986), or Tough Love (Neff, 1982) are suited to families in which an adult has ADHD or LD.

In regard to parenting children with ADHD, S. Goldstein and Goldstein (1992, 1995) offer a model with nine guidelines that can be incorporated into any parenting program (see Figure 9.1). The model focuses on helping parents understand what ADHD is and is not, developing effective behavioral strategies, and maintaining a close parent-child relationship despite the child's disruptive behavior.

Figure 9.2 presents the Adult Self-Evaluation of Child Behavior form developed by Braswell and Bloomquist (1991). It has been well demonstrated that the attributions parents hold about themselves, their children, the operation of their family, and the future exert a powerful influence on their present motivation and behavior. Thus, the clinician may wish to use this form before planning intervention. Specific attributions, beliefs, and expectations that parents hold about their children, especially those that are inaccurate, can and will undermine even the best clinical intervention.

Fisher, Ury, and Patton (1991) offer guidelines for negotiation as part of family functioning. These include separating the person from the problem, focusing on interests rather than positions, generating a variety of options before acting, and measuring results in an objective manner. Negotiation and problem solving usually take place in a natural setting as problems occur. However, the concept of family meetings as a time and place specifically for negotiating, compromising, and problem solving has become very popular in parent training programs. K. Kelly and Ramundo (1993) list the following principles and rules of conduct for family meetings:

1. Recognize the good things that are happening in the family, *not* just the bad.
2. Schedule a regular time and planned duration of meetings.
3. Share responsibility for running the meetings among all family members, children and adults.
4. Share responsibility for keeping track of what takes place during meetings.
5. Keep an agenda for the meeting that anyone can add to.
6. Review "old business" and evaluate previous decisions as well as unresolved issues during family meetings.
7. Institute a policy of allowing everyone equal opportunity to participate.
8. Use effective communication and reflective listening skills.
9. Focus on the group rather than on any one member to avoid making someone feel that he or she is the problem.
10. Develop chore and related lists through consensus.
11. Use brainstorming techniques to identify possible solutions. Allow everyone the opportunity to make a suggestion without criticizing. Listen to and list all suggestions and

To effectively parent a child with ADHD you must be an effective manager. Your interactions with your ADHD child must be consistent, predictable and most importantly, understanding of the chronic difficulties this child likely will experience. The following guidelines are essential:

1.   *Education.* You must become an educated consumer. You must thoroughly understand this disorder, including developmental, scholastic, behavioral and emotional issues.

2.   *Incompetence vs. Non-compliance.* You must develop an understanding of incompetence (non-purposeful problems that result from the child's inconsistent application of skills leading to performance and behavioral deficits) and non-compliance (purposeful problems which occur when children do not wish to do as they are asked or directed). ADHD is principally a disorder of incompetence. However, since at least 50% of children with ADHD also experience other disruptive, non-compliant problems. Parents must develop a system to differentiate between these two issues and have a set of interventions for both.

3.   *Positive Directions* (telling children what to do rather than what not to do or giving them a start rather than a stop direction). This provides the most effective type of commands for the ADHD population.

4.   *Rewards.* Remember that children with ADHD need more frequent, predictable and consistent rewards. Both social rewards (praise) and tangible rewards (toys, treats, privileges) must be provided at a higher rate when the ADHD child is compliant or succeeds. Remember, it is likely that the ADHD child receives less positive reinforcement than siblings. Make an effort to keep the scales balanced.

5.   *Timing.* Consequences (both rewards and punishment) must be provided quickly and consistently.

6.   *Response Cost.* A modified response cost program (you can lose what you earn) must be utilized with this child at home. This system can provide the child with all the reinforcers starting the day and the child must work to keep them or can start the child with a blank slate, allowing the child to earn at least three to five times the amount of rewards for good behavior versus what is lost for negative behavior (earn five chips for doing something right, lose one chip for doing something wrong).

7.   *Planning.* Understanding the forces that affect your ADHD child, as well as the child's limits, should be used in a proactive way. Avoid placing the child in situations in which there is an increased likelihood the child's temperamental problems will result in difficulty.

Figure 9.1   Guidelines for successfully parenting children with ADHD

Note. By S. Goldstein and M. Goldstein. Copyright 1994 by Neurology, Learning and Behavior Center, Salt Lake City, UT. Used with permission.

8. *Take Care of Yourself.* Families with one or more children experiencing ADHD are likely to experience greater stress, more marital disharmony, potentially more severe emotional problems in parents and often rise and fall based upon this child's behavior. It is important to understand the impact this child may have upon a family and deal with these problems in a positive, preventative way rather than a frustrated, angry and negative way after you have reached your tolerance.

9. *Take Care of Your Child.* Remember that your relationship with this child is likely to be strained. It is important to take extra time to balance the scales and maintain a positive relationship. Find an enjoyable activity and engage in this activity with your child as often as possible, at least a number of times per week.

Figure 9.1 *(Continued)*

then allow the person responsible for the problem to comment, observe, and ask further questions.
12. Pinpoint real rather than contrived issues.
13. Work for consensus and agreement.
14. Clarify, summarize, and acknowledge commitment at the close of family meetings.
15. Acknowledge that all agreements are in effect until the next family meeting.
16. Follow through on all agreements.
17. Plan fun activities at the end of every meeting.

Braswell and Bloomquist (1991) offer guidelines for family problem solving grouped into five steps.

1. Stop! What is the problem we are having?
   - Try to avoid blaming individuals
   - Focus on how each family member is interacting and causing problems together.
   - State specifically what the problem is so that everyone agrees.
2. What are some plans we can use?
   - Think of as many alternative plans as possible.
   - Don't evaluate or criticize any family members' ideas.
3. What is the best plan we could use?
   - Think of what would happen if the family used each of the alternatives.
   - Think about how each alternative would make each family member feel.
   - Decide which alternative is most likely to succeed.
   - Reach an agreement by most or all family members if possible.
4. Do the plan.
   - Try the plan as best the family can.
   - Don't criticize or say "I told you so," etc.
5. Did our plan work?
   - Evaluate the plan.
   - Determine if everyone is satisfied with the way the problem was solved.
   - If the solution didn't work, repeat the entire family problem-solving process again.

Child's Name: _____

Parent's Name: _____ Date: _____

DIRECTIONS: Listed before are a variety of thoughts that parents may have about their children and themselves. Read each thought and indicate how frequently that thought typically occurs for you over an average week. Ask the person giving you the form to clarify any questions you don't understand. Add up all the numbers for a total score.

1	2	3	4	5
Not at all	Sometimes	Moderately often	Often	All the time

I.   Attributions about the child
    ____   A.   This child is a brat.
    ____   B.   This child does it intentionally.
    ____   C.   This child is the cause of all the family's problems.
    ____   D.   This child is just trying to get attention.

II. Attributions about self/others
    ____   A.   It's my fault that this child is that way.
    ____   B.   If I wasn't such a poor parent this child would be better off.
    ____   C.   It's his/her (other parent's) fault that this child is that way.
    ____   D.   If he/she (other parent) wasn't such a poor parent, this child would be better off.

III. Beliefs/expectations about the child
    ____   A.   This child's future is bleak. When he/she grows up, he/she will probably be irresponsible, a criminal, high school dropout, etc.
    ____   B.   This child should behave like other children. I shouldn't have to teach this child how to behave.
    ____   C.   This child must do well in school, sports, scouts, etc. It is unacceptable if this child does not do as well in these activities as any other child.
    ____   D.   This child is defective. This child has many problems. This child does not fit in with other children.

IV. Beliefs, expectations about self and/or family
    ____   A.   Our family is a mess.
    ____   B.   I can't make mistakes in parenting this child.
    ____   C.   I give up. There is nothing more I can do for this child.
    ____   D.   I have no control over this child. I have tried everything.

V.   Beliefs/expectations about medications
    ____   A.   He/she needs medications. He/she can't function without medications.
    ____   B.   Medications are the answer. This child's problems will be greatly diminished or gone when he/she is on medications.

VI. Beliefs/expectations about therapy
    ____   A.   Therapy will fix or cure this child.
    ____   B.   My child is the focus of therapy.
    ____   C.   Therapy will not really help.

Figure 9.2   Adult self-evaluation of child behavior

Note. From *Cognitive Behavioral Therapy of ADHD Children* (p. 130), by L. Braswell and M. L. Bloomquist, 1991, New York: Guilford. Used with permission.

Note: Try to stay focused on the here and now. Do not bring up old issues when trying to do family problem-solving.*

S. Goldstein (1991) provides a Problem Solving Worksheet as a means of facilitating this process (see Figure 9.3).

In regard to making contracts, K. Kelly and Ramundo (1993) offer the following suggestions:

1. Contracts must be specific, current, and written. They should contain a statement of who is responsible for a task and how often the task is to be done. The statement should include a description of all requirements of the task and should be signed by all family members.
2. Goals must be attainable. There must be a match to the age and ability of family members, a statement of exceptions to the task performance (e.g., the job of removing extra garbage from spring cleaning will be shared with everyone), and an allowance for altering any part of the agreement if it is not working.
3. Finally, the contract must be positive. It must contain a description of reward—how much, when it will be given, and by whom; a statement of the consequences for nonperformance—for example, loss of the opportunity for reward; and an agreement that is fair and beneficial for all family members.

A set of guidelines for effective communication skills during problem solving is summarized in Figure 9.4.

H. M. Walker and Walker (1991) offer a set of guidelines for helping parents develop compliance at home (Figure 9.5). Though not a substitute for a parenting program, these guidelines offer a general, straightforward overview and should be easy for adults with ADHD or LD to follow, as well.

Finally, Hallowell and Ratey (1994) suggest 10 ways parents who may have ADHD can help their children with ADHD, or without ADHD for that matter, understand the disorder:

1. Tell the truth.
2. Provide accurate vocabulary.
3. Offer a nonthreatening set of analogies or metaphors.
4. Answer questions.
5. Explain what the problem is rather than what it is not.
6. Provide supportive history and current examples.
7. Inform extended family members.
8. Make certain the ADHD or LD is not used as an excuse.
9. Be prepared to deal with misinformation.
10. Build self-esteem by helping the child prepare in advance to deal with potential problems.

It is beyond the scope of this text to review parent training programs or to outline an extended parent training program. Appendix B lists a number of popular parenting programs. Once again these may be of benefit to families dealing with ADHD or LD, so long as adjustments are made for the manner in which the disorder affects an adult's ability to follow through or a child's ability to respond.

*From *Cognitive Behavioral Therapy of ADHD Children* (p.300), by L. Braswell and M. L. Bloomquist, 1991, New York: Guilford Press. Used with permission.

What is the problem?

1._____
2._____
3._____
4._____

Which is it?   1   2   3   4

What solutions are available?

1._____
2._____
3._____
4._____

What is the best solution?   1   2   3   4

What steps will this solution require?

1._____
2._____
3._____
4._____
5._____
6._____

How will I check to see if it's working?_____
_____
_____
_____
_____

Figure 9.3   Problem solving worksheet

Note. From *It's Just Attention Disorder* [User's manual], by S. Goldstein, 1991, Salt Lake City, UT: Neurology, Learning and Behavior Center. Copyright 1991 by Neurology, Learning and Behavior Center, Salt Lake City, UT. Unlimited copies of this form may be made for personal use.

Counseling

In an insightful discussion of psychotherapy for children with ADHD, H. F. Smith (1986) pointed out that the adjustment problems that children with ADHD face result not only from the interaction of development and environmental demand but also from the child's ego development. Smith argued that children with ADHD experience cognitive impairments that require modification of traditional psychotherapeutic techniques, regardless of the therapist's specific orientation. Further, Smith suggested that psychotherapy be part of an integrated approach to treating ADHD. Individual psychotherapy has been found to be an effective intervention in a multitreatment program for the related problems children with ADHD experience (Satterfield, Cantwell, & Satterfield, 1979).

Most children with ADHD do not exhibit problems requiring long-term psychotherapy. Most do, however, experience repeated failure, which places them at greater risk to develop an external locus of control, feelings of helplessness, and an inability to understand why they

I. **Be brief**
   A.   Make statements very short, preferably ten words or less.

II. **Make "I" statements**
   A.   Stay away from "you" statements like "You should do...."
   B.   Instead, say things like "I would like it if you...."

III. **Be direct**
   A.   State exactly what you want or need from another person. Avoid being vague or confusing in stating what you want.
   B.   State specific behaviors you want someone else to do. For example, "I want you to be in at 10:30 and, if you will be late, you will have to call me."

IV. **Congruence**
   A.   Communicate the same message on verbal and nonverbal levels. For example, the statement "I love you" should be said in a calm, sensitive manner, and not by yelling and pounding one's fist on a table.

V. **Give feedback**
   A.   After someone has spoken to you, say it back to him/her. This will let the other person know that you understood him/her. This also gives the other person a chance to clarify anything you did not understand correctly.

VI. **Make impact statements**
   A.   Tell the other person what effect his/her behavior or statements have on you. For example, "When you do..., I feel...."

VII. **Be an active listener**
   A.   When someone is speaking to you, let him/her know you are really listening. This can be done by maintaining good eye contact, nodding, leaning forward, and giving feedback.

Figure 9.4   Communication skills

Note. From *Cognitive Behavioral Therapy of ADHD Children* (p. 268), by L. Braswell and M. L. Bloom-quist, 1991, New York: Guilford. Used with permission.

experience so much difficulty meeting the demands of their environment. This pattern likely exists for children with LD as well. For children with ADHD or LD, short-term counseling that focuses on helping them understand their difficulties and develop a sense of hope is recommended (S. Goldstein & Goldstein, 1990). Counseling gives children with ADHD or LD the opportunity to feel less helpless, increase motivation, and improve coping skills. These are appropriate goals for adults with these disorders as well. These goals can often be approached through the careful implementation of daily successes. Further, it is clear that children and adults with ADHD or LD often have feelings about themselves, family members, and school or work that can be dealt with very effectively in counseling. These same issues likely compound, intensify, and continue to affect the daily lives of adults with histories of LD or ADHD. Some writers suggest that these issues can be addressed in group therapy, although no empirical evidence exists that this is a particularly beneficial intervention for this population (Hallowell & Ratey, 1994).

It is beyond the scope of this book to describe in detail the different schools of counseling.

One of the most important skills you can teach your child is to comply promptly with appropriate adult requests. Child compliance with adult commands and directives is a very important factor in facilitating normal development and socialization. The persistently non-compliant child who continually resists adult attempts to instruct, manage, or influence him or her is likely to experience conflict and later adjustment problems of a serious nature. Compliance with teacher instructions, directions, and commands is one of the single most important factors affecting school success. It is an absolute requirement for children to do well in school and to maximize the opportunities of the schooling process. Some tips and guidelines are provided below to assist you in developing appropriate compliance in your child that can affect both the parent-child relationship and the teacher-student relationship.

1. It is important to have a positive relationship with your child so he or she will want to comply with your requests and commands. Making this relationship as positive as you can will increase the likelihood of your child's compliance with your requests.

2. It is important to distinguish requests from commands. A request carries with it the option of child refusal; a command is more authoritative and does not allow the option of refusal. Thus, if you give a command, you need to be prepared to follow through to ensure that compliance occurs or some acceptable compromise is reached with your child.

3. Although children should be trained and encouraged to comply with adult commands, you should not give commands indiscriminately or excessively. Each command is essentially a demand for the child to do something and may be perceived as a burden or as an unpleasant chore. Only give necessary commands and use requests when you can accept appropriate refusal by the child.

4. When making requests or giving commands, you should observe the following rules:
    a. Give only one request or command at a time.
    b. Be specific and exact in your description of the request/command.
    c. Use language the child can understand.
    d. Be sure the child understands exactly what he or she is to do.
    e. Be sure the child is capable of responding as you expect.
    f. Allow a reasonable amount of time for compliance before reissuing the command or request.
    g. Praise the child and give positive attention for prompt compliance with your requests and commands.
    h. If the child does not comply in a reasonable time, reissue the command and wait for compliance.
    i. If compliance still does not occur, either leave the child's presence and wait until compliance occurs or put the child in timeout for a brief period (2 to 3 minutes).

Figure 9.5   Tips for parents in developing compliance at home

Note. From *Coping with Noncompliance in the Classroom: A Positive Approach for Teachers* (p. 96), by H. M. Walker and J. E. Walker, 1991, Austin, TX: PRO-ED. Used with permission.

j. Do not try and force the child's compliance if he or she is reluctant to do so. Explain what the choices are and wait for the child's decision.

k. Use commands only if they are necessary; use requests when they are appropriate to the situation.

l. Once you have given a command, do not verbalize about it while waiting for compliance unless it is appropriate to negotiate about the nature or conditions of the command.

m. Do not argue with the child about the command or request. Generally, you should not respond to questions designed to get you to withdraw or terminate the command.

5. Stress with your child the importance of complying promptly and appropriately to teacher commands at school. Monitor your child's school performance carefully and work cooperatively with teachers if compliance problems develop. Children who are cooperative and positive with their teachers generally do better in school and get more out of it.

Figure 9.5 (*Continued*)

The interested reader is referred to Corey (1991). Table 9.1 presents an overview of the more popular therapeutic and counseling approaches. There are no data to indicate which, if any, of these methods is effective with adults experiencing ADHD or LD and related emotional or life problems.

A brief description of the four major schools of therapy into which these different models fall offers a starting point for discussion. *Psychodynamic therapy* emphasizes the unconscious processes developed in childhood that lead to certain thoughts, feelings, and behaviors. A psychodynamic therapist attempts to help affected individuals relive these processes in the hope that the insight so gained will lead to change. *Behavioral therapy* focuses on what the individual is doing to create problems, helping to identify certain behaviors that are more or less likely to lead to increasing discomfort. The therapist concentrates on what the individual needs to do to change rather than on how he or she developed the problems. *Cognitive therapy* focuses on the thoughts and beliefs that lead to faulty behavior in the belief that the development of new thoughts will lead to more adaptive behavior. Finally, *humanistic therapy* focuses on thoughts and feelings, relying on support and encouragement to help the affected individual feel wanted and worthwhile.

The remainder of this section will discuss the cognitive model. Again, no research has yet shown the cognitive model to be better than other approaches to assisting individuals with ADHD or LD experiencing life or emotional problems. However, the proven benefits of cognitive therapy in the treatment of depression and anxiety (disorders frequently co-occurring with ADHD and LD) make it an attractive choice.

Cognitive psychology emphasizes cognitive activity as the means by which people learn, manage their behavior, and experience emotions. Beginning with the work of Lewin (1935) and Tolman (1935), thoughts have been viewed as the primary forces affecting behavior. G. A. Miller, Galanter, and Pribram (1960) articulated a cognitively based model accounting for human thoughts, feelings, and behavior. This computer model was a precursor of the cognitive model of human psychological adjustment and disturbance later developed. According to the latter model, human behavior is a function of different types of information-processing abilities (e.g., attention, encoding, storage, and retrieval).

Although the cognitive model of therapy has diverse orientations, all theories have three basic commonalities: 1. Human beings develop adaptive and maladaptive behavior and

Table 9.1   Therapeutic and Counseling Approaches

Approach	Founders/Leaders	Methods	Goals
Behavioral	Bandura, Eysenck, Wolpe, Pavlov, Skinner	Counterconditioning, modeling, operant conditioning, functional analysis, successive approximation, small sequential steps, self-management training	Decrease maladaptive behavior, increase and maintain appropriate behavior, acquisition of new behavior
Client centered	Rogers	Empathy, congruence, genuineness, unconditional positive regard, active listening, transference relationship, insight	Clarification of life plans and tasks, increase in life focus and self-awareness, improvement in overall functioning and interpersonal relationships
Cognitive	Beck, Ellis, Meichenbaum	Analysis and modification of maladaptive cognitions and beliefs underlying emotional distress and behavioral disorders, verbal persuasion and other behavioral methods, stress inoculation emotive therapy	Change in client's appraisal of self and world, development of coping skills
Developmental	Dinkmeyer, Havighurst	Highly collaborative client-therapist relationship emphasizing client-centered approaches, self-examination, problem solving and decision making techniques	Development of human potential and ability to plan, responsibility, maturity in social relationships
Existential	Frankl, May, Moustakas	Verbal persuasion, paradoxical intention, deflection, insight through inward searching moving from self-awareness to decision making	Help client find meaning in life, client's realization of potential through elimination of constraints, openness

Table 9.1 *(Continued)*

Approach	Founders/Leaders	Methods	Goals
Gestalt	Perls	Confrontation with here and now, therapist confrontation and encounter with client, interpretation of body language, awareness expanding and self-discovery exercises differentiating reality from fantasy, empty chair technique	Help client move from environmental to self-support, increase ability to use one's senses and personal responsibility, full personality integration, cultivate individuality, be fully present
Individualistic	Adler, Driekurs	Development of good client-therapist relationship, data gathering by therapist about client's role in family and self-perception of purposes of behavior, interpretation, active reconstruction and redirection of client by therapist	Change client's self-concept, correct perceptions of client, help client recognize mistakes in living, change in life goals
Multimodal	Keats, Lazarus	Pragmatic technical eclecticism, including anxiety, management training, imagery, cognitive, drug, and interpersonal treatments, assertion training, biblio- and audiotherapy, operant conditioning, desensitization, modeling, gestalt techniques	Improvement in client's life functioning through changes in behavior, affect, sensations, imagery, cognitions, interpersonal relationships, drugs and diet
Perceptual	Snygg, Combs	Accurate empathy, self-disclosure, facilitating process of furthering client's perceptions	Change or reorganization of client's self-concept, and in turn perception of world
Play therapy	Axline, A. Freud, S. Freud, Klein	Free play situation where child acts out	Diagnosis of areas and the degree of

Table 9.1   *(Continued)*

Approach	Founders/Leaders	Methods	Goals
		fantasies and conflicts, use of a variety of toys that provide for creative and aggressive activities, development of close therapist-child therapeutic relationship	child's problems, understanding of child's fantasies, thoughts and feelings about him/herself and others, catharsis, reality testing by child, communication of human values, social learning
Psychopharmacological	Employed by many child therapists since 1940s	Variety of psychostimulants, antipsychotics and tricyclics	Removal of physiological cause of maladaptive behavior, changing psychological state of client to facilitate use of other therapies, increase child's functional capacity
Reality therapy	Glasser	Warm client-therapist relationship, verbally active focusing on present behavior, help client to make own value judgments, make realistic plans to enhance self-worth and make commitments	Helping client make better choices and fulfill needs within constraints of reality
Transactional analysis	Berne, Freed	Teaching parent-child-adult model, analysis of verbal interactions and recurrent life plans and role play	Help client to understand self to strengthen functioning of child's adult state and to become more aware of life's options

Note. From *Rational-Emotive Therapy* (pp. 14–15), by M. E. Bernard and M. R. Joyce, 1984, New York: Wiley. Used with permission.

affective patterns as a result of their thoughts. 2. These thoughts can be functionally activated and modified. 3. The task of the therapist is, as a diagnostician-educator, to assess maladaptive thought processes and arrange learning experiences that alter cognition and the behavior and affective patterns with which they correlate (Mahoney & Arnkoff, 1978). A central assumption of cognitive models is that perception, representation, interpretation, and appraisal of external influence in an idiosyncratic fashion affects the psychological adjustment of the human organism (Bernard & Joyce, 1984). Through the operation of thought factors such as expectation, attribution, interpretation, belief, and reasoning, individuals interact with the world in a very personal way. Feelings and behaviors depend on the content of these thoughts. As Marzillier (1980) noted, cognitive therapy is directed toward making cognitive modifications. This approach varies from the psychoanalytic model, which attributes problems to early childhood experience and unconscious forces, and the behavioral model, which attributes dysfunctional emotional states, thoughts, and behaviors to the unfortunate pairing of conditioned and unconditioned stimuli. As Mahoney (1974) writes:

> One of the cardinal characteristics of the cognitive learning perspective is its view of man as an active element in his own growth and development. He is a both controlled and controlling organism, a product and producer of environmental forces. (p. 146)

Three distinct classes of cognitively based interventions form the framework for various theoretical models. These have been defined by Mahoney and Arnkoff (1978) quite well. *Cognitive-restructuring approaches* attempt to teach individuals more adaptive thought patterns that will alleviate uncomfortable emotions and aid the acquisition of practical coping skills. Self-instruction training (Meichenbaum, 1974) and rational-emotive therapy (Ellis, 1962), as well as cognitive therapy (Beck, 1976), are examples of this model. *Coping skills therapies* include a variety of procedures designed to teach individuals to cope with daily stress. The stress inoculation model of Meichenbaum (1975a) is an example of such a treatment. Finally, the third set of theories involves *problem-solving therapies* that attempt to teach individuals how to go about solving interpersonal difficulties in everyday life. Mahoney's (1974) personal science and the behavioral problem solving of D'Zurilla and Goldfried (1971) are examples of this type of treatment. As Braswell (1995) noted, the three broad classes of cognitive approaches encompass areas involving self-regulation, cognitive restructuring, and problem-solving training.

Cognitive therapies have been shown to be extremely effective for a variety of adult life problems (for a review, see Mahoney, 1977), so it is likely that these therapies can help the adult experiencing LD or ADHD with emotional problems, as well. Nonetheless, it is important to repeat that there is no consistent body of research evaluating the benefits of the majority of these therapies with children, adolescents, or adults suffering from ADHD or LD. However, the intuitive match between the focus of these therapies and the types of difficulties the ADHD and LD populations experience suggests the potential for benefit. Cognitive therapies offer preventive as well as therapeutic models for working with adults struggling with ADHD or LD.

GENERAL COGNITIVE MODELS FOR ADHD AND LD COUNSELING

Goldstein and Goldstein. S. Goldstein and Goldstein (1990) outlined a three-step approach to counseling individuals with ADHD. The model can be extended to LD as well. First, individuals must understand how their inattentive, impulsive, hyperactive, and consequential difficulties lead to their persistent failure to meet the demands of their environment. Individuals must have a commonsense understanding of what ADHD or LD is and be able to apply that definition in order to understand daily failure. This ability helps individuals observe how these problems affect daily functioning. The goal is to use ADHD or LD, not as an excuse, but rather as a benign, nonthreatening explanation of the difficulty they experience. For those with LD, psychotherapy provides an excellent opportunity to discuss how specific skill deficits can cause specific types of learning problems and to emphasize that learning-disabled individuals are neither bad nor stupid if they struggle to learn.

Second, individuals must build motivation and develop a sense of internal control. The cognitive model that places cognition intermediate between action and response offers a mechanism to facilitate change. Third, counseling must address the means by which other treatments (e.g., educational support and medication) may or may not help a particular individual. The focus on the individual as his or her own treatment manager is essential in working with adults with ADHD or LD. Without such a focus, a situation may develop similar to that found by Whalen and Henker (1976) in which a group of children with hyperactivity came to view the medication they were taking as completely responsible for their success. If an individual believes and is reinforced in the belief that an external force is responsible for changing and controlling his or her behavior, that individual is unlikely to take responsibility for changes, internalize success, or generalize from treatment benefits.

Douglas. Over 15 years ago, Douglas (1980) suggested a three-level program to develop an internal locus of control in children with ADHD or LD. Level 1 is designed to help the child understand the nature of his or her deficits and the ways in which learning alternative ways of behaving and thinking can help. During this stage, the counselor explains the problem to the child, discusses how the problem affects the child, and introduces the attributional concept that problems can be modified. In level 2, the child's motivation and capacity to solve problems is expanded. Children are taught specific strategies, such as breaking tasks into components. Successful experiences are sought by picking small, everyday challenges that can be managed and modified. The concepts of self-monitoring and self-evaluation are taught. Finally, in level 3, children are taught problem-solving strategies for specific problems. These might include scanning and attention techniques, active listening, and strategies to inhibit impulsive responding or facilitate problem solving.

Covey. Among the more popular self-help works are those of Stephen Covey (1989). His basic model, referred to in his text as "the seven habits," appears to meet the needs of adults with ADHD or LD. Covey hypothesized that these habits relate to knowledge, skills, and desire. Developing and managing these habits leads to life satisfaction and success. The seven habits are

1. Acting in a proactive rather than reactive manner when dealing with problems
2. Planning actions and beginning activities with the end in mind
3. Ranking problems and dealing with issues of greatest importance first
4. Relating to others in a win-win rather than win-lose manner
5. Seeking first to understand then to be understood
6. Focusing on synergy, which Covey defines as "the relationship which the parts have to each other [which] is a part in and of itself. It is not only a part, but the most catalytic, the most empowering, the most unifying and the most exciting part." (p. 263)
7. Reformulating, redesigning, and setting new goals involving the other six habits, which Covey calls "sharpening the saw"

Though untested scientifically, this model has greatly attracted the public and the business community. The model is intuitively appealing, especially in light of the kinds of problems adults with LD or ADHD reportedly experience in regard to inner thoughts, self-esteem, relations to others, and life goals. The interested reader is referred to Covey's book (Covey, 1989).

Kelly and Ramundo. K. Kelly and Ramundo (1993) offered a 12-step model, similar to that proposed for alcoholics, as a way to assist "personal recovery" from ADHD. Without a research base, these authors wrote that "although this program specifically refers to alcohol and alcoholics, it is possible to substitute virtually any chronic problem or disability" (p. 128). The 12-step model developed for Alcoholics Anonymous is a systematic plan for acknowledging one's limitations to oneself and others, making amends to others, and achieving greater self-acceptance (*Alcoholics Anonymous,* n.d.). Kelly and Ramundo argued that in order to deal with ADHD in their lives, adults with this disorder must recognize that they are powerless, that the problem is not anyone's fault, and that it cannot be cured. They should work, not to eliminate their deficits, but rather to identify, accept, and manage them. Finally, these authors suggested that helping affected individuals relabel their qualities in positive ways is an important and effective intervention. For example, people who may have experienced difficulty dealing with rules and authority can be encouraged to see these traits as ones that allow them to solve problems creatively.

Weiss. L. Weiss (1992) argued that people with ADHD must restructure all aspects of their lives, redefining relationships, pacing work, developing appropriate work space, dealing with family problems, gaining control of temper, and planning for the long term. Without a specific research base, Weiss proposed a therapy model that uses visualization to help individuals with histories of ADHD "go back" and relive some of their most frustrating and disturbing childhood and life experiences and then relabel those experiences in more positive ways. An application of Weiss's suggested model is presented below.

> In a quiet place, sit in a comfortable chair that has arms, close your eyes, and take a step back from your experience. Think of something that makes you feel secure, very secure, safe, and protected. It might be sitting in the lap of your grandmother. Or it might be feeling the sun on your shoulder while you walk through a forest filled with the smell of springtime, a soft breeze against your cheek. Choose your own brand of safety—and feel the arm of the chair.
>
> Imagine projecting your experience onto a movie screen, and view it as you might a movie. As you do this, grasp the arm of the chair that you're sitting in while watching the movie and feel the security of it. You can even see yourself watching the movie.
>
> (If you feel resistant to doing this exercise, don't do it. Your psyche is telling you: "Whoa, I'm not ready for this. It's not good for me." You may wish to do this work with a counselor or not at all. Your psyche knows best; trust it.)
>
> Now, let's all get ready to change history.
>
> Let your mind drift back to a time in your youth when you feel misunderstood, inadequate, out of control. Visualize that part of you in your mind's eye. You will probably feel a sensation within you that reflects how you felt at the time. Pay particular attention to that feeling, its shape, its location in your physical body, and its size and substance. Is it hot or cold, hard or soft, solid or porous? Attach a color to it.
>
> Immediately after defining it, squeeze the arm of the chair and find that nice, warm secure feeling. As you neutralize the sensation that causes you discomfort, realize that you can grow beyond your history.
>
> Remember, if you are projecting this experience on a movie screen, keep it there while you watch yourself sitting and watching the movie.
>
> Next, let your mind drift back to an earlier time in your life when you encountered a similar feeling. Locate its presence in your body again and visualize where you were standing as a

child when it happened. What were you doing? Squeeze the arm of the chair. Remember to keep the vision on your movie screen.

Now, go back and seek the earliest experience you can recall when the same constellation of events or feelings took place. You may have been four, five, or six years old. Once more, squeeze the arm of the chair and check your movie screen if you need to.

It is now time to rewrite history:

Pretend you are a script writer. You have the capability to rewrite your childhood history any way you want. You can give your child words and understanding that realistically he or she would not have had. In this rewriting job, anything is possible. Also allow the others in your drama to have words, skills, and understanding they didn't actually have but that you can give them since you are recreating their characters.

Visualize the child with the out-of-control, inadequate feelings and let the child say what he or she needs: Understanding? Support? A sense of control? Your child might say something like: "I feel overwhelmed. I need you to understand that I'm trying as hard as I can." Squeeze the arm of the chair you're sitting in. Feel it holding you up.

Visualize the grownups in the child's life reassuring the child, giving him understanding, knowledge, whatever was needed. Hear them teaching the child: "You have ADD. It's no big deal. I can help you learn to overcome its effects. You are smart. You are okay. I love you. I'm here with you and I'll help you learn to pay attention. See, you are already doing it. You're a fast learner. I love you."

If you like, feel the warm arm of the adult around the child's shoulders. Watch the adult walk the child into school and explain to the teachers what is needed. See the teachers pass the message on. And see your child grow assured, secure, capable, and able to be in control.

If the adults in your early life were particularly abusive, see the child on the movie screen stop them. Have them freeze, like the child's game "Freeze," where no one can move without permission of the game leader. Let the child be the leader and call "freeze." Then let a special, understanding adult teach them about ADD.

Next, watch the abusive adults change their level of understanding, becoming enlightened. Let them say, "I am so sorry. I didn't mean any harm. I didn't know any better. Please forgive me."

Watch the child on the screen take as long as he needs to do that. No rush. If the child needs to vent some anger, fine. If the child wants to scold, fine. When the feeling is vented and the child sees the adults for what they were—frightened, helpless, frustrated—forgiveness will come. But let it come in its own time as you again squeeze the arm of your chair, feeling the security it offers, the support and comfort.

Feel the child's growing sense of control. Realize that the feeling will spread and grow to be used daily as you go about your business in confidence, knowing that you are now understood and strong.

You can change each recalled experience this way. Give the child what is needed. Provide the child with the power of information and the support of understanding. Watch the child, adolescent, and adult in you grow in confidence before your mind's eye. Forgive those who hurt you out of ignorance and feel the confidence build within you to be in control of yourself as someone who has ADD. Simply make room for it when planning your activities. (L. Weiss, 1992, pp. 73–76)

Beck, Rush, Shaw, and Emery. Cognitive therapy finds its roots in the original work of Aaron Beck and colleagues at the University of Pennsylvania (Beck, Rush, Shaw, & Emery, 1979). This school of therapy hypothesizes that maladaptive ways of thinking are both shaped by and shape feelings and behavior. For example, individuals suffering from depression and other forms of emotional distress appear to develop cognitive distortions or maladaptive ways of thinking about themselves, the world, and their future. These negatively toned thoughts lead to feelings of hopelessness, despair, and depression. Given the history and daily lives of adults with LD or ADHD, it is likely that this type of cognitive approach will be beneficial in alleviating some of their emotional distress. The types of cognitive distortions affected individuals may form fall into three distinct classes:

1. *Negative self-evaluation.* Individuals with ADHD or LD often believe they are defective and unworthy, lacking in what it takes to be successful and happy. They may be self-critical, quick to blame themselves, and certain that there is nothing much that will help.

2. *Negative worldview.* They may have a propensity to see anything positive as transient and limited and anything negative as a certain sign of more bad things to come. They may misinterpret the actions of others, taking offense at even tiny slights and attributing malice when none is intended.

3. *Negative view of the future.* It has been suggested that when adults with ADHD or LD look into the future, they perceive limited opportunity for change or success. This is a pattern found among adults with histories of depression as well.

Beck et al. (1979) identified a number of systematic patterns of thinking that appear to be characteristic of people with depression. These patterns may also be characteristic of adults struggling with ADHD or LD. They include the following:

1. *Arbitrary inference* refers to the process of drawing a specific conclusion in the absence of evidence to support the conclusion or when the evidence is contrary to the conclusion (e.g., I haven't tried to do it yet but I just know I won't succeed).

2. *Selective abstraction* consists of focusing on a detail taken out of context, ignoring other more salient features of the situation, and conceptualizing an entire experience based only on analysis of a small part (e.g., if my efforts today were unsuccessful, any future efforts will be unsuccessful).

3. *Overgeneralization* refers to the pattern of drawing a general rule or conclusion on the basis of one or more isolated incidents and applying the concept in all related or even unrelated situations (e.g., since this particular person did not want to be my friend, anyone else whom they know will also not want to be my friend).

4. *Magnification and minimization* reflect errors in evaluating the significance or magnitude of an event, distorting a particular event, and giving it more meaning than it is worth (e.g., if I failed a quiz I am likely to fail the test).

5. *Personalization* refers to an individual's tendency to relate external events to him or herself when there is no basis for making such a connection (e.g., if someone couldn't see me, it wasn't because they were busy; it was just because they didn't want to see me).

6. *Absolutistic, dichotomous thinking* is manifested by a tendency to place all experiences in black or white categories and then choose the negative category as reflecting the truth (e.g., good or bad).

The therapeutic application of this model will be described later, as rational-emotive therapy.

Mufson, Moreau, Weissman, and Klerman. Interpersonal psychotherapy (IPT) is a more recently researched and developed cognitive treatment for depression. IPT may offer an alternative model for dealing with the psychosocial issues of adults with LD and ADHD. This program was originally developed to treat depression in adults (Mufson, Moreau, Weissman, & Klerman, 1993) and has been adapted for use with adolescents as well. IPT is a time limited, 12–16-week therapy based on the premise that depression occurs within the context of the ongoing interpersonal relationships in an individual's life. The goals of IPT are to identify and treat depression-related symptoms as well as problem areas associated with the onset of depression. Five areas, all of which appear relevant to the lives of adults with ADHD or LD, lie at the focus of treatment:

1. *Prolonged grief.* It has been repeatedly suggested that adults with ADHD and LD struggle with grief over their perceived incompetence and lifetime difficulty with meeting everyday expectations.

2. *Interpersonal role disputes.* Adults with LD or ADHD have been hypothesized to have more daily conflicts with family members, friends, and employers than do unaffected adults.

3. *Role transitions.* Many adults with histories of LD or ADHD are reported to have had difficulty making a successful transition into adulthood.

4. *Developing necessary interpersonal skills.* A lack of effective interpersonal skills has been demonstrated in children with histories of LD or ADHD and hypothesized to occur in adults with these disorders.

5. *Family issues.* It has been suggested that families in which one of the adults has ADHD or LD do not operate effectively or efficiently.

IPT seeks to help the individual understand how problems with interpersonal relationships affect emotions. The emphasis is on current relationships rather than those that existed in the past. Techniques used in treatment include rehearsal and role play. The interested reader is referred to Mufson et al. (1994).

Ellis. The basic premise of the rational-emotive model is that between an activating event and an emotional or behavioral consequence comes a rational or irrational belief that drives the emotional or behavioral consequence (Ellis, 1979b). Ellis (1973) described the emotional and cognitive goals for rational-emotive therapy as follows:

> My main goals in treating any of my psychotherapy clients are simple and concrete; to leave the client, at the end of the psychotherapeutic process, with a minimum of anxiety (or self-blame) and of hostility (or blame of others and the world around him) and just as importantly, to give him a method of self-observation and self-assessment that will ensure that, for the rest of his life, he will be minimally anxious and hostile. (p. 147)

Thus, Ellis argued that people who struggle in their daily lives, such as those with LD or ADHD, develop self-defeating beliefs that inevitably produce negative emotions such as rage, guilt, anxiety, and depression and eventually translate into maladaptive behavior (Ellis, 1962).

Ellis (1979b) described a variety of environmental and innate influences that account for human behavioral patterns and emotionality. These provide a good overview of the forces that likely affect the lives of adults with ADHD or LD:

1. Ongoing relationships with other people

2. Specific teaching by others, beginning with parents, teachers, clergymen, and peers

3. What is learned through the mass media (radio, television, films, books, etc.)
4. Group influences (peers, community organizations, and religious organizations)
5. Biological and innate forces. This is especially important in regard to ADHD and LD.
6. Positive reinforcers in one's life, including those that are tangible, such as money and success, as well as inner feelings of satisfaction
7. Negative consequences, disapproval, anxiety, depression, even poverty
8. Self-perceptions and attribution
9. Analysis of one's own behavior and the conclusions that are drawn
10. Modeling others, particularly those admired
11. Identification with certain groups or individuals and acceptance or imitation of their behavior
12. Formulation of goals, purposes, and ideals and attempts to achieve them
13. Superstitious beliefs
14. Impressionability to the persuasions and ideas of others
15. The need for individuality

The primary irrational beliefs people hold that cause or create emotional and behavioral consequences, according to Ellis, fall in three basic categories (Ellis, 1980):

1. The individual must do well and win approval; otherwise, he or she is unworthy.
2. Others in the world must treat the individual kindly and precisely in the way he or she wants to be treated. If not, the world should suffer.
3. The conditions under which the individual lives should be arranged so that everything goes his or her way.

Ellis and Harper (1975) described a number of irrational beliefs that likely have relevance in therapeutic work with people with ADHD or LD:

1. A person must be loved and approved of by everyone in his or her life.
2. If one is not competent, intelligent, and excessively achieving, one is not worthwhile.
3. Life is terrible if one does not obtain all of one's goals.
4. The world should treat everyone in a fair and just manner.
5. Life should be entirely pleasant and free of pain or discomfort.
6. People need to excessively depend or rely on others.
7. Human worth can be judged and values assigned to others.
8. Past negative experiences ruin present experiences and cannot be overcome.
9. Emotional discomfort comes almost exclusively from external forces, and individuals have little ability to manage and control their feelings.
10. The problems and disturbances of each person should be upsetting to everyone.
11. Worry is a means by which people can change their behavior and themselves.
12. All problems have perfect solutions.
13. Individuals must be able to control the attitudes and beliefs of others.
14. It is easier to avoid than face life's difficulties.

The clinician, as part of counseling work, may wish to use specific rating scales to identify irrational thoughts or beliefs. Such scales include the Self-Rating Scale (Bard, 1973), the Adult Irrational Ideas Inventory (Fox & Davies, 1971), and the Rational Beliefs Inventory (Shockey &

Whiteman, 1977). Meichenbaum (1977) suggested that the therapist work to identify the style and occurrence of an individual's thoughts and the relationship of the thoughts to behavior and feelings. There are four basic ways to assess thoughts (Kendall & Hollon, 1981):

1. *Recording methods* record conversations and transcribe or code them into various categories.

2. *Endorsement methods* use inventories containing a predetermined series of items (e.g., sample self-statements) that can be used to assess rational and irrational thoughts. For example, subjects can perform certain tasks and then complete the inventory, indicating the types of thoughts they had and the frequency of these thoughts as they completed the task.

3. *Production methods* ask subjects to retrospectively produce thoughts they had either during a particular interval of time or immediately preceding a particular time. The subjects or the judges must then read over the list of thoughts and categorize them along certain dimensions. This method has been called "thought listing."

4. *Sampling methods* are a way to assess self-statements. They require subjects to provide a thought sample when cued by a sampling device. The process is akin to behavioral time-sampling procedures used to observe and code behavior. Thought-sampling procedures attempt to obtain an accurate picture of a subject's self-statements by randomly sampling thoughts at a variety of different times and on different days. Thought sampling seeks a representative sample of a subject's self-statements while in the process of everyday living.

Many therapists have difficulty explaining the concept of irrational beliefs or thoughts to clients. Whalen and Henker (1980) have defined the concept of rational belief as follows:

1. *A rational belief is true.* Such a belief is consistent with reality in kind and degree; it can be supported by evidence; it is empirically verifiable, logical, and internally consistent.

2. *A rational belief is not absolutistic.* Instead, it is conditional, stated as a desire, hope, want, wish, or preference and reflects a desiring rather than a demanding philosophy.

3. *A rational belief results in moderate emotion.* Rational beliefs lead to feelings that may range from mild to strong but are not upsetting to the individual.

4. *A rational belief helps you attain your goals.* They are congruent with satisfaction in living, minimal intrapsychic conflict, and minimal conflict with the environment. They are directed at growth toward some personally fulfilling endeavor.

The rational-emotive model of therapy for those with ADHD or LD experiencing life problems offers a workable set of strategies clustered in four basic areas. Although research verifying the benefits of these treatments for ADHD or LD has yet to be conducted, research with related populations, such as adults with depression, suggests that this mode of intervention can be an important component of psychotherapy for the adult ADHD and LD populations. The four areas into which strategies can be grouped are:

1. *Cognitive restructuring.* It has been suggested that adults with histories of LD or ADHD need to be taught to identify specific negative thoughts and beliefs that result in feelings of hopelessness, despair, and depression (e.g., even if I try my best I will fail since I have failed before). They must be helped to challenge the accuracy of their thoughts (e.g., I believe that even if I try my best I will fail. Has that always happened? Have I ever succeeded?) and to generate more adaptive alternative thoughts (e.g., if I try my best I might fail but I also might succeed).

2. *Attribution training.* Attribution, as previously discussed, refers to the means by which people explain events in their lives. People who attribute their successes to their own skills and efforts rather than to outside forces such as luck are described as having an internal locus of control (Nowicki & Strickland, 1973). People with histories of ADHD or LD are reported to be more likely to develop an external locus of control (S. Goldstein & Goldstein, 1990). That is, they blame themselves for all bad things that happen but dismiss any achievements or successes as random occurrences. They minimize and overgeneralize. Attribution training teaches individuals to choose more adaptive attributions and to use these attributions to solve problems effectively.

3. *Self-control training.* To facilitate the change from negative and maladaptive patterns of thinking to more functional ones, people should be taught to monitor and evaluate their thoughts on an ongoing basis. A process of self-reward to strengthen new patterns of thoughts, feelings, and behaviors is instituted.

4. *Adjunctive techniques.* Given the myriad of life problems that adults, including those with ADHD or LD, may experience, social skills development, problem solving, interpersonal relationships, and even issues related to intimacy and money management will likely need to be addressed with many of the adults with ADHD or LD seeking help.

From a therapeutic perspective, the basic work in rational-emotive therapy involves disputation. In disputation, individuals employ cognitive, emotional, and behavioral techniques to challenge and debate within themselves the irrational beliefs they hold. This process allows them to reason through and develop an understanding of the relationship between specific ideas and beliefs they hold and their actions (Bard, 1980). Disputation requires individuals to internalize the following view of their thoughts, feelings, and behavior:

1. If I am upset, I am largely responsible.
2. There is something about what I am saying to myself and how I am evaluating this situation that is causing me to be overly upset.
3. I had better be prepared to accept another point of view about what is going on.
4. I must be prepared to question my thoughts and beliefs about the world and not rigorously hold on to those that do not have any relationship with reality or my goals (Bernard & Joyce, 1984).

Finally, Ellis and Harper (1975) and Whalen and Henker (1980) offered a list of rational beliefs and ideas that, on face value, appear to be useful for adults with histories of ADHD or LD to incorporate into their everyday lives:

1. It would be desirable and productive to concentrate on achieving self-respect, on winning approval for practical purposes, and on loving instead of being loved.
2. It is advisable to accept myself as an imperfect creature with human limitations and fallibilities. It is better to do than to do well.
3. While I prefer things to go my way, there is nothing awful about not getting what I want.
4. The world is often unfair. People may behave stupidly or unethically, and it would be better if they were helped to change their ways.
5. There's seldom gain without pain. I can tolerate discomfort, although I might not enjoy it.
6. While I enjoy the company of intimate others, I do not need anyone to help me get along in life; I can always rely on myself.
7. People are extremely complex. It is impossible to measure self-worth.

8. I can overcome the effects of past experience by reassessing my perceptions of the past and reevaluating my interpretations of its influence.

9. I am largely responsible for my own emotional upsets. I can control my feelings by changing the way I view and evaluate events.

10. The only way I am going to be of any help to others is by remaining calm, judging specific situations to see what I can do to help, and offering assistance. If nothing can be done, I will not surrender my personal peace to an impossible situation.

11. Worrying will not magically make things disappear. I will do my best to deal with potentially distressing events, and when this proves impossible, I will accept the inevitable.

12. The world is an uncertain place to live. To fully enjoy life, I will have to make decisions and take risks without having any guarantees.

13. While I would like to have the affection and respect of others, there is no law of the universe that says everyone must like me and follow what I say.

14. Problems are seldom made to go away by my sticking my head in the ground.

Troubleshooting Tips

A useful axiom for the clinician to remember is What is beneficial therapeutically for the needs of all people will likely be beneficial for the emotional and life needs of people with ADHD or LD until proven otherwise. It has been well documented in the childhood literature that psychotherapy for symptoms of ADHD and LD is ineffective in changing the core problems of these disorders. However, clinicians are also well aware that the comorbid, or accompanying, problems that the adult ADHD and LD populations experience are similar to the problems other adults experience and will likely respond to general therapeutic approaches. Further, while there may be some benefit to short-term information-focused counseling when an adult is initially diagnosed with ADHD or LD, there is no data to suggest that long-term counseling concentrating on the symptoms of these disorders is particularly helpful.

It is important to keep in mind that after a diagnosis of adult ADHD or LD is made there may be people in the affected person's life unwilling to accept this explanation who respond by subtly or openly working to undermine any change. Spouses may feel the diagnosis is an excuse. Parents may perceive their children as lazy or unmotivated. Clinicians are well aware that in such circumstances confronting the disbelieving individuals is more likely to lead to greater skepticism, antagonism, and a rift in family functioning than to improvement. Patience and education would appear to be the best solution.

Clinicians also report that often when a diagnosis of adult LD or ADHD is made, affected individuals listen but do not hear. They may reject the diagnosis, accept it but not completely understand the implications, seek a single treatment or cure, or in many cases take the diagnosis and not return. The clinician must be patient, honest, persistent, and hopeful when discussing the client's diagnosis and problems.

Clinicians also must help affected individuals recognize that a diagnosis may provide hope and insight but treatment requires hard work and in the case of ADHD or LD is often compensatory rather than remedial. Without this preparation, what begins with a fast start may end quickly because the affected individual does not see "enough change." Further, psychosocial treatment may be affected by an individual's limited support system or by other, more extensive psychiatric problems, such as serious depression. Very clearly, in such circumstances, the more serious psychiatric disorder must be aggressively treated before issues related to ADHD or LD can be adequately addressed. Appendix A contains a list of resource organizations and currently available self-help texts dealing with adult ADHD and LD.

It has been suggested that the types of daily organization and life efficiency problems reported by adults with ADHD or LD are similar to the organizational difficulties reported by unaffected adults (Kristan, 1995). Kristan thus suggested that a generic repertoire of techniques used by all adults to assist with organization and functioning in daily life may be especially helpful for adults with ADHD.

Kravetz (1994) suggested that the following points be addressed when counseling young adults with ADHD who are preparing to enter college. These are likely also to be useful when counseling young adults with LD.

1. *Acceptance.* The student must be willing to accept his or her ADHD symptoms and the fact that compensatory strategies and interventions are going to be necessary in college.
2. *Prioritizing.* Efforts should be made to identify and rank the most important criteria for college selection. These criteria might include a smaller college, smaller classrooms, core substitution, available advocacy and tutoring, even extracurricular activities.
3. *Assessment.* Is the chosen college willing to recognize and accept credits from modified courses and so forth?
4. *Disclosure.* Colleges must be willing not to view disclosure of LD or ADHD problems negatively.
5. *Testing.* How will ACT or SAT scores or college grades be used in the admissions process?
6. *Recommendations of college counselors.*
7. *Interviewing.* The student should be willing to participate in a college interview and should ask questions about the philosophy of the college regarding students with LD or ADHD.
8. *Understanding efficient procedures.* Some colleges admit to blindly using a fixed formula; others are more flexible and will make special allowance for students with certain disabilities.

CHAPTER 10

College Programs and Services

Mary McDonald Richard

T HIS CHAPTER examines a number of topics related to the college experience of students with ADHD or LD and provides information for professionals about the specific needs of this group. Among the subjects addressed are academic concerns, psychosocial issues, and institutional services. All contribute to an understanding of college students with ADHD or LD and the campus resources available to them.

Students with ADHD or LD who have the intellectual potential and commitment to achieve a postsecondary degree are enrolling in college in record numbers. For these students, colleges and universities offer an environment in which they can expand their personal, social, and academic abilities and so gain access to a greater range of career options (Javorsky & Gussin, 1994). Institutions are responding to this growing population with a wide range of services, including assistive technology, tutorial services, counseling programs, assistance with advocacy, and academic accommodations. The majority of these services are required by federal laws intended to protect the educational rights of qualified students with disabilities in postsecondary education.

Health care professionals who provide services for students with ADHD or LD must have information about these legal issues and institutional resources. Their clinical summaries convey recommendations to campus service providers critical in determining student eligibility for modifications and accommodations. Decisions concerning the provision of specific academic adjustments depend on detailed knowledge of students' disabilities and the ways they affect learning. Such knowledge allows student affairs practitioners not only to provide assistance to students but to provide effective consultation with faculty and promote fair practices in higher education.

Incidence in the College Population

As reviewed in Chapter 4, the number of students with ADHD or LD entering colleges and universities has burgeoned in the past 10 years, and this trend is expected to continue. According to recent HEATH statistics, over 100,000 students with LD graduate from high school annually (American Council on Education, 1993). A significant proportion of these students, as many as 67%, plan to pursue some kind of postsecondary education (W. White et al., 1982). Students from this pool of potential freshmen, combined with those diagnosed with LD after college enrollment, have produced substantial demographic results. Available data indicate that between 160,000 and 300,000 students with LD are currently part of the college population (American Council on Education, 1993).

While statistical research on the numbers of students who have disclosed LD to colleges and universities is somewhat inexact, the numbers for students primarily diagnosed with ADHD are purely a matter of estimation. The prevalence of ADHD within the college population has not been precisely determined, although it has been estimated at 1%-3% (Barkley, 1993c). One way of estimating the potential number of students with ADHD in postsecondary education is to consider the statistics on students with conditions that coexist at high rates with ADHD, such as learning and psychological disabilities (Cantwell & Baker, 1992a; Semrud-Clikeman et al., 1992). ADHD seldom exists alone, and while this lone occurrence is possible, ADHD more often appears with other neurobiological disabilities (Barkley & Murphy, 1993b; Gersh, 1993; M. Stein, 1993). Since LD and ADHD often occur together, it is probable that the incidence of ADHD has been subsumed into the statistics documenting the LD category. Statistics for students with psychological disabilities may also be counting students who have ADHD.

When considering these figures, it is important to take into account the population of students with undiagnosed ADHD or LD. Student Disability Service (SDS) offices indicate that a significant number of the students they serve are not identified until after enrollment in college (Richard, 1995b). However, as inexact as statistics or estimates may be, they do not obscure the reality of a growing population of students eligible for access to services under Section 504 (Rehabilitation Act, 1973) and the Americans with Disabilities Act (1990).

Eligibility Standards for Services

Section 504 of the Rehabilitation Act of 1973 directs postsecondary institutions to protect the educational rights of qualified students with disabilities under Subpart E of the statute. While its language provides a broad foundational definition of disability, it does not describe ADHD, LD, or any other specific disorder or condition. It defines an individual with a disability as anyone who 1. has a physical or mental impairment that substantially limits one or more major life activities (e.g., learning), 2. has a history of such an impairment, or 3. is regarded as having such a condition. It states that if an individual with a disability meets the academic standards and requirements for admission to a college that receives federal funding or is qualified to participate in a federally funded college's programs or activities, then equal access must be ensured.

Colleges require verification of disability(ies) from students for the purpose of determining eligibility for services. Documentation of psychoeducational testing for LD by licensed school or clinical psychologists is accepted.

In the case of ADHD, medical and psychological reports from a multidisciplinary assessment are recommended. Comprehensive evaluations combining information from the areas of medicine and psychology are more likely to correctly identify ADHD and distinguish it from other medical, psychiatric, and psychological disorders that produce similar symptoms. SDS offices often receive documentation from licensed school or clinical psychologists, as well as from physicians in such areas as family practice, internal medicine, neurology, pediatrics, and psychiatry.

Documentation of disability is released voluntarily by the student to the institution's SDS office or designated person, where it is kept in confidential files separate from academic records. In the case of ADHD or LD, institutions usually request that the information be recent (no more than two to three years old). The report should provide the results of a comprehensive evaluation, including details about the process of assessment, the diagnosis of disability(ies), and the impact of the disability(ies) on learning processes. It includes 1. descriptions of the student's presenting problems, 2. a developmental and educational history, 3. information on cognitive ability, and 4. information on academic strengths and weaknesses. Finally, the summary should include recommendations for accommodations, such as taped reading materials, examination modifications, note takers, and course substitutions. This information is important in selecting appropriate services and planning for their delivery.

Institutional Resources

Among the factors contributing to the increasing awareness at colleges and universities of students with ADHD or LD is the sharp increase in their numbers on campus. It is widely recognized at postsecondary institutions that this group of students has grown more rapidly than any other disability population. Since 1985, the proportion of college freshmen who have disclosed LD has increased from 15% to 25% of the entire disability population (American Council on Education, 1993).

In response to the numbers and needs of these students, many institutions have identified an individual or developed SDS offices to serve students with disabilities. SDS offices work to facilitate campuswide compliance with federal nondiscrimination mandates and institutional policies on equal educational opportunity. On many campuses, SDS offices operating under student or academic affairs departments assist in reducing physical, programmatic, and attitudinal barriers that might otherwise impede student success (Kravets & Wax, 1992). Many institutions consider SDS programs to be among their frontline efforts to increase the retention and graduation rates of their students.

Some SDS offices offer special programs and services for students with ADHD or LD. Many of these services are relatively new. Programs for students with physical and sensory disabilities were the foundation for early programs for students with LD. More recently, some, but not all, LD programs have included services for students diagnosed with ADHD (without a coexisting LD). In addition to accommodations required by law, some SDS offices also offer supplemental or remedial programs designed to address the academic problems experienced by some students with ADHD or LD (Richard, 1992). The University of Connecticut Program for College Students with Learning Disabilities (UPLD) offers three tiers of services designed to assist students in performing successfully while becoming more self-sufficient (University of Connecticut School of Education, 1995). The first tier of UPLD emphasizes direct instruction and high involvement in reaching out to students. The second focuses on applications of skills, with less staff involvement; the third on student self-management, with consultation available. While no charges should be made for services that are required by law, additional enrollment fees may be required for participation in these supplemental programs. The description of UPLD provided to interested parties appears in Appendix E.

Academic and Behavioral Characteristics

Like their classmates, college students with ADHD or LD may possess a wide range of talents. They display a variety of personality traits and learning styles. They have learned to use their strengths in these areas to compensate for weaknesses. Informational materials provided to colleges and universities by the Association for Higher Education and Disability (AHEAD) describe a number of academic and behavioral deficits, related to study and social skills, attention, and concentration, that are characteristic of students with ADHD or LD (Association for Higher Education and Disability, 1991):

1. Reading skills
   - Slow reading rate or difficulty in modifying reading rate in accordance with material's level of difficulty
   - Uneven comprehension and retention of material read
   - Difficulty identifying important points and themes
   - Incomplete mastery of phonics, confusion of similar words, difficulty integrating new vocabulary
   - Skipping words or lines of printed material
   - Difficulty reading for long periods of time

2. Written language skills
   - Difficulty planning a topic and organizing thoughts on paper
   - Difficulty with sentence structure (e.g., incomplete sentences, run-ons, poor use of grammar, missing inflectional endings)
   - Frequent spelling errors (e.g., omissions, substitutions, transpositions), especially in specialized and foreign vocabulary
   - Difficulty effectively proofreading written work and making revisions
   - Compositions often limited in length
   - Slow written production
   - Poor penmanship (e.g., poorly formed letters, incorrect use of capitalization, trouble with spacing, overly large handwriting)
   - Inability to copy correctly from a book, overhead transparency projections, or the chalkboard

3. Oral language skills
   - Inability to concentrate on and comprehend spoken language when presented rapidly
   - Difficulty speaking grammatically correct English
   - Trouble telling a story in the proper sequence
   - Difficulty following oral directions

4. Mathematical skills
   - Incomplete mastery of basic facts (e.g., multiplication tables)
   - Tendency to reverse numbers (e.g., 123 to 321 or 231)
   - Confusion of operational symbols, especially + or ×
   - Difficulty copying problems correctly from one line to another
   - Difficulty recalling the sequence of operational concepts

- Difficulty comprehending word problems
- Difficulty understanding key concepts and applications to aid problem solving

5. Organizational and study skills
   - Difficulty with organizational skills
   - Time management difficulties
   - Slowness in starting and completing tasks
   - Repeated inability, on a day-to-day basis, to recall what has been taught
   - Lack of overall organization in taking notes
   - Difficulty interpreting charts and graphs
   - Inefficient use of library and reference materials
   - Difficulty preparing for and taking tests

6. Attention and concentration
   - Trouble focusing and sustaining attention on academic tasks
   - Fluctuating attention span during lectures
   - Easily distractible by outside stimuli
   - Difficulty juggling multiple task demands, becoming overloaded quickly
   - Hyperactivity and excessive movements may accompany difficulty focusing or maintaining attention

7. Social skills
   - Difficulty detecting the difference between sincere and sarcastic comments or inability to recognize other subtle changes in tone of voice
   - Difficulties in interpreting nonverbal messages, resulting in lowered self-esteem and difficulty meeting people or working cooperatively

While the skill deficits associated with LD are generally pervasive, appearing consistently across a variety of these situations, those who assist students with ADHD will recognize that "the most consistent thing about ADHD is inconsistency" (Barkley, 1991). These students do not display impairment at all times, nor do their difficulties necessarily arise from skill deficits. Instead, ADHD appears to be a performance deficit, a problem of "not doing what one knows," rather than "not knowing what to do" (S. Goldstein & Goldstein, 1990). When these students encounter tasks that offer high interest, novelty, immediate feedback, or risk and danger, they may focus and keenly attend. In contrast, when they are faced with tasks that are routine, repetitive, and require attention to detail, they may demonstrate great difficulty voluntarily focusing and maintaining attention (S. Goldstein, 1995). Thus, those working with students with ADHD can apply this observation to interpret students' tendency to earn better grades in classes that intrinsically interest them or are taught by instructors who use attention-holding teaching methods (Zentall, 1993).

Attention and skill deficits may also cause students to be at risk for a variety of secondary problems that can hinder college performance. Jarvorsky and Gussin (1994) described five risk areas that they believed may jeopardize students' educational, social, and emotional development:

1. *Substance abuse.* Students with ADHD may use alcohol and marijuana more often than the average, possibly as a result of impulsivity or attempts to self-medicate (Barkley, 1990b; Biederman, Faraone, et al., 1993).

2. *Financial management.* Problems related to impulsivity and inattention may contribute to significant difficulties in the management of money and credit practices. Students may have problems following through with financial aid procedures (e.g., meeting deadlines or picking up checks).

3. *Academic responsibilities.* Problems with organization may compromise students' performance of timely registration responsibilities, meeting course deadlines, and class attendance. They may find the selection of and subsequent commitment to a major area of study difficult.

4. *Employment.* Since students with ADHD tend to become bored in jobs that are repetitive or routine (e.g., most work-study jobs), they may be at risk for poor performance and subsequent loss of employment and needed income.

5. *Legal concerns.* Students with ADHD may be at risk for increased incidence of parking tickets, traffic violations, and accidents. Those who have coexisting conduct or personality disorder may also have a higher incidence of aggressive behavior or other activities that result in problems with authorities.

Although not all students with ADHD experience these difficulties, college service providers must be aware of these risk areas and their relationship to students' adjustment and accommodation needs.

Adjustment and Treatment Compliance

Even before their first day on campus, students with ADHD or LD may be concerned about meeting the increased demands of postsecondary study (Richard, 1995b). Given their learning difficulties, students with ADHD or LD may have underdeveloped, or undeveloped, social, living, and study skills. The anxiety level of students with ADHD may also be raised as a result of the stress intolerance associated with the significant maturational lag in many activities of daily living found among this group (Barkley, 1993c). If their prior school performance has not been strong, their doubts about their chances of success may have foundation. Moreover, those who have had poor high school experiences with unhelpful or unfair teachers may have little faith that college personnel will demonstrate any more interest in assisting them in their education.

Students who have had years of special education services may have little experience in making decisions about their academic programs. Related to this, at the outset of college few situations provoke more anxiety for these students than their first registration for classes. Professionals may advise students to consult the SDS office (or another office designated to fulfill this function) at their college and disclose their disability and request accommodations in the registration process. As a part of disclosure, they should also provide a copy of their diagnostic summary and treatment recommendations to verify their eligibility for services. First-semester registration is often conducted as a part of orientation programs for freshman and transfer students. If this is the case, the student should also inform the office of orientation of their needs.

Some entering freshmen seek to "graduate" from disability by denying any need for continued support after high school (F. Leonard & McCormack, 1994). They may also make an internal decision to stop taking medication prescribed for ADHD. The underlying issue in noncompliance often originates in students' needs for "reality checks" related to the presence of their disability and the relative benefits of interventions. While this appears to be "a step in the wrong direction" to parents and professionals who have been working for their success, such behavior is not unusual, and for some students it probably manifests their desire for greater independence. In the event that rejection of treatment and academic support results in problems for students, it is important that they are received with understanding when they seek assistance. By this time, they are likely to recognize their need for services. They will benefit more from a problem-solving approach than from lectures, scoldings, or "I told you so's."

Another set of external issues related to continuing medication and services at college are circumstantial. Students who have not developed a clear understanding of their disability(ies) and the role of interventions are less likely to seek out and use support services. Medication compliance is often compromised when students have not been trained to obtain and administer their own medication dependably, or when they encounter difficulty in obtaining and filling prescriptions. For example, although many students are required to pay student health service fees, some campus providers of student health services are not willing to prescribe or monitor the medications used in the treatment of ADHD. Barkley (1993c) noted that although research has repeatedly demonstrated that medication is highly effective for the majority of young adults with ADHD, they are generally compliant with medication treatment only for a period of six months to a year. This seems to contradict fears that student health service providers may have about students' abusing or becoming addicted to their medications. Rather, compliance and symptom management are much greater concerns for SDS staff members and other professionals working with college students who have ADHD.

Ideally, students should receive a unified message about the benefits of treatment and compliance from the health care and education professionals assisting them. It is important to convey to students that ADHD is often a life-span disability and that practical skills are needed to manage its symptoms. Students need to be well trained in medication self-management during high school in order to reduce the occurrence of problems caused by ADHD symptoms in college.

By the time they enter college, traditional-age students with ADHD have often experienced some of the psychosocial problems that frequently accompany the disorder. These include inaccurate self-perception and low self-esteem in a variety of areas and reduced motivation. Students may respond to these feelings by developing depression or anxiety (Werry, Reeves, & Elkind, 1987). Both internal and external factors affect the degree to which students display these problems. Among the internal factors are the severity of the disability(ies), response to treatment, and attributes such as personality, intelligence, and talent. External factors include the availability of appropriate education and treatment and the presence of understanding and supportive adults during childhood and adolescence.

Students with ADHD or LD encounter a number of challenges in their freshman and sophomore years. They are often especially vulnerable in the social and academic situations that hold risk potential for all students. These situations include living independently away from parental support and supervision, organizing for academic work, and making choices about relationships and activities. Students with ADHD or LD often must address these areas of concern with less developmental maturity and fewer skills than most of their age mates. Consequently, in order to provide effective support, those assisting these students prior to college, and the student affairs practitioners who work with them during the college years, need to take into account the individual transitional issues and needs of each student.

Most colleges and universities encourage students to select and declare a major area of study after the freshman year (or after about 30 semester hours of credit). A few students with

ADHD or LD accomplish this choice quickly. The academic interests of these students may be narrowly defined because they have foreclosed any other options. If their choices are indeed well suited to their abilities and corresponding institutional resources are available, early declaration of a major may result in successful outcomes.

A greater number of students with ADHD and LD find the selection of a major to be especially difficult. Some believe, realistically or not, that ADHD or LD automatically disqualifies them from some areas of study. Others have difficulty focusing on an area of ongoing interest. For these students, a class such as "Making an Educational-Vocational Choice" may help them to evaluate their interests and options. They may also be encouraged to participate in career counseling and advising programs offered by their campus SDS office, or by counseling and placement centers.

Although juniors and seniors have progressed beyond most of the transition-to-college adjustments, they encounter the greater demands of upper level classes and need to address many transition-to-career issues. If ADHD or LD has been a hindrance in the past, these students may perceive it as a barrier to their graduation and career goals, just as they may have once felt their disabilities made the selection of a major difficult. Some externalize their frustration, blaming their problems on faculty members or advisors. Others may take it out on themselves in a manner that results in feelings of anger or depression. If students have not gained insight into the symptoms of their disability, they may struggle with unrecognized transition issues by finding fault and reacting with anger to every situation that poses challenges. This is often especially true if ADHD or LD impairs their ability to move into new situations, learn "unwritten rules," and readily integrate different or more complex procedures. Students may react by thinking that new situations are "awful" and that the people they meet in these situations are untrustworthy or are working against them. Responses such as anxious displays of overtalkativeness, outbursts of temper, or withdrawal into depression are not uncommon. If in any of these situations students have come to blame others in an unrealistic way, professionals assisting them will need to gain their cooperation and trust through the use of caring and careful communication and clear, well-founded information. Students may be advised to investigate various career options by serving internships in areas associated with their major. These firsthand experiences allow students to evaluate their interests and skills in a real-world setting. They provide students with concrete situations and structure that help them focus on career goals and options.

College Admissions Issues

Some students have been diagnosed with ADHD or LD prior to college enrollment. They should be advised that students who disclose their disability(ies) at the time of admission, seek assistance early, and use appropriate accommodations are more likely to achieve academic success (Richard & Chandler, 1994). However, those assisting these students must recognize that although accommodations may be valuable, the decision to self-identify is a personal one and a student's choice not to do so should be respected.

Examples of accommodations at the outset of college include 1. support during orientation programs (e.g., extended time on placement examinations), 2. assistance in the registration process, 3. an interview to initiate SDS services, and finally, 4. referral to other offices and, if needed, to state and federal agencies that may offer assistance.

Early intervention and support can be critical in dealing with the problems of high school students with ADHD or LD who are applying to colleges (Mangrum & Strichart, 1984). Students (especially those who were not diagnosed until secondary school) are often hindered by lags and discontinuous development in academic, social, and emotional functioning. Their risk factors may include an inadequate concept of the nature or difficulty of the college experience and unrealistic expectations about their future performance at college based on their high school achievement. Vulnerability to underachievement, interpersonal problems, low self-esteem, stress intolerance, and depression may hamper independent long-term planning. Symptoms such as procrastination and disorganization may further compromise their progress toward self-determination (Brinckerhoff, Shaw, & McGuire, 1993).

With respect to academic matters, as they relate to college selection, students with ADHD or LD need information about the sufficiency or insufficiency of their preparation for college. High schools vary in their practices for preparing students with disabilities. Some students with ADHD or LD are not encouraged to take classes that are routinely part of the college-bound curriculum in spite of the fact that any transcript deficiencies (e.g., missing high school requirement courses) must usually be made up at college without benefit of credit toward graduation.

It is important to mention that some students with ADHD or LD may be unable to successfully complete the required courses in such areas as mathematics and foreign language. Psychoeducational testing may demonstrate that LD coexisting with ADHD prevents a student from mastering these subjects. If this is the case, it is important that this information be placed in the psychoeducational report and that a clear recommendation be made that the student be allowed to complete the college graduation requirement compromised by the disability through the substitution of approved courses.

College Selection Issues

Professionals working with students and their parents may advise them that in addition to requesting information from admissions offices, they should ask SDS offices for materials about institutional services for students with ADHD or LD. Following their review of all the information, they may be advised to make appointments to meet with SDS staff members on the campuses they plan to visit (Richard, 1992).

Applicants should be able to obtain the following information from college offices of admissions:

1. What criteria are considered in the admissions process (ACT or SAT scores, class rank, or grade point average)?

2. Are there special considerations for admission of students who have documented ADHD or LD? Is there an admissions deadline for applications that request special admissions consideration?

3. Is there an SDS office at the school? If so, what is the name, address, and phone number of the contact person for students with ADHD or LD?

Applicants may also want to obtain the following information from staff at SDS offices. Answers are often readily available in the print materials published by these offices. If more information is needed, applicants may want to make an appointment to talk by phone or meet with a staff member. The schedules of most counselors are very full, and appointments are necessary for extended discussions.

1. Does the institution accept the applicant's current diagnosis? What kind of verification is needed? Are there guidelines about the recency of the documentation?
2. What kinds of recommendations about eligibility for specific services (e.g., note takers, course substitutions, textbook taping, reduced course loads, and test accommodations) must be stated in the student's documentation?
3. How many credit hours must be taken to be a full-time student? Are students with disabilities such as ADHD and LD permitted to take reduced course loads and still be considered full-time students?
4. Does the institution accommodate students who need to substitute courses for curriculum requirements in areas such as foreign language and mathematics?
5. What are the qualifications and size of the staff? What training and experience do they have in assisting students who have ADHD or LD?
6. Do any staff members belong to professional and general associations such as the Association of Higher Education and Disability (AHEAD), Children and Adults with Attention Deficit Disorder (CHADD), or the Learning Disabilities Association (LDA)?
7. Are students assigned a staff counselor? How accessible are counselors to students?
8. How many students with ADHD or LD are now actively receiving services from the office?
9. What do students need to do to obtain needed services?
10. How cooperative are faculty members in providing academic accommodations?
11. Are there specific programs and services for students with ADHD or LD? Is there a charge for these services?

Colleges and universities may not discriminate against qualified applicants in their admissions policies on the basis of ADHD or LD. In general, these students are considered for admission to college on the same basis as all other applicants and must meet the same academic requirements. However, some admissions offices recognize that extenuating circumstances related to disabilities have impaired a student's ability to meet admissions standards. They carefully evaluate the overall performance of these applicants for evidence of the ability needed to pursue studies successfully at their college or university (Barron, 1993).

Students may not be required on the application form to disclose whether they have a disability. In fact, such preadmission inquiries are illegal. However, disclosing this information may have benefits if a student wants to be referred quickly for services or if he or she does not meet admissions criteria and wants to request special consideration in the admissions process. When applying to an institution, prospective students should ask the office of admissions about its procedures. In the event students want to initiate a request for special consideration in the admissions process, they should also ask about procedures for this. While each institution has its own policies and instructions, applicants are usually asked to submit a letter to the director of admissions disclosing the disability. Additional information that may be requested includes

1. A statement requesting special consideration in the admissions process
2. A description of how the ADHD or LD affects the applicant
3. A description of how the student has compensated for any academic deficits
4. Resources used to compensate for these deficits (e.g., resource room, tutors, word-processing software, calculators, extended time for testing, taped textbooks)
5. Discussion of the student's involvement in self-advocacy

6. Information about any high school course requirements for college admission that are missing and why the applicant was unable to complete them. This should be verified by a psychologist's written assessment or by a letter from the student's school guidance counselor.

7. A diagnostic report and summary of treatment recommendations related to the student's ADHD or LD and any other disabilities

8. Copies of recent educational plans if the student has been served under Section 504 or the Individuals with Disabilities Education Act.

Assessment Issues

A number of students with ADHD or LD are not identified prior to college enrollment. Of this group, those who are diagnosed reach help in a number of ways. Some are self-referred or referred by parents or friends to private resources. Others seek assistance for behavior or learning problems from SDS offices or campus counseling centers. Although postsecondary institutions are not mandated by law to identify students with disabilities, some have clinical psychologists on staff who are qualified to perform assessments for ADHD and LD and are able to make accommodation recommendations.

Frequently, before a referral is made, students are screened by an SDS counselor who is trained to look for indications that a student should be assessed to rule out ADHD or LD. Screening usually includes a structured interview to obtain a developmental history and a description of the problems the student is currently experiencing. The process usually consists of 1. the student's completion of an information form or inventory and 2. a one-hour interview with a staff counselor. The use of simple assessment tools, such as inventories, in combination with structured interviews is helpful in screening for the symptoms of ADHD and LD and other concerns that underlie academic problems, difficulty with concentration, disorganization, and impulsive behavior. Even so, students are not always forthcoming with information, and those assisting them must be aware that defensiveness, or anxiety, frustration, or depression, may both result from and conceal ADHD or LD.

If a student's symptoms of attentional or learning disabilities are substantial, the counselor should recommend a comprehensive evaluation. To encourage follow-up, counselors should explain to the student that the evaluation report will be helpful because it will profile weaknesses and provide clues to methods of mitigating them, as well as identify areas of strength that the student may use in overcoming difficulties. While students' responses to referral vary, many are encouraged when they find their difficulties being taken seriously and being addressed. The findings from the screening interview may be released to the psychologist or psychiatrist performing the formal assessment upon a release of information by the student to the SDS office.

It is essential that clinicians recognize the importance of providing concrete recommendations about academic accommodations as part of their formal assessment. An example follows:

Recommendations for academic accommodations: The following modifications are appropriate academic accommodations of this student's disability:

1. The substitution of approved, alternative courses in foreign civilization and culture for the student's foreign language graduation requirement

2. Textbooks (and other reading materials) on tape
3. Double time and a private, low-stimulus room for examinations. If the examination exceeds two hours when double time is given, then student should have a supervised break of 30 minutes at the midpoint of the exam period
4. Note takers for lecture classes
5. Tutoring
6. Access to a computer with a spell-check program for all papers and essay examinations
7. Use of a simple calculator during examinations for computation

A multidisciplinary evaluation is important in the diagnosis and treatment of ADHD and LD. Physicians are often first involved in checking for other conditions that might account for the presenting symptoms. If they diagnose ADHD, they may subsequently prescribe and monitor medication therapy on an ongoing basis.

Summaries may be provided to the SDS office by the student or sent directly by the clinician following release by the student. If a relationship has not been established with the office, they may be provided by the student to the institution at a later time for the purpose of verifying disability and supporting eligibility for services. SDS counselors use this information both for academic purposes and to help students to understand and cope with the impact of ADHD or LD on their personal lives. Counselors focus not only on the cognitive aspects of the disabilities but on their effects on students' relationships and activities of daily living. Students are often receptive to counseling and programming that provides sound information about ADHD and LD through a variety of media, including fact sheets, periodical literature, booklets, books, and videotapes. These materials can be provided in the context of individual or group counseling (Appendix A contains a summary of these materials).

Issues in Late Diagnosis

When students who have undiagnosed ADHD or LD are identified and provided appropriate assistance in college, their chances for a successful outcome often improve. Effective intervention can improve self-esteem, academic achievement, and general adjustment. An accurate diagnosis can help students put their difficulties into perspective. Prior to evaluation, many feel they are to blame for their difficulties with learning and attention or incorrectly attribute them to low intelligence. These students are often relieved by the diagnosis. Uncertainty over what was "wrong" or what led to the referral is replaced with information and hope for the future (Children and Adults with Attention Deficit Disorder, 1993).

In spite of the benefits of diagnosis, it is important to acknowledge the problems connected with late identification. Often, students with ADHD or LD have long been misunderstood by themselves and others. In order to gain acceptance some students have struggled to control their symptoms, expending a great deal of energy in their efforts to "pass for normal." Others have acted out their frustration, adopting the persona of class "clown" or "rebel." As a result, they may have records of impaired social, academic, and emotional functioning. College students often report that, in spite of their best efforts, throughout their school years they have been told by parents and teachers that they are "not trying hard enough." Many have been labeled in school records as "having a bad attitude," "a slow learner," "unmotivated," "immature," "lazy," "spacey," or "self-centered." Many students with undiagnosed ADHD or LD have developed negative self-perceptions as a result of underachievement and social failures (G. Weiss & Hechtman, 1993). While students who have unidentified ADHD or LD are relatively successful, others experience difficulty to the degree that they abandon their efforts to complete a college education. It is not uncommon for students with ADHD or LD to experience adjustment problems related to social behavior. Some act out, while others withdraw in order to avoid criticism or hurt (Werry, Reeves, & Elkind, 1987). Others are chronically distrustful or behave cynically or manipulatively.

Professionals working with college students frequently ask how students with significant attention and learning disabilities have passed undetected through the educational and health care delivery systems. It appears that for a number of reasons, many students with disabilities that are not visible "fall through the cracks" of the systems charged with their identification and treatment. Among the causes of late identification is the lack of preservice and in-service training for mainstream educators and health care providers regarding the identification of children at risk for disorders of learning and attention.

Among the current college population are students who completed their secondary education prior to the enactment of laws requiring school-based assessment services for children suspected of LD. Others who attended primary or secondary school after the implementation of these laws may not have received services because they did not meet the eligibility criteria of substantial academic failure or problematic behavior. For example, state regulations for eligibility have often required that students score two to three years below grade level in mathematics or reading in order to qualify for services. Among those students who were evaluated, some were missed or misdiagnosed because of service providers' lack of information about identifying students at risk for ADHD or LD.

Students with ADHD or LD meeting college admission standards are in general of average or above average intelligence and have developed a range of compensatory strategies. Thus, it is not surprising that they were not identified on the basis of academic failure or persistent misbehavior. In addition, those students meeting criteria related to a primary attention deficit disorder without the presence of specific LD, may have erroneously been considered ineligible for educational services. It was not until the U.S. Department of Education issued a memo of clarification on 16 September 1991 that the law was clear on the point that students whose educational progress is impaired by ADHD are eligible for accommodations and services under Section 504 of the Rehabilitation Act of 1973 or the Individuals with Disabilities Education Act.

Responsibilities of Students and Institutions

Postsecondary institutions should be prepared to provide program access through appropriate accommodations and modifications for students who are diagnosed with ADHD or LD. Federal law mandates that otherwise qualified students who have disabilities be permitted to use alternative methods to meet educational requirements as long as these methods do not alter the essential components of the course or program or create an undue burden on the institution. Disability is defined as a condition that impairs an individual's ability to carry out a major life function, such as learning. Accommodations that are reasonable and appropriate do not lower academic standards; they simply provide alternative ways for students to meet graduation requirements.

Contrary to the perception that accommodations and modifications for students with ADHD or LD give these students an advantage over others, their purpose is to reduce or eliminate any disadvantages that may exist because of the disability. Institutions are not required by law to waive specific courses or academic requirements considered essential to a particular program or degree. Rather, they are mandated to modify requirements on a case-by-case basis to ensure that the requirements do not discriminate on the basis of disability. The purpose of accommodations is to ensure that students with disabilities have equal opportunity to benefit from institutional programs. However, the law does not require that these adjustments produce achievement identical to that of students without disabilities (Frank & Wade, 1993).

Students who want to use access services must identify themselves and provide appropriate verification of their disability. Eligibility for reasonable and appropriate accommodations is individually determined (Latham & Latham, 1993). Not all students with ADHD or LD need or benefit from identical modifications and accommodations, nor do they necessarily use them to the same degree. Actual use of services is the student's choice, and it is the responsibility of each individual to determine whether to use available services.

Issues and Practices

Students with ADHD or LD have diverse profiles of strengths and areas of need. The following "menu of services" lists accommodations for which students may be eligible, as determined on a case-by-case basis (Richard, 1992). Details will be discussed later in the chapter.

- Assistance during orientation services
- Priority registration
- Testing accommodations
- Advocacy with staff and faculty
- Tutorial services
- Note-taking services
- Assistance with time management
- Extended assignment deadlines
- Recorded reading materials
- Degree requirement substitutions
- Assistance with academic skills
- Individual and group counseling
- Technological tools and auxiliary aids

Students with ADHD or LD may want to use additional services, such as transcription or word processing, that are not required under Section 504. Some SDS offices maintain lists of persons or services available as assistants for hire by students with disabilities. In general, assistants are paid directly by the student, who makes arrangements regarding hours and payment.

Effective practices for students with ADHD or LD include the provision of individualized, cooperatively planned accommodations that are structured yet integrated with existing university services. SDS counselors or other designated student services or counseling center personnel advise students about obtaining the assistance they require. Eligibility for accommodations and services is determined by student and counselor and is guided by the information in the student's disability evaluation.

Institutional practices that affect the learning and development of students with ADHD or LD fall into five areas: 1. transition to college, 2. institutional involvement, 3. student involvement, 4. academic accommodations and support services, and 5. career development assistance.

TRANSITION TO COLLEGE

The transition from high school to college may be facilitated for students with ADHD or LD by a preadmissions meeting with an SDS counselor. If students schedule campus tours, they should consider requesting an appointment on the day of their visit. Others can benefit from participation in a summer program or orientation session designed to address their needs. Many schools offer general summer orientation sessions, which range from one to several days in length, for students who have been accepted for enrollment. Some of these, such as the two-day program at the University of Iowa, insert into their traditional schedule of events additional sessions for students with ADHD or LD and their parents.

A growing number of institutions offer specialized summer programs for high school students planning to attend college after graduation. Students who participate in these programs are introduced to the college experience. They may be given opportunities to learn study skills and self-advocacy, find out how to obtain support services, and become familiar with campus technology resources. Students in some of the programs attend classes and earn college credits.

Students learning to negotiate the postsecondary system need information and support in order to handle the shifting of responsibility to students. At the elementary and secondary levels, federal statutes state that schools are responsible for identifying and serving students with disabilities. At the postsecondary level, the law places the responsibility on students to identify themselves and request services. Most students are unprepared for this abrupt change in procedures. Professionals assisting students must help them not only to become more articulate in discussing their disability but also to understand and face any attitudinal barriers they may encounter, and to implement strategies for dealing with them (Association for Handicapped Student Services Programs in Postsecondary Education, 1987).

While many faculty members cooperate in serving students, a number still hold erroneous notions about ADHD and LD—from denying that these disorders exist to attributing them to emotional disturbance or mental retardation. Since instructors vary in their personal reactions to disclosure, it is critical to successful transition that students become capable and comfortable in self-advocacy. They must be able to speak for themselves in order to 1. make appointments with instructors to disclose the disability, 2. discuss any relevant information about the disability, 3. request any classroom accommodations that are needed, and 4. request the examination accommodations that will help them to demonstrate knowledge of course material (Nadeau, Dixon, & Biggs, 1994; Richard, 1995b).

Students with ADHD or LD should also be involved in requesting the accommodations they need. Learning and implementing the skills of self-advocacy is critical during college and will likely be important later, in the workplace. While SDS counselors work in a variety of ways to assist students, they do not reduce the need for student self-advocacy. At the request of students, SDS offices at a number of campuses provide students with letters or forms to give to their instructors that verify their needs for specific accommodations. Counselors may instruct or coach students in specific self-advocacy skills, such as making requests of faculty members, and provide information about the organization of the institution and its academic departments.

INSTITUTIONAL INVOLVEMENT

The collaborative involvement of college and university administrators, staff, and faculty in policies and practices appropriate for students with ADHD or LD is often an important factor in their outcome.

Support staff and disability services. The availability of an SDS office and staff who are trained about ADHD or LD, who are experienced in assisting students with these disabilities, and who have excellent interpersonal skills is one key to student retention and success.

Verification policies and procedures. Campuses must have reliable and confidential procedures for conveying information about student eligibility for specific accommodations to the instructors of classes in which disabled students are enrolled. This exchange of information may be accomplished in several ways. One method is the use of a student accommodation request form, printed on a carbon triplicate (Kennedy, Shinkunas, & Richard, 1995). Students actively participate in the process of obtaining accommodations by meeting with their counselors to discuss appropriate accommodations for each of their classes. When the accommodations have been determined, counselors enter this information on the form and sign it, certifying eligibility. Accommodation forms should also be signed by students, in recognition of their responsibility to follow through on arrangements in a timely manner. Students deliver their forms to their instructors, who are directed to sign them, agreeing to provide the accommodations indicated or contact the SDS counselor within 48 hours to discuss them. The instructor, student, and SDS counselor (in the student's SDS file) each keep one copy of the triplicate form.

Faculty and staff awareness. Faculty members, administrators, and student services practitioners who have some training about ADHD or LD as disabilities and are aware of students' legal rights are more likely to help students obtain access. They may both assist students who have disclosed their disabilities and refer to the SDS office students who demonstrate characteristics of an undiagnosed disorder. Information about the needs of students with ADHD or LD can be used to improve instructional practices and facilitate student learning. SDS staff should be available to provide staff development and consultation in order to enhance faculty and staff awareness and promote effective teaching.

Effective instructional practices. The following list of teaching practices for assisting students with ADHD or LD in classes has been adapted from several sources (Association for Higher Education and Disability, 1991; Vogel, 1993a):

- Encourage students with disabilities who need accommodations to talk to the instructor on the first day of class to make arrangements.
- Supply a list of course readings a semester in advance for students who need to have materials tape recorded.

- Provide students with a detailed course syllabus that includes specific information about grading and due dates prior to or on the first day of class.
- Start lecture classes with an outline of the material to be covered, and conclude each class with a summary of the main concepts.
- Prepare student handouts and examinations in at least a 12-point typeface and with adequate white space on each page.
- Introduce new vocabulary by displaying new words on the chalkboard, the overhead projector, or a student handout. Use these terms in context to associate meanings with the new words.
- During lectures, pause periodically and invite questions.
- Permit the tape-recording of lectures.
- Provide study questions for exams that model the test format and content.
- Offer review sessions prior to examinations.
- Explain what components the instructor expects to find in a good answer, paper, or project and why these are considered important.
- Provide test accommodations for individual students when indicated, including modifications in time allowed, test location, and environment, use of assistive devices (e.g., word-processing equipment, calculators, speller's dictionaries, and scratch paper), and format.

Student Involvement

Students who are encouraged to meet regularly with their SDS counselors and use the programs and accommodations available to them are more likely to be successful. Since students with ADHD or LD often experience a sense of acute boredom that is symptomatic of their disorder, it is especially important that they be encouraged to participate in programs of residence life, academic advising, and other campus activities and affiliations. If they work, an on-campus part-time job of not more than 10–15 hours per week may enable students to remain connected to school while earning money. Volunteering in a campus service program may also increase student commitment to staying in college.

Academic Accommodations and Support Services

A list of accommodations and services appeared earlier in this chapter. The following descriptions offer more information about many of them.

Degree requirement substitutions. When ADHD or LD prevents students from completing degree requirements in such areas as mathematics or foreign language, the SDS office may help them obtain a course substitution from an approved list of courses. Students with ADHD or LD may be eligible, on a case-by-case basis, for these accommodations. To accomplish the substitution, SDS counselors often work with students in cooperation with an academic review committee in the college of liberal arts. The process usually involves a meeting at which the student and SDS counselor discuss the student's eligibility for this accommodation and the process through which it may be requested. Academic review committees often ask the student to write a letter or complete a petition requesting the substitution and providing information about the need for it. This letter or petition is submitted together with a letter of support from the SDS counselor and a clinical recommendation that the proposed modification is an appropriate accommodation. The recommendation is usually contained in the student's diagnostic report from an educational specialist, school or clinical psychologist, neuropsychologist, developmental pediatrician, or psychiatrist.

Testing accommodations. Examination accommodations are frequently requested by postsecondary students with ADHD or LD to help them compensate for their disability-related symptoms. Based on their individual needs, students may be able to take exams in a private or semiprivate room, have extended time limits, or be assisted by a reader or scribe. Other assistive devices that students may be eligible to use include a calculator, speller's dictionary, proofreader, and word-processing equipment. Some students may be eligible to request the substitution of specific exam formats (e.g., essay, multiple choice, or short answer) through arrangements with the SDS office and faculty members. While some students with ADHD or LD make these arrangements with their instructors independently, others do so through the SDS office. Students who plan to use examination accommodations should discuss them with their instructors ahead of time so that arrangements can be made in a timely manner. Some SDS offices have reservation forms to facilitate arrangements for tests that will be proctored through the office and accommodation forms for students to use when arranging their tests with faculty members.

Note-taking services. Depending on their profiles of abilities and deficits, some students with ADHD or LD may qualify for the use of note-taking services because they are unable to concentrate on listening and processing simultaneously with transcribing. A student may be supplied with the instructor's notes, may make copies of another student's notes by formal arrangement, or may be provided with notes by a paid note taker. Since notes are only as good as the note taker, their usefulness and accuracy may vary. Programs should provide training to note takers to establish consistent note-taking practices and quality.

Recorded reading materials. Students who have severe reading disabilities are eligible to receive their textbooks and reading assignments on tape. Tapes may be available through the SDS office or through other national and campus resources. SDS counselors can certify student application forms for membership in the Recording for the Blind (RFB) Master Tape Library. RFB is a nonprofit agency that supplies taped materials to persons with specific disabilities. Students are responsible for obtaining lists of required readings from instructors, gathering books and materials, taking them to the recording drop-off site, and completing any recording request forms. Another way to obtain taped texts is to use a reading machine, available on many campuses. These devices, which look like personal copiers, have optical character readers and voice synthesizers. They are used to electronically scan and read text aloud, onto tape, or onto computer disk.

Technological tools and auxiliary aids. Students with ADHD or LD may be able to use a number of technological tools to help them compensate for their problems with organization and planning. Among materials currently available are electronic spellers and personal organizers, calculators, tape player-recorders, and computers with word-processing, spread sheet, database, and time management software. Students may own these items or, in some cases, gain access to items through campus loan services.

Priority registration. Many institutions offer priority enrollment for students with disabilities. This accommodation allows access to enrollment in classes during the initial period of registration, when more classes and sections are open at more times. Students with ADHD or LD should use this accommodation to schedule classes at effective times.

Reduced course load. Students with ADHD or LD who are entering college are often advised to schedule no more than 12–13 hours of credit per semester. This load is recommended because some family health insurance plans will only continue to carry college students when they are enrolled in 12 or more hours of college credit per semester (usually until age 24) and some forms of student financial aid require that students carry at least 12 hours of credit. If, after a semester or two at a reduced course load, a student's grades are good to excellent (in the 3–4-point range on a 4-point scale) and the student believes these grades can be maintained, he or she may consider enrolling in an additional three hours of credit.

STUDENT SUPPORT AND ASSISTANCE PROGRAMS

Tutorial and learning assistance programs. Institutions vary in their mechanisms for delivering content-based tutorial services. Some programs are located within the SDS, while others are delivered under the auspices of a campus learning center, departmental learning labs, counseling centers, or a tutorial service. Some students with ADHD or LD hesitate to use tutorial services, waiting until they are in trouble to ask for assistance. Embarrassment about needing help and denial of problems may contribute to the tendency of these students to procrastinate in arranging for and using tutorial services. Counselors should emphasize that using tutorial services is a common practice in college and does not imply that a student is incompetent. Training for tutors should include information about the cardinal characteristics of ADHD and LD and should emphasize that every student has a different pattern of academic strengths and weaknesses. It is important that students participate actively in their learning. Strategies that tutors can use to encourage this process include starting each session by asking the student for a "success story" related to the tutoring teamwork, making miniassignments related to the material, and administering practice tests. Tutors should ask new students what methods of studying have helped them in the past. Tutors need to recognize the importance for students of task mastery and the consequent rewards of accomplishment. Even though some students display learned helplessness, tutors must not do a student's work.

Self-management instruction. Interviews with college graduates with ADHD reveal that they have used a number of cognitive strategies to gain insight into and regulate their attention and productivity. While most describe difficulty with the symptoms of stress intolerance and cognitive fatigue and many say that they have continuing problems with inconsistency, strategies such as "self-talk," note-taking systems, and time management tools are considered helpful. Some college students have written personal essays about growing up and living with ADHD or LD. By telling their stories, students may reflect on where they have been and where they are going in their personal and academic development. This is a valuable exercise for developing insight, especially for students who process information well through writing.

Support groups. Support groups meet the needs of students who process information well through discussion and are validated by group support. Groups for students with ADHD or

LD can be time limited (e.g., four to five 90-minute sessions) or ongoing. They may target any student with ADHD or LD who would like to attend, or they may be limited to those who are newly diagnosed. Some are self-help in nature; others are facilitated by a trained counselor or psychologist.

Individual counseling. Students with ADHD or LD have more concerns about college and career than other students. Coping with a disability requires a good deal of effort, and this may reduce the effort that students are able to put into achieving their goals. Individual sessions with a counselor who is knowledgeable about ADHD and LD can help students to overcome feelings of frustration and being "stuck" or helpless and can aid in identifying strengths, resources, and opportunities. Students may need guidance in choosing a major, an intern- or externship, relationships, and careers. Services may be available through SDS programs or counseling services.

Mentoring program. Studies have found that the most successful adults with LD have a number of characteristics in common (Gerber et al., 1992). One of the most important was the presence of a positive role model or mentor. Because of their characteristic developmental lag, many college students with ADHD or LD are reassured and can benefit by anchoring themselves to a counselor, SDS staff person, faculty member, or successful older student with ADHD or LD. Having such a person available can greatly help students recover from setbacks and avoid prolonged downward spirals in academic performance or emotional adjustment. Some SDS offices offer mentoring programs in which a faculty member or another student is paired with a student who requests this assistance.

Status of Research on Interventions for the College Population

Additional research on the status of the population of college students with ADHD or LD should examine their needs, progress, and development. A number of questions must be answered about how well these students are being served by the allocation of institutional resources and the implementation of policies and practices. Such research might allow services to be improved so that they provide students with better chances of success and practitioners with a stronger foundation for justifying their recommendations. The development of a greater base of empirical information about "best" practices for students with ADHD or LD is an area worthy of continuing professional study.

Summary

While nondiscrimination related to college students with disabilities is mandated by law, the proactive implementation of supportive policies and practices also reflects the ethics of postsecondary institutions and their commitment to providing access. As a part of the diverse student body in postsecondary education, students with ADHD or LD should be valued for their differences and accommodated with accessible programs and learning environments.

As the number of students who are disclosing their disabilities and requesting services increases, practitioners are being challenged to understand the nature and characteristics of these disabilities and to respond appropriately. Students and those who assist them should be aware of the educational rights of students with disabilities and of the services offered at the postsecondary level. These services include disability and resource information, advocacy, tutorial and other supportive services, and academic accommodations. Professionals who understand ADHD and LD and the related resources can recommend and design services and accommodations that help students obtain access to programs and develop academic and life skills. Combined with staff and faculty awareness of ADHD and LD and provision of appropriate accommodations, the campus community can contribute to the retention and graduation outcomes of students in the ADHD and LD populations.

CHAPTER 11

Vocational Programs and Practices

Rob Crawford

T HIS CHAPTER provides an overview of vocational assessment and guidance issues. An overview of the Life Development Institute model of vocational training for people with ADHD or LD is presented. Vocational strategies for college graduates and possible accommodations in the workplace are also discussed.

Vocational Assessment and Guidance

Most employment and educational reform initiatives continue to neglect or ignore adults with ADHD or LD. Yet adults with these disorders represent the largest single identified population of special needs learners seeking employment. Many of these individuals are nontraditional learners. They often do not present their best capabilities with assessment approaches that rely on traditional, norm-referenced measurements. In order to make a vocational assessment that reflects the individual's true interests, abilities, and aptitudes, the clinician and client should thoroughly investigate the following areas: 1. level of client involvement, 2. methods used in securing previous employment, 3. background information from previous employers and co-workers, 4. level of functional skills required for targeted employment, and 5. availability of support services.

LEVEL OF CLIENT INVOLVEMENT

The most important user of the vocational assessment is the client, and therefore, the client must be the focus of the assessment process. Many assessments reviewed by this writer revealed an approach in which superficial information was collected, demonstrating the presenting level of self-advocacy, level of age-appropriate peer relationships, previous testing experience, perception of what constitutes the individual's view of quality of life, and stress and personal conflict issues present at the time of assessment in making career decisions.

Making assessments client centered is a method of teaching self-advocacy. The person being assessed becomes primarily responsible for the direction and quality of choices rather than relying on the clinician, a teacher, or a parent to make decisions. Assessments that lack meaningful consumer input run the risk of creating an entitlement mentality as opposed to an empowerment mentality.

Previous studies examining vocational guidance and career education approaches for the LD and ADHD populations suggest that career development needs to be an experiential learning process that gives the client opportunities to make logical connections between his wants and needs and to understand the demands of the work setting (Rosenthal, 1989; Schaller, 1994). When an assessment is conducted *for* the client rather than *by* the client, the client does not learn how to use community information sources.

A client can learn important basic advocacy skills by, for example, 1. interviewing local employers to gain an understanding of the basic skills needed for entry-level positions, 2. determining the level of literacy required to benefit from a vocational-technical training program, and 3. recognizing the time management requirements for scheduling, confirming, and conducting informational interviews at local community-based resources.

Competency in advocating for oneself should also involve social competency, especially as it relates to interpersonal relationships. Young adults with ADHD or LD, becoming independent for the first time, often equate advocacy with pushiness. Frequently, they are reluctant to speak up strongly on their own behalf for fear of seeming too aggressive or to avoid retaliation from coworkers, parents, and professionals—for example, being asked, "What do you know? You're just a dishwasher," or being told, "You know you're not good at math."

During assessments, clients often behave in a way that indicates their unawareness of social graces, making "off the wall" comments unrelated to the conversation, avoiding eye contact in conversations, or exhibiting poor taste in personal hygiene or grooming habits (e.g., picking nose or playing with hair). Many times, the client is unaware of how this behavior affects the positive development of peer relationships because he lacks experience interacting with older adults.

When asked specific questions—such as What is your medication for? What is your social security number? Why did you leave your last job? How long were you employed at your last job?—the client frequently defers to her parents for the answers. In this situation, the client loses valuable practice in responding to an "authority figure" and continues to depend on others to handle things instead of assuming that responsibility.

Adults living outside of their parents' residence interact with many types of personalities and communication situations each day. Collecting information about how the client handles day-to-day interactions with adults in a variety of situations (recreation, work, and home) can make it possible to discover what seems to upset the client. This method is helpful in ascertaining how capable he is of filtering information, organizing possible responses, and choosing the best way to handle a conflict. It is not unusual for the young adult with ADHD or LD to have had limited dating experience and casual opposite-sex conversations (outside of family members) or to know how to initiate these interactions.

Obtaining this type of information in the assessment allows the practitioner to understand how the client will handle social interaction in the workplace. Social situations are potentially more difficult to deal with than any learning or attentional barrier.

Moya and O'Malley (1994) noted the shortcomings of limited client involvement in assessments controlled by the clinician. Some of the limitations that result from single-measured approaches are that 1. low scores yield little information about strengths to build upon, 2. attention is focused on lower level skills, 3. the process fails to take into account thought processes and reasons for the answers given, and 4. quantitative outcomes are emphasized more than instructionally useful feedback.

Attention should also be paid to what constitutes "quality of life" in the eyes of the client, and from more than just the employment perspective. Additional values related to what Halpern (1992a) and others identified as a holistic conceptual quality-of-life model are found in Figure 11.1. This model emphasizes personal choices and needs (the subjective perspective) versus social norms and expectations (the objective perspective) in identifying quality-of-life outcomes.

Putting this model into practice allows the clinician to understand the subjective dimensions of the client's idea of quality of life. A full array of psychological issues, including but not limited to employment options, is considered. Halpern (1992a) identifies the following 15 types of outcomes from the three basic quality-of-life domains. Most of these outcomes can be measured objectively (e.g., is the person living independently?) and subjectively (is the person satisfied with where she lives?).

Physical and material well-being

- Physical and mental health

- Food, clothing, and lodging

- Financial security

- Safety from harm

Personal fulfillment

- Happiness

- Satisfaction

- Sense of general well-being

Performance of adult roles

- Mobility and community access

- Vocation, career, and employment

- Leisure and recreation

- Personal relationship and social networks

- Educational attainment

- Spiritual fulfillment

- Citizenship (e.g., voting)

- Social responsibility (e.g., doesn't break laws)*

*From "Quality of Life as a Conceptual Framework for Evaluating Transition Outcomes," by A. Halpern, 1992, *Interchange, 12* (2), p. 1–3. Used with permission.

Figure 11.1   Objective and subjective dimensions of quality of life

Note. From "Quality of Life amongst Handicapped Adults," by R. Brown, M. Bayer, and C. MacFarlane, 1988, in *Quality of Life for Handicapped People: A Series in Rehabilitation Education,* edited by R. Brown, London: Croom Helm. Used with permission.

Examining these areas allows the practitioner to help the client achieve the highest quality of life possible from his individual frame of reference and from the perspective of what is considered socially appropriate. This collaborative approach avoids situations in which the assessment team does a great deal of developmental work to place the client in a training or employment setting and the client sabotages the placement because he is not "happy" with the way he is expected to perform.

Impulsive behavior leading to job or program termination can be minimized by taking the time to understand what constitutes job satisfaction from the point of view of the client and by explaining that employers expect *all employees* to perform certain job functions in specific ways. Stress is inevitable when an individual unaccustomed to being involved in or responsible for critical decisions about her own life tries to make correct decisions that are both personally satisfying and acceptable to other adults involved in the process. Each decision that a client must make about her vocational future requires her to take a chance and risk failure.

The amount of vocational stress the adult with ADHD or LD experiences is directly related to his uncertainty about employment goals and his perceived needs associated with those goals. If the expectations of the client are not met and the alternatives proposed do not seem viable to either client or practitioner, avoidance behavior on the part of the client usually results. The client may miss scheduled appointments, be hypersensitive to the "messenger" bringing the bad news, and fail to follow through with school and work requirements.

Janis and Mann (1977) contend that in their conflict model of career decision making, the process of choosing the best vocational path threatens the decision maker. By working to remove as many of the risks of "failing" as possible, the practitioner can help the client to objectively consider the positive and negative consequences of various alternatives. This writer frequently witnesses clients who are struggling to make wise career choices fall victim to the "eight career myths":

1. *I want to be sure I choose exactly the right career.* While it is understandable for a client to want to make a sound career choice, the simple truth is that there is no such thing as the "right" choice. Not only is this approach stifling and self-limiting, it allows for procrastination and indecision because the client's expectations are too high. The best way to refocus an individual who insists on finding a career using this approach is to point out that there are no more perfect jobs than there are perfect people. Each workplace offers both good and bad conditions that must be compared to the client's wants and needs. A client must look at the overall picture of the job in question. If she sees more positive aspects than negative ones in relationship to areas of personal job satisfaction, the choice can be a sound one.

2. *When I choose my career, I'm deciding for a lifetime.* Given the likelihood that the client lacks extensive exposure to the world of work, this writer would explain that what looks good now may not be satisfying 10, 20, or 30 years from now. People change their priorities and interests over time. A substantial body of statistics shows that people change jobs many times over the course of a lifetime. This would also be a good time to suggest that the client interview parents, employers, or administrators of training programs who have frequently changed jobs themselves on this issue.

3. *Most people have made a definite decision about what they want to do when they have reached my age.* This writer believes that each person has an "internal alarm clock" and that the time when a client will be ready to make a career decision is unique to the client. Often the client does not know what he *really* wants to do with his life, and because of this apparent indecision, he feels something is wrong with him because everyone in his family or peer group seems to know exactly where they fit in the job market.

   This writer has heard numerous invalid comparisons by clients who try to measure their life progress against that of their parents, siblings, or peers at the same age. The clients often come from very successful, affluent families. Most of their family members have graduated from prestigious colleges or are attending college, have excellent paying jobs, and are solidly independent. The pressure to "catch up" with people who seem better than they are many times drives clients to make vocational choices that reflect someone else's life rather than their own deeper interests, abilities, and aptitudes.

4. *I would like to take a test that will tell me what I should do.* No such test exists! Testing can only take a client *part* of the way in making a good career decision. In the interests of enhancing personal responsibility, the client must understand that the ultimate answer to what is workable lies within him.

5. *I think that if I like to do something, I should be good at it.* Many times adults with ADHD or LD with whom this writer has been conducting job placement activities have been ready to take a job with a company that has placed a classified ad promising to pay $20.00 an hour to start, no experience necessary. Obviously, the money is attractive to someone who does not understand that if a job looks too good to be true, it probably is! If good pay and the lack of a work experience requirement are the primary motivators for the client, however, this writer would acknowledge that those two factors are a good starting point for job exploration. This writer would ask the client to compare her personal abilities and aptitudes with the daily requirements of the job. Also, if the job does not work

out, what does she propose for plan B or plan C? It never hurts to prequalify the prospective employer by conducting an informational telephone interview to find out what specifically the company does, the basic skills needed for entry-level employment, and the opportunities for growth in the future.

This writer would advise the client that if the company has what she is looking for and she is qualified, she should schedule a trip to the place of business where she can discuss her qualifications in person. In this way, the client can make an informed decision about the suitability of the company and at the same time find out from the employer what level of effort would be needed to succeed in that employment setting.

6. *I must develop all of the stages in my career plan as soon as possible.* Impulsive, "do it now" planning with "kamikaze" follow-through is typical of the client who subscribes to this myth. Clients may place undue or unnecessary pressure on themselves to have a plan, without having a clear idea of the steps needed to develop a thorough plan. The local community has many types of vocational and educational resources. In order to find the best one to commit to, the client must undertake a certain amount of deliberate investigation first.

7. *If I don't succeed in reaching my career goals, then I have failed.* Many clients approach vocational choices with an "all or nothing" attitude. The practitioner should ask, "What would your life be like if you hadn't tried at all?" The client may then acknowledge that most people do not even try to define specific career goals, let alone pursue them. Making an effort required the client to take a chance on himself, and while he might not have achieved his specific career objective, he is a better person for the attempt. Recognizing incremental personal successes toward achieving a career objective and developing an increased awareness of the targeted career leaves the door open to discovering other occupational possibilities that would accomplish the purpose originally intended.

8. *Since I am confused about my career plans, I'll take "time out" so I'll know when it's the right time to come back.* Practitioners should ask these clients two questions: When and how will you know what the right time to come back to your career plan is? What productive use will you make of your extra time? Lengthy experience working in assessment situations with adults who are unaccustomed to filtering and synthesizing vocational information has taught this writer to push for a specific action plan that justifies a course of nonaction on the part of the client. If she is able to outline solid reasons for taking time off, such as analyzing the potential risks involved in making a job change, then it is probably appropriate to grant her that time.

Frequently, these individuals face time limitations due to lack of funding or unemployment. In these cases, procrastination often results in job plans and vocational assessments that are practitioner-driven because the client is unwilling or unable to commit to a specific course of action. When a practitioner has a client engaged in avoidance behaviors, an approach that Janis and Mann (1977) call "bolstering" can assist the process of decision making.

In reviewing all information collected by the client, the practitioner can suggest that the client objectively consider all the positive and negative consequences of different choices. During this review, the client will begin to recognize that he has truly covered all the aspects of the decision and has done his best in arriving at a decision that makes sense in terms of his career choice. For example, a client who has lost a successful position will likely approach getting a new position from a decidedly defensive posture. If he has pressing financial concerns, he may take the first job that is offered to him or may find reasons to reject opportunities because they are not exactly like the position he held previously. Although no decision is perfect, getting the client to review objectively all of his perceived risks and gains makes him more likely to reach a satisfactory decision.

Whether the client obtaining the vocational assessment is just entering the adult world or whether she is an older, more vocationally mature person looking toward a career change, it is imperative that she be the center of the learning process. By minimizing the risks of change and eliminating her need to have others tell her what to do, the adult with ADHD or LD comes to see herself as a capable, self-directed learner.

METHODS USED IN SECURING PREVIOUS EMPLOYMENT

Noticeably absent from most vocational reports is information about how the adult with ADHD or LD conducted job search activities in the past. Such information allows the practitioner to identify the approaches that were successful in securing the client employment and the client's level of involvement in the search process.

The National Longitudinal Transition Study of Special Education Students published findings on job search activities that detailed the methods used by young adults with disabilities to identify and secure employment opportunities (D'Amico & Blackorby, 1992). The good news is that 60% of these youth conducted their job searches themselves. The bad news is that their primary sources of information were reading the classified section of the newspaper and walking in off the street and filling out an application for employment. Relying primarily on these resources overlooks the larger "hidden job market" of unadvertised employment openings. Youth using this approach were in direct competition with all job applicants for these advertised positions and were likely hard-pressed to find a suitable job because they lacked specific information about employers' requirements.

The single largest resource available to job seekers with ADHD or LD is the local yellow pages. The yellow pages list every company doing business in the local area and should be used in conjunction with the want ads to cluster a group of employers. The job seeker will then ask each of these employers for background information on what his or her company does, what requirements it has for entry-level positions, and what its opportunities for growth in the future are. In this way, a job seeker can obtain a tremendous amount of useful information about vocational possibilities and the expectations of employers for each position. In addition, the job seeker is able to make direct contact with the key decision maker of the company. This is an advantage that allows the job seeker to prequalify the company and ask, Do I want to work for them? rather than, Will they want me to work for them? The job-seeking adult with ADHD or LD is in a much better negotiating position using this direct approach than randomly applying for the first position that comes his way.

A large percentage of job seekers depend on job leads and contacts coming from family, friends, and outside agencies. It is important to document the level of involvement of these other individuals in the job development process. In particular, to what extent did they identify acceptable employment, provide transportation to the interview, make sure that all necessary identification was present, correct spelling on the application, fill in all the "blanks" on the application, and participate on behalf of the client in the interview phase of the application process? Many well-meaning individuals actually detract from the abilities of the job seeker by "fixing" the interview and application until the adult with ADHD or LD is virtually guaranteed a job. In this case, unfortunately, the ownership of the job lies with the individuals working with the job seeker rather than with the client himself.

It is important to determine whether the client went through a true interview, was given the job as a result of outside involvement, or simply showed up at the right time when the employer was desperate for a "warm body" and would hire anybody with a pulse. If all job search activities were performed by others for the client, the client will lack functional expertise in conducting an independent job search.

Developing independent search capabilities is critical to the successful implementation of the vocational assessment. Time and attention will need to be devoted to facilitating experiential learning activities such as how to use public transportation, how to summarize personal qualifications, and how to answer various interview questions.

BACKGROUND INFORMATION FROM PREVIOUS EMPLOYERS AND COWORKERS

Many adults with ADHD or LD are capable of conducting successful job searches independently but are unable for any number of reasons to maintain job stability. In contrast, many adults in this population experience excellent job stability and retention but feel they are underemployed and need better vocational opportunities. In order to measure individual competency and identify probable stumbling blocks, this writer has found it useful to survey the opinions of employers and coworkers who are familiar with the work habits and functional social skills displayed by the client in the work setting.

For both un- and underemployed adults with ADHD or LD, the practitioner should identify how the client was trained, how long the training took, what shifts the client worked, how many hours the client worked per shift, how many hours the client worked per week, and how much support coverage the client received from coworkers and employers. This information may uncover strategies and techniques that the client used successfully at the work site that resulted in enhanced work performance. If the interventions used by coworkers and employers required a high level of supportive maintenance, that particular work experience would be difficult to replicate without a similarly broad-minded employer willing to invest the extra time and attention. Also, for the adult hoping to upgrade his present work situation, job accommodations requiring extensive coworker assistance may negate the applicant's ability to perform the essential functions of a more responsible position.

Other important background information the practitioner should obtain includes coworkers' and employers' opinions about the types of training methods that seem to be most or least effective for the client. Depending on the particular kind of job, training and instructions are usually provided through demonstration, orally, or from a written manual. A comparison of baseline psychometric information with feedback from the work site often shows discrepancies between what the testing indicates to be the functional levels of the client and how she performs in an actual work setting. Some individuals work very well in quiet, controlled test situations but fall apart when asked to make decisions based on multiple priorities in the face of a lot of extraneous auditory and visual stimuli. Others thrive in a work environment characterized by high levels of stress but may not be able to demonstrate these skills in the assessment process. Talking to people who know the client outside of an assessment setting can provide an extra dimension of knowledge that may encourage investigation of other vocational possibilities that would not have been suggested by traditional testing procedures.

While they cannot be expected to have specialized knowledge about ADHD and LD, previous employers and coworkers can fill in some of the missing background information on a client's work performance by providing objective recollections. One area of particular interest would be their evaluation of the client's work-related social skills. Did the client work better alone or as part of a team? If the organizational culture places a premium on being a team player and the client tended to keep to herself, she may not have fared very well with that company. In another case, the organization may prefer self-directed workers, whereas the client was a social butterfly frequently found visiting coworkers rather than tending to business.

Former coworkers and employers can also give practitioners "before and after" snapshots of the relative improvement of the client's social skills at the workplace. Many adults with ADHD or LD present themselves to their peers as being somewhat immature or different because they lack experience with workplace social situations. As the client adjusted to the new work setting, did coworkers and employers observe a leveling out of behavior? This adjustment is common with younger individuals or those new to the workforce.

The practitioner also needs to find out whether the client started out on a good footing but developed increasingly disruptive behaviors that interfered with his job performance or that of his coworkers. Many adults with ADHD or LD get themselves into trouble with their coworkers and employers by being too relaxed or becoming overly familiar. The client's perceptions of how people felt about him usually differ sharply from information gathered from the perspective of coworkers at the receiving end of these behaviors. Especially damaging to the client are reports of disruptive social habits that went unremediated, such as interrupting others, correcting others by pointing out their mistakes, or being unable to accept responsibility for doing a job a certain way without complaining about it. The client and practitioner have their work cut out for them if these situations consistently recur throughout the client's work history.

Minimizing the likelihood of future occurrences of this sort will require prior knowledge of the specific expectations of the targeted work site. In addition, the client must learn what constitutes fair and reasonable treatment of coworkers, perhaps by scripting or role playing situations similar to those that occurred at previous work sites. A major benefit of this exercise is to provide practice time for the client to identify the conditions and circumstances in which it is appropriate for her to assert her opinions. This practice time also allows the client to learn how to accept work-related criticism of her performance gracefully and use it to improve her work quality without personalizing it.

Many adults with ADHD or LD derive their primary social relationships from their jobs. When they sense or experience failure, rejection, or exclusion at work, the effect is similar to the feelings of social failure they may have experienced in school. A significant number of adults who have suffered humbling social experiences at work would rather interact with people like themselves than be "mistreated" by people who do not understand. It makes little difference to this subgroup that they may have brought their social isolation on themselves; all they know is that they are not comfortable with their coworkers and it is easier for them to take fewer risks by remaining alone or being with a similar peer group.

Finally, the practitioner should obtain a thorough description of all tools and equipment that the client used to perform essential work tasks. Sometimes a client believes that because he once started a forklift he has mastered all operational aspects of its use! Previous employers can give a much clearer picture of all work technologies that were introduced to and mastered by the client. It is also useful to know examples of the client's best and worst performance areas and the conditions or situations in which work rate or quality was affected.

Every employee on the job today has a wide range of work performance depending on the events in his life and on the job. When debriefing the employer about the client's performance in different work situations, the clinician should interpret this information in the context of what was happening in that client's life at the time. In some cases, the client was experiencing emotional upheaval that affected him on the job. This type of experience affects *all* employees, not just those who have ADHD or LD. The goal for the client and clinician is not so much to review the past as to develop effective coping strategies that enable the client to achieve greater emotional control while maintaining satisfactory job performance.

LEVEL OF FUNCTIONAL SKILLS REQUIRED FOR TARGETED EMPLOYMENT

Employers must be able to supply products and services of the highest quality if they are to compete, survive, and grow in the global market. This means that, increasingly, entry-level employees will find themselves in work settings committed to excellence, product quality, and customer satisfaction. In order to translate these abstract ideas of quality into usable vocational data, the clinician must go beyond traditional job descriptions as the basis of summary recommendations and use information from other sources to identify the specific skills needed for employment in these high-performance workplaces.

One source is the report of the Secretaries' Commission on Achieving Necessary Skills (1991b). This report provides a broad conceptual framework for the generic skills required in the workplace, as well as a description of how the skills are used in a variety of tasks the client is likely to encounter. In recommending that performance be assessed in a way that recognizes incremental progress toward a level of mastery, the commission suggested the following six criteria for an effective assessment system:

1. It defines and communicates what is to be learned—the expected outcomes of the knowledge and skills of the students. In effect, these outcomes become standards for all. A useful assessment does not merely indicate success or failure in meeting the standards but identifies the degree of progress made in meeting them.

2. It assures [that] students are taught what the system calls for and that teachers are significantly involved in determining educational standards, outcomes, and goals.

3. It permits comparison of local performance to national benchmarks.

4. It protects students against sorting and labeling by moving away from distinguishing between "good" and "bad" to measuring performance against standards of what students should know and be able to do.

5. It is dynamic, meaning [that] it can be improved on the basis of experience and of advances in knowledge.

6. It motivates students who believe that the assessment will count in the world beyond school because they see that employers make decisions based on the assessment. (Secretaries' Commission on Achieving Necessary Skills, 1991a, pp. 60–62)

The clear and consistent assessment standards for all individuals recommended by the commission would be an excellent first step toward identifying specific marketable skills and would remove the stigma of being a low achiever from the adult with ADHD or LD. The design of a vocational assessment system that provides more than one way to evaluate performance and measure success for adults with special learning needs was identified by the commission as an area that still needed to be addressed.

The need to develop alternative assessment packages acceptable to employers that do not rely only on traditional academic measurements of skills is critical to overcoming the barriers inherent in presenting oneself as a qualified applicant capable of performing the essential functions of the targeted job but not able to demonstrate this proficiency in test-taking situations.

A major national electronics firm in Arizona is a good example of an otherwise outstanding corporation that needs to overhaul its screening methods. A candidate applying for a job would first be required to fill out a six-page application. Many applicants do not successfully complete this initial task, according to the corporation's human resource department. The human resource officer reports that the department has a bank of filing cabinets filled with thousands of applications missing such basic items as work history information (e.g., duties and dates of employment), containing misspelled words, and missing whole sections of the application. But presuming the interested applicant can successfully pass this hurdle, the next step of the process involves taking a timed battery of academic tests encompassing reading comprehension, mathematical computation, tracking the path of an electrical circuit, inventory process control, and a videotape of "what if" situations. The videotape section asks the applicant to determine the proper action to take from three different perspectives: 1. what your supervisor would want you to do, 2. what your coworkers would do, and 3. what you should do. Typical accommodations, such as having a test reader or getting more time to respond to some or all of the test battery, can be granted if they are formally requested at the beginning of the application process.

The applicant is not required to provide proof of a disability, and the corporate psychologist decides whether a requested accommodation is workable within the context of the test situation. The functional level of literacy required to comprehend test questions is at approximately the sixth-grade level. The applicant must pass all components of this battery to demonstrate the ability to learn and perform effectively in a manufacturing environment. This firm offers no alternative assessments for prospective employees (with or without disabilities) seeking to demonstrate that they can perform the essential functions of the job. This deficiency stands in sharp contrast to the amount of individualized training that occurs at the work site. Most of the technology that this company uses to fabricate semiconductor chips has been developed in-house. Each manufacturing order requires custom production engineered for specific applications of that chip. This means that for most entry-level assembly positions, no technical schools exist to train future employees in the specific skills needed to fabricate semiconductor chips. Since formal training must be conducted by members of the work team and training divisions, one might ask how a traditional battery of academic tests can truly reflect the workplace capabilities of a prospective employee with ADHD or LD. This Malcolm Baldridge Award–winning company has a workforce diversity program that is extensively involved with employees who are disabled and have successfully surmounted the existing application process. One hopes that at some time in the future, the successful job modifications and accommodations that have been implemented on the shopfloor will be incorporated into an alternative assessment package for applicants who are nontraditional learners.

Another example illustrating the need for the client and clinician to familiarize themselves with how a company evaluates prospective employees is found in the screening process used when filling stock clerk positions at a large Phoenix-area store chain. When applying for this entry-level position, the applicant must take a timed mathematics test structured at the sixth-grade level of literacy. Some questions ask the job seeker to make computations such as changing fractions into percentages. If the applicant is unable to demonstrate competency on this screening device, he is considered unable to stock the shelves of the store. He would probably be offered a job bagging groceries and shagging carts at minimum wage and without benefits. Again, one must ask how this test proves that an applicant can or cannot do this job. Certainly the ability to serve the customer promptly and courteously is as important as mathematical proficiency and the physical ability to perform the tasks associated with this position. At present, this store has not investigated ways to assess this related skill area.

Neither of the corporations discussed, at present, provide alternative assessments for potential employees who are nontraditional learners and come from culturally diverse backgrounds or have limited proficiency in English. Predicting job success for this subpopulation will require the development of assessments that address learning differences and are respectful of linguistic and cultural differences as well. The 1990 U.S. census shows that the largest percentage of immigrants to the United States come from countries where Spanish, Asian, or Pacific Island languages are spoken. This trend is expected to continue well into the 21st century, resulting in a workforce that will have significant literacy development and training needs. This changing workforce will require considerable retooling of the assessment and hiring methods presently in use in corporate America. As employers are compelled to modify their hiring practices, alternative assessment packages will be developed that will benefit individuals currently penalized by employment decisions based on traditional assessments.

Employer interviewing, hiring, and evaluation practices for nontraditional learners have changed as a result of the Americans with Disabilities Act (1990), which requires the focus of these activities to be on what the job involves and not on the disability of the applicant or employee. The Alexander Hamilton Institute (1993) published a booklet outlining practices that are both effective and legal that human resource professionals can use in determining the capabilities of the members of their workforce who are disabled. For example, the institute points out that in order to avoid discrimination charges of disability bias, three interview practices are essential:

1. *All questions should be job related.* Do not ask questions such as How would you get to work? or Are you taking any medications that could make you drowsy?

2. *Do not jump to conclusions about whether a disabled person can perform the job or not.* Some disabled persons are able to come up with ideas that might make accommodation easy and inexpensive. Others may remove themselves from contention after they realize the physical or mental demands of the job.

3. *Let applicants visit the job site.* This will allow them to judge the accessibility and comfort level of the workplace. It will also let them decide whether reasonable accommodation will allow them to do the job. This process is particularly effective when combined with a detailed job description that identifies and assesses the employer's functional job requirements for that specific work site. From the job seeker's point of view, for each targeted employer there will need to be an investigation of what constitutes a complete job description. Such a description should contain the following components:

   - *Essential duties.* Obtain a description of what is to be accomplished, in terms of both guidelines and methods of performing duties. For example, "communicating information" could mean writing information on a notepad. It also could mean that an opportunity exists to perform this task in an another way, such as typing or tape-recording the information, if the applicant with ADHD or LD has problems with writing. It may not have occurred to the employer that tasks accomplished through written communication can be dispatched as effectively through alternative strategies. Part of the process of determining whether the client is suitable for a specific job is to find out whether certain job tasks can be modified to accommodate the applicant's learning needs without raising objections from others about perceived special treatment.

   - *Mental functions.* Obtain a list of all required job elements, such as coordinating, analyzing, and synthesizing, so the client can determine what abilities are required. For instance, if the job requires providing emergency medical treatment to accident victims, the ability to handle stress is required.

- *Physical functions.* Each task should be broken down into elements such as standing, squatting, reaching, lifting, and grasping. The duration and frequency of these tasks should be part of this analysis.

- *Methods, techniques, and procedures.* Obtain a list of the procedures for accomplishing the essential duties of the job, for example, the amount of time spent working as a member of a team, the type of in-house communications used for memoranda, and the procedure for seeking help with specific job tasks.

- *Working conditions.* Obtain information about such factors as work site locations (indoors or outdoors), potential work hazards, safety considerations, and level of auditory and visual stimuli.

- *Technology, equipment, and work materials.* Establish what types of tools or knowledge of work-specific technologies are needed for the applicant to perform the job effectively. Ascertain the possibility of modifying, replacing, or adjusting products and materials used to perform the job without affecting the quality of work performed (Alexander Hamilton Institute, 1993, pp. 8–10).

AVAILABILITY OF SUPPORT SERVICES

Both client and clinician must familiarize themselves with available community resources that could provide direct services in the areas of job development and job placement, vocational-technical training, work-related literacy, and independent living. These adult agencies and service providers have different eligibility criteria and funding priorities. Those who seek these services should familiarize themselves with the jargon, application procedure, and referral process that is unique to each agency. A vocational rehabilitation (VR) counselor working in a rural location quite often is responsible for job development, job placement, and job maintenance efforts. The lack of local service providers means that rural VR counselors must accept a higher level of personal involvement than do their counterparts situated in urban and suburban settings where there are ample vocational opportunities, public transportation, and private contractors to provide support services.

Appropriate services for adults with ADHD or LD in most communities are either nonexistent or fragmented. Individuals seeking to tap into public or private resources can expect to go to one agency for vocational assessment, another for job training, and still another for job placement and job crisis intervention. Most service providers have limited resources—as measured in both time and money. Vocational guidance efforts must focus on providing a clear picture of the specific nature and manifestations of a client's disability in terms of its potential vocational impact while demonstrating how the client meets the demands of a targeted job or training opportunity for a specific employer. In addition, the knowledgeable consumer takes the time to become familiar with regional and national resources and programs that address the specific needs of the adult with ADHD or LD. Resources such as the National Adult Literacy and Learning Disability Center, the Learning Disabilities Resource and Training Center, and the Job Accommodation Network (JAN) are examples of programs that specifically address the employment, literacy, and training needs of adults with ADHD or LD. They provide a wealth of user-friendly information on how to access local and national programs, they identify best practices in assessment and employment, and they conduct numerous training sessions disseminating information to both the public and private sector about the unique nature of the adult with ADHD or LD. Advocacy groups such as the Learning Disabilities Association of America (LDA), Children and Adults with Attention Deficit Disorder (CHADD), and the National Association of Adults with Special Learning Needs (NAASLN) offer other excellent resources for individuals seeking support groups, knowledgeable consumers who understand the rights and responsibilities assigned to the public by various federal mandates, and state and national conferences spanning the full continuum of issues facing adults with ADHD or LD.

Local resources specializing in direct service provision include state departments of VR, JTPA programs, Adult Basic Education/GED (ABE/GED) programs, and private vendors providing specialty services (supported employment, psychological testing, etc.). The ABE/GED programs offer literacy instruction free of charge to individuals 16 years of age and older. Relying primarily on traditional paper-and-pencil approaches to education, most ABE/GED programs provide some adult contextually related instruction that updates rusty literacy skills and can be beneficial when it is time to draft a cover letter, fill out a job application, or write a résumé.

JTPA programs have both private vendors and comprehensive centers that provide opportunities for subsidized on-the-job training, vocational-technical training, and direct job placement with some minimal follow-up support to allow for job retention. Individuals seeking services through this agency must qualify for them primarily on the basis of economic need. This means that individuals must meet income guidelines indicating either that they themselves have limited financial resources or that they come from a family that has limited financial resources. Placement into employment or training settings is determined on the basis of standardized assessments and in few instances takes into account the latent abilities of the nontraditional learner. Consequently, even if the adult with ADHD or LD qualifies under the economic criteria, she may be unable to secure training or may be placed in a job that does not use her capabilities because she cannot demonstrate the "tested" ability to succeed in another setting.

VR services are available to anyone covered under the Americans with Disabilities Act who has a documented or suspected disabling condition. Assessment, diagnostics, counseling, training, job placement, and educational opportunities are some of the funded services available through this agency. Recently, the Rehabilitation Services Administration (1990) initiated an order of selection process giving priority to those clients considered severely disabled. Many VR counselors tend to view adults with ADHD or LD as being only mildly disabled by their condition. Dowdy (1995) points out that this misconception about the severity of these conditions is difficult to dispel in the presence of diagnostics that lack in scope and sensitivity and fail to pinpoint specific functional limitations and their vocational effects on the adult with ADHD or LD. A specific LD task force established through the Rehabilitation Services Administration (1990) sought a way to measure the serious vocational barriers faced by adults with ADHD or LD. The task force identified specific vocational limitations that could be encountered by these individuals and tied them to seven major life functions identified in the Americans with Disabilities Act as a way of documenting the severity of these limitations and of establishing a rationale for service provision. In order to be considered severely disabled, two or more of the major life functions must be significantly affected by the condition to warrant consideration for VR services.

The client and clinician should carefully review the following list in preparation for making a case for service provision through VR:

1. *Mobility.* Problems reading and interpreting bus or train schedules, road maps, and signs; problems budgeting and paying for public transportation; impaired sense of direction

resulting in getting lost; deficient sense of time resulting in chronic tardiness; inability to arrange transportation (e.g., taking the wrong bus, getting off at the wrong stop, taking wrong turns while driving, and forgetting landmarks and directions); gross motor coordination problems causing difficulties in using elevators and escalators

2. *Communication.* Difficulties in following oral and written instructions; difficulty interpreting written materials, particularly job manuals, work orders, diagrams, and signs; difficulty understanding complex sentences or language subtleties, including work-related items such as job applications; difficulty learning new tasks or procedures from written materials or verbal instructions; difficulty remembering multistep directions; difficulty differentiating important from unimportant information; tendency to transpose words and delete parts of language such as prepositions, articles, and connectors; illegible handwriting; difficulties in using the telephone; inability to repeat instructions to coworkers and others

3. *Self-care.* Problems with reasoning, processing, and cognition that may cause the individual to repeatedly make poor decisions about basic life activities (health, safety, grooming, dressing, and managing finances); difficulty with shopping and banking; impulsive and explosive behaviors; distractibility

4. *Self-direction.* Lack of insight; inability to monitor performance; tendency to shift from one activity to another without purpose; lack of follow-through; inability to set up and implement a study schedule or job search

5. *Interpersonal skills.* Inability to interact in a mature, socially acceptable manner with peers and supervisors; inability to accept supervisory monitoring and criticism; inappropriate behaviors and language; lack of inhibitions; explosiveness; withdrawal; low frustration; task avoidance; unpredictability

6. *Work tolerance.* Inability to carry out required physical and cognitive work tasks in an effective manner over a sustained period of time; feelings of restlessness or tendency to flee the job site; distractibility on the job; inability to adjust to increased production demands or unexpected changes in job duties

7. *Work skills.* Inability to benefit from training and to perform job tasks that rely on written instructions or materials; inability to take messages or develop written reports; difficulty recalling instructions or following task sequence language; high-level conceptual deficits; deceptive language deficits; expressive language deficits; inability to understand multistep instructions; tendency to transpose words and delete less concrete parts of language; inability to repeat or relay instructions

Documenting or specifying how the ADHD or LD interferes with the adult's daily activities and will impose severe functional limitations throughout the individual's life creates a compelling case for services through VR.

The Life Development Institute Approach to Vocational Assessment

THE PROGRAM

Since 1982, the Life Development Institute (LDI), a private, nonprofit organization, has conducted a community-based program in a residential setting in Phoenix, Arizona. The purpose of the program is to help individuals with ADHD or LD and other related conditions gain skills in order to be workplace literate, achieve careers by finding employment commensurate with their capabilities, and attain independence. LDI conducts two different two-year programs for adolescents and adults, 16 years of age and older. One program focuses on secondary education, and the other focuses on postsecondary literacy, social skills, and job placement.

The institute is authorized under federal law to enroll nonimmigrant client students. LDI also has contracts with the State of Arizona Rehabilitation Services Administration and Administration for Children, Youth and Families and, in addition, receives private referrals from a variety of sources. Extensive interagency linkages with area employers, adult education providers, the community college system, and state agencies enables LDI to provide holistic services to program participants. LDI is recognized nationally for its exemplary literacy program for adults with learning and literacy disorders. In 1992, it was a recipient of the coveted Presidential Points of Light award (one of the 21 selected from among 4,500 nominees) presented by President and Mrs. Bush.

LDI program participants are housed in a complex of 44 two-bedroom, two-bath apartments located in a central Phoenix middle-class, culturally diverse neighborhood. The complex has two clubhouses, a swimming pool with a jacuzzi, one half basketball court, washers and dryers and telephones in many apartments, training rooms, and computer labs.

The unique residential setting gives program participants the opportunity to live in an apartment community with a minimum of staff supervision and a moderate amount of structure. LDI is part of the community, not an "island." The usual limitation of most residential training situations is that they are "sheltered" or "institutional" in their orientation. At LDI, the setting is an actual apartment complex and not a dormitory, institutional setting, or group home.

PROFILE OF PROGRAM PARTICIPANTS

For most program participants entering LDI, educational and employment success have been elusive. Their educational and employment difficulties have adversely affected how many view themselves and their opportunities for the future.

As stated earlier, LDI's population is 16 years old and older. Participants come primarily from three referral sources. The first group are referrals from the Arizona Foster Care Young Adult Program. These individuals are dependent wards of the court who have not finished high school and are required to pursue continuing education opportunities leading to a high school diploma or a GED. Most of these young people make progress toward graduation but possess limited marketable skills. Once they obtain a GED, high school diploma, or reach 21 years of age, they lose the support system they have depended on.

The second group of participants are referrals from the Arizona and Navajo Nation departments of VR. The majority of these individuals are from rural areas that lack the educational, employment, and residential options needed to facilitate successful transition into adult life.

The third group of program participants have been referred through educational consultants, advocacy organizations, or parents who have adult children in the program. This group of individuals is privately funded for services offered through LDI. These people have been unable to succeed in traditional learning environments. Their needs include remediation, improvement in learning abilities and processing, postsecondary training and education, and competitive employment commensurate with their individual capabilities.

A "typical" program participant would have many or all of the following characteristics:

1. Qualified for VR services according to the guidelines for eligibility established by the specific LD task force

2. 16–44 years old
3. Little or no work history
4. Little or no clearly defined vocational objectives
5. Approximately fifth-grade mathematical and sixth-grade English levels of literacy
6. Social, emotional, and behavioral ages lower than chronological age
7. Never lived away from home
8. Never managed money before
9. Little, if any, experience dating or establishing age-appropriate peer relationships
10. Unable to define his LD, learning style, or coping and compensatory strategies
11. Tested IQ averaging from low 80s to 110s
12. Does not know how to advocate for self
13. Does not drive or have access to reliable transportation
14. Home and family situation unstable or dysfunctional
15. Lack of or limited appropriate local community resources and economic opportunities available
16. Unable to meet the minimum literacy requirements of the American worker as outlined in Goals 2000 and Workforce 2000

Referral sources with prospective LDI program participants recognize that LDI's job placement component pursues only competitive employment opportunities *without* job coaching. Vocational assessment and exploration targeting individual education, training, and employment needs are pursued through the completion of a vocational research project. This project establishes a career ladder, justifies future vocational-technical training, addresses individual vocational deficits and barriers, and matches the individual's transferable skills with appropriate employment and training opportunities.

Assessment Process

Each group of new program participants goes through a highly structured two-week orientation designed to familiarize them with the LDI staff and the expectations of the program. Nominal group technique is used to identify vocational issues from the participants' perspective and to establish consensus within the group about areas of instructional focus and the scope of vocational guidance.

New members of the LDI program bring with them a complete psychoeducational evaluation containing all diagnostic reports and test records. LDI uses both norm-referenced and criterion-referenced assessments to individualize a vocational-skilled sequence of tutorial instruction. Through self-assessment, each program participant identifies his or her preferred learning style, identifies characteristics that affect academic and employment performance, and develops knowledge of basic work skills and potential barriers to success. These results are used collectively in conjunction with job-specific aptitudes, interests, and employment history to develop a career plan.

The Vocational Research Institute's APTICOM AF System (Vocational Research Institute, 1988) is used to provide initial information concerning individual interests, abilities, and aptitudes. The system consists of three test batteries: the Aptitude Test Battery, the Occupational Interest Inventory, and the Educational Skills Development Battery. The APTICOM Aptitude Test Battery and General Aptitude Test Battery (GATB; Goals 2000, 1993) are designed to assess cognitive, perceptual, and motor skills. The relationships between aptitude scores and jobs are established using the Occupational Aptitude Pattern (OAP) structure. OAPs are closely related to the work groups of the *Guide for Occupational Exploration* (*GOE*, 1989). The Educational Skills Development Battery screens for levels of General Educational Development as defined by the U.S. Department of Labor's *Dictionary of Occupational Titles* (*DOT*). Every job in the *DOT* has been rated in terms of required levels of mathematical development and language development. Scores derived from the Educational Skills Development Battery allow for a general estimate of an individual's ability to handle the workplace literacy requirements of a given job. Both aptitude and educational skills batteries are important indicators of where an individual is performing relative to all other job seekers. Very few employers are willing to allow a worker unlimited time to perform the essential functions of a job. A qualified worker, with or without disabilities, must expect to do the same job with the same quality and rate of output as everyone else in order to earn the same wage.

The APTICOM Occupational Interest Inventory measures individuals' interests according to the *GOE*, which classifies all Department of Labor titles recognized in the *DOT.* The goal of this measurement is to assist an individual's vocational exploration by identifying occupational possibilities that are compatible with expressed personal preferences. Since many applicants are unsure of their vocational direction, information derived from this inventory gives many opportunities for exploration of their vocational future. A person with a future is much more inclined to investigate, consider alternatives, and take responsibility for a vocational plan than an individual unwilling to express her preferences. The results from these test batteries and interest inventories are subsequently entered into the Occupational Awareness System (OASYS) program (Vertek, 1989). OASYS is a computer-aided counselor support system that matches a person's skills and abilities to employer job demands. The database in OASYS contains the entire *DOT,* including all the *DOT* job descriptions, job performance criteria, and operational definitions of job performance variables. The version used at LDI complies with Americans with Disabilities Act criteria, which establish essential job functions, physical demands, environmental conditions, and the frequency with which tasks or functions are performed.

A case record is opened by the LDI program participant (LDI staff members act as facilitators) by entering his work history and personal skill and work ability profile. He then asks the computer to conduct a search for job matches. The type of job matches found in this search depends on the individual's highest demonstrated skill profile from his work history, levels of demonstrated performance from the aptitude and educational batteries, and identified areas of occupational interest from the inventory.

Each job match contains a complete description of all tasks required to perform the job and of related jobs listed under alternative titles. This information allows the development of a career ladder made up of an occupational cluster of jobs directly related to the targeted position. Each job match states the Specific Vocational Preparation (SVP) required to learn the techniques, acquire the information, and develop the facility needed for average performance in a specific work situation. The nine SVP levels range from unskilled jobs requiring a short demonstration only to skilled positions requiring over 10 years to master.

OASYS can compare an individual's skills and abilities to *DOT* job performance variables. In situations where the person has a career goal or knows about a possible job opening, Occupational Goal Analysis (OGA) allows comparisons of the person's skills and aptitudes to each job performance variable required for the job. This comparison makes it possible to identify potential barriers to employment that may exist for a particular job. The barrier may be significant, such as the client's having a much lower level of literacy than the job requires, or may be minor, such as his having no demonstrated work history for the particular job.

Combining career ladder and OGA information allows the client and LDI staff to explore "hunches" about different kinds of jobs the client could perform. Frequently, individuals at LDI need a career goal reality check in order to be candid with themselves about whether their abilities meet the job requirements. Their initial career goal may involve more training or experience than they presently possess, and it is important to identify any vocational barriers involving academic enrichment, job modification, or skill development that must be overcome in order to achieve their career goal. This realization must come primarily from the individual's investigating the occupation, allowing him to recognize his present limitations with respect to this choice and encouraging him to develop alternative vocational strategies.

Following the hypothetical case of a job seeker with previous experience working as a diet clerk in a nursing home can clarify this process. This person is interested in staying in the same occupational cluster but is not sure what career path she should take. When OASYS is asked to construct a career ladder for health-related occupations that take no more than one to two years of training and experience to master, it produces the ladder shown in Table 11.1. This career ladder contains occupations identified by *DOT* code number, occupational title, SVP level, strength required (STR), and General Educational Development (GED) needed to fulfill the literacy requirements of this position.

This hypothetical career seeker decides that being a paramedic looks interesting. She decides to find out what the National Employment Outlook is for this occupational category. Table 11.2 represents an employment growth projection based on three scenarios assuming low, moderate, and high GNP growth, respectively. Annual growth or decline in the number of jobs is projected from 1992 to 2005, and nationwide employment in this category by industry is broken out by the number of individuals actually employed in 1992, percentage of the total workforce

Table 11.1   Career Ladder

DOT Code	Occupational Title	SVP	STR	GED
079.374-014	Nurse, licensed practical	6	M	434
079.364-026	Paramedic	6	V	434
079.362-014	Medical record technician	6	L	434
079.374-026	Psychiatric technician	6	M	434
079.374-010	Emergency medical technician	5	M	434
245.362-010	Medical record clerk	4	L	433
355.354-010	Physical therapy aide	4	M	323
355.377-014	Psychiatric aide	4	M	322
355.674-014	Nurse's assistant	4	M	322
074.382-010	Pharmacy technician	3	L	333
079.364-022	Phlebotomist	3	L	323
245.587-010	Diet clerk	3	S	333
323.687.010	Cleaner, hospital	2	M	212
355.677-014	Transporter, patients	2	M	212

Note. From Occupational Awareness System (OASYS), 1989, Vertek, Inc., Bellevue, WA. Used with permission.

Table 11.2 OASYS National Employment Outlook Projection, 1992–2005

OES Category:	Emergency Medical Technician	Code: 32508
Includes DOT:	PARAMEDIC	Code: 079.364-026
OES Comprised of:	2 DOTS	
OES Employment in 1992:	114,114	

OES Employment Growth Projection	Low	Moderate	High
Annual growth or decline (−)	2,145	3,152	3,409
Growth or decline through period	27,889	40,977	44,326
Projected employment in 2005	142,003	155,091	158,440

No.	Code	Industry Title	Actual 1992 Employment		Estimated Change by 2005	
			Number	Percentage	Number	Percentage
1	411	Local and suburban transportation	47,498	41.6	14,549	30.6
2	930	Local government, exc educ/ hospital	33,042	29.0	13,249	40.1
3	806	Hospitals, public and private	28,847	25.3	10,111	35.1
4	801	Offices, physicians and osteopaths	1,552	1.4	1,098	70.7
5	809	Health and allied services, NEC	677	.6	424	62.6
6	805	Nursing & personal care facilities	632	.6	373	59.0
7	920	State government, exc educ/hospital	586	.5	72	12.3
8	808	Home health care services	581	.5	655	112.7
9	804	Offices, other health practitioner	570	.5	469	82.3
		Total	113,985	99.9	41,000	36.0

in this category employed in that industry, and the estimated change by 2005 in terms of additional jobs gained or lost.

Local listings of educational and training organizations and employers who can be sources of information about the targeted occupation will be identified after the client has conducted an OGA. The OGA will correlate national employment demographics found in the *DOT* with local requirements for the desired position.

The next step is to compare the job performance requirements to the person's current abilities (Table 11.3). This information is organized as follows: occupational variables analyzed are in the first column, the person's work traits are in the second column (Person), job performance variables are in the third column (Occupation), and the fourth column comments on the comparison of the Person and Occupation variables.

All searches conducted in the OGA are based on federal definitions of skills transferability. Our hypothetical career seeker is considered to have transferable skills when the work activities she performed in past jobs can be used to meet the requirements of skilled or semiskilled work activities in other jobs or kinds of work. The extent to which transferable skills are identified in the OGA depends on the similarity between occupationally significant work activities in the individual's work history and those in the targeted occupation.

Machines, Tools, Equipment and Work Aids (MTEWA) describes the instruments and de-

Table 11.3 Occupational Goal Analysis for Paramedic

	Variables Analyzed		Work Traits		
Level	Work Field	MPSMS	Person	Occupation	Comment
1	Same	Same			No match
2	Similar	Same			No match
3	Same	Similar			No match
4	Similar	Similar			No match
5	Different	Same			No match
6	Same	Different	SVP Level 3	SVP Level 6	Underqualified
7	Different	Similar			No match
8	Similar	Different	SVP Level 3	SVP Level 6	Underqualified

	Work Traits		
Variables Analyzed	Person	Occupation	Comment
Specific Vocational Preparation			
Person minimum	Level 1	Level 6	
General education			
Reasoning	Level 5	Level 3	Exceeds demand
Math	Level 3	Level 3	
Language	Level 5	Level 4	Exceeds demand
Strength			
Lift, Carry, Push, Pull	Very heavy	Very heavy	
Physical demands			
Climbing	Constantly	Occasionally	Exceeds demand
Balancing	Constantly	Occasionally	Exceeds demand
Stooping	Constantly	Frequently	Exceeds demand
Kneeling	Constantly	Frequently	Exceeds demand
Crouching	Constantly	Occasionally	Exceeds demand
Crawling	Constantly	Occasionally	Exceeds demand
Reaching	Constantly	Frequently	Exceeds demand
Handling	Constantly	Frequently	Exceeds demand
Fingering	Occasionally	Frequently	Underqualified
Feeling	Constantly	Occasionally	Exceeds demand
Talking	Constantly	Frequently	Exceeds demand
Hearing	Constantly	Frequently	Exceeds demand
Environmental conditions			
Exposure to weather	Constantly	Frequently	Exceeds demand
Nonweather extreme cold	Constantly	Never	Exceeds demand
Nonweather extreme heat	Constantly	Never	Exceeds demand
Wet-humid	Constantly	Never	Exceeds demand
Vibration	Frequently	Never	Exceeds demand
Atmospheric conditions	Frequently	Never	Exceeds demand
Moving mechanical parts	Constantly	Never	Exceeds demand
Electrical shock	Occasionally	Never	Exceeds demand

Table 11.3   *(Continued)*

| | Work Traits | | |
Variables Analyzed	Person	Occupation	Comment
High, exposed places	Occasionally	Never	Exceeds demand
Radiant energy	Occasionally	Never	Exceeds demand
Explosives	Occasionally	Never	Exceeds demand
Toxic/caustic chemicals	Frequently	Never	Exceeds demand
Other hazards	Constantly	Constantly	
Noise	Moderate	Loud	Underqualified
DOT aptitudes			
G: General learning ability	3 (34%–67%)	2 (68%–90%)	Underqualified
V: Verbal	3 (34%–67%)	3 (34%–67%)	
N: Numerical	3 (34%–67%)	3 (34%–67%)	
S: Spatial perception	3 (34%–67%)	3 (34%–67%)	
P: Form perception	4 (11%–33%)	2 (68%–90%)	Underqualified
Q: Clerical perception	3 (34%–67%)	2 (68%–90%)	Underqualified
K: Motor coordination	3 (34%–67%)	2 (68%–90%)	Underqualified
F: Finger dexterity	3 (34%–67%)	2 (68%–90%)	Underqualified
M: Manual dexterity	3 (34%–67%)	2 (68%–90%)	Underqualified
E: Eye-hand-foot coordination	3 (34%–67%)	3 (34%–67%)	
C: Color discrimination	4 (11%–33%)	3 (34%–67%)	Underqualified

Note. The top panel shows at which level(s) transferability of skills occurs between the person's SVP, Work Fields, and MPSMS and the occupational requirements. Each level of transferability contains different inferences concerning 1. the amount of training required to perform the job goal and 2. the suitability of the job goal for the person. Levels 1–4 are "skill transfer" levels according to the definition. Levels 5–8 do not reflect the operational definition of transferability. Transferability is further qualified by the analysis of each worker trait in the following table. From Occupational Awareness System (OASYS), 1989, Vertek, Inc., Bellevue, WA. Used with permission.

vices that are commonly used to carry out the specific functions of a job. MTEWA should be thought of as "what you do on a job."

Material, Products, Subject Matter and Services (MPSMS) describes the end results on which the work activities are performed. MPSMS characteristics can be viewed as "what you do it to" on a job and the type of business.

The transferability of a person's skills is most probable and meaningful among jobs in which

- The same or a lesser degree of skills (SVP) is required
- The same or similar tools and machines (MTEWA) are used
- The same or similar raw materials, products, processes, or services (MPSMS) are involved

The person reviewing the OGA would see that while an exact match between her abilities and the demands of the occupation is not present, there is indication that she should consider further career exploration in this area based on matches at Level 6 and Level 8. Job matches identified at Level 6 include the same work activities as in previous jobs, but with a different type of employer. Occupation-specific training in this area and strategies on how to use past skills will most likely be necessary. Job matches at Level 8 include similar work activities as in previous jobs, but again with a different type of employer. Extensive training in both job-specific work activities and a thorough orientation to the business type will be necessary for success.

Further exploration of this OGA (which lists over 130 traits, each with a one to two para-graph description) reveals that the individual's General Educational Development exceeds the reasoning and language requirements for this position and her present mathematical compe-tence is at an appropriate level of literacy. Therefore, the client has the academic competence to learn the job requirements. Because she is young and lacks work experience, this client has not had the opportunity to pursue this type of employment. The potential to benefit from a learning environment offering a job-specific course of instruction seems evident.

Reviewing the physical demands required by this position raises only one red flag. The client is recorded to be capable of using her fingers only occasionally to perform essential physical functions, whereas the position would require her to use them frequently. Work situations re-quiring fine motor finger skills pertinent to this occupation, such as finding a vein to give an injection or ascertaining a pulse or heart rate, would be explanations of the importance of this particular demand.

The client's capacity to perform effectively in various environmental conditions shows high transferability to the requirements of being a paramedic, except that her recorded level of per-formance under the condition of *noise* is found to be underqualified. Noise levels and situations typical of crime and accident scenes would require the individual to be able to handle pande-monium and extreme auditory stimuli. It turns out, however, that our career seeker is a semi-professional rock musician accustomed to the above-mentioned noise levels. This additional information would be used to change the previous response to one that better indicates the client's present level of ability. If a person with ADHD or LD (or anyone) is unable to handle the noise level involved in working as a paramedic, a severe vocational limitation would be identified because of the possibility that a life-threatening mistake could be made by a person with this deficit.

DOT aptitudes indicate that some significant review will be required to determine whether the dexterity, perception, and coordination qualifications can be met at the level needed to perform essential functions of this job. On closer questioning, our career seeker acknowledges that she just "worked to get them over with" and wants to have another chance to give her best performance. This is a fairly common occurrence among people who have been extensively tested throughout their lives and who have come to see little connection between these mea-sures and their wants and needs.

At all stages of this analysis, the emphasis is on the prospective candidate's capabilities. Employers hire, train, and employ workers based on their abilities to make them money, fit in, and be functioning members of the company. The focus, then, should first be on the bigger picture of what the applicant *can* do for the employer and should then circle back to any areas in the OGA found lacking or in need of further development.

Now that the client has a detailed description of her targeted career, her next step is to undertake a sequence of vocational-skilled tutorial instruction emphasizing contextual literacy, which promotes learning by doing. Incorporating technical industry-specific terminology, acro-nyms, jargon, and other vocabulary into computer-assisted instruction and learning strategies allows the development of career-related projects and demonstrations that mirror the world of work that she would experience in her desired occupation. Strategies developed by the Univer-sity of Kansas Institute for Research in Learning Disabilities are taught in order to enhance the client's ability to acquire information for later use, to express information in writing, and to demonstrate competence on tests and assignments.

Computer-assisted instruction is provided through the Invest Learning System (Josten's Learning, 1994) and through a program developed by Pennsylvania State University's Institute for the Study of Adult Literacy and Curriculum Associates, A Day in the Life . . . (Pennsylvania State University, 1993). Both programs are specifically designed for adult learners and span a literacy range from grade 1 to grade 12. These programs build on the learner's prior knowledge and learning strengths, establish objectives for learning tasks, break the tasks down into small and manageable units, use actual work-related materials, and provide opportunities for transfer and application with follow-up tutorials and activities. In A Day in the Life . . . , six different modules representing a variety of occupation-specific work situations guide the user through a typical day on the job complete with numerous "what if" situations requiring critical thinking skills and problem-solving abilities germane to that industry.

The Health Care Provider module allows the individual interested in becoming a paramedic the opportunity to learn some of the basic skills necessary to be a nurse's assistant, a position one level higher than her current position on the career ladder. The job scenarios are typical of daily situations experienced by health care providers and guide the learner through the tasks of taking a patient's vital signs, feeding a patient, providing direct patient care, and being supervisor for the day. Each section of the job scenario module has a Build Your Vocabulary section and a Making a "To Do" Checklist section. These enrichment activities help to review specific tasks completed in the module. Before the client can become a paramedic, she must master the basic skills needed to be a nurse's assistant. Any difficulty she might have with this level of material (fourth-grade reading level) would indicate that alternative vocational options should be investigated. In contrast, mastery of these materials indicates that she is heading in the right vocational direction. Familiarity with occupation-specific vocabulary and jargon will allow her to "talk the talk" and will provide a greater measure of comfort when she interviews with potential training or employment personnel.

Additional literacy enhancement is provided by a customized curriculum supported through the Invest Learning System, designed to teach specific skills in subject areas in which the client needs improvement. Occupational objectives are grouped without regard to instructional level. This allows for complete instruction based on the individual's skill. Third-party software such as OASYS can be combined with this program to correlate the results of computer-assisted instruction with occupational objectives for the targeted career.

As one of several related written and oral projects, the client reviews a checklist (Dowdy, 1995) that screens for ADHD or LD characteristics, determines what effect these characteristics might have in her desired occupation, and identifies specific strategies or techniques that could be implemented to work around the barriers presented by her condition. She then drafts a cover letter to a potential employer, outlining the position she wants, mentioning the potential impact of her condition, suggesting training interventions she will implement to minimize this impact, and stressing her desire to be evaluated by the same standards as coworkers. This disclosure letter uses the sentence-writing, paragraph-writing, and paraphrasing strategies developed by the University of Kansas Institute for Research on Learning Disabilities. When the letter is completed, the client presents it orally to her program peers, and the presentation is videotaped for playback and review of content. This exercise is very important because many individuals who come to LDI are unable or reluctant to identify their specific ADHD or LD. This exercise helps them to recognize that the interference caused by ADHD and LD is selective, and not global, in nature.

At this point the program emphasizes that being comfortable with what makes one a unique human being allows others to feel comfortable with one's uniqueness. An empowered person is strong enough to recognize both his personal strengths and his personal weaknesses and still be able to respect himself as a whole human being capable of performing as well as anyone on the job. This abilities-based approach is at the center of this communication, and it permeates all interaction between LDI staff and program participants. The consistent and persistent message presented to program members is that they are responsible for determining their quality of life.

In 1995, the Phoenix metropolitan area had over 300 vocational-technical schools, 16 universities, 12 community colleges, and 80,000 companies conducting education, training, and employment or business activities. Field investigations into which of these settings is the most appropriate for the LDI participant are now initiated and are limited only by the individual's intellectual capabilities, her desire to succeed, and the thoroughness of her research plan. Site visits of various programs and schools that offer vocational training are scheduled and conducted by the program participant—for example, there are eight schools and vocational-technical programs in Phoenix that offer training leading to emergency medical technician or paramedic certification. Information gathered from these visits would include but should not be limited to

- Levels of literacy required for admissions test
- Levels of literacy in classroom instruction
- Methods of instruction used in classroom or lab
- Accommodations for ADHD and LD
- Tutorial support available
- Qualifications of staff providing tutorial assistance
- Length of training, cost, and financial aid availability
- Personal observations about condition of campus and facilities
- Any and all promotional literature regarding program of instruction
- A list of current students and graduates willing to provide testimonials
- A list of employers who have hired graduates

Once these tours have been completed, the client follows up by interviewing consumers of the program's educational or training services. It is at this stage that the client would compare local labor market information with that gathered from the OASYS program. Interviews are conducted with persons who have finished training and with local employers who have hired graduates from these programs. These interviews allow the LDI program participant to gauge the market value potential of training, the qualifications employers are looking for, training satisfaction among current students, factors constituting job satisfaction among current employees, average wage information, and other pertinent information affecting her career choice.

The participant then develops a multimedia presentation using Microsoft's Power Point (Microsoft, 1993) program to evaluate and synthesize the pros and cons of each education or training program. The presentation incorporates the information identified by the program participant as being essential to making an informed, intelligent decision. This information is divided into slides on which the participant may use words, designs, pictures, photographs, video, audio, and many other options to present the results of her vocational investigation.

The end result of this investigation is that the individual looking for the right training program—leading to paramedic certification, for example—becomes the expert on all available and appropriate opportunities. Now in possession of a high-quality vocational plan, the program participant can act on it with a high degree of personal confidence.

Vocational Strategies for College Graduates

Adults with ADHD or LD should feel great satisfaction in completing the degree requirements of a specific program of study. The difficulty of completing a college program for many individuals in this population makes the success of those who do finish very inspiring.

The next challenge is applying theoretical concepts to workplace situations and problems. In the workplace, standards of acceptable performance are measured quite differently than in the college environment. Employer expectations about the ability of college graduates to handle multiple tasks and priorities smoothly and effectively require advance preparation on the part of the job-seeking college graduate.

The following are suggested guidelines, strategies, and accommodations that clinicians can use to help the college graduate with ADHD or LD make a successful transition from education to employment (Lieb, 1995; Payne, 1993, pp. 2–6):

1. Seek employment that uses identified abilities and college education. Decide on a job or career after carefully looking at what is required both during training and on the job. Avoid job searches that are too narrowly or broadly focused. Resist the impulse to go after employment opportunities because of primarily financial motivations; instead, concentrate on the opportunities inherent in the position itself.

2. Assess the targeted employer's awareness of and efforts to work with employees who have ADHD or LD. Ascertain whether personal work habits (e.g., messy desk, need to walk around, need for quiet work area, receptivity to practical jokes) are compatible with company culture.

3. Develop a long-term career ladder that includes the estimated amount of time needed to move up to successive levels of responsibility, the number of potential openings in the targeted area, and anticipated future learning needs. It is in the best interests of the career-minded job applicant to focus on companies that offer in-house continuing education programs. Once competency and capabilities have been established, many academic difficulties can be dealt with much more flexibly on the part of the employer because the individual has proved himself.

4. Find out how companies that offer continuing education programs deliver these services. Find out whether service delivery is by traditional paper-paper techniques or whether it is industry specific and taught in the context of the job. Be aware of the accommodations the individual used successfully in school and do not assume that they will automatically be allowed on the job.

5. Ask for specific time lines for performance evaluations and understand when and how performance will be evaluated. If accommodations will be needed, propose an evaluation process through which the employee and supervisor can review the effectiveness of the accommodations and the possibility of adjustments.

Suggested Accommodation Strategies for Success in the Workplace

College graduates with ADHD or LD need to have compensatory strategies ready to offer employers once they succeed in securing employment. The following are accommodations for specific deficits easily operationalized in just about any work setting at little or no cost to the employer:

- *Needs oral directions.* Provide written copy or picture, model, flow chart, or diagram; shorten directions; use simple sentences and explain one step at a time; have employee repeat directions in own words; have trainer physically demonstrate the task
- *Learns erratically.* Have model of finished product available for review; record or videotape instructions; repeat activity until learning is accomplished
- *Is distracted by irrelevant details.* If unable to focus, clarify directions and provide clear, reasonable expectations; underline or number key points using color; break activities or tasks into small, sequenced steps
- *Struggles with expression of ideas.* Keep responses simple (yes or no choices); keep questions short and direct, clearly expressed; focus on the order of events; use clues to help person get through steps or explanation (e.g., first, second, third)
- *Perseverates—has trouble moving to new tasks.* Identify time frames or limits for tasks; help create lists, checking off completes; design a task chart with time frames; keep a calendar with start and end dates; give regular feedback
- *Is unorganized—has difficulty planning.* Provide concise directions; spell out all steps of tasks; specify time limitation for activities; organize work spatially so sequence and structure are more visible
- *Is easily frustrated—lacks self-confidence.* Make task assignment short to promote quick success; teach to self-rate quality; give or repeat work tasks person enjoys; praise
- *Is impulsive—rushes tasks.* Emphasize intent or purpose of task; concentrate on accuracy rather than deadlines
- *Lacks time orientation.* If person has difficulty tracking time or staying on time, check to see whether he or she has difficulty telling time; identify which time-telling device is best—digital or analog clock; encourage use of a watch with an alarm or use of a stop watch; have person time activities to experience completion time; give task assignments time frames; monitor time, eventually have person monitor own time; team up with coworker with similar schedule
- *Struggles with attention—is easily distracted.* Place person in stimulus-free environment; use time chart; identify expected and actual finish times; minimize distractions (visual or auditory); have person focus on supervisor's or trainer's eyes when giving or receiving instructions
- *Lacks direction orientation.* Encourage person to ask questions when confused; suggest he or she carry small notepad; use landmarks or color when giving directions; use maps and models with landmarks and street names
- *Has spatial judgment difficulties that interfere with reading.* Suggest use of a ruler as a guide; cut a window in a piece of cardboard; use magnifiers, colored markers, and overlays
- *Struggles with writing and copying tasks.* Have person copy from notes or outline, not the board, flip chart, or overhead; carbon copy or photocopy another's notes; photocopy or duplicate worksheets; encourage use of outlines
- *Struggles with written directions.* Tape-record or read the printed information; demonstrate directions in an oral and hands-on fashion if possible; print directions on 3 × 5 cards with step-by-step instructions (one instruction per card)
- *Struggles with integration of work tasks.* Have example of finished product; demonstrate how parts fit into a meaningful whole
- *Struggles when coping with changing environments.* Try to keep tasks and activities highly structured; minimize changes and distractions whenever possible

- *Has poor social judgment.* Create buddy system with senior employee in same section who will advise and explain hidden rules, nonverbal communication, and culture of the organization; role play or discuss group situations; reinforce positive behaviors; help person identify and respond to nonverbal cues and information
- *Is vulnerable to auditory distractions.* Try to eliminate open, noisy spaces; place person in small quiet office or room; utilize headsets or earphones; supplement information with written instructions and outlines
- *Struggles with handwriting and forms.* Make sure person can read supervisor's handwriting; provide person with samples or examples of forms, worksheets, and timesheets; color code similar tasks for processing (colored baskets, folders, or labels; Payne, 1994, pp. 52–54)

Summary

Many adults with ADHD or LD seeking vocational assessment lack or cannot demonstrate competency in the skills they need to show employers. These adults must learn to recognize the abilities that will enable them to perform the essential functions of a desired job and the aptitudes that will help them acquire the new job skills needed to be part of a self-directed work team.

This task is made more difficult by a shortage of appropriate training programs providing services to this population, limited understanding of how to make reasonable accommodations in the workplace, and lack of insight of many adults with ADHD or LD into how they can cope with and compensate for their deficits.

This writer's experience as a treatment provider and as an adult with ADHD and LD has taught that when reasonable expectations of personal performance are combined with appropriate treatment, individuals with ADHD or LD can and do succeed at levels of accomplishment commensurate with their nondisabled peers.

Society has expected too little from those with special learning needs, and sadly, it has not been disappointed. These individuals are chronically un- and underemployed and at risk of becoming involved in the welfare, criminal justice, and mental health systems as consumers of public resources instead of providers to the community.

Clinicians must approach vocational planning by dealing with the characteristics and demands of tomorrow's workplace and workforce within an aggressively developed consumer-directed vocational assessment. Consumer-directed vocational assessments provide depth and meaning to background information on the individual's interests, abilities, and aptitudes. Targeted occupational clusters can be examined in order to identify a career ladder, tasks essential to a desired job, and general literacy requirements.

Because the occupational goals identified in this process are set by the consumer with clinician support, the consumer can take ownership of and thus responsibility for the action plan. Discovering a personally satisfying occupational niche and learning how one can achieve it produces dramatic positive changes in one's life. The goal for those of us who work with this population must be to provide the tools and techniques necessary to start and to complete this vocational journey successfully.

CHAPTER 12

Legal Rights

Patricia H. Latham and
Peter S. Latham

THE UNITED STATES has a long tradition of respecting the civil rights of its citizens. Civil rights were originally viewed as the rights each citizen had to be safe from governmental misconduct. Among the most important of these were the rights conferred by the Fifth and Fourteenth Amendments to the Constitution. Both amendments have been interpreted to require that disadvantaged minorities (including individuals with disabilities) be afforded equal access to public education (*Brown v. Board of Education*, 347 U.S. 483 (1954)).

The Fifth and Fourteenth Amendments apply only to governmental actions. In order to ensure that employment, education, and public accommodations were truly open to all citizens, the Congress enacted legislation that implemented these fundamental rights and extended them to apply to the private sector. Three key federal statutes were adopted.

The Rehabilitation Act of 1973 (RA; 29 U.S.C. § 701 *et seq.*) made discrimination against individuals with disabilities unlawful in three areas: 1. employment by the executive branch of the federal government, 2. employment by most federal government contractors, and 3. activities that are funded by federal subsidies or grants. The last category includes all public elementary and secondary schools and most postsecondary institutions. The statutory section that prohibits discrimination in grants was numbered § 504 in the original legislation and the Rehabilitation Act of 1973 is often referred to simply as "Section 504." Other sections, for example, create a limited requirement for affirmative action in the hiring of individuals with disabilities by the executive branch of the federal government and most federal government contractors.

In 1975, the Congress enacted a statute titled the Education for All Handicapped Children Act. That statute (now called the Individuals with Disabilities Education Act, or IDEA; 20 U.S.C. § 1400 *et seq.*) provided funds to state and local elementary and secondary schools for public education, including the education of children with disabilities. It represents a unique approach to civil rights in that the IDEA provides at least a part of the funds that enable these school systems to comply with federal disability-based civil rights laws. Comparable financing does not exist for compliance with race- and gender-based civil rights laws.

In 1990, the Congress enacted the Americans with Disabilities Act (ADA; 42 U.S.C. § 12101 *et seq.*). This act extended the concepts of Section 504 to 1. employers with 15 or more employees (Title I), 2. all activities of state and local governments, including but not limited to employment and education (Title II), and 3. virtually all places that offer goods and services to the public—termed "places of public accommodation" (Title III). In addition, the ADA extended the antidiscrimination provisions of the RA to employment by the Congress.

Legal Principles

The RA and ADA have collectively created the right to be free from discrimination based on one's disability. The protection of these laws extends to those who 1. are individuals with disabilities under the law; 2. are otherwise qualified, with or without a reasonable accommodation; 3. are being excluded from employment or education solely by reason of their disability; and 4. are covered by applicable federal or state law. These basic principles differ somewhat in their application to postsecondary education, licensing, and employment.

POSTSECONDARY EDUCATION AND LICENSING

Individual with a Disability

The protection of the RA and ADA applies only to an "individual with a disability," which is

any individual who:

    (i) has a physical or mental impairment which substantially limits one or more of such person's major life activities,

    (ii) has a record of such an impairment, or

    (iii) is regarded as having such an impairment. (29 U.S.C. § 706(8)(B))

The second and third definitions are intended to protect individuals who 1. previously had a disability but do not now and 2. are treated as though they had a disability but do not. The most important category for our purposes is the first, and it is discussed below. The ADA contains definitions that are "equivalent" to those contained in the RA. The discussion that follows applies to both statutes unless otherwise specified.

Impairments covered. The definition of a "physical or mental impairment" includes "any mental or psychological disorder, such as mental retardation, organic brain syndrome, emotional or mental illness, and specific learning disabilities" (29 C.F.R. § 1613.702(b)(2)). Note that "specific learning disabilities" are expressly covered by the regulations. The courts have indicated that they will utilize the definition of a "specific learning disability" as it appears in the IDEA when construing this regulation (*Argen v. New York State Board of Law Examiners,* 860 F. Supp. 84 (S.D. N.Y. 1994)).

    ADHD is not specifically mentioned in the regulations. (For convenience, in the following we will use the term "ADD" because its use is so common.) ADD, however, has been recognized as a "mental or psychological disorder." In *Gaston County School District* (Letter of Findings [LOF], OCR Docket No. 04-90-1617), the Department of Education's Office of Civil Rights ruled that the Gaston County School District of North Carolina (which received federal funding) failed to identify, evaluate, and provide the complainant's child who had ADD with a free public education appropriate to his disorder and thereby violated the RA (29 U.S.C. § 794). There are similar holdings under the ADA.

Thus, the RA and ADA potentially apply to individuals with LD and ADD. However, the LD or ADD in question must also substantially limit a major life activity.

Substantially limits. The impact of the impairment must be severe enough to result in actual substandard performance. The regulations provide that the term "substantially limits" means that an individual is either 1. "[u]nable to perform a major life activity that the average person in the general population can perform" or 2. "[s]ignificantly restricted as to the condition, manner or duration" of the major life activity in question, when measured against the abilities of the "average person in the general population" (29 C.F.R. ¶¶ 1630.2(j)(1)(i)-(ii)).

Major life activities. An impairment must substantially limit a major life activity before it can be considered a "disability" under the law. The major life activities are considered to be caring for oneself, performing manual tasks, walking, seeing, hearing, speaking, breathing, learning, and working (29 C.F.R. ¶ 1630.2(i)). Note that the regulations provide that learning and working are major life activities, and these are the ones that most concern us. However, working is treated differently from all other major life activities for purposes of considering whether an individual with an impairment is substantially limited. In order to determine whether a substantial limitation on working exists, the individual's impairment must bar him or her from significant *classes* of jobs and not just a particular job. Only disabilities with the former (and broader) impact are considered substantially to limit working.

Otherwise Qualified

Under both the RA and ADA, an "individual with a disability" must be one who is "otherwise qualified." An "otherwise qualified" individual is one who, though possessed of a disability, would be eligible for the job, education, or program benefit with or without a reasonable accommodation. The institution or employer must either provide the accommodation or justify in detail the refusal to provide it (*Fitzgerald v. Green Valley Area Education Agency,* 589 F. Supp. 1130 (S.D. Iowa 1984)).

Testing Modifications and Accommodations

Education revolves around testing. Students spend their academic lives either being tested on their knowledge or acquiring the knowledge to be tested. Testing is used for admissions, course completion, graduation, and expulsion. Testing modifications and accommodations are therefore of central importance to individuals with disabilities.

Discriminatory testing is prohibited under both the RA and ADA. There are four further questions to be answered in deciding whether a test is discriminatory:

- Does the test measure a relevant academic skill or an irrelevant disability?
- If the test results may reflect the existence of a disability, is the measured skill one that is essential to obtaining the education offered?
- Are there alternative methods of measuring an essential academic skill?
- Is the process of providing alternatives unreasonably expensive, given the postsecondary institution's resources?

Testing accommodations are required for individuals with disabilities unless the accommodations would alter the essential nature of the course materials or create an undue hardship (these concepts are discussed below).

Delivery of Course Materials

A right to testing modifications and accommodations would be meaningless if the student were prevented by a disability from acquiring the knowledge to be tested. Most recently, in *United States v. Becker C.P.A. Review* (CV 92–2879 (TFH) D. D.C. 1994), the U.S. District Court for the District of Columbia issued an order that addresses several issues of importance to postsecondary institutions.

In that case, the defendant, Becker C.P.A. Review ("Becker"), had adopted a policy of providing only limited auxiliary aids and services for its hearing-impaired students, consisting of instructor notes, transcripts of prerecorded audio lectures, and transparencies known as "J-notes." The Department of Justice sought a mandatory injunction, contending that these measures were not effective means of ensuring full class participation by hearing-impaired students and thus that Becker's policies denied those students "the full and equal enjoyment of the privileges of a place of public accommodation" in violation of Title III of the ADA.

Following discovery, the parties agreed to the issuance of an injunction (termed a "consent order") that stated in part that 1. "[i]t is a violation of the Americans with Disabilities Act to maintain a policy of providing auxiliary aids and services that does not recognize individual communication needs" and that 2. the "effective communication" required of Becker means "contemporaneous communication of the breadth of the Becker educational experience, among all participants, in a manner that can be understood by each individual with a hearing impairment and that allows for equal participation in the educational experience offered by the Becker course" (Order, ¶¶ A (1)-(2)).

The order then required (among other things) that Becker provide at no additional expense "appropriate auxiliary aids and services" consisting of "qualified interpreters (sign language interpreters, oral interpreters, cued speech, etc.), computer-aided transcription (CAT) services, assistive listening devices, notetakers, transcripts, special seating locations including a reserved seat in the front row of a class, student transcript assistants, staff persons assigned to assist a student in following 'J-notes,' and other similar aids and services or combinations thereof" (Order, ¶ C.(6)(a)).

While the consent order is not, strictly speaking, a legal precedent, it is instructive because it makes clear three points: 1. A place of public accommodation may not, alone, determine which aids and services are appropriate for a student with a disability. 2. The aids and services provided must be "effective" in achieving "contemporaneous communication" of the "educational experience, among all participants, in a manner that can be understood by each individual" and that allows for "equal participation in the educational experience" offered by the institution. 3. Effectiveness is determined *primarily* by specific consideration of the needs of the students affected.

Types of Auxiliary Aids and Services

Reasonable accommodations, including auxiliary aids and services, are required by the RA and ADA to be made available to students with LD who need these services in order to access the institution's courses, examinations, and activities. Required reasonable accommodations, auxiliary aids, and services include taped examinations, large-print examinations, large-print answer sheets, qualified readers, transcribers, interpreters, taped texts, and other similar accommodations, aids, and services. Alternative arrangements may be used, including videotaped lectures, cassettes, and prepared notes. The governing principle is that the methods of instruction provided to the student with LD must be "effective" in achieving "contemporaneous communication" of the "educational experience, among all participants, in a manner that can be understood by each individual" and that allows for "equal participation in the educational experience" offered by the institution. These must be provided at no extra charge to the student (*University of Arizona*, Letter of Findings (LOF), OCR Docket No. 09-91-2402; 2 N.D.L.R. ¶ 285; *United States v. Board of Trustees for the University of Alabama*, 908 F.2d 740 (11th Cir. 1990)).

Accommodations, aids, and services that focus on increasing the skill level of the student in the area of the disability are not required by the ADA and the RA. For example, an institution would not be required to provide developmental reading courses or remedial tutoring services free of charge to a student with dyslexia (*Halasz v. University of New England*, 816 F. Supp. 37 (D. Me. 1993)).

Institutions may offer separate programs (which may include separate courses and services) for students with LD, provided that qualified students are clearly informed that they have a choice between 1. the separate program and 2. regular programs offered with suitable modifications and auxiliary aids at no additional charge. Institutions may limit students to entry into separate programs only if these students are truly not qualified for regular programs offered with suitable modifications and auxiliary aids at no additional charge.

Limitations on the Duty to Accommodate

A postsecondary institution has no obligation to provide accommodations that will alter the fundamental nature of the course materials or course of study being offered (*Wynne v. Tufts University School of Medicine*, 976 F.2d 791 (1st Cir. 1992); see also *Pandazides v. Virginia Board of Education et al.*, 946 F.2d 345 (4th Cir. 1991)). Nor does such an institution have an obligation to provide accommodations that will result in an economic hardship to the institution. Economic hardship is measured by the impact on the institution's financial resources, not its relationship to the size of the requesting student's tuition. For this reason, few institutions argue that accommodations will provide an economic hardship.

EMPLOYMENT

Individual with a Disability

Earlier in this chapter, we noted that—legally speaking—a "disability" is a physical or mental impairment that substantially limits a major life activity. This definition governs accommodations in the workplace as well as accommodations in postsecondary education. As to major life activities, in March 1995 the Equal Employment Opportunity Commission (EEOC) released ADA guidance adding to the list of major life activities mental and emotional processes, such as thinking, concentrating, and interacting with others (EEOC Compliance Manual § 902: Definition of the Term Disability).

What Is a Job?

To begin with, it is important to consider just what we mean by job requirements. Most job "requirements" fall into at least five separate categories: 1. academic qualifications; 2. required on-the-job experience; 3. competence in the work itself; 4. general standards of cooperativeness in the work situation; and 5. compliance with "good citizenship" rules—for example, being on time and no unauthorized absences. Moreover, requirements 3–5 become increasingly subjective as the seniority and pay of the positions increase. All of these factors must be considered in selecting a job and deciding whether and how to deal with a disability.

Two case studies may be helpful. In *Dazey v. Department of the Air Force* (54 M.S.P.R. 658 (1992)), a GS-12 auditor was removed in major part for using abusive language in the office. She suffered from mood changes caused by manic depression and an "apparently irrational dislike for her supervisor." Her psychiatrist prescribed lithium and Prozac and testified that the treatment would prevent bizarre disruptive behavior if the auditor returned to the workplace even without accommodations. However, the auditor displayed some of these symptoms at the trial notwithstanding medication. The administrative judge found that she had not shown that medication was a sufficient answer. Accordingly, the judge found that she "could not perform the essential functions of her position because such essential functions included not engaging in the bizarre behavior previously engaged in, and getting along with her supervisor." Clearly, having the 1. academic qualifications, 2. required on-the-job experience, and 3. competence in the work itself, while failing to meet general standards of cooperativeness in the work situation and comply with good citizenship rules, was not sufficient.

In *Mancini vs. General Electric Co.* (820 F. Supp. 141 (D. Vt. 1993)), the court held that an employee with a disability, who had developed a personality conflict with his supervisor resulting in a failure to comply with the supervisor's directions to work in particular places that made him uncomfortable, was properly discharged under the Vermont Fair Employment Practices Act (similar to the RA and ADA). The court held that the employer had no duty to transfer the employee in order to avoid a conflict with the supervisor. In so ruling, the court said that "employees must be present and willing to obey their supervisors to perform the essential functions of their job" (820 F. Supp. 141 at 147). Had the employee identified himself as an individual with a disability and employed appropriate strategies it is entirely possible that the work situation would not have deteriorated to the point of disobedience and firing.

Essential Features

An individual with a disability is required to perform the essential features of a job with or without a reasonable accommodation. All job features that are not essential are considered marginal and therefore capable of being restructured as a reasonable accommodation.

All of the five job elements discussed above may be considered essential features of jobs. As noted above, meeting general standards and rules becomes increasingly important as the seniority of the position increases. However, these elements can be highly subjective and, in some cases, can serve as a pretext for discrimination. The regulations and EEOC Interpretive Guidance analyze the essential features of a job by considering primarily the role the job plays in the employer's operations rather than the individual skills necessary to perform the job. However, the case law suggests that the broader factors considered in this section also apply.

Case studies. Most jobs actually involve several sets of duties. Often it is necessary to decide whether all of these sets of duties should be considered essential requirements of a single job. Compare the following cases.

1. In *Fitzgerald v. Green Valley Area Education Agency* (589 F. Supp. 1130 (S.D. Iowa 1984)), the court held that a school district's requirement that all teachers take turns driving school buses was not an essential part of the teaching function. Accordingly, the school district was required to restructure its job requirements to permit the hiring of a qualified teacher whose dyslexia and other impairments prevented him from driving a school bus.

2. In *DiPompo v. West Point Military Academy et al.* (960 F.2d 326 (2nd Cir. 1992)), the court held that dispatcher duties that were required of all firemen on a rotational basis and involved the use of computers were an essential part of the work of a fireman and refused to order job restructuring. The U.S. Court of Appeals for the Second Circuit affirmed the trial court.

Reasonable Accommodations

Reasonable accommodations are of three general types: 1. those required to ensure equal opportunity in the job application process, 2. those that enable the individual with a disability to perform the essential features of a job, and 3. those that enable individuals with disabilities to enjoy the same benefits and privileges as those available to individuals without disabilities (EEOC Interpretive Guidance at 408). Reasonable accommodations for ADD and LD can include any of the following:

- Providing or modifying equipment or devices

- Job restructuring

- Part-time or modified work schedules

- Reassignment to a vacant position

- Adjusting or modifying examinations, training materials, or policies

- Providing readers or interpreters

- Making the workplace readily accessible to and usable by people with disabilities (Equal Employment Opportunity Commission, 1991, p. 3)

Despite this sweeping description, the accommodations actually required for individuals with ADD and LD are generally not extensive or expensive. The President's Committee on Employment of People with Disabilities (1993) has pointed out that

- Thirty-one percent of accommodations cost nothing.
- Fifty percent cost less than $50.00.
- Sixty-nine percent cost less than $500.00.
- Eighty-eight percent cost less than $1,000.00.

The bar against employment discrimination covers all employment activities of the firms to which it applies. It applies to recruitment, advertising and job application procedures, hiring, upgrading, promotion, award of tenure, demotion, transfer, layoff, termination, right of return from layoff, rehiring, rates of pay, compensation, changes in compensation, job assignments, job classifications, organizational structures, position descriptions, lines of progression, seniority lists, leaves of absence, sick leave, other leaves, fringe benefits, selection and financial support for training, including apprenticeships, professional meetings, conferences, and other related activities, selection for leaves of absence to pursue training, activities sponsored by a covered entity including social and recreational programs and any other term, condition, or privilege of employment (29 C.F.R. ¶¶ 1630.4 (a)-(i)). The number of potential reasonable accommodations is as large as the number of activities to which the ban on discrimination applies.

The EEOC recommends a four-step process in determining whether a reasonable accommodation is required.

1. Analyze the particular job involved and determine its purpose and essential functions.
2. Consult with the individual with a disability to ascertain the precise job-related limitations imposed by the individual's disability and how those limitations could be overcome with a reasonable accommodation.
3. In consultation with the individual to be accommodated identify potential accommodations and assess the effectiveness each would have in enabling the individual to perform the essential functions of the position.
4. Consider the preference of the individual to be accommodated and select and implement the accommodation that is most appropriate for both the employee and employer (EEOC Interpretive Guidance at 415).

Note the central role played by the definition of the essential features of the job. Essential features are discussed below.

Case studies. Many jobs (such as writing this chapter) need not be performed during a specific eight-hour period. Others (such as operating an emergency hotline) must be. Often it is necessary to decide whether the essential requirements of a job preclude the use of flexible schedules. Compare the following cases.

1. In *Lynch v. Department of Education* (52 M.S.P.R. 541 (1992)), a GS-13 trial attorney was dismissed for unsatisfactory work and excessive absences due to an epileptic condition that was treated with medication. The medication, however, affected her memory and ability to concentrate. As a reasonable accommodation she requested: 1. training in legal drafting, 2. specific structured assignments including clear written assignment instructions and increased supervisory assistance, and 3. the opportunity to make up hours missed by late arrivals. These accommodations were found to be reasonable, in our view, because they increased only marginally, if at all, the burden on the employer. Specifically, the agency needed legal drafting done. Further, it already had in place supervisors whose very purpose was to make sure that work flowed smoothly. Finally, the opportunity to make up missed work functioned very much like the flextime programs many employers (including the agency) already had in place. As a result, the individual was found to be a "qualified handicapped person" under the RA whose proposed accommodation was reasonable and was ordered reinstated.
2. In *Guice-Mills v. Derwinski* (967 F.2d 794 (2nd Cir. 1992)), a nurse who suffered from depression and sedating medication that required her to report two hours late was not an

otherwise qualified person. Whether schedule or job description changes are reasonable accommodations depends on the facts.

Generally speaking, an employer is entitled to enforce rules whose purpose is to reduce workplace friction by requiring polite behavior on the job. In general, these requirements are also considered essential features of a job that must be complied with. Compare the following cases.

1. In *Ross v. Beaumont Hospital et al.* (687 F. Supp. 1115 (E.D. Mich. 1988)), a hospital terminated the privileges of a surgeon who suffered from narcolepsy despite the fact that her narcolepsy was largely controlled through medication. However, the surgeon had also verbally abused nurses over a seven-year period. There was no evidence that the abuse was related to narcolepsy. Accordingly, the termination was held to be lawful under the RA because it was based in major part on her unacceptable conduct.

2. In *Shartle v. Motorola, Inc.* (No. 93 C 5508 (N.D. Ill. 1994)), a dyslexic security guard who had difficulty writing reports and who was insubordinate was properly fired for insubordination. The anti-insubordination policy was uniformly applied. The guard did not show that the policy was applied as a result of her request for an accommodation.

Undue Hardship

A "reasonable accommodation" is one that does not either 1. alter the essential nature of a job or 2. result in "significant difficulty or expense" to the employer. A proposed accommodation that does either of these things creates an "undue hardship" and need not be made (EEOC Interpretive Guidance at 409).

In judging whether a proposed accommodation creates an "undue hardship," the particular circumstances of the employer's situation must be considered. What is an undue hardship for one employer may not be an undue hardship for another. The EEOC gives as an example the case of an individual with a disabling visual impairment that makes it extremely difficult to see in dim lighting. If such an individual were to seek employment as a waiter in a nightclub, the club would not be required to provide bright lighting for the dining and lounge areas even though it would involve nothing more than turning up the lights. The nightclub relies on dim lighting to create an "ambiance" that attracts customers, and bright lighting would destroy the nightclub's trade. Providing it would be an undue hardship (EEOC Interpretive Guidance at 409).

Affirmative Action

The duty to undertake affirmative action differs from the duty to avoid discrimination. Affirmative action is the positive obligation to adopt and implement a plan (acceptable to the government) for the employment of individuals with disabilities. It is required of 1. the federal government, 2. federal government contractors, and 3. some recipients of federal funding under the IDEA. In contrast, the duty to avoid discrimination is the obligation to refrain from discriminatory conduct.

Disclosure

There is no duty to disclose a disability and none to accommodate a disability that has not been disclosed. The conventional wisdom is that there is no need to disclose unless accommodation is sought. However, that is a half-truth at best. Many individuals with ADD or LD have some difficulty responding to the social requirements of the workplace. As a result, it is often the case that they are the last to see trouble coming. Where this appears to be a substantial possibility for an individual, it may be wise to disclose even when no specific accommodation is at issue. There can be another reason for disclosure. Mandatory drug testing that is justified by business necessity and is uniformly administered is lawful. Mandatory drug tests can identify drugs such as Ritalin or Dexedrine. If such testing is used, disclosure of the lawful circumstances under which these medications are being taken is essential.

Issues for Individuals and Professionals

DOCUMENTATION

Most documentation involves three steps: diagnosis, evaluation of impact, and recommendation. Together they establish 1. the existence of a disability; 2. the areas of functioning affected by that disability; and 3. the specific strategies and accommodations in school, testing, workplace, and personal living made necessary by that disability.

How much documentation is enough?

The ADA addresses the question of documentation in connection with academic and license testing. The Preamble to Regulation on Nondiscrimination on the Basis of Disability by Public Accommodations and in Commercial Facilities, which provides guidance on the proper interpretation of the ADA and its implementing regulations, provides that: 1. "requests for documentation must be reasonable," 2. "such requests must be limited to the need for the documentation or aid requested," and 3. "the applicant may be required to bear the cost of providing such documentation" (28 C.F.R. Pt. 36, App. B, p. 626 (1995); Preamble to Regulation on Nondiscrimination on the Basis of Disability by Public Accommodations and in Commercial Facilities).

That raises a key point. A principal purpose of documentation is the establishment of an individual's entitlement to special education and reasonable accommodations in education, testing, and employment. With few exceptions, the "requirements" for documentation are really dictated by the rules governing burden of proof in a civil action. Here is what this means. If a person asserts a claim for reasonable accommodation based on her disability, the school, test giver, or institution with whom she is dealing can do one of two things: 1. accept her claim or 2. reject it. There are no legal rules that prevent an institution from recognizing and accommodating disabilities generously. In dealing with such an institution, the amount of documentation required will be virtually nonexistent. Agreement will be quick. However, if there is no agreement, if the claim is resisted by the institution, then the individual is faced with the necessity of proving her claim to a third party. This may be done informally to an EEOC or other federal compliance officer, semiformally in an administrative proceeding, or formally to a court.

In asserting a claim, the individual will act as a plaintiff. In that case, she will be required to prove her claim by a preponderance of the evidence. This is legal language that means that her evidence must be substantially more convincing and persuasive than that of her opponent. In other words, most of the convincing evidence must support her claim.

As a practical matter then, a disability must be "documented" by either: 1. presenting that amount of evidence necessary to persuade the pertinent firm or 2. proving entitlement by a preponderance of the evidence, whichever is the lesser standard. Since an individual can never know for certain when he will be called on to prove his case, his documentation should be developed with care in the event that he may one day need to prove his case.

CONFIDENTIALITY

Preemployment inquiries. Everyone expects confidentiality to be respected. Most people never have occasion to consider that it might not be. There are several sources of requirements that define when and on what terms confidential information must be shared with others.

The rules governing preemployment inquiries concerning disabilities are quite definite. A prospective employer who is subject to the ADA "shall not conduct a medical examination or make inquiries of a job applicant as to whether such applicant is an individual with a disability or as to the nature or severity of such disability" (42 U.S.C. § 12112(d)(2)(A)). The prospective employer may, however, "make pre-employment inquiries into the ability of an applicant to perform job-related functions" (42 U.S.C. § 12112(d)(2)(B)).

After a prospective employer makes an offer, but before the start of employment, he may require an "employment entrance examination" if 1. "all entering employees are subjected to such an examination regardless of disability," 2. certain confidentiality restrictions (discussed below) are observed, and 3. the "results of such examination" are used only in accordance with the ADA (42 U.S.C. § 12112(d)).

Confidentiality restrictions are worth considering at some length. The postoffer, preemployment medical examination must meet the requirement that information obtained regarding the medical condition or history of the applicant is collected and maintained on separate forms and in separate medical files and is treated as a confidential medical record, except that

- "[S]upervisors and managers" may be "informed regarding necessary restrictions on the work duties of the employee and necessary accommodations."
- First aid and safety personnel "may be informed, when appropriate, if the disability might require emergency treatment."
- State workmen's compensation offices may be provided with the medical information.
- Insurance companies may be informed where the firm requires a medical examination to provide health or life insurance to employees (A Technical Assistance Manual on the Employment Provisions (Title I) of the Americans with Disabilities Act, U.S. Equal Employment Opportunity Commission at VI-11-12).

The legitimate scope of the medical examination is not defined, but if it is the standard medical examination given to all employees, it will not necessarily elicit information about specific LD. However, it will almost certainly require discussion of one's medication. In the case of most individuals with adult ADD, the examination will require disclosure of that condition, even if no disability is claimed.

Job accommodation information. An employer may require a medical examination to confirm the existence of a claimed disability and the appropriateness of a proposed reasonable accommodation. An employer may also be entitled to require a medical examination if an employee is unable to perform his or her job effectively (A Technical Assistance Manual on the Employment Provisions (Title I) of the Americans with Disabilities Act, U.S. Equal Employment Opportunity Commission at VI-13-14).

Drug testing. Under the ADA an employer or prospective employer may test for the illegal use of drugs. These tests may, of course, identify the lawful use of prescription medications such as Dexedrine or Ritalin as well as illegal drugs. Information about the lawful use of prescription medications and disabilities "must be kept confidential, in the same way as any medical record" (A Technical Assistance Manual on the Employment Provisions (Title I) of the Americans with Disabilities Act, U.S. Equal Employment Opportunity Commission at VIII-7).

Asserting Legal Rights

REHABILITATION ACT OF 1973

The RA contains various enforcement mechanisms. Most important for our purposes, it may be enforced by civil suit, either by itself or, in appropriate cases, with civil rights statutes. Most private actions are for injunctive relief, whose purpose is to prevent discrimination or to correct its effects. Civil actions may also be brought by the United States for the same purpose. The Department of Justice can, in some cases, pursue fines and penalties. Individuals may recover attorneys' fees in appropriate cases.

AMERICANS WITH DISABILITIES ACT OF 1990

The ADA contains various enforcement mechanisms. These include actions by the EEOC and Justice Department, as well as private actions. The ADA enforcement provisions are borrowed from the Civil Rights Act of 1964. They permit civil suits by individuals for relief, including injunctive relief, back pay, and, sometimes, damages. However, the Department of Justice, on behalf of an individual, can pursue fines and penalties. The ADA also encourages the use of alternative dispute resolution, fact finding, minitrials, and arbitration to the extent they are appropriate and authorized by law. Individuals may recover attorneys' fees in appropriate cases.

Summary

Individuals with ADD and specific LD are considered individuals with disabilities under federal law when their conditions are of sufficient severity to substantially limit a major life activity such as learning or working. Individuals with these disabilities enjoy the right to be free from discrimination and to receive reasonable accommodations in the classroom and workplace under federal law.

CHAPTER 13

Drugs Affecting Learning, Attention, and Memory

Sam Goldstein and Michael Goldstein

I N 1937, CHARLES BRADLEY first reported the benefits of stimulant medications for a range of disruptive behaviors in adolescents. Stimulants were then tried as a way to improve intellectual functioning (Cutler, Little, & Strauss, 1940). Benefits have been consistently shown, primarily for disruptive behaviors. A review of the thousands of studies using stimulants primarily with children finds that the majority of dependent variables include disruptive behavior problems (J. M. Swanson, 1993; J. M. Swanson et al., 1993). These behaviors have included restlessness, hyperactivity, off-task behavior, aggression, talking out, out-of-seat behavior, irritability, inability to follow directions, poor cooperation, oppositionality, and noncompliance with rules. In children, reduction of these problems has been shown to lead to a decrease in complaints of disruptive behavior in many settings, including the playground, the home, and the classroom. Concomitantly, stimulants have been shown to increase the ability to sit still, control impulses, delay gratification, comply with rules, follow directions, and complete assigned work. There has been less research primarily with children on a number of other classes of medications, including the antidepressants, targeting disruptive problems as well as problems related to depression and anxiety. Surprisingly, studies of antidepressant use with children have failed to demonstrate efficacy for treatment of depression (Ambrosini, Bianchi, Rabinovich, & Elia, 1993). The findings about the ability of these medicines to treat nondisruptive problems have simply not been as convincing in children as they are in adults (R. P. Greenberg & Fisher, 1989). However, the study of antidepressants, principally the tricyclics, has shown them to be excellent second-choice medications for the treatment of ADHD problems. In fact, some researchers have suggested that the antidepressants should be the treatment of choice for ADHD (Huessy, 1988).

Research on the use of these medications for adult ADHD and LD problems constitutes a very small percentage of the overall research literature. In contrast, the use of these medications with the adult population in clinical practice has been increasing dramatically, far exceeding the research-based, scientific foundation. It is important, therefore, for the clinician to understand the history of these medications, beginning with their use in the childhood population prior to a review of their use with adults. This chapter will begin with an overview of general principles concerning psychotropic medications. Research with stimulants, antidepressants, and other medications, as well as issues related to medicines, including mechanism of action, side effects, and use with special populations, will be reviewed. The primarily experimental research on the potential benefits of medications for learning and memory problems in children and adults will then be discussed. The chapter will conclude with a review of a model to facilitate the nonmedical clinician's interaction with physicians. Guidelines for clinical practice with adults are offered.

Children with ADHD constitute by far the largest group receiving medications for disruptive behavior. The three behaviors most powerfully affected when stimulants are used with this population are general conduct, the ability to remain on task, and the overall quality of work completed (DuPaul & Rapport, 1993). It is obvious that increases in task efficiency and time on task likely reflect decreases in disruptive, noncompliant, or inappropriate behaviors. Nondisruptive symptoms of social isolation, anxiety, or unhappiness may characterize some children with ADHD without hyperactivity, but in general these are considered to be minor problems in the ADHD and LD populations. Thus, it is not surprising that groups of internalizing, nondisruptive symptoms have only been minimally targeted for medication treatment in these populations.

From the clinician's perspective, it is the specific behavior, not necessarily the type or class of medication used to treat the behavior, that is of primary interest. Thus, as noted in other publications (S. Goldstein & Goldstein, 1995), it makes intuitive sense to organize a chapter such as this by behavior. However, most research studies target multiple behaviors, making it difficult to review the literature in that framework without a significant degree of redundancy. For this reason, this chapter is organized by class and type of medication rather than by behavior. While this may make reading somewhat more difficult, it enables a more direct and thorough review of the available literature.

General Principles

COMMUNICATING WITH PHYSICIANS

For many nonmedical clinicians, physicians—either primary care physicians or specialists such as neurologists and psychiatrists—may appear distant and unreachable. Yet the medications these physicians prescribe are often directly focused on modifying behaviors and problems initially identified and primarily dealt with by the clinician.* Therefore, it is vital that physicians be provided accurate data on general behavior and response to medications.

There are three key points for clinicians to keep in mind when communicating with physicians. First, while verbal communication may be helpful, it is not always possible. Direct written communication between the clinician and physician is most likely to provide the physician with needed information. Further, as in the game "Telephone," information relayed through the patient from clinician to physician may become distorted. Oral communication between clinician and physician, if possible, is effective, but even in these situations a written follow-up provides data for the chart and needed information about behaviors to be targeted and benefits and adverse side effects from medication.

---

*In the remainder of this chapter, "clinician" will refer to nonmedical professionals including psychologists, social workers, and educators.

Clinicians must remember that most physicians are not trained in behavioral assessment. Lengthy psychological evaluations may be of only peripheral interest to a prescribing physician. On the other hand, one or two brief sentences loosely describing the adult's behavior are unlikely to be thorough enough for the physician. Many physicians use specific rating scales with which they are familiar. There are a number of excellent scales available for children. As reviewed in an earlier chapter, the development of such scales for adults is in its infancy. Thus, when prescribing medications for ADHD, most physicians will rely solely on patient report. It is helpful for the clinician to offer quantifiable data (e.g., from the BAADS or Wender checklists). The clinician must also recognize that when a physician suggests a specific measure (e.g., Conners), it is important to try to provide that measure with an accompanying explanation of what the data may actually mean. Further, if the clinician believes the measure is inadequate or incomplete, providing additional data is ethical and is the clinician's responsibility. When the clinician provides measures for instruments the physician may not be familiar with (e.g., questionnaires or testing), a brief explanation of the scores and their meaning is often helpful.

Given the infant state of affairs in the use of medications for adults with ADHD, it is likely that in most situations, referral for a medication trial will come from a clinician. At the conclusion of this chapter we will provide a step-by-step model to help the clinician initiate this process and assist the physician by providing well-defined, operationalized, and measured behaviors to assess the need for and benefits of medication. The importance of this process cannot be underestimated. The clinician must understand these target behaviors and the encompassing disorder that they may reflect. Further, clinicians must have a basic understanding of the primary medications used to modify ADHD behavior, as well as the negative or side effects that can and often do occur. Finally, it often falls on the clinician's shoulders to integrate medication treatment as part of a more comprehensive intervention plan.

TIME COURSE

Time course in regard to medication effectiveness reflects the change in target behaviors from the time medication is taken until after the time the medication has cleared the body. Consistently, after a medication to affect behavior is taken, positive and negative effects increase until they reach a peak, at which point they slowly and steadily decrease. Some medicines may have their strongest effect one or two hours after ingestion; other medicines have peak effects that occur sooner, later, or for longer periods of time. Further, as the body withdraws from certain medications, unwanted behavioral effects may occur. For example, withdrawal from stimulants results in rebound irritability in some people: Over a brief period of time, the person appears to be more hyperactive, irritable, and inattentive than usual.

Understanding the time course of a particular medication used to affect behavior allows the clinician to choose the optimal time to observe improvement in behavior as well as potential unwanted side or withdrawal effects. These types of data are critical to physicians as they make decisions about medications, particularly those requiring multiple daily doses.

BRAND NAMES AND GENERICS

All medications begin with a generic or chemical name. The pharmaceutical company developing or initially marketing the medication chooses a trade or brand name to market the medication to the public. For 17 years after a medication is registered with a specific brand name the manufacturer holds a patent, or exclusive right to distribute that medication. When the patent expires the manufacturer continues to maintain the exclusive use of the copyrighted brand name but can no longer claim exclusive use of the chemical or generic substance. Thus, during the first 17 years, only one company can produce and sell the medication. From that point on, other companies may manufacture the medication, choosing to market it under its generic name or choosing another brand name. For example, methylphenidate was developed and first marketed by CIBA Geigy as a treatment for attention deficit disorder and narcolepsy. CIBA Geigy chose the brand name Ritalin and marketed the drug under that name. Once the patent exclusivity expired, other companies began manufacturing the drug, marketing it under the generic name methylphenidate. At this time, several pharmaceutical companies manufacture generic-form methylphenidate.

In general, the medication sold under the original brand name commands a higher price than the medication sold under the generic chemical name or a new brand name. The original manufacturer attempts to recover the enormous cost of researching the drug prior to obtaining permission for its release. The permission process required by the Food and Drug Administration is often lengthy and can cost millions of dollars. In contrast, the generic manufacturer does not have to recover research and development costs.

The Food and Drug Administration carefully regulates generic and brand-name medications at the federal level. The bioavailability (how quickly the medication enters the blood) in the generic drug must be within 20% of that in the brand-name substance. There are also regulations on what materials in addition to the active substance can be present in the tablet. For example, chemicals may be used to bind the medication into pill form or to provide a more appealing color or taste. These may, however, be chemicals that could change the positive effect or produce side effects. Most manufacturers of brand-name and generic medications attempt to stay well within the tolerances allowed by the federal government. However, it is possible in the case of methylphenidate that the generic preparation has 20% less bioavailability. The manufacturer states that this is not the case. Hypothetically, this could represent a difference in the amount of drug entering the bloodstream and available to the brain. For some sensitive individuals, slight changes in dosage may lead to more modest changes in behavior. For example, the American Academy of Neurology (1990) recommends that particular brands of anticonvulsant medications (the Dilantin brand of phenytoin and the Tegretol brand of carbamazepine) be used to assure that change from one month to the next does not occur, because some individuals are very sensitive to slight changes in dosages in these particular medications. In regard to Ritalin, although no clear research data are available, clinicians often report groups of children who are responsive to Ritalin but unresponsive or responsive only at a higher dosage when changed to the generic preparation.

For most medications, the advantage of lower price outweighs the potential disadvantage of dosage variation. For medications primarily used to modify ADHD symptoms, only the issue of generic methylphenidate versus Ritalin has caused concern. Clinicians, physicians, and patients should be aware that dosage may fluctuate and should be cautious about dosage variability that may occur with the generic formulation of methylphenidate, as well as with other medications used to modify behavior.

Nonmedical Clinicians' Knowledge of Psychotropic Medications

A literature search made prior to this text's going to press did not reveal any studies that have attempted to evaluate the general opinions and knowledge of nonmedical mental health clinicians in regard to psychotropic medication, specifically stimulants. Such a literature does exist, however, about educators' knowledge of these medications. This literature may or may not be directly applicable. Nevertheless, a brief review may be valuable to the clinician. Although S. S. Robin and Bosco (1973) concluded that it is uncommon for educators to possess specific and accurate knowledge about the characteristics of stimulant medications, teachers are the best source of information about children's responses to these medications (Sprague & Gadow, 1976). It can be argued that in regard to adults who are not attending school, clinicians likely offer the best source of information about medication response because of their communication with the patient and family members. The clinician must recognize that medications designed to affect daily behavior cannot be easily adjusted by physicians who see patients only in the examination room (Rizzolo, 1976).

In general, educational professionals often report feeling uncomfortable or poorly trained in communicating with physicians (Epstein, Singh, Luebke, & Stout, 1991). Epstein et al. polled 104 teachers of learning-disabled students about medication use. Less than 15% of the teachers indicated that their professional preservice training had given them enough information on the use of medications by children with behavior problems. Less than 20% felt that the in-service training they had received was enough. These educators also thought that physicians use global impressions and observation during visits with the child to assess the effects of medication, although most physicians reported preferring observations of classroom behavior and rating scale data for these decisions. Although there has been a movement to train clinical psychologists to qualify for prescription privileges (DeLeon, 1995), in general, most doctoral-level clinical training programs include only bare minimum course work on psychotropic medications.

In a recent study, Kasten, Coury, and Heron (1992) polled 322 regular and special education teachers. Ninety-six percent stated that they had received too little or no training about the use of stimulants by children, as part of their undergraduate education program. An almost equal number reported that they had had limited in-service training as well. Yet over 50% of the regular classroom teachers in this study reported that they had been asked by parents whether a particular child should receive stimulant medication! Fifty percent of the regular classroom teachers and up to 30% of the special education teachers responded that they did not understand or recognize the physical and behavioral benefits, or the side effects, that might result from the use of stimulants. For example, only 8% of regular education teachers were aware that tics may be caused by stimulants. Up to 20% of the educators believed that prescribed stimulants could be addictive in children and might result in drug addiction in adulthood.

The data also suggest that physicians retain a healthy skepticism about the quality of the information teachers give them in regard to the benefits of medication (Kasten et al., 1992). This observation might be generalized to indicate that physicians feel the same way about the information they receive from other nonmedical professionals. As clinicians provide physicians with precise, well-defined data concerning target behaviors to be modified by medications, however, there is little doubt that physicians will come to rely on and respect these data.

TRENDS IN MEDICATION USE

Stimulants are by far the most frequently prescribed medications for ADHD (Safer & Krager, 1988; for a review, see S. Goldstein, 1995; S. Goldstein & Goldstein, 1990). Thus, tracking the trends in stimulant use for ADHD provides the largest body of data to review. Unfortunately, there are no survey data concerning the use of stimulants by adults. In contrast, there are numerous surveys of the use of stimulants by children with ADHD. A survey of an elementary and two middle schools in Baltimore County concluded that 1. three-fourths of the 176 students receiving stimulant medication in 1987 had pretreatment ratings consistent with moderate to severe hyperactivity or inattentiveness; 2. over 90% of the students evidenced at least

50% improvement initially after stimulant treatment, according to teacher ratings; 3. 76% of the medicated students continued to show this level of improvement at the end of the 1987 school year; 4. medication improvement and compliance declined in middle school; 5. 15% of the students receiving stimulant medication in 1987 were inattentive but not hyperactive at baseline ratings, but their degree of improvement with stimulants was equivalent to that of the hyperactive students; and 6. in the county-run hyperkinesis clinic, the population of inattentive but not hyperactive students receiving stimulants rose from 7% to 18% of the total between 1976 and 1987 (Safer & Krager, 1988). These results have potentially important implications in regard to adults. As an increasing number of children treated with stimulants for ADHD enter adulthood, their medication history provides important longitudinal baseline data. The improvements reported for the inattentive but not hyperactive group gives reason for optimism that these medications will help adults as well.

Interestingly, Safer and Krager (1988) also reported that in the close to 25-year period leading up to 1987, the use of Ritalin to treat symptomatic problems increased to over 90% while the use of Dexedrine decreased dramatically from 40%. The use of nonstimulants to treat ADHD problems declined from 20% to only 1% by the close of this period. In this same study, almost 7% of third-graders were receiving stimulant medication in the 1987 school year. The peak time of diagnosis appeared to parallel the peak time of treatment. The use of stimulants to treat ADHD problems in children appears to have doubled every seven years over the past fourteen years (Safer & Krager, 1991). Given the increased interest in and awareness of ADHD problems in adulthood, an even more dramatic increase in stimulant use might be expected over the coming years for the adult population.

While the clinical use of nonstimulants, principally tricyclics, to treat ADHD symptoms as well as internalizing symptoms of anxiety and depression is increasing, especially with adults, there continues to be a dearth of epidemiologic research on the incidence and use of these medications. Given the studies reviewed, it is likely that a very small percentage of children, well below 1% of children treated for ADHD, receive these medications for either disruptive or nondisruptive problems (Safer & Krager, 1991). The incidence in adults is unknown. It might be suspected that since a number of well-known professionals in the adult ADHD field have promoted the use of tricyclics, their use with adults may be somewhat higher than with children (Hallowell & Ratey, 1994).

With the increasing interest in using medications to modify ADHD symptoms, there has also been growing controversy surrounding the use of medications, specifically stimulants, along with interest among clinical and research professionals in setting standards for the use of these medicines. Similar controversies are sprouting in the adult field. In general, stimulant treatment for ADHD has been the subject of substantial debate. Inflammatory comments have been an integral part of the discussion. Some critics believe that stimulant treatment for behavior deprives children of the opportunity to use their natural disposition to regulate their behavior (Simms, 1985). Other critics fuel the fears of already vulnerable families by describing the use of medications for ADHD as a tragedy (Bosco, 1975). Bosco cautioned that before looking to medications to modify behavior, other aspects of children's environments such as parent and teacher behavior, should be evaluated and modified. This suggestion is certainly reasonable given the available data on the benefits of efficient contingency management for children with ADHD. The limited but developing base of knowledge about adult ADHD, as well as continuing questions about the specificity of diagnosis, makes these arguments pertinent to adult ADHD as well, with critics describing many adults with these problems seeking benefits through medication as the "worried well."

Yet those interacting daily with children and adults suffering from ADHD consistently report benefits from medication. In an interesting survey, Kasten et al. (1992) found that over 65% of regular and special education teachers believed that stimulants were useful for the treatment of ADHD behaviors in the classroom. Teachers' belief in the benefits of medications to modify classroom behavior decreased with increasing grade. Further, elementary school teachers in this study tended to believe that stimulants were not overprescribed, while middle school teachers believed they were. It is not surprising that elementary school teachers are more enthusiastic advocates of stimulants because they are often the first educators to observe the marked improvements in student behavior and class work.

Barkley (1990b) argued that six factors must be considered when deciding whether to use these medications to regulate a child's behavior. It is likely that these factors can be generalized to adults. They include 1. the severity of the child's symptoms and disruptive behavior; 2. prior use of other treatments (nonmedication intervention should be attempted initially); 3. anxiety disorder symptoms that might result in a lower likelihood of positive response to stimulant medication (Pliszka, 1989); 4. parental attitude toward the use of medication; 5. adequacy of adult supervision; and 6. the child's or adolescent's attitude toward medication. Generalizing these to adults, one might conclude that when stimulants are being considered as a treatment for adult ADHD, the following factors must be carefully assessed: 1. the severity of the adult's symptoms in disrupting his or her ability to meet daily life expectations, and in disturbing and disrupting the lives of people with whom he or she lives, interacts, or works; 2. prior use of other treatments; 3. related anxiety or mood disorders that might be fueling ADHD symptoms and that might lower the likelihood of positive response to stimulant medication; 4. the individual's interest in using the medication as part of a cohesive treatment plan; 5. the co-occurrence of alcohol or substance abuse problems, which must also be treated; and 6. the stability of the adult's marriage (if applicable).

A national survey of pediatricians found that slightly less than half employed objective teacher and parent ratings to determine medication efficacy (Copeland, Wolraich, Lindgren, Milich, & Woolson, 1987). Copeland et al. proposed that an optimal medication dose be established within the context of a double-blind placebo-controlled assessment paradigm, including multiple measures collected across several settings. However, such an approach is often difficult, costly, and time consuming. A less conservative but certainly effective approach for children has been suggested. It includes several steps: 1. dosage sequences are prescribed in which the child receives one of several doses, including baseline with a week between each dose; 2. objective measures of treatment and response are collected across these conditions (e.g., classroom observation and work completed); 3. parent and teacher perceptions are evaluated for evidence of side effects; and 4. communication is maintained between the physician, the clinician, and teachers (S. Goldstein, 1995; S. Goldstein & Goldstein, 1990). With some modifications, this model can certainly be applied to adults, relying somewhat more, however, on the patient's own perceptions of medication effectiveness. Nevertheless, some effort should be made to collect observations about medication response from spouses, significant others, and, if feasible, employers.

Methylphenidate

Since most children receiving stimulant medication for ADHD behaviors receive methylphenidate, the research on this drug and its impact on childhood behavior will be the focus of this section. For an in-depth review on the use of methylphenidate to modify children's behavior, the reader is referred to Greenhill and Osman (1991).

MECHANISM OF ACTION

ADHD symptoms appear to decrease when children receive methylphenidate. Methylphenidate and other drugs used to treat ADHD have consistently been found to increase the amount of available catecholamines in the brain, thereby increasing the inhibitory effects of nerve cells served by these catecholamines (Hynd et al., 1991). There has been interest in the research literature, however, in localizing the effect of these catecholamines to specific parts of the brain. Lou et al. (1984) suggested that increased blood flow to the frontal lobes of the brain results from stimulant administration. These authors implied that methylphenidate works by making the planning centers (frontal lobes) of the brain more active and efficient. Zametkin et al. (1990) showed that adults with histories of ADHD in childhood manifested low glucose metabolism in parts of the frontal lobes. This abnormality was at least partly modified by methylphenidate. Moreover, brain metabolism research in females found further evidence of brain metabolism differences in the ADHD group (Ernst et al., 1994). Interestingly, in a population of adolescents with ADHD, these brain metabolic differences were noted in the female but not the male population. S. Goldstein and Goldstein (1990) reviewed the available literature on neurotransmitters and concluded that there is reason to believe that the stimulants produce at least a modest change in the catecholamines dopamine and noradrenaline. These neurotransmitters are produced in the central area of the brain (brain stem). Zametkin and Rapoport (1987) reviewed studies attempting to identify neuroanatomical and functional differences between the brains of children with ADHD and those of unaffected children. The hypotheses included disruptions in the function of the thalamus, hypothalamus, reticular activating system, locus coeruleus, caudate region, medial septum, hippocampus, and the nigrostriatal tract.

Semrud-Clickeman et al. (1994) reported additional data reflecting physiological and likely physical differences in the brains of children with ADHD. These authors found a smaller splenial area of the corpus callosum. They hypothesized that this smaller area may relate to commonly seen sustained attention deficits in children with ADHD. Further data reported by Giedd et al. (1994) added significantly to this body of research. In a study of boys with and without ADHD, two anterior regions of the corpus callosum, the rostrum and rostral body, were found to have significantly smaller areas in the ADHD group. These differences correlated in the expected direction with teacher and parent ratings of hyperactivity-impulsivity.

The exact means by which methylphenidate or other stimulants alleviate ADHD symptoms is unknown. The preponderance of the research literature more strongly suggests a chemical than a neuroanatomical effect. Certainly, medications used to modify ADHD symptoms affect the chemical systems of the brain and not the physical structures.

POSITIVE EFFECTS OF METHYLPHENIDATE ON BEHAVIOR

Ritalin is the brand name of the chemical generic methylphenidate. Methylphenidate is also used appropriately to treat narcolepsy (a rare disorder characterized by the irresistible urge to sleep) and geriatric depression. It is rarely if ever appropriate to use methylphenidate to help normal people stay awake or lose weight.

Methylphenidate reduces irrelevant movement during work situations (Cunningham & Barkley, 1979). Problems with aggression, disruptive classroom behavior, and noncompliance with teachers also improve. It has been suggested that effects on behavioral control and sustained attention are stronger at higher doses. Rapport and Kelly (1991) suggest the following doses for cognitive tasks: low doses of methylphenidate for tasks requiring quick responding, moderate doses for tasks involving vigilance and response inhibition, and higher doses for tasks requiring extended effort. A large volume of data also suggests improvements in academic productivity and accuracy among samples of children with ADHD treated with methylphenidate (Douglas, Barr, O'Neil, & Britton, 1986; Pelham, Bender, Caddell, Booth, & Moorer, 1985; Rapport et al., 1987, 1988). For many behaviors, the child with ADHD demonstrates improvement with methylphenidate to the point that he or she is indistinguishable from normal peers. DuPaul and Rapport (1993) reported that in a population of 31 children with ADHD treated with methylphenidate, measures of attention to task and academic efficiency improved to the point that their behavior no longer deviated statistically from that of the normal controls. When examined individually, however, only 75% of the children with ADHD showed normalized behavioral levels. Thus, the need for ancillary school-based interventions was eliminated for this group but not for the remaining 25% of methylphenidate-treated children.

Methylphenidate significantly improves the quality of children's social interactions with parents, teachers, and peers. Children's compliance with parent or teacher commands and responsiveness to others improves. Negative and off-task behaviors are reduced. Compliant situations resulted in a reduction in the frequency of commands by teachers and an increase in positive adult attention to child behavior (Barkley, Karlsson, Strzelecki, & Murphy, 1984; Whalen & Henker, 1980). Other researchers report improvements in peer relations. The child with ADHD treated with methylphenidate demonstrates a reduction in aggressive behavior that appears to result in greater peer acceptance (Cunningham, Siegel, & Offord, 1985; Pelham & Hoza, 1987; Whalen & Henker, 1980).

Cunningham, Siegel, and Offord (1991) thoroughly reviewed the research on the peer interactions of children treated with methylphenidate. They reported that the literature indicated that methylphenidate reduced aggressive behavior and controlling-negative interactions in both laboratory and community settings. These reductions in negative behaviors were readily detected by the other children. The trend in these data suggested that a reduction in these disruptive behaviors improved the social status of the child with ADHD. These authors concluded that methylphenidate significantly improved the quality of social interactions with parents, teachers, and peers.

In part, reports of improvement in social interactions may stem more from the reduction of inappropriate, disruptive behavior than from an increase in appropriate behavior. Methylphenidate has consistently been found to increase compliance with parent and teacher commands. Reduction in off-task behavior results in fewer negatively reinforcing interactions with adults. Reduction in aggressive, disruptive behavior leads to a greater degree of acceptance, whether or not these reductions coincide with an improvement in appropriate social behavior (Whalen & Henker, 1991). The data also suggest that methylphenidate-related improvements in social behavior are more easily observed in structured laboratory settings than in free play settings. There are also data to suggest that while the child with ADHD demonstrates marked reductions in disruptive behaviors, his or her social perception is unchanged (Milich & Okazaki, 1991).

Reduction in aggressive behavior has been a particular focus of the use of methylphenidate. In general, problems with disruptive, aggressive, and noncompliant behavior, principally with authority figures, are reduced with methylphenidate (DuPaul, Barkley, & McMurray, 1991). S. L. Kaplan, Busner, Kupietz, Wasserman, and Segal (1990) found that for six adolescent boys with aggressive conduct problems, methylphenidate significantly reduced aggressivity and hyperactivity. In a group of 11 aggressive, hyperactive children, methylphenidate suppressed nonphysical aggression in the classroom, and a moderate dose of medication decreased physical aggression and verbal aggression on the playground (Gadow, Nolan, Sverd, Sprafkin, & Paolicelli, 1990). This group of children received either a low (0.3 mg/kg) or a moderate (0.6 mg/kg) dose under double-blind conditions. The levels of appropriate social interaction on the high dose were the same or higher than on the placebo. Both doses of methylphenidate reduced the levels of motor activity, off-task behavior, noncompliance, and general disruptiveness.

Carlson, Pelham, Milich, and Dixon (1992) found that methylphenidate may in fact replace the need for behavior modification. Twenty-four boys in a summer program were treated with behavior modification, a token economy, time out, and a daily report card. This group was also provided with methylphenidate. A low dose of methylphenidate was approximately equivalent to these behavioral interventions in improving behavior and academic productivity. A combination of the behavioral interventions and the methylphenidate resulted in maximal behavioral improvement. However, the improvements this combination produced were nearly identical to those obtained with a slightly higher dose of methylphenidate alone. That methylphenidate treatment alone provides benefits close or equal to those obtained by a combination of methylphenidate and behavioral or cognitive interventions with children and adolescents has been found consistently (Abikoff & Klein, 1992). Nonetheless, multitreatment approaches continue to be the most popular with all age groups, with myriad unproven psychosocial interventions touted for adults (for a review, see S. Goldstein & Goldstein, 1995).

Some combined treatments have been found to produce added effect, however. W. F. Horn and Ialong (1988) made a strong case that single-modality treatment is generally not effective in dealing with the wide range of problems experienced by children with ADHD. While methylphenidate may in and of itself deal with the majority of ADHD problems, medicine alone is thought to be ineffective in dealing with the many related problems that disruptive children experience. These authors concluded that the failure of some researchers to find positive additive effects for stimulant medication and behavioral treatments (Abikoff & Klein, 1992; R. T. Brown, Borden, Wynne, Schleser, & Clingerman, 1986) may result from their exclusion of either the parent or child therapeutic component. As noted in Chapter 9, issues related to locus of control and self-esteem are important for all at-risk populations. Studies that have used medication together with a combination of behavior management and education for parents and children consistently report statistically positive results from treatment (Horn & Ialong, 1988; Satterfield et al., 1981). The findings of Carlson et al. (1992) and others, however, cannot be disregarded. Specifically, in classroom and home settings, methylphenidate alone at the appropriate dose appears to reduce disruptive ADHD behaviors as effectively as the combination of methylphenidate and behavioral interventions.

Based on a review of the available literature, S. Goldstein and Goldstein (1990) argued that problems with attention span are dealt with most effectively through the use of stimulant medication, problems with impulse control may require medication and behavior management, and academic achievement problems require both of those components and educational interventions. These authors suggested that this multitreatment approach is logical given a hypothesis that difficulty with attention span is primarily a physiological modulation problem. Difficulty with impulse control results from a combination of inattention, difficulty with inhibition, and a lack of higher cerebral problem-solving skills. Impulsivity and inattention can create or compound difficulties with scholastic achievement over time, resulting in the lack of an academic foundation on which to build further achievement.

Impact on the Family

Consistently, interactions between children with ADHD and their parents have been reported to improve dramatically and quickly with stimulant treatment. Schachar, Taylor, Weiselberg, Thorley, and Rutter (1987) described a group of 35 boys with attention deficit treated with methylphenidate. Eighteen were found to be methylphenidate responders. In this group, interactions between the child, his siblings, and his parents improved dramatically. The mothers of these children demonstrated increased maternal warmth, decreased maternal criticism, and greater frequency of maternal contact. Fewer negative sibling encounters were reported. These positive changes were not observed in the non–methylphenidate responders. Interestingly, in this study mothers reported significantly greater improvements than fathers. Methylphenidate responders also did not appear to be more likely to be isolated within the family, as previously reported by other authors (Barkley & Cunningham, 1979). The findings of increased maternal warmth and contact, increased positive encounters with siblings, and decreased maternal criticism in the families of children responding to methylphenidate led the authors to conclude that "methylphenidate treatment of the hyperactive child may be a useful means of initiating improvement in function in the family system and that families of children who respond to methylphenidate might be more amenable to other types of intervention than before this treatment" (Schachar et al., 1987, p. 731).

Similar improvement in interactions between children with attention deficit and their mothers was reported by Barkley et al. (1984) and Barkley (1988). In the first study, Barkley et al. found that "mothers decrease their control and negative behavior towards children during high dose conditions" (p. 750). This change resulted in reports of improved mother-child interactions. The effect was not related to the age of the child. Conners and Wells (1986) reported, however, that in many instances decreased negative parenting behavior was not associated with an increase in positive parenting behaviors for children treated with stimulants in a playroom setting. Barkley (1988) reported that 27 preschool children with attention deficit "decreased their off task and non-compliant behavior and significantly increased their rates of compliance as well as the length of sustained compliance with maternal commands while receiving methylphenidate" (p. 336). These studies suggest that stimulant treatment for ADHD consistently decreases negative parent behaviors, especially among mothers, and in some settings may lead to an increase in positive parent behaviors.

Effect on Self-Esteem

Though studies on self-esteem in children being given methylphenidate are few, P. C. Kelly, Cohen, Walker, Caskey, and Atkinson (1989) in a study of twenty-one 8–12-year-old children with ADD reported self-esteem improvements. Multimodal management, including 5–10 mg of methylphenidate twice daily, was used for treatment. Improved general as well as academic self-esteem as measured by the culture-free Self-Esteem Inventory for Children was seen for the 12 children in the long-term (average 16 months) follow-up group. No significant improvement in self-esteem was seen after only one month, however. The authors concluded that long-term multimodal management, including methylphenidate, appeared to improve self-esteem in children with attention deficit.

It has also been hypothesized that improved daily functioning exerts a long-term positive impact on self-esteem, locus of control, and receptivity to adult suggestions (S. Goldstein, 1995). Since improved daily interactions occur with methylphenidate and since easy temperament has been described as a powerful resilience factor (Werner, 1994), it would not be surprising if the daily improvements achieved with stimulant medication led to improved self-esteem as well.

Impact on Academic Skills

Barkley (1979), on reviewing 18 studies using 55 objective measures of scholastic achievement and productivity in children with hyperactivity, concluded that stimulants, principally methylphenidate, resulted in a positive impact on these variables of less than 17%. Thus, early studies did not find consistent positive effects on learning. Certainly, the impact of methylphenidate on disruptive behavior is much more dramatic than its impact on learning. This difference may occur for a number of reasons; for example, disruptive behavior is much easier to define operationally, observe, and measure immediately than are improvements in academic achievement. It is likely that earlier studies evaluating stimulant impact on achievement secondary to reductions in disruptive behavior did not find improvements because trials were too brief, dose response was poorly evaluated, individual differences affected group outcome data, children were not provided with instruction at optimal times during medication effectiveness, or compliance with medication administration was poor. More recent, better controlled studies have found improvements in academic achievement for children with ADHD receiving methylphenidate (Richardson, Kupietz, & Maitinsky, 1987). Concomitant research has yet to be generated at the postsecondary level.

In an extensive review of the literature related to the effects of methylphenidate on learning in children with attention disorder, J. M. Swanson, Cantwell, Lerner, McBurnett, and Hanna (1991) found that in well-controlled studies of academic productivity, stimulants improved the academic performance of children with ADHD on tasks designed to resemble classroom assignments. The effect was substantial (25%–40% improvement) and had been replicated across studies. Figure 13.1 shows the results from a well-controlled study demonstrating significantly better progress in reading grade equivalent for learning-impaired children with ADHD who were good responders to methylphenidate than for learning-impaired children with ADHD who were not good responders. Over a 28-week period the good responders made almost eight months more progress in reading grade equivalent (Richardson et al., 1987).

The preponderance of the data makes undeniable the fact that methylphenidate reduces disruptive behavioral problems. Does improvement in disruption alone result in a long-term beneficial effect on learning or academic achievement? This is still a subject of debate. J. M. Swanson et al. (1991) suggested there are two types of ADHD medication responders in terms of cognitive improvements: favorable and nonfavorable. The nonfavorable group is divided further into groups demonstrating adverse and nonsignificant cognitive responses. In empirical testing, favorable responders were defined as improving 25% or more on a simple cognitive laboratory task. Adverse responders were those in whom cognitive performance actually declined despite improvements in disruptive behaviors. Some researchers suggest that all stimulant responders demonstrate a general improvement in cognitive functioning. Balthazor, Wagner, and Pelham (1991) found that among 19 boys treated with methylphenidate, an improvement in academic processing occurred through general rather than specific aspects of information-processing skills. Thus it was not a specific skill, such as selective attention or retrieving name codes, that was responsible for the improvement in achievement but rather a generalized increase in cognitive efficiency. Forness, Cantwell, Swanson, Hanna, and Youpa (1991) found that methylphenidate improved reading comprehension for boys with ADHD and

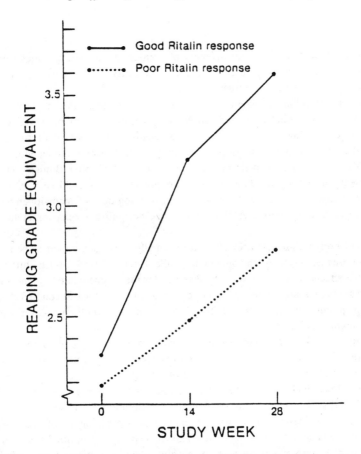

Figure 13.1   Reading grade scores of good and poor Ritalin responders

Note. From "What Is the Role of Academic Intervention in the Treatment of Hyperactive Children with Reading Disorders?" by E. Richardson, S. Kupietz, and S. Maitinsky, 1987, in *The Young Hyperactive Child: Answers to Questions about Diagnosis, Prognosis and Treatment* (p. 87), edited by J. Loney, New York: Haworth. Copyright 1987 by Haworth Press. Used with permission.

conduct disorder but not for boys with ADHD without conduct disorder. Only 4 of the 56 boys studied in each of the two groups met the discrepancy criteria for LD. When reading recognition and comprehension were studied, no significant medication effects were found in the attention-disordered group alone.

What is the clinician to make of this brief review of the literature on the impact of methylphenidate on learning? It is fair to conclude that—especially among populations of children and adolescents with comorbid ADHD and LD, or comorbid ADHD and conduct disorder, or all three—the stimulants indirectly produce improved academic achievement and not just performance. J. M. Swanson et al. (1991) concluded that when a higher than optimal dose of methylphenidate is administered, mild cognitive impairments on laboratory tasks occur for some children. These authors suggested that there are greater cognitive impairments with larger doses and raised the possibility that several lower doses spread across the day may negate this problem. For the clinician, observation of changes in behavior with methylphenidate must be accompanied by careful collection of data on quantity and quality of work completed.

Optimal Dosage

Clinicians know that there is a great diversity of opinion about the adjustment and optimal dosage of methylphenidate given to children and adolescents. Typical questions have involved dosage by weight, preset factors, target symptoms, and type of medication. These are all important issues for the clinician to understand. However, characteristics inherent in the child, or adult, may also be predictive of medication effect. For example, higher severity of inattentiveness, younger age, lower rates of comorbid problems, and higher intellectual ability have been posited as the best predictors of good methylphenidate response independent of dosage (Buitelaar, Van der Gaad, Swaab-Barneveld, & Kuiper, 1995). Further, Buitelaar et al. suggest that the benefits of methylphenidate treatment are greater among children 6–13 years of age than among younger children. In this study, a single 10 mg dose of methylphenidate was extremely effective in ameliorating ADHD symptoms, normalizing behavior at home and at school.

The issue of body weight has been studied repeatedly. It is not thought to be a significant predictor of dose response to methylphenidate (DuPaul et al., 1991; Rapport, DuPaul, & Kelly, 1989). Dosage effects, however, have been observed for methylphenidate in comorbid populations. For example, research with a group of children with ADHD and conduct disorder suggests that this population may require a higher dose of medication than children with ADHD alone (Cunningham et al., 1985).

Sprague and Sleator (1977) identified a 0.3 mg/kg dose of methylphenidate as optimal for children with ADHD. Clinically optimized improvements in laboratory tasks were reported by Kinsbourne and Swanson (1979) at a dose of 0.5 mg/kg. Rapport, DuPaul, Stoner, Birmingham, and Massey (1985) reviewed and evaluated dose response function for 12 children with ADHD and concluded that an absolute dose in milligrams was superior in addressing target behaviors than a relative dose provided in milligrams per kilogram of body weight. J. M. Swanson et al. (1991) found that in regard to cognitive response, the optimal dose of methylphenidate is obtained more effectively with an absolute dose than with one provided by body weight. Children in this study on an absolute dose of methylphenidate obtained positive responses with a wide variation in body weight. It is now consistently recommended that in clinical practice, the absolute dose method and not the milligram per kilogram dose method be used for methylphenidate (S. Goldstein & Goldstein, 1990).

For most areas of classroom functioning, including cognitive, social, and behavioral functioning, dose response effects have been linear, with higher doses leading to the greatest change. However, a child may show the greatest improvement in academic performance at a dose different from the one found optimal for a laboratory task emphasizing impulse control over sustained attention. Consistently, individual children have been found to vary with respect to behavior change across dosage (Douglas et al., 1986; Rapport et al., 1987, 1988). Some children exhibit a linear dose response, while others do not.

The greatest level of improvement has consistently been found to occur in the mid (10–15 mg) or high (20 mg) dosage of methylphenidate, for all ages (DuPaul & Rapport, 1993). Both attention and academic efficiency at these doses improve to near normal levels. Conduct improves more than any other behavior but still deviates somewhat from that observed in the normal group. In this study, the greatest overall level of change observed in attention and reduction in day-to-day variability and behavior occurred under the higher medication dosage.

The issue of dose response differences between primarily inattentive and primarily hyperactive-impulsive children with ADHD was addressed by Barkley, DuPaul, and McMurray (1991).

The children with ADHD-HI were rated as having more pervasive behavior problems at home and more serious conduct problems in the classroom. In laboratory testing this group showed problems with vigilance. The ADHD-I group appeared to be more impaired in retrieval of verbal information and were not as disruptive in the classroom. The ADHD-HI group was more likely to respond to methylphenidate than the other group. The ADHD-I group had a higher percentage of nonresponse (24%) or responding best at a lower dose of methylphenidate (35%).

S. Goldstein and Goldstein (1990) suggested a model to facilitate a physician's ability to identify the optimal dosage of methylphenidate. Initially, behaviors are targeted, operationally defined, and measured through questionnaires and direct observation. Target behaviors are those that have been found to respond to methylphenidate. A low dose of methylphenidate is administered, and behavioral observations are obtained daily and summarized weekly. As a result of these data, the physician decides which dose has the greatest overall effect on the target symptoms with the least side effects. In some situations a higher dose of methylphenidate will be prescribed in the morning than in the afternoon based on the pattern of target behaviors. The optimal dose of methylphenidate is determined logically, as the result of measurable rather than anecdotal data.

Negative and Side Effects

Negative and side effects are unwanted effects that medications may have on behavior or physical functioning while the medicine is effective or during withdrawal. For example, the development of a tic or obsessive behavior has been suggested as a side effect of psychotropic medications in some children (Borcherding, Keysor, Rapoport, Elia, & Amass, 1990). Few of the negative effects of methylphenidate treatment are behavioral effects. One of the most common negative behavioral effects observed is rebound irritability. As the child withdraws from methylphenidate, there is a period of increased activity and irritability. This is an effect of withdrawal rather than a direct side effect of the active substance. Although there are anecdotal reports of children becoming "zombie-like" or oversedated as the result of stimulants, large-scale side effect studies have not shown this phenomenon to be widespread.

Probably the most thorough evaluation of side effects was undertaken by Barkley, McMurray, Edelbrock, and Robbins (1990). These authors studied 83 children for 7–10 days at each of three conditions—placebo, low dose (0.3 mg/kg), and high dose (0.5 mg/kg)—with twice daily dosage and random selection for each of six medication orders. Measurable side effects included 1. decreased appetite with significantly increased dose; 2. insomnia, which increased from placebo to low dose but not significantly from low to high dose; 3. stomachaches, which increased significantly from placebo to low dose and again to high dose; and 4. headaches, which increased significantly from placebo to low dose but not from low to high dose. Nonsignificant changes included a tendency toward crying, tics and nervous movements, dizziness, drowsiness, nail biting, more talking, anxiety, lack of interest in others, euphoria, irritability, nightmares, sadness, and staring. These results are summarized in Table 13.1.

Waltonen et al. (1993) found a very similar pattern of side effects due to methylphenidate, including insomnia, decreased appetite, stomachache, headache, and dizziness. Decreased appetite was related to the level of dosage, with children being nearly twice as likely to have decreased appetite at a higher dose. The other symptoms did not appear to be dose related. In this study, daydreaming, irritability, anxiety, and nail biting actually decreased from pretreatment frequency with both low- and high-dose Ritalin therapy. No dose effect was noted for

Table 13.1   Placebo "Side Effects" and Ritalin

| Possible Side Effect | Drug Condition | | | | | |
| | Placebo | | Low Dose | | High Dose | |
	%	Sev.[a]	%	Sev.	%	Sev.
Decreased activity	15	0.4	52	1.8	56	2.6
Insomnia	40	1.5	62	2.7	68	3.1
Stomachaches	18	0.5	39	1.0	35	1.5
Headaches	11	0.3	26	0.6	21	0.8
Prone to crying	49	1.8	59	2.3	54	2.0
Tics and nervous movements	18	0.7	18	0.9	28	1.2
Nail biting	22	1.1	26	1.1	29	1.3
Talks excessively	16	0.4	20	0.6	22	0.9
Irritable	72	3.2	65	2.6	66	2.7
Sadness	43	1.6	48	1.9	41	1.8
Stares excessively	40	1.3	38	1.2	38	1.0

Note. Table reports percentage of 82 children with ADHD experiencing each side effect of Ritalin at two dose levels: low (0.3 mg/kg twice daily) and high (0.5 mg/kg twice daily). From "Side Effects of Methylphenidate in Children with Attention Deficit Hyperactivity Disorder: A Systematic, Placebo-Controlled Evaluation," by R. A. Barkley, M. B. McMurray, C. S. Edelbrock, and K. Robbins, 1990, *Pediatrics, 86,* p. 789. Used with permission.
[a]Sev. = Severity rating of this side effect using a scale from 0 (*not at all*) to 9 (*severe*)

anxiety. Age and sex of the child, methylphenidate response, and occurrence of side effects were not found to be significantly related. These authors also did not report an increase in either motor or vocal tics in this population of 234 children between 5 and 15 years of age. Clinicians must recognize that many of the behaviors typically associated with methylphenidate treatment have not been consistently reported in adults.

In summary, common side effects, when they occur, include appetite reduction while the medicine is active and insomnia, with occasional increased irritability, headaches, stomachaches, and, in rare cases, motor and vocal tics (DuPaul et al., 1991). Similar data have yet to be consistently generated in adults receiving methylphenidate. As noted, rebound irritability is a common effect and appears to occur in approximately one-third of children treated with methylphenidate. It is an effect of withdrawal from the active substance. The magnitude of rebound, however, varies considerably from one day to the next for individual children. Late afternoon administration of an additional, at times lower, dose of methylphenidate has been found to be effective in reducing the severity of rebound behaviors.

Other concerns have been raised about methylphenidate. One pressing issue is whether the use of methylphenidate causes already impaired children to be at greater risk for substance abuse or drug addiction. DuPaul et al. (1991) stated the case very strongly when they argued that viewing drug addiction, depression, and other emotional difficulties as side effects of methylphenidate has "no basis in the empirical literature and [they] should not be considered as viable treatment risks" (p. 210). Although there is a trend toward tobacco, alcohol, and substance abuse among children with comorbid ADHD and conduct disorder, there have been no controlled studies suggesting that methylphenidate is a moderator variable responsible for this trend (Fischer, Barkley, Edelbrock, & Smallish, 1990). In fact, the opposite has been suggested (for a review, see Barkley, 1990b; S. Goldstein & Goldstein, 1990).

There has been concern that methylphenidate slows growth and eventually suppresses height in treated children. Studies of the long-term use of methylphenidate, however, have not found this to be a consistent trend. Growth suppression occurs in relation to dose during the first year of treatment (Greenhill, 1984; Mattes & Gittelman, 1983). A recovery in growth following discontinuation of treatment or habituation to this effect seems to occur thereafter, with little appreciable alteration in eventual adult height and weight predicted prior to methylphenidate initiation (Greenhill, 1984). Reviews of long-term follow-up studies of children treated with methylphenidate have failed to find significant negative effects on height or weight (for a review, see S. Goldstein & Goldstein, 1990; Greenhill & Osman, 1991).

Although Safer, Allen, and Barr (1972) suggested that the discontinuation of methylphenidate over the summer might allow increased weight and height gain, the evidence for this once popular belief is limited. In fact, it has consistently been dextroamphetamine, not methylphenidate, that has been found to decrease height and weight growth over the short term. Furthermore, the significant rebound of growth with discontinuation of methylphenidate over the summer initially reported was not replicated in a later study by these same authors (Safer & Allen, 1973). The American Academy of Pediatrics (1987) Committee on Drugs Report summarized the available information and reported, "There was fear that stimulant medications would lead to growth retardation; however, growth suppression is only minimally related to stimulant dosage. Results of the study indicate that no growth suppression occurred in doses of methylphenidate up to 0.8 mg/kg during a prolonged period" (p. 759).

Despite the data, the misconception persists that stimulant medications can and regularly do cause growth and weight suppression and that discontinuation over the summer prevents this problem. The available data suggest that children treated with stimulants, primarily dextroamphetamine, may have a transient decrease in weight and may have slightly slowed growth for a period lasting two to three years. Studies do not demonstrate a risk of long-term effects on height and weight. Nevertheless, clinicians must recognize that there are likely individual children whose stature is initially short and who may be affected, at the very least, in the short term. The decision to use methylphenidate or other stimulants to modify behavior, however, should not be based on the unproven hypothesis that methylphenidate treatment results in long-term decreases in height or weight.

Concern exists that methylphenidate may induce motor or vocal tics in children. Multiple motor tics associated with one or more vocal tics are the criteria for Gilles de la Tourette's syndrome. Tourette's syndrome is a combination of recurrent, involuntary, repetitive, rapid, purposeless motor and vocal movements. Age at onset is between 2 and 15 years, and the tics must be present for more than one year before the diagnosis can be made (APA, 1994). The peak onset of the disorder is five years of age, with the age at onset usually between four and nine years (McDaniel, 1986). Severity of the disorder is variable. Vocal outbursts and coprolalia characterize some of the more severe cases. Individuals with Tourette's syndrome manifest a higher incidence of other disruptive and nondisruptive disorders. One-half of children diagnosed with Tourette's syndrome are treated for ADHD symptoms one to two years before their first tic appears (G. S. Golden, 1977; E. A. K. Shapiro, 1989). Children and adolescents with Tourette's syndrome also appear prone to obsessions and compulsions. In approximately one-third of these children, this pattern progresses by young adolescence to a full-blown obsessive/

compulsive disorder. The *Physician's Desk Reference* (1995) recommends that if a child manifests a tic or if there is a family history of tics or Tourette's syndrome, stimulant treatment is contraindicated. If a child, while treated with methylphenidate develops a tic, physicians usually discontinue the medication. However, the relationship between methylphenidate and tics is not clearly understood. Since ADHD presents in a significant group of children prone to Tourette's syndrome, it is not surprising that there are children with ADHD who begin demonstrating tics after methylphenidate is initiated. The consensus among researchers is that methylphenidate does not cause Tourette's syndrome but might accelerate the onset of symptoms if the treated child is at risk. Barkley (1988) in a large-scale study found that 1 out of 100 children develop a visible motor or vocal tic when treated with methylphenidate. Nineteen out of 20 of these children demonstrate a cessation in tics when the methylphenidate is discontinued. In possibly the most extensive study of tics associated with methylphenidate, Denckla, Bemporad, and MacKay (1976) reported that among more than 1,500 children treated with methylphenidate, 20 developed tics (1.3%). One out of these 20 cases proceeded to develop Tourette's syndrome, even when the stimulant was withdrawn. Onset of Tourette's syndrome has also been associated with other stimulants, including pemoline (Bachman, 1981; Mitchell & Matthews, 1980). For approximately 1 out of 2,000 children treated with stimulants, the tics remain when medication is discontinued and progress to Tourette's syndrome.

One study that watched children closely for development of minor tics and compulsive behavior found that 70% of children treated with moderate doses of methylphenidate developed tics and almost 50% developed compulsive behaviors (Borcherding et al., 1990). However, in this inpatient study, only one child in the population developed symptoms severe enough to require cessation of the medication. For the majority of these children, these symptomatic side effects were seen only on close observation. It is essential that clinicians help others become sensitive to the definition and types of tic behaviors. Observation for tics should be part of the protocol for evaluating the modification in children's behavior when methylphenidate is introduced.

Erenberg, Cruse, and MacKay (1985) studied 200 children with Tourette's syndrome. Of the 200 studied, 48 had received stimulants at some time. Nine had been treated with stimulants before the onset of their tics. Only 4 were still receiving stimulants when tics began. Therefore, only 4 of the 200 manifested their first symptoms of Tourette's syndrome while they were taking stimulant medications. Thirty-nine of the children had tics before their treatment with stimulant medication. Of these 39 children, 11 demonstrated worsening of tics on stimulant medication, 26 had no change in their tics when treated with stimulants, and 2 actually experienced improvement. Obviously, the relationship of tics to stimulants is far from clear at this time. Gadow, Nolan, and Sverd (1992) in double-blind treatment of 11 prepubertal boys with ADHD and tic disorder found that methylphenidate not only reduced hyperactive, disruptive behaviors in the classroom and aggression in the lunchroom and on the playground but also reduced the occurrence of vocal tics. Only one boy experienced an exacerbation of motor tics with the stimulant. Methylphenidate was also found to reduce tics compared with initial placebo treatment in a group of four boys with Tourette's syndrome and ADHD (Sverd, Gadow, & Paolicelli, 1989). Clinical ratings and playroom observations showed clear improvements in ADHD symptoms for these boys treated with methylphenidate. Sverd et al. (1989) concluded that tic frequency in this population of boys was unrelated to methylphenidate and that the methylphenidate was clearly effective in treating this group of children with comorbid ADHD.

Gadow, Nolan, Sprafkin, and Sverd (1995) added to their studies of comorbid tic disorder in ADHD treatment with stimulants by evaluating 34 prepubertal children with ADHD and tic disorder. Three doses of methylphenidate, 0.1, 0.3, and 0.5 mg/kg, were evaluated twice daily for two weeks under double-blind conditions. There were no nonresponders in this study. Marked reductions in hyperactive, disruptive, and aggressive behavior were evident even at the low dose. Findings supported the conclusion that methylphenidate suppresses ADHD behaviors in the classroom and aggressive behavior in all settings. It was also found that a low dose of stimulant may weakly exacerbate the frequency of motor tics, but the majority of this group of children did not experience clinically significant tic worsening with methylphenidate.

The data suggest that methylphenidate can bring out latent symptoms of Tourette's syndrome in children who might eventually develop these symptoms without stimulant medication. It has not been proved that methylphenidate is a primary cause of Tourette's syndrome. Therefore, it is prudent to summarize the available information by stating that methylphenidate is rarely, if ever, a primary cause of Tourette's syndrome. As of this writing there are no available data on the onset of tics in adults treated with stimulants.

The *Physician's Desk Reference* warns that the use of methylphenidate carries with it a risk of epileptic seizures. Adequate information is not available to allow accurate determination of the likelihood that seizures will result from the dosages of methylphenidate commonly used to treat ADHD. What increased risk, if any, is present in children or adults with histories of epilepsy, family history of epilepsy, or abnormal EEG is unknown. It should be noted, however, that seizures were not a reported side effect in an extensive review by Barkley (1976) of over 2,000 reported cases of children with hyperkinetic symptoms treated with stimulants. Thus, the available information indicates that the risk of epileptic seizures resulting from methylphenidate treatment for ADHD, if it exists at all, is quite low. H. Feldman, Crumrine, Handen, Alvin, and Teodori (1989) found that in 10 children being treated with a single antiepileptic drug for seizures who also demonstrated symptoms of ADHD, methylphenidate was associated with significant improvements in disruptive behavior. There were no significant changes in eliptiform features or background activity on EEGs and no alterations in antiepileptic drug levels. These authors concluded that methylphenidate may be a safe and effective treatment for certain children with seizures and concurrent ADHD.

It has also been reported that methylphenidate, when used in a population of young adults with post-traumatic seizures and disruptive behavior, led to improvements. All but two of this population were also receiving anticonvulsants. This group demonstrated behavioral improvements with methylphenidate, and interestingly a lesser incidence of seizure activity was noted during methylphenidate administration (Wroblewski, Leary, Phelan, & Whyte, 1992).

Issues Related to Methylphenidate Administration

Time course. As with all medications affecting behavior, an understanding of time course—time of onset, time period for optimal effect, and withdrawal effect—is critical in evaluating medication benefits. Typically, methylphenidate has little effect during the first half-hour following administration. By the end of the first hour, its benefits can often be clearly observed. The greatest or peak effectiveness for methylphenidate is reached between one and two hours following administration and continues in most children for a period of two to three hours. There is a gradual loss of effectiveness over the next one to two hours. Thus, standard methylphenidate has a positive impact for most children lasting between three and five hours. Some children have exaggerated problems four to eight hours after medication administration. As previously discussed, this is considered a withdrawal or rebound effect. Given these data, the optimal time to evaluate methylphenidate benefits is approximately two to three hours after administration.

Given the short action of methylphenidate, most children require a second dose during the typical six-hour school day. Physicians often routinely have the second dose administered four hours after the morning dose. Data obtained at school, however, show that some children may not need a second dose of medication, while others experience a period of withdrawal causing rebound irritability when the initial dose wears off before the second dose takes effect. Many families use a third, often smaller, dose of methylphenidate after school to facilitate homework and evening routine. A third dose of methylphenidate has been found to be effective in reducing afternoon behavioral problems for this population (Barkley, 1990b). As noted, the magnitude of rebound irritability varies considerably from day to day for individual children (Johnston, Pelham, Hoza, & Sturges, 1987). S. Goldstein and Goldstein (1990) recommend titrating dosage individually for each time of the day to determine the most effective levels. For reasons that are not well understood, some children require the same dosage at every administration while others demonstrate similar behavioral improvements with smaller second and third doses during the day.

Clinicians must realize that the duration of medication effect is not the same for all children. As noted, for some children methylphenidate loses its effectiveness before the typical four-hour period. For others, a single dose may be effective throughout the entire school day. This phenomenon may exist among adults as well.

Because appetite suppression is a consistent side effect for many children, methylphenidate may cause appetite suppression at lunch. Clinicians should counsel parents and school personnel not to be alarmed if a child treated with methylphenidate is not interested in eating lunch. Often reporting this to the physician will allow him or her to adjust the amount or timing of the dose of methylphenidate, which may improve the child's appetite.

Change of dosage with time and weight. Even as children with ADHD grow older the dosage of methylphenidate that appears to be beneficial remains fairly constant into adulthood. In fact, adjusting methylphenidate dosage to a child's weight has been found to lead to overdosage (Safer & Allen, 1989). While the effective dose of methylphenidate may increase slightly as children become older, it does not increase as fast as children's height and weight do. It has been consistently suggested based on reviews of the literature that the most effective way of determining the optimal beneficial dose of methylphenidate for behavior is to observe children in a natural setting (Barkley, 1990b; S. Goldstein & Goldstein, 1990).

Sustained-release methylphenidate. Sustained-release methylphenidate was developed to provide beneficial effects over an eight-hour rather than four-hour period by releasing the substance into the body slowly. Clinical reports suggest that this preparation of methylphenidate does not improve behavior as much as two equal doses four hours apart. There have been a number of research studies addressing this issue, but unfortunately, taken together, the results are inconclusive.

Whitehouse, Shah, and Palmer (1980) evaluated 30 children between 6 and 14 years of age with attention deficit. Standard methylphenidate was effective in controlling ADHD symptoms in all of these children. Sixteen of the children were given sustained-release methylphenidate over a two-week period. There was no significant overall difference in reports of behavioral improvements and reduction in conduct problems between the sustained-release group and the standard methylphenidate group. However, the second group demonstrated fewer adverse reactions than the first.

In a group of 13 boys treated with placebo, methylphenidate, or sustained-release methylphenidate, no statistical differences were found between the effects of the two active substances. Both resulted in improvements well beyond those reported with placebo. However, as in the Whitehouse et al. (1980) study, there appeared to be more children demonstrating adverse effects to the sustained-release preparation than to the standard preparation. Pelham and Hoza (1987) also suggested, based on time course data for this population, that the standard methylphenidate produced the greater effect earlier in the day but that the sustained-release and regular preparation were equally effective by the end of the day. Dosage was certainly an issue in all of these studies. In this study, a 20 mg dose of sustained-release methylphenidate was compared with a twice daily 10 mg dose of regular preparation.

Birmaher, Greenhill, Cooper, Fired, and Maminski (1989) provided pharmacokinetic data in part consistent with Pelham and Hoza's behavioral observation. The sustained-release preparation appeared to take longer to reach maximum plasma levels. Moreover, it did not reach the same maximum concentration as an identical dose of standard methylphenidate, nor did the blood level concentration last for an eight-hour period. The latter finding is consistent with clinical observations that for a significant group of children, the sustained-release preparation was not as beneficial as two doses of the regular preparation.

Finally, Fitzpatrick, Klorman, Brumaghim, and Borgstedt (1992) evaluated 19 children 6–11 years of age, comparing a 20 mg dose of sustained-release methylphenidate with a twice daily 10 mg dose of standard methylphenidate. Multiple measures of academic and behavioral performance were evaluated, including CPTs, paired associate learning, and evoked responses. Trials of each preparation and placebo lasted two weeks. Both medications were found to be significantly more effective than placebo. Statistical differences between the two preparations were not observed.

The studies described above had several shortcomings. The time on medication observed was very short (at most, two weeks), and no attempts were made to adjust dosage even though all of these studies used fairly low doses of methylphenidate. Individual dosage adjustment and longer trials may well demonstrate significant differences between these two preparations. Moreover, a lack of statistical difference is not the same as demonstrating that the two preparations are equivalent. Subjective judgments, when presented, show substantial differences in both benefits and side effects that were rarely reflected quantitatively. A study allowing for dosage adjustment and allowing children to take each preparation for a longer period of time could well demonstrate substantial differences between the sustained-release and the standard preparation similar to those observed in clinical practice. Certainly, a larger scale study evaluating 100 rather than 15 children is needed.

It has been recommended that standard methylphenidate be titrated dose by dose initially, except when administering a noontime dose at school is not possible, for example, because an adult is not available to dispense the medication as required by law in many states (DuPaul et al. 1991; S. Goldstein & Goldstein, 1990). After a dose-by-dose titration is determined using brand-name methylphenidate, a trial of a sustained-release preparation can be attempted if necessary. Further, once baseline improvements are observed using the brand-name preparation, a trial of generics may be considered if finances are an issue. Observations from clinical practice indicate that most families prefer the regular preparation to the sustained-release preparation despite the inconvenience of extra doses. In fact, it is the authors' experience that even when the sustained-release preparation is used, a noontime dose is often administered as well.

METHYLPHENIDATE WITH SPECIAL POPULATIONS

Preschoolers

According to the guidelines of the Food and Drug Administration, methylphenidate is not recommended for children under six years of age. A higher likelihood of side or unwanted effects and a lower likelihood of positive effects have been reported for this population. Conners (1975a) and Schlieper et al. (1975) found the effectiveness of methylphenidate relative to placebo with preschool children with hyperactive symptoms to be less dramatic, consistent, and positive than with older children. Conners (1975a) did not report significant or serious side effects in this preschool population and suggested that methylphenidate may be an effective treatment for preschoolers. Schlieper et al. (1975), however, observed more side effects in this population than in the older population, including irritability and solitary play. These authors recommended that methylphenidate not be considered as a treatment for preschoolers because of the side effects.

The use of stimulants in children under the age of six has not been well studied in general. One cannot state with certainty the likelihood of positive effects or negative side effects in this age group. Further studies are needed to produce additional information for this group. S. B. Campbell (1985) cautions that the use of stimulants or other psychotropic medications with preschoolers should be considered only in extreme cases, with careful monitoring and close supportive work with the child's family.

Adolescents

The preponderance of the data suggests that symptoms of ADHD continue and for some intensify in the adolescent years (Barkley, Fischer, et al., 1990; Evans & Pelham, 1991; Gittelman et al., 1985; Satterfield et al., 1982; G. Weiss & Hechtman, 1986). The need to continue medication is often a source of disagreement, however, between the adolescent and his or her parents. Often the adolescent says that he "does not need" the medication, that it makes no difference in his grades or social relationships. Although this observation is sometimes accurate, more often when the medication is discontinued, a marked deterioration in classroom behavior and productivity quickly becomes apparent to everyone, though sometimes not to the adolescent.

Klorman, Brumaghim, Fitzpatrick, and Borgstedt (1990) evaluated 48 adolescents with ADHD, 12–18 years of age, treated for the first time with methylphenidate. Parent and teacher ratings of hyperactivity, inattention, and oppositionality dropped significantly over a three-week period. Even the adolescents rated themselves on clinical measures as improved and reported elevated subjective mood. Comorbid problems related to conduct or oppositional disorder did not appear to impair medication benefits, nor did present or past internalizing symptoms related to depression. Korman et al. (1990) concluded that "these results support the continued effectiveness of stimulant therapy for attention deficit disorder in adolescents. However, the magnitude of clinical effectiveness reported was smaller than previously found in younger patients" (p. 702).

Other authors, however, have demonstrated that the effects of methylphenidate are as dramatic in adolescents as in younger children. A series of studies by Pelham and colleagues found methylphenidate to be as efficacious with adolescents as with younger children when effects were measured during a summer treatment program using a classroom format (Pelham et al., 1985, 1990; Pelham, Walker, Sturges, & Hoza, 1989). This series of studies found improvements in grades and class work with modest doses of methylphenidate.

Often, a critical task for the clinician is to help the adolescent with ADHD recognize and accept that the disability has a negative effect on classroom functioning and behavior. A number of print (H. C. Parker, 1992) and multimedia (S. Goldstein, 1991) resources are available to facilitate this part of the consultation process. Encouraging the adolescent with ADHD to be active in data collection and medication trials often results in positive acceptance of the need for medication and active participation in medication use.

Autistic Children

The use of methylphenidate targeted specifically at the disruptive symptoms of autistic children may run a higher risk of adverse side effects. Cantwell and Baker (1987b) suggested that treating some autistic children with methylphenidate may further narrow an already narrow attention span. This finding, however, was disputed by Strayhorn, Rapp, Donina, and Strain (1988). Strayhorn et al. presented a case of a six-year-old autistic boy treated with methylphenidate and concluded that the negative effects on mood and tantrums were outweighed by the positive effects on attention, activity, destructive behavior, and stereotypic movements. This single case study failed to support statements that stimulants are contraindicated for autistic children.

Improvement in a group of autistic children with methylphenidate treatment was also reported by Birmaher, Quintana, and Greenhill (1988). Eight of the nine children studied showed significant improvement on all rating scales. No major side effects or worsening of stereotypic movements were seen.

Intellectually Handicapped Children

It has been suggested that as many as 10%–20% of intellectually handicapped children and adults receive psychotropic medications for behavioral problems (Cullinan, Epstein, & Lloyd, 1983). In a thorough review of the literature on psychopathology and psychopharmacologic treatment of the intellectually handicapped, Bregman (1991) reported that most psychopharmacologic agents prescribed to the intellectually handicapped are used entirely to reduce disruptive behaviors, principally those involving aggression, hyperactivity, and stereotypies. These studies reported that 95% of treated children respond to medication, demonstrating moderate to substantial improvement in clinical symptoms. Across studies, clinical response does not appear to be affected by the presence of a particular psychiatric diagnosis. However, as Aman and Singh (1988) noted, there continues to be marked weakness, particularly in regard to methodological soundness and diagnostic rigor, in available psychopharmacologic studies with the intellectually handicapped.

Intellectually handicapped children have been considered candidates for stimulant medication to improve both cognitive functioning and behavior. Gillberg, Persson, Grufman, and Temner (1986) report that approximately 10%–20% of intellectually handicapped children exhibit developmentally inappropriate degrees of hyperactivity, inattention, and impulsivity, warranting an additional diagnosis of ADD. Although there have been few systematic studies addressing the benefits of stimulants with this population, the available research suggests that intellectually handicapped children with ADD benefit to some extent from stimulant treatment

(Gadow, 1985). Gadow also reported that approximately 7.5% of mildly intellectually handicapped children were receiving stimulant medication, a rate considerably higher than the approximately less than 1% of the intellectually normal population receiving stimulant treatment.

Earlier studies of the effects of stimulants on cognitive functioning for the intellectually handicapped did not yield positive results (Cutler et al., 1940). Payton, Burkhart, Hersen, and Helsel (1988) reported on three male children with intellectual handicap and ADHD treated with methylphenidate. These authors found that excessive movement was reduced and on-task behavior increased in these three children in response to methylphenidate.

More recent research has attempted to evaluate the effects of methylphenidate on a select population of intellectually handicapped individuals who in comparison to their developmental level exhibit an excess of symptoms consistent with ADHD (Helsel, Hersen, & Lubetsky, 1989). Helsel et al. reported an idiosyncratic response to dosage level and negative changes in social behavior, resulting in increased social isolation. They suggested that this idiosyncratic response may reflect observational difficulty in accurately differentiating attention deficit from other deficits caused by the intellectual handicap. In a study of 27 mildly intellectually handicapped children, rates of irritability, anxiety, moodiness, and activity decreased significantly when the children were treated with methylphenidate (Handen, Feldman, Gosling, Breaux, & McAuliffe, 1991). However, in six children methylphenidate was discontinued when motor tics or symptoms of severe social withdrawal appeared. These data suggest that intellectually handicapped children with ADHD symptoms may be more likely to develop side effects to methylphenidate than are non–intellectually handicapped children with ADHD.

A study of 12 mildly intellectually handicapped children with ADHD treated with methylphenidate found that 75% demonstrated improved behavior in the classroom (Handen, Breaux, Gosling, Ploof, & Feldman, 1990). Significant increases were noted in work output, on-task behavior, and general attention in the classroom. No significant increases in appropriate social interactions during free play were noted. These authors went so far as to conclude from this limited study that children with intellectual handicaps and comorbid ADHD respond to methylphenidate at a similar rate and in a similar domain to non-intellectually handicapped children with ADHD.

Twenty-seven children with below-average intellectual functioning and ADHD or conduct disorder were treated with methylphenidate and thioridazine by Aman, Marks, Turbott, Wilsher, and Merry (1991). Methylphenidate improved accuracy on a memory task, reduced omission errors on an attention task, and reduced seat movements in the classroom. These authors concluded that the methylphenidate was likely to enhance sustained attention and motivation in appropriately selected children with ADHD and mild intellectual handicaps.

Finally, Handen et al. (1992) administered methylphenidate to 14 children with mild intellectual handicap and ADHD. Sixty-four percent of this population were methylphenidate responders based on objective measures in the classroom. Significant gains in on-task behavior were noted in comparison to placebo. Again, as noted in earlier studies, there were no improvements in social interaction or on measures of learning.

Children with Bipolar Disorder

While it is accepted that a small group of children suffer from bipolar depressive disorder, this condition is not well understood and no clearly defined set of diagnostic criteria exist for children. G. A. Carlson, Rapport, Kelly, and Pataki (1992) reported on seven psychiatrically hospitalized children with ADHD and bipolar disorder. These children were treated with a combination of methylphenidate and lithium. Clinical observation found that neither the methylphenidate nor the lithium alone significantly improved or worsened classroom symptoms of hyperactivity and inattention. Together, however, the two medications appeared to act synergistically to improve performance on a learning task and to improve behavioral measures of attention. As G. A. Carlson et al. (1992) noted, lithium treatment alone for children with ADHD and comorbid depressive disorders tends to worsen performance on cognitive tasks and behavioral ratings compared with initial placebo levels but not at a statistically significant rate. Recent preliminary research suggests that stimulants may act as short-term, fast-acting antidepressants when used in conjunction with other medications (Gwirtsman, Szuba, Toren, & Feist, 1994).

Other Stimulants

Information on other drugs that affect behavior will be briefly reviewed, divided into sections on treatment benefits, dosage and time course, side effects, and related issues. Since the majority of disruptive behaviors treated are either directly related to ADHD or frequently occur comorbidly with ADHD, Table 13.2 contains a summary chart of the most common medications used to treat ADHD symptoms.

DEXTROAMPHETAMINE

Dextroamphetamine (Dexedrine) is used to treat the same disorders as methylphenidate.

Benefits. The potential benefits of dextroamphetamine are similar to those described for methylphenidate. Studies of dextroamphetamine in children are reviewed in S. Goldstein and Goldstein (1990). It was estimated in a large epidemiologic study that approximately 3% of children with ADHD received dextroamphetamine (Safer & Krager, 1988).

Dosage and time course. In general, the milligram dosage of dextroamphetamine used to treat ADHD is approximately 50% that of methylphenidate (*Physician's Desk Reference,* 1993). Ten milligrams of methylphenidate may have the same effect as a 5 mg tablet of dextroamphetamine. Dextroamphetamine also comes in a sustained-release tablet (Dexedrine Spansule) of 5, 10, or 15 mg. There have not been enough studies to determine whether dextroamphetamine spansules are more effective than regular dextroamphetamine.

Side effects. The side effects of dextroamphetamine are similar to those of methylphenidate. As previously noted, negative impact on height and weight may be greater with dextroamphetamine than methylphenidate.

METHAMPHETAMINE

Methamphetamine (Desoxyn) is similar to methylphenidate in its effects and is used to treat similar disorders.

Benefits. Methamphetamine has potential benefits similar to methylphenidate. It has been only minimally studied in children.

Table 13.2 Medications to Treat Attention Deficit Disorders

Drug	Form	Dosing	Common Side Effects	Duration of Behavioral Effects	Pros	Precautions
Ritalin (methylphenidate)	Tablet 5 mg 10 mg 20 mg	Start with a morning dose of 5 mg/day and increase up to 0.3–0.7 mg/kg of body weight. 2.5–60 mg/day[a]	Insomnia, decreased appetite, weight loss, headache, irritability, stomachache	3–4 hours	Works quickly (within 30–60 minutes); effective in 70% of patients; good safety record	Not recommended in patients with marked anxiety, motor tics, or family history of Tourette's syndrome
Ritalin-SR (methylphenidate)	Tablet 20 mg	Start with a morning dose of 20 mg and increase up to 0.3–0.7 mg/kg of body weight. Sometimes 5 or 10 mg standard tablet added in morning for quick start. Up to 60 mg/day[a]	Insomnia, decreased appetite, weight loss, headache, irritability, stomachache	About 7 hours	Particularly useful for adolescents with ADHD to avoid noontime dose; good safety record	Slow onset of action (1–2 hours); not recommended in patients with marked anxiety, motor tics, or family history of Tourette's syndrome
Dexedrine (dextroamphetamine)	Tablet 5 mg Spansule 5 mg 10 mg 15 mg Elixir	Start with a morning dose of 5 mg and increase up to 0.3–0.7 mg/kg of body weight. Give in divided doses 2–3 times per day. 2.5–40 mg/day[a]	Insomnia, decreased appetite, weight loss, headache, irritability, stomachache	3–4 hours (tablet) 8–10 hours (spansule)	Works quickly (within 30–60 minutes); may avoid noontime dose in spansule form; good safety record	Not recommended in patients with marked anxiety, motor tics, or family history of Tourette's syndrome

Cylert (pemoline)	Tablet (long acting) 18.75 mg 37.5 mg 75 mg 37.5 mg chewable	Start with a dose of 18.75–37.5 mg and increase up to 112.5 mg as needed in a single morning dose. 18.75–112.5 mg/day[a]	Insomnia, agitation, headaches, stomachaches; infrequently, abnormal liver function tests have been reported	12–24 hours	Given only once a day	May take 2–4 weeks for clinical response; regular blood tests needed to check liver function
Tofranil (imipramine hydrochloride)	Tablet 10 mg 25 mg 50 mg	Start with a dose of 10 mg in evening if weight <50 lb and increase 10 mg every 3–5 days as needed. Start with a dose of 25 mg in evening if weight is >50 lb and increase 25 mg every 3–5 days as needed. Give in single or divided doses, morning and evening. 25–150 mg/day[a]	Dry mouth, decreased appetite, headache, stomachache, dizziness, constipation, mild tachycardia	12–24 hours	Helpful for ADHD patients with comorbid depression or anxiety; lasts throughout the day	May take 2–4 weeks for clinical response; to detect preexisting cardiac conduction defect, a baseline ECG may be recommended; discontinue gradually

Table 13.2   (Continued)

Drug	Form	Dosing	Common Side Effects	Duration of Behavioral Effects	Pros	Precautions
Norpramin (desipramine hydrochloride)	Tablet 10 mg 25 mg 50 mg 75 mg 100 mg 150 mg	Start with a dose of 10 mg in evening if weight <50 lb and increase 10 mg every 3–5 days as needed. Start with a dose of 25 mg in evening if weight is >50 lb and increase 25 mg every 3–5 days as needed. Give in single or divided doses, morning and evening. 25–150 mg/day[a]	Dry mouth, decreased appetite, headache, stomachache, dizziness, constipation, mild tachycardia	12–24 hours	Helpful for ADHD patients with comorbid depression or anxiety; lasts throughout day	May take 2–4 weeks for clinical response; to detect preexisting cardiac conduction defect, a baseline ECG may be recommended; discontinue gradually
Catapres (clonidine hydrochloride)	Tab .1 mg .2 mg .3 mg Patch TTS-1 TTS-2 TTS-3	Start with a dose of .025–.05 mg/day in evening and increase by similar dose every 3–7 days as needed. Give in divided doses 3–4 times per day. .15–.3 mg/day[a]	Sleepiness, hypotension, headache, dizziness, stomachache, nausea, dry mouth, localized skin reactions with patch	3–6 hours (oral form) 5 days (skin patch)	Helpful for ADHD patients with comorbid tic disorder or severe hyperactivity or aggression	Sudden discontinuation could result in rebound hypertension; to avoid daytime tiredness starting dose given at bedtime and increased slowly

Note. From *Medication and Classroom Guide,* by H. C. Parker, 1993, Plantation, FL: Impact Publications.

[a]Daily dosage rate.

Dosage and time course. Methamphetamine has a similar time course to methylphenidate. Often the milligram dosage is approximately 50% that of methylphenidate, so that 5 mg of methamphetamine may have the same effect as 10 mg of methylphenidate (*Physician's Desk Reference,* 1993). Methamphetamine also comes in a time-release Gradumate form. This form may last twice as long as regular methamphetamine, but there have not been enough studies to determine whether the time-release form of methamphetamine is as effective as two doses of regular methamphetamine.

Side effects. The side effects of methamphetamine are similar to those of methylphenidate.

PEMOLINE

Pemoline (Cylert) is used to treat ADHD.

Benefits. Pemoline has positive effects, and side effects, similar to those of other stimulants (Pelham, Swanson, Bender, & Wilson, 1980). It has been estimated that fewer than 6% of children with ADHD who are medically treated receive pemoline (Safer & Krager, 1988). Pemoline is a long-acting stimulant often given once a day for ADHD symptoms. This dosage has the benefit of avoiding a noontime dose at school. In clinical settings, however, most children receiving pemoline take a second dose (Collier et al., 1985). In Collier et al.'s study, the treatment of 70% of the children taking pemoline was adjusted to a twice daily dosage.

When compared to placebo and methylphenidate, pemoline has been found to be significantly more effective than placebo but for some children not as effective as methylphenidate (Dykman, McGrew, Harris, Peters, & Ackerman, 1976). In Dykman et al.'s study, pemoline was also found to be less desirable than methylphenidate because of a delay of eight to nine weeks in the onset of full benefits. However, it must be noted that a small group of children in this study responded better to pemoline than to methylphenidate, based on a reduction of disruptive behavior. Moreover, pemoline has a long history of benefiting approximately 70%–80% of children with ADHD symptoms (Conners, 1972).

Pemoline offers the additional benefit of a lower level of regulation by the Drug Enforcement Administration (*Physician's Desk Reference,* 1993). As a result, pemoline can be prescribed by telephone and prescriptions can be refilled five times.

Dosage and time course. Pemoline is usually effective for eight hours, allowing once-a-day dosage. Pemoline is made in dosage strengths of 18.75, 37.5, and 75 mg, as well as in a chewable 37.5 mg tablet. The dosage is usually one to three 37.5 mg tablets. Some studies suggest it takes six to eight weeks for pemoline to become fully effective (Dykman et al., 1976). In comparison, methylphenidate, dextroamphetamine, and methamphetamine become fully effective on the first day of use.

Side effects. In general, the side effects of pemoline are similar to those of methylphenidate. Pemoline has been reported to cause more side effects of insomnia and anorexia than other stimulants (Page, Bernstein, Janicki, & Michelli, 1974). The finding of a high degree of variability in pemoline metabolism has been suggested as a possible explanation of rare negative reactions, including liver problems. A 600% interindividual variation in elimination and 300% variation in total body clearance of pemoline was discovered by Sallee, Stiller, Perel, and Bates (1985) in a study of 10 children 5–12 years of age. This finding may explain the unpredictable significant side effects, including sleep and appetite disruption, seen in some children treated with pemoline.

Possibly the greatest disadvantage of pemoline is the concern that it may cause liver failure. There have been reports of hepatic dysfunction, including elevated liver enzymes, hepatitis, and jaundice in individuals receiving pemoline. Although no causal relationship has been established, S. L. Jaffe (1989) reported two pemoline-related deaths. The first was a 10-year-old who died in 1977; this child had experienced liver-related problems prior to starting the pemoline. The second was a 12-year-old boy who died in 1981 after taking pemoline for three years; death was attributed to toxic hepatitis secondary to an overdose of pemoline. As a result, laboratory tests for liver function are recommended. They should be performed prior to and periodically during treatment with pemoline. Page et al. (1974) in a study of 288 children receiving pemoline for over 50 weeks found that nine required discontinuation of the pemoline because of elevations in liver enzymes. There were no clinical signs or symptoms present in any of the individuals demonstrating the enzyme elevation. Drug administration was discontinued when the elevations were found, and the enzyme levels returned to normal. Two patients were rechallenged with pemoline, and serum liver enzymes rose again. The authors suggested that this represents an individual delayed hypersensitivity to pemoline that is reversible on discontinuation of the medication. They reported an overall incidence of this reaction in all studies in the range of 1%–2% of children treated.

ADDERALL

Adderall, a medicine previously marketed under a different trade name for weight loss, is similar to methylphenidate in its effects and is used to treat similar disorders. Adderall contains one-fourth of each of the following: dextroamphetamine saccharate, amphetamine aspartate, dextroamphetamine sulphate, and amphetamine sulphate.

Benefits. Adderall has potential benefits similar to methylphenidate. It has been marketed as an alternative for individuals with ADHD who may not respond to other medications.

There are no peer-reviewed studies available on Adderall. An unpublished retrospective clinical profile (Jones, 1994) reports that in comparison to methylphenidate, Adderall was found to be safe and efficacious and produced "similar patient response." Side effect profiles were similar for methylphenidate and Adderall, with anorexia and insomnia being most frequently observed.

Dosage and time course. It has been suggested that because of the combination of amphetamine-based salts it contains, Adderall will last six to eight hours, reducing the need for a noontime dose. Because of the hypothesized longer action, Adderall may need to be given only once or at most twice per day. It is manufactured in 10 and 20 mg tablets.

Side effects. Side effects of Adderall are reported to be similar to those of methylphenidate.

Antidepressants

TRICYCLICS

The tricyclic antidepressants have been used primarily as second-line drugs to treat disruptive problems related to ADHD. Although there is a literature attesting to their clinical use in adults for anxiety and depressive problems, the childhood literature has not found benefits for these internalizing symptomatic problems in double-blind placebo-controlled studies (for a review, see S. Goldstein, 1995). In regard to disruptive symptoms, the tricyclic antidepressants desipramine (Norpramin), imipramine (Tofranil), nortriptyline (Pamelor), and amitriptyline (Elavil) have been shown to produce reductions in disruptive classroom problems of children with ADHD (see Pliszka, 1987, for a review). Improved teacher ratings of inattention, hyperactivity, and aggression have been found for up to 70% of treated children. Some studies suggest that the tricyclics may be particularly helpful for children who are nonresponders to stimulants (Biederman, Baldessarini, Wright, Knee, & Harmatz, 1989).

Benefits. Huessy and Wright (1970) suggested that tricyclic antidepressants were safe and effective based on clinical global impressions, objective measures of cognitive function, and improvement in behavioral rating scales. Garfinkel, Wender, Sloman, and O'Neill (1983) compared imipramine, desipramine, and methylphenidate in a crossover double-blind study of a group of 12 boys with ADD. The tricyclic antidepressants were found to be more useful in treating affective symptoms and less likely to disturb sleep than the methylphenidate. However, behavior ratings by teachers and child care workers indicated that methylphenidate was more effective than the tricyclics. These authors concluded that different medications can have differential effects on specific components of ADD. This and other studies suggest that methylphenidate is more effective in reducing classroom problems than are the tricyclics.

Stimulant medications were judged superior to tricyclics for the treatment of ADD symptoms by Pliszka (1987), as a result of his review of five quantitative studies of imipramine reported between 1972 and 1983. Pliszka discounted earlier conclusions by Huessy and Wright (1970) that imipramine should be the drug of choice for ADD. He did conclude that for children who do not respond to stimulants, imipramine or a similar tricyclic is an appropriate choice. However, Huessy (1988) continued to report that tricyclics should be the drug of choice for ADHD symptoms. In Huessy's study, 90% of individuals with ADHD were reported to respond to tricyclic antidepressants without side effects. This author argued that methylphenidate should therefore be the drug of last resort. However, most authors agreed with Pliszka's (1987) contention that the scientific literature does not support Huessy's conclusions and that the tricyclic antidepressants are not as effective as stimulants over the long term.

Wilens, Biederman, Geist, Steingard, and Spencer (1993) conducted a chart review of 58 children and adolescents with ADHD treated with the tricyclic nortriptyline. Over 76% of this population was considered to experience moderate to marked improvement in overall behavior, including classroom functioning. Mildly adverse effects were reported in 20 children, however.

Children with ADHD and comorbid disorders appear to benefit from tricyclics as much as children with ADHD alone (Biederman, Baldessarini, Wright, Keenan, & Faraone, 1993). Biederman et al. evaluated data from a study published in 1989 of 62 children and adolescents. This population was treated for six weeks with 4–5 mg/kg of desipramine. Biederman et al.'s reevaluation of the cases specifically focused on children experiencing ADHD with comorbid conduct disorder, depression, anxiety, or family history of ADHD. ADHD behavior improved in these populations at a rate similar to that of the ADHD group with no comorbid disorders. The presence of other disorders did not cause a negative response rate. These authors concluded that the tricyclic antidepressant was just as effective for children with ADHD and comorbid problems as for children with ADHD alone.

Tricyclics have also been found to be beneficial for the treatment of ADHD symptoms in children with tics or Tourette's syndrome (Spencer, Biederman, Wilens, Steingard, & Geist, 1993). In a chart review of 12 children with chronic motor tics or Tourette's syndrome as well as ADHD, tic symptoms were found to have improved in 60% of the population and ADHD symptoms to have improved in 92% without major side effects in an average follow-up period of 19 months. These authors concluded that their chart review indicated a therapeutic role for tricyclics in the treatment of ADHD complicated by chronic tics or Tourette's syndrome.

Dosage and time course. The tricyclics remain active in the blood for up to 20 hours, allowing most children to take one dose per day. These medicines are usually taken before bed as they often induce drowsiness initially. Although there has been some debate in the literature about how best to determine dosage for the tricyclics, a review of available research suggests that a dose of approximately 3 mg/kg adjusted by blood level is optimal (Biederman, Baldessarini, et al., 1993; S. Goldstein & Goldstein, 1990).

Side effects. The most common reversible side effects of the tricyclic antidepressants are drowsiness, dry mouth, upset stomach, constipation, and headache. Among other side effects is an increase in blood pressure and heart rate, as well as possible slowing of intracardiac conduction. In fact, four children treated with the tricyclic desipramine have died from sudden heart failure. The first three cases were reported in 1990 ("Sudden Death in Children," 1990). In a review of these cases and the mechanism of action for the tricyclics, Biederman (1991) found that treatment with tricyclics at high doses may increase the risk of electrocardiographic changes; however, he also stated that the full clinical implications of these findings are not yet clear and require further investigation. Biederman (1991, p. 497) concluded that "until more is known, a cautious approach" to the use of tricyclics in children, with a careful risk versus benefit analysis, is best.

Bupropion

In a double-blind crossover study of 15 subjects with ADHD between 7 and 17 years of age, methylphenidate and bupropion (Welbutrin) produced equivalent and significantly greater than placebo improvement in parent and teacher ratings (Barrickman et al., 1995). In this six-week study with a two-week washout phase, the same pattern of improvement observed by parents and teachers was also noted on a global impression scale and a number of structured test instruments, including a CPT. Thus, these two medicines did not appear to differ in their overall efficacy as a treatment for ADHD. Further research with bupropion is ongoing.

Prozac

The specific serotonin uptake inhibitor fluoxetine (Prozac) was evaluated by Barrickman, Noyes, Kuperman, Schumacher, and Verda (1991) as a treatment for ADHD. Following treatment of 19 children in an open study, nearly 60% were judged to be at least moderately improved, a rate above placebo but not approaching the benefits reported with stimulants. No effects on appetite or weight were observed and side effects were minimal. The typical dose was 20 mg given once per day.

Antihypertensives

CLONIDINE

Clonidine (Catapres) is a medication developed to treat high blood pressure. Clonidine, a noradrenergic agonist, has been documented to be beneficial in the treatment of highly active, oppositional, and aggressive patients with ADHD when compared to placebo (Hunt, Mindera, & Cohen, 1985) and to methylphenidate (Hunt, 1987). Hunt's research group considers clonidine to be a promising medication for the treatment of aggressive children with ADHD. Clonidine has also been used to treat severe aggression, cruelty to others, and destruction of property in the absence of ADHD symptoms. Kemph, DeVane, Levin, Jarecke, and Miller (1993) treated 17 aggressive children with clonidine in an open pilot study. Aggression decreased in 15 children with minimal side effects. These authors concluded that, while lithium and haloperidol have been demonstrated to be effective in reducing aggressive behavior (M. Campbell et al., 1984), significantly fewer side effects were reported with clonidine, suggesting this may be a more effective pharmacologic treatment for serious aggression. Moreover, clonidine has been found to benefit nonaggressive children with ADHD, as well as children experiencing comorbid tic disorders. Steingard, Biederman, Spencer, Wilens, and Gonzalez (1993) conducted a retrospective chart review of 54 children with ADHD, with and without comorbid tic disorders, treated with clonidine. Clonidine treatment resulted in improvement in 72% of the population for ADHD symptoms and 75% of the total population for tic symptoms. Ninety-six percent of the children with ADHD and comorbid tic disorders showed a positive response for ADHD symptoms, suggesting that they have a more frequent positive behavioral response to clonidine than do children with ADHD without comorbid tic disorders. These authors noted that there has been some disagreement among researchers about the benefits of clonidine for this population. In this study, sedation was the most common side effect. This report contributes to the literature documenting clonidine as moderately effective in the treatment of ADHD.

Singer (1994) compared children with ADHD and Tourette's syndrome treated with clonidine with those treated with desipramine. Singer found that desipramine produced better response and fewer side effects. When given in combination with methylphenidate, clonidine has been reported to reduce activity, aggression, and oppositionality at a lower dose of methylphenidate, thereby reducing overall side effects (Hunt, 1988). However, the clinical usefulness of clonidine is somewhat limited by side effects of sedation and hypotension and its relatively short half-life (2.5 hours; Hunt, Capper, & O'Connell, 1990).

T. E. Brown and Gammon (1994) reported that low doses of clonidine before bed may be an effective treatment for children with ADHD experiencing severe problems falling asleep. The group of children studied did not demonstrate any negative side effects from the clonidine, and parents reported significant improvements in their children's settling down to sleep and sleeping through the night.

GUANFACINE

Guanfacine (Tenex) is a noradrenergic agonist similar to clonidine. It has a longer excretion half-life, estimated to be nearly 18 hours (Sorkin & Heel, 1986). It has also been reported to be less sedating and less hypotensive than clonidine (Kugler, Seus, Krauskopf, Brecht, &

Raschig, 1990). In animal research it has been shown to enhance cognitive functioning in regard to working memory and attention (Arnsten & Contant, 1992).

Hunt, Arnsten, and Asbell (1995) evaluated 13 subjects ranging in age from 4 to 20 years, with a mean age of 11 years. Eleven were male; two were female. All met the *DSM-III-R* criteria for ADHD, with three demonstrating comorbid oppositional defiance and one demonstrating LD. Guanfacine was administered in an initial dosage of 0.5 mg per day, increasing to as much as 4 mg per day in 0.5 mg increments every third day. Dose amounts were individually titrated for optimum clinical response. The results of this preliminary clinical study indicated that guanfacine was beneficial and useful in the treatment of ADHD. Major beneficial effects were noted in behaviors reflecting high levels of arousal and activity, as well as in cognitive aspects of inhibition and selective attention. A reduction in hyperactive behavior with an enhancement of frustration tolerance and affect modulation was reported. Although this was an open trial, the experimenters were impressed with the reported benefits and the scarcity of side effects. Hunt et al. (1995) concluded that "the predominant behavioral effects of calming and improved frustration tolerance—occurring at the expense of only slight sedation—appeared most beneficial in highly aroused, irritable, hyperactive children" (p. 53). At their two research sites in Nashville, Tennessee, these authors continue to experiment with antihypertensive medications.

Propranolol

Propranolol (Inderal) is a medication used to relax the muscles around blood vessels. This is helpful in treating migraine, high blood pressure, and certain heart disorders. Propranolol has also been studied as a treatment for behavioral problems in children. D. T. Williams, Mehl, Yudofsky, Adams, and Roseman (1982) studied 32 patients who had suffered from uncontrolled rage outbursts over a period of at least six months in childhood or adolescence and who had failed psychotherapy. The population ranged from 7 to 35 years of age and included 11 children, 15 adolescents, and 4 adults. The authors concluded that 75% of the patients demonstrated moderate to marked improvement in their ability to control rage outbursts and aggressive behavior with propranolol. Maximum doses of propranolol were 50 to 1,600 mg per day. Duration of treatment was 1–30 months with a median of 3.5 months.

Neuroleptics

Neuroleptic medications, including haloperidol (Haldol), thioridazine (Mellaril), and chlorpromazine (Thorazine), are among the medications used to treat major psychiatric disorders. Haloperidol has also been used to control tics associated with Tourette's syndrome and, on occasion, has been studied as a medicine to control disruptive behaviors, including aggression and hyperactivity. L. T. Anderson et al. (1984) suggested that haloperidol is probably the most effective of the neuroleptics in reducing disruptive behaviors and the most extensively studied in well-designed double-blind placebo studies. These authors concluded that severe behavioral symptoms associated with autism often targeted for pharmacologic treatment, including self-injury, aggression, hyperactivity and stereotypy, and affective instability, improve with haloperidol treatment. This finding is reflected in the work of others as well (M. Campbell, Anderson, Meier, Cohen, & Small, 1978).

M. Campbell et al. (1984) found that haloperidol was successful in controlling severe conduct and aggression in 61 treatment-resistant psychiatrically hospitalized children. However, there was a high incidence of side effects such as sleeplessness and loss of spontaneous activity. Thioridazine has been found to be more effective than methylphenidate for children with IQs below 45 in improving conduct and hyperactivity problems based on teacher ratings (Aman et al., 1991).

Side effects. Neuroleptics can have significant side effects. Their use may cause stiffness of movement and flattening of emotional responses. Of greatest concern in the use of haloperidol and other neuroleptics is the development of tardive dyskinesia. This is a spontaneous movement disorder, most commonly of the face and lips but also involving the jaw, tongue, arms, neck, shoulders, and at times legs. In 41 patients withdrawn from neuroleptic treatment because of tardive dyskinesia, more than half continued to demonstrate the dyskinesia after the neuroleptics ceased (T. Gualitieri, Quade, Hicks, Mayo, & Schroeder, 1984). While uncommon, the possibility of tardive dyskinesia should discourage the use of neuroleptics for all but the most serious problems.

Epilepsy Medications

Medications commonly prescribed to control epileptic seizures include phenobarbital (Luminal), carbamazepine (Tegretol), phenytoin (Dilantin), and valproate (Depakote). Clinicians and educators are rarely given enough information about epilepsy and its treatment. Based on interview data, Gadow (1982) concluded that teachers were often poorly informed about the overt features of seizures, the side effects of medication, and seizure management. Even when students experienced seizures or medication side effects at school, teachers were often poorly informed. For 70% of the children in this study, teachers were involved either in evaluating response to treatment, administering medication, or managing and coping with seizures in the classroom. Side effects from these anticonvulsants are common. Over one-third of the children in this study were rated as more drowsy or sleepy than their peers, and according to teachers, drug-induced impairments in adaptive behavior were common problems.

It is important to recognize that, independent of treatment, epileptic children are more likely to have behavior and developmental problems. Aldenkamp, Alpherts, Dekker, and Overweg (1990) concluded that learning problems occur in approximately 5%-50% of children with epilepsy. In this study, 30% of epileptic children required special education services compared with 7% of a matched nonepileptic control group.

In a careful review of the available scientific literature, Trimble (1979) suggested that confusion about the negative effects of anticonvulsants on cognition and behavior was due to a lack of accurate assessment of behaviors. More careful studies clearly demonstrate a correlation between use of the anticonvulsant phenobarbital and impaired performance on subtests of the WISC. This suggests that the medication was in fact responsible for the deterioration. Trimble concluded that phenobarbital and chemically related medications primidone (Mysoline) and phenytoin (Dilantin) produce an insidious deterioration of mental state characterized by progressively falling intellectual levels.

Children treated for febrile seizures with phenobarbital frequently develop a reversible pattern of hyperactivity. Often this pattern includes irritability, tantrums, disobedience, lethargy, or insomnia. The behavioral effects appear to be unrelated to drug blood levels, and many of these children demonstrated behavioral problems prior to their initial convulsion. Some concern has been raised, however, that these effects, including lower IQ, may not be resolved after the medication is discontinued.

It has been widely reported that mental slowing occurs with the use of valproate, phenytoin, and phenobarbital. However, Forsythe, Butler, Berg, and McGuire (1991) in a study of 64 cases of newly diagnosed childhood epilepsy found that only carbamazepine in moderate doses negatively affected memory. Phenytoin and valproate did not. None of these three drugs were reported to affect behavior negatively. It has been demonstrated that carbamazepine may cause impairment in motor speed. Phenytoin has been reported to produce nystagmus or ataxia, delirium, or psychosis as symptoms of intoxication or overdosage. Involuntary movements and thinking difficulty have also been reported. These side effects may be more likely to occur when the child has a preexisting history of intellectual handicap (C. R. Reynolds, 1983). Valproate, while not as well studied, has been reported to produce behavioral side effects similar to those of phenytoin.

Although there has been interest in the use of anticonvulsants to treat certain behavior disorders, in general these drugs have not been found beneficial for typical childhood behavioral problems. The most popular anticonvulsant drug now prescribed for disruptive behavior is carbamazepine. Although it has been proved to benefit individuals with rapid cycling mood disorder, some individuals experience severe side effects and all other beneficial reports are anecdotal (Pleak, Birmaher, Gavrilescu, Abichandini, & Williams, 1988).

Medications to Treat ADHD in Adults

STIMULANTS

Until recently, most available medication treatment studies for adults have been characterized by the use of low doses (similar to those given to children), inconsistent diagnostic criteria, unclear target symptoms, poor control, and a lack of a longitudinal population to evaluate. Further, adults with core symptoms of ADHD were rarely the subject of medication treatment trials until 1976 (Wood et al., 1976). Wood et al. initially studied four patients in an open clinical trial and then 11 individuals given the diagnosis of adult residual attention deficit disorder in a placebo-controlled pilot study with methylphenidate. In these adults, methylphenidate produced a statistically significant therapeutic effect on target symptoms of nervousness, poor concentration, fatigue, and hot temper. A 10-month follow-up found that two-thirds of the responders demonstrated continued moderate to good response. No development of tolerance, abuse, or significant side effects were reported.

In general, studies of stimulant medication have shown them to be the most efficacious of all classes of drugs studied at improving ADHD symptoms in adults (Fargason & Ford, 1994). Double-blind controlled studies as well as case studies have consistently reflected the benefits of stimulants for adult symptoms of ADHD, with only one controlled study finding negative results (Mattes et al., 1984). Among the stimulants, methylphenidate has been the most widely studied and the most popular (Matochik et al., 1994; Wood et al., 1976; Yellin, Hopwood, & Greenberg, 1982). Representative of these studies is the work of Mattes et al. (1984). Twenty-six individuals meeting the adult criteria for ADD with a childhood history of the disorder and 35 meeting the criteria in adulthood with no childhood history were treated with methylphenidate. Approximately 25% of the sample appeared to benefit clinically from the methylphenidate, but no clear-cut predictors of drug response were identified. History of drug abuse

Table 13.3 Dosages of Methylphenidate Studied for Adult ADHD

Author	Dosage
Matochik et al., 1994	28 mg average dose
Varley, 1985	10–60 mg per day
Wood et al., 1976	Less than 60 mg per day
Ernst et al., 1994	30 mg twice a day or 20 mg three times a day
P. H. Wender & Reimherr, 1990	40–80 mg per day
P. H. Wender, Wood, & Reimherr, 1985	40 mg average dose
Fargason & Ford, 1994	20–90 mg per day
Matochik et al., 1993	.35 mg/kg average dose
C. T. Gualitieri et al., 1985	.1–.5 mg/kg

appeared to be the best predictor of treatment success. Even among the responders, however, the authors reported that benefits were generally not as clinically valuable or distinct as in children with ADHD. Mattes et al. (1984) concluded from their study that "it appears most reasonable to assume that methylphenidate is not generally helpful in adults with residual ADD" (p. 1063). They hypothesized that stimulants might activate relatively different pathways in childhood and adulthood and that this might account for their differential results. However, it has been reported in the majority of adult studies that, as in children, approximately two-thirds of adults with ADHD symptoms show good response to stimulant treatment (for a review, see Fargason & Ford, 1994). Forty milligrams of methylphenidate per day spread across several doses appears to be the most common treatment regime for adults. However, up to 90 mg per day has been reported (see Table 13.3).

As with children, the treatment effectiveness of methylphenidate has been demonstrated by improvement in the symptoms used to diagnose the disorder (Wood et al., 1976), laboratory performance (Satterfield, Satterfield, & Schell, 1987), and rating scales (Mattes, 1985). In fact, rating scales of ADHD symptoms have been found to be an excellent means of identifying those individuals most likely to respond to medication treatment (Mattes et al., 1984).

There is disagreement about whether strong indices of ADHD in childhood indicate greater likelihood of medication response in adulthood (Mattes et al., 1984; Yellin et al., 1982). Unfortunately, studies to date do not allow a decisive resolution of this issue.

Dextroamphetamine, which has a stimulant action similar to that of methylphenidate, has also been considered beneficial in the treatment of adult ADHD (P. H. Wender, Wood, & Reimherr, 1985). Maximum dosages of Dexedrine have been reported to be 30 mg per day or less for adults (see Table 13.4).

The beneficial effects of dextroamphetamine appear to be similar to those of methylphenidate. Side effects have been reported to be somewhat greater. The sustained-release form of Dexedrine is believed to work more effectively than the sustained-release form of methylphenidate (Fargason & Ford, 1994), but this belief has not been supported by scientific study. There have been no published studies on the use of sustained-release dextroamphetamine for ADHD in adults.

Pemoline has also been reported to be helpful for symptoms of adult ADHD (R. D. Weiss, Pope, & Mirin, 1985; P. H. Wender et al., 1981; Wood et al., 1976). Dosages of pemoline for

Table 13.4   Dosage of Dextroamphetamine Studied for Adult ADHD

Author	Dosage
Matochik et al., 1994	19 mg per day (average)
P. H. Wender & Reimherr, 1990	20–30 mg per day
P. H. Wender, Wood, & Reimherr, 1985	Less than 30 mg per day
Matochik et al., 1993	.25 mg/kg

adults have been reported to be as high as 225 mg per day (R. D. Weiss et al., 1985). P. H. Wender, Wood, and Reimherr (1985) reported an average dose of 65 mg. These authors evaluated 48 adults with histories of residual attention deficit disorder in a random-assignment, parallel double-blind placebo-controlled study (P. H. Wender et al., 1981). The trial lasted six weeks. A number of assessment procedures were used. It is important to note that medication benefits were not considered significant until physicians' observations were added to the assessment measures. Physicians' observations were used to separate the study subjects into two groups: basically those with more severe and those with less severe attention deficit symptoms. The adults with less severe symptoms did not respond to the pemoline. The adults with more severe symptoms did. These authors noted as well that pemoline was not a treatment of choice because even at low doses side effects, including agitation, headaches, stomachaches, and insomnia, were noted. Pemoline has been reported to be advantageous because of its longer therapeutic action, which is possibly even more important for adults (Fargason & Ford, 1994; R. D. Weiss et al., 1985; P. H. Wender, Wood, & Reimherr, 1985). In addition, the less restrictive classification of pemoline as a Schedule IV controlled substance allows less restrictive prescription writing. Prescriptions for pemoline can be telephoned to a pharmacy and may be refilled for six months.

Pemoline has been associated with abnormal liver function studies in adults, as well as children. Two percent of adults receiving pemoline are reported to have demonstrated evidence of liver toxicity (Fargason & Ford, 1994). While there is agreement among physicians that liver enzyme must be monitored when pemoline is prescribed, there are no specific recommendations for the frequency with which blood work should be performed or liver function studies followed in adults. Nonetheless, there is a consensus that if liver function studies are abnormal, pemoline treatment should be discontinued (Fargason & Ford, 1994).

The side effects of stimulant treatment in adults appear to be similar to those in children (Mattes et al., 1984). The most common side effects reported are anorexia, sleeplessness, and restlessness. Often these do not outweigh the benefits reported. Feelings of anxiety, rebound, or "ups and downs," and ineffectiveness of medication caused six of eight patients in one study to choose not to continue methylphenidate treatment (Gualitieri et al., 1985). Studies of amphetamine use in adults have also shown increased blood pressure (Ernst et al., 1994). Long-term studies are not available to indicate whether prolonged use of stimulants in adults produces symptoms due to this elevation in blood pressure.

ANTIDEPRESSANTS

Antidepressants have been demonstrated to be efficacious in reducing symptoms of adult ADHD (Wood et al., 1976). Ten to twenty milligrams of imipramine was reported to be helpful by Shekim et al. (1990). Twenty-five milligrams of nortriptyline twice per day was reported to be helpful by Saul (1985). Among the other antidepressants reported to be beneficial for symptoms of adult ADHD are pargyline at a dose of 10–15 mg (P. H. Wender, Wood, Reimherr, & Ward, 1983), nomifenisne (Shekim, Masterson, Cantwell, Hanna, & McCracken, 1989), deprenyl (P. H. Wender et al., 1983), tranylcypormine at a dose of 40 mg, and bupropion (Barrickman et al., 1995; P. H. Wender & Reimherr, 1990). It has been suggested that if an individual has difficulty sleeping at night or is restless as the result of a stimulant, an antidepressant may be the treatment of choice. Anxiety has been reported to be a common comorbid problem with adult ADHD. As reviewed above, stimulants are less effective at treating symptoms of childhood ADHD when anxiety disorders are also present. Whether this is the case for adults remains to be demonstrated. Antidepressants may help alleviate anxiety symptoms in adults with comorbid ADHD. It is difficult to be certain which of the antidepressants is the most effective, however, because no studies directly compare one against another. Some information can be obtained by comparing one study with another, but such a comparison is not entirely valid scientifically. Given the lack of data, many clinicians choose to allow patients to choose a medication after trials with several medicines. Without a systematic comparison of the antidepressants, it cannot be scientifically determined which of the many antidepressants available is most effective for ADHD symptoms. Further, there is little data to guide the physician in determining the dosage of antidepressants and dose response for ADHD. In general, lower doses, often considered nontherapeutic for depression, have been suggested for ADHD.

OTHER MEDICATIONS

In addition to stimulants and antidepressants, there are several other medications that have been studied as treatments for adult ADHD. Propranolol (Inderal) has been reported to be beneficial in high doses (528 mg/day; Mattes, 1986). Clonidine has been demonstrated to improve ADHD behavior in children. Its main side effects are sleepiness. It has been shown to be less effective than the tricyclic antidepressant desipramine in treating ADHD associated with Tourette's syndrome in children (Singer, 1994). It has not been studied in adults. Nevertheless, it may be considered in some refractory adult cases.

Other medications, including L-dopa, a combination of L-dopa and carbidopa, phenylalanine, and tyrosine, have been reported to be marginally helpful (P. H. Wender & Reimherr, 1990). Bromocriptine (Cavanagh, Clifford, & Gregory, 1989; Cocores et al., 1986), S-adenosyl-L-methionine (Shekim et al., 1990), and other medications have been shown to be helpful in limited studies. The anticonvulsant Dilantin has been recommended without controlled study at 100 mg per day for three days to prevent premenstrual restlessness (Bellak & Black, 1992). Another anticonvulsant, carbamazepine, has been described as helpful for hyperactive, mentally retarded children in dosages of 400 and 600 mg per day (A. H. Reid, Naylor, & Kay, 1981). Lithium has been described as helpful (Crabtree, 1981), as has an experimental stimulant, MK-801 (Reimherr, Wood, & Wender, 1986). Lithium is a useful medication for the treatment of bipolar illness. While found to be ineffective for children with ADHD, lithium may be effective for ADHD symptoms that are part of a bipolar disorder. Antianxiety medications such as diazepam (Valium) or Xanax have not been demonstrated to be helpful for childhood ADHD and may actually aggravate some of its symptoms.

If taking one medication is good, is taking two medications better? The combination of 10 mg of methylphenidate twice per day and 40 mg of nadolal was found to decrease temper outbursts (Ratey, Greenberg, & Lindem, 1991). The combination of fluoxetine and methylphenidate was found to be helpful for a group of adults with ADHD (Fargason & Ford, 1994). Crabtree (1981) found the combination of lithium and tricyclic antidepressants helpful for adult ADHD. Ratey et al. (1991) found methylphenidate and nadolol helpful for temper outbursts. Lorazepam treatment of .5–1 mg twice a day was recommended without study for additive control of anxiety symptoms with ADHD (Bellak & Black, 1992). However, studies of multiple drug usage in children with epilepsy have shown clearly that the addition of a second medication will improve the likelihood of seizure control slightly but will substantially increase the likelihood and severity of side effects. There have not been enough studies of multiple drug treatments for ADHD either in children or in adults. It is difficult to determine how common this practice is in the treatment of ADHD in adults. However, in the absence of evidence that multiple medications substantially improve the likelihood of success without substantially increasing the likelihood of side effects, medications are usually best administered one at a time. Some combinations are clearly contraindicated, such as the combination of a monamine oxidase inhibitor such as pargyline and a stimulant such as methylphenidate. Three medications are not likely to be three times as good as one but are likely to cause three times as many side effects. Many patients present with a complex diagnosis. In addition to symptoms consistent with ADHD, other psychiatric conditions may be present as well. Anxiety and depression are possibly the most common. The presence of bipolar disorder or borderline personality may prevent the accurate diagnosis of ADHD and preclude treatment for ADHD until these disorders are addressed. Thorough diagnostic evaluation is essential in order to determine the presence of comorbid disorders and to identify which has the most pressing need for treatment. Use of multiple medications requires further study. It is our recommendation that medications be used one at a time for most adults with ADHD.

After a treatment regimen is selected, a method of follow-up evaluation to determine the effect of treatment must be chosen. Reevaluation is most helpful long enough after treatment has begun to be able to see an effect but soon enough after to be able to determine whether side effects or serious problems are present. Follow-up intervals of between two and four weeks are usually chosen. Follow-up usually involves the evaluation of questionnaire data from the patient. Questionnaires completed by peers or a spouse are also helpful when available. These have, in some studies, proved sensitive to treatment effects. Global rating scales, direct patient observation, and qualitative reports from the patient are also used to determine the effectiveness of treatment.

Medications to Improve Memory and Learning

In an attempt to identify clinically relevant means of enhancing memory and learning, researchers have studied myriad psychoactive and neuroactive substances for potential therapeutic effect. Despite the large volume of research, only limited data have been generated to suggest that at this time any class of substance or any specific substance might facilitate this process. Nearly all forms of pharmacologic intervention that affect the workings of the brain have been studied, including drugs that interact with cholinergic (Bartus, 1980), dopaminergic (J. A. Davies, Jackson, & Redfern, 1974), noradrenergic (Lian, Juler, & McGaugh, 1986), and serotonergic (Altman, Nordy, & Oegren, 1984) neurotransmission to modify the memory and learning performance of humans and laboratory animals. Even peptide-sensitive neurons (McGaugh, 1989) and excitatory and inhibitory amino acids (Mondadori, Preiswerk, & Jaekel, 1992) have been found to affect memory and learning. All of these systems have been studied in one way or another in an effort to discover how to facilitate memory and learning.

Further, studies have demonstrated that interventions affecting other physiological processes can affect learning and memory, including those involving protein synthesis (H. P. Davies & Squire, 1984), steroids (Flood, Bennett, Orme, Vasquez, & Jarvik, 1978), and modulation of enzyme functions (Ali, Bullock, & Rose, 1988). Yet, manipulation of these systems has yielded very little that is promising.

It is also important to note that despite the significant behavioral benefits of the stimulant medications for those with ADHD and the reports of improved targeted academic achievement in laboratory and related settings, neither these drugs nor others used principally to treat ADHD have demonstrated anything more than mild impact on memory and learning (for a review, see Barkley, 1990b; S. Goldstein & Goldstein, 1990; Greenhill & Osman, 1991).

A promising line of recent research has focused on a group of drugs referred to as nootropics. These drugs are almost inert in humans and animals and have almost no toxic effects. Although to some absence of toxicity may suggest lack of pharmacologic action, the research argues otherwise (Mondadori, 1993). Piracetam, the first identified nootropic, and other related drugs in this family have been demonstrated to improve memory and related behavioral functioning in animals (Bhattacharya, Upadhyay, & Jaiswal, 1993) and humans (Wilsher, 1986).

Piracetam is a gamma amino butyric acid (GABA) derivative. It was first developed in a mechanism-based approach to discovering novel hypnotic agents (Nicholson, 1989). The drug has been shown to lack sedative, analeptic, analgesic, neuroleptic, or tranquilizing properties (Branconnier, 1983). Nootropics have been proposed as drugs to improve or restore brain functions rather than to treat pathology (Deberdt, 1994). Deberdt argues that brain functions may be trained using a variety of nonmedical treatments such as memory training, speech therapy, or cognitive enhancement. Treatment with nootropics, such as piracetam or ginko biloba extractum (GBE), may yield similar results. Reviewers acknowledge existing data that suggest that reading accuracy and comprehension are enhanced in nearly 50% of those with LD treated with piracetam. Dysphasic patients have also been reported to make greater progress in speech therapy. It has been suggested that the nootropic drugs act by restoring or enhancing neurotransmitter systems closely related to learning and memory functioning. Results of animal research indicate that piracetam restores the availability and function of muscarinic and N-methyl-D-aspartate (NMDA) receptors in aging animals, possibly through a modulation of the neuronal membrane. Piracetam appears to improve short-term memory, which then may have a significant impact on the acquisition of other academic skills. In adults it has been studied principally with the geriatric population.

In animals and healthy volunteers, piracetam is said to improve the efficiency of the higher telencephalic functions of the brain, involving cognitive processes such as learning and memory. Piracetam's actions are considered pharmacologically unusual. Studies suggest it may protect against various physical and chemical insults to the brain. Piracetam appears to facilitate learning and memory in both healthy animals and animals whose brain functions have been compromised. These reports indicate that high doses enhance interhemispheric transfer of information via the corpus collosum. Since piracetam is reported to be devoid of any sedative, analeptic, or autonomic activity, it can be administered with little worry. The exact mechanism by which piracetam operates is still unclear. Peak serum levels of piracetam are observed within 30–45 minutes of oral administration. It does not appear to be metabolized in the body, and it is therefore excreted unchanged in the urine. Its elimination half-life is reported to be five to six hours (Tacconi & Wurtman, 1986).

Piracetam achieves high concentrations in brain tissue, primarily in the cerebral cortex. It is found in the olfactory bulb at a much higher concentration than in the brain stem (Tacconi & Wurtman, 1986). Piracetam has also been reported to be beneficial for myoclonus (Obeso et al., 1988), sickle cell anemia (de Araujo & Nero, 1977), and alcoholism (Barns et al., 1990). It is thought that piracetam facilitates central nervous system efficiency of cholinergic neurotransmission (for a review, see Vernon & Sorkin, 1991).

Trials with elderly patients with senile cognitive disorders have been equivocal, but some studies have produced favorable results. As yet, although the drug appears to have a definite effect on children with LD, especially in regard to improving reading speed, there is not enough information about the specific types of problems for which it has significant and reproducible clinical benefit. Nonetheless, a brief review of the available literature will illustrate the work in this area.

Herrmann and Stephan (1991) studied three chemically different cognitive enhancers, piracetam, acetyl-L-carnitine, and nimodipine (NIM). In general, improvements with these drugs reached or exceeded the baseline variability of the assessment measures used with Alzheimer's patients. In a double-blind randomized trial involving 162 individuals with age-associated memory impairment, Israel, Melac, Milinkevitch, and Dubos (1994) evaluated placebo (following placebo washout), low-dose piracetam, and high-dose piracetam. The best memory improvements were obtained with the higher dose of piracetam, suggesting a dose-response effect. Medication effectiveness, interestingly, was enhanced when cognitive training was introduced after six weeks of drug treatment. This line of research suggests additive benefits of skill building and medication treatment in a multitreatment model.

There have been a limited number of studies researching piracetam with learning-disabled children. Ackerman, Dykman, Holloway, Paal, and Gocio (1991) evaluated 60 children (two-thirds of them boys) between 9 and 13 years of age in a 10-week summer program. The children were randomly and blindly assigned to receive placebo or piracetam. In this group of 60 children, two-thirds were classified as dysphonetic, with the rest classified as phonetic in their LD. The phonetic group improved significantly more in word recognition ability than the dysphonetic group. Overall, the children receiving piracetam did not improve more than the nonmedicated children in any aspect of reading. The phonetic subgroup receiving piracetam gained more in word recognition than any subgroup but did not improve significantly more than the phonetic subgroup receiving placebo.

Helfgott, Rudel, and Kairam (1986) evaluated the effects of piracetam on short- and long-term verbal retrieval in 60 dyslexic boys between 8 and 14 years of age. The children were evaluated over a 12-week period. Those with intellectual, sensory, psychiatric, or neurological impairments were screened out of the study. There were no changes at the end of the 12 weeks to distinguish the medicated from the nonmedicated group in accuracy or comprehension of reading. However, short-term memory gains were noted for the medicated group on tests of digit span and immediate and delayed recall.

Tallal, Chase, Russell, and Schmitt (1986) evaluated a variety of academic variables in a group of 55 boys, 8–13 years of age, treated with piracetam over a 12-week period. Reading speed and number of words written in a given time period were significantly enhanced in the group receiving piracetam. Effective reading and writing ability, taking both rate and accuracy into consideration, were also significantly improved in the piracetam group compared to the placebo group. Further, as expected, the medication was well tolerated, with no adverse side effects reported.

In what is probably the largest and most extensive study in this area, 225 dyslexic children between 7 1/2 and 13 years of age were enrolled in a multicenter, 36-week, double-blind placebo-controlled study of piracetam (Wilsher et al., 1987). As with other well-controlled studies, children with intellectual, neurological, or psychiatric problems were screened out. Piracetam again was well tolerated. Piracetam-treated children showed significant improvements in reading ability, including reading comprehension. Treatment effects were evident after 12 weeks and were sustained for the 36-week follow-up.

Newer nootropic agents derived from the original studies with piracetam (Klawans & Genovese, 1986) have been initially reported as more potent and possibly more effective in their impact on learning and memory (Nicholson, 1990). The newer nootropic agents include oxiracetam, aniracetam, etiracetam, and pramiarcetam.

Although this group of medications shows great potential to improve memory, it is important to note that this group's impact on academic achievement appears to be mediated through its effects on memory. There does not appear to be a group of medications or other agents that has been identified as significantly affecting learning through other mechanisms (e.g., attention or visual perception).

A Model to Consult with Physicians

In this chapter we have provided a thorough overview of the use of stimulant medications as the treatment of choice for children, adolescents, and adults with ADHD symptoms. We have also reviewed the much smaller, less developed literature on nonstimulants as medications for ADHD, as well as the experimental literature on medications to improve learning. Since there is high comorbidity of other problems potentially responsive to medication in the ADHD and LD populations (e.g., depression and anxiety), it is important for the physician and nonmedical clinician to be aware of these medications and the role they may play in the treatment of people with ADHD or LD. It is beyond the scope of this chapter to provide a thorough overview. The interested reader is referred to A. R. Green and Costain (1981).

The clinician must know and understand the data provided in this chapter when working with adults receiving one or more of these medications. For example, when an individual reports an abrupt change in his or her functioning while taking medication, one of the issues the clinician needs to address immediately is appropriate use. Further, by understanding the types of behaviors that medications have been proved to improve as well as other life stresses for adults, clinicians play a critical role in identifying people who may be candidates for medication intervention, defining and measuring target behaviors, and providing a comprehensive summary of that information to physicians. Clinicians then play a major role in assisting the physician by collecting data as medication is adjusted. These issues determine the basic model proposed here to facilitate the clinician's work with the physician.

It is important for clinicians to recognize that, following the trend with children, it is likely that most adults receiving medication for ADHD will do so from their family practitioner, internist, or in some cases gynecologist. The prescribing physician's knowledge of adult ADHD and the methods used to evaluate medication benefits may be limited. The relative infancy of the adult ADHD field also means that many psychiatrists either do not believe in or possess limited information about this disorder and the potential benefits of medication. It is therefore strongly recommended that clinicians take the time to provide physicians with comprehensive information and to answer their questions. When a referral is made for medication evaluation, data should also include a summary of nonmedication efforts that have been undertaken to treat these problems. The referral should not be a request to prescribe medication but rather a request for the physician to determine whether the adult's problems have a medical explanation and whether in the physician's opinion the symptoms presented warrant medication treatment.

Although physicians may be well informed about certain behavior checklists and other tests used for childhood ADHD, it is likely they will know much less about the use of checklists or related measures for adults. It is the clinician's job to provide target behaviors defined in an operational manner. These data should be contrasted with a brief explanation of the magnitude of these behaviors in comparison to other adults. Further, clinicians should explain the effects of these problems on the individual and his or her family members and in the workplace.

In some situations, consultants may not be approached until the physician has already decided to pursue medication treatment. In such cases, it is strongly recommended that efforts be made to obtain at least a few weeks of baseline observations of the behaviors the medications are intended to affect. It cannot be too strongly emphasized that without baseline data, decisions to continue, discontinue, or modify medication usage end up being made arbitrarily.

Guidelines for Prescribing Medications for ADHD

Although there is some general agreement on the criteria for a diagnosis of ADHD in adults, there are few guidelines for determining which individuals should receive medication treatment. The standard medical model for decision making requires that the risks and benefits of treatment be compared with the alternatives. Several factors may contribute to the decision to use medication for symptoms of adult ADHD. As noted earlier in this chapter, these factors include severity of symptoms, presence of comorbid disorders, effectiveness of nonmedication interventions, the individual's ability to follow through with the treatment plan, family circumstances, and interest and desire for medication. As the severity of ADHD symptoms increases, medication intervention becomes a more attractive option. However, when ADHD symptoms become severe, the affected adult's ability to follow through with medication and to accept the responsibility necessary for medication treatment may be limited. Severely affected children can often count on parents to remember their medications. Adults with ADHD cannot. The need for ADHD medication treatment is also influenced by the presence of other disorders. For example, if an adult with ADHD is also suffering through a severe episode of depression, medication might focus on depressive symptoms.

When medication treatment for adult ADHD is undertaken, physicians must choose the medications. Stimulants and antidepressants are the most widely accepted medications for treatment of ADHD in adults and children. As reviewed, studies indicate that stimulants are far more effective than tricyclic antidepressants in childhood (Garfinkel et al., 1983). Practice surveys also suggest that stimulants are the overwhelming favorites of physicians treating children and adolescents (Safer & Krager, 1988). In contrast, antidepressants have been recommended as the initial treatment of choice for adults (Hallowell & Ratey, 1994). It is important to note that no controlled research supports this course. Why is the less effective treatment so widely recommended? First, a number of clinicians relate that in their personal experience, low-dose tricyclic antidepressants are most effective for adults with ADHD. There is also an undercurrent of suspicion that stimulants for adults are dangerous. Methylphenidate is highly regulated by the Drug Enforcement Administration. Prescribing controlled substances based on patient report may lead to drug abuse and addiction. This concern is heightened by anecdotal reports of children selling their Ritalin pills on the school playground ("90s Teens Find a New High," 1995). Many physicians consider it inappropriate to prescribe a controlled substance to individuals for whom drug and alcohol addiction is a common problem. In order to determine whether these concerns are warranted, a review of some of the data on drug addiction and methylphenidate may be helpful.

Although unrelated chemically, methylphenidate has clinical effects similar to those of the amphetamines. In 1971 several amphetamines were classified by the Drug Enforcement Administration as Schedule II controlled substances. This is the most restrictive category of prescribable medications. Medications on Schedule II are considered to have high abuse potential. It seemed logical to the Drug Enforcement Administration in 1971 (U.S. Department of Justice, 1971; cited in U.S. Department of Justice, 1987) that because methylphenidate had a clinical action similar to the amphetamines it must also have substantial abuse potential and warrant similar classification. As a result, methylphenidate became a Schedule II controlled substance. In 1986, as a result of an administrative action, the Justice Department submitted evidence on methylphenidate (U.S. Department of Justice, 1987). It acknowledged that according to the three methods used to determine the degree to which a drug is abused—surveys of high school seniors, evaluation of chemical substances found in drug raids, and lists of drugs producing emergency room admissions—methylphenidate is not highly abused. High school seniors do not recognize methylphenidate as a recreational drug of choice, drug raids do not produce quantities of illicitly manufactured or stored methylphenidate, and illicitly ingested methylphenidate is not a common reason for drug-related emergency room admission. Many of the drugs that do appear on these lists, such as diazepam (Valium) or hydrocodone (Lortab), are Schedule III or IV substances much less regulated than methylphenidate.

Because ADHD is a long-term chronic disorder, there may be concern that long-term treatment with a controlled substance is likely to produce abuse. Two cases of parents using their children's medication have been reported (Fulton & Yates, 1988). Many authors have expressed concern about stimulant medications and drug addiction (Denckla, 1991). But how likely is an adult ADHD patient to abuse stimulant medication? P. H. Wender, Reimherr, and Wood (1985) found no evidence of drug addiction in this population. Varley found only a single case report in the literature (Varley, 1985). Vinson (1994) found that euphoria was absent with methylphenidate, arguing, nevertheless, that pemoline was less likely to cause drug addiction. Langer, Sweeney, Bartenbach, Davis, and Menander (1986) found that by 1986 only four reports of pemoline withdrawal symptoms and no cases of pemoline abuse had been recorded. Nevertheless, the potential for abuse is a subject of substantial concern in studies of psychopharmacologic treatment of adult ADHD (Shaywitz & Shaywitz, 1988b).

Several studies have looked at treatment of patients with ADHD with comorbid drug abuse problems. While some have argued that nonstimulant medications should not be used with this population (Cavanagh et al., 1989; Cocores et al., 1986), other authors have looked at the effects of stimulants on adults with ADHD who were also drug addicts. Merrill and Garfinkel (1987) and G. Weiss et al. (1985) showed improvement in drug-dependent behavior with pemoline. Rifkin, Wortman, Reardon, and Siris (1986) presented subjects whose conduct disorder improved on stimulant medication, with no evidence that the subjects were abusing or obtaining a high from the medication.

Anecdotes about abuse, addiction, or inappropriate disposal of methylphenidate together with governmental classification of methylphenidate as a dangerous drug with high abuse potential have raised concern about its use. However, there appears to be neither a scientific basis for this concern nor evidence that methylphenidate has been or will likely be abused when prescribed for treatment of adult ADHD.

Do stimulants have a specific effect on ADHD, or do they simply improve everyone's ability to concentrate and pay attention? Rapoport et al. (1980) showed that normal subjects had improvements in concentration, vigilance, and attention. However, Satterfield et al. (1987) showed that methylphenidate did not improve the performance of normal subjects on CPTs but did improve the performance of adults with ADHD. As a result of these studies, it would appear that, in general, while the performance of normal subjects improves somewhat, subjects with ADHD show greater improvement as the result of stimulant treatment.

Given the above information, what is the optimal treatment regime? Physicians must first determine which medication to prescribe initially. The choice is usually between stimulants and antidepressants. In some situations, this choice will be easy. Adults with a major depressive disorder or anxiety disorder are more likely to benefit from antidepressants. However, adults whose primary disorder is ADHD are more likely to benefit from stimulants. For these adults, the physician will need to determine his or her comfort level with concerns about substance abuse and drug addiction. The physician may decide not to consider stimulant medications because of concern about drug addiction or may carefully consider the individual patient's risk for abuse.

When stimulant medication is chosen, the next decision concerns the particular stimulant to prescribe. While there is no scientific basis to determine which stimulant is best for adults, the most common choice is methylphenidate. It has been abused infrequently and is the most extensively studied. The average dose for children is between 10 and 20 mg. Usually, this dose is administered two to three times a day. For adults the dosage may be substantially higher and three dosage administrations per day may be needed. Beginning with a 10 mg tablet in the morning and at noon, an increase of 5 mg once a week to a maximum of 30 mg per dose is suggested. Follow-up should be conducted in one month, with questionnaires, global ratings, direct observation, and qualitative reports from the patient to determine the effectiveness of treatment. Additional follow-up information from peers or a spouse is also helpful. An afternoon dose can be added if symptoms recur, and an evening dose may be needed. Side effects are likely to include mild and temporary appetite suppression and sleeplessness. Increases in symptoms of anxiety may also be present. Experience with children suggests that when the optimal dosage is established it is not likely to change. A patient who appears to have been successfully treated but subsequently requires increasing dosages should raise concern about abuse or inappropriate use. Reevaluation intervals of no longer than six months are recommended. While there is a sustained-release preparation of methylphenidate, evaluation of this preparation in children has yielded mixed results. It is recommended that initial treatment for adults be undertaken with regular methylphenidate. If a longer duration of action is then desired, a change to the sustained-released preparation for comparison with regular methylphenidate may be appropriate. There is little data to determine whether generic preparations are as effective as the brand name Ritalin.

If an antidepressant is chosen, the next decision concerns which antidepressant to prescribe. Generic tricyclics (e.g., desipramine) are much less expensive than the specific serotonin reuptake inhibitors (e.g., Prozac). The generic tricyclics have been widely studied and proved efficacious for ADHD, the specific serotonin re-uptake inhibitors have not. It is recommended that dosage start with 25 mg desipramine tablets, beginning with one at night, and be increased one tablet every three days to 75 mg. Expected side effects may include dryness of the mouth, stomach pain, constipation, and sleepiness. If no effect is seen after one month, a blood level reading should be taken and the medication increased. If side effects permit, dosage should increase to obtain a blood level within the range considered therapeutic for treatment of moderate depression. If insufficient positive effect or side effects are present, a change in medication should be considered. Stimulants should be reconsidered as an alternative. If antidepressants are again chosen, consider a specific serotonin re-uptake inhibiter such as fluoxetine (Prozac). The initial dose is 20 mg once in the morning. If substantial results have not been obtained in one month, an increase to 40 mg should be considered. Side effects include sleeplessness, loss of sexual orgasm, irritability, and headache.

Once a medication is initiated for ADHD symptoms, the clinician should try to collect qualitative and, if possible, quantitative data (e.g., questionnaires) at least a few times during the first two weeks of medication usage and later during any adjustments. At the very least, standardized self-report and possibly spousal report sets of questionnaires should be completed during the first week of medication and compared with baseline observations. Clinicians should also be aware that data collected during assessment may not always make the best baseline information given a tendency toward regression to the mean with further assessment.

Any change in medication dosage should be followed by more data collection. These data should be summarized in writing and given to the physician. As noted earlier, clinicians sensitive to the potential side effects of medications are in a much better position to observe and report on these issues.

Because medications are likely to play an important role in the treatment of adult ADHD, clinicians must help physicians recognize that ADHD is diagnosed through a logical process based on measurable, observable behavior and that the risks and benefits of medication usage are evaluated according to a logical system. As S. Goldstein and Goldstein (1990) note, "By understanding the risks of medication and how to decrease them, the benefits of medication and how to increase them, and the alternatives to medication and how to use them, it is possible to make a reasoned and reasonable decision concerning medication intervention" (p. 266). The use of medications in the treatment of adult ADHD offers a potentially powerful treatment modality.

CHAPTER 14

Concluding Remarks

THE PATH TO SUCCESS IN LIFE is not easy. It requires focus, opportunity, commitment, and, most important, ability. Even when commitment, focus, and opportunity are present, weak learning and attentional abilities can and do create insurmountable hurdles. Life success takes many forms—vocational, family, religious, academic, social, community. For individuals with LD or ADHD, success in these important areas of life has been an elusive and, for some, quixotic quest. The available data suggest that the burdens of LD and ADHD throughout the life span far outweigh any potential benefits. Although it is the liabilities that most interest educators and clinicians, the assets of some of these individuals and their tenacity have certainly led to life success (Gerber & Reiff, 1991). For most, however, success often comes at a very high personal and emotional cost.

The outcome and profiles of adults with histories of LD or ADHD vary. The problems these two disabilities cause are clearly not outgrown but become part of these children grown up. In some cases, problems metamorphosize and change. In other cases, they are managed. They are, however, part of the living organism. Just as one cannot outgrow a body part, one does not outgrow LD or ADHD.

Individuals with LD or ADHD are affected by the same forces that affect and shape the lives of all of us. However, the data are clear. As the severity of LD and ADHD, and of comorbid problems, increases, the daily family, vocational, and interpersonal problems these people experience become a significant handicap. Further, for a large minority in the ADHD population, ADHD symptoms appear to be catalytic, increasing vulnerability in the face of other stressors to more serious adult life problems such as antisocial personality and substance abuse.

As our society becomes increasingly complex, the liabilities of living with LD and ADHD grow at an alarming pace. Although there are more regulations, there are fewer vocational opportunities, especially in blue-collar work, for adults with LD or ADHD. Even minimal-skill jobs today require what was considered a modest level of training a few years ago.

In the midst of this great period of change, there is still much not known about ADHD and LD in adulthood. Yet as scientist-practitioners, clinicians must balance continued research with appropriate, conscientious care. The issues needing future research are many:

374

- Accurate estimates of the adult LD and ADHD populations, symptom presentation, severity, and comorbidity
- The effects of other life factors, such as low socioeconomic status, weak intellect, or other family variables, on the adult outcome of children with LD or ADHD
- The employment-related problems the LD and ADHD populations face and the true benefits of compensation in the workplace
- The actual success of LD individuals with the intellectual capacity to attend college and the effect that attending and graduating from college has on their future vocational attainment
- The best means of providing vocational training for adults with LD or ADHD
- Understanding and helping to alleviate the daily life and emotional problems of individuals with LD or ADHD

The responsibility of balancing what is known and what is not known with what can realistically be done falls on the shoulders of clinicians. To be effective, a clinician must be aware of and must believe a number of facts:

- Children with ADHD or LD grow up to be adults with ADHD or LD.
- Adults with ADHD or LD can and do experience more life and vocational problems than others. For some, these problems are pervasive and intrusive. For others, they are fairly subtle. Data suggest that no one with a history of LD or ADHD is completely unaffected as an adult.
- Many people with LD or ADHD use other strengths to compensate for their disabilities and develop a variety of coping strategies that allow them to function better, but they do not outgrow their problems.
- Adult vocational and college programs for people with ADHD or LD are being developed. Nevertheless, clinicians are going to find themselves playing the increasingly important role of advocate, helping students with LD or ADHD make the transition to college and vocational programs.
- Despite increasing knowledge and greater availability of programs, demand outpaces supply. The number of individuals with LD or ADHD is increasing as quickly as the ability to identify these problems accurately in childhood improves. This increases demand for services and programs as these children and adolescents become adults. For example, recent estimates indicate that the number of children being treated for ADHD has more than doubled since 1990 (Williams, Lerner, Wigal, & Swanson, 1995).
- The adult ADHD and LD populations, as they become defined, offer excellent target markets for all of the fads, mythical treatments, and unproven remedies that have been aggressively marketed to parents of children with LD or ADHD. Clinicians will find themselves becoming sources of information.

Knowledgeable clinicians can give their clients a powerful sense of hope by being available and providing accurate information, understanding, and support. Much of the science remains in the future, but common sense and clinical judgment are undeniable. Identification through careful assessment, intervention and accommodation through careful treatment, and implementation and support through advocacy and education are making and will continue to make a positive difference in the lives of adults with ADHD and LD.

APPENDIX A

Resources for Late Adolescents and Adults

Organizations/Information Resources

ACT Assessment Special Testing—61
ACT Universal Testing
P.O. Box 4028
Iowa City, IA 52243-4028
319-337-1332

ADDult Support Network
2620 Ivy Place
Toledo, OH 43613
419-472-1286

Association for Higher Education and Disabilities (AHEAD)
P.O. Box 21192
Columbus, OH 43221-0192
614-488-4972

Children and Adults with Attention Deficit Disorder (CHADD)
499 NW 70th Avenue, Suite 308
Plantation, FL 33317
305-587-3700

Council for Learning Disabilities (CLD)
P.O. Box 40303
Overland Park, KS 66204
913-492-8755

Educational Testing Services (SAT tests)
SHEP Administration (Carnegie)
Rosedale Road
Princeton, NJ 08541

609-771-7137
609-951-1090 (fax)

Equal Employment Opportunity Commission
11305 Reed Hartman Highway No. 219
Cincinnati, OH 45241
800-669-3362

HEATH Resource Center
One DuPont Circle, Suite 670
Washington, DC 20036-1193
202-939-9320
800-544-3284

Information Center for Individuals with Disabilities (ICID)
20 Park Plaza, Room 330
Boston, MA 02116
617-727-5540

Learning Disabilities Association of America (LDA; formerly Association for Children and Adults with Learning Disabilities)
4156 Library Road
Pittsburgh, PA 15234
412-341-1515
412-341-8077

Learning Resources Network
1550 Hayes Drive
Manhattan, KS 66502
800-678-5376

National Attention Deficit Disorder Association (ADDA)
P.O. Box 1610
Valparaiso, IN 45384
219-462-5141 (fax)

National Center for Learning Disabilities
(formerly Foundation for Children with
Learning Disabilities)
99 Park Avenue
New York, NY 10016
212-687-7211

National Center for Research in Vocational
Education
2150 Shattuck Avenue, No. 1250
Berkeley, CA 94704
800-762-4093

National Library of Education at the U.S.
Office of Educational Research and
Improvement
800-424-1616

National Library Services for the Blind and
Physically Handicapped

291 Taylor Street NW
Washington, DC 20542

National Network of LD Adults (NNLDA)
808 North 82nd Street
Scottsdale, AZ 85257

Orton Dyslexia Society (ODS)
Chester Building, Suite 382
8600 LaSalle Road
Baltimore, MD 21204-6020
301-296-0232

President's Committee on Employment of
People with Disabilities
1111 20th Street NW, Room 600
Washington, DC 20036
202-653-5010

Rebus Institute
198 Taylor Blvd., Suite 201
Millbrae, CA 94030

Recording for the Blind and Dyslexic, Inc.
20 Roszel Road
Princeton, NJ 08540
800-221-4792

Organizations/Newsletters

ADDedum
5041-A Backlick Road
Annandale, VA 22003

ADDult News
c/o ADDA
2620 Ivy Place
Toledo, OH 43613

Adult ADD Association
1225 East Sunset Drive, No. 640
Bellingham, WA 98226

Adult ADDult Support Network
2620 Ivy Place
Toledo, OH 43613

Attention Deficit Disorders Association
P.O. Box 972
Mentor, OH 44061

Attention Deficit Information Network
475 Hillside Avenue
Needham, MA 02194

Challenge, Inc.
Box 488
West Newbury, MA 01985

Children and Adults with Attention Deficit
Disorder (CHADD)
499 NW 70th Avenue, No. 109
Plantation, FL 33317

JKL Communications
P.O. Box 40157
Washington, DC 20016

Learning Disabilities Association of America
(LDA)
4156 Library Road
Pittsburgh, PA 15234

National Center for Learning Disabilities
381 Park Avenue South, Suite 1420
New York, NY 10016

National Information Center for Children
and Youth with Disabilities
P.O. Box 1492
Washington, DC 20013-1492

National Institute for Attention Deficit Disorder
407 Resor Avenue
Cincinnati, OH 45220

National Network of Learning Disabled
   Adults
808 West 82nd Street, F-2
Scottsdale, AZ 85257

Orton Dyslexia Society
Chester Building, Suite 382
8600 Lasalle Road
Baltimore, MD 21204-6020

Neurology, Learning and Behavior Center
230 South 500 East, Suite 100
Salt Lake City, UT 84102

Books

Fielding, P., & Moss, J. R. (Eds.). (1989). *A national directory of four year colleges, two year colleges and post high school training programs for young people with learning disabilities (6th ed.).* Tulsa, OK: Partners in Publishing.

Gerber, P. J., & Reiff, H. B. (1991). *Speaking for themselves: Ethnographic interviews with adults with learning disabilities.* Ann Arbor, MI: University of Michigan Press.

Gerber, P. J., & Reiff, H. B. (Eds.) (1994). *Learning disabilities in adulthood: Persisting problems and evolving issues.* Boston: Andover.

Gordon, M., & McClure, F. D. (1995). *The down and dirty guide to adult attention deficit disorder.* DeWitt, NY: GSI Publications.

Hallowell, N., & Ratey, J. (1994). *Driven to distraction.* New York: Pantheon.

Hayes, M. L. (1993). *You don't outgrow it: Living with learning disabilities.* Novato, CA: Academic Therapy Publications.

Kravets, M., & Wax, I. (1991). *The K and W guide to colleges for the learning disabled.* New York: Harper Collins.

Latham, P. S., & Latham, P. H. (1992). *Attention deficit disorder and the law: A guide for advocates.* Washington, DC: JKL Communications.

Lipkin, M. (1992). *Private schools with programs or services for students with learning disabilities.* Schoolsearch, 127 Marsh Street, Belmont, MA 02178.

Lipkin, M. (1993). *Colleges with programs or services for students with learning disabilities (2nd ed.).* Schoolsearch, 127 Marsh Street, Belmont, MA 02178.

Liscio, M. A. (1984). *A guide to colleges for learning disabled students.* Orlando, FL: Harcourt Brace Jovanovich.

Mangrum, C., & Strichart, S. (Eds.). (1988). *Peterson's guide to colleges with programs for learning disabled students (2nd ed.).* Princeton, NJ: Peterson's Guides.

Nadeau, K. (1994). *Survival guide for college students with ADD or LD.* New York: Brunner/Mazel.

Nadeau, K. (1995). *ADD in adults: Research, diagnosis and treatment.* New York: Brunner/Mazel.

Nadeau, K. (1996). *A user-friendly guide to understanding adult ADD.* New York: Brunner/Mazel.

Sciafani, A. J., & Lynch, M. J. (1988). *College guide for students with learning disabilities.* Farmingville, NY: SPEDCO Associates.

Skyer, R., & Skyer, C. (1986). *What do you do after high school? The nationwide guide to residential, vocational, social and collegiate programs serving the adolescent, young adult, and adult with learning disabilities.* Rockaway Park, NY: Skyer Consultation Center. (To order, write to the ACLD Bookstore, 4156 Library Road, Pittsburgh, PA 15234)

Straughn, C. T. (Ed.). (1988). *Lovejoy's college guide for the learning disabled.* New York: Monarch.

Weiss, L. (1992). *Attention deficit disorder in adults.* Dallas, TX: Taylor.

Wender, P. H. (1987). *The hyperactive child, adolescent and adult: ADD through the life span.* New York: Oxford University Press.

APPENDIX B

Resources for Parents

Books

Barkley, R. A. (1987). *Defiant children: A clinician's manual for parent training.* New York: Guilford.

Bloomquist, M. L. (1996). *Skills training for children.* New York: Guilford.

Bramer, J. S. (in press). *ADD goes to college: Issues and strategies for students, counselors and educators.* Plantation, FL: Specialty Press.

Clark, L. (1986). *SOS: Help for parents.* Bowling Green, KY: Parent's Press.

Clarke, J. I., & Dawson, C. (1989). *Growing up again.* New York: Harper Collins.

Dendy, C. A. (1995). *Teenagers with ADD: A parent's guide.* Rockville, MD: Woodbine House.

Dinkmeyer, D., & McKay, G. D. (1982). *Systematic training for effective parenting: The parent's handbook.* Circle Pines, MN: American Guidance Service.

Goldstein, S., & Goldstein, M. (1992). *Hyperactivity: Why won't my child pay attention?* New York: Wiley.

Goldstein, S., & Ingersoll, B. (1995). *Lonely, sad and angry: A parent's guide to depression in children and adolescents.* New York: Doubleday.

Ingersoll, B. (1988). *Your hyperactive child.* New York: Doubleday.

Ingersoll, B., & Goldstein, S. (1993). *Attention deficit disorder and learning disabilities: Realities, myths and controversial treatments.* New York: Doubleday.

Parker, H. C. (1988). *The ADD hyperactivity workbook.* Plantation, FL: Impact Publications.

Patterson, G. R. (1975). *Families: Applications of social learning to family life.* Champaign, IL: Research Press.

Patterson, G. R., & Forgatch, M. S. (1987). *Parents and adolescents living together: Part 1. The basics. Part 2. Family problem solving.* Eugene, OR: Castalia.

Phelan, T. (1984). *1-2-3-Magic.* Child Management, 800 Roosevelt Rd., Glen Ellyn, IL 60137, 708-699-0484.

Popkin, M. (1986). *Active parenting.* Atlanta, GA: Author

Robin, A. L., & Foster, S. L. (1989). *Negotiating parent-adolescent conflict.* New York: Guilford.

Videotapes

Barkley, R. A. (1993). *ADHD—What can we do?* New York: Guilford.

Barkley, R. A. (1993). *ADHD—What do we know?* New York: Guilford.

Barkley, R. A. (1994). *ADHD in adults.* New York: Guilford.

Barkley, R. A. (1994). *ADHD in the classroom.* New York: Guilford.

Goldstein, S. (1989). *Why won't my child pay attention?* Salt Lake City, UT: Neurology, Learning and Behavior Center.

Goldstein, S. (1991). *It's just attention disorder.* Salt Lake City, UT: Neurology, Learning and Behavior Center.

Goldstein, S. (1993). *Why isn't my child happy?* Salt Lake City, UT: Neurology, Learning and Behavior Center.

Goldstein, S., & Goldstein, M. (1990). *Educating inattentive children.* Salt Lake City, UT: Neurology, Learning and Behavior Center.

Lavoie, R. (1974). *Understanding LD: How difficult can this be?* The FAT City Workshop, 508–888–0489.

Phelan, T. (1984). *1-2-3-Magic.* Child Management, 800 Roosevelt Rd., Glen Ellyn, IL 60137, 708–699–0484.

APPENDIX C

Adult Questionnaire Used at the Neurology, Learning and Behavior Center

Please bring this completed form with you at the time of your next appointment on

_____ at _____.

Name _____ Birthdate_____

Address _____
             Street   City   State   Zip

Home Phone ( ) _____ Work Phone ( )_____

Occupation _____

By whom were you referred? _____

With whom are you now living? (List people) _____

_____

_____

Do you live in a house, hotel, room, apartment, etc? _____

Marital Status: ☐ Single   ☐ Engaged   ☐ Married

                      ☐ Remarried   ☐ Separated   ☐ Divorced

                      ☐ Widowed

CLINICAL HISTORY

1.   State in your own words the nature of your problems and their duration. _____

      _____

2.   Give a brief account of the history and development of your complaints (from onset to present). _____

      _____

      _____

Note. Adult History Form, by S. Goldstein, 1993, Unpublished form, Neurology, Learning and Behavior Center, UT.

381

3. On the scale below please estimate the severity of your problem(s).

| Mildly upsetting | Moderately severe | Very severe | Extremely severe | Totally incapacitating |

4. Whom have you previously consulted about your present problem(s)?_____
   _____
   _____

DEVELOPMENTAL HISTORY

1. As far as you know, were there any problems with your mother's pregnancy or delivery of you? Yes ____ No ____
2. Was it a full term pregnancy? Yes ____ No ____
3. Did your mother use alcohol or other drugs during the pregnancy?
   Yes ____ No ____
   Details: _____
4. Did your mother smoke cigarettes during the pregnancy?
   Yes ____ No ____
   Details: _____
5. Did you have any developmental delays, i.e., in walking, talking or sitting up?
   Yes ____ No ____
   Details: _____
6. Did you have any childhood illnesses/diseases/major surgery?
   Yes ____ No ____
   Details: _____
7. Did you have any problems getting along with your peers as a child?
   Yes ____ No ____
   Details: _____
8. Did you have any temperament or mood difficulties as a child?
   Yes ____ No ____
   Details: _____
9. Underline any of the following that applied during your childhood:

Night terrors	Bed wetting	Sleeping
Thumb sucking	Nail biting	Stammering
Fears	Happy childhood	Unhappy childhood
Any other:		

10 Health during childhood (list illnesses) _____

_____

11. Health during adolescence (list illnesses) _____

_____

12. What is your height? _____ Your weight? _____

13. Any surgical operation (please list and give age at time) _____

_____

14. When were you last examined by a doctor? _____

_____

15. Any accidents _____

HEALTH HISTORY

1. Have you ever had any of the following:

		NEVER	PAST	PRESENT
1.	Allergies			
2.	Heart Problems			
3.	Epilepsy or Seizures			
4.	High Blood Pressure			
5.	Head injury with loss of consciousness			
6.	Lead Poisoning			
7.	Broken Bones			
8.	Surgery			
9.	Migraine Headaches			
10.	Thyroid Condition			
11.	Any Other Chronic Illness			

2. Are you currently taking any medications? Yes _____ No _____
Details _____

3. Please describe any other health difficulties you have experienced now or in the
past._____

4.   Underline any of the following that apply to you.

Headaches	Dizziness	Fainting Spells
Palpitations	Stomach Trouble	No Appetite
Bowel Disturbances	Fatigue	Insomnia
Nightmares	Take Sedatives	Alcoholism
Feel Tense	Feel Panicky	Tremors
Depressed	Suicidal	Take Drugs
Unable to Relax	Sexual Problems	Shy with People
Don't like weekends or vacations	Over Ambitious	Can't Make Decisions
	Inferiority Feelings	Home Conditions Bad
Can't Make Friends	Memory Problems	Unable to have a good time
Financial Problems	Concentration difficulties	Other:
Can't Keep a Job		

EMPLOYMENT HISTORY

1.   Current employment status (circle):

Full time	Unemployed	Homemaker
Part time	Student	Disabled

2.   Occupation: _____
       Current employer: _____
3.   Length of time in present job: _____
4.   History of previous employment:

<u>Job Title</u>   <u>Length of Time</u>   <u>Reason for Leaving</u>

MARITAL HISTORY

1.   How long have you been married? _____ Husband's/wife's age _____
2.   How long did you know your marriage partner before engagement? ____
3.   Occupation of husband or wife _____
4.   Personality of husband or wife (in your own words) _____
       _____
5.   In what areas is there compatibility _____
       _____

6. In what areas is there incompatibility _____
_____

7. How do you get along with your in-laws? (This includes brothers-in-law and sisters-in-law) _____
_____

8. How many children do you have? _____ Please list their sex and age(s)
_____

9. Do any of your children present special problems? _____
_____

10. Give details of any previous marriage(s) _____
_____

FAMILY DATA

1. Father:
   Living or deceased _____ If deceased, your age at the time of his death __
   Cause of death _____
   If alive, father's present age _____ Health _____
   Occupation _____

2. Mother:
   Living or deceased _____ If deceased, your age at the time of her death __
   Cause of death _____
   If alive, mother's present age _____ Health _____
   Occupation _____

3. Siblings:
   Number of brothers _____ Brother's ages _____
   Number of sisters _____ Sister's ages _____
   Relationship with siblings:
   (a) Past _____
   _____

   (b) Present _____
   _____

4. Give a description of your father's personality and his attitude toward you (past and present) _____
_____

5.   Give a description of your mother's personality and her attitude toward you (past and present) _____

6.   In what ways were you punished by your parents as a child? _____

7.   Give an impression of your home atmosphere (i.e., the home in which you grew up. Mention state of compatibility between parents and between parents and children) _____

8.   Were you able to confide in your parents? _____

9.   If you have a step-parent, give your age when parent remarried _____

10.   If you were not brought up by your parents, who did bring you up and between what years? _____

11.   Has anyone (parents, relatives, friends) ever interfered in your marriage, occupation, etc.? _____

12.   Who are the most important people in your life? _____

13.   Does any member of your family suffer from alcoholism, epilepsy or anything which can be considered a "mental disorder?" Give details_____

14.   Are there any other members of the family about whom information regarding illness, etc., is relevant? _____

15.   Recount any fearful or distressing experiences not previously mentioned _____

16.   List any situations that make you feel particularly anxious _____

17.   List the benefits you hope to derive from therapy _____

18.   List any situations which make you feel calm or relaxed _____

19.   Have you ever lost control (e.g., temper or crying or aggression)? If so, please describe _____

SOCIAL HISTORY

1. Do your moods change **very** frequently, abruptly, and/or unpredictably?
    Yes _____ No _____

2. Do you have trouble making friends? Yes _____ No _____

3. Do you have trouble keeping friends? Yes _____ No _____

4. Do you have trouble in your relationships with others?
    Yes _____ No _____

5. Do you have problems with your temper? Yes _____ No _____
    Details _____

6. Do you have a driver's license? Yes _____ No _____

7. Has your license ever been suspended? Yes _____ No _____
    Details _____

8. How many speeding/moving violation tickets have you ever gotten?_____

9. Have you ever been arrested for DUI? Yes _____ No _____

10. How many car accidents, regardless of fault, have you ever been in? _____

11. How many times have you moved since leaving high school? _____

12. In what ways do your ADHD symptoms interfere in your life? _____
    _____

13. In what ways have you tried to compensate for or cope with your deficits? ____
    _____

14. Underline any of the following words which apply to you.

worthless	useless	a "nobody"	life is empty
inadequate	stupid	incompetent	naive
morally wrong	horrible thoughts	guilty	evil
anxious	agitated	hostile	full of hate
panicky	aggressive	cowardly	unassertive
unattractive	repulsive	ugly	deformed
unloved	misunderstood	depressed	lonely
confused	unconfident	bored	restless
worthwhile	sympathetic	in conflict	full of regrets
confident	considerate	attractive	intelligent
"can't do anything right"		others	

15. Present interests, hobbies, and activities _____
    _____

16.   How is most of your free time occupied? _____

_____

17.   What is the last grade of schooling that you completed? _____
18.   Scholastic abilities; strengths and weaknesses _____

_____

19.   Where you ever bullied or severely teased? _____

_____

20.   Do you make friends easily? _____ Do you keep them? _____

Use the space below to add any information you feel is important or to finish answering any questions that required more space.

List names and addresses of any other professionals consulted (including family doctor)

1. _____
2. _____
3. _____
4. _____

APPENDIX D

The Transition Profile: A Guide to Transition Planning

INTRODUCTION

The Transition Profile is an effective tool for developing plans for transition services for students with disabilities. The Profile provides a basis for recognizing student strengths and preferences and for determining present and future needs of students eligible for transition services. It can be used by teachers, parents, students, community resource personnel, and employers to create a realistic appraisal of student strengths, competencies and vocational needs. Based on this individualized appraisal, transition services can be created that will enable students to achieve desired postschool outcomes.

The Transition Profile was developed to provide a structured, systematic way to consider the choices available when projecting the postschool outcomes for individual students. The basic components are divided into two areas: Basic Skill Competencies for Employment and Postschool Outcomes. The Basic Skill Competencies for Employment are based on the legal requirement that instruction be an integral part of transition planning and service. The additional categories of Learning Styles, Computer Literacy and Study Skills extend the categories beyond the realm of basic academics. The remaining required areas of community experiences, employment objectives, adult living objectives, acquisition of daily skills, and functional vocational evaluation are included in Postschool Outcomes.

The Transition Profile is recommended for use as a pre-IEP planning document in the initial stage of the planning process, the profile provides a summary of categories that should be considered for each student. As each category is considered, there is a continuum of possible choices for each student. For example, within the areas of development employment, the choices can range from career exploration to gainful employment. Each category contains skills that have been mastered, skills targeted at the present time, items to be included at a future date, items that require further evaluation before a decision can be made, and items and categories not appropriate for a given student. The Profile can assist the planning team by targeting areas where more information is needed or where further assessment is necessary. It can help identify which community agencies need to be involved at the IEP Meeting and can be used to prepare for the IEP meeting where transition needs and projected postschool outcomes will be discussed. The Profile can be a planning document that provides the information base for both short-term and long-term transition goals. For the transition planning team, the Transition Profile can become the bridge needed between the regular IEP and the transition IEP.

The development nature of the Transition Profile can be easily adapted to portfolio assessment. Documentation of achievements and completion of transition activities can form the basis of an individualized student portfolio which helps to personalize the transition process. Each student can take responsibility for helping to provide documentation of transition goals met and activities completed. The portfolio can be presented by a student to a prospective employer as a record of the student's background and experiences. The portfolio creates new opportunities for the student to increase personal responsibility and to develop communication skills. In effect, development of the portfolio can become a transition activity.

EVALUATION CRITERIA FOR THE TRANSITION PROFILE

Within the area of Basic Skill Competencies for Employment, each category states a long-term goal. The goal is then analyzed into tasks that are the subskills necessary to achieve the goal. Each subskill can be evaluated according to four criteria:

Evaluation Criteria for Basic Skill Competencies for Employment:

1. MASTERY: Student can demonstrate mastery of this skill. Enter current date to show skill was discussed and evaluated.

2. N/A: The skills is not appropriate for this student. Enter date that this skill was reviewed.

3. IEP: If the skill is on the present IEP, write R-IEP and note page number, e.g., R-IEP, p. 3, or objective number, e.g., R-IEP, #7. If the skill is appropriate for the student and will be included in the Transition IEP, it will e addressed at the IEP meeting.

4. FUTURE: If the skill is appropriate for the student but will be addressed at a later date in the planning process, estimate date that the skill be included and the agency responsible.

While the Transition Profile provides a wide range of objectives and skills, adjustments and additions will be required for some students whose needs are not adequately described in the profile. Each category includes an extra line for additional objectives. However, it may be necessary to add some other

categories and objectives to meet specific needs of some students or to include goals of a specific technical nature.

In the area of Postschool Outcomes, the categories represent environments, services, and skill competencies. Different criteria are used in this section of the profile to reflect the differing natures of the categories.

Evaluation Criteria for Postschool Outcomes:

1. PARTICIPATION: Student has already been enrolled in program. Enter dates of participation, e.g., 93-94.

2. N/A: Not appropriate for this student. Enter date profile was reviewed, e.g., 5-93.

3. CONCERN: This area is a possible concern for this student. Enter date profile was reviewed, e.g., 5-93.

4. AWARENESS: Student demonstrates awareness of need in this area. Enter date profile was reviewed, e.g., 5-93.

5. ELIGIBLE: Student is already eligible for this service. Enter date profile was reviewed, e.g., 5-93.

6. APPROPRIATE: This choice is appropriate for this student. Enter date profile was reviewed, e.g., 5-93.

7. MASTERY: Student can demonstrate mastery of this skill. Enter date skill was evaluated, e.g., 5-93.

8. IEP: If the skill is on the present IEP, write R-IEP and note page number, e.g., R-IEP, p. 3 or objective number, e.g., R-IEP, #7.
If the skill is appropriate for the student and will be included in the Transition IEP, it will be addressed at the IEP meetings.

9. FUTURE: If the skill is appropriate for the student but will be addressed at a later date, estimate date that the skill will be included and the agency responsible.

TRANSITION PROFILE	Background Information

BACKGROUND INFORMATION

Student Name: _____ DOB: _____ Age: _____ Social Security: _____

School: _____ School Year/Grade: _____

Disabling Condition(s): _____

Program Placement (REPT)*: _____ (REPT) _____ Sp. Ed. Class _____ Other _____

Anticipated Date of Public School Exit: Month: _____ Year: _____ Date Profile Initiated: _____

Name/Title of Transition: _____

The Transition Profile was discussed/reviewed on these dates: Name/Title of Participants:

_____   _____

_____   _____

_____   _____

_____   _____

_____   _____

_____   _____

*REPT - Regular Education Part Time

1

TRANSITION PROFILE   Area I: Basic Skill Competencies for Employment

CATEGORY A: READING
GOAL: The student will locate, understand, and interpret information in written form.

	Mastery	N/A	IEP	Future
1. Locates information in books, magazines, newspapers				
2. Answers factual questions from material in books, magazines, newspapers				
3. Sequences events in a story, book, or movie				
4. Makes inferences, chooses main idea, predicts outcomes, identifies cause and effect, draws conclusions				
5. Distinguishes fact and opinion				
6. Identifies author bias				
7. Recognizes propaganda				
8. Follows assembly instructions				
9. Locates information in a manual				
10. Follows directions in a manual				
11. Answers questions from interpreting a graph				
12. Locates information on a schedule				
13. Other (Describe)				

2

393

CATEGORY B: WRITING

GOAL: The student communicates thoughts, ideas, information, and messages in writing and creates documents such as letters, directions, reports and graphs.

	Mastery	N/A	IEP	Future
1. Applies appropriate rules of grammar to writing.				
2. Produces written work with correct spelling.				
3. Arranges sentences in logical order to form coherent paragraph.				
4. Composes a paragraph on a given topic that has correct punctuation, spelling and grammar and expresses clear thought.				
5. Communicates thoughts, ideas, information, and messages clearly.				
6. Can write summaries of stories, articles and movies.				
7. Prepares instructions in writing.				
8. Summarizes oral instruction in written form.				
9. Composes social letters.				
10. Composes business letters in correct form.				
11. Writes a report on a given topic.				
12. Writes a speech to inform, persuade.				
13. Creates graphs to present information.				
14. Produces written documents using a computer/word processor.				
15. Transfers information into written form to complete reports, summaries.				
16. Takes notes on oral presentations.				
17. Evaluates own performance in written form according to preestablished criteria.				
18. Correctly completes job application form.				
19. Creates resume for job application.				
20. Records progress in personal portfolio.				
21. Other (Describe)				

3

CATEGORY C: ARITHMETIC/MATHEMATICS

GOAL: The student performs basic computations and solves practical problems using a variety of techniques.

	Mastery	N/A	IEP	Future
1. Performs addition, subtraction, multiplication and division on whole numbers, fractions, and decimals.				
2. Performs addition, subtraction, multiplication and division on whole numbers, fractions, and decimals using a calculator.				
3. Solves multistep story problems using addition, subtraction, multiplication, and division.				
4. Uses formulas to derive area, perimeter, volume and circumference.				
5. Demonstrates mastery of money, concepts and making change.				
6. Understands application of time in story problems.				
7. Determines hours worked at regular time and overtime.				
8. Determines cost of materials needed for a project.				
9. Determines total amount due for sale of goods.				
10. Figures sales tax due on a given figure.				
11. Converts unit measures to metric system.				
12. Applies math skills to measuring tasks.				
13. Can apply math skills in budgeting.				
14. Applies math skills to wages, withholding.				
15. Completes time sheet correctly for hours worked.				
16. Completes records of financial transactions.				
17. Schedules oneself on daily, weekly, monthly basis.				
18. Figures percentage of increase, decrease.				
19. Figures sale price when discount and original price are given.				
20. Computes interest amounts on installment sales.				
21. Reconciles checking and/or savings account.				
22. Creates graph to display financial information.				
23. Other (Describe).				

4

CATEGORY D: LISTENING

GOAL: The student will attend to, interpret and respond appropriately to verbal messages and nonverbal cues.

	Mastery	N/A	IEP	Future
1. Listens with a purpose in both small and large group situations.				
2. Understands and follows multistep directions.				
3. Repeats and/or summarizes directions and asks for clarification when needed.				
4. Forms sensory images (visualizes) from oral directions.				
5. Translates oral directions into a series of steps (1st, 2nd, 3rd, etc.)				
6. Interprets and evaluates information obtained from resource -- people, books, tapes, radio and video presentations.				
7. Listens and takes notes on important points.				
8. Recognizes nonverbal cues such as body language, eye contact, facial expressions.				
9. Can infer from others' behavior and nonverbal cues.				
10. Listens carefully to questions to determine form of answer or type of response needed.				
11. Other (Describe)				

CATEGORY E: SPEAKING

GOAL: The student organizes ideas and communicates effectively with peers, supervisors, and others in the workplace.

	Mastery	N/A	IEP	Future
1. Communicates orally using good standard English.				
2. Communicates well with adults and peers.				
3. Participates as a member of a team.				
4. Formulates and asks questions when needed.				
5. Evaluates and answers questions.				
6. Explains schedules.				
7. Explains procedures.				
8. Describes problem to teacher/supervisor.				
9. Organizes and communicates ideas in conversations and in groups.				
10. Organizes ideas and communicates oral messages appropriate for listeners.				
11. Gives instructions to a group of peers.				
12. Develops and states a point of view to individuals and groups.				
13. Presents view with purpose of convincing or persuading.				
14. Introduces self and others.				
15. Demonstrates courteous telephone behaviors appropriate for home or work.				
16. Answers questions appropriately in interview situation.				
17. Handles complaints in a polite, courteous manner with appropriate voice tone and body language.				
18. Coordinates verbal language with nonverbal cues such as body language.				
19. Choose verbal language appropriate in style, tone, and level of complexity for target audience.				
20. Verbally states personal rights and responsibilities.				
21. Other (Describe)				

6

397

CATEGORY F: LEARNING STYLES

GOAL: The student will be able to apply knowledge of Learning Styles to career choices and environments.

	Mastery	N/A	IEP	Future
1. Explains his/her major learning styles				
2. Identifies learning environments that complement his/her style.				
3. Analyzes new skills to be learned and then uses his/her major learning style to master the material.				
4. Identifies characteristics of his/her learning from a list or right-brained, left-brained, and whole-brain descriptors.				
5. Identifies random, sequential, concrete and abstract characteristics.				
6. Evaluates job descriptions and work environments to see which one match his/her learning styles.				
7. Other (Describe)				

7

CATEGORY C: COMPUTER LITERACY
GOAL: The student will demonstrate a working knowledge of word processing programs and computer software and hardware.

		Mastery	N/A	IEP	Future
1.	Demonstrates basic keyboarding skills.				
2.	Identifies meaning of words considered to be the specialized language of computer jargon.				
3.	Understands the phases of the computer information cycle (input, process, output, and storage).				
4.	Explains difference between hardware and software.				
5.	Demonstrates the steps to follow in the proper care and handling of software disks.				
6.	Correctly uses technical terms related to computer systems.				
7.	Matches software to situations using terms: spreadsheet, graphics, program, word processor, accounting program, desktop publisher, computer games.				
8.	Runs software programs effectively.				
9.	Operates a word processing program to produce text and written documents.				
10.	Identifies different types of printers.				
11.	Other (describe).				

8

399

CATEGORY H: STUDY SKILLS
GOAL: The student will use appropriate study skills to prepare for tests.

	Mastery	N/A	IEP	Future
1. Uses a system to maintain organization of class notes, assignments, completed homework, and important dates.				
2. Takes notes during class discussion.				
3. Copies what teacher writes on board.				
4. Recognizes teacher cues for important information and writes down information.				
5. Uses stars, underlining, and the like, to emphasize important information.				
6. Utilizes a study buddy or gets copies of class notes to complete personal notes.				
7. Obtains note for classes missed.				
8. Writes down all assignments and due dates.				
9. Saves homework and studies to review for tests.				
10. Reads questions at end of assignment before reading material.				
11. Identifies boldface words as important.				
12. Writes definitions or facts for all boldface words.				
13. Studies all charts, pictures, and captions.				
14. Looks up any words he/she doesn't understand.				
15. Can use index to obtain information.				
16. Uses glossary to find meanings of words.				

9

CATEGORY H: STUDY SKILLS   (CONTINUED)

	Mastery	N/A	IEP	Future
17. Identifies words in questions.				
18. Locates key words by skimming material.				
19. Formulates answers using key words.				
20. Uses a teacher-made study guide to prepare for tests.				
21. Creates own study guide to prepare for tests.				
22. Creates flashcards to prepare for tests.				
23. Develops word associations to aid memory.				
24. Uses pneumonic devices to aid memory.				
25. Applies strategies to true-false questions.				
26. Applies strategies to true-false correction questions.				
27. Applies strategies to multiple choice questions.				
28. Use key words to answer essay questions.				
29. Applies time management skills to assignments.				
30. Applies time management skills to test taking.				
31. Other (Describe).				

10

TRANSITION PROFILE   Area II: Postschool Outcomes

CATEGORY A: JOB TRAINING AND PLACEMENT
GOAL: The student will complete training programs and hold a job of his/her own.

Check Services/Programs that will be needed by this student	Participation	N/A	IEP	Future
1. Prevocational Education				
2. Vocational Evaluation				
3. Vocational (Career) Education				
4. Vocational Technical Center				
5. Rehabilitation Facilities				
6. Volunteer Work				
7. In-School Work-Study Experience				
8. Summer Employment				
9. Ongoing Supported Work: Workcrew/Enclaves/Workshops				
10. Community Work Experience (Daily Support)				
11. Community Work Experience (Limited Support)				
12. Employment Placement Assistance and Counseling (Bureau of Employment Programs)				
13. Community Employment Programs - Specify program:				
14. On the Job Training				
15. Competitive Employment With No Assistance				
16. Military Service				
17. Other (describe)				

11

CATEGORY B: LIMITS TO EMPLOYABILITY
GOAL: The student will understand the need for special consideration in job placement in areas indicated.

	Concern	N/A	IEP	Future
1. Intellectual				
2. Physical				
3. Motor-Sensory				
4. Communication				
5. Environmental Stress				
6. Mobility/Transportation				
7. Other (Describe)				
8. No Anticipated Limits to Employability				

12

CATEGORY C: POSTSECONDARY EDUCATION
GOAL: The student will enroll in postsecondary course of study.

	Appropriate	N/A	IEP	Future
1. Community College				
2. College/University				
3. Adult Continuing Education				
4. Technical Training				
5. 2 + 2 Program				
6. Other (describe)				

13

404

CATEGORY D: MEDICAL SERVICES AND THERAPIES
GOAL: The student will demonstrate an understanding of his/her needs for medical services and therapies.

	Awareness	N/A	IEP	Future
1. Behavioral				
2. Occupational				
3. Physical				
4. Speech/Language/Hearing				
5. Vision				
6. Drug/Alcohol Abuse				
7. Family Planning				
8. Sex Education				
9. Genetic and Family Counseling				
10. Crisis Intervention				
11. Other (describe)				

14

CATEGORY E: MEDICAL RESOURCES
GOAL: The student will follow proper procedures to handle medical need and expenses.

Check Service/Programs that will be needed by this student.

		Eligible	N/A	IEP	Future
1.	Group Policy				
2.	Individual Policy				
3.	Medicaid				
4.	Dental Care				
5.	Accident Insurance				
6.	Other (describe)				

15

406

CATEGORY F: INCOME
GOAL: The student will have sufficient financial support to live adequately.

	Appropriate	N/A	IEP	Future
1. Family Support				
2. Supplemental Security Income				
3. Earned Income				
4. Unearned Income				
5. Insurance				
6. General Public Assistance				
7. Food Stamps				
8. Other (describe)				

CATEGORY C: HOUSING/RESIDENTIAL
GOAL: The student will live short-term/long-term in the following situation:

	Appropriate	N/A	IEP	Future
1. With Family				
2. Adult Foster Care				
3. Group Home				
4. Accessible Housing				
5. Subsidized Housing				
6. Independent Living (Daily Support)				
7. Independent Living (Infrequent Support)				
8. Independent Living (Time-Limited Support)				
9. Independent Living (No Support)				
10. Other (describe)				

16

CATEGORY H: COMMUNITY LEISURE AND RECREATIONAL ACTIVITIES
GOAL: The student will participate in community activities.

	Appropriate	N/A	IEP	Future
1. Specialized/Recreational Activities				
2. Community Centers				
3. Community Colleges				
4. Independent Activities				
5. Clubs/Groups: Social, Hobby, Church				
6. Volunteers				
7. Other (describe)				

17

408

CATEGORY I: INDEPENDENT LIVING SKILLS
GOAL: The student will meet and handle the demands of daily independent living.

	Mastery	N/A	IEP	Future
(1) HOUSEHOLD MANAGEMENT: The student will locate an appropriate living situation and manage the household responsibilities.				
1. Reads local newspaper ads to find available housing				
2. Researches other sources for housing to buy or rent				
3. Identifies personal housing needs				
4. Evaluates available housing in relation to needs				
5. Determines price range for rent/payments				
6. Demonstrates behaviors needed to arrange opportunity to view housing				
7. Computes estimated cost of rent, utilities, food and other expenses				
8. Compares estimated expenses to income				
9. Understands terms of lease or rental agreement				
10. Identifies steps needed to establish utilities				
11. Lists household chores and creates schedule				
12. Develops menus and shopping lists				
13. Other (Describe)				

18

CATEGORY I: INDEPENDENT LIVING SKILLS				CONTINUED

	Mastery	N/A	IEP	Future
(1) MONEY MANAGEMENT				
1. Understands earnings: Net and Gross Wages/Withholding				
2. Creates list of monthly expenses				
3. Opens personal savings/checking account				
4. Manages personal savings/checking account				
5. Understands how to share costs with roommate				
6. Creates monthly budget for income/expenses				
7. Creates monthly calendar for payment of bills				
8. Understands value of checks and money order to pay bills				
9. Files receipts in personal file				
10. Evaluates costs of major purchases				
11. Understands meaning of good credit rating				
12. Other (Describe)				
(3) PERSONAL AND FAMILY RELATIONS				
1. Identifies steps needed to maintain contact with family				
2. Develops and maintains friendships with peers, roommates, and support groups				
3. Makes healthy lifestyle choices				
4. Understands rights of others to privacy, respect, safety				
5. Explains role of individuals in relationships				

19

CATEGORY I: INDEPENDENT LIVING SKILLS

CONTINUED

	Mastery	N/A	IEP	Future
6. Identifies individual responsibilities in relationships				
7. Understands cooperative role of roommates				
8. Identifies steps needed for conflict resolution and problem solving				
9. Explains essential elements of relationships: Communication, Trust, Caring and Respect				
10. Identifies resource people for personal loss and handling grief				
(4) SAFETY				
1. Identifies characteristics of a safe living environment				
2. Identifies characteristics of a safe work environment				
3. Explains/demonstrates emergency procedures for home, school, and the workplace				
4. Other (describe)				
(5) WELLNESS/PERSONAL HYGIENE				
1. Establishes daily schedule that promotes physical fitness and exercise				
2. Plans meals that represent balanced diet				
3. Include regular mealtimes in daily schedule				
4. Shows awareness of basic health care needs				
5. Understands stress management strategies				
6. Other (Describe)				

20

	Mastery	N/A	IEP	Future
(6) TRAVEL/TRANSPORTATION				
1. Travels from his/her home to work, school, medical services, shopping, recreation, and social events				
2. Travels independently (car, bicycle, walk)				
3. Travels independently on public transportation				
4. Understands how to set up a carpool				
5. Travels with specialized equipment and/or transportation				
6. Other (describe)				
(7) CITIZENSHIP				
1. Identifies and explains responsibilities of citizenship				
2. Understands need to file and pay taxes				
3. Demonstrates awareness/understanding of laws of community				
4. Obeys laws of community				
5. Demonstrates awareness/understanding of rules of workplace/school				
6. Obeys rules of workplace/school				
7. Anticipates consequences for noncompliance				
8. Understands the significance of voting				
9. Knows procedures necessary to register and vote				
10. Other (describe)				

21

CATEGORY J: SELF-ADVOCACY SKILLS

GOAL: The student will behave and speak in a manner which represents and protects his/her interests.

	Mastery	N/A	IEP	Future
1. States rights mandated under Public Law 101-476				
2. States rights mandated under Section 504 of the Rehabilitation Act				
3. States differences between IDEA and Section 504 of the Rehabilitation Act				
4. Identifies support service staff of postsecondary institutions				
5. Defines the terms "assertive," "passive," and "aggressive"				
6. States example of his/her own assertive, passive, and aggressive behaviors				
7. Responds assertively in a given situation				
8. Identifies and requests accommodations needed for a course or job				
9. Works with a personal care attendant appropriately				
10. Communicates with parents and teachers to determine realistic goals				
11. Follows up on Transition Plan objectives for which he/she is responsible				
12. Completes job applications appropriately				
13. Develops and completes a job resume				
14. Develops and compiles an Exit File/Portfolio				
15. Demonstrates needed behaviors for job interview				
16. Other (Describe)				

22

CATEGORY K: SOCIAL COMPETENCIES
GOAL: The student will demonstrate needed social skills to make a positive adjustment in the school, the workplace and the community.

	Mastery	N/A	IEP	Future
(1) INTRAPERSONAL SKILLS				
1. Demonstrates acceptance and respect for self				
2. Identifies and interprets feelings of fear, anger, happiness and sadness				
3. Understands the relationship between self-esteem and behavior				
4. Understands personal interests, preferences, and aptitude and relates these to career options				
5. Sets standards and goals appropriate for level of ability				
6. Evaluates personal behavior in relation to set of standards				
7. Evaluates personal work performance in relation to established standards				
8. Sets personal goals				
9. Develops strategies to achieve personal goals				
10. Implements strategies to achieve personal goals				
11. Adjusts strategies as needed				
12. Recognizes personal mistakes and failures				
13. Recognizes when to seek support people and ask for help				
14. Assess/anticipates results of personal actions				
15. Accepts personal responsibility for school work				
16. Accepts personal responsibility for actions in workplace				
17. Accepts personal responsibility for actions in home and community				
18. Evaluates personal behavior in relation to standards of school, workplace, and community				
19. Other (describe)				

23

414

	Mastery	N/A	IEP	Future
(2) INTERPERSONAL SKILLS				
1. Demonstrates acceptance and respect for others and their opinions				
2. Respects the rights of others and their property				
3. Respects cultural differences				
4. Respects individual differences				
5. Is sensitive to feelings and problems of others				
6. Creates personal analogy to identify with feelings of others				
7. Offers assistance to others				
8. Considers, accepts alternative points of view				
9. Provides constructive criticism to others				
10. Communicates concerns about behaviors/problems of others				
11. Accepts constructive criticism from others; teachers, peers, coworkers, supervisors				
12. Contributes/facilitates decision making in a group				
13. Understands need for authority and respects authority				
14. Meets behavior standards of school, workplace, and community				
15. Applies/maintains personal standards in group situation				
16. Other (describe)				

24

	Mastery	N/A	IEP	Future
(3) PROBLEM SOLVING SKILLS				
1. Can identify a problem				
2. Evaluates possible causes of problem				
3. Develops a list of possible actions to take				
4. Lists pros and cons of different choices				
5. Evaluates possible consequences of each action				
6. Chooses a course of action				
7. Implements a course of action				
8. Evaluates outcome of decision				
9. Revises plan if needed				
10. Other (describe)				

25

APPENDIX E

The University of Connecticut Program for College Students with Learning Disabilities (UPLD) Brochure

---

Joan M. McGuire, Director

A. Vivienne Litt, Assistant to the Director

Nanette Hatzes

The University of Connecticut is committed to assuring equal educational opportunity for students with learning disabilities who have the potential for success in a highly competitive university setting. Since 1984, a comprehensive program has been available to assist qualified students with learning disabilities to become independent and successful learners within the regular University curriculum. The University Program for College Students with Learning Disabilities (UPLD) is designed to complement and support, but not duplicate, the University's existing campus services and programs. UPLD is located in the Gentry School of Education and is part of the A. J. Pappanikou Center on Special Education and Rehabilitation. This brochure is designed to cover several areas related to UPLD: the process of applying for admission as an incoming freshman or transfer student, accessing UPLD services which are provided by a staff of trained Learning Specialists, and questions which are often asked about services at the University of Connecticut for students with learning disabilities.

ADMISSIONS PROCESS

Students with learning disabilities may voluntarily self-identify on the application for admission or in a cover letter. Upon self-identification, applicants are sent a letter from the Admissions Office outlining documentation which can be voluntarily submitted for consideration in the admissions process. At the University of Connecticut, a thorough review process is conducted to determine if a student with a learning disability is qualified. Typically, the profile of students offered admission is as follows:

- High school rank in the upper third in competitive, college preparatory coursework
- Performance in another college at a 2.5 or higher grade point average
- Combined SAT scores of 800 and above (nonstandard administration of this test is encouraged)
- Above average intellectual potential
- Strong personal motivation for college study

If a student does not meet the standard University criteria for admission, voluntarily submitted documentation is considered through a cooperative procedure between the Admissions Office and UPLD. Guidelines for documentation are included in this brochure. A personal interview is not a required component of the admission process. *All documentation should be sent to the Director of UPLD.*

ACCESSING SERVICES

Any student with a documented learning disability is eligible to receive services from UPLD. To access services, students must refer themselves to UPLD and provide adequate documentation. Since the purpose of the documentation is to assist the student and the University in determining reasonable academic adjustments as stipulated under Section 504 of the Rehabilitation Act of 1973 (e.g., extended test time, reduced courseload, auxiliary aids), the following guidelines should be followed to assure that the diagnostic evaluation report is appropriate for verifying accommodation needs:

1. Testing must be comprehensive and must include more than one test. Minimally, domains to be addressed include aptitude, achievement, and information processing.
2. Testing must be current. In most cases, this means within the past three years.
3. There must be clear and specific evidence and identification of a learning disability. A "unique learning style" or "learning differences" in and of itself does not constitute a learning disability.
4. Actual test scores or data should be included.
5. Professionals conducting the assessment must be qualified to do so. Experience in working with an adult population is essential.
6. Diagnostic reports must include the names and titles of the evaluators as well as the date(s) of testing. Background information regarding the student's history with respect to age at diagnosis and educational interventions is very helpful.

All materials submitted to UPLD to verify eligibility and determine reasonable academic adjustments are treated as confidential information.

PROGRAM SERVICES

Three types of program services are offered along a continuum leading to independence. Components of Direct Instruction, Monitoring, and Consultation are illustrated in the UPLD Continuum of Services.

A trained staff of Learning Specialists (graduate students pursuing Masters and Doctoral degrees) are available to work with students on developing learning strategies to apply to their

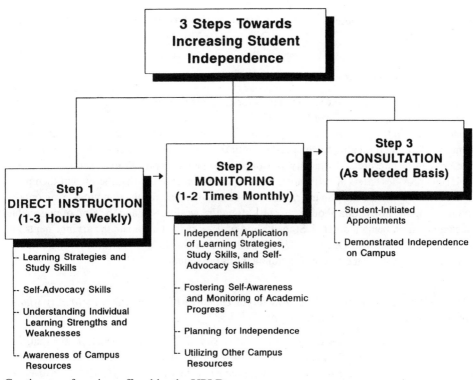

Continuum of services offered by the UPLD

college coursework. Individual structured sessions are planned on a weekly, biweekly, or monthly basis. Students are encouraged to plan their coursework in a way which affords an opportunity for success which may include a reduced courseload and extending the time period for degree completion. Accommodations including, but not limited to, alternative testing, use of a tape recorder for notetaking, and taped textbooks are facilitated by program staff.

Learning Specialists also assist students with learning disabilities to identify and make use of existing campus resources such as the Center for Students with Disabilities, Counseling Services, the Speech and Hearing Clinic, Writing Resource Center, Math Center, Mental Health Services and Career Services. UPLD staff work closely with students to empower them to plan and implement a successful academic experience. Training in self-advocacy skills encourages students to consult directly with faculty regarding modifications and alternative testing procedures. Learning Specialists are available to assist students to identify and monitor their needs for additional support services. This process culminates in the development of an individualized, comprehensive, educational plan which is cooperatively generated by the student, the Learning Specialist, and UPLD administrative staff.

Learning Specialists also assist students with learning disabilities to identify which level of program services will best meet their individual needs. Most students find that it is beneficial to access services at the Direct Instruction level, and to progress at an individual rate through the UPLD Continuum as they experience increasing confidence and competence. Support services are available at no cost, and for as long as a student needs them.

FREQUENTLY ASKED QUESTIONS ABOUT SERVICES FOR STUDENTS WITH LEARNING DISABILITIES

How are reasonable testing accommodations provided?

Students should discuss their specific needs for testing accommodations (e.g., extended time, separate location, or use of word processing) with UPLD staff *within the first two weeks of a semester.* It is in the student's best interest to self-identify to professors at the beginning of the semester. Waiting until after the first test or until the end of the semester to request accommodations can be interpreted by faculty as avoidance or lack of motivation.

UPLD provides letters of verification based upon documentation that the student then presents to faculty. This initiates an interaction between student and faculty that provides an opportunity to share information about a student's strengths, weaknesses, and the kind of reasonable accommodation being requested. Students and professors then negotiate the arrangements for testing accommodations. Of course, UPLD staff are available to assist students throughout this process for as many semesters as accommodations are required.

Are students assured priority registration for courses which are taught by faculty who are helpful to students with learning disabilities?

There are over 1,000 courses offered at the University of Connecticut which means that it is unrealistic to "handpick" faculty and classes. Furthermore, the better able a student is in working with a variety of instructors the more prepared he or she will be to work within the diversity of workplace environments.

Are students assisted in choosing which courses to take?

Staff of UPLD are not qualified to serve as academic advisors since there are nearly 100 possible majors offered. However, students often do identify themselves as having a learning disability when meeting with an advisor through the University's system of advisement. UPLD staff are trained to assist students in their understanding of strengths and weaknesses which is important when planning a semester. For example, if reading is slow and challenging, it is helpful to balance a semester so that it does not include four courses which have heavy reading demands.

Are there smaller classes for students with learning disabilities?

All students with learning disabilities are fully integrated within every program at the University of Connecticut. There are no separate classes. Academic standards are in no way modified.

Can students use a tape recorder in classes?

Many students find that tape recorders are helpful in reviewing and adding to class notes. As a common courtesy, students are encouraged to speak with professors about using a tape recorder before appearing in class ready to tape.

Can students request a single room in a dormitory?

Because there is a limited number of single dormitory rooms on campus, priority is based upon the nature and severity of a student's disability. There are students with physical disabilities who must have access to the accommodation of a single room. Very rarely does the student with a learning disability require a single room since there are many places on campus which provide quiet, nondistracting study environments (e.g., study rooms designated for students with disabilities in the Homer Babbidge Library). Of course, each case is considered on an individual basis.

How long does it typically take a student with learning disabilities to complete an undergraduate program at the University of Connecticut?

It is reasonable for students to plan a course of study in a way which will promote success. Many students with learning disabilities spread their coursework over a longer period of time, taking an average of four courses each semester. By "overloading" a schedule, it is possible to jeopardize the ability to maintain a grade point average of at least 2.0 which is required for satisfactory academic standing. Matriculated students can carry whatever courseload is reasonable without losing access to dormitory facilities.

Does the University permit course substitutions (e.g., foreign language)?

The University of Connecticut has a formal course substitution policy for students with learning disabilities. UPLD staff assist students in completing the petition process which is based upon strong diagnostic evidence that the nature and severity of the learning disability precludes completion of course requirements in either foreign language or mathematics despite the provision of accommodations.

Can students with attention deficit disorders (ADD or ADHD) or other disabilities receive services from UPLD?

Any student who has a documented, specific learning disability is eligible for services from UPLD. In a case where the disability does not include a specific learning disability, students can receive support services from the Center for Students with Disabilities. In instances where a student has a diagnosed learning disability and another disability (e.g., ADD or ADHD), services can be coordinated through UPLD and the Center for Students with Disabilities.

Is there an office for students with all disabilities at the University of Connecticut?

The Center for Students with Disabilities provides generic accommodation services to students with all disabilities in accordance with Section 504 regulations. Students with learning disabilities may access services through the Center if they desire an alternative to UPLD. Documentation is required to verify accommodation needs. UPLD staff work closely with the Center for Students with Disabilities in instances where services from both programs are appropriate for and desired by students with learning disabilities. The Center is located in the Wilbur Cross Building.

For additional information please contact:

Joan M. McGuire, Ph.D., Director
University of Connecticut Program for College Students with Learning Disabilities
A. J. Pappanikou Center on Special Education and Rehabilitation:
A University Affiliated Program
U-64, 249 Glenbrook Road
Storrs, CT 06269-2064
203-486-0178

References

Alcoholics Anonymous. (n.d.). New York: Alcoholics Anonymous.

Abbott, H. (1978). *Classroom strategies to aid the disabled learner.* Cambridge, MA: Educators Publishing Service.

Abikoff, H. (1985). Efficacy of cognitive training interventions in hyperactive children: A critical review. *Clinical Psychology Review, 5,* 479–512.

Abikoff, H. (1987). An evaluation of cognitive behavior therapy for hyperactive children. In B. B. Lahey & A. E. Kazdin (Eds.), *Advances in clinical child psychology* (Vol. 10, pp. 171–216). New York: Plenum.

Abikoff, H. (1991). Cognitive training in ADHD children: Less to it than meets the eye. *Journal of Learning Disabilities, 24,* 205–209.

Abikoff, H., Courtney, M., Pelham, W. E., & Koplewicz, H. S. (1993). Teachers' ratings of disruptive behaviors: The influence of halo effects. *Journal of Abnormal Child Psychology, 21,* 519–533.

Abikoff, H., Ganeles, G., Reiter, G., Blum, C., Foley, C., & Klein, R. G. (1988). Cognitive training in academically deficient ADDH boys receiving stimulant medication. *Journal of Abnormal Child Psychology, 16,* 411–432.

Abikoff, H., Gittelman-Klein, R., & Klein, D. F. (1977). Validation of a classroom observation code for hyperactive children. *Journal of Consulting and Clinical Psychology, 45,* 772–783.

Abikoff, H., & Klein, R. G. (1992). Attention-deficit hyperactivity and conduct disorder: Comorbidity and implications for treatment. *Journal of Consulting Clinical Psychology, 60,* 881–892.

Achenbach, T. M. (1975). Longitudinal study of relations between association of responding, I.Q. changes, and school performance from grades 3 to 12. *Developmental Psychology, 11,* 653–654.

Achenbach, T. M., & Edelbrock, C. (1991). *Normative data for the Child Behavior Checklist—Revised.* Burlington, VT: University Associates in Psychiatry.

Achenbach, T. M., Howell, C. T., McConaughy, S. H., & Stanger, C. (1995). Six-year predictors of problems in a national sample: III. Transitions to young adult syndromes. *Journal of the American Academy of Child and Adolescent Psychiatry, 34,* 658–669.

Achenbach, T. M., McConaughy, S. H., & Howell, C. T. (1987). Child/adolescent behavioral and emotional problems: Implications of cross informant correlations for situational specificity. *Psychological Bulletin, 101,* 213–232.

Ackerman, P. T., Dykman, R. A., Holloway, C., Paal, N. P., & Gocio, M. Y. (1991). A trial of piracetam in two subgroups of students with dyslexia enrolled in summer tutoring. *Journal of Learning Disabilities, 24,* 542–549.

Ackerman, P. T., Dykman, R. A., & Oglesby, D. M. (1983). Sex and group differences in reading and attention deficit disordered children with and without hyperkinesis. *Journal of Learning Disabilities, 16,* 407–415.

Ackerman, P. T., Dykman, R. A., & Peters, J. E. (1977). Teenage status of hyperactive and non-hyperactive learning disabled boys. *American Journal of Orthopsychiatry, 47,* 577–596.

Ackerman, P. T., McGrew, J., & Dykman, R. A. (1987). A profile of male and female applicants for a special college program for learning disabled students. *Journal of Clinical Psychology, 34,* 67–78.

Adams, W., & Sheslow, D. (1990). *Wide Range Assessment of Memory and Learning.* Wilmington, DE: Jastak Wide Range.

Adelman, H. S., & Taylor, L. (1986). The problems of definition and differentiation and the need for classification schema. *Journal of Learning Disabilities, 19,* 514–521.

Adelman, P. B., & Vogel, S. A. (1990). College graduates with learning disabilities: Employment attainment and career patterns. *Learning Disability Quarterly, 13,* 154–166.

Adelman, P. B., & Vogel, S. A. (1993). Issues in the employment of adults with learning disabilities. *Learning Disability Quarterly, 16,* 219–231.

Administration for Children, Youth and Families (1993). *The effects of the Head Start program on children's cognitive development (preliminary report): Head Start evaluation, synthesis and utilization project.* Washington, DC: U.S. Department of Health and Human Services. (ERIC Document Reproduction Service No. ED 248 989)

Aiello, N. (1981). A meta-analysis comparing alternative methods of individualized and traditional instruction in science (Doctoral dissertation, Virginia Polytechnic Institute and State University, 1981). *Dissertation Abstracts International, 42,* 977A.

Aiello, N., & Wolfe, L. M. (1980). *A meta-analysis of individualized instruction in science.* (ERIC Document Reproduction Service No. ED 190 404)

Aldenkamp, A. P., Alpherts, W. C. J., Dekker, M. J. A., & Overweg, J. (1990). Neuropsychological aspects of learning disabilities in epilepsy. *Epilepsia, 31,* S9–S20.

Alessandri, S. M. (1992). Attention, play, and social behavior in ADHD preschoolers. *Journal of Abnormal Child Psychology, 20,* 289–302.

Alexander Hamilton Institute. (1990). *What every manager should know about the Americans with Disabilities Act.* Maywood, NJ: Author.

Algozzine, B., & Ysseldyke, J. (1983). Learning disabilities as a subset of school failure: The over-sophistication of a concept. *Exceptional Children, 50,* 242–250.

Ali, S. M., Bullock, S., & Rose, S. P. R. (1988). Protein kinase C inhibitors prevent long-term memory formation in the one-day-old chick. *Neuroscience Research Communications, 3,* 133–140.

Altman, H. J., Nordy, D. A., & Oegren, S. O. (1984). Role of serotonin in memory: Facilitation by alaproclate and zimelidine. *Psychopharmacology, 84,* 96–502.

Amado, H., & Lustman, P. J. (1982). Attention deficit disorders persisting in adulthood: A review. *Comprehensive Psychiatry, 23,* 300–314.

Aman, M. G., Marks, R. E., Turbott, S. H., Wilsher, C. P., & Merry, S. N. (1991). Clinical effects of methylphenidate and thioridazine in intellectually subaverage children. *Journal of the American Academy of Child and Adolescent Psychiatry, 30,* 246–256.

Aman, M. G., & Singh, N. N. (1988). *Psychopharmacology of developmental disabilities.* New York: Springer.

Ambrosini, P. J., Bianchi, M. D., Rabinovich, H., & Elia, J. (1993). Antidepressant treatments in children and adolescents: I. Affective disorders. *Journal of the Academy of Child and Adolescent Psychiatry, 32,* 1–6.

American Academy of Neurology. (1990). Assessment: Generic substitution for anti-epileptic medication. *Neurology, 40,* 1641–1643.

American Academy of Pediatrics. (1987). Committee on drugs report: Medication for children with an attention deficit disorder. *Pediatrics, 80,* 5.

American Council on Education. (1993). *College freshman with disabilities. Information from HEATH, 12,* 4.

Americans with Disabilities Act of 1990, P.L. 101–336.

American Psychiatric Association. (1968). *Diagnostic and statistical manual of psychiatric disorders* (2nd ed.). Washington, DC: Author.

American Psychiatric Association. (1980). *Diagnostic and statistical manual of psychiatric disorders* (3rd ed.). Washington, DC: Author.

American Psychiatric Association. (1987). *Diagnostic and statistical manual of psychiatric disorders* (3rd ed. rev.). Washington, DC: Author.

American Psychiatric Association. (1994). *Diagnostic and statistical manual of psychiatric disorders* (4th ed.). Washington, DC: Author.

Anastopoulos, A. D., Spisto, M., & Maher, M. C. (1994). The WISC-III third factor: A preliminary look at its diagnostic utility. *The ADHD Report, 1*(6), 4.

Anderson, C. W. (1994). Adult literacy in learning disabilities. In P. J. Gerber & H. B. Reiff (Eds.), *Learning disabilities in adulthood.* Stoneham, MA: Butterworth-Heinemann.

Anderson, J., Williams, S., McGee, R., & Silva, P. (1989). Cognitive and social correlates of DSM-III disorders in preadolescent children. *Journal of Child Psychology and Psychiatry, 28,* 842–846.

Anderson, L. T., Campbell, M., Grega, D. M., Perry, R., Small, A. M., & Green, W. H. (1984). Haloperidol in infantile autism: Effects on learning and behavioral symptoms. *American Journal of Psychiatry, 141,* 1195–1202.

Arcia, E., & Gualitieri, C. T. (1994). Neurobehavioral performance of adults with closed-head injury, adults with attention deficit and controls. *Brain Injury, 8,* 395–404.

Arcia, E., & Roberts, E. (1993). Brief report: Otitis media in early childhood and its association with sustained attention in structured situations. *Developmental and Behavioral Pediatrics, 14,* 181–183.

Arnsten, A. F. T., & Contant, T. A. (1992). Alpha-2 adrenergic agonists decrease distractibility in aged monkeys performing a delayed response task. *Psychopharmacology, 108,* 159–169.

Asencio, C. E. (1984). Effects of behavioral objectives on student achievement: A meta-analysis of findings. *Dissertation Abstracts International, 45,* 501A. (University Microfilms No. 84–12499)

Association for Handicapped Student Services Programs in Postsecondary Education. (1987). *Unlocking the doors: Making the transition to postsecondary education.* Columbus, OH: Author.

Association for Higher Education and Disability. (1991). *College students with learning disabilities.* Columbus, OH: Author.

Astin, A., Green, K., Korn, W., Schalit, M., & Bertz, E. (1988). *The American freshman: National norms for 1988.* Los Angeles: University of California.

August, G. J., & Garfinkel, B. D. (1989). Behavioral and cognitive subtypes of ADHD. *Journal of the American Academy of Child and Adolescent Psychiatry, 28,* 739–748.

August, G. J., Ostrander, R., & Bloomquist, M. J. (1992). Attention deficit hyperactivity disorder: An epidemiological screening method. *American Journal of Orthopsychiatry, 62,* 387–396.

Aune, E. (1991). A transition model for postsecondary-bound students with learning disabilities. *Learning Disabilities Research and Practice, 6,* 177–187.

Aviles v. Brown, 715 F. Supp. 509 (S.D. N.Y. 1989).

Bachman, D. S. (1981). Pemoline-induced Tourette's disorder: A case report. *American Journal of Psychiatry, 138,* 1116–1117.

Badian, N. A. (1984). Reading disability in an epidemiological context: Incidence and environmental correlates. *Journal of Learning Disabilities, 17,* 129–136.

Baker, D. P., Knight, K., & Simpson, D. D. (1995). Identifying probationers with ADHD related behaviors in a drug abuse treatment setting. *Criminal Justice and Behavior, 22,* 33–43.

Baker, L., & Cantwell, D. P. (1987). A prospective psychiatric follow-up of children with speech/language disorders. *Journal of the American Academy of Child and Adolescent Psychiatry, 26,* 546–553.

Bakker, D. J. (1979). Hemisphere differences and reading strategies: Two dyslexias? *Bulletin of the Orton Society, 29,* 84–100.

Balow, B., & Bloomquist, M. (1965). Young adults ten to fifteen years after severe reading disability. *Elementary School Journal, 66,* 44–48.

Baltes, P. B., Reese, H. W., & Lipsitt, L. D. (1980). Lifespan developmental psychology. *Annual Review of Psychology, 31,* 65–110.

Balthazor, M. J., Wagner, R. K., & Pelham, W. E. (1991). The specificity of the effects of stimulant medication on classroom learning-related measures of cognitive processing for attention deficit disorder children. *Journal of the Association for Persons with Severe Handicaps, 17,* 67–76.

Bangert, R. L., Kulik, J. A., & Kulik, C. C. (1983). Individualized systems of instruction in secondary schools. *Review of Educational Research, 53,* 143–158.

Bangert-Drowns, R. L., Kulik, J. A., & Kulik, C. C. (1983). Effects of coaching programs on achievement test performance. *Review of Educational Research, 53,* 571–585.

Bangert-Drowns, R. L., Kulik, J. A., & Kulik, C. C. (1985). Effectiveness of computer-based education in secondary schools. *Journal of Computer-Based Instruction, 12,* 59–68.

Barbaro, F., Christman, D., Holzinger, S., & Rosenberg, E. (1985). Support services for the learning-disabled college student. *Journal of the National Association of Social Workers, 30,* 12–18.

Bard, J. A. (1973). Rational proselytizing. *Rational Living, 8,* 13–15.

Bard, J. A. (1980). *Rational-emotive therapy in practice.* Champaign, IL: Research Press.

Barkley, R. A. (1976). Predicting the response of hyperkinetic children to stimulant drugs. A review. *Journal of Abnormal Child Psychology, 4,* 327–348.

Barkley, R. A. (1979). Using stimulant drugs in the classroom. *School Psychology Digest, 8,* 412–425.

Barkley, R. A. (1981a). *Hyperactive children: A handbook for diagnosis and treatment.* New York: Guilford.

Barkley, R. A. (1981b). Hyperactivity. In E. Mash & L. Terdal (Eds.), *Behavioral assessment of childhood disorders.* New York: Guilford.

Barkley, R. A. (1988). The effects of methylphenidate on the interactions of preschool ADHD children with their mothers. *Journal of the American Academy of Child and Adolescent Psychiatry, 27,* 336–341.

Barkley, R. A. (1990a). *ADHD adolescents: Family conflicts and their treatment* (Grant No. MH41583). Washington, DC: National Institute of Mental Health.

Barkley, R. A. (1990b). *Attention deficit hyperactivity disorder: A handbook for diagnosis and treatment.* New York: Guilford.

Barkley, R. A. (1990c). A critique of current diagnostic criteria for attention deficit hyperactivity disorder: Clinical and research implications. *Journal of Developmental and Behavioral Pediatrics, 11,* 343–352.

Barkley, R. A. (1991). *Attention deficit hyperactivity disorder: A clinical workbook.* New York: Guilford.

Barkley, R. A. (1993a). *Adult ADHD history form.* Unpublished, University of Massachusetts, Worcester, MA.

Barkley, R. A. (1993b). *Attention deficit hyperactivity disorder: A clinical workbook.* New York: Guilford.

Barkley, R. A. (1993c). *Attention deficit hyperactivity disorder: Workshop manual.* Worcester, MA: Author.

Barkley, R. A. (1994). *ADHD in adults* [Videotape]. New York: Guilford.

Barkley, R. A. (1995a). ADHD in I.Q. *ADHD Report, 3*(2), 1–3.

Barkley, R. A. (1995b). Focus on DSM-IV. *ADHD Report, 3,* 1–5.

Barkley, R. A., Anastopoulos, A. A., Guevremont, D. C., & Fletcher, K. E. (1991). Adolescents with ADHD: Patterns of behavioral adjustment, academic functioning and treatment utilization. *Journal of the American Academy of Child and Adolescent Psychiatry, 30,* 752–761.

Barkley, R. A., & Cunningham, C. (1979). The effects of methylphenidate on the mother-child interactions of hyperactive children. *Archives of General Psychiatry, 36,* 201–208.

Barkley, R. A., DuPaul, G. J., & McMurray, M. B. (1991). Attention deficit disorder with and without hyperactivity: Clinical response to three dose levels of methylphenidate. *Pediatrics, 87,* 519–531.

Barkley, R. A., Fischer, M., Edelbrock, C. S., & Smallish, L. (1990). The adolescent outcome of hyperactive children diagnosed by research criteria: I. An 8-year prospective follow-up study. *Journal of the American Academy of Child and Adolescent Psychiatry, 29,* 546–557.

Barkley, R. A., & Grodzinsky, G. M. (1994). Are tests of frontal lobe functions useful in the diagnosis of attention deficit disorders? *Clinical Neuropsychologist, 8,* 121–139.

Barkley, R. A., Guevremont, D. C., Anastopoulos, A. D., DuPaul, G. J., & Shelton, T. (1993). Driving-risks and outcomes of attention deficit hyperactivity disorder in adolescents and young adults: A three-to-five follow-up survey. *Pediatrics, 92,* 212–218.

Barkley, R. A., Karlsson, J., & Pollard, S. (1985). Effects of age on the mother-child interactions of hyperactive children. *Journal of Abnormal Child Psychology, 13,* 631–638.

Barkley, R. A., Karlsson, J., Strzelecki, E., & Murphy, J. V. (1984). Effects of age and Ritalin dosage on the mother-child interactions of hyperactive children. *Journal of Consulting and Clinical Psychology, 52,* 750–758.

Barkley, R. A., McMurray, M. B., Edelbrock, C. S., & Robbins, K. (1990). Side effects of methylphenidate in children with attention deficit hyperactivity disorder: A systematic, placebo-controlled evaluation. *Pediatrics, 86,* 184–192.

Barkley, R. A., & Murphy, K. (1993a). Differential diagnosis of adult ADHD: Some controversial issues. *ADHD Report, 4,* 1–3.

Barkley, R. A., & Murphy, K. (1993b). Guidelines for written clinical report concerning ADHD adults. *ADHD Report, 1,* 8–9.

Barns, C., Miller, C., Ehrmann, H., et al. (1990). High versus low-dose piracetam in alcohol organic mental disorder: A placebo-controlled study. *Psychopharmacology, 100,* 361–365.

Barrickman, L., Noyes, R., Kuperman, S., Schumacher, E., & Verda, M. (1991). Treatment of ADHD with fluoxetine: A preliminary trial. *Journal of the American Academy of Child and Adolescent Psychiatry, 30,* 762–76.

Barrickman, L. L., Perry, P. J., Allen, A. J., Kuperman, S., Arndt, S. V., Herrman, K. J., & Schumacher, E. (1995). Buproprion versus methylphenidate in the treatment of attention-deficit hyperactivity disorder. *Journal of the American Academy of Child and Adolescent Psychiatry, 34,* 649–657.

Barron, M. (1993). *Admissions decisions.* Paper presented at the National Association of College Admission Counselors workshop, Understanding Learning Disabilities, Northwestern University, Evanston, IL.

Barton, R. S., & Fuhrman, B. S. (1994). Counseling and psychotherapy for adults with learning disabilities. In P. J. Gerber & H. B. Reiff (Eds.), *Learning disabilities in adulthood.* Stoneham, MA: Butterworth-Heinemann.

Bartus, R. T. (1980). Cholinergic drug effects on memory and cognition in animals. In L. W. Poon (Ed.), *Aging in the 1980s: Psychological issues.* Washington, DC: American Psychological Association.

Bassett, D. S., Polloway, E. A., & Patton, J. R. (1994). Learning disabilities: Perspectives on adult development. In P. J. Gerber & H. B. Reiff (Eds.), *Learning disabilities in adulthood.* Stoneham, MA: Butterworth-Heinemann.

Battle, E. S., & Lacey, B. (1972). A context for hyperactivity in children, over time. *Child Development, 43,* 757–773.

Bauermeister, J. (1992). Factor analyses of teacher rating of attention deficit hyperactivity and oppositional defiant symptoms in children aged four through thirteen years. *Journal of Clinical Child Psychology, 21,* 27–34.

Baumgaertel, A., Wolraich, M. L., & Dietrich, M. (1995). Comparison of diagnostic criteria for attention deficit disorders in a German elementary school sample. *Journal of the American Academy of Child and Adolescent Psychiatry, 34,* 629–638.

Baumrand, D. (1991). The influence of parenting style in adolescent competence and substance use. *Journal of Early Adolescence, 11,* 56–95.

Beck, A. T. (1976). *Cognitive therapy and the emotion disorders.* New York: International Universities Press.

Beck, A. T. (1978). *The Beck Depression Inventory.* New York: Psychological Corporation.

Beck, A. T., Rush, A. J., Shaw, B. F., & Emery, G. (1979). *Cognitive therapy of depression.* New York: Guilford.

Becker, B. J. (1990). Coaching for the Scholastic Aptitude Test: Further synthesis and appraisal. *Review of Educational Research, 60,* 373–417.

Beitchman, J. H. (1987). Language delay and hyperactivity in preschoolers. *Canadian Journal of Psychiatry, 32,* 683–687.

Beitchman, J. H., Hood, J., Rochon, J., & Peterson, M. (1989b). Empirical classification of speech/language impairment in children: I. Identification of speech/language categories. *Journal of the American Academy of Child and Adolescent Psychiatry, 28,* 112–117.

Beitchman, J. H., & Inglis, A. (1991). The continuum of linguistic dysfunction from pervasive developmental disorders to dyslexia. *Pervasive Developmental Disorders, 14,* 95–111.

Beitchman, J. H., Nair, R., Clegg, M., Ferguson, B., & Patel, P. G. (1986). Prevalence of psychiatric disorders in children with speech and language disorders. *Journal of the American Academy of Child Psychiatry, 25,* 528–535.

Bellak, L. (Ed.). (1979). *Psychiatric aspects of minimal brain dysfunction in adults.* New York: Grune & Stratton.

Bellak, L., & Black, R. B. (1992). Attention-deficit hyperactivity disorder in adults. *Clinical Therapeutics, 14,* 138–147.

Ben-Amos, B. (1992). Depression and conduct disorders in children and adolescents: A review of the literature. *Bulletin of the Menninger Clinic, 56,* 188–208.

Benton, A. L. (1975). Developmental dyslexia: Neurological aspects. In W. J. Friedlander (Ed.), *Advances in Neurology* (Vol. 17, pp. 1–47). New York: Raven.

Benton, A. L., & Pearl, D. (1978). *An appraisal of current knowledge.* New York: Oxford University Press.

Berger, M. (1981). Remediating hyperkinetic behavior with impulse control procedures. *School Psychology Review, 10,* 405–407.

Bernard, M. E., & Joyce, M. R. (1984). *Rational-emotive therapy.* New York: Wiley.

Berry, C. A., Shaywitz, S. E., & Shaywitz, B. A. (1985). Girls with attention deficit disorder: A silent minority? A report on behavioral and cognitive characteristics. *Pediatrics, 76,* 801–809.

Bhattacharya, S. K., Upadhyay, S. N., & Jaiswal, A. K. (1993). Effect of piracetam on electroshock induced amnesia and decrease in brain acetylcholine in rats. *Indian Journal of Experimental Biology, 31,* 822–824.

Biederman, J. (1991). Sudden death in children treated with tricyclic antidepressant. *Journal of the American Academy of Child and Adolescent Psychiatry, 30,* 495–498.

Biederman, J., Baldessarini, R. J., Wright, V., Keenan, K., & Faraone, S. (1993). A double-blind placebo controlled study of desipramine in the treatment of ADD: III. Lack of impact on comorbidity and family history factors on clinical response. *Journal of the American Academy of Child and Adolescent Psychiatry, 32,* 199–204.

Biederman, J., Baldessarini, R. J., Wright, V., Knee, D., & Harmatz, J. S. (1989). A double-blind placebo controlled study of desipramine in the treatment of ADD: I. Efficacy. *Journal of the American Academy of Child and Adolescent Psychiatry, 28,* 777–784.

Biederman, J., Faraone, S. V., Keenan, K., Benjamin, J., Krifcher, B., Moore, C., Sprich, S., Ugaglia, K., Jellinek, M. S., Steingard, R., Spencer, T., Norman, D., Kolodny, R., Kraus, I., Perrin, J., Keller, M. B., & Tsuang, M. T. (1992). Further evidence for family-genetic risk factors in attention deficit hyperactivity disorder (ADHD): Patterns of comorbidity in probands and relatives in psychiatrically and pediatrically referred samples. *Archives of General Psychiatry, 49,* 728–738.

Biederman, J., Faraone, S. V., Keenan, K., Knee, D., & Tsuang, M. T. (1990). Family-genetic and psychosocial risk factors in DSM-III attention deficit disorder. *Journal of the American Academy of Child and Adolescent Psychiatry, 29,* 526–533.

Biederman, J., Faraone, S. V., Keenan, K., & Tsuang, M. T. (1991). Evidence of familial association between attention deficit disorder and major affective disorders. *Archives of General Psychiatry, 48,* 633–642.

Biederman, J., Faraone, S., Mick, E., & Lelon, E. (1995). Psychiatric comorbidity among referred juveniles with major depression: Fact or artifact? *Journal of the American Academy of Child and Adolescent Psychiatry, 34,* 579–590.

Biederman, J., Faraone, S. V., Spencer, T., Wilens, T., Norman, D., Lapey, K. A., Mick, E., Lehman, B. K., & Doyle, A. (1993). Patterns of psychiatric comorbidity, cognition and psychosocial functioning in adults with attention deficit hyperactivity disorder. *American Journal of Psychiatry, 150,* 1792–1798.

Biederman, J., Munir, K., & Knee, D. (1987). Conduct and oppositional disorder in clinically referred children with attention deficit disorder: A controlled study. *Journal of the American Academy of Child and Adolescent Psychiatry, 26,* 724–727.

Biederman, J., Munir, K., Knee, D., Armentano, M., Autor, S., Waternaux, C., & Tsuang, M. (1987). High rate of affective disorders in probands with attention deficit disorders and their relatives: A controlled family study. *American Journal of Psychiatry, 144,* 330–333.

Biederman, J., Newcorn, J., & Sprich, S. (1991). Comorbidity of attention deficit hyperactivity disorder with conduct, depressive, anxiety, and other disorders. *American Journal of Psychiatry, 148,* 564–570.

Biggs, S. H. (1995). Neuropsychological and psychoeducational testing in the evaluation of the ADD adult. In K. Nadeau (Ed.), *A comprehensive guide to attention deficit disorder in adults.* New York: Brunner/Mazel.

Bingham, M. B. (1989). *Learning differently: Meeting the needs of adults with learning disabilities.* Knoxville, TN: University of Tennessee, Center for Literacy Studies.

Bird, H. R., Canino, G., Rubio-Stipec, M., Gould, M. S., Ribera, J., Sesman, M., Woodbury, M., Huertas-Goldman, S., Pagan, A., Sanchez-Lacay, A., & Moscoso, M. (1988). Estimates of the prevalence of childhood maladjustment in a community survey in Puerto Rico. *Archives of General Psychiatry, 45,* 1120–1126.

Birmaher, B., Greenhill, L. L., Cooper, T. B., Fired, J., & Maminski, B. (1989). Sustained release methylphenidate: Pharmakinetic studies in ADDH males. *Journal of the American Academy of Child and Adolescent Psychiatry, 28,* 768–772.

Birmaher, B., Quintana, H., & Greenhill, L. L. (1988). Methylphenidate treatment of hyperactive autistic children. *Journal of the American Academy of Child and Adolescent Psychiatry, 27,* 248–251.

Black, M. M., & Sonnenchein, S. (1993). Early exposure to otitis media: A preliminary investigation of behavioral outcome. *Developmental and Behavioral Pediatrics, 14,* 150–155.

Blalock, J. (1981). Persistent problems and concerns of young adults with learning disabilities. In W. Cruickshank & A. Silver (Eds.), *Bridges to tomorrow* (Vol. 2, pp. 3–56). Syracuse, NY: Syracuse University Press.

Blalock, J. (1982). Residual learning disabilities in young adults: Implications for rehabilitation. *Journal of Applied Rehabilitation Counseling, 13,* 9–13.

Blick, D. W., & Test, D. W. (1987). Effects of self-recording on high-school students' on-task behavior. *Learning Disability Quarterly, 10,* 203–213.

Bluestone, C. D. (1989). Recent advances in the pathogenesis, diagnosis and management of otitis media. *Pediatric Clinics of North America, 28,* 727–756.

Boder, E. (1973). Developmental dyslexia: A diagnostic approach based on three atypical reading patterns. *Developmental Medicine and Child Neurology, 15,* 663–687.

Bogart, S. K., Eidelman, L. J., & Kujawa, C. L. (1988). Helping learning disabled students in college. *Education Digest, 53,* 48–51.

Borcherding, B. G., Keysor, C. S., Rappoport, J. L., Elia, J., & Amass, J. (1990). Motor/vocal tics and compulsive behaviors on stimulant drugs: Is there a common vulnerability? *Psychiatry Research, 33,* 83–94.

Borland, B. L., & Hechtman, H. K. (1976). Hyperactive boys and their brothers: A 25-year follow-up study. *Archives of General Psychiatry, 33,* 669–675.

Bosco, J. (1975, March). Behavior modification drugs and the schools: The case of Ritalin. *Phi Delta Kappan,* pp. 489–492.

Bradley, C. (1937). The behavior of children receiving benzedrine. *American Journal of Psychiatry, 94,* 577–585.

Branconnier, R. J. (1983). The efficacy of the cerebral metabolic enhancers in the treatment of senile dementia. *Psychopharmacology Bulletin, 19,* 212–219.

Braswell, L. (1995). Cognitive-behavioral approaches in the classroom. In S. Goldstein (Ed.), *Understanding and managing children's classroom behavior.* New York: Wiley.

Braswell, L., & Bloomquist, M. L. (1991). *Cognitive-behavioral therapy with ADHD children: Child, family and school interventions.* New York: Guilford.

Breen, M. J., & Altepeter, T. S. (1990). *Disruptive behavior disorders in children: Treatment focused assessment.* New York: Guilford.

Bregman, J. D. (1991). Current developments in the understanding of mental retardation. II: Psychopathology. *Journal of the American Academy of Child and Adolescent Psychiatry, 30,* 861–872.

Brinkerhoff, L., Shaw, S., & McGuire, J. (1993). *Promoting postsecondary education for students with learning disabilities in higher education: A handbook for practitioners.* Austin, TX: Pro-Ed.

Broca, P. (1861). Nouvelle observation d'aphemia produite par une lésion de le moitié postérieure des deuxième et troisième circonvolutions frontales. *Bulletin de la Société Anatomie, 6,* 398–407.

Broden, M., Hall, R. V., & Mitts, B. (1971). The effect of self-recording on the classroom behavior of two eighth-grade students. *Journal of Applied Behavior Analysis, 4,* 191–199.

Brown, D. (1980). *Career opportunities for learning disabled adults.* Paper presented at the international convention of the Association of Children with Learning Disabilities.

Brown, D. (1984). Employment considerations for learning disabled adults. *Journal of Rehabilitation, 2,* 74–77, 88.

Brown, L., Sherbenou, R. J., & Johnsen, S. K. (1990). *Test of Nonverbal Intelligence* (2d ed.). Austin, TX: Pro-Ed.

Brown, R. T., Borden, K. A., Wynne, M. E., Schleser, R., & Clingerman, S. R. (1986). Methylphenidate and cognitive therapy with ADD children: A methodological consideration. *Journal of Abnormal Child Psychology, 14,* 481–497.

Brown, T. E. (1995). *Brown Attention Deficit Disorder Scales.* New York: Psychological Corporation.

Brown, T. E., & Gammon, G. D. (1994). Attention deficit disorder without hyperactivity in adults: Instruments for assessment. Unpublished manuscript.

Brown, V. L., Hammill, D. D., & Wiederholt, J. L. (1995). *Test of reading comprehension* (3rd ed.). Los Angeles: Western Psychological Services.

Bruck, M. (1985). The adult functioning of children with specific learning disabilities: A follow-up study. In I. E. Siegel (Ed.), *Advances in applied developmental psychology* (Vol. 1, pp. 91–129). Norwood, NJ: Ablex.

Bruck, M. (1986). Social and emotional adjustments of learning disabled children: A review of the issues. In C. S. Hillsdale (Ed.), *Handbook of cognitive, social and neuropsychological aspects of learning disabilities* (Vol. 1). Hillsdale, NJ: Erlbaum.

Bruck, M. (1989). The adult outcome of children with learning disabilities. *Annals of Dyslexia, 39,* 252–263.

Bruck, M. (1990). Word recognition skills of adults with childhood diagnoses of dyslexia. *Developmental Psychology, 26,* 439–454.

Bruck, M. (1992). Persistence of dyslexics' phonological awareness deficits. *Developmental Psychology, 28,* 874–886.

Bruck, M. (1993). Component spelling skills of college students with childhood diagnoses of dyslexia. *Learning Disability Quarterly, 16,* 171–184.

Bryan, T. (1976). Peer popularity of learning disabled children: A prediction. *Journal of Learning Disabilities, 9,* 307–311.

Buchanan, M., & Wolf, J. (1986). A comprehensive study of learning disabled adults. *Journal of Learning Disabilities, 19,* 34–38.

Buchsbaum, M. S., Haier, R. J., Sosteck, A. J., Weingartner, H., Zahn, T. P., Siever, L. J., Murphy, D. L., & Brody, L. (1985). Attention dysfunction and psychopathology in college men. *Archives of General Psychiatry, 42,* 354–360.

Buitelaar, J. K., Van der Gaad, R. J., Swaab-Barneveld, H., & Kuiper, M. (1995). Prediction of clinical response to methylphenidate in children with attention deficit hyperactivity disorder. *Journal of the American Academy of Child and Adolescent Psychiatry, 34,* 1025–1032.

Burns, P. K. (1982). A quantitative synthesis of research findings relative to the pedagogical effectiveness of computer-assisted instruction in elementary and secondary schools (Doctoral dissertation, University of Iowa, 1981). *Dissertation Abstracts International, 42,* 2946A.

Bursuck, W. D., & Jayanthi, M. (1993). Strategy instruction: Programming for independent study skill usage. In S. A. Vogel & P. B. Adelman (Eds.), *Success for college students with learning disabilities.* New York: Springer.

Bursuck, W. D., Rose, E., Cowen, S., & Yahaya, M. A. (1989). Nationwide survey of postsecondary education services for students with learning disabilities. *Exceptional Children, 56,* 236–245.

Butler-Nalin, P., & Wagner, M. (1991). Enrollment in postsecondary schools. In M. Wagner, L. Newman, R. D'Amico, E. D. Jay, P. Butler-Nalin, C. Marder, & R. Cox, *Youth with disabilities: How are they doing? The first comprehensive report from the National Longitudinal Transition Study of Special Education Students.* Menlo Park, CA: SRI International.

Byrne, T. P., & Crawford, A. (1990). Some theoretical and practical issues in counseling the learning disabled student. *Journal of College Student Psychotherapy, 5,* 75–85.

California Community College Chancellor's Office. (1992). *Disabled students programs and services: Annual report 1990–91.* Sacramento, CA: California Community College Chancellor's Office, Disabled Students Programs and Services.

Campbell, J. W., D'Amato, R. C., Roggio, D. J., & Stephens, K. D. (1991). Construct validity of the computerized continuous performance test with measures of intelligence, achievement and behavior. *Journal of School Psychology, 29,* 143–150.

Campbell, M., Anderson, L., Meier, M., Cohen, L., & Small, A. (1978). A comparison of haloperidol and behavioral therapy and their interaction with autistic children. *Journal of Child Psychiatry, 17,* 640–655.

Campbell, M., Small, A. M., Green, W. H., Jennings, S. J., Perry, R., Bennett, W. G., & Anderson, L. (1984). Behavioral efficacy of haloperidol and lithium carbonate. *Archives of General Psychiatry, 41,* 640–656.

Campbell, S. B. (1985). Hyperactivity in preschoolers: Correlates and prognostic implications. *Clinical Psychology Review, 5,* 405–428.

Campbell, S. B., & Cluss, P. (1982). Peer relationships of young children with behavior problems. In K. H. Rubin & H. S. Ross (Eds.), *Peer relationships and social skills in childhood.* New York: Springer.

Campbell, S. B., Endman, M. W., & Bernfeld, G. (1977). A three-year follow-up of hyperactive preschoolers into elementary school. *Journal of Child Psychology and Psychiatry, 18,* 239–249.

Campbell, S. B., & Paulauskas, S. (1979). Peer relations in hyperactive children. *Journal of Child Psychology and Psychiatry, 20,* 233–246.

Cantwell, D. P. (1972). Psychiatric illness in the families of hyperactive children. *Archives of General Psychiatry, 27,* 414–417.

Cantwell, D. P. (1985). Hyperactive children have grown up: What have we learned about what happens to them? *Archives of General Psychiatry, 42,* 1026–1028.

Cantwell, D. P., & Baker, L. (1977). Psychiatric disorder in children with speech and language retardation. *Archives of General Psychiatry, 34,* 583–591.

Cantwell, D. P., & Baker, L. (1985). Psychiatric and learning disorders in children with speech and language disorders: A descriptive analysis. *Advances in Learning and Behavioral Disabilities, 4,* 29–47.

Cantwell, D. P., & Baker, L. (1987a). *Developmental speech and language disorders.* New York: Guilford.

Cantwell, D. P., & Baker, L. (1987b). Differential diagnosis of hyperactivity/response to commentary. *Journal of Developmental Pediatrics, 8,* 159–165, 169–170.

Cantwell, D. P., & Baker, L. (1988). Issues in classification of child and adolescent psychopathology. *Journal of the American Academy of Child and Adolescent Psychiatry, 27,* 521–533.

Cantwell, D. P., & Baker, L. (1992a). Association between attention deficit hyperactivity disorder and learning disorders. In B. Shaywitz & S. Shaywitz (Eds.), *Attention deficit disorder comes of age: Toward the twenty-first century.* Austin, TX: Pro-Ed.

Cantwell, D. P., & Baker, L. (1992b). Attention deficit disorder with and without hyperactivity: A review and comparison of matched groups. *Journal of the American Academy of Child and Adolescent Psychiatry, 31,* 432–438.

Cantwell, D. P., Baker, L., & Mattison, R. (1981). Prevalence, type and correlates of psychiatric disorder in 200 children with communication disorder. *Journal of Developmental and Behavioral Pediatrics, 2,* 131–136.

Cantwell, D. P., & Satterfield, J. H. (1978). The prevalence of academic underachievement in hyperactive children. *Journal of Pediatric Psychology, 3,* 168–171.

Carey, W. B. (1970). A simplified method for measuring infant temperament. *Journal of Pediatrics, 77,* 188–194.

Carlberg, C., & Kavale, K. (1980). The efficacy of special versus regular class placement for exceptional children: A meta-analysis. *Journal of Special Education, 14,* 295–309.

Carlson, C. L., Lahey, B. B., & Neeper, R. (1986). Direct assessment of the cognitive correlates of attention deficit disorders with and without hyperactivity. *Journal of Psychopathology and Behavioral Assessment, 8,* 69–86.

Carlson, G. A. (1987). *Social and academic outcomes of cooperative learning in the mainstreamed classroom: A meta-analysis.* Unpublished manuscript, Claremont Graduate School, Claremont, CA.

Carlson, G. A. (1993). Bipolar effective disorder in childhood and adolescence. In D. P. Cantwell & G. A. Carlson (Eds.), *Affective disorders in childhood and adolescence.* New York: Spectrum.

Carlson, G. A., Pelham, W. E., Milich, R., & Dixon, J. (1992). Single and combined effects of methylphenidate and behavior therapy on the classroom performance of children with attention deficit hyperactivity disorder. *Journal of Abnormal Child Psychology, 20,* 213–232.

Carlson, G. A., Rapport, M. D., Kelly, K. L., & Pataki, C. S. (1992). The effects of methylphenidate and lithium on attention and activity level. *Journal of the American Academy of Child and Adolescent Psychiatry, 31,* 262–270.

Casto, G., & White, K. (1984). The efficacy of early intervention programs with environmentally at-risk infants. *Journal of Children in Contemporary Society, 17,* 37–50.

Cavanagh, R., Clifford, J. S., & Gregory, W. L. (1989). The use of bromocriptine for the treatment of attention deficit disorder in two chemically dependent patients. *Journal of Psychoactive Drugs, 21,* 217–220.

Centra, J. A. (1986). Handicapped student performance on the Scholastic Aptitude Test. *Journal of Learning Disabilities, 19,* 324–327.

Cherkes-Julkowski, M., & Stolzenberg, J. (1983). The learning disability of attention deficit disorder. *Learning Disabilities, 2,* 8–15.

Chess, S., & Thomas, A. (1986). *Temperament in clinical practice.* New York: Guilford.

Children and Adults with Attention Deficit Disorder. (1993). ADD in adulthood: Not just for children anymore. *CH.A.D.D.ER, 7*(2), 19–21.

Christensen, S. L., Rounds, T., & Gorney, D. (1992). Family factors and student achievement: An avenue to increase student's success. *School Psychology Quarterly, 7,* 178–206.

Christie, D. J., Hiss, M., & Lozanoff, B. (1984). Modification of inattentive classroom behavior: Hyperactive children's use of self-recording with teacher guidance. *Behavior Modification, 8,* 391–406.

CITE Inventory. (1995). In F. J. Krieg, P. Brown, & J. Ballard (Eds.), *Transition: School to work. Models for effective transition planning.* Bethesda, MD: National Association of School Psychologists.

Clement-Heist, K., Siegel, S., & Gaylord-Ross, R. (1992). Simulated and *in situ* vocational social skills training for youths with learning disabilities. *Exceptional Children, 58,* 336–345.

Closer Look. (1981). *Work is for everyone.* Washington, DC: Parents Campaign for Handicapped Children and Youth.

Cocores, J. A., Davies, R. K., Mueller, P. S., & Gold, M. S. (1986). Cocaine abuse and adult attention deficit disorder. *Journal of Clinical Psychiatry, 48,* 376–377.

Cohen, N. J., Davine, M., Horodezky, N., Lipsett, L., & Isaacson, L. (1993). Unsuspected language impairment in psychiatrically disturbed children: Prevalence, language and behavioral characteristics. *Journal of the American Academy of Child and Adolescent Psychiatry, 32,* 595–603.

Cohen, N. J., Davine, M., & Meloche-Kelly, M. (1989). Prevalence of unsuspected language disorders in a child psychiatric population. *Journal of the American Academy of Child and Adolescent Psychiatry, 28,* 107–111.

Cohen, N. J., & Lipsett, L. (1991). Recognized and unrecognized language impairment in psychologically disturbed children. Child symptomatology: Maternal depression and family dysfunction. *Canadian Journal of Behavioral Science, 23,* 376–389.

Cohen, N. J., Sullivan, S., Minde, K. K., Novak, C., & Helwig, C. (1981). Evaluation of the relative effectiveness of methylphenidate and cognitive behavior modification in the treatment of kindergarten-aged hyperactive children. *Journal of Abnormal Child Psychology, 9,* 43–54.

Cohen, P. A., Ebeling, B. J., & Kulik, J. A. (1981). A meta-analysis of outcome studies of visual-based instruction. *Educational Communication and Technology, 29,* 26–36.

Cohen, P. A., Kulik, J. A., & Kulik, C. C. (1982). Educational outcomes of tutoring: A meta-analysis of findings. *American Educational Research Journal, 19,* 237–248.

Coleby, M. (1995). The school-aged siblings of children with disabilities. *Developmental Medicine and Child Neurology, 37,* 415–426.

Collier, C. P., Soldin, S. J., Swanson, J. M., MacLeod, S. M., Weinberg, F., & Rochefort, J. G. (1985). Pemoline pharmacokinetics and long-term therapy in children with attention deficit disorder and hyperactivity. *Clinical Pharmacokinetics, 10,* 260–278.

Collins, R. C. (1984). *Head Start: A review of research with implications for practice in early childhood education.* Washington, DC: American Educational Research Association. (ERIC Document Reproduction Service No. ED 245 833)

Collins, T. (1990). Evaluating spell checkers, thesauruses, dictionaries and grammar editors for the community college student with learning disabilities. In H. J. Murphy (Ed.), *Proceedings of the fifth annual conference on technology and persons with disabilities, 5,* 163–175.

Collins, W. L. (1987). Psychological/affective interventions with under-prepared adult learners: A meta-analytic and triangulation study (Doctoral dissertation, Union for Experimenting Colleges, University without Walls and Union Graduate School, 1987). *Dissertation Abstracts International, 42,* 4272A.

Conners, C. K. (1972). Rating scales for use in drug studies with children. *Psychopharmacology Bulletin: Special Issue. Pharmacotherapy with Children,* pp. 24–84.

Conners, C. K. (1975a). Control trial of methylphenidate in preschool children with minimal brain dysfunction. *International Journal of Mental Health, 4,* 61–74.

Conners, C. K. (1975b). Minimal brain dysfunction and psychopathology in children. In A. Davids (Ed.), *Child personality and psychopathology: Vol. 2. Current topics.* New York: Wiley.

Conners, C. K. (1989). *Conners Parent Rating Form.* Toronto, ON: Multi-Health Systems, Inc.

Conners, C. K. (1992). *The neurology of reading.* Grand Round Presentation, University of Utah School of Medicine.

Conners, C. K. (1994a). Conners Continuous Performance Test (Version 3.0) [Computer software]. Toronto, ON: Multi-Health Systems, Inc.

Conners, C. K. (1994b). Conners Continuous Performance Test (Version 3.0) [User's manual]. Toronto, ON: Multi-Health Systems, Inc.

Conners, C. K., Eisenberg, L., & Barcai, A. (1967). Effective dextroamphetamine on children: Studies on subjects with learning disabilities and school behavior problems. *Archives of General Psychiatry, 17,* 478–485.

Conners, C. K., Erhardt, D., & Sparrow, E. (1995). *Conners Adult ADHD Rating Scale—Self.* North Tonawanda, NY: Multi-Health Systems, Inc.

Conners, C. K., & Rothchild, G. H. (1968). Drugs and learning in children. In J. Helmuth (Ed.), *Learning disorders* (Vol. 3, pp. 192–223). Seattle, WA: Special Child Publications.

Conners, C. K., & Wells, K. C. (1986). *Hyperkinetic children: A neuropsychosocial approach.* Beverly Hills, CA: Sage.

Cook, S. B., Scruggs, T. E., Mastropieri, M. A., & Casto, G. C. (1986). Handicapped students as tutors. *Journal of Special Education, 19,* 483–492.

Coons, H. W., Peloquin, L. J., Klorman, R., Ryan, R. M., Bauer, L. D., Perlmutter, R. A., & Salzman, L. F. (1981). Effect of methylphenidate on young adults' vigilance and event-related potentials. *Electroencephalography and Clinical Neurophysiology, 51,* 373–387.

Copeland, L., Wolraich, M., Lindgren, S., Milich, R., & Woolson, R. (1987). Pediatricians' reported practices in the assessment and treatment of attention deficit disorders. *Journal of Developmental and Behavioral Pediatrics, 8,* 191–197.

Cordoni, B. K. (1993). Commentary on "An approach to meeting the needs of medical students with learning disabilities." *Teaching and Learning in Medicine, 5,* 36.

Cordoni, B. K., & Goh, D. (1989). A comparison of the performance of college students with learning disabilities on the Stanford-Binet Intelligence Scale, fourth edition, and the Wechsler Adult Intelligence Scale—Revised. *Learning Disabilities, 1,* 35–39.

Corey, G. (1991). *Theory and practice of counseling and psychotherapy.* Pacific Grove, CA: Brooks/Cole.

Costello, E. J. (1989). Developments in child psychiatric epidemiology [Special section]. *Journal of the American Academy of Child and Adolescent Psychiatry, 28,* 836–841.

Cotugno, A. J. (1993). The diagnosis of attention deficit hyperactivity disorder (ADHD) in community mental health centers: Where and when. *Psychology in the Schools, 30,* 338–344.

Covey, S. (1989). *The seven habits of highly effective people.* New York: Simon & Schuster.

Cowen, E., Pederson, A., Babigan, H., Izzo, L., & Trost, M. (1973). Long-term follow-up of early detected vulnerable children. *Journal of Consulting and Clinical Psychology, 41,* 438–446.

Crabtree, L. H. (1981). Minimal brain dysfunction in adolescents and young adults: Diagnostic and therapeutic perspectives. In *Hyperactives as young adults.* University of Chicago, Chicago.

Critchley, M. (1964). *Developmental dyslexia.* London: Heinemann.

Cullinan, D., Epstein, H., & Lloyd, J. (1983). *Behavioral disorders.* Englewood Cliffs, NJ: Prentice-Hall.

Cummings, D. E. (1995). The role of genetic factors in conduct disorder based on studies of Tourette's Syndrome and attention deficit hyperactivity disorder in probands and their relatives. *Journal of Developmental and Behavioral Pediatrics, 16,* 142–157.

Cunningham, C. E., & Barkley, R. A. (1979). The interactions of normal and hyperactive children with their mothers in free play and structured tasks. *Child Development, 50,* 217–224.

Cunningham, C. E., Siegel, L. S., & Offord, D. R. (1985). A developmental dose-response analysis of the effects of methylphenidate on the peer interactions of attention deficit disordered boys. *Journal of Child Psychology and Psychiatry, 26,* 955–971.

Cunningham, C. E., Siegel, L. S., & Offord, D. R. (1991). A dose-response analysis of the effects of methylphenidate on the peer interactions and simulated classroom performance of ADD children with and without conduct problems. *Journal of Child Psychology and Psychiatry, 32,* 439–452.

Cutler, M., Little, J. W., & Strauss, A. A. (1940). The effect of benzedrine on mentally deficient children. *American Journal of Mental Deficiency, 45,* 59–65.

D'Amico, R. (1991). The working world awaits: Employment experiences during and shortly after secondary school. In M. Wagner, L. Newman, R. D'Amico, E. D. Jay, P. Butler-Nalin, C. Marder, & R. Cox, *Youth with disabilities: How are they doing? The first comprehensive report from the National Longitudinal Transition Study of Special Education Students.* Menlo Park, CA: SRI International.

D'Amico, R., & Blackorby, J. (1992). *Trends in employment amongst out-of-school youth with disabilities: The second comprehensive report from the National Longitudinal Transition Study of Special Education Students* (OSEPS Contract No. 300-87-0054. Washington, DC: U.S. Department of Education.

Dalke, C., & Franzene, J. (1988). Secondary-postsecondary collaboration: A model of shared responsibility. *Learning Disabilities Focus, 4,* 38–45.

Dalke, C., & Schmitt, S. (1987). Meeting the transition needs of college-bound students with learning disabilities. *Journal of Learning Disabilities, 20,* 176–180.

Davidson, L. L., Taylor, E. A., Sandberg, S. T., & Thorley, G. (1992). Hyperactivity in school age boys and subsequent risk of injury. *Pediatrics, 9,* 697–702.

Davies, H. P., & Squire, L. R. (1984). Protein synthesis and memory: a review. *Psychopharmacology Bulletin, 96,* 518–559.

Davies, J. A., Jackson, B., & Redfern, P. H. (1974). The effect of amantadine, L-dopa (+) amphetamine and apomorphine on the acquisition of the conditioned avoidance response. *Neuropharmacology, 13,* 199–204.

de Araujo, J. T., & Nero, A. S. (1977). Piracetam and acetamide in sickle-cell disease. *Lancet, 2,* 411.

Deberdt, W. (1994). Interaction between psychological and pharmacological treatment in cognitive impairment. *Life Science, 55,* 2057–2066.

deBettencourt, L. J., Zigmond, N., & Thornton, H. (1989). Follow-up postsecondary-age rural learning disabled graduates and dropouts. *Exceptional Children, 56,* 40–49.

Decker, T., Polloway, E., & Decker, B. (1985). Help for the LD college student. *Academic Therapy, 20,* 339–345.

DeFries, J. C. (1985). Colorado reading project. In D. B. Gray & J. F. Kavanaugh (Eds.), *Behavioral measures of dyslexia.* Parkton, MD: York.

DeFries, J. C., & Decker, S. N. (1982). Genetic aspects of reading disability: A family study. In R. N. Malatesha & P. G. Aaron (Eds.), *Reading disorders: Variations and treatments.* New York: Academic.

DeFries, J. C., & Fulker, D. W. (1985). Multiple regression analysis of twin data. *Behavior Genetics, 15,* 467–473.

DeFries, J. C., & Fulker, D. W. (1988). Multiple regression analysis of twin data: Etiology of deviant scores versus individual differences. *Acta Geneticae Medicae et Gemellologiae: Twin Research, 37,* 205–216.

Dekkers, J., & Donatti, S. (1981). The integration of research studies on the use of stimulants as an instructional strategy. *Journal of Educational Research, 74,* 424–427.

DeLeon, P. H. (1995). Prescription privileges and state legislation: Indiana, Montana and California. *Register Report (Newsletter for Health Service Providers in Psychology), 21,* 19–21.

Denckla, M. B. (1972). Clinical syndromes in learning disabilities: The case for splitting versus lumping. *Journal of Learning Disabilities, 5,* 401–406.

Denckla, M. B. (1977). The neurological basis of reading disability. In F. G. Roswell & G. Natchez (Eds.), *Reading disability: A human approach to learning.* New York: Basic Books.

Denckla, M. B. (1991). Attention deficit hyperactivity disorder—residual type. *Journal of Child Neurology, 6,* S44–S48.

Denckla, M. B., Bemporad, J. R., & MacKay, M. C. (1976). Tics following methylphenidate administration. *Journal of American Medical Association, 235,* 1349–1361.

Denman, S. B. (1984). *Denman Neuropsychology Memory Scale.* (Available from S. B. Denman, Ph.D., 1040 Fort Sumter Drive, Charleston, SC)

DerSimonian, R., & Laird, N. M. (1983). Evaluating the effect of coaching on SAT scores: A meta-analysis. *Harvard Educational Review, 53,* 1–15.

Deshler, D. D. (1978). Psychoeducational aspects of learning disabled adolescents. In L. Mann, L. Goodman, & J. L. Wiederholt (Eds.), *Teaching the learning disabled adolescent.* Boston: Houghton-Mifflin.

Deshler, D. D., & Schumacher, J. B. (1986). Learning strategies: An instructional alternative for low-achieving adolescents. *Exceptional Children, 52,* 583–590.

Deshler, D. D., Schumacher, J. B., Lenz, B. K., & Ellis, E. (1983). Academic and cognitive interventions for LD adolescents, II. *Journal of Learning Disabilities, 17,* 170–179.

de Sonneville, L. M., Nijokiktjien, C., & Vos, H. (1994). Methylphenidate and information processing. *Journal of Clinical and Experimental Neuropsychology, 16,* 877–897.

Dexter, B. L. (1982). Helping learning disabled students prepare for college. *Journal of Learning Disabilities, 15,* 344–346.

Dickstein, E., & Warren, D. (1980). Role-taking deficits in learning disabled children. *Journal of Learning Disabilities, 13,* 378–382.

Doehring, D. G. (1968). *Patterns of impairment in specific reading disability.* Bloomington, IN: Indiana University Press.

Dole, A. A., Rockey, P. B., & DiTomasso, R. (1983). *Meta-analysis of outcome research in reducing test anxiety: Interventions, rigor, and inertia.* Washington, DC: American Educational Research Association. (ERIC Document Reproduction Service No. ED 231 844)

Dopkin, P. L., Tremblay, R. E., Masse, L. C., & Vitaro, F. (1995). Individual and peer characteristics in predicting boys' early onset of substance abuse: A seven year longitudinal study. *Child Development, 66,* 1198–1214.

Douglas, V. I. (1972). Stop, look and listen: The problem of sustained attention and impulse control in hyperactive and normal children. *Canadian Journal of Behavioral Science, 4,* 359–282.

Douglas, V. I. (1980). Treatment and training approaches to hyperactivity: Establishing internal or external control. In C. K. Whalen and B. Henker (Eds.), *Hyperactive children: The social ecology of identification and treatment.* New York: Academic.

Douglas, V. I. (1985). The response of ADD children to reinforcement: Theoretical and clinical implications. In L. N. Bloomingdale (Ed.), *Attention deficit disorder: Identification, course and rationale.* Jamaica, NY: Spectrum.

Douglas, V. I., Barr, R. G., Desilets, J., & Sherman, E. (1995). Do high doses of stimulants impair flexible thinking in attention-deficit hyperactivity disorder? *Journal of the American Academy of Child and Adolescent Psychiatry, 34,* 877–885.

Douglas, V. I., Barr, R. G., O'Neil, M. E., & Britton, B. G. (1986). Short-term effects of methylphenidate on the cognitive, learning and academic performance of children with attention deficit disorder in the laboratory and classroom. *Journal of Child Psychology and Psychiatry, 27,* 191–211.

Douglas, V. I., & Peters, K. G. (1979). Toward a clearer definition of the attentional deficit of hyperactive children. In G. A. Hale & M. Lewis (Eds.), *Attention and the development of cognitive skills.* New York: Plenum.

Dowdy, C. (1990). *LD characteristics checklist.* Birmingham, AL: University of Alabama at Birmingham.

Dowdy, C. A. (1995). Attention deficit rating scale. In C. A. Dowdy, J. R. Patton, T. E. C. Smith, & E. A. Polloway (Eds.), *Attention-deficit/hyperactivity disorder in the classroom: A practical guide for teachers.* Austin, TX: Pro-Ed.

Dowdy, C. A., Carter, J. F., & Smith, T. E. C. (1990). Differences in transitional needs of high school students with and without learning disabilities. *Journal of Learning Disabilities, 23,* 343–353.

Driscoll, M. S., & Zecker, S. G. (1991). Attention deficit disorder: Are there subtypes? A review of the literature from 1980 to 1989. *Learning Disabilities, 2,* 55–64.

Duane, D. D. (1991). Biological foundations of learning disabilities. In J. E. Obrzut & G. W. Hynd (Eds.), *Neuropsychological foundations of learning disabilities* (pp. 7–27). New York: Academic.

Dulcan, M. K. (1986). Comprehensive treatment of children and adolescents with attention disorders: The state of the art. *Clinical Psychology Review, 6,* 539–569.

Dunivant, N. (1982). *The relationship between learning disabilities and juvenile delinquency.* Washington, DC: U.S. Department of Justice, National Institute for Juvenile Justice and Delinquency Prevention.

Dunn, L. M., & Dunn, L. M. (1981). *The Peabody Picture Vocabulary Test—Revised.* Circle Pines, MN: American Guidance Service.

DuPaul, G. J., Barkley, R. A., & McMurray, M. B. (1991). Therapeutic effects of medication on ADHD: Implications for school psychologists. *School Psychology Review, 20,* 203–219.

DuPaul, G. J., Guevremont, D. C., & Barkley, R. A. (1992). Behavioral treatment of attention-deficit hyperactivity disorder in the classroom: The use of the Attention Training System. *Behavior Modification, 16,* 204–225.

DuPaul, G. J., & Rapport, M. D. (1993). Does methylphenidate normalize the classroom performance of children with attention deficit disorder? *Journal of the American Academy of Child and Adolescent Psychiatry, 32,* 190–198.

DuPaul, G. J., & Stoner, G. (1994). *ADHD in the schools: Assessment and intervention strategies.* New York: Guilford.

Dykman, R. A., McGrew, J., Harris, T. S., Peters, J. E., & Ackerman, P. T. (1976). Two blinded studies of the effects of stimulant drugs on children: Pemoline, methylphenidate and placebo. In R. T. Anderson & C. G. Halcomb (Eds.), *Learning disability/minimal brain dysfunction syndrome.* Springfield, IL: Thomas.

Dykman, R. A., Peters, J. E., & Ackerman, P. T. (1973). Experimental approaches to the study of minimal brain dysfunction: a follow-up study. *Annals of the New York Academy of Science, 205,* 93–108.

D'Zurilla, T. J., & Goldfried, M. R. (1971). Problem solving and behavior modification. *Journal of Abnormal Psychology, 78,* 107–126.

Eisenberg, L. (1966). Reading retardation: I. Psychiatric and sociologic aspects. *Pediatrics, 37,* 352–365.

Ellis, A. (1962). *A reason and emotion in psychotherapy.* New York: Stuart.

Ellis, A. (1979). *New developments in rational emotive therapy.* Monterey: Brooks/Cole.

Ellis, A. (1973a). *Humanistic psychotherapy: The rational-emotive approach.* New York: Julian.

Ellis, A. (1979b). Rational-emotive therapy. In A. Ellis & J. M. Whiteley (Eds.), *Theoretical and empirical foundations of rational-emotive therapy.* Monterey, CA: Brooks/Cole.

Ellis, A. (1980). Overview of the clinical theory of rational-emotive therapy. In R. Grieger & J. Boyd (Eds.), *Rational-emotive therapy: A skills based approach.* New York: Van Nostrand Reinhold.

Ellis, A., & Harper, R. A. (1975). *A new guide to rational living.* Englewood Cliffs, NJ: Prentice-Hall.

Epps, S., Ysseldyke, J., & McCue, M. (1984). I know one when I see one: Differentiating learning disorder and non-learning disorder students. *Learning Disability Quarterly, 7,* 89–101.

Epstein, M. H., Singh, N. N., Luebke, J., & Stout, C. E. (1991). Psychopharmacological intervention: II. Teacher perceptions of psychotropic medication for students with learning disabilities. *Journal of Learning Disabilities, 24,* 477–483.

Equal Employment Opportunity Commission. (1991). *The Americans with Disabilities Act: Your rights as an individual with a disability* (EEOC-BK-18). Washington, DC: Author.

Erenberg, G., Cruse, R. P., & MacKay, M. C. (1985). Gilles de la Tourette's Syndrome: Effect of stimulant drugs. *Neurology, 35,* 1346–1348.

Erikson, E. (1950). *Childhood and society.* New York: Norton.

Ernst, M., Zametkin, A. J., Matochik, J. A., Liebenauer, M. A., Fitzgerald, G. A., & Cohen, R. M. (1994). Effects of intravenous dextroamphetamine on brain metabolism in adults with attention-deficit hyperactivity disorder (ADHD): Preliminary findings. *Psychopharmacology Bulletin, 30,* 219–225.

Evans, S. W., & Pelham, W. E. (1991). Psychostimulant effects on academic and behavioral measures for ADHD junior high school students in a lecture format classroom. *Journal of Abnormal Child Psychology, 19,* 537–552.

Evelo, S., & Price, L. (1991). The transition of students with learning disabilities: A case study. *Journal of Postsecondary Education and Disability, 9,* 207–218.

Eyestone, L. L., & Howell, R. J. (1994). An epidemiological study of attention deficit hyperactivity disorder and major depression in a male prison population. *Bulletin of the American Academy of Psychiatry and the Law, 22,* 181–193.

Faas, L. A., & D'Alonzo, B. J. (1990). WAIS-R scores as predictors of employment success and failure among adults with learning disabilities. *Journal of Learning Disabilities, 23,* 311–316.

Fairweather, J. S., & Shaver, D. M. (1991). Making the transition to postsecondary education and training. *Exceptional Children, 57,* 264–270.

Faraone, S. V., Biederman, J., & Milberger, S. (1995). How reliable are maternal reports of their children's psychopathology. One-year recall of psychiatric diagnoses of ADHD children. *Journal of the American Academy of Child and Adolescent Psychiatry, 34,* 1001–1008.

Fargason, R. E., & Ford, C. V. (1994). Attention deficit hyperactivity disorder in adults. Diagnosis, treatment and prognosis. *Southern Medical Journal, 87,* 302–309.

Farrington, D. P., Loeber, R., & Van Kammen, W. B. (1990). Long-term criminal outcomes of hyperactivity-impulsivity-attention deficit and conduct problems in childhood. In L. N. Robins & M. Rutter (Eds.), *Straight and devious pathways to adulthood.* New York: Cambridge University Press.

Feldman, E., Levin, B. E., Lubs, H., Rabin, M., Lubs, M. L., Jallad, B., & Kusch, A. (1993). Adult familial dyslexia: A retrospective developmental and psychosocial profile. *Journal of Neuropsychiatry and Clinical Neurosciences, 5,* 195–199.

Feldman, H., Crumrine, P., Handen, B. L., Alvin, R., & Teodori, J. (1989). Methylphenidate in children with seizures and attention-deficit disorder. *American Journal of the Disabled Child, 143,* 1081–1086.

Feldman, S., Denhoff, E., & Denhoff, E. (1979). The attention disorders and related syndromes outcome in adolescence and young adult life. In E. Denhoff & L. Stern (Eds.), *Minimal brain dysfunction: A developmental approach.* New York: Musson.

Felton, R. (1986). *Bowman-Gray follow-up study.* Paper presented at the Orton Dyslexia National Conference.

Ferdinand, R. F., & Verhulst, F. C. (1994). The prediction of poor outcome in young adults: comparison of the Young Adult Self-Report, the General Health Questionnaire, and the Symptom Checklist. *Acta Psychiatrica Scandinavica, 89,* 405–410.

Ferdinand, R. F., Verhulst, F. C., & Wiznitzer, M. (1995). Continuity and change of self-reported problem behaviors from adolescence into young adulthood. *Journal of the American Academy of Child and Adolescent Psychiatry, 34,* 680–690.

Finucci, J. M., & Childs, B. (1981). Are there really more dyslexic boys than girls? In A. Ansara, N. Geschwind, A. Galaburda, M. Albert, & N. Gartrell (Eds.), *Sex differences in dyslexia.* Baltimore, MD: Orton Dyslexia Society.

Finucci, J., Gottfredson, L. S., & Childs, B. (1985). A follow-up study of dyslexic boys. *Annals of Dyslexia, 35,* 117–136.

Fischer, M., Barkley, R. A., Edelbrock, C. S., & Smallish, L. (1990). The adolescent outcome of hyperactive children diagnosed by research criteria: II. Academic, attentional and neuropsychological status. *Journal of Consulting and Clinical Psychology, 58,* 550–588.

Fischer, M., Barkley, R. A., Fletcher, K. E., & Smallish, L. (1993). The adolescent outcome of hyperactive children: Predictors of psychiatric, academic, social and emotional adjustment. *Journal of the American Academy of Child and Adolescent Psychiatry, 32,* 324–332.

Fisher, R., Ury, W., & Patton, B. (1991). *Getting to yes: Negotiating agreement without giving in.* New York: Penguin.

Fishlock, D. J. (1987). Variety of services now available for students with "hidden" handicaps. *Chronicle of Higher Education, 34,* 40.

Fitzpatrick, P. A., Klorman, R., Brumaghim, J. T., & Borgstedt, M. D. (1992). Effects of sustained release and standard preparations of methylphenidate on attention deficit disorder. *Journal of the American Academy of Child and Adolescent Psychiatry, 31,* 226–234.

Fletcher, J. D. (1990). *Effectiveness and cost of interactive videodisc instruction in defense training and education* (IDA Report No. R2372). Arlington, VA: Institute for Defense Analysis. (ERIC Document Reproduction Service No. ED 326 194)

Fletcher, J. M., & Satz, P. (1985). In B. P. Rourke (Ed.), *Neuropsychology of learning disabilities: Essentials of subtype analysis.* New York: Guilford.

Fletcher, J. M., Satz, P., & Morris, R. (1984). The Florida longitudinal project: A review. In S. A. Mednick & N. A. Harway (Eds.), *U.S. longitudinal projects.* New York: Praeger.

Flicek, M. (1992). Social status of boys with both academic problems and attention-deficit hyperactivity disorder. *Journal of Abnormal Child Psychology, 20,* 353–366.

Flood, J. F., Bennett, E. L., Orme, A. E., Vasquez, S., & Jarvik, M. E. (1978). Memory facilitating and anti-amnesic effects of corticosteroids. *Pharmacological Biochemical Behavior, 8,* 81–87.

Flynn, J. M., & Rahbar, M. H. (1994). Prevalence of reading failure in boys compared with girls. *Psychology in the Schools, 31,* 66–71.

Fonagy, P., Steele, M., Steele, H., Higgitt, A., & Target, M. (1994). The Emanuel Miller Memorial Lecture 1992: The theory and practice of resilience. *Journal of Child Psychology and Psychiatry, 35,* 231–257.

Fordyce, D. J. (1983). *Psychometric assessment of denial of illness in brain injured patients.* Paper presented at the 91st annual convention of the American Psychological Association, Anaheim, CA.

Forness, S. R., Cantwell, D. P., Swanson, J. M., Hanna, G. L., & Youpa, D. (1991). Differential effects of stimulant medication on reading performance of boys with hyperactivity with and without conduct disorder. *Journal of Learning Disabilities, 24,* 304–310.

Forsythe, I., Butler, R., Berg, I., & McGuire, R. (1991). Cognitive impairment in new cases of epilepsy randomly assigned to carbamazepine, phenytoin and sodium valproate. *Developmental Medicine and Child Neurology, 33,* 524–534.

Fourquean, J. M., Meisgeier, C., Swank, P. R., & Williams, R. E. (1991). Correlates of postsecondary employment outcomes for young adults with learning disabilities. *Journal of Learning Disabilities, 24,* 400–405.

Fox, E. E., & Davies, R. L. (1971). Test your personality. *Rational Living, 5,* 23–25.

Frank, K., & Wade, P. (1993). Disabled student services in postsecondary education: Who's responsible for what? *Journal of College Student Development, 34,* 26–30.

Franklin Learning Resources, 122 Burrs Road, Mt. Holly, New Jersey 08060.

Fraser, S. (Ed.). (1995). *The bell curve wars: Race, intelligence and the future of America.* New York: Basic Books.

Frauenheim, J. G., & Heckerl, J. R. (1983). A longitudinal study of psychological and achievement test performance in severe dyslexic adults. *Journal of Learning Disabilities, 16,* 339–347.

Frick, P. J., Kamphaus, R. W., Lahey, B. B., Loeber, R., Christ, M. A. G., Hart, E. L., & Tannenbaum, L. E. (1991). Academic underachievement and the disruptive behavior disorders. *Journal of Consulting and Clinical Psychology, 59,* 289–294.

Frick, P. J., Lahey, B. B., Applegate, B., Kerdyck, L., Ollendick, T., Hynd, G. W., Garfinkel, B., Greenhill, L., Biederman, J., Barkley, R. A., McBurnett, K., Newcorn, J., & Waldman, P. D. (1994). DSM-IV field trials for the disruptive behavior disorders: Symptom utility estimates. *Journal of the American Academy of Child and Adolescent Psychiatry, 33,* 529–539.

Fuerst, D. R., Fisk, J. L., & Rourke, B. P. (1989). Psychosocial functioning of learning-disabled children: Replicability of statistically derived subtypes. *Journal of Consulting and Clinical Psychology, 57,* 275–280.

Fuerst, D. R., & Rourke, B. P. (1993). Psychosocial functioning of children: Relations between personality subtypes and academic achievement. *Journal of Abnormal Child Psychology, 21,* 597–607.

Fuerst, D. R., & Rourke, B. P. (1995). Psychosocial functioning of children with learning disabilities at three age levels. *Child Neuropsychology, 1,* 38–55.

Fulton, A. L., & Yates, W. R. (1988). Family abuse of methylphenidate. *AFB, 38,* 143–145.

Funk, J. B., & Ruppert, E. S. (1984). Language disorders and behavioral problems in preschool children. *Developmental and Behavioral Pediatrics, 6,* 357–360.

Gaddes, W. H. (1985). *Learning disabilities and brain function: A neuropsychological approach* (2nd ed.). New York: Springer.

Gadow, K. D. (1982). School involvement in the treatment of seizure disorders. *Epilepsia, 23,* 215–224.

Gadow, K. D. (1985). Prevalence and efficacy of stimulant drug use with mentally retarded children and youth. *Psychopharmacology Bulletin, 21,* 291–303.

Gadow, K. D., Nolan, E., Sprafkin, J., & Sverd, J. (1995). School observations of children with attention-deficit hyperactivity disorder and comorbid tic disorder: Effects of methylpheni-date treatment. *Developmental and Behavioral Pediatrics, 16,* 167–176.

Gadow, K. D., Nolan, E. E., & Sverd, J. (1992). Methylphenidate in hyperactive boys with comorbid tic disorders: II. Short-term behavioral effects in school settings. *Journal of the American Academy of Child and Adolescent Psychiatry, 31,* 462–471.

Gadow, K. D., Nolan, E. E., Sverd, J., Sprafkin, J., & Paolicelli, L. (1990). Methylphenidate in aggressive hyperactive boys: I. Effects on peer aggression in public school settings. *Journal of the American Academy of Child and Adolescent Psychiatry, 29,* 710–718.

Gajar, A., Salvia, J., Gajria, M., & Salvia, S. (1989). A comparison of intelligence achievement discrepancies between learning disabled and non-learning disabled college students. *Learning Disabilities Research, 4,* 119–124.

Gajar, A. H., Schloss, P. J., Schloss, C. N., & Thompson, C. K. (1984). Effects of feedback and self-monitoring on head trauma youths' conversational skills. *Journal of Applied Behavioral Analysis, 17,* 353–358.

Galaburda, A. M. (1985). Developmental dyslexia: A review of biological interactions. *Annals of Dyslexia, 35,* 21–33.

Galaburda, A. M. (1989). Ordinary and extraordinary brain development: Anatomical varia-tion in developmental dyslexia. *Annals of Dyslexia, 39,* 67–80.

Galaburda, A. M. (1991). Anatomy of dyslexia: Argument against phrenology. In D. D. Duane & D. B. Gray (Eds.), *The reading brain: The biological basis of dyslexia.* Parkton, MD: York.

Garfinkel, B. G., Wender, P. H., Sloman, L., & O'Neill, I. (1983). Tricyclic antidepressant and methylphenidate treatment of attention deficit disorder in children. *Journal of the American Academy of Child Psychiatry, 22,* 343–348.

Gerber, P. J. (1978). *A comparative study of social perceptual ability of learning disabled and nonhandicapped children.* Unpublished doctoral Dissertation, University of Michigan, Ann Arbor.

Gerber, P. J. (1983). Conference summary and generation of final research priorities. In *Special rehabilitation needs of learning disabilities adults* (pp. 50–61). Washington, DC: National In-stitute for Handicapped Research.

Gerber, P. J. (1984). *A study of the school to work transition for learning disabled students and the learning disabled adult in society in the Netherlands and Denmark.* New York: World Re-habilitation Fund.

Gerber, P. J. (1988). *Highly successful learning disabled adults: Insights from case interviews.* Paper presented at the annual conference of the Association for Handicapped Student Ser-vices Programs in Postsecondary Education, New Orleans.

Gerber, P. J., & Brown, D. (1990). Report of the pathways to employment consensus conference on employability of persons with learning disabilities. *Learning Disabilities Research and Practice, 6,* 475–487.

Gerber, P. J., Ginsberg, R. J., & Reiff, H. B. (1992). Identifying alterable patterns in employ-ment success for highly successful adults with learning disabilities. *Journal of Learning Disa-bilities, 25,* 475–487.

Gerber, P. J., & Mellard, D. (1985). Rehabilitation of learning disabled adults: Recommended research priorities. *Journal of Rehabilitation, 51,* 62–64.

Gerber, P. J., & Reiff, H. B. (1991). *Speaking for themselves: Ethnographic interviews with adults with learning disabilities.* Ann Arbor, MI: University of Michigan Press.

Gerber, P. J., & Reiff, H. B. (1994). *Learning disabilities in adulthood: Persisting problems and evolving issues.* Boston: Andover.

Gerber, P. J., Schneiders, C. A., Paradise, L. V., Reiff, H. B., Ginsberg, R., & Popp, P. A. (1990). Persisting problems of adults with learning disabilities: Self-reported comparisons from their school age years. *Journal of Learning Disabilities, 23,* 570–573.

Gersh, F. (1993). Treatment of ADD in college students. *CH.A.D.D.ER Box, 6,* 10–11.

Getzel, E. E. (1990). Entering postsecondary programs: Early individualized planning. *Teaching Exceptional Children, 23,* 51–53.

Gibbs, D. P., & Cooper, E. B. (1989). Prevalence of communication disorders in students with learning disabilities. *Journal of Learning Disabilities, 22,* 60–63.

Giedd, J., Castellanos, G., Eckburg, P., Marsh, W., Kozuch, P., King, A., Hamburger, S., Ritchie, G., & Rapoport, J. (1994). Quantitative morphology of the corpus callosum in attention deficit hyperactivity disorder. *American Journal of Psychiatry, 151,* 655–669.

Gillberg, C., Persson, U., Grufman, M., & Temner, U. (1986). Psychiatric disorders in mildly and severely mentally retarded urban children and adolescents: Epidemiological aspects. *British Journal of Psychiatry, 149,* 68–74.

Gilligan, C. (1982). *In a different voice: Psychological theory and women's development.* Cambridge, MA: Harvard University Press.

Gillingham, M. G., & Guthrie, J. T. (1987). Relationships between CBI and research on teaching. *Contemporary Educational Psychology, 12,* 189–199.

Gilmore, J. N., & Gilmore, E. S. (1968). *Gilmore Oral Reading Test.* New York: Harcourt Brace & World.

Ginsberg, R., & Gerber, P. (1990). *Conquering success: Patterns of highly successful learning disabled adults in the workplace.* Paper presented at the annual meeting of the American Educational Research Association.

Gittelman, R., Mannuzza, S., Shenker, R., & Bonagura, N. (1985). Hyperactive boys almost grown up. *Archives of General Psychiatry, 42,* 937–947.

Glasser, J. M. (1995). Differential diagnosis of ADHD and bipolar disorder. *ADHD Report, 3,* 8–10.

Glow, R. A., & Glow, P. H. (1980). Peer and self-rating: Children's perception of behavior relevant to hyperkinetic impulsive disorder. *Journal of Abnormal Child Psychology, 8,* 471–490.

Goals 2000. (1993). *General Aptitude Test Battery (GATB).* Washington, DC: U.S. Department of Education.

Golden, C. J., Hammeke, T. A., & Purisch, A. D. (1980). *The Luria-Nebraska Neuropsychological Battery: A manual for clinical and experimental uses.* Lincoln, NE: University of Nebraska Press.

Golden, G. S. (1977). Tourette's syndrome: The pediatric perspective. *American Medical Journal of Diseases in Children, 131,* 531–534.

Goldring, E. B., & Presbrey, L. S. (1986). Evaluating preschool programs: A meta-analytic approach. *Educational Evaluation and Policy Analysis, 8,* 179–188.

Goldstein, G., Katz, L., Slomka, G., & Kelly, M. A. (1993). Relationships among academic, neuropsychological, and intellectual status in subtypes of adults with learning disability. *Archives of Clinical Neuropsychology, 8,* 41–53.

Goldstein, S. (1989). *Observation Checklist.* Salt Lake City, UT: Neurology, Learning and Behavior Center.

Goldstein, S. (1991). *It's just attention disorder* [Videotape]. Salt Lake City, UT: Neurology, Learning and Behavior Center.

Goldstein, S. (1994). *Attention-deficit hyperactivity disorder in adults: Symposium handbook.* Salt Lake City, UT: Neurology, Learning and Behavior Center.

Goldstein, S. (1995). *Understanding and managing children's classroom behavior.* New York: Wiley.

Goldstein, S., & Goldstein, M. (1990). *Managing attention disorders in children: A guide for practitioners.* New York: Wiley.

Goldstein, S., & Goldstein, M. (1992). *Why won't my child pay attention?* New York: Wiley.

Goldstein, S., & Goldstein, M. (1994). *Childhood history form.* Salt Lake City, UT: Neurology, Learning and Behavior Center.

Goldstein, S., & Goldstein, M. (1995). Attention-deficit hyperactivity disorder in adults. *Directions in Psychiatry, 15*(18), 1–8.

Goldstein, S., & Hinerman, P. (1988). *A parent's guide: Language and behavior problems in children.* Salt Lake City, UT: Neurology, Learning and Behavior Center.

Gomez, R. L., Janowsky, D., Zetin, M., Huey, L., & Clopton, P. L. (1981). Adult psychiatric diagnosis and symptoms compatible with the hyperactive syndrome: A retrospective study. *Journal of Clinical Psychiatry, 42,* 389–394.

Goodyear, H. P., & Hynd, G. W. (1992). Attention deficit disorder with and without hyperactivity: Behavioral and neuropsychological differentiation. *Journal of Clinical Psychology, 21,* 273–305.

Gordon, M. (1988). *Gordon Diagnostic System.* DeWitt, NY: Gordon Diagnostic Systems.

Gordon, M. (1994). *Database of CPT research.* DeWitt, NY: Gordon Diagnostic Systems.

Gordon, M., & McClure, F. D. (1983). *The objective assessment of attention deficit disorders.* Paper presented at the 91st annual convention of the American Psychological Association, Anaheim, CA.

Grammatik [Computer software]. San Francisco: Reference Software.

Grane, M. E., Weinstein, T., & Walbert, H. J. (1983). School-based home instruction and learning: A quantitative synthesis. *Journal of Educational Research, 76,* 351–360.

Grant, D. A., & Berg, E. A. (1984). *Wisconsin Card Sorting Test.* Odessa, FL: Psychological Assessment Resources, Inc.

Green, A. R., & Costain, D. W. (1981). *Pharmacology and biochemistry of psychiatric disorders.* New York: Wiley.

Green, P., & Brightman, A. J. (1990). *Independence day: Designing computer solutions for individuals with disability.* Allen, TX: DLM.

Greenberg, L. M., & Crosby, R. D. (1992). *Specificity and sensitivity of the Test of Variables of Attention (TOVA).* Manuscript submitted for publication.

Greenberg, R. P., & Fisher, S. (1989). Examining antidepressant effectiveness: Findings, ambiguities and some vexing problems. In S. Fisher & R. P. Greenberg (Eds.), *The limits of biological treatments for psychological distress.* Hillside, NJ: Erlbaum.

Greenberg, L. M., & Waldman, I. D. (1991). *Developmental normative data on the Test of Variables of Attention.* Unpublished manuscript.

Greenhill, L. L. (1984). Stimulant related growth inhibition in children: A review. In L. Greenhill & B. Shopsin (Eds.), *The psychobiology of childhood.* New York: Spectrum.

Greenhill, L. L., & Osman, B. B. (1991). *Ritalin theory and patient management.* New York: Liebert.

Grilo, C. M., Becker, D. F., Walker, M. L., Levy, K. N., Edell, W. S., & McGlashan, T. H. (1995). Psychiatric comorbidity in adolescent inpatients with substance use disorders. *Journal of the American Academy of Child and Adolescent Psychiatry, 34,* 1085–1091.

Grodzinsky, G. (1990). *Assessing frontal lobe functioning in 6 to 11 year old boys with attention deficit hyperactivity disorder.* Unpublished doctoral dissertation, Boston College, Chestnut Hill, MA.

Gronwall, D. (1977). Paced auditory serial addition task: A measure of recovery from concussion. *Perceptual and Motor Skills, 44,* 367–373.

Gronwall, D., & Wrightson, P. (1981). Memory and information processing capacity after closed head injury. *Journal of Neurology, Neurosurgery and Psychiatry, 44,* 889–895.

Gruenberg, D. E. (1983). College basic skills program: A national survey. *Journal of Developmental and Remedial Education, 6,* 2–5.

Gualitieri, C. T., & Evans, R. W. (1988). Motor performance in hyperactive children treated with Imipramine. *Perceptual and Motor Skills, 66,* 763–769.

Gualitieri, C. T., Ondrusek, M. G., & Finley, C. (1985). Attention deficit disorders in adults. *Clinical Neuropharmacology, 8,* 343–356.

Gualitieri, T., Koriath, U., Van Bourgondien, M., & Saleeby, N. (1983). Language disorders in children referred for psychiatric services. *Journal of the American Academy of Children and Adolescent Psychiatry, 22,* 165–171.

Gualitieri, T., Quade, D., Hicks, R. E., Mayo, J. P., & Schroeder, S. R. (1984). Tardive dyskinesia and other clinical consequences of neuroleptic treatment in children and adolescents. *American Journal of Psychiatry, 141*, 20–23.

Guide for Occupational Exploration (GOE). (1989). Washington, DC: U.S. Department of Labor.

Guskey, T. R., & Pigott, T. D. (1988). Research on group-based mastery learning programs: A meta-analysis. *Journal of Educational Research, 81*, 197–216.

Gwirtsman, H. E., Szuba, M. P., Toren, L., & Feist, M. (1994). The antidepressant response to tricyclics in major depressives is accelerated with adjunctive use of methylphenidate. *Psychopharmacology Bulletin, 30*, 157–164.

Haenlein, M., & Caul, W. F. (1987). Attention deficit disorder with hyperactivity: A specific hypothesis of reward dysfunction. *Journal of the American Academy of Child and Adolescent Psychiatry, 26*, 356–362.

Hagerman, R. J., & Falkstein, A. R. (1987). An association between recurrent otitis media in infancy and later hyperactivity. *Clinical Pediatrics, 26*, 253–257.

Hagerman, R., Kemper, M., & Hudson, M. (1985). Learning disabilities and attentional problems in boys with the fragile x syndrome. *American Journal of Diseases in Children, 139*, 674–678.

Hall, L. E. (1989). The effects of cooperative learning on achievement: A meta-analysis (Doctoral dissertation, University of Georgia, 1988). *Dissertation Abstracts International, 50*, 343A.

Hallahan, D. P., Marshall, K. J., & Lloyd, J. W. (1981). Self-recording during group instruction: Effects on attention to task. *Learning Disability Quarterly, 4*, 407–413.

Hallahan, D. P., & Sapona, R. (1983). Self-monitoring of attention with learning-disabled children: Past research and current issues. *Journal of Learning Disabilities, 16*, 616–620.

Hallowell, E. M., & Ratey, J. J. (1994). *Driven to distraction*. New York: Pantheon.

Hallowell, E. M., & Ratey, J. J. (1995). *Understanding attention deficit disorder and addiction*. Center City, MN: Hazelden.

Halperin, J. M., & Gittelman, R. (1982). Do hyperactive children and their siblings differ in I.Q. and academic achievement? *Psychiatry Research, 6*, 253–258.

Halperin, J. M., Gittelman, R., Klein, D. F., & Rudel, R. G. (1984). Reading-disabled hyperactive children: A distinct subgroup of attention deficit disorder with hyperactivity? *Journal of Abnormal Child Psychology, 12*, 1–14.

Halperin, J. M., Matier, K., Bedi, G., Vandsheep, S., & Newcorn, H. J. (1992). Specificity of inattention, impulsivity and hyperactivity to the diagnosis of attention-deficit hyperactivity disorder. *Journal of the American Academy of Child and Adolescent Psychiatry, 31*, 190–196.

Halperin, J. M., Newcorn, J. H., Matier, K., Sharma, V., McKay, K. E., & Schwartz, S. (1993). Discriminant validity of attention-deficit hyperactivity disorder. *Journal of the American Academy of Child and Adolescent Psychiatry, 32*, 1038–1043.

Halperin, J. M., O'Brien, J. D., Newcorn, J. H., Healey, J. M., Pascualvaca, D. M., Wolf, L. E., & Young, J. G. (1990). Validation of hyperactive, aggressive and mixed hyperactive/ aggressive childhood disorders: A research note. *Journal of Child Psychiatry and Psychology, 31*, 455–459.

Halpern, A. (1992). Transition: Old wine in new bottles. *Exceptional Children, 58*, 202–213.

Halpern, A. (1993). Quality of life as a conceptual framework for evaluating transition outcomes. *Exceptional Children, 59*, 486–498.

Halpern, A. S., & Fuhrer, M. J. (1984). *Functional assessment in rehabilitation*. Baltimore, MD: Brooks.

Halstead, W. C. (1947). *Brain and intelligence*. Chicago: University of Chicago Press.

Hammill, D. D., & Larsen, S. C. (1996). *Test of written language—3 (TOWL-3)*. Los Angeles: Western Psychological Services.

Hammill, D. D., Leigh, J. E., McNutt, G., & Larsen, S. (1981). A new definition of learning disabilities. *Learning Disabilities Quarterly, 4,* 336–342; reprint, *Learning Disabilities Quarterly, 11,* 217–223.

Hamsher, K. (1987). Adult norms for a short vigilance task. *ADD/Hyperactivity Newsletter, 7,* 2.

Handen, B. L., Breaux, A. M., Gosling, A., Ploof, D. L., & Feldman, H. (1990). Efficacy of methylphenidate among mentally retarded children with attention deficit hyperactivity disorder. *Pediatrics, 86,* 922–930.

Handen, B. L., Breaux, A. M., Janosky, J., McAuliffe, S., Feldman, H., & Gosling, A. (1992). Effects and non-effects of methylphenidate in children with mental retardation and ADHD. *Journal of the American Academy of Child and Adolescent Psychiatry, 31,* 455–461.

Handen, B. L., Feldman, H., Gosling, A., Breaux, A. M., & McAuliffe, S. (1991). Adverse side effects of Ritalin among mentally retarded children with ADHD. *Journal of the American Academy of Child and Adolescent Psychiatry, 30,* 241–245.

Haring, K. A., Lovett, D. L., & Smith, D. D. (1990). A follow-up study of recent special education graduates of learning disabilities programs. *Journal of Learning Disabilities, 23,* 108–113.

Harnadek, M. C. S., & Rourke, B. P. (1994). Principal identifying features of the syndrome of non-verbal learning disabilities in children. *Journal of Learning Disabilities, 27,* 144–154.

Harris, K. R. (1986). Self-monitoring of attentional behavior versus self-monitoring of productivity: Effects on-task behavior. An academic response rate among learning disabled children. *Journal of Applied Behavior Analysis, 19,* 417–423.

Harris, M. M. (1988). Meta-analyses of test anxiety among college students (Doctoral dissertation, Ohio State University, 1987). *Dissertation Abstracts International, 49,* 543B.

Hartman, R. C., & Krulwich, M. T. (1983). *Learning disabled adults in postsecondary education.* Washington, DC: Department of Education.

Hartman, R. (1991). LD among high achieving students. *Information from HEATH, 10,* 2–12.

Hartocollis, P. (1968). The syndrome of minimal brain dysfunction in young adult. *Bulletin of the Menninger Clinic, 32,* 102–114.

Hartsough, C. S., & Lambert, N. M. (1985). Medical factors in hyperactive and normal children: Prenatal, developmental, and health history findings. *American Journal of Orthopsychiatry, 55,* 190–210.

Harvey, J. R., & Wells, M. (1989). *Diagnosis of adult learning disabilities and vocational rehabilitation: A descriptive analysis.* Paper presented at the ACLD International Conference, Miami, FL.

Hathaway, S. R., & McKinley, J. C. (1989). *Minnesota Multiphasic Personality Inventory—II (MMPI-II).* Circle Pines, MN: NCS Assessments.

Hauser, P., Zametkin, A. J., Martinez, P., Vitiello, B., Matochik, J., Mixson, J., & Weintraub, B. (1993). Attention deficit hyperactivity disorder in people with generalized resistance to thyroid hormone. *New England Journal of Medicine, 328,* 997–1001.

Healy, J. M. (1990). *Endangered minds: Why children don't think and what we can do about it.* New York: Simon & Schuster.

Heaton, R. K. (1981). *A manual for the Wisconsin Card Sorting Test.* Odessa, FL: Psychological Assessment Resources.

Heaton, R. K., & Pendleton, M. G. (1981). Use of neuropsychological tests to predict adult patients' everyday functioning. *Journal of Consulting and Clinical Psychology, 49,* 807–821.

Hechtman, L. (1981). Families of hyperactives. *Research in Community and Mental Health, 2,* 275–292.

Hechtman, L. (1989). Attention-deficit hyperactivity disorder in adolescence and adulthood: An updated follow-up. *Psychiatric Annals, 19,* 597–603.

Hechtman, L., Weiss, G., & Metrakos, K. (1978). Hyperactive individuals as young adults: Current and longitudinal electroencephalographic evaluation and its relation to outcome. *Canadian Medical Association Journal, 118,* 919–923.

Hechtman, L., Weiss, G., & Perlman, T. (1978). Growth and cardiovascular measures in hyperactive individuals as young adults and in matched normal controls. *Canadian Medical Association Journal, 118,* 1247–1250.

Hechtman, L., Weiss, G., Perlman, T., Hopkins, J., & Wener, A. (1979). Hyperactive children in young adulthood: a controlled perspective ten-year follow-up. *International Journal of Mental Health, 8,* 52–66.

Helfgott, E., Rudel, R. G., & Kairam, R. (1986). The effect of piracetam on short and long term verbal retrieval in dyslexic boys. *International Journal of Psychophysiology, 4,* 53–61.

Helsel, W. J., Hersen, M., & Lubetsky, M. J. (1989). Stimulant medication and the retarded. *Journal of the American Academy of Child and Adolescent Psychiatry, 28,* 138–139.

Hembree, R. (1988). Correlates, causes, effects, and treatment of test anxiety. *Review of Educational Research, 58,* 47–77.

Herjanic, B. M., & Penick, E. C. (1972). Adult outcomes of disabled child readers. *Journal of Special Education, 6,* 397–410.

Hern, K. L., & Hynd, G. W. (1992). Clinical differentiation of the attention deficit disorder subtypes: Do sensorimotor deficits characterize children with ADD/WO? *Archives of Clinical Neuropsychology, 7,* 77–83.

Herrmann, W. M., & Stephan, K. (1991). Efficacy and clinical relevance of cognition enhancers. *Alzheimer Disease and Associated Disorders, 5*(Suppl. 1), S7–S12.

Herrnstein, R. J., & Murray, C. (1994). *The bell curve: Intelligence and class structure in American life.* New York: Free Press.

Herzog, J. E., & Falk, B. (1991). A follow-up study of vocational outcomes of young adults with learning disabilities. *Journal of Postsecondary Education and Disability, 9,* 219–226.

Hill, J. W. (1984). Unrecognized learning disabilities in adulthood: Implications for adult education. Paper presented at the annual meeting of the American Association of Mental Deficiency.

Hinshaw, S. P. (1992). Externalizing behavior problems and academic underachievement in childhood and adolescence: Causal relationships and underlying mechanisms. *Psychological Bulletin, 111,* 127–155.

Hinshaw, S. P., & Erhardt, D. (1991). Behavioral treatment of attention deficit hyperactivity disorder. In V. B. Van Hasselt & M. Hersen (Eds.), *Handbook of behavior therapy and pharmacotherapy for children: A comparative analysis.* New York: Grune & Stratton.

Hinshaw, S. P., Lahey, B. B., & Hart, E. L. (1993). Issues of taxonomy and comorbidity in the development of conduct disorder. *Development and Psychopathology, 5,* 31–50.

Hinshaw, S. P., Morrison, D. C., Carte, E. T., & Cornsweet, C. (1987). Factorial dimensions of the Revised Behavior Problem Checklist: Replication and validation within a kindergarten sample. *Journal of Abnormal Child Psychology, 15,* 309–327.

Hoffman, F. J., Sheldon, K. L., Minskoff, E. H., Sautter, S. W., Steidle, E. F., Baker, D. P., Bailey, M. B., & Echols, L. D. (1987). Needs of learning disabled adults. *Journal of Learning Disabilities, 20,* 43–52.

Hogenson, D. L. (1974). *Reading and juvenile delinquency.* Towson, MD: Orton Dyslexia Society.

Hohman, L. B. (1922). Post-encephalitic behavior disorders in children. *Johns Hopkins Hospital Bulletin, 33,* 372–375.

Holborow, P. L., & Berry, P. S. (1986a). Hyperactivity and learning disabilities. *Journal of Learning Disabilities, 19,* 426–431.

Holborow, P., & Berry, P. (1986b). A multinational, cross-cultural perspective on hyperactivity. *American Journal of Orthopsychiatry Association, 56,* 320–322.

Hollingshead, A. B. (1975). *Four-factor index of social status.* New Haven, CT: Yale University, Department of Sociology.

Hood, D. F. (1991). Using meta-analysis for input evaluation (Doctoral dissertation, Florida State University, 1990). *Dissertation Abstracts International, 51,* 4099A.

Horak, V. M. (1981). A meta-analysis of research findings on individualized instruction in mathematics. *Journal of Educational Research, 74,* 249–253.

Horn, W. F., & Ialong, N. (1988). Multi-modal treatment of attention deficit hyperactivity disorder in children. In H. Fitzgerald, B. Lester, & M. Yogman (Eds.). *Theory and research in behavioral pediatrics, Vol. 4.* New York: Plenum.

Horn, W., O'Donnell, J., & Vitulano, L. (1983). Long-term follow-up studies of learning disabled persons. *Journal of Learning Disabilities, 16,* 542–555.

Houck, C. K., Englehard, J., & Geller, C. (1989). Self-assessment of learning disabled and nondisabled college students: A comparative study. *Learning Disabilities Research, 5,* 61–67.

Howlin, P., & Rutter, M. (1987). *Treatment of autistic children.* New York: Wiley.

Hoy, C., & Gregg, N. (1985). Appraisal and assessment of learning disabilities, including a special bibliography. In *Academic assessment and remediation of adults with learning disabilities: A resource series for adult basic education teachers.* Atlanta, GA: Georgia State Department of Education, Adult and Community Education Unit.

Hoy, C., & Gregg, N. (1986). Learning disabled students: An emerging population on college campuses. *Journal of College Admissions, 112,* 10–14.

Huessy, H. R. (1988). Behavior disorders and the Ritalin controversy. *Journal of the American Medical Association, 260,* 2219.

Huessy, H. R., & Wright, A. I. (1970). The use of imipramine in children's behavior disorders. *Acta Paedopsychiatrica, 37,* 194–199.

Hugdahl, K., Synnevag, B., & Satz, P. (1990). Immune and autoimmune diseases in dyslexic children. *Neuropsychologia, 28,* 673–679.

Hughes, C. A., & Smith, J. O. (1990). Cognitive and academic performance of college students with learning disabilities: A synthesis of the literature. *Learning Disabilities Quarterly, 13,* 66–79.

Hunt, R. D. (1987). Treatment effects of oral and transdermal clonidine in relation to methylphenidate: an open pilot study in ADDH. *Psychopharmacological Bulletin, 23,* 111–114.

Hunt, R. D. (1988). Attention deficit disorder: diagnosis, assessment and treatment. In C. Kestenbaum & D. Williams (Eds.), *Handbook of clinical assessment of children and adolescents: A biopsychosocial approach, Vol. 2.* New York: Oxford University Press.

Hunt, R. D., Arnsten, A. F. T., & Asbell, M. D. (1995). An open trial of guanfacine in the treatment of attention deficit hyperactivity disorder. *Journal of the American Academy of Child and Adolescent Psychiatry, 34,* 50–54.

Hunt, R. D., Capper, L., & O'Connell, P. (1990). Clonidine in child and adolescent psychiatry. *Journal of Child and Adolescent Psychopharmacology, 1,* 87–101.

Hunt, R. D., Mindera, R. B., & Cohen, D. J. (1985). Clonidine benefits children with attention deficit disorder and hyperactivity: Report of a double blind placebo-controlled crossover. *Journal of the American Academy of Child and Adolescent Psychiatry, 24,* 617–629.

Hynd, G. W., Hern, K. L., Voeller, K. K., & Marshall, R. M. (1991). Neurobiological basis of attention deficit disorder (ADD). *School Psychology Review, 20,* 174–186.

Illinois program helps learning disabled graduate from college. (1990). *Education of the Handicapped, 16,* 9–10.

Implementation of Part B of the Education of the Handicapped Act, 42 Fed. Reg. 42474–42518 (1977).

Individuals with Disabilities Education Act of 1975, 20 U.S.C. § 1400 *et seq.*

Ingersoll, B., & Goldstein, S. (1993). *Attention deficit disorder and learning disabilities: Realities, myths and controversial treatments.* New York: Doubleday.

Interagency Committee on Learning Disabilities. (1987). *Learning disabilities: A report to the U.S. Congress.* Washington, DC: U.S. Department of Health and Human Services.

Israel, L., Melac, M., Milinkevitch, D., & Dubos, G. (1994). Drug therapy and memory training programs: a double-blind randomized trial of general practice patients with age-associated memory impairment. *International Psychogeriatrics, 6,* 155–170.

Jacobson, J. W., Mulick, J. A., & Schwartz, A. A. (1995). A history of facilitated communication: Science, pseudo science and anti-science. *American Psychologist, 50,* 750–765.

Jaffe, P. (1993a). Howe case stirs controversy. *ADDendum, 11,* 6–9.

Jaffe, P. (1993b). Randi Rosenthal, J.D. *ADDendum, 11,* 14.

Jaffe, S. L. (1989). Pemoline and liver function. *Journal of the American Academy of Child and Adolescent Psychiatry, 28,* 457–458.

Janis, I. L., & Mann, L. (1977). *Decision making: A psychological analysis of conflict, choice and commitment.* New York: Free Press.

Javorsky, J., & Gussin, B. (1994). College Students with ADHD: An overview and description of services. *Journal of College Student Development, 35,* 170–177.

Jenkins, J. R., Pious, C. G., & Peterson, D. L. (1988). Categorical programs for remedial and handicapped students: Issues of validity. *Exceptional Children, 55,* 147–158.

Jessor, R. (1992). Risk behavior in adolescence: A psychological framework for understanding and action. *Developmental Review, 12,* 374–390.

Johnson, C. (1981). LD adults: The inside story. *Academic Therapy, 16,* 435–442.

Johnson, D. J. (1987a). Assessment issues in learning disabilities research. In S. Vaughn & C. S. Bos (Eds.), *Research in learning disabilities: Issues and future directions.* Boston: College-Hill.

Johnson, D. J. (1987b). Disorders of written language. In D. J. Johnson & J. W. Blalock (Eds.), *Adults with learning disabilities: Clinical studies.* Orlando, FL: Grune & Stratton.

Johnson, D. J. (1993). Professional preparation of specialists to work in postsecondary learning disability programs. In S. A. Vogel & P. B. Adelman (Eds.), *Success for college students with learning disabilities.* New York: Springer.

Johnson, D. J., & Blalock, J. (Eds.). (1987). *Adults with learning disabilities.* Orlando, FL: Grune & Stratton.

Johnson, D. W., & Johnson, R. T. (1987). Research shows the benefits of adult cooperation. *Educational Leadership, 45,* 27–30.

Johnson, D. W., Johnson, R. T., & Maruyama, G. (1983). Interdependence and interpersonal attraction among heterogeneous and homogeneous individuals: A theoretical formulation and a meta-analysis of the research. *Review of Education Research, 53,* 5–54.

Johnson, D. W., Maruyama, G., Johnson, R., Nelson, D., & Skon, L. (1981). Effects of cooperative, competitive, and individualistic goal structures on achievement: A meta-analysis. *Psychological Bulletin, 89,* 46–62.

Johnston, C. J., & Pelham, W. E. (1986). Teacher ratings predict peer ratings of aggression at 3 year follow-up in boys with attention deficit disorder with hyperactivity. *Journal of Consulting and Clinical Psychology, 54,* 571–572.

Johnston, C., Pelham, W. E., Hoza, J., & Sturges, J. (1987). Psychostimulant rebound in attention deficit disordered boys. *Journal of the American Academy of Child and Adolescent Psychiatry, 27,* 806–810.

Jones, R. (1994). *A retrospective clinical evaluation: Adderall and methylphenidate.* Unpublished manuscript.

Jorm, A. F., Share, D. L., Matthews, R., & MacLean, R. (1986). Behavior problems in specific reading retarded and general reading backward children: A longitudinal study. *Journal of Child Psychology and Psychiatry, 27,* 33–43.

Joschko, M., & Rourke, B. P. (1985). Neuropsychological subtypes of learning-disabled children who exhibit the ACID pattern on the WISC. In B. P. Rourke (Ed.), *Neuropsychology of learning disabilities: Essentials of subtype analysis.* New York: Guilford.

Josten's Learning (1994). Invest learning system [Computer software]. San Diego, CA: Author.

Kanfer, F. H. (1970). Self-regulation: Research, issues, and speculations. In C. Neuringer & J. L. Michel (Eds.), *Behavior modification in clinical psychology.* New York: Appleton-Century-Crofts.

Kaplan, H. K., Wamboldt, F., & Barnhardt, R. D. (1986). Behavioral effects of dietary sucrose in disturbed children. *American Journal of Psychology, 7,* 143.

Kaplan, S. L., Busner, J., Kupietz, S., Wasserman, E., & Segal, B. (1990). Effects of methylphenidate on adolescents with aggressive conduct disorder and ADDH: A preliminary report. *Journal of the American Academy of Child and Adolescent Psychiatry, 29,* 719–723.

Kashani, J., Chapel, J., & Ellis, J. (1979). Hyperactive girls. *Journal of Operational Psychiatry, 10,* 145–149.

Kasten, E. F., Coury, D. L., & Heron, T. E. (1992). Educators' knowledge and attitudes regarding stimulants in the treatment of attention deficit hyperactivity disorder. *Journal of Developmental and Behavioral Pediatrics, 13,* 215–219.

Katz, L., & Goldstein, G. (1993). The Luria-Nebraska Neuropsychological Battery and the WAIS-R in assessment of adults with specific learning disabilities. *Rehabilitation Counseling Bulletin, 36,* 190–198.

Kaufman, K. F., & O'Leary, K. D. (1972). Reward, cost and self-evaluation procedures for disruptive adolescents in a psychiatric hospital school. *Journal of Applied Behavior Analysis, 5,* 293–309.

Kavale, K. A. (1984). A meta-analytic evaluation of the Frostig test and training program. *Exceptional Child, 31,* 134–141.

Kavale, K. A. (1988). The long-term consequences of learning disabilities. In M. C. Wang, M. C. Reynolds & H. J. Walberg (Eds.), *Handbook of special education: Research and practice.* Oxford: Pergamon.

Kavale, K. A., & Forness, S. R. (1987). Substance over style: Assessing the efficacy of modality testing and teaching. *Exceptional Children, 54,* 228–239.

Kavale, K., & Mattson, P. D. (1983). One jumped off the balance beam: Meta-analysis of perceptual-motor training. *Journal of Learning Disabilities, 16,* 165–173.

Kavanaugh, J. (1988). *New federal biological definition of learning and attentional disorders.* Speech given at the 15th annual conference of the New York Branch of the Orton Society.

Kavanaugh, J. F., & Truss, T. J. (1988). *Learning disabilities: Proceedings of the national conference.* Parkton, MD: York.

Kelly, K., & Ramundo, P. (1993). *You mean I'm not lazy, stupid or crazy: A self-help book for adults with attention deficit disorder.* Cincinnati, OH: Tyrell & Jerem.

Kelly, P. C., Cohen, M. L., Walker, W. O., Caskey, O. L., & Atkinson, A. W. (1989). Self-esteem in children medically managed for attention deficit disorder. *Pediatrics, 83,* 211–217.

Kemph, J. P., DeVane, C. G., Levin, G. M., Jarecke, R., & Miller, R. L. (1993). Treatment of aggressive children with clonidine: Results of an open pilot study. *Journal of the American Academy of Child and Adolescent Psychiatry, 32,* 577–581.

Kendall, P. C., & Hollon, S. D. (1981). *Assessment strategies for cognitive-behavioral interventions.* New York: Academic.

Kennedy, R., Shinkunas, T., & Richard, M. (1995). *Student Academic Accommodations Request Form.* Iowa City, IA: University of Iowa.

Keough, B. K., & Barkett, C. J. (1980). An educational analysis of hyperactive children's achievement problems. In C. K. Whalen & B. Henker (Eds.), *Hyperactive children: The social ecology of identification and treatment.* New York: Academic.

King, C., & Young, R. D. (1982). Attentional deficits with and without hyperactivity: Teacher and peer perceptions. *Journal of Abnormal Child Psychology, 10,* 483–495.

Kinsbourne, M., & Swanson, J. M. (1979). Models of hyperactivity: Implications for diagnosis and treatment. In R. G. Trites (Ed.), *Hyperactivity in children: Etiology, measurement and treatment implications.* Baltimore: University Park Press.

Kirby, E. A., & Grimley, L. K. (1986). *Understanding and treatment attention deficit disorder.* New York: Pergamon.

Kirby, E. A., VandenBerg, S. P., & Sullins, W. (1993). *Evaluation of the continuous performance test for assessing ADHD.* Poster session presented at the 101st annual convention of the American Psychological Association, Toronto, ON.

Kirk, S. A. (1962). *Educating exceptional children.* Boston: Houghton-Mifflin.

Klawans, H. L., & Genovese, N. (1986). Pharmacology of dementia. *Neurologic Clinics of North America, 4,* 459–467.

Klee, S. H., Garfinkel, B. D., & Beauchesne, H. (1986). Attention deficits in adults. *Psychiatric Annals, 16,* 52–56.

Klein, R. G. (1987). Pharmacology of childhood hyperactivity: An update. In H. Y. Meltzer (Ed.), *Psychopharmacology: The third generation of progress.* New York: Raven.

Klein, R. G., & Mannuzza, S. (1991). Long-term outcome of hyperactive children: A review. *Journal of the American Academy of Child and Adolescent Psychiatry, 30,* 383–387.

Klorman, R., Brumaghim, J. T., Fitzpatrick, P. A., & Borgstedt, A. D. (1990). Clinical effects of a controlled trial of methylphenidate on adolescents with attention deficit disorder. *Journal of the American Academy of Child and Adolescent Psychiatry, 29,* 702–709.

Kramer, J. R. (1987). What are hyperactive children like as young adults? In J. Loney (Ed.), *The young hyperactive child.* New York: Haworth.

Kravets, M., & Wax, I. (1992). *The K and W guide to colleges for the learning disabled (4th edition).* Deerfield, IL: Kravets, Wax and Associates, Inc.

Kravetz, M. (1994). Choosing the best college when you have ADD. *Attention, 1,* 22–25.

Kristan, P. (1995). Getting it together: Notes from a personal organization skill consultant to adults with ADHD. *ADHD Report, 3,* 10–12.

Kugler, J., Seus, R., Krauskopf, R., Brecht, H. M., & Raschig, A. (1990). Differences in psychic performance with guanfacine and clonidine in normotensive subjects. *British Journal of Clinical Psychopharmacology, 99,* 803–809.

Kulik, C. C., Kulik, J. A., & Bangert-Drowns, R. L. (1984). *Effects of computer-based education on elementary school pupils.* Washington, DC: American Educational Research Association. (ERIC Document Reproduction Service No. ED 244 616)

Kulik, C. C., Kulik, J. A., & Bangert-Drowns, R. L. (1990). Effectiveness of mastery learning programs: A meta-analysis. *Review of Educational Research, 60,* 265–299.

Kulik, C. C., Kulik, J. A., & Cohen, P. A. (1980). Effectiveness of computer-based college teaching: A meta-analysis of findings. *Review of Educational Research, 50,* 525–544.

Kulik, C. C., Schwalb, B. J., & Kulik, J. A. (1982). Programmed instruction in secondary education: A meta-analysis of evaluation findings. *Journal of Educational Research, 75,* 133–138.

Kulik, J. A., Bangert, R. L., & Williams, G. W. (1983). Effects of computer-based teaching on secondary school students. *Journal of Educational Psychology, 75,* 19–26.

Kulik, J. A., Bangert-Drowns, R. L., & Kulik, C. C. (1984). Effectiveness of coaching for aptitude tests. *Psychological Bulletin, 95,* 179–188.

Kulik, J. A., Cohen, P. A., & Ebeling, B. J. (1980). Effectiveness of programmed instruction in higher education: A meta-analysis of findings. *Educational Evaluation and Policy Analysis, 2,* 51–63.

Kulik, J. A., Kulik, C. C., & Bangert, R. L. (1984). Effects of practice on aptitude and achievement test scores. *American Educational Research Journal, 21,* 435–447.

Kulik, J. A., Kulik, C. C., & Cohen, P. A. (1979). Research on audiotorial instruction: A meta-analysis of comparative studies. *Research in Higher Education, 11,* 321–341.

Kulik, J. A., & Kulik, C. L. C. (1987). Review of recent research literature on computer-based instruction. *Contemporary Educational Psychology, 12,* 222–230.

Kussmaul, A. (1877). Die Storungen der Sprache. *Ziemssen's Handbuch der Speciellen Pathologie und Therapie, 12,* 1–300.

LaDoux, C. (1986). Sensory systems and emotions. *Integrative Psychiatry, 4,* 237–248.

Lahey, B. B., Applegate, B., McBurnett, K., Biederman, J., Greenhill, L., Hynd, G. W., Barkley, R. A., Newcorn, J., Jensen, P., Richters, J., Garfinkel, B., Kerdyk, L., Frick, P. J., Ollendick, T., Perez, D., Hart, E. L., Waldman, I., & Shaffer, D. (1994). DSM-IV field trials for attention deficit/hyperactivity disorder in children and adolescents. *American Journal of Psychiatry.*

Lahey, B. B., Piacentini, J. C., McBurnett, K., Stone, P., Hartdagen, S., & Hynd, G. (1988).

Psychopathology in the parents of children with conduct disorder and hyperactivity. *Journal of the American Academy of Child and Adolescent Psychiatry, 27,* 163–170.

Lahey, B., Schaughency, E., Frame, C., & Strauss, C. (1985). Teacher ratings of attention problems in children experimentally classified as exhibiting attention deficit disorders with and without hyperactivity. *Journal of the American Academy of Child and Adolescent Psychiatry, 24,* 613–616.

Lahey, B. B., Schaughency, E. A., Hynd, G. W., Carlson, C. L., & Nieves, N. (1987). Attention deficit disorder with and without hyperactivity: Comparison of behavioral characteristics of clinic-referred children. *Journal of the American Academy of Child and Adolescent Child Psychiatry, 26,* 718–723.

Lahey, B., Schaughency, E., Strauss, C., & Frame, C. (1984). Are attention disorders with and without hyperactivity similar or dissimilar disorders? *Journal of the American Academy of Child Psychiatry, 23,* 302–309.

Lambert, N. M., & Sandoval, J. (1980). The prevalence of learning disabilities and a sample of children considered hyperactive. *Journal of Abnormal Child Psychology, 8,* 33–50.

Lambert, N. M., Sandoval, J., & Sassone, D. (1978). Prevalence of hyperactivity in elementary school children as a function of social system definers. *American Journal of Orthopsychiatry, 48,* 446–463.

Lamminmaki, T., Ahonen, T., Narhi, V., Lyytinen, H., & Todd de Barra, H. (1995). Attention deficit hyperactivity disorder subtypes: Are there differences in academic problems? *Developmental Neuropsychology, 3,* 297–310.

Langer, D. H., Sweeney, K. P., Bartenbach, D. E., Davis, P. M., & Menander, K. B. (1986). Evidence of lack of abuse or dependence following pemoline treatment: Results of a retrospective study. *Drug and Alcohol Dependence, 17,* 213–227.

LaPouse, R., & Monk, M. A. (1958). An epidemiologic study of behavior characteristics in children. *American Journal of Public Health, 48,* 1134–1144.

Larsen, J. P., Høien, T., Lundberg, I., & Ødegaard, H. (1990). MRI evaluation of the size and symmetry of the planum temporale in adolescents with developmental dyslexia. *Brain and Language, 39,* 289–301.

Lassiter, K. S., D'Amato, R. C., Riggio, D. J., Whitten, J. C. M., & Bardos, A. N. (1994). The construct specificity of the continuous performance test: Does inattention relate to behavior and achievement? *Developmental Neuropsychology, 10,* 179–188.

Latham, P. S., & Latham, P. H. (1992). *Attention deficit disorder and the law: A guide for advocates.* Washington, DC: JKL Communications.

Latham, P. S., & Latham, P. H. (1993). *ADD and the law.* Washington, DC: JKL Communications.

Latham, P. S., & Latham, P. H. (1994). *Succeeding in the workplace—Attention deficit disorder and learning disabilities in the workplace: A guide for success.* Washington, DC: JKL Communications.

Latham, P. S., & Latham, P. H. (1995). Legal rights of the ADD Adult. In K. G. Nadeau (Ed.), *Attention deficit disorder in adults: Research, diagnosis and treatment.* New York: Brunner/Mazel.

Lee, W. C. (1990). The effectiveness of computer-assisted instruction and computer programming in elementary and secondary mathematics: A meta-analysis (Doctoral dissertation, University of Massachusetts, 1990). *Dissertation Abstracts International, 51,* 775A.

Leonard, F., & McCormack, A. (1994). In P. Quinn (Ed.), *ADD and the college student: A guide for high school and college students with attention deficit disorder.* New York: Magination.

Leonard, F. C. (1991). Using Wechsler data to predict success for learning disabled college students. *Learning Disabilities Research and Practice, 6,* 17–24.

Lerner, J. (1985). *Learning disabilities: Theories, diagnosis, and teaching strategies* (4th ed.). Boston: Houghton-Mifflin.

Lerner, J. (1993). *Learning disabilities: Theories, diagnoses, and teaching strategies.* Boston: Houghton-Mifflin.

Levin, H. S., Benton, A. L., & Grossman, R. G. (1982). *Neurobehavioral consequences of closed head injury.* New York: Oxford University Press.

Levine, M. (1990). *Keeping a head in school.* Cambridge, MA: Educators Publishing Service.

Levine, M. D. (1989). Learning disabilities at 25: The early adulthood of a maturing concept. *Learning Disabilities, 1,* 1–11.

Levinson, E. (1986). School psychology and college learning disabled students: Training and service responsibilities. *Psychology in the Schools, 23,* 295–302.

Lewin, K. (1935). *A dynamic theory of personality.* New York: McGraw-Hill.

Lewis, R. D., & Lorion, R. P. (1988). Discriminative effectiveness of the Luria-Nebraska Neuropsychological Battery for LD adolescents. *Learning Disability Quarterly, 11,* 62–69.

Lewis, R. J., & Vosburgh, W. T. (1988). Effectiveness of kindergarten intervention programs: A meta-analysis. *School Psychology International, 9,* 265–275.

Lewison, P. N., Gottlieb, I. H., & Seeley, J. R. (1995). Adolescent psychopathology: IV. Specificity of psychosocial risk factors for depression and substance abuse in older adolescents. *Journal of the American Academy of Child and Adolescent Psychiatry, 34,* 1221–1229.

Lezak, M. D. (1995). *Neuropsychological assessment* (3rd ed.). New York: Oxford University Press.

Lian, K. C., Juler, R. G., & McGaugh, J. L. (1986). Modulating effects of post-training epinephrine on memory: involvement of the amygdala noradrenergic system. *Brain Research, 368,* 125–133.

Licht, B. G., Kistner, J. A., Ozkaragoz, T., Shapiro, S., & Clausen, L. (1985). Causal attributions of learning disabled children: Individual differences and their implications for persistence. *Journal of Educational Psychology, 77,* 208–216.

Lieb, V. (1995). *Choosing careers.* St. Louis, MO: People Achieving Results Together.

Lieberman, L. M. (1987). Is the learning disabled adult really necessary? *Journal of Learning Disabilities, 20,* 64.

Lipsey, M. W., & Wilson, D. B. (1993). The efficacy of psychological, educational, and behavioral treatment: Confirmation from meta-analysis. *American Psychologist, 48,* 1181–1209.

Literacy for All Americans Act of 1990, H.R. 5115.

Litowitz, B. (1987). Problems of conceptualization and language: Evidence from definitions. In D. J. Johnson & J. W. Blalock (Eds.), *Adults with learning disabilities: Clinical studies.* Orlando, FL: Grune & Stratton.

Loeber, R., Brinthaupt, V. P., & Green, S. M. (1990). Attention deficits, impulsivity and hyperactivity with or without conduct problems: Relationships and delinquency and unique contextual factors. In R. J. McMahon & R. D. Peters (Eds.), *Behavior disorders of adolescence: Research intervention and policy in clinical and school settings.* New York: Plenum.

Loeber, R., Green, S. M., Keenan, K., & Lahey, B. B. (1995). Which boys will fare worse? Early predictors of the onset of conduct disorder in a six-year longitudinal study. *Journal of the American Academy of Child and Adolescent Psychiatry, 34,* 499–509.

Loeber, R., Green, S. M., Lahey, B. B., & Stouthamer-Loeber, M. (1989). Optimal informants on childhood disruptive behaviors. *Development and Psychopathology, 1,* 317–337.

Loeber, R., Stouthamer-Loeber, M., Van Kammen, W., & Farrington, D. P. (1991). Initiation, escalation and desistance in juvenile offending and their correlates. *Journal of Criminal Law and Criminology, 82,* 36–82.

Loney, J. (1974). The intellectual functioning of hyperactive elementary school boys: A cross sectional investigation. *American Journal of Orthopsychiatry, 44,* 754–762.

Loney, J. (1986). Hyperactivity and aggression in the diagnosis of attention deficit disorder. In B. B. Lahey & A. E. Kazdin (Eds.), *Advances in Clinical Child Psychology.* New York: State University of New York Press.

Loney, J., Kramer, J., & Milich, R. (1981). The hyperactive child grows up: Predictors of symptoms, delinquency and achievement at follow-up. In K. D. Gadow & J. Loney (Eds.), *Psychosocial aspects of drug treatment for hyperactivity.* Boulder, CO: Westview.

Loney, J., Langhorne, J. E., Patternite, C. E., Whaley-Klahn, M. A., Blair-Broeker, C. T., & Hacker, M. (1980). The Iowa Habit: Hyperkinetic/aggressive boys in treatment. In S. Sells, R. Crandall, M. Roff, J. Strauss, & W. Pollin (Eds.), *Human functioning and longitudinal perspective: Studies of normal and psychopathic populations.* Baltimore: Williams & Wilkins.

Loney, J., & Milich, R. S. (1981). Hyperactivity, inattention, and aggression in clinical practice. In M. Wolraich & D. K. Routh (Eds.), *Advances in behavioral pediatrics.* Greenwich, CT: JAI.

Lorys, A. R., Hynd, G. W., & Lahey, B. B. (1990). Do neurocognitive measures differentiate attention deficit disorder with and without hyperactivity? *Archives of General Neuropsychology, 5,* 119–135.

Lou, H. C., Henriksen, L., & Bruhn, P. (1984). Focal cerebral hypoperfusion in children with dysphasia and/or attention deficit disorder. *Archives of Neurology, 41,* 825–829.

Love, A. J., & Thompson, M. G. G. (1988). Language disorders and attention deficit disorders in young children referred for psychiatric services: Analysis of prevalence and a conceptual synthesis. *American Journal of Orthopsychiatry, 58,* 52–64.

Lovitt, T. C., & Curtiss, K. A. (1969). Academic response rate as a function of teacher- and self-imposed contingencies. *Journal of Applied Behavior Analysis, 2,* 49–53.

Lubar, J. (1992, October). *Is EEG neurofeedback an effective treatment for ADHD?* Paper presented at the 4th annual conference of Children and Adults with Attention Deficit Disorder, Chicago.

Luria, A. R. (1959). The directive function of speech in development. *Word, 15,* 341–352.

Luria, A. R. (1961). *The role of speech and the regulation of normal and abnormal behaviors.* New York: Liveright.

Lynam, D., Moffitt, T., & Stouthamer-Loeber, M. (1993). Explaining the relation between I.Q. and delinquency: Class, race, test motivation, school failure, or self-control? *Journal of Abnormal Psychology, 102,* 187–196.

Lysakowski, R. S., & Walberg, H. J. (1980). Classroom reinforcement. *Evaluation in Education, 4,* 115–116.

Lysakowski, R. S., & Walberg, H. J. (1981). Classroom reinforcement and learning: A quantitative synthesis. *Journal of Educational Research, 75,* 69–77.

Lysakowski, R. S., & Walberg, H. J. (1982). Instructional effects of cues, participation and corrective feedback: A quantitative synthesis. *American Educational Research Journal, 19,* 559–578.

Mackworth, N. H. (1957). Some factors affecting vigilance. *Advancements in Science, 53,* 389–393.

Mahoney, M. J. (1974). *Cognition and behavior modification.* Cambridge, MA: Ballinger.

Mahoney, M. J. (1977). Reflections on the cognitive-learning trend in psychotherapy. *American Psychologist, 32,* 5–13.

Mahoney, M. J., & Arnkoff, D. B. (1978). Cognitive and self-control therapies. In S. L. Garfield & A. E. Bergin (Eds.), *Handbook of psychotherapy and behavior change* (2nd ed.). New York: Wiley.

Malcolm, C. B., Polatajko, H. J., & Simons, J. (1990). A descriptive study of adults with suspected learning disabilities. *Journal of Learning Disabilities, 23,* 518–520.

Malter, R., & Frank, L. M. (1995). *Freedom from distractibility or auditory processing problems: A critical look at the WISC-III third factor.* Paper presented at the annual convention of the Learning Disabilities Association, Orlando, FL.

Manganello, R. (1990). The learning disabled college student: Balancing the 3 Rs and the 3Ds. In *Latest developments: A publication for the learning disabilities special interest group.* Columbus, OH: Association for Handicapped Student Services Programs in Postsecondary Education.

Mangrum, C. T., & Strichart, S. S. (1984). *College and the learning disabled student.* New York: Grune & Stratton.

Mangrum, C. T., & Strichart, S. S. (1988). *College and the learning disabled student* (2nd ed.). Orlando, FL: Grune & Stratton.

Mannuzza, S., Gittelman-Klein, R. G., Bessler, A. A., Malloy, P., & LaPadula, M. (1993). Adult outcome of hyperactive boys: Education achievement, occupational rank, and psychiatric status. *Archives of General Psychiatry, 50,* 565–576.

Mannuzza, S., Klein, R. G., Bonagura, N., Konig, P. H., & Shenker, R. (1988). Hyperactive boys almost grown up: II. Status of subjects without mental disorders. *Archives of General Psychiatry, 45,* 13–18.

Mannuzza, S., Klein, R. G., Bonagura, N., Malloy, P., Giampino, T. L., & Addalli, K. A. (1991). Hyperactive boys almost grown up: V. Replication of psychiatric status. *Archives of General Psychiatry, 48,* 77–83.

Mariani, M., & Barkley, R. A. (1995). *Neuropsychological and academic functioning in preschool children with attention deficit hyperactivity disorder.* Submitted for publication, University of Massachusetts Medical Center, Worcester, MA.

Marsh, G. E., & Price, B. J. (1980). *Methods for teaching the mildly handicapped adolescent.* St. Louis, MO: Mosby.

Martin, C. S., Earleywine, M., Blackson, T. C., & Vanyukov, M. M. (1994). Aggressivity in attention, hyperactivity and impulsivity in boys at high and low risk for substance abuse. *Journal of Abnormal Child Psychology, 22,* 177–203.

Marzillier, J. S. (1980). Cognitive therapy and behavioral practice. *Behavior Research and Therapy, 18,* 249–258.

Mash, E. J., & Johnston, C. (1983). Sibling interactions of hyperactive and normal children and their relationship to reports of maternal stress and self-esteem. *Journal of Clinical Child Psychology, 12,* 91–99.

Mather, N., & Healey, W. C. (1990). Deposing aptitude-achievement discrepancy as the imperial criterion for learning disabilities. *Learning Disabilities: A Multi-Disciplinary Journal, 1,* 40–48.

Matochik, J. A., Liebenauer, L. L., King, A. C., Szymanski, H. V., Cohen, R. M., & Zametkin, A. J. (1994). Cerebral glucose metabolism in adults with attention deficit hyperactivity disorder after chronic stimulant treatment. *American Journal of Psychiatry, 151,* 658–664.

Matochik, J. A., Nordahl, T. E., Gross, M., Semple, W. E., King, A. C., Cohen, R. C., & Zametkin, A. J. (1993). Effects of acute stimulant medication on cerebral metabolism in adults with hyperactivity. *Neuropsychopharmacology, 8,* 337–386.

Mattes, J. A. (1985). Stimulant therapy of "adult hyperactivity": In reply. *Archives of General Psychiatry, 42,* 840.

Mattes, J. (1986). Propranolol for adults with temper outbursts and residual attention deficit disorder. *Journal of Clinical Psychopharmacology, 6,* 299–302.

Mattes, J. A., Boswell, L., & Oliver, H. (1984). Methylphenidate effects on symptoms of attention deficit disorder in adults. *Archives of General Psychiatry, 41,* 1059–1063.

Mattes, J. A., & Gittelman, R. (1983). Growth of hyperactive children on maintenance regimen of methylphenidate. *Archives of General Psychiatry, 40,* 317–321.

Matthews, P. R., Anderson, D. W., & Skolnick, D. B. (1987). Faculty attitudes toward accommodations for college students with learning disabilities. *Learning Disabilities Focus, 3,* 46–52.

Matthews, R. M., Whang, R. L., & Fawcett, S. B. (1982). Behavioral assessment of occupational skills of learning disabled adolescents. *Journal of Learning Disabilities, 15,* 38–41.

Mattis, S., French, J., & Rapin, I. (1975). Dyslexia in children and young adults: Three independent neuropsychological syndromes. *Developmental Medicine and Child Neurology, 17,* 150–163.

McCarney, S. B. (1989). *The transition behavior scale, IEP and intervention manual: Goals, objectives and intervention strategies for behavior necessary for success and independent living and employment.* Columbia, MO: Hawthorne.

McCue, M. (1994). Clinical diagnostic and functional assessment of adults with learning disabilities. In P. J. Gerber & H. B. Reiff (Eds.), *Learning disabilities in adulthood.* Boston: Andover.

McCue, M., Shelly, C., & Goldstein, G. (1986). Intellectual, academic and neuropsychological performance levels in learning disabled adults. *Journal of Learning Disabilities, 19,* 233–236.

McCue, M., Shelly, C., Goldstein, G., & Katz-Garris, L. (1984). Neuropsychological aspects of learning disability in young adults. *Clinical Neuropsychology, 6,* 229–233.

McDaniel, K. D. (1986). Pharmacologic treatment of psychiatric and neurodevelopmental disorders in children and adolescents. II. *Clinical Pediatrics, 25,* 143–146.

McDermid, R. D. (1990). A quantitative analysis of the literature on computer-assisted instruction with the learning-disabled and educable mentally retarded (Doctoral dissertation, University of Kansas, 1989). *Dissertation Abstracts International, 51,* 1196A.

McGaugh, J. L. (1989). Involvement of hormonal and neuromodulatory systems in the regulation of memory storage. *Annual Review of Neuroscience, 12,* 255–287.

McGee, R., & Share, D. L. (1988). Attention deficit hyperactivity disorder and academic failure: Which comes first and what should be treated? *Journal of the American Academy of Child and Adolescent Psychiatry, 27,* 318–325.

McGee, R., Williams, S., & Feehan, M. (1992). Attention deficit disorder and age of onset of problem behaviors. *Journal of Abnormal Child Psychology, 20,* 487–503.

McGee, R., Williams, S., & Silva, P. A. (1984). Behavioral and developmental characteristics of aggressive, hyperactive and aggressive-hyperactive boys. *Journal of the American Academy of Child and Adolescent Psychiatry, 23,* 270–279.

McGee, R., Williams, S., & Silva, P. A. (1987). A comparison of girls and boys with teacher-identified problems of attention. *Journal of the American Academy of Child and Adolescent Psychiatry, 26,* 711–716.

McGuire, J. M., Norlander, K. A., & Shaw, S. F. (1990). Postsecondary education for students with learning disabilities: Forecasting challenges for the future. *Learning Disabilities Focus, 5,* 69–74.

McNeil, B. J., & Nelson, K. R. (1990). *Meta-analysis of interactive video instruction: A 10-year review of achievement effects.* (ERIC Document Reproduction Service No. ED 321 761)

Mehrabian, A., & Ferris, S. R. (1967). Inference of attitudes from nonverbal communication in two channels. *Journal of Consulting Psychology, 31,* 248.

Meichenbaum, D. (1974). Self-instruction methods. In F. H. Kanfer & A. P. Goldstein (Eds.), *Helping people change.* New York: Pergamon.

Meichenbaum, D. (1975a). A self-instructional approach to stress inoculation training. In I. Sarason & C. D. Spielberger (Eds.), *Stress and anxiety, Vol. 2.* New York: Wiley.

Meichenbaum, D. (1975b). Self-instructional methods. In F. H. Kanfer & A. P. Goldstein (Eds.), *Helping people change.* New York: Pergamon.

Meichenbaum, D. (1977). *Cognitive-behavior modification.* New York: Plenum.

Meichenbaum, D. H., & Goodman, J. (1969). Reflection-impulsivity and verbal control of motor behavior. *Child Development, 40,* 785–797.

Meichenbaum, D. H., & Goodman, J. (1971). Training impulsive children to talk to themselves: A means of developing self-control. *Journal of Abnormal Psychology, 77,* 115–126.

Melekian, B. (1990). Family characteristics of children with dyslexia. *Journal of Learning Disabilities, 23,* 386–391.

Mellard, D. F. (1987). Educational issues surrounding severe discrepancy: A discussion. *Learning Disabilities Research, 3,* 50–56.

Mellard, D. F. (1990). The eligibility process: Identifying students with learning disabilities in California's community colleges. *Learning Disabilities Focus, 5,* 75–90.

Menkes, M. H., Rowek, J. S., & Menkes, J. H. (1967). A 25-year follow-up study on the hyperkinetic child with MBD. *Pediatrics, 39,* 393–399.

Merrill, R. D., & Garfinkel, G. (1987). Unexpected consequence of treatment for attention deficit disorder. *American Journal of Psychiatry, 144,* 250.

Messick, S., & Jungeblut, A. (1981). Time and method in coaching for the SAT. *Psychological Bulletin, 89,* 191–216.

Meyers, G. S., & Messer, J. (1981). The social and vocational adjustment of learning disabled/behavior disordered adolescents after h.s.: A pilot survey. In *Proceedings from the International Conference on the Career Development of Handicapped Individuals* (pp. 70–83). Washington, DC: National Institute of Education.

Michaels, C. A. (1987). Assisting students with learning disabilities in transition from high school to college. In D. Knapke & C. Lendman (Eds.), *Capitalizing on the future.*

Microsoft. (1993). Power Point [Computer software]. Bellevue, WA: Author.

Milich, R., & Dodge, K. A. (1984). Social information processing in child psychiatric populations. *Journal of Abnormal Child Psychology, 12,* 471–490.

Milich, R., & Loney, J. (1979). The role of hyperactive and aggressive symptomatology in predicting adolescent outcome among hyperactive children. *Journal of Pediatric Psychology, 4,* 93–112.

Milich, R., & Okazaki, M. (1991). An examination of learned helplessness among attention-deficit hyperactivity disordered boys. *Journal of Abnormal Child Psychology, 19,* 607–623.

Milich, R., & Pelham, W. E. (1986). Effects of sugar ingestion on the classroom and playgroup behavior of attention deficit disordered boys. *Journal of Consulting and Clinical Psychology, 54,* 714–718.

Miller, G. A., Galanter, E., & Pribram, K. N. (1960). *Plans and the structure of behavior.* New York: Holt, Rinehart & Winston.

Miller, R. J., Snider, B., & Rzonca, C. (1990). Variables related to the decision of young adults with learning disabilities to participate in postsecondary education. *Journal of Learning Disabilities, 24,* 188–191.

Millon, T. (1987). *Millon Clinical Multiaxial Personality Inventory (MMPI).* Minneapolis, MN: NCS Assessments.

Millon, T., Green, C. J., & Meagher, R. B. (1982). *Millon Adolescent Personality Inventory (MAPI).* Circle Pines, MN: NCS Assessments.

Minde, K. K., Lewin, D., Weiss, G., Lavigueur, H., Douglas, V., & Sykes, E. (1971). The hyperactive child in elementary school: A five year controlled follow-up. *Exceptional Children, 38,* 215–221.

Minde, K., Weiss, G., & Mendelson, N. (1972). A five-year follow-up study of ninety-one hyperactive school children. *Journal of the American Academy of Child Psychiatry, 11,* 595–610.

Minskoff, E. H. (1994). Post-secondary education and vocational training: Keys to success for adults with learning disabilities. In P. J. Gerber & H. B. Reiff (Eds.), *Learning disabilities in adulthood.* Boston: Andover.

Minskoff, E. H., & DeMoss, S. (1993). Facilitating successful transition: Using the trace model to assess and develop academic skills needed for vocational competence. *Learning Disability Quarterly, 16,* 161–170.

Minskoff, E. H., Hawks, R., Steidle, E. F., & Hoffman, F. J. (1989). A homogeneous group of persons with learning disabilities: Adults with severe learning disabilities in vocational rehabilitation. *Journal of Learning Disabilities, 22,* 521–528.

Minskoff, E. H., Sautter, S. W., Hoffman, F. J., & Hawks, R. (1987). Employer attitudes toward hiring the learning disabled. *Journal of Learning Disabilities, 20,* 53–57.

Minskoff, E. H., Sautter, S., Sheldon, K. L., Steidle, E. F., & Baker, D. P. (1988). A comparison of learning disabled adults and high school students. *Learning Disabilities Research, 3,* 115–123.

Mirsky, A. F. (1987). Behavioral and psychophysiological markers of disordered attention. *Environmental Health Perspectives, 74,* 191–199.

Mirsky, A. F. (1989). The neuropsychology of attention: Elements of complex behavior. In E. Perecman (Ed.), *Integrating theory and practice in clinical neuropsychology.* Hillsdale, NJ: Erlbaum.

Mitchell, E., & Matthews, K. L. (1980). Gilles de la Tourette's disorder associated with pemoline. *American Journal of Psychiatry, 34,* 740–754.

Moffitt, T. E. (1993). Adolescence-limited and life-course persistent anti-social behavior: The developmental taxonomy. *Psychological Review, 100,* 674–701.

Mondadori, C. (1993). The pharmacology of the nootropics; new insights and new questions. *Behavioral Brain Research, 59,* 1–9.

Mondadori, C., Preiswerk, G., & Jaekel, J. (1992). Treatment with a GABA receptor blocker improves the cognitive performance of mice, rats, and rhesus monkeys. *Pharmacology Communications, 2,* 93–97.

Morgan, W. P. (1896). A case of congenital word blindness. *British Medical Journal, 2,* 1378.

Morrison, J. R. (1979). Diagnosis of adult psychiatric patients with childhood hyperactivity. *American Journal of Psychiatry, 136,* 955–958.

Morrison, J. R. (1980). Adult psychiatric disorders in parents of hyperactive children. *American Journal of Psychiatry, 137,* 825–827.

Morrison, J. R., & Minskoff, K. (1975). Explosive personality as a sequel to the hyperactive-child syndrome. *Comprehensive Psychiatry, 16,* 343–348.

Morrison, J., & Stewart, M. (1971). A family study of hyperactive child syndrome. *Biological Psychiatry, 3,* 189–195.

Morrison, J., & Stewart, M. (1973). The psychiatric status of the legal families of adopted hyperactive children. *Archives of General Psychiatry, 23,* 888–891.

Moya, S. S., & O'Malley, J. M. (1994). A portfolio assessment model for English as a second language. *Journal of Educational Issues of Language Minority Students, 13,* 13–36.

Mufson, L., Moreau, D., Weissman, M. M., & Klerman, G. L. (1993). *Interpersonal psychotherapy for depressed adolescents.* New York: Guilford.

Mufson, L., Moreau, D., Weissman, M. M., Wickramaratne, P., Martin, J., & Samoilov, A. (1994). Modification of interpersonal psychotherapy with depressed adolescents (ITP-A): Phase I and II Studies. *Journal of the American Academy of Child and Adolescent-Psychiatry, 33,* 695–705.

Murphy, K., & Barkley, R. A. (1995a). ADHD preliminary normative data on DSM-IV criteria for adults. *The ADHD Report, 3(3),* 6–7.

Murphy, K., & Barkley, R. A. (1995b). Norms for the DSM IV symptom list for ADHD in adults. Study in progress, University of Massachusetts Medical Center, Worcester, MA.

Murphy, K. R., & LeVert, S. (1995). *Out of the fog: Treatment options and coping strategies for adult attention deficit disorder.* New York: Hyperion.

Murphy, K., & Vervock, J. (1995). *Adult ADHD Questionnaire.* New York: Brunner/Mazel.

Myklebust, H. R., & Boshes, B. (1969). *Final report: Minimal brain damage in children.* Washington, DC: U.S. Department of Health, Education and Welfare.

Nabuzoka, D., & Smith, P. K. (1993). Sociometric status and social behavior of children with and without learning difficulties. *Journal of Child Psychology and Psychiatry, 34,* 1435–1448.

Nadeau, K. G. (1995). *A comprehensive guide to attention deficit disorder in adults: Research, diagnosis and treatment.* New York: Brunner/Mazel.

Nadeau, K., Dixon, E., & Biggs, S. (1994). *School strategies for ADD teens.* Bethesda, MD: Chesapeake Psychological Publications.

National Advisory Committee on Handicapped Children. (1968, January 31). *Special education for handicapped children* (First annual report). Washington, DC: U.S. Department of Health, Education and Welfare.

National Joint Commission on Learning Disabilities. (1983). *Learning disabilities: The needs of adults with learning disabilities.* Washington, DC: U.S. Government Printing Office.

National Joint Commission on Learning Disabilities. (1987). Adults with learning disabilities: A call to action. *Journal of Learning Disabilities, 20,* 172–175.

National Literacy Act of 1989, S.1310.

Naugle, R. I., & Chelune, G. J. (1990). Integrating neuropsychological and "real life" data: A neuropsychological model for assessing every day functioning. In D. E. Tupper & K. D. Cicerone (Eds.), *The neuropsychology of everyday life: Assessment and basic competencies.* Boston: Kluwer.

Naylor, C. E., Felton, R. H., & Wood, F. B. (1990). Adult outcome in developmental dyslexia. In G. T. Pavlidis (Ed.), *Perspectives in dyslexia, Vol. 2.* Chichester, England: Wiley.

Needleman, H. L., Gunnoe, C., Leviton, A., Reed, R., Peresie, H., Maher, C., & Barrett, P. (1979). Deficits in psychologic and classroom performance of children with elevated dentine lead levels. *New England Journal of Medicine, 300,* 689–695.

Neff, P. (1982). *Tough Love.* Abingdon, VA: Abingdon.

Nelson, J. R., Dodd, J. M., & Smith, D. J. (1990). Faculty willingness to accommodate students with learning disabilities: A comparison among academic divisions. *Journal of Learning Disabilities, 23,* 185–189.

Ness, J., & Price, L. A. (1990). Meeting the psychosocial needs of adolescents and adults with LD. *Intervention in School and Clinic, 26,* 16–21.

Newcorn, J. H., Halperin, J. M., Healey, J. M., O'Brien, J. D., Pascualvaca, D. M., Wolf, L. E., Morganstein, A., Vanshdeep, S., & Young, J. G. (1989). Are ADDH and ADHD the same or different? *Journal of the American Academy of Child and Adolescent Psychiatry, 285,* 734–738.

Newill, B. H., Goyette, C. H., & Fogarty, T. W. (1984). Diagnosis and assessment of the adult with specific learning disabilities. *Journal of Rehabilitation, 8,* 188–189.

Nichols, P. L., & Chen, T. C. (1981). *Minimal brain dysfunction: A prospective study.* Hillsdale, NJ: Erlbaum.

Nicholson, C. D. (1989). Nootropics and metabolically active compounds in Alzheimer's disease. *Biochemical Society Transactions, 17,* 83–85.

Nicholson, C. D. (1990). Pharmacology of nootropics and metabolically active compounds in relation to their use in dementia. *Psychopharmacology, 101,* 147–159.

Niemiec, R. P. (1985). The meta-analysis of computer assisted instruction at the elementary school level (Doctoral dissertation, University of Illinois at Chicago, 1984). *Dissertation Abstracts International, 45,* 3330A. (University Microfilms International No. 85–01250)

Niemiec, R., Sampson, G., Weinstein, T., & Walberg, H. J. (1987). The effects of computer based instruction in elementary schools: A quantitative synthesis. *Journal of Research in Computing in Education, 20,* 85–103.

90s teens find a new high by abusing Ritalin. (1995, March 14). *USA Today,* p. 1-D.

Nowicki, S., & Strickland, B. R. (1973). A locus of control scale for children. *Journal of Consulting and Clinical Psychology, 40,* 148–154.

Nussbaum, N. L., Grant, M. L., Roman, M. J., Poole, J. H., & Bigler, E. D. (1990). Attention deficit disorder and the mediating effect of age on academic and behavioral variables. *Developmental and Behavioral Pediatrics, 11,* 22–26.

Obeso, J. A., Artieda, J., Quinn, N., et al. (1988). Piracetam in the treatment of various types of myoclonus. *Clinical Neuropharmacology, 11,* 529–536.

O'Bryan, V. L. (1985). The treatment of test anxiety: A meta-analytic review (Doctoral dissertation, Ohio University, 1985). *Dissertation Abstracts International, 46,* 2818B. (University Microfilms International No. 85–23654)

Occupational Aptitude Profile (OAP). (1989). Washington, DC: U.S. Department of Labor.

O'Donnell, J. P., Kurtz, J., & Ramanaiah, N. V. (1983). Neuropsychological test findings for normal learning disabled and brain damaged young adults. *Journal of Consulting and Clinical Psychology, 51,* 726–729.

Oestreicher, J. M., & O'Donnell, J. P. (1995). Validation of the general neuropsychological deficit scale with non-disabled, learning disabled and head injured young adults. *Archives of Clinical Neuropsychology, 10,* 185–191.

Office of Special Education and Rehabilitation Services. (1986). *Eighth annual report to Congress on the implementation of the Education of the Handicapped Act.* Washington, DC: Author.

O'Neal, P., & Robins, L. E. (1958). The relation of childhood behavior problems to adult psychiatric status: A 30-year follow-up study of 150 subjects. *American Journal of Psychiatry, 114,* 961–969.

Ostertag, B. A., Baker, R. E., Howard, R. F., & Best, L. (1982). Learning disabled programs in California community colleges. *Journal of Learning Disabilities, 15,* 535–538.

Ostrom, N. N., & Jenson, W. R. (1988). Assessment of attention deficits in children. *Professional School Psychology, 3,* 253–269.

Ottenbacher, K. (1982). Sensory integration therapy: Affect or effect. *American Journal of Occupational Therapy, 36,* 571–578.

Ottenbacher, K. J., Muller, L., Brandt, D., Heintzelman, A., Hojem, P., & Sharpe, P. (1987). The effectiveness of tactile stimulation as a form of early intervention: A quantitative evaluation. *Journal of Developmental and Behavioral Pediatrics, 8,* 68–76.

Ottenbacher, K. J., & Petersen, P. (1984). The efficacy of vestibular stimulation as a form of specific sensory enrichment. *Clinical Pediatrics, 23,* 428–433.

Page, J. G., Bernstein, J. E., Janicki, R. S., & Michelli, F. A. (1974). A multi-clinical trial of pemoline in childhood hyperkinesis. *Excerpta Medica, 48,* 99–124.

Palkes, H. S., & Stewart, M. A. (1972). Intellectual ability and performance of hyperactive children. *American Journal of Orthopsychiatry, 42,* 35–39.

Palkes, H. S., Stewart, M. A., & Freedman, J. (1971). Improvement in maze performance of hyperactive boys as a function of verbal-training procedures. *Journal of Special Education, 5,* 337–342.

Palkes, H. S., Stewart, M. A., & Kahana, B. (1968). Porteus Maze: Performance of hyperactive boys after training in self-directed verbal commands. *Child Development, 39,* 817–826.

Paradise, J. L. (1981). Otitis media during early life: How hazardous to development? A critical review of the evidence. *Pediatrics, 68,* 869–873.

Parker, H. C. (1992). *The ADD hyperactivity handbook for schools.* Plantation, FL: ADD Warehouse.

Parker, J. G., & Asher, S. R. (1987). Peer relations and later personal adjustment: Are low-accepted children at risk? *Psychological Bulletin, 102,* 357–389.

Parks, A. W., Antonoff, S., Drake, C., Skiba, W. F., & Soberman, J. (1987). A survey of programs and services for students with learning disabilities in graduate and professional schools. *Journal of Learning Disabilities, 20,* 181–188.

Paschal, R. A., Weinstein, T., & Walberg, H. J. (1984). The effects of homework on learning: A quantitative synthesis. *Journal of Educational Research, 78,* 97–104.

Pasuraman, R. (1994). Sustained attention and detection in discrimination. In R. Pasuraman & R. Davies (Eds.), *Varieties of Attention.* New York: Academic.

Patterson, G. R., DeBaryshe, B. D., & Ramsey, E. (1989). A developmental perspective on antisocial behavior. *American Psychologist, 44,* 329–335.

Patton, J. R., & Polloway, E. A. (1992). Learning disabilities: The challenges of adulthood. *Journal of Learning Disabilities, 25,* 410–416.

Payne, N. (1993). *What employers want in an employee.* Olympia, WA: Payne and Associates.

Payne, N. (1994). *Building learning power for children and adults who have special learning needs.* Olympia, WA: Payne and Associates.

Payton, J. B., Burkhart, J. E., Hersen, M., & Helsel, W. J. (1988). Treatment of ADDH mentally retarded children: A preliminary study. *Journal of the American Academy of Child and Adolescent Psychiatry, 28,* 761–767.

Pelham, W. (1991, Spring). ADHD and alcohol problems: Related disorders of childhood and adulthood. *Parents of ADD/Hyperactive Children Newsletter,* pp. 1–3.

Pelham, W. E., Atkins, M. S., Murphy, H. A., & White, K. S. (1981). *Operationalization and validation of attention deficit disorders.* Paper presented at the annual meeting of the Association for Advancement of Behavior Therapy, Toronto, ON.

Pelham, W. E., & Bender, M. E. (1982). Peer relationships and hyperactive children: Description and treatment. In K. Gadow & I. Bailer (Eds.), *Advances in learning and behavioral disabilities, Vol. 1.* Greenwich, CT: JAI.

Pelham, W. E., Bender, M. E., Caddell, J., Booth, S., & Moorer, S. H. (1985). Medication effect on arithmetic learning. *Archives of General Psychiatry, 42,* 948–951.

Pelham, W. E., Gnagy, E. M., Greenslade, K. E., & Milich, R. (1992). Teacher ratings of DSM-III-R symptoms for the disruptive behavior disorders. *Journal of the American Academy of Child and Adolescent Psychiatry, 31,* 210–218.

Pelham, W. E., Greenslade, K. E., Vodde-Hamilton, M., Murphy, D. A., Greenstein, J. J., Gnagy, E. M., Guthrie, K. J., Hoover, M. D., & Dahl, R. E. (1990). Relative efficacy of long-acting stimulants on children with attention deficit-hyperactivity disorder: A comparison of standard methylphenidate, sustained release methylphenidate, sustained release dextroamphetamine and pemoline. *Pediatrics, 86,* 226–237.

Pelham, W. E., & Hoza, J. (1987). Behavioral assessment of psychostimulant effects on ADD children in a summer day treatment program. In R. Prinz (Ed.), *Advances in behavioral assessment of children and families, Vol. 3.* Greenwich, CT: JAI.

Pelham, W. E., & Milich, R. (1984). Peer relations of children with hyperactivity/attention deficit disorder. *Journal of Learning Disabilities, 17,* 560–568.

Pelham, W. E., Swanson, J., Bender, M., & Wilson, J. (1980). *Effects of pemoline on hyperactivity: Laboratory and classroom measures.* Paper presented at the annual meeting of the American Psychological Association, Montreal.

Pelham, W. E., Walker, J. L., Sturges, J., & Hoza, J. (1989). The comparative effects of methylphenidate on ADD girls and boys. *Journal of the American Academy of Child and Adolescent Psychiatry, 28,* 773–776.

Pennington, B. F. (1991). *Diagnosing learning disorders.* New York: Guilford.

Pennington, B. F., Grossier, D., & Welsh, M. C. (1993). Contrasting cognitive deficits in attention deficit hyperactivity disorder versus reading disability. *Developmental Psychology, 29,* 511–523.

Pennington, B., McCabe, L., Smith, S., Lefly, D., Bookman, M., Kimberling, W., & Lubs, H. (1986). Spelling errors in adults with a familial dyslexia. *Child Development, 57,* 1001–1013.

Pennington, B. F., Smith, S. D., Kimberling, W. J., et al. (1987). Left-handedness and immune disorders in familial dyslexics. *Archives of Neurology, 44,* 634–639.

Pennsylvania State University. (1993). A Day in the Life . . . [Computer software]. University Park, PA: Author.

Petrauskas, R., & Rourke, B. P. (1979). Identification of subgroups of retarded readers: A neuropsychological multivariate approach. *Journal of Clinical Neuropsychology, 1,* 17–37.

Phillips, G. W. (1983). Learning the conservation concept: A meta-analysis (Doctoral dissertation, University of Kentucky). *Dissertation Abstracts International, 44,* 1990B. (University Microfilms International No. 83–22983)

Physician's Desk Reference. (1995). Montvale, NJ: Medical Economics.

Physician's Desk Reference. (1993). Montvale, NJ: Medical Economics.

Pickering, E., Pickering, A., & Buchanan, M. (1987). LD and nonhandicapped boys' comprehension of cartoon humor. *Learning Disability Quarterly, 10,* 45–51.

Platzman, K. A., Stoy, M. R., Brown, R. T., Coles, C. D., Smith, I. E., & Falek, A. (1992). Review of observational methods in attention deficit hyperactivity disorder (ADHD): Implications for diagnosis. *School Psychology Quarterly, 7,* 155–177.

Pleak, R., Birmaher, B., Gavrilescu, A., Abichandini, A., & Williams, D. (1988). Mania and neuropsychiatric excitation following carbamazepine. *Journal of the American Academy of Child and Adolescent Psychiatry, 27,* 500–503.

Pliszka, S. R. (1987). Tricyclic antidepressants in the treatment of children with attention deficit disorder. *Journal of the American Academy of Child and Adolescent Psychiatry, 26,* 127–132.

Pliszka, S. R. (1989). Effect of anxiety on cognition, behavior and stimulant response in ADHD. *Journal of the American Academy of Child and Adolescent Psychiatry, 28,* 882–887.

Pliszka, S. R. (1992). Comorbidity of attention-deficit hyperactivity disorder and overanxious disorder. *Journal of the American Academy of Child and Adolescent Psychiatry, 31,* 197–203.

Polirstok, S. R. (1987). Training handicapped students in the mainstream to use self-evaluation techniques. *Techniques: A Journal for Remedial Education and Counseling, 3,* 9–18.

Polloway, E. A., Schewel, R., & Patton, J. R. (1992). Learning disabilities in adulthood: Personal perspectives. *Journal of Learning Disabilities, 25,* 520–522.

Popkin, M. (1986). *Active parenting.* Atlanta, GA: Author.

Poplin, M. (1988). The reductionist fallacy in learning disabilities: Replicating the past by reducing the present. *Learning Disability Quarterly, 7,* 389–400.

Porteus, S. D. (1950). *The Porteus Maze Test and intelligence.* Palo Alto, CA: Pacific Books.

President's Committee on Employment of People with Disabilities. (1993). *Job accommodation ideas.* Washington, DC: Author.

Price, L. (1988). Effective counseling techniques for LD adolescents and adults in secondary and postsecondary settings. *Journal of Postsecondary Education and Disability, 23,* 466–471.

Primus, C. (1990). *Computer assistance model for learning disabled* (Grant No. G008630152–88). Washington, DC: U.S. Department of Education, Office of Special Education and Rehabilitation Services.

Prinz, R. J., & Loney, J. (1974). Teacher-rated hyperactive elementary school girls: An exploratory developmental study. *Child Psychiatry in Human Development, 4,* 246–257.

Racine, J. D., & Campbell, D. (1995). Adult attention deficit disorder: What's in a name? *Bulletin of the National Academy of Neuropsychology, 12,* 7–8.

Rapoport, J. L., Buchsbaum, M. S., Weingartner, H., Zahn, T. P., Ludlow, C., & Mikkelsen, E. J. (1980). Dextroamphetamine: Its cognitive and behavioral effects in normal and hyperactive boys and normal men. *Archives of General Psychiatry, 37,* 933–943.

Rapport, M. D., DuPaul, G. J., & Kelly, K. L. (1989). Attention-deficit hyperactivity disorder and methylphenidate: The relationship between gross body weight and drug response in children. *Psychopharmacological Bulletin, 25,* 285–290.

Rapport, M. D., DuPaul, G. J., Stoner, G., Birmingham, B. K., & Massey, G. (1985). Attention deficit disorder with hyperactivity: Differential effects of methylphenidate on impulsivity. *Pediatrics, 76,* 938–943.

Rapport, M. D., Jones, J. T., DuPaul, G. J., Kelly, K. L., Gardner, M. J., Tucker, S. B., & Shea, M. S. (1987). Attention deficit disorder and methylphenidate: Group and single subject analyses of dose effects on attention in clinic and classroom settings. *Journal of Clinical Child Psychology, 16,* 329–338.

Rapport, M. D., & Kelly, K. L. (1991). Stimulant effects on learning and cognitive function: Findings and implications for children with attention-deficit hyperactivity disorder. *Clinical Psychology Review, 11,* 61–92.

Rapport, M. D., Stoner, G., DuPaul, G. J., Kelly, K. L., Tucker, S. B., & Schoeler, T. (1988). Attention deficit disorder and methylphenidate: A multilevel analysis of dose response effects on children's impulsivity across settings. *Journal of the American Academy of Child and Adolescent Psychiatry, 27,* 60–69.

Raskin, M. (1993). Assistive technology and adults with learning disabilities: A blueprint for exploration and advancement. *Learning Disability Quarterly, 16,* 185–196.

Ratey, J. J. (1991, Fall/Winter). Paying attention to attention in adults. *CH.A.D.D.ER Newsletter,* pp. 13–14.

Ratey, J. J., Greenberg, M. S., Bemporad, J. R., & Lindem, K. J. (1992). Unrecognized attention-deficit hyperactivity disorder in adults presenting for outpatient psychotherapy. *Journal of Child and Adolescent Psychopharmacology, 2,* 267–275.

Ratey, J. J., Greenberg, M. S., & Lindem, K. (1991). Combination of treatment for attention deficit hyperactivity disorders in adults. *Journal of Nervous and Mental Disease, 179,* 699–701.

Ratey, J. J., Hallowell, E. M., & Miller, A. C. (1995). Relationship dilemmas for adults with ADD. In K. Nadeau (Ed.), *A comprehensive guide to attention deficit disorder in adults.* New York: Brunner/Mazel.

Rawson, M. (1968). *Developmental language disability.* Baltimore, MD: Johns Hopkins University Press.

Reader, M. J., Harris, E. L., Schuerholz, L. J., & Denckla, M. B. (1994). Attention deficit hyperactivity disorder and executive function. *Developmental Neuropsychology, 10,* 493–512.

Reeves, J. C., Werry, J. S., Elkind, G. S., & Zametkin, A. (1987). Attention deficit, conduct, oppositional, and anxiety disorders in children: I. A review of research on differentiating characteristics. *Journal of the American Academy of Child and Adolescent Psychiatry, 26,* 144–155.

Rehabilitation Act of 1973, P.L. 93–112.

Rehabilitation Services Administration. (1985, January 24). Program policy directive (RSA-PPD-85-3). Washington, DC: U.S. Department of Education, Office of Special Education and Rehabilitation Services.

Rehabilitation Services Administration (1990). Program assistance circular. Washington, DC: U.S. Department of Education, Office of Special Education and Rehabilitation Services.

Reid, A. H., Naylor, G. J., & Kay, D. S. G. (1981). A double-blind, placebo controlled, crossover trial of carbamazepine in overactive, severely mentally handicapped patients. *Psychological Medicine, 11,* 109–113.

Reid, M. K., & Borkowski, J. G. (1987). Causal attributions of hyperactive children: Implications for teaching strategies and self-control. *Journal of Educational Psychology, 79,* 296–307.

Reiff, H. B. (1987). Cognitive correlates of social perception in students with learning disabilities. Unpublished doctoral dissertation.

Reiff, H. B., & Gerber, P. J. (1989). Social cognition and cognitive processing in students with learning disabilities. *Learning Disabilities: A Multidisciplinary Journal, 1,* 56–62.

Reiff, H. B., & Gerber, P. J. (1994). Social/emotional and daily living issues for adults with learning disabilities. In P. J. Gerber & H. B. Reiff (Eds.), *Learning disabilities in adulthood.* Boston: Andover.

Reiff, H. B., Gerber, P. J., & Ginsberg, R. (1993). Definitions of learning disabilities from adults with learning disabilities: The insiders' perspective. *Learning Disability Quarterly, 16,* 114–125.

Reimherr, F. W., Wood, D. R., & Wender, P. H. (1980). An open clinical trial of L-dopa and carbidopa in adults with minimal brain dysfunction. *American Journal of Psychiatry, 137,* 73–75.

Reimherr, F. W., Wood, D. R., & Wender, P. H. (1986). The use of MK-801, a novel sympathomimetic in adults with attention deficit disorder, residual type. *Psychopharmacology Bulletin, 22,* 237–242.

Reitan, R. M. (1986). Theoretical and methodological bases of the Halstead-Reitan Neuropsychological Test Battery. In I. Grant & K. Adams (Eds.), *Neuropsychological assessment of neuropsychiatric disorders.* New York: Oxford University Press.

Reitan, R. M., & Wolfson, D. (1985). The Halstead-Reitan Neuropsychological Test Battery. Tucson, AZ: Neuropsychology Press.

Reitan, R. M., & Wolfson, D. (1988). *Traumatic brain injury: Recovery and rehabilitation.* Tucson, AZ: Neuropsychology Press.

Resnick, R. J., & McEvoy, K. (Eds.). (1995). *Bibliographies in psychology: Vol. 14. Attention deficit hyperactivity disorder: Abstracts of the psychological and behavioral literature, 1971–1994.* Washington, DC: American Psychological Association.

Reynolds, C. R. (1983). *Critical measurement issues in learning disabilities.* Unpublished report, U.S. Department of Education, Special Education Programs Work Group on Measurement Issues in the Assessment of Learning Disabilities.

Reynolds, C. R. (1985). Critical measurement issues in learning disabilities. *Journal of Special Education, 18,* 451–476.

Reynolds, C. R., & Richmond, B. O. (1985). *Revised Children's Manifest Anxiety Scale.* Los Angeles: Western Psychological Services.

Reynolds, W. M. (1986). *Reynolds Adolescent Depression Scale.* Odessa, FL: Psychological Assessment Resources.

Rhode, G., Morgan, D. P., & Young, K. R. (1983). Generalization and maintenance of treatment gains of behaviorally handicapped students from resource rooms to regular classrooms using self-evaluation procedures. *Journal of Applied Behavioral Analysis, 16,* 171–188.

Rich, D. (1992). *MegaSkills: Effective family educational involvement.* New York: School Administrators Association of New York State.

Richard, M. M. (1992). Considering student support services in college selection. *CH.A.D.-D.ER Box, 5,* 6–7.

Richard, M. M. (1995a). *Recommended assessment instruments for cognitive processing evaluation.* Iowa City, IA: University of Iowa, Office of Disability Services.

Richard, M. M. (1995b). Students with ADD in postsecondary education. In K. Nadeau (Ed.), *A comprehensive guide to attention deficit disorder in adults.* New York: Brunner/Mazel.

Richard, M. M., & Chandler, D. (1994). *Student handbook: Student disability services.* Iowa City, IA: University of Iowa, Office of Student Disability Services.

Richardson, S., Kupietz, S., & Maitinsky, S. (1987). What is the role of academic intervention in the treatment of hyperactive children with reading disorders? In J. Loney (Ed.), *The young hyperactive child: Answers to questions and diagnosis, prognosis and treatment.* New York: Haworth.

Richters, J. E., Arnold, L. E., Jensen, P. S., Abikoff, H., Conners, C. K., Greenhill, L. L., Hechtman, L., Hinshaw, S. P., Pelham, W. E., & Swanson, J. M. (1995). NIMH collaborative multisite multimodal treatment study of children with ADHD: I. Background and rationale. *Journal of the American Academy of Child and Adolescent Psychiatry, 34,* 987–1000.

Riddle, K. D., & Rapoport, J. L. (1976). 2-year follow-up of 72 hyperkinetic boys: Classroom behavior and peer acceptance. *Journal of Nervous and Mental Disease, 162,* 126–134.

Ridloff, L. S. (1977). CES-D Scale. *Applied Psychological Measures, 1,* 385–401.

Rifkin, A., Wortman, R., Reardon, G., & Siris, S. G. (1986). Psychotropic medication in adolescents: A review. *Journal of Clinical Psychiatry, 47,* 400–408.

Rizzolo, J. K. (1976). Building better communication between the educational and medical professions with respect to learning disabled children. *Illinois School Research, 12,* 25–33.

Robin, A. L. (1992). *ADHD in adulthood: A clinical perspective* [Videotape and manual]. Paxton, MA: Professional Advancement Seminars.

Robin, A. L., & Foster, S. L. (1989). *Negotiating parent and adolescent conflict.* New York: Guilford.

Robin, S. S., & Bosco, J. J. (1973). Ritalin for school children: the teacher's perspective. *Journal of School Health, 43,* 624–628.

Robins, L. N. (1991). Conduct disorder. *Journal of Child Psychology and Psychiatry, 32,* 193–212.

Roff, M., Sells, S., & Golden, M. (1972). *Social adjustment and personality development in children.* Minneapolis, MN: University of Minnesota Press.

Rogan, L. L., & Hartman, L. D. (1976). *A follow-up study of learning disabled children as adults.* Washington, DC: U.S. Department of Health, Education, and Welfare, Office of Education, Bureau of Education for the Handicapped.

Rogan, L. L., & Hartman, L. D. (1990). Adult outcomes of learning disabled students ten years after initial follow-up. *Learning Disabilities Focus, 5,* 91–102.

Roman, N., Nussbaum, N. L., & Bigler, E. (1988). Assessment of a case of residual ADHD first identified in adulthood. *ADHD/Hyperactivity Newsletter, 10,* 4–6.

Rooney, K. J., Hallahan, D. P., & Lloyd, J. W. (1984). Self-recording of attention by learning-disabled students in the regular classroom. *Journal of Learning Disabilities, 17,* 360–364.

Rose, E. (1991). Project TAPE: A model of technical assistance for service providers of college students with learning disabilities: *Learning Disabilities Research and Practice, 6,* 25–33.

Rose, E., & Sloan, L. (1990). *Teaching note-taking strategies to adults with learning disabilities.* Unpublished manuscript, Northern Illinois University, DeKalb, IL.

Rosenberg, B., & Gaier, E. (1977). The self-concept of the adolescent with learning disabilities. *Adolescence, 12,* 489–498.

Rosenthal, I. (1989). Model transition programs for learning disabled high school and college students. *Rehabilitation Counseling Bulletin, 33,* 54–66.

Rosevald, H. E., Mirsky, A. F., Sarason, I., Branson, E. D., & Beck, L. H. (1956). A continuous performance of brain damage. *Journal of Consulting Psychology, 20,* 343–350.

Ross, D. M., & Ross, S. A. (1982). *Hyperactivity: Current issues, research and theory* (2nd ed.). New York: Wiley.

Rothstein, L. (1986). Section 504 of the Rehabilitation Act: Emerging issues for colleges and universities. *Journal of College and University Law, 13,* 229–265.

Rourke, B. P. (1978). Neuropsychological research in reading retardation: A review. In A. Benton & D. Pearl (Eds.), *Dyslexia: An appraisal of current knowledge* (pp. 139–172). New York: Oxford University Press.

Rourke, B. P. (1982). Central processing deficiencies in children: Toward a developmental neuropsychological model. *Journal of Clinical Neuropsychology, 4,* 1–18.

Rourke, B. P. (1985). *Neuropsychology of learning disabilities: Essentials of subtype analysis.* New York: Guilford.

Rourke, B. P. (1989). *Nonverbal learning disabilities: The syndrome and the model.* New York: Guilford.

Rourke, B. P., & Fuerst, D. R. (1991). *Learning disabilities and psychosocial functioning: A neuropsychological perspective.* New York: Guilford.

Routh, D. K. (1978). Hyperactivity. In P. R. Magrab (Ed.), *Psychological management of pediatric problems.* Baltimore: University Park Press.

Rowe, K. J., & Rowe, K. S. (1992). The relationship between inattentiveness in the classroom and reaching achievement (Part B): An explanatory study. *Journal of the American Academy of Child and Adolescent Psychiatry, 31,* 357–368.

Rudel, R. G., Holmes, J. M., & Pardes, J. R. (1988). *Assessment of developmental learning disorders.* New York: Basic Books.

Rugel, R. (1974). WISC subtest scores of disabled readers: a review of Bannatyne's recategorization. *Journal of Learning Disabilities, 7,* 57–64.

Rutter, M. (1978). Prevalence and types of dyslexia. In A. L. Benton & D. Pearl (Eds.), *Dyslexia: An appraisal of current knowledge.* New York: Oxford University Press.

Rutter, M. (1988). Biological basis of autism: Implications for interventions. In F. J. Menolascino & J. A. Stark (Eds.), *Preventative and curative intervention in mental retardation.* Baltimore, MD: Brookes.

Rutter, M., Graham, P., & Birch, H. G. (1970). *Clinics in developmental medicine: Vol. 35/36. A neuropsychiatric study in childhood.* London: SIMP/Heinemann.

Rutter, M., Tizard, J., & Whitmore, K. (1970). *Education, health and behavior.* London: Longman.

Ryan, A. W. (1991). Meta-analysis of achievement effects of microcomputer applications in elementary schools. *Educational Administration Quarterly, 27,* 161–184.

Safer, D. J., & Allen, R. P. (1973). Factors influencing the suppressant effects of two stimulant drugs on the growth of hyperactive children. *Pediatrics, 51,* 660–667.

Safer, D. J., & Allen, R. P. (1976). *Hyperactive children: Diagnosis and management.* Baltimore, MD: University Park Press.

Safer, D. J., & Allen, R. P. (1989). Absence of tolerance to the behavioral effects of methylphenidate in hyperactive and inattentive children. *Journal of Pediatrics, 115,* 1003–1008.

Safer, D. J., Allen, R. P., & Barr, E. (1972). Depression of growth in hyperactive children on stimulant drugs. *New England Journal of Medicine, 287,* 217–220.

Safer, D. J., & Krager, J. M. (1988). A survey of medication treatment for hyperactive/inattentive students. *Journal of the American Medical Association, 260,* 2256–2258.

Safer, D. J., & Krager, J. M. (1991). Hyperactivity and inattentiveness: School assessment of stimulant treatment. *Clinical Pediatrics, 28,* 216–221.

Sallee, F., Stiller, R., Perel, J., & Bates, T. (1985). Oral pemoline, kinetics and hyperactive children. *Clinical Pharmacology Therapy, 37,* 606–609.

Samson, G. E. (1985). Effects of training in test-taking skills on achievement test performance: A quantitative synthesis. *Journal of Educational Research, 78,* 261–266.

Sandoval, J., & Lambert, N. M. (1984–85). Hyperactive and learning disabled children: Who gets help? *Journal of Special Education, 18,* 495–503.

Sanford, J. A. (1994). *Intermediate visual and auditory continuous performance test.* Richmond, VA: Brain Train.

Sassone, D., Lambert, N. M., & Sandoval, J. (1982). The adolescent status of boys previously identified as hyperactive. In D. M. Ross & S. A. Ross (Eds.), *Hyperactivity: Current issues, research and theory* (2nd ed.). New York: Wiley.

Satin, M. S., Winsberg, B. G., Monetti, C. H., Sverd, J., & Ross, D. A. (1985). A general population screen for attention deficit disorder with hyperactivity. *Journal of the American Academy of Child Psychiatry, 24,* 756–764.

Satterfield, J. H., Cantwell, D. P., & Satterfield, B. T. (1979). Multi-modality treatment. *Archives of General Psychiatry, 36,* 965–974.

Satterfield, J. H., Hoppe, C. M., & Schell, A. M. (1982). A perspective study of delinquency in 110 adolescent boys with attention deficit disorder and 88 normal adolescent boys. *American Journal of Psychiatry, 139,* 795–798.

Satterfield, J. H., Satterfield, B. T., & Cantwell, D. P. (1981). Three-year multi-modality treatment study of 100 hyperactive boys. *Journal of Pediatrics, 98,* 650–655.

Satterfield, J. H., Satterfield, B. T., & Schell, A. E. (1987). Therapeutic interventions to prevent delinquency in hyperactive boys. *Journal of the American Academy of Child and Adolescent Psychiatry, 26,* 56–64.

Satz, P., & Fletcher, J. M. (1980). Minimal brain dysfunctions: An appraisal of research, concepts and methods. In H. Rie & E. Rie (Eds.), *Handbook of minimal brain dysfunctions.* New York: Wiley.

Satz, P., & Morris, R. (1981). Learning disability subtypes: A review. In F. J. Priozzolo & M. C. Wittrock (Eds.), *Neuropsychological and cognitive processes in reading.* New York: Academic.

Saul, R. C. (1985). Nortriptyline in attention deficit disorder. *Clinical Neuropharmacology, 4,* 382–383.

Saykin, A. (1989). Preliminary data on application of GDS tasks to adult neuropsychological assessment. *ADHD/Hyperactivity Newsletter, 13,* 2.

Scarborough, H. (1984). Continuity between childhood dyslexia and adult reading. *British Journal of Psychology, 75,* 329–348.

Schachar, R. (1991). Childhood hyperactivity. *Journal of Child Psychology and Psychiatry, 32,* 155–191.

Schachar, R., Logan, G., Wachsmuth, R., & Chajczyk, D. (1988). Attaining and maintaining preparation: A comparison of attention in hyperactive, normal, and disturbed control children. *Journal of Abnormal Child Psychology, 16*, 361–378.

Schachar, R., Sandberg, S., & Rutter, M. (1986). Agreement between teachers' ratings and observations of hyperactivity, inattentiveness and defiance. *Journal of Abnormal Child Psychology, 14*, 331–345.

Schachar, R., & Tannock, R. (1995). Test of four hypotheses for the comorbidity of attention-deficit hyperactivity disorder and conduct disorder. *Journal of the American Academy of Child and Adolescent Psychiatry, 45*, 649–658.

Schacher, R., Taylor, E., Wieselberg, M. B., Thorley, G., & Rutter, M. (1987). Changes in family function and relationships in children who respond to methylphenidate. *Journal of the American Academy of Child and Adolescent Psychiatry, 26*, 728–732.

Schacher, R., & Wachsmuth, R. (1990). Hyperactivity and parental psychopathology. *Journal of Child Psychology and Psychiatry, 31*, 381–392.

Schaller, J. (1994). Vocational assessment, career education, and students with learning disabilities. *LD Forum, 19* (4), 20–22.

Schaughency, E., McGee, R., Nadaraja, S., Fehen, M., & Silva, P. A. (1994). Self-reported inattention, impulsivity and hyperactivity at ages fifteen and eighteen years in the general population. *Journal of the American Academy of Child and Adolescent Psychiatry, 33*, 173–184.

Schaughency, E. A., & Rothlind, J. (1991). Assessment and classification of attention deficit hyperactive disorders. *School Psychology Review, 20*, 187–202.

Schermer, J. D. (1984). Visual media and attitude formation and attitude change in nursing education (Doctoral dissertation, Wayne State University, 1983). *Dissertation Abstracts International, 44*, 3581A. (University Microfilms International No. 84–06022)

Schimmel, B. J. (1983, April). *A meta-analysis of feedback to learners in computerized and programmed instruction.* Paper presented at the annual meeting of the American Educational Research Association, Montreal. (ERIC Document Reproduction Service No. ED 233 708)

Schlieper, M., Weiss, G., Cohen, N. J., Elman, M., Cvejic, H., & Kruger, E. (1975). Hyperactivity in preschoolers and the effect of methylphenidate. *American Journal of Orthopsychiatry, 45*, 35–50.

Schloss, P. J., & Smith, M. A. (1990). A futures oriented curriculum for adolescents with learning disabilities. *Learning Disabilities. A Multidisciplinary Journal, 1*, 128–136.

Schmidt, J. P., & Tombaugh, T. N. (1995). *The learning and memory assessment battery manual (LAMB).* North Tonawanda, NY: Multi-Health Systems.

Schmidt, M., Weinstein, T., Niemiec, R., & Walberg, H. J. (1986). Computer-assisted instruction with exceptional children. *Journal of Special Education, 19*, 493–502.

Schonhaut, S., & Satz, P. (1983). Prognosis for children with learning disabilities: A review of follow-up studies. In M. Rutter (Ed.), *Developmental neuropsychiatry.* New York: Guilford.

Schumacher, J., & Hazel, S. (1984). Social skills assessment and training for the learning disabled: Who's on first and what's on second? *Journal of Learning Disabilities, 17*, 422–431.

Scruggs, T. E., Bennion, K., & White, K. (1984). *Teaching test-taking skills to elementary grade students: A meta-analysis.* Salt Lake City: Utah University, Developmental Center for the Handicapped. (ERIC Document Reproduction Service No. ED 256 082)

Secretaries' Commission on Achieving Necessary Skills (SCANS) (1991a). *Learning and living: A blueprint for high performance.* Washington, DC: U.S. Department of Labor, Employment and Training Administration.

Secretaries' Commission on Achieving Necessary Skills (SCANS) (1991b). *What work expects of school.* Washington, DC: U.S. Department of Labor, Employment and Training Administration.

Seidenberg, P. L. (1986a). *The high school-college connection: A guide for the transition of learning disabled students* (Document No. 8). Greenvale, NY: Long Island University Transition Project.

Seidenberg, P. L. (1986b). *The unrealized potential: College preparation for secondary learning disabled students. A guide for secondary school administrators, faculty and parents.* (Position Paper Series, Document No. 10). Greenvale, NY: Long Island University Transition Project.

Seligman, M. E., Peterson, C., Kaslow, N. J., Tanenbaum, R. L., Alloy, L. B., & Abramson, L. Y. (1984). Attributional style and depressive symptoms among children. *Journal of Abnormal Child Psychology, 93,* 235–238.

Semrud-Clikeman, M., Biederman, J., Sprich-Buchminster, S., Lehman, B., Faraone, S. V., & Norman, D. (1992). Comorbidity between ADHD and learning disability: A review and report in a clinically referred sample. *Journal of the American Academy of Child and Adolescent Psychiatry, 31,* 439–448.

Semrud-Clikeman, M., Filipek, P. A., Biederman, J., Steingard, R., Kennedy, D., Renshaw, P., & Bekken, K. (1994). Co-morbidity between ADDH and learning disability: A review and report in a clinically referred sample. *Journal of the American Academy of Child and Adolescent Psychiatry, 31,* 439–448.

Shaffer, D., & Schonfeld, I. (1984). A critical note on the value of attention deficit as a basis for a clinical syndrome. In L. M. Bloomingdale (Ed.), *Attention deficit disorders: Diagnostic, cognitive and therapeutic understanding.* Long Island, NY: Spectrum.

Shafir, U., & Siegel, L. S. (1994). Subtypes of learning disabilities in adolescents and adults. *Journal of Learning Disabilities, 27,* 123–134.

Shapiro, E. A. K. (1989). Teaching self-management skills in learning disabled adolescents. *Learning Disabilities Quarterly, 12,* 275–287.

Shapiro, E. S., & Lentz, F. E. (1991). Vocational-technical programs: Follow-up of students with learning disabilities. *Exceptional Children, 58,* 47–59.

Shaw, S. F., Byron, M. A., Norlander, K. A., McGuire, J. M., & Anderson, P. (1987). *Preparing learning disabled high school students for postsecondary education.* Paper presented at the 65th annual conference of the Council for Exceptional Children, Chicago, Illinois.

Shaw, S. F., Norlander, K. A., & McGuire, J. M. (1987). Training leadership personnel for learning disability college program: Pre-service and inservice models. *Teacher Education and Special Education, 10,* 108–112.

Shaywitz, S. E. (1986). Prevalence of attentional deficits and an epidemiologic sample of school children [Unpublished raw data]. In J. F. Kavanagh & T. J. Truss (Eds.), *Learning disabilities: Proceedings of the National Conference.* Parkton, MD: York.

Shaywitz, S. E., & Shaw, R. (1988). The admissions process: An approach to selecting learning disabled students at the most selective colleges. *Learning Disabilities Focus, 3,* 81–86.

Shaywitz, S. E., & Shaywitz, B. (1988a). Attention deficit disorder: Current perspectives. In J. Kavanaugh & T. Truss, Jr. (Eds.), *Learning disabilities: Proceedings of the National Conference.* Parkton, MD: York.

Shaywitz, S. E., & Shaywitz, B. A. (1988b). Increased medication used in attention deficit hyperactivity disorder: Regressive or appropriate? [Editorial]. *Journal of the American Medical Association, 260,* 2270–2272.

Shaywitz, S. E., Shaywitz, B. A., Fletcher, J. M., & Escobar, M. D. (1990). Prevalence of reading disability in boys and girls: results of the Connecticut Longitudinal Study. *Journal of the American Medical Association, 264,* 998–1002.

Shekim, W. O. (1990, Spring/Summer). Adult attention deficit hyperactivity disorder, residual state. *CH.A.D.D.ER Newsletter,* pp. 16–18.

Shekim, W. O., Antun, F., Hanna, G. L., McCracken, J. T., & Hess, E. B. (1990). S-adensoly-L-methionine (SAM) in adults with ADHD, RS: Preliminary results from an open trial. *Psychopharmacology Bulletin, 26,* 249–253.

Shekim, W. O., Masterson, A., Cantwell, D. P., Hanna, G. L., & McCracken, J. T. (1989). Nomifensine maleate in adult attention deficit disorder. *Journal of Nervous and Mental Disease, 177,* 296–298.

Sheldon, K. L., & Prout, H. T. (1991). Vocational rehabilitation and learning disabilities: An analysis of state policies. *Journal of Rehabilitation, 51,* 59–61.

Shockey, C., & Whiteman, V. (1977). Development of the rational behavior inventory: Initial validity and reliability. *Educational and Psychological Measurement, 37,* 527–534.

Shwalb, B. J. (1987). Instructional technology in American and Japanese schools: A meta-analysis of achievement findings (Doctoral dissertation, University of Michigan). *Dissertation Abstracts International, 48,* 370A.

Silver, A. A., & Hagin, R. A. (1985). Outcomes of learning disabilities in adolescence. In S. Feinstein (Ed.), *Adolescent psychiatry* (pp. 197–213). Chicago: University of Chicago Press.

Silver, A. A., & Hagin, R. A. (1990). *Disorders of learning in childhood.* New York: Wiley.

Silver, L. B. (1981). The relationship between learning disabilities, hyperactivity, distractibility and behavioral problems. A clinical analysis. *Journal of the American Academy of Child Psychiatry, 20,* 385–397.

Silver, L. B. (1990). Attention deficit hyperactivity disorder: Is it a learning disability or a related disorder? *Journal of Learning Disabilities, 23,* 394–397.

Simms, R. B. (1985). Hyperactivity and drug therapy: What the educator should know. *Journal of Research and Development in Education, 18,* 1–7.

Singer, H. S. (1994). Neurobiological issues in Tourette Syndrome [Special article]. *Brain & Development, 16,* 353–364.

Sitlington, P., & Frank, A. R. (1990). Are adolescents with learning disabilities successfully crossing the bridge in adult life? *Learning Disability Quarterly, 13,* 97–111.

Slavin, R. E. (1987). Mastery learning reconsidered. *Review of Educational Research, 57,* 175–213.

Slavin, R. E., & Madden, N. A. (1989). What works for students at risk: A research synthesis. *Educational Leadership, 46,* 4–13.

Smith, H. F. (1986). The elephant on the fence: Approaches to the psychotherapy of attention deficit disorder children. *American Journal of Psychotherapy, 40,* 252–264.

Smith, J. O. (1992). Falling through the cracks: Rehabilitation services for adults with learning disabilities. *Exceptional Children, 58,* 451–460.

Smith, S. D., Kimberling, W. S., Pennington, B. F., & Lubs, M. A. (1983). Specific reading disability: Identification of an inherited form through linkage analysis. *Science, 219,* 1345–1347.

Snowling, M., & Hulme, C. (1991). Speech processing and learning to spell. In W. Ellis (Ed.), *All language and the creation of literacy.* Baltimore: Orton Dyslexia Society.

Snyder, S., & Sheehan, R. (1983). Integrating research in early childhood special education: The use of meta-analysis. *Diagnostique, 9,* 12–25.

Social Security Act, 42 U.S.C.

Sonuga-Barke, E. J., Lamparelli, M., Stevenson, J., Thompson, M., & Henry, A. (1994). Behavior problems and pre-school intellectual attainment: The associations of hyperactivity and conduct problems. *Journal of Child Psychology and Psychiatry, 35,* 949–960.

Sorkin, E. M., & Heel, R. C. (1986). Guanfacine: A review of its pharmacodynamic and pharmacokinetic properties, and therapeutic efficacy in the treatment of hypertension. *Drugs, 31,* 301–336.

Spencer, T., Biederman, J., Wilens, T., Steingard, R., & Geist, D. (1993). Nortriptyline treatment of children with attention deficit hyperactivity disorder and tic disorder or Tourette's syndrome. *Journal of the American Academy of Child and Adolescent Psychiatry, 32,* 205–210.

Spitzer, R. L., Williams, J. B. W., Gibbon, M., & First, M. B. (1990). *Structured clinical interview for DSM-III-R—Non-patient edition (SCID-NP)* (Version 1.0). Washington, DC: American Psychiatric Press.

Sprague, R. L., & Gadow, K. D. (1976). The role of the teacher in drug treatment. *School Review,* 109–140.

Sprague, R. L., & Sleator, E. K. (1977). Methylphenidate in hyperkinetic children: Differences in dose effects on learning and social behavior. *Science, 198,* 1274–1276.

Spreen, O. (1981). The relationship between learning disability, neurological impairment and delinquency: Results of a follow-up study. *Journal of Nervous and Mental Disorders, 169,* 791–802.

Spreen, O. (1982). Adult outcomes of reading disorders. In R. N. Malatesha & P. G. Aaron (Eds.), *Reading disorders, varieties and treatments.* New York: Academic.

Spreen, O. (1984). A prognostic view from middle childhood. In SRI International (1990). *The National Longitudinal Transition Study of Special Education Students: Vol. 2. Youth categorized as learning disabled.* Washington, DC: U.S. Department of Education, Office of Special Education Programs.

Spreen, O. (1987). *Learning disabled children growing up: A follow-up into adulthood.* Lisse, Netherlands: Swets & Zeitlinger.

Spreen, O., & Haaf, R. G. (1986). Empirically derived learning disability subtypes: A replication attempt and longitudinal patterns over 15 years. *Journal of Learning Disabilities, 19,* 170–180.

Sprich-Buckminster, S., Biederman, J., Milberger, S., Faraone, S. V., & Lehman, B. K. (1993). Are perinatal complications relevant to the manifestation of ADD? Issues of comorbidity and familiality. *Journal of the American Academy of Child and Adolescent Psychiatry, 32,* 1032–1037.

SRI International. (1990). *The National Longitudinal Transition Study of Special Education Students: Vol. 2. Youth categorized as learning disabled.* Washington, DC: U.S. Department of Education, Office of Special Education Programs.

Stanovich, K. E., & West, R. (1989). Exposure to print and orthographic processing. *Reading Research Quarterly, 24,* 402–433.

Stark, K. D., Bernstein, L. E., & Condino, R. (1984). Four-year follow-up study of language impaired children. *Annals Dyslexia, 34,* 50–69.

Stein, M. (1993). Has hyperactivity grown up yet? *CH.A.D.D.ER Box, 6,* 6–7.

Stein, M. A., Sandoval, R., Szumowski, E., Roizen, N., Reinecke, M. A., Blondis, T. A., & Klein, Z. (in press). Wender Utah Rating Scale (WURS): Reliability and factor structure for men and women. *Psychopharmacology Bulletin.*

Steingard, R., Biederman, J., Doyle, A., & Sprich-Buckminster, S. (1992). Psychiatric comorbidity in attention deficit disorder: Impact on the interpretation of child behavior checklist results. *Journal of the American Academy of Child and Adolescent Psychiatry, 31,* 449–454.

Steingard, R., Biederman, J., Spencer, T., Wilens, T., & Gonzalez, A. (1993). Comparison of clonidine response in the treatment of attention-deficit hyperactivity disorder with and without comorbid tic disorders. *Journal of the American Academy of Child and Adolescent Psychiatry, 32,* 350–353.

Stevens, R. J., & Slavin, R. E. (1991). When cooperative learning improves the achievement of students with mild disabilities: A response to Tateyama-Sniezek. *Exceptional Children, 57,* 276–280.

Stewart, M. A. (1980). Genetic, perinatal, and constitutional factors in minimal brain dysfunction. In H. E. Rie & E. D. Rie (Eds.), *Handbook of minimal brain dysfunctions.* New York: Wiley.

Stewart, M. A., & Olds, S. W. (1973). *Raising a hyperactive child.* New York: Harper & Row.

Stewart, M. A., Thatch, B. T., & Freidin, M. R. (1970). Accidental poisoning in the hyperactive child syndrome. *Diseases of the Nervous System, 31,* 403–407.

Stone, A. C. (1987). Abstract reasoning and problem solving. In D. J. Johnson & J. W. Blalock (Eds.), *Adults with learning disabilities: Clinical studies.* Orlando, FL: Grune & Stratton.

Stone, R. (1985). Students with invisible handicaps. *College Board Review, 127,* 22–27.

Stott, D. H. (1981). Behavior disturbance and failure to learn: A study of cause and affect. *Educational Research, 23,* 163–172.

Strang, J. D. (1981). *Personality dimensions of learning disabled children: Age and subtype differences.* Unpublished doctoral dissertation, University of Windsor, Windsor, ON.

Strang, J. D., & Rourke, B. P. (1985). Arithmetic disability subtypes: The neuropsychological significance of specific arithmetical impairment in childhood. In B. P. Rourke (Ed.), *Neuropsychology of learning disabilities: Essential subtype analysis.* New York: Guilford.

Strauss, A. A., & Kephart, N. C. (1955). *Psychopathology and education of the brain-injured child: Vol. 2. Progress in theory and clinic.* New York: Grune & Stratton.

Strauss, A. A., & Lehtinen, L. E. (1947). *The psychopathology and education of the brain-injured child, Vol. 1.* New York: Grune & Stratton.

Strayhorn, J. M., Rapp, N., Donina, W., & Strain, P. S. (1988). Randomized trail of methylphenidate for an autistic child. *Journal of the American Academy of Child and Adolescent Psychiatry, 27,* 244–247.

Strichart, S., & Mangrum, C. (1985). Selecting a college for the LD student. *Academic Therapy, 20,* 475–479.

Strober, M., & Carlson, G. (1982). Bipolar illness in adolescents with major depression: Clinical, genetic, and psychopharmacologic predictors in a three-to-four year prospective follow-up investigation. *Archives of General Psychiatry, 39,* 549–555.

Succimarra, D. J., & Speece, D. L. (1990). Employment outcomes and social integration of students with mild handicaps: The quality of life two years after high school. *Journal of Learning Disabilities, 23,* 518–520.

Sudden death in children treated with a tricyclic antidepressant. (1990). *Medical Letter, 32*(819).

Sulzbacher, S., Thompson, J., Farwell, J. R., Temkin, N. R., & Holubkov, A. L. (1994). Crossed dominance and its relationship to intelligence and academic achievement. *Developmental Neuropsychology, 10,* 473–479.

Sverd, J., Gadow, K. D., & Paolicelli, L. M. (1989). Methylphenidate treatment of attention-deficit hyperactivity disorder in boys with Tourette's syndrome. *Journal of the American Academy of Child and Adolescent Psychiatry, 28,* 574–579.

Swanson, H., & Trahan, M. (1986). Characteristics of frequently cited articles in learning disabilities. *Journal of Special Education, 20,* 167–182.

Swanson, H. L. (1993). Developmental study of vigilance in learning-disabled and non-disabled children. *Journal of Abnormal Child Psychology, 16,* 361–378.

Swanson, J. M. (1993). *The UCI ADD Center: Final report. The effects of stimulant medication on children with ADD.* Washington, DC: U.S. Department of Education; University of California, Irvine, Attention Deficit Disorder Center.

Swanson, J. M., Cantwell, D., Lerner, M., McBurnett, K., & Hanna, G. (1991). Effects of stimulant medication on learning in children with ADHD. *Journal of Learning Disabilities, 24,* 219–230.

Swanson, J. M., McBurnett, K., Wigal, T., Pfiffner, L. J., Lerner, M. A., Williams, L., Christian, D. L., Tamm, L., Willcutt, E., Crowley, K., Clevenger, W., Khouzam, N., Woo, C., Crinella, F. M., & Fisher, T. D. (1993). Effect of stimulant medication on children with attention deficit disorder: A "Review of reviews." *Exceptional Children, 60,* 154–162.

Swartz, G. A. (1974). *The language-learning system.* New York: Simon & Schuster.

Szatmari, P., Boyle, M., & Offord, D. R. (1989). ADDH and conduct disorder: degree of diagnostic overlap and differences among correlates. *Journal of the American Academy of Child and Adolescent Psychiatry, 28,* 865–872.

Szcrurek, M. (1982). Meta-analysis of simulation games effectiveness for cognitive learning (Doctoral dissertation, Indiana University, 1982). *Dissertation Abstracts International, 43,* 1031A. (University Microfilms International No. 82–20735)

Tacconi, M. T., & Wurtman, R. J. (1986). Piracetam: Physiological disposition and mechanism of action. *Advances in Neurology, 43,* 675–685.

Tallal, P., Chase, C., Russell, G., & Schmitt, R. L. (1986). Evaluation of the efficacy of piracetam in treating information processing, reading and writing disorders in dyslexic children. *International Journal of Psychophysiology, 4,* 41–52.

Tannock, R., Ickowicz, A., & Schachar, R. (1995). Differential effects of methylphenidate on working memory in ADHD children with and without comorbid anxiety. *Journal of the American Academy of Child and Adolescent Psychiatry, 34,* 885–896.

Tarter, R. E., McBride, H., Buonpane, N., & Schneider, D. U. (1977). Differentiation of alcoholics. *Archives of General Psychiatry, 34,* 761–768.

Tarter, R. E., Van Thiel, D. H., & Edwards, K. L. (1988). *Medical neuropsychology: The impact of disease on behavior.* New York: Plenum.

Taylor, H. G. (1989). Learning disabilities. In E. J. Mash & L. G. Terdal (Eds.), *Behavioral assessment of childhood disorders* (2nd ed.). New York: Guilford.

Taylor, J. (1990). *Helping your hyperactive child.* Salem, OR: Prima.

Taymans, J. M. (1982). Career/vocational education for handicapped students: A joint venture throughout the school years. *Pointer, 26*(4), 13–17.

Technology-Related Assistance for Individuals with Disabilities Act of 1988, P.L. 100–47, 29 U.S.C. 2201, 2202 (1988).

Teele, D. W., Klein, J. O., & Chase, C. (1990). Otitis media in infancy and intellectual ability, school achievement, speech and language at age seven years. *Journal of Infectious Diseases, 162,* 685–694.

Teele, D. W., Klein, J. O., & Rosner, B. A. (1980). Epidemiology of otitis media in children. *Annals of Otology Rhinology and Laryngology, 68,* 5–6.

Terestman, N. (1980). Mood quality and intensity in nursery school children as predictors of behavior disorder. *American Journal of Orthopsychiatry, 50,* 125–138.

Thomas, A., & Chess, S. (1977). Temperament and development. New York: Brunner/Mazel.

Thomas, B. H., Byrne, C., Offord, D. R., & Boyle, M. H. (1991). Prevalence of behavioral symptoms and the relationship of child, parent and family variables in 4- and 5-year-olds: Results from the Ontario Child Health Study. *Developmental and Behavioral Pediatrics, 12,* 177–184.

Thompson, J. M. (1987). A meta-analysis of test anxiety therapy outcome studies (Doctoral dissertation, Texas Christian University, 1986). *Dissertation Abstracts International, 47,* 3570B.

Thompson, R. J., Lampron, L. B., Johnson, D. F., & Eckstein, T. L. (1990). Behavior problems in children with the presenting problem of poor school performance. *Journal of Pediatric Psychology, 15,* 3–20.

Tolman, E. C. (1935). Psychology versus immediate experience. *Philosophy and Science, 2,* 356–380.

Trillo, S. J. (1995). *Attention deficit disorder scales for adults.* New York: Brunner/Mazel.

Trillo, S. J., & Murphy, K. (1995). *The manual for scoring and interpretation of the attention deficit scales for adults.* New York: Brunner/Mazel.

Trimble, M. (1979). The effect of anti-convulsant drugs on cognitive abilities. *Journal of Pharmacology Therapeutics, 4,* 677–685.

University of Connecticut School of Education (1995). *The university program for college students with learning disabilities.* Storrs, CT: University of Connecticut.

U.S. Department of Education. (1987). *Profile of handicapped students in postsecondary education* (National Center for Education Statistics, 1987 National Postsecondary Student Aid Study, Report No. 0065–000–00375–9). Washington, DC: U.S. Government Printing Office.

U.S. Department of Health and Human Services. (1990). *Family support administration. Federal regulations for the job opportunities and basis skills program.* Washington, DC: Author.

U.S. Department of Justice. (1987). *In the matter of methylphenidate quotas* (Docket No. U.S. 86–52). Washington, DC: Author.

U.S. Department of Labor. (1991). *The learning disabled in employment and training programs* (Research and Evaluation Report No. 91-E). Washington, DC: U.S. Government Printing Office.

U.S. Department of Labor, Bureau of Labor Statistics. (1987). *Occupational outlook handbook.* Washington, DC: U.S. Government Printing Office.

Utah State University Exceptional Child Center. (1983). *Early intervention research institute: Final report, 1982–83 work scope.* Logan, UT: Utah State University. (ERIC Document Reproduction Service No. ED 250 845)

Valdez, K. A., Williamson, C. L., & Wagner, M. M. (1990). *The National Longitudinal Transition Study of Special Education Students, statistical almanac: Vol. 2. Youth categorized as learning disabled.* Palo Alto, CA: SRI International.

Varlaam, A. (1970). Educational attainment and behavior at school. *Greater London Council Intelligence Quarterly, 29,* 29–37.

Varley, C. K. (1985). A review of studies of drug treatment efficacy for attention deficit disorder with hyperactivity in adolescents. *Psychopharmacology Bulletin, 21,* 216–221.

Velez, C. N., Johnson, J., & Cohen, P. (1989). A longitudinal analysis of selected risk factors for childhood psychopathology. *Journal of the American Academy of Child and Adolescent Psychiatry, 28,* 861–864.

Vernon, M. W., & Sorkin, E. M. (1991). Piracetam. An overview of its pharmacological properties and a review of its therapeutic use in senile cognitive disorders. *Drugs Aging, 1,* 17–35.

Vertek, Inc. (1989). Occupational Awareness System (OASYS) [Computer software]. Bellevue, WA: Author.

Viller, E. F. (1985). *Understanding and guiding the career development of adolescents and young adults with learning disabilities.* Springfield, IL: Thomas.

Vinson, D. C. (1994). Therapy for attention-deficit hyperactivity disorder. *Archives of Family Medicine, 3,* 445–451.

Vocational Research Institute (VRI). (1988). APTICOM [Computer software]. Philadelphia: Author.

Vogel, S. A. (1985). Learning disabled college students: Identification, assessment, and outcomes. In D. D. Duane & C. K. Leong (Eds.), *Understanding learning disabilities: International and multidisciplinary views.* New York: Plenum.

Vogel, S. A. (1986). Levels and patterns of intellectual functioning among LD college students: Clinical and educational implications. *Journal of Learning Disabilities, 19,* 71–79.

Vogel, S. A. (1987a). Eligibility and identification considerations in postsecondary education: A new but old dilemma. In S. Vaughn & C. Bos (Eds.), *Research in learning disabilities: Issues and future directions.* Boston: Little Brown.

Vogel, S. A. (1987b). Issues and concerns in LD college programming. In D. J. Johnson & J. W. Blalock (Eds.), *Adults with learning disabilities: Clinical studies.* Orlando, FL: Grune & Stratton.

Vogel, S. A. (1990a). *College students with learning disabilities: A handbook for college LD students, admissions officers, faculty and administrators* (3rd ed.). Pittsburgh: National Learning Disabilities Association.

Vogel, S. (1990b). Gender differences in intelligence, language, visual-motor abilities, and academic achievement in students with learning disabilities: A review of the literature. *Journal of Learning Disabilities, 23,* 44–52.

Vogel, S. A. (1993a). *College students with learning disabilities: A handbook for college students with learning disabilities, university admissions officers, faculty and administration* (4th ed.). Pittsburgh: Learning Disabilities Association.

Vogel, S. (1993b). Postsecondary education for LD students. In S. A. Vogel & P. B. Adelman (Eds.), *Success for college students with learning disabilities.* New York: Springer.

Vogel, S. (1995). *College students with learning disabilities: A handbook for students with LD, admissions officers, faculty/staff, administrators* (5th ed.). Northern Illinois University, DeKalb, IL.

Vogel, S. A., & Adelman, P. B. (1990a). Extrinsic and intrinsic factors in graduation and academic failure among LD college students. *Annals of Dyslexia, 40,* 119–137.

Vogel, S. A., & Adelman, P. B. (1990b). Intervention effectiveness at the post-secondary level for the learning disabled. In T. Scruggs & B. Wong (Eds.), *Intervention research in learning disabilities* (pp. 329–344). New York: Springer.

Vogel, S. A., & Adelman, P. B. (1993). *Success for college students with learning disabilities.* New York: Springer.

Vogel, S., & Moran, M. (1982). Written language disorders in learning disabled college students. A preliminary report. In W. Cruickshank & J. Lerner (Eds.), *Coming of age: The best of ACLD 1982.* Syracuse, NY: Syracuse University Press.

Vygotsky, L. (1962). *Thought and language.* New York: Wiley.

Waddell, K. J. (1984). The self-concept and social adaption of hyperactive children and adolescents. *Journal of Clinical Child Psychology, 13,* 50–55.

Wagner, M. (1989). *Youth with disabilities during transition: An overview of descriptive findings from the National Longitudinal Transition Study.* Menlo Park, CA: SRI International.

Walker, H. M., & Walker, J. E. (1991). *Coping with non-compliance in the classroom: A positive approach for teachers.* Austin, TX: Pro-Ed.

Walker, J. L., Lahey, B. B., Hynd, G. W., & Frame, C. L. (1987). Comparison of specific patterns of antisocial behavior in children with conduct disorder with or without coexisting hyperactivity. *Journal of Consulting and Clinical Psychology, 55,* 910–913.

Wallace, T. A. (1990). The effects of enrichment on gifted students: A quantitative synthesis (Doctoral dissertation, University of Illinois at Chicago, 1989). *Dissertation Abstracts International, 50,* 1A.

Walters, J. A., & Croen, L. G. (1993). An approach to meeting the needs of medical students with learning disabilities. *Teaching and Learning in Medicine, 5,* 29–35.

Walters, L. W. (1987). *Mathematics learning disabilities in college-aged adults.* Unpublished master's thesis, Georgia State University, Atlanta, GA.

Waltonen, S. J., Ahmann, P. A., Theye, F. W., Olson, K. A., Van Erem, A. J., & LaPlant, R. J. (1993). Placebo-controlled evaluation of Ritalin side effects. *Pediatrics, 91,* 1101–1106.

Wang, M. C., & Baker, E. T. (1986). Mainstreaming programs: Design features and effects. *Journal of Special Education, 19,* 503–523.

Ward, F. F., Wender, P. H., & Reimherr, F. W. (1993). The Wender Utah Rating Scale: An aid in the retrospective diagnosis of childhood attention deficit hyperactivity disorder. *American Journal of Psychiatry, 150,* 885–889.

Warren, R. P., Odell, J. D., Warren, W. L., Burger, R. A., Maciulis, A., & Torres, A. R. (1995). Is decreased blood plasma concentration of the compliment C4B protein associated with ADHD? *Journal of the American Academy of Child and Adolescent Psychiatry, 34,* 1009–1014.

Wechsler, D. (1974). *Wechsler Intelligence Scale for Children—Revised.* New York: Psychological Corporation.

Wechsler, D. (1981). *Wechsler Adult Intelligence Scale—Revised.* New York: Psychological Corporation.

Wechsler, D. (1987). *Wechsler Memory Scale: Revised.* New York: Psychological Corporation.

Weinberg, W., & Brumback, R. A. (1976). Mania in childhood. *American Journal of Diseases in Children, 130,* 380–385.

Weintraub, S., & Mesulam, M. M. (1983). Developmental learning disabilities of the right hemisphere. *Archives of Neurology, 40,* 463–468.

Weiss, G. (1992). *Attention-deficit hyperactivity disorder.* Philadelphia: Saunders.

Weiss, G., & Hechtman, L. (1986). *Hyperactive children grown up.* New York: Guilford.

Weiss, G., & Hechtman, L. T. (1993). *Hyperactive children grown up* (2nd ed.). New York: Guilford.

Weiss, G., Hechtman, L., Milroy, T., & Perlman, T. (1985). Psychiatric status of hyperactives as adults: A controlled prospective 15 year follow-up of 63 hyperactive children. *Journal of the American Academy of Child Psychiatry, 23,* 211–220.

Weiss, G., Hechtman, L., & Perlman, T. (1978). Hyperactives as young adults: Social employer and self-rating scales obtained during ten-year follow-up evaluation. *American Journal of Orthopsychiatry, 48,* 438–445.

Weiss, G., Hechtman, L., Perlman, T., Hopkins, J., & Wenar, T. (1979). Hyperactives as young adults: A controlled prospective 10-year follow-up of the psychiatric status of 75 children. *Archives of General Psychiatry, 36,* 675–681.

Weiss, G., Minde, K., Werry, J., & Douglas, V. (1971). Studies on the hyperactive child: VII. Five year follow-up. *Archives of General Psychiatry, 24,* 409–414.

Weiss, L. (1992). *Attention deficit disorder in adults.* Dallas, TX: Taylor.

Weiss, R. D., Pope, H. G., & Mirin, S. M. (1985). Treatment of chronic cocaine abuse and attention deficit disorder, residual type, with magnesium pemoline. *Drug and Alcohol Dependence, 15,* 69–72.

Wender, E. H. (1986). The food additive-free diet in the treatment of behavior disorders: A review. *Developmental and Behavioral Pediatrics, 7,* 35–42.

Wender, E. H. (1995). Attention-deficit hyperactivity disorders in adolescence. *Journal of Developmental and Behavioral Pediatrics, 16,* 192–195.

Wender, P. H. (1975). The minimal brain dysfunction syndrome. *Annual Review of Medicine, 26,* 45–62.

Wender, P. H. (1979). The concept of adult minimal brain dysfunction. In L. Bellak (Ed.), *Psychiatric aspects of minimal brain dysfunction in adults.* New York: Grune & Stratton.

Wender, P. H., & Reimherr, F. W. (1990). Buproprion treatment of attention-deficit hyperactivity disorder in adults. *American Journal of Psychiatry, 147,* 1018–1020.

Wender, P. H., Reimherr, F. W., & Wood, D. R. (1981). Attention deficit disorder ("minimal brain dysfunction") in adults: A replication study of diagnosis and drug treatment. *Archives of General Psychiatry, 38,* 449–456.

Wender, P. H., Reimherr, F. W., & Wood, D. R. (1985). Controlled study of methylphenidate in the treatment of attention deficit disorder, residual type in adults. *American Journal of Psychiatry, 142,* 547–552.

Wender, P. H., Wood, D. R., & Reimherr, F. W. (1985). Pharmacological treatment of attention deficit disorder, residual type (ADD, RT, "minimal brain dysfunction"), hyperactivity in adults, *Psychopharmacology Bulletin, 21,* 222–231.

Wender, P. H., Wood, D. R., Reimherr, F. W., & Ward, M. (1983). An open trial of pargyline in the treatment of attention deficit disorder, residual type. *Psychiatry Research, 9,* 329–336.

Wentzel, K. R., & Asher, S. R. (1995). The academic lives of neglected, rejected, popular and controversial children. *Child Development, 66,* 754–763.

Werner, E. E. (1989). High-risk children in young adulthood: A longitudinal study from birth to 32 years. *American Journal of Orthopsychiatry, 59,* 72–81.

Werner, E. E. (1993). Risk and resilience in individuals with learning disabilities: Lessons learned from the Kauai Longitudinal Study. *Learning Disabilities Research and Practice, 8,* 31–38.

Werner, E. E. (1994). Overcoming the odds. *Developmental and Behavioral Pediatrics, 15,* 131–136.

Werner, E. E., & Smith, R. S. (1977). *Kauai's children come of age.* Honolulu, HI: University of Hawaii Press.

Werner, E. E., & Smith, R. S. (1992). *Overcoming the odds: High risk children from birth to adulthood.* Ithaca, NY: Cornell University Press.

Werry, J. S. (1988). In memoriam—DSM-III [Letter to the editor]. *Journal of the American Academy of Child and Adolescent Psychiatry, 27,* 138–139.

Werry, J. S., Elkind, G. S., & Reeves, J. S. (1987). Attention deficit, conduct, oppositional, and anxiety disorders in children: III. Laboratory differences. *Journal of Abnormal Child Psychology, 15,* 409–428.

Werry, J., Reeves, J., & Elkind, G. (1987). Attention-deficit, conduct, oppositional and anxiety disorders in children: A review of research on differentiating characteristics. *Journal of the American Academy of Child and Adolescent Psychiatry, 26,* 133–143.

Whalen, C. K., & Henker, B. (1976). Psychostimulants and children: A review and analysis. *Psychological Bulletin, 83,* 1113–1130.

Whalen, C. K., & Henker, B. (1980). The social ecology of psychostimulant treatment. A model for conceptual and empirical analysis. In C. K. Whalen & B. Henker (Eds.), *Hyperactive children: The social ecology of identification and treatment.* New York: Academic.

Whalen, C. K., & Henker, B. (1991). Social impact of stimulant treatment for hyperactive children. *Journal of Learning Disabilities, 24,* 231–241.

Whalen, C. K., Henker, B., Castro, J., & Granger, D. (1987). Peer perceptions of hyperactivity and medication effects. *Child Development, 58,* 816–828.

Whalen, C. K., Henker, B., Collins, B. E., McAuliffe, S., & Vaux, A. (1979). Peer interaction in structured communication task: Comparisons of normal and hyperactive boys and of methylphenidate (Ritalin) and placebo effects. *Child Development, 50,* 388–401.

Whalen, C. K., Henker, B., & Dotemoto, S. (1981). Teacher response to methylphenidate (Ritalin) versus placebo status of hyperactive boys in the classroom. *Child Development, 52,* 1005–1014.

Whalen, C. K., Henker, B., Collins, B. E., Fick, D., & Dotemoto, S. (1979). A social ecology of hyperactive boys: Medication efforts in structured classroom environments. *Journal of Applied Behavior Analysis, 12,* 65–81.

White, J. L., Moffitt, T. E., Caspi, A., Jeglum, D., Needles, D., & Stouthamer-Loeber, M. (1994). Measuring impulsivity and examining its relationship to delinquency. *Journal of Abnormal Psychology, 103,* 192–205.

White, W., Alley, G., Deshler, D., Schumaker, J., Warner, M., & Clark, F. (1982). Are there learning disabilities after high school? *Exceptional Children, 29,* 273–274.

White, W. A. T. (1987). The effects of direct instruction in special education: A meta-analysis (Doctoral dissertation, University of Oregon, 1986). *Dissertation Abstracts International, 47,* 1A.

White, W. J. (1985). Perspectives on education and training of learning disabled adults. *Learning Disability Quarterly, 8,* 231–236.

Whitehouse, D., Shah, U., & Palmer, F. B. (1980). Comparison of sustained release and standard methylphenidate in the treatment of minimal brain dysfunction. *Journal of Clinical Psychiatry, 41,* 282–285.

Wiederholt, J. L. (1982). Lifespan instruction for the learning disabled. *Topics in Learning and Learning Disabilities, 2,* 1–89.

Wiederholt, J. L., & Bryant, B. R. (1992). *Gray Oral Reading Tests—Third Edition (GORT-3).* Los Angeles: Western Psychological Services.

Wiig, E. H., & Semel, E. M. (1976). *Language disabilities in children and adolescents.* Columbus, OH: Merrill.

Wilczenski, F. L. (1991). Comparison of academic performances, graduation rates, and timing of drop out for LD and non-LD college students. *College Student Journal, 7,* 184–194.

Wilczenski, F. L., & Gillespie-Silver, P. (1992). Challenging the norm: Academic performance of university students with learning disabilities. *Journal of College Student Development, 33,* 197–202.

Wilens, T. E., Biederman, J., Geist, D. E., Steingard, R., & Spencer, T. (1993). Nortriptyline in the treatment of ADHD: A chart review of 58 cases. *Journal of the American Academy of Child and Adolescent Psychiatry, 32,* 343–349.

Wilens, T. E., Biederman, J., Spencer, T. J., & Frances, R. J. (1994). Comorbidity of attention deficit hyperactivity disorder and the psychoactive substance use disorders. *Hospital and Community Psychiatry, 45,* 421–435.

Wilens, T. E., & Lineham, C. E. (1995). ADD and substance abuse: An intoxicating combination. *Attention, 1*(2), 25–31.

Wilkinson, G. S. (1993). *Wide Range Achievement Test—3.* Wilimington, DE: Jastak Associates.

Wilkinson, P. C., Kercher, J. C., McMahon, W. M., & Sloane, H. N. (1995). Effects of methylphenidate on rote strength in boys with attention-deficit hyperactivity disorder. *Journal of the American Academy of Child and Adolescent Psychiatry, 34,* 897–901.

Will, M. (1984). *Bridges from school to working life.* Washington, DC: U.S. Department of Education, Office of Special Education and Rehabilitation Services.

Willerman, L. (1973). Activity level and hyperactivity in twins. *Child Development, 44,* 288–293.

Williams, D. T., Mehl, R., Yudofsky, S., Adams, D., & Roseman, B. (1982). The effect of propranolol on uncontrolled rage outbursts in children and adolescents with organic brain dysfunction. *Journal of the American Academy of Child Psychiatry, 21,* 129–135.

Williams, L., Lerner, M., Wigal, T., & Swanson, J. (1995). Minority assessment of ADD: Issues in the development of new assessment techniques. *Attention, 2*(1), 9–15.

Williams, W. V. L. (1990). A meta-analysis of the effects of instructional strategies delivered to the mathematically disadvantaged (Doctoral dissertation, George Peabody College for Teachers of Vanderbilt University, 1989). *Dissertation Abstracts International, 51,* A.

Wilsher, C. R. (1986). Effects of piracetam on developmental dyslexia. *International Journal of Psychophysiology, 4,* 29–39.

Wilsher, C. R., Bennett, D., Chase, C. H., Conners, C. K., Dilanni, M., Feagans, L., Hanvik, L. J., Helfgott, E., Koplewicz, H., & Overby, P. (1987). Piracetam and dyslexia: Effects on reading tests. *Journal of Clinical Psychopharmacology, 7,* 230–237.

Winokur, G., Coryell, W., Endicott, J., & Akiskal, A. (1993). Further distinctions between manic-depressive illness (bipolar disorder) and primary depressive disorder (unipolar depression). *American Journal of Psychiatry, 150,* 1176–1181.

Wood, D. R., Reimherr, F. W., Wender, P. H., & Johnson, G. E. (1976). Diagnosis and treatment of minimal brain dysfunction in adults. *Archives of General Psychiatry, 33,* 1453–1460.

Woodcock, R. W. (1987). *The Woodcock Reading Mastery Tests—Revised.* Circle Pines, MN: American Guidance Service.

Woodcock, R. W., & Johnson, M. B. (1989). *The Woodcock-Johnson Psycho-Educational Battery—Revised.* Allen, TX: DLM Teaching Resources.

Wooten, S., & Wooten, C. (1987). *A process for transition from secondary to postsecondary studies for students with learning disabilities.* Paper presented at the 65th annual conference of the Council for Exceptional Children, Chicago, IL.

Wozniak, J., & Biederman, J. (1994). Prepubertal mania exists and co-exists with ADHD. *ADHD Report, 2,* 5–6.

Wroblewski, B. A., Leary, J. M., Phelan, A. M., & Whyte, J. (1992). Methylphenidate and seizure frequency in brain injured patients with seizure disorders. *Journal of Clinical Psychiatry, 53,* 86–89.

Yanok, J. (1985). Modifying academic requirements for learning disabled students enrolled in teacher education programs. *Teacher Educator, 21,* 19–27.

Yanok, J. (1992). College students with learning disabilities enrolled in developmental education programs. *College Student Journal,* 166–174.

Yanok, J., & Broderick, B. (1988). Program models for serving learning disabled college students. *Review of Research in Developmental Education, 6,* 1–4.

Yanow, M. (1973). Report on the use of behavior modification drugs on elementary school children. In M. Yanow (Ed.), *Observations from the treadmill.* New York: Viking.

Yellin, A. M., Hopwood, J. H., & Greenberg, L. M. (1982). Adults and adolescents with attention deficit disorder: Clinical and behavioral responses to psychostimulants. *Brief Reports, 2,* 133–136.

Zametkin, A. J., Nordahl, T. E., Gross, M., King, A. C., Semple, W. E., Rumsey, J., Hamburger, S., & Cohen, R. M. (1990). Cerebral glucose metabolism in adults with hyperactivity of childhood onset. *New England Journal of Medicine, 323,* 1361–1366.

Zametkin, A. J., & Rapoport, J. L. (1987). Neurobiology of attention deficit disorder with hyperactivity: Where have we come in 50 years? *Journal of the American Academy of Child and Adolescent Psychiatry, 26,* 676–686.

Zentall, S. (1993). Research on the educational implications of attention deficit hyperactivity disorder. *Exceptional Children, 60,* 143–155.

Zentall, S. S., & Ferkis, M. A. (1993). Mathematical problem solving for youth with ADHD with and without learning disabilities. *Learning Disability Quarterly, 16,* 6–18.

Zentall, S. S., Smith, Y. N., Lee, Y. B., & Wieczorek, C. (1994). Mathematical outcomes of Attention-Deficit Hyperactivity Disorder. *Journal of Learning Disabilities, 27,* 510–519.

Zigmond, N., & Thornton, H. (1985). Follow-up of postsecondary age learning disabled graduates and dropouts. *Learning Disabilities Research, 1,* 50–55.

Author Index

478

Subject Index

Challenging Democracy

This is a time when the very meaning of democracy and citizenship is contested. This makes *Challenging Democracy* an even more important volume. It demonstrates the power of feminist voices in providing new ways of thinking about and practicing democracy in education and the larger society.

Michael W. Apple, John Bascom Professor of Education, University of Wisconsin, Madison

This ground-breaking book establishes a highly topical, new, international field of study: that of gender, education and citizenship. It brings together for the first time important cutting-edge research on the contribution of the educational system to the formation of male and female citizens. It shows how gender relations operate behind apparently neutral concepts of liberal democratic citizenship and citizenship education.

Madeleine Arnot and Jo-Anne Dillabough asked leading international educationalists to describe the theoretical frameworks and methodologies they used to research gender and citizenship. The diversity and richness of their accounts set out the parameters of this new and growing field of educational research.

Challenging Democracy goes to the heart of the contemporary debate about the nature of democratic education. It suggests ways in which the educational system in the new century could help develop genuinely inclusive democratic societies in which men and women play an equal role in shaping the meaning of citizenship. This book is essential reading for anyone involved in the fields of gender and education, women studies, curriculum studies, cultural studies, teacher education or the sociology of education.

Madeleine Arnot is a Fellow of Jesus College and University Lecturer in the School of Education at Cambridge University. Recent publications include co-editing *Feminism and Social Justice in Education: international perspectives* (1993) and co-authoring *Closing of the Gender Gap: postwar education and social change* (1999).

Jo-Anne Dillabough is an Assistant Professor at the Ontario Institute for Studies in Education, University of Toronto. She has published widely on gender theory and teacher education and is currently writing a book on cultural identities and political communities in Canadian schools.

Challenging Democracy
International Perspectives on
Gender, Education and Citizenship

**Edited by
Madeleine Arnot and
Jo-Anne Dillabough**

London and New York

First published 2000 by
RoutledgeFalmer
11 New Fetter Lane, London EC4P 4EE

Simultaneously published in the USA and Canada
by RoutledgeFalmer
29 West 35th Street, New York, NY 10001

RoutledgeFalmer is an imprint of the Taylor & Francis Group

Typeset in Galliard by Florence Production Ltd, Stoodleigh, Devon
Printed and bound in Great Britain by
TJ International Ltd, Padstow, Cornwall

British Library Cataloguing in Publication Data
A catalogue record for this book is available from the British Library

Library of Congress Cataloging in Publication Data
Challenging democracy : international perspectives on gender, educaton
and citizenship/edited by Madeleine Arnot and Jo-Anne Dillabough.
    p.cm.
  Includes bibliographical references and index.
    1. Citizenship—Study and teaching—Cross-cultural studies.
  2. Feminisim and education.   3. Women in education—Cross-cultural
  studies.   I. Arnot, Madeleine.   II. Dillabough, Jo-Anne, 1963–
  LC1091 .C43 2000   00-030438
  370.11′5—dc21

ISBN 0–415–20316–3 (pbk)
ISBN 0–415–20315–5 (hbk)

Contents

Contributors

Helena C. Araújo is an Associate Professor in the Faculty of Psychology and Education at Porto University, Portugal. As a sociologist of education working in women studies and gender studies, she has published widely on girls' education, women teachers, citizenship, social and human rights and education. She teaches courses on gender, education and citizenship and her research team developed *Values and Roots: education and women's citizenship* (1997), a video and guide book for teacher training programmes in Portugal.

Madeleine Arnot is a Fellow of Jesus College and teaches in the School of Education in the University of Cambridge, England. She is a sociologist of education specialising in gender, class and race relations in education. She has published extensively on these themes and received a Leverhulme Research Fellowship to study gender, democracy and education. Her recent books include: *Feminism and Social Justice in Education* (edited with K. Weiler, Falmer Press, 1993) and *Closing the Gender Gap* (with G. Weiner and M. David, Polity Press, 1999). She directed the European Council funded project *Women as Citizens: promoting equality awareness* and has been actively involved in promoting citizenship education for teacher training.

Gloria Bonder was the founding Director of the first women's studies NGO in Argentina, the Centro de Estudios de la Mujer (CEM). From 1991 to 1995, she co-ordinated the National Program for Women's Equal Opportunities in Education. Since 1987 she has also been the Director of the Interdisciplinary Postgraduate Program in Women's Studies at the University of Buenos Aires, Argentina. She has conducted research on gender and educational issues both at the national and regional levels and has acted as a consultant for mainstreaming gender perspectives into educational policies for several Latin American countries. She co-ordinates the Postgraduate Seminar on Gender and Public Policies in FLACSO (Latin American Postgraduate Institute for Social Science).

Ann Brooks is a Senior Lecturer in the School of Sociology and Women's Studies at Massey University, New Zealand. Her teaching and research interests cover: feminism, cultural theory and post-colonialism; citizenship and social justice; and gender and international labour market policy issues in tertiary education. She has published widely in these areas including two books, *Academic Women* (Open University Press, 1997) and *Postfeminisms: feminism, cultural theory and cultural forms* (Routledge, 1997). She has just completed a sequel to the latter entitled *Postcolonial Feminisms* (forthcoming 2000) and is currently working on *Gender and the Restructured University* (Open University Press, forthcoming 2000) with Alison Mackinnon.

Christine Callender is a Lecturer in Primary Education at the London Institute of Education, University of London. She has research interests in the areas of Black teaching styles and in the underperformance of Black pupils. Her book *Education for Empowerment: the practice and philosophies of black teachers* (Trentham, 1997) considers teacher–pupil interaction amongst Black teachers and Black pupils.

Lynn Davies is a Professor of Education and Director of the Centre for International Education and Research at the University of Birmingham, England. She has lived and worked in Mauritius and Malaysia and has conducted shorter term research and consultancy in many parts of Africa, Asia and Latin America. She has focused on issues of equity and social justice in the management of education, and has published widely on gender, school effectiveness and democratisation. Her recent books include *School Management and Effectiveness in Developing Countries* (with C. Harber, Cassell, 1997), *Beyond Authoritarian Management: the challenge for transparency* (Education Now, 1994), *Equity and Efficiency? School Management in an International Context* (Falmer, 1990). Having just finished a project on the relationship of school councils and pupil exclusion in UK, she is currently engaged in a research project on education for democracy and citizenship in four European countries.

Kiki Deliyanni is an Associate Professor in the Department of Psychology in the Aristotle University of Thessaloniki, Greece. She teaches courses on feminist perspectives in psychology and the sociology of education and on women and citizenship. She has recently directed European research projects on gender and citizenship, masculinity and gender identities, marginalised youth, and gender and occupational choices and has published widely on these themes, including two books entitled *Gender and School Praxis* (Vanias, 1997) and *Women and Citizenship: perspectives on gender and democracy in teachers' education* (Vanias, 1998). She is currently researching Greek pupils' perspectives on citizenship.

Jo-Anne Dillabough is an Assistant Professor at the Ontario Institute for Studies in Education of the University of Toronto (OISE/UT), Canada and teaches courses in feminist theory in the Department of Curriculum, Teaching and Learning. Prior to her post at OISE/UT, she worked as a Post-doctoral Fellow at the University of Cambridge in the UK. Her doctoral thesis, which won the national Ph.D. award in Curriculum Studies in 1996 (Canadian Association of Curriculum Studies), is to be published by UBC Press as *Cultural identities and political communities in Canadian schools*. Recent publications include articles on feminist methodology and theory in *Theory and Research in Social Education*, *British Journal of Educational Studies*, and *Curriculum Inquiry* (with M. Arnot) and research on gender and teacher education in the *British Journal of Sociology of Education*.

Penny Enslin is a Professor of Education in the School of Education at the University of the Witwatersrand in South Africa, where she teaches philosophy of education. Her research and teaching interests are in the fields of democracy and citizenship education, with particular reference to liberal democracies. She has published locally and internationally on civic education in South Africa, nation-building and citizenship, the family and democracy education, and Political Liberalism. With colleagues in the School of Education, she has participated in an international comparative study on human rights and democratic education.

Victoria Foster teaches courses on gender studies and on gender and citizenship in the Faculty of Education at the University of Wollongong, Australia. She is a Visiting Scholar in the Faculty of Education at the University of Canberra, where she is a consultant for the Civics and Citizenship Research Group, and a Visiting Scholar at Umea University, Sweden. A former teacher, she has directed several national and international curriculum projects on gender and education. Her research interests include interdisciplinary studies and curriculum theory and practice in education.

Tuula Gordon is a Professor of Women's Studies and Social Sciences in the Department of Women's Studies, University of Tampere. She has also taught in the University of Helsinki. She has published extensively on issues of gender, education and citizenship, including: *Democracy in One School? Progressive Education and Restructuring* (Falmer Press, 1986); *Feminist Mothers* (Macmillan, 1990); *Single Women: on the margins?* (Macmillan, 1994); *Making Spaces: citizenship and difference in schools* (with J. Holland and E. Lahelma, Macmillan, 2000).

Janet Holland is a Professor of Social Research and Director of the Social Sciences Research Centre at South Bank University, London. Her recent publications include: *Making Spaces: citizenship and difference in schools* (with T. Gordon and E. Lahelma, Macmillan, 2000); *Sexual Cultures* (edited with J. Weeks, Macmillan, 1996); *Sex, Sensibility and the Gendered Body* (edited with L. Adkins, Macmillan, 1996) and *The Male in the Head* (with C. Ramazanoglu, S. Sharpe and R. Thomson, Tufnell Press, 1998).

Gabrielle Ivinson is a Lecturer in the new School of Social Sciences at Cardiff University. Prior to this post, she was research Fellow in the Centre of Curriculum and Teaching Studies at the Open University (UK) where she co-ordinated the Equity and the Curriculum Research Group. She is a social and developmental psychologist whose main interest is in the field of social representations. Her research projects are extensive and she has a particular interest in the role that gender plays in shaping children's social representations in school. Her doctoral thesis was entitled *The Construction of the Curriculum* (Cambridge 1998). She was also research associate on the EC Project 'Women as Citizens' with M. Arnot during the 1990s, and has worked with Patricia Murphy at the Open University researching pedagogic strategies introduced into secondary schools in the UK to address boys' underachievement.

Jane Kenway is a Professor of Education in the Language and Literacy Research Centre in the School of Education, University of South Australia. Her research expertise is in educational policy sociology in the context of wider social and cultural change. She has a specific interest in issues of social justice. Her most recent book is the co-authored title *Answering Back: girls, boys and feminism in schools* (Routledge, 1998). She is currently working on *Selling Education: consumer cultures, consuming kids* (Open University Press, 2000).

Elina Lahelma is Docent in Sociology of Education in the Department of Education, University of Helsinki. Currently she works as Senior Fellow at the Academy of Finland. She has written extensively on gender and education, including *Making Spaces: citizenship and difference in schools* (with T. Gordon and J. Holland, Macmillan, 2000).

Diana Langmead works as a Researcher at the Deakin Centre for Education and Change, Deakin University, Geelong, Australia. She has been actively involved in the women's movement, the community and the university. Her research interests centre around women, work and education. She is planning to commence doctoral studies investigating *The Art of Foreignness: international postgraduate women's diasporic identities.*

Sue Lees is a Professor of Women's Studies at the University of North London. Her research interests centre around the social control of young women and the influence of the criminal justice system. Her recent publications include: *Carnal Knowledge: rape on trial* (Penguin 1997); *Ruling Passions: sexual violence, reputation and the law* (Open University Press 1997); *Policing Sexual Assault* (with J. Gregory, Routledge 1999) and *Sugar and Spice: sexuality and adolescent girls* (Penguin, 1993). In 1998, she was a Visiting Professor at the University of Wisconsin and Duke University, North Carolina, USA. She has been the British representative on two recent European Daphne projects investigating interventions to combat violence against women.

Heidi Safia Mirza is a Professor of Racial Equality Studies at Middlesex University, London, where she is also Head of the Centre for Racial Equality Studies. Her academic career includes teaching African-American Studies at Brown University, USA, and research on race and gender issues in Britain, Europe, and the Caribbean. Her current research is on Black women in higher education and the educational strategies of the Black community in Britain and South Africa. She is the author of *Young, Female, and Black* (Routledge, 1992). Her latest book is an edited collection entitled *Black British Feminism* (Routledge, 1997).

Diane Reay is a Senior Research Fellow at the School of Education, King's College, University of London. She has been a primary school teacher in Inner London for 20 years. Her current research interests are on issues of social justice in relation to access to higher education and children's relationships to space and place. Her recent book is *Class Works: mothers involvement in their children's primary schooling* (London, University College Press, 1998).

Lynda Stone is an Associate Professor, Philosophy of Education at the University of North Carolina at Chapel Hill, USA. Her interests include feminism and social theory as they relate to education. She has published internationally in such journals as *Teachers College Record, Journal of Curriculum Studies,* and *Studies in Philosophy and Education,* and is editor of *The Education Feminism Reader* (Routledge, 1994).

Amparo Tomé teaches Sociology of Education in the Autonomous University of Barcelona and is working in the area of gender studies. She has published widely on girls' education, women teachers, and citizenship and education. She recently directed two European Council funded projects on women as citizens, and on masculinities and gender identities. She has also directed several national projects funded by the National Women's Institute on Gender and Education. She is an international consultant on gender to the Ministry of Education of the Panamanian government. She is the director of a series of texts on gender for primary and secondary teachers, entitled *Cuadernos para la Coeducación.* She is currently editing a book entitled *Can schools democratise gender relations?* (forthcoming 2000).

Elaine Unterhalter is a South African who has been living and working in the UK for 20 years. She lectures at the London Institute of Education and has published extensively on education and international development and has a special interest in gender in this context. She has focused on historical and contemporary educational policy transformations in South Africa. Recent publications include a chapter on the ways in which citizenship and education are related in *Women, Citizenship and Difference* (N. Yuval-Davis and P. Werbner [eds], Zed Press, 1999) and an analysis of the treatment of gender and citizenship issues in South African education policy texts (*Curriculum Journal,* forthcoming, 2000).

Kathleen Weiler teaches in the Education Department at Tufts University, Boston, USA and has written widely in the field of women's education. She employs a variety of disciplinary approaches to explore the meaning of teaching as women's work and the possibilities and parameters of education. Among her books are *Country Schoolwomen* (Stanford University Press,

1998), *Pedagogies of Resistance* (M. Crocco and P. Munro, Teachers College Press, 1999), and *Telling Women's Lives: narrative inquiries in the history of women's education* (co-edited with S. Middleton, Open University Press, 1999).

Cecile Wright is a Reader in Sociology at the Nottingham Trent University in the UK. Her research interests include 'race', gender and class in education. She has recently directed a project funded by the Runnymede Trust, UK: *Improving Practice: A Whole School Approach to Raising the Achievement of African Caribbean Youth* (with D. Weekes) and *'Race', Class and Gender in Exclusion from School* (with D. Weekes and A. McGlauglin, Falmer Press, 2000).

Acknowledgements

We wish to thank all the contributors to this collection for tackling some of the difficult challenges presented in the study of gender and citizenship and for their patience throughout the editorial process. A number of authors presented their chapters at international conferences at the American Educational Research Association (1999, 2000), International Gender and Education Conference (1998), British Educational Research Association (2000), and the European Education Research Association (1997). Discussants and colleagues who read and commented on our own work include Jane Gaskell, Kathleen Weiler, Wendy Luttrell, Kiki Deliyanni, Helena Araújo, Amparo Tomé, Michael Apple and Phil Gardner. We are grateful for their thoughtful questioning and editorial comments on our joint and individual work.

We are grateful for the support given to Jo-Anne Dillabough by the Social Sciences and Humanities Research Council of Canada and The Connaught Fund at the University of Toronto; and the Leverhulme Trust for the research fellowship granted to Madeleine Arnot for the development of her work on citizenship, gender and education.

We also wish to thank our colleagues and friends for additional support provided while editing the various articles in this collection, Sandra Acker, Patrick Brindle, Wendy Luttrell, Chris Mann, Terry McLaughlin, P. S. Robinson, Barbara Shannon and M. C. Zak, who, each in their own way, were particularly helpful in providing intellectual guidance and support throughout this period. Susanne Tombs and Nancy Fortin provided all the essential secretarial support for which we are grateful. We also wish to thank Heather Berkeley for additional editorial assistance.

Finally our deep appreciation is also extended to Robin Young and Louis Lefebvre, our partners, and to our children Kathryn and Adam Arnot Drummond and Dominique and Pascal Dillabough-Lefebvre for providing us with the space necessary to complete the editorial work on the book. Without their patience and good humour, completing this task would have been impossible.

1 Introduction

Madeleine Arnot and
Jo-Anne Dillabough

> The identity of every 'we' depends on a power structure; collectivities consti-
> tute themselves not only by excluding, but also by oppressing others, over and
> against whom they define themselves.
>
> (Benhabib, 1995: 33)

The primary aim of the book is to cross the threshold from studies of gender
relations in schooling to the feminist study of citizenship in education. It locates
gender and educational studies within the framework of citizenship studies and
draws critically and constructively upon the latter field. One way to achieve this
aim is to explore the challenges that feminist educationists have offered to the
concept and the practices of liberal democracy and liberal democratic education.
The task we have given ourselves is a demanding one, since such feminist challenges are wide-ranging, covering diverse and sometimes conflicting theoretical,
methodological, and epistemological issues. Feminist educational theorising has
been shaped directly and indirectly by local, national, international and global
contexts and must be viewed within such contexts. In an attempt to capture
such diversity, a primary goal of this collection is therefore not only to bring
together examples of the leading feminist academics in this field internationally
but also to encourage cross-fertilisation of ideas. This volume represents the first
attempt to identify the parameters of this new field of study.

Our intention is to move beyond a simple engagement with citizenship and
citizenship education in order to examine the discursive framing of such terms,
the ways in which they become part of the everyday practice of education
and the consequences they have for the positioning of men and women in
society. The contradictory effects and the tensions associated with such
social/political constructions are therefore of considerable interest, as are the
forms of political agency associated with them.

Two key themes provide a focus for the book. The first theme concerns
the relationship between male power and the construction of the modern
citizen in schools. The second relates to the part played by feminist theory
itself in affecting contemporary educational concepts and curricular practices
such as citizenship and citizenship education. In this book, we explore such
issues critically and reflexively by:

- examining contemporary definitions of democracy and citizenship as they impact on gender relations in different national education contexts;
- analysing citizenship and liberal democratic schooling from the diverse perspectives of feminist political and social theorists and education feminists;
- exploring the role of education in framing citizenship identities and identifications which are gendered and developed in relation to, for example, race, class and sexuality.

In short, the chapters in this volume describe a new political landscape for linking feminist theory with the study of citizenship and education.

A new political landscape for the study of gender and education

The starting point for many of the analyses of gender, education and citizenship represented in this anthology is well described by Seyla Benhabib's observation that:

> feminism and women's movements [concerned with citizenship] have always struggled with dilemmas of equality and difference: equality with males versus being different from them, preserving women's separate sphere versus becoming full members of existing society by giving up women's traditional spaces. These tensions constitute what the women's struggle is all about; what will change from period to period is the construction and contestation around these oppositions, but not the fact that women will always be aware of such oppositions, dichotomies, and conflicts.
>
> (1995: 29–30)

As Benhabib (1995) suggests, a female citizen is embedded in a set of tensions which illustrate the struggles women have waged in relation to the exclusive elements of liberal democratic citizenship. Citizens, therefore, become subjects within a symbolic order which is premised upon a particular notion of rights, duties and responsibilities. At the same time, in order to become a speaking 'I' in the symbolic space identified as citizenship, the social processes of identification with others are also significant. This concerns what Weir (1997: 189) refers to as 'the problem of the identity of the self'. She writes: 'the problem of the identity of the self is bound up with the problem of the identity of meaning, and with the problem of identification with, or relationship to, others.' The task, then, for feminists is to consider how, and in what contexts, schooling shapes the processes of gender identification and citizenship identification in the broadest sense.

But there are broader issues to consider when examining the relationship between identification and citizenship. The politics of citizenship (as a struggle to belong in a collective ('we')) is not only about the politics of identity or about identity struggles (Benhabib, 1995). It is also about the struggle for self-definition amidst conflicting and sometimes contested notions of state citizenship. In such a contested political arena, individuals (the 'I') are expected to identify with particular concepts of citizenship as members of the collective 'we', to position themselves in relation to them and gain a sense of moral and political belonging. Yet paradoxically, even though 'the people' are thought to 'speak' as citizens, citizenship is not a position which can be spoken from. It functions largely as an abstract concept which rests at the heart of liberal democratic thought. The citizen *per se*, therefore, has no substantial identity because he/she can only be viewed within the context of an abstract understanding of liberal democractic practice (Donald, 1996: 174).

The concept of citizenship, thus, denotes an empty space that in theoretical terms could be occupied by anyone, assuming that anyone and everyone has the power to occupy such a place (Donald, 1996). And even though, as history tells us, only particular and privileged identities can and have occupied the place of citizenship, the concept nevertheless emerges as a nameless, faceless, entity.

Cynthia Cockburn (1998: 9) recently described the politics of the 'identity work' central to citizenship as the 'knitting together, the unravelling, texturing and tearing of the space' between people. She argues that this is precisely the sort of identity work (10) which, when fashioned upon hegemonic state discourses, functions to sustain unequal power relations:

> It is important to stress that inequalities are felt first and foremost materially, through the appropriation and squandering of wealth by a few, the exploitation by some of others' labour power and the abuse of others' bodies. Identity processes matter precisely because they are second only to force as the means by which power is effective in oppressed and exploitative systems . . .
>
> When control by any group is capable of being maintained without direct force it is always because compliance has been won through processes of identification. Those who benefit from class domination and male power make sure that the working class and women 'know their place'.

Yet the processes of gender identification, like other equivalent processes, are now understood not as unchangeable acts of oppression but rather as 'lived by individuals as changeable and unpredictable' (Cockburn, 1998: 212). The way they take shape and change is not static but relational in character. As Cockburn argues, both social forces and lived experiences 'shape the range of identities at play' (212). Most identities are created through both discursive and structural processes rather than through direct force. As the various chapters of this collection illustrate, collective and individual male and female identities are shaped by a variety of official, educational and academic discourses.

When reading the contributions in this volume it is evident that the social relations and relations of power which shape such identities tend to be masked by the abstractness, rationality and principles of universality which define citizenship in modern Western European nations. For example, the concept of the autonomous individual in liberal democracy masks the social conditions of its production (Pateman, 1988). As a consequence, this abstract notion of 'citizenship' comes to represent (albeit falsely) a democratic social order – a society in which the collective 'we' is an inclusive form of citizenship where the multiplicity of citizen identities are thought to be represented.

The power of such abstractness for the 'people' has meant that citizenship is traditionally thought to be emblematic of equal freedom as well as a bond between people within and across often hierarchically structured and ethnically diverse societies. The concept of citizenship offers liberal democracies 'a direct sense of community membership based on loyalty to a civilisation which is a common possession' (Marshall, 1965: 101 quoted in Wexler, 1991). Citizenship education, in turn, offers a citizenry schooled to display 'enthusiastic loyalty' to the nation state; or it prepares a citizenry to use its vote rationally and with understanding; or it acts to destabilise vested power relations and establishments (Heater, 1990: 76).

Such an abstract concept of the citizen masks its deeply undemocratic social relations and institutions. As Lyotard (1984) argues, in the Enlightenment, not only was the concept of humanity constructed as 'the hero of liberty' – the subject of history – but so too was a legitimating consensus among the people (again abstractly defined) and a 'mirage of freedom' to which all people could aspire. The educational system was directly implicated in sustaining this illusory process whilst also regulating citizens. As Lyotard (1984) argues: 'The State resorts to the narrative of freedom every time it assumes direct control over the training of the "people", under the name of "the nation", in order to point them down the path of progress' (quoted in Gilbert 1992: 54).

Women and those individuals and groups who were defined as 'others' or outside this definition of 'the people' were deeply affected by such abstract concepts of citizenship. Therefore, as far as women were concerned, liberal democratic philosophy was that which had to be transcended so that women could become citizens (Lloyd, 1986). For those with the status of 'second class citizens' (minority groups, refugees, migrant workers, etc.), the challenge was to expose not only the discriminatory assumptions which lay behind such abstractions, but the ways in which the construction of 'other' acted as the mechanism for social exclusion and marginalisation. It is in this context that we begin to understand the emergence of new social movements of the 1960s and 1970s in the industrialised nations and the development of post-colonial discourses and strategies. The very abstractness of the concept of citizenship was contested terrain.

Feminist campaigns, particularly those which focused upon white women's positioning in the nation state, did not adequately address women's formal exclusion from citizenship but rather the terms under which they were to be included. Political theorists such as Pateman (1980, 1988) and Phillips (1991, 1992) point out, however, that women were both included in and excluded from formal citizenship simultaneously. As a woman it was virtually impossible to enter the space called citizenship in Western industrialised countries. For example, Foster (1996) argues that women were viewed as 'space invaders' as they began to affiliate formally with the male public world. It was, therefore, difficult to imagine the shape of female citizen identities, particularly if the sphere of their greatest activity – that of the private sphere – was precisely that which was outside the political/public sphere of citizenship. The distinction and separation between public and private spheres, constructed by European political philosophers, was described as synonymous with the distinction found in the natural order between men and women (cf. Dillabough and Arnot, this volume).

Thus, according to Pateman (1988), underlying the concept of the social contract within liberal democracies was a sexual contract which circumscribed male power over women. This sexual contract, symbolised *par excellence* by the marriage contract, was rarely recognised by male political theorists even though it represented as pivotal a set of social relations which legitimated (through liberal democracy) female subordination. Implicated in the sexual contract were women's sexual, economic and political dependencies on men, their exclusion from the public realm, the control of their childbearing and sexuality through marriage, and their domesticity (Arnot et al., 2000).

Elshtain's seminal text *Public Man, Private Woman* (1981) and Pateman's (1988) *The Sexual Contract* argue that the gendered relationship between the public and private spheres is critical to the positioning of men and women. This arbitrary separation excluded family life from the public realm and marriage/motherhood was therefore deemed irrelevant to the development of citizenship identities and, even more significantly, democracy itself. Critical analyses of schooling, therefore, were also likely to neglect the political significance of 'female' spheres, or indeed women's political agency within such spheres. Indeed any analysis which drew upon conventional notions of citizenship would most likely fail to take account of women as citizens.

In contrast to this tradition, the authors in this collection recognise the role of discursive practices, social constraints, contemporary gender relations, and social and cultural reproduction (the manifestation of symbolic and material relations) as key to the framing of female citizenship. Drawing in different ways upon such feminist political theory, they attempt to understand how schools have shaped and structured a gendered citizenry. As Pateman (1997) points out, the impact of social contract theory was particularly strong in major social institutions between the 1840s and the 1970s – the historical period which saw the founding of the modern educational system. Although challenged by various social movements, such discursive framings of citizenship leave legacies in the institutional cultures which divide and differentiate pupils and shape their citizenship identities and those of others. As a number of the contributors to this volume demonstrate, such institutional cultures still play an important role in shaping contemporary male–female relations and, it naturally follows, male and female citizenship. In this book, some of those legacies and the fate of challenges to such legacies are described.

The various examples of empirical and theoretical work in this book will demonstrate how education has become a site of conflict over the meaning of citizenship, particularly as it concerns girls and women, and in relation to claims about the constitution of national identity. Contributors also identify, drawing upon diverse feminist methods, the problems associated with the many state projects which are now being developed in different national contexts. They show, for example, the ways in which educational institutions and their participants (teachers and pupils) draw upon national and often masculine narratives around democracy, equality and identity.

When addressing such concerns, many of the authors describe empirical data that have been generated by a range of different methodologies. These methodologies attempt to capture an elusive concept which, as Wexler (1991) suggests, is not part of the linguistic currency in use in lived experience and everyday life. The concept of citizenship is filled with meanings and great portent in different cultural contexts and exploratory research is clearly an important beginning. The use of open-ended group discussions, narratives of memories, oral history and critical ethnography which takes account of transitions and time-space paths, the use of social representation theory and discursive analysis of policy texts, are all represented in the collection. Each approach offers more insights into how citizenship, as a social construct, plays itself out in the everyday lives of differently positioned individuals and groups.

Choosing how to organise such examples of research and theorising in a complex field involves making decisions about the parameters which shape the structure, levels and types of analysis. The way in which we have organised the contributions to this new field of study is described below.

The structuring of the field

The contributions have been organised into four contemporary themes which concern the gendered nature of citizenship and citizenship education in the twenty-first century, with each part offering a range of disciplinary, national and international perspectives. These four themes are:

1   Discursive framings of female citizenship and female education;
2   Teachers' identities and public identifications;
3   Schooling and the construction of the gendered citizen; and,
4   Citizenship education and new democratic agendas.

Part 1, for example, offers a selection of current discursive framings of the nature of citizenship and, on occasion, female citizenship. The purpose here is to illustrate a range of relevant contemporary debates about the construction of the female citizen and female education in relation to it. One of the central debates amongst feminist political theorists is the extent to which liberal democratic forms can ever offer women full citizenship. A key theme amongst education feminists is, therefore, the tension in the women's movement between arguing for equal citizenship with men, and the maintenance of a complementary yet different basis for female citizenship. Some of the questions our contributors address are, for example: 'How can feminist political theory assist us in addressing questions of difference and identity in any modern conception of citizenship?' and 'What political concepts and related arguments can be drawn upon to expose the gendered nature of citizenship and citizenship education?'.

Parts 2 and 3 focus on the relationship between gender, citizenship and the construction of teachers', teacher educators' and pupils' political identities in secondary and tertiary education. For example, contributors illustrate the reasons why 'citizenship education' has not been successful in eradicating gender inequality for female students and teachers. Historical and sociological research demonstrates how teachers (and teacher educators) and pupils negotiate the conflicts associated with gender and citizenship in education. Some of the issues which are addressed include the conflicts between equal rights in public and private spheres, and pupil resistance to negative (and gendered) representations of themselves as 'other', or as marginal, citizens.

Part 2 focuses specifically on women as teacher educators and as teachers. Given women's key role in servicing national educational systems as teachers and their identifications with issues of citizenship, the lack of research on their political identifications and professional/personal identities is surprising. Examples of historical and sociological/social psychological research suggest ways in which such absences might be addressed.

Part 3 focuses on the national and local construction of the citizen and its impact on contemporary gender relations in education. For example, each of our contributors attempts to expose the 'gendered' nature of the modern education project and its impact on current understandings of the democratic state and the 'citizen'. The relationship between gender and citizenship is therefore examined in relation to specific educational policies and national/cultural identities to be promoted in schools. Contributors revisit traditional understandings of gender differences in schools, and their relation to class and ethnicity, by considering, for example, the notion of pupils as learner citizens, the tensions between disciplining pupils and democracy, and young people's understanding of social change.

Finally, in Part 4, the focus is upon the future and the ways in which new and more radical understandings of democracy and citizenship might be used to promote more just social practices in relation to gender, particularly through national or international educational initiatives which take account of feminist concerns. Key themes here are democratic forms of sexuality education, the organisation and management culture of schooling, the relationship of gender equality to broader customary traditions and the disruptions caused by cyberspace politics to the public's understanding of rights, democratic social relations and the political imaginary. Below we describe the specific contributions in more depth.

Part 1: Discursive framings of female citizenship and female education

There are now numerous debates within feminism about the nature of democracy and democratic education. In a recent article, we reviewed a range of

modernist, poststructuralist and postmodern feminist perspectives on democratic values in education and came to the view that, although such work was
sophisticated and important, it nevertheless failed, on some level, to address
systematically the gendered nature of the democratic education project (Arnot
and Dillabough, 1999). We also argued that different feminist perspectives
have contributed unique insights into the liberal democratic education project.
However, the lack of integration of feminist theory and research, combined
with a neglect of the broader field of feminist social and political theory, has
meant that some of our original goals of challenging the manifestation of the
public/private split in education have gone unrecognised.

In our chapter in this collection (ch. 2), we argue that there is not sufficient
dialogue between the work of feminist educationists and the work of feminist political theorists. We point to three theoretical problematics raised by
feminist political theorists which we believe make an important contribution
to the field of feminist educational theory and encourage interesting theoretical dialogue between the two fields. These three problematics are
summarised as: the study of the public/private split in education; education,
gender and the nation state; the concept of women as a political category
and the implications for political collectivities of women in brokering social
change in education.

Mapping a field of study is always controversial, not least because of its
modernist overtones. Inevitably, the project itself oversimplifies, sorts and cate-
gorises highly complex theoretical lines whilst simultaneously excluding others.
Ann Brooks' and Lynda Stone's chapters are, therefore, invaluable comple-
ments to our own overview since they remind us of the powerful national
specificity of feminisms and the different disciplinary and political influences
on the shaping of feminist discourse itself. Debates about, for example, post-
colonialism in relation to feminism have become vitally important components
of the feminist debates in the 1990s in such post-colonial contexts as Australia
and New Zealand.

In Ann Brooks' analysis of the discursive framing of citizenship in the
academy (ch. 3), we see the complex interface between postmodernism, post-
colonialism and feminism and the ways in which such perspectives are brought
to bear on new forms of 'emancipatory' politics, first in the context of Maori
struggles and the framing of bipolar politics in New Zealand and, second, in
the context of the Australian Labor Government's 'politics of inclusion'. Here,
citizenship is understood not as a singular, abstract universal entity which
represses difference, but as a mechanism for identifying with multiple and
diverse identities. In this way, female citizenship is thought to emerge as a
fluid and transitory state rather than as a simple question of state membership. Thus, rather than working on the politics of inclusion and exclusion,
Brooks argues that new articulations between the universal and the particular
are critical in understanding new perspectives on female citizenship.

In Lynda Stone's analysis of the 'American Girl' (ch. 5), we are reminded
first and very importantly that schooling has only a limited part to play in
the education of citizens. As she argues, the formation of young girls' citizen

identities is also heavily influenced by consumer and popular cultures. Her argument suggests that female narratives which are constructed around the 'American Girl' – a multi-cultural doll which invokes an image of femininity in the US) – prescribe the discursive limits and possibilities of femininity and female citizenship. Stone also identifies what she calls 'particularist' feminist theories that challenge conventional notions of citizenship which are premised upon an abstract understanding of the individual as the criteria of citizenship. Such conventions, she argues, focus on the 'citizen mind' and ignore female questions about the 'body'. Particularist feminist theories counterpose such male-centred concepts of citizenship by recuperating the body, which is now understood as the 'home' of citizen life and the new understandings of political action. Such feminist discourses which concern the 'body' reveal their distance from the socio-political constructs described in our own chapter.

Two other chapters (chs 4 and 6) play a key role in opening up the analysis of citizenship. Heidi Mirza and Diane Reay (ch. 4) draw upon their empirical research to describe how Black African-Caribbean communities in the UK have forged new notions of citizenship in what the authors call a 'third space'. They argue that the classical notions of citizenship (the distinction between public and private spheres) is disrupted by the concept of community and political cohesiveness. In this 'third sphere', Black women educators demonstrate new and inclusive forms of 'real citizenship'. The creative contingent engagement of Black women thus 'effectively subverts the subjectisation and individualisation inherent within the processes of postmodern fragmentation'. They decentre fixed notions of citizenship and create a third space of radical opposition.

Elaine Unterhalter's chapter (ch. 6) also places us firmly in the contemporary context by encouraging us to examine how international educational platforms shape our understandings of the female citizen. For example, by exploring the range of 'redemptive declarations' put forward by international agencies such as the World Bank and UNESCO, and alternative declarations put forward by the Jomtien Conference in 1990 and the Beijing World Conference on Women in 1995, Unterhalter considers how the education of women and girls is circumscribed by sometimes traditional understandings of the female citizen and the private sphere. She reveals, through textual analyses of such key policy documents, the need to address the essentialism and passivity ascribed to women's citizenship in the 'developing world' and to challenge the ways in which investment in female education is restrained by the limited notions of stakeholding and citizenship used by such agencies.

Part 2: Teachers' identities and public identifications

In Part 2, a number of authors consider the ways in which women educators within mainstream schooling or the college/university system are positioned in relation to citizenship. Women as teachers and teacher educators find themselves, on the one hand, excluded from mainstream debates about democracy and education and, on the other hand, positioned as the key agents in the project of cultivating, through education, society's future citizens. Whilst often denied political agency themselves, their task nevertheless is both to ensure the creation of tomorrow's obedient citizens and to promote a more democratic society. Their individual histories, values and identities as women and as teachers are often absent from histories of citizenship education and taken for granted in relation to the implementation of citizenship values. In this section of the book such contradictions are explored empirically in a range of different national contexts.

Helena Araújo's historical analysis of the period 1919 to 1933 identifies just how problematic women's citizenship has been in Portugal (see ch. 7). Drawing upon the themes of motherhood and citizenship, she explores the Portuguese political context and the tensions about female citizenship between the Republicans, anarchists, feminists and Catholics in this period. She focuses particularly on how women's citizenship (women's right to work outside the home, their political rights and the relationship between citizenship and motherhood) was understood and the tensions and conflicts it created in the Portuguese state. The conflicts between these particular discursive framings – as the feminist, the anarchist, etc. – suggest that women primary teachers were subjected not merely to pedagogic discourses but to shifting and contradictory gendered discourses articulated through social structures and practices in the state. Araújo argues that these competing definitions of femininity affected women teachers who were given carefully prescribed roles in the creation of a gendered citizenry.

Progressive female teacher educators, many of whom were keen to promote democratic citizenship, as Kathleen Weiler points out in her chapter (ch. 8), were a contradiction in terms since such women were defined conventionally as close to nature and thus naturally excluded from citizenship. This process was particularly painful for leading women, progressive educators in America – such internationally renowned figures as Willystine Goodsell, Patty Smith Hill, Mabel Carney, Fannie Dunn and Leta Hollingsworth. Promoting the education of women was a controversial goal in a setting where women educators were excluded from the male intellectual forum (such as that around the journal *The Social Frontier*). Kathleen Weiler's analysis of such women – in particular, Willystine Goodsell – illustrates the story of how progressive education came to be split between child-centred and more conservative forces. The relationship of female educationists to the Progressive Education Association and the more radical social reconstructionists was thus, in part, a result of particular concepts of citizenship and the associated undemocratic and exclusionary practices of male progressive theorists, followers paradoxically of John Dewey.

James Donald argues that one of the ways in which individuals acquire a citizenship identity is by 'identifying with some master signifier guaranteeing its place in the symbolic network' (Donald, 1996: 175). As a result, the processes of identification become enmeshed in histories of parties, sects, movements, and national and communal self-definitions. At the same time, individuals are connected to a political imaginary (a symbolic world) – 'to *become* a citizen is therefore to become a subject within the symbolic order and to be subjected to it' (175). Therefore, the desire and need for identification, he argues, does not 'reduce the symbolic order of citizenship or the habits and rhetorics it generates to the absolutism of identity politics' (176).

When describing the research data from a comparative European project, Gabrielle Ivinson and her colleagues in chapter 9 also point to the importance of symbolic structures when they explore the relationship of gender to citizenship representations. They argue that gender becomes the symbolic network which exposes the premises upon which female citizenship is based. By uncovering the ways in which student teachers, who are about to enter the school system, express anxiety about social and economic transitions, the authors reveal how such concerns vary across contexts. They also vary according to student teachers' gender and their social representations of the gendered citizen. Ivinson and her colleagues suggest that when these young professionals adjust to social change (e.g. shifts in public and private boundaries caused by women's transitions into the labour market and political life), they represent female sexuality as transgressive, potent and dangerous. Such representations act as a form of symbolic armour to mask social anxieties about personal and social change. Degendering citizenship in the cause of democracy arguably will not necessarily engage with teachers' deeper connections to gender and citizenship.

Similarly, Jo-Anne Dillabough (ch. 10) digs deeper into the political identifications of female workers in education (student teachers, female researchers, and teacher educators) and the world in which they must operate (i.e. their lived experience) as educators. Here, women's role as 'educator' is described in terms of their long-standing and symbolic affiliation to, on the one hand, the private sphere, whilst still remaining responsible, both theoretically and practically, for cultivating liberal democratic citizenship. She argues that the reproduction of the gender spheres of work in teacher education can be identified through a critical and historical analysis of female citizenship. Her aim is to identify the way teacher education, as a social instittiion, is premised on the gendered principles of liberal democratic thought and Pateman's concern about the public/private split. Through the use of oral history methods, she therefore draws upon teacher educators' memories of how their own gender, racial and class-based identities have been shaped to act in concert with women's servicing role in the private sphere.

Part 3: Schooling and the construction of the gendered citizen

In 1980, Joel Spring produced an insightful book entitled *Educating the Worker Citizen* in which he argues that nineteenth-century political goals for school evolved around concepts of patriotism, nationalism and good citizenship. Schools were to serve 'the people' (i.e. popular sovereignty) by creating loyal citizens. The challenge was to create a form of political loyalty to the state but not in such a way that children would become 'servants of power'.

In reality, this triple task was hard to achieve, and in 1975 Dan C. Lortie found in his famous study of American school-teachers that, although some teachers emphasised 'the desirability of independence of mind', most teachers' allusions to 'moral outcomes and citizenship emphasised compliance and obedience' (quoted in Spring, 1980: 19). In actuality, Lortie found that most teachers' notions of good citizenship were directly related to their own interests in maintaining classroom control rather than developing a sense of social responsibility for others in the state.

> Connecting compliance with classroom norms to future citizenship authenticates the teacher's control effect. Thus discipline becomes more than mere forbidding and ordering; the dross of classroom management is transformed into the gold of dependable citizenship.
>
> (113–114, quoted in Spring, 1980: 19)

The concept of citizenship therefore raises many critical questions in relation to educational theory and research. In what ways, we might ask, are citizens constructed in schools? How do the overt and hidden aspects of schooling influence the child as a 'learner citizen' and as future 'worker citizens'? What role does gender play in the formation of such 'dependable' citizenship identities? What potential is there in schooling today for the development of precisely this independence of mind, a sense of political agency rather than subordination?

The analyses of schooling in this volume offered by Tuula Gordon and her colleagues, by Victoria Foster, and by Christine Callender and Cecile Wright reveal a far more complex account of the significance of schooling in the education of citizens than that described in the 1970s and 1980s. In chapter 11, Tuula Gordon, Janet Holland and Elina Lahelma describe how in English and Finnish schools, notions of nationhood and citizenship identity are reconciled. In the route from pupil to citizen, young people (initially occupying the 'empty space' of citizenship) pass through and occupy a space in the official school, the informal school and the physical school. The route through these forms of schooling is differentiated in such a way that boys and girls pass through varied time-space paths. They learn a 'curriculum of the body' and thus achieve what Stone referred to as 'embodied identities'. At the same time they are offered only limited public and private spaces in which to exercise their agency. Boys are provided with more popular physical and emotional space to do this than girls; the process of what Gordon and her colleagues call 'agentic embodiment' is thus prefigured by gender inequalities.

The gendered notion of the 'learner citizen' is now key to understanding contemporary gender politics in education. For example, the processes of social transformation associated with women's changing position in society can also be found by examining the considerable change in girls' educational patterns of performance. The movement of young women into traditional male spheres in schooling (male subjects such as a science and mathematics) and into traditionally male forms of elite education (universities, professional training) can be interpreted, as Victoria Foster demonstrates (ch. 12), as a major threat to the education processes which have been designed to create 'male learner-citizens'. Describing the backlash in Australia over girls' educational success, Foster raises important questions about the relationship between the school's promotion of the male 'learner citizen' and the gender relations which prefigure female citizenship. She also identifies key concerns about radicalising and extending the significance of female citizenship education as a curricular subject which must ultimately challenge the de-gendering of citizenship.

Whilst school and learning processes such as those described by Gordon et al. and Foster are critical to the formation of citizens, no analysis of gender would be complete without more explicit reference to the regulatory role of discipline in schools. As Lortie argued twenty-five years ago, classroom management may have its own agenda separate from the concerns of an emancipatory civic curriculum. Therefore, in Wright and Callender's chapter (ch. 13), the tensions Lortie identified between discipline on the one hand, and empowerment on the other, are explored. The chapter compares findings from two programmes of research – one on white teachers with Black secondary school pupils and the other with Black African-Caribbean primary teachers and Black pupils. These two projects highlight the difficult task of capturing the tensions between discipline and democracy. In the former case, gender differentiation is used as a mechanism of differentiation and control within a racialised set of disciplinary procedures. In the latter case, discipline is used as force for solidarity and empowerment in ways not dissimilar from the 'third space' described by Mirza and Reay (ch. 4 above).

The theme of diversity and citizenship is one which is taken up by a number of authors. Dillabough, Brooks and Enslin also draw our attention to the critical relationships between race, gender and citizenship. Dillabough, for example, illustrates how teacher educators' and teachers' collective memories of racism in their school days and their experiences of racism within teacher training affect their struggles for inclusion and their concepts of political agency. Brooks gives an account of how feminist theory itself has had to come to terms with the politics of multiple and diverse citizenship identities. Such identity struggles provide the basis for political agency which is grounded in community experiences. Drawing on the recent South African experience of building a democracy, Enslin (in Part 4), considers what is the most appropriate relationship between community customs and state education policies. The tensions associated with state and community-based gender values should be important aspects of any discussion of citizenship education.

Similarly, a number of projects focus on the significance of youth and citizenship. Research on the impact of schooling on young people's social attitudes is quite common, with many projects highlighting levels of political literacy (e.g. Wilkinson, 1994, Hahn, 1999). Such analyses suggest that generational gaps are quite considerable in the post-war years when many young people's experience of gender relations has been transformed. Critical sociological analyses of such attitudes, however, have been rare, with most of the writing on citizenship education focused upon the curriculum rather than the perspectives of those for whom the curriculum is designed. Gloria Bonder's report of an open-ended study of young women's representations of citizenship in Argentina is, therefore, unique. In chapter 14, Bonder reports how she and her colleagues found that young women's lives were profoundly affected by transformations in Argentinian social structures and how concerns about nationality and identity dovetail into anxieties around social change and women's changing position. The process of individualisation which Gordon et al. (ch. 11) referred to, and as well as the impact of conventional family values, suggest again female desires for greater participation as citizens in forms which allow their 'freedom and individuality to be respected'.

Part 4: Citizenship education and new democratic agendas

Given many of the traditional associations of citizenship with nationalism, few feminist educationalists engage with citizenship education; Foster's (1996) and Weiler's (this volume) work are some of the key exceptions. Many recent texts on citizenship education, in turn, give only passing attention to concerns about gender, or indeed about sexuality or ethnicity (Quicke, 1999 is the exception here). Therefore, citizenship education is often portrayed as straddling the worlds of political literacy and moral/religious discourses, rather than the more critical political terrain of feminism, anti-racism, social and cultural reproduction theory, socialism and poststructuralism. Indeed, despite the role it could play as critical pedagogy (Giroux 1980), many citizenship education textbooks fail to make explicit their political stance.

The development of citizenship education as a curriculum subject can never be seen as uncontested or indeed lacking in controversy given the concerns of liberal democracy for independence of thought and the development of government for social order. Different audiences are interested in the teaching of citizenship in the curriculum and in the school as a whole. Teachers, for example, need to consider how they themselves are placed in the curriculum – what expertise will the subject require, how will teachers deal with controversial issues (e.g. sexuality, moral concerns, racism), how will they work with such an abstract concept without repressing difference? Schools wishing to promote democracy in its fullest sense will consider how best to organise their instructional discourses: teaching styles, curriculum, assessment or their regulative discourses (Bernstein 1996) around pupil organisation, disciplinary codes, rituals and values, etc. What values and political issues would they wish to express and how, within the institution as a whole? Campaigning pressure groups too are interested in citizenship education as a means of maintaining traditional values or encouraging social transformations. Many of these audiences already appreciate the political significance of citizenship education, but not necessarily its gendered aspects.

As a result, some feminist educationists have found themselves commenting on national programmes of civic education or international developments. In this part of the collection, four important examples of this programmatic work are described. The ways in which the education of the citizen can be used to promote greater gender equality are explored, for example, in the context of sexuality education, democratic schooling, government programmes for nation-building in South Africa, and feminist responses to the gender politics of cyberspace.

Sue Lees and Lynn Davies both address the theme of women's freedom explored at the Beijing World Conference for Women in 1995. Sexuality is one of the means by which women are denied full rights as citizens in many countries. Women experience violence, bullying, and personal interference in school, in the workplace and in the family. At the same time, women are encouraged to learn about their rights as citizens within a form of schooling that may even encourage such harassment. Such contradictions are explored by Lees in chapter 15 where she demonstrates the various ways in which sexuality is linked to citizenship and why citizenship education needs to engage with the hegemonic dominance of heterosexuality (and the gendered power relations it entails) as a social institution. She argues that 'it is only when citizenship education and sex education adopt a wider framework which problematises the relations of power underlying sexual relations that progress in relation to more equal citizenship can be made'.

Taking violence and sexuality seriously is central to democratic education. In chapter 16, Lynn Davies describes how the liberal democratic education project needs to be challenged and transformed if such gender regimes are to be tackled. In her chapter, Davies describes how the curriculum and the organisation and management of schooling (with its principles of conflict and power) would need restructuring if schools were to become what she calls 'civil schools' – a model of schooling which represents a more radical and effective democratic institution. Drawing upon her research on democratic practices in the 'developing' world, Davies outlines the elements of a 'gender-inclusive' model of democratic schooling and the key issues necessary to address if it were to educate a 'just citizenry'.

Concern about the development of a gender-inclusive democracy are also reflected in Penny Enslin's discussion of post-apartheid education in South Africa (see chapter 17). In this particular case, where the government, at least on the face of it, is attempting to develop a new society – a new nation in which there is social justice for all – Enslin describes the tensions between definitions of liberal citizenship in terms of *rights* and citizenship defined as *membership* (of nation or as defined by custom). Citizenship defined in terms of membership of a community with strong customary traditions, she argues, tends to confine issues of gender equity to the private sphere. In such post-colonial contexts, tensions between indigenous, and Western and non-Western patriarchal forms need to be confronted such that any notion of female citizenship does indeed emerge in the name of women's political interests and relevant collectivities rather than as a male-centred notion of democratic practice.

Such nation-building, however, may well be overtaken by global developments. In chapter 18, Jane Kenway and Diana Langmead are right to remind us of the ever encroaching nature of cyberspace. In their description of the various feminist positionings in relation to cyberspace, Kenway and Langmead highlight the distinction between conventional cyberfeminism and avant-garde cyberfeminism. Cyberfeminism focuses on women gaining equal access to new technologies and drawing upon such technologies for the purposes of their own emancipation. By contrast, avant-garde cyberfeminism seeks to challenge the social relations which are constructed in this new 'political imaginary'. In this new 'space', democratic citizenship is being redefined and new gender regimes and relationships are cultivated. The implications for female citizenship and citizenship education are therefore challenging, not least because they move beyond the agendas set by modernist feminist educational analyses. As Kenway and Langmead argue, cyberspace provides a new realm for the study of female citizenship where novel concepts of the public/private, women as political actors and nationhood emerge.

Reflections

The chapters in this collection challenge contemporary understandings of the location and significance of gender relations in education. What these chapters also attempt to demonstrate is the relationship between gender relations and other political relations – those of, for example, sexuality, nationhood, 'race' and citizenship. Embedded within a contested notion of citizenship are issues of ethnicity, gender and class, although all too often we have divided them. Such issues are more clearly integrated within an analysis of citizenship where the multiple positioning of individuals has been addressed and recognised (see for example, Mirza and Reay, Bonder, Dillabough, Callender and Wright, and Enslin in this volume) within contemporary educational literature.

Citizenship, as a concept, allows us access to the contested terrain of democracy and the very nature of democratic schooling. It also allows us to analyse, from a feminist perspective, critical educational policies as well as the discursive frameworks used by national and international governmental agencies and to consider the impact of global developments more generally. As a concept, it is precisely what needs to be signified, since its very abstractness allows it to become both the object of study and the focus of political action. As Donald rightly argued, citizenship has no substantial identity until it is located within a set of social and symbolic social relations. The radical potential of the concept is, therefore, as important as its discriminatory political history (cf. Heater, 1990).

The authors in the collection attempt to close the gap between political theory, feminist theory and feminist educational theory (Dillabough and Arnot, chapter 2). They have engaged at a theoretical level with a range of important feminist debates around the concept of citizenship, an embodied citizenship, the politics of difference, the nature of the public/private binary, the third sphere, and the processes of individualisation and differentiation and the political imaginary. A new language, therefore, is emerging with which to talk about gender relations and citizenship in education.

In short, the contributors to this volume argue that current conceptions of citizenship and democratic schooling not only endorse particular forms of masculinity, but serve, at least in part, to regulate the production of the citizen. They also suggest that the ideas which currently underlie the drive for citizenship and citizenship education are gendered in ways which may serve to further marginalise, rather than emancipate, women. Tackling these gendering processes, therefore, implies a feminist analysis of citizenship and citizenship education. To recapture the political and more radical dimensions of citizenship, then, is one of the main tasks of the book.

Bibliography

Arnot, M. (1982) 'Male hegemony, social class and women's education', *Journal of Education*, 164, 1: 64–89.

Arnot, M. (1999) 'Gendered citizenry: new feminist perspectives on education and citizenship', *British Education Research Journal*, 23, 3: 275–295.

Arnot, M. and Dillabough, J. (1999) 'Feminist politics and democratic values in education', *Curriculum Inquiry*, 29, 2: 149–158.

Arnot, M., Araújo, H., Deliyanni, K. and Ivinson, G. (2000) 'Changing femininity, changing concepts of citizenship in public and private spheres', *European Journal of Women's Studies* 7, 2, May, 149–168.

Benhabib, S. (1995) 'From identity politics to social feminism', in D. Trend (ed.) *Radical Democracy: identity, citizenship and the state*, New York: Routledge.

Bernstein, B. (1996) *Pedagogy, Symbolic Control and Identity: theory, research, critique*, London: Taylor and Francis.

Cockburn, C. (1998) *The Space Between Us: negotiating gender and national identities in conflict*, London: Zed Books.

Dillabough, J. and Arnot, M. (2000 forthcoming) 'Feminist sociology of education: dynamics, debates and directions', in J. Demaine (ed.) *Sociology of Education Today*, London: Macmillan.

Donald, J. (1996) 'The citizen and the man about town', in S. Hall and P. du Gay (eds) *Questions of Cultural Identity*, London: Sage.

Elshtain, J. Bethke (1981) *Public Man, Private Woman: women in social and political thought*, Princeton, N.J.: Princeton University Press.

Foster, V. (1996) 'Space invaders: desire and threat in the schooling of girls', *Discourse: studies in the cultural politics of education*, 17: 43–63.

Gilbert, R. (1992) 'Citizenship, education and postmodernity', *British Journal of Sociology of Education*, 13: 51–68.

Giroux, H. (1980) 'Critical theory and rationality in citizenship education', *Curriculum Inquiry*, 10: 329–336.

Gordon, T., Holland, J. and Lahelma, E. (1996) 'Nation space: the construction of citizenship and difference in schools', paper presented at the British Sociological Association Conference, Reading.

Hahn, C. L. (1999) *Becoming Political: comparative perspectives on citizenship education*, Albany: State University of New York Press.

Heater, D. (1990) *Citizenship: the civic ideal in world history, politics and education*, London: Longman.

Lloyd, G. (1986) 'Selfhood, war and masculinity' in C. Pateman and E. Gross (eds) *Feminist Challenges: social and political theory*, London: Allen and Unwin.

Lortie, D. C. (1975) *Schoolteacher: a sociological study*, Chicago: University of Chicago Press.

Lyotard, J. F. (1984) *The Postmodern Condition: a report on knowledge*, Manchester: Manchester University Press.

Marshall, T. H. (1965) 'Citizenship and social class', in *Class, Citizenship and Social Development*, New York: Anchor Books.

Pateman, C. (1980) *The Disorder of Women*, Cambridge: Polity Press.

Pateman, C. (1988) *The Sexual Contract*, Cambridge: Polity Press.

Pateman, C. (1997) 'Beyond the sexual contract', in J. Dench (ed.) *Rewriting the Social Contract*, London: Institute of Community Studies.

Phillips, A. (1991) *Engendering Democracy*, Cambridge: Polity Press.

Phillips, A. (1992) *Democracy and Difference*, Cambridge: Polity Press.

Quicke, J. (1999) *Curriculum for Life: schools for a democratic learning society*, Buckingham: Open University Press.

Spring, J. (1980) *Educating the Worker Citizen: the social, economic and political foundations of eduation*, New York: Longman.

Voet, R. (1998) *Feminism and Citizenship*, London: Sage.

Weir, A. (1997) *Sacrificial Logics: feminist theory and the critique of identity*, New York: Routledge.

Wexler, P. (1991) 'Citizenship in the semiotic society', in B. Turner (ed.) *Theory of Modernity and Postmodernity*, London: Sage.

Wilkinson, H. (1994) *No Turning Back: generations and the genderquake*, London: Demos.

Part 1

Discursive framings of female citizenship and female education

2 Feminist political frameworks
New approaches to the study of gender, citizenship and education

Jo-Anne Dillabough and
Madeleine Arnot

The liberal democratic state, together with the patriarchal discourses which shape its central doctrines, has became a particularly powerful global force in the industrialised world. At the same time, liberal democracy has incorporated within itself the standard mechanisms for challenging its own political machinery. This makes liberal democracy and its central feature – a gendered notion of the rational citizen – an extremely complex political idea when compared to other patriarchal formations. Various feminist academic fields have recognised this complexity and its profound implications for the social order, yet the insights gained from such feminist critiques have not necessarily been brought together to form a coherent political analysis of the state.

In the present chapter, we bring together questions about female citizenship and liberal democracy within two fields of feminist analysis: feminist socio-political theory and feminist educational theory. Put simply, our argument can be summarised as follows: important links between feminist political theory and feminist educational theory have not always been made explicit. As a consequence, education feminism (see Stone, 1994) has not had sufficient impact on the restructuring of citizenship and the formation of citizenship education. The goal here, therefore, is to forge links between these two domains of thought so that key issues about the relationship between gender, citizenship and education can be addressed.

Engaging feminist political and educational theories of citizenship

There are a number of similarities between feminist political theory and 'education feminism' (see Stone, 1994), each of which attempts to critique liberal democratic discourses and practices. Feminist educational theorists in Western industrialised nations have explored the social construction, recontextualisation and reproduction of gender relations and gender inequalities within liberal democratic educational systems. At the same time, feminist political theorists (especially in the UK, Australia and the US) have examined the sources of female oppression which are still embedded in the language of political liberalism (Pateman, 1988, 1989; Phillips, 1992; Young, 1995). They have exposed male-centred versions of traditional liberal democratic thought (Elstain, 1981) and identified the complex ways in which liberal political discourse itself framed gender relations. This has led to an awareness of the ways in which the concept of citizen has been constructed as male and the 'other' as female. In both frameworks, the processes of degendering liberal democratic institutions have been discussed. There have also been attempts in both fields to resolve the key dilemma of how to include women as equals in social institutions, with the same entitlement as men, whilst still recognising women's different material conditions and experiences.[1]

Yet gender issues in education were not, until very recently, explicitly linked to theoretical questions about female citizenship (Arnot and Dillabough, 1999; Foster, this volume). Such issues have been neglected largely because citizenship has been considered by many feminists to be too strongly associated with conservative politics in the formal sense (government, law, etc.), or associated with nationalist or modernist movements. As a result, the educational debate about similarity and difference between the sexes and the implications for male and female entitlements has tended to focus upon the *cultural* rather than the *political* nature of the gendered patterns of schooling in contemporary society. For example, feminist debates here highlighted the controversy about co-education or single sex schools, whether girls should be entitled to school subjects which reflected their interests, whether school culture should address female values (competition versus hierarchy) or whether the different forms of authority used by women teachers (caring ethic etc.) should be validated (Arnot and Dillabough, 1999). Consequently, key political concepts and theoretical arguments used by feminist political and social theorists to dissect the state and liberal democratic practices – such as critiques of the 'public citizen' or the 'autonomous subject' – remained on the margins of education feminism.

Where feminist political and educational theorists could usefully have disagreed was in relation to the possibilities of liberal democratic educational institutions. First, Pateman (1988) argued, for example, that the social order underlying liberal democracy was premised upon a 'fraternal pact' which failed to acknowledge women as political equals and undermined their rights to full citizenship. Instead, social institutions presumed and enforced the subordination of women. In contrast, education feminists argued for the importance of using education as a means of promoting gender equality, social justice and egalitarianism.

Second, unlike feminist political theorists, feminist educationalists who worked with educational practitioners in schools were more interested in the formulation of practice/praxis which was thought to reflect the interests and rights of women. They saw the necessity of associating feminist theory with 'insider' reform (Weiner, 1989). Pressure was therefore put upon education feminism to respond to the immediate problems of policy-making as well as the more abstract critical analyses of liberal democracy. The relationship of feminist educationalists to liberal democracy was, therefore, always likely to be different from, and sometimes in conflict with, the concerns of feminist political theorists.

As a result of the distinctiveness of these two domains of feminist thought, such similarities and tensions between them have remained unexplored. Our primary goal, therefore, is to consider how such work might usefully be brought together – to bridge the gap between the work of feminist scholars in education and feminist theorists in social and political theory.

In attending to this task, we begin our analysis by first positioning feminist educational theories within the different strands of feminist political thought. We then describe three themes that have emerged in feminist political and social theory about democracy and citizenship. These themes are not only highly relevant to educational theory but they also provide a conceptual framework for re-evaluating the basis of the liberal democratic education project. We draw upon these three themes – what we refer to here as *theoretical problematics* – to locate and contextualise the contribution of feminist political theory to our understanding of liberal democracy and the democratic education project.

Positioning feminist educational theories of citizenship

Education feminism, like feminist political theories, has actively engaged with the tensions between concepts of universality and particularism, between unity and plurality and between equality and difference (Voet, 1998). It also has hopes and ideals in relation to, for example, unity, plurality, justice, freedom and equality (Arnot and Dillabough, 1999). The variation of responses accounts for the range of feminist educational theories and the momentum behind their development in the Western industrialised world in the last twenty years. Such differences in education feminism have been 'mapped' (not uncontroversially) by a number of authors (see Acker, 1994; Weiner, 1994; Middleton, 1987; Arnot and Weiner, 1987). For example, in a recent paper (see Arnot and Dillabough, 1999) we show how diverse strands of education feminism take up or reject the principles of liberal democracy in competing and conflicting ways.

Interestingly, Voet (1998) clusters feminist political thought into three different conceptualisations of female citizenship which she refers to as *humanist feminist* theories, *women-centred* theories and *deconstructionist feminist* theories.[2] She describes how the *humanist feminist*, for example, works on the tension beween individualism and humanism, focusing on the notion of equal rights and duties for all. In terms of citizenship, humanist feminists (e.g. liberal, socialist and radical) struggle for women's inclusion in the state as citizens rather than critiquing the analytical category 'woman'. By contrast, *women-centred* theorists call for the acceptance of 'women' as women, who have the right to be recognised as citizens with their own sets of values over and above the needs of equal treatment, equality of voice and access. Such theories do not promote a gender neutral citizenship. Indeed, women-centred feminists urge us to rethink citizenship from the viewpoint of the female citizen who nurtures and cares for the state and its members. In this model, women would be granted special collective rights and treament and there would be special concern for women's needs. The nurturing element of citizenship and new meanings and values (e.g. the ethics of care associated with womanhood) would be incorporated into political thought.

In contrast, the third group of feminist theorists – *the deconstructionist feminists* – recognise more plurality in politics and society and focus on key questions around voice, identity, and discourse. However, they remain sceptical about liberal democratic concepts such as equal rights and any notion of a gender differentiated citizenship. In fact, even a notion of differentiated citizenship could be considered dangerous since it might lead to the stigmatisation of one sex or promote a false notion concept of equality which leads to the repression of difference. Rather than providing a set of political goals in relation to citizenship, deconstructionist feminists therefore offer a methodology for critiquing concepts of citizenship and liberal democracy.

Voet's (1998) description of the linking of political feminism to the broader questions of citizenship allows us to view education feminism in a different way. For example, clustering the range of 'modernist' 'rational' theories of education (see Dillabough and Arnot, 2000 forthcoming) allows us to highlight humanist feminist concerns about promotion of women's citizenship through education. Here questions about women's agency, rights and autonomy are developed within the framework of liberal democratic citizenship. By contrast, the women-centred feminist education tradition (e.g. maternal feminism) is concerned with the nature and character underlying the ideal female citizen, as possessing traditionally female values such as kindness, openness, caring and nurturance. It is thought that such values challenge the liberal notion of the rational and abstract male citizen. In the deconstructionist feminist education tradition, the diversity and plurality of human subjects come to the fore, the category 'woman' is challenged and the premises upon which citizenship are built come into question.

Using this set of distinctions we can now consider how each tradition addresses what we identified as three major *theoretical problematics* derived largely from the work of eminent feminist political theorists. In a previous paper (Arnot and Dillabough, 1999), we argued that such problematics set an agenda for educationalists, only a part of which has been addressed to date. The three problematics are:

- The 'fraternal pact' in feminist political and educational theory;
- The gendering of nationhood and national educational systems; and
- 'Woman' as a political category.

Below we describe each of the following problematics and consider 'humanist', 'women centred' and 'deconstructionist' feminist educational responses to them. In our view, these theoretical problematics contribute substantial weight to unanswered yet intriguing questions about gender, democracy and citizenship in education.

The fraternal pact in feminist political theory and education

Carol Pateman, a feminist political theorist, constructed a new theoretical agenda for the study of democracy and citizenship (Pateman, 1988, 1989 and 1992). She argued, for example, that traditional, liberal views on citizenship negated the possibility of female citizenship through its promotion of masculinity as the basis for the democratic state. Liberal democracy, therefore, privileged the ontology of maleness and the 'epistemic' dominance of masculinity in liberal political thought.

What lay behind the concept of the individual in the liberal state, with its rational autonomous selfhood and its universal and objective social principles, was a Western European version of masculinity. Men, for the predominantly male European political philosophers, exemplified the potential of humans to create a social order that was based on rationality and truth. Male forms of autonomy and rational thought were, thus, thought to define order in the state. On the other side of the equation, that of disorder, women were portrayed as psychologically unbalanced and unable to articulate a political consciousness. Pateman (1992: 19) writes:

> Women, our bodies and distinctive capacities, represented all that citizenship are not. 'Citizenship' has gained its meaning through the exclusion of women, that is to say (sexual) difference.

The combination of women's psychological disabilities and sexual characteristics led to their exclusion from the original social contract, or in effect, the 'fraternal pact' (Pateman, 1989). However, according to Pateman, the relationship of women to liberal democratic citizenship moved beyond a case of simple exclusion from the state. For example, women were included as cultivators of the moral order within the liberal democratic project because of their symbolic link to the private sphere. However, as a consequence of such links, they were excluded from possessing political power, and, as it naturally follows, from the realm of citizenship (e.g. enfranchisement). Therefore, one of the greatest weaknesses of liberal democracy was the political settlement which ultimately legitimised gender inequality within its formal principles and practices. In constructing a civic brotherhood as the basis of the social order, men legitimated their autonomic right to that power in public life, and, at the same time, their sexual rights over women:

> The brothers made a sexual contract. They established a law which confirms masculine sex right and ensures that there is an orderly access by each man to a woman.
>
> (Pateman, 1989: 109)

The concept of the social and sexual contract, at first glance, may seem far removed from educational concepts and the terrain of educational feminists. However, a number of these issues relate to the nature of liberal democratic education. For example, Pateman's work suggests that a tension exists between the extent to which schooling establishes the separation of the public and private spheres and the ways in which such separations have become associated with the historical distinction between male and female as antagonistic universalising (and liberal democratic) categories. Women (both students and teachers), if associated only with the private sphere, become symbols of emotion, natural feeling and caring. Consequently, they cannot emerge as active citizens; they are simply viewed as the moral vessel through which a notion of citizenship is cultivated. This conception of women thus raises interesting questions about the terms upon which women and girls have been included in the liberal democratic education project. What role, for example, has gender played in shaping our understandings of democratic education and, ultimately, the most appropriate forms of identities which schools are expected to promote?

The association of gender difference with the public and private spheres also encourages us to ask what is education's contribution to the gendered nature of the public/private separation? And what happens to the social order (and the fraternal pact) when girls start to acquire access to male public spheres through schooling, through qualifications and through access to traditional male employment spheres? Below we briefly describe some of the contributions of education feminism to these questions.

Education, gender and civic spheres

The development of education feminism (Stone, 1994), particularly since the 1960s, has to a large extent involved challenging gender inequalities in what might be called the *civic* or *public* (as opposed to the economic) *sphere*. Such work has been instrumental in exposing women's uneasy relationship to public decision-making, to patriarchal machineries and modes of regulation in education and to male public discourses in schools. As a result of liberal humanist educational initiatives, women have found a place in the public sphere (Arnot and Dillabough, 1999). Such initiatives have taken the form of educational reforms (e.g. educational policies, curricular initiatives, affirmative action), but they have also involved political activism (e.g. campaigning against discrimination).

Much humanist feminist research in education (e.g. liberal and socialist feminism) still remains concerned with women's and girls' public achievement even though it also reveals the enduring stability of the patriarchal state and the need to address men's position within the private sphere. Similarly, although some feminists (e.g. socialists) recognised the exploitative nature of the public/private distinction by exposing its associations and functions within capitalist social formations, paradoxically, they too tended to work only with the concept of the 'public' in education, failing on some level to investigate the political and social significance of the 'private'. They also failed to define what democratic participation would mean in the home. As Jagger (1983) argued, a more equal division of domestic labour and women's control over biological reproduction should be essential to the achievement of democracy. Some, however, argued for community control over biological reproduction in the name of the common good as a radical ideal. Deeply problematic issues such as public coercion versus private rights and the role of the state in relation to domestic relations were, thus, never fully resolved.

Such feminist educational work usefully focused on the most overt contradictions of capitalist democracy – the gap between, for example, equal opportunity as a principle and the reality of differential treatment. At the same time, it failed to identify far deeper obstacles to gender equality such as the role of schooling in relation to competitive and rationalised performances in the market. Post-war concepts of liberal democratic education emphasised its competencies, excellence, marketability and technical skills each of which (at least in theory) were thought to apply equally to men and women. Seen in this light, democratic schooling was used as the 'training ground for the [female] entrepreneur' (see Deitz, 1985, our addition), and was seen as the institutional form capable of granting women an equal chance in the race towards individual progress. Thus whilst liberal feminists in particular (Dillabough and Arnot, 2000) argued for equality of opportunity, they supported rather than challenged this economic project of inclusion. The concept of the public therefore was disassociated from male forms of power and the social contracts which underlie such economic contracts.

The desire to challenge the public–private split and the dominance of male culture in schools re-emerges when considering the success of feminist educational initiatives such as critical pedagogy (Ellsworth, 1997; Luke and Gore, 1989). For example, while still humanist in focus, an image of democratic educational practice was put forward which implied the celebration of a radical consciousness, through alternative curricular forms and feminist critical pedagogy (Arnot and Dillabough, 1999). However, despite the value of such work, it stopped short of seriously destabilising the forms of male authority which supported the dominance of a masculinised bourgeois culture (Bourdieu and Passeron, 1977).

Radical feminist concerns about sexuality and the sexual control of women by men and maternal feminist celebration of female values (such as caring and ethics) got closer to challenging the gendered relations of the public/private domains. Radical feminist analysis of schooling, for example, demonstrated how schools both regulated and controlled girls in terms of their use and ownership of physical space, linguistic space and educational space (Mahoney, 1985). They worked on the complexity of male control of female sexuality – through the language of the school, through female representations in school curricula and cultures, through sex education and parenthood education, and through the sexual underworld of schooling (e.g. Lees this volume). Their analysis highlighted how the processes of exclusion in the public sphere were paralleled by girls' internalisation of male norms. Holland and her colleagues (1998) labelled this practice the 'male in the head' with its associated devaluation of female norms and cultures.

Maternal feminist responses (or what Voet calls women-centred theorising) addressed the notion of the social and sexual contracts by encouraging the celebration of the private 'female' sphere over and above public patriarchy. The solutions they offered privileged the caring ethic as an essential female attribute which could replace the hierarchical, elitist, competitive (and often militaristic) cultures of the male public realm. For educationalists, this would mean working on the reform of the social contract (the abstract public male) and subverting the sexual contract (male domination in the private sphere) in accordance with women's ethics.

One might wish to suggest that maternal feminism addressed Carole Pateman's concerns about the exclusion of 'female values' from the definition of citizenship by arguing for their inclusion in the reconstruction of demo-cratic educational practice. However, as Deitz (1985) suggests, maternal feminism failed to treat as problematic either the essentialisation of women as mothers (i.e., 'political' category of 'women') or the differentiation of women's experiences. In other words, women-centred theorists universalised the importance of the private sphere in ways which may have further demeaned women. Therefore, whilst liberal feminism – as a humanistic initiative – failed to question female subordination in the private sphere, maternal feminists essentialised women as mother (Arnot and Dillabough, 1999).

In seeking to address the relationship between public and private spheres, post-structural feminists created a more active association of the public and private by using Foucault's concept of discourse, where language, knowledge, and power are seen as linked (Walkerdine and Lucey, 1989). From the perspec-tive of deconstructionist education theory, the shaping of privacy, sexuality and the marriage contract, described by Pateman and other feminist political theorists (see Benhabib, 1995), is significant to the analysis of modern educa-tional systems because they are part of the framing, through state and local discourses, of the public or ideal citizen. The deconstruction of the distinc-tion between public and private spheres thus becomes the task at hand for educationalists, rather than the promotion of women or men in either sphere.

In retrospect, education feminists to some extent have recognised the signif-icance of the public/private distinction but at the same time have tended on the whole to work with it rather than against it. Often a unitary category of 'woman' was described. Engagement with this essentially modernist distinction was left up to deconstructionist feminists who documented the *performative* and gendered elements of difference, identity and subjectivity within such a structure. Their analyses began to expose other systems of iden-tification (e.g. race, class, sexuality) as central elements at work in the production of female subordination.

The gendering of nationhood and national educational systems

A second theoretical problematic to be found in feminist political and social theory also contributes to our understanding of female citizenship in education. This problematic is tied largely to questions about the relationship between difference and concepts such as nationhood, social inclusion/exclusion, culture and identity. Using these concepts, feminist political theorists have critiqued democratic citizenship and exposed diverse forms of female marginalisation resulting from allegedly democratic practice.

In this model of analysis, feminist political theorists do not simply view citizenship as a masculine entity as it appears in the work of Carol Pateman. Rather, the goal is to examine how questions of nationhood, identity and the civil society impact on the nature and constitutive elements of women's marginalisation in an era of increasing globalisation and advanced modernisation. An additional goal is to explore the internal gendered dynamics of national politics and its impact on the political and social identities (and experiences) of culturally oppressed and differently positioned women (e.g. class, sexuality).

Some of the most interesting work in this area has been conducted by Nira Yuval-Davis (1997), Yuval-Davis and Anthias (1989) and Pieterse and Parekh (1995). Yuval-Davis (1997), for example, suggests that women are represented in nationalist discourses as romantic symbols of cultural morality who do not possess political agency, but who instead function as maternal catalysts of national identity in the broadest sense. She writes:

> Women are required to carry this burden of representation – the symbol bearers of the collectivity's identity and honour, both personally and collectively.... Girls did not need to act: they had to become the national embodiment.
>
> (Yuval-Davis, 1997: 105)

In this representation of identity, women are not given any formal role in the construction of the state; they are instead seen as keeper and cultivators of it. This implies a certain responsibility which is placed upon women to reproduce and cultivate in democratic subjects those dominant cultural values that are endorsed by those who dominate the political machinery (and indeed political memory) of the state. This 'reproductive' process leads to a cultural privileging that exalts not only the state's position on national identity but also women's position within it. In so doing, nationalist rhetoric not only privileges the dominance of male super-ordinance in state hierarchies but also represses, both epistemically and politically, the many cultural and national understandings that reside on the margins of the state. This legitimised practice of privileging also means that women who oppose or resist the dominant view of culture and nationhood are viewed as 'non-persons' or 'non-citizens'. The non-citizen ultimately comes to signify difference. As Yuval-Davis (1997: 5) writes:

The study of citizenship should consider the issue of women's citizenship not only by contrast to that of men but also in relation to women's affiliation to dominant or subordinate groups, their ethnicity, origin, and urban or rural residence. It also should take into consideration global and transnational positioning of these citizenships.

The work of Yuval-Davis (1997) raises key questions for feminist educationalists. First, such work focuses attention on the role of national rhetoric and symbolism in the formation of gender and cultural identities in education. It also exposes a link between the liberal democratic schooling project, globalisation, and gender in the broadest sense. It raises questions, for example, about the relationship between the social exclusion of particular groups of women (e.g. migrant women, indigenous women) through education and the restructuring of schooling in response to the modernisation of the nation-state and globalisation of the national economy.

Such political theory can also be used to consider the ways in which civic nationalism (as educational discourse) or neo-colonialism, which is manifested in liberal democratic practice, simultaneously conditions and undermines the cultural identities and representations of differently positioned women and men (girls and boys). It also sheds light on the ways in which political socialisation in education (e.g. patriotism through civic/citizenship education) is implicated in traditional and indeed racialised patterns of gender identity-formation.

In short, as was the case with Pateman's analysis of the public/private split, Yuval Davis (1997) and her colleagues pose some interesting questions for education feminists. We now turn to look at how educational research and theory has attempted to address feminist political and social theorist concerns with the question of gender, difference and national identity.

Education and national narratives

It goes without saying that questions about the female identity, difference and selfhood have preoccupied education feminists for at least a decade or so; this notwithstanding, such topics are typically viewed as unrelated to citizenship and/or nationhood. However, the most obvious place where such work can be found is in historical and feminist analyses of national, imperial and colonial education. For example, historians of education have exposed the role of national values in educating the 'daughters of the nation'. Anna Davin's (1978) analysis of imperialism and motherhood is an excellent example of this tradition. She argues that the reasons for educating women were not given in terms of their suffrage, nor their economic role, but as mothers of the nation, bearers of soldiers, workers and citizens. At the turn of the twentieth century, schools were specifically set up to educate mothers in the national interest of creating healthier workers and soldiers. The legacies of such ideologies were to be found in the official schoolgirls' curriculum, and in the forms of civic education developed after the Second World War even though women had defied such ideologies to contribute to the war effort themselves (Brindle and Arnot, 1999).

The construction, for example, of Englishness or indeed of the British Nation, was understood even more critically by Black writers and Black feminists working at the interface between humanist feminist models and deconstructionist models. The Centre for Contemporary Cultural Studies' (1982) text *The Empire Strikes Back* and Paul Gilroy's (1986) seminal text *There Ain't No Black in the Union Jack* set a new agenda for the political analysis of national identity and schooling. In this context, both Black and post-colonialist feminists began to explore the relationship between the liberal democratic education project, the multiple forms of racialised exclusions and the contruction of racialised 'otherness'. They also exposed the limits of the democratic education project in providing Black and minority ethnic youth with both a foundation and opportunity structure for full citizenship. These themes have been followed up by work conducted by Callender and Wright (this volume) and Mirza and Reay (this volume), who identify challenges posed to the colonial legacy of education by Black educators and Black cultural politics in local school settings. The concept of 'nation-space' has recently been taken up by white feminists aware of the ways in which schooling and its representations of nation construct gendered and racialised imaginaries (Gordon et al., this volume).

It could be argued that more recent feminist policy analyses of New Right educational reforms have highlighted similar concerns about the role of education in the construction of national identity. For example, feminist studies in education have exposed the ways in which state policies have constructed a notion of the teacher as male 'citizen worker' (see Dillabough, this volume) and the student as the 'male learner citizen' (see Foster, 1997). Such analyses identify the reinstatement of male-centred ideals through the implementation of teacher reforms and state regulating bodies. For example, the image of an ideal pupil and an ideal teacher emerging from state-centred assessments of the 'Standards Teacher' and the 'Competent Student' in the UK represent a view of 'citizen worker' and 'learner citizen' as the white rational, competent male.

These reform initiatives serve also to reconstitute the professional teacher as the moral authority on issues of 'nationhood' and national identity. This authority is visible to the extent to which 'difference' is denied in reform documentation and thus pushed to the margins of many national curriculum agendas (see Dillabough, 2000). For example, questions of gender, race, class, and/or sexuality and disability and the kinds of national identities he/she is expected to shape are not addressed in the context of the 'standards/competent' teacher.

Such issues are important and they do speak, at least indirectly, to feminist political theorists' concerns about, for example, those who are defined by the nation-state as 'deviant', 'other' and the 'non-citizen'. Education feminism has therefore diverted attention away from the racist notion that cultural pluralism is a social ill which needs remediation. This has involved challenging curriculum and reforms which imply a de-gendered and 'static national culture' and instead identifying the state (particularly black, post-colonial and deconstruction feminism) 'as a condition in itself [made up] of complex multiple identities – a situation which increasingly reflects the global human condition' (Pieterse and Parekh, 1995, our addition)

Arguably, many of the critical questions raised by feminist political theorists still remain unanswered, particularly those which concern the nation-state and its impact on the role of education for citizenship. For example, whilst humanist feminists and, to some extent, deconstructionist feminists have addressed difference and national identity, they have not examined how gender politics evolve within dynamic educational cultures in the nation-state, especially those national contexts associated with rapid social and political change. As a consequence, there is still no certainty that new models of liberal democratic education serve as an appropriate social mechanism for providing diverse forms of female citizenship, particularly for differently positioned women constructed as 'other'. In fact, one could argue that all three feminist traditions identified by Voet (1998) (humanist, women-centred, deconstructionist) have failed to build a stronger and more emancipated school structure because of their preoccupation with identity and 'self' over and above a concern for the development of a political citizenship which accounts for women's differences.

'Woman' as a political category

The third theoretical problematic which we identified within feminist political theory is a concern with the ways in which women's roles and social practices have been represented as political categories in the polity, especially those associated with the democratic state. Does the state support a formal view of women as political agents, or do women have historically determined 'apolitical' roles in a democracy? Are women still seen, as they were at the early stages of the suffragist movement, as 'benevolent philanthropists'[3] or are they political actors who possess agency in their own right?

Such questions are addressed by feminist political theorists and philosophers who are concerned with the epistemological significance of women's representation in both political theory and the state. For example, the feminist political philosopher Roland Martin argues that the category 'woman' has been erased from politics and political theory:

> Women, children and the family dwell in the 'ontological basement', outside and underneath the political structure. This apolitical status is due not to historical accident or necessity but to arbitrary definition [...]. Since the subject matter of political theory is politics and since reproductive processes have been traditionally assigned to women and have taken place within the family, it follows that women and the family are excluded from the very subject matter of the discipline.
>
> (1994: 107–108)

Roland Martin's description of women's 'apolitical status' in the state leads to a historically determined and socially constructed vision of womanhood – that of *benevolent actor* and *virtuous being*. In this context, women, as mothers and care-givers, are constructed against the grain of formal political action and are, therefore, seen as outsiders to the political process.

By contrast, the category 'woman', as described by Iris Marion Young (1995), not only illuminates a vision of women as 'political' in the formal sense but also points to women's collective resistance to more conventional definitions of political participation. Women are, therefore, seen as motivated political actors in their own right. Young writes:

> One reason to conceptualize women as a collective, I think, is to maintain a point of view outside of liberal individualism [. . .] Without conceptualizing women as a group in some sense, it is not possible to conceptualize oppression in a systematic, structured institutional process.
>
> (1995: 192)

Women are thus placed at the centre of democratic politics as a form of gendered resistance to masculine conceptions of the state. This oppositional practice is designed to challenge those liberal assumptions which view women as the 'victim', conflate the categories 'women' and 'domesticity' and ultimately function to exclude women from full political participation.

In such polarised representations, we find binary images of the category 'women': on the one hand, a daughter of the nation state thought to instill a moral 'ethics of care' (Gilligan, 1982, 1986) in society through her connection to the private sphere; and on the other hand, an active *social* agent with membership in a political collectivity. At first glance, such contemporary visions appear irreconcilable and indeed contradictory. Nevertheless, they bear some relevance to current understandings of democracy. For example, the notion of women as daughters of the nation state invokes symbolic images of care in the maintenance of democratic relations. At the same time, Young's description of the feminist collectivity points to an image of female agents who actively participate in the reconstruction of a democracy.

Both humanist and deconstructionist political theorists have justifiably exposed both these images as problematic because they essentialise women in unacceptable ways. However, revealing such problems does not necessarily lead to a stronger theoretical analysis of women's political position in the state or state education. It is our argument therefore that a feminist political/social analysis (rather than simply a deconstructionist analysis) of the varied and sometimes conflicting categories of 'womanhood' provides an alternative lens through which to examine the relationship between gender and democracy. This kind of analysis implies the need to unravel the complex web of relations which underpin questions about women's inclusion and participation in a democracy. However, in confronting such issues, one must go beyond a simple examination of 'woman' as a gender category in order to address Iris Young's (1995) interest in *women's relation to the 'political'*. The simplest and arguably most powerful mechanism for achieving this end is to examine the potential links between the *feminist project* and *democratic principles.* In so doing, one learns that democratic concepts, such as equality, do not necessarily converge at the centre of all feminist projects and do not apply to the history of all women's struggles. Nor is it necessarily the case that all women define their politics in relation to the liberal democratic project. Wilson (1995: 8) writes:

> It is not . . . possible to say that [feminism] is a commitment to equality, since some feminists have argued, both in the past and today, for separate spheres of influence, emphasizing difference and complementarity rather than equality.

In short, feminist political theorists have raised questions about the suspected and elusive character of 'equality' and its contradictory role in the 'emancipation' of women. They have also exposed the gendered classifications which manifest the 'male-oriented' trajectory of liberal democratic thought. Indeed, such efforts have called into question the very structures of liberal democratic thinking and their role in the formation of gender identities. In our view, such insights can be used, for example, to critique state education and its regulation of women and girls' (and men and boys') political identities. We might also ask how a political and social analysis of gender categories might force us to question the very precepts of democratic educational practice.

Deconstructionist feminism and the political category 'woman'

The notion of 'woman' as a political category has had much exposure in education, although both humanist feminists and women-centred feminists have focused less on the study of the category itself (as feminist political theorists have) and more on facilitating its representation in schools and education. Within education, the feminist tradition most concerned with critiquing the category 'woman' is feminist deconstruction. Our discussion focuses largely on this tradition and assesses whether it has addressed concerns raised by feminist political theorists about the category 'women' and its link to liberal democratic theory.

Feminist post-structuralists have attempted to take up the questions posed by Foucault (1977) about liberal democracy by assessing the degree to which education had emerged as a state form of identity regulation. For example, such work sought to confirm the assumption that schools, as local sites, play a significant role in reconstituting the nature of gender politics in society (see Walkerdine and Lucey, 1989) and what we understand democracy to be. It also challenged the normative and universalistic assumptions thought to characterise 'democratic' schooling and its apparent role in women/girls' emancipation. In that sense, it has responded precisely to the problematic which emerges in endorsing either a unitary category of womanhood (e.g. women centred feminism) or feminist positions which are more deterministic in their explanations about women's marginal status in the state (e.g. humanist feminisms).

For example, Valerie Walkerdine and Helen Lucey (1989) illustrated how modern education fosters the development of normative liberal ideals which regulate women's and girls identities, and ultimately, democratic citizenship. They demonstrated, for example, that primary school teachers are positioned within liberal discourses which not only construct, but regulate, the 'good female teacher' and 'student'. Using Foucault, they described the female teacher as one who monitors and regulates the development of democratic concepts such as 'free-will' through educational discourse, thus encouraging support for the democratic order using 'non-coercive strategies'. The promotion of this discourse is a 'management technique' in which students are encouraged to accept, as 'normal', modern forms of liberal democratic governance and the ideal of the 'bourgeois individual'. Walkerdine (1986: 63) writes:

> It is women, whose sexuality itself is regulated to produce 'normal femininity', who become the central prop of the new form of pedagogy. Teachers trained in psychology, were to assume the entire responsibility for the 'freedom' of children, and for the continuous maintenance of the bourgeois democratic order. I want, therefore, to demonstrate that women, positioned as teachers, mothers, carers and caring professionals are held absolutely necessary for the moral order. [. . .] It places them as responsible for ensuring the possibility of democracy, and yet as deeply conservative. My argument is that . . . women of all classes have been placed as guardians of an order which is to difficult to escape. If you are told you are totally responsible for the nature of the child and with it, therefore, the possibility of freedom, of democracy – how much guilt and pain is involved resisting such a notion?

The circulation of liberal democratic ideals (e.g. freedom) in schools positioned women teachers within a discourse of 'correct mothering' which *ultimately* cast responsibility upon them for the reconstitution of gender identities in schools, only one of which was 'the right citizen'.

Much deconstructionist feminist educational research has also highlighted, through individualised narratives, the processes of social exclusion, particularly in relation to those constructed as 'other' (lesbian, gay, disabled). At the same time, such research has resisted the categorisation of public/private, or classifications such as male and female, preferring to report them as discursive entities, which permanently shift and are reconstituted. Consequently, for many feminist post-structuralists in education, to claim a political identity, to lay the foundations of a new democratic project for women, or even engage in identity politics as part of democratic practice is to engage in an act of *repression*: 'the subject is an instance of mastery, of narrative closure, of the freezing of a process of difference/differance' (see Weir, 1997: 25). Identities must therefore be seen as discursively constructed through the language of democracy rather than shaped directly by democratic relations or social forces. In this context, identities must always be seen as sites of 'open political contest' (see Butler, 1995) and as a struggle to identify with political hierarchies which are framed by democratic discourse in school spaces. Such approaches are useful reminders of the none too simple relationship between the official *discourses* which underlie the democratic education project and gender identity-formation.

Whilst post-structural work has had an enormous impact on how gender is conceptualised in education, we wish to suggest that it also poses difficulties for any feminist conceptualisation of citizenship. For example, it appears as though the incompatibilities revealed between what Voet called humanist feminist political theory (liberal, radical and socialist feminists) and theories of citizenship more generally are not necessarily resolved by contemporary post-structural and post-modernist narratives about democratic schooling. Indeed, the contemporary versions of gender, often described as a free-floating linguistic entity, were no less problematic politically. This is largely because in feminist theories of deconstruction any notion of women's action or agency was viewed as a liberal commitment to masculine forms of autonomy and freedom. Women could no longer act politically in their own name.

One could also argue that deconstructionist feminists have failed to address key concerns about the role of a collective citizenry in challenging state practices because of an intense preoccupation with the study of the female 'self' extracted out of a meaningful social context. Post-structuralism, in emphasising the authentic identity, has therefore sometimes inadvertently aligned itself with neo-liberal views which ignore the potential for seeing the self as part of a social or collective element of the polity. As Weir (1997: 1990) writes:

> once we get to the point where we reject any abstraction of the individual from contexts, and reject any postulation of the individual's capacity for reflection on contexts, we effectively deny any capacity of agents to criticize and change those contexts.

The ability of feminists to speak on behalf of, and in the name of, women thus becomes more difficult. Clearly, socialist feminists and their counterparts in education (i.e. the humanist strand) had very different agendas.

A feminist framework for the study of citizenship

Voet argues that citizenship theorists in education tend to dismiss feminist concerns on the basis that they have little to do with matters of citizenship. Feminist political theories are sometimes understood to be concerned with the private, personal and the particular and therefore have little relevance to such 'public' issues. The distanced relationship between feminist political theorists and feminist educationalists can only add to the marginalised position in which feminists find themselves in relation to public political discourses. The lack of dialogue between feminist political and educational theorists has also meant that important research questions about the political role of schooling in late modernity are not being addressed sufficiently at a time when issues concerning, for example, identity, social exclusion and new forms of government are at the centre of international public concern.

Feminist social and political theory, we have argued, provides invaluable conceptual tools for re-examining liberal democracy and the democratic education. Critiques of liberal democracy encourage educationalists to address key questions about female citizenship which have been neglected in education feminism to date. They also highlight precisely where education feminists have made important political contributions to the study of a gendered citizenry.

The three theoretical problematics derived from a feminist political analysis of liberal democracy suggest that female citizenship, as a concept, has largely been constructed within a male logic and has therefore remained on the outside of a relevant and just understanding of female participation in the state. The female citizen within such political discourses (and problematics) has, on the whole, been constructed as marginal. The dismantling of such a concept requires, therefore, more than a dialogue with feminist political thought. It suggests the need for alternative concepts of female citizenship, outside the 'master narratives' of liberal democratic logic.

It is with these concerns in mind that we may wish to ask what we have learnt from political theory which help us engage afresh with educational issues. In our view, such lessons are both practical and epistemological since they demand consideration not only in educational theory, but in the context of schooling. Some of the most transformative feminist engagements with schooling have been the development of such practices as feminist critical pedagogy, women-centred education, and the development of feminist educational policy. However, it is still not clear how we might theorise such initiatives, the development of women's collective forms of consciousness as a result of such educational reforms, or the role of female political strategies in the formation of women's citizenship.

Understanding female citizenship in education requires, first, a study of the ways in which both women and men and girls and boys attempt to resolve contradictions about the public, private and nationhood within schools from the point of view of consciousness and social collectives. This demands that we posture female citizens within educational theory as active agents who engage in the act of mutual recognition through a process we refer to as *reflexive solidarity*. Such recognition necessitates social mediation and solidarity with a collective form of female consciousness (however diverse) which ultimately allows women, through reflection upon others' social circumstances, to make sense of their own position in the state.

Second we need to recognise, as deconstructionist feminists have suggested, that gender is not a singular identity and, therefore, cannot be viewed in isolation when studying the female citizen in education. This implies the recognition of the processes of differentiation within identity formation (the creation of what we might call *differentiated identities*) where women acknowledge their relationship to others as central to defining themselves as citizens

(Lister, 1997). To simply conceptualise identity as an authentic subject may lead to a negative conception of female citizenship, one which cannot account for social difference on a broad scale, but also one that ignores social consciousness and the act of reflection and social mediation.

In raising these conceptual issues we wish to suggest that it is no longer possible for educational feminism to take for granted definitions of democracy based upon liberal principles, nor can we base democratic politics on the interests of women as women in the simplest of senses. As Chantal Mouffe (1992) argues, old versions of citizenship have become an obstacle to making democracy work for women in a more genuinely inclusive way. It is time to change the ways in which we struggle for democracy in education – to abandon the 'lion's skin' and construct new definitions of citizenship which are based upon the needs of contemporary women. Clearly, this work must move beyond a feminist engagement with voice, subjectivity and difference. It must also examine how political formations and social constraints structure the relationship between gender and democracy in education. One task for feminists is, therefore, to problematise the gendered premises of democratic education drawing upon the concerns raised by feminist political theorists, whilst still defending a 'radical democracy' (Fraser, 1996) which accords women political agency and the possibility of solidarity without repressing difference. This is no easy task but we believe it is one well worth defending as we move forward in the study of gender, citizenship and democracy.

Acknowledgements

We are grateful for the support given to Jo-Anne Dillabough by the Social Sciences and Humanities Research Council of Canada, and to the Leverhulme Trust for the research fellowship granted to Madeleine Arnot for this work. We would also like to thank Jane Gaskell and Wendy Luttrell for comments on an early draft of this paper. The arguments in this paper are described more extensively in Arnot and Dillabough (1999).

Notes

1   Phillips (1992) calls this Wollstonecraft's dilemma.
2   Voet's goal in identifying these strands is to frame feminism within broader political processes, but the classification is also helpful in pointing to historical shifts in the relation of feminist theory to citizenship. This set of distinctions is not dissimilar from that which we constructed between, on the one hand, *rationalistic*, and on the other, *relational* feminist theories of education (Dillabough and Arnot, 2000 forthcoming). We too consider the shift, which Voet outlines, away from modernist towards deconstructionist (post-modernist and post-structuralist) analyses as highly significant – in this case for the framing of feminist democratic discourses in education.
3   See Ryan (1997) on the subject of 'benevolent philanthropy'.

References

Acker, S. (1994) *Gendered Education: sociological reflections on women*, Buckingham: Open University Press.

Arnot, M. and Dillabough, J. (1999) 'Feminist politics and democratic values in education', *Curriculum Inquiry*, 29, 2: 159–190.

Arnot, M. and Weiner, G. (eds) (1987) *Gender and the Politics of Schooling*, London: Hutchinson.

Benhabib, S. (1995) 'Feminism and postmodernism', in S. Benhabib, J. Butler, D. Cornell and N. Fraser (eds) *Feminist Contentions: a philosophical exchange*, New York: Routledge.

Bourdieu, P. and Passeron, C. (1977) *Reproduction in Education, Society and Culture*, London: Sage.

Brindle, P. and Arnot, M. (1999) 'England expects every man to do his duty: the gendering of the citizenship textbook 1940–1966', *Oxford Review of Education*, 25, 1&2: 103–123.

Butler, J. (1995) 'Contingent foundations. in S. Benhabib, J. Butler, D. Cornell and N. Fraser (eds) *Feminists Theorise the Political*, London and New York: Routledge.

Centre for Contemporary Cultural Studies (1982) *The Empire Strikes Back: race and racism in 70s Britain*, London: Hutchinson.

Davin, A. (1978) 'Imperialism and motherhood', *History Workshop Journal*, 5: 9–65.

Dietz, M. G. (1985) 'Citizenship with a feminist face: the problem with maternal thinking', *Political Theory*, February: 19–37.

Dillabough, J. (1999) 'Gender politics and conceptions of the modern teacher: women, identity, and professionalism', *British Journal of Sociology of Education*, 20, 3: 373–394.

Dillabough, J. (2000) 'Degrees of freedom and deliberations of "self"'. In P. Trifonds (ed.), *Revolutionary Pedagogies: cultural politics, instituting education, and the discourse of today*, Routledge Falmer: New York.

Dillabough, J. A. and Arnot, M. (2000 forthcoming) 'Feminist sociology of education: dynamics, debates and directions', in J. Demaine (ed.) *Sociology of Education Today*, London: Macmillan.

Ellsworth, E. (1997) *Teaching Positions: difference, pedagogy and the power of address*, New York: Teachers College Press.

Elshtain, J. Bethke (1981) *Public Man, Private Woman: women in social and political thought*, Princeton, N.J.: Princeton University Press.

Foster, V. (1997) 'Feminist theory and the construction of citizenship education', in K. Kennedy (ed.) *Citizenship, Education and the Modern State*, London: Falmer Press.

Foucault, M. (1977) *Discipline and Punish: the birth of the prison*, London: Allan Lane.

Fraser, N. (1996) 'Equality, difference and radical democracy', in D. Trend (ed.) *Radical Democracy: identity, citizenship and the state*, New York: Routledge.

Gilligan, C. (1982) *In a Different Voice: psychological theory and women's development*, Cambridge, Mass.: Harvard University Press.

Gilligan, C. (1986) 'Moral orientation and moral development' in E. Kitty and D. Meyers (eds) *Women and Moral Theory*, New Jersey: Rowman and Littlefield

Gilroy P. (1986) *There Ain't No Black in the Union Jack*, London: Hutchinson.

Holland, J., Ramazanoglu, C., Sharpe, S. and Thomson, R. (1998) *The Male in the Head: young people, heterosexuality and power*, London: Tufnell.

Jagger, A. M. (1983) *Feminist Politics and Human Nature*, Rowman and Allanheld. Sussex: Harvester Press.

Lister, R. (1997) *Citizenship: feminist perspectives*, London: Macmillan Press.

Luke, C. and Gore, J. (eds) (1989) *Feminisms and Critical Pedagogy*, New York: Routledge.

Mahoney, P. (1985) *Schools for the Boys*, London: Hutchinson.

McInnes, J. (1998) *The End of Masculinity: the confusion of sexual genesis and sexual difference in modern society*, Buckingham: Open University Press.

Middleton, S. (1987) 'Sociology of Women's Education', in M. Arnot and G. Weiner (eds) *Gender and the Politics of Schooling*, London: Hutchinson.

Mouffe, C. (1992) 'Feminism, citizenship and radical democratic politics', in J. Butler and J. W. Scott (eds) *Feminists Theorise the Political*, New York: Routledge.

Pateman, C. (1988) *The Sexual Contract*, Cambridge, Polity Press.

Pateman, C. (1989) *The Disorder of Women*, Cambridge, Polity Press.

Pateman, C. (1992) 'Equality, difference, subordination: the politics of motherhood and women's citizenship', pp. 17–31, in G. Bock and S. James (eds) *Beyond Equality and Difference: citizenship, feminist politics and female subjectivity*, London: Routledge.

Phillips, A. (1992) *Democracy and Difference*, Cambridge: Polity Press.

Pieterse, J. N. and Parekh, B. (eds) (1995) *The Decolonisation of Imagination: culture, knowledge and power*, London: Zed Books.

Roland Martin, J. (1994 [1982]) 'Excluding women from the educational realm', in L. Stone (ed.) *The Education Feminism Reader*, New York: Routledge.

Ryan, B. (1997) *Feminism and the Women's Movement: dynamics of change in social movement ideology and activism*, New York: Routledge.

Stone, L. (1994) (ed.) *The Education Feminism Reader*, New York: Routledge.

Voet, R. (1998) *Feminism and Citizenship*, London: Sage.

Walkerdine, V. (1986). 'Post-structuralist theory and everyday social practices', in V. Walkerdine (ed.) *Feminist Social Psychology*, Milton Keynes: Open University Press.

Walkerdine, V. and Lucey, H. (1989) *Democracy in the Kitchen*, London: Virago.

Weiner, G. (1994) *Feminism in Education: an introduction*, Buckingham: Open University Press.

Weiner, G. (1989) 'Professional self-knowledge versus social justice: a critical analysis of the teacher-researcher movement', *British Educational Research Journal*, 15, 1: 41–51.

Weir, A. (1997) *Sacrificial Logics: feminist theory and the critique of identity*, New York: Routledge.

Wilson, E. (1995) first published 1986. *Hidden Agendas: theory, politics and experience in the women's movement*, London: Tavistock Publications.

Young, I. M. (1995) 'Gender as seriality: thinking about women as a social collective', in L. Nicholson and S. Seidman (eds) *Social Postmodernism*, Cambridge: Cambridge University Press.

Yuval-Davis, N. (1997) *Gender and Nation*, London: Sage.

Yuval-Davis, N. and Anthias, F. (1989) *Woman-Nation-State*, London: Macmillan.

3   Citizenship, identity and social justice

The intersection of feminist and post-colonial discourses

Ann Brooks

This chapter examines the intersection of feminist and post-colonial discourses for debates in the areas of citizenship, identity, social justice and difference. In particular, it explores the centrality of concepts such as citizenship and identity in understanding the challenges posed by feminist and post-colonial perspectives to modernist Western conceptions of liberal democracy and social justice. It also explores the intersection of postmodernism with feminism in framing these challenges, and shows how, recently, these concepts have provided the tools for the understanding of difference. The chapter also attempts to demonstrate how questions of citizenship have become increasingly complex, requiring new frameworks of analysis and new conceptualisations of subjectivity and political subjecthood. The focus of the chapter is, therefore, first on how feminists construct new frameworks for the analysis of citizenship and, second, on what post-colonial perspectives offer feminist writers attempting to understand the politics of citizenship.

The first part of the chapter explores the intersection of feminism and post-colonialism, and examines the relationship of these two theoretical traditions to postmodernism. It also considers the impact that all three theoretical perspectives have had on the reconsideration of the concept of selfhood and empancipatory politics in late modernity. Drawing on these theoretical debates, the political dilemmas generated by these theories are examined in two post-colonial contexts – that of New Zealand and of Australia. In the case of New Zealand, I examine the conflicts associated with the position of contemporary struggles of Maori and the bipolar politics which frame contemporary politics in Aotearoa[1]/New Zealand. I then go on to consider Australian feminist debates around the 'politics of inclusion' in relation to issues of citizenship, diversity and difference. Throughout the chapter, consideration is given to the theoretical and political impact of 'post-colonial thinking' on issues which concern gender, education and citizenship.

The intersections of feminism, post-colonialism and postmodernism

Post-colonialism and feminism have parallel yet distinct theoretical histories and concerns. Ashcroft et al. (1995: 249) comment:

Feminist and post-colonial discourses both seek to reinstate the margin-alised in the face of the dominant, and early feminist theory, like early nationalist post-colonial criticism, was concerned with inverting the structures of domination, substituting for instance, a female tradition or traditions for a male dominated canon. But like post-colonial criticism, feminist theory has rejected such simple inversions in favour of a more general questioning of forms and modes, and the unmasking of the spuri-ously author/itative on which such canonical constructions are founded.

One of the contributions of post-colonial thinking is its critique of those Second Wave feminisms which suggested that patriarchal and imperialist oppressions were universally experienced oppressions. Gunew and Yeatman (1993) show how post-colonialism, which they describe as a loosely defined body of theories, created a theoretical space in which those who had been excluded from Western metaphysics could speak. They argue that together with poststructuralism, post-colonialism 'gives us the tools to deconstruct these homogenizing categories so that it is possible to admit difference, not simply as the self confirming other, but as the admission and recognition of incom-mensurabilities' (ibid.: xiii). This new 'politics of difference' does not support pluralism *per se* but rather 'implies incommensurable differences which cannot be subsumed under one universal category' (ibid.). There is a need therefore to 'organise around local allegiances in order to dismantle once again the universal models, which however benign they may appear, work ultimately to confirm the old power structures, whether these be patriarchies or neo-imperialisms' (Gunew and Yeatman 1993: xiv). Feminism, therefore, 'repre-sents one interesting possibility within the politics of difference that has emerged as an important site of political mobilisation' (Spoonley 1995a: 64) in late modernity.

Feminism, post-colonialism and postmodernism have all experienced an upsurge of theoretical development in the last two decades (Ashcroft et al. 1995: 117). They share the goal of dismantling or subverting dominant hege-monic discourses, challenging traditional epistemologies and re-establishing marginal discourses. For example, intersections of feminist and post-colonialist theoretical debates have challenged existing disciplinary boundaries and paradigms and established a new political and cultural agenda for the 1990s. Their challenges to liberal humanist conceptions of subjectivity have, in turn, been accelerated by the postmodern critique of the Enlightenment discourses of modernity and 'their foundation in universal reason'. Yeatman (1994) contends that an acceptance of the reality of the postmodern condition neces-sitates a relinquishing of any nostalgic commitment to modern(ist) standards of reflection and critique. However, she also argues that postmodernism's emancipatory politics is fundamentally pragmatic, oriented as it is to the 'contemporary politics of movements which have adopted and reshaped the modern(ist) imaginary of self-determination' (Yeatman 1994: 6). The paral-lels between postmodernism and post-colonialism are most clearly demarcated when they operate critically. As Yeatman (1994: 9) notes, such linkages have led to a postmodern and post-colonial feminist analysis, and reformulations of, for example, the institutional infrastructure of modern capitalism within a postmodern frame of reference and the univocalism and monoculturalism of the modernist rationalist project. They have invoked, in turn, a politics of voice and representation establishing 'creative forms of positive resistance to various types of domination'.

Seen from a different perspective, the contribution of feminism to post-colonialist (and postmodernist) discourses arguably has given these traditions an even more critical edge. For example, Hutcheon (1995: 130) suggests that while post-colonialism emphasises the relationship between imperialism and the construction of identities, and postmodernism stresses the relationship between liberal humanism and subjectivity, 'feminists point to the patriarchal underpinnings of both'. Hutcheon goes on to argue that post-colonialism and feminism have 'political agendas and often a theory of agency that allows them to go beyond the post-modern limits of deconstructing (on its own) existing orthodoxies into the realms of social and political action' (ibid.). Feminism, therefore, has the capacity to expose major differences in the orientation and discourses of post-colonialism and postmodernism (Hutcheon 1995: 131). Although some similarities can be found in these two traditions, as Hutcheon observes, 'this does not mean that the two can be conflated unproblematically as many commentators seem to suggest' (Slemon 1988). The relationships, therefore, between these three theoretical discourses are complex and interactive and arguably are seen more visibly in some political contexts than others.

Citizenship, social justice and emancipatory politics

Yeatman (1993, 1995a) has taken the lead in exploring the impact of postmodernism and post-colonialism on feminist emancipatory politics, especially in forcing it to investigate both 'the genealogy' and 'status of oppression as a category of a modern politics of emancipation' (1995a: 45). She notes that Second Wave feminism initially subscribed to an 'emancipatory politics which made claims to the idea of a universal conception of oppression and oppressed subject' (ibid.). This stance confirmed the view of Second Wave feminism that humanist values of freedom and equality should be 'inclusive' of all emancipatory movements. And, as Yeatman argues, 'when working-class, feminist and anti-colonial movements are oriented in this way, they subsume the specificity of their struggles within the general project of advancement of humanity' (1995a: 51).

Recent shifts of emphasis towards a politics of difference have had implications for issues of citizenship, social justice and such politics. For example, the interpellation of different identity groups (for example, women, the colonised), drawing upon modernist discourses of liberty, freedom and equality, has shaped emancipatory movements. Arguably, the work of such movements has led to a very high degree of formal inclusion in the state (Yeatman 1995a: 49). It could, therefore, be argued that discriminatory discourses 'against any subject on the basis of characteristics unrelated to capacities for citizenship: sex, religion, ethnicity, race, age, sexual preference' (ibid.) are no longer tolerated in contemporary society at least as far as the formal rhetoric of legislation is concerned. Yeatman goes on to note that: 'ours is the age of the formal completion of the modern ideal of a universalistic humanity' (ibid.). The implications of this are that exclusionary practices still operate but in more subtle ways. As a consequence, while the dominant modes of social participation have become open to the 'excluded subjects of modernity' (ibid.), in reality only a minority from marginalised or excluded subject groups actually find a political voice.

'Interlocking oppressions'[2]

The study of what Yeatman called a system of 'interlocking oppressions' (the interlinking of a range of oppressions experienced by women, the colonised and indigenous groups) has been facilitated considerably by the intersection of the discourses around feminism, postmodernism and post-colonialism in the 1980s. This discursive intersection has provided an intellectually vibrant landscape in which it has become possible to develop a pluralist model in which multiply oppressed-subjects, according to Yeatman, can now claim the 'multiplicity of their oppressed subject status' (Yeatman 1995a: 53). The new 'feminist pluralism' of the 1990s, with its emphasis on multiplicity, heterogeneity and difference, also suggests that both the universal subject and the national community are 'internally fractured'. At the same time, such fracturing can be found in feminism's own identity as a movement representing the interests of diverse women.

The nature of a humanist emancipatory politics has in the past meant that a person could be positioned, for example, as both black and female but she most likely had to subscribe to 'the most heavily marked of these identities and its politics' (ibid.: 53). A black woman or a working-class woman therefore had to subscribe to either a Black or working-class status and to the 'contestation' of one of these identities. In each case, 'the feminine subject within the oppressed race or class was asked to subordinate her own distinctive claims to what would further the well being and good of the whole race or class' (ibid.: 53). The implications of these 'positionings' for a feminism dominated by white, middle-class women were clear; they were the only group 'whose subject status threw into relief the condition of women as a marked term and oppressed group' (ibid.). The form of politics which emerged from this version of emancipatory politics valorised separatism since it advanced 'an identity claim on behalf of a group in a way which denies reciprocity or respect for its others' (Yeatman 1995b: 197).

This type of 'separatist' or 'identity politics' can be identified in both feminist and bicultural movements. An example of biculturalism, despite the contested nature of the territory, can be applied to the concept of cultural difference in Aotearoa/New Zealand and the relations between Maori and Pakeha.[3] For example, Wilson and Yeatman, in their text *Justice and Identity: Antipodean Practices* (1995), claim that 'Maori and Pakeha constantly run the risk of overlooking both New Zealanders who fall outside this binary and the complexities within these two identities'. They also raise the question of how adequate a bicultural policy and practice can be without being part of a 'multi-cultural policy and practice' (Wilson and Yeatman 1996: viii).

Within a framework of Maori separatism, there were claims to the privilege of sovereign selfhood which were not dissimilar to the claims for privileged subject status from privileged groups. What is at issue, and what is problematic about such a politics is, as Yeatman contends, that such claim to sovereign selfhood seems to 'deny reciprocal respect for that same claim on behalf of others' (Yeatman 1995b: 97). In similar ways, feminist separatists appear to have denied the rights of men to sovereign selfhood:

> Feminist separatists who have designed a moral universe that excludes men operate in such a way as to deny justice. The same occurs when Maori separatists make identity claims that seem to deny the historical fact of Maori co-existence with Pakeha.
>
> (ibid.)

Both movements – feminism and bicultural politics – offer alternative conceptions of selfhood which are characterised by what Bartky (1990) calls an 'ethical ambiguity'. Interestingly both feminist and post-colonial theorists of difference reject the concept of the unified sovereign self in favour of 'a selfhood that is contradictory, hybridised and disjunctive' (Yeatman 1995b: 208). At the same time, as Yeatman shows, feminist and post-colonial theorists do not 'abandon the claim to sovereign selfhood with claims for a post-colonial or feminist self' (ibid.: 208). The newer concept of self contests 'the oppressed subject positioning that specifies the terms of the selfhood' (ibid.). Post-colonial and feminist theorists of difference thus challenge the very conception of 'modern sovereign selfhood' by rejecting 'the premise of indivisibility' (Yeatman 1995b: 209) which is expressed in a notion of the free and sovereign identity.

Finally, in discussing the issue of intersubjectivity as pivotal for an inclusive conception of citizenship, Yeatman explores the notion of intersubjectivity in the context of Maori/Pakeha relations in post-colonial Aotearoa/New Zealand. She argues that:

> . . . the historically sustained and complex imbrication of Maori and Pakeha histories, one in the other, in New Zealand/Aotearoa marks the identities of both Maori and Pakeha in virtually all contexts of life. It is not just the reciprocal imbrication of these histories in a practical sense that is at issue. For this imbrication to constitute the basis of an intersubjective relationship, both subjects have to make a positive acceptance of this imbrication, and of the differentiation of identity, on which it is predicated. The relationship of difference and identification between Maori and Pakeha is enormously complex, and it implicates the histories of kin, localities, regions, institutions as of nation itself.
>
> (Yeatman 1996: 3)

The 'politics of difference' as outlined by Gunew and Yeatman (1993) is one which alleges a strict binary oppositional logic. A number of feminist theorists working in the area of feminism and post-colonialism have come to similar conclusions. Larner (1993), in her analysis of bicultural politics in New Zealand, suggests that New Zealand needs to move beyond the bicultural model of Maori–Pakeha differences. Trinh T. Minh-ha, an American Vietnamese feminist theorist, deconstructs the Western model of 'individuated subjectivity' which posits a conception of the 'self' in opposition to, and in hierarchical relation to, 'other'. Trinh (1989) suggests that, 'in a society where they remain constantly at odds on occupied territories, women can only situate their social spaces precariously in the interstices of diverse systems of ownership'. She goes on to state that women need to cut across borders rather than fetishising themselves 'in a spectacle of difference' which, in the end, 'disavows difference'.

Increasingly, therefore, feminists have argued for the conception of the 'sovereign self' (see Brooks, 1997) to be 'replaced by much more constrained and localised notions of "subject"' (Flax, 1998b). As a consequence, a new language has developed around the relationship between subject, subjectivity and subject position. There is now a recognition that the subject's autonomy is more than a mutual recognition of the subjectivity of others; it is based upon the subject's independence from others (see Yeatman, 1996: 9). If emancipatory politics is to involve a 'democratic politics of co-existence' of the sort proposed by Yeatman, then the subject must be capable of achieving intersubjective[4] relations with others (see Benjamin 1995). Implicit in this conception of intersubjectivity is a subject who acknowledges and addresses difference. As Yeatman (1996: 4–5) comments:

> In our current postcolonial and postpatriarchal world, those who the sovereign subject cast as its others to know and master have insisted on their becoming subjects in their own right. When women and indigenous peoples insist on their own subject presence within the life of the democratic polity they radically illuminate the fact that political subjects can be very different from each other in who they are, and what they demand of politics. In doing so, they put on the table so to speak this conception of politics as a project of working out the terms of co-existence between differently positioned subjects.

The essence of a democratic politics based on intersubjectivity is an understanding and accommodation of difference which is situated within particular personal histories. Emancipatory politics, Yeatman (1996: 15) argues, therefore becomes 'a bond or tie of citizenship' – 'a politico-ethical orientation' which can form the basis of the intersubjectivity of subjects.

In the next two sections, the themes of intersubjectivity and inclusion are further explored in relation to specific national examples of emancipatory politics. The first section looks at Maori–Pakeha relations in post-colonial Aotearoa/New Zealand;[5] the second section focuses on the 'politics of inclusion' as a dimension of the Australian political framework.

Indigenous feminist theorising and bicultural politics in Aotearoa/New Zealand

The 'politics of difference' as advocated by Gunew and Yeatman (1993) is not necessarily one subscribed to by those adopting an indigenous feminist perspective in Aotearoa/New Zaland or elsewhere. As Larner (1995: 177) points out 'many New Zealand feminists both Maori and Pakeha have become concerned with the task of establishing an autonomous existence premised on unique identities'. The historical particularities of Maori/Pakeha relations in New Zealand and the specificity of the Treaty of Waitangi[6] in constructing those relations has influenced the nature of political relations in New Zealand, establishing bicultural forms of nationalism and feminism. As Larner comments:

> . . . 'difference' in New Zealand is often understood as involving a distinction between the experiences of Maori women, who are descendants of indigenous tribal groups, and Pakeha women, who are the descendants of colonising settlers. This bipolar understanding, which emphasises cultural and ethnic differences, reflects the specificity of developments within local versions of feminism. Maori feminists have forced the majority of Pakeha feminists to acknowledge, and to understand, that there is more than one way of interpreting gender relations . . . Integral to these discussions have been deliberations over the forms that feminist politics and theorising should take in a bicultural society.
>
> (1995: 177–178)

While recognising the importance of historical and cultural specificity in understanding feminist theorising, the implications of the bipolarity of perspectives can lead to a position which 'accepts the notion of pre-given, or pre-constituted identities and rests on assumptions about the authenticity of experience' (ibid.: 178). The distinction made by Meaghan Morris (1992) is an important one here. Morris, an Australian cultural studies critic who combines feminist, post-colonial and poststructuralist elements in her work, draws a distinction 'between an essentialist cultural politics *dependent* on inherited notions of identity and community, and a differential or "diasporic" identity politics understood as an historical, as well as cultural *production* carried out in the midst of, precisely, flux and change' (1992: 207).

This distinction is central to understanding culturally oppressed women's struggles in challenging issues of citizenship on a global basis. The critiques which emerged from a range of Black women, women of colour, Third World women, indigenous women and post-colonial feminists in the 1980s challenged white Eurocentric models of feminism (Carby 1982; Amos and Parmer 1984; Awatere 1984). In New Zealand the challenges came primarily from Maori women. As Larner comments:

> Maori women were also organising, but around different issues and in different forums. As Te Awekotuku (1991) points out, one of the reasons

why so few Maori women joined 'women's liberation' during this period was because there were so many other struggles which were seen as having a higher priority. The 1970s were the years in which young Maori activists, many of whom were women, were combining long-standing grievances about land, culture and language with new protest strategies and goals adapted from international civil rights and feminist movements.

(1995: 182)

Significant points of tension emerged between Maori and Pakeha feminisms, particularly around the issue of Maori women seeing themselves as part of a unified struggle with Maori men. As Irwin (1992: 12) noted: 'Maori women work with all Maori people including men, a principle that stands Maori feminism apart from some other expressions of feminism'. In the 1980s, tensions between Maori and Pakeha feminism were amplified by the growth of Maori nationalism and demands for Maori sovereignty. The publication of Donna Awatere's *Maori Sovereignty* articulated the central premise of Maori sovereignty as 'the desire to gain control over those economic and social resources which would contribute to a form of Maori self-determination within the New Zealand nation state, [and] was identified as a fundamental goal for feminists' (Larner 1995: 182–183).

The framing of Maori sovereignty in terms of '*te tino rangatiratanga*' (self-determination) signalled not just a new vocabulary for Maori self-determination but also an increased emphasis on indigenous forms of feminism and identity and a rejection of theory which referenced colonisation. As Irwin notes, 'the development of Maori feminist theories, in which *mana tane* and *mana wahine* are equally powerful, is crucial if our culture is to retain its *mana* as Maori culture and not a hybrid version of international patriarchy' (1992: 19)[7] (my italics).

Coincidentally, Pakeha feminists have also distanced themselves from overseas feminist theoretical perspectives and have identified issues such as an identification with the land and a culture specific to New Zealand as significant elements in the emergence of a 'post-colonial Pakeha feminism' (Dann 1991; Middleton 1992; Larner and Spoonley 1995)' (Larner 1995: 184). For example, Middleton's work has articulated the need for 'programmes and pedagogies which are authentic to our personal and collective history' (Middleton 1992: 36). However, as Middleton also notes, Maori and Pakeha feminisms operate as discrete identities and 'the result thus far is two sets of theoretical positions and, as yet, little analysis of relationships, conflicts and contradictions between them' (1992: 34). Larner also points to the emergence of 'strong, politically grounded, bipolar variants of feminist scholarship' (see Du Plessis et al. 1992; Alice and Du Plessis et al., 1998). The direction of Maori feminism in the 1990s has served to reinforce this position, strongly asserting that 'academic work about Maori women should only be promoted and undertaken by Maori women (Irwin 1992: 7)' (Larner 1995: 185). The work of Johnston and Pihama (1993), Irwin (1992) and Smith (1992) confirms this view, thus:

The challenge for Maori women in the 1990s is to assume control over the interpretation of our (Maori) struggles and to begin to theorise our experiences in ways which make sense for us and which may come to make sense for other women . . . One of the difficulties in subsuming our struggle as Maori women under existing feminist analyses is that we deny the centrality of our identity and the specific historical and cultural realities we endure.

(Smith 1992: 34–35)

Larner maintains that the bicultural framing of feminism in New Zealand and the emphasis on indigenous forms of scholarship can be seen as 'expressions of progressive forms of politics based on self-defined identities and reflecting local sensitivities' (Larner 1995: 185). These theoretical and political struggles can be seen as one aspect of the emergence of new identities and new forms of feminist theorising in the space opened up by post-colonialism.

Citizenship, diversity, difference

The interface between feminism and post-colonialism not only has implications for issues of gender and citizenship but also contributes to a critical analysis of the politics of inclusion and exclusion. Not only is there concern that the 'abstract individual' implied in modernist conceptions of the nation state is white and male, but also that minority women who are even more likely than white women to be excluded from this category cannot, therefore, participate in the liberal nation state (see Flax 1996 quoted in Kaplan 1997: 46).[8] This is largely because the liberal definition of citizenship 'constructs all citizens as basically the same and considers the differences of class, ethnicity, gender, etc., as irrelevant to their status as citizens' (Yuval-Davis 1997: 8). Broadly speaking, some of the literature on citizenship supports the claim that citizenship is inclusive. Alternatively, it portrays 'citizenship as a force for exclusion which creates non or partial citizens' (Lister 1997: 36). In the latter case, the analysis fails to address the fact that citizenship can exclude those 'from without' as well as those excluded 'from within' specific citizenship communities or nation states (Yeatman 1994: 80). Not surprisingly, such universalistic conceptualisations of citizenship have been confronted time and again by challenges from the 'margins'. As Yuval-Davis states, 'in virtually all contemporary states there are migrants and refugees, "old" and "new" minorities and in settler societies there are also indigenous people who are not part of the hegemonic national community (Stasuilis and Yuval-Davis 1995)' (Yuval-Davis 1997: 7). These marginalised 'others' challenge both the ethos of inclusion and the perpetuation of exclusion.

As is evident in the realm of political theory, feminists have also explored and challenged the relationship between citizenship rights and individualised social differences. They have confronted not only what they see as 'the false universalism of citizenship', but also universalistic conceptions of 'woman'. Feminist political theory has therefore focused on the need for 'a conception of citizenship which would accommodate all social cleavages simultaneously' (Leca 1992: 30). Iris Young (1989) has gone further, suggesting that representative democracy should treat people not as individuals but as members of groups. She argues that a discourse of universal citizenship which ignores group differences enhances the domination of groups which are already dominant and could potentially silence the marginal and oppressed groups (Yuval-Davis 1997: 17–18). However, post-colonial theorists have put forward the concept of 'trans-culturalism', which as Lister notes 'neither reduces people to cultural groups nor ignores cultural identities' (Lister 1997: 37).

This tension between citizenship rights and the politics of inclusion and exclusion is particularly significant for women. Sangal and Yuval-Davis (1992) show how 'women often suffer from the acceptance by the state of the definition of what constitutes "the cultural needs of the community" in matters of education, marriage and divorce and other provisions such as women's refuges' (quoted in Yuval-Davis 1997: 11).

Citizenship and the *'politics of inclusion'*

This theme is taken up by Johnson (1996a: 102) who maintains that the last two Labour governments in Australia (the Hawke and Keating Labor governments) have practised what she describes as 'a politics of inclusion'. Yet Johnson maintains that this process has marginalised women and other traditionally oppressed groups, even though such groups were seen to be strategic in the 'new internationally competitive Australian economy of the twenty-first century' (ibid.). Below, we consider how such politics of inclusion have been analysed by Australian feminists.

On the one hand, Johnson points out that an Australian politics of inclusion (supported by the last Australian Labor governments) offered feminists some opportunities for advancement, particularly in areas such as affirmative action and equal opportunities. On the other hand, women made little headway in terms of any significant economic intervention. She notes, for example, that 'the "economic" sphere has functioned as a meta-category which dissolves difference and conflict' (ibid.). Thus much of the legislation introduced by these Labor governments, particularly around Equal Employment Opportunities, has been conceived within a 'managerialist framework':

> The Hawke government introduced new equal employment opportunities measures and Affirmative Action and Sex Discrimination legislation, justifying it partly on the grounds that it would enable Australian business to mobilize both sexes for economic restructuring (Australian Parliamentary Debates, 1986: 862).
>
> (Johnson 1996a: 105)

Such policies nevertheless were preferable in terms of the opportunities provided to feminists and other socially marginalised groups, especially in contrast with Thatcherism in the UK:

One could argue that Australian Labor governments propagated an inclusivist model for restructuring capitalism while Thatcherism and its successors propagated an exclusionist version based on a more individualistic rather than cooperative conception of enterprise culture, and attacks on diverse groups from women and unions to gays and lesbians.

(Johnson 1996a: 104)

The implications of these government policies for broader questions of feminist analysis have been profound, especially in relation to issues of citizenship, difference and national identity. Johnson argues that 'many critics have been deeply suspicious of Keating's politics of inclusion', quoting Ien Ang in support:

As Ien Ang says, when deconstructing both mainstream conceptions of Australian national identity and western, middle-class white feminist accounts of the politics of difference, the 'politics of inclusion' is born of a liberal pluralism which can only be entertained by those who have the *power* to include' (Ang 1995: 73).

(Johnson 1996a: 106)

The liberal pluralist model which offers a discursive basis to the politics of inclusion is one which draws on a laissez-faire ideology of market-driven principles. This dominant model of 'economic citizenship' has therefore been promoted by Australian Labor governments who, as Johnson (1996a: 110) claims, have 'successfully utilized right-wing economics to appeal to a multiplicity of identities'. While superficially acknowledging issues of the fragmentation of identity around gender, sexuality, race and ethnicity within the context of mainstream political discourse:

the predominant identity being privileged seems to be Labor's version of capitalist rational economic man with other social groups tacked on as an afterthought and in a way that does not adequately transform the gendered (Johnson 1996b, 1995) or, indeed, heterosexist, racist and ethnicist nature of the original category.

(Johnson 1996a: 110)

Thus, a politics of inclusion (as enunciated by Australian Labor governments), while celebrating difference, at the same time assimilates difference within this broader model of 'economic citizenship'. As a consequence, 'the forms of citizen identity being constructed in Labor Party discourse, workplaces and educational institutions (among other locations) look very like a variant of traditional right wing liberal economic ideology' (Johnson 1996a: 110).

In short, the types of critiques that have emerged from Australian feminist, postmodernist and poststructuralist theories around identity and difference have not fully addressed how these issues have been incorporated into mainstream political and economic discourses of citizenship. To a large extent, contemporary feminists' concerns with questions of identity and difference underscore some of their political assumptions. However, to date such debates, according to Johnson, have not been extended into economic policy and theory. Johnson therefore maintains that:

> Much of the more innovative feminist theorizing in Australia has occurred in postmodernist influenced writings on history, the body, literature and popular culture. It is only relatively recently that writers from these perspectives have begun to engage with mainstream party political debates such as debates over national identity.
>
> (Johnson 1996a: 111)

Feminists who have taken issue with feminist postmodern and poststructural discourses maintain that such debates ignore the way civic identities are constructed by market-driven factors. For example, poststructuralist analysis which draws upon a Foucauldian analysis of government discourse is problematic because as Johnson (1996a: 100) points out, 'the private sector is privileged and the state plays an increasingly limited role in terms of regulation or ownership of capital (even if it may be "interventionist" in terms of influencing constructions of personal practices and identity)'. The reduced role of the state in shaping the economy resembles New Right economic policy and does indeed impact on the construction of a gendered identity.

Conclusion

The interface between feminism and post-colonialism has provided another alternative mechanism for the study of liberal democracy. Such intertextuality is important for the development of critically reflexive perspectives of any modernist conception of 'emancipatory politics' based on one or both traditions. As I have shown elsewhere (Brooks 1997), the effects of postmodernism on feminist and post-colonial discourses have challenged both of these traditions and their assumptions about identity, subjectivity, inclusion and rights. The framing of discourses around the 'politics of difference' reflects such an engagement with postmodernism. This form of politics is found particularly and rather interestingly in Australia and New Zealand.

To what extent the particular inflection of these debates in these two post-colonial contexts reflects a distancing on the part of these countries from Western European philosophical and political dominance must remain, at this juncture, purely speculative. However, there is little doubt that the impact of these debates is significant in terms of issues of gender, citizenship and education. Feminist theorising about questions of citizenship is still working on the politics of inclusion and exclusion, universalism and particularism, and subjectivity and selfhood. As Lister (1997: 39) notes:

> . . . our goal should be a universalism which stands in creative tension to diversity and difference and which challenges the divisions and exclusionary

inequalities, which can stem from diversity. We might call this a 'differentiated universalism' drawing on contemporary radical political theory which is attempting to 'particularize' the universal in the search for 'a new kind of articulation between the universal and the particular' (Mouffe 1993: 13; Yeatman 1993: 229). Universalism is understood here not as false impartiality but as a 'universality of moral commitment' to the equal worth and participation of all (Young, 1990).

Notes

1 Aotearoa is the Maori name for New Zealand and is politically important in its post-colonial identity. Aotearoa means 'Land of the long white cloud'.

2 See A. Yeatman (1995) Interlocking Oppressions in B. Caine and R. Pringle (eds) *Transitions: new Australian feminisms*, Sydney: Allen and Unwin.

3 The term 'Pakeha' is a contested one in New Zealand. It is used to apply to those of white European descent who were born in New Zealand. It is also used to apply more generally to the white European-born immigrant who has 'settled' in New Zealand, but whose cultural reference points are European. It is sometimes used by Maori in more general terms to refer to white non-Maori.

4 Yeatman draws on Jessica Benjamin's (1995) use of the Habermasian concept of intersubjectivity which Benjamin states was 'brought into psychoanalysis from philosophy'. Benjamin shows how 'intersubjectivity was formulated in deliberate contrast to the logic of subject and object, which predominates in Western philosophy and science. It refers to that zone of experience or theory in which the other is not merely the object of the ego's need/drive or coginition/perception but has a separate and equivalent center of self. (Benjamin 1995: 30). Yeatman indicates that Benjamin's psychoanalytic model is 'influenced not only by object relations theory but by the contemporary problematics of feminism and the politics of difference' (Yeatman 1996: 2 n. 2).

5 In discussing the basis of an 'intersubjective' relationship between Maori and Pakeha, Yeatman recognises the significance of Maori protocol and oratory on Pakeha institutions:

> It is this which has come to constitute the polity of New Zealand, and it is the reason the Treaty of Waitangi is regarded by many as the fundamental law of the unwritten constitutional reality of this polity. The Mabo decision in Australia is the foundations of the beginnings of an intersubjective relation between settler and Aboriginal Australians but this is still a highly fraught and contested development . . . All of this said, the interpenetration of the ethos of being Maori and of being Pakeha respectively, is not to suggest some sentimental kind of togetherness. On the contrary, the politics of the colonizers and the colonized settling their fates in a postcolonial polity is neither a sentimental nor a gentle politics . . .
>
> (Yeatman 1996: 4 n. 3)

6 The Treaty of Waitangi (1840) was signed by Maori chiefs and in the process ceded sovereignty of Aotearoa to the British Crown. In return it was guaranteeed that they would retain *rangatiratanga* (local authority) over their affairs. On the basis of this document, Hobson, the first Governor, annexed New Zealand to Great Britain, thus opening the way to a radical transformation of Maori political life.

7 Larner notes that while Maori words are part of an everyday vocabulary for Maori and Pakeha, they are often difficult to translate directly. *Wahine* and *tane* are women and men respectively while *mana* has spiritual and cultural connotations.

8 In a lecture entitled 'The Clarence Thomas Hearings and the Revenge of the Repressed: changing subjects, and the limits of liberal political institutions' (1996), Jane Flax explores issues to do with 'slavery and the American liberal nation-state . . . Flax argues that the real possibility of slavery, as the plantation owners knew firsthand, determined the specific form of the American concept of the liberal nation-state. In this model the individual exists prior to the state . . . These individuals are claimed to have rights and to be free and sovereign *just because* in America . . . other humans were not free and did not have property rights – that is, they were slaves, a state that defined them as such' (Kaplan 1997: 26 n.13). Jane Flax's lecture on this subject was a precursor to the publication of *American Dream in Black and White: The Clarence Thomas Hearings*, Ithaca, Cornell University Press, 1998a.

References

Alice, L. and Du Plessis, R. (eds) (1998) *Feminist Thought in Aotearoa/New Zealand*, Auckland: Oxford University Press.

Amos, V. and Parmer, P. (1984) 'Challenging imperial feminism', *Feminist Review*, No. 17: 3–20.

Anderson, B. (1983) *Imagined Communities: reflection on the origins and spread of nationalism*, London: Verso.

Ang, I. (1995) 'I'm a feminist but . . . "Other women" and postnational feminism', in B. Caine and R. Pringle (eds) *Transitions: new Australian feminisms*, Sydney: Allen and Unwin.

Arnot, M. (1992) 'Feminist perspectives on education for citizenship', Paper presented at the International Sociology of Education Conference, Citizenship, Democracy and the Role of the Teacher, Birmingham: Westhill College.

Arnot, M. and Weiler, K. (1993a) 'Introduction', in M. Arnot and K. Weiler (eds) *Feminism and Social Justice*, London: Falmer Press.

Arnot, M. (1993b) 'A crisis in patriarchy? British feminist educational politics and state regulation of gender', in M. Arnot and K. Weiler (eds) *Feminist and Social Justice*, London: Falmer Press.

Arnot, M. and Weiler, K. (eds) (1993) *Feminism and Social Justice*, London: Falmer Press.

Ashcroft, B., Griffiths, G. and Tiffin, H. (eds) (1995) *The Post-colonial Studies Reader*, London: Routledge.

Awatere, D. (1984) *Maori Sovereignty*, Auckland: Broadsheet Publications.

Bartky, S. L. (1990) *Femininity and Domination: studies in the phenomenology of oppression*, New York/London: Routledge.

Benjamin, J. (1995) *Like Subjects, Love Objects: essays on recognition and sexual difference*, New Haven/London: Yale University Press.

Blackmore, J. and Kenway, J. (eds) (1988) *Gender Issues in the Theory and Practice of Educational Administration and Policy*, Waurn Ponds, Victoria: Deakin University.

Brooks, A. (1997) *Postfeminisms: feminism, cultural theory and cultural forms*, New York/London: Routledge.

Carby, H. (1982) 'White woman listen! Black feminism and the bounds of sisterhood', in Centre for Contemporary Cultural Studies *The Empire Strikes Back*, London: Hutchinson.

Connell, R. W. (1990) 'The state, gender and sexual politics', *Theory and Society*, 19: 507–544.

Curthoys, A. (1993) 'Feminism, citizenship and identity', *Feminist Review*, No. 44: 19–38.

Dann, C. (1991) 'In love with the land', in M. King (ed.) *Pakeha: the quest for identity*, Auckland: Penguin.

Du Plessis, R. with Bunkle, P., Irwin, K., Laurie, A. and Middleton, S. (eds) (1992) *Feminist Voices: women's studies texts for Aotearoa/New Zealand*, Auckland: Oxford University Press.

Eisentein, H. (1990) 'Femocrats, official feminism and the uses of power', in S. Watson (ed.) *Playing the State: Australian feminist interventions*, London: Verso Press.

Eisenstein, H. (1991) *Gender Shock: practising feminism on two continents*, Boston, Mass.: Beacon Press.

Flax, J. (1990) *Thinking Fragments: psychoanalysis, feminism, postmodernism in the contemporary West*, Berkeley: University of California Press.

Flax, J. (1996) 'The Clarence Thomas Hearings: the revenge of the repressed', paper given at The Humanities Institute, SUNY Stony Brook, 7 March.

Flax, J. (1998a) *American Dream in Black and White: the Clarence Thomas hearings*, Ithaca: Cornell University Press.

Flax, J. (1998b) 'Changing the subject: contemporary theories and practices of subjectivity in the postmodern West', Seminar given at The School of Sociology and Women's Studies, Massey University, New Zealand, 16 October.

Franzway, S., Court, D. and Connell, R.W. (eds) (1989) *Staking a Claim: feminism, bureaucracy and the state*, Sydney: Allen and Unwin.

Gelb, J. (1989) *Feminism and Politics*, Berkeley, Calif.: University of California Press.

Grewal, I. and Kaplan, C. (eds) (1994) *Scattered Hegemonies: postmodernity and transnational feminist practice*, Minneapolis: University of Minnesota Press.

Gunew, S. and Yeatman, A. (eds) (1993) *Feminism and the Politics of Difference*, N.S.W.: Allen and Unwin.

Hall, S. (1988) *The Hard Road to Renewal: Thatcherism and the crisis of the Left*, London: Verso.

Hutcheon, L. (1995) 'Circling the downspout of Empire: post-colonialism and postmodernism', in B. Ashcroft et al., op. cit.

Irwin, K. (1992) 'Towards theories of Maori feminism', in R. Du Plessis with P. Bunkle, K. Irwin, A. Laurie and S. Middleton (eds) (1992) *Feminist Voices: women's studies texts for Aotearoa/New Zealand*, Auckland: Oxford University Press.

Johnson, C. (1990) 'Whose consensus? women and the ALP', *Arena*, 93: 85–104.

Johnson, C. (1995) 'Women and economic citizenship: the limits of Keating's inclusive social democracy', *Just Policy: A Journal of Australian Social Policy*, No. 2: 11–16.

Johnson, C. (1996a) 'Negotiating the politics of inclusion – women and the Australian Labor Governments 1983–1995', *Feminist Review*, No. 52, spring: 102–117.

Johnson, C. (1996b) 'Shaping the future: women, citizenship and Australian political discourse', in B. Sullivan and G. Whitehouse (eds) *Governing Gender: sex, politics and citizenship in the 1990s*, Sydney: University of New South Wales Press.

Johnston, P. and Pihama, L. (1993) 'The marginalisation of Maori women', *Hecate*, 20, 2: 83–97.

Kaplan, E. A. (1997) *Looking for the other: feminism, film and the imperial gaze*, New York/London: Routledge.

Kenway, J. (1994) *Economising Education: the post-Fordist direction*, Victoria: Deakin University Press.

Kenway, J. (1995) *Marketing Education: some critical issues*, Victoria: Deakin University Press.

56   *A. Brooks*

Larner, W. (1993) 'Changing contexts: globalization, migration and feminism in New Zealand', in S. Gunew and A. Yeatman (eds) *Feminism and the Politics of Difference*, Sydney: Allen and Unwin.

Larner, W. (1995) 'Theorising "difference" in Aotearoa/New Zealand', *Gender, Place and Culture*, 2, 2: 177–190.

Larner, W. and Spoonley, P. (1995) 'Post-colonial politics in Aotearoa/New Zealand', in D. Stasiulis and N. Yuval-Davis (eds) *Unsettling Settler Societies*, London: Sage.

Lather, P. (1991) *Getting Smart: feminist research and pedagogy within the postmodern*, London: Routledge.

Leca, J. (1992) 'Questions on citizenship', in C. Mouffe (ed.) *Dimensions of Democracy*, London: Verso.

Lister, R. (1997) 'Citizenship: towards a feminist synthesis', *Feminist Review*, No. 57, autumn, pp. 28–48.

McClintock, A. (1995) *Imperial Leather: race, gender and sexuality in the colonial context*, New York/London: Routledge.

Middleton, S. (1988) 'Researching feminist educational life histories', in S. Middleton (ed.) *Women and Education in Aotearoa*, New Zealand: Allen and Unwin.

Middleton, S. (1992) 'Towards an indigenous university women's studies for Aotearoa: a Pakeha educationalist's perspective', in R. Du Plessis with P. Bunkle, K. Irwin, A. Laurie and S. Middleton (eds) *Feminist Voices: women's studies texts for Aotearoa/New Zealand*, Auckland: Oxford University Press.

Middleton, S. (1993a) *Educating Feminists: life histories and pedagogy*, New York: Teachers College Press.

Middleton, S. (1993b) 'A post-modern pedagogy for the sociology of women's education', in M. Arnot and K. Weiler (eds) *Feminism and Social Justice*, London: Falmer Press.

Morris, M. (1992) 'The man in the mirror: David Harvey's condition of post-modernity', *Theory, Culture and Society*, 9: 253–279.

Mouffe, C. (1993) *The Return of the Political*, London: Verso.

Pateman, C. (1980) 'Women and consent', *Political Theory* 8, 2: 227–239.

Pere, R. (1983) *Ako: concepts and learning in Maori traditions*, Monograph, Hamilton: University of Waikato.

Pringle, R. and Watson, S. (1990) 'Fathers, brothers, mates: the fraternal state in Australia', in S. Watson (ed.) *Playing the State*, London: Verso.

Pringle, R. and Watson, S. (1992) '"Women's interests" and the post-structuralist state', in M. Barrett and A. Phillips (eds) *Destablizing Theory*, Cambridge: Polity Press.

Sangal, G. and Yuval-Davis, N. (1992) *Refusing Holy Orders: women and fundamentalism in Britain*, London: Virago.

Slemon, S. (1988) 'Magic realism as post-colonial discourse', *Canadian Literature*, 116: 47.

Smith, L. (1992) 'Maori women: discourses, projects and Mana Wahine', in S. Middleton and A. Jones (eds) *Women and Education in Aotearoa 2*, Wellington: Bridget Williams Books.

Spoonley, P. (1995a) 'The challenges of post-colonialism', *Sites*, No. 30, autumn: 48–68.

Spoonley, P. (1995b) 'Constructing ourselves: the post-colonial politics of Pakeha', in M. Wilson and A. Yeatman (eds) *Justice and Identity, Antipodean Practices*, Wellington: Bridget Williams Books.

Stasiulis, D. and Yuval-Davis, N. (eds) (1995) *Unsettling Settler Societies: articulations of gender, ethnicity, race and class*, London: Sage.

Te Awekotuku, N. (1991) *Mana Wahine Maori*, Auckland: New Women's Press.

Trinh, T. Minh-ha (1989) *Woman, Native, Other*, Bloomington: Indiana University Press.

Watson, S. (1992) 'Femocratic feminisms', in M. Savage and A. Witz (eds) *Gender and Bureaucracy*, Oxford: Blackwell Publishers/The Sociological Review.

Watson, S. (ed.) (1990) *Playing the State: Australian feminist interventions*, London: Verso Press.

Weiler, K. (1993) 'Feminism and the struggle for a democractic education: a view from the United States', in M. Arnot and K. Weiler (eds) *Feminism and Social Justice*, London: Falmer Press.

Weiner, G. (1989) 'Feminism, equal opportunities and vocationalism: the changing context', in H. Burchell and V. Millman (eds) *Changing Perspectives on Gender*, Milton Keynes: Open University Press.

Wilson, M and Yeatman, A. (1996) (eds) *Justice and Identity: antipodean practices*, Wellington: Bridget Williams Books/St Leonards: Allen & Unwin.

Yates, L. (1990) *Theory/Practice Dilemmas: gender knowledge and education*, Waurn Ponds, Victoria: Deakin University Press.

Yates, L. (1993) 'Feminism and Australian state policy: some questions for the 1990s', in M. Arnot and K. Weiler (eds) *Feminism and Social Justice*, London: Falmer Press.

Yeatman, A. (1990) *Bureaucrats, Technocrats, Femocrats: essays on the contemporary Australian state*, Sydney: Allen and Unwin.

Yeatman, A. (1993) 'Voice and representation in the politics of difference', in S. Gunew and A. Yeatman (eds) *Feminism and the Politics of Difference*, N.S.W.: Allen and Unwin.

Yeatman, A. (1994) *Postmodern Revisionings of the Political*, New York/London: Routledge.

Yeatman, A. (1995a) 'Interlocking oppressions', in B. Caine and R. Pringle (eds) *Transitions: new Australian feminism*, N.S.W.: Allen and Unwin.

Yeatman, A. (1995b) 'Justice and the Sovereign Self', in M. Wilson and A. Yeatman (eds) *Justice and Identity: antipodean practices*, Wellington: Bridget Williams Books/St. Leonards: Allen and Unwin.

Yeatman, A. (1996) 'Democratic theory and the subject of citizenship', Keynote address, *Culture and Citizenship Conference*, 30 September-2 October.

Young, I. (1989) 'Polity and group difference: critique of the ideal of universal citizenship', *Ethics*, No. 99: 250–74

Young, I. (1990) *Justice and the Politics of Difference*, Oxford: Princeton University Press.

Yuval-Davis, N. (1997) 'Women, citizenship and difference', *Feminist Review*, No. 57, autumn: 4–27.

4 Redefining citizenship

Black women educators and 'the third space'

Heidi Safia Mirza and Diane Reay

Feminist scholars have argued that a genuine politics of inclusion is impossible to achieve so long as the mechanisms which exclude the demands of minority or marginal groups are not explored. Moreover, feminist theorising on who becomes accepted and treated as a citizen suggests that the pervasive modernist assumption of universalism and sameness that suppresses group difference in the public realm means excluded groups are measured according to the norms derived from and defined by the patriarchally privileged group (Young 1990). The consistent exclusion of women from the public sphere through restrictions on paid employment, threats of violence, restrictions on speaking in public spaces, and confinement to domestic duties in the feminised private sphere critically affects equal participation and hence the citizenship status of women (Lister 1990; Walby 1994). However, since the starting point of much feminist theorising is the gendered exclusion of women from the patriarchal discourse of citizenship (especially from definitions of who counts as a citizen), such theorising becomes preoccupied with issues of gender equality, and the acceptance and membership of women in the masculine civic polity. The terrain of feminist academic discourse thus slips into the revalorisation of difference and the celebration of the private sphere rather than considering the more challenging position of 'acts of citizenship'.

New forms of engagement have emerged as the socially marginal, and in particular as Black women (who are defined and excluded through their gendered racialisation) adjust their strategies to accommodate a changing variety of racially contested public and private spaces (Hill Collins 1998). These acts of citizenship, which require 'other ways of knowing', are rarely given legitimacy in the classical political and social discourse on citizenship.

The classical notion of citizenship, in terms of universalist inclusion, and participation in a stable political community require rethinking in postmodern times. In the context of global economic and political change and increasing social fragmentation, the centrality and stability of traditional forms of belonging and solidarity that bind citizens together in a common public culture have been undermined by the increasing subjectivisation of social actors who are occupied with the politics of self-actualisation and hence the nature of 'the self' (Lash 1996; Mouffe 1993). Inequality now, it is argued, can be explained by how adept some groups are in adjusting to the fluidity of social change. Active participants, the 'new citizens', are reflexive autonomous 'clever people' capable of changing expert systems and reconstructing new solidarities across time and space (Giddens 1994: 94). Those who are successful advocates of their social and political rights in the public sphere advance the claims of the 'reflexive winners' (Beck 1992). It is suggested that the 'reflexive losers' are those who adapt to their increasing exclusion by ceasing to participate as citizens. In a process of strategic disengagement from the public sphere, they defensively withdraw collectively and individually from public participation (Ellison 1997). It is in this latter marginal disengaged category that Black women are so often inappropriately positioned as members of the passively constructed 'socially excluded'.

In this paper, our intention is to highlight the ways in which Black women's participation as both mothers and educators sheds new light on traditional conceptualisations of citizenship. First, we argue that their active engagement in Black supplementary schools demonstrates the paradoxical relationship between individual educational achievement and collective community commitment that characterises Black female citizenship. Second, in their gendered/racialised version of citizenship, the women combine their social capital and emotional capital skills of resourcefulness and networking thus enabling them to become collective transformative agents. Finally, we suggest their radical forms of 'giving back' and their 'educational desire' open up a 'third space' of strategic engagement. This 'third space' has hitherto remained invisible, as the traditional gaze on the public and private dichotomy in current citizenship theorising has obscured 'other ways of knowing' and thus 'other ways of being' a citizen.

Black supplementary schools: a study of Black female agency

Black women's educational strategies and struggles to support their children within increasing social and educational exclusion in Britain call for the necessity to redefine what is meant by 'real citizenship' in late/postmodernity . In this analysis of Black women's participation in Black supplementary schools, our intention is to develop an understanding of citizenship within the context of the dynamics of race and gender. As the data from this study reveal, Black women's grassroots activism is not rooted in 'defensive engagement'. On the contrary, Black women have actively evolved gendered/racialised forms of community solidarity and collective voice which refuse to privilege dominant definitions of a decentred, multiply-positioned, self-articulating postmodern citizen.

Our small-scale study of African-Caribbean supplementary schooling focused on just four Black supplementary schools: three London-based schools (Colibri, Community Connections and Ohemaa) and one in a provincial city, Scarlet Ibis. The six Black women educators, whose in-depth interviews form the main data for this study, had been involved in supplementary schooling for periods ranging from four to sixteen years. They had often started out as a member of a small group of Black parents, talking in terms of themselves and a few other mothers getting together. Their narratives reveal a 'real' commitment to community through the complex and strategic rationalisation of both their own and their children's educational aspirations. Our findings, arising as they do out of a very small-scale investigation based on qualitative interviews and three days of participant observation, are necessarily exploratory and tentative. However, we hope our data show that the participation and commitment reveals a very different vision of citizenship from prevailing orthodoxies which give primacy to the traditional forms of collective social participation.

Black supplementary schools are for the most part self-funding, organic grassroots organisations consciously hidden away from the public 'gaze' of funders and local authorities. These schools, which were set up by and for the Black community and which are mainly run by women, have a history that reaches back into the 1950s, ever since the first wave of post-war Black migrants arrived and settled in Britain (Reay and Mirza 1997). The supplementary schools are small concerns which run in after-school hours and on Saturdays or Sundays, and are difficult to locate as they exist deep within the informal Black community and are supported by the Black church networks. These small, local, often community-based schools are not regarded in the same light as the voluntary-aided separate religious 'ethnic' schools movement. Unlike established Muslim, Jewish or Seventh Day Adventist schools, the supplementary school is based on a philosophy of inclusion rather than exclusiveness. A notable characteristic of these Black schools is that regardless of whether the school's orientation is Methodist, Evangelical, Pentecostal, Rastafarian, or Afrocentric (rooted in Garveyism), other children, including white working-class children and children from other denominations or ethnic backgrounds, are welcomed. Their open community membership means that these schools place themselves outside of the contentious discourse for separate religious 'ethnic schools'. Black supplementary schools are, in that sense, an anomaly within 'ethnic education'.

Ironically, the ambiguous status of Black supplementary schools has meant that they have been for the most part left alone. The schools are not seen to represent a 'critical mass' in terms of numbers and voice. What is regarded as their fragmented, localised and contingent formation is not perceived as constituting any threat to the mainstream. As funding through local authority or the voluntary sector has always been small, unreliable or resisted, the self-sufficiency and genesis of these schools in community activism have placed them outside the gaze of the local authority. For the most part, the schools rely on parental contributions and community donations. As many as 1,000 schools have been reported in London (Abdelrazack et al. 1999). In our small-scale study, which we carried out in 1995, we uncovered the presence of 60 supplementary schools in Inner and Greater London alone. By the time the study ended, through personal and social networks and word of mouth, we were hearing of more and more schools every day. Sometimes there would be several supplementary schools on one council estate or in one neighbourhood. They appeared to spring up 'unofficially' in houses, community centres, and unused schoolrooms. The average size of the schools was between 30 and 40 pupils. However, some schools had as few as 15 children and others as many as 90. The age range of pupils was anywhere between 3 and 18 years old, though the average age range for most schools was 5–16 years.

Of the 60 schools in our research, over 65 per cent of the teachers were women. Even where men ran the school, women's daily work as teachers and carers was clearly the majority input. Mac An Ghaill writes that in the Black education movement, 'it is important to emphasise that Black women were at the forefront of the implementation of these strategies of resistance' (1991: 134). Similarly, Black women writers, Bryan, Dadzie and Scafe argue, 'for Black women challenging education has been part of a wider struggle to defend the rights and interests of the Black community as a whole . . . education struggles have been central to our political development' (1985: 59). In the four supplementary schools focused on in our research, Black children discovered 'really useful knowledge' (Johnson 1988) which allowed them 'to step outside the white hermeneutic circle and into the black' (Gates in Casey 1993: 110).

Each of the four schools in our study was distinct, but they were all underpinned by two main pedagogies. Some focused more on Black images, Black history and Black role models. Others focused more on 'back to basics', the formal teaching of the 3 Rs. Some did both. In the same way as the schools were paradoxically radical and conservative in their aims, so too were the teachers both radical and conservative in their praxis. On the one hand, the women, who were for the most part, voluntary unpaid teachers, talked of their 'joy' in what they do, the 'gift of giving back', and of their work to 'raise the race'. Many had been giving up their weekends for 20 years. Others had become ill from overwork and dedication. On the other hand, the same teachers saw themselves as complementing mainstream education. They were concerned about 'fitting in', assisting parents with home–school relations and getting the children to do better. On the surface, these schools appeared conformist and conservative, with their focus on formality and a commitment to 'buying into' the liberal democratic ideal of meritocracy.

However, our thesis is that Black supplementary schools should be seen as more than simply a response to exclusion and evidence of good practice. These schools embody, in their presence and praxis, an evolving organic critique of what mainstream education 'lacks'. In mapping Black supplementary schools' hidden history, what emerges is a picture of collective Black educational agency that challenges taken-for-granted assumptions embodied within the rationale of mainstream education. In the words and actions of the heterogeneous Black female educators involved in these schools, we find evidence of a radical Black agency from which has evolved a unified collective consciousness. It could be argued that such conscious forms of female collective action should be recognised as constituting a new social movement (Mirza 1997b; Mirza and Reay 2000), and that such female collective action offers a new direction in the investigation of Black social movements where for too long Black female agency has remained invisible. In the masculinist discourse of 'race' and social change, the assumption has always been that the struggle against racist exclusion is contested and fought over in the masculine arena of streets – riots, rebellion and violent confrontation characterise the struggle of the (male) youth in the city. In privileging such a gendered analysis, the subversive and covert transformative action of women is rarely valorised as an act of social change. However, Black women struggle for educational inclusion in order to transform their opportunities and so in the process subvert racist expectations and beliefs. In our study, the women were found collectively to have opened up transformative possibilities for their community through their pragmatic recognition of the power of education to transform and change the hegemonic discourse. Similar processes can also be seen in the educational aspirations and identities of younger women in the African-Caribbean community.

From personal desire to collective radicalism: Black women's stories of community and commitment

In *Young, Female and Black* (Mirza 1992), British African-Caribbean women tell stories of their educational commitment and desire to do well. They talk of passing exams, going to college, and proving their worth. On the surface their instrumental credentialism appears to be grounded in traditional values of meritocracy. However, an alternative reading of such credentialism, which acknowledges the circumstances in which it is developed, reveals that what these young women do is to strategically redefine success. Following in the footsteps of their mothers and grandmothers, they predictably follow the generational line that links back to an apparently traditional pattern of inclusive educational practice. However, what the young women are actually doing by their inclusive acts of 'doing well' is subverting the individualism of the mainstream educational system. They do so by their pragmatic refusal, using the educational structures and systems that exist, to achieve occupational mobility and academic success on their own terms. The young Black women work individually, on their own, at the back of noisy run-down classrooms. In their actions they are not 'resisting through accommodating', as is so often believed, they are refusing to fulfil racist expectations by being labelled underachievers. The underlying discourse they identify with is to 'raise the race' – to do well for others in the community through their own achievements. The racialised reality of their world means they recognise that a Black person is located very differently from a white person. Thus to be educated is to engage in a radical act, as Kathleen Casey observes:

> In a racist society for a black child to become educated is to contradict the whole system of racist signification ... to succeed in studying white knowledge is to undo the system itself ... to refute its reproduction of black inferiority materially and symbolically.
>
> (Casey 1993: 123)

This paradoxical pattern of personal educational desire and collective community commitment is mirrored in other research. Signithia Fordham's research in the USA reveals that young Black students reject the achievement-orientated individualism of formal schooling in favour of a collective individualism, which valorises the 'Black Self's commitment to the imagined or fictive Black community. Fordham explains that in hostile contexts controlled by the 'white (an)Other' it was necessary to behave as a collective 'Black Self', suppressing the desire to promote the individual 'self'. Presenting an identity that minimises individual distinctions strengthens the possibility of community stability, promoting survival in a system not designed for Black survival:

> The commitment of African American students to the Black fictive kinship system sanctions individual competition only if it compels the individual to give competitively, to use his or her skills to connect or reconnect him or herself to an imagined Black community. If individuals possess skills and expertise in an area external to what their peers construct as the Black community, people who share or have access to them assume that they will be willing to share this 'gift' or skill unconditionally.
>
> (Fordham 1996: 91)

What is also marked in the research on Black educational orientation is the gendered nature of this educational commitment. Our finding that running Black supplementary schools was primarily women's work is supported by a growing body of research both here and in the US which asserts that children's education is predominantly the concern and responsibility of mothers (Reay 1998a). Often, as in this study, collective Black agency is generated through the efforts of particular women:

> The translation of common experience into collective action requires some additional impetus. That impetus frequently comes from one or more pioneer women. These women have a catalytic impact on the women in a given community or locality and begin the process of awareness raising and mobilisation.
>
> (Sudbury 1998: 87)

The narratives of Black women educators in our study mirrored this finding of covert gendered agency, as Charity a mother and teacher in a Black supplementary school explains:

> It's mainly women who are the ones who are involved in education in this country. Within the Afro-Caribbean community it tends to be mainly women. In my family that was the case and at Colibri it was mainly women who came and that was fine. Obviously, there were a few fathers who were involved and there were a couple of men on the committee but it was mainly women.

Charity's narrative not only highlights the key contribution of women, it also presents a very different version of urban Black community to those endemic in popular media and political discourses:

> There was a group of about six parents, who like myself as a Black teacher, were dissatisfied with what was happening to Black pupils. They felt if they had been in the Caribbean their children would be much further on academically and they decided something had to be done, schools weren't doing anything so it had to be them. I really wish someone had the time to chart the enormous amount of work they put in those first few years. It was immense. The school started off in someone's front room on Saturday mornings. The parents doing all the teaching themselves to start with and it was very much focused on what was their main concern; their children not being able to read and write properly. Then these parents found the group of children grew from 10 to 15 and soon it was 20 and at this point it was unmanageable running a Saturday school in someone's front room so they petitioned the council for accommodation and finally got one of the council's derelict properties. They spent their spare time shovelling rubbish out of the room, tramps had been living there, doing building, repair work, getting groups of parents together to decorate. They pulled together and did all this work themselves, used the expertise they had to get the school on its feet and it was mainly the women organising things, making sure it got done, although in those early days quite a few men were involved as well.

As Charity's words indicate, these four Black supplementary schools generate rich opportunities for contesting prevalent discourses about contemporary urban communities.

There is none of the apathy, recalcitrance, fecklessness and aggression which permeate both popular and political discourses on the 'socially excluded'. Dominant discourses of the urban working class, both black and white, paint pictures of apathetic masses, the inactive and uninformed. Once named 'the underclass' by the socially and politically privileged, and now renamed the 'socially excluded' by the New Labour elite, these urban communities have been ritually pathologised as disengaged, disadvantaged and inherent under-achievers (SEU 1998).

However, Charity tells a very different story: it is a story about Black women's effective agency. The agency she speaks of is not the individualised agency of the white middle classes (Jordan et al. 1994; Reay 1998b), but rather a collectivised agency grounded in communal responses to a main-stream educational system which is perceived to be failing Black children. Similarly in Verna's narrative we hear commitment, reciprocity and continuity:

> I really wanted to do Saturday school because so much was given to me when I was a child. I had so much positive input I wanted to give some of it back. I also wanted to challenge this Government's views on community – that community isn't important. Not that I'm interested in

politics. I keep my head down. My work is on the ground with children, doing my bit here and it has been rewarding, very rewarding. Children have gone through the school that others have given up on and they are doing very well. Matthew, who was so very, very difficult when he came, could not sit down for more than thirty seconds. I see him now on his way to college. Perhaps it is alright, you know, that this is a stage. The school has done a great deal for a number of children. I can see the fruits of my labour.

Verna is not 'interested in politics'. Rather, her focus is intensive work 'on the ground with children'. She is engaged in, dare we say, a variant of motherwork (Hill Collins 1994), but one, despite her protestations, which ultimately has a political edge. Verna's text also speaks of community – one that is grounded in her own labour. Community, as a concept, may be out of favour within academic circles (cf. Young 1990), but all the women used the term extensively in their narratives as something they were not simply a part of, but were also actively engaged in constructing through their work as educators. As Rose stated emphatically, 'An important part of Saturday school is about creating community. That's part of what we're here for'.

In order to make sense of the enormous chasm between popular and elite prejudices in relation to urban communities and the actual practices going on within them, we need to inject a gendered analysis (Burlet and Reid 1998). So many successful communities across all fields of society are founded on women's invisible unpaid labour despite the high profile of male leaders. In her exemplary work on 'reading the community', Valerie Hey differentiates between male strategies of commandeering social resources and female strategies of constructing social capital in order to develop effective community links (Hey 1998). The Black women educators had minimal possibilities of commandeering social resources. Rather, they all worked incredibly hard to generate a sense of community and develop social capital out of friends and neighbour social relationships. As Hey succinctly puts it, 'There are at least two versions of community – his and hers' (1998: 2) and these six Saturday schools were all built on 'her version'.

Similarly, Patricia Hill Collins makes a case for appreciating the specific nature of Black female 'community connectedness'. She suggests we rearticulate Black women's experiences with Afrocentric feminist thought in order to challenge prevailing definitions of community. She writes:

> The definition of community implicit in the market model sees community as arbitrary and fragile, structured fundamentally by competition and domination. In contrast, Afrocentric models stress connections, caring, and personal accountability . . . Denied access to the podium, Black women have been unable to spend time theorising about alternative conceptualisations of community. Instead through daily actions African American women have created alternative communities that empower.
>
> (Hill Collins 1990: 223)

Hill Collins shows that through reconceptualising the work of mothers, women educators, church and union leaders, community power is not about domination in the Eurocentric sense, but about energy which is fostered by creative acts of resistance. Bourdieu has developed the concept of social capital which illuminates this point of gendered community participation. He defines social capital as: 'contacts and group memberships which, through the accumulation of exchanges, obligations and shared identities, provide actual or potential support and access to valued resources' (Bourdieu 1993: 143). Social capital is underpinned by practices of sociability which require specific skills and dispositions. However, we suggest that there are gender implications which Bourdieu ignores but which would point to a connection between social capital and Helga Nowotny's concept of emotional capital.

Nowotny (1981) defines emotional capital as 'knowledge, contacts and relations as well as the emotionally valued skills and assets, which hold within any social network characterised at least partly by affective ties' (Nowotny 1981: 148). As Virginia Morrow points out, 'this concept should alert us to the invisibility of women's work in creating and sustaining social networks and hence social capital' (Morrow 1999: 795). The Black women, through their involvement in supplementary schooling, were producing resources to compensate for perceived deficits in state educational provision and thereby enhancing the Black community's stock of both social and cultural capital.

All six women were extensively involved in the wider Black community, as well as the community they saw themselves as actively constructing through Black supplementary schooling. They were all facilitating Black parents' groups and working with local Black arts and business collectives. Two of the women were involved in national Black women's networks. The social capital generated through such contacts was fed back into the school. This benefited the pupils in a variety of ways; through, for example, additional funding, sponsorship and curriculum enhancement. For example, in Scarlet Ibis, a local Black business had paid for computing equipment, while members of the Black arts collective had volunteered their services and provided sessions on pottery making, set design and printing.

Black women reimagining, reinventing 'community'

There are a variety of competing tensions within representations of Black supplementary schools as forms of private-sector schooling and evidence of Black enterprise. They can be depicted as autonomous self-sufficient organisations which are part of a vibrant, growing (largely unacknowledged) Black enterprise culture which spans commerce, the voluntary sector, and arts and education fields. Aligned with such understandings of Black supplementary schools are views of them as predominantly community self-help projects. Such representations coalesce around New Right, and increasingly, New Labour, emphases on enterprise and local initiatives. Yet, at the same time, there are other images which cut across and powerfully contradict such representations: for example, the association of Black supplementary schooling with the political Left's project of anti-racism and the rediscovery of marginalised groups' histories.

In addition to extensive links within and beyond the immediate community, the women were firmly rooted in the localities their supplementary schools served. Both Rose and Verna lived on the large sprawling council estate that Scarlet Ibis was situated on, while Charity, Nadine and Maxine all lived within walking distance of the schools they helped run. The women's narratives, with their emphases on material notions of community grounded in a specific geographical locale, render problematic new notions of 'community' in which the developing agenda of communitarianism has detached understandings of community from its grassroots connotations. In this model, the linking of community with groups of working-class workers has been prised apart and into the gap has been inserted a 1990s view of 'diasporic collectivities' made up of individuals (communities) who have one or maybe two or three characteristics in common (Etzioni 1993). It is important not to overlook the work of regulation and governance such changes achieve:

> One of the ways the discourse of the new works to maintain the symbolic order is through a strategy of transference. Under pressure from overdetermined shifts in the social formation, modes of thinking and desiring which had been thoroughly sanctioned in one ideological formation become inadequate to the reproduction of social subjects in another.
>
> (Hennessy 1993: 104)

As a result, the circulation of new modes of thinking and desiring in the social imaginary must be publicly inhibited and repressed. Community, in any 'true' sense of collectivity, has been discursively reworked to fit the competitive individualism of the 1990s.

Through the 'third way' rhetoric of self-help, choice, and individual and family responsibility, community has been remodelled and appropriated by the intellectual elite and white middle classes (cf. SEU 1998). It is in this ironic reversal of 'community', which obscures the unspoken self-interested individualism that has always accompanied middle-class activities (Jordan et al. 1994), that any understanding of a middle-class community is problematic. The classic ethnography of a working-class English community described Bethnal Green in the 1950s as:

> a community which has some sense of being one. There is a sense of community that is a feeling of solidarity between people who occupy the common territory which springs from the fact that people and their families have lived there a long time.
>
> (Young and Willmott 1957: 113)

The associations implicit in Young and Willmott's work, of family, kinship, rootedness, localism and collectivity, are no longer apparent in contemporary understandings of community. Community, in the Young and Willmott sense, is perceived to have disappeared. Yet, paradoxically, it is in the 1990s Bethnal Green that we actually do have a community in the Young and Willmott mould. The difference is that this community is no longer only white working class but also made up of a new urban Bengali working class.

We argue that similar notions of working-class community are to be found in the discourses of both Black women educators and parents whose children attend supplementary schools. The use of community in the discourses of these Black women educators operates as a challenge to the consumerist individualism of the late 1990s communitarianism. Ferree has argued that women, working-class people, and Black groups in society are especially likely to reject competitive individualism as a feasible value, instead emphasising the construction and maintenance of viable networks of relationships (Ferree 1992: 37).

The sense of community engendered through these Black women's activities, embracing as it does an interdependency of the individual and the necessity of the communal, is very different to the sterility of academic injunctions of communitarianism. It is also a gendered form of Black activism quietly taken up by women which sharply contrasts with the far more high-profile agitations valorised by Black male activism. However, we would argue Black female activism shares neither the inherent ephemerality usually attributed to the men nor the self-defeating qualities often assumed of women. Iris Marion Young warns against the tendency to ascribe essentialist male and female ways of working to notions of individualism and community respectively. She argues that modern political theory and bourgeois culture,

> identifies masculinity with values associated with individualism – self-sufficiency, competition, separation of the formal equality of rights. The culture identifies femininity, on the other hand, with the values associated with community-affective relations of care, mutual aid, and co-operation. Asserting the value of community over individualism, the feminine over the masculine does have some critical force with respect to dominant ideology and social relations. [But] merely revising their valuation does not constitute a genuine alternative to capitalist patriarchal society.
>
> (Young 1990: 306–307)

Black supplementary schools paradoxically embody elements of both masculine individualism and feminine co-operation. Within a wider social context in which British consciousness, whether black or white, is currently preoccupied with individualism, Black supplementary schools are places of collectivity at the same time as they focus on individual achievement. bell hooks discusses the trend in the USA for Black people to buy into liberal individualism and cease to see their fate as in any way linked to a notion of a collective fate (hooks 1995). Similar discursive shifts are happening in Britain across racial divisions and within all sectors of society. According to Shotter (1993), processes of postmaterialism are breaking down traditionally homogeneous notions of culture and identity, thus allowing individuals to free themselves from the constraints of religion, class and traditional community bonds.

However, the ability to surrender the familiarity of the (national, ethnic, religious) community in favour of unknown, individualistic autonomy appears to be the preserve of the few. It is these few (for example, web surfers and nomadic academics) who used to justify postmodern explanations of the obsolescence of traditional means of social organisation. Yet, contrary to the fragmenting forces of postmodernity, the traditional means of community organising used by Black supplementary schooling can be seen to be flourishing. It would seem that:

> In spite of postmodernism, little has changed for the majority of Black women, globally and nationally. For them power is not diffuse, localised and particular. Power is as centralised and secure as it has always been, excluding, defining and self-legitimating.
>
> (Mirza 1997a: 20)

Conclusion: grassroots citizenship and the 'third space'

Black women educators in Black supplementary schools work for the reinscription and revitalisation of traditional notions of community. The idea of 'community' as practised among the women was less about creating symbolic markers and more about the conscious, pragmatic construction of a 'Black home'. While the schools themselves were set up as physically bounded 'spaces of safety', these 'sacred spaces of Blackness' were not just symbolic. They were a lived reality in which the women's energy and creativity generated 'social capital' (Bourdieu 1993). Notions of community were thus grounded in the women's own labour. They were not simply a part of the community. They were also actively engaged in constructing it through their work as radical Black educators. Hidden from view, in covert quiet ways, Black women work to keep alive the Black communities' collective desire for self-knowledge and 'belief in the power of schooling to mitigate racial barriers . . . and make dreams come true' (Fordham 1996: 63).

Feldman et al. (1998) argue that the realm of community which women create through their everyday activities becomes the 'third element' that mediates between the public and the private spheres and provides the base for a new politics. However, we would argue that Black women's agency and strategic self-determination does not simply mediate between the public and the private spheres but instead disrupts the static modernist distinction between the public and the private which dominates feminist theorising on citizenship. As Patricia Hill Collins demonstrates, the racialised context of public and private means that the Black female experience is different from that of white women. Though they enjoy formal legal citizenship, for Blacks in America the public has become a place of danger characterised by the containment and surveillance of the 'private lives' of the so-called Black 'underclass', through welfare regulation and racist institutionalised market inequalities (Hill Collins 1998: 35).

In this context of public danger, Black female participatory politics has to be strategic and contingent, using formal institutional structures that are advantageous and finding ways around those that are not. However, Black female agency has remained invisible in the emerging masculine discourse on post-modern citizenship. Gilroy suggests that spontaneous Black grassroots schools which, as this study shows, are led primarily by women, are 'defensive organisations with their roots in a radical sense of powerlessness' (1987: 230). Similarly, Ellison argues that marginal groups (who are unable to deal in the public realm with the fragmenting effects of social change) take up positions of defensive engagement. He suggests they resort to fundamentalist solidarities and recidivist social forms in an attempt to mitigate the effects of exclusion:

> The limitation of effective citizenship to those with the personal or collective resources – material cultural and intellectual – to construct solidarities and imagine new identities and modes of belonging carries the danger that those excluded from the sphere of reflexive engagement could be forced into a 'non-reflexive' defence of interests.
>
> (Ellison 1997: 715)

What both Gilroy and Ellison fail to understand is the creative contingent engagement of Black women who effectively subvert the subjectivisation and individualisation inherent within the processes of postmodern fragmentation. Operating in the interstices of a range of constituting identifications and subject positions, the women decentre fixed notions of citizenship that still prevail by simultaneously employing the contradictory discourse of individual self-achievement and educational self-improvement in an ingenious patchwork quilt of collective community reciprocity.

In our study, what the Black women appeared to have learnt is an awareness of the need for social support and collaborative action through their experience of marginality in a white racist society. From this awaking of consciousness and socio-analysis (Bourdieu 1990: 116) the women created their own cultural capital. Their habitus embodied 'real intelligence' in their ways of knowing and understanding (Johnson 1988; Luttrell 1992). As their words show, this ultimately led to collective action and social change through self-determination and educational urgency to succeed within the mainstream.

Black women's community action creates, in effect, a 'third space' of radical opposition. In the context of white hegemony, this 'third space' constitutes a subaltern counter-public. Nancy Fraser writes about hidden counter-public spheres which have always existed, including women's voluntary associations and working-class organisations. She describes such subaltern counter-hegemonic spaces as 'parallel discursive arenas where members of subordinated social groups invent and circulate counter discourses, which in turn permit them to formulate oppositional interpretations of their identities, interests and needs' (Fraser 1994: 84).

It is in the 'third space', a de-essentialised but invisible counter-hegemonic space, where the marginal and the excluded – those situated as such through their gender and radicalised construction – find a voice. That voice, as the Black women's narratives show, is subversive and radical. In the 'third space', Black women educators' acts of belonging and sustenance of community demonstrate new and inclusive forms of 'real citizenship' that deserve to be recognised.

Note

This research was made possible only by the kind and open participation of the Black women interviewed. Their names and the names of the schools have been changed.

References

Abdelrazack, M. and Kempadoo, M. (eds) (1999) *Directory of Supplementary and Mother-tongue Classes 1999–2000*, Resource Unit for Supplementary and Mother-tongue Schools, Department for Education and Employment, School Inclusion Division.

Beck, U. (1992) *Risk Society*, London: Sage.

Bryan, B., Dadzie, S. and Scafe, S. (1985) *The Heart of the Race: Black women's lives in Britain*, London: Virago Press.

Bourdieu, P. (1990) *In Other Words: essays towards a reflexive sociology*, Cambridge: Polity Press.

Bourdieu, P. (1993) *Sociology in Question*, London: Sage.

Burlet, S. and Reid, H. (1998) 'A gendered uprising: political representation and minority ethnic communities', *Ethnic and Racial Studies*, 21, 2: 270–287.

Casey, K. (1993) '*I Answer with My Life*': life histories of women teachers working for social change, New York: Routledge.

Ellison, N. (1997) 'Towards a new politics: citizenship and reflexivity in late modernity', *Sociology*, 31, 4: 697–717.

Etzioni, A. (1993) *The Spirit of Community*, New York: Crown.

Feldman, R., Stall, S. and Wright, P. (1998) 'The community needs to be built by us', in N. Naples (ed.) *Community Activism and Feminist Politics*, New York: Routledge.

Ferree, M. M. (1992) 'The political context of rationality: rational choice theory and resource mobilisation', in A. D. Morris and C. McClurg Mueller (eds) *Frontiers in Social Movement Theory*, New Haven: Yale University Press.

Fordham, S. (1996) *Blacked-Out: dilemmas of race, identity and success at Capital High*, Chicago: University of Chicago Press.

Fraser, N. (1994) 'Rethinking the public sphere: a continuation to the critique of actually existing democracy' in H. A. Giroux and P. McLaren (eds) *Between Borders: pedagogy and the politics of cultural studies*, pp. 74–98, New York: Routledge

Giddens, A. (1994) *Beyond Left and Right: the future of radical politics*, Oxford: Polity Press.

Gilroy, P. (1987) *There Ain't No Black in the Union Jack*, London: Hutchinson.

Hargreaves, I. and Christie, I. (eds) (1998) *Tomorrow's Politics: the third way and beyond*, London: Demos.

Hennessy, R. (1993) *Materialist Feminism and the Politics of Discourse*, London: Routledge.

Hey, V. (1998) 'Reading the community: A critique of some post/modern narratives about citizenship and civil society', in P. Bagguley and G. Hearn (eds) *Transforming the Political*, London: Macmillan.

Hill Collins, P. (1990) *Black Feminist Thought: knowledge, consciousness and the politics of empowerment*, London: Routledge.

Hill Collins, P. (1994) 'Shifting the centre: race, class and feminist theorising about motherhood', in D. Bassin, M. Honey and M. Kaplan (eds) *Representations of Motherhood*, New Haven: Yale University Press.

Hill Collins, P. (1998) *Fighting Words: Black women and the search for justice*, Minneapolis: University of Minnesota Press.

hooks, b. (1995) *Killing Rage: ending racism*, London: Penguin Books.

Johnson, R. (1988) 'Really Useful Knowledge 1790–1850: memories for education in the 1980s', in T. Lovett (ed.) *Radical Approaches to Education: a reader*, New York: Routledge.

Jordan, B., Redley, M. and James, S. (1994) *Putting the Family First: identities, decisions, citizenship*, London: UCL Press.

Lash, S. (1996) 'Tradition and the limits of difference', in P. Heelas, S. Lash and P. Morris (eds) *Detraditionalisation*, Oxford: Blackwell.

Lister, R. (1990) 'Women, economic dependency and citizenship', *Journal of Social Policy*, 21, 1: 445–468.

Luttrell, W. (1992) 'Working-class women's ways of knowing: effects of gender, race and class', in J. Wrigley (ed.) *Education and Gender Equality*, London: Falmer Press.

Luttrell, W. (1997) *School-smart and Mother-wise: working-class women's identity and schooling*, London: Routledge.

Mac an Ghaill, M. (1991) 'Black voluntary schools: the "invisible" private sector', in G. Walford (ed.) *Private Schooling: tradition, change and diversity*, London: Paul Chapman Publishing.

Mirza, H. S. (1992) *Young, Female and Black*, London: Routledge.

Mirza, H. S. (1997a) *Black British Feminism: a reader*, London: Routledge.

Mirza, H. S. (1997b) 'Black women in education: a collective movement for social change', in H. S. Mirza (ed.) *Black British Feminism: a reader*, London: Routledge.

Mirza, H. S. and Reay, D. (2000) 'Spaces and places of Black educational desire: rethinking Black supplementary schools as a new social movement', *Sociology*, August, vol 34, no. 3.

Morrow, V. (1999) 'Conceptualising social capital in relation to health and well-being for children and young people: a critical review', *Sociological Review*, 47, 4: 744–765.

Mouffe, C. (1993) *The Return of the Political*, London: Verso.

Nowotny, H. (1981) 'Women in public life in Australia', in C. Fuchs Epstein and R. L. Coser (eds) *Access to power: cross national studies of women and elites*, London: George Allen and Unwin.

Reay, D. (1998a) *Class Work: mothers' involvement in their children's primary schooling*, London: University College Press.

Reay, D. (1998b) 'Rethinking social class: qualitative perspectives on class and gender', *Sociology*, 32, 2: 259–276.

Reay, D. and Mirza, H. S. (1997) 'Uncovering genealogies of the margins: Black supplementary schooling', *British Journal of Sociology of Education*, 18, 4: 477–499.

Shotter, M. (1993) *The Cultural Politics of Every Day Life*, Buckingham: Open University Press.

Social Exclusion Unit (1998) *Bringing Britain Together: a national strategy for neighbourhood renewal*, Report by the Social Exclusion Unit CD 4045, London: HMSO.

Sudbury, J. (1998) *'Other Kinds of Dreams': Black women's organisations and the politics of transformation*, London: Routledge.

Walby, S. (1994) 'Is citizenship gendered?', *Sociology*, 28, 2: 379–395.

Young, I. M. (1990) 'The ideal of community and the politics of difference', in L. Nicolson (ed.) *Feminism/Postmodernism*, London: Routledge.

Young, M. and Willmott, P. (1957) *Family and Kinship in East London*, Harmondsworth: Penguin.

Young, S. (1997) *Changing the World: discourse, politics and the feminist movement*, London: Routledge.

5 Embodied identity

Citizenship education for American girls

Lynda Stone

The essay that follows is situated, significantly, in the context of contemporary life in the US, a situating that is at once complex and enigmatic. The country is huge and very diverse with conflict between unity and plurality evident everywhere. This plays out as individuals and groups each struggle with complex personal and public needs and desires. For example, out of this diversity, young males and females are expected to become citizens 'in common', to assume responsible places in society. From the perspective of conventional formal education, there seems little attention given to how commonality in the form of citizenship is to be enacted. However, there are also a number of significant, although less formal, influences on the development of citizens. One is the immense power of the consumer culture – a site explored in this chapter. Also important is the amount and character of attention to democracy itself, surprisingly strong in places outside of the US today but not very prevalent (except in times of political and military crisis) within the country. Paradoxically, this lack of public attention to citizenship and democracy exists alongside a very vibrant scholarly tradition. Writing on liberal democratic theory is widespread by 'Americans', and some even consider education therein (e.g. Barber 1992; Gutmann 1987). Part of this scholarship is represented by the considerable interest of feminist theorists in citizenship.[1]

This chapter is written from the perspective of an 'education feminist' (Stone 1994), and in a style somewhat different from others in the present collection. It works with both cultural studies and feminist theory, beginning with a discussion of citizenship and turning to a current consumer-based 'educational effort'. It then outlines the diverse interest in citizenship from various feminist theoretical positions. Importantly, there is no attempt to achieve any reconciliation of these positions, but rather there is a celebration of their difference. Overall, a two-part thesis frames the structure of the chapter: in the first part, contemporary citizenship is discussed as embodied in an 'identity' that has come to be linked to body as well as mind; thus, in effect, to reinterpret the traditional reliance on 'citizen mind' or rationality. Moreover consumed popular culture today, which strongly influences the construction and maintenance of identity, is described as helping to educate and create 'embodied' citizens. In the second part, this thesis is substantiated, first by calling on 'traditional' feminist treatments of citizenship, then by focusing on recent feminist writings about the body. The result is a significant contrast between what the consumer culture treats as embodied citizenship and contributions from feminist theorists, with interesting emergent lessons. In order to set out this two-part thesis, the chapter is organised into the following sections: Citizenship and education; *American Girl*™; Feminist citizenship; Particularist bodies; and, Embodied citizenship.

Citizenship and education

A rather bold premise was put forward above that little formal citizenship education exists today in the USA. This statement merits further consideration and elaboration both as a complex history and a specific present 'reality'. Two points are significant: first, what constitutes citizenship has changed over the past century; and second, what constitutes citizenship education – or even better, the place of citizenship in education – has also changed over time.

Citizenship in the US is first and foremost linked to democracy and to ideals of democratic governance. The rhetoric of the ideal is largely what matters, not, ironically, whether there is widespread and authentic democracy or not. Such governance is multi-leveled and multi-layered and extends from the family outward into many different organizational forms. Governance, moreover, is usually defined in terms of emphasis and balance between the one and the many, in the vernacular, 'me', 'them', and the 'government', the latter a catch-all for anything connected to bureaucracy. Unlike many other Western societies, in the US there is very little reference to 'the state', whatever its ubiquity in people's lives. In a conflation that incorporates personal history and ideological orientation, citizens today base their affiliation to democracy (and sometimes to country in times of crisis) on *identity*. Americans are always conscious of personal and familial background which, for some, includes group membership based in ethnic/racial origin. And, depending on this group attribution and how it relates to a 'mythical' American mainstream, one's personal identity is virtually always more important than being American. One is African-American, Latino and American and so forth. Whites, and those of Euro-American background, continue to call themselves (merely) 'American', but today their whiteness (and Eurocentrism) is being challenged.

This emphasis on individual identity characterises much of American cultural life and surely it makes the definition of citizenship different today than in the past: few expect everyone to be 'the same' as Americans. Sameness used to mean accepting and practicing a set of values that were White, male, Protestant, and republican. This is not to say that there were not conflicting values but rather that consent to the hegemonic culture was the societal expectation. Yesterday citizenship meant common socialisation, enculturation, and assimilation. Today assimilation is 'given up', at least as a publicly stated expectation, and what the other processes mean is not clear. Yesterday, new citizens wanted to be like older ones; today the lure of 'nativism' is not so compelling. Today, to emphasise, difference and not sameness characterises identity and, with it, citizenship.

An important aspect of citizenship concerns males and females. It is at the site of gender, as feminists amongst others note, that citizenship becomes *embodied*. It mattered and still matters whether one is female or male: women have had the vote for only about eighty years, women are only now military combatants, etc. The point is that a citizen has an identity that incorporates a specific body. As discussed subsequently, both identity and body change the traditional philosophical conception of citizenship as that which formerly resided in mind and its rationality, and, most significantly, as that which was male in origin and practice.

Another change from yesterday to today in the US concerns citizenship education. Overall there is less emphasis on educating for citizenship, largely because, paradoxically, public affiliation is a private matter of identity. Here there is a distinction between moral and political education, what constitutes both and what constitutes their relationship. In the nation's earliest public schooling, the moral and political were one with education itself: schooling was to ensure moral, God-fearing, loyal citizens. This has changed over time, especially in the second half of the twentieth century. Today emphasis is placed on the separation of morality and politics, with these kept separate from 'the basics' of curriculum. Children in contemporary classrooms learn the mechanisms of government in lessons which appear to be of little relevance; who remembers or needs to remember these processes (when one can turn to the internet for information and quick answers). A wrinkle in the curricular fabric of today is that some children are being taught 'character' as part of a national movement that claims no political status within schools. Even if for some, morality is receiving a little more attention in schooling, politics is receiving less; the importance of practical politics to the social studies curriculum is typically negligible. At most, citizenship enters through a back-door in courses which focus on US history. This curriculum, by the way, is still predominately White and male in spite of additions of the many women and minorities (typically in textbook sidebars). Identity and embodiment figure here too.

Two brief examples serve to illustrate the general point: 'Character education', as it is now called, takes the form of instruction in values wherein children define and practise specific daily or weekly virtues, like honesty. Furthermore, education for patriotism – as proposed in at least one State – takes the form of daily student recitation of sections of *The Declaration of Independence*. At the same time social studies – for example, the study of national holidays – if taught at all is relegated to time in the school day and week when the basics are completed. In a national movement of 'high stakes' standardised testing, in which social studies is not tested, this means very infrequent engagement with any social studies curriculum.[2]

Yet even though citizenship, democracy and citizenship education are largely taken for granted, a central premise of this chapter is that the informal education of citizens exists. This form of education uses what Australian feminist, Carmen Luke, calls 'pedagogies of everyday life' (Luke 1996). The central 'media' of these pedagogies are media itself, such as magazines and television, along with other forms of popular culture. As the exemplar of this chapter demonstrates, dolls, stories, artifacts, and the social practices related to them comprise a significant segment of popular culture for young girls. Now, this pedagogical form is not new – many people can recall dolls and story heroines of previous eras. What seems new, or at least more insistent, is the immense commercialisation of these products. Several decades ago, a small number of dolls (often 'European' and White in origin) were available – and affordable for most families – and a small number of story heroines were significant also. Not too long ago, parents and children went to the local bookstore or library to get the books and maybe in some cases dolls and books were presents for birthdays and Christmas. And, young girls had one 'good' doll, a special present. Over the past generation, accessibility as well as expense has changed as, it also seems, desirability has increased. Today there are numerous doll characters and story heroines for young girls *to identify with*, an identification that strongly contributes to individual identity development of which citizenship is a part. Importantly, the products girls buy influence who they become – *consumered citizenship* is constructed. Using *American Girl*™, the notion of consumered citizenship is now explored.

American Girl™

A prominent exemplar of popular culture is *American Girl*™. The enterprise is the brainchild of educator and entrepreneur, Pleasant Rowland, founder of the Pleasant Company in 1986 (bought in 1998 by Mattel, the world's largest toy manufacturer).[3] The company's catalogue, aimed at girls aged 7–12, offers a huge range of goods and supporting items: as well as three ranges of dolls (the *American Girls Collection*™ of 'six historically, racially and ethnically differentiated girl characters', *American Girl Today*™, 'contemporary dolls of various combinations of skin tones, facial features and hair types', with *Bitty Baby*™ providing the 'infant dolls representing major ethnic groups to teach about child care'), pre-adolescent girls are tempted by a variety of accessories and support goods. These include educational project books for the *Collection*, 'to recreate meals, crafts and costumes' (*American Girls Pastimes*™); pre-teens' own *American Girl*™ magazine 'advertising-free alternative to teen magazines'; *American Girl Library*, 'article collections including games, money makers and advice', and a 'reasonably priced' clothes range, *A. G. Gear*. This *American Girl*™ world is wide enough to include *American Girl Place*, '35,000 feet of things girls love' in Chicago, which includes *The Theater – The American Girls Revue*, and *The Café*. While *American Girl Events* promises the delights of a fashion show, ice cream social . . . and trip into history to raise money for charity', *The American Girls Museum Programs* (tours of six 'living history sites' in the US) and *America at School*™ and *Six Plays* ('easy to use teaching materials') offer more educational packages. To ensure optimum utility of the *American Girl*™ range, the last comes 'with rentals available of all other products to complement'.

Consumered identities: three stories

Much can be said about this exemplar, by the way existing along with product counterparts such as *Barbie*™ and *GI Joe*™ with decades of their own commercial and ideological histories. What is significant is the collection's influence on the engendering of specific girls. As prices of the products indicate, these are girls of the middle classes (or upper middle classes); for example, each doll with six paperbacks is $104 US; with single paperbacks at $6. The starter set of doll, books and accessories for the character Addy (on sale for Christmas 1998) is $280 while the complete collection is $1,000 (× 6 for all characters).

What are these 'American Girls' to be like? Who are they as 'citizens'? Obviously, they like 'things' to buy and to have, to play with, and to share. Given the product emphasis on historical characters, girls have histories as well as lives which are culturally diverse. They are White, African-American and Hispanic with lives that today's girls can emulate in their own ways.[4] Such girls do things: they are members of families, they go to school, they baby-sit. As persons, they make money, need advice, enjoy cultural events, and visit historic places. More importantly, as stories from the *American Girl*™ collection reveal, they also have personal dilemmas about which they must make choices and decisions.

Three stories, selected from a total of thirty, further illustrate the character of *American Girl*™ citizens. They are *School Stories*, one for each of the six historical characters chosen herein because of the traditional value placed on school as the site of formal citizenship education. The first is the story of Josephina set in the territory of New Mexico in 1824 (and available in Spanish). Out of a set of family crises that focus on the death of her mother, Josephina learns to weave and to read and write. Her teacher is an aunt who becomes a favourite and the learning process is one of enculturation. The second is the story of Samantha, a (White) suburban resident and student at a private academy for girls in 1904. Raised by her grandmother, she learns that friends from different backgrounds can teach each other. She helps a servant girl to catch up to her grade level in public school and in turn comes to understand the lives of others – perhaps less fortunate economically but not in other important ways.

The third story is of Addy, an African-American ex-slave in Philadelphia in 1864. A bit more detail about her story highlights some of the ideological underpinnings of the *American Girl*™ collection. In the first book, Addy's family is separated as the males are sold to a new plantation; however, the women escape to freedom. In the follow-up school story, Addy and her mother receive help from fellow churchpersons as well as find work and shelter with a White, somewhat stern seamstress. Addy begins formal education for the first time in a Freedman's school. She also learns about friendship by discriminating between true and false friends; tied to this is material wealth and social status as well as valuing one's own beliefs. In the books that follow, the lives of Addy and her mother undergo changes which incorporate them into a non-slave society. Finally, with the escape of her father and brother, the family is reunited.

American Girl ™ *'citizens'*

The stories of Josefina, Samantha and Addy portray specific lives of historical girls, each of which is different and is located in a different time. These stories give contemporary girls a sense of history and of their own histories, since they 'share' common interests and problems. They identify with and learn who they are today from these stories of yesterday. But, in these accounts, girls are 'produced' in some ways and not others. Striking is the ideology that their public lives are extensions of private lives but ones bounded in personal and familial concerns. Exemplified is a modification of the central feminist maxim, 'the personal is public, but not political, not civic'.[5]

If these stories are typical, all girls appear to care about are matters that affect them very directly, as relatively traditional young women. Given primacy, for instance, are interactions with peers in which friendships do have implications of class and race but whose implications are not developed in girls' minds. Here, as a lesson for citizenship, the potential of such stories remains inchoate and unexplored. But in fairness, there are other potential civic influences in these stories as well. The girls encounter new people within the sphere of bounded semi-public places such as neighborhood and school. They acquire new tools of communication that can enable decision-making. They enlarge their acquaintance, at least a little, with people different from themselves. They begin to acquire a sense of self-awareness, accomplishment, and confidence within limited environs. However, relevant to the theme of this chapter, girls in these stories do not have experiences in what is traditionally considered 'the public arena' – the larger world beyond the relatively private domain.[6] Significantly, in the consumered identity created by *American Girl*™, there is no education, implicit or explicit, for young girls to acquire *identities as citizens*. Moreover, anticipating the concerns of feminist theory on citizenship described in the next sections, there is no specific attention to girls' bodies.

Feminist citizenship

Much of the feminist writing in this volume is positioned within Western European political thoughts, some with specific ties to Liberal and Marxist traditions. For the purposes of this chapter, another, more comprehensive way of organizing feminist contributions to citizenship is outlined. This outline begins with a brief introduction to a category of particularist feminisms.

'Particularism' (Stone 1994: 6) characterises diverse feminist writings situated in this historical moment. Most important theoretically are the notions of distinction, differences between positions and approaches to issues as well as political and other concrete differences among groups of women. A consideration of the literature reveals two overarching perspectives: one that works from a broad or generic identification and the other that is very specific. Two kinds of the general formulations are cultural and postmodern feminisms, on the one hand, and ecological and theological, on the other. These contrast with more focused and direct links in the second overarching perspective. Again there are two kinds: a first kind that is theoretical and philosophical such as socialist or poststructuralist feminisms, and another kind that is related to specific cultural identities such as African-American or Lesbian feminisms. There is no need in what follows to keep these categorical distinctions in mind but to retain the idea of the diverse – and vibrant – sub-traditions that describe feminist theory today. Where pertinent, specific feminist orientations will be mentioned.

The tradition and the body

Over the last several decades, a feminist response to standard philosophical treatments of citizenship has developed with attention given first to the concept of mind and rationality. One tactic of this work has been to focus on what Australian Genevieve Lloyd names 'the maleness of reason' (Lloyd 1984). Posited down through the ages, she argues, is a singularity of the rational mind that is male in origin: these origins begin with systematically organised philosophy. A central figure is Aristotle who theorised different male and female minds (based significantly in different bodies) and different societal functions that were naturalised, normalised and 'hierarchised'. In this classical era – with a misogyny that continues into the present century – a dichotomous social order and definition of 'citizenship' was established and perpetuated. With different mental capacities, *man* was superior to *woman*. Importantly, even modern reinterpretations from Locke, Rousseau and others maintained the hierarchy in which, in effect, man is citizen and woman is non-citizen.

A first tactic of feminist response was to reinterpret and modify the concept of male rationality, often however retaining the historical discriminatory categories. A second tactic was to work directly with the conceptualisation and the language of misogyny in which 'woman' and 'gender' receive attention in terms of the connections made between public and private, sameness and difference, and independence and dependence (Stone 1996). In some of this work, and relatively recently, the body has begun to be considered. One classic example comes from Marxist-inspired feminist, Catharine MacKinnon as she relates the concept of 'the state' to embodied ownership. She asks, 'what, in gender terms, are the state's norms of accountability, sources of power, real constituency? Is the state to some degree autonomous of the interests of men or an integral expression of them?' (MacKinnon 1991: 185). Taking a 'conceptual route', she further tackles the issue of 'privacy', often in terms of the way the state regulates sexuality. She writes, 'Privacy . . . [has been] everything women as women have never been allowed to be or to have; at the same time the private is everything women have been equated with and defined in terms of *men's* ability to have' (1991: 194, emphasis in original). MacKinnon's contribution thus is to assert that the private has always been public and – when viewed in terms of state function – has always been 'bodily' as well.

Another set of body 'treatments' is found in the writings of Australian, Moira Gatens (1997) and American, Kathleen Jones (1993). Their source is Hobbes's 'body politic'. For Hobbes and other seventeenth-century philosophers, the metaphor of the body functioned by analogy, first with man as God's representative and second as 'the political body', the former's creation. But here one political body – and that male – comes to stand for many bodies. Further, the male/female hierarchy ensures that the civic male body operates 'on the back' of the female in the private sphere; women service men so that they may pursue their public, civic functions. Jones's contribution is to question 'authority' in the Hobbesian picture in which, paradoxically, the body of the father as disciplinarian is wedded to the mind of the mother as caretaker (1993: 87).

This brief review of the feminist theoretical interest in citizenship within Western political theory and philosophy reveals that there has been movement towards conceptualising 'the body' as well as 'the mind' as the 'home' of citizen life and action. This movement suggests still one more tactic by feminist theorists in which mind/body becomes attached to identity and action. Jones suggests that today citizenship is conceived as 'a particular type of action performed by people with a common political identity in a specific locale ... [but to be] a citizen is to trade one's particular identity for an abstract, public self' (1997: 2). Significantly, this process of abstraction represents a contemporary 'problem' of citizenship, that is, if the consumered personal identity of pre-adolescent girls described above is taken into account. The problem is that identity on the whole is concrete and specific but citizenship identity 'remains' conceptually abstract and therefore impersonal.

Particularist bodies

Within contemporary American feminist theory, an emphasis on 'the body' comprises an addition to (or perhaps an undercutting of) traditional feminist writings. Attention to the body has not just occurred in Anglo-America but has also been significant in another cultural context, that of French feminism. Arleen Dallery (1989: 52–53) claims that the chief distinction between the two 'cultural' approaches is the recognition of the empirical, irreducible reality of women's experience in the American context in contrast with the turn to discourse as the basis for experience in the French context. However within the past decade or so, some American feminists have followed their French counterparts into the realm of discourse, text, and writing (see Trinh 1989). American contributions on the body in relation to citizenship are discussed below in relation to the following: *generational* body; *comporting* body; *disciplined* body; *symbolic* body; and, *writing* body. These 'stories' are followed by one more, about *body erasure*.

Patricia Williams, for example, as a feminist legal scholar and Black 'identity' feminist takes up the issue of history in her writings. Williams' own body is '*generational*', as she traces back personal history to roots of a great-great-grandmother. She begins:

I like so many blacks, have been trying to pin myself down in history, place myself in the stream of time ... To be without documentation is too unsustaining, too spontaneously ahistorical, too dangerously malleable in the hands of those who would rewrite not merely my past but my future as well.

(Williams [1988] 1991: 165)

Her approach is genealogical in the standard sense based on the 'body texts' of family members and herself. In her story, literal body debasement takes place through slavery, enforced impregnation and enforced sterilization; figurative body debasement takes place through the discourse of law which disguises 'the brutality of enforced arrangements ... [in which women's] anatomy, their flesh and blood, were locked away in word vaults' (Williams 1991: 171). In conclusion she documents herself: 'Patricia Joyce, born of parents named Williams ... delivered into the world "colored"' (176).

Iris Marion Young, a political philosopher who is identified as a postmodern feminist, contributes a narrative about a '*comporting body*'. She writes in 1977 about 'the basic modalities of feminine body comportment, manner of moving, and relation in space ... for women situated in contemporary, advanced, urban, and commercial society' (Young 1990: 143). Working from roots in existentialism and phenomenology, she describes a general picture of female body use and identity that points to differences from that of males. Females are confined and do not make use of the total spatial and lateral potential of their bodies. They are more guarded and shielding and do not employ the body with ease and naturalness. Women, thus, are frustrated and self-conscious. As Young puts this, 'a woman lives her *body* as a thing ... [that] exists as looked at and acted upon' (1990: 150, emphasis in original). Paradoxically, women also come to believe that better use of their bodies potentially subjects them to even more objectification (155) since extension means more opportunity for constraint. She suggests, as Foucault so well understood, that constraint is not only other-imposed but also self-imposed.

Indeed, a Foucauldian reading of the body is available from Sandra Lee Bartky (1990) in a third story of a '*disciplined body*'. Her theme is stronger than body constraint; it is of the body disciplined through practices socially defined as 'feminine'. As a poststructuralist feminist, Bartky works towards a 'genealogical' portrait of contemporary body style which is connected to diet and exercise. From her analysis, the body that is evoked is 'taut, small-breasted, narrow-hipped, and of a slimness bordering on emaciation' (Bartky 1990: 66). Connected to body discipline are social practices used for its disciplining. Here is one example: Because '[a] woman's skin must be soft, supple, hairless, and smooth ... [hair] must be removed not only from the face but from large surfaces of the body as well ... [This is accomplished by shaving, buffing with fine sandpaper or foul-smelling depilatories. Some procedures] are painful and expensive' (69). Two Foucauldian aspects of body discipline are present. One is the connection of discourse in the way bodies are talked and written about, and the other, connected above to forms of constraint, is sanction to women for not 'being disciplined'.

Body shape and image figure in a fourth rendering from contemporary popular culture. African-American, Doris Witt presents a provocative account of the '*symbolic body*' in her theorisation of the remaking of the figure of Aunt Jemima in advertisements based in the womanist perspective of Alice Walker. The occasion is the relatively recent 100th birthday of the icon of nourishment, Aunt Jemima, as a powerful symbol of food, its preparation and its value as sustenance. She undergoes what might be called a 'body lift'. Witt writes, 'Noticeably different . . . is a new, stylish grey-streaked hairdo, and her headband has been removed. Other changes . . . [in the makeover from lower-class servant to middle-class consumer] include cosmetic touches such as a different collar and the addition of earrings' (Witt 1994–1995: 98, citing *Quaker Oats*™). As Witt points out, the old Aunt Jemima now looks like Oprah Winfrey! The general analytical contribution is to point to the power of the image and what it says both about the appetite of African-American females and about Black female health problems. The present situation, furthermore, is tinged with irony as change from potentially new discourses comes 'via the inscription of their oppression' (1994–1995: 113).

The fifth particularist account focuses on the '*writing body*', from immigrant and post-colonial feminist, Trinh Minh-ha. She is influenced by the French feminists mentioned previously. Woman, she begins, has been both '[dissolved] on the walls of silence . . . [and] warned of the risk she incurs . . . [by writing]' (Trinh [1989] 1995: 264). In what seems a contradiction, this author warns against authorship – returning to the kind of warning of potential oppression described by Young above (see Trinh 1989: 35). Her body writing has a specific politics, one tied to the openness of writing itself:

> [Writing] is that abstract–concrete, personal–political realm of excess not fully contained by writing's unifying structural forces. Its physicality (vocality, tactility, touch, resonance), or edging or margin, exceeds the rationalised 'clarity' of communicative structures . . . It is a way of making theory in gender, of making a politics of everyday life, thereby re-writing the ethnic female subject as a site of differences.
>
> (1989: 44)

Being positioned as different is especially important for Third World Women although, according to Trinh, writing is open to all women (and all who are oppressed).

Each of these five particularist feminists has attempted to recuperate the body as part of identity and citizenship. Among them, they acknowledge the dangers of recuperation; in other words, practices that reinscribe societal and gender hierarchies, that are often linked in several of their 'stories' to race and class. One more move among recent feminist writings makes a contribution through the critique of body stories which suggest body presence; this is writings on '*body erasure*' from Donna Haraway and Peggy Phelan. In 1985, Haraway creates the image of the cyborg, a new body ontology that is not human. She explains, '[a] cyborg is a cybernetic organism, a hybrid of machine and organism . . . a matter of fiction and lived experience that changes what counts as women's experience' (Haraway 1985: 65). *We* are all cyborgs, claims Haraway, engaged in struggles over life and death at the borders of production, reproduction, and imagination. Her call is for a cyborg politics in a post-gender (and post-'body') world. In a complementary way, influenced by Lacan, Phelan (1993) theorises a different undercutting of the body in writing from psychoanalytic roots and construction of the fictional body in performance art. One example offered by her is of New York City's Guerrilla Girls, feminist artists who appear in gorilla masks to protest about the art establishment (1993: 19). For Phelan, their masking resists the marking of identity – and control – in art. Furthermore the politics of performance rests on ironic disappearance of the body, of giving up the unity of the self. This means too that control of the other's controlling gaze is also denied.

Embodied citizenship

Up to this point, a 'story' of contemporary citizenship education for girls has been set out: citizenship in a US context refers to democracy in a form of allegiance that appears uniquely individualistic among Western nations. Individuals are 'American' in their own personal ways, and identity is the basis of this attachment. Moreover, identity is contested today since personal difference (for some in terms of ethnic group) is valued. 'I' is the most prominent word in US public discourse – and the 'we' of family is taken in the same individualistic sense.

Given the personal nature of identity, difference rather than sameness has a stronger rhetorical hold: 'pluribus' in the current vernacular 'rules'. The contemporary nature of US society contributes two not-surprising aspects of citizenship education: first, citizenship education about what is held in common – how *we* must all act – has little actual relevance; and second, citizenship education in order to 'succeed' ought to emphasise individual identity. Currently, citizenship education does not attend to individual identity and thus it matters little. Enter upon this 'scene' both popular culture/commerce and feminist theory with distinct emphases on *identity development*.

If *American Girl™* is exemplary, 'stories' about historical characters (described above) reveal four important dimensions of education for *consumered identity* – and for citizenship. Indeed, because of specific engendering from popular culture, they demonstrate a new 'form' of informal citizenship education. The first dimension is the message that for all the difference in historical time, girls' personal desires and interests have changed little: they value family and friendship even as personal achievement differs and its possibilities improve over time. The second dimension is that perennial personal conflicts among girls can be worked out because girls have much in common, indeed, they are more alike than different.[7] The third dimension is especially significant for pre-adolescent girls: while the bounds of experience have extended a little, the centre of life remains the personal. Now the 'personal is public'. The fourth and final dimension is that girls are still ill-prepared for civic life, although they do gain some potentially useful skills. One reason for the present state of American girls' citizenship implied in the writings of particularist feminists is the lack of attention to female *embodiment as citizens*. Herein, embodiment is literal, as *body* is integral to identity and as significant surely as mind. The integrity of body as a basic part of identity and now of citizenship is surely an important feminist contribution!

The focus of this chapter has implicitly been a changed conception of citizenship *for* American girls. The analysis suggests the relevance of body to identity and identity to citizenship; and furthermore, the salience of popular culture as a significant site (possibly the most important one) to the engendering and the construction of citizenship today. For example, in her analysis of 'body politic' and authority, American feminist Kathleen Jones ponders the sovereignty of 'the menstruating body, the body-with-a-womb, the birthing, fecund body, the lactating body, the menopausal body, the more docile and more specular or to-be-looked-at body' (Jones 1993: 81). The connection of this 'body' to traditional male-inspired citizen rationality seems heretical at best!

As writings from US feminists attest, there is much to be said about the body – and important connections to be made. Importantly, one notes that consideration of the body does have its own historical situating today. This is largely a result of the women's movement and of the natural centrality of bodies in women's lives: as we seem to agree today, bodies are actual as well as active – and actually the 'homes' of mind. As bodies *qua* bodies they are concrete and lived: they come into being, take up space and exist over time, change constantly, enact movement, leave waste, create progeny, construct edifices and leave artifacts, stand side by side with other bodies, are constrained within a natural and social world and 'escape' it, in imagination and death. It seems commonsense in the late twentieth century to acknowledge the prominence of the body in women's lives.

But, more can be implied about bodies from above – and implied as a 'unity' of body/mind for citizenship and education. First, drawing from Young (1990), bodies are not just 'things'. They have meaning and they matter. They matter in what is today a significant intermingling of traditionally private and public realms. This traditional split has, in effect, disappeared even if minimally so for young girls. Other general implications are these: bodies are personal, diverse, and integral to identity. It matters whether one 'disciplines' one's own body shape, how one reacts to 'symbols' of ethnic bodies, or if one connects to a 'generational' history through body identity. Second, these matters are of public (and not just private) concern. As the example from MacKinnon (1991) above relates, the state 'regulates' sexuality – and with it privacy. This began with the inception of the nation state and remains today. Importantly, in a country like the US without a strong state discourse, much of this regulation is either explained away or hidden. Third, to focus on diversity, bodies are both individually and culturally different and, as such, have distinct, public implications. It matters 'bodily' whether one 'sees' oneself in the public culture – whether in a somewhat outdated way of putting this, one is part of a 'majority' or 'minority'. Pluralism through identity is vital in current conceptions of citizenship. What constitutes pluralism remains the open and indeed the still vibrant contemporary question.

Conclusion

There are three parts to the story of citizenship and its education in this chapter. A first is an almost missing school story of formal citizen education which is replaced by popular culture. To this, two other contrasting stories devolve: one is that of the identity formation of young girls heavily influenced by consumer culture and specific messages about who girls are to be. At least in pre-adolescence, they are to live relatively bounded 'semi-public' (at best) but not civic lives – and they are to exist without bodies. In contrast, adult women, as particularlist feminists have argued, are 'embodied' in lives which substantially alter the scope and interests of females in contemporary society. They alter who they are as citizens, and what has public import for them. How girls, consumerised as they are, become fully-functioning civic women is the question. Related to this question is how formal education is to contend today with its informal cultural counterparts (if not competitors). One 'educational' contribution may indeed be this chapter's description of the central and still contrasting stories of embodiment from *American Girl*™ and from American particularist feminists.[8]

Notes

1 Although using 'American' throughout as does the doll company, I recognise the wider context of many different American regions and countries and the ethnocentrism of use in the USA.
2 These examples are taken from New Jersey and North Carolina in 1999. One notes also that in American high schools, social studies has historically been the least favorite subject.
3 This description is from company materials. The public relations department was most generous with time and information.
4 Recent catalogues include Asian girls.
5 The well-known maxim is 'the personal is political'.
6 They do not consider the lessons of facing problems of a conventionally public civic nature and of taking public stands; consider having opinions about and criticizing 'government' actions.
7 One notes the absence of 'boys', thus of emerging sexuality, and with it – as mentioned – that of the body.
8 A special thanks to Madeleine Arnot and Jo-Anne Dillabough for the invitation to contribute to this volume and for care and patience with this chapter. Contributions on the initial draft came from researcher Kathleen Martin, with references from Jennifer Kretchner and Hannah Tavares, with suggestions for references and content ideas from James Cunningham, Michael Gunzenhauser, Ashley Larsen, Dixie Speigel, and Christine Titone and finally from Elizabeth McHugh, Media Specialist, Grady Brown School, Pittsboro NC who led me to *American Girl*™.

References

Barber, B. (1992) *An Aristocracy for Everyone: the politics of education and the future of America*, New York: Oxford University Press.

Bartky, S. ([1988] 1990) *Femininity and Domination: studies in the phenomenology of oppression*, New York: Routledge.

Dallery, A. (1989) 'The politics of writing (the) body: ecriture feminine', in A. Jaggar and S. Bordo (eds) *Gender/Body/Knowledge: feminist reconstructions of being and knowing*, New Brunswick, N.J.: Rutgers University Press.

Gatens, M. ([1991] 1997) 'Corporeal representation in/and the body politic', in K. Conboy, N. Medina, and S. Stanbury (eds) *Writing on the Body: female embodiment and feminist theory*, New York: Columbia University Press.

Gutmann, A. (1987) *Democratic Education*, Princeton: Princeton University Press.

Haraway, D. (1985) 'A manifesto for cyborgs: science, technology, and socialist feminism in the 1980s', *Socialist Review* (No. 80) 15, 2: 65–107.

Jones, K. (1993) 'What sort of body is the body politic?', in *Compassionate Authority: democracy and the representation of women*, New York: Routledge.

Jones, K. (1997) 'Introduction', in the Special Issue 'Citizenship in Feminism: identity, action, locale', *Hypatia*, 12, 4: 1–5.

Lloyd, G. (1984) *The Man of Reason: 'male' and 'female' in Western philosophy*, Minneapolis: University of Minnesota Press.

Luke, C. (ed.) (1996) *Feminisms and Pedagogies of Everyday Life*, Albany, N.Y.: State University of New York Press.

MacKinnon, K. ([1983] 1991) 'Feminism, marxism, method, and the state: toward feminist jurisprudence', in K. Bartlett and R. Kennedy (eds) *Feminist Legal Theory: readings in law and gender*, Boulder, Colo.: Westview.

Phelan, P. (1993) *Unmarked: the politics of performance*, London: Routledge.

Stone, L. (ed.) (1994) 'Introducing education feminism', in *The Education Feminism Reader* (with G. Boldt), New York: Routledge.

Stone, L. (1996) 'Feminist political theory: contributions to a conception of citizenship', *Theory and Research in Social Education*, 24, 1: 36–53.

Trinh, T. Minh-ha (1989) *Woman, Native, Other: writing postcoloniality and feminism*, Bloomington, Ind.: Indiana University Press.

Trinh, T. Minh-ha ([1989] 1995) 'Writing postcoloniality and feminism', in B. Ashcroft, G. Griffiths and H. Tiffin (eds) *The Post-Colonial Studies Reader*, London: Routledge.

Williams, P. ([1988] 1991) 'On being the object of property', in K. Bartlett and R. Kennedy (eds) *Feminist Legal Theory: readings in law and gender*, Boulder, Colo.: Westview.

Witt, D. (1994–1995) 'What never happened to Aunt Jemima: eating disorders, fetal rights, and Black female appetite in contemporary American culture', *Discourse*, 17, 2: 98–122.

Young, I. (1990) *Throwing Like a Girl and Other Essays in Feminist Philosophy and Social Theory*, Bloomington, Ind.: Indiana University Press.

6 Transnational visions of the 1990s

Contrasting views of women, education and citizenship

Elaine Unterhalter

The 1990s have been a decade characterised as much by visionary hope as by apocalyptic despair. In the face of, and indeed because of, extensive global poverty, environmental catastrophes, and pervasive inequalities, national and international commissions and conferences were convened which undertook to chart a better course for humanity. They were also designed, at least in part, to formulate policies that offered a promise that the next century might start to heal some of the wounds inflicted by the old. In the declarations emerging from these conferences and commissions, education was given a central role in cementing the plans for securing justice and building social cohesion. This approach is typified by that of Jacques Delors[1] when he drew on a fable by La Fontaine to call learning 'the treasure within' (Delors 1996a: 35). Through this metaphor of 'treasure', Delors argued that education should mediate between an inheritance from the past, the value invested in individual autonomy, and a sense of the untold potential promised to the world.

Women and girls play a particular role in these 'redemptive' declarations. Out of all the groups who have suffered in the twentieth century, their experiences are drawn upon and identified in such reports. On one level, this is a welcome development for feminists, who have long criticised the absence of any international recognition of the educational demands of girls and women. On the other hand, the special significance given to women by such diverse bodies as the World Bank and small NGOs (non-governmental organisations) raises questions about such a consensus. What purpose is being signalled in visionary statements which highlight the need for heightened international concern with the education of girls and women? Do these aim to respond to women's demands or dictate to women what their demands should be? Through what processes of consultation have globalised agendas on women's education been formulated? What notions about citizenship and the state do they utilise?

This chapter considers these questions through an examination of four documents (produced by international bodies in the 1990s) which position women's education as key to global transformation. The texts analysed are the *World Declaration on Education for All* adopted by an international conference at Jomtien in Thailand in 1990 (WCEFA 1990) (henceforth called the Jomtien Declaration); the World Bank's policy paper of 1995, *Priorities and Strategies for Education* (World Bank 1995); the Report of the UNESCO International

Commission on Education for the Twenty-first Century chaired by Jacques Delors that deliberated between 1993 and 1996 (Delors 1996b) (called here the Delors Commission Report); and the Beijing Declaration adopted at the World Conference on Women in 1995 (WCW 1995a). The chapter considers the processes through which these international statements came to be formulated, exploring the ways in which the four texts discursively situate the education of women and girls, and drawing out the notions of citizenship that underpin the different framings. It also considers the implications of the ways in which women's education and citizenship are linked.

The chapter is divided into four sections. The first section describes the background to the four texts and the basic ideas and themes inherent in each document; the second section utilises textual analysis to draw out different conceptions of women's education in the four documents. In the concluding sections, discursive framings of women's education are linked with different views of citizenship, and each of the four texts is examined in order to determine its influence on national and international educational agendas.

Women's education and the dream of global redemption: who dreams for whom?

No period since the end of World War II saw such widespread international concern with the expansion of education as that displayed in the 1990s. The decade opened with the World Conference on Education for All, convened by UNESCO, UNDP (United Nations Development Program), UNICEF and the World Bank in Jomtien. It was attended by delegates and officials from 155 governments, 20 intergovernmental bodies and 150 nongovernmental organisations (Little 1994: 1). This conference adopted the *World Declaration on Education for All* (the first text I shall discuss), which had a particularly strong impact on international education policy, especially on the expansion of basic education (Buchert 1995).

The Jomtien Conference was the largest and most representative education conference of the decade. However, it had not been preceded by any structured process of debate or consultation across a range of constituencies. The Declaration was formulated largely by a transnational community of what Chabbott has termed 'international development professionals' (Chabbott 1998). Little responsibility for policy formulation at Jomtien rested with teachers or trainers; even less was delegated to learners. Shotton has argued that major inputs at Jomtien were made by governments and high-profile northern NGOs and their southern partners; less well-connected southern NGOs found it impossible either to get to Jomtien or to intervene in a debate whose discursive parameters were already set (Shotton 1998: 37).

In 1995, the World Bank published its own education policy document, *Priorities and Strategies for Education*, the second text I will discuss. The Bank had come to exercise enormous influence on international education policy, not so much because of the total amount it spent, but because of its link to the IMF, and the leverage it exercised over governments facing financial crisis. *Priorities and Strategies* was written by the World Bank's education policy advisors and drew on much World Bank commissioned research on education and international development. In arguing for expanded access to basic education, it reiterated ideas contained in the Jomtien Declaration. This was hardly surprising, as many of the same international education policy professionals who had helped shaped the *World Declaration* contributed to *Priorities and Strategies*.

The International Commission on Education for the Twenty-first Century Commission, appointed in 1993 by UNESCO, was made up of 15 members, only five of whom came from Northern or Western contexts. Ten commissioners were, or had been, government ministers; there was no formal representation of grassroots organisations. The Delors Commission's report, entitled *Learning: the treasure within* (the third document analysed here) was published in 1996 (Delors 1996b).

The most representative of all the conferences and commissions discussed in this paper is the Fourth World Conference on Women, convened by the United Nations in Beijing in 1995 with a parallel NGO Forum attended by thousands. The Beijing conference adopted a *Declaration and Platform for Action* with a substantial education chapter (WCW 1995a; WCW 1995b). The NGO Forum, despite its own divisions and debates, had an impact on the framing of both documents (Baden and Goetz 1998).

It is evident that the visions for education of the 1990s were generally formulated by governments, international organisations and their policy advisors. Ideas from a wider range of constituencies were generally not included, except to a small extent at Jomtien, and on a somewhat larger scale at Beijing. However, despite the general homogeneity of authorship of the four texts, they represent different discourses regarding women's education and citizenship. In the next section, some of these discourses will be analysed and discussed in relation to gender and the politics of citizenship.

Women's education: basic needs, social solidarity or autonomy?

The four texts discuss women's education within different discursive frameworks. The *World Declaration on Education for All* and *Priorities and Strategies* situate the importance of women's education in relation to meeting basic needs and developing human resources. By contrast, the UNESCO Commission overlays notions of human resources or basic needs with a concern that women's education should serve not biological necessity but social solidarity. To some extent there is a conflation in this text of the distinction Molyneux has elaborated between needs and interests (Molyneux 1998). The Beijing Declaration, on the other hand, utilises neither the conception of needs, nor interests, but instead stresses education in terms of autonomy and rights, signalling that the fulfilment of rights will realise social and economic potential.

Biological essentialism and the discourse of basic educational needs

The discourse of basic educational 'needs' which characterises the main part of the *World Declaration on Education for All* and the World Bank's *Priorities and Strategies* echoes the discourse of 'basic needs' that was developed in the 1960s in order to put forward a theory of development which examined problems of poverty linked to capitalist growth. This theory, like much of the literature it criticised, argued that societies must satisfy and foster the growth of human needs which are given by the necessity for biological survival. Basic needs thus comprise the satisfaction of hunger and thirst, provision of shelter, the maintenance of health and the developing knowledge of the world. These universalised 'needs' are often taken to be a proxy for political, economic and cultural interests and therefore scant attention is paid to the analysis of 'interests'. In the theorisation of basic needs, the space in which interests might be formulated or contested evaporates (Molyneux 1998). Interests come to be seen as a biological imperative, and therefore classed as a 'needs'-based imperative.

The preamble in the 1990 Jomtien Declaration bases its argument for 'Education for All' on notions of education as follows: (1) a fundamental right for all people; (2) a tool to secure a safer, healthier and more prosperous world; and (3) a way to recognise that education is a necessary, but insufficient, condition for 'personal and social improvement' (WCEFA 1990: 231). According to Chabbott, this gesture towards conceptualising education in terms of rights – and using the language of rights to moderate instrumental claims for what education might accomplish (for the economy and social change) – was part of a strategy to construct an educational consensus amongst international development professionals (Chabbott 1998: 211–214). But despite this resonance with familiar international documents on human rights, the Jomtien Declaration frames all its subsequent sections (or Articles) in terms of 'meeting basic learning needs'. This practice links education and learning to the survival of an essentialised human subject whose needs are mediated by biology. Article 1[2] praises the empowerment of individuals which is thought to emerge from the *satisfaction* of basic learning needs (WCEFA 1990: 232); the word 'satisfaction' connotes instincts or desires which originate in the physical body being fulfilled. A different meaning might have been signalled had terms been used that referred to interests being met/advanced or rights being vindicated. Article 5[3] stresses the necessity to take into account 'the culture, *needs* and opportunities of the community' (WCEFA 1990: 233). This suggests that needs stand outside culture, but must in some sense be moderated by a liberal notion of opportunity. The Jomtien Declaration ends with the statement: 'Only a stable and peaceful *environment* can *create* the conditions in which every *human being*, child and adult alike, may benefit from the goals of this Declaration' (WCEFA 1990: 236, my italics).

The place in which educational goals are realised is called an 'environment', a word which connotes the world of biology or geography. The beneficiaries of education are human beings, essentialised subjects. Social spaces and social

subjects do not appear. The Jomtien Declaration thus slips from th
of its preamble, with socially and politically constructed rights, to i
tive Articles which stress a naturalised version of 'basic needs'. In th'
slide, what is lost is the sense of politics as conflictual, a realm of smiting
alliances. The documents instead construct a notion of 'society' or 'culture'
which is both homogenised and static, whereby different elements all function together. Citizenship, although not mentioned by name, is implied as
part of the glue which generates this cohesion; it emerges as a form of undifferentiated social bonding.

   In this structural-functionalist version of 'educational needs', the specificity
of education for girls and women is noted in two ways. First, girls' and
women's education deficits are identified as a marker of the scale of the
problem of global illiteracy, itself a major concern of the Jomtien Declaration.
The Declaration notes in its preamble that at least 60 million out of the estimated 100 million children without access to schooling are girls. In addition,
women account for two-thirds of the estimated 960 million illiterate adults
(WCEFA 1990: 230). What is the significance of highlighting *female* illiteracy, and not that of, say, the landless or the exploited who might amount
to similar large proportions of the total number of illiterates? Perhaps the
emphasis given to women illiterates speaks to the demands of feminist activists
who began to voice their concerns in UN organisations after the Nairobi
Conference on Women in 1985. However, it appears more likely that the
identification of women as the major component of the world's population
of illiterates is part of the process of essentialising women, which runs through
the whole Declaration. It is implied that the 'basic learning needs' of a very
large but homogenised group of women 'are not being met'. The women
were seen as passive. Their needs, it seems, merely wait to be satisfied. The
concept of 'women' is used descriptively; it does not signal any political relationship or highlight any injustice.

   The second way in which the specific conditions of girls and women are
noted is, at another level, not quite so negative. In Article 3, improving access
and quality of education for girls and women is identified as 'the most urgent
priority'. This article talks of expanding 'basic education *services*' and equitable provision through attention to questions of access, quality, participation
and the elimination of stereotypes. This second mention of girls and women's
education, in contrast to much of the Jomtien Declaration, does focus on
social relations, rather than biologistic needs. However, it is hard to separate
this particular clause from other elements in Article 3. It is followed by a
discussion of the need for 'active commitment' to 'underserved groups'. These
groups are identified as 'the poor; street and working children; rural and
remote populations; nomads and migrant workers; indigenous peoples; ethnic,
racial and linguistic minorities; refugees; those displaced by war; and people
under occupation ... the disabled' (WCEFA 1990: 233). The necessity for
an expansion of educational services for girls and women is thus placed alongside the obligation to help other 'underserved' groups. Here again women
and girls appear as homogeneous, discursively linked with all the other

homogenised 'outsiders' referred to in the text. There is an implication of marginality and minority in the description of girls, although in all regions (except China and South Asia) women and girls constitute 50 per cent or more of the population. They, like the poor and many indigenous peoples, are actually the majority and central to their societies. However, the discussion of their education in Article 3 constructs women as outsiders who reside at the margins of society. Moreover, the interrelationship between gender and other markers of inequity which affect relations between educationally excluded populations in particularly complicated ways is not noted. Thus, in keeping with the largely biologistic framing of the *World Declaration of Education for All,* the education of girls and women is noted as a priority on the grounds of feminine essentialism and not because of questions of rights or the complexities of interlocking oppressions.

Women and civic order

The essentialism of the Jomtien Declaration, with its homogenising framing of women's needs for education was utilised and streamlined in 1995 in the World Bank's *Priorities and Strategies for Education.* Like the Jomtien Declaration, *Priorities and Strategies* begins with an affirmation of the political dimension of education, although what is noted here are not rights, but 'civic order' linked with economic growth. The document opens with the words: 'Education produces knowledge, skills, values and attitudes. It is essential for civic order and citizenship and for sustained economic growth and the reduction of poverty' (World Bank 1995: xi).

Like the Jomtien Declaration, this text also abandons complex discussions of education, citizenship and the political realm, having as its major focus an outline of human capital theory. The analysis made in the text is that investment in human capital is the only means to alleviate poverty, because labour is the chief resource of the poor. For the World Bank, 'the poor' have an excess of potentially productive labour. Therefore, common to both this document and the Jomtien Declaration is a kind of essentialism which understands society and citizenship in terms of their productive capacities and natural rules. For example, the early chapters of *Priorities and Strategies* serve as a classic statement of evolutionism which is mapped onto an analysis of the economy. The sequence of links which are most important is as follows:

> Education, especially basic (primary and lower secondary) education also contributes to poverty reduction by increasing the productivity of the poor's labour, by reducing fertility and improving health, and by equipping people to participate fully in the economy and society. In addition, education contributes to the strengthening of the institutions of civil society, to national capacity building, and to good governance, all of which are increasingly recognised as critical elements in the effective implementation of sound economic and social policies.
>
> (World Bank 1995: 19)

Education is important in this analysis largely because it focuses on increasing productivity, reducing fertility and improving health. It widens participation in the economy, society and lastly the polity. (The ordering is worth noting.)

Priorities and Strategies situates its discussion of girls' and women's education largely in terms of the alleged link between women's level of education and their reduced fertility (World Bank 1995: 28). Although aggregated population data suggest a statistical correlation between the numbers of girls who complete a certain level of schooling and a fall in the fertility rate, more detailed regional and local studies have raised doubts about whether schooling is no more than a form of contraception which delays child-bearing (Jeffery and Basu 1996; Jeffery and Jeffery 1998). It seems hard to believe that schooling alone, regardless of its content or organisation, can be responsible for a decrease in fertility. Yet the inferred link forms a major part of the argument for prioritising the education of girls and women in *Priorities and Strategies.*

Other elements of the argument made in *Priorities and Strategies* for expanding provision for education to girls and women form a cruder version than that of the Jomtien Declaration. Here girls are explicitly and not just implicitly linked with marginal groups:

> Girls, the rural poor, children from linguistic and ethnic minorities, nomads, refugees, street and working children, and children with special needs go to school less than others. In part, this reflects limited access, in part, lower demand.
>
> (World Bank 1995: 43)

Here girls are positioned within 'fringe' populations with no acknowledgement that this marginality is socially constructed. Categories which essentialise girls are drawn upon, and part of the problem is depicted as originating in the 'victim's' deviant 'lower demand' for education. The importance of the education of girls in this analysis is primarily in terms of the breeding function of mothers:

> Parents, especially mothers, with more education provide better nutrition to their children, have healthier children, are less fertile, and are more concerned that their children be educated. Education – in particular female education – is key to reducing poverty and must be considered as much part of a country's health strategy as, say, programs of immunisation and access to health clinics.
>
> (World Bank 1995: 92)

In this text women appear primarily as mothers. Their education is important not because of any concerns with human rights or personal autonomy, but as a form of vaccination which society can give against poverty.

Both the Jomtien Declaration and *Priorities and Strategies* highlight the lack of access of women and girls to education, but they do so in ways which describe women and girls primarily as homogeneous categories. Both texts obscure the existence of political demands or the interests of differing groups. Indeed the discourse of basic needs and human resources positions education in ways which mask the existence of a social or political terrain upon which demands of different constituencies might be articulated.

Education for social solidarity

The Delors Commission Report framed an alternative approach to education in terms of social inclusion. Here education is not confined to formal schooling, but encompasses lifelong learning. It is not simply a tool for economic growth, but a force for developing social solidarity in a globalising world. Education develops democratic participation and is responsible for 'fitting humanity to take control of its own development'. This is to be achieved by enlarging people's choices, particularly choices for a long and healthy life, acquiring knowledge, and access to resources necessary for a decent living (Delors 1996b: 78–9).

This analysis differs substantially from the essentialism of the Jomtien Declaration and *Priorities and Strategies*. In place of 'basic needs', there are active choices; in place of the stress on developing human resources, there is the need to foster social solidarity. Nonetheless the Delors Commission Report repeats selected elements from both the earlier documents, particularly those regarding the need for the education of women and girls. Despite a concern with the realm of the social, as opposed to the biological, when the document comments specifically on the education of women it links this to women's role as mothers who will, it is asserted, provide improved nutrition and health to all children if they are educated. Delors also stresses the need for mothers to be educated for the sake of their daughters, that is, to break a cycle of female illiteracy (Delors 1996b: 75–6). In these passages women are singled out for education because they are mothers. Elsewhere in the Report women are subsumed within general formulations regarding 'local community', 'world society' or 'democracy'.

The Delors Commission Report also avoids positioning girls alongside an arbitrary group of children who are viewed as outcasts. But it does not adapt the subtlety of its analysis of the purposes of education to a consideration of the gendered, racialised and ethnicised divisions of global and local polities. Similarly the Commission develops a strong notion of social solidarity, but fails to consider the impact of gender and other divisions on projects for social inclusion.

In developing its major theme around the relationship between education and social solidarity, the Report neglects to make any specific comment on gender. And when it does consider women, it does so, not out of any rigorous development of its theorisation of social inclusion, but rather by uncritically borrowing formulations regarding women's education and motherhood from Jomtien and the World Bank Review.

Women as agents and beneficiaries of education and development

The Beijing Declaration is the fullest UN statement of the decade regarding women's rights and acknowledges 'the voices of all women and . . . the diversity of women and their roles and circumstances' (WCW 1995a: 154). The Declaration commits itself to the social and political project of promoting 'the goals of equality, development and peace for all women everywhere in the interests of all humanity' (WCW 1995a: 154). Social concepts of human rights and human dignity replace 'needs'. A position regarding liberal democratic rights and women's rights to education is thus formulated. These are seen in terms of the empowerment which is thought to emerge from the sequence represented at one end by rights and at the other by freedom of thought (a sequence not necessarily found in formal education settings, although not exclusively outside them either). The Beijing Declaration affirms a commitment to:

> The empowerment and advancement of women, including the right to freedom of thought, conscience, religion and belief, thus contributing to the moral, ethical, spiritual and intellectual needs of women and men, individually or in community with others, and thereby guaranteeing them the possibility of realising their full potential in society and shaping their lives in accordance with their own aspirations.
>
> (WCW 1995a: 155)

Here the primary goal proposed for thought, belief, and ethics is one of personal autonomy within a community or a society. Unlike the other documents analysed the stress is not on women's obligations as mothers, their labour as human resources, or their invisibility in a generalised social solidarity.

Women's and girls' education is also referred to in relation to the expansion of 'people-centred sustainable development'. This is seen to include 'sustained economic growth through the provision of basic education, life-long education, literacy and training and primary health care for girls and women' (WCW 1995a: 157). Women must therefore gain equal access to this economic growth, expanded education and health provision but no strong causal links between these different elements of development are suggested. Development programmes are not intended to utilise women as a tool for a greater good (for example, lower fertility or expanded growth). The Declaration instead stresses the need for policy on the eradication of poverty which links sustained economic growth, social development, environmental protection and social justice (WCW 1995a: 156). It also emphasises how projects working towards people-centred development need to involve 'women and men as agents and beneficiaries' (WCW 1995a: 157). The stress on agency as opposed to passivity therefore stands in contrast to the other documents.

The Platform of Action, also adopted at Beijing, set out a detailed agenda for realising the goals of the Declaration. Education and training of women was ranked second to the elimination of poverty in the list of strategic objectives (WCW 1995b). The Platform of Action notes that education is a human right and 'essential for achieving the goals of equality, development and peace' (WCW 1995b: 181). The document therefore makes the case for the importance of establishing equality of educational access and attainment largely to ensure that greater numbers of women become 'agents of change'; it makes the link between 'improving health, nutrition and education *in the family*'; and it recognises the necessity to empower women in decision-making in society (ibid.). The Platform of Action does not replicate the reductive assumptions of the other three documents. For example, the benefits of women's education are not discussed in relation to children and the general expansion of economic growth in the society. Where the link between education and health is noted, it is with respect to a particular site – the family. This conception of education, linked as it is to agency rather than passive, 'basic needs' or invisible 'social solidarity', has important consequences for understanding women's citizenship. It does indeed imply that women are a social group that must be seen as both active and capable of reflection.

It should also be noted that the Platform of Action conceptualises the problem of women' and girls' lack of education not in terms of their 'fringe' or marginal location, or their failure to register demand. It notes instead (more forcefully) that girls' and women's exclusions are shaped by customs such as early marriage, violence (often entailing sexual harassment), or educational factors such as gender-biased curricula, assessment procedures or the lack of financial resources (WCW 1995b: 181–183). This naming of the processes entailed in women's exclusion from education shifts the 'blame' from female 'victims' with 'low demand' for education, unsatisfied 'basic needs', or a homogenised marginality. Social conditions that can lead to exclusion and violence are indicated, particular processes are singled out, and certain agents with key responsibilities for challenging the status quo and for promoting change are identified. Thus, much more direct action is advocated in this document compared to the other texts discussed above. Women's political agency is of key importance, as women are no longer conceptualised in this declaration as passive sufferers.

In short, what seems clear is that each document frames the purposes of women's education in diverse and sometimes contradictory ways. This diversity of conception has important consequences for female citizenship. It is to discussion of this theme that I now turn.

Contrasting conceptions of citizenship

Citizenship, as a concept, appears most explicitly in the Delors Commission Report. All the other documents utilise a notion of citizenship which is more implicit. In each document, there is also a recognition of the ways in which the interrelationship between the citizen and the state is mediated by other

forms of association. However, only in the Beijing Declaration
recognition of a gendered political terrain which makes citizen⟨
for women to claim.

Three different notions of citizenship are associated with the different understandings of women's education outlined above. First, the Jomtien Declaration
and *Priorities and Strategies* weave together the notion of basic education
needs with that of developing human resources. Citizenship thus confers a
mutual obligation on the citizen and the state to develop *human resources*.
Second, the notion of social solidarity utilised by the UNESCO commission
draws upon a notion of citizenship as *stakeholding*, although paradoxically,
this notion of stakeholding is also used by the World Bank. However, a weaker
form of association and obligation as 'stakeholder' is put forward in the World
Bank document compared to that used by Delors. Lastly, the Beijing
Declaration formulates a notion of citizenship linked to *human rights* and
social participation, which resonates with its conception of education for
autonomy and empowerment.

Human resources, women's citizenship and the private sphere of the household

In the Jomtien Declaration and the World Bank's *Priorities and Strategies*,
there is a minimal notion of citizenship. Government under the guidance of,
or in partnership with, international agencies provides education to citizens
(and possibly non-citizens) on the grounds of their 'basic education needs'.
The special needs of women are thus defined in relation to traditional activities associated with motherhood (e.g. as providers and nurturers of 'human
resources'). It is therefore through this interpellation that their minimal citizenship is recognised.

In both these texts, citizenship is a passive acknowledgement of need and
the state is the most important agent in satisfying that need. Women's needs
must therefore be satisfied primarily in the private sphere of the household,
where women continue to provide food and shelter, health and education to
their children. No importance is attached to women's participation in the
public sphere. Hence, little attention is paid to women's education in these
documents, except insofar as it, like their claims on citizenship, is located in
the domestic realm of motherhood.

Stakeholding and social solidarity

A contrasting notion is that citizenship, conceived of as social solidarity and
the enactment of democracy, is better secured through education. In this
model, education and citizenship are strongly intertwined. This is the notion
touched on in the World Bank's *Priorities and Strategies*, but fully discussed
by the Delors Commission. Much of this analysis is gender neutral. Citizenship
and education are the outcomes of a realisation of rights and are seen as
instruments to secure gender equality. Where the specific exclusions of women

and girls from education are addressed, these are seen as violations of rights; that is, an inadmissible denial of citizenship and its reflexive counterpoint of education. However, as Delors draws explicitly on Jomtien for this section of the Commission Report, what he emphasises is the economic 'investment' which should be realised through the education of citizenship. Alongside women's representation as citizens bearing gender neutral rights, they are also portrayed as economic assets, who as mothers will secure the health of their children, and as productive workers, who will contribute to the economic growth of their societies (Delors 1996b: 179). It is through women's participation that the provision of education and the enactment of social development emerges. Social solidarity is an unquestionable good.

In the Jomtien Declaration, there is a call for 'partnerships at all levels' to be strengthened in order to revitalise the provision of basic education (WCEFA 1990: 234). The partnerships identified are a loose assemblage of participants in education which include 'local communities' and families. However, the gender politics of such forms of association are not examined. In contrast, the World Bank's *Priorities and Strategies* replaces the rather amorphous notion of partnership with the concept of 'stakeholder'. Policy formulation will need 'to consult key stakeholders . . . In increasingly decentralised contexts, the stakeholders will include not only central governments but also other levels of government, as well as communities, parents, teachers and employers' (World Bank 1995: 15).

The Jomtien Declaration and the World Bank's *Priorities and Strategies* are both strongly influenced by liberal democratic thought. The concepts of stakeholders and partners draw on liberal notions of civil society, where socially defined groups of stakeholders express private political interests (McClure 1992). The influence of Gramscian and feminist scholars on reshaping notions of civil society, and recasting understandings of the 'private' have had very little influence on these texts (Mouffe 1992; Young 1990).

Some writers on stakeholding have extolled its potential to build bridges across the fault lines of political theory, thus attempting to reconcile personal autonomy, civil society and the regulatory state (Kelly, Kelly and Gamble 1997). However, the use of the concept in practice by large international agencies in documents like *Priorities and Strategies* does not indicate anything beyond an expression of particularistic interests. In this formulation, education is understood as an unproblematic realm for the simultaneous satisfaction of private need and public good. State education policy organises and adjudicates between these two concepts. Feminist scholarship has therefore questioned the possibility of this simultaneous satisfaction, but both the Jomtien Declaration and *Priorities and Strategies* fail to address this debate, despite their concern with the education of women and girls.

The notion of stakeholding is also utilised by Delors. While for the World Bank, stakeholding appears as a means of articulating citizenship and participating in consultative processes to shape policy (although also implying little further action and no sense of accountability), the Delors Commission Report describes stakeholding as a means of winning support for public policy reform and putting change into practice. Citizenship is treated as a given and stake-holding is the way in which citizenship is enacted. The relationship is revealed in this passage:

> One of the main aims of education reform – and probably the best means of going about it – is to involve the stakeholders in decision-making. This is the context – relating both to public policy and to process – within which the Commission stresses the importance of decentralisation measures in education.
>
> (Delors 1996b: 158)

Thus, while for the World Bank consultation with stakeholders is a form of market research on public policy, for Delors the process of consultation moves beyond the formulation of policy and makes the involvement of stakeholders central to implementation.

The Delors Commission Report is largely an articulation of republican and communitarian ideals of citizenship and an argument for education as an expression of communal solidarity. The notion of stakeholders is used more as a proxy for community and less as an index of the private realm of civil society. The Report links communitarianism to a notion of human rights and global solidarity. This avoids the exclusionary and essentialising notions of the nation which can often accompany communitarian writing (Yuval-Davis 1997). But, because the conception of global citizenship utilised by Delors remains gender neutral and fails to account for difference, it is unable to address the extent to which solidarity and education might be at one and the same time exclusionary and inclusionary. Women might be stakeholders, but the difficulties and barriers they experience in claiming their stake remain unacknowledged.

Human rights and social participation

A third notion of citizenship suggests that women are neither passive receivers of education nor compelled into education because of the obligations to the state. The Beijing Declaration and the Platform of Action pivot on a notion of the centrality of personal autonomy, which citizenship and education may regulate and guarantee, but where the voice and action of women (singly or collectively) are of equal importance. This is potentially a much more subversive notion of citizenship than either the minimal notion encapsulated by the Jomtien Declaration, or the more republican notion of the 'general will' expressed by Delors. It is noteworthy that in this third formulation women are not represented exclusively as mothers, although the family as a site of subordination, as well as possible emancipation, is noted.

The Beijing Declaration makes no mention of stakeholding. The state is conceived in two roles, both as the active initiator of programmes for reform that will carry out the strategies assigned by the Platform of Action, and as a regulatory body facilitating actions that take forward the vision of the

Declaration by institutions, organisations, social groups like families, and individuals (see for example WCW 1995b: 183–187). Citizenship is not conferred by stakeholding, but by human rights and an enactment of social participation, particularly in 'women's groups and networks and other non-governmental organisations and community based organisations' (WCW 1995a: 156).

Of all the documents, only the Beijing Declaration grapples with the contradictory, problematic and gendered nature of citizenship which feminist scholarship has identified – that citizenship is the necessary condition for the realisation of personal autonomy and emancipatory projects but is also an exclusionary instrument creating privileged spaces for some and not for others (Lister 1997). Agency and 'people-centred sustainable development', rather than passivity and 'basic' need or communal action for the greater good, are emphasised. But the clauses on education, while constituting a useful agenda, do not acknowledge that education might stand against emancipation. The ambiguous influences of education (like that of citizenship), which can be both potentially emancipatory for some and subjugating for others, are not referred to, thus highlighting the challenge of formulating strategic demands that recognise women's difference that a number of scholars have drawn attention to since Beijing (Molyneux 1998; Yuval-Davis and Werbner 1999).

Conclusion

Different and sometimes contested understandings of women's citizenship and the purposes of their education characterise the documents discussed in this chapter. In the Jomtien Declaration and the World Bank's *Priorities and Strategies*, education is conferred upon women because of a relatively passive form of citizenship, only minimally recognised in terms of stakeholding. But, in the Beijing Declaration, education is a necessary component of empowerment, itself an enactment of citizenship by autonomous bearers of rights and articulators of demands. The Delors Commission Report leans in both directions.

In these documents political relationships are either barely defined (e.g. just sketched in as 'partnerships' in the Jomtien Declaration) or strongly circumscribed in terms of stakeholding and citizenship as in the Delors Commission Report. In the Beijing Declaration a complex role for the state is formulated suggesting multiple locations for political encounters.

Of the three positions, the Jomtien Declaration has been most extensively utilised by governments and international donor agencies in the formulation of policy. The Delors Commission has had virtually no visibility outside UNESCO. The pre-eminence of the Jomtien Declaration appears likely to continue into the next century. This is partly because of the powerful consensus that surrounded its 'Education for All' initiative which Chabbott noted (Chabbott 1998), and partly because of the minimal challenges its agenda presents to entrenched gender regimes and dominant political, economic and cultural interests. The Jomtien Declaration is the text with the weakest notion of women's citizenship, agency or autonomy. The challenge for feminists as theorists and activists in the coming decades is to build on some of the more emancipatory understandings of education and citizenship (e.g. women's agency and collective action) articulated at Beijing to challenge the essentialism and passivity ascribed to women in the 'developing world'. Such a challenge may ultimately lead to a new and more evolved understanding of women's citizenship and its impact on education.

Notes

1   Jacques Delors chaired the 1993 UNESCO Commission on Education for the Twenty-first Century.
2   Article 1 on meeting basic learning needs defines what these needs are for every person, and the individual and social reasons why they should be satisfied.
3   Article 5 deals with broadening the means of delivery of basic education and the imperative to reach people of all ages.

References

Baden, S. and Goetz A. M. (1998) 'Who needs [sex] when you can have [gender]? Conflicting discourses on gender at Beijing', in C. Jackson and R. Pearson (eds) *Feminist Visions of Development: gender analysis and policy*, London: Routledge.

Buchert, L. (1995) *Recent Trends in Education Aid: towards a classification of policies. A report for the International Working Group on Education*, Paris: International Institute for Educational Planning.

Chabbott, C. (1998) 'Constructing educational consensus: international development professionals and the World Conference on Education for All', *International Journal of Educational Development*, 18, 3: 207–218.

Delors, J. (ed.) (1996a) 'Education: the necessary Utopia', *Learning: the treasure within. Report of the International Commission on Education for the twenty-first century*, Paris: UNESCO Publishing.

Delors, J. (1996b) *Learning: the treasure within. Report of the International Commission on Education for the twenty-first century*, Paris: UNESCO Publishing.

Jeffery, P. and Jeffery, R. (1998) 'Silver bullet or passing fancy? Girls' schooling and population policy', in C. Jackson and R. Pearson (eds) *Feminist Visions of Development: gender analysis and policy*, London: Routledge.

Jeffery, R. and Basu A. (eds) (1996) *Girls' Schooling, Women's Autonomy and Fertility change in South Asia*, New Delhi: Sage.

Kelly, G., Kelly, D. and Gamble, A. (eds) (1997) 'Conclusion: stakeholder capitalism', *Stakeholder Capitalism*, Basingstoke: Macmillan.

Lister, R. (1997) *Citizenship: feminist perspectives*, London: Macmillan.

Little, A. (1994) 'The Jomtien Conference and the implementation of primary education projects', in A. Little, W. Hoppers and R. Gardner (eds) *Beyond Jomtien: implementing primary education for all*, Basingstoke: Macmillan.

McClure, K. (1992) 'On the subject of rights: pluralism, plurality and political identity', in C.Mouffe (ed.) *Dimensions of Radical Democracy: pluralism, citizenship, community*, London: Verso.

Molyneux, M. (1998) 'Analysing women's movements', in C. Jackson and R. Pearson (eds) *Feminist Visions of Development: gender analysis and policy*, London: Routledge.

Mouffe, C. (ed.) (1992) *Dimensions of Radical Democracy: pluralism, citizenship, community*, London: Verso.

Shotton, J. (1998) *Learning and Freedom: policy and paradigms in Indian education and schooling*, New Delhi: Sage.

World Bank (1995) *Priorities and Strategies in Education. A World Bank review*, Washington: World Bank.

World Conference on Education for All (WCEFA) (1990) 'World Declaration on Education for All: meeting basic learning needs', in A. Little, W. Hoppers and R. Gardner (eds) (1994) *Beyond Jomtien: implementing primary education for all*, Basingstoke: Macmillan.

World Conference on Women (WCW) (1995a) 'Beijing Declaration', *Women's Studies Quarterly*, 24, 1&2: 154–158.

World Conference on Women (WCW), (1995b) 'Platform of Action', *Women's Studies Quarterly*, 24, 1&2: 159–361.

Young, I. M. (1990) *Justice and the Politics of Difference*, Princeton: Princeton University Press.

Yuval-Davis, N. (1997) *Gender and Nation*, London: Sage.

Yuval-Davis, N. and Werbner, P. (eds) (1999) *Women, Citizenship and Difference*, London: Zed Press.

Part 2

Teachers' identities and public identifications

7 Motherhood and citizenship
Educational conflicts in Portugal

Helena C. Araújo

Classical political theorists as different as Locke or Rousseau have conceptualised motherhood in ways that tie women to the state of nature (see Coole 1988; Okin 1980; Philips 1991). In consequence, women as mothers were considered to be separate from the public sphere of citizenship, which was commonly understood in terms of political and civil rights (Joaquim 1998). This chapter focuses on the relationship between the different political perspectives on motherhood and women's citizenship in Portugal in the final phase of the Republican period (1919–1926) and the period of transition (1926–1933) to the authoritarian State (the so-called New State). The analysis describes the conflictual images which confronted women in society and more specifically women primary teachers who, at the time, already constituted the majority in the profession. The central concern of Republicanism in Portugal was the construction of the polity guided by the ideals of 'freedom, equality and fraternity'. Yet, as I shall show, there were considerable tensions between the perspectives on women's citizenship adopted by various political groupings within the Republic and immediately after which had consequences for the construction of women's role as teachers.

Carole Pateman's (1988) feminist analysis of the male-centric state provides an interesting framework for understanding women's citizenship. For example, she points out that women were, paradoxically, both excluded and included by liberal concepts of citizenship even though they possessed the same abilities and attributes as men. On the basis of sexual difference, women were excluded from participating in political life and public citizenship at the same time as they were 'included' as subordinates in the domestic sphere, with duties towards the nation-state as mothers and reproducers of the nation (see Arnot 1997; Arnot et al. 1996; Yuval-Davis 1997). In Portugal, as we shall see, a form of 'symbolic motherhood' was also promoted – as a means of transmitting republican ideals.

The first section of the chapter briefly describes the Portuguese political context in these particular historical periods. It is followed by an analysis of the gendered perspectives of Republicans, anarchists, feminists and Catholics, focusing particularly on their ways of understanding women's citizenship: women's right to work outside the home; women's political rights; and the relationship between citizenship and motherhood. The final section of the chapter discusses how such contradictory pressures impinge upon women teachers and leave legacies which are still (now seventy years later) being experienced by women teachers today.

The Portuguese context

The Portuguese Republican period (1910–1926) is often characterised as a period of 'democratic instability'. After the military coup of 28 May 1926, such political instability continued during the early years of the Military Dictatorship (1926–1933), until the authoritarian state of Salazar was able to dominate the political process. Portuguese women were also affected by a society undergoing a slow process of industrialisation and by the powerful influence of a conservative Catholic Church which was supported by a large peasantry and rural bourgeoisie. As far as women's position in the world of work was concerned, Ana Osório, a well-known feminist, argued that their situation was worse in Portugal than in other countries. In her view, an atmosphere of 'moral asphyxia' was applied to the lives of Portuguese women (Osório 1918: 19) and the prejudices in girls' convent education at that time contributed to a situation where it was 'as if they [women] were incarcerated in a prison from which they can only escape by scaling the walls' (ibid.: 111).

By examining the various perspectives on citizenship, we gain a sense of how these particular historical periods (both the Republican era and the later transition to an authoritarian state) were crucial to the formation of gender politics around the questions of women's citizenship and motherhood and women's role as teachers of a new generation. While gender and citizenship issues were often perceived as mutually exclusive, there were attempts, mainly during the military dictatorship, to establish a greater connection between women and the nation-state. In this analysis, the contradictions surrounding women's citizenship and images of mothering in Portuguese society in Republican and dictatorial years become more visible.

Throughout the first decades of the twentieth century, as we shall see, Republicanism embraced and reworked many of the perspectives of positivism (Catroga 1991). The images of femininity which stemmed from positivism, especially from the theories of Auguste Comte, clearly had an impact. Other perspectives on women's citizenship, during the same period, included those of anarchists ('anarco-sindicalistas') who represented one of the most influential traditions within the trade union movement. Also, during this period feminists, who were organised in their own groups whilst simultaneously belonging to masonic lodges and Republican parties, expressed views on such matters. One of these groups, the League of Portuguese Republican Women, had more than three-hundred names on its roll. The most traditional perspective, supported by sectors connected with the Catholic Church as well as by other conservative sectors, dominated from 1926 onwards. Given the intensity and influence of their contribution to the debate, it was mainly the Catholic proposals of the Academic Centre for Christian Democracy (CADC) which attracted university students of Coimbra during the Republican years.

The analysis of these four different perspectives on women's citizenship thus follows the logic of political events through this key period of political transition in the early twentieth century.

Republican views of women

In the early twentieth century, positivism[1] as a European philosophy of knowledge (Catroga 1991; Mayeur 1979) generated a range of negative images of women especially since women were assumed to be still at the 'metaphysical' stage (Manieri 1978). Reason was portrayed as the territory and the capacity of men. In the Republican period, women were often mentioned as an impediment to progress and civilisation. The influence of the Catholic Church was critical here. The division between husband and wife was based on religion, because the wife was understood as a 'believer' and the husband was guided by 'reason'. A second powerful division as expressed through education was the notion of the wife as ignorant, as lacking in 'instruction', whereas the husband had the potential intelligence to gain access to university education. Françoise Mayeur writes: 'As far as the Republicans are concerned, the main question lies in the husband who works and does not find any understanding, but only hostility, from the women of his family, who are united against him' (Mayeur 1979: 16).

However, if women's 'expressiveness' was seen as negative in relation to the political field, it was also proclaimed as the distinctive quality which differentiated women from men. Rosaria Manieri (1978), in her analysis of Comte's perspective, demonstrates that women were thought to be determined by their 'nature'. As a result, women's supposed physical weakness was contrasted to the assumed physical strength of men:

> [Comte constructs his theory] according to the Hobbesian notion of human nature as essentially aggressive and competitive, aided by the concept of *homo economicus* from classical economists, and applying to the civil world the Darwinist biological principle of the survival of the fittest. . . . [Hence] he states that, being the economic, social and political world constructed on the basis of the natural world (that is, being regulated by the law of the fittest), the woman shall be subjected to a fierce daily competition with the stronger sex, a competition that she will not be able to bear . . . The price will be [the loss of] her own femininity, the delicacy of her feelings, which is her essential merit and the source of her value.
>
> (Manieri 1978: 26)

This kind of male theorising implied that women were to be excluded from material production which was conceptualised as a male domain. Women were responsible instead for providing care and solicitude in the home, making it a haven (for men) away from the competitiveness and aggressiveness of the public world. They were expected to use their 'weapons of sentiment' to help men find a solution to their dilemmas, to help the bourgeois, i.e. by encouraging a more humanitarian treatment of the workers, or to help the proletariat, via 'sweeter and more realistic means', to overcome their opponents.

Voices such as Barreiro (1912) contested this crude view of women's role:

> ... the natural selection that, in Darwin's opinion, explains the muscular superiority of men ... cannot demonstrate in any way the organic or intellectual superiority of either of the sexes. For this, it would be necessary to know previously which one needed more organic capacity and intelligence: whether it was the woman who had to feed the children, educate them and govern the household, or the man who was restricted to the role of warrior, shepherd or peasant. The problem does not give clear clues and is not in accordance with Darwin's solution which stresses that the men's intellectual average is higher than women's, and for that reason, men would be predetermined to hold the monopoly of 'instruction'.
>
> (Barreiro 1912: 15–16)

Nevertheless, Barreiro himself went on to emphasise the 'high mission of a woman ... the management of the household, the education of her children, and as far as possible, [her being] of some support to her husband' (ibid.: 41).

Many Republican leaders stated that the best place for women was the domestic sphere, with the expectation that Republican mothers and housewives would build support for the Republic in their families and networks of personal relationships thus contributing to the hegemony of the State over the Catholic Church. Somewhat paradoxically, women's 'expressiveness' was seen as potentially useful to the Republican struggle. António J. Almeida expressed this quite clearly:

> The modern Christ, which is the People, needs to be himself rescued, by women's contribution, as the constant and careful beings they are. ... It is necessary that liberal women stand up to fanatical women, who are under the influence of priests, and, with the seductive power of their words, promote the true ideals of liberation ... We do not aim to bring women into the streets or into clubs, involving them in great agitation, from which Portuguese women have distanced themselves so well. What is needed is that they exert their influence and republican propaganda in the family, in kinship relations.
>
> (Almeida, quoted in Esteves 1992: 40–41)

Some of the traditions within Republicanism referred to women's rights in the family as *equal* to men's. Afonso Costa (a prominent Republican leader) explained that the Republican regime 'ha[d] transformed the wife into a partner for her husband':

[the wife is able] to assume more delicate functions, and is in a better position as an educator of children . . . She is not only granted the government of the household, the superior administration of the family. She is the careful custodian of family unity, the main educator of those who will be the main leaders of the destiny of the country. The wife is the defender of her husband's patrimony which she needs to administer and multiply.

(1913: 53)

To be man's equal meant to be a 'partner', which, in turn, meant to be in charge of domestic duties in a subordinate position. Within the Republican law, married women were granted some rights. They were no longer defined as obedient and compliant beings, subordinate to their husbands. They were able to get a civil divorce based on the same grounds as men. They were also able to publish their own work without their husband's permission. However, these gains were jeopardised by a legal system where men owned the economic assets of the family (including those of wives and children). Geraldine Scanlon (1986), writing about Spain, maintains that although there was much rhetoric in Republican discourse emphasising the equality between married partners, primarily during the period after the 1868 Republican Revolution: 'The patriarchal structure of the family was never seriously questioned. . . . And even the introduction of civil marriage was basically anticlerical and not a feminist measure' (ibid.: 8/9).

Paradoxically, women were still denied the vote. Republicans, on the whole, feared that if women were granted the vote, monarchists, Catholics and other conservative forces would be able to defeat the Republicans as well as the project of secularisation, seen as the project of *modernity* for Portugal. As a Republican MP claimed in Parliament, women's vote should be denied since in the countries where it had been introduced, 'the effects were bad, because almost all women are conservatives' (quoted in Catroga 1991: 292). Political democracy implied a form of rationalised participation which was, by implication, autonomous of the Catholic Church.

Certainly the denial of women's franchise presented some difficulties for the Republican politicians who, before the emergence of the Republic, had defended universal enfranchisement as one of their first priorities. After its emergence, however, they began to query who had the 'capacity' to vote. 'Lunatics' and the 'insane' were to be excluded, as well as the 'illiterate' and women – not only illiterate women, but women *per se*, because of their 'expressiveness' and 'irrationality'. Afonso Costa's rhetorical statement, in a parliamentary session on the women's vote, clearly articulated this view:

We, who have ended slavery [meaning 'wives' slavery'], who have granted equality to men [*sic*], who have turned women into partners for men, we have reversed our position concerning women's political capacity to vote in similar terms to men. This is because the problem needs to be confronted with the question of the dispositions and even structures of such capacities [i.e. the capacity for voting] ... The only thing necessary to require is *the development of reason, it is a psychological phenomenon* ... The State needs more and more active, superior, prepared leaders ... The Republic wants conscious. defined, confident, reflexive minds.

(Costa 1976: 531/533, emphasis added)

The dominant republican-positivist perspective on women's main mission in the home as mothers and educators, wives and housekeepers disguised the fact that the Republican government was denying women the rights that it was granting to men. Republican militants (i.e. the radical sectors) who supported the fight for suffrage for women were also most likely to be those who supported women's autonomous lodges against the masonic leadership. Some even made speeches at the *Feminist and Educational Congress*, in 1924. The President of the Republic, in the opening session, stated that because women were the educators of their children, they should have the right to intervene in political affairs. Another Republican leader stated that just because women had great domestic virtues, this should not imply their 'slavery outside the family' (Bernardino Machado). Others were conscious that the Republic still had not given women what was promised to them (for instance, Magalhães Lima).[2]

Anarchist views on women's role

Emilio Costa, a unionist and political militant,[3] was an anarchist who expressed strong views on women's position in society at that time. In 1928, he wrote a book entitled *Women and Feminism*, where he debated many of the current issues. He too emphasised that the main role of woman in society was 'to start a family, do the housework and educate her own children' (Costa 1928: 49). Yet these sentiments did not imply that he disagreed with female employment outside the home. Women had a right to work, he argued, to gain their autonomy from men. At the same time, he appeared to speak in the name of those men who were feeling 'domestic unrest' (Costa 1928: 50) caused by the work of 'their' women outside the home. 'It is the duality of [women's] occupations that is one of the greatest problems of our times' (ibid.).

> Family life tends to disappear ... I belong to those who consider this a bad thing, although it is risky to say so because I will be considered a conservative ... For a while, I have not favoured the woman going out to work, that woman who does not have time to go home to eat and instead goes to restaurants with (or without) her husband and children. As a result, she looks at her home as a dull place, which is natural ... What do the husband and children gain from such family life? I have never obtained a satisfactory answer.
>
> (Costa 1928: 68–69)

Costa's preferred formula was that women should work outside the home, but not once they were married. His argument was captured in the phrase – 'Not at the same time' – meaning that a housewife should not be a professional, a white-collar or factory worker at the same time. He also warned women against their many illusions about paid work.

Using the same arguments, Costa advised the feminist movement of its main tasks. He distanced himself from feminist suffrage campaigns since, in his view, political rights were not as important as major questions about the economy. First, Costa argued that the feminist movement should value manual work amongst women who were at risk of forming an army of 'declassées'. Second, Costa supported women's rights, as individuals, to receive education. Women's education was important because it would better prepare them for their role as mothers and educators of children. Third, Costa argued that it was necessary to campaign to promote those occupations which he considered to be those most appropriate for women's natural qualities. Portugal, for example, needed good nurses. At the same time, he argued that the garden, the orchard, the vegetable-garden were 'magnificent' places for women to work. Feminists, according to Costa, should organise the education of women for such occupations. At the same time, an amelioration of the conditions in which housework was done was necessary. Electricity should be provided for households at low prices so that the domestic servant could be dispensed with. 'It is better for women's emancipation to get electricity at low cost, than to multiply the number of women lawyers, engineers or deputies, however talented they might be (Costa 1928: 69). Finally, and most important of all, in Costa's view, the feminist movement should fight for the 'male breadwinner's wage', so that women would not have to work. This appeared, in his view, to be one of the best means of overcoming 'domestic unrest' and of restoring family life – which he praised so highly.

An analysis of the anarchist daily newspaper *A Batalha* (*'The Battle'*), published between 1919 and 1927, reveals that although gender issues were clearly not a central concern, women's equality in the 'workplace' was supported.[4] It was stressed that economic exploitation was common for both men and women. For that reason, feminist issues did not exist: 'we are firmly convinced that there is not a feminist problem to solve, but only a social question, i.e. the moral and political emancipation of the female gender depends on the economic liberation of the people'. Despite this statement, anarchists sent a message supporting the 1924 *Feminist and Educational Congress* and arguing that the equality of sexes should be considered only 'as a stage in the journey that men and women need to go through to attain happiness'.[5] A slightly different version was supported in another article in 1925 entitled 'The victories of feminism depend mainly upon the economic situation of women in society'. Here it was maintained that the aim of feminism was not the emancipation of women: 'one sex cannot be emancipated alone'. The purposes of feminism were instead designed to end the 'monstruous inequality between men and women'.

In many anarchist writings, the emphasis put on economic contradictions as a way of explaining women's situation downplayed the importance of the struggles and movements to change patriarchal relations at the political level. In contrast, the anarchist Adolfo Lima, an editor who wrote quite often in the education journal *Educação Social*, did not embrace such views and addressed the equal importance of women's social, political and economic rights. As a lecturer in the Lisbon Teacher College, Lima (along with some other members of the anarchist movement) supported women teachers in much the same way as they supported their male counterparts. They were also strong defenders of co-education arguing that, in this way, women teachers would not be differentiated in terms of their functions in the school from male teachers (Lima 1925).

Feminist views of women's role

Feminism was not a unified movement in the country in the periods under consideration. The first organisation to emerge, the League of Portuguese Republican Women, had, as its first priority, civil and economic rights as well as support for republican ideals. The attempt to reconcile Republican aims with feminist objectives undoubtedly produced many tensions and defeats for the feminist movement. The discourse on women's rights supported the view that women were human beings who should be granted the same rights as men; at the same time, the attempt to involve women politically in the Republican movements could also have been instrumental as a way to counteract the influence of the Church and the 'fanatical women' under its influence. A similar process took place within the masonic lodges which initially invited women to join and yet subsequently expelled them (see Costa n.d.).

Protesting against the subordinate status of women within marriage, Osório argued:

> The girl who is to be married is maintained in the most complete ignorance, compelled to such naivety, taught to be submissive to man. Man does not find in marriage a loyal partner and collaborator, but only searches to destroy a virginity and finds ignorance which amuses him.
>
> (Osório 1911: 31)

In the view of such militant feminists, the struggle for divorce would grant women equal status with men, at least in the family, which from their perspective would lead to the granting of other rights. Even within Republican ranks, feminists had to demonstrate that divorce was not leading women to misery. Ana Osório recorded the polemical dispute between herself and the well-known male republican writer and politician, Raul Proença. According to Osório, Proença wrote a newspaper article in which he stated that a divorced woman was despised by society because she had already lived with a man and, if she married a second time, her new husband would be thinking about her first husband all the time. Osório used the occasion to re-emphasise women's right to be considered autonomous persons, not solely the sexual property of men (Osório 1911: 17).

The right to work was the backbone of the equality argument. Autonomous life could be achieved given access to the 'workplace', and doing 'honest work'. Women should participate in the same way in the workplace, 'in every field of activity, according to their intellectual capacities . . . and their own ambitions' (Osório 1912). The opening of new areas of the 'workplace' for women and equal pay therefore would also be required: 'Probably, we, Portuguese women, will have to strike . . . in order to be considered as human beings, with the right to paid work, since we have – something which till now has not been contested – the right to live' (Osório 1918: 43). Women's citizenship, Osório argued, should be constructed through work. In that way, liberal versions of citizenship which were concerned mainly with the public sphere could be challenged. For other members of the League, the right to work applied only to single women. The majority of women were seen first as mothers, wives and housekeepers. The emphasis of the League on the domestic duties of women was therefore clearly ambivalent.

Women's right to vote was even more problematic. Political rights were viewed as important, but in their first negotiations with the new-born Republican government, Republican-feminists declared that political rights would be dealt with later because they did not want to disrupt the Republican struggle against the monarchy and the Church. Their struggle for the vote was such a sensitive issue that Republican feminists treated it as secondary to main Republican aims. Although such feminists held a widespread view that political rights should be won, such rights were considered to be the product of evolution, rather than revolution. The feminist emphasis on the vote became more central when the Chamber of Deputies debated women's vote (already approved in the Senate), and also following the defeat of the campaign for women's right to vote in the Chamber in 1913. Feminist campaigns for the vote were expected to transmit the idea to the Portuguese people that 'the meaning of universal does not consist only of a male reality' (Osório 1915: 61; cf. also Velleda 1912). Many feminists even accepted women's right to vote on a restricted basis of certification, as a preliminary strategy towards extending this right to other women later.

Adelaide Cabete, a more pro-republican feminist, and President of the National Council of Portuguese Women, claimed that women's vote was a useful way of moralising social life through the 'protection of childhood, social hygiene, the amelioration of economic life, and the abolition of laws permitting prostitution' and that this would be the aim of women's intervention in Parliament (Cabete 1923: 33). Women's vote was not incompatible with the domestic duties of women; on the contrary, women could better serve the nation if they brought women's issues to Parliament to be debated. Women in politics would be a means of counterbalancing 'man's instinct of domination, moderating his selfishness, . . . revealing that other beings exist on the earth – women' (Cabete 1925: 50).

A more sophisticated view was supported by the lawyer Aurora C. Gouveia.

In opening the *Feminist and Educational Congress* (1924), she focused feminism on women's rights and democracy as part of the modernising of Portugal. She argued in favour of a democratic Republic, stressing that this could only be achieved when democracy was constructed in three spheres: the state, the 'workplace', and, the family. Gouveia was clear about the crucial importance for democracy of the very different ways in which women and men were incorporated as citizens. She argued that because women had obtained equality in the family, the time had come for its extension into the 'citizenplace'. Her discourse, however, appeared to fall into the trap of using the language of legal reform when considering social and political change for democracy. For instance, she argued that with the new republican laws, women were already equal to men in the family, since they were granted equal rights regarding children and their own status as citizens in the family. But in so doing, she failed to refer to the subordinate economic status of wives vis-à-vis their husbands within marriage.

Other feminist groupings, not affiliated with the feminist associations referred to above but nevertheless close to Catholicism, also made their views known on women's issues. One of them was Emília de S. Costa, who declared herself a Catholic as well as a supporter of feminist ideas (but not a 'suffragette'). Belonging to a traditional sector of Republican feminism, she strongly supported women's duties in the home. She was clearly emphasising the notion of 'woman's nature' as more suited to domestic duties which were seen as being her 'natural mission', 'imposed by God'. It was because of this divine attribution that women had to suffer the (albeit gratifying) pains of maternity. At the same time, they possessed great sensitivity and spirituality which was a compensation for their 'inability to rise to the pinnacles of genius' (Costa 1923: 57). But women were not 'beings short of ideas', as Schopenhauer (cf. Costa 1922: 11) had contended. If society claimed that women were the best educators, it should grant them respect and approval for their femininity (Costa 1922: 11). In particular, women's work outside the home was justified for those who were not able to find the necessary means of support. If women had to earn a living, they should only pursue activities seen as 'suitable for their own sex'. Some such activities might be as shop assistants in fashion stores, or in bakeries, thus replacing men. Women tram drivers, such as those found in Oporto, were considered unacceptable (Costa 1923: 39).

Using the same line of argument, Costa argued that politics should not be of concern to women. Any intervention in politics was only justified when they were heads of household. Husbands and fathers should be in charge of public issues because mothers' and daughters' lives should be devoted to the issues relating to their homes, especially to the 'interior world' (Costa 1923). The main emphasis of Costa's Catholic-feminist perspective therefore was divine law and female nature, with the language of women's rights being far less prominent. Paradoxically, however, Costa was also a supporter, against her own Church, of divorce and the other changes that Republicanism had brought into the family and women's situation.

With the emergence of the Military Dictatorship, feminist voices expressed themselves less easily. The National Council of Portuguese Women held its last Congress in 1928 (Silva 1983). Lamy (1935) suggested that there was increasing hostility to the issue of women's work outside the home. In her view, women at the time wanted to be seen as equal to men, and no more the 'unnoticed housekeeper, with a subordinate position'. Female subordination was even referred to as 'the state of domestic slavery . . . in which women are oppressed by domestic duties and their lives are chained to the kitchen and children' (Lamy 1935: 4).

Other voices were also struggling with questions of equality and difference in relation to changes in women's lives. Probably as a consequence of the frequent criticisms against feminists, Cândida Ferreira (1935) distanced herself from what she called *masculinisation*. It was not this process that women were striving for when refusing their subordinate situation in Portuguese society. What women needed, she argued, was to develop their own potential and 'natural abilities' and to correct 'negative' traits (such as 'hysteria'). Ferreira argued that since women and men had different 'natural abilities', this should influence the organisation of social life.

It is curious to note that some feminists, whether pro-Republican or pro-Catholic, praised the Republic for granting women extended civil rights, when a more critical stance might have been expected. Could this stance be interpreted as a strategy to convince people of the moderate intentions of feminism, implying that feminism did not want to dissociate women from motherhood? Feminists could be interpreted as negotiating the boundaries of their struggle. For example, while attempting to gain wider support for women's right to work outside the home, feminists often insisted that women did not want to ruin family life by diluting their domestic duties. It is such a frequent argument in feminist writings that one is tempted to interpret it more as a strategy to reassure a society hostile to feminist issues, rather than a political platform. Feminists knew only too well that the domestic sphere continued to be legally defined in terms of women's subordination, especially economically. Hostility in Portugal at that time towards feminists and independent women was intense and widespread partly because of the frequent caricatures of feminists with sexist overtones that many writers reproduced (e.g. way of dressing, hairstyle, smoking of cigarettes and wearing a monocle as well as shortened skirts). There was clearly a hostile stereotype of the feminist and independent woman spreading throughout Portuguese urban society during this period. The widespread fear of appearing as 'viragos' was expressed in the testimony of a woman student of medicine (Passos 1924), who attempted to distance herself from this model as a way of negotiating her position and social standing in Portuguese urban society.

Women's role and the Catholic perspective

At the time, Catholic sectors in Portugal supported the conventional consensus about women's main duties in the home, incorporating all the rhetorical

s for the true and great mission for women in the home. The most
Catholic writers emphasised that it was the Catholic Church which
contributed most to the dignity of women, praising their role as wives and
mothers as their real 'mission'. The perspectives supported by the Church on
these matters, however, went further than this. Mary Daly (1969) noted that,
at the end of the nineteenth century, Pope Leo XIII produced several documents which attempted to confront the persistent contradiction in the Catholic
view that, on the one hand, women were made in the image of God and,
on the other hand, they were thought to be inferior beings. In several encyclical
documents (*Quod Apostolici Muneris*, 1878, *Arcanum Divinae*, 1880, *Rerum
Novarum*, 1891), the Pope stressed that women needed to be subordinate
to men. The husband was to be the head of the family in the same way as
Christ was the head of the Church. Women's nature suited motherhood and
other domestic duties and they should dedicate their lives to the well-being
of their families. As Daly points out, to say that women were partners of their
husbands but, at the same time, obliged to submit themselves to their will,
constituted another obvious contradiction (1969: 76).

One Portuguese writer, Gonçalves Cerejeira, who was a member of the right-
wing youth organisation at Coimbra University, the Catholic Centre of
Christian Democracy (CADC) published several articles in the organisation's
journal in which he explained how canon law constructed women's situation
and mission in society. The two main assumptions in Catholic legal regulations
regarding family life were: 'subordination to hierarchy and equality regarding
duties' (Cerejeira 1922: 163). Nature was very important in such explanations
for women's subordination. In Cerejeira's words, women's social position was
to be framed according to their 'identity with nature'.

After the Military Dictatorship was established, the voices of Catholic writers
on women's position increased, once again guided by the publication of a
'papal encyclical'. In *Divini Illius Magistri* (1929), Pope Pius XI wrote that
women, given their nature, were not seen as equal to men. The same line of
argument was maintained in his subsequent encyclical, *Casti Connubi* (1930),
where he clearly condemned women's emancipation stating that only 'bad
educators' supported equal rights for women.

However, one of the writers from the Catholic Centre of Christian
Democracy was Pimpão (1926). He presented feminism as a movement which
forced men to recognise women's rights as human beings. Women were feeling
oppressed under 'virile autocracy' and their revolt against 'virile despotism'
was righteous since men were blocking women from 'their legitimate and
natural desire to make a living for themselves' (Pimpão 1926: 506). He went
on to question the wider assumption that women were born to be wives and
mothers. 'What would we say if we stated that men were born to be husbands
and fathers?' (ibid.: 507). He put forward the following views: (1) reason had
no sex; (2) women were, albeit in a distinct way, as clever as men; and (3)
women's education was to blame for their 'inferiority'.

In his second article, Pimpão changed his position. Although he maintained
an historical explanation for women's subordination, he criticised women who

were too erudite, who knew too much and who showed off their knowledge. (Molière's *Les Précieuses Ridicules* surely influenced him.) He went on to repeat Cavaleiro de Oliveira's statement that: 'knowledge for women should be used in the same way as salt in the kitchen – in the right measure' (ibid.: 555). In his third article, Pimpão quotes Pope Pius XI's statement that women had a right to make a living, but then goes on to argue that feminism could only attain its aims through 'charity' and that while women should have the right to vote they must still be compelled to obey the Catholic Church and be submissive to their husbands (ibid.: 827).

In later years, right-wing discourse on women was more consistent with its own traditional lines of argument. Vale (1934), writing in the same journal, was no longer talking about women's rights. He acknowledged the major changes that Portuguese society had undergone in recent years that had pushed women to work outside the home. He characterised these changes as being 'ruinous' to the family and causing 'an infinite social disturbance' (Vale 1934: 162). Women's work resulted, in his view, in women competing with men, contributing to greater competitiveness in the 'workplace', the lowering of salaries and an increase in unemployment. Second, children were abandoned with the lack of parental vigilance and protection leading them to a future life of 'crime' and 'vice'. Third, 'female professionalism' was harmful for women themselves because, with a diploma, they would become dissatisfied with marriage and domestic life. Therefore, the best thing that a married professional woman could do was to leave her job because, surely, domestic duties, the education of her children, and 'everything which constitutes the perfect management of the home is not compatible with any other occupation' (ibid.: 216).

Clearly, from this right-wing (conservative) perspective, the moral corruption of women had been caused by Republican education which had allowed them the same freedom as men (Viana 1927). Women and their families had become morally degraded because there was too much freedom. Such freedom was associated with free love, modern dances, 'negro fashions', night clubs, 'the artistic nude and everything which pleases Russia'. Women were the 'best propagandists of Russian beliefs'.[6]

Increasingly Republican (and feminist) notions of marriage as a contract were replaced by the emphasis on the family as a central institution. The family was the institution 'which we fight for as it is the foundation stone of a well organized society' (*Salazar*, by A. Ferro, quoted in Mónica 1978: 275). Indeed, the *1933 Constitution* stressed that the family was central to the 'Estado Novo' and women were to be defined within the State according to their 'nature' and their main duties within the family. The emphasis on the family as central to the 'Estado Novo' and to Portuguese society as a whole had important consequences. Women were inevitably construed in even more repressive 'images of femininity', and could be defined as a '*socia subordinata*' (i.e. not having the same rights as men) (Mónica 1978: 275). This did not mean that progress in legal regulations concerning women was irretrievably lost. A restricted number of women (21+ years old, and with a higher education degree, or the head of a household) even won the right to vote in 1931. However, the emphasis on 'family life' and women's subordination certainly had a significant influence on the construction and trajectories of women's lives.

Conflicts around women teachers and their professional status

When summarising these different perspectives on women's citizenship in such an unstable political period, it is important to recognise that, in addition to the basic consensus on women as mothers, wives, and housekeepers, images of women as *citizens* also emerged. Gender politics became an arena of heated debate. Even within left-wing parties, there was no consensus on the access of women to the 'workplace' and to 'citizenplace', and the democratisation of the 'household'. The feminist movement was not able to gain wide acceptance. The majority of these groups shared a broad consensus on motherhood, wifehood and domestic work as the 'natural' stages of women's lives – a consensus which explains a good deal about the social conditions structuring women's lives today.

However, the language of women's rights was also heard during this time and this influenced Republican policies. Hence, the image of a mother as citizen was mainly a Republican one. At this time more human rights were becoming women's rights and women were beginning to be regarded as caring citizens, bringing their tenderness and human concerns to the service of the community. There was, however, also a growing Catholic concern, as we have seen, to re-emphasise women's place in the family and this view overshadowed Republican attempts to broader women's inclusion as citizens in the public sphere. Women's position as a 'socia subordinata' was being re-emphasised.

Such contradictory views about women in the inter-war years were reflected in the images of women teachers and also had implications in terms of the development of government policy in relation to the teaching profession. Women, by virtue of their female nature and their position as mothers, were seen as having the special and intrinsic qualities necessary for teaching children. Women teachers were to mother younger pupils so that they would not find the transition from home to school too painful. As far as older boys were concerned (those 10 years old and above), precisely the reverse logic applied. Those same nurturing qualities were understood to have a harmful effect on boys, putting at risk the construction of their masculinity. Some Republicans believed that female teachers' presumed compassion, affection and delicacy would contribute to boys becoming too effeminate and men would be in danger of becoming what were called 'eternal losers'. Boys would be unable to develop their strength and energy, their capacity for decision-making, or would fail to acquire the courage normally associated with the male character.

Female teachers were also expected to behave according to established models of womanhood at the same time as contributing to social transformations in line with Republican ideals. They were expected to become involved in school activities but, because they were women, they were also expected to limit their involvement to subordinate positions within school. The social imagery associated with women teachers was one of 'care', 'tenderness' and 'patience' but at the same time male teachers feared them as 'competitors'.

For women teachers, being autonomous professionals meant that they were also not likely to be praised by Catholic sectors, especially given the growing emphasis on women's place in the family as an 'altar of sacrifice' and the expression of their major duties. Teaching children was associated, if anything, with mothering rather than with educating them and therefore it was not associated with women's contribution to the promotion of a wider citizenship amongst pupils.

Militant feminists in comparison did not necessarily distance themselves from the argument that women's capacity for mothering was central for the modernisation of Portuguese schools and society. They coupled this female capacity, however, with an expectation that women teachers would also be the best elements for wakening 'the Portuguese people from depression and routine' (Osório 1918: 58), for giving 'moral help' especially to the poorest children (ibid.: 77) and for promoting national reconstruction 'as women missionaries' (ibid.: 61).

Such contradictory pressures on women help to explain the 'stormy' social tensions which have enveloped women teachers in Portugal. The situation of men in primary schools was not addressed with the same intensity, nor even questioned. The Republican image of the teacher, at the level of educational policy-making, was a male image. Yet the increasing presence of women in primary schools meant that it was no longer possible to ignore the reality that women constituted the majority within the profession. Women's increasing presence was perceived as a threat by those who had viewed teaching as a male preserve. Not surprisingly, the presence of women was questioned by these sectors.

The debate about women's status within teaching appears, first, to have revolved around the distinctive character of female teaching in contrast with that of men. Much of the discourse on *maternalism* from the turn of the century, resurfaced in the 1920s (cf. Araújo 1992). This time however there were hints that women's *specificity* in primary schools could be defined in terms of a 'moral' role. Second, Republican concerns could also be heard in this debate among educators who suggested that women were politically conservative. Ideally women should help promote a modern and Republican community and society. Third, the issue of marriage in relation to female teachers came to the forefront in Portugal after the military coup of 1926, thus echoing the debate about the marriage bar implemented in countries such as England. However, this strategy was never implemented in Portugal. Finally, this period in Portuguese history saw the debate about women teachers extended by their own responses to questions about their expertise to teach the final years of primary school. They challenged the accusations of conservatism made against them. Women headmistresses of girls' schools, for example, contested the 1919 regulations which adversely affected their rights regarding their professional status.

The debates, therefore, about women's position among the various political groups we have looked at had a special resonance for women teachers. They helped to structure women teachers' lives to conform to strict rules of moral behaviour and to images of their role as mothers. At the same time, discourses on women's rights, which encouraged more open opportunities in the 'workplace' and the 'citizenplace', made women's position more contradictory than the prevailing consensus on women's domestic duties would lead us to think.

Notes

1   Briefly, positivism refers here to an epistemological tradition that sees social processes as similar to laws of the physical world – in other words they can be measured, quantified and as such objectified (cf. for instance Stanley and Wise 1983; Giddens 1996).

2   *Alma Feminina*, 1924, VII (May-August), 23–24.

3   Emilio M. Costa (1877–1952) joined the anarchist movement, editing political journals, writing articles, giving speeches and teaching in union schools. He maintained close relations with the international anarchist movement and wrote several articles for the French journal *Les Temps Nouveaux*. Emilio Costa was also the private secretary of Francisco Ferrer, a radical educator executed by the Spanish in 1909. During the years in which he lived under the 'Estado Novo', he joined the political opposition. He wrote about anarchism, unionism, Karl Marx and the education of the proletariat.

4   See, for instance, *A Batalha* 1924, V (1593), 6 February, and VI (1673), 10 May.

5   In *A Batalha* 1924, VI (1673), 10 May.

6   *A Educação Nacional*, 1, 2nd phase (11), 15 May 1927.

References

Araújo, H. C. (1992) 'The emergence of a "new orthodoxy": public debates on women's capacities and education in Portugal (1880–1910)', *Gender and Education*, 4, 1&2: 7–24.

Arnot, M. (1997) '"Gendered citizenship": new feminist perspectives on education and citizenship', *British Educational Research Journal*, 23, 3: 275–295.

Arnot, M., Araújo, H. C., Deliyanni, K., Rowe, G. and Tomé, A. (1996) 'Teachers, gender and the discourses of citizenship', *International Sociological Studies of Education*, 6: 3–35.

Barreiro, A. (1912) *O Feminismo (principalmente do ponto de vista do ensino secundário)*, Porto: Tipografia Empresa Literária e Tipográfica.

Cabete, A. (1923) 'Relatório do Congresso Internacional Feminista de Roma', *Alma Feminina*, July 2–4.

Cabete, A. (1925) 'Discurso de abertura do I congresso feminista e de educação', in A. Brazão (ed.) *O Primeiro Congresso Feminista e de Educação*, Lisbon: Edição Spartacus.

Catroga, F. (1991) *O Republicanismo em Portugal – da formação ao 5 de Outubro de 1910*, 2 vols, Coimbra: Faculdade de Letras.

Cerejeira, G. (1922) 'Da influência do cristianismo na reabilitação da mulher', *Estudos – Revista Mensal do CADC*, 6: 161–167.

Coole, D. (1988) *Women in Political Theory*, Hertfordshire: Harvester Wheatsheaf.

Costa, A. (1976) *Discursos Parlamentares*, Lisbon: Livraria Bertrand.

Costa, E. de S. (1922) *A Mulher Educadora*, Lisbon: Editora Universo.

Costa, E. de S. (1923) *A Mulher Educação Infantil*, Rio de Janeiro: Álvaro Pinto.

Costa, E. (1928) *As Mulheres e o Feminismo*, Lisbon: Tipografia Seara Nova.

Costa, F. M. (n.d.) *A Maçonaria Feminina*, Lisbon: Editorial Vega.

Daly, M. (1969) *Le Sexe Conteste*, Paris: MAME.

Esteves, J. G. (1992) *A Liga Republicana das Mulheres Portuguesas – uma organização política e feminista*, Lisbon: ONG/ CIDM.

Ferreira, C. F. (1935) *A Mulher Portuguesa Contemporânea*, Lisbon: Sociedade Nacional de Tipografia.

Giddens, A. (1996) *In Defence of Sociology: essays, interpretations and rejoinders*, Cambridge: Polity Press.

Gouveia, A. C. (1924) 'Discurso pronunciado na sessão Inaugural do 1° Congresso Feminista e de Educação', *Alma Feminina* VII 9–12: 65–69.

Joaquim, T. (1998) 'Social citizenship and motherhood', in V. Ferreira (ed.) *Shifting Bonds, Shifting Bounds: women, mobility and citizenhip in Europe*, Oeiras: Celta.

Lamy, E. (1935) 'A igualdade dos sexos perante o trabalho', *Alma Feminina* XX 5–6, May-June: 4–5.

Lima, A. (1925) 'A Educação da Mulher', *Educação Social* II 29–30: 87–94.

Manieri, R. (1978) *Mujer y Capital*, Madrid: Editorial Debate.

Mayeur, F. (1979) *L'Éducation des Filles en France au XIX siecle*, Paris: Hachette.

Mónica, M. F. (1978) *Educação e Sociedade no Portugal de Salazar*, Lisbon: Presença.

Okin, S. M. (1980) *Women in Western Political Thought*, London: Virago.

Osório, A. de C. (1911) *A Mulher no Casamento e no Divórcio*, Lisbon: Guimarães.

Osório, A. de C. (1912) 'A Propaganda Feminista', *A Muher Portuguesa*, 1: 17–18.

Osório, A. de C. (1915) *A Mulher na Agricultura, nas Indústrias Regionais e na Administração Municipal*, Lisbon: Editora 'Para as Crianças'.

Osório, A. de C. (1918) *Em Tempo de Guerra*, Lisbon: Editora Ventura.

Passos, M. (1924) 'A Mulher nas Profissões Liberais', *Revista Escolar*, 4, 10: 441–445.

Pateman, C. (1988) *The Sexual Contract*, Cambridge: Polity Press.

Philips, A. (1991) *Engendering Democracy*, Oxford: Polity Press.

Pimpão, Á. C. (1926) 'O feminismo e a igreja católica', *Estudos – orgão do CADC*, 55, 56, 57: 503–513; 553–559; 822–829.

Scanlon, G. (1986) *La Polemica Feminista en la España Contemporanea (1868–1974)*, Madrid: Ediciones Akal.

Silva, M. R. T. da (1983) 'Feminismo em Portugal na voz de mulheres escritoras do início do sec. XX', *Análise Social*, vol. XIX: 875–907.

Stanley, L. and Wise, S. (1983) 'Back into the personal or: our attempt to construct "feminist research"', in G. Bowles and R. D. Duelli (eds) *Theories of Women's Studies*, London: RKP.

Vale, A. L. (1934) 'Aspectos actuais da condição social da mulher', *Estudos – orgão do CADC*, 123, 150–162.

Velleda, M. (1912) 'Orientação e fins da nossa revista', *A Mulher Portuguesa*, 1, June: 13.

Viana, M. G. (1927) 'Sintomas . . . desoladores', *A Educação Nacional*, 1, 2ª fase (34), 23 October: 16.

Yuval-Davis N. (1997) *Gender and Nation*, London: Sage.

8 No women wanted on the social frontier
Gender, citizenship and progressive education

Kathleen Weiler

Citizenship education in the United States has most frequently been conceived of as a means of inculcating patriotism and loyalty to the nation, of constructing a shared political identity. This process can be seen in the iconography of the flag, the pledge of allegiance, and required high school courses in US history and civics. Although this view of citizenship education has been dominant, alternative visions of citizenship education as preparation for participation in a more inclusive vision of democracy have also come to the fore at different points in history. Before the Civil Rights movement of the 1950s and 1960s, probably the best-known and most influential conception of democratic citizenship education emerged from the progressive education movement and in particular from the self-conscious group of progressive educators associated with Teachers College, Columbia who came to be known in the 1930s as the 'social reconstructionists'. The social reconstructionists, whose ideas were most powerfully put forward in the brief-lived radical journal *The Social Frontier*, challenged a conception of citizenship as unquestioning loyalty to the state and, instead, argued that citizens should be active participants in an evolving social democracy. In this conception, schools were seen as potential sites for educating such democratic citizens.

Using a feminist political critique of the idea of citizenship, in this chapter I examine the work of men and women progressive educators at Teachers College, the center of the social reconstructionist movement.[1] I first provide a brief history of the social reconstructionist movement, focusing on the academic culture of Teachers College. I then explore the social reconstructionists' conceptions of democratic citizenship, contrasting the vision of citizenship of the male social reconstructionist theorists with that of Willystine Goodsell, professor of history and philosophy of education at Teachers College. By exploring the ways patriarchal privilege shaped both the careers and theoretical understandings of these figures, I connect the private world of personal relationships and the academic culture of Teachers College to their political and theoretical visions of democracy, education, and citizenship.

In my analysis, I build on the work of feminist political theorists who have critiqued the idea of citizenship from the perspective of gender. Numerous feminist theorists have addressed the question of women and citizenship in the past two decades. Although classic European political theorists spoke of universal women's rights, feminist political theorists point out that these classic ideas of citizenship in fact were shaped by assumptions about the differences between men and women. Joan Scott points out that central to traditional liberal ideas of citizenship was the idea of a citizen who acts in the public sphere and who is conceived of in purportedly gender-neutral terms – the universal citizen.[2] Women, defined as close to nature and naturally domestic, were in such theories defined as 'naturally' excluded from citizenship. Carole Pateman describes the paradox of women's inclusion into the political order in these ideas of citizenship, in which 'women were incorporated differently from men, the "individuals" and "citizens" of political theory; women were included as subordinates, as the "different" sex, as "women"'.[3] And Iris Young speaks of the problematic conception of the independent, autonomous, reflective citizen in liberal conceptions of citizenship. As Young argues, this autonomy is nurtured by 'the loving attention of particularist mothers who devote themselves to fostering this sense of self in their children'.[4] Because mothers are seen as 'emotional and oriented to particular needs and interests instead of to the general good', they cannot make good citizens. Feminist analyses of the gendered nature of the liberal idea of citizenship (with its unexamined assumptions of public and private) thus provide a useful framework for an examination of democratic citizenship education in the social reconstructionist movement of the 1930s.

The social reconstructionists at Teachers College

The social reconstructionists were part of the wider movement of progressive education, a somewhat amorphous and ill-defined movement which originated with educational reformers in the progressive era of 1890–1920, and which became more clearly delineated as a recognised movement with the founding of the Progressive Education Association (PEA) in 1919 and the establishment of the journal *Progressive Education* in 1924. It is generally agreed to have ended as a coherent movement with the dissolution of the Progressive Education Association in 1955. The accepted view of the progressive education movement is that by the early 1930s it had become sharply divided between child-centered progressives and more radical and politicised social reconstructionists. Moreover, the argument goes that this split was gendered, with women progressive educators concerned with the domestic world of early childhood and elementary education while male educational philosophers grappled with the broad questions of citizenship and democracy.

This history rests on three key historical studies, all published in the 1960s, and all sharing a kind of liberal consensus. These works are Lawrence Cremin's *The Transformation of the School*, C. A. Bowers' *The Progressive Educator and the Depression*, and Patricia Graham's *Progressive Education: from arcady to academe*.[5] The picture these books provide is similar. In his classic study, *The Transformation of the School*, Cremin identifies three strands of progressive education: the administrative progressives, influenced by the scientific method and advocated by figures such as Edward Thorndike, who argued for institutional and bureaucratic reform; the child-centered progressives, influenced by the work of G. Stanley Hall and the child study movement, who emphasised the importance of the development of the individual child but who, according to Cremin, lacked a clear social or political vision; and in the 1930s, the more politically radical figures around *The Social Frontier*, who demanded that the schools build a new social order.[6] Bowers and Graham agree. The gendered nature of these splits between administrative, child centered and socially committed progressive educators is never questioned in the accounts of Cremin, Graham, or Bowers. Nor do they engage the political and social criticism of women progressive educators working at the time. In the historical accounts expounded by all three historians, progressive women educators are presented as primarily concerned with the welfare of individual children, while the public world, with its administrative, theoretical, and political interests, is the domain of men.

The narratives of Cremin, Bowers, and Graham accept at face value the understanding of the social reconstructionists themselves as radical educators. The key figures in the social reconstructionist movement were all men who taught at Teachers College, Columbia. John Dewey, without doubt the most impressive intellectual figure among progressive educators, was appointed to the philosophy department at Columbia in 1905, but also taught courses at Teachers College. His protégé William Heard Kilpatrick joined the Teachers College faculty in 1913, after completing his doctorate with Dewey. Kilpatrick was a charismatic teacher, who lectured to classes of over six hundred and was estimated to have taught over thirty-five thousand students in his career.[7] Kilpatrick rose quickly at Teachers College, being promoted to associate professor in 1915 and full professor in 1918.[8] Other figures, among them Harold Rugg and George Counts, joined the Teachers College faculty in the 1920s. By the late 1920s, a self-conscious group of left-leaning educators began to form. What was called the Kilpatrick Discussion Group met first on 8 May 1928. It is not clear whether a decision was actually made to exclude women, but in practice the group was made up exclusively of men. Kilpatrick's biographer notes that 'each man (the inclusion of women was apparently not considered) brought to the group a series of issues he was personally interested in, there being few, if any, limitations on the subjects to be discussed'.[9] Cremin describes the development of the group:

> One by one, other like-minded progressives began to join the Teachers College faculty: George S. Counts, John L. Childs, R. Bruce Raup, Goodwin Watson, Edmund de S. Brunner, Jesse Newlon, Harold F. Clark, and F. Ernest Johnson. Regularly from 1927 to 1934, intermittently from 1934 to 1938, and then regularly again for several years, this group – joined by Dewey and others for varying periods of time – carried on bimonthly discussion under the chairmanship of Kilpatrick.[10]

In their meetings, the group engaged with contemporary questions of politics and society. All, with the exception of Isaac Kandel, were considered to be on the left. Counts, Dewey, and Kilpatrick all travelled to the Soviet Union in the late 1920s and were welcomed by Soviet educators eager to hear of progressive education.

The stock market crash of 1929 and the onset of world-wide depression led the members of the group to have deepening doubts about capitalism and to have more radical views about the possible role of education in creating an alternative social order. In February 1932 at the Progressive Education Association convention in Baltimore, George Counts delivered his famous speech 'Dare Progressive Education Be Progressive?' in which he attacked the lack of social and political commitment of the PEA. In the following months Counts gave similar speeches before the National Education Association and the National Council of Education and, later that year, his pamphlet *Dare the Schools Build a New Social Order?* was published. In it Counts proclaimed:

> If Progressive Education is to be genuinely progressive, it must emancipate itself from the influence of this class [the ruling class], face squarely and courageously every social issue, come to grips with life in all of its stark reality, establish an organic relation with the community, develop a realistic and comprehensive theory of welfare, fashion a compelling and challenging vision of human destiny, and become less frightened than it is today at the bogies of imposition and indoctrination.[11]

Along with *The Educational Frontier*, a collection of essays edited by William Kilpatrick, *Dare the Schools Build a New Social Order?* announced a radical shift to the left in educational thinking.

The ideas of the social reconstructionist group found further expression with the founding of the journal *The Social Frontier* in 1934. The key figures associated with *The Social Frontier* were all sympathetic to socialism by the early 1930s. Although their definition of what exactly 'socialism' meant tended to be somewhat vague, they argued, following Counts, that schools could and should help build a new social order, one based on collectivist and democratic principles; the obligation of progressive teachers was both to create democratic classrooms and to encourage social critique. The site of political activism and, by implication, active citizenship was located in the political and economic spheres. Although the social reconstructionists' calls for progressive education tended to focus on the class struggle and called for teachers to lead this struggle, the social reconstructionists of Teachers College had few interactions with actual classroom teachers.

By 1936 differences began to surface within the editorial board of *The Social Frontier*. Raup, Rugg, Dewey, and Kilpatrick began to question the Marxist tone of the many articles and Dewey became increasingly distant, particularly around the key issue of 'indoctrination'.[12] In the face of political differences and a growing financial crisis, in 1937 the board turned to the Progressive Education Association for help. At first the PEA refused to consider a merger, but in 1939, in even more desperate financial circumstances, *The Social Frontier* editors again came to the PEA for help. This time, the leaders of the PEA agreed to take over the publication of the journal, but insisted that the name be changed to *Frontiers of Democracy*. Although *Frontiers of Democracy* was published for another four years, its focus soon turned to the challenges raised by the war against fascism. In 1943, the executive committee of the Progressive Education Association voted to abolish the journal. In the post-war period, with the rise of McCarthyism and the Red Scare, the social reconstructionists' vision of the public schools as the site for building democratic citizenship in a new social order disappeared from public discourse and figures such as George Counts themselves engaged in anti-Communist attacks on former colleagues and associates.

Gender and citizenship on the social frontier

This narrative of the rise and fall of the social reconstructionists is well known. But if we examine this history through the lens of gender, a somewhat different picture emerges. Men still dominate the story, but women progressive educators committed to social and political change are not so much absent as they are ignored and silenced. And the causes of the growing isolation of the social reconstructionists and their failure to build a movement among public school teachers can be seen not only as the result of a changing social and political landscape but of the narrowness of their own understanding of politics and teaching. The progressive male educators associated with *The Social Frontier* and *Frontiers of Democracy* approached the idea of citizenship education from a commitment to radical social change, but their work was highly abstract and conceived of citizenship in conventional gendered ideas of public and private spheres. A closer examination of their ideas and lives reveals both their acceptance of this gendered distinction and their seeming lack of awareness of their own patriarchal privileges. Although most of them supported the suffrage movement and thus accepted the entry of women into the public sphere of voting, they failed to address the patriarchal structure of public schools in the United States or the male privileges they enjoyed at Teachers College itself. That lack of attention served to reproduce and intensify male dominance and to silence women's voices. Instead, they assumed that men were naturally concerned with politics and the economy, while women cared for children in the home or the school.

In the same way as the earlier political theorists of the classic European liberal tradition, progressive male educators saw the educated citizen as free to act in the public sphere without concern for emotion, home, or family. But as Iris Young argues: 'Holding independence as a norm not only renders dependent people and their caretakers second-class citizens, but it also tends to make them invisible.'[13] When citizenship is conceived of as activity in the public world but at the same time traditional gender divisions of public and private remain unchallenged, both women teachers and girls as students are essentially excluded from the sphere of citizenship and political action.[14] The failure of the social reconstructionists to challenge the binary divisions of gender was not only a serious theoretical weakness, but a weakness in terms of practice as well, since they rarely acknowledged that four-fifths of the teachers they were calling upon to lead a social revolution were women. The lack of attention given to teachers' working conditions or the fact that the majority of teachers were young single women forced by the widespread practice of the marriage bar to give up their jobs when they married meant that the calls of the Teachers College professors to teachers to 'build a new social order' were seriously out of touch with the realities of American schools.

The male-dominated nature of the social reconstructionist movement can be seen not only in the writings of the leading figures, but also in the gender composition of the editorial boards of *The Social Frontier* and *Frontiers of Democracy* and the authors they published. The board of directors of *The Social Frontier* listed in its first volume in October 1934 included one woman (Lois Meek, the secretary of the American Association of University Women and a former student of Kilpatrick's) in a group of twenty-seven. The second and expanded editorial board in 1935 was somewhat more representative, with eight women in a group of forty-four. Two women (Laura Zirbes of Ohio State and the anthropologist Ruth Benedict) were listed on the editorial board of *Frontiers of Democracy*. But even more telling than this imbalance is the nature of the articles published in these two journals. The eighty-one issues of *The Social Frontier* and *Frontiers of Democracy* included a little over four-hundred articles. Of these, twenty were written by women – approximately five percent. But even more significantly, of those four-hundred articles (those written by women as well as men) only one addressed the question of the education of women – a 1940 article in *Frontiers of Democracy* entitled 'Opportunities of American Women in Education and the Professions', by the then retired Teachers College professor Willystine Goodsell.

Progressive women at Teachers College

With some significant exceptions, women faculty members at Teachers College tended to focus on early childhood or rural education. They seem to have supported one another through informal clubs and discussion groups similar to the all-male groups that dominated the College. In response to early men's clubs, for example, a 'women's discussion club' met from its founding in 1911 throughout the 1920s.[15] As we have seen, when Kilpatrick's discussion group was formed (a group that formed the nucleus of the social reconstructionist movement), only men were asked to participate. But the women of Teachers College, although excluded from administrative positions or full professorships and isolated from the powerful all-male discussion groups, were highly accomplished and deeply concerned with the social and political role of education. In the years before the First World War, many of these women had been active in the settlement house movement or in rural school reform, areas in which women predominated. In the 1930s, they expanded their work to address not only the general crisis of the Depression but more specific issues such as the impact of poverty or racism on children and families – questions ignored in the social reconstructionists' call for class struggle.

Such figures as Patty Smith Hill, Mabel Carney, Fannie Dunn, and Leta Hollingsworth had published widely and were active in national and international organizations.

The most important educational theorist among the women of Teachers College in this period was undoubtedly Willystine Goodsell, who taught philosophy and history of education. But other women contributed valuable social criticism and were actively engaged in progressive projects. Patty Smith Hill and Mabel Carney are two prime examples. As head of the Kindergarten Department at Teachers College for thirty years, Patty Smith Hill was an internationally recognized progressive educator. Although she was influenced by Thorndike's behaviorist psychology, Hill also advocated a focus on the child as opposed to a set curriculum or 'apparatus' and in the 1920s was a follower of Kilpatrick's project method, with its emphasis on the child's ability to define and carry out projects as the core of the curriculum.[16] In the late 1920s, she traveled to the Soviet Union, where she visited nursery schools and kindergartens in Moscow and where her books were being translated into Russian and used in normal school classes. Kilpatrick was visiting Moscow at the same time, and they were both treated as major progressive educators and both had interviews with Krupskeya.[17] Hill was concerned to make early childhood education available to all families, not just the wealthy. After she retired from Teachers College in 1935, she created Hilltop Community Center, a federal nursery school program 'which provided nurses, doctors, dietitians, parent workers, and teachers drawn from the unemployed'.[18]

Mabel Carney came to Teachers College in 1918 from the Illinois State Normal University, already well known for her 1912 book, *Country Life and the Country School*, in which she argued for the opportunities presented by rural schools for democratic education. Like Kilpatrick and Dewey, Carney lectured widely on educational issues throughout the twenties.[19] In the 1920s, she became interested in 'negro education' in the South. In 1924, she spent a month visiting segregated Black schools in the South under the auspices of the General Education Board. In 1926, she was sent to Africa for eight months by the International Institute of Teachers College. When she returned, she continued her work with the General Education Board, making frequent trips to the South and visiting Black normal schools and colleges and becoming involved with the Southern Mountain Workers project. In the early 1930s she directed a series of lectures on race relations sponsored by the Julius Rosenwald Fund which brought speakers like Walter White and W.E.B. DuBois to Teachers College. Her stature in the areas of both progressive rural education and Black education can be seen in the invitation offered to her, along with John Dewey and Harold Rugg, to speak at educational conferences held in Capetown and Johannesburg in South Africa in 1934. Although these educational projects for Black students in both the United States and South Africa may have been framed by paternalistic attitudes, they were at the same time attempts to expand educational opportunities for Africans and African Americans and, in Carney's vision, an attempt to create greater possibilities of democratic participation.[20]

Although both Hill and Carney were colleagues of the male social reconstructionists at Teachers College and were treated internationally as leading progressive educators, they were not part of the informal networks and discussion groups of the male progressives at Teachers College; nor did they appear on the editorial boards or in the pages of *The Social Frontier* and *Frontiers of Democracy*. The only woman on the Teachers College faculty included (although peripherally) in the social reconstructionist group was Willystine Goodsell, the most prominent scholar exploring issues of women's education in the 1930s.[21] Goodsell's career at Teachers College is instructive in terms of the opportunities and limitations available to women academics in this period. After teaching in Normal Schools for several years, Goodsell entered the doctoral program at Teachers College at the age of thirty-six. She took her preliminary Ph.D. examination in philosophy of education in May 1909. Of nine candidates, she was the only one to receive an 'A' on all three questions.[22] Isaac Kandel, who also took his exams that year and who later became one of the strongest critics of progressive education on the Teachers College faculty, was second. After completing her doctorate in philosophy under the direction of John Dewey, Goodsell was immediately hired as an assistant professor at Teachers College, the same year that Kandel and Kilpatrick joined the faculty. Like Kandel and Kilpatrick, she taught both history and philosophy of education, but although both Kilpatrick and Kandel were made full professors quite early in their careers, Goodsell never moved beyond the rank of associate professor, to which she was named in 1927. In 1913, she introduced a course on the education of women, which she continued to teach until her retirement in 1936, one year before Kilpatrick.

Goodsell's first book, *The Conflict of Nationalism and Humanism* (1910), was based on her doctoral dissertation. She then focused her writing on various aspects of women's education, an interest which resulted in 1924 in *The Education of Women* and, in 1931, *Pioneers of Women's Education in the United States*, a collection of writings of Emma Willard, Catherine Beecher, and Mary Lyon. Her exploration of women's traditional sphere in the home and family led her to write *A History of the Family as a Social and Educational Institution* (1927), *Problems of the Family* (1930), and *A History of Marriage and the Family* (1935). She was also concerned with broader issues of social justice. She was Chair of the Program Committee for the World Democracy Movement at Teachers College and was a member of the American Civil Liberties Union. In the 1930s, Goodsell became interested in eugenics. Her only article in *The Social Frontier* was a defense of what she called 'the new eugenics' which she saw as rejecting social class as a marker of superior heredity but which emphasised women's right to birth control and choice about whether to bear children.[23] In 1935, one year before her retirement, she was made a member of the board of *The Social Frontier*. She published her last article on women's education in 1940 in *Frontiers of Democracy*.

In her central concerns with education and democracy, Goodsell clearly can be placed in the social reconstructionist camp. She saw education as meaningful only if it contributed to a social, not just an individual good. Like the male social reconstructionists, she was critical of capitalism, but unlike their emphasis on the dignity of labour and the need for collective ownership of the means of production, her emphasis was on the need for a gender-sensitive socialism that would support universal childcare and family planning. She was suspicious of a higher education for women that focused only on their individual desires and not on the demands of citizenship in a democracy. As she wrote in 1919, immediately after the First World War:

> Have these young women, sifted like wheat through fifteen years of schooling, justified, as a body, the high hopes of society with respect to original, constructive work and social leadership? If the answer be no, is it not possible that the education of girls and women is in need of a thoroughgoing re-organization which shall bring it into sympathetic touch with the purposes and problems of a democracy in the process of remaking itself?[24]

Goodsell's analysis of women's education for citizenship rested on an understanding of the competing claims of seeing women, on the one hand, in terms of civic equality and, on the other, in terms of their sexual and reproductive difference from men, a tension central to present-day feminist theories of democracy and citizenship.

Goodsell's most important work is doubtless *The Education of Women*, published in 1924. In this wide-ranging book, Goodsell addressed the relationship of women's education and democratic citizenship. She began with a sharp critique of the sexist psychologies of G. Stanley Hall and Edward Thorndike, who asserted that women were innately emotional and nurturing (and intellectually inferior) because of their biological role as mothers. She then turned to a discussion of the ways in which women should be educated in order to participate as full and equal citizens in a democracy. Throughout the book, she grappled with the tension between women's reproductive and sexual difference from men and the assumptions of equality implicit in conceptions of universal democratic citizenship. In her focus on women's difference, Goodsell forecast the concerns of later feminist theorists like Jacqui Alexander and Chandra Mohanty. Alexander and Mohanty, for example, ask:

> How do we understand the idea of universal citizenship (for us, citizenship which is defined through and across difference) and the way the state mobilizes a citizenship machinery which excludes and marginalizes particular constituencies on the basis of their 'difference'?[25]

It is precisely this tension between assumptions of difference and claims of universal citizenship that Goodsell addressed in *The Education of Women*.

However contemporary Goodsell's concern with balancing women's difference and a demand for political equality, it is important not to exaggerate the extent of her critique of ideas of citizenship education of her time. She was hardly calling for social revolution in her demand for education for democracy; her conception of citizenship education for high school students, for example, focused upon alliances with business people and participation in such activities as the Junior Red Cross, the Junior Good Citizenship League, the Boys and Girls Schools, military training and student government.[26] Citizenship here thus implies a kind of loyalty to the government and economic system of the United States. The extent to which this system itself reproduced existing class, race, and gender hierarchies is unaddressed in her work. Nonetheless, her call for women's education to prepare them for full citizenship explores questions in the inter-war period completely ignored by the male social reconstructionists.

Goodsell argued that the biological fact of motherhood had to be addressed in any theory of women's citizenship. She wrote:

> At the very outset of human history woman's peculiar function was marked out for her. She was destined by Nature to be the mother of the race – to bear and bear again that humanity might perpetuate itself in the midst of an inhospitable environment.[27]

Motherhood, Goodsell argued, kept women in the domestic sphere, where they performed economically essential but unrecognized labour. With the industrial revolution, which held the promise of freeing women from the obligations of domestic work and with enlightenment ideas of democracy and human rights, the possibility of a new society based on the equal participation of men and women became possible. But the historical legacy of women's place in the domestic sphere as wives and mothers did not in fact disappear with industrialisation and democracy. Assumptions of women's innate difference (and inferiority) from men continued to dominate. This assumption of innate difference can be seen in education where boys are educated for future roles as citizens and girls are educated to be wives and mothers:

> The full and free development of the individuality of young women is too often subordinated to conventional conceptions of what women are and what they ought to contribute to society. As we have seen, the prevailing theory that 'Woman' represents an easily recognizable domestic type, together with the firm conviction that her best work for the world can only be done in the home *as it is presently organized*, are responsible for the attempts of educators to differentiate the education of women from that of men. [italics in the original][28]

In passages like these, Goodsell emphasises the historical and social construction of ideas of womanhood and denies the inevitability of society 'as it is presently organized'. This analysis is similar to that of contemporary feminist political theorists, who argue for the need to analyse the construction of gender difference, who try to bring to light the hidden assumptions of universal conceptions and shaping narratives of citizenship, and ask whether women can imagine themselves within them.

For Goodsell, education was the key to women's full participation as citizens. Because women have been kept in the domestic world, they have had much less opportunity than men to engage with political issues. But with suffrage, women for the first time gain full citizenship and thus may escape 'the cramping effects of the restrictions that have been imposed upon them' and leave what Goodsell called their 'social isolation'.[29] She was highly critical of the kind of maternal feminism that assumes women's higher moral nature:

> There seems not much reason to regard women as more 'moral' than men, except in the realm of sex and family relations, where it has been in their interest to develop and conserve certain values and where powerful social pressure has tended to make them conform to rigid social standards. Already there is some evidence to show that women in business and politics can be quite as self-seeking and unscrupulous, quite as blind to the inhumane phases of their vocation, as their husbands and brothers. The sooner women get rid of the notion that a peculiar moral sanctity hovers about them the sooner will they face squarely and honestly the danger of their becoming, like some men, driving machines, deaf to the call of beauty, blind to the fundamental rights of men and women, pushing ahead ruthlessly to their goal of wealth or power or prestige.[30]

But, at the same time, Goodsell still wanted to hold onto the idea that women attach a great value to human life. Like contemporary educational theorists such as Nel Noddings and Jane Roland Martin, she is highly critical of educational theories that ignore the emotional work of women.[31] She cited the work of women social reformers, who were motivated by a powerful sense of responsibility toward others: 'On this humane and nurturing sentiment in women, rising almost to a passion in the few, rests much of the world's hope of progress toward more healthful, happy, and beautiful living'.[32] This 'nurturing sentiment' in women may have resulted from their socially imposed roles, but the sentiment itself, says Goodsell, is vital to a humane society and should be celebrated.

Goodsell's strongest defense of the social reconstructionist movement came in her 1933 *Teachers College Record* article responding to Isaac Kandel's attack on the social reconstructionists. Kandel, who had disliked and disapproved of the more radical progressive educators for years, was outraged at George Counts' 1932 pamphlet, *Dare the Schools Build a New Social Order?* Kandel accused the social reconstructionists of hypocrisy and asserted that their own earlier emphasis on the individual child was in part responsible for what he called 'social disorder'.

> One point is clear: in analyzing the causes of the social crisis the progressives must honestly recognize the consequences of their own doctrines and concern themselves not with a new social order but with the removal of those causes of social disorder which were, until recently, inherent in their philosophy of education.[33]

Goodsell, who may have had a long-standing dislike for Kandel given their parallel careers, responded, defending Counts and the social reconstructionists and citing Dewey in *Democracy and Education*:

> From its inception the progressive education movement has never lost sight of its social purposes and goals, even though an individual teacher here and there may have emphasized personal development of the child without sufficient regard for the formation of social attitudes and habits.[34]

Kandel, she argued, had conflated the progressive educators' focus on the value of each individual child with a theory of economic laissez-faire individualism.[35]

It is instructive, given her treatment at Teachers College, that although Goodsell presents a strong defense of the social reconstructionists, she made no claim to be included among them. Consider her own location in this passage defending progressive education:

> So far as the writer knows, no progressive educator believes that he can build a society which shall be the 'New Jerusalem'. These men understand too well the intricacy and delicate adjustments of our complex economic order. All they are claiming is that education can help youths and adults better to understand the situations and the tested facts of our economic and social order and better to cooperate, wherever concerted action is called for, in bringing about improved conditions in the interests of all.[36]

Here, Goodsell carefully located herself as an outsider, as not part of the group. She was 'the writer', they were 'these men'; she referred to the group as 'they' and not 'we'. This passage recalls her sharp comment in *The Education of Women* regarding the blindness of male progressive educators to their own privilege:

> It is the author's belief that the widening of opportunities for women, both educational and social, the gradual breaking down of the traditional conceptions of woman's nature and woman's sphere, will proceed without serious hindrance. Unquestionably, however, the movement could be hastened as well as more intelligently directed were individuals immediately interested in women's education to examine in a critical spirit their own educational philosophy respecting the larger purposes, the procedures and the available means in the education of women to enable them to play a larger and more useful part in the life of the twentieth century.[37]

This criticism of the failure of progressive educational philosophers to examine their blindness to gender certainly reflected her own experience of being excluded and marginalised. Goodsell's last published piece was an attack on the discrimination faced by women in colleges, universities, graduate and professional schools. In it she wrote,

American schools and universities have gone far toward equalizing the educational opportunities of men and women. But the higher institutions of learning have still a long road to travel before equality of opportunity is offered to women. That goal, if it arrives at all, must wait upon profound social change.[38]

This brief piece and this passage in particular could be a comment on her own career and on the inherent limitations of theories of democratic education which uncritically accept male privilege and dominance.

Conclusion

The social reconstructionists put forward a powerful argument for education as a means for progressive social change. But their vision was deeply flawed. The inability of the social reconstructionists to move beyond their own narrow experience led them to slight central questions of gender that were being explored by their own women colleagues. The well-known split between the child-centered and more conservative figures associated with the Progressive Education Association and the more radical social reconstructionists was in part a gendered division, but it was encouraged by the social reconstructionists themselves, who failed to include women in the pages of *The Social Frontier* or to address the concerns of women scholars and classroom teachers. Instead of encouraging an expanded discussion of citizenship education, the social reconstructionists accepted the divide between what they saw as their own serious concerns with the universal arena of democracy and citizenship and the concerns of the women educators at Teachers College with 'women's issues' – the world of young children (Patty Smith Hill), subordinate African Americans (Mabel Carney), or women and the family (Willystine Goodsell).

For the social reconstructionists, as for other male educational theorists, only women bore 'difference'. In their conception of education for democracy, future citizens were not conceived of as embodied or sexed beings, but as abstractions. Women, on the other hand, were both sexed and embodied. The social reconstructionist ideas of citizenship thus built upon a liberal tradition in which citizens were conceived of as purportedly gender-neutral but implicitly male. Women, defined as close to nature and naturally domestic, were in such theories defined as 'naturally' excluded from citizenship, or, if included, were not imagined as active agents. Like Willystine Goodsell, contemporary feminist political theorists argue that it is necessary to explore traditional conceptions of difference between women and men if a persuasive and inclusive theory of democratic citizenship is to be constructed. As Chantal Mouffe argues:

> If the category 'woman' does not correspond to any unified and unifying essence, the question can no longer be to try to unearth it. The central issues become: how is 'woman' constructed as a category within different discourses? how is sexual difference made a pertinent distinction in social

relations and how are relations of subordination constructed through such a distinction?[39]

In following this line of argument, we can problematise not only conceptions of 'woman', but of 'man' as well and suggest the need for what Mouffe calls 'a radical democratic conception of citizenship', one that both critiques the liberal idea of citizenship (the unexamined claim that all individuals are born free and equal) and at the same time holds on to its fundamental assertion of the goal of 'liberty and equality for all'.[40] The social reconstructionists shared the assumptions of gender difference and male privilege of their time. Those unexamined assumptions distorted and limited their conceptions of both education and democracy. A re-reading of the gendered story of the progressive educators of Teachers Colleges not only reveals the limitations of social reconstructionist ideas of education and citizenship, it challenges the accepted history of progressive education itself.

Notes and References

1 Very little historical work has addressed the involvement of women or conceptions of women's education in the social reconstructionist movement. The absence of women in this narrative is in striking contrast to the increasing interest in activist women educators in the years before the achievement of national suffrage for women in 1920, particularly Ella Flagg Young and Margaret Haley. One obvious reason for this lack of attention to this question by historians is the lack of concern with women's issues by the social reconstructionists themselves and their own gendered conceptions of citizenship and democracy. One exception to this lack of attention to the treatment of women in the progressive education movement more broadly is S. Biklen, 'The Progressive Education Movement and the Question of Women', *Teachers College Record* 80, 2 (December, 1978) pp. 216–235. As Biklen comments, 'Though education was still a concern of feminists, feminism was not a concern of the progressive education movement', 216.
2 J. Scott, *Only Paradoxes to Offer*, Cambridge, MA, Harvard University Press, 1996.
3 C. Pateman, 'Equality, difference, subordination: the politics of motherhood and women's citizenship', in G. Bock and S. James, Eds *Beyond Equality and Difference: Citizenship, feminist politics, female subjectivity*, London, Routledge, 1992, 19.
4 I. Young, *Intersecting Voices: dilemmas of gender, politics, philosophy and policy*, Princeton: Princeton University Press, 1997, 123.
5 L. Cremin, *The Transformation of the School*, New York, Vintage Books, 1964; C. A. Bowers, *The Progressive Educator and the Depression*, New York, Random House, 1969; P. Graham, *Progressive Education: from Arcady to Academe*, New York, Teachers College Press, 1967.
6 Cremin, *Transformation of the School*, 1964.
7 Bowers, *The Progressive Educator and the Depression*, 12.
8 J. Beineke, *And There were Giants in the Land*, New York, Peter Lang, 1998, 94–96.
9 J. Beineke, *And There Were Giants in the Land*, 178.
10 L. Cremin, *Transformation of the School*, 228.
11 G. Counts, *Dare the Schools Build a New Social Order?*, New York, John Day, 1932, 9.
12 R. Westbrook, *John Dewey and American Democracy*, Ithaca, Cornell University Press, 1991, 507.

13 I. Young, *Intersecting Voices: dilemmas of gender, political philosophy, and policy*, Princeton, Princeton University Press, 1997, 124.

14 See V. Foster, 'Feminist theory and the construction of citizenship education', in K. Kennedy, Ed. *Citizenship Education and the Modern State*, London, Falmer Press, 1997.

15 W. Goodsell, 'Mary Adelaide Nurring: educator and builder', *Teachers College Record* XXVII 5 (Jan. 1926) 382–393.

16 Barbara Beatty is critical of the influence of Thorndike and his followers on Hill. See B. Beatty, *Preschool Education in America*, New Haven, Yale University Press, 1995, 118.

17 'Patty Smith Hill Visits Russia', *Teachers College Record* XXI2 (Nov. 1929) 179.

18 L. Cremin, *A History of Teachers College, Columbia University*, New York, Columbia University Press, 1954, 50.

19 A typical account is from *Teachers College Record* in 1918: 'Miss Carney spent the interval between spring and summer sessions on a western trip speaking fifty-four times on rural school conditions and needs in war time.' Engagements were filled at normal schools, rural conferences, and state educational associations in West Virginia, Tennessee, Illinois, Minnesota, Michigan, Idaho, and Washington. 'Rural Education News', *Teachers College Record* XIX 5 (Nov. 1918) 496.

20 See J. Anderson, *The Education of Blacks in the South*, Chapel Hill, University of North Carolina Press, 1988, for an analysis of paternalism in the work of the General Education Board.

21 Goodsell is now remembered for the Willystine Goodsell Award, given annually to a member of the American Educational Research Association who furthers the interests of women in education. Discussions of her work can be found in R. Engel, 'Willystine Goodsell: feminist and reconstructionist educator', *Vitae Scholasticae*, Vol 3, No. 2 (Fall, 1984) pp. 355–80 and S. Biklen, 'Willystine Goodsell', in M. Seller, Ed. *Women Educators in the United States*, New York, Greenwood, 1994, 227–232. Biklen sees Goodsell's challenge to the sexism of G. Stanley Hall and Edward Thorndike in *The Education of Women* as 'perhaps her greatest intellectual contribution to the history of American education', 229.

22 Reports of Professors on Examinations of Students for the Ph.D. Degree 1905–1909. Department of Special Collections, Milbank Memorial Library, Teachers College, Columbia University, New York.

23 W. Goodsell, 'The New Eugenics and Education', *The Social Frontier IV*, 31 (January, 1938) 113–117.

24 W. Goodsell, 'The Effects of the War in Women's Colleges', *Teachers College Record* XX 1 (Jan. 1919) 35.

25 M. J. Alexander and C. Mohanty, 'Introduction: Genealogies, Legacies, Movements', in M. J. Alexander and C. Mohanty, Eds *Feminist Genealogies, Colonial Legacies, Democratic Futures*, London, Routledge, 1997, xxxi.

26 W. Goodsell, *The Education of Women*, New York, MacMillan, 1924, 255.

27 Goodsell, *The Education of Women*, 3.

28 Goodsell, *The Education of Women*, 347.

29 Goodsell, *The Education of Women*, 7.

30 Goodsell, *The Education of Women*, 341.

31 Nel Noddings, *Caring*, Berkeley, University of California Press, 1984; Jane Roland Martin, *Changing the Educational Landscape*, New York, Routledge, 1993.

32 Goodsell, *The Education of Women*, 342.

33 I. L. Kandel, 'Education and Social Disorder', *Teachers College Record* XXXIV, 5 (February 1933) 367.

34 W. Goodsell, 'The New Education As It Is: A Reply to Professor Kandel', *Teachers College Record* XXXIV, 7 (April, 1933) 542.

35 Kandel responded to Goodsell with a brief, labored parody, 'Alice in Cloud-

Cuckoo-Land', *Teachers College Record* XXXIV, 8 (May, 1933) 627–634. There is no further published exchange between the two of them.

36 Goodsell, 'The New Education As It Is', 550.

37 Goodsell, *The Education of Women*, 350.

38 W. Goodsell, 'Opportunities of American Women in Education and the Professions', *Frontiers of Democracy* (April 15, 1940), 117.

39 C. Mouffe, 'Feminism, citizenship and radical democratic politics', in J. Butler and J. Scott, Eds. *Feminists Theorize the Political*, New York, Routledge, 1992, 373.

40 Mouffe, 'Feminism, Citizenship and Radical Democratic Politics', 378.

9 Student teachers' representations of citizenship

A comparative perspective

G. Ivinson with M. Arnot, H. Araújo,
K. Deliyanni and A. Tomé

In this chapter, we contend that educational debates about citizenship, and whether or not it should be taught as a formal aspect of the curriculum, have to start from an understanding of common sense assumptions that people hold about what it means to be a citizen in a particular country. Assumptions about citizenship circulate in societies at large and are likely to enter schooling as part of the 'hidden curriculum' of schooling. Educationalists, therefore, have to ask not only what they should teach in relation to citizenship but also how critical thinking in this area can be achieved. The first stage in achieving a critical approach to the study of citizenship is to make explicit common sense assumptions about what is currently understood as citizenship within a particular society.

The study of common sense knowledge is central to the theory of social representations[1] (Moscovici 1976, 1981, 1984, 1998). The emphasis on the dynamic aspect of everyday knowledge in the theory allows us to investigate how ideas are transformed through everyday communication as groups strive to make sense of their world(s). Yet, the process of transformation often involves a conservative element. Ideas or representations that have deep historical roots become ossified as they are incorporated into the language used by a speech community (cf. Heider 1958). Thus when groups recycle old ideas to make sense of contemporary crises, associations rooted in the past are drawn into the present.

Notions about citizenship, for example, are constantly being produced and transformed in everyday conversations and through the media. Some aspects are bound up with representations of national identity and, therefore, have implications for the way social meaning and coherence are maintained. Other aspects are transformed as a result of social, political and material changes. For example, technological advances, changes in the labour market and changes in family structures challenge traditional gender representations. In particular, the activities of women who are searching for independence often blur the symbolic boundaries that separate work and family and public and private life. Debates concerning working mothers, for example, demonstrate that questions of access to public arenas are controversial. As symbolic boundaries become blurred, anxieties arise and groups often attempt to re-establish a sense of order by drawing on familiar, conservative representations of gender.

It can be seen, then, that citizenship and the assumptions that we hold about it cannot be isolated from social representations of gender.

In this chapter, we describe how we drew on cross-cultural data to develop a typology of citizenship that allowed us to unearth some of the hidden assumptions about citizenship held by student teachers in four European countries – Britain, Greece, Portugal and Spain. The typology allowed us, first, to consider the different social representations of citizenship in each country and, second, to investigate divergent views between men and women within each country. The typology provided the basis upon which we could begin to think critically about some of the commonsense notions of citizenship that are circulating in different countries. Further, it allowed us to recognise how gender, itself a social representation, was used by groups to sustain positions on controversial issues (e.g. working mothers) which were more favourable to them than other possible positions.

In the first section of the chapter, we consider the emergence and significance of concepts of public space and the implications for women as citizens from the perspective of political and feminist theory. In the sections which follow, we describe the typology of citizenship that was constructed from student teachers' focus group discussion across the four countries and then we use it to illustrate national differences in the social representation of citizenship. We then go on to describe how different groups of student teachers mobilised gender as a symbolic network to make sense of tensions around the public–private boundary.

Representations of the public domain

Jurgen Habermas (1985, 1990) and the feminist political theorists who critique his work, such as Carole Pateman (1988), often look back to Arendt's (1958) vision of the public domain as the place where individuals congregate as equals to make decisions aimed at transforming the ideal of public freedom into tangible social reality. Habermas' central tenet was to define the public sphere as a social structure within civil society. His goal was to move beyond a narrow definition of 'the state' to consider a broader conception of the political system (cf. Landes 1995: 92). In his critical analysis of the history of the public/private divide, he identified the genesis of the public realm as part of changes made in the organisation of society and forms of communication present in the early modern era. He focused largely on the rise of the bourgeoisie during the age of Enlightenment and Revolution and on new cultural practices in Britain, Germany and France in the eighteenth century. Social activities carried out in coffee houses, salons, theatres, lending libraries, lecture halls and through journals and the commercial press became associated with bourgeois public space. Habermas argued that because these social spaces were insulated from religious and social hierarchies, new forms of communication were able to evolve. The shift relied upon a form of individualism linked to a patriarchal family structure which afforded opportunities for private intimacy. The new meeting places thus allowed individuals to reflect publicly on novel, private experiences and this, he suggested, provided the grounds for a new debate which had the potential to challenge the established authority of the monarchy. He viewed this activity as the precursor of a new political public sphere.

Feminist political theorists have argued that the very existence of the bourgeois public sphere was founded on inequality and exclusion because women and dependants were often, both socially and legally, excluded from political life. Habermas addressed this problem by distinguishing between literary and political bourgeois spaces, yet as Joan Landes (1995) argues, the bourgeois public space never came to actualise its utopian potential.

Pateman (1988) maintains that political theory constructed a story about the progress towards greater freedom through the establishment of the social contract. According to Pateman, one consequence of the social contract was that the difference arising from being born a man rather than a woman acquired the status of 'political difference'. The fact that women were considered subordinate to men purely by being women constituted a fundamental contradiction at the heart of the social contract. To accommodate this, patriarchal civil society was divided into two spheres, the private and the public. According to Pateman (1988), the two spheres were separate yet mutually dependent. The public realm cannot be properly understood without the private, hence Pateman's premise that civic freedom was dependent on patriarchal right (ibid.: 4). She therefore argues that we need to understand patriarchy in order to understand both modern Western institutions and the social construction of the citizen.

Arguably, Habermas' account of the emergence of public space is too narrowly conceived to provide any grounds for the possibility of gender equality (Fleming 1993/1995; Pateman 1988). However, some feminists maintain that Habermas' (D'Entreves and Benhabib, 1996) vision of the public space as a truly democratic place can be salvaged if we reconsider the criteria that underpins public debate and hence public domains (Fraser 1987, 1995). For example, feminist political theorists argue that the strict criteria required for rational debate, such as the ability to take the position of the 'generalised other' (cf. Benhabib 1992; Young 1987)[2] are untenable and cannot fulfil the functions Habermas requires them to. Feminists argue for a greater awareness of the social, situated and emotive aspects of language, on the one hand, and the embodied aspects of public actors, on the other (cf. Outram 1989). As a consequence, they advocate a wider understanding of communicative debate to include, for example, personal narrative, rhetoric and gesture as ways of achieving empathetic understanding with others based on solidarity and community. In this respect, feminist political theorists have proposed a model of the public grounded in the socially mediated aspects of communication rather than in the abstract rules of language and debate and in doing so have tried to find ways to feminise and radicalise public space.

By contrast Jovchelovitch (1995), a social psychologist, emphasised the importance of the psychological processes involved in material and symbolic changes in public space. She argues that the progressive growth of intimate space has created new tensions between the state and the individual. She distinguishes intimacy and subjectivity inside and 'a space of discussion, debate and citizenship outside' (Jovchelovitch 1995: 96). She argues that mass media have made it virtually meaningless for individuals to come together to engage in conversation as a means of accessing information. The lack of need to congregate in public spaces removes a mediating space between the state and the individual. As the need for public meetings diminishes and mass society produced via the media increases, the individual paradoxically, becomes more isolated, confined as it were to the private space of the home. Jovchelovitch draws attention to the psychological processes involved in changes in public space which afford new grounds for the emergence of human subjectivity and, by implication, her work forces us to think anew about women (and men) as citizens.

Each of these accounts of public space entails a representation of the citizen. The issues raised by feminist political theorists suggest that it is important to consider who can legitimately take part as a citizen, in what kinds of space, using which forms of communication; and, supported by what kinds of social, linguistics and material resources? These points beg the question: who counts as a citizen and by extension, who is included in, or excluded from, full participation in social life? The questions we asked, when analysing the data, follow from these concerns and can be stated as follows:

- How is public space represented by student teachers in different countries?
- Who do they envisage as the 'ideal citizen'?
- What social, political and civic requirements are thought to guarantee or maintain citizenship and access to what kind of public space?

Parameters of citizenship

In order to map commonsense notions associated with the term 'citizenship'[3] we engaged student teachers in each of the four countries in focus group discussions. These discussions gave us the opportunity to tap student teachers' social representations of citizenship and of public and private space. It is likely that aspects of citizenship that were talked about at length within a group were aspects that caused concern or tension. As Bruner (1990) argues, it is when the constituted beliefs embedded in folk psychology are violated that narratives are constructed and it becomes necessary to speak. By conducting focus groups in different countries we were able to identify issues that were of concern, and by looking across countries, to identify aspects of citizenship that were not mentioned at all by some groups.

In order to map the explicit and the unspoken aspects of the social representation of citizenship in each of the four countries we constructed a typology of citizenship from the data across all four countries. The value of a typology of citizenship is that is allows differences between countries to be detected and this in turn points to aspects of citizenship that were hidden in some countries yet visible in others. One feature of a social representation is that aspects that are taken for granted become hidden. That is, in some situations commonsense knowledge is simply not available for articulation. Another reason why aspects of citizenship mentioned in one country were absent in others is that they were less problematic or troublesome to student teachers in those countries.

Cross-cultural research of this sort is never unproblematic. We conducted the interviews in single-sex groups between May and July in 1994. The semi-structured interview schedule and the focus group settings both facilitated and limited what was spoken about. In addition, the different cultural settings provided specific types of discursive contexts which, again, will have shaped what was said. For these reasons, we recognise that the typology of citizenship is a crude model and we do not claim validity for its use beyond the very specific context of this study.

Constructing the typology of citizenship

The typology of citizenship was constructed from the transcripts of group discussions with student teachers[4] in the following ways. Initially, all the issues and ideas that arose in the focus groups in response to questions relating to citizenship were recorded (the full list amounted to 240 items). Second, themes or topics were identified through an interpretative process which relied on subjective judgements, although this was informed by theoretical debates relating to the emergence and transformation of public space outlined above. The full typology is included in Appendix 9.1. The classification allowed seven overarching themes to be identified which we refer to as the parameters of citizenship. These are:

1   representations of public space;
2   representations of the citizen;
3   representations of forms of citizenship;
4   representations of the social contract (structures and resources that support citizenship);
5   forms of communication and social exchange relating to citizenship;
6   representations of inclusion and exclusion; and,
7   sentiments relating to citizenship.

Table 9.1 provides a summary of the parameters of citizenship in each country based on this typology. Elements in each cell were determined by referring to the full range of items mentioned by student teachers across focus groups in one country. The summary is designed to give an overview of differences among countries.

In the following sub-sections we describe the parameters of citizenship in each country in more detail focusing on the issues which student teachers were concerned about in relation to citizenship and highlighting the issues that were either invisible or absent. Points of tension and anxiety relating to

Table 9.1 Student teachers' representations of citizenship in four European countries

	Britain	Greece	Portugal	Spain
Representations of public space	Global	State (rural/city)	State (rural/city)	State (rural/city)
Representations of the citizen	Individualistic	Collective	Collective, moral	Collective, moral
Representations of forms of citizenship	Absent Active	Critical Active	Active	Active
Representations of the social contract	Laws, Rights, Citizens' Charter, United Nations Charter	Laws, Political, Social and Civic Rights, participate in state decision making	Laws, Bill of Rights, participation in State decision-making	Rights
Forms of communication and social exchange	Mass media Consumer economy	Access to healthcare, education, work and leisure provision. Protection from the state	Access to education, financial obligations, respect for others	Lack of economic resources
Representations of inclusion and exclusion	Inclusion – middle class. Exclusion – race, colour, class, Aids/HIV, carers gender, ignorant of rights, few academic qualifications	Inclusion – men, having a voice. Exclusion – class, ethnicity, gender, carers, diseased, unemployed, uneducated, in rural areas, the poor	Inclusion – having a voice Exclusion – class, gender, race, gypsies, carers, the poor, victims of violence	Exclusion – gender, carer, immigrant, uneducated, poor, Aids/HIV
Sentiments relating to citizenship	Shame, pride scepticism, apathy	Solidarity, love of fatherland, insecurity	Solidarity, loyalty	Harmony, community spirit, apathy

citizenship in particular countries are also identified. In the later sections, we describe how gender as a social representation was mobilised by different groups to resolve social tensions resulting from changes in the social representation of citizenship.

Parameters of citizenship in Britain

In the British data, the parameter of public space tended towards the global. Student teachers spoke of being involved in ecological and environmental issues and made references to the planet and the universe. There was little variation in what was mentioned in the men's or women's groups in relation to citizenship. However, student teachers in Britain were relatively young (in their early 20s) and, therefore, had little experience of life outside the family, home and university. Prominent themes were the importance of access to information via new technologies, such as satellite communication, and the role of the media, including television, radio and the press. Britain was the only country in which being a consumer and buying British or European goods was mentioned as an expression of citizenship.

There was practically no mention of local communities although social participation was referred to through concrete, local acts such as 'helping an old lady across the road'. A sense of the citizen as someone who was politically active, which was articulated at length in Greece, was all but absent from the British data.

Apart from the right to equality, gay rights and women's rights, no other political, social or civil right was mentioned. The only social responsibility mentioned was to pay taxes. Some respondents pointed to the fact that the British are 'subjects' rather than 'citizens'. Revolution and communism were presented as antithetical to citizenship.

A sense of national identity was articulated in relation to the 'outsider' such as 'the foreigner', and this was linked with travelling abroad. In these contexts, participants spoke of the need to make a good impression, of having a sense of pride, a sense of community and a sense of representing the nation. However, student teachers also spoke of a sense of shame relating to Britain's reputation for hooliganism abroad.

Groups with access to public school education were said to be more likely to become involved in state and social affairs than other groups and one reason given for this was 'the old boy network'. Lack of educational qualifications, lack of information and lack of knowledge about rights were mentioned as sources of social marginalisation. It was notable that the ordinary citizen referred to as 'the man in the street' was also spoken of as a marginal social participant. Social exclusion was associated with race, ethnicity, colour, gender, sexual orientation and, unique to British data, having an Irish nationality. The ideal citizen was said to be honest, responsible, reliable, balanced and confident. Because few personal qualities were mentioned in other countries, this gave a particularly strong impression of the individualistic nature of the citizen in Britain.

However, contrary to what we might have predicted, British student teachers exhibited little sense of isolation and instead expressed a sense of belonging, albeit to something rather amorphous or global. They mentioned 'being part of something', 'world citizens', 'plurality', 'a network of people' and belonging to a 'culture', 'Europe', 'democracy' and 'a community'.

Parameters of citizenship in Greece

Laws were mentioned as the principal structures of citizenship in Greece. Public space was often mentioned in place of, or synonymous with, the state and few participants spoke of belonging to Europe and to another culture. An impression of the overpowering authority of the state in relation to the citizen emerged from the data. This became noticeable because of the extensive talk about rights and concern with personal freedom in comparison with other countries. Although some confusion was expressed about the meaning of the term 'citizenship', it was associated with being critical and active. This notion of the citizen was linked to concerns about establishing and maintaining the social structures which support democracy. Rights to education, health, work and leisure were stressed, as were rights to different types of personal freedom and to protection from the state. Responsibilities to vote, to pay taxes, to be productive and to treat others with dignity were mentioned.

Inclusion in Greek society was considered a matter of living in an organised state and women participants stressed men's privileged social position. Marginal groups included those discriminated against according to class, race and gender as well as immigrants and mothers. Men spoke about military service as a form of social inequality. Lack of economic resources, access to education, healthcare provision and information, as well as living in rural areas were all mentioned as exclusionary influences.

There was a greater polarisation in the topics mentioned by male and female student teachers than in Britain. Men, in particular, spoke about the 'right to be elected', 'building a democracy', 'helping to modernise the country', 'taking political action', 'intervening in governors' decisions', 'fighting for rights', 'leading', 'managing and organising' and 'being politicised'. Women spoke about specific laws that had been introduced to protect women against rape, sexual abuse and harassment at work. They also mentioned women's double burden of domestic and paid work.

Male student teachers referred to a love of the fatherland and both men and women spoke about solidarity. Authoritarian rule, conformity and insecurity were given as examples that were opposite to citizenship. Domestic and state oppression were spoken about at length by women. The characteristics of the citizen included altruism and having a specific mentality. Male student teachers, in particular, mentioned the weak-willed as a threat to society and spoke of the citizen as 'a warrior'.

Recent Greek history, which involves transition from authoritarian rule to a democratic society, appeared to have influenced student teachers' representations of citizenship. Both men and women in Greece expressed a greater sense of mistrust towards those in power than in other countries. Apart from qualities of leadership and the ability to manage, individual attributes were spoken of less than communal attributes such as those required to foster political involvement. Solidarity and a willingness to mobilise for the common good were stressed, yet this sense of communality was restricted to talk of the state and European or global citizenship were rarely mentioned.

Parameters of citizenship in Portugal

Although there were fewer data available from Portugal it was still possible to extract, in a preliminary fashion, the parameters of citizenship. The representation of public space mapped onto a representation of the state although, as in Greece, differences between rural and city dwelling were mentioned. Laws and the constitution were cited as the primary structures supporting citizenship. More social responsibilities, primarily relating to the rights of others, were referred to in Portugal than in the other countries. Also, a wide range of expectations such as legal rights, the political right to intervene in decision-making, the social right to health and civic rights relating to personal freedom were mentioned.

Social integration, having a voice and protection from the state were given as forms of social inclusion. Participants spoke of a sense of belonging to 'somewhere', to 'society' and to 'a culture'. Solidarity and loyalty were mentioned and one person expressed anxiety over hero-worshipping. Marginal participation was related to social class, colour, gender, gypsies, violence and a lack of economic resources.

The citizen was described by student teachers as someone who had a specific mentality, particular habits, a particular world-view, a particular religious belief and an attitude of social participation. The importance of relating to others through 'co-operation', 'acceptance' and 'sensitivity' was stressed. Attributes of the ideal citizen included autonomy, responsibility, respect, adopting an ethical or moral position, having a sense of good and evil, having a 'conscience' and being 'daring'.

Portugal is a Catholic country and religious influences were apparent in the way the parameters of citizenship were described by student teachers. The citizen was represented as a collective being strongly connected to, and recognised within, social and family groups. An emphasis on tolerance and acceptance of others demonstrated further that the social whole (body-politic) was more highly valued than individuality. The family provided a metaphor for the polis which had implications for the way gender, as a social representation, was used: for example, to support role differences, as we report later.

Parameters of citizenship in Spain

Very limited data were available from Catalonia in Spain (where the research was conducted) which made it difficult to identify the key parameters of citizenship with any confidence. However, exploratory analysis suggested that the right to vote and the right to elect governors were key features of citizenship for these student teachers. As in Greece and Portugal, public space appeared to map onto the state and the divide between rural and city dwellers was mentioned. Citizenship was linked to active participation. Some expressed confusion about what the word 'citizen' meant. Spanish men, in particular, mentioned social commitment and the need to act in a professional manner while women referred to mothering, socialising children and the double burden of domestic and paid work.

Peripheral groups identified by the Spanish group of student teachers were immigrants, those not well educated, those awarded unequal pay for equal work, those who lacked economic resources, those in poverty and those afflicted with disease (e.g. HIV/Aids).

Sentiments relating to citizenship were harmony and a sense of community spirit as well as apathy. Attributes such as having individual values, independence, the need to lead and to show a good example were mentioned. In terms of social relations, participants included being a good neighbour and being friendly.

To summarise, there was cross-cultural consensus that men and women function differently in public space. Findings point to a pattern in which representations of public space are linked to specific representations of the citizen. In Britain, a global representation of public space corresponded to an individualistic representation of the citizen characterised by autonomy and independence. There was little sense of local communities as fora for public debate and instead the role of the media was stressed. The absence of a political sense of the citizen in Britain, particularly in comparison with Greece, suggests that democratic processes were taken for granted. In Greece, the representation of public space was commensurate with the state. An image of the political citizen who was watchful and sceptical about progress towards democracy emerged. However, men and women spoke about this in different ways. Male student teachers described the citizen as an active, alert warrior while women focused on social mechanisms such as laws that protect vulnerable citizens. The family and society emerged as mirror images in Portugal. Here the representation of the citizen was characterised by altruism, anchored by family membership and social roles, and a balance between expectations and duties. While in Portugal the role of mothers was not spoken of as a burden and gender differences were under-represented, in Catalonia a greater distinction in the way men and women were spoken of as citizens pointed to anxiety over women's emancipation.

Gender as a symbolic network

The parameters of citizenship were represented differently in each country. Social changes, such as those already referred to, potentially generate anxiety. In this section, we provide examples of how gender was mobilised in each country to make sense of changes in social representations of the public/private boundary as it was functioning in each country at the time of the study.

Issues that were spoken about at length by student teachers in each country suggested points of anxiety within groups. However, the ways anxieties manifest themselves may well be gendered. From their material positions, men and women may view social change and its effects differently. In consequence, when social representations of gender are used to mask anxiety they may be mobilised in different ways by men and women. Below, we illustrate how the interaction of social representations of gender and social change were talked about differently by male and female focus groups in each country.

Britain – gender, power and the media

The previous description of the parameter citizenship revealed the high social value placed on access to information in Britain. Mass media inform public debate, and in this sense, constitute a contemporary public domain. As Jovchelovitch (1995) has pointed out, the relation between public and private is undergoing rapid change as mass media penetrate the intimate, previously private, space of the home through television. The emphasis that female and male student teachers placed on the media suggested some social anxiety about the way the boundary between public and private was being disturbed. However, the greatest point of tension was identified by the way female student teachers spoke about women in the media.

Female student teachers spoke of the media as a remote domain in which the rules for access and participation were almost totally exclusionary. They contrasted the way men and women in the media were represented within society. For example, they stated that men in the media were listened to and taken seriously while women were not. They objectified women in the media in contradictory ways resulting in problematic portrayals of femininity. On the one hand, they agreed that women should 'say what they think' and yet, on the other hand, they recognised that this is a dangerous position for a woman to take in comparison with a man. This tension is illustrated in the comment below in which a student teacher describes Nina Mishkoff (a television presenter of a current affairs programme) as someone she both admires and dislikes.

> And anyone who's slightly different and stands up for what she thinks, I mean I don't like her particularly, like Nina Mishkoff, who does actually say what she thinks, which I think is fair enough. That's a valid thing to do, most men do that all the time, she gets shot down in flames. They'll pick up on what she looks like rather that what she said . . .
>
> (UK female student teacher)

By using the phrase, 'I mean I don't like her particularly', the student teacher distances herself from a representation of female assertiveness. In the most extreme examples, women in the media were described as 'out to get what they want'. Assertive women were described as having masculine traits and Margaret Thatcher, who had then been the prime minister for thirteen years, was referred to at these points in the discussions. In particular, these student teachers mentioned a portrayal of her in the television programme, *Spitting Image*, in which a puppet of Thatcher appeared dressed as a man. Tensions around male–female, powerful–weak, and assertive–composed binaries were revealed through the way female student teachers spoke of women in the public realm of television media.

Notions of the encroaching spread of the media had been transposed onto representations of women in public life, and specific features such as clothing, looks, ways of speaking and gestures were appropriated for projections of fears and anxieties. Representations oscillated between images of women as objects of sexual desire and as over-assertive:

> I also think it's the public image we get of women as either very strong and forthright, I'm going to get what I want anyway, or they're start-lingly beautiful and they're all like film stars and there is no sort of female role model that make young girls think, 'yeah, I could be like that'.
>
> (UK female student teacher)

In the comment below the degrading reference to a 'cow' links assertiveness to a lack of sexual attractiveness:

> . . . he's strong and he's . . . whereas a woman's perceived as being a bit ridiculous or a cow if she is like this.
>
> (UK female student teacher)

Other comments revealed an opposition between intelligence and sexual attrac-tiveness. Actresses, icons of feminine beauty, were accused of gaining access to the media by compromising their autonomy.

> I think that even people who are in professions like acting and singing, they are always, women, I feel, are portrayed as being bimbos. You have to be gorgeous, you have to be skinny . . . for a woman you have to be under 35, have long hair and be fantastically good-looking and you're just something on someone's arm.
>
> (UK female student teacher)

The characteristics of a 'bimbo' as 'just something on someone's arm' linked lack of intelligence, desirability and women as male possessions. Female student teachers were making secondary adjustments (Goffman 1961) as a possible reaction to loss of control. We found discordant images of women in the media which were full of ambiguity, doubts and uncertainties. Historically, social representations of middle-class femininity legitimated the linkage between attractiveness and gaining power in private and domestic life (cf. Skeggs 1997). Television literally inserts images of powerful or attractive women in public life into the private space of the sitting room or the bedroom. Actresses and politicians represented two extreme forms of femininity opposed to traditional domestic femininity. 'Old' binaries such as ugly–beautiful, cow–bimbo, clever–stupid and active–passive were being reappropriated to counteract the encroaching power of the media which was disrupting the public–private boundary and challenging student teachers' understandings of their own femininity.

Greece – gender, nostalgia and the family

One point of tension in the Greek data focused on the authoritarian power of the state. The new era of Greek democracy has fostered expectations that the state would deliver greater social equality. Doubts about the state's capacity to deliver greater social equity were evident in the contrasting images of Greek family life that emerged from the male and female focus groups. Whilst both male and female student teachers spoke of the centrality of women in the family, male participants displayed anxiety over the changing role of women in society.

The Greek data provided an example of what Doane and Hodges (1987) have identified as nostalgia around the loss of the idealised family. Historically, the representation of the bourgeois family was sharply separated from the domain of work. Within the idealised family setting, a specific representation of the mother provided an organising principle at the centre of a segregated, strongly bounded, private space. Within this representational network, the mother both constructs and maintains private space through the processes of nurturing. The stable psychic structures essential to the formation of children as strong characters develop within this insulated space. Therefore, the very cradle that fosters the autonomous, rational, independent qualities of the citizen, imbued with an ethic of responsibility, is neglected, if not abandoned, by women who go out to work. The family as the site of order and stability provides an important image of social stability. Accordingly, mothers who work threaten the foundations upon which liberal democracy is built. Such anxiety was evident in the way male Greek student teachers talked about the activities of working mothers.

> . . . the family needs a woman in the house: if the woman does not stay home, then the family is lost.
>
> (Greek male student teacher)

> There are many couples that are faithful to tradition: inside the house and the family, the man should be real man and the woman the real woman. In general the woman should not lift her head up.
>
> (Greek male student teacher)

They drew upon biological metaphors such as women's ability to 'suckle young' to justify women's position at the centre of the family. Men projected anxieties around social change onto women. For example, they spoke about feminine beauty as a mechanism that women use for feminine advancement:

> Women today have a very important arm that they can use in the labour market and in social life if you like, their beauty. The fact that they are the beautiful sex. It is then much easier for a woman to find a job, she is able to mobilise the mechanisms.
>
> (Greek male student teacher)

> *Question.* What happens when the appointment is for a director or a manager?

> If the candidate is a woman who knows the topic of the work well, if she is considered to be very smart, a sly fox, then she will get the job.
>
> (Greek male student teacher)

Men described themselves as in danger of being manipulated by women, illustrated through the metaphor of 'the sly fox'. Their anxiety was projected outside and located in the imagined dark recesses of femininity. Women were spoken of as if they were endowed with powerful internal forces, which were articulated as sexuality and emotionality.

> Women do what they want in the family. They are the heads in what concerns the organisation, the upbringing of the children, everything. Even in the emotional level, please tell me who can say no to the tears of a woman.
>
> (Greek male student teacher)

> A woman will do what she likes, sometimes with the grizzling, sometimes with complaints, she will manage to persuade you to do what she wants. She is much more sly or smarter in some cases.
>
> (Greek male student teacher)

These male student teachers held a representation of women as endowed with a latent (sexual) force that could propel them into positions of political power without exerting the kind of effort and hard work required by men to gain public positions.

There was also a sense that in the home, children were not being raised in the environment required for the development of the kind of individual needed to build a liberal democracy. The expression of loss over the mother, as a symbolic referent at the heart of the family home, was possibly linked to a fear of social instability. As the symbolic boundary separating work–family, public–private transgressed, conventional family life can appear relative, rather than as a fixed and secure, social foundation.

Portugal – gender, belonging and the political body

The relation between the citizen and the state in Portugal was reflected in representations of the family identifiable through the way groups discussed roles and responsibilities. According to this representation, what children learn in the family is replicated in their attitudes and behaviour as members of the *polis*. Attributes of autonomy and solidarity formed the heart of this representation of citizenship and intrinsic to this was an image of the family or social unit as an entity whose whole transcended the sum of its parts. Thus, talk about moral responsibilities and duties relating to family life slipped easily into talk about political and social responsibilities. Democracy was represented as a form of social balance. One student teacher commented that:

> Citizenship implies democracy and this in turn implies equality, and all this depends on the way it will be materialised in social terms; therefore a social balance is necessary.
>
> (Portuguese male student teacher)

Members have specific functions within any organised whole. This kind of social representation of the family and of society implies significant consequences for people who step out of line or who do not support the prevailing view. This might explain why the focus group discussions in Portugal reflected a greater consensus than in other countries and why there was little talk about social conflict (between men and women). It was not surprising, therefore, that biological explanations of gender role difference were given. Yet even here, there was a representation of human beings as a homogenous group:

> The fact that human beings are biological beings belonging to the same species.
>
> (Portuguese male student teacher)

> Cultural diversity is an obstacle to the materialisation of an ideal of citizenship which is both social and worldwide.
>
> (Portuguese male student teacher)

The role of a teacher was presented as similar to the role of the parent in socialising children.[5] This may have been behind the relative lack of discussion concerning the role of teachers in educating the citizen. Student teachers' discussions revealed an understanding that the relation between teacher and student was a moral relationship involving respect, trust and collaboration that extended beyond the classroom to public life and could equally be taught in the home. An underlying metaphor of the whole functioning as a series of interrelated parts seemed to lie behind talk about the family, society, the world and indeed the human species. This representation appeared to have suppressed debate about gender inequality and may have ensured a level of agreement among men and women on gender issues that was greater than in any of the other countries. This does not mean that gender inequalities, particularly relating to working life, went unrecognised yet this was not articulated at length. In Portugal, gender as a symbolic network was overshadowed by a symbolic representation of the individual embedded within interconnected, mirror representations of public and private domains across each layer of social life. Thus, the idea that citizenship should be included as a formal subject in the curriculum not only seemed to be a contradiction in terms but also threatened to rob the teacher of his or her professional identity. Student teachers' discussions in Portugal were marked by an absence of debate around gendered aspects of citizenship.

Spain – gender: blaming the victim

Spain has had a constitution only since 1978 and between 1939 and 1975 it was under dictatorship. An awareness of social transition in Spain and the need to establish democratic practices were particularly noticeable in focus group discussions. Both male and female student teachers spoke about women's continuing inequality in the relatively young Spanish democracy. Proposals from student teachers about how to change social inequality were infused with Catholic morality. This may have contributed to the relative lack of debate about the structural issues that perpetrate discrimination. Instead, a notion of personal blame pervaded discussions. Both male and female student teachers accused women of being the most significant barrier to equality. They spoke of women's submissive tendencies as a reason for this and some went so far as to describe this as a sin. Female student teachers spoke in ways that suggested that they had internalised this representation. For example, in focus group discussions they did not project their anxieties onto external symbolic objects. Therefore, women became symbolically both the subject and object of social inequality. While projection and objectification can, in some cases, demonise the 'other', to internalise social blame prevents the kind of objectification required to grasp social issues and bring them to the surface for conscious debate. And in Spain, women were represented as culpable, first for capitulating to a representation of 'the sexual contract' and second, for not fighting against its presence in contemporary life.

Gender and citizenship

Since the Enlightenment, access to resources, to social spaces and to forms of communication has been constantly shifting, yet the ways societies represent these changes to themselves are imbued with historical legacies. MacInnes (1998) has argued that there is a need to recognise that the 'sexual contract' is part of a historical legacy such that aspects of contemporary ways of thinking may still bear the imprint of history. By using the typology of citizenship as a framework, it was possible to recognise issues that were causing student teachers anxiety. These anxieties were likely to be related to social and economic transitions in each country. Our research reveals how groups in different national contexts called upon gender as a social representation in different ways to make sense of social tensions by changing the unfamiliar into something familiar.

For example, we have suggested that in Portugal investment in a representation of social membership as family membership suppressed talk of inequality in terms of gender and heightened the use of naturalistic and biological explanations of gender role difference. In Spain, both men and women projected anxieties about social change onto representations of femininity and used a language of blame. In Greece, women were also represented in this way, but particularly by men who imagined femininity as sexual and economic power. Accordingly, they expressed a sense of injustice that women were able to short-circuit routes to power and prestige that they considered should be a legitimate reward for men's effort and labour. In Britain, anxiety over social change was projected onto women in the media, particularly by women. Here, conflicts surrounding representations of gender and power were expressed as tensions within forms of femininity rather than between men and women. The presence of extreme and contradictory images of femininity in the British data might have been related to the expansion of the power of the media which was disrupting the public–private boundary.

We have shown how some of the most conservative aspects of social representations of gender resurface as people attempt to adjust to changes that affect their everyday lives. Different sets of tensions around the representation of public space emerged in the three Mediterranean countries when compared with Britain. In the former, there was a need for student teachers to reaffirm themselves within idealised family and local community life. This can be contrasted with a local–global polarisation found in the British data. The struggle for gender equality in Greece and Spain may have been competing with the struggle to establish democracy and self-rule. Social change often challenges previous understandings of gender roles, citizenship and the processes of inclusion and exclusion.

Widely held beliefs or social representations derive from and mask social and political tensions in specific societies at particular times. When they enter teachers' classroom discourse they constitute the invisible pedagogy of citizenship. While people often carry these views unconsciously, they are apt to resurface and become visible at critical moments. Amrita Chachhi (cf. Ward et al. 1992) has suggested that profound social change and the development of capitalist market relations can lead to the rise of fundamentalist movements as people seek refuge from anomie and uncertainty. Yuval-Davis reminds us that, 'Conservative and dogmatic positions are often fostered by the state itself at these moments as a means of maintaining social order' (cf. Ward et al. 1992: 15). The 'lynch-pin' (Yuval-Davis 1992: 15) for drives towards actual and symbolic social order often involves the control of women.

Our data suggest that social representations of female sexuality as transgressive, potent and dangerous were being used as symbolic armour to mask social anxieties concerning shifts in the public–private boundary. Feminists have argued that a de-gendered notion of citizenship provides an inadequate starting point for furthering the cause of democracy and social justice. We contend that any form of education claiming to teach citizenship should start with an understanding of the assumptions which circulate in societies at large and in particular the symbolic values attached to gender and women. Further we need to recognise that both women and men actively reconstruct representations of gender through their everyday practices and discourse.

We are all implicated in the social representations that circulate in the societies in which we live. The nature of public space is linked to the possibilities for making meaning. What we have tried to show is that public debate takes place in those areas where individuals feel they are free to speak. If people carry with them a perception of a limited sense of freedom this is likely to influence how they speak, if at all, and what they say:

> The human infant becomes a person through contingent processes of socialisation, acquires language and reason, develops a sense of justice and autonomy, and becomes capable of projecting a narrative of which she is not only the author but the actor as well.
>
> (Benhabib and Dallmayr 1990: 175)

The ways the self is reflected back to the student via the teacher will influence the kinds of citizens and assumptions about citizenship that are made possible in the classrooms of our schools.

Acknowledgements

Gabrielle Ivinson was the lead author for this chapter. The other authors, international directors of the project, were responsible for the design and the co-ordination of the research in their various countries. Financial support for this project was gratefully received from the European Commission and the Levehulme Trust (for M. Arnot). For other reports on the project see Arnot et al. (1996) and Arnot et al. (2000).

Notes

1   The term 'social representation' refers to both the 'structures' that allow communication to take place through inter-subjective shared meanings and the 'process' whereby shared meanings are created. Societies could not operate without these collective systems of meaning (Moscovici 1976; Moscovici and Hewstone 1983). '[social] sic representations also evoke what is absent from the world, they form it rather more than they simulate it' (Moscovici, 1998, p 245)

2   Benhabib introduced the notion of 'the concrete other' in place of Habermas' 'generalised other' and Young (1987) has suggested that this revision still does not go far enough.

3   Moscovici (1981) makes a distinction between the reified world of scientific discourse and the consensual universe of social representations. Here we are concerned to map commonsense ideas about citizenship which belong to the latter.

4   The numbers of participants involved in focus group discussions in each country varied. In Britain there were eight single-sex focus groups (4 female and 4 male

with an average of 5 student teachers in each); in Greece there were five focus groups (2 male and 3 female); in Spain (Catalonia) there were two focus groups (1 male and 1 female); and in Portugal there were two focus groups (1 male and 1 female). The student teachers in England and Wales were on average 24 years old. In contrast, female Greek student teachers were on average, approximately 35 years old.

5   Walkerdine's (1990) research points to a link between teaching, childcare and the cultivation of the good citizen.

References

Arendt, H. (1958) *The Human Condition*, Chicago: University of Chicago Press.

Arnot, M., Aráujo, H., Deliyanni-Kouimtzis, K., Rowe, G. and Tomé, A. (1996) 'Teachers' gender and the discourses of citizenship', *International Studies in Sociology of Education*, 6, 1: 3–35.

Arnot, M., Aráujo, H., Deliyanni, K. and Ivinson, G. (2000) 'Changing femininity, changing concepts of citizenship in public and private spheres', *European Journal of Women's Studies*, 149–168.

Benhabib, S. (1992) *Situating the Self: gender, community and postmodernism in contemporary ethics*, Cambridge: Polity Press.

Benhabib, S. and Dallmayr, F. (1990) *The Communicative Ethics Controversy*, Cambridge, MA; London: MIT Press.

Bruner, J. (1990) *Acts of Meaning*, Cambridge, Mass.: Harvard University Press.

D'Entreves, M. P. and Benhabib, S. (1996) *Habermas and the Unfinished Project of Modernity: critical essays on the philosophical discourse of modernity*, Cambridge: Polity Press.

Doane, J. and Hodges, D. (1987) *Nostalgia and Sexual Difference: The resistance of contemporary femininism*, New York and London: Methuen.

Fleming, N. (1993/1995) 'Women and the "Public Use of Reason"', in J. Meehan (ed.) *Feminists Read Habermas: gendering the subject of discourse*, New York and London: Routledge.

Fraser, N. (1987/1995) 'What's critical about critical theory', in J. Meehan (ed.) *Feminists Read Habermas: gendering the subject of discourse*, New York and London: Routledge.

Goffman, E. (1961) *Asylums*, Garden City, New York: Anchor.

Habermas, J. (1985) *The Theory of Communicative Action*, Vol. 2, Boston: Beacon Press.

Habermas, J. (1990) *The Structural Transformation of the Public Sphere: an inquiry into a category of bourgeois society*, London: Polity Press.

Heider, F. (1958) 'The Psychology of Interpersonal Relations', New York: Wiley.

Jovchelovitch, S. (1995) 'Social representations in and of the public sphere: towards a theoretical articulation', *Journal of the Theory of Social Behaviour*, 25, 1: 81–102.

Landes, J. B. (1995) 'The public and the private sphere: a feminist reconsideration', in J. Meehan (ed.) *Feminists Read Habermas: gendering the subject of discourse*, New York and London: Routledge.

MacInnes, J. (1998) *The End of Masculinity: the confusion of sexual genesis and sexual difference in modern society*, Buckingham: Open University Press.

Moscovici, S. (1976) *La Psychanalyse, son image et son public*, 2nd edn Paris: Presses Universitaires de France.

Moscovici, S. (1981) 'On social representation', in J. Forgas (ed.) *Social Cognition*, London: Academic Press.

Moscovici, S. (1984) 'The phenomenon of social representations', in R. M. Farr and S. Moscovici (eds) *Social Representations*, Cambridge: Cambridge University Press.

Moscovici, S. (1998) 'The history and actuality of social representations', in U. Flick (ed.) *The Psychology of the Social*, Cambridge: Cambridge University Press.

Moscovici, S and Hewstone, M. (1983) 'Social representations and social explanations: from the 'naïve' to the 'amateur' scientist', in M. Hewstone (ed.) *Attribution Theory: social and functional extensions*, Oxford: Basil Blackwell.

Outram, D. (1989) *The Body and the French Revolution*, New Haven, Conn.: Yale University Press.

Pateman, C. (1988) *The Sexual Contract*, Cambridge: Polity.

Skeggs, B. (1997) *Formations of Class and Gender: becoming respectable*, London: Sage.

Walkerdine, V. (1990) *Schoolgirl Fictions*, London: Verso

Ward, A., Gregory J., and Yuval-Davis, N. (eds) (1992) *Women and Citizenship in Europe*, Stoke: Trentham Books/European Forum of Socialist Feminists.

Young, I. (1989) 'Impartiality and the civil public: some implications of feminist critiques of moral and political theory', in S. Benhabib and D. Cornell (eds) *Feminism as Critique: on the politics of gender*, Minneapolis: University of Minneapolis Press.

Yuval-Davis, N. (1992) 'Introduction', in A. Ward, J. Gregory and N. Yuval-Davis (eds) *Women and Citizenship in Europe*, Stoke: Trentham Books/European Forum of Socialist Feminists.

Appendix 9.1 Typology of citizenship with examples taken from focus group interviews in four European countries

Parameter	Sub-section within parameter	Examples from focus group interviews
Representations of public space	Global:	The planet, the world, multi-cultural, multi-national
	Nation/State:	Country
	Local community:	City, town or rural dweller, belonging to a community, an organisation, an institution, a club
	Belonging to:	'something', 'what's going on', world citizenry, a culture, a network of people. Europe, a democracy, an organised state
	Family:	Being related to mother, father, brothers, sisters, other relatives
	Intimate relations:	Being a partner, wife, husband, mother, father, son, daughter
Representations of the citizen	Towards the collective/ society:	Participate, collaborate, share, co-operative, social attitude, shared values, shared religion, shared ideology, shared habits
	Towards other individuals	
	– distanced:	Tolerant, not prejudiced, accepting, respectful, not authoritarian, non-intrusive
	– near:	Friendly, neighbourly, involved, sensitive, caring, aware of problems
	Personal attributes	
	– distanced	Leadership qualities, individualistic, autonomous, independent, ability to manage, ability to organise, showing a good example
	– near	Rounded, balanced, sensible, confident
	– moral	Not corrupt, good, ethical, honest
Representations of forms of citizenship	Absent:	e.g. 'I can't relate to the word', 'it's vacuous', 'it does not exist' or those who expressed confusion
	Conforming:	Obey rules, conform to social norms, accept your social role, accept family role

Appendix 9.1 (continued)

Parameter	Sub-section within parameter	Examples from focus group interviews
	Participatory:	Participate in international, cultural, social and/or family relations
	Active:	Build democracy, make political decisions, elect governors, lead, be prepared to fight, be productive, act professionally, help modernise, help improve efficiency, bring up children, influence young people, teach, organise meetings, be on committees, take care of the environment, pick up litter, help old ladies, be involved in charity work, buy e.g. British or European goods
	Critical:	Question the law, question those in authority, intervene in political decision making, define social orientation, challenge stereotypes, take political action, make your view known, take risks, fight for rights, mobilise
Representations of the social contract	Supporting structures:	Laws, constitution, Bill of Rights, Charters (United Nations, European and National)
	Responsibilities:	Vote, pay taxes, obey the laws, work hard
	Expectations:	Rights – political (to vote, to elect governors, to intervene in political decision making), social (access to education, to a health system, to work, to equal pay for equal work), civic (personal freedom, freedom of speech, of information, of conscience)
Forms of communication and social exchange	Media – information:	Access to – television, satellite communication, newspapers, radio, amateur radio, telephone
	Finance:	Money
	Consumerism:	Consumer choice – e.g. to choose to buy goods made in Europe, Britain

Appendix 9.1 (continued)

Parameter	Sub-section within parameter	Examples from focus group interviews
Representations of inclusion and exclusion	Inclusion:	Having a passport
		Those belonging to elite groups (e.g. public-school educated), those in positions of power, professional occupation, the rich, living in a nice place, good lifestyle
	Exclusion:	Due to overpowerful authorities
		Through – social class, gender, race, ethnicity, colour, sexuality
		Through role – carers, mothers, those with children
		Through lack of resources – not well-educated, poor, lacking health provision
		Through ignorance – not knowing your rights, inadequate access to information
		By location – rural dwellers, immigrants, travellers, gypsies, 'the man in the street'
		Through oppression – victims of violence and rape, those sexually abused, harassed at work
		Through disease – Aids, HIV
	Sense of belonging:	Sense of security, sense of harmony, living in peace, sense of solidarity, sense of commitment, community spirit, altruism
Sentiments relating to citizenship		In relation to the nation
	– positive:	Pride, loyalty, love
	– negative:	Shame (e.g. related to hooliganism), apathy, scepticism, weariness, alienation, fear, anxiety
	In opposition to the 'other':	Having a sense of citizenship when abroad, in relation to foreign visitors, representing the nation abroad or at home to foreigners

10 Women in teacher education

Their struggles for inclusion as 'citizen-workers' in late modernity

Jo-Anne Dillabough

It has been customary among feminist theorists to assert that women have been both hidden and excluded from the subject of citizenship and the nation state in the modern era. Feminist political theorists have, therefore, placed considerable emphasis upon the study of women's exclusion from full citizenship and their political status over time and across national contexts. In so doing, this work has signalled the substantial conflict between male-centered understandings of liberal democratic thought and women's participation as citizens in the public and political sphere. It has also exposed those elements of liberal democracy which presume a view of the ideal citizen as possessing a range of qualities traditionally affiliated with masculinity, such as rationality, objectivity, and abstractness. Underlying these arguments are long-standing and more general feminist concerns about the exclusion of women from politics and civic life and the subordination of women in both public and private spheres. One way that exclusion and such subordination have been revealed is through an analysis of women's work, in particular, women's labours in the feminised professions such as teaching and/or teacher education (see Acker, 1994; Walkerdine and Lucey, 1989).

In this chapter, I consider the issue of women's work as an element of citizenship. In so doing, I extend the arguments I have made elsewhere regarding the positioning of female service work in the larger political and historical arena of state politics and gender relations (see Dillabough, 1999). Here I examine the relationship between women's citizenship and teachers' labours and experiences in teacher education. Drawing upon the work of eminent feminist political theorists (see Benhabib, 1996; Pateman, 1988), my central argument runs as follows: traditionally women have been shaped by the 'democratic' state to fulfil the role of caregiver and to cultivate the qualities and characteristics of 'the good citizen' through acts of motherhood and/or nurturance (see Walkerdine and Lucey, 1989). For the liberal state, this role has been legitimated by long-standing distinctions between the public and private spheres and the association of particular gender relations with each sphere. This has meant that women have been socially constructed as 'non-citizens' because of their supposed 'natural affiliation' with the private sphere. But despite this, they have been and remain expected to socialise citizens in each new generation, mainly through their work in the service professions and domestic labour.

Yet female labour in education, although analysed by feminists, has not been associated with larger questions about female citizenship – a separation which has many implications. Arguably, its most critical implication is that female workers are simply viewed as low-status educators to whom it falls to keep intact the political machinery of liberal democracy rather than to acquire citizenship status themselves. Arguably, then, women teachers' responsibility for the cultivation of citizenship is precisely what is required in order to sustain social and sexual contracts in the liberal democratic state. Women must therefore accept as natural the distinctions legitimated by the restructuring of the social and patriarchal order. Moreover, their own professional status and the symbolic activities in which they must engage themselves function to sustain the gender binary – male power over women – in education (see Dillabough, 1999).[1] The fields of teaching and teacher education constitute important sites where such gendered responsibilities for cultivating citizenship are very prominently deployed. It should not surprise us, therefore, that female teachers and teacher educators have come to be regarded as the 'keepers of liberal democracy' (Walkderdine and Lucey, 1989). And yet women remain precluded from citizenship status themselves (see Dillabough, 1999).

In the abstract, such an argument could unwittingly imply that the reproduction of the gendered spheres of work in teacher education is a substantially straightforward procedure premised largely on activities assigned to the female worker. Given the historical construction of women teachers' work and the ample evidence of gendered hierarchies in teacher education, such a case can be convincingly made (see Acker, 1994; Acker, 1995; Acker and Feuerverger, 1997; Dillabough, 1999; Steedman, 1986). However, as I will attempt to show in this chapter, such gendered reproduction through teaching or teacher education is by no means as straightforward as it might initially seem. Women workers, as I shall demonstrate, carry with them their personal memories of ill-treatment in schools, their inadequate working conditions, and a critical understanding of the operation of gender and race hierarchies in schools and higher education (see Acker and Feuerverger, 1996). Such experiences provide many women with appropriate and instructive tools not just for understanding the problem of social inequality and injustice in the workplace but also for their awareness of the need for change.

I will begin this chapter by introducing three key themes that have emerged as prominent issues within feminist political and social theory and which can usefully be drawn upon to explore women's struggles for inclusion in teacher education. I will then go on to discuss the concerns of a diverse group of female workers (including the work of student teachers) in teacher education whose memories and stories reveal something of the ways in which traditional notions of the 'public' and 'private', and the structures and experiences of social exclusion, are inscribed within women's lives as workers in teacher education.

In following Weir's (1997) feminist concerns about the formation of social identities, I wish to put foward key questions which underpin my central argument. These questions are:

- What is the relationship between how women construct their past and how they interpret their status as citizens in teacher education? Is there an element of *collective* or *social* memory to be tapped here and, if so, what might this mean for the ways in which teachers' gender identities are mediated?
- How do female workers in teacher education address the question of gender politics and their conditions of work in the professional world of teacher education?
- What role does feminism play in shaping differently positioned women workers' understanding of agency and resistance in teacher education? What bearing does feminism have on women's understanding of themselves as political agents in the workplace?

These questions have offered helpful guidelines for examining women's work in teacher education more generally and in exploring how contemporary feminist concepts might shed light on how race, gender and class hierarchies are normalised 'through the category of women's work' (see Mohanty, 1997).

Feminist political theory and the study of female workers in teacher education

Here, I consider three interlocking themes which have regained some prominence in social and feminist theory in recent years. These I describe as the 'limits of the private', 'gender, exclusion and social differentiation' and 'women's collective memory'. Each contributes to the ways in which we can interpret women's status as female workers in teacher education and their struggles for inclusion as 'real' citizen workers.

The limits of the private

It has now been well established by feminist political theorists that women's citizenship has been constituted as a feeble enterprise in most Western nations, precisely because 'to be a women' has typically implied the opposite of citizenship, that is, the non-citizen (see Pateman, 1988). This is largely to do with the long-standing and traditional distinction in liberal democratic theory between the public and private and the homologous categories of 'male' and 'female'. As Mary O'Brien (1981: 93) writes: 'Men are somehow separate from and in antagonistic relation to Nature, while women are in some even vaguer sense unified and indeed imprisoned by Nature'.

The central argument here is that women have been linked, both traditionally and ideologically, to the private sphere and domesticity. To engage in the work of the private sphere or 'Nature' – motherhood, caring, service – has therefore been to invoke the status of non-citizen, or non-worker.

These liberal distinctions have a long history in political thought and have emerged largely because it was thought that the activities of the private – activities Habermas referred to as *symbolic activities* and *symbolic reproduction* – did not require the work of the intellect or of 'reason' (see Habermas, 1974, 1993; Fraser, 1989; Pateman, 1988, 1989). They do not call for, in other words, the highly rationalised thinking required of the 'citizen worker'. The consequence has been that women are not seen as rational thinkers, as individuals capable of contributing to the public order. Instead, they are seen as the medium through which the state and its members might be nurtured. They cannot, therefore, be seen as citizens on a par with men because their traditional roles in the state (and within accompanying social discourse) have been defined in accordance with that pervasive private/public split which privileges objectivity over subjectivity, mind over body, and reason over emotions (Benhabib, 1996).

A further consequence of this division dictates that men and women must ultimately be regulated by state discourses which lead to the performance of different social functions (see Fraser, 1989). For example, if women are to be affiliated with the private sphere, then their role as citizens must be linked, both symbolically and normatively, to practices which are ultimately devalued because they are not defined in relation to the work of the 'citizen worker' (Fraser, 1989). This, of course, does not imply that women and men always engage with the polity in gender-specific ways. The primary concern here is with public discourse about women as citizens and the consequences of these very traditional and constraining distinctions.

By contrast, the activities which have been traditionally considered part of the public, rational sphere are seen, as Habermas has characterised them, as 'social labour and serve the function of material production' (Fraser, 1989: 33). This position of power in the state is that of the male 'citizen worker' and is associated with *material production* – those activities which lead to capitalist production and rational organisation of the state. Since this species of power is given super-ordinate status in the state, women are placed in a rather contradictory position; to be successful, they must submit to a larger symbolic discourse which circulates about them, at the same time as trying to enact a notion of self which separates them from such symbolic gestures. Consequently, the only option is to accept the premises of liberal democratic citizenship – a premise which dates back to Kantian assumptions about the 'citizen worker' – as possessing a form of rationality and objectivity which only men are thought to possess. The acquisition of female citizenship must involve, therefore, conformity to the moral imperatives of a masculine epistemology, that is, a rejection of the private sphere in favour of the more productive, public sphere of material production (Fraser, 1989).

Such contradictions, together with the traditional ties which regulate the production of female identity, have been critiqued by feminist theorists for more than three decades. Within the field of education, however, there is still limited understanding of how such a split has influenced the development of female workers in the service professions (of which teacher education is such a prominent representative). More important yet, in recent years we have moved away from an analysis of women's labour largely due to a preoccupation with questions of identity. This postmodern preoccupation has been fruitful in many ways. However, as Seyla Benhabib (1996) has noted, this preoccupation may have kept women from challenging the splits thought to be maintained through patriarchal practice in late modernity. This has been accomplished largely through the destabilisation of the notion of female agency. For example, a central assumption underlying the post-modern preoccupation with identity is that female identities are constructed through linguisitic devices (i.e. discourse) and 'knowledge–power' matrices and relations; in this model, identities are not always viewed as socially mediated and notions of female agency or critical reflection are rejected as a male form of liberal autonomy and another element of liberal democratic ideology. The very idea of women as reflective agents is therefore viewed within some postmodern feminist theories as implausible.

Paradoxically, however, the most extreme consequence of such a stance is that the female subject cannot speak because she has been robbed (at least theoretically) of her reflexive capacity to do so in an epistemological sense. This is indeed a problematic outcome of current feminist theoretical debates since one of the original arguments made by feminists at the turn of the nineteenth century was that women did not possess the power to speak in their own name. Their struggles were designed to rectify this problem. Yet, a hundred years on we are still struggling with these same political and theoretical dilemmas.

Therefore, in attending to questions about the *limits of the private sphere* for understanding female citizenship, I have to agree substantially with Benhabib (1996) about what this might mean for the future of feminist theory and women's citizenship. She writes:

> Contemporary feminist theory is bordering on incoherence if it cannot clarify a consistent and intelligible view of agency. . . . Distinctions between 'constitution' and 'determination' . . . do not clarify the question as to what views of agency or subjectivity are possible within the framework of radically constructionist theory. If these agents retain a capacity for resistance . . . or for subverting gender codes, from where do these capacities derive? What are the sources of spontaneity, creativity and resistance in agents? (1996: 34)

In all of these respects, much of the critical assessment of the private–public split is founded upon the work of feminist political theorists such as Benhabib who have not, to date, strongly influenced the work of feminist educationists (see Arnot and Dillabough, 1999). However, many of Benhabib's (1996) arguments indirectly suggest that teacher education mirrors the public/private split inherent in liberal democratic ideals. The conditions of women teachers' work in the academy and schools illustrate this point well (see Acker, 1994,

1995; Acker and Feuerverger, 1997), since they expose the ways in which teacher education has developed as a symbolic reflection of traditional understandings of female citizenship over time. Simultaneously, however, an assessment of these conditions may also highlight the active attempts women workers have made to redefine not only their professional image but also the very premise of gender politics in the state.

Gender, exclusion and social differentiation

Another contemporary theme in feminist theory is the question of women's social *inclusion* and *exclusion* in the state (see Dillabough and Arnot, ch. 2, this volume). For example, some feminist theorists argue that national policy and state practices exclude women from the possibility of full political participation as citizens. These might include national public policy on, for example, women's work, schooling (see Bickmore, 1996), family and child welfare, and immigration and human rights issues, all of which indirectly or directly pertain to citizenship issues for women.

The ways in which women in any national context are configured as 'included' or 'excluded' citizens are also significantly influenced by societal change. For example, shifts in economic and social formations can have a differential impact on men and women and their abilities to acquire political agency. Similarly, national rhetoric and policies construct women symbolically (for example, within political discourses) and these in turn will have a differential impact on the material lives and the political identities of differently positioned groups of women.

The current feminist interest in women, the nation state and public discourses is highly relevant for the study of female workers in teacher education, not least because of the ways in which their own schooling will have been shaped by such national discourses and policies. Memories of social exclusion in schools and the ways in which their identities are constructed in relation to imaginary notions of 'the nation' are likely to affect the ways in which female educators interpret their role as workers. Although national identities appear to be far removed from the work of teacher educators, the process of inclusion and exclusion associated with the formation of such identities will be shown to be integral to teacher educators' political and work identites.

The theoretical character of such an argument assumes that in accordance with liberal democratic theory, the state and its citizenry come into view as an essentially featureless realm – a realm in which female identities and indeed women's history are erased by neglecting social differentiation between women. It thus dismisses differences of gender, race and class and treats them as an artefact of the private, and one which does not warrant interference from the state. In this context, difference is scarcely politically relevant. This kind of abstraction and neutrality is often found in teacher education. However, through the study of women's experiences as differently positioned workers, difference is rendered as a compelling and important aspect of women's work as citizens in teacher education.

Women's collective memory

Memory, as a mechanism for uncovering both individual and collective social practices, has also taken on a renewed significance in feminist and social theory in recent years (Gardner, 1999; Luttrell, 1997; Rosenberg and Simon, 1999). Amongst the variants of theory now circulating, two critical elements of memory emerge. The first of these concerns an *individual memory* of an event which is clearly particular to one's life, locality and context. As Gardner (1999: 12) suggests, its core elements are premised on the existence of an individual's private life and the maintenance of his/her 'narrative identity'. The second concerns a form of *social* or *collective memory* which may be particular to one's life or locality but, at the same time, may expose something about social practices which members of a group share in some manifest form – for example, memories of the Holocaust, of war and of some sustained institutional injustice. From this standpoint, the existence of a social or collective memory implies that any history of events or ideas is characterised by what Rosenberg and Simon (1999) refer to as a 'pedagogical intent'. Collective memory therefore leaves behind not just a 'legacy' of shared knowledge but also encourages a proactive social response to it in the future.

This notion of collective memory resonates substantially with what women across time and location have put forward about their subordinate positioning in the state. In so doing, collective memory as it pertains to women has the capacity to render explicit women's place in the construction of knowledge. It also exposes the manner in which women's social memory might influence female agency in a state premised on the public/private divide.

For example, women's memories might reveal historically grounded, normative assumptions about women and broader social relations as they are expressed in fields such as philosophy or political thought. Such assumptions may constrain, for example, women's actions because they circulate as a form of historical morality or truth about who women should be as subjects in a liberal democracy. At the same time, women's memories may also expose the sometimes hidden ways in which women have constructed their own political agency over time; that is, such memories may provide the conditions for acting as agent of change and serve as the basis for political resistance to practices which marginalise women as citizens. In this case, memory serves to reveal particular social moralities, ethical notions and indeed something about women themselves. As Luttrell (1997: 8) argues, 'women's stories [*as a retrospective view*] are about the events and conditions of their lives' (*italics my addition*). Uncovering such conditions, as embedded in collective memory, thus becomes central to questions about women's inclusion in the state.

It seems appropriate, therefore, to explore *collective* or *social* memory in the study of women's work in teacher education. Indeed, one may wish to ask 'what role does women's collective memory play in women's responses to the construction of femininity in the private sphere, to current conceptions of inclusion and to gender politics in teacher education?' Drawing upon empirical data, I now turn to an empirical exploration of such issues as they pertain to women's labour in teacher education.

Women's work in teacher education

In this section, I present a piece of exploratory data drawn from a longitudinal, ethnographic study of women workers in teacher education conducted in the UK between 1996 and 1999. This study examined the role that contemporary gender relations and gender hierarchies play in shaping the political identities of women in a teacher education college. As one part of this study, student teachers, women teachers, teacher educators and teacher education researchers (on contract) were interviewed about their working conditions, their understanding of gender hierarchies in teacher education, and their concerns about their inclusion as professionals in the workplace. Women also described the political framework they use to characterise women teachers' work in modern society. The ways in which they see themselves as political agents in their working context, and the impact that race and class have on such conceptions, were also explored. The goal was to acquire some understanding of how such women were constructing their own political agency in relation to, and often against, institutional forms and practices which shaped their status as citizens in teacher education.

The study

The interview data reported here were collected from a sub-sample of twenty women teachers/teacher educators and contract researchers over a period of two-and-a-half years in a teacher-training college in a major city in England.[2] The college is located in a large, culturally diverse sector of the city. Like other education departments, this department had experienced a significant degree of change over the last four to five years, including loss and/or reform of many of its programmes, increased numbers of part-time contracts and the implementation of regular national inspection exercises. There were also substantial changes in the institutional management just prior to the onset of the study, which led to substantial academic downsizing.

I drew upon three different interview forms in the study: oral and life history interviews; more general open-ended interviews; and interviews concerning teachers' political beliefs about working conditions, their inclusion in the institution, and their interests in feminist politics. From the larger sample of twenty female workers, I selected a sub-sample of six women with whom I worked with in a greater capacity over the entire duration of the ethnography. I interviewed these women on as many as four occasions, in some cases observed their teaching, attended their classes, and sometimes followed them (in the case of the teacher educators) to school visits where they met with student teachers.

Below I explore the stories of three different groups of female workers in teacher education, locating concerns about their experiences of marginality in a historical context and drawing upon a collection of women's memories of their past.

Marginal citizenship: memories of racism, sexism and classism

> There was one time in my class when I had to go up to my English Teacher and I said 'excuse me sir. I have to go for my career interview now', and he looked at me and he said 'Ohh, you're not going to have a career' ... Even to this day, I don't know why he said that. Maybe because I was a girl or an ethnic minority but that was so real and it affected me ever since.
>
> (Sally, Minority Ethnic Teacher Educator/Contract researcher, Interview 1, 1998)

> I remember doing house craft, needlecraft ... I also remember my first experience of racism. My friends and I ... got into trouble and the head mistress looked at us (there were three of us, all ethnic minority) and she said 'if you don't behave yourself and you don't study you will all end up seamstresses, just like your mothers'.
>
> (Sophia, Minority Ethnic Teacher Educator/Contract researcher, Interview 1, 1998)

It is still commonplace to say that education is the mechanism for achieving what the liberal democratic state proposed in the post-war period: equality of opportunity, equality of condition and education for a more just and egalitarian society. Post-war state schooling was meant to be more progressive and sympathetic to the concerns of all students, regardless of their position in the social and economic world. And schooldays, at least as they have been expressed through the eyes of the traditional historian, were meant to be some of the happiest memories of one's youth. However, as many sociologists and critical theorists of education have asserted, one must be clear about precisely the kind of educational experiences we are referring to and for whom.

The words of both Sally and Sophia, both ethnic minority workers in teacher education, force us to consider such a question. They also provide a template for understanding the history of women's exclusion in education and the relation of such exclusions to women's citizenship and cultural identities. For example, Sophia's memory of her teacher's claim about her own future – 'you will all end up seamstresses, just like your mothers' – highlights the diminished status of the private sphere and motherhood, and the prominent place such images have in the living memories of such women.

But Sally's and Sophia's memories tell us a good deal more about schooling. For example, the social reproductions of racial and gender inequality in schools are central themes in their memories. Such themes expose a normative hegemonic discourse which regulates who (and what identity) belongs in education. This discourse is not only grounded in dominant cultural assumptions about the ideal citizen (or ideal pupil, see Callender and Wright, this volume); it is also premised upon the patriarchal division of private and public and highlights the many symbolic roles assigned to diverse women early on in their educational careers. Another of Sally's memories of school experience highlights this:

> We were seen as *gentle little flowers*. The white girls would comment on our black hair . . . but my brothers said they had a really bad time . . . When [my brother] was at school he was smart and some of the other students got jealous of his grades and . . . they actually shot some chilli into his eyes. Things like that happened – so he got physical abuse but my sisters and I got a different kind of abuse – more gentle.
>
> (Sally, Minority Ethnic Teacher Educator/Contract researcher, Interview 2, 1998)

Here, one begins to see how race relations and popular ideas about masculinity and femininity are intimately connected to the ways in which culturally oppressed women are constructed as marginal citizens in schools. For example, Sally's reference to emotional or 'gentle' elements of abuse has important links to historical and symbolic constructions of culturally oppressed women (images of fragility and national symbols of sexuality) in the private sphere and indeed to images of domesticity and sexuality. Sally's comments also suggest that 'difference' is often equated with 'deviance' in the social world of schools. Yuval-Davis (1997) tells us that such symbolic gestures are central to the maintenance of a masculine form of the 'civil society', hegemonic forms of citizenship, and nationhood.

Another dimension of women's marginalisation, as recounted through women's stories of their past, is that of class. In this case, a white working-class female teacher educator is charting the memory of her early teaching career in the UK after leaving her home country. In this quote, she is reflecting upon the expectations which she felt were put upon working-class female teachers:

> There were the same attitudes to [working-class] women working as though you could be put upon, you could be asked to do things, you didn't necessarily answer back and if you did you were seen as stroppy. I always disliked that.
>
> (Susan, Teacher Educator, Interview 3, 1998)

Susan's expression of concern speaks directly to the lives of women workers and the ways in which they have been constructed in the fields of teaching and teacher education: as something to be 'put upon' and as passive subjects who do not or cannot speak in their own name. As Benhabib (1996) suggests, in a patriarchal structure such images of women dominate the public sphere and are expressed as uniformly characteristic. Susan's view, which she spoke about often throughout the course of the study, was that women must counter their own image of 'domestic servant' in the workplace. This meant educating the academic community at large about the problems associated with the reproduction of gender inequalities and in some cases refusing requests which led to the symbolic reproduction of such female service in the workplace.

From Susan's perspective, drawing upon one's experience of working-class life became critical to transforming the workplace. The comments of Brianne, another working-class teacher educator, certainly imply this:

> You were a nuisance if the baby cried. It was your fault. So when I went back to work (which I had to) I actually really enjoyed that and I realized that the next time I gave up work [as a teacher], I would make sure that I would not go down that road as being seen as a vegetable, excluded from my group of friends who didn't have children who could all go on holidays and had access to money . . . washing machines going round and round and getting your identity off by who gets the cleanest clothes.
>
> (Brianne, Teacher Educator, Interview 3, 1998)

The degree to which women educators spoke about the role of domesticity and motherhood in their working life was astounding. It was used to explain set-backs and the deleterious conditions of their labours in research, teaching and teacher education over time. It was also used as a metaphor for exploitation, as represented in memories of schooling and work in teacher education. This sphere – the realm of the private and/or domestic/biological reproduction – appeared to regulate women's memories of their marginal status regardless of how they were positioned in relation to race or class.

In moving this issue beyond women's accounts to the question of theory, one might wish to argue that women's memories of injustice have a *collective* or *social* element which is ultimately linked to very traditional understandings – in particular, liberal democratic understandings – of citizenship. For example, women's memories of school exclusions and work mirror many aspects of the patriarchal division of labour and highlight women's exclusion from full citizenship. This emerges in myriad forms but the most common memories come forward as a notion of women/girls as service providers or cultural deviants who cannot speak in their own name. The question as to what kind of self-understandings such women come to possess (as political agents) cannot be answered by examining such exploratory data. However, what does seem clear is that Habermas's notion of symbolic reproduction is alive and well in the memories of both white working-class and culturally-oppressed female workers in teacher education. This element of social reproduction points to a stable element of the gender order in women's lives despite the many other aspects of social change which have formed part of their lives and influenced the face of gender relations in recent years. The examination that follows aims to bring this aspect of women's working lives more clearly into view.

The marginal 'citizen worker'

In this section, I move beyond women's memories of marginal status in schools and the workplace to look more closely at women's accounts of their marginalization in teacher education. I do so with the purpose of analysing the link between the working conditions of female workers in teacher education and women educators' political identities as professionals.

There are a numerous ways in which women experience exclusion in teacher education, although the specifics are often particular to a woman's circumstances and the social and cultural context she operates in. It thus becomes more difficult to recognise precisely how the structure of gender relations is manifest in women's accounts of their working conditions. Nevertheless, the broader hierarchy of gender relations can be found in women's stories. For example, many women's stories reflected a strong emphasis on gender conflict which was almost always related to male expectations about female labour. As Sophia, an minority ethnic teacher educator, comments:

> I remember when I got my first job. It was a male teacher looking quite a lot older than me. I was only about 22–23 . . . I remember I asked for a room. He assumed I was a student and told me to get out. So that was one experience being both a women and [culturally oppressed]. So I thought he was making an assumption in terms of my age, my colour and my being a woman. When I told him I was a teacher, he said 'well it shouldn't be allowed to have teachers so young'. So it was one experience, if you like, but I always felt I was in competition [with the men].
>
> (Sophia, Minority Ethnic Teacher Educator/Contract researcher,
> Interview 2, 1998)

A similar experience is echoed in the words of Kate, a white working-class teacher educator in the same institution, who is reflecting on her experience of work in a previous post:

> When the Head of Department job became permanently available the female Headteacher said 'it would be too difficult for someone as young as you, for a woman as young as you to have credibility with the older male members of staff'. Basically, I left the job for that reason. I didn't get the Head of Departmentship.
>
> (Kate, Teacher Educator, Interview 2, 1996)

Sophia's and Kate's words do not only speak to the uncomfortable position of female work in education and its link to female sexuality in a broad sense. They also highlight the ways in which women are constructed as a man's competitor in the professional world. This is not neutral competition in an equal workforce; it is a competition premised upon a notion of sexuality which places women on the defence in many aspects of their lives. This not only impacts on women's conditions of work but also imposes a definition of women's labour which is premised upon the 'mainstay of capitalist patriarchal cultures' (Mohanty, 1997: 13).

Knowledge of such circumstances was at the core of many women's stories and served as the basis for understanding their own marginalisation. As Luttrell

(1997) notes, such self-knowledge is necessary for self-protection; however, it is wrong to see it as so valuable that we ignore the costs incurred to women as a result of their positioning. Luttrell (1997: 35) writes: 'while they may value their common sense as "real intelligence", there are few arenas in which women have been allowed to exercise their power and authority'. In other words, the actual costs to women's lives are greater than the true benefit of knowing one is oppressed.

There are numerous ways in which such costs become visible in women's working lives. For example, Sophia's and Kate's remarks point to the competitive gender relations women must confront as they struggle for inclusion and acceptance in the workplace. Women workers often feel obliged to enter into the competition for fear of losing out (or losing their jobs) in the institution (see Acker and Feuerverger, 1997). As a consequence, they are sometimes forced to operate as the marginal citizen worker who is attempting to gain legitimacy to a male-centered institution.

Sophia's remarks also reveal the ways in which 'gender codes' (Arnot, 1982) are represented in the working lives of culturally-oppressed women in education. These codes often serve as social markers for the emotional consequences such women face in the workplace over time. Such issues can be detected in the concerns expressed by Rali, a minority ethnic teacher educator, when reflecting on her own working conditions:

> I suppose you blank a lot of it out because they are not very positive experiences. Where my language was never acknowledged, my identity was never acknowledged. I think through those experiences my own self-esteem dipped, it has taken a knocking.
> (Rali, Minority Ethnic Teacher Educator, Interview 1, 1996)

According to Rali, such racial and gender codes, it seems, undermine women's belief in their own abilities as competent professionals. Such codes may also impede women's ability to function as political agents in their own right; in other words, such codes further resemble the gendered and racialised structure of the state. These experiences reflect the problems many women face once they are employed in teacher education, including whether or not they will gain access to permanent employment or get promoted (eg., securing a permanent post) (see Acker and Feuerverger, 1997). As Sophia points out:

> I always felt I had to fight for my job and I think it was because I was part-time, and then I became temporary and then I had to fight for it again, and in fact, I'm still fighting ... I fight for this work, to mainstream this work, not just to mainstream the work so that it becomes part of mainstream factors but also because of the people who work within it. Because those people that work within it are generally people from [a minority ethnic] community.
> (Sophia, Minority Ethnic Teacher Educator/Contract researcher, Interview 2, 1998)

But there are other costs beyond competition which affect the lives of female teachers and teacher educators. Lorna, a black student teacher, reflects, for example, on the gendered working conditions in her practice teaching school:

> They give a harder time to the women and not just to me . . . to all the female staff and sometimes some of the men teachers made it harder for the women because so much of the men's thing with the boys is very physical . . . Like 'I'm stronger physically' . . . and that made it even worse for us.
>
> (Lorna, Black Student Teacher, Interview 1, 1997)

The work of female teachers is not only affected by what is understood as the traditional male/female divide or other male members of staff. It is also connected to cultural contexts in schools. As Lorna goes on to suggest when discussing her practicum placement during her teacher training:

> [The school I was in] was mainly Afro-Carribbean kids so everybody spoke English as their main language. The second one – it was white upper-class kids and it was completely different because they were much more aggressive . . . the white kids . . . The boys weren't that bad really. They weren't really nasty but the girls were.
>
> (Lorna, Black Student Teacher, Interview 1, 1997)

Lorna's comments serve, as Omni and Winant (1986: 161) point out, to 'signify race culturally, to interpret its meaning in terms of practical and political terms'. They also provide some evidence, it would seem, of the hegemonic norms which guide the treatment, in this case, of Black female teachers in schools. Lorna's comments also reveal the role that dominant groups of marginalised communities might play in reproducing these conditions – for example, middle-class white girls – and the complicated ways in which gender, race and class play themselves out in teacher education.

When Lorna was questioned about any other gender politics present in the classroom, particularly in relation to working conditions, she responded by saying, 'No there wasn't anything apart from the fact that he [my mentor] called me and the other student teachers his girls, so he kept apologizing and saying I'm sorry I shouldn't' (Lorna, Black Student Teacher, Interview 1, 1997). In our discussion, Lorna did not view the comments of her mentor as something which might marginalise women teachers. Perhaps when the issue was extracted out of the race dimension, the consequences appeared less severe, at least in Lorna's case. This did not appear to be the case for Sohali, another Black student teacher who reflected on the gender and race relations of her own training placement:

> I noticed in the staff room that the Black teachers were sitting on their own . . . the whites were sitting on their own. I don't know whether this was consciously or sub-consciously . . . but I also noticed that the Black

teachers were not very happy with the way they were being treated. The Black girl I was working with I could sense the Head did not have any respect for. I think this was the case more so for Black teachers because they were very subtly telling me things about trying to stand on my own two legs ... When we left we did not get a thank you from the Head, whereas I remember there were two other [white] trainee students in the school ... The Head flattered [one of them] and said 'you'll be a wonderful teacher' ... But when we went we didn't get a thank you from her, nothing at all ... I think deep down it was something to do with racism.

(Sohali, Black Student Teacher, Interview 1, 1997)

Sohali's account provides an insider's view of what it means to be 'different' in an educational context which does not reward 'difference' and makes 'otherness' seem inappropriate, alienating or strange. As Mohanty (1997) suggests, when women workers are labelled 'other', they are often seen as 'unskilled' and therefore unworthy of praise or support. However, Sohali's account also reveals an opposition between the worker as skilled and women as service provider (and therefore unskilled). For example, people who go unrecognised in the workplace or who are expected to serve are not seen as workers at all; they simply make it possible for the 'real workers' to be recognised. This idea is reflected in the words of Sandy, a white working-class teacher educator:

A group of women teachers ... we all became very much like a Wendy House and my friends would say 'we're his harem' because we worked for this young man that had been promoted after three years of teaching and he didn't know how to do it. We basically carried him and he knew it ... so we just got totally fed up and we went to the local authorities and said we wanted something different but the authorities wouldn't let us ... [so] we just went round trying to meet others in schools ... We were seen as the ringleaders ... We had quite a strong network of women who weren't teaching ... women who were active in the women's movement.

(Sandy, Teacher Educator, Interview 2, 1998)

The image of the 'harem' is indeed a revealing one; it points to the sexualised nature of women's work and demonstrates precisely how women emerge symbolically as non-workers in teaching and teacher education. As Mohanty (1997: 13) writes: 'ideologies of seclusion and the domestication of women are clearly sexual, drawing as they do on masculine and feminine notions of protectionism and property'.

The kinds of support women are often expected to provide to male colleagues in teaching and teacher education illustrate some of the clear effects of a social definition of female work firmly positioned in the private sphere. Unfortunately, this definition of the female worker means that men, by default, are re-established normatively as skilled workers (see Mohanty, 1997) and that the labours of teacher educators operate within the confines of the image of the white, male worker. As Mohanty (1997: 14) writes:

the effect of this definition of labour is not only that it makes women's labor and its costs invisible, but that it undercuts women's agency by defining them as victims of a process of pauperization or of 'tradition' or 'patriarchy', rather than as agents capable of making their own choices.

Noteworthy, however, is that many female workers resisted any definition of victim status and struggled to define themselves as agents. This meant pushing male workers beyond an understanding of women as mothers and challenging any symbolic references which invoke patriarchal images of 'conjugal family life' in the workplace. Sandy remarks:

> People are now [talking] much more openly about the differences between how men in schools are treated and how they treat us. I have male colleagues who say to me I know you won't approve and I say (a) I'm not your mother and (b) I am not teaching on your course. Why are you wasting my time? I won't engage in these discussions. [As far as I can tell] they want you to shout and scream. Just don't play the game.
>
> (Sandy, Teacher Educator, Interview 2, 1998)

For Sandy, there are ways to challenge the public-private divide. However, women cannot do this without costs, and one's citizen status may be compromised in challenging dominant gender hierarchies.

We may also wish to reconsider women's responses to their working conditions, at least as far as theories of women's actions are concerned, in light of the broader issue of politics and social change more generally. For example, the data suggest that women are more active in the political sphere of work than many feminist theories of society currently suggest (see also Walby, 1997):

> Gender issues are coming up [in the workplace] now because I keep moaning about them which is why I lead them. I do the gender lecture which annoys me. I tried to get them [the men] to some gender lectures, but they won't. They chickened out. I knew they were going to because I said we need a male and a female here.
>
> (Sandy, Teacher Educator, Interview 2, 1997)

As Walby (1997: 154) writes, 'women are not as quiescent in their subordination as contemporary theories suggest. Women do resist, and theories of gender must take this into account rather than presuming or trying to explain female passivity'. In the section which follows, I draw upon data that charts such resistance and the role that women's communities play in encouraging what could be referred to as an *intersubjective agency* in the workplace. Such agency is premised upon the formation of a political identity grounded in feminist principles generated by membership in small women's groups and female workers' historical links to feminism.

Feminism and intersubjective agency

The vast majority of women educators I interviewed viewed their political agency in relation to women's groups, gender politics and feminism. Their affiliation to a collective and/or social notion of agency demonstrated, empirically, the ways in which women's identities are socially mediated in political communities. The data also resolve in some sense current opposing debates about identity in feminist theory: on the one hand, of seeing women's identity as a free-floating form of fluidity (post-modernism) which cannot speak in its own name or, on the other hand, a firmly entrenched notion of women as existing solely as part of a homogeneous, universal collective. Instead, the data suggest that women who have been committed to feminism are neither of these two extremes. Their accounts are suggestive of a much more complex social identity which is based on a strong social affiliation to women's groups, an explicit commitment to a collective (although a heterogeneous one), and to political action in their own working contexts.

Many women in the larger study had not been well served by a traditional notion of female citizenship – that is, a notion of women as part of a universal female category. Notwithstanding this difficulty, they remained committed to the construction of a social identity premised upon the idea of attempting to reconcile multiple and competing identities in the gender order. As Weir (1997: 186) writes:

> Ideally, these reconciliations are achieved not through the imposition of an identity which excludes or represses difference and nonidentity (the concern of postmodernists), but through a capacity to reflexively and practically accept, live with and make sense of difference and complexity.

Weir's words are suggestive of the idea that any capacity for social reflection may only be possible within the limits of a social community which recognises difference as a normative element in the development of political understanding. In part, women's accounts support such a view. For example, as the women in this study argue, difference is the tie that binds the actual group. It also leads to a sense of belonging which has implications for women's ability to create an inclusive space for themselves as citizen workers in teacher education. In the remaining part of the chapter, I describe data which highlight such themes of group solidarity, female agency and intersubjectivity.

One of the most profound and recurring themes present in the data was female workers' commitment to women's groups within the institution. This commitment emerged as a necessary aspect of working life which protected women from discrimination in their jobs but also supported the female students they served. As Sophia, an ethnic minority teacher educator and researcher, reported:

> We had the women's group there and [therefore] we were always challenging them, both the students and the staff . . . That's why the women's

group was so good because they were so active both informally and informally. There was clearly discrimination against female students, whether it was directly or indirectly in courses, because it was coming back to us. These were the kinds of issues that we discussed in the women's group and we tried to come up with strategies for dealing with it. In terms of action, I felt a bit stronger there. We even felt stronger to challenge it [the discrimination].

(Sophia, Minority Ethnic Teacher Educator/
Contract Researcher, Interview 2, 1998)

As Sophia described it later in greater detail, this group was composed of culturally diverse women who saw their basic concerns around gender exploitation and racism as the common elements which brought them together. Their differences were seen as strengths which evolved within the group. Sophia's own notions of agency and self-control thus appeared linked to the idea of difference as a form of social consciousness. Her remarks also illustrate the role of the group in sustaining feminist action and women's ability to make changes in their working life.

Sandy, a white working-class teacher educator, expressed a similar affiliation with the idea of feminism, and its role in her emotional survival on the job:

[Feminism] . . . I would say that it saved my sanity because it made me realize a shared expression. It made me realise that (a) it wasn't just me and (b) when I hear other women, especially when I am working with all these women who have childcare expenses and I think when you have childcare responsibilities you really see things. It is bad enough not getting jobs but parallel to what was going on in my private life . . . None of my friends got the jobs they deserved. [In my job] I felt totally patronised. 'She is good in teaching' but not worth more because they wanted men for management if you look at the career structure there.

(Sandy, Teacher Educator, Interview 1, 1997)

Here, as Sandy suggests, the endless contradictions for women re-emerge. It seems that women often feel shortchanged by their experiences of service work. They must experience their working 'lives as largely out of control, as victims of oppression and misogyny, and to a large extent must then become the sole agent for personal and social change' (see Pitt, 1995: 164). At the same time, they can only be 'teachers' or contract researchers; they cannot be 'citizen workers'.

But, as Sandy's remarks imply, feminism has been an important social force in her own life. Her views on feminist politics and her ability to reflect upon her own marginalisation resonate with other culturally oppressed women's views. There seems to be an affinity, at least among the women I interviewed, that there was a way of seeing and acting collectively as diverse women. Such collective action had important political consequences for women's social inclusion:

I think as a woman we look at things from a woman's point of view. We're more perceptive to gender issues, we're more perceptive to discrimination. The way that I have worked with women is that we would challenge, you know, the sexism and racism issue. We look at the strategy and see how we can make things better. You have a common goal and sometimes it's unspoken. I'm not saying it's like that with all women in institutions because there was a women manager in a previous job, and I don't think she was involved in the women's group and we were in constant conflict with her as a woman. You can't make that assumption. You work from a particular perspective.

> (Sophia, Minority Ethnic Teacher Educator/
> Contract Researcher, Interview 1, 1998)

I was totally committed to the idea that 'Black is beautiful'. Suddenly, I fit in with other like-minded women.

> (Phoebe, Black Teacher Educator, Interview 1, 1998)

While it is clear from earlier excerpts that Black and minority ethnic female workers do indeed encounter different meanings associated with gender and racialized forms of oppression, Sophia's and Pheobe's commitment to a notion of women as a social entity is important in understanding that it is not the collective *per se* which dominates women and leads to the repression of difference. Rather, it may be the nature of such collective groups and the ways in which they construct themselves in relation to others that becomes salient.

The central point here is clear: the social element of identity formation has both an implicit and explicit role in facilitating the development of a feminist political identity and agency. However, the goals of such action or self-understandings are, to a large extent, socially determined. This is not, as many feminists might wish to argue, a simple case for a liberal form of consciousness-raising. Rather, it concerns the social processes which influence and shape one's thinking about feminism in social contexts.

Ironically, many of the women workers saw education as a way out of involvement and affiliation with the private sphere, despite the reproduction of the 'domestic sphere' in their own working lives. Sandy states:

When I started teaching I also started having my family so I gave up teaching and became a housewife which again was a very oppressed political position to be in . . . The difference in being at home was that I was seen as worthless with no access to any real power and being back at work and being given more status . . . I was told constantly that when I went back to work that this was for pin money which is a concept that you work part-time to keep your husband in holidays . . . [Then] I became very interested [in gender]. The first course I did was to do with sociology and standing in society. We talked about her-story and his-story and it made me more politicized and gave me access to reading and *discussion* that I'd never analysed at home . . . I was also at College . . . when we were all part of a struggle to give oppressed peoples their voices. It was a very important time for me to become a teacher.

(Sandy, Teacher Educator, Interview 2, 1997).

The ways of getting beyond the gender paradox is to affiliate, belong and develop a social community outside the private sphere and, in some cases, within the workplace:

> The women's movement gave me a huge boost in my confidence and then I made friends who obviously thought like me ... It was a good time for me to have an alternate avenue rather than just becoming obsessed with housework ... I deliberately kept that for me. I kept going ... and my husband really resented that and I said I am still going and I stuck to it or got my friends to babysit.
>
> (Sandy, Teacher Educator, Interview 1, 1997)

Conclusion

In this chapter, I have argued that women's memories of schooling and work and their reflections on teacher education as a gendered workplace provide vantage points for making explicit the racialised, classed and gendered hierarchies which are embedded in the 'analytical category of women's work'.[4] As a secondary goal, I have explored data which illustrate the important role of women's memory in exposing differently positioned women workers' exclusion from full citizenship in teacher education, the power of social collectives in the formation of female agency and the role of feminist movements in challenging images of female subordinance in teacher education.

In committing to such issues, a number of theoretical issues come to the fore. First, it appears as though women do experience themselves as marginal citizens in the workplace, despite their commitments to social change. However, at the same time, these commitments serve not as examples of female passivity or service, but as social actions which push women beyond their marginal status. They are therefore not solely confined to, or symbolically represented in, the private; women do see themselves as part of the public sphere, not just as catalysts in symbolic reproduction but as citizen workers and agents involved in the political machinery of the state. Indeed many of their struggles are concerned with getting beyond the symbolic reproduction of the gendered spheres of work.

Second, the data suggest that women's views and perspectives on schooling and work are not discrete and isolated. Women in teacher education share many things in common, all of which are linked to the abstract idea of females as non-workers or as subordinates who must provide service to others. It is at this juncture that one begins to see how closely women's work may function to regulate and, in some cases, reproduce gender hierarchies. For example, if much of what women are expected to do in their jobs conforms to traditional understandings of the private, then it seems clear that such work will be devalued. However, even if their work challenges the gender codes of the private sphere, women are still held accountable to such activities in the symbolic sense.

I think it is also fair to say that female workers in teacher education engage in political actions not only to protect themselves from any further discrimination (i.e. the liberal view), but to represent and act out a social view of female experience. In other words, their experiences represent a broader social category of experience ('my experience includes the experiences of others')[3] (Bar-On, 1993). It is therefore part of the social character of female knowledge which defines, in part, how women come to know themselves as reflective agents in teacher education. The social element of knowledge emerges in the accounts women provide not only of their experiences as marginal citizen workers, but of their memories of school and work experience in the past.

Such a view stands against some postmodern feminist perspectives which suggest that all experience is fluid in character and grounded in the power of construction and discourse. Rather, the more modest view represented here suggests that women's experiences do at some point intersect with other women's experiences even if only around one central theme – that of exploitation. I do not wish to argue, however, that women's experience should be constitutive of a dominant form of knowledge or discourse. I merely wish to suggest that women are often constructed as passive observers who do not engage in political actions. Charting diverse women's experience of work in teacher education suggests the contrary; a view which points to a more comprehensive picture of women's political life as so-called 'agents' or 'worker citizens' in teacher education.

I have also tried to make a case for viewing women's agency as contingent upon the actions of others in particular (and indeed feminist) contexts. Clearly, agency is not something women simply possess or do not possess in teacher education. It is cultivated locally in social groups and in such contexts women begin to see the potential for social change. The premise for such action in social institutions is based upon the fact that women feel there is enough social and political support amongst themselves as workers to act upon their social beliefs.

In short, I have argued that the 'category of women's work' in teacher education is still grounded in a sexualised notion of women as service providers. However, women have a vested interest in getting beyond such a notion to claim their stake to citizenship in the larger society. They tell us, through their own accounts, that social inclusion in the workplace cannot be understood without an assessment of women's experiences and connections to broader social movements, only one of which is feminism. I therefore wish to reclaim the significance of the 'social' in women's working lives and argue that female agency in teacher education involves two central elements of intersubjectivity: the ability, through social and cultural mediation in groups, to reflect upon the normative conditions of teacher education and the capacity to act as political interlocuters through 'an affective investment in discourse with others' (Weir, 1995: 279). Considering such issues not only points to the salience of women's memories of injustice. It requires what Hannah Arendt has referred to as an 'enlarged mentality' (as cited in Benhabib, 1996: 38):

> And this enlarged way of thinking . . . cannot function in strict isolation or solitude; it needs the presence of others 'in whose place' it must think, whose perspective it must take into consideration, and without whom it never has the opportunity to operate at all.

Acknowledgements

I wish to extend my appreciation to the Social Sciences and Humanities Research Council of Canada (SSHRC) for the necessary funding to conduct this work. I also wish to thank Phil Gardner, Heather Berkeley and Madeleine Arnot for comments on an earlier draft of this chapter. I also extend my appreciation to the participants of this study. Without their participation, this work would not have been possible.

Notes

1   See Fraser (1989) for a feminist analysis of Habermas's notion of symbolic repro-
    duction.
2   Only a portion of the interview data from the sub-sample is reported here.
3   See Bar-On (1993) on the epistemological significance of women's experience.
4   See Mohanty (1997).

References

Acker, S. (1994) *Gendered Education: sociological reflections on women, teaching and feminism*, Buckingham: Open University Press.

Acker, S. (1995) 'Carry on caring: the work of women teachers', *British Journal of Sociology of Education*, 16: 21–36.

Acker, S. and Feuerverger, G. (1997) 'Doing good and feeling bad: the work of women university teachers', *Cambridge Journal of Education*, 26(3): 401–422.

Arnot, M. (1982) 'Male hegemony, social and women's education', *Journal of Education* 164(1): 64–89.

Arnot, M. (1997) 'Gendered citizenry: new feminist perspectives on education and citizenship', *British Educational Research Journal*, 23, 4: 275–295.

Arnot, M. and Dillabough, J. (1999) 'Feminist politics and democratic values in education', *Curriculum Inquiry*, 19(2): 159–190.

Bar-On, B. (1993) 'Marginality and epistemic privilege', in L. Alcoff and E. Potter (eds) *Feminist Epistemologies*, Routledge: New York.

Benhabib, S. (1996) 'From identity politics to social feminism: a plea for the nineties', in D. Trend (ed.) *Radical Democracy: identity, citizenship and the state*, New York: Routledge.

Bickmore, K. (1996) Women in the world, women in the classroom: gender equity in the social studies', *High School Journal* 79(3, February-March): 231–241.

Dillabough, J. (1999) 'Gender politics and conceptions of the modern teacher: women, identity, and professionalism', *British Journal of Sociology of Education*, 20(3): 373–394.

Fraser, N. (1989) 'What's so critical about critical theory? The case of Habermas and Gender', in N. Fraser (ed.), *Unruly Practices: power, discourse and gender in contemporary social theory*, Minnesota Press: Minneapolis.

Gardner, P. (1999) 'Great experiment and great transformation: revisiting wartime evacuation in England 1939–1940'. Paper presented to the American Educational Research Association, Montreal, Quebec.

Habermas, J. (1974) 'On social identity', *Telos*, 19: 91–103.

Habermas, J. (1993) in T. McArthy (trans.) *The theory of communicative action*, Vol. 2, Boston, Mass.: Beacon Press.

Luttrell, W. (1997) *Schoolsmart and Motherwise: working class women's identity and schooling*, Routledge: New York.

Mohanty, C. (1997) 'Women workers and capitalist scripts: ideologies of domination, common interests and the politics of solidarity', in M. J. Alexander and C. T. Mohanty (eds), *Feminist Genealogies, Colonial Legacies, Democratic Futures*, New York: Routledge.

Mouffe, C. (1992a) 'Feminism, citizenship and radical democratic politics', in J. Butler and J. Scott (eds) *Feminists Theorise the Political*, New York: Routledge.

O'Brien, M. (1981) *The politics of reproduction*, London: Routledge.

Omni, M. and Winant, H. (1986) *Racial Formation in the United States: from the 1960's to the 1980's*, New York: Routledge.

Pateman, C. (1988) *The Sexual Contract*, Cambridge, Polity Press.

Pateman, C. (1989) *The Disorder of Women*, Cambridge, Polity Press.

Pitt, A. (1995) 'Subjects in tension: engaged resistance in the feminist classroom', Unpublished Dissertation, OISE/UT, Toronto, Ontario.

Rosenberg, S. and Simon, R. (1999) 'Beyond the logic of emblemization: remembering and learning from the Montreal Massacre'. Unpublished Manuscipt.

Steedman, C. (1986) *Landscape for a Good Woman*, New Brunswick, N.J.: Rutgers University Press.

Stone, L. (1994) (ed.) *The Education Feminism Reader*, New York: Routledge.

Walby, S. (1997) *Gender Transformations*, Routledge: London.

Walkerdine, V. and Lucey, H. (1989) *Democracy in the Kitchen*, London: Virago.

Weir, A. (1995) 'Toward a model of self-identity: Habermas and Kristeva', in J. Meehan (ed.), *Feminists Read Habermas: gendering the subject of discourse*, New York: Routledge.

Weir, A. (1997) *Sacrificial Logics: feminist theory and the critique of identity*, New York: Routledge.

Yuval-Davis, N. (1997) *Gender and Nation*, London: Sage.

Part 3

Schooling and the construction of the gendered citizen

11 From pupil to citizen

A gendered route

Tuula Gordon, Janet Holland
and Elina Lahelma

The relationship between the individual and the nation state is encapsulated in the elusive concept of citizenship, an organising principle which signals at one and the same time inclusion and exclusion. In the development of the Western nation-state the individual, abstracted from his or her social location, became the citizen through the social contract which structured the state of culture (contrasted with the state of nature; cf. Pateman, 1988). This citizenship was literally exclusive and ethnocentric; the white, able-bodied, propertied men upon whom it was based excluded women, children, working-class men, and men from minority ethnic groups from full citizenship.

As European welfare states developed in the post-war period, formal rights became increasingly inclusive, although equality in social citizenship (Marshall, 1963; Jones, 1990; Prokhovnik, 1998) has not been achieved, and there are still groups excluded from formal citizenship rights (e.g. registered alien workers, lesbians and gays, children). Arguably, social citizenship should take account of cultural, sexual, reproductive and embodied lives (i.e. those who are likely to be excluded from the state). Equality between men and women, for example, is difficult to achieve if cultural processes and representations of women emphasise femininity, and the feminine is constructed as subordinate in relation to the masculine. Similarly, we shall argue that, without what we have called 'agentic embodiment' (Gordon, Holland and Lahelma, 2000a) – that is, making decisions about one's own circumstances and acting upon such decisions – the possibilities for realising formal rights are limited.

Education prepares children to take up their place as future citizens. A process of normalisation takes place in schools, which is based on conceptions of proper adulthood and the rights and duties of citizens. In this process, children and young people are seen as abstract 'pupils', abstracted from diverse social and cultural contexts, and trained equally to become the future citizens. Historically schools have been expected to confirm, reproduce, and challenge social divisions. A continuous strand in educational thinking has emphasised schools as sites of emancipation, and channels for advancing social change (Davies, 1990; Green, 1990; Donald, 1992). Thus, schools are sites with multiple levels and practices, some of which are contradictory. However, within schools there are also spaces for agency, negotiation, avoidance, opposition, and resistance. These spaces are limited, but significant, in the context of tensions between emancipation and regulation, control and agency. Educational policies have addressed these spaces by redrawing the map of possibilities and limitations for individual citizens.

In this chapter, we draw on data from the project *Citizenship, Difference and Marginality in Schools, with Special Reference to Gender,*[1] a comparative, cross-cultural study of secondary education in Finland and Britain. We trace the trajectory of education policy from the macro level of the broad social context in which it is generated, through to an analysis of curriculum documents and statements (vehicles for carrying policy into practice) and the micro level of its realisation in the classroom. We then go on to investigate school processes and teacher and pupil practices in an ethnographic study of two secondary schools in London and two in Helsinki.[2] Within each school we distinguish between three layers: the official school, the informal school, and the physical school (Gordon, Holland and Lahelma, 2000a). The route from pupil to citizen is constructed through dynamic and intertwined processes which can be located within and/or across all of these layers. Using our ethnographic material collected among groups of 13- and 14-year-old students, we try to illustrate how, within the school, 'neutral' pupils are socially and culturally differentiated *en route* to citizenship. Our starting point for differentiation is gender, placed in the broader theoretical context of an analysis of citizenship. We begin by focusing on what we call the 'official school'.

A map for teachers – the curriculum

Changes have been taking place in education politics and, policies in recent years; New Right policies have been influential in the restructuring of education in the USA, and have spread to many European countries as well as to Canada, Australia and New Zealand. Raising *future citizens* capable of carrying out their duties and responsibilities, and exercising their rights, is still an important educational goal in these countries. Thus, implicit notions of citizenship and increased concern for *individualisation* and *differentiation* inform both education debate and policy in each of the two countries we examined. With an increasing emphasis on individuals and individualisation, the relationship between citizenship and individuality is in a process of reformulation. Within the New Right position, neo-liberalism contains strong arguments supporting choice, competition and autonomy, and has brought the 'market' into education (Gordon, Holland and Lahelma, 2000a; Arnot and Gordon, 1996). Although traditional values are encouraged in neo-conservatism, the combination of neo-liberalism and neo-conservatism nevertheless extracts school students from their social and cultural locations and relations. In our research, we explore the impact of these influences on everyday life at school.

Britain and Finland no longer have New Right governments, but education policies put in place by former governments continue to be pursued. Before analysing educational policies, it is important to draw attention to some relevant differences between Finland and Britain. In Finland, women's participation in the labour market has long been sustained at a higher level than in Britain, but horizontal and vertical gender segregation is stronger in Finland. Finnish girls have outnumbered boys in upper secondary schools since the 1940s. An important difference is the existence of a fully comprehensive education system in Finland (since the 1970s) and much more differentiation between schools in England and Wales.[3] It is also important to note that, whilst schools in Britain (particularly in London) cater to students from diverse minority ethnic groups, schools in Finland, like Finland itself, remain relatively homogeneous as far as culture is concerned. Traditionally, the other ethnic groups in Finland are a Swedish-speaking minority, Romany and native Sami people. Only recently has there been increased immigration from, for example, Somalia and the former Soviet Union. Finland is a Nordic welfare state, where democratic structures and social citizenship are expected to redress inequality. In contrast, Britain has a stronger liberal tradition with more hierarchical structures, but attempts have been made to develop social justice in education through policies addressing, for example, sexism and racism (e.g. Arnot, David and Weiner, 1996, 1997).

Although recent policy changes and developments seem diametrically opposed, the two education systems have in fact become more similar with these changes (Lahelma, 1993). In England and Wales, a national curriculum was introduced in 1988 which increased centralisation of a decentralised curriculum. In Finland, the movement in recent decades has been towards decentralisation, with more power for schools to prepare their own curricula on the basis of a Framework Curriculum. In Finland, it has been more common to address structures rather than cultural and social processes, and so equality has been sought through a comprehensive education system, with less attention paid to everyday life in schools. In Britain, in the context of a more divided system, the decentralised legacy gave teachers scope for a great deal of grassroots action, and more attention was given to school processes in the context of equality work.

In terms of the curriculum, students are regarded as *citizens-to-be*, with equal rights and responsibilities. In Finland, the *Framework Curriculum for the Comprehensive School* (NBE, 1994: 13) states that citizens' 'mutual equality and people's willingness to participate actively in attending to common affairs are some of the characteristics of a functioning society of citizens'. Equality is mentioned as one of the starting points for any consideration of basic values, and gender, ethnicity and social background are mentioned as dimensions of equality. The school's responsibility for promoting gender equality is incorporated into legislation. In the curriculum document it is interpreted as enabling students to function with equal rights and responsibilities in family life, in working life, and in society (NBE, 1994). Our analysis of the document, however, suggests that the individualisation (cf. Lukes, 1973; Abercombie, Hill and Turner, 1986) that is highlighted in the text is more related to celebrating the possibilities of choice and competition than addressing diversity based on gender, ethnicity, and social class (Gordon, Holland and Lahelma, 2000a).

In comparison, the British curricular document *Education for Citizenship* (NCC, 1990: 6), emphasised the fact that Britain is a pluralist society.[4] Pupils must be made aware 'that all citizens can and must be equal ... Citizen's rights include civil, political, social and human rights and how these may be violated by various forms of injustice, inequality and discrimination, including sexism and racism'. Citizenship could be taught through subjects in the national curriculum, and through immersion in the corporate life of the school, which could provide training in the skills, knowledge and capacities which would produce the *good citizen*. Most of the current documentation in Britain cannot be faulted with regard to its use of non-sexist, non-racist language. But as far as subject curricula are concerned, difference and diversity are less apparent. Both the English and the History curricula have been criticised for being nationalistic (McKiernan, 1993; File, 1995). In English, for example, there was a requirement that pupils should be taught to read, analyse and evaluate a wide range of texts, including literature from the English literary heritage and from other cultures and traditions (NCC, 1990: 2). However, the range of authors from which the texts were drawn represented a narrow view of the English literary heritage, and included very few women and no black authors or works in translation (Garside, 1995).

Curriculum documents do not speak with one voice, and some of the ideals put forward may not reach the practices of the schools, particularly if other government policies undermine both the material and ideological base of such practices. The abstract aims and contents of national documents are adopted differently by individuals, reflecting the ideas of the head teachers and other staff, and the ethos and patterns of the everyday life of the school (see e.g. Mahony, 1992; Middleton, 1992; Ball and Bowe, 1992). In the following sections, we consider how boys and girls are steered in the official school towards adult citizenship. In so doing, we also consider whether gender or other dimensions of difference are signs which send boys and girls in different kinds of political direction, for example, towards more or less autonomous citizenship, or positions with more or less agency.

Following the signposts: gender and citizenship in the official school

'I think we are, we are trying to create citizens, but we are trying to create thinking citizens, or citizens who, erm ... it's not autocratic, I think that's what I am trying to say' (John, MTL).[5] This English school teacher did not talk about *males* or *females* as *thinking citizens*. Both girls and boys are supposed to follow the same route to equal citizenship. Gender also tended to be rather muted in the curricula of our research schools in Helsinki where equality was often regarded as a self-evident fact. Both of the London schools, however, have produced (or were producing) written policies on a range of issues including equal opportunities. The dissimilar histories of both countries in relation to grassroot policies of equal opportunities (Gordon, Holland and Lahelma, 2000a) is reflected in this difference.

Teachers' sensitivity to gender is therefore particularly important for the way in which they steer students towards citizenship. Such sensitivity can be reflected in open or more hidden ways in the processes and practices at school (Ruddock, 1994; Riddell, 1992). In the Helsinki schools, essentialist notions of gender difference were apparent, and some teachers admitted that they had not really thought about gender. Whilst teachers in London schools were determined not to discriminate in relation to gender, they also regarded girls and boys as different. Many teachers in both countries took differences between the sexes to be self-evident, and while they talked about 'pupils' in general, in particular contexts (e.g. when discussing work habits) differences between girls and boys were often taken for granted.

These taken for granted positions reflect prevalent notions of gender. Boys were seen as more relaxed, bohemian, inventive, straightforward and usually more interesting than girls. Many teachers saw girls as more mature, more sensible and easier to teach. One teacher argued that 'all girls are sweet, all boys are a nightmare, whatever age'. There were pupils who were identified as exceptions and contrasted with the expected norm. One teacher was familiar with the research on girls and boys being treated differently in schools, and as a trainee she had undertaken her own study on the topic. She was determined not to give the boys more attention than the girls. But she felt that this might have led to her discriminating against the boys and that the students might have experienced it that way (as it was clear that they did from their interviews). She was still attempting to adjust her teaching to get the balance right.

Teachers also held contradictory views about gender and 'citizens-to-be'. For example, one female teacher argued that the school system favoured 'niceness' and 'obedience', and that girls adapted more easily to the system. But later in the same interview she argued that girls were teased and harassed and their life at school was difficult. She states: '. . . and boys are approved of although they know nothing, and boys are allowed to be kind of wild [. . .] and they get grades almost for nothing' (Aila, FTH). Another teacher realised that she did not encourage girls enough, explaining that in the hustle and bustle of the classroom, she was constantly occupied by assisting assertive, vocal boys, and as a result was grateful that at least the girls were quiet. She was, however, interested to find out how such problems could be addressed.

Boys' underachievement has emerged recently as an issue in the UK and Australia (Arnot, David and Weiner, 1996, 1997; Yates, 1997; Epstein et al., 1998) whereas in Finland it has long been known that girls, on average, have higher achievement in schools than boys. Since the 1980s public discussion in Finland has focused on the educational problem of boys. Teachers in our study were therefore aware of gender differences in achievement, and often took it as an unquestioned backdrop: 'Well, it's the traditional difference that girls are conscientious and knowing students . . . but then there is somebody, somebody who is extremely interested, some boy, who brings extra material' (Eila, FTH); 'Comprehensive school is more suitable for girls, of course, they concentrate better in what they are supposed to do here' (Erkki, MTH).

Underlying these statements was a view prevalent in all of our schools (and much of the literature on gender differences in school), that girls are more conscientious, work harder and produce neater work than boys. This is often paired with the view that conscientiousness is the only reason that girls do achieve. As a result teachers, parents and the students themselves may not look for excellence in girls (Walkerdine, 1989). One English male teacher described the difference, speaking first of the girls:

> If you ask them to write a story, they will take a long time over it. It'll be . . . well presented, neat handwriting, and they'll obviously have thought it through and they will have spent . . . quite often a long time, over and above the homework time that they've been set. Whereas I get the feeling quite often, some of the boys will dash off the work, to a fairly . . . minimal standard. Erm, it won't be as accurate as the work is required to be, and there won't the same sense of . . . pride or pleasure in the work.
>
> (Sean MTL)

Gender differentiation was constantly present in the 'official school', even if teachers held a range of views and aims in relation to gender equality and social justice. Many of them wanted to address gendered processes, although some regarded such work as superfluous and unnecessary. This should not be too surprising given that work on feminist practices in Australian schools, for example, demonstrates that introducing change can be fraught with difficulties (Kenway et al., 1998). Our ethnographic research with students also suggested that cultural notions of gender were still important in everyday paths at school.

Gender differences in achievement were self-evident for many students. According to their perceptions, girls work more dutifully, raise their hand more often, listen more carefully and know more than boys. Both boys and girls regarded boys generally as more wild than girls, having a tendency to fool around in the class. Boys are also seen as becoming easily bored:

> *Janet:* And how do you know they're bored?
> *Rachel:* Well they start making jokes and stuff. Amongst themselves. And just, mucking about.

Rachel went on to say the following about the ways girls behave in class:

> The way we act. We, some, we usually do our homework, right, and sometimes they don't. And we, I don't know, we, it's just, I don't know, everything. It's the way we act in lessons as well. Whereas we can get on with work, they have to, like, chuck things at people and that.
>
> (Rachel, FSL)

Some of the girls were annoyed with teachers who did not stop the boys. Auli, for example, said:

Well, in general it's just boys who spoil everything. Everything is ruined when they start to fool around over there . . . It depends on the teacher who lets them fool around . . . then I told her that you should shout louder, you must hit your fist on the table!

(Auli, FSH)

Although girls' achievement was often higher than boys, the differences were not so apparent in student's descriptions of themselves. Girls often compared themselves with other girls, and boys with other boys. Justus (MSH) explained this clearly when he described himself as 'quite an ordinary male pupil'. Both girls and boys usually saw themselves as average students, fairly quiet, and reasonably well behaved. This was the case regardless of how they actually achieved or behaved in the classroom.

Gendered processes differed across groups in our research schools, but largely followed the well known patterns that previous research has demonstrated: in general boys were at the centre of teachers' gaze and observation more often than girls, and teachers interacted more with boys than with girls (cf. Clarricoates, 1978; Delamont, 1990). Many teachers made a conscious effort in classroom interaction to treat girls and boys in the same manner. We saw this effort in observations, and in follow-up interviews many of the pupils supported our observations. One student remarked, 'There's no sexism here' and another stated, that 'They treat us basically all the same'. But others reported (as our observations confirmed) that teachers' differentiated expectation of boys and girls affected the ways in which they taught, responded and behaved towards students.

Gender was often unproblematised during lessons, although there were instances of teachers attempting to involve both girls and boys. For example, a teacher might argue that there are no jobs that are specific for girls and boys. Different synonyms for the words 'girl' and 'boy' were discussed in one lesson, and sexualised ways of addressing girls was taken up as an issue by the teacher. But more often than not gender was taken for granted, and often in this taken for granted discourse 'human being' meant male. For example, in a history lesson in a Helsinki school the teacher said, 'Boers took their wives and children with them' when relating the history of South Africa, and a teacher of religious education noted that 'In India you all would already be monks' when explaining Hinduism. During one lesson, gender equality was discussed by a teacher in the following manner: 'You should be satisfied, girls, that you are women here in Finland where we do have gender equality' and contrasted the situation with some other countries. We also observed cases where a teacher did not discuss gender bias when some students had questioned it. The example below is taken from a lesson where the teacher showed an overhead of a well-known series of pictures which portrayed evolution. The image is of an ape transforming into a *man*. A discussion between a female student and the teacher followed:

Pinja: Why do they always use a man?
Teacher: It just happens to be.
Pinja: They *always* use a man!
Teacher: The author has happened to have made this choice. I haven't got any pictures of women.

In this dialogue – which was not typical – a girl questioned the male bias in our culture. However, the teacher did not pursue a discussion on this issue. In the interview, Tuula asked Pinja about this incident:

I don't experience it as a threat or sort of – women should stand up – because I know anyway what the position of women is, and in my opinion women are as good as men. And in my opinion, again, men are not worse than women, they are on an equal level, and it all depends on your own personality. It just occurred to me that it's always [the same]. That there isn't even one exception, as there should be in this day and age. Now there is a lot of talk about that equality business. Now everyone should be terribly equal, but nevertheless they make graphics like this all the time or teaching materials and it still remains always the same.

(Pinja, FSH)

As such discussions imply, gender still circulates as a social construct which reproduces very particular forms of gender division in the school curriculum, despite the fact that overt gendered classifications have become less prevalent in both countries (Wolpe, 1974; Arnot, 1991; Kaarninen, 1995). But, within this ostensible gender neutrality, lurk assumptions that are seldom questioned. Clearly, there was a desire for gender balance in the classroom (Gordon, Holland and Lahelma, 2000a) with the assumption that the presence of girls counteracted the behaviour of 'wild' boys. Assumptions about girls and boys having differing interests stubbornly persisted as an explanation for gendered choices that steer them to gendered paths – especially in Finland.

In short, the production of individual citizens takes place simultaneously in the official, the informal and the physical school. In the official school, students are constructed as *knowing citizens*, and national curricula define the knowledge a citizen should possess. The official level also includes the inculcation of ways of being for citizens as responsible adults, ready to step into the world of work and the heterosexual family.

Diversions, shortcuts and roundabouts: the informal school

The inculcation of the notion of a *good citizen* in the official school emphasises duties and responsibilities. Students should be well-behaved, must acquire the knowledge required of them, and prepare themselves for responsible adulthood. But the *individual citizen* should also be able to make autonomous judgements as a *critical citizen*. Interaction with others is therefore deemed necessary, since as *future citizens* students will need to be able to co-operate with others. Students learn to be active in negotiating the classroom order, and a degree of informalisation of classroom activities is desirable. 'Nobody is happy among a row of statues', suggests Salli (FSH), and most teachers and students would agree with this.

The informal school is therefore also intertwined with official ends in the construction of a route from pupil to citizen. But the informal school is also potentially a place where the responsible citizen is criticised. Students construct their own practices of co-operation and differentiation; they are constantly engaged in forming communities as well as hierarchies. The informal school exists alongside and inside the official school, but also in opposition to it. It is viewed as a potential source of danger and chaos (Gordon, Holland and Lahelma, 2000a).

In the Helsinki schools we studied, relatively little scope was provided for informal activities; the school timetable was tightly constructed, and students had to seek opportunities to insert informal activities and practices into its processes. By contrast, in the London schools there were more attempts to integrate the informal school with the official; time was available for informal activities, but these activities could be subjected to official guidance and control (Gordon, Holland and Lahelma, 2000a). Students, through their own activities, made inroads into the official school, whilst teachers and other staff, through their activities, made inroads into the informal school.

Teachers, to varying degrees, create informal relationships with students in order to gain better rapport, to encourage learning and a willingness to co-operate and to make their own work pleasant. Informal styles within the classroom can also reflect differences, since not all students are prepared or able to take part in such informal interactions. In our observations, we noted that some teachers were more inclined to engage in this type of activity with boys, whilst, for others, girls were the focus. In these processes, it was often lively, talkative students who were drawn into the interaction, and in this way students with lower achievement but accomplished social skills could be brought into the centre of the classroom.

Important parts of the informal school are the special activities which punctuate routinised school processes, and which often provide an arena of training for the skills of the *cultural citizen* (e.g. official celebrations, sports days, concerts, theme days and school trips). During these events gender can assume particular visibility or can fade into the background (cf. Thorne, 1993). In Finland, for ritual celebrations such as Christmas and end of term events, students, as well as teachers, are more likely to dress in a festive manner, and often such clothes are more gender differentiated than every-day wear. The ritual celebrations are formal in nature, and good manners must be on display (Lahelma and Gordon, 1997). Classical music and formal speeches are typical. During such a celebration in one of the schools in our study, students were already buzzing, and a performance by a group of girls who, by inverting traditional texts, employed irony to criticise consumerism, racism and sexism incited the audience to further merrymaking.

Teachers were extremely critical of the students' behaviour in an assembly the following day.

Such special days can be quite diverse. The Helsinki schools organised more special days than London schools, probably as there were less opportunities for informal activities on normal days. Although London schools had more open and committed equal opportunities policies, Nordic notions of democratic schooling were displayed on such special days. For example, sports days were not structured around competition. Instead, the aim was to familiarise students with as many activities as possible, such as roller skating, bowling and oriental dancing. These kinds of activities (e.g. sports days) have long been regarded as providing a grounding in some of the basic skills of citizenship. In London, sports days encourage both competition and collaboration (for example in team games).

Other special days in Finland included, for example, a Tender Day, an Occupational Day, an induction of new students and two days of school being run by male teachers. During the Tender Day, the aim was to increase tolerance of difference, and to encourage students to treat each other with tender affection. Music chosen by students was played during the lessons, students brought in soft toys and could have their faces painted. The wide range of activities culminated in a film which portrayed difference in an empathetic way. Although special events take place under the teachers' gaze, and disagreements about the limits of the acceptable occur, the organisation of special events and special days suggests that whilst control and emphasis on behaviour are prevalent in the classroom, an individual citizen also needs to be able to exercise agency in more open situations.

While the official school included diversions, students also construct their own routes through short cuts and roundabouts through the official school. These informal student activities can be based on, or constructed by, similarities amongst and between students, but they can also be based on difference. Such activities can result in the marginalisation of those regarded as different. In their discussions, the students suggest that processes of informal differentiation were most often based on individual characteristics which made a student stand out, but our analysis of the data suggests that complex sociocultural processes are embedded in their practices. Students construct gender differentiation by calling girls 'slags' or 'whores', remarking on their bodies, clothes and appearance. Many of these characterisations are made by boys, but such terms can be evoked by girls. The sexual terms addressed to girls suggest that 'making the difference' is sexualised as well as gendered. The policing of the boundaries of proper gender and sexuality among boys typically takes place through naming others as 'queers' or 'homos' (Nayak and Kehily, 1997). Although such naming can appear to be, and can be detached from the sexuality or sexual orientation of those so named, it is also addressed to those boys who are not considered to be appropriately masculine or who display gender-blending characteristics (Lehtonen, 1998). Students suggest that naming can be joking and it is not to be taken seriously, but they also know that being named can be part of a process of marginalisation, and that a marginal positioning in the informal student hierarchies is a position which gives its carrier very little agency.

Making differences also included racist processes, as was evident particularly in 'cussing' contests in London. In Helsinki schools, there were fewer students of minority ethnic groups, but ethnic and racist differences could be built as symbolic markers of marginalisation among white boys who might call each other names using foreign names such as José, or by counteracting (felt) discrimination by asking teachers 'are we Somalians?'.

Official processes were constantly informalised in schools and whilst such processes included making connections among students or between students and teachers too, students were also active in using and displaying the differentiations they observed in the cultural and social processes around them.

Moving on down the road: citizenship, space and embodiment in the physical school

The school's dual and contradictory task of regulation and emancipation, and the fraught progress from child to adult, pupil to citizen over which they are played out, are writ large upon the body and its deployment in space in the school. At times it seems as if the major objective of the school is to constrain, contain and control the bodies of the young people who move within its spaces, and that the search for agency expressed through the body will find little realisation (Gordon, Holland and Lahelma, 2000b). And the urgency of bodily control is easy to understand. The route from unruly child/adolescent to responsible adult, from pupil to citizen, is predicated on appropriate bodily comportment and control, and the school is a major site for the collective construction of this conformity. But the task is not easy. The chaos which lurks behind control, and which is feared by both teachers and students in our study, can be seen in a school during break times. The impression to an outsider is of movement and sound, embodiment and physicality, with large numbers of young people walking, running, playing, talking, shouting, and laughing. Bodies may interact in a relatively confined space, or be released to run exuberantly onto outside playing space. This sound and movement contrast with the stillness and silence required, and often attained, in many lessons in classrooms, and characteristic of corridors during lessons.

The practical problems of channelling and controlling the movement of large numbers of young people are paralleled by expectations of problems generated at the level of individual bodily change. Dominant discourses of adolescence, often emanating from psychology, stress turbulent bodily change in these years, with concomitant emotional turmoil, and those charged with educational responsibility for young people often draw upon these discourses. For example, reaching or passing through puberty can be used to explain particular behaviours. Routes through puberty and its effects are highly gender specific in this discourse and cloak the normative requirements of heterosexuality, as these requirements cloak gendered power relations. At no time is the hold of heterosexual values more powerfully pursued and enforced than during adolescence (Prendergast, 1995). As we have attempted to demonstrate, the official and informal school contributes to such processes.

Control and surveillance of the body in the school is aimed at producing the docile bodies of Western societies (Foucault, 1980). As Foucault has pointed out, the most efficient way for this to be accomplished is for external surveillance to become internalised such that individuals control their own behaviour, and external control is no longer required. Considerable effort is expended when new students arrive at secondary school and become familiar with the requirements of bodily control, laid out in the rules and regulations, specified and constantly reiterated by the teachers, and formalised in the time-space paths which the students are required to follow (Gordon et al., 1999). These time-space paths dictate when and where students are to be at any time in the school day, which spaces they must be in or may not enter, and when. They are descriptions of how physical space is socially organised; school and individual timetables provide maps to this temporal, spatial and social domain. It is not just movement in space which is defined by the time-space paths, but bodily presentation and comportment: 'sit up straight'; 'walk, don't run'; 'silence, speak only when I say you can' are typical injunctions from teachers. The school has rules prohibiting running, eating, making loud noises in unacceptable places, gum chewing, and in the case of England and Wales specifying dress and bodily decoration.

The specification of school uniform is also gendered, with different clothing prohibited or allowed for girls and boys in the two London schools in the study. All of these rules were flouted, skirted or played with by students, and these practices were also gender differentiated. In relation to the uniform, for example, boys wore trainers when prohibited, and were more often seen with their shirts hanging out (a disciplinary matter). Some girls made changes to the standard uniform or wore make-up and jewellery to produce a more sexualised and feminine image. In both countries girls groomed each other, usually in breaks, but often in the classroom during lesson time. In Finland there is no school uniform and comfort and ease are important in the choice of clothing. Jeans, loose pullovers, sweatshirts and trainers are popular, but there is nevertheless subtle differentiation between appropriate wear for boys and girls. We observed teachers, too, being less concerned about constraining or controlling clothing and decoration when students conformed along traditional gendered lines.

In our observations (like those of other school ethnographers), girls tend to make less noise, are less disruptive and expansive in their movements and their claims on space than boys in school. Despite years of research pointing to this differentiation, the outside recreational spaces of the two London schools during break were almost a parody of the separation, with boys dominating most of the space and girls pushed to the margins. When girls in one school agitated to have some of the tennis courts reserved for their use during breaks, since 'a first come first served' approach had resulted in boys claiming all the tennis courts, the boys objected on the grounds of discrimination.

Within school, the girls' restraint is often a relief to teachers, and remarked upon if it does not occur by both teachers and boys, who may challenge or ridicule noisy or loud girls. Similar behaviour from boys and girls is interpreted differently by teachers, students and researchers (Gordon et al., 1997). Heli commented on this bodily control, 'I mean it's more than just being brought up or educated' (FSH). And she is right – it is being guided down a particular route.

Conclusion

In this chapter, we have attempted to demonstrate that there is a relationship between the construction of the abstract pupil in educational policy and in school, and the abstract citizen required in a nation state. Pupils as citizens should be autonomous, knowing, responsible and aware of their culture, but the emphasis is on future citizenship. We have discussed some of the processes of differentiation which lead to the construction of differences between individuals and groups, and which characterise the secondary school in its production of the abstract pupil and the resulting citizen. Much of this differentiation is conducted through spatial praxis. Spatial praxis establishes the comportment of bodies in space through time-space paths (control of movement in time and space, typified by the student's timetable) and the curriculum of the body (explicit in rules about what the body may do or wear, but also implicit in setting limits on acceptability of bodily manifestations) (Giddens, 1985; Lesko, 1988; Gordon, Holland and Lahelma, 2000b). These processes of spatial praxis entail ritual display in a space such as the school and point to how one is expected to act in another space, in particular, the social worlds of citizenship and work.

The context for this ritual is constructed through the dual tasks of education and schooling. First, schools are expected to confirm the social, political and cultural order of the nation state by regulating ways in which students prepare and are prepared to take their place as future adults. Second, schools have been expected to ensure social justice, social mobility and emancipation of both social groups and individuals. As a result, ideologies of equality of opportunity have been part of educational politics and policies – though the implications of such inclusion may not have been pursued more than superficially. These contradictory dual expectations create tensions at the level of school processes and practices. Such expectations are transmitted through rules which coexist alongside a requirement for agency on the part of students who must take charge of their own lives and futures. Students are expected to behave well and be industrious without undue questioning of, or challenges to, school organisation. But they are also supposed to conduct themselves as autonomous individual citizens, making decisions and engaging actively and creatively with tasks in school. They must operate in ways which indicate that they can fit into work organisations and relations. But they must also be prepared to act as responsible citizens capable of reflection with regard to the exercise of their duties, responsibilities and rights.

In schools, students are inscribed into particular subject positions, but they are also able to play with ways of locating themselves in these positions. In this way, they can exercise agency. But the exercise of agency can also be a site for constructing difference. Some students can claim more space than others. For example, those pushed to the margins will always have less space and less autonomy. Those with more space to exercise control are more likely to be boys (but not all boys) and those with less space to do so are likely to be girls (but not all girls). Patterns of student agency are thus prefigured by existing gender inequalities. A boy who is able to exert control over other boys and possibly most girls may in turn be in a vulnerable position in the hierarchies of achievement in the official school since such hierarchies may provide more powerful sites for some of the students over whom he exerted control.

It is therefore more difficult for girls to develop the capacity to control their own lives if their autonomy in relation to their own bodies, and the space surrounding them, is curtailed. Foster (1996: 43; see also chapter 10, this volume) argues that in order to pursue equal rights as citizens, women must enter 'a particular space – social, psychological and existential – between and beyond that which is prescribed for women'. If those defined as members of 'racial'/ethnic minorities are constructed as 'present others', this has implications for their positioning. Those students who are marginalised in relation to several dimensions of socially structured inequalities – gender, social class, 'race'/ethnicity, sexual orientation, dis/ability – are more likely to carry a heavier burden, and the achievement of space in one site can be counteracted by losses in other sites.

Notes

1   Other members of the Finnish project team were Pirkko Hynninen, Tuija Metso, Tarja Palmu and Tarja Tolonen. In England Janet Holland worked together with Nicole Vitellone and Kay Parkinson.
2   In each context, we chose two schools, one of which was predominantly middle class and the other predominantly working class.
3   In Finland there are very few private special schools, e.g. Steiner schools; in England and Wales there is much more differentiation, with a private sector in education, and grant-maintained schools in the state sector.
4   The Advisory Group on Citizenship has produced a report (QCA, 1998) on the basis of which education for citizenship is included in the revised National Curriculum, 2000. Citizenship education at the secondary level will become statutory from August 2002 (QCA 2000).
5   In this chapter we identify quotes from respondents by a pseudonym, plus gender (M/F), whether a student or a teacher (S/T), and whether in Helsinki or London (H/L).

References

Abercombie, N., Hill, S. and Turner, B. (1986) *Sovereign Individuals of Capitalism*, London: Allen and Unwin.

Arnot, M. (1991) 'Equality and democracy: a decade of struggle over education', *British Journal of Sociology of Education*, 12, 4: 447–465.

Arnot, M., David, M. and Weiner, G. (1996) *Educational Reforms and Gender Equality in Schools*, Manchester: Equal Opportunities Commission.

Arnot, M., David, M. and Weiner, G. (1997) 'Educational reform, gender equality and school cultures', in B. Cosin and M. Hales (eds) *Families, Education and Social Differences*, London and New York: Routledge in association with The Open University.

Arnot, M. and Gordon, T. (1996) 'Gender, citizenship and marketisation: a dialogue between Madeleine Arnot and Tuula Gordon', *Discourse: studies in the cultural politics of education*, 17, 3: 377–388.

Ball, S. J. and Bowe, R. (1992) 'Subject departments and the "implementation" of National Curriculum Policy: an overview of the issues', *Journal of Curriculum Studies*, 24, 2: 97–115.

Clarricoates, K. (1978) 'Dinosaurs in the classroom: a re-examination of some aspects of the hidden curriculum in primary schools', *Women's Studies International Quarterly*, 1, 4: 353–364.

Davies, B. (1990) 'Agency as a form of discursive practice: a classroom scene observed', *British Journal of Sociology of Education*, 11, 3: 341–361.

Davies, B. and Hunt, R. (1994) 'Classroom competencies and marginal positioning', *British Journal of Sociology of Education*, 15, 3: 389–408.

Delamont, S. (1990) *Sex Roles and the School*, London: Routledge.

Donald, J. (1992) *Sentimental Education: schooling, popular culture and the regulation of liberty*, London and New York: Verso.

Epstein, D., Elwood, J., Hey, V. and Maw, J. (eds) (1998) *Failing Boys?: issues in gender and achievement*, Buckingham: Open University Press.

File, N. (1995) 'Surviving the National Heritage Curriculum', *Multicultural Teaching*, 13, 3: 23–25.

Foster, V. (1996) 'Space invaders: desire and threat in the schooling of girls', *Discourse: studies in cultural policies of education*, 17, 1: 43–46.

Foucault, M. (1980) *Power/Knowledge*, London: Harvester Wheatsheaf.

Garside, R. (1995) 'Whose heritage, sir? and other issues: the new English National Curriculum', *Multicultural Teaching*, 13, 3: 6–8.

Giddens, A. (1985) 'Time, space and regionalisation', in D. Gregory and J. Urry (eds) *Social Relations and Spatial Structures*, London: Macmillan.

Gordon, T., Holland, J., Lahelma, E. and Tolonen, T. (1997) *Hidden from Gaze: problematising action in the classroom*, Paper presented at the British Sociological Association Annual Conference, York.

Gordon, T., Holland, J. and Lahelma, E. (2000a) *Making Spaces: citizenship and difference in schools*, London: Macmillan, and New York: St. Martin's Press.

Gordon, T., Holland, J. and Lahelma, E. (2000b) 'Moving bodies/still bodies: embodiment and agency in schools', in L. McKie and N. Watson (eds) *Organising Bodies*, London: Macmillan.

Gordon, T., Lahelma, E., Hynninen, P., Metso, T., Palmu, T. and Tolonen, T. (1999) 'Learning the routines: "professionalisation" of newcomers in secondary school', *International Journal of Qualitative Studies in Education*, 12, 6: 689–706.

Green, A. (1990) *Education and state formation: the rise of education systems in England, France and the USA*, London: Macmillan.

Jones, K. (1990) 'Citizenship in a woman-friendly polity', *Signs*, 15, 4: 781–812.

Kaarninen, M. (1995) *Nykyajan tytöt, Koulutus, luokka ja sukupuoli 1920 – ja 1930 – luvun Suomessa* (Modern girls. Education, social class and gender in Finland in 1920–1930), Helsinki: Suomen Historiallinen Seura.

Kenway, J. and Willis, S. (with Blackmore, J. and Rennie, L.) (1998) *Answering Back*, London: Routledge.

Lahelma, E. (1993) *Policies of Gender and Equal Opportunities in Curriculum Development: discussing the situation in Finland and Britain*, Research Bulletin 85, Department of Education, University of Helsinki.

Lahelma, E. and Gordon, T. (1997) 'First day in secondary school: learning to be a professional pupil', *Educational Research and Evaluation*, 3: 119–139.

Lehtonen, Jukka (1998) 'Young people's definitions of their non-heterosexuality', in H. Helve (ed.) *Integrated or Marginalized Youth in Europe*, Nuorisotutkimus 2000, 6/98, Helsinki: Nuorisotutkimusseura.

Lesko, N. (1988) 'The curriculum of the body: lessons from a Catholic high school', in L.G. Roman and L.K. Christian-Smith with E. Ellsworth (eds) *Becoming Feminine*, London: Falmer Press.

Lukes, S. (1973) *Individualism*, London: Basil Blackwell.

Mahony, P. (1992) 'Which way forward? Equality and schools in the 1990s', *Women's Studies International Forum*, 15, 2: 293–302.

Marshall, T. H. (1963) *Sociology at Crossroads*, London: Heinemann.

McKiernan, D. (1993) 'History in a national curriculum: imagining the nation at the end of the 20th century', *Journal of Curriculum Studies*, 25, 1: 33–51.

Middleton, S. (1992) 'Equity, equality, and biculturalism in the restructuring of New Zealand schools: a life-history approach', *Harvard Educational Review*, 62, 3: 301–322.

Nayak, A. and Kehily, M. J. (1997) 'Masculinities and schooling: why are young men so homophobic?', in D. L. Steinberg, D. Epstein and R. Johnson (eds) *Border Patrols: policing the boundaries of heterosexuality*, London: Cassell.

NBE (1994) *Framework Curriculum for the Comprehensive School 1994*, Helsinki: National Board of Education.

NCC (National Curriculum Council) (1990) *Curriculum Guidance & Education for Citizenship*, London: HMSO.

Pateman, C. (1988) *The Sexual Contract*, Cambridge: Polity Press.

Prendergast, S. (1995) 'With gender on my mind: menstruation and embodiment at adolescence', in J. Holland and M. Blair (with S. Sheldon) (eds) *Debates and Issues in Feminist Research and Pedagogy*, Cleveland: Multilingual Matters in association with the Open University.

Prokhovnik, R. (1998) 'Public and private citizenship: from gender invisibility to feminist inclusiveness', *Feminist Review*, 60: 84–104.

QCA (Qualifications and Curriculum Authority) (1998) *Education for Citizenship and the Teaching of Democracy in Schools*, London: QCA.

QCA (Qualifications and Curriculum Authority) (2000) *Education 3–16*, http://www.qca.org.uk

Riddell, S. I. (1992) *Gender and the Politics of the Curriculum*, London and New York: Routledge.

Ruddock, J. (1994) *Developing a Gender Policy in Secondary Schools*, Buckingham and Philadelphia: Open University Press.

Thorne, B. (1993) *Gender Play: girls and boys in schools*, Buckingham: Open University Press.

Walkerdine, V. (1989) *Counting Girls Out*, London: Falmer Press.

Wolpe, A. M. (1974) 'The official ideology of education for girls', in M. Flude and J. Ahier (eds) *Educability, Schools and Ideology*, London: Croom Helm.

Yates, L. (1997) 'Gender equity and the boys' debate: what sort of challenge is it?', *British Journal of Sociology of Education*, 18, 3: 337–347.

12 Is female educational 'success' destabilising the male learner-citizen?

Victoria Foster

This chapter examines the implications of the relationship between two contemporary international trends in education for women's equality as citizens. The first trend is that in most Western countries girls are now achieving statistically slightly better average school-leaving results than boys. This success has led to a hostile populist 'backlash' in contemporary Western culture (Foster, 2001 forthcoming; Martino and Meyenn, 2001 forthcoming). For example, a recent international collection (Mackinnon, Elgqvist-Saltzman and Prentice, 1998) argues that education in the twenty-first century will be 'dangerous terrain' for women. The second trend is the revival of interest in participatory democratic theory which is reflected in the strong current focus on civics and citizenship education in education systems.

The specific question of what happens to the social and educational order when girls begin to gain access to the traditional masculine public spheres of male-dominated curriculum areas is addressed here. The chapter develops the argument that in the present international climate it is impossible for girls to be equal with boys as learner-citizens. Instead, girls must still function as an appendage to the male learner-citizen, a problem which is not addressed in current models of citizenship education. These two trends are therefore discussed as contradictory – positioning girls within a dialectic of desire and threat simultaneously in their quests for citizenship (see Foster, 1996b, 1998).

The chapter has three sections. In the first section I offer a brief overview of the theoretical literature on the gendered nature of citizenship, and its relevance to gender and citizenship education as a field of study. The second section describes what has developed into an international backlash against girls' alleged success in education, and goes on to analyse the exact nature of this success. I argue that the backlash is fuelled by two rhetorical shifts in the discourses of disadvantage relating to both boys and girls. In the concluding section I discuss the public taboos and private imperatives which operate to circumscribe girls' desires to be equal learner-citizens with boys.

The gendered nature of citizenship and citizenship education in the modern state

There is considerable literature[1] on the gendered nature of citizenship, and 'the problem of women's standing in a political order in which citizenship has been made in the male image' (Pateman, 1989: 14). Much of this literature focuses on women's exclusion from the ideal of the civic public realm of citizenship which is both normatively masculine, and relies on an opposition between the public and private dimensions of human life. This broad ranging literature has demonstrated that women are in fact outside the frame of patriarchal citizenship and that there is an enormous gulf between the apparent guarantee of full citizenship for women and women's actual lived experience of that guarantee (Leech, 1994: 81). Pateman (1988) argues that women's status as citizens is underwritten by a sexual contract which denies them free and equal status on a par with that of men. Feminist legal theory in particular[2] shows that the burden of women's responsibility for work associated with the private sphere has implications for their legal status as citizens.

The substance of feminist critiques of citizenship is that equality for women is not, and will not, be delivered merely by attempting to include women in the normative conception of man as citizen by 'laundering some of its ideals' (Young, 1987: 58). And as feminist theorists such as Pateman (1989: 14) suggest, women, *as women*, cannot meet the criteria for citizenship. Her observation that 'women are incorporated into a sphere that both is and is not in civil society' (1988: 11) underlines women's ambiguous relationship with citizenship. It is this contradiction and ambiguity which poses a dilemma for contemporary female citizenship. Can women be inserted into existing conceptions of citizenship? Although this contradiction is addressed in detail by feminist critiques, it is largely ignored in the development of curricula for citizenship education.

In earlier work (Foster, 1997), using examples from Australia, the Netherlands and Scandinavia, I explored some of the ways in which the school curriculum mirrors the modern state's valorisation of public life and devaluing of the private. The citizen-as-male has his counterpart in the learner-as-male. For example, in Australia, curriculum development in citizenship education has not yet adequately addressed the public–private dialectic in social life. Consequently, it has not succeeded in incorporating private life into the curriculum. Thus, despite the current revival of interest in citizenship education in Australia and other countries, education continues to perpetuate women's and girls' lack of citizenship status.

There are two further problems which need to be addressed in the development of citizenship curriculum. The first problem is the low curriculum status which is accorded to the knowledge and skills related to the private, domestic sphere of life. In the Netherlands, a curriculum reappraisal involving the introduction of the compulsory subject 'Care' saw the status of these same skills and knowledge fiercely contested (ten Dam and Volman, 1996; Volman, 1997). In addition, women tend to be marginalised as a group with special needs. This is seen for example in Australian curriculum documents (Foster, 1997) which attempt merely to add women to the normative conception of the citizen-as-male in an 'add women but don't stir' approach (Foster, 1996a).

Girls' status as learner-citizens: an international backlash

Over the past few years, in most Western countries we have witnessed what Weiner, Arnot and David (1997: 620) refer to as a 'moral panic' over claims, largely promulgated through the media, that boys are suffering from new forms of educational disadvantage. Common representations are 'girls are outperforming boys'; 'girls are succeeding at the expense of boys'; 'boys are struggling'; 'boys are in deep trouble'. However, as Mahony and Smedley (1998: 41) point out, these kinds of claims are not new, and have a long history.

Media reporting of the 1998 New South Wales Higher School Certificate results frequently referred to girls' apparent success as 'dangerous'. Such comments bring to mind Rousseau's claim that 'never has a people perished from an excess of wine; all perish from the disorder of women' (Pateman, 1989: 17). As Pateman further points out, Rousseau is not the only social or political theorist to regard women as a permanently subversive force within the political order. She elaborates:

> Although women have now been granted citizenship in the liberal demo-cracies, it is still widely believed that they are unfitted for political life and that it would be dangerous if the state were in their hands. This belief is very complex.

Clearly, such a belief has some resonance in contemporary Australian society. Women are not only believed to be unfit for political life, a fact that is demonstrated by women's low representation (13 per cent) in Australian parliaments. Women are also deemed to be unfit to share equally in the decision-making and higher status positions in civil and social life, that is, public life. In Australia, women are seriously under-represented in a range of occupations as diverse as corporation director, writing and the arts, chef, engineer and academic. In New South Wales, while women are 75 per cent of primary school teachers, they represent only 25 per cent of principals and senior executive staff in schools (NSW Department of Education and Training, 1999).

Similar problems are also encountered by girls in Australian schools. To date, girls have experienced only the *appearance* of success in schooling outcomes since this success is yet to have any impact on post-school employment patterns. Australian research[3] shows that the school-leaving credential has quite a different value for boys and girls, and that while boys design their curriculum choices around the 'male career trajectory', girls remain 'over-represented in subjects with poor vocational linkages' (Teese, Davies, Charlton and Polesel, 1995). It is paradoxical that while girls demonstrate a stronger attachment to, and dependence on, school credentials, this is not paying off for them as it does for boys. In Australia currently, one-third of male early school-leavers go directly into apprenticeships (Lamb and McKenzie, 1999) while 28 per cent of female early leavers go to no form of employment, education or training (Foster, 2000) or else leave school because they are pregnant (Milne-Home, 1996).

Despite the lack of post-school rewards, the strong reaction to girls' improved performance at school suggests that this success is challenging deeply held assumptions about girls' and women's status as learner-citizens, and their proper relationship with education. If equal participation in education and its outcomes is fundamental to one's status as a future citizen, then the construction of girls' success as dangerous and threatening poses serious consequences for their relationship with citizenship and civil society. I address this issue in greater detail later in the chapter.

It is significant that in Australia the most contested curriculum areas are the high prestige male-dominated areas of Mathematics and Science. It was only in 1997 that a girl topped 4-Unit Mathematics, the most difficult level of study, for the first time in Australia. Nevertheless, this was widely misconstrued in the media as girls collectively beating boys at maths and science, and over a longer period of time. Certainly, a significant factor in the recent politicisation of girls' school performance is the nature of the contested areas themselves and the casting of girls as interlopers and 'space invaders' (Foster 1996b, 1998) in high-status educational terrain assumed to be the natural preserve of males. One wonders about the news value of girls beating boys in the curriculum areas of Life Management or Child and Family Studies or Care, for example!

In fact, while a small, highly select group of Australian girls is achieving equally with, or better than, boys in male-identified subject areas, girls' participation in these subjects remains very low, and in some cases, is diminishing. Girls continue to have low participation rates in higher level Mathematics, Physics (where in some states their participation has declined) and Technology and Engineering Science subjects where they are a tiny fraction of students (NSW Board of Studies, 1999, unpublished data)

Of particular concern is the dramatic decline in girls' participation in Information Technology and Computer Studies, particularly in New South Wales where the backlash has been the strongest. In 1991 there were many more girls in Computer Studies than there were in 1998, and in 1998 boys outnumbered girls by more than 2:1 in 2-unit, and by 5:1 in the highest level, 3-unit[4] (NSW Board of Studies, 1999, unpublished data). These low participation rates have clear implications for women's entry into technology-related growth areas of the labour market, as well as their influence on the increasing globalisation and construction of knowledge via technology. Women are virtually absent from this important aspect of citizenship.

Rhetorical shifts in the discourses of disadvantage

Two interrelated shifts in the discourses of disadvantage relating to gender can be identified, especially in Australia. The first is in the construction of girls themselves and the second, as we have seen, is in the rhetoric alleging that boys are the new disadvantaged. It is interesting that much of the recently emerging academic literature on boys' education tends to decontextualise boys and men from their asymmetrical power relations with girls and women in society, and in education. For instance, in an entire 1998 issue of the journal *Change: Transformations in Education* which was devoted to boys' education and published by the University of Sydney, discussion of girls' continuing inferior post-school outcomes was virtually non-existent, as was a consideration of the unchanging nature of the sexual division of labour in private domestic life (Bittman and Pixley, 1997; Dempsey, 1997; Wolcott and Glezer, 1995). These are serious issues for citizenship education.

Just as serious is the general lack of challenge to the rhetoric of 'presumptive equality' (Foster, 1995) on which the concept of male disadvantage is founded. Related to this is the general lack of a critique of the enormous resources currently being poured into compensatory programs for boys (NSW Department of School Education, 1994), and support for the gendered hierarchy of teaching itself (NSW Department of Education and Training, 1999). An exception, however, is the critique of Mahony and Smedley (1998). Current issues concerning boys and their education are entirely political and are intimately bound up with assumptions about boys and girls as learners.

In Australia, initial attempts to achieve greater educational equality for girls centred on positioning girls within a deficit framework, in which they were seen as lacking in relation to male norms of the educated person. Equity policies encouraged girls to measure up to those norms (Foster 1992). The following *Education and Training Strategy for Women* of the NSW Ministry of Education and Youth Affairs (1989: 3) is an example of this deficit framework formulated as policy. It states that in school girls:

- have a low level of participation in technical and key science subjects and in highest level mathematics and science courses;
- consider a narrow range of options in making career choices;
- have lower levels of self-esteem.

It is clearly a major discursive shift from this earlier deficit framework to the current depiction of girls as actively succeeding, and even beating boys, in male educational terrain. The hostility on the part of some to ideals of equality in schooling for girls has taken the form of a refrain around *What about the boys!* in an attempt to reassert the primacy of male educational interests (Foster, 1995). This refrain is echoing internationally (Mackinnon, Elgqvist-Saltzman and Prentice, 1998; Martino and Meyenn, 2001 forthcoming).

It is interesting that this refrain is endemic in countries which have experienced quite different policy contexts. For instance, Mahony and Smedley (1998: 49) note significant differences between the British 'particularly hard version of economic rationalism' and the Australian policy framework which is to some degree underpinned by social justice and equity principles. The subtext of the refrain is that notions of educational equality for girls entail taking something very crucial away from boys: their supremacy as learners, as well as the caretaking resources of women and girls, to which boys are thought to be entitled. By contrast, male educational interests had earlier been strongly supported by a construction which emphasised girls as lacking, rather than viewing boys themselves as being advantaged (Eveline, 1995).

The construction of boys' continuing advantage in education, particularly in relation to curriculum participation, access to school resources and post-school outcomes (Teese et al., 1995) as 'disadvantage', is a rhetorical twist which has been used to great effect both in Australia and Britain in simplistic and emotive accounts (Connell, 1994; Foster 2000). These accounts have been stated and restated by a handful of very vocal individuals, who have been content to argue their case through the media, rather than in academic or other professional forums. Gilbert (1998: 21) describes this as 'a conservative and potentially divisive men's movement, which rejected feminism and wanted boys' work to be seen as separate from the broader project of the democratic reform of schooling'. The result is a climate in which the notion of male disadvantage can be stretched to extremes. For example, Michael Brown, who teaches at a prestigious Sydney boys' independent school, argues (1994: 9) that we are creating a new 'underclass': gifted males! He urges that advocacy is needed for the white, male, Caucasian, non-migrant child.

Connell (1994: 2) describes this process in the following way:

> In places where feminist work has created women's studies programs or affirmative action programs (e.g. encouraging girls into science and mathematics), the idea that it is 'boys' turn' for attention and resources is easily spread. This can be reinforced by calling attention to ways in which boys are less successful in schooling than girls: for instance in regard to reading and in higher drop-out rates. Combined with statistics about men's earlier death, men's greater rates of injury by violence etc., this can be worked up into a claim that men are the *truly disadvantaged group*. [author's emphasis]

Connell (1995: 208) persuasively argues that this process, which he calls 'masculinity therapy', relies on 'a redefinition of power by shifting from the public world to the inner world of emotion' and 'a preoccupation with emotional relationships, a speculative method and a satisfaction with snippets of evidence' (210).

The notion of male disadvantage is further bolstered by the rhetoric of 'presumptive equality' (Foster, 1995) which includes the widely popular beliefs that women have achieved equality with men in society, and are therefore the same as men. The asymmetry of men's and women's social relations (for example in relation to employment) is quickly dispensed with, and the conclusion is easily reached that it is men and boys who are now suffering inequality, reflected in catchy media grabs such as 'men are the future second sex'.

Desire and threat as dialectical experiences in girls' schooling

The rhetorical shift which has occurred in the construction of girls as learners can be explained by two quite different philosophical approaches to the question of desire. Grosz (1989: xvi) distinguishes the first tradition, which conceives of desire as a 'fundamental lack in being, an incompletion or absence within the subject', from the second tradition in which desire is conceived not as a lack but as a positive force of production and self-actualisation. In this second sense, at the level of the subject, desire functions insofar as the subject 'desires the expansion or maximisation of its power ... it is not an unactualised or latent potential; it is always active and real'.

Policy discourse concerning the desirable educational achievements of girls has, at different times, encompassed both the senses of desire which Grosz has delineated. Earlier, girls were constructed as lacking the necessary masculine learner subjectivity as well as the necessary male-defined knowledge. The very meaning of 'girl' included a negativity or lack (Jones, 1993: 12). In this construction, girls' inadequacies were to be addressed by increasing their access to masculine knowledge areas but not, it transpired, by enhancing their achievement relative to boys in those areas. This first sense of desire as addressing an inadequancy resonates with the philosophical and social construction of femininity as 'other' to the masculine.

The second sense of desire referred to by Grosz is, however, much more problematic for girls because it invokes a more normative male orientation to desire, that of actively seeking and pursuing achievement, and to some extent, power. For example, even more problematically for girls, their achievement has centred specifically on predominantly masculine curriculum areas and subject domains. Although the discourse of reform is couched philosophically in Grosz's first sense, the implications for girls of following that discourse, as well as the outcomes, relate more directly to Grosz's concern with self-actualisation. In concrete terms, this has resulted in the perception that girls are interlopers or 'space invaders' (Foster, 1996b) in male educational terrain, depriving boys of their prior rights as learners. The crucial point here, then, is that for girls to possess desire ultimately places them not only in a contradictory position as 'educated women' (Martin, 1991), but also in a position of threat, which is both actual in school, and potential in relation to post-school life. It is significant that the *What about the boys!* movement in Australia emerged at the precise moment (and not a moment earlier) when girls were perceived to be outstripping boys in the areas of male power and privilege. This point is obvious if one asks whether there would have been such concern about boys and their schooling if the contested areas had been different.

The first sense of desire as lacking, in which girls are seen as disadvantaged, is relatively safe for girls, posing no threat to hegemonic masculinity and possibly reinforcing it. It is the second form of desire – that of self-actualisation – in the educational setting which (by challenging male educational privilege) becomes threatening for girls and women.

This discussion of desire and threat in girls' schooling raises several questions. For instance, what might happen if girls move outside the frame of their construction as inadequate in relation to boys? How could girls be the caretakers of boys if they are equal (or better) achievers? Such a prospect could be very threatening for girls and their education. For example, the current reaction to girls' perceived advances in maths and science may well make it very difficult for girls to pursue excellence in those subjects particularly if they are seen as depriving boys of their rights as the high achievers in those areas. In fact, girls' performance in those subjects actually declined from 1993 to 1994 (NSW Board of Studies 1996), when the backlash period was beginning to gain momentum. The interesting question is also raised of whether, and to what extent, girls and women use caretaking as an accommodative strategy to control the threat against them which is posed by greater equality. Finally, given that the value-added dimensions (to use an economic rationalist concept) of care and caretaking are vastly different according to whether they are done by men or women, where does this leave care as a curriculum issue? This question is very pertinent in Australia where care-related matters have been relegated to the bottom of the curriculum hierarchy, with serious implications for the education of both boys and girls as future citizens (Noddings, 1992).

Public taboos: space invaders in the space-between

In this section I argue that girls cannot be equal as learner-citizens when they are constructed as 'space invaders' in male educational terrain (Foster, 1996b, 1998). The notion of the 'space between' is a heuristic device to analyse and explain girls' experiences of contemporary events in education. In particular, it explains the lack of change in post-school outcomes for girls, the insignificant degree of change in girls' participation in male-dominated curriculum areas (despite their successes in those areas), the endemic nature of sexual harassment and the inequitable use of school resources by girls.[5]

For women and girls, pursuing equal educational and citizenship rights, entails entering a particular space – social, psychological and existential – between and beyond that which is prescribed for women, that is, women's 'place', and that which is proscribed to women (Foster, 1994, 1996b). This is a space of lived experience, mediating between private and public spheres, where women and girls attempt to negotiate the conflicting, contradictory (at best), or violent and destructive (at worst), demands of a neo-liberal framework of equality – a framework which retains a masculinist subject at its centre (Leck, 1987; Martin, 1991). Both the individual learner-subject and the epistemological foundations of the curriculum are male-defined (Martin, 1981). Girls are to be given equal opportunity to achieve parity in an education system which is defined normatively as masculine (Foster, 1992).

The patriarchal power relations of schooling, and their connection with the public–private dialectic in society, make the lived curriculum of schools a complex site of both desire and threat for girls. Equality-directed curriculum reforms require girls to transpose themselves from private realm status to a relatively different position as the equals of males in the public realm of the school. In this process, girls' status is defined and redefined as the 'other' in relation to males, in various ways which frequently define girls physically or sexually in terms of their bodies, and provide constant reminders of gender difference.

Both the idea and the concrete reality of 'public woman' violate public–private norms, requiring women to give up the (dubious) protection of the private sphere, and expose themselves to the threat of violence in the public sphere. Similarly, for girls to take up the promises of reforms towards equality in education in their present form entails the threat of violence in one form or another.

Education for women is both contradictory (Martin, 1991) and, inasmuch as it entails movement into male terrain, potentially threatening and dangerous. Noting that it is not uncommon for women to experience male violence in connection with educational participation, Rockhill (1987: 316) observes that 'we know little about how it is lived in women's lives'. The mass murder in 1989 of 14 female engineering students at the University of Montreal is a stark example of this violence (Malette and Chalouh, 1991).

Private imperatives: caretaking boys in the classroom

This final section discusses one of the most profound aspects of the 'space between': that both girls' and boys' schooling experiences are situated in what Griffith and Smith (1987: 96) refer to as a 'mothering discourse'. This discourse, they suggest, operates according to a 'paradigm of the ideal mother', which can be traced back to Rousseau's prescriptions for Sophie's primary function as Emile's helpmate and nurturer in *Emile*. For example, in contemporary educational discourse, the 'social benefits' and 'reality' often attributed to the co-educational school setting are, in fact, conflated with the injunction on women and girls to take care of and nurture the interests of others. Brady (1998) provides a detailed historical analysis of the role of women teachers as mother-nurturers and carers.

The phenomenon of girls as caretakers of boys in the classroom has not received any extended, formal discussion in Australian education policy, although Lewis (1990) discusses this dynamic in relation to the university classroom setting. It is, however, one of the most powerful, albeit subtle, determinants of girls' day-to-day schooling experiences. It is powerful because of its location in the public–private nexus and, specifically, as part of the unspoken sexual contract whereby the patriarchal meaning of femininity entails the provision of service, sexual and otherwise, to men (Pateman, 1988: 126). Within the sexual contract, the functions of caring, nurturance and emotional support are seen as women's functions. Women are seen as the keepers and cultivators of the nation state and its development (Yuval-Davis, 1997: 5). Women, as Benhabib (1987: 95) puts it, are the 'housekeepers of the emotions'. Men may carry out these functions but they are valued differentially according to whether they are done by men or women. The ways in which both female and male students live the curriculum reinforces this sexual contract. In general, boys eschew any association with the feminine or curriculum areas related to the private, domestic sphere where, by contrast, girls are thought to dominate this sphere (Collins, Batten, Ainley and Getty, 1996).

Education is concerned primarily with the initiation of young men as citizens into the 'productive' processes of society and its culture (Foster, 1992: 58). Conversely, through its devaluing of the private sphere, education underwrites the natural 'non-citizenship of women' (Castles and Davidson, 1999: 142) and women's consequent 'deviant' status (Yuval-Davis, 1997: 5). A clear example of the latter point is the case of pregnant schoolgirls whose rights as learner-citizens are withdrawn when they are routinely labelled by society as deviant and unfit for school life (Milne-Home, 1996).

Conclusion

In this chapter I have raised questions about the ways in which girls may experience and resolve for themselves the simultaneous desire to be 'somebody' which education for citizenship implies, and the potential threat to them from those who in turn feel threatened by girls' living out of this desire. The very processes in schooling which aim to empower boys place girls in a contradictory and paradoxical relationship with the rhetoric of equal and democratic participation which characterises much citizenship education discourse. An unspoken question is, what would happen to boys if girls do become boys' equals and stop being their caretakers? Interestingly, during the current backlash period in Australia, there has been no acknowledgement that girls' achievement in male-dominated subjects may be beneficial for boys. For example, boys would have an opportunity to see girls in a new, healthier light as peers and equals. Even more profoundly, how would both boys' and girls' development as learner-citizens be enhanced by a citizenship education curriculum which foregrounded the values of caring in both public and private life?

Notes

1 For example, Benhabib, 1992; Cass, 1994; Leech, 1994; Pateman, 1988, 1989, 1992; Shanley and Pateman, 1991; Young, 1987.
2 For example, Charlesworth, 1992; Gavison, 1992; Graycar, 1992, 1993.
3 Foster, 2000; NSW Board of Studies, 1996; Teese, Davies, Charlton and Polesel, 1995; Yates and Leder, 1996
4 The term 'unit' denotes the degree of difficulty of levels of study. The higher the unit, the more advanced is the level of study.
5 Australian Education Council, 1992; Collins, Batten, Ainley, and Getty, 1996; Foster, 2000; Teese et al., 1995.

References

Australian Education Council (1992) *Listening to Girls*, Melbourne: Australian Education Council.

Benhabib, S. (1987) 'The generalized and the concrete other: the Kohlberg-Gilligan controversy and feminist theory', in S. Benhabib and D. Cornell (eds) *Feminism as critique: essays on the politics of gender in late-capitalist societies*, pp. 77–95, Cambridge UK: Polity Press.

Benhabib, S. (1992) *Situating the Self: gender, community and postmodernism in contemporary ethics*, Cambridge UK: Polity Press.

Bittman, M. and Pixley, J. (1997) *The Double Life of the Family: myth, hope and experience*, Sydney: Allen and Unwin.

Brady, K. (1998) 'Teaching as women's work', *Teaching and Teachers' Work: a publication on professional and pedagogical issues*, 6, 4: 1–12, Adelaide: Flinders University of South Australia.

Brown, M. (1994) 'Educational opportunities for gifted and talented boys', *Gifted*, NSW Association for Gifted and Talented Children.

Cass, B. (1994) *The State and Economy in Australia: an overview of work, welfare and the position of women*, Social Politics, No. 1: 19–25, Sydney: Social Policy Research Centre.

Castles, S. and Davidson, A. (1999) *Citizenship and Migration: globalisation and the politics of belonging*, London: Macmillan.

University of Sydney (1988) *Change: Transformations in Education*, Vol 1, No. 2, November.

Charlesworth, H. (1992) 'Has the United Nations forgotten the rights of women?', *Research and Information Series*, Canberra: Australian Council for Overseas Aid.

Collins, C., Batten, M., Ainley, J., and Getty, C. (1996) *Gender and School Education*, Canberra: Australian Council for Educational Research.

Connell, R. W. (1994) 'Knowing about masculinity, teaching boys and men: education implications of the new sociology of masculinity and the old sociology of schools', Paper for Pacific Sociological Association conference, San Diego.

Connell, R. W. (1995) *Masculinities*, Sydney: Allen and Unwin.

Dempsey, K. (1997) *Inequalities in marriage: Australia and beyond*, Melbourne: Oxford University Press.

Eveline, J. (1995) 'The (Im)possible reversal: advantage, education and the process of feminist theorising', in *Lararutbildning och forskning i Umea (Teacher education and research in Umea)*, 3–4, 2: 29–46, Sweden: Umea University.

Foster, V. (1992) 'Different but equal? Dilemmas in the reform of girls' education', *Australian Journal of Education*, 36, 1: 53–67.

Foster, V. (1994) 'Making women the subject of educational change: an interdisciplinary and comparative study', unpublished doctoral dissertation, Macquarie University.

Foster, V. (1995) 'What about the boys!': Presumptive equality in the education of girls and boys', Vol. 1: 81–97. Published proceedings of the National Social Policy Conference, 'Social Policy and the Challenges of Social Change', University of New South Wales.

Foster, V. (1996a) '"Whereas the People" and civics education: Another case of "add women and stir?"', in *Curriculum Perspectives*, Special Issue, 'Reconstructing Civics Education: *Whereas the People* as a prescription for the new civics', 16, 1: 52–56. Canberra: Australian Curriculum Studies Association.

Foster, V. (1996b) 'Space Invaders: desire and threat in the schooling of girls', *Discourse: Studies in the Cultural Politics of Education*, 17, 1: 43–63.

Foster, V. (1997) 'Feminist theory and the construction of citizenship education in the modern state', in K. Kennedy (ed.) *Citizenship Education and the Modern State*, London: Falmer Press.

Foster, V. (1998) 'Education: a site of desire and threat for Australian girls', in Elgqvist-Saltzman, I., Prentice, A. and Mackinnon, A. (eds) *Dangerous Terrain for Women?: education into the twenty-first century*, London: Falmer Press.

Foster, V. (2000) 'Gender, schooling achievement and post-school pathways: Beyond statistics and populist discourse', in Dinham S. and Scott C. (eds) *Teaching in Context*, Canberra: Australian Council for Educational Research .

Foster, V. (forthcoming 2000) 'What about the boys! The Australian case', in Martino, W. and Meyenn, B. (eds) *Teaching Boys: issues of masculinity in schools*, UK: Open University Press.

Gavison, R. (1992) 'Feminism and the public/private distinction', *Stanford Law Review*, 45, 1: 1–45.

Gilbert, P. (1998) 'Gender and schooling in new times: the challenge of boys and literacy', in *The Australian Educational Researcher*, Vol. 25, No. 1, April: 15–37.

Graycar, R. (1992) 'Before the high court: women's work, who cares?, *Sydney Law Review*, 14, 86: 86–105.

Graycar, R. (1993) 'Legal categories and women's work: explorations for a cross-doctrinal feminist jurisprudence', *Canadian Journal of Women and the Law*, 6: 23–29.

Griffith, A. I. and Smith, D. E. (1987) 'Constructing cultural knowledge: mothering as discourse', in Gaskell J. S. and A. T. McLaren (eds), *Women and Education: a Canadian perspective*, pp. 87–103. Calgary: Detselig Enterprises Limited.

Grosz, E. (1989) *Sexual subversions: three French feminists*, Sydney: Allen & Unwin.

Jones, A. (1993) 'Discourses of disadvantage: the construction of girls at school', keynote address for National Transition Conference, Christchurch, New Zealand, 23 August.

Lamb, S. and McKenzie, P. (1999) *Patterns of Success and Failure in the Transition from School to Work in Australia*, Canberra: Australian Council for Educational Research.

Leck, G. M. (1987) 'Review article – feminist pedagogy, liberation theory and the traditional schooling paradigm', *Educational theory*, 37, 3: 343–354.

Leech, M. (1994) 'Women, the state and citizenship: "Are women in the building or in a separate annex?"', *Australian Feminist Studies*, No. 19: 81.

Lewis, M. (1990) 'Interrupting patriarchy: politics, resistance and transformation in the feminist classroom', *Harvard Educational Review*, 60, 4: 467–488.

Mackinnon, A., Elgqvist-Saltzman, I. and Prentice, A. (1998) *Education into the 21st century: dangerous terrain for women?*, London: Falmer Press.

Mahony, P. and Smedley, S. (1998) 'New times old panics: the underachievement of boys', in *Change: Transformations in Education*, Vol. 1. No., 2. November, The University of Sydney.

Malette, L. and Chalouh, M. (eds) (1991) *The Montreal Massacre*, Canada: Gynergy Books.

Martin, J. R. (1981) 'The ideal of the educated person', *Educational Theory*, 31, 2: 97–109.

Martin, J. R. (1991) 'The contradiction and the challenge of the educated woman', *Women's Studies Quarterly*, 1&2: 6–27.

Martino, W. and Meyenn, B. (forthcoming 2001) *Teaching Boys: issues of masculinity in schools*, Buckingham: Open University Press.

Milne-Home, J. (1996) *Pregnant Futures: barriers to employment, education and training amongst pregnant and parenting adolescents,* Canberra: Australian Government Publishing Service.

Noddings, N. (1992) *The Challenge to Care in Schools: an alternative approach to education,* New York: Teachers College Press.

NSW Board of Studies, (1996) *The Report of the Gender Project Steering Committee,* Sydney: NSW Board of Studies.

NSW Board of Studies (1999) Unpublished data, Sydney: NSW Board of Studies.

NSW Department of Education and Training (1999) *10th Annual Equal Employment Opportunity Report,* Sydney.

NSW Department of School Education (1994) *Evaluation of Educational Outcomes for Girls in NSW Government Secondary Schools,* Sydney.

NSW Ministry of Education and Youth Affairs (1989) *Education and Training Strategy for Women,* Sydney.

Pateman, C. (1988) *The Sexual Contract,* Cambridge UK: Polity Press.

Pateman, C. (1989) *The Disorder of Women: democracy, feminism and political theory,* Cambridge UK: Polity Press.

Pateman, C. (1992) 'Citizen Male', *Australian Left Review,* March: 1–6.

Rockhill, K. (1987), 'Literacy as threat/desire: longing to be somebody', in J. S. Gaskell and A. T. McLaren (eds), *Women and education: A Canadian perspective,* Calgary: Detselig Enterprises Limited.

Shanley, M. L. and Pateman, C. (1991) *Feminist Interpretations and Political Theory,* Cambridge, UK: Polity Press.

Teese, R., Davies, M., Charlton, M. and Polesel, J. (1995) *Who Wins at School?: boys and girls in Australian secondary education,* Melbourne: University of Melbourne.

ten Dam, G. and Volman, M. (1996) 'Women's history and the subject "Care"', *The High School Journal,* 79, 3: 262–270, University of North Carolina.

Volman, M. (1997) 'Care, computers and the playground: gender and identity in education', in *Discourse: Studies in the Cultural Politics of Education,* 18, 2: 229–241.

Weiner, G., Arnot, M. and David, M. (1997) 'Is the future female?: female success, male disadvantage and changing gender patterns in education', in A. H. Halsey, P. Brown and H. Lauder (eds) *Education, Economy, Culture and Society,* Oxford University Press.

Wolcott, I. and Glezer, H. (1995) *Work and Family Life: achieving integration,* Melbourne: Australian Institute of Family Studies.

Yates, L. and Leder, G. (1996) *The Student Pathways Project: a review and overview of national databases,* Report to the Gender Equity Task Force of the Ministerial Council on Education, Employment, Training and Youth Affairs, La Trobe University.

Young, I. M. (1987) 'Impartiality and the civic public: some implications of feminist critiques of moral and political theory', in S. Benhabib and D. Cornell (eds), *Feminism as critique: essays on the politics of gender in late-capitalist societies,* Cambridge UK: Polity Press.

Yuval-Davis, N. (1997) *Gender and Nation,* London: Sage Books.

13 Discipline and democracy
Race, gender, school sanctions and control

Christine Callender and Cecile Wright

> Citizenship contributes to the school curriculum by giving pupils the knowledge, understanding and skills to enable them to participate in society as active citizens of our democracy ... Citizenship encourages pupils to become helpfully involved in the life of their schools, neighbourhoods, communities and the wider world. It promotes their political and economic literacy through learning about our economy and our democratic institutions, with respect for its varying national, religious and ethnic identities ... It shows pupils how to make themselves effective in the life of the nation, locally, regionally, nationally and internationally.
>
> (Qualifications and Curriculum Authority 1999: 28)

The statement above from the review of the National Curriculum consultation document (QCA 1999) identifies citizenship education as an integral part of the statutory curriculum in the UK and promotes broad societal values such as democracy, equality of opportunity, effort and achievement and respect for others. At the same time, citizenship education has been designed to promote more narrowly defined educational values such as the pursuit of knowledge and the acquisition of key skills. The notion of 'social citizenship' underlying this broad conception of citizenship education thus comprises basic social rights that are parallel to civil and political rights (Marshall 1981) and assumes that education serves as the social foundation upon which adults become full citizens.

Yet current recommendations for a citizenship education curriculum in England and Wales and, indeed, most of the recent educational literature on citizenship education and democratic schooling[1] are silent on questions relating to children's educational experiences. Little attention, for instance, has been given to the educational contexts in which teaching and learning about citizenship is to take place. Arguably, the various ways in which diverse groups of children experience schooling should be an integral concern of the project to educate citizens and create democratic schools.

Research studies have shown that schooling experiences are differentiated by social class (e.g. Aggleton 1987; Willis 1977) and gender (e.g. Weiner and Arnot 1987); Walkerdine 1989). Furthermore, research has consistently highlighted the vulnerability of Black[2] pupils in UK schools. African-Caribbean boys, for instance, are more at risk than other groups of experiencing academic under-performance and exclusion from school.[3]

Exclusions[4] of Black pupils from both primary and secondary schools in the UK, which have escalated dramatically in the 1990s, represent a significant factor in the low achievement levels of some Black children in mainstream schooling (e.g. Social Exclusion Unit 1998; Ofsted 1999; Runnymede 1998). The denial of educational opportunities which follows permanent exclusion from school ultimately results in a lack of job opportunities and material prospects, thus effectively reducing these pupils' opportunity to participate fully in mainstream society. Critical to this over-representation of Black pupils in the school exclusion statistics are the relations between white teachers and Black pupils which have often been characterised by conflict.[5] This is clearly demonstrated in a number of recent empirical studies of teacher–pupil interaction.[6] Bound up with this conflict are the white teacher's perceptions of Black male and female pupils as the 'other' (Gordon 1992)[7] and, as a consequence, 'not fitting the concept of the 'ideal pupil'.[8]

In this chapter, we draw upon qualitative data from two separate programmes of research. The first of these focuses on white teachers' interactions with Black African-Caribbean pupils (Wright, Weekes and McGlaughlin 2000). The second of these explores Black African-Caribbean teachers' classroom philosophies and practices, particularly in their interactions with Black pupils (Callender 1997). In discussing these projects side by side, we begin to see how Black pupils can experience the effects of both inclusion and exclusion as a racialised group. In one case, they symbolise 'others' who are excluded from school because they are perceived as threatening and do not fit the implicit codes of conduct. In another case, they symbolise 'others' who are to be empowered because they are 'unlike others' (i.e. more likely to experience discrimination in schooling as a result of 'race' and/or socio-economic position). Thus, 'otherness' predominates even when teachers actively engage in more inclusionary school practices.

In the discussion which follows, we outline (in exploratory fashion) some of the findings of these two separate research studies on teacher–pupil relations in the light of the theme of citizenship. We focus, in particular, on the relationship between school discipline and democracy as contested aspects of schooling. The first section of the chapter reports on a recent study conducted by Wright, Weekes and McGlaughlin (2000) in five multi-racial secondary schools within a large multi-racial education authority in the UK. The second section of the chapter reports on a recent ethnographic study of six Black primary school teachers in two multi-racial primary schools (Callender 1997). In particular, we highlight Black male and female pupils' experiences of teachers' authority and school sanction systems and what these experiences tell us about the pupils' status as citizens. We also explore the ways in which Black and white teachers differentiate between students' identities through their application of school discipline and control procedures in the classroom.

When discussing these studies, we suggest ways in which race shapes gender relations. We suggest that, as far as questions concerning school inclusions, exclusion and citizenship are concerned, African-Caribbean boys and girls have a good deal in common. Whilst their responses and experiences in schooling can differ in subtle ways, the underlying construction of their 'otherness', even though gendered, reveals many similar characteristics. We explore these similarities and differences by considering first how white teachers construct notions of non-conformity and disruption and use school sanctions in five multi-racial secondary schools in England.

Teacher authority, school sanctions and the construction of 'otherness'

Many studies of classroom interaction have highlighted the existence of a highly structured system of attitudes and behaviours which together aim to promote children's learning. Furthermore, the processes by which these multi-layered understandings are established and mediated is heavily dependent upon the systems of management and control present both in the classroom and the school. McCadden (1998), for instance, notes that contemporary approaches to classroom management and discipline are inextricably linked to the teacher's perception of instructional goals and 'organisational morality'. Instructional goals are achieved through a strong management style and a clear articulation of the skills children need to perform effectively in school, whilst organisational morality incorporates the identification of acceptable behaviours, linking children's work with the purpose(s) of school and explicit teacher modelling of organisational routines.

The complex interplay of such management styles and organisational morality with racialised and gendered discourses is demonstrated vividly in Wright et al.'s (2000) research in School A. This school was situated in the middle of an upper-middle-class suburb of a city, and performs very well within the education authority in terms of five higher grade GCSEs.[9] The majority of the pupil population was drawn from the immediate vicinity and, therefore, many of the pupils came from professional families. There was a small (but increasing) African-Caribbean and Asian population, both in the area and the school. However, these pupils were perceived as being highly visible by many teachers. Black male and female pupils, in turn, were aware of their numerical minority status and of their visibility within the school, and therefore often grouped together for mutual support. A central feature of many of these pupil's difficulties in the school related to the perceived or experienced authoritarianism embedded within the school ethos. Alex, aged 14, for example, was part of a larger group of Black male and female pupils in Years 9 and 10. His feelings about his school were generally negative:

> *Alex:* I don't like [my Drama] teacher. He picks on you. Like if you've got a bad reputation then he'll try and pick on you. If someone else was talking and so were you, they'd point out you . . . 'cause in the

first week of school, when I was in Year 7, I got done on a [school] trip 'cause I was running off. And then ever since then, the teachers have not liked me because they thought I was a troublemaker.

Researcher: What sort of things do you get into trouble for?

Alex: I've been put on report for answering back and being cheeky.

At its most literal level, Alex was concerned about teachers who consistently brought up the past whenever they interacted with him as it did not allow him to move beyond conflictual relationships with teachers. His response was to challenge teachers verbally by using 'cheekiness', a strategy which has been noted by many researchers as representative of pupils' disaffection and subculture (Willis 1977; Mac an Ghaill 1988; Gillborn 1990; Eggleston et al. 1986). It is also used here by Alex to emphasise that, as a pupil, he could respond to teachers on equal terms – if 'cheekiness' is worthy of school sanction when used by a pupil, it can also be condemned by pupils when used by teachers. In this sense, Alex contests (rather than resists) teacher power. Although Alex had never experienced a school exclusion, he had been subject to labelling (Mac an Ghaill 1988) and reported being perceived as a 'troublemaker' by senior teachers. As he comments:

'Cause sometimes they just say 'you've been into trouble before so we're going to make it harder on you this time, and then the next we'll go harder and next time we'll go harder', just so they can prove a point.

Alex conceded that he was high spirited and often talked and 'messed about' with friends in the classroom. However, he suggested that sanctions had been used excessively by school staff to 'prove the point' that they had the ability to exert control over students.

Although he did not articulate this himself, Alex's experience was further mediated by his racial background. His membership of a friendship group of Black boys affected teachers' perceptions of him, as the group he was part of was already deemed a 'cause for concern'. One teacher revealed:

I have noticed that we have . . . the West Indian groups of lads grouping together as Black kids and running around. I say running because they are ever so gregarious . . . of course you get White kids but they don't seem to be . . . they [Black pupils] are always singing and dancing and they're much more physically expressive. Now that in itself makes them noticed more, and they're really keen on developing an identity. And there's a special uniform that they wear and if they can possibly help it, they'll get it into school . . . But when they are walking around with scarves across their face, with all of them [faces] hidden. That's fine, that's brilliant. Come into the classroom, coats off and sit down, but they'll bring it into the classroom. And we've got one or two of these groups with strong leaders who are actually coming out with the racist thing.

Like 'it's because I'm Black that you're doing this'. And that really irritates me because it's not, it's because they're not taking their bloody scarves off.

(Teacher 'A', School A)

Even though scarves were worn by a large number of Black, white and Asian pupils in the school (often pulled up over mouths and noses), the teacher assumed that Alex and his friends sang, danced and wore specific clothing because of a natural disposition and the need for a specific racial identity. The teachers who expressed concern thus constructed the wearing of scarves as a racial signifier for a group of friends and as indicative of a racialised identity as well as a physical presence. In some senses, then, the conflictual relationship between white teachers and African-Caribbeans resulted in both the boys and the teacher constructing a notion of 'otherness' in relation to Black pupils in general. Further, the 'separateness' of such pupils was perceived by teachers as an act of resistance, in a context where pupil mixing was understood to be more conducive to learning:

To be honest, we've got some Black kids, not lots, and they seem, not all, but a lot of them, seem to hang around with their own peers within a group. They have their own subculture. Try to bend the uniform so they can dress in whatever way and so when they're together, some of them don't perform as well as they should do, because, yet again, they want to be one of the boys. And they're bright, there's no problem in that respect, it's just they want to be different – that's understandable perhaps – but it does affect the way they learn . . . They do group together, they want to have their own personal identity and that's how the uniform changes a bit. They wear woolly hats and we say no woolly hats in school etc. and you have to keep on and on . . . I suppose if they hang around together, it can be a bit intimidating perhaps for other kids. You know, we've got some other Black kids, lads particularly, who will just do their own thing . . . hang around with everybody else and just, y' know, *mix in.*

(Teacher 'B', School A)

The assumption here is that Black children who achieve well do so because they integrate, and that those who do not integrate are likely to underachieve because of the racial identity which is fostered within the group.

Similar racialised constructions of 'otherness' were found also by Wright, Weekes and McGlaughlin amongst African-Caribbean girls in the school. One Black female pupil in this group identified racism as part of teachers' practice and related this to the fact that their friendship groups were seen by teachers in racially negative terms. African-Caribbean girls responded by actively promoting particular racialised identities and using each other to resist the desire for classroom integration. This was a challenge both to teachers' attempts to control friendship groupings, and to the wider social relations which construct racialised groups as separatist.

In contrast, some pupils found it easier to submit to the forms of teacher control within schools, because of the implicit power imbalance embedded within the teacher–pupil relationship. For Johnny, an African-Caribbean Year 11[10] pupil who had moved to the school at the start of the year from another city, the form of pupil contestation he employed at his former school had not proved satisfactory, and it is here that the transformative possibilities of pupil resistance came into question. Johnny had previously lived in an area where the British National Party was very active, and because his father had been fairly well known, Johnny had been subject to racial and physical attacks. This experience had affected his behaviour in school where he felt that teachers were not supportive:

> A lot of teachers, sometimes they're scared of Black boys. My form tutor was scared of me, you could tell. I was probably big for my age and . . . he wouldn't tell me to sit down and take my jacket off. He'd wait till I'd do it. He wouldn't ask for homework. If he told me something and I disagreed with it, he'd back down straight away. And I took that to my advantage.

Johnny had employed various types of resistance in school, answering back and fulfilling what he felt to be teacher expectations of Black male behaviour. However, whilst he was aware that the same stereotypes were in operation at this new school as they were in his former school, he no longer wished to contest them. As he commented:

> Over here, every Black person is a 'rude boy', if they dress a certain way. That's how they [teachers] see them. Here it's just more blatant, probably because they haven't got much Black people in the school. Because when I came here I had long plaits and I kept hearing people say to me 'oh he's a rude boy'. So I cut it all off. Just to give me a new image and start afresh.

Gendered responses

Such shared concerns about racialised identities may result in similar gender responses. A previous study undertaken by Wright (1987) in two Midland comprehensive schools revealed that since African-Caribbean boys and girls were singled out as an 'other group', both voiced similar concerns about teacher behaviour in the classroom and were prepared to confront and challenge teachers.

The similarities in Black male/female interaction with white teachers are exhibited, for example, in the following extracts taken from a metalwork class. The first class was taught by Mr Craig.

Mr Craig was talking to the class. Whilst he wrote on the blackboard, a group of four white boys sat talking in an ordinary tone of voice. The teacher, annoyed by the noise level in the room, threw a piece of chalk at one African-Caribbean boy (Peter) who was not particularly noisy:

> *Teacher:* (shouted): Pay attention. (To an Asian boy). Could you get me that piece of chalk?
>
> *Peter:* (African-Caribbean): Why don't you use black chalk?

Here Peter responds with a challenge to the teacher:

> *Teacher:* (Turning to the researcher): Did you hear that? Then I would be accused of being a racist. Take this for example, I was down at Lower School, I had a Black girl in my class. She did something or another. I said to her, if you're not careful I'll send you back to the chocolate factory. She went home and told her parents. Her dad came up to school, and decided to take the matter to the Commission for Racial Equality. It was only said in good fun, nothing malicious.

Similarly African-Caribbean girls were confronted by processes of 'othering' and excluded from normative classroom practices by Miss Simms, another teacher at the school who tended to blame a group of Black girls for the threat they posed to classroom management. As she commented: 'If this group of African-Caribbean girls were not in the class, I feel I'd be able to do a much more effective teaching job with the others . . .' Consequently, when there was general classroom noise, it was the Black girls who were singled out for disciplining. The following vignettes from classroom observations illustrate this:

> Pupils began talking among themselves. The teacher looks up from her marking as a result of the increasing classroom noise. She looks to the back of the classroom where four African-Caribbean girls sit, talking among themselves.
>
> *Miss Simms:* (in a raised voice): Will you four girls stop talking and get on with your work.
>
> *Barbara:* (African-Caribbean): We are working, we're just talking about the question.
>
> *Jean:* (African-Caribbean): It's not only us talking. What about her (pointing to Kulwinder) shouting? Why do you always pick on us?

While the teacher was talking to the African-Caribbean girls, three white boys sat playing with a pocket computer game, which the girls had noticed.

> *Miss Simms:* Whenever I look up you're always talking.
>
> *Barbara:* That's 'cause you only see us, everybody else is talking. Look at them (pointing to the boys playing with the computer game) they're not even working. (Turning to the other African-Caribbean girls and talking in a loud whisper) Damn facety.

The African-Caribbean girls burst into laughter at Barbara's comment to them.

> *Miss Simms:* (shrill): Barbara and Jean will you leave the room?

The girls left the room, closing the door loudly behind them.

Subtle differences in such confrontations/challenges to teachers, however, were perceived by Vera, another female pupil. It was her view that the African-Caribbean boys were not disciplined in the same way as the girls and that, as a result, the boys' responses and interaction with teachers were different. 'The boys I know don't get the same treatment because most of the lads are quicker to box the teachers-dem than the girls, you see.'

African-Caribbean boys also vividly described how their classroom experiences of discipline were linked to prejudice and injustice and how they were understood as not just racialised but also as gendered subjects. An example relating specifically to Black masculinity was implicated in the teachers' excessive use of discipline (in this case expulsion):

Mullings: The teachers here are too facety, they don't give you a chance.

Michael: For example, Hill [Anglo African-Caribbean boy], who was expelled.

Paul (Williams): That just prejudice, he never did nothing wrong.

Michael: He never done nothin much you know. He's half-caste, but he was more to the coloured people-dem.

Researcher: Why was he expelled?

Michael: What it is I think, he got suspended three times and he was on report, kept getting bad grade, they just put him in front of the Governors. Yet a big skinhead [white boy] boy right, he go in front of the Governors three times already, right, they expelled him. He came back, and dem let him back in a de school yesterday.

Errol: We were messing 'bout right, he said something about Black people. So I called him a mother fucker, he looked at me.

Michael: He said, him going to dash you out of the school in'it?

Errol: He could have but he didn't.

Paul: I'm not saying that we cause trouble, but I'm just saying the teachers think Black boys are always going round causing trouble. That's what they think ...

There were subtle differences in the boys' and girls' responses to such marginalisation. The male pupils often responded to teachers with 'face winning' contests, viewing teachers' lack of respect for them as a central feature of their interaction with teachers. Female pupils did not directly confront teachers. Instead they refused, through verbal challenges, to reveal or accept an identity of helplessness in the presence of teachers.

The stance taken by Black girls can be seen in the accounts of two female pupils, Chantel and Donna, in School B – a school situated near a large housing estate in the centre of the city. Its student population contained excluded pupils from a nearby technology school and housed a greater number of Black pupils than School A. It also appeared as though there was a greater focus on 'race', as expressed, for example, in wall displays. The school had recently introduced a change in classroom discipline which some of the pupils felt had an adverse effect on the experiences of Black pupils. For example,

Chantel, a Year 10 pupil of mixed parentage, felt that racism was one such consequence:

> Do you know how many Black pupils he's [the head teacher] excluded? Seventeen last time I looked. I was the first Black girl to be excluded. It was all boys and then we . . . it was like we was putting up a stubborn way. If he spoke to us we would just walk off and kiss our teeth after him. He started excluding White people to style it out. He said 'we're going to kick all the clowns out . . .'

Chantel, and the other Black pupils she spoke of, had developed various forms of resistance against the threat of school exclusion employed by the head teacher. For example, they employed racial signifiers (such as 'kissing their teeth') which had a similar effect on school staff to the wearing of woolly hats and scarves by the Black boys described above. However, such confrontations clearly had emotional consequences for the Black girls:

> She's [teacher] got a big problem. She said something racist to me, I can't remember the words but I reported it and [the headteacher] says 'you'll find that Miss Beverage is not racist because she is in the Black bullying group'. [My Science teacher] said [to us] 'Didn't they bring you up with manners where you two come from?' We tried to get him done, but we swore at him. Sometimes we just go in the room and cry our eyes out. We just cry, because we report it, report it and no one does anything. So they wonder why we turn bad. [They say] 'the best thing to do with Chantel is to chuck her out before the lesson starts'. I go home and I feel like . . . I've just started my period.
>
> Donna started crying when she walked out of his office because she was saying sorry for no reason.
>
> (Chantel, Year 10 pupil)

Both Donna and Chantel felt powerless, yet importantly, they avoided displaying these feelings in the presence of teachers' sanctions. Chantel went into a separate room, and Donna waited until she had left the head teacher's office before crying. Thus both Donna and Chantel extracted some power from their interactions with teachers.

African-Caribbean girls, on the whole, have been found to be more committed to working hard in class and acquiring qualifications despite their dissatisfaction in schools. Evidence from this study and related work (e.g. Mac an Ghaill 1988; Mirza 1992) suggests that on the whole African-Caribbean girls tend to behave in a conciliatory manner towards a teacher following a confrontation. In contrast African-Caribbean boys who were also committed to education found their classroom experiences were demotivating and as a consequence they worked erratically in class. Their more overt stance triggered the use of the disciplinary framework rather than inclusionary strategies.

One of the reasons for this difference has been found in the relationship of Black masculinity to school achievement (Sewell 1997; Wright et al. 2000). It is now clear that Black boys are disproportionately excluded from UK schools (e.g. Social Exclusion Unit 1998) and that the construction of Black masculinity in schools plays an important part in this process of marginalisation. Definitions of masculinity within education are now understood to relate closely to schools' definitions of educational success and failure in ways that are also class and race specific (Willis 1997; Gillborn 1990; Mac an Ghaill 1995; Wright 1987; Sewell 1997). Thus, working-class boys' masculinities, particularly that of 'macho-lads' (Mac an Ghaill 1995), conflict with white teachers' concepts of a successful pupil and, having been labelled as failures, such boys tend to become alienated. Similarly, by engaging in masculine behaviours, Black boys do not conform to hegemonic understandings of educational success.

McCadden (1998) reports that the actions of teachers may well disadvantage Black pupils, particularly boys (cf. Biggs and Edwards 1991). He argues that teachers' emphasis on hard work, task orientation and product orientation effectively 'stifle' Black boys 'apparent creativity, collectivism, energy and artistic aptitudes' (116). According to McCadden, this also has the effect of preventing the boys from expressing their Blackness.

Black boys in Wright et al.'s (2000) study recognised that they were more likely to experience negative attention from teachers because of their masculinity. They appeared to respond forcefully to the label of 'marginalised other' (through interactions and school treatment) and admitted to more vehement responses to such treatment than those of their female contemporaries, as the following dialogue demonstrates:

> *Paul:* The school don't respect Black pupils. We are treated badly, we are forever hassled . . . I can remember the time I was in [subject], Mr X keep saying to me 'Why you've got a tan?' – I say, 'Well I was born like this'. He say, 'Well you should go back to the chocolate factory and be remade' or something like that. To me that wasn't a nice thing to say.
>
> *Kevin:* We are treated unfairly, because we are Black. They look after their flesh not ours.
>
> *Michael:* They look after fe [for] them white people-dem, you know what I mean, but we get dash at the back all the time.

Traditionally, masculinity has been associated with access to high status academic knowledge. However, Black male pupils are over-represented as 'academic failures' rather than 'academic successes'. Consequently, they have adopted other forms of masculinity to gain high status such as sporting prowess and aggression. However, these forms of activity do not have equal legitimacy in schools because not all male pupils' identities have equal validity (Aggleton 1987). It is the adoption of these latter forms of masculinity that seem to justify teachers' expectations of African-Caribbean pupils and their characterisation as highly aggressive and sexualised subjects. Arguably then, when Black male pupils attempt to exercise some influence over the conditions of their powerlessness by constructing masculine identities that exert some power over others (especially in relation to females: see Eggleston et al., 1986; Wright 1987), they reinforce their teachers' characterisation.[11]

Channelling their masculinity into sport can also have other negative effects for Black male pupils as, for example, Bernadette (the mother of an African-Caribbean pupil) found. She recognises that her son's school, by encouraging his sporting activity, may have inadvertently resulted in her son's exclusion from the academic mileu of schooling:

> To me, they're not supporting him in his education, his academic education. Sports, they're quick fe do anything for him and to me personally, me tell him already 'me never bring you in the world fe kill out yourself running for no school, no country, no nothing, right?
>
> (Bernadette, mother of Shante, aged 14)

Young Black boys who refuse to take part in team sports are doubly excluded from an acceptable and indeed 'normal' schooling identity. This is largely because the lack of both a sporting and an academic identity produces no 'true' sense of masculinity. Thus, it is clear that 'race' acts to position Black masculinities as illegitimate, rather than simply subordinate. It is on this basis that young Black men find themselves excluded from the schooling process and distanced from the definitions of various forms of (white) masculinity found there. As previous studies suggest, Black males wish to achieve but they are rarely able to move beyond the idea that Black masculinity is strongly linked to conflict and confrontation. Such limitations for Black male students emerge in response to teachers' expectations of Black student behaviour, much of which appears to be grounded in misguided assumptions about the gender identities of Black students.

The data drawn on in this section suggest that school sanctions signify a process by which Black male and female pupils are constructed as the excluded 'other' in the education system and that there are a variety of ways in which pupils respond to teachers' indiscriminate use of punitive sanctions. The pupils interviewed in these two schools did not hold anti-education sentiments. However, their goals were to resist the constructed and indeed stereotypical position of the powerless pupil. Noteworthy is how much pupils were aware of teachers' perceptions of them. Clearly, this kind of awareness raises questions about Black students' right to belong in the school community and the ways in which schools construct, through the transmission of very particular race relations, the ideal citizen (Gillborn 1992).

Black teachers, school discipline, control and empowerment

In contrast to the school experiences of Black pupils, particularly as they relate to the authority of mainly white teachers who rely heavily upon the school sanction systems, we shall now focus on the experiences of Black pupils who are taught by Black teachers. Qualitative data are used to describe the complex and multi-layered fusion of classroom interaction (community, traditional and school knowledge) and the intersection of race and gender in Black teacher–pupil relationships.

Within the UK, Black and ethnic minority teachers make up a very small percentage of those practitioners in mainstream schools (approximately 2 per cent). In fact, close analysis of the statistics on ethnic male teachers currently practising in schools and students in training shows that there has been a steady decline over the past few years.[12] Concern about this trend is such that the Teacher Training Agency (TTA), the national body responsible for the recruitment of teachers in the UK, spearheaded a recruitment drive which explicitly targets people from Black and ethnic minority communities such that the teaching profession becomes more reflective of the community it serves. As part of this strategy the TTA introduced national targets for teacher training institutions.

The teachers who participated in this study, therefore, were part of a small group of Black practitioners, who up until very recently have remained invisible in the British research literature.[13] The teachers and pupils who took part in the study were drawn from two primary schools. Both schools were located in urban multi-ethnic areas and the local communities were reflected in the composition of teaching and non-teaching personnel. Both schools were performing well in terms of local and national norms with many children attaining an average of level 4 in the core subjects in national assessments at 11 years old (Key Stage 2). The Black teachers interviewed were fully committed to education in its broadest sense, and to the development of all children in their care. One very experienced African-Caribbean male teacher, who was very popular with pupils and parents alike, exposes his commitment in the following excerpt:

> I do a lot of home visits because I know it's the basis of a good education. Know the child to be educated. You cannot educate a child unless you know him. You must know his background, his environment and how his parents are guiding him.
>
> (Callender 1997: 120)

For this teacher and the other teachers in the study, it was vitally important to establish links with parents. Such a link provided the foundation upon which a sound educational experience would be built. Other teachers stated that their role was akin to that of the parent – not just simply acting *in loco parentis* but instead extending their educative role to the wider development of the child. Many, nonetheless, were acutely aware of the precarious nature of schooling for Black pupils, particularly boys, and were very conscious of the inequitable outcomes for many Black pupils.

Within Callender's study, although sanctions were a particularly noticeable aspect of the day-to-day management and organisation of learning, here they functioned in the opposite fashion to the ways described earlier. For example, in McCadden's study, sanctions acted as the vehicle through which Black children were motivated, educated and empowered both in their learning and in their preparation as citizens. This observation is similar to that of Noblit (cited in McCadden 1998: 119) who observed that Pam, a Black teacher, was firm with her Black pupils and had higher than average expectations of them. In fact,

> she saw her position as being imbued with a moral responsibility to be in charge of guiding what her pupils could and could not do, and rather than be repelled by this, her pupils embraced her and her standards.

One could argue, therefore, that the place of discipline within the process of schooling involves issues concerning the racial identity of teachers. Clearly, to discuss discipline without reference to racial identities is to deny the experiences of Black teachers. Gender similarly plays a part in shaping teachers' understanding of their role. It is to a discussion of some of these issues that we now turn.

Black teachers, Black pupils and discipline

> If I am to discuss my role as a teacher it is very difficult. I can't divorce my role as a mother. It's still a continuity . . .

This statement was drawn from the teacher interviews which were carried out as part of a wider study on Black teaching styles (Callender 1997). It exemplifies the emergence and continuing maintenance of kin-like relationships that often exist between Black teachers, Black pupils and their parents which Foster (1991), writing in the USA, refers to as 'connectedness' – the extent to which the connections between the teacher, community, home and school actively supports the cognitive, social and emotional growth of the child. In the UK, Osler (1997) noted that Black teachers' commitment often incorporates any pupil who may be disadvantaged because of gender or race. Moreover, she states that their practice is underpinned by principles of equity and justice (see also Dillabough, this volume, chapter 10).

Black teachers, in Callender's study, expressed their solidarity with Black pupils both in words and deeds. Close examination of their pedagogical practice and classroom management identifies a complex system of sanctions where Black students are encouraged and challenged both in their learning and in their preparation as citizens of the wider society. Discipline in these classroom contexts extends beyond the transmission of school rules – instead discipline incorporates the fundamental skills and understandings that Black students require for them to comprehend their existence both within and outside of the school.

Interview data, collected as part of the study, suggested that Black teachers' regulatory practices were characterised by a set of behaviours ranging from *directness* and *shaming* through to *truth-telling*. These sanctions limited the effects of unacceptable behaviour whilst, at the same time, acting as a liberating force for Black pupils. The approach often meant that Black practitioners found themselves challenging negative attitudes amongst other teachers and supporting students in their understandings of Blackness. Winston, a Black teacher, found it necessary and empowering to draw pupils' attention to their ethnicity, through regular reminders of their Blackness. He went on to explain how this strategy operated in the classroom context: 'I hit them hard [the pupils], knock them down and try to build them up again. When they realise you are building them up again, they will come and say "remember you're Black" . . .'. For Winston, the explicit criticism of Black pupils served to build resilience and a strong sense of identity. As his strategies appeared unorthodox, he recognised that these practices were not necessarily accepted by his colleagues. However, he and his colleagues had come to an unspoken agreement about the nature of his disciplinary repertoire (cf. Noblit 1993). Cited in McCadden 1998.

Black teachers' interactions with Black pupils not only related to matters concerning the school, but also extended to issues outside education. The role of 'significant adult' was closely related to the role of adults within the wider Black community. In the classroom observations, it was not unusual for adult members to act as an external locus of control, providing guidance and support. For example, during the study, Evadne, a Year 4[14] teacher was observed. She had several years teaching experience and was a former head teacher in the Caribbean. Evadne noticed that Devante, an African-Caribbean boy in her class, had worn an eye-catching shirt to school, which exposed his back and chest. Concerned by this and the fact that he had been talking in class, Evadne registered her disapproval in front of the class stating:

> Just keep yourself quiet. Do you see me come to class and sit down like that in front of you? Well don't do it in front of me. You put on your clothes . . .
> Next thing you'll be coming here naked.

Later, when Devante returned to class without his jacket, she again returned to the topic of his inappropriate dress. However, this time Evadne not only admonished him and asked him to leave the class but informed him that she would be notifying his mother of his choice of school attire. Whilst Devante had not broken school rules *per se*, he had contravened what Evadne regarded as appropriate dress for a pupil in Year 4. In order to bring home the message more forcefully, she included parental sanction as part of the process of disciplining Devante.

Perhaps one of the most striking aspects of Black teachers' regulatory behaviour in this study was their use of verbal sanctions to limit inattentiveness and to reduce misbehaviour in class. Shaming, for example, a recognised feature of the oral culture that has developed in Black communities (Labov 1972;

Edwards and Sienkewicz 1990), is used by pupils so that they can verbally outdo their opponents. This verbal interplay may incorporate rhythmic and/or poetic qualities and its main intention is to embarrass. Truth-telling, on the other hand, involves the critical analysis of the individual (hooks 1993). Here the intention is that the recipient engages in self-reflection as a part of the truth-telling process.

Pupil interviews revealed that many Black pupils were aware of the purposes of shaming and truth-telling *and* that they recognised the function(s) of these strategies. Instead of creating and/or reinforcing Black pupils 'otherness', these sanctions promoted community and oneness. In the classroom, African-Caribbean teachers were observed using these strategies as part of their everyday practice. There were, however, important similarities and differences in the ways in which boys and girls both received and perceived these public admonishments.

Gender and race in Black teacher–pupil relationships

Unlike the research findings reported earlier in this chapter about white teachers' relations with Black pupils, Callender's study found no major differences in the ways in which Black male and female teachers interacted with such pupils. All of the teachers were concerned about patterns of achievement and gave personal insights as to how they perceived the differential academic outcomes of Black boys and girls. Both male and female teachers in the sample commented on the ways in which girls responded to schooling, stating that they showed a more positive attitude and that they demonstrated more enthusiasm. Fuller (1980) noted a similar phenomenon in her work on the school-based subcultures of Black girls. Although Black girls displayed ambivalence towards school in her study, they nonetheless had a firm commitment to education.

In Callender's study, boys were reported to be less involved academically and did not show the same levels of engagement in school as the girls. For example, an African-Caribbean male Year 6 teacher stated:

> There is a distinct difference between the boys and girls. The girls will listen and try to improve – not the boys . . .when I look at them I know they have academic potential but they don't care about it. The Black girls are moving on much better than the Black boys.
>
> (Callender 1997: 143)

Osler (1997) drew attention to the ways in which Black teachers in her study perceived Black boys as behaving in a 'self-defeating' way, arguing that Black boys' conceptualision of Black identity was often in opposition to the way they perceived, and responded to, Black male teachers. In Osler's study, Black male teachers were seen as 'acting white' through their involvement with the process of formal schooling. She also suggests that:

It is possible that both Black and white teachers have experienced fewer difficulties or conflicts with African-Caribbean girls whose approach to school appears more utilitarian and whose understandings of Black female identity may be broader and more positive.

(Osler 1997: 112).

In Callender's study, several teachers commented that Black girls appeared more motivated in school, whilst Black boys were disinterested. This observation became more apparent in the upper stages of primary schooling (Years 5 and 6)[15] where the peer group was a much stronger influence.

> I find that with the Black girls there is a more positive response to work. They are very enthusiastic about their work, whereas Black boys have a lackadaisical attitude. They are not as concerned about education as the girls are.
>
> (Callender 1997: 143)

Similar concerns were raised by Eustace Braithwaite, a teacher of pupils in Years 5 and 6.

> There is a distinct difference between the girls and boys. The girls will listen and try to improve – not the boys. The boys are more concerned with what he thinks of him as a footballer, etc. When I look at them I know they have academic potential but they don't care about it. The Black girls are moving on much better than the Black boys.
>
> (Callender 1997: 143)

Both male and female pupils in Callender's study experienced positive relationships with Black *and* white teachers. Pupils commented particularly on how differently they interacted with Black teachers, equating their criticisms with care and concern. Moreover, they were acutely aware of the 'hidden messages' contained in Black teachers' discourse. Rather than debilitate or stifle pupil development in school, Black teachers' interactions with Black pupils appeared to increase their motivation, improve attitudes and enhance the learning process. Significantly, Black pupils perceived such teachers to be more effective in classroom management: 'Most Black teachers are strict and if the class goes wrong they can put it back' (Rosalind, African-Caribbean girl). Teachers' and school sanctions were viewed not as generating conflict but rather as behaviours that were an integral part of the Black teachers' disciplinary repertoire.

> He's different from all the other teachers . . . like he says he's going to hit you. In Jamaica if you do anything like talk you get beaten with the cane or the ruler, I find it different to some of the white teachers. Like Nzinga said, some of the white teachers are soft.
>
> (Carolyn, dual heritage pupil)

Both boys and girls regretted for instance, the limited experiences they had of being taught by Black practitioners, and pointed to the fact that Black teachers represented role models for them. In contrast, they perceived white teachers as being unable to 'control' the class and not providing sufficiently challenging tasks.

Unlike Wright et al.'s (2000) research findings (described above) which showed how Black boys engage in 'face winning' episodes, as a way of exercising some control over their powerlessness, the young Black male pupils in Callender's study displayed a high level of camaraderie with both male and female teachers. Similarly Black girls responded equally positively to their interactions with Black teachers. In the following vignette we will see how a potential face-threatening episode is acted out by the teacher, and the pupil's subsequent response to it.

The class is having a maths session. Nzinga, an African-Caribbean girl, is not paying attention and is caught by her class teacher, Mr Braithwaite, fiddling with a calculator:

> *Teacher:* So now we've got our statement, what is the next thing we do? Sixth year come on. Nzinga stand up and tell me what is the next thing we do (she stands uncomfortably). Come on Nzinga, come and show me, come (she moves towards the board). Come on girl, move man, sitting down there playing with calculator (she is handed the chalk). Show me what is the next stage we'd take, you've got your statement written out (Nzinga stares at the board). Come on *don't you know?*
>
> *Nzinga:* No.
> *Teacher:* Because you weren't listening. Now stand right there please. Move out of the way and pay attention.
> Nzinga is left standing in front of the class for a full 25 minutes.

Whilst it would be reasonable for Nzinga to be embarrassed and hurt by her teacher's actions, she is somewhat unconcerned as the following interview extract, which occurred after the episode, reveals: 'He's much stricter [than White teachers], he gives you harder work and he teaches you better, and if you get to go in his class I think you're lucky'.

In the case of Black primary teachers in Callender's study, the intersection of gender and race with teacher–pupil interaction appeared to be less confrontational and, therefore, less problematic in the context of school sanctions. There may be several reasons for this, some of which may be to do with the ages of the pupils and the very different ethos to be found in primary and secondary schools, although, of course, some Black pupils may still have negative schooling experiences with teachers during the primary years (Bourne, Bridge and Searle, 1994).

The girls in Callender's study also shared some similarities with the girls reported in Wright et al.'s (2000) recent work. They tended not to 'act out' negative teacher perceptions of them. They worked diligently in class and held high aspirations for the future. On the other hand, the boys, whilst being perceived as less interested in schooling, did not attempt to challenge overtly teachers' authority, or indeed, exhibit anti-school behaviour.

The significance of Black masculinity was not as apparent as that which was reported in the secondary school studies described above. Whilst Callender's study did not highlight teachers' gendered responses to Black pupils, nevertheless it drew attention to the question of race and gender in Black teacher–pupil relationships. Much of the previous work concentrates on Black female educators and whilst such work provides valuable insights, it clearly needs to be balanced with similar work which addresses the interactions between Black male teachers and Black boys (Mac an Ghaill 1988)

We have seen the ways in which Black teachers' regulatory behaviour may promote inclusion and empowerment. Such practices and strategies were central to their notions of *political empowerment*. Whilst the Black teachers did not achieve this through the spoken word, they were nevertheless achieving their goals through discipline and through strategies to motivate African-Caribbean pupils.

The application of familiar community methods of discipline such as truth-telling serve to prepare young African-Caribbean pupils for full citizenship. The Black teachers in the study recognised the failure of Black boys to engage fully with the process of education but did not, as a result, differentiate in their responses to them. They also highlighted the motivation of Black girls, but again it was not possible to identify differential treatment across gender. Mirza's (1992) suggestion in her work on young Black girls that African-Caribbean families do not tend to apply Eurocentric distinctions between genders may be relevant here in the context of African-Caribbean teachers.

Conclusion

> The role of democratic education 'does not mean getting to vote on the form of oppression to which you will be subjected'.
>
> (McEwan 1998: 274)

Questions of discipline and democracy within schools present complex and conflicting illustrations of the experiences of Black pupils in school. This seems particularly clear in the case of boys. The studies reported here reflect the twin processes of inclusion and exclusion as they are being played out in the same educational arena. As a consequence, when Black pupils move from school to school, classroom to classroom and teacher to teacher they are positioned, repositioned and position themselves according to their racialised and gendered identities.

Pupils in different schools experience both exclusion and empowerment. On the one hand, they are subject to the regulatory controls mediated by white teachers where they are controlled, sanctioned and excluded from schooling. On the other hand, they may be part of a collective group where

Black teachers promote community knowledge and understandings which, in turn, lead to solidarity, community and empowerment. One context results in the use of school sanctions where Black pupils are constructed as the 'other' and where Black pupils are positioned to assert various forms of masculinity and femininity in school, whilst the other context utilises school and community sanctions as a mechanism for reinforcing a strong sense of individual and collective identity and achievement.

In relation to broader questions of school inclusion and citizenship, a number of issues have been raised. For example, the implementation of a formal citizenship curriculum and the creation of democratic schools will not be possible without reference to the social and educational processes of racialisation, gender formations, identities and teachers' expectations of diverse pupil groups. Moreover, the school processes and related educational contexts which lead to both the exclusion and inclusion of Black pupils need and deserve careful examination, particularly in relation to teacher practices and the many ways in which Black students are excluded. Clearly, the study of such contexts is crucial to understanding what it means to develop a more inclusive form of political citizenship, and to support the potential for democratic schooling.

Notes

1 It is not the intention here to explore and problematise the notion of citizenship, since this is undertaken elsewhere in this book (e.g. see chapter 2, Dillabough and Arnot). But it is worth noting that contemporary debates and critiques of traditional discourse on citizenship include uncovering the gendered nature of the concept (Gordon 1992; Walby 1994; Lister 1997), laying bare its national and racialised dimensions (Anthias and Yural-Davis 1992) and the notion of sexual or intimate citizenship (e.g. Weekes 1998).

2 Black refers to children of African/Caribbean heritage (see Eggleston et al.; Gillborn and Gipps 1996; McGaill 1988; Mirza 1992; Sewell 1997).

3 (e.g. Social Exclusion Unit 1998; Runnymede Trust 1998; Ofsted 1999; Wright Weekes and McGlaughlin 2000).

4 (e.g. Social Exclusion Unit 1998; Runnymede Trust 1998; Ofsted 1999; Wright Weekes and McGlaughlin 2000).

5 See for example Eggleston et al. 1986, 1987; Gillborn 1990, Gillborn and Gipps 1996; Mac an Ghaill 1988; Mirza 1992.

6 Eggleston et al. 1986, 1987; Wright et al. 1998; Wright et al. 2000; Sewell 1997.

7 Gordon (1992), in her discussion of 'gender, democracy and education' employs the concept of 'otherness' in her analysis of gender, education and marginalisation. In this chapter, the concept is used to refer to both race and gender dimensions of schooling.

8 The term 'ideal pupil' is an adaptation of Becker's (1952) original concept of the 'ideal client'. Becker suggests that teachers operate with the implicit concept of the 'ideal client', which is based on particular cultural norms and values. Consequently, white teachers tend to view much of the behaviour of Black children as deviant. Educational policy over the last 15 years has reinforced the concept of the 'ideal' pupil by emphasising lost efficiency, examination and marketisation in schools (e.g. see Ball 1993).

9 GCSE: This is the General Certificate of Secondary Education, expected to be taken in up to ten academic subjects by the vast majority of school pupils, usually

at age 16. It is the end of compulsory schooling qualification. It is graded from 'A'-star to 'G', with grades 'C' and above referred to as higher grades. Although there are no pass and fail grades, it is grade 'C' that is generally accepted as the requirement for advanced study and employment qualification. There is also a grade 'U' for those not achieving any grade. In most subjects, 55 per cent of pupils taking the examination obtain grade 'C' and above.

10 Refers to secondary school pupils, aged 16.

11 However, within Black communities, such characteristics are usually seen as more abhorrent than the sexism and male domination that pervade the culture as a whole (hooks 1991).

12 National Union of Teachers.

13 Notable exceptions are Callender (1997), Ghuman (1995) and Osler (1997).

14 Year 4 refers to Primary School children, aged 8–9.

15 Pupils aged 10–11.

16 Year 10 refers to pupils, aged 15.

References

Aggleton, P. (1987) *Rebels Without a Cause: middle class youth and the transition from school to work*, London: Falmer Press.

Anthias, F. and Yuval-Davis, N. (1992) *Racialised Boundaries: race, nation, gender, colour and class, and the anti-racist struggle*, London: Routledge.

Ball, S. (1993) 'Education policy, power relations and teachers' work', *British Journal of Education Studies*, 41, 2: 106–121.

Becker, H. (1952) 'Social class variations in the teacher–pupil relationships', in B. R. Cosin et al. (eds) (1977) *School and Society*, London: Routledge and Kegan Paul.

Biggs, N. and Edwards, V. (1991) 'I treat them all the same: teacher–pupil talk in multiethnic classrooms', *Language and Education*, 5, 3: 161–176.

Blyth, E. and Milner, J. (1996) *Exclusion from school: inter-professional issues for policy and practice*, London: Routledge.

Bourne, J., Bridge, L. and Searle, C. (1994) *Outcast England: how schools exclude black children*, London: Institute of Race Relations.

Callender, C. (1997) *Education for Empowerment: the practice and philosophies of black children*, Stoke on Trent: Trentham.

Davies, L. (1984) *Pupil Power: deviance and gender in education*, Lewes: Falmer Press.

Dewey, J. (1938) *Experience and Education*, New York: Macmillan.

Durkheim, E. (1961) *Moral Education*, Glencoe: The Free Press.

Edwards, V. and Sienkewicz, T.J. (1990) *Oral Cultures Past and Present: rappin' and Homer*. Oxford: Basil Blackwell.

Eggleston, J., Dunn, D., Anjali, M. and Wright, C. (1986) *Education for Some: the educational and vocational experiences of 15–18 year olds, members of minority ethnic groups*, Stoke on Trent: Trentham Books.

Foster, M. (1991) 'Constancy, connectedness and constraints in the lives of African-American Teachers', *NWSA Journal* 3, 2: 233–261.

Fuller, M. (1980) Black girls in a London comprehensive school, in R. Deem (ed.) *Schooling for Women's Work*. London: Routledge and Kegan Paul.

Ghuman, P. (1995) *Asian Teachers in British Schools: a study of two generations*, Clevedon: Multilingual Matters.

Gillborn, D. (1990) *Race, Ethnicity and Education: teaching and learning in multi-ethnic schools*, London: Unwin Hyman.

Gillborn, D. (1992) 'Citizenship, "Race" and the hidden curriculum', *International Studies in Sociology of Education*, 2, 1: 57–75.

Gillborn, D. and Gipps, C. (1996) *Recent Research on the Achievement of Ethnic Minority Pupils*, London: HMSO.

Gordon, T. (1992) 'Citizens and Others: gender, democracy and education', *International Studies in Sociology of Education*, 2, 1: 23–57.

Harrell, P. (1995) 'Do teachers discriminate? Reactions to pupil behaviour', in *Sociology*, 29, 1: 59–73.

hooks, B. (1991) *Yearning: Race, Gender and Cultural Politics*, London: Turnaround.

hooks, B. (1993) *Sisters of the Yam: black women and self-recovery*, London: Turnaround.

Horvat, E. (1997) 'Structure, standpoint and practices: the construction and meaning of the boundaries of Blackness for African-Caribbean female High School services in the college choice process', paper presented at the Annual Conference of the American Educational Research Association, March 1997.

Labov, W. (1972) *Language in the Inner City*, Philadelphia: University of Pennsylvania Press.

Lister, R. (1997) *Citizenship: feminist perspectives*, Basingstoke: Macmillan.

McCadden, B. (1998) 'Why is Michael Always Getting Timed Out?: race, class and the disciplining of other people's children', in R. Butchart and B. McEwan (eds), *Classroom Discipline in American Schools: problems and possibilities for democratic education*, New York: State University of New York Press.

McEwan, B. (1998) Conclusion in R. Butchart and B. McEwan (eds), *Classroom discipline in American schools: problems and possibilities for democratic education*, New York: State University of New York Press.

Mac an Ghaill, M. (1988) *Young, Gifted and Black*, Milton Keynes: Open University Press.

Mac an Ghaill, M. (1995) *The Making of Men: masculinities, sexualities and schooling*, Buckingham: Open University Press.

Marshall, T. (1981) *The Right to Welfare and Other Essays*, London: Heinemann.

Mirza, H. (1992) *Young, Female and Black*, London: Routledge.

Noblit, (1999) G. W. (1993) 'Power and caring', *American Education Research Journal*, 1, 30: 23–38.

Office for Standards in Education (1999) *Raising the Attainment of Minority Ethnic Pupils: school and LEA responses*, London: Ofsted Publications Centre.

Osler, A. (1997) *The Education and Careers of Black Teachers: changing identities, changing lives*, Milton Keynes: Open University Press.

Qualifications and Curriculum Authority (1999) *The Review of the National Curriculum in England: the Secretary of State's Proposals*, London QCA.

Runnymede Trust (1998) Improving Practice: a whole school approach to raising the achievement of African-Carribean youth. London: The Runneymede Trust.

Sewell, T. (1997) *Black Masculinities and Schooling: how Black boys survive modern schooling*, Stoke-on-Trent: Trentham Books.

Social Exclusion Unit (1998) *Truancy and School Exclusion*, London: The Stationery Office.

Torres, R., Mirza, L. and Xavier Inda, J. (1999) *Race, Identity and Citizenship: a reader*, Oxford: Blackwell Publishers.

Walby, S. (1994) 'Is Citizenship Engendered?', *Sociology*, 28: 379–395.

Walker, J. (1986) 'Romanticising resistance, romanticising culture: problems in Willis' theory of cultural production', in *British Journal of Sociology of Education*, 7: 59–80.

Walkerdine, V. (1989) *Counting Girls Out*, London: Virago.

Watson, I. (1993) 'Education, class and culture: the Birmingham ethnographic tradition and the problem of the new middle class', *British Journal of Sociology of Education*, 14: 179–197.

Weekes, J. (1998) 'The Sexual Citizen', *Theory, Culture and Society*, special issue on Love and Eroticism, 2, 4: 35–57.

Weiner, G. and Arnot, M. (eds) (1987) *Gender Under Scrutiny: new inquiries in education*, London: Hutchinson.

Willis, P. (1977) *Learning to Labour: how working-class kids get working-class jobs*, Aldershot: Saxon House.

Woods, P. (1990) *The Happiest Days?: how pupils cope with school*, Lewes: Falmer.

Wright, C. (1987) 'The relations between teachers and Afro-Caribbean pupils: observing multi-racial classrooms', in G. Weiner and M. Arnot (eds), *Gender Under Scrutiny: new inquiries in education*, London: Hutchinson.

Wright, C., Weekes, D. and McGlaughlin, A. (2000) *'Race', Class and Gender in Exclusion from School*, London: Falmer Press.

Wright, C., Weekes, D., McGlaughlin, A. and Webb, D. (1998) 'Masculinised discourses within education and the construction of Black male identities amongst African-Caribbean youth', *British Journal of Sociology of Education*, 19, 1.

14 Young women in Argentina

Citizenship representations and practices in the context of transition

Gloria Bonder

According to contemporary observers, Argentina is becoming a 'dualistic society' with some sectors of society integrated into its mainstream political structure (although with profound socio-economic differences between them), whilst other sectors are being excluded or marginalised by the social and economic politics. As a consequence, according to Isuani and Filmus (1998), important progress in the demand for, and exercise of, relatively sophisticated rights may be made by those who belong to and are included in society (for example, protection of women's and children's rights, preservation of the environment and defense of the rights of sexual minorities). At the same time, there is likely to be a reduction in the rights of those who are excluded from access to basic health, education, housing and even food services.

In this national context, it is hard to explain the passive stance being adopted by many Argentinians towards measures which seriously erode those civil rights which were enshrined historically. This passivity can only partially be explained by what Garcia Delgado (1996) called 'the dilemmatic disciplining' device – that is, the paralysing effect of political discourses which are labelled democratic and yet have been used to justify specific political and economic reforms. Such reforms were presented by politicians as if they were the only possible means of avoiding more serious misfortunes or dilemmas – such as returning to hyper-inflation or anarchic situations which could again give rise to new military *coups d'état* (Garcia Delgado, 1998).

Within this new social climate, there are some important exceptions to such political passivity in Argentina. For example, there have been massive demonstrations against the use of violence by police or 'political caudillos'[1] towards young people.[2] These exceptions notwithstanding, some researchers wonder whether current political passivity and lack of civic engagement is cyclical or permanent, whether it is linked to the particular circumstances of the country and region or whether it is a structural characteristic of post-modern societies, or all of these. Unfortunately much of the published literature does not apply to the Argentinian context. Cansino and Sermeno (1999) argue that it is inappropriate to find explanations in the conventional theoretical debates in Europe about liberal, participatory, formal and substantial democracy, since in Latin American nations democracy has had to be created from scratch. In Argentina this entails not only developing a particular form of government, but also ensuring the development of a new democratic lifestyle.

In this paper I hope to contribute to this debate by considering how one group of young Argentinians conceptualise their role as citizens. I report on the ways in which young women attribute meaning to the concept of citizenship and their rights in relation to this unstable and complex political and economic context. Related questions emerge such as: what are the socio-economic and cultural conditions under which young women live in Argentina? What are their opinions and values in relation to political and social institutions and leaders? Do they perceive gender discrimination in social and school environments, and if so how do they react to it? Do they even consider themselves to be citizens? Do they know and understand their rights and attempt to defend them actively?

Such questions, along with many others, guided the project, *Possible Futures: conditions, lifestyles and citizenship among young Argentinian women*. This project[3] which aimed to explore, on the one hand, young women's concepts of citizenship as well as their understanding of the role of the school in forming citizens and, on the other hand, how such economic and political changes have affected young women's concepts of citizenship. The recent reform of the secondary school curriculum in Argentina introduced a new curriculum subject called 'ethical and civic education', and one of the aims in conducting empirical research was that it could encourage those responsible for the development of this new subject to be sensitive to the needs, culture and values of young Argentinian women.[4]

The new syllabus for ethical and civic education proposed by the Ministry of Education in 1991 triggered a range of polemic discussions. The rather weak original proposal put forward by specialists in charge of curricular transformations was aimed at creating an 'ethical subject' that would have moral autonomy and be capable of making rational choices in defense of human rights, democracy and the dignity of the human being. These goals, however, were severely attacked by the Catholic Church because they were seen as anti-spiritual, constructivist and materialistic in nature. In the end, the Church imposed its view emphasising 'the spiritual nature of the human being', transcendence through religion, and moral submission to hierarchical values. The Church demanded that the inclusion of gender issues in the curriculum be abolished, attacking its dangerous relativism in understanding so-called 'normal' sexual identities, its probable incitement to, or legitimisation of, homosexuality, and its contribution to the breakdown of the family structure. All this occurred some months before the Fourth Women's World Conference at Beijing in 1995. The government's obedience when responding to such demands can be explained by its strategic alliance with the Vatican's position on matters of gender, sexual and reproductive rights. However, after Beijing, the political climate became more relaxed and modern ideas prevailed in the daily practices of schools and in public opinion. The opportunities, therefore, for intervention in relation to gender have been much improved.

In the first section of the paper, I describe some characteristics of the process of democratisation of Argentinian society, setting the context which shaped (and continues to shape) young women's representations of citizenship, and their values and ideals. The following sections draw upon analysis of interview data from a sample of young Argentinian working-class and middle-class women (aged 15 to 20), revealing how they represented this period in their lives, their understanding of generational change and their responses to dominant discourses circulating in Argentina about appropriate identities and social roles for young women. In the final section, I report their views and suggestions for a form of citizenship education which is meaningful to them.

Learning democracy in an exclusive society

In 1983, Argentina returned to democracy after eight years of a particularly cruel and repressive military dictatorship. This was followed by a process usually referred to as a 'transition to democracy'.[5] At the beginning of the 1990s, another equally important transition period began, only this time in the economy. The government tried to solve a long-lasting economic crisis, which had reached its most critical stage in the 1980s and had been associated with a considerable decline in production, and rampant inflation. So began a period in which growth and redistribution were based on the privatisation of key public services, anti-inflationary policies, deregulation of broad sectors of the economy and major amendments to the labour laws. All these measures had the explicit purpose of re-establishing macro-economic balances and increasing competition at an international level, by decreasing public expenditure and attracting new capital.

These reforms had dramatic social consequences. Despite the considerable global increase in economic activity, the problems of the 1980s were aggravated by unemployment, a reduction in salaries and income redistribution, all of which accelerated the exclusion of an important sector of the population from the goods and services necessary for preserving their basic status as citizens. Since 1983, there have been three constitutional governments. Numerous legislative changes have been made, such as the approval of a new National Constitution, the creation of new institutions and the reform of others with the intention of developing a democratic order appropriate to 'modern' societies.

The violation of human rights during the military dictatorship between 1976 and 1983 was an important focus of discussion during this period of transition in the Argentinian society. It gave rise to an increasing antagonism towards the state by organisations which stood for human rights such as *Madres y Abuelas de Plaza de Mayo*. But this period also saw the enactment of laws (such as *Obediencia Debida* and *Punto Final*) which limited, for example, the responsibility for murder committed by the subordinated sectors within the military establishment, prevented trials against members in the highest military ranks, and encouraged political agreements with the military sector for the sake of governability. All these, together with a noticeable increase in the importance and influence of the mass media in public opinion, motivated a vivid public debate about emerging social problems and the desirability of modernisation and democratisation.[6]

One of the greatest threats to social order is unemployment. By 1997, unemployment in Argentina reached 17 per cent of the economically active population, a level not recorded since the critical years of the 1930s. Underemployment (both open and hidden) has also increased, thus raising the number of Argentinian people who experienced employment problems to approximately half the labour force. At the same time, the total public expenditure declined from 33 per cent in the 1980s to 25 per cent in the 1990s considerably decreasing the cover and quality of basic social services such as medical assistance, housing, retirement pensions, etc.

Statistics show that at the beginning of the 1980s, 11 per cent of Argentinian homes were below the poverty line. This percentage increased to 24 per cent by 1996. Moreover, an unexpected phenomenon took place: the appearance of the so-called 'new poor'. At the beginning of the 1980s, only 3.2 per cent of the population were described as the new 'poor'. However, by May 1997 this percentage had increased to 26.7 per cent (Minujin, 1993). It has been suggested that the generation classified as the 'newly impoverished' (which was the result of the breakdown of the middle classes and the old industrial working groups) had become a structural trend (Palomino, 1996).

Young people during this period, as a matter of course, had to come to terms with high levels of unemployment, informal employment and illegal work.[7] Between the ages of 15 to 24, unemployment was twice that of the adult population, and young women's unemployment rate was twice that of young men's. It is estimated that 48 per cent of Argentinian young women worked in unskilled jobs and 26 per cent of this group were employed as maids, without legal protection.

In a country that was formed largely by European groups immigrating to Argentina in search of a better lifestyle and ways of ensuring the well-being of their children, such economic and cultural changes had considerable impact. The fear of unemployment, which according to opinion polls is the main concern for Argentinians, differs from the deep-rooted assumption that 'the one who does not work is the one who does not want'.

The political context is also changing with the state acquiring a new role in Argentinian society. Historically, the country was organised around a strong interventionist and centralist state which led to the formation of a weak and state-dependent civil society. However, by the end of the 1990s, this had partially changed. The neo-liberal model adopted by the government was linked to the need to stabilise a 'minimal' state for the sake of economic transparency and efficiency. At the same time the prevalent discourse stressing the importance of citizenship rights and participation generated important changes at the legal level such as the introduction of new 'semi-direct' democratic mechanisms (e.g. referendum and social audit measures) within the Constitutional Amendment of the 1990s.

However, very few people knew about and used these political devices. There was still a tendency to delegate almost all political responsibility to the government, while special efforts were not made by the political sector to increase citizens' participation in decision-making. Instead they conceived of civil society as a resource for delegating responsibility for social services. As O'Donnell (1996) explains, after a period of dictatorial governments in Latin America, the democratic regimes seem to have consolidated, but only as fragmented or restricted democracies.

In this context, the prevailing social atmosphere is one of unease, uncertainty and concern. There is a feeling of dissatisfaction with the political system, a distrust of the political leaders and the institutions in charge of justice and national security, and disappointment with economic reform. However, this dissatisfaction has not led to strong public mobilisation. Instead there is a feeling of apathy and a tendency either to privatise social life by keeping it sheltered in the most intimate personal environments or, in recent years, to manifest common interests and demands in massive cultural events.[8]

Obviously the ways in which young women in our study constructed their notions of citizenship and exercised their rights cannot be separated from this unstable and complex political and economic context. Below, I present some of the findings of the project, focusing on the ways in which young women conceptualised their concerns, political ideals, the restrictions on their lives and their future ambitions.

The study

The research, carried out between 1996 and 1998, involved a study of young women's representations of citizenship. Socio-demographic information on the position of young women was used to contextualise a qualitative study (in-depth interviews and focus groups) with forty middle-class and working-class young women who lived in Buenos Aires or its suburbs.

Three fundamental premises shaped the design of our research regarding the representations of, and values associated with, young women's notions of citizenship. First, we did not want to restrict our understanding of citizenship identities and practices to a view which implies that such identities and practices may either be or not be present in young women. The research team preferred to conceptualise the formation of citizenship identities as an ongoing process, closely related to the socio-economic and political contexts in which young women live and project their futures. We therefore wanted, on the one hand, to explore the different conditions and opportunities (both material and symbolic) which promote or prevent young women from conceptualising themselves as citizens and, on the other hand, to describe the kind of social and political ideals and civic actions which they accept and respect.

The second premise underlying the project was a concern not to construct young people as bearers of an original culture or set of behaviours. As Sidicaro and Tenti (1998) state, 'There is no "youth planet", neither are there communities of young people totally isolated from the global society'. Young people's opinions and, in particular, those related to citizenship, democracy, politics and social change are strongly influenced by dominant discourses as well as by the role which society offers to youth in the governance and development of their community.

Our third premise was that youth is neither a statistical age group nor a homogeneous generation. Young people's life conditions and lifestyles are heterogeneous; thus, it is more appropriate to speak of a plurality of youth, with diverse positions in the state (for example, gender, social class, age).[9] In this sense, we conceptualised young women as belonging to a range of different socio-economic and cultural backgrounds.

Decoding dominant discourses of femininity and youth

According to Griffin (1993), youth is both a reality (that is, a particular age group) and a category of analysis discovered at the beginning of this century. But it is also a social representation associated with certain attitudes and behaviours. Discursive configurations and treatment regimes stabilise what is normal, troubled or deviant youth according to categories such as gender, race, social class or sexual orientation. Such discourses have a powerful influence on the self-definitions of young people and on the way they behave and are treated by society. In the study, therefore, we explored how young women reacted to some of the 'common sense' opinions or stereotypes about youth which are currently circulating in Argentina. We wanted to know to what extent they identified with the current representations of post-modern youth (in particular, female youth) that circulate in the media and also in public opinion; did they recognise such discourses as forms of social control and were they able to set themselves apart from such pressures? As a methodology, therefore, we chose to ask young women to comment on some common statements about youth, society, politics, and their visions of the future. Below I report some of our findings.

Almost all of the young women we interviewed described this stage of their lives in terms of a progressive accumulation of responsibilities. They felt they had left behind their childhood and their early adolescence in which they had few worries and experienced absolute dependence on their families.[10] Characteristics that are usually attributed to youth, such as the achievement of greater independence, pleasure and joy, were almost non-existent in their representations of this stage of their lives. Clearly, this did not mean that these young women did not have such positive experiences, but that these aspects of life did not constitute a priority for, nor a identifiable feature of, their lives. Responsibility was perceived as a burden but also as a value which might have positive consequences for their present behaviour and their futures.

At an imaginary level, responsibility represented a sort of 'moral card'; a mark of distinction that might help these young women integrate into 'normal' adult society. Although these attitudes were in no way conscious, their rationality could be explained in the following way: with so few opportunities for young people, they were much more likely to be marginalised if they behaved in a way that departed from the standard rules. Therefore, obeying accepted rules (such as studying, not being sexually promiscuous, not rebelling dramatically against the family norms) was seen as increasing one's self-esteem and acceptance by others. Such moderated or strategically calculated attitudes contrasted sharply with the idealisation of cultural rebellion by youth in the 1960s which was predicated upon the breakdown of the sexual order, or the youth of the 1970s who fought for the rupturing of the political order.

Pleasure, adventure, power, fame or success did not appear to be high priorities for the young people in the study. From their point of view, to keep on studying, to get a steady job with a decent salary, to give oneself some pleasure, and to be able to take care of one's children seemed to be enough achievement for their generation. Most young women felt that their current possibilities were much better than those of their mothers. Expressing themselves freely and even discussing ideas with their parents was seen as one of the major achievements of their generation. Girls from the poorest families also highlighted the opportunities to study – a possibility that the majority of their mothers did not have – and, more generally, the chance of having a better life.

However, not everything in their present life was seen as more positive than their parents' experiences. Some young girls longed for the times when their parents as young people could actively participate in political struggles to change society. They admitted not knowing enough about the military dictatorship and having only 'flashing' images rather than clear information that would enable them to understand properly why the dictatorship had happened and what the consequences had been. Regardless of what they actually knew about this period in Argentinian history, they gave us the impression that the image of the dictatorship had a symbolic influence on the ways in which they represented what they could and could not do to contribute to social change.

'Young people of today have no ideals'

The first statement that the young women responded to, 'young people of today have no ideals', illicited a number of interesting themes. For example, all of the young women strongly rejected this statement. They affirmed that they had their own ideals which related to caring for others in a much closer and more concrete way. As Alicia (16) stated, 'It is a lie that we do not have ideals; they are different, they may not be so great, so big, but we do have them.'

Young women did not speak about freedom *per se* (perhaps because they thought they already had it) and only some of them talked about justice. Rather than hold absolute values, they seemed to place great importance on interpersonal relations: friendship, sensitivity about other people's needs and suffering, and authenticity. Getting their friends' love, self-reliance, and co-operating to create family harmony were very important for them.

They also rejected the view that young people were individualistic and not interested in any social cause. Their answers were complex and elaborate, involving discussion of ethical dilemmas and social and political practices that prior generations had seemed to accept without question. They denied separating their personal interest from their concern about others, setting themselves apart from an 'ethics of sacrifice' that has been transferred from religion to many modern political ideologies. Looking for happiness as well as trying to make their families and friends happy were examples of a 'virtuous' life. They did not appear to be motivated by 'abstract' and rhetorical ethical discourses.

Family comes first

When the sample of young women were asked what they cared most about in their lives, almost all answered, 'I want my family to be all right'. This implied that family well-being was not something they took for granted. In fact, many of them described painful or problematic family situations to which they reacted with compassion and, once again, feelings of responsibility. They were worried about economic problems and the unemployment that many of their parents faced, as well as their parents' divorce, quarrels, and painful decisions such as whether to migrate to other countries or move to smaller or poorer homes.

Since many of the young women described the contemporary social context as hostile and threatening, the family, in spite of its problems, was conceived of as one of the few places in which they expected security and support. They often had an idealised picture of their family, hardly criticised their parents' ideas and behaviour and were quite conscious of the acceptable degree of conflict that they might cause in their homes. Though many of them talked in detail about their strategies for negotiating more autonomy, they reported finally accepting most of their family's control over their lives, which they interpreted as an indication of love, protection and/or overprotection.

Personal autonomy in the public sphere

A preliminary analysis of the data suggests that young women in Argentina move in restricted public areas carefully selected by their parents and themselves, according to the degree of danger. They go to their friends' houses, to school, to clubs, to shopping centres and to country clubs, if they are rich. They go to music concerts in stadiums. But they are almost never alone (parents typically bring them home or send taxis to pick them up). In contrast, girls from the poorest families move in a much more limited area: many of them live further than 30 kilometres from Buenos Aires or within 10 kilometres of another important city. However, the girls in our study had been to both places three or four times, usually taken by their schools. If the practice of citizenship is related to personal autonomy in public spheres, the picture we received helped us understand some of the constraints young women face in learning and practising citizenship in Argentina. At the same time, the violence of the police against young people, and incidents of riotous behaviour in discos, for example, discourages them from circulating in public places and at the same time encourage acceptance of their family restrictions. For many others, the perception of this risky context and their need for security leads them to value their homes as precious 'shelters'.

Almost all of the young women interviewed considered work to be an essential dimension in their lives. They were worried about the problems they might have finding a job and keeping it and they were terrified of becoming unemployed. Many expressed indignation at the level of verbal abuse, harassment and discrimination they were likely to be exposed to when looking for a job. However, they also seemed to have very limited knowledge about current working conditions and predicted labour market trends; they persevered in pursuing a miraculous 'formula': if they continued studying, they would find a job and avoid marginalisation.

Young women's life experiences and the information about the labour market which they had gleaned from the mass media suggested a poor scenario with only limited possibilities. When planning their future, these young women imagined themselves working in a formal and steady job, with a decent salary and social security. They also wanted to be mothers and to work at the same time and thought that they would be able to cope with both responsibilities without major difficulties. In short, they moved from a frightening vision of the present to an unrealistic vision of the future. At the same time, they could not explain how one situation would transform itself into the other.

Approximately 30 per cent of all the young women we interviewed worked, and some of them had temporary jobs. Most of those who had jobs came from working-class families and the stories they told about the working conditions they were subjected to involved extended working hours, economic exploitation, harassment and discrimination. One young women commented:

> The employers tell you what they expect you to do at work. Then they want you to do other tasks and eventually you end up doing everything, but you cannot complain, because if you quit there is a line of people after you for the same job.
>
> (Mariana, 18)

All the young women in the study regarded education as an essential value in the process of socialisation and integration into society. The ones who had dropped out of school regretted the decision and wished they had other opportunities to return. High school is obviously a privileged space for interacting with one's peers, for making friends, and for having intellectual and emotional exchanges not available in other social institutions. For many girls, especially those who belonged to the lower social classes, school was the only space outside the family in which they could participate and feel safe, protected and supported by their parents' confidence. They believed that if they were to finish high school they would have a safety net, a wall protecting them from the dangers of social marginalisation.

None of the respondents harshly criticised school. They valued the efforts of their teachers, the respectful and supportive 'climate' some teachers created, the educational reforms that were attempting to make schools more democratic and, most importantly, the enriching peer interchange. Such 'tolerant' attitudes were particularly evident amongst young working-class women who felt grateful to receive some basic cultural capital from school: 'High school is important to be aware of what is going on, to understand the news broadcasts in the media' (Adriana, 17).

Politics and power: frontiers, institutions, actors

As other studies on youth have shown,[11] young women expressed great distrust in political institutions and political leaders. Moreover, any discourse or social practice associated with politics tended to be interpreted in terms of abuse of power and was also rejected. As these young women remark:

> I think they [politicians] live in another world, they are not here, they do not live with people, they do not know what happens to people . . . they do not have the slightest idea.
>
> (Raquel, 15)

> Beyond the phrase that goes 'I am going to save you', there is nothing.
>
> (Veronica, 18)

The young women told us how they wished that their political leaders would have a more accurate vision of reality, be sincere, honest and ethical, listen to and work for people and account for their behaviour. Some of the girls had more trust in female political leaders, suggesting that they are less corrupt, more able to put themselves in other people's shoes, and keep their word more firmly.[12] But most of the girls did not differentiate between male and female politicians.

It is not clear how we should understand these opinions which, after all, are expressed by youth in many other countries. In Argentina, the media have played a complex role: its members have helped consolidate democracy by exposing corruption and abuse of power in government and in the political parties; they have also promoted political scepticism and discredited political institutions in Argentina. Indeed, when the girls were asked what 'sources of information' they used to judge political leaders many of their opinions were based on news broadcasts and on some kind of 'common sense' which they do not question:

> *Question:* Why don't you like politics?
> *Answer:* (Rocio, 19) Because I listen (in radio or TV) to what happens in the government and I realise everything goes wrong with politics.

> They [the politicians] do not do anything. Each day there are more and more poor people.

> (Lucia, 17) Everyone knows that the one (politician) who is not corrupt is a thief, and has no interest in people at all, nor in this country.

Not one of the young women in our study was satisfied with the current socio-economic and political situation in Argentina. However, all of them appreciated living in a democratic system and they felt themselves to be the beneficiaries. They remarked upon the fact that democracy brought about freedom of expression and less fear than in the previous period. Paradoxically, their representations of democracy did not include the idea of conflict, negotiation, participation, institutions and collective responsibility. They conceived of Argentina as a 'quasi-natural' society, regulated almost exclusively by periodic elections of representatives whom they did not consider trustworthy.

In 'reading' young women's accounts, it is possible to design a sort of imaginary 'political map', with its actors and the different channels of participation and decision. Within this space there are two territories. On the one hand, 'the President' is pictured as a patriarchal authority with omnipotent power. As a father, he is held responsible for all the problems of society, such as unemployment, retired people's low pensions, education, violence, etc.; he is also considered to be the one who could solve these problems, 'if he wanted to', without having to negotiate the different interests at stake. On the other hand, there is a 'discontented society' which, whilst still maturing, depends upon a form of quasi-direct participation to limit the Presidential authority. In this context, public mobilisation, demonstrations and media accusations are the privileged devices which the young women attributed to society. The traditional mediation institutions, such as political parties, the parliament, social organisations and trade unions were not viewed as playing any major role. Only (some) journalists and social leaders were seen to be capable of mediating between the President and society.

Young women's participation in civic life: desires and contraints

In general, the level of female participation in political institutions, and in social organisations, was low. Many of the young women in the study argued that, although they would like to be more committed to social causes, they could not find the appropriate channels for a higher level of participation. Their parents' fears and their own, in terms of the advisability of attending public demonstrations, were described as one possible cause.

> I think there are ideals today, but it is really difficult to go on to the street and complain. I mean, if you complain against the government, you don't know if you will be able to go back home . . . I think I would be afraid of that.

> (Violeta, 16)

There were also important differences between girls of different social classes. Many of the middle-class girls had attended some recent public demonstrations, but young working-class women, who usually lived in the suburbs, had less opportunity to do so, in part because they lived far away from the capital and they did not have money to travel.

Both the young women who had participated in public demonstrations and the ones who had not held positive opinions about these forms of active citizenship were in some ways committed to social involvement. But they made a clear distinction between the occasional and voluntary nature of public demonstrations and being part of stable organised initiatives. In relation to the latter, they were somewhat suspicious of most social organisations, supporting only those that 'are not interested in power or money, as political parties are'.

None of the girls perceived any difference between men and women in terms of their participation in social causes, nor, for that matter, did they perceive gender inequality in their generation. Yet, when they referred to generational difference, they felt they identified more than the older generation with the struggle to defend democracy and they defined themselves as much more realistic and cautious. They did not approve of violence, nor did they idealise risk. In contrast with their parents' generation, they are not attracted by 'heroic' discourses. At the same time, they recognised that, unlike previous generations of Argentinians, they had far more possibilities in terms of being free to express their views and to settle social conflict through communication rather than violence. As one young women commented:

> I think that in the past young people used to exceed their own limits. They used to plant bombs, things like that. Maybe they were not allowed to be different. Instead young pople talk today. We are more objective . . . we are more open-minded, we are civilised.
>
> (Carla, 19)

Defining good citizenship

During the interviews and group discussions, girls were encouraged to describe the concepts, attitudes and practices they associated with citizenship. We were interested in knowing what they knew about citizenship and where they had learnt it; what dimensions of social life they associated with it; how they defined active citizenship; what their image of a 'good' citizen was; and finally what role the school should play in educating young people in relation to citizenship.

The young women who were interviewed appeared to know very little about citizenship. As two interviewees said:

> No idea . . . I must have been taught that thousands of times during my Civic Education Classes but . . .
>
> (Clara, 15)

Yes, I think we studied that at school, but it seems that I do not remember much, because I can't even tell you what it is.

(Carola, 17)

Others vaguely associated citizenship with 'national identity', with 'being an inhabitant of a city, with 'one's roots', with 'the heritage' and with 'political and civil rights'. The association of citizenship with the concept of rights was still prevalent. However, these young people had very limited knowledge about their own rights (in general and, specifically, as young women) and they appeared to be completely unaware of the recent changes that had taken place as a consequence of the amendment of the National Constitution and the Constitution of the City of Buenos Aires. Yet, in some sense, young women felt they had 'the right to have rights'. It is interesting to note that once these young women conceived of themselves as citizens, they articulated demands mainly in relation to the authorities, and questioned those who, in their opinion, were constantly subjugating them – namely, the police and the government.

The majority of the girls in our study appeared unable to avoid prevailing gender, class, age and cultural stereotypes when describing the ideal citizen: they imagined a good citizen to be an adult man, in a sound financial position; a good neighbour, and an heir to the male civic tradition of 'boy scouts' and civic campaigners.

I imagine a citizen as the father of a middle-class family, kind, helpful, tidy, wearing a suit, who crosses the street on the corners and throws the trash into the garbage can.

(Sonia, 18)

A man who walks his dog with a little shovel and the newspaper.

(Alba, 16)

None of the respondents established a relationship between good citizenship and active participation, least of all the notion of making decisions relating to the public interest.

It is hard to explain this gendered and class concept of an obedient and dependent citizen. Young women in the study seemed to ignore state mechanisms and the rights and powers of the government and civil society. However, their opinions appear to be the result of the inertia which, after ten years of democracy, has seen a national history characterised by successive dictatorships, by authoritarian paternalism and the absence of daily democratic practices. Furthermore, the fear of these young girls was associated with everything that is public, with institutions that are supposed to protect them, with the adult world which (beyond their own small family or friendly space) was not considered trustworthy, and with an uncertain future.

Education for citizenship: demands and proposals

Arguably, the young women in this study believed that schools should provide them with an adequate education for citizenship. They were not satisfied with the ways civic education was taught at school, having found it very formal, disconnected from reality and based on rote learning. They agreed that the subject should be included in the high school syllabus, as a special course or as a cross-section area in Social Sciences. However, they criticised the traditional assessment methods, proposing instead that education for citizenship should be rooted in the everyday experiences of school life. For example, it should teach young people how to participate in the process of making decisions about issues such as dress code and discipline rules.

One of the most interesting results of this project was the way in which the young women expressed their wish to be educated as citizens in relation to those dimensions of personal and collective life that are not usually considered 'public'. As Susana commented:

> Young women should be empowered by teaching them about their rights and their possibilities of participating in so many places ... I am afraid of leaving school, of not finding a job, of the university, of being in a couple and how to cope with all that. It is not easy and nobody talks about it at school.
>
> (Susana, 18)

Articulating a discourse that we could call 'spontaneous feminism', many of the girls in the study understood citizenship as a set of rights and social practices that should include public and private aspects of daily life. They wanted to learn how to deal with situations such as adolescent pregnancy and maternity, unemployment, sexual harassment at work, family and urban violence, the violation of their rights by companies and state services, etc. They wished there was a closer relationship between what was taught in school and the problems of the real world which were being revealed daily in the media. To sum up, they wanted the school to transmit a 'grounded' knowledge that was sensitive to their anxieties and helpful for the elaboration of their own life project.

They thought that citizenship education should start in the primary school and that their parents should be taught as well. During the focus group discussions, the girls put forward more creative pedagogic proposals for citizenship education. For example, Zulema (a young women of 18) suggested that citizenship education should contain 'a little of psychology and real life experiences'. Children should be expected to be shown, and to observe, the world around them:

> Children should understand citizenship beginning with oneself and considering the people who are around us. We should try to help someone in our neighbourhood if they need clothes, food or any other basic

necessities of life, and we ought to see what we can do to help them since society does not help much nowadays. There are many people who are starving, most of them. We should find the way to survive and help others survive, as well.

(Zulema, 18)

Rather than teaching the formal facts of citizenship, this young women argued for the value of some kind of 'therapy' in schools, encouraging young people to express their visions of the future and their feelings about their lives:

We should try to pour out what we have inside or what we would like to do, and understand what we would like the world to be like ... I think young people have a vision of a better future, but we are not sure whether we will achieve it; and then the adults tell us that we will never be able to succeed, that we had better forget about it and resign to live the way people do today. That hurts. I would like people to help each other, I do not want to give up.

(Roxana, 19)

When asked how the school might address such demands for a closer relation between ethics and citizenship, between illusions and the desire for a better society, a range of suggestions emerged. For example:

At school people should be taught how to relax and do yoga so that they are not a complete wreck when they get to an older age. In former times, people did not use to live as we do now ... that is why it would be good to have a healthy lifestyle.

(Marcela, 17)

The young women seemed almost to be overwhelmed by the tensions they found in their families. Their views revealed the hidden aspect of the current economic system (an aspect not recorded in statistics) – the effects on subjectivity and intersubjective relationships of the current socio-economic system. Not apparently familiar with feminist theory *per se*, they nevertheless related citizenship to sexuality. Below are some examples:

I would like to be taught how to take care of my health and I would like to be given information on contraception and AIDS prevention, because all this has to do with citizenship.

(Marian, 17)

If we do not have sex education at school and we do not talk about those girls who have abortions, what is the use in knowing about the Constitution?

(Mercedes, 18)

We should have sexual education at school, but not the nonsense and lies some teachers tell us.

(Paula, 17)

Politicians must be aware that first of all, young women should avoid getting pregnant or dying as a consequence of having an abortion performed. Girls from lower classes do not have time to go to a hospital, so they do not go. All this has to do with the rights workers are given ... people who work in factories are treated like slaves, they do not have time to go to a hospital, and those who do not work, do not have any money.

(Mónica, 17)

Conclusions

A preliminary analysis of the data suggests that young Argentinian women's lives may have been profoundly affected by the transformation of the social structure; by the drastic, and maybe irreversible restriction of present and future opportunities to which each socio-economic sector could have access, and by the emergence of unexpected problems such as the impoverishment of middle-class sectors, adult and juvenile unemployment and intergenerational competition for jobs. The break from traditional representations of Argentinian society also lies at the centre of concerns about national identity and generational change, as does the decline of the value of high school education in improving young people's chances of employment.

New devices for the social control of youth and especially of young women are in place. Unemployment has had a disciplinary effect on these girls' subjectivity. Apart from the 'statistical' reality of unemployment, we have also identified an alarmist but also 'impotent' discourse, particularly in the media, which promotes an oppressive and repressive cycle of ambition, anger and vindication, but also transforms girls' fear of becoming forced into submission and resignation.

Another aspect of social control is the influence which the previous dictatorship still has on the representations of social conflict and the ways in which young people of today are to promote social change. The message today appears to be no more heroes, martyrs or utopias – a message that contributes to young women's vision of their own political participation.

AIDS, drugs, and social concern about adolescent pregnancy are other realities that underlie the discursive limits about the nature of social trespass, the punishment to be imposed on 'sinners', and consequently the assumptions about what young girls should be like and what they should do to deserve the approval and support of society. Urban violence similarly represented for these young women an undeniable reality, but was also another controlling discourse which restricted their autonomy and self-determination – an impediment to the process of becoming a female citizen.

The key question which derives from the study is what kind of female subjectivities arise from this symbolic order? What resistances have young women developed and how we can increase their capacity to create new symbolic references? How can we help them to integrate, without renouncing change in a world they considered to be demanding, unfair, threatening, and insensitive?

We learned that their goals for the future in relation to family life were imbued with a mixture of traditionalism and innovation that do not always follow a coherent progressive direction. The young women in this study were eager to affirm traditional values and ideals that challenge current or postmodern discourses on youth which imply youth are sceptical, individualistic, pragmatic and hedonistic.[13] Instead, they felt moved by injustice, particularly if it affected people they knew, they were sensitive to pain and inequality, and they looked for authenticity and honesty in their relationships. They appreciated tolerance, valued friendship and the care of others and nature.

The findings from this small-scale study provide support to Lipovetsky's (1996) argument about the need to make a distinction between individualism and immorality in contemporary culture. The young women we interviewed spoke about what he called 'prudent ethics'.

In the world we live in today, there coexists a feeling of disaffection towards the huge ideological and political odysseys, the great collective projects, the absolute positions, and the growing desire for specific commitments made with freedom for the sake of near others (Lipovetsky, 1996: 145).

When these young women were asked what suggestions they would give to government and/or politicians about improving young people's situation, many offered realistic, concrete and intelligent proposals, giving priority to sexuality, health and employment. They emphatically defended their right to be listened to, the need for their personal and generational singularity, and their absolute rejection of any truth that could be imposed on them, including feminism. They represented themselves as flexible enough to 'take' all the opportunities they were given and in which they trusted, and they would not refuse to participate as citizens, provided that their freedom and individuality were respected.

Notes

1 We are referring here to political leaders who usually are to be found in the less developed provinces or communities, using a charismatic and paternalistic political style and sometimes even violence in order to maintain their power.
2 These led to cases of murder, rape and kidnapping.
3 The research was carried out between 1996 and 1998 by a group of researchers from the Women's Study Centre (Centro de Estudios de la Mujer: CEM) directed by Gloria Bonder and financed by the European Union. Madeleine Arnot acted as advisor to the project and the methodology developed by her and her European colleagues Helena Aráujo, Kiki Deliyanni, Gabrielle Ivinson, Amparo Tomé and Roula Ziogou provided the basis for a number of the themes and questions for which we are grateful.

4 Throughout the history of the Argentinian school system, citizenship education has been one of its fundamental components. Ironically it has been part of the school syllabus even during the dictatorship periods when citizens' rights were suppressed! However, the educational reform that was introduced in 1991 represented a chance to influence the civic education of a new generation of young women in a context which emphasised the need for a stable democracy.

5 The previous 30 years of Argentinian political history were characterised by the succession of elected governments which failed to relinquish power and which were eventually overthrown by military *coups d'état* who then ruled through authoritarian regimes.

6 UNICEF, Argentina. 1998 Data. Buenos Aires.

7 The statistics from the 1991 Census showed that 20 per cent of young people of both sexes aged between 15 and 24 worked illegally, which accounted for approximately 1 million people.

8 The impressive attendance at all kinds of cultural events organised by private and governmental bodies, especially by young people, is a remarkable characteristic of Argentine society and highly noticeable in big cities like Buenos Aires. One example is the attendance of more than a million young people at an event especially devoted to youth called '*Buenos Aires no duerme*', which has been held annually since 1997.

9 As Griffin (1993) argued, 'Youth itself is constructed in monolithic terms as a relatively uniform age stage . . . [which] obscure[s] differences between groups of young people and especially those based on social relations around gender, "race", class, sexuality or disability.'

10 Only the youngest girls (who were very few in number) highlighted the freedom and the possibility of thinking differently, and being able to talk to their parents about things that were not allowed to be spoken of, or were never spoken about at all, during their childhood.

11 J. Hoy. *Segundo estudio sobre juventud en Argentina* (1999), Deutsche Bank, Planeta; R. Sidicaro and E. Tenti (eds) (1998).

12 As a matter of fact, they knew very few politicians' names, and even less about the Argentinian female politicians' careers. With the exception of Evita and two or three women who in the late 1990s were shown regularly in the media, they were not aware of how many women participated in the Congress or who were in decision-making positions. Above all, they did not seem to have great expectations regarding women's contribution to the improvement of society.

13 During recent years, different authors have reacted to these interpretations of youth. For example, Stainton Rogers et al. (1997) states: 'some politicians and social commentators seem to be quite ready to label young people as "individuals who have no values as a consequence of their own alienation in those which are traditional". Therefore, they accept that young people are lost, confused, disaffected and indifferent. This not only discredits young people, but also reveals a lack of sensitivity and will to recognise that young people have constellations of values' (in Roche, J. and S. Tucker (1997), op. cit.).

References

Cansino, C. and Sermeno, A. (1999) *Democracia y Sociedad Civil en Latinoamérica*, presentación de un curso de especialización: Material publicado por Internet.

Garcia Delgado, D. (1996) 'La reforma del Estado en la Argentina: de la hiperinflación al desempleo estructural', ponencia presentada en el *I Congreso Interamericano del Consejo Latinoamericano de Administración del Desarrollo (CLAD)*, Río de Janeiro, Brasil.

Garcia Delgado, D. (1999) 'Crisis de representación en la Argentina de fin de siglo', in A. Isuani and D. Filmus (eds) *La Argentina que Viene: Análisis y propuestas pra una sociedad en transición*, UNICEF-FLACSO. Buenos Aires: Editorial Grupo Norma.

Griffin, C. (1993) *Representations of Youth: the study of youth and adolescence in Britain and America*, Cambridge, UK: Polity Press.

Isuani, A. and Filmus, D. (eds) (1998) *La Argentina que Viene. Análisis y propuestas pra una sociedad en transición*, UNICEF-FLACSO, Buenos Aires: Editorial Grupo Norma.

Lipovetsky, G. (1996) *El Crepúsculo del Deber: La ética indolora de los tiempos democráticos*, Barcelona: Anagrama.

Minujin, A. (ed.) (1993) *Del Progreso al Abandono: Demandas y carencias de la nueva pobreza*, Documento de Trabajo No. 16, Buenos Aires, Argentina: UNICEF.

O'Donnell, G. (1996) *Contrapuntos: Ensayos sobre Autoritarismo y Democracia*, Buenos Aires: Editorial Paidos.

Palomino, H. (1996) *Las Nuevas Relaciones entre el Capital y el Trabajo en la Argentina*, Mimeo.

Roche, J. and Tucker , S. (eds) *Youth in Society*, The Open University, SAGE.

Sidicardo, R. and Tente, E. (eds) (1998) *La Argentina de los jóvenes: Entre la indiferencia y la indignación*, Buenos Aires: UNICEF-LOSADA.

Stainton Rogers, W., Stainton Rogers, R. and Uyrost y Ladislav Lovás, J. (1997) 'Worlds Apart: young people's aspirations in a changing Europe', in J. Roche and S. Tucker (eds) *Youth in Society*, The Open University, SAGE.

Part 4

Citizenship education and new democratic agendas

15 Sexuality and citizenship education

Sue Lees

Citizenship education is now on the agenda in England since it is to be integrated into the national curriculum. However, the proposed remit is far too limited drawing as it does on the conventional political view of citizenship which focuses largely on the public sphere. Such narrowly political terms have been criticised by a number of authors in the last decade for their neglect of key issues relating to gender difference (for example: Arnot et al. 1996, Prokhovnik 1998, Rahman 1998, Richardson 1998). As David Evans (1993) points out, one consequence is that while questions about sexuality and citizenship have been central to government and institutional policy concerns, they are detached from concerns about mainstream power relations and political interests.

The same can be said about discussions of citizenship education, which have tended to focus on the realm of the political at the expense of sexuality and the family (see Inman and Buck 1995, Osler 1995). For example, definitions of citizenship have reflected the analytic separation of the public world of politics and employment from the private sphere of the family and interpersonal relations. Yet, this separation between the private and the public sphere has been at the core of most feminist critiques of the concept of citizenship. Prokhovnic (1998), in her review of different critiques of citizenship, suggests that feminist challenges to the public/private dichotomy has highlighted, paradoxically, both the need to assess gendered power within the family, marriage and sexuality, and to provide an alternative to the public/private split. Therefore, in order to understand why the concept of citizenship should address issues of sexuality specifically (issues that are often relegated to the private sphere), the relation between the social/political and the sexual order needs to be addressed.

In this chapter, I demonstrate how sexuality is related to citizenship and why citizenship education requires an analysis of gendered power relations which are rooted in the dominance of heterosexuality as a social institution. I argue that current sociological analysis of sex education curriculum should be expanded to make it relevant to the needs of contemporary society where relations between men and women and between different ethnic groups are undergoing rapid change. I shall begin the chapter by discussing the relation between the social and the sexual order, and then outline three major themes which need to be embraced within a wider version of citizenship education which attempts to account for such concerns about sexuality.

The relation of the social to the sexual order

The 'personal is political' was one of the core slogans of the women's liberation movement of the 1960s. This slogan has been employed in a variety of ways, but most commonly it has been used to argue that general political ideals, such as equality and challenging male domination, should not be held up as abstract ideals but should be put into practice in one's personal life (see Gould 1984: 9). In this chapter, however, I shall limit my discussion to the way in which the slogan was used to illustrate how the structure of domination within the public domains of political and economic life carries over into personal life and the family.

Feminist writers (see for example: Millett 1972, Siltanen and Stanworth 1984, Rowbotham 1986) have long argued that it is not only within the public sphere that women are oppressed, but sexual desire and heterosexual relations, seen as part of 'private' rather than public life, involve similar relations of dominance and submission.

Adrienne Rich (1980: 648) was one of the first to challenge the way heterosexuality is constructed, arguing that 'the failure to examine heterosexuality as an institution is like failing to admit that the economic system called capitalism or the caste system of racism is maintained by a variety of forces, including both physical violence and false consciousness'. She demonstrated that young women are coerced into, for example, marriage and domestic circumstances through social and economic considerations. She argued, therefore, that heterosexuality and marriage are not actively chosen by girls, but are seen as 'compulsory'. In other words, the choice of getting married becomes a negative one – of avoiding being left on the shelf. She concluded that:

> within the institution exists, of course, qualitative differences of experience, but the absence of choice remains the great unacknowledged reality ... and the individual will have no collective power to determine the meaning and place of sexuality in their lives.
>
> (659)

My research (Lees 1993) into adolescent girls' attitudes to marriage[1] in the early 1980s confirmed the way that marriage was seen as inevitable, despite the grave reservations held by girls about its potential value. One girl, for example, epitomised the servitude she was expecting through marriage by commenting, 'I will get married when I've had my life'. More recently, Holland et al. (1998) have suggested that the invisibility of heterosexuality as an institution allows women's absence of choice over their sexuality to go unrecognised. This often means that women are unable to identify their own sexual needs.

During the 1970s, the family and the sexual division of labour within it was seen by feminists as the primary cause of women's subordination. In *The Sexual Contract*, Carol Pateman (1988) analyses how the social contract, on which democratic governance rests, is premised on the sexual control of women by men. She traces the development of relationships which were based upon equality – the *social* contract – and discusses the distinction between social contracts that are typical of labour relations and sexual contracts that are typical of marriage relationships. She also attempts to demonstrate how sexual contracts are based upon relationships which have been grounded in female subordination and slavery. Since old domestic contracts between a master and his slave and servants were labour contracts, she points out that the marriage contract can also be seen as a form of labour contract. Indeed, over the past three centuries feminists have compared wives to slaves, servants and workers.

With the separation of production from the family, male domestic labourers were viewed as 'workers'. What Pateman (1988), therefore, argues is that the wage labourer (in contrast to the domestic labourer) stands as a civil equal with his/her employer in the public realm of the capitalist market. A housewife thus remains in the private domestic sphere, but since unequal relations in domestic life are 'naturally so', women's position in the private sphere does not rebut the universal equality of the public world. The marriage contract therefore reflects the patriarchal ordering of nature embodied in the original contract through which a sexual division of labour is constituted. Or as Delphy and Leonard (1992) suggest, household and caring take place within a domestic or patriarchal mode of production, where men exploit women's labour and benefit from it. The consequence is that women still do not have equal access to citizenship rights with men, due to their position in the family as wives and as caregivers. Women still bear the main responsibility for childcare, domestic services and care of the elderly (McMahon 1999). Even when men and women both spend the same amount of time at work, women do more housework (see Gershuny et al. 1994).

Pateman (1988) perceptively points out that women cannot be inserted into the public sphere without generating a complete upheaval of the private sphere. This is because women will no longer be prepared to accept subordination based on a sexual contract. One potential outcome of female employment could be that young women will not find marriage attractive, particularly if young men are not breadwinners. With the decline in male full-time employment 'for life' and the rise in female employment especially of married women, the dramatic rise in the divorce rate can be seen as an indication that this is already occurring (see Lees 1999). More children are born out of wedlock than ever before. By the early 1990s, 27 per cent of births were to unmarried mothers (Muncie et al. 1995). Women are marrying later and divorcing earlier. Three-quarters of divorces are now initiated by women and divorce has increased sixfold in England and Wales over the past 30 years, a higher increase than in any other European country. Women living outside marriage may well be more autonomous, if childless and with an independent income. However, if they are lone parents, it is likely that their access to citizenship rights will be limited. Indeed the Labour government's Social Exclusion Unit (1999) designates them as an excluded group.

There are, however, important economic and physical constraints placed upon women to remain married. Research on the feminisation of poverty has highlighted the considerable difference which women's economic dependence on men and divorce can make on women's standard of living (see Richardson 1996: 51). Research on domestic violence has also indicated that women are at greater risk of violence following separation or divorce, which leads many to remain married through fear of violent partners. Women who leave proprietary husbands are pursued, harassed, and threatened and sometimes killed (Wilson and Daly 1998).

We have seen how the social order depends on what Connell (1995) referred to as the 'gender order', or on power relations between men and women. Instead of viewing the family and sexual identities as biologically 'natural', this approach views the heterosexual nuclear family as an institution which has been legitimised by such essentialist discourses, but is also subject to change.

In the remainder of the chapter I address this theme by exploring three ways in which sexuality (as part of the gender order) and citizenship have been linked within education. First, I analyse the ways in which heterosexual identities are constructed, especially in relation to the mechanisms of conformity and resistance, and to bullying and sexual violence. I then go on to discuss the contradictions in the way sex education is now taught. I conclude by suggesting a new focus for citizenship education which accounts for sexuality.

Sexual identity, sexual violence and citizenship

If citizenship education is to provide a forum for contesting gendered power relations and their differential effect on girls and boys from different class and racial groups, it needs to address how sexual identities are constructed and how choices are constrained. Such an education would consider the role of desire and sexuality along the lines suggested by Hanson and Patrick who argued that young people should be provided with 'an understanding of their sexuality, the choices that flow from it and the knowledge, understanding and power to make those choices positive, responsible and informed' (quoted in Inman and Buck 1995: 76). A starting point for such an education could address the relevant evidence which has been collected by researchers on male and female sexual identities.

Having said that, until recently, the relationship between sexual identity and concerns about social justice was neglected by academics. Feminists, in the early 1980s, had pointed out that the ways in which sociologists had analysed the strategies which young working-class men used to resist a class-based educational system had ignored the ways in which such strategies oppressed young women and Asian and African-Caribbean young people (McRobbie 1978, Amos and Parmar 1981, Carby 1982). There was little connnection, therefore, between such forms of sexual/gender oppression and concerns about class injustices. By the 1990s, however, the relation between education and the development of sexual identities became an important focus of research and, as I shall show, is now considered more relevant to the issue of citizenship rights.

What emerges from this recent research are the ways in which constructions of masculinity and femininity are both dynamic and intimately related to the private/public sphere. For example, there has been little shift in the burden of housework and childcare carried by women, both young and old, which are identified as women's work (McMahon 1999). Carrying such responsibilities is a major barrier to taking part in the public sphere as a citizen in the wider society. For a man to care for children or to undertake domestic work is to render him 'feminine' and open him up to ridicule. Such constructions are embedded in the fabric of the school culture.

Connell (1995, 1996), for example, showed how different gender regimes in schools are embodied in the very hierarchy of educational institutions and that education thus produces different forms of masculinity. For example, in a study of Australian schools, Connell (1989) identified social dynamics where the sporting 'bloods' claimed superiority over the academic 'Cyrils', and in a rural high school where the 'cool guys' distinguished themselves from the 'swots' and 'wimps'. He argued that the institutional structure of schooling is central to the production of such masculine subjectivities. In response, Connell put forward the concept of *hegemonic masculinity* which he saw as constructed both in relation, and in opposition, to femininity and subordinated forms of masculinity. As Hearn and Morgan (1990: 11) have suggested, hegemonic masculinity is also 'white, heterosexist, middle class, Anglophone and so on . . .'.[2]

Similarly, in *The Making of Men*, Mac an Ghaill (1994) took up this theme and explored how British boys learn to be men and how schools actively produce, through official and hidden curriculum, a range of masculinities. His work supported Connell's view that dominant forms of hegemonic masculinity are linked to heterosexuality. As a consequence, a number of researchers now agree that the construction of an ideal *heterosexuality* is a crucial element of the structured gender relations in social institutions, of which education is one (see Mac an Ghaill 1994, 1996, Connell 1995, 1996, Richardson 1996, Jackson and Salisbury 1996, Griffin and Lees 1997).

There is also greater recognition that sexual performance and the domination of young women is a crucial attribute of hegemonic masculinity. Powerful young men in Joyce Canaan's (1998) study of young working-class men's masculinity, for example, were referred to as 'cocks' whereas the softest young men were referred to as 'wankers', indicating that male genitals played a central role in young men's constructions of masculine identity. Women were defined as 'soft' and therefore as subordinate. They could not choose their partners and once they entered into relationships with young men, they were seen as objects to be controlled.

A number of studies have also focused on the way that girls are constrained by this hegemonic form of sex/gender relations (see Halson 1989, Lees 1993,

Holland et al., 1998). For example, Mac an Ghaill (1994: 115) argued that 'at the cultural level the promoted institutionalised modes of masculinity and femininity constructed in everyday social practices, provide the bases of women's subordination'. Such gendering of everyday practices results in female exclusion from certain citizenship rights (and the exclusion of young men who do not meet the requirements of the heterosexual ideal (i.e. gay men)). Connell (1987) regarded 'emphasised femininity' (organised around heterosexual appeal, desire and subordination) as a response to the dominance of hegemonic masculinity.

In my own research (Lees 1986, 1993), adolescent girls were constrained by slurs on their reputation from both girls and other boys. I found that female identity involved distinguishing the difference between 'slags' (whores, promiscuous girls) and 'drags' (marriageable respectable girls). I argued that sexuality is not seen as natural for women, and can only reside in the negative discourses which circulate about girls' sexuality (e.g. 'the slag'). There were no positive words for the sexually active girl. The criteria for assessing reputation, from appearance (such as wearing your skirt too short or your top too low) to acting independently (for example, going places on your own or being a single mum), are ambiguous. As Cain (1989) points out, the solidarity and collective denial of the validity of these criteria have not even occurred to the girls. They accept the criteria and end up assisting the boys in the policing of other girls; thus girls are as likely to call each other 'slags' as boys are. The lack of a specific definition of the term 'slag' means that girls are in a permanent state of vulnerability and its actual usage is such that *any unattached girl* is vulnerable to being categorised as a slag. Their only defence is to deny the truth of the allegation or to revert to the protection of a boyfriend *by getting attached.*

This research indicates that the development of both boys' and girls' identities are constrained by compulsory heterosexuality. For boys to adopt characteristics that are seen as feminine, to develop reciprocal rather than sexually dominating relationships with young women or to come out as gay, renders them vulnerable to bullying and abuse. For young women, their lives are still constrained by the double standard which positions them as subordinate to male desire and constructs their bodies as primarily sexual. This profoundly effects the development of their identity and limits their autonomy, both of which depend upon their participation in, and possession of, citizenship rights.

The effects are not, of course, identical across different social classes and ethnic groups. Some young women will have more opportunity to subvert the discourses on which their subordination rests. For example, Madonna named her video company 'Slutco' (Lees 1993: 287), and the American black pop group named themselves 'Hoes wit Attitude' ('Hoes' being American slang for prostitute). Similarly, young women in Skeggs' (1994: 134) study felt able to adopt regular confrontational stands which sexualised classroom interaction in order to embarrass and humiliate male teachers by, for example, goading them about the size of the penises. Girls' comments therefore challenged the prerogatives of male power by refusing to take masculinity seriously. These young women were able to use their knowledge of masculinity to subvert the regulatory mechanisms. Subverting such discourses, or acting autonomously does, however, carry risks. Developing the necessary independence to enable participation in political, social and sexual relationships may mean that girls run the risk of being labelled 'unfeminine' or 'promiscuous' and subsequently being ostracised.

Sex education, arguably, should concentrate far more on the relation between young men and women and their mutual responsibilities. Citizenship education should therefore enable both boys and girls to be more aware of the way relations of power are embedded in their relationships and the implications this has for the changing family. Boys, when adult, need to be encouraged to take on far more responsibilities for children and for their sexual relationships if women are to obtain citizenship rights. If this does not occur, the consequences for the next generation, many of whom will be brought up in poverty-stricken single-parent households, deprived of the rights for citizenship, will be dire.

School bullying and sexual violence

A second way in which sexuality can be related to citizenship education in contemporary society is through a consideration of bullying and violence. Bullying and violence amongst teenagers are now recognised. However, they are rarely linked to the mechanisms by which the gender order (and hetero-sexuality) is both developed and maintained. Yet both, as I shall show, are intricately connected to the way sexual identities are formed and maintained in the heterosexual gender order (or, in Pateman's terms, the sexual contract).

Since the 1980s and 1990s, there has been growing concern amongst teachers, parents, educational policy-makers and researchers about the incidence of bullying in schools (Mahony 1985, Tattum and Lane 1989, Pitts and Smith 1995, Arnot et al. 1998, Duncan 1999). The UK government's proposals (QCA 1999) for citizenship education, although worthy, treat these issues in a superficial way. The proposals include such platitudes as 'helping pupils to develop effective and fulfilling relationships and learn to respect differences between people' (19). In order to achieve this, the report suggests that pupils should be taught 'to recognise that there are different forms of teasing and bullying, that bullying is wrong: and about how to seek help in resisting bullying' (19) and to learn 'the consequences of racism, teasing, bullying and violent behaviour, to respond appropriately to them and ask for help, to recognise and challenge stereotypes' (21). The phrasing of these aims fails to address why bullying occurs, and gives little indication of the contribution that educational practices themselves could have in supporting, rather than contesting, such behaviour. Therefore, it is not clear how pupils will be taught to respond 'appropriately' (21).

Bullying and violence need to be understood within the context of the gender and ethnic order. School policies can either encourage or discourage such phenomena and are closely related to the 'gender/racial order' of particular schools. A major problem is that the prevalence of bullying which pervades many classrooms and playgrounds is often undetected by teachers and parents. Davies (1996), in her study of primary school children, makes two important points about how gender differences are maintained in groups, and how bullying and the construction of sexual identities are interdependent. First, she suggests that the dichotomy between 'male' and 'female' requires collective activity to maintain it. She calls this collective activity 'category maintenance work', which is primarily aimed at maintaining the category (i.e. 'male' or 'female') as meaningful. Second, it is the boundaries of male and female behaviour in which this category maintenance work occurs. Girls and boys do not always behave in sex appropriate ways, nor do men and women. Often the boundaries between male and female appropriate behaviour are violated. This leads to behaviour designed to bring the deviant back into line (Davies 1989: 29) and takes the form of bullying, of teasing and at the extreme, of violence.

Any deviant behaviour (e.g. a boy behaving like a girl) leads to other members of the group letting the deviant know they have done wrong. If a boy bursts into tears, he is called a 'cry-baby'. If a girl does the same, she is behaving 'just like a girl should' and she is comforted. Teasing is usually about bringing category deviants back into line. Though individuals can deviate from prescribed forms of masculinity and femininity, their deviance gives rise to category maintenance work, in order to maintain the category as meaningful in the context of dominant roles. Girls who behave like tomboys and boys who like to talk to girls are teased and disapproved of by the more conforming groups.

Category maintenance work is more important for a boy than a girl, as masculinity only reflects superiority if differentiated from femininity. For boys to hang around with girls is to acknowledge their similarity. To be similar to girls is to be associated with a lower status group which means that it may be worse for a boy to show feminine characteristics than for girls to show masculine characteristics. Hegemonic heterosexual masculinities are, therefore, constructed and defined in terms of the subordination of girls, which reflects sexual rights (and later on, marriage involves other rights such as rights to being serviced by women).

Bullying is, therefore, a strategy for maintaining strong gender categories and is supported by the gender regime of the school. When an individual deviates from their sex category they are teased, or violence may result. It is not only pupils that bully, teachers can also be involved in similar activity. One of the most thorough studies of school violence was undertaken by Beynon (1989) who found that violence towards boys was deeply embedded in teachers' practices of crowd control in the 'tough' school he studied. He began by observing teachers and those pupils who were in the process of transition to secondary school. He observed a number of staff employing threats as part of the institutional welcome. Boys were hit, pushed and shaken. In the early years of secondary schooling, a hard core of male teachers regarded coercive measures as synonymous with 'good' teaching, and a virtue to be upheld. Beynon argued that most violence threatens personal rights, under-mines social order and is illegal. However, some violence can be deemed acceptable. The manhandling increased the more Beynon became accepted as a member of staff. The fact that there was so much violence in the lower secondary school was attributed by both staff and pupils to the need for boys to 'be a man' in a context in which 'weaklings go under'. Men and boys expected to put up with a certain amount of manly behaviour if they were to win the accolade of 'good teacher' or 'good lad'. Beynon argues that violence is at the heart of contemporary masculinity and contemporary schooling.

Male sexual bullying takes the form of calling girls 'slags' or 'too tight' which implies that on the one hand that they are promiscuous, or, on the other hand, calling them 'lesbian' as a term of abuse. In either case, they are not conforming to the image of the conventional woman, dependent on a man. For boys, 'poof' and 'gay' are used as insults, not just to imply that a boy has a homosexual orientation, but that he does not fit into the model of hegemonic masculinity. The linguistic insults point to the reality that there are real penalties for breaches of social behaviour that no girl or boy can afford to disregard. As Maureen Cain writes:

> There are real rewards for conventional living, and real penalties for eschewing it. It is therefore necessary for researchers to recognise these realities and the discourse of sexually appropriate behaviour which expresses and constitutes them . . . it is clear that discourses can be used to autho-rise and justify painful and even penal practices, and that sometimes the use of language can constitute a pain itself.
>
> (Cain 1989: 7)

The roots of the racial and sexual violence can therefore be found in the institutional and normative cultures and discursive framing of schools, even primary schools. Connolly (1995), in his study of different racial groups in English primary schools found, for example, that sexuality, especially its emphasis on violence and power, manifested itself most frequently in terms of verbal abuse and insults. However, fighting or physical bullying also occurred. Some of the group who were labelled the 'bad boys' (predomi-nantly African-Caribbean low achievers) were observed in the playground abusing girls physically, pushing them over, swinging them round and kick-ing them. Young people's discussions about girls' relationships were highly racialised: for example, having an Asian boyfriend was grounds for abuse. Emphasising the active role that very young children play in constructing and negotiating their identities, Connolly argues for the need to locate the forging of black masculinities, for example, within the specific contexts in which racism pervades. He also points to the central role of teachers and the school in developing and reinforcing racist constructions especially when it involves the labelling of African-Caribbean boys as 'bad' and the consequent self-fulfilling prophecy which results. Citizenship education arguably could play a key role in deconstructing not just these stereotypes but also in challenging such institutional school cultures.

Sexual violence amongst boys can also be found in their later behaviour when dating girls (Roscoe and Kelley 1986, Lloyd 1991). It is estimated that 50 per cent of rapes in the US are perpetuated against adolescents, mainly between those who know or are dating each other (Levy 1991). Death can result, as shown by FBI estimates that 20 per cent of female homicide victims in the United States are between the ages of 14 and 24 (Spaid 1993). In an English study (Holland et al. 1991, 1998) of young women aged 16 to 20, nearly a quarter reported having had unwanted sex in response to pressure varying from mild insistence to intercourse with threats, physical assault, and child abuse. The researchers identified the difficulties young women had when negotiating the use of contraception. They argued that when women negotiate safer sexual practices, they question the conventional basis of sexual activity in which it is boys and men who determine the meanings and practices of standard heterosexuality.

A survey by the Zero Tolerance Charitable Trust on young people's attitudes towards violence against women showed that some young men had a high acceptance of sexual violence (see Burton et al. 1998). The pressure to achieve an identity which conforms to notions of hegemonic masculinity could explain why, in a socially unequal society, so many young men are pushed into economic marginality. As Hudson (1998: 247) comments, 'those who cannot demonstrate the affluence of successful masculinity will be likely to exaggerate through violence their claims that they are racially superior, heterosexual and macho'. Not only is this pattern destructive for men but research has shown that male violence in the family has devastating effects on women and children and leads to psychological disturbances and, at the extreme, homocide and suicide (see Koss and Harvey 1991, Lees 1997). Braithwaite and Daly (1994), along with others, suggest that therefore vigorous social education is needed to ensure that domestic violence and social and racial violence are challenged and perpetrators are shamed. Arguably, such social education should be one of the main tasks of citizenship education in schools.

Sexuality and citizenship education

Various other suggestions have been put forward about how to widen the remit of the national curriculum to encompass citizenship education in England. In this section, I focus more specifically on how sex/sexuality education could be related to citizenship education. Osler (1995: 3) suggests that citizenship education should cover forms of social exclusion and discrimination based on racism and sexism and should 'prepare young people for European citizenship and most effectively confront racism, xenophobia, sexual inequality and other challenges to social justice'. Others have argued for the inclusion of sexuality into citizenship education: Edwards and Fogelman (1993), for example, argued that the formation of sexual identity and sex education should be an important element, and Inman and Buck (1995) suggest that citizenship education should include sexuality education rather than sex education (which is grounded in a biological frame of reference).

This leads us to a third way in which sexuality is related to conceptions of citizenship and which citizenship education should address. Introducing an analysis of gendered heterosexual power into the curriculum would involve dealing with the gender regimes of schooling and the bullying and violence referred to earlier. It would also include promoting acceptance of gays and lesbians. This agenda, however, presents the government with a dilemma. Education has always been concerned with fitting individuals into the status quo which is generally assumed to be the heterosexual two-parent family. Both the last Conservative and present Labour governments have been concerned about the growing disintegration of the traditional family and have been anxious to avoid being seen as encouraging promiscuity and immorality (see Kelly 1992, Thomson and Holland 1994). For this reason government attitudes to sex education have fluctuated and the scope for intervention has been both restricted and narrow (see Sex Education Forum 1992, Corlyon and McGuire 1997).

An example of this is the way in which schools reinforce the suppression of female autonomy and desire by constantly presenting girls as potential victims rather than as initiators of sexuality. Michelle Fine (1988), in her research on sex education, found that girls were taught to define themselves against disease, pregnancy and 'being used'. Female desire was tied to negative emotions and seen as having moral and reproductive consequences. Male desire, on the other hand, was typically represented as a normal biological process consisting of such phenomena as wet dreams and ejaculation. Fine called for a more open discussion where girls could therefore become subjects of their own desires rather than simply objects of male desire. Instead of adopting such an approach, under the Education Act 1986 it was specified that sex education should be placed 'in a moral and family framework' (Durham 1991) and the controversial clause 28 of the Local Government Act (1988) went so far as to make it illegal for local authorities to intentionally promote homosexuality or the acceptability of homosexuality (as described in the Act) as 'a pretended relationship' (in other words a family relationship).

Similar contradictions are reflected in the government's approach to Britain's record of the highest teenage conception and motherhood rates in Western Europe (Cabinet Office 1998, Dollomore 1989, Hudson and Ineichen 1991). Teenage mothers are a particularly poverty-striken group and are considered by New Labour as socially excluded (Bradshaw and Millar 1991, Millar 1994, Mann and Roseneil 1999, Social Exclusion Unit 1999). Caring for children at such a young age can be seen as a deprivation of young women's rights as a citizen to a full education and the freedom to make life choices. Yet despite such realities, as Fox Harding (1999) points out, government education circulars in the late 1980s and 1990s cautioned teachers against giving contraceptive advice to under-16s without parental knowledge or consent even though a major study of 37 countries found that adolescent pregnancy rates are lower in countries where there is greater availability of contraceptive services and sex education (Jones et al. 1985). Similarly, a more recent study of the World Health Organisation (Baldo et al. 1993) indicated that knowledge of sex and contraception does not encourage or increase sexual activity among the young but may, in fact, be instrumental in delaying sexual activity and promoting safer sex.

Rather than addressing the inadequacy of sex education and the lack of choices available to young women, a high degree of consensus developed among policy-makers in hostility towards single parents, and, in particular, to unmarried mothers who were seen as a particular burden on the state. Such women were periodically attacked by politicians for 'jumping the Council housing queue', deliberately becoming pregnant in order to do so, and being 'wedded to welfare'. Mann and Roseneil (1994) analysed the ways that single parents have been blamed for what Charles Murray (1990, 1994), American right-wing social scientist, depicted as the disintegration of the nuclear family, which he saw as the principal source of social unrest and rising crime. Murray gained much publicity in England by propagating the idea that the rise in single mothers is linked to the threat of an 'underclass', whose three characteristics are illegitimacy, violent crime and unemployment. The link between illegitimacy (i.e. fatherless families) and crime, however, is far from proven. It is the presence of family discord which seems to be far more related to crime rather than the presence or absence of the mother or father from the home (Brown 1998).

Although teenagers today, according to a statistical analysis by Corlyon and McGuire (1997), are far less likely to have a baby than 20 years ago, New Labour continued to target them and announced a 10-year strategy to halve the rate of teenage pregnancies by 2010. The Social Exclusion Unit (1999), set up by the government to address problems of poverty and social exclusion, published a special report arguing that pregnancy prevents young women from gaining an education and has implications for both themselves and their children's ability to participate fully as citizens in society. Although single parenthood is associated with poverty and can be seen as connected to social exclusion in a number of respects (such as the interruption of schooling, further social exclusion from the work force, and transmission of poverty to children), for some young women, parenthood may well give them more status than employment without prospects.

So, if the overall numbers of teenage mothers are decreasing, why is the government defining them as a 'socially excluded group' and setting targets to reduce their numbers? It seems likely that the real concern is how to limit the rise of single-parent households. The proportion of single mothers is increasing overall, with young fathers appearing to take a peripheral role in childcare, even when they are unemployed. This poses problems both for the state – in so far as single mothers are usually on benefit – and for the future of the traditional heterosexual family. According to Castells (1999), single-parent families are the fastest growing category in the United States, followed by single people and then by couples without children, where today only 25 per cent fit the model of the traditional family (or married couple and children).

The contradictions implicit in addressing sexuality education at the same time as supporting the traditional family, however, are still evident. I remember the primary school class which my son attended, at least half of whom were from single-parent families, being asked to write about a 'family outing' and all the children fabricating images of 'ideal' families for the teacher. The significance of this for citizenship rights is that the potential to address the real problems that emerge in a rapidly changing society is lost. There is a vagueness about the role of schools in relation to such issues and concern about the lack of measures to improve the availability of contraception, in particular with regard to providing contraceptive advice to young people (*Guardian*, 15 June 1999). There is anxiety that the new guidance on prescribing contraception to under 16s will require health professionals to discuss 'the arguments for delaying sexual activity'. This is reminiscent of comments made by Tessa Jowell, Public Health Minister, who suggested in 1998 that under-age girls requesting contraceptives from the doctor should be given a lecture on the dangers of promiscuity (Nicoll 1998).

How can schools intervene?

As we have seen, the concept of citizenship is closely associated with the institutionalisation of heterosexual as well as male privilege (Richardson 1998). Citizenship education should, therefore, begin with a critique of 'the gender order' (Connell 1987) whereby the social, legal and institutional processes through which citizenship rights are established and maintained can be exposed as gendered. If the subject of sexuality is to be addressed effectively, citizenship education needs to include an awareness of gendered power relations which create *the constraints on autonomy and choice.*

Second, citizenship education should address current debates about what constitutes the rights of citizenship. It is argued that the right to choose and express your sexuality is a basic human right. In this sense certain groups such as lesbians or gay men have been denied equal social benefits as married couples (Evans 1993, Richardson 1998).[3]

Sexuality has been conspicuously absent in citizenship education initiatives.[4] As we have seen, the remit of sex education remains severely limited and it fails to address the complexity of the way sex gender relations are structured. It is here that citizenship education in the broad sense could be a crucial tool for improving sex education. Citizenship in this sense is seen as a set of rights, where educating young men and women about the way sexual identities are constructed, about sexual behaviour/orientation and contraception, and about parenting responsibilities should be considered as important as the mechanics of contraceptive devices. Issues of responsibility and moral choice are mentioned in the government reports on citizenship education (see Advisory Group report 1998) but not related to questions of sexual power relations. It is not enough, for example, to give young men and women information about contraception without examining the social context in which negotiation between young women and men takes place in regard to its use and the power relations between them. A consideration of Gilligan's (1982) *In a Different Voice*, where the forms of male and female moral reasoning were compared, would be a beginning. Gilligan contrasted the reasoning of teenage girls and boys when judging moral dilemmas concerning whether or not to have an abortion. By analysing their replies, she showed moral reasoning arose from conflicting responsibilities rather than absolute rights. Previous analysis by psychologists had assumed that boys reached a higher level of moral reasoning (by referring to abstract principles as the 'right to life'). Discussing such issues in citizenship education would enable pupils to grasp the way discourses around sex are gendered and reflect power differences between the sexes.

Challenging gender regimes in schools is no easy task, but there have been some developments. In the 1980s a few schools had developed whole school policies on various forms of discrimination, and by the close of the 1990s most schools had coherent policy requirements operating across all areas of institutional practice (see Arnot et al. 1998, Smith and Sharpe 1994). Some schools are developing more active policies to reduce sexism, racism and bullying, and various resource packs have been developed. *Hands off*, for example, is a resource pack for teachers and youth workers to facilitate workshops with 11–14 year olds on stereotyping, bullying and domestic violence, developed by Welsh Women's Aid (see Women's Unit report 1999: 47). However, there needs to be much more recognition of the contexts in which bullying takes place. Complaints about, and indicators of, bullying need to be heard and recorded. Effective and appropriate liberating action needs to be taken. Schools need to recognise the way they perpetuate patterns of dominance and subordination, and conformity and exclusion.

The Advisory Group on Education for Citizenship and the Teaching of Democracy in Schools (1998) has examined the most effective way of providing citizenship education. The three strands identified by the committee were social and moral responsibility, political literacy and community involvement. In 1999, the Advisory Group developed a national framework as part of the wider review of the national curriculum which led to proposals by the Qualifications and Curriculum Authority (QCA) for citizenship education. These proposals argued that citizenship education should be combined with personal, social and health education (PSHE), within which sex education is now taught. Both reports address relationship issues in terms such as 'encouraging self respect' and 'non-conflictual conflict resolution'. They aim to help develop communication and negotiation skills in a range of contexts including citizenship and human rights education.

A possible approach that could be introduced into schools under this rubric involves more participatory methods of dispute resolution. A useful model is that suggested by prison abolitionists of the ideal of restorative justice or the setting up of 'alternative dispute settlements' (Braithwaite and Daly 1994). This conference model allows the victim to have representatives to urge the victim's view of events, in which a feminist or racial ethnic standpoint can be accommodated. So, for example, if a pupil had been bullied, the victim's definition of harm or threat would be at the centre of proceedings. She/he is transformed from the humiliated victim to an active claimant, identifying her/his own requirement and drawing her/his own lines in future contacts with the perpetrator.[5] This could well be linked with other community dispute settlements involving violence in the family, issues of equal pay, reproductive rights, and more conventional political disputes around, for example, environmental issues. Role-play and drama could be used effectively to bring to life the way power is gendered.

In summary, citizenship education offers an opportunity to develop more integrated and critical approaches to gender relations of schooling. It provides an opportunity for schools to develop whole school policies which would address problems of sexism, homophobia, bullying and violence which are endemic in the present structure of hegemonic heterosexuality. It is only when citizenship education and sex education adopt a wider framework which problematises the relations of power underlying sexual relations that progress can be made.

Notes

1   A hundred 15–17-year-old girls from a range of ethnic and social class backgrounds at four comprehensive schools in London were interviewed and group discussions were held (see Lees, 1993). The girls were asked about five areas of their lives: their views of same-sex friends, opposite-sex friends, school, sexual relations and marriage, and how they saw the future. Marriage was seen as anything but romantic – rather it brought in its train subordination and loneliness. Yet despite this, most of them saw a future without marriage as unimaginable. Only three girls said they did not want to get married.

2   Indeed a UK government report published in the late 1980s, the Macdonald Inquiry Report, revealed the connections between a school's perpetuation of a white supremacist ethos and its failure to deal with harassment (Kelly 1991).

3   This should not, in Rahman's (1998) view, lead groups to seek equal rights (to marry for example) since the equal rights agenda takes the normality of heterosexuality as given and hence fails to question the legitimacy of its institutionalisation.

4   For example, the Advisory Group on Education for Citizenship and the Teaching of Democracy in Schools (1998) and the QCA's Review of the National Curriculum (1999).

5   One can see why feminists are such a threat and so often reviled in schools and in the wider society. They are not only arguing that categories should be broken down, but that female subordination should be opposed. Examples of resistance to such strategies among teachers are given by Cunnison (1989) and Kenway (1998).

Bibliography

Advisory Group on Education for Citizenship and the Teaching of Democracy in Schools (1998) London: Qualifications and Curriculum Authority.

Amos, V. and Parmar, P. (1981) 'Resistances and responses, the experiences of black girls in Britain', in A. McRobbie and T. McCabe (eds) *Feminism for Girls: an adventure story*, London: Routledge and Kegan Paul.

Arnot, M., Araújo, H., Deliyanni-Kouimtzi, K., Rowe, G. and Tomé, A. (1996) 'Teachers, gender and discourses of citizenship', *International Studies in Sociology of Education*, 6, 1: 3–35.

Arnot, M., Gray, J., James, M. and Ruddock J. (1998) *Recent Research on Gender and Educational Performance*, Office for Standards in Education: London: HMSO.

Baldo, A., Aggleton, P. and Slutkin, E. (1993) *Does Sex Education Lead to Earlier or Increased Sexual Activity in Youth?*, Report PO-DO2–3444, World Health Organisation.

Beynon, J. (1989) 'A school for men: an ethnographic case study of routine violence in schooling', in L. Barton and S. Walker (eds) *Politics and the Processes of Schooling*, Milton Keynes: Open University Press, pp. 191–217.

Bradshaw, J. and Millar, J. (1991) *Lone Parent Families in the UK*, London: DSS Research Report No. 6, HMSO.

Braithwaite, J. and Daly, K. (1994) 'Masculinities, violence and communitarian control', in T. Newburn and E. Stanko (eds) *Just Boys Doing Business: men, masculinities and crime*, London: Routledge.

Brown, S. (1998) *Understanding Youth and Crime*, Buckingham: Open University Press.

Burton, S., Kitzinger, J. with Kelly, L. and Regan, L. (1998) *Young People's Attitudes Toward Violence Sex and Relationships*, Executive Summary, Zero Tolerance Charitable Trust.

Cain, M. (1989) 'Introduction: feminist transgress criminology', in M. Cain (ed.) *Growing Up Good*, London: Sage.

Canaan, J. (1998) 'Is "doing nothing" just boys' play?', in K. Daly and L. Maher (eds) *Criminology at the Crossroads*, Oxford: Oxford University Press.

Carby, H. (1982) 'Schooling in Babylon', in P. Gilroy et al. (eds.) *The Empire Strikes Back: race and racism in 1970s Britain*, London: Hutchinson.

Castells, M. (1999) *Flows, Networks, Identities in Critical Education in the New Information Age*, Oxford: Rowman and Littlefield.

Connell, R. W. (1987) *Gender and Power*, Cambridge: Polity Press.

Connell, R. W. (1989) 'Cool guys, swots and wimps: the interplay of masculinity and education', *Oxford Review of Education*, 15, 3: 291–303.

Connell, R. W. (1995) *Masculinities*, Oxford: Polity Press.

Connell, R. W. (1996) 'Teaching the boys: new research on masculinity and gender strategies for schools', *Teacher College Record* 98, 2: winter, Columbia University.

Connolly, P. (1995) 'All lads together?: racism, masculinity and multicultural anti-racist strategies in a primary school', *International Studies in Sociology of Education*, 4, 2: 191–211.

Corlyon, J. and McGuire, C. (1997) *Young Parents in Public Care*, London: National Children's Bureau.

Cunnison, S. (1989) 'Gender joking in the classroom', in *Teachers, Gender and Careers*, London: Falmer Press.

Currie, E. (1985) *Confronting Crime*, New York: Pantheon.

Davies, B. (1989) *Frogs and Snails and Feminist Tales*, Sydney: Allen and Unwin.

Davies, B. (1996) 'Constructing and deconstructing through critical literacy', *Gender and Education*, Special Issue on Masculinities and Education.

Delphy, C. and Leonard, D. (1992) *Familiar Exploitation: a new analysis of marriage in contemporary western societies*, Cambridge: Polity.

Dollomore, G. (1989) 'Live births in 1988', *Population Trends*, 57: 20–6.

Duncan, N. (1999) *Sexual Bullying in UK Secondary Schools*, London: Routledge.

Durham, M. (1991) *Sex and Politics: the family and morality in the Thatcher years*, Basingstoke: Macmillan.

Edwards, J. and Fogelman, K. (eds) (1993) *Developing Citizenship in the Curriculum*, London: David Fulton Publishers.

Evans, D. (1993) *Sexual Citizenship*, London: Routledge.

Fine, M. (1988) 'Sexuality, schooling, and adolescent females: the missing discourse of desire', *Harvard Educational Review*, 58: 29–53.

Fox Harding, L. (1999) '"Family values" and Conservative government policy', in G. Jagger and C. Wright (eds) *Changing Family Values*, London: Routledge.

Gershuny, J., Godwin, M. and Jones, S. (1994) 'The domestic labour revolution: a process of lagged adaptation', in M. Anderson, F. Bechofer and J. Gershuny (eds) *The Social and Political Economy of the Household*, Oxford: Oxford University Press.

Gilligan, C. (1982) *In a Different Voice*, Cambridge, Mass.: Harvard University Press.

Gould, C. (1984) 'Private rights and public virtues: women, the family and democracy', in C. Gould (ed.) *Beyond Domination*, New Jersey: Rowman & Littlefield, pp. 3–21.

Griffin, C. and Lees, S. (eds) 1997 Special Issue: Masculinities and Education, *Gender and Education*, 9: 1.

Halson, J. (1989) 'The sexual harassment of young women', in L. Holly (ed.) *Girls and Sexuality*, Buckingham: Open University Press.

Hanson, B. and Patrick, P. (1995) 'Towards some understanding of sexuality education', in S. Inman and M. Buck (eds) *Adding Value?: schools' responsibility for pupils' personal development*, Exeter: Trentham Books.

Hearn, J. and Morgan, D. (eds) (1990) *Men, Masculinities and Social Theory*, London: Unwin Hyman.

Holland, J., Ramazanoglu, C., Sharpe, S. and Thomson, R. (1991) *Pressured Pleasure*, 47 Dalmeny Rd, N7: Tufnell Press.

Holland, J., Ramazanoglu, C., Sharpe, S. and Thomson, R. (1998) *The Man in the Head*, 47 Dalmeny Rd, N7: Tufnell Press.

Hudson, B. (1998) 'Restorative justice: the challenge of sexual and racial violence', *Journal of Law and Society* 25, 2, June: 247.

Hudson, F. and Ineichen, B. (1991) *Taking it Lying Down: sexuality and teenage motherhood*, London: Macmillan.

Inman, S. and Buck, M. (1995) *Adding Value: schools' responsibility for pupils' personal development*, Stoke on Trent, Staffordshire.

Jackson, D. and Salisbury, J. (1996) 'Why should secondary schools take working with boys seriously?', *Gender and Education* 8, 1: 103–115.

Jones, E. F. et al. (1985) 'Teenage pregnancy in developed countries: determinants and policy implications', *Family Planning Perspectives* 17, 2: 53–63.

Kelly, E. (1991) 'Bullying and racial and sexual harassment in schools', *Multicultural Teaching* 10, 1.

Kelly, E. (1993) 'Gender issues in education for citizenship', in G. K. Vernon and P. D. Penfrey (eds) *Cross Cultural Contexts*, London: Falmer Press.

Kelly, L. (1992) 'Not in front of the children: responding to right wing agendas on sexuality and education', in M. Arnot and L. Barton (eds) *Voicing Concerns: sociological perspectives of contemporary education reforms*, Bristol: Triangle.

Kenway, J. (1995) 'Masculinities in schools: under siege, on the defensive and under reconstruction?', *Discourse*, 16, 1: 58–79.

Kenway, J. (1998) *Answering Back: girls, boys and feminism in schools*, London: Routledge.

Koss, M. and Harvey, M. (1991) *The Rape Victim: clinical and community interventions*, London: Sage.

Lees, S. (1986) *Losing Out: sexuality and adolescent girls*, London: Unwins.

Lees, S. (1993) *Sugar and Spice*, Harmondsworth: Penguin.

Lees, S. (1997) *Ruling Passions: sexual violence, reputation and the law*, Buckingham, Open University Press.

Lees, S. (1999) 'Will boys be left on the shelf', in C. Wright and G. Jagger (eds) *Changing Family Values*, London: Routledge.

Levy, B. (1991) *Dating Violence: young women in danger*, Seattle: The Seal Press.

Lloyd, S. (1991) 'The darkside of courtship: aggression and sexual exploitation', *Family Relations*, 40: 14–20.

Mac an Ghaill, M. (1994) *The Making of Men: masculinities, sexualities and schooling*, Buckingham, Open University Press.

Mac an Ghaill, M. (ed.) (1996) *Understanding Masculinities*, Buckingham: Open University Press.

Mahony, P. (1985) *Schools for the Boys*, London: Hutchinson.

Mann, K. and Roseneil, S. (1994) ' "Some mothers do 'ave 'em": backlash and the gender politics of the underclass debate', *Journal of Gender Studies*, 3, 3: 79–98.

Mann, K. and Roseneil, S. (1999) 'Poor choices?: gender, agency and the underclass debate', in G. Jagger and C. Wright (eds) *Changing Family Values*, London: Routledge.

McMahon, A. (1999) *Taking Care of Men*, Cambridge: Cambridge University Press.

McRobbie, A. (1978) 'Working-class girls and the culture of femininity in women's studies groups', in Centre for Contemporary Cultural Studies (eds) *Women Take Issue: aspects of women's subordination*, London: Hutchinson.

Messerschmidt, J. (1993) *Masculinities and Crime*, Lanham, MD: Rowman and Littlefield.

Millett, K. (1972) *Sexual Politics*, London: Abacus.

Millar, J. (1994) 'State, family and personal responsibility: the changing balance for lone mothers in the UK', *Feminist Review*, 48, Autumn.

Muncie, J., Wetherell, M., Dallos, R., and Cochrane, A. (eds) (1995) *Understanding the Family*, London: Sage.

Murray, C. (1990) *The Emergent British Underclass*, London: IEA Health and Welfare Unit.

Murray, C. (1994) *Underclass: the crisis deepens*, London: IEA Choice in Welfare Series, No. 20.

Nicoll, R. (1998) 'Underage sex lectures by GPs', *Guardian*, 19 January.

Osler, A. (1995) 'Introduction: citizenship, schooling and teacher education', in A. Osler, H. Rathenow and H. Starkey (eds) *Teaching for Citizenship in Europe*, Exeter: Trentham Books, 3–15.

Pateman, C. (1988) *The Sexual Contract*, Oxford: Polity.

Pitts, J. and Smith, P. (1995) *Preventing School Bullying*, Policy Research Group, Crime Detection and Prevention Series, Paper 63.

Prokhovnik, R. (1998) 'Public and private citizenship: from gender invisibility to feminist inclusiveness', *Feminist Review* No. 60, autumn: 84–104.

Qualifications and Curriculum Authority (May-July 1999) *The Review of the National Curriculum in England: the Secretary of State's proposals*, London, DEE.

Rahman, M. (1998) 'Sexuality and rights: problematising lesbian and gay politics', in T. Carver and V. Mottier, *Politics of Sexuality*, London: Routledge.

Rich, A. (1980) 'Compulsory sexuality and lesbian existence', in C. Stimpson and S. Person (eds), *Women Sex, and Sexuality*, Chicago: University of Chicago Press.

Richardson, D. (1996) 'Heterosexuality and social theory', in D. Richardson (ed.) *Theorising Heterosexuality*, Buckingham: Open University Press.

Richardson, D. (1998) 'Sexuality and citizenship', *Sociology*, Vol. 32, No. 1, February.

Roscoe, B. and Kelley, T. (1986) 'Dating violence among high school students', *Psychology*, 23, 1: 53–59.

Rowbotham, S. (1986) 'Feminism and democracy', in D. Held and C. Pollitt (eds) *New Forms of Democracy*, London: Sage.

Sex Education Forum (1992) *A Framework for School Sex Education*, National Children's Bureau.

Siltanen, J. and Stanworth, M. (1984) *Women and the Public Sphere*, London: Hutchinson.

Skeggs, B. (1994) 'Refusing to be civilised: "race, sexuality and power"', in H. Afshar and M. Maynard (eds) *The Dynamics of Race and Gender*, London: Taylor and Francis.

Smith P. and Sharpe, E. (eds) (1994) *School Bullying: insights and perspectives*, London: Routledge.

Social Exclusion Unit (1999) *Teenage Pregnancy*, London: Cabinet Office.

Social Exclusion Unit (1999) *Women's Unit Fact Sheet 2*, London.

Spaid, E. (1993) 'Justice: young activist defends abused woman', *Christian Science Monitor*, 85: 12–13.

Tattum, D. P. and Lane, D. A. (1989) *Bullying in Schools*, Stoke on Trent: Trentham Books.

Thomson, R. (1994) 'Moral rhetoric and public health pragmatism: the recent politics of sex education', *Feminist Review*, 48, Autumn.

Thomson, R. and Holland, J. (1994) 'Young women and safer (hetero) sex', in S. Wilkinson and C. Kitzinger (eds) *Women and Health: feminist* perspectives, London: Taylor & Francis.

Wilson, M. and Daly, M. (1998) 'Sexual rivalry and sexual conflict: recurring themes in fatal conflicts', *Theoretical Criminology*, 2, 3: 291–311.

Women's Unit (1999) *Living Without Fear*, Cabinet Office: Home Office.

16 The civil school and civil society

Gender, democracy and development

Lynn Davies

Shifts in gender regimes and the processes which lead towards democracy always involve transformations in power relations. The movements are interlinked, in that tackling gender injustice can be central to major social concerns of peace and the development of civil society. In moves towards democratisation which are occurring in many parts of the world, the role of education becomes at one and the same time more conspicuous and more complex. In school contexts, the desire for democratisation is often becoming tied up with education for citizenship. In theory, such education should include an analysis of how women and men may – historically or currently – be differentially positioned with regard to their roles or rights as citizens. In practice, there may be different sets of discourses operating such that the intersections between democracy, citizenship, rights and gender are not fully revealed. This apparent distinctiveness is sometimes symbolised internationally through different agencies or non-governmental organisations, which deal primarily with themes such as 'pro-democracy', women in development, human rights, or adult literacy.

This chapter focuses on the organisation and management of schooling with the aim of outlining, in this context, how international agendas of democratisation and citizenship are linked to questions about gender equity and feminism. The key themes I shall explore are those of conflict and power. The questions of who is a citizen and who is included in the state are crucial contemporary concerns not only with regard to nationalism, but also to civil war, violence and ethnic cleansing. Political instabilities in other parts of the world affect us all, and education for peace and for the formation of civil society are not simply national issues. Therefore, in the first section, I examine the invisibility of gender in writings on democracy and democratic education. I then outline what could or should be at the heart of feminist citizenship in the creation of an effective school. I focus on, for example, representative models of citizenship, participation, educational institutions as micropolitical cultures, effective schools, and conflict and education. I conclude with a discussion of how to promote what I call a 'civil school'.

The exclusion of women from democracy

A major problem in Europe is the continued disregard for concerns about gender in writings on democracy, and the uncritical acceptance of some version of democracy as uniformly desirable. For example, Baechler's (1995) book *Democracy: an analytical survey* begins in a promisingly open way:

> [I]t is difficult to reach a common understanding of what the word means. Democracy is a free regime? Undoubtedly. But what is freedom? A regime of equality? Perhaps. But how many crimes have been committed in the name of equality? A regime of majority rule? And suppose the majority favours absurdities and outrageous acts? And, to begin with, is democracy a political regime, a form of social organisation, a state of mind or a set of behaviour patterns? Or is it all of them and still more?
>
> (Baechler 1995: 9)

And yet when we turn to the first chapter on the nature of the political order we find that the first heading is 'Man'. 'Since we are trying to define the "good" political regime, we begin with man, because if the regime is good, it is good for everybody. Thus, we must adopt the viewpoint of all men, that is of man' (13). Admittedly, the book is translated from the French, but what is UNESCO (the publisher) doing to permit such language in the mid-1990s? More significantly, how can the subsequent discussion of peace, violence, virtue and equality ignore gender?

An equally astonishing invisibility is in Giddens' influential book *The Third Way: the renewal of Social Democracy* (1998). There is one reference to women participating in the voluntary sector, and a discussion of 'equality of the sexes' in the section on the 'democratic family'. His analyses of globalisation, of the state and civil society and of poverty contain no references to gender. This is the case despite two decades of feminist analysis which reveals, for example, the differential impact of structural adjustment policies and the operation of markets on women, and explores why women are still over-represented in the poorer sections of society (Stromquist 1999).

Such sidelining of gender concerns in the writings on democracy has a long tradition, and is an international phenomenon. In her book on *Gender in Third World Politics*, Waylen (1996) convincingly illustrates how the conventional social science literature on democracy, democratisation and the role of social movements in transitions has, by and large, had little to say about gender relations. Top-down approaches which define democracy as competitive electoral politics ignore the activities of women outside the formal political arena. Even analyses which concentrate on the activities of social movements, and the challenge to militaristic rule, often remain ungendered despite the fact that the majority of participants are women.

It therefore becomes important to draw upon a wider definition of 'the political' when thinking about democracy and gender relations in education, and return to the debate about the public and private sphere (Davies 1984).

As we know, policy areas linked to the public sphere such as state-defined politics, war, foreign policy, international trade, resources extraction and long-distance communication have excluded women. Instead, women feature in areas related to the private sphere of reproduction, welfare, housing, health, and education. In her analysis of feminist theory and international relations, Sylvester (1994: 16) identified the 'evacuation' of women from the theoretical fields of international relations:

> Contractarian liberalism excluded 'women' from the originative myth of civic society and installed a notion of democracy that put an imprimatur on pre-existing conditions of sexual (and, for a while, racial) slavery . . . 'Women' still does not fit the image of combatant citizens in most western societies.

This absence of women begs the question of whether we need to seek out – or establish – some permanent international principles of democracy which would be non-sexist or even anti-sexist, or whether democracy can only ever be the contemporary and regional construction placed upon it. Is democracy an umbrella word, debased through over-use, and an excuse for continued invisibility of women's concerns through the emphasis on 'the people'?

Democracy has become one of the current indices of human development in a country. The 1995 UNDP (United Nations Development Program) Human Development Index has 'participation in decision-making in the public sphere' as one of its indicators. Gender equality is often, however, a separate index so that gender and democracy are presented as additive rather than interwoven. In some reports, the two concepts are juxtaposed. For example, the UNICEF report *The State of the World's Children* (1995: 49) speaks of the 'Kerala factor'. Within India, while the State of Kerala falls below the average in India for wealth in social progress, it is considerably more advanced:

> Along with Kerala's long history of progressive social policies, two of the most powerful factors are a tradition of participatory democracy and a strong commitment to female education. Almost all girls complete secondary as well as primary education.

Yet it is significant that the focus here is on *completion* of education rather than the *content* of that education.

An analysis of this UNICEF report also exposes an important discourse. It draws attention to the World Bank's admission in 1993 that a major redirection of public resources is needed and that such change would be difficult, since an array of interest groups may stand to lose. The UNICEF report lists at length the vested interests leading to particular economic decisions and donor aid priorities, for example, the imported over the locally produced, the expansion of airlines over the improvement of local bus services, central teaching hospitals over local health centres, universities over primary schools. While recognising the power in these vested interests, and flaws in democracies, the report settles firmly on democracy as the only corrective to persistent economic distortions and injustices in a society.

> Despite the setbacks, the march towards democracy across so much of the world in recent years therefore represents the beginning of a change which, if sustained, could fundamentally alter the prospects for development in the years ahead. But this is a two-way relationship. Democracy makes the sustained achievement of social goals more likely, and social progress makes more likely the survival and development of democracy.
>
> (UNICEF, 1995: 47)

It is this 'two-way relationship' between democracy and development which is the cornerstone of thinking about gender. The UNICEF report portrays women and children as *recipients* or victims of unjust or powerful interests; yet it does not enter the debate over the *composition* of those groups making socially unjust decisions. We do not know whether an equal gender balance in government, industry, aid agencies or religion would mean fairer decisions. However, attempting such equity would have to be at least an indicator of an adequately functioning democracy. Participation within, and outcomes of, democracy are therefore inextricably linked.

The invisibility of gender in democratic education

In terms of education, democratisation has been taken to mean a variety of things: equal access and education for all, a discourse of participation, or some notion of 'empowerment' for women (Davies 1994a). Rarely, however, is there a clear political definition which makes any kind of link between the democratic governance of a country and democratic processes in schools. Bunwaree (1997: 305), for example, in talking about the marginalisation of girls in Mauritius, writes:

> Mauritius, unlike a number of countries within the 'developing world' group, can boast of a democratic system of government but the quality of that democracy can be questioned. Mauritius is experiencing increasing pockets of poverty, exclusion and frustration by certain marginalised groups.

Her discussion of gender within schools, however, focuses on gender stereotyping of subjects and of textbooks, and on the dual labour market, but does not return directly to female participation in democracy or in structures of power. Her implication is that a 'quality' democracy would minimise social exclusion; but my concern would be whether it is sufficient in schools to aim at a 'gender-sensitive curriculum' or whether the governance of school and society should be tackled directly.

I have argued elsewhere that the state of gender relations in a school is a good benchmark for how effectively democracy has been embraced by that school (Davies 1994b; 1997a). Equity is not the same as democracy, as one refers to the achievement of social justice and the other to a political process, but they come together in the areas of equal rights and in access to participation in decision-making. The UNESCO book, *Introducing Democracy* (Beetham and Boyle 1995: 1), offers a conventional definition of democracy that links the two: 'Democracy ... entails the twin principles of popular control over collective decision-making and equality of rights in the exercise of that control.' A democratic school, therefore, would have mechanisms for both managing popular control and for monitoring whether there is equality of rights – including gender equality.

Much feminist analysis of gender disparity in education has focused on classrooms, interpersonal relations and curriculum at the expense of analysis of processes of decision-making and agenda-building in the organisation. Although there is a good deal of writing on women in educational management, there are few studies that link citizenship rights of pupils in the school to gender subordination. Different waves of feminism since the 1890s have, at times, tackled the nature of political organisation, for example, with radical feminism refusing formal delegated structures and stressing participation rather than representation. However, the emphasis within theory on consciousness and women's subjectivity has served in many cases to draw attention away from the basic political education necessary for students to understand how power can be legitimately used.

It is significant that Weiner's (1994) list of the 'demands of a feminist critical praxis' in education draws heavily on experience, reflexivity and change rather than on transforming an organisation. 'Feminist organizational practice grounded in equality, non-hierarchy and democracy' is demanded 'within the classroom' (1994: 130). However, the concern with democracy appears to remain at the classroom level. A feminist theory of citizenship in education must, therefore, begin with the notion of the *school* as a micropolitical organisation, and examine how students (and teachers) are organised for learning and living. Generating equal opportunities policies is not the same as seeing each student and teacher as a citizen of the school with an equal right to a voice, to a vote, to representation, to active responsibility and to a full understanding of how the collectivity works.

Feminist citizenship and effective schooling

Feminist citizenship would not initially focus on women, but on inclusion in the structures by which all can exercise their rights and responsibilities. The remainder of this paper argues that a feminist citizenship for education has four purposes:

1   to mount a critique of simple 'representative' models of citizen participation;
2   to analyse educational institutions as micropolitical sites of power;
3   to provide indicators of, and preconditions for, a gender-inclusive democratic institution; and
4   to confront major social issues such as conflict and violence and their relation to education.

I now take each of these in turn, beginning with the question of 'representation' of teachers.

Representative models of citizenship participation in schools

It could be argued that teachers, particularly female teachers, are not full citizens of the school. International research exposes large differences in the gender composition of the teaching workforce, from under 10 per cent of teachers in countries like Nepal to over 80 per cent in Seychelles; yet whatever the base, women become consistently under-represented as seniority increases, or as the age or status of the student increases (Davies and Gunawardena 1992). Their representation is important at four levels: so that both boys and girls see women in decision-making capacities; as a question of equal career rights for teachers; to query masculinist definitions of appropriate management; and finally to challenge male domination of the selection of school knowledge and curricula. It is not just in the interests of girls for women to hold educational power; it is in the interests of both sexes that there is progress towards democratic and radical education as a whole.

Our research into female teachers' under-representation in countries in Africa and South-East Asia (Davies and Gunawardena 1992) did not find differential qualifications as good predictors of future positions, although participation and selection for management training certainly was. The 'dual-role' thesis was also challenged: there were no significant sex differences in perceptions of a conflict between school careers and home life. Both men and women appeared to want the same things from the organisation, such as constructive criticism, recognition for doing a good job, social contact with colleagues and efficient administration that made their work smooth. Girls are often encouraged to choose teaching because it is a job which will fit in with family life. Contrary to this myth, we found that women did not primarily enter teaching for the long hours and holidays. Interestingly, neither sex seemed to put 'participation in management' as a high priority, an initial puzzle for us, although more men than women described management as a 'duty' for them.

The most convincing 'sex differences' found in this research were that:

- male teachers performed more of the administrative tasks in school in general;
- male teachers assumed more of the 'hard' and visible managerial tasks which anticipate public decision-making;
- male teachers were more confident (or arrogant?) about their capacity to do managerial tasks, *whether or not they actually performed them;*
- some male teachers utilised the dominant discourse of competition, material reward, and status.

Therefore, what emerged was not so much broad 'gender roles' but the actual workings of an institution where the management discourse was being 'captured' by men who saw life in competitive, hierarchical and status terms. The aim of equity interventions for teachers, therefore, should not necessarily be 'entryism' – getting more women into management – but challenging existing concepts of how schools should be run, and in whose interests. Many men are equally disadvantaged and frustrated by the typical bureaucratic pyramid which is the conventional way of seeing workplaces and rewards for work. More importantly, pupils are disadvantaged by the way management and careers are conceptualised. The reward for good teaching is often to leave the classroom and pupils and enter 'management'. There is no guarantee that good teachers make good administrators, nor that women managers necessarily bring superior styles with them. Women can be just as authoritarian or bureaucratic as men, and single-sex girls' schools can be just as rigid and non-transparent as single-sex boys' schools. Structures are needed which enable good teachers to stay teaching and which ensure full participation and ownership of decisions, whether by staff or students. Such structures also would prevent intentional and unintentional discrimination in terms of who assumes which sorts of power and authority. The summative term for this is democracy.

A gender analysis within educational management theory or practice is not, therefore, about identifying fundamental differences in teachers or administrators, or to go down the blind alley of the 'women in leadership' analyses. It is not about providing female access to a male-dominated or male-defined occupational hierarchy. Instead it is about locating what women and men teachers bring to education and what they want from the school or workplace. It is about returning to a sociology of work, and arguing for a management ethos that takes account of the 'total' individual with all their roles in and out of school. The areas for concern are: the vertical division of labour (who occupies which rank); the horizontal division of labour (the academic/pastoral split, the science/arts divide); the allocation of mentoring, encouragement and in-service training; the provision of flexibility so that family concerns do not induce guilt or cover-ups; and the dynamics of meetings and discussion which decide informal power processes. As I have argued elsewhere (Davies 1997b), models of 'leaderless' schools, or at least those with rotational heads, share power more equitably and avoid tokenism or quotas for females in senior positions.

Further evidence that a feminist management stance is not just about enabling women to enter higher positions in schools, or to 'participate' more in education, comes from analyses of destinations after formal education. The statistics on the representation of women in executive and legislative bodies, in positions of authority on management and in academic leadership, do not indicate a positive relationship between the participation of women in higher education and access to such positions (UNDP 1995). I would argue that this is, at least in part, because the education individuals have received does not actively tackle politics or political skills and duties. Jones (1997) reports on non-formal education in small island countries, and found that programmes that focused purely on technical skills were less successful. Women acknowledged that they needed new attitudes, business skills and the confidence to break into rapidly emerging centralised economies: 'they need to participate in decision-making at the national level, but expressed frustration that they did not have the skills and political support to achieve this' (1997: 285).

The famous women leaders in India, Bangladesh and Sri Lanka indeed came to power through the democratic process, but belonged to relatively elite families; the educational level of the population or their own educational attainments were irrelevant to their emergence to power (Jayaweera 1997). I am therefore uneasy about this currently popular notion of the 'glass ceiling' for women: it implies that women have moved rapidly upwards only to find a one-off barrier at some point. Instead, I would argue that the process of incorporation into or exclusion from the polity begins very early, and schools are responsible not just for academic attainments but for orientations to power and politics.

Sometimes this may mean examining, perhaps in the history classroom, previous pre-colonial patterns of community power. For example, Waylen has an interesting discussion of the female networks of organisation and solidarity among the Igbo of Southern Nigeria:

> The women had their own structures of power which dealt with issues which concerned them, including the regulation of markets. These structures were headed by a female official, the *omu*, who had her own council of elders paralleling that of the male official, the *obi*. Meetings named *mikiri* were held where women could resolve issues arising from their roles particularly as traders, but also as farmers, wives and mothers. Women could also resort to taking sanctions both on other women and on men to resolve individual or collective grievances. 'Making war on' or 'sitting on a man' – surrounding his hut and protesting at his behaviour – was recognized by men as a legitimate and effective course of action for women to take, as was the strike – refusing to cook meals and provide other services for men.
>
> (1996: 52)

I have quoted this in full because it demonstrates both the strength and fragility of political life: female networks were very powerful and innovative, but were overtaken by colonial patterns. Education in the political process has to be a continuous effort, which in the formal sector means that it must begin at the primary level and continue through to higher education.

Outside the formal sector, interesting work is being conducted with women, by agencies such as the British Council, to train in advocacy and political skills. In Jordan, for example, women have been trained to manage an election campaign as candidates, campaign managers, press officers, fund-raisers and co-ordinators. The participants also received a 'candidate kit' which included criteria for choosing campaign team members, and useful guidelines for organising a grassroots campaign. Also in the 'kit' were tips on preparing press releases and effective television and radio presentations. (British Council 1997b). The Women's College in Cape Town, South Africa, takes a similar approach in preparing female candidates at election time. Literacy programmes (using participatory Freirian techniques) for women in Brazil have also shown a degree of success in increasing their control over their daily lives, fighting to improve conditions of employment and entering community politics (Stromquist 1997). Yet how far are such initiatives confined only to women attending non-formal education? I turn now to the political nature of formal schooling.

Schools as micropolitical sites of power

In order to see who becomes incorporated as citizens in school, a micro-political analysis is needed which examines both formal and informal organisations. In terms, first, of the formal structure, schools the world over show features of typical bureaucracies, demonstrating both vertical and horizontal divisions (Harber 1989; Harber and Davies 1997). In theory, bureaucracies should be exemplary sites for equity. An 'ideal type' bureaucracy in a civil service avoided the favouritism and personalisation of monarchies or feudal systems – often patrimonial ones. 'Scientific' or 'classical' management theorists in North America in the early 1900s were firm advocates of bureaucratisation, attempting to make organisations run as efficiently as machines (Morgan 1986). To achieve targets and goals, rationality and efficiency were the key, with workers selected on the basis of their ability to do a predetermined job in the most efficient way. Nowadays, the emphasis on merit, on impersonal relations and on unified rules ought to mean that neither men nor women are able to gain advantage because of traditional power.

However, it would appear that educational bureaucracies and the way they are now interpreted remain good sites for the play of gender power. Many are not bureaucracies in the 'ideal' sense, but use the trappings of rules and conformity in order to mask the play of power. The hidden gendering of bureaucracies and male versions of 'rationality' were revealed over two decades ago (Kanter 1977) and have indeed been strengthened in contemporary management discourse.

Ianello (1992), in her book, *Decisions Without Hierarchy: feminist interventions in organisation theory and practice* contrasts the typical line management with a more radical and equitable circular model of an organisation. In the circle there is a combination of permanent elected co-ordinators and other positions which are rotational. Critical decisions are reserved for the entire membership; routine decisions are delegated horizontally to the co-ordinators. Routine decisions have the potential to become critical, in which case they can be reconsidered by the entire group. No one works 'for' anyone else, although co-ordinators have additional authority in their areas of expertise. Clearly, this would need much unpacking in a large organisation such as a school, but it is an interesting concept which has worked well in collectives, and makes us question the inevitability of lines and pyramids.

There are indeed times when a strong direction is needed, particularly in times of crisis or externally driven change, and it would be foolish to say that all decisions should be democratic, consultative or participative. The point made in our book on *School Management and Effectiveness in Developing Countries* (Harber and Davies 1997) is that many apparent bureaucracies are in fact bureaucratic facades. They are hierarchical without being necessarily efficient, power is concentrated at the top without decisions being made, and subordinates are frightened to break rules while superiors mismanage and bend rules to their advantage. This has clear implications for an understanding of greater hierarchies in education. Even apparently democratic structures within bureaucracies, such as committees, may mask the fact that the 'gate-keepers' are predominantly male. In her study of teacher education in Botswana, Mannathoko (1995) explored the flatter 'professional' bureaucracy of the University. A series of committees replaced top-down management, in a structure thought to represent full participation. Yet the reality was that policies, plans and regulations had to go through the various committees and as they moved up the ladder and got cleared, they did not necessarily go back down again. The top (predominantly male) management could quite easily use the committees to delay or block implementation of policies and programmes they did not favour. This was done by arguing that proper procedures had not been followed or consultation had not been done.

Is bureaucracy then used as a cloak for authoritarianism (management by decree) and/or patriarchy (the exercise of power through the 'father' head)? Clues to the latter can also be found in thinking about how far the organisational ethos either *prevents or sustains* abuses of power such as violence (bullying or corporal punishment) and sexual harassment. This leads on to the micropolitics of informal cultures.

In theory, effective schools teach both sexes the rights and responsibilities of a citizen. Responsibility for reproduction and sexuality, for example, is supposed to be part of educational socialisation, for school is one of the few places which is thought to question the traditional cultures which reproduce power relations. Research in Uganda on the results of AIDs education, for example, shows that it is not enough to teach the facts about AIDs; teachers must simultaneously empower young people, especially girls, to think about sexual behaviour, and who controls it (Mirembe 1998). For example, a particular feature of Mirembe's ethnographic research in Uganda was the exposure of the power cultures of the school, which acted to undermine girls' self esteem and sense of control. Men dominated the staff and boys dominated the prefect system; boys were able to 'call' the girls to empty classrooms after school, and very much dominated sexual encounters, including choices about condom use. This parallels Morell's comment about South African schools, where patriarchal, tough, sporting values impact on sexual relationships, 'where male entitlement to the female body is still the norm', and where there are very high rape and sexual harassment rates in school (1998: 109). In Uganda, Mirembe's action research showed that pupils already knew a fair amount about AIDs and its transmission; what was of value in her intervention was less the 'delivery' of new knowledge and more the opportunity for pupils to voice their concerns about uneven relationships and about harassment, and receive support from peers and teachers.

Such research shows a clear relationship between the micropolitics of the school and the gender relations which prefigure it. Hierarchical, authoritarian institutions block efforts to challenge power relations between males and females; conversely, more democratic, transparent institutions can provide the framework where the unspeakable can be spoken. Raising questions of sexuality in school is not easy, but it is being done in countries such as Uganda and Malawi.

What is important then is to deconstruct how teachers and policy makers are talking about democracy – or its supposed antithesis, authoritarianism – and how their definitions surround or legitimise certain sorts of behaviours. Recent ethnographic work in Pakistan, for example, asking head teachers about their definitions of democracy (Quraishi 1999) reveals some clearly gendered stances. A boys' school Head responds:

> Our aim here is to educate young men who are intellectually, emotionally and technically prepared to meet the challenges of the 21st century. We have to make them competent and worthy leaders who will be able to compete at all levels . . .

In a girls' school, in contrast, a Head states: 'Democracy in schools is about inculcating discipline and lawful behaviour in students . . . here we train our girls to be better citizens . . .'.

Another girls' school Head saw democracy as the provision of extra-curricular activities where girls could 'share'. Democracy in a culture such as Pakistan appears to be interpreted very differently for boys and girls. More importantly, according to these Heads, democracy does not seem to be about social justice or a challenge to the system for either sex. 'Citizenship' here would be about social reproduction, social control and competition, not about rights.

Indicators of, and preconditions for, democratic schooling

Ethnographic work such as the above can reveal continuing barriers to full citizenship education. Yet, together with moves towards political democracy in many parts of the developing world is a long-standing recognition for the need of such education. As Wamahiu writes:

> Education in the contemporary context must be transformative . . . Both genders must learn that to be socially responsible is not incompatible with being free, that to be successful does not necessarily require aggressiveness, that a true leader does not rule with force. This can only happen within the context of a democratic school culture that replaces slavish allegiance to authority with critical thinking, creativity and flexibility.
>
> (1996: 56)

In schools, visible signs of transformatory moves towards popular control of collective decision-making by pupils would be structures such as student councils, circle time, peer mediation, grievance procedures, involvement of pupils in appointments of teachers and head teachers, representation on governing bodies, and linkages between student forums and wider student parliaments or regional/national councils. To establish equality of rights, such indicators of democratic practice in schools would have to be further broken down to see whether girls and boys participated equally and whether both sexes experienced a practical political education which prepared them for future active participation in civil society.

As in the wider polity, there would still be questions of the balance between participatory and representative democracy, that is, how far each individual student can directly contribute and negotiate, and how far decisions are made through a system of elected representatives and delegation. Whatever the formal processes, the indicators above would be based on the notion that key components of democracy – and thus a democratic school – would be participation, legitimacy, accountability and respect for human rights (British Council 1993). Translated into educational terms, and with an eye on gender, we would first look to see whether people in authority in schools or Ministries of Education were properly appointed or elected, and whether there are formal channels for open protest. Second, we would look for proper audit procedures, to expose nepotism, corruption and abuses of power (accountability); third, we would want to see management with the skills to make and implement policy, to communicate it, and to distribute resources fairly (competence); and finally, we would look for recognition of children's and teachers' rights (for example, freedom of thought, expression, freedom to participate in decisions affecting them, and freedom from mental or physical violence).

A parallel set of tenets for democracy would be *transparency, participation and challenge*, that is, a system where:

- the ways of operating are open and clear to everyone, and those in power are accountable;
- there are mechanisms for people to participate in decisions on matters that affect them; and,
- the organisation is continuously open to criticism and change through legitimised formal and informal processes of challenge, such as opposition parties or a free press.

Democracy by definition thus carries within it the seeds of resistance and the possibilities of change. It can be seen that democracy is not just about 'levels' of participation (as these were fairly high even in Nazi Germany) but about *how* we participate. Values of tolerance of diversity, of respect for others, and of laying decisions open to criticism might be central.

Conventionally, two forms of democracy are distinguished, 'weak' and 'strong'. Weak (or representative) forms of democracy are characterised by people voting for others to represent their interests, but devolving power upwards to expertise or authority vested in that representative. Strong (or participative) forms of democracy entail participation at an appropriate level. This has been called 'statistical democracy'. This means that *everyone* with a legitimate interest in a decision has a right to representation in respect of that decision; and, *only* those with a legitimate interest in a decision have a right to representation. In terms of schooling this means a system of small groups, committees or 'houses' in which all students and staff can participate, *but in forums appropriate to them.*

Both forms of democracy, weak and strong, might be in operation in an educational institution, depending on scale or size; but it has been found important to correct two possible misapprehensions. First, democracy is not just about voting or automatic majority rule. There is often the assumption that democracy is only about the process whereby a conflict is resolved by recourse to the referendum. Yet voting carries with it the problems of how minority views are heard, of how voters are persuaded, and of whether the issue being voted on is indeed what is important to people. If an organisation is unbalanced in terms of gender or ethnicity, then straightforward voting – especially on an equity issue – may not ameliorate power interests. Other forms of consensual conflict resolution, mediation, channels for grievance procedures, representation and mandating are equally important. This is why structures such as committees need review, in terms of how they operate as well as who is represented.

Some teachers may be reluctant to take on controversial issues in a perceptibly crowded formal curriculum in some national contexts. Quraishi (1999) is finding, for example, that teachers in Pakistan are firmly resistant to the idea of any political education in the school. Yet, as a report on Pakistan shows (British Council 1997a), while women have the right to vote and stand for elective or public office, in practice fewer women are registered voters. Voting is conditional on the possession of a national identity card; many women do not possess these, or with changes of names on marriage, their names do not match the voters' list. Political education therefore does not have to be formal introductions to national constitutions; it can be as simple as reminding students about national identity cards and the right to vote.

It is possible to legislate either for political education or for democratic structures in schools, or both. Countries such as Denmark and Poland have student councils as compulsory; South Africa has also incorporated recommendations on democracy into its constitution and its White Papers for schools (see ch. 17, by Enslin). Systems that have student participation in school decision-making have found that, as with student mediators, there must be training before democracy is implemented fully. This training is also a useful life-long skill, and possibly of more benefit than quadratic equations.

Conflict and violence

I now turn to the matter of conflict as a key issue in the establishment of feminist citizenship education internationally. Violence is a highly gendered

issue, both at the intimate, domestic level and in the national and international arena. If one of the purposes of democracy is to work towards a
sustainable peace, then children must be exposed to the nature of conflict
while in school. Taking the lead in teaching conflict resolution and mediation skills is seen as the role of some schools in Europe as well as the UK
(Davies and Kirkpatrick, 2000), but it is not typically a national requirement.
A focus on gender enables questions of male violence to surface, and both
boys and girls, and male and female teachers to learn assertiveness rather than
aggression, advocacy rather than authoritarianism, and mediation rather than
domination.

Education for non-violence does not mean 'protecting' children from
viewing the conflictual nature of the societies we live in. All sorts of projects
are currently in place around domestic violence, for example, providing refuges
and telephone help-lines in countries such as China and Pakistan; yet these
issues curiously do not always find their way into the formal programme of
schools before such strategies become necessary. A particularly disturbing
feature which has emerged from research into violence against women
(UNICEF 1995) is the possibility of a link between domestic violence and
progress towards equality for women. The suspicion is that the risk of violence
rises when male partners feel that their traditional position of superiority and
control is being threatened. Gender equity can thus evoke backlash unless
accompanied by skills acquired by both sexes in peaceful conflict resolution.

This requires a shift both in the hidden and official curriculum. Schools in
many parts of the world are still physically brutal places for girls (Harber and
Davies 1997). Mehran writes on pupil drop-out in Iran:

> Inappropriate behaviour of the teacher remains a bitter reality in rural
> and nomadic schools. Physical punishment, psychological degradation,
> imposition of too many restrictions, excessive discipline, and creating an
> atmosphere of fear and anxiety, especially by younger, inexperienced
> teachers, is a problem for both boys and girls. Parents, however, reported
> that their daughters 'begin to hate their school and their teacher' imme-
> diately upon encountering any of the above.
>
> (1997: 271)

Similarly, Geissinger (1997: 290) (writing about Papua New Guinea) noted
the concern of the Council of Education Ministers regarding the problems
of tribal and random violence that children face, the lack of enforcement of
laws and double standards, and the resulting restrictions on the deployment
of female professional staff:

> Unfortunately, even though the ministers were influential members of
> their provincial governments, they offered no solution to the problem of
> violence against either children or women teachers, so it has continued
> to restrict girls' access to school at every level.

Again, a social contract which includes women seems to be missing.

On the other hand, one of the spin-offs of the current concern in other parts of the world about the 'underachievement' of boys is the recognition of schools as brutalising places, and of male 'laddish' cultures which promote boys' deviance and rejection of learning. The hidden curriculum of rules and repression is coming under scrutiny, particularly in transforming societies such as Namibia and South Africa (see Harber 1998), and this has profound implications for gender relations.

Violence is a gendered problem, not just a women's problem. Women are more often seen to be the subject of violence, and at the same time are less likely to have a role in the decisions leading to armed conflict. In a revealing paper 'Masculinities and education for democracy in the new South Africa', Morell (1998) first examines the work of the Gender Education Task Team. Identifying violence as a major problem of schooling, GETT had made recommendations which went further than protecting women and providing better rehabilitation and trauma facilities, and did not automatically locate girls as victims and boys as perpetrators. However,

> what the report didn't say was that most of the victims of violence are boys. From this follows that boys also have an interest in confronting violence. The matter is complex, not least because constructions of masculinity frequently emphasise the ability to be violent and uncomplainingly to endure pain. For our purposes, it is necessary to make a very simple statement: democratic education cannot occur in violent schools. In order to create environments which are conducive for democratic education, it is necessary to tackle masculinity.
>
> (Morell 1998: 107)

Morell, therefore, argues for an approach which tackles the structural features of the gender regime together with personal, anti-sexist, therapeutic work with boys: 'not only does this have the advantage of taking boys seriously and dignifying their humanity, it also develops the communication skills essential for mediation' (110).

In the formal curriculum, too, issues of violence, war and the role of women can surface. Waylen (1996), for example, documents the long history of women in different countries of Latin America mobilising both on behalf of the Right, and in oppositional movements demanding human rights. While some of these movements can be seen as part of the 'patriarchal bargain' (Kandiyoti 1988) which supports the status quo for the short-term protection of women's interests, others directly challenge existing regimes and notions of womanhood, using public and private space in protests. It is not appropriate here to enter the debate about whether women's liberation movements are in the end essentialist and regressive or whether they are transformative in terms of demanding an 'ethic of care'. I merely wish to argue that the history and social science curriculum should contain an analysis of women's resistance to colonialism, to military regimes or indeed to socialist regimes, in order to portray both women's power and their varied responses to political control.

Finally, a feminist analysis of citizenship education must address the role of women in war and conflict. An African Rights Report argued in 1995:

> Thousands of women were killed by other women. They often died at the hands of educated women, the very women who had access to political power, economic means and education ... The extent to which women took an active role in the killings is unprecedented. This is not accidental. The architects of the holocaust sought to involve as much of the population as possible – men, women and even children as young as eight. They set out to create a nation of extremists bound together by the blood of genocide. If everyone was involved ... there would be no one to point an accusing finger.
>
> (Quoted in McGreal 1995)

As Aguilar and Richmond point out, the active involvement of women, children and young people in carrying out acts of violence, sometimes against their teachers and fellow pupils, raises further questions about the kind of education they had received:

> For those preparing educational responses appropriate to the post-genocide situation, it was clear that Rwanda's education could never be the same again; it was evident that such themes as peace, reconciliation, human rights and tolerance would have to figure in the 'values education' of all Rwanda's children and young people in the future.
>
> (Aguilar and Richmond 1998: 123)

Questions about gender, particularly with regard to post-conflict education, should not be limited to female literacy; they relate to the brutalisation of both boys and girls and the education which promotes intolerance. The seeds are there in any divided and segregated education, whether in Northern Ireland or the Balkans. In Kosovo after 1989, schools were physically divided, often with brick walls, so that Serb and Albanian children did not mix, and had education in their own language. Given existing hostilities and feelings of discrimination, such an education would only have added to suspicion, distrust and more conflict. As Pigozzi points out, too much peace education comes after the fact:

> [M]uch peace education tends to use conventional approaches – telling children how to act, how to 'be nice and better people' rather than demonstrating and living those elements that are essential for peaceful and productive lives on a large scale.
>
> (1998: 346)

Conclusion

This chapter has tried to show how a school – whether in a peace or a war zone – can engage in an education which promotes a just citizenry. In this model, a combination of gender-inclusion and a democratic approach is crucial. Historically, and despite formal equality as voters, women have been 'differentially incorporated as citizens of the state' (Waylen 1996: 14). I would also argue that, despite inroads into curriculum and pedagogy, girls have been differentially incorporated as citizens of the school. However, this is largely because of an insufficient focus on citizenship itself and its key elements and egalitarian processes. A feminist citizenship programme for a school would include ensuring democratic structures of decision-making and participation and the tackling of rights and responsibilities through the formal curriculum. A 'gender-sensitive' curriculum is not one that simply depicts more females in textbooks. It is one that includes the vital political skills required to challenge gender and class relations. This means a learning programme which includes a direct focus on conflict and conflict resolution. Such a programme would teach human rights and legal rights and the skills of participating in the political process, such as advocacy, lobbying, and the different workings of representative and participatory democracy (see for example Harber 1995).

Feminist analyses have demonstrated how unchallenged neo-patrimonial regimes hinder the development of a civil society. I would claim that a sustained focus on gender relations means the recognition of how education as rights and responsibilities will ultimately benefit both women and men, and directly impact on that civil society. Schools are often highly undeveloped civil societies which are linked to their own patriarchal and bureaucratic regimes. Our task is to generate feminist models of citizenship education which can create a '*civil school*', in turn to aid in social development. By constantly juxtaposing gender with democracy and citizenship in our analysis and our educational practice, we might establish international principles for social change as well as local strategies to develop a more ideal civil society.

References

Aguilar, P. and Richmond, M. (1998) 'Emergency educational response in the Rwandan crisis', in G. Retamol and R. Aedo-Richmond (eds) *Education as a Humanitarian Response*, London: Cassell.

Baechler, J. (1995) *Democracy: an analytical survey*, Paris: UNESCO.

Beetham, D. and Boyle, K. (1995) *Introducing Democracy*, Paris: UNESCO.

British Council (1993) *Development Priorities and Guidelines*, Manchester: British Council.

British Council (1997a) *Network Newsletter* 13.

British Council (1997b) *Network Newsletter* 14.

Bunwaree, S. (1997) 'Education and the marginalisation of girls in post-GATT Mauritius', *Compare*, 27, 3: 297–318.

Davies, L. (1984) 'Political education, gender and the art of the possible', *Educational Review*, 35, 2: 187–197.

Davies, L. (1994a) *Beyond Authoritarian School Management: the challenge for transparency*, Nottingham: Education Now.

Davies, L. (1994b) 'Can students make a difference?: international perspectives on transformative education', *International Studies in Sociology of Education*, 4, 1: 43–56.

Davies, L. (1997a) 'Democratic schooling, transformation and development', in C. Modgil and J. Lynch (eds) *Education and Development: tradition and innovation*, London: Cassell.

Davies, L. (1997b) 'The case for leaderless schools', in K. Watson, C. Modgil and S. Modgil (eds) *Educational Dilemmas: debate and diversity*, Vol. 3 *Power and Responsibility in Education*, London: Cassell.

Davies, L. and Gunawardena, C. (1992) *Women and Men in Educational Management: an international enquiry*, Paris: IIEP.

Davies, L. and Kirkpatrick, G. (2000) *A Review of Pupil Democracy in Europe*, Research Report, London: Children's Rights Alliance.

Geissinger, H. (1997) 'Girls' access to education in a developing country', *Compare*, 27, 3: 287–296.

Giddens, A. (1998) *The Third Way*, Cambridge: Polity Press.

Harber, C. (1989) *Politics in African Education*, London: Macmillan.

Harber, C. (ed.) (1995) *Developing Democratic Education*, Nottingham: Education Now.

Harber, C (ed.) (1998) *Voices for Democracy: a North – South dialogue in education for sustainable democracy*, Nottingham: Education Now/British Council.

Harber, C. and Davies, L. (1997) *School Management and Effectiveness in Developing Countries: the post-bureaucratic school*, London: Cassell.

Ianello, K. (1992) *Decisions Without Hierarchy: feminist interventions in organisation theory and practice*, London: Routledge.

Jayaweera, S. (1997) 'Higher education and empowerment of women in Asia', *Compare*, 27, 3: 245–261.

Jones, A. (1997) 'Training for empowerment? A comparative study of nonformal education for women in small island countries', *Compare*, 27, 3: 277–286.

Kandiyoti, D. (1988) 'Bargaining with patriarchy', *Gender and Society*, 2, 3: 271–290.

Kanter, R. (1977) *Men and Women of the Corporation*, New York: Basic Books.

Mannathoko, C. (1995) 'Gender, Ideology and the State in Botswana's Teacher Education', unpublished thesis, Unversity of Birmingham.

McGreal, C. (1995) 'Women "took part in killings"', *Guardian Weekly*, 3 September: 1.

Mehran, G. (1997) 'A study of girls' lack of access to primary education in the Islamic Republic of Iran', *Compare*, 27, 3: 263–276.

Mirembe, R. (1998) 'AIDs Education and Gender in Uganda', unpublished Ph.D thesis, University of Birmingham.

Morell, R. (1998) 'Masculinities and education for democracy in the New South Africa', in C. Harber (ed.) *Voices for Democracy: a North–South Dialogue in education for sustainable democracy*, Nottingham: Education Now/British Council.

Morgan, G. (1986) *Images of Organization*, Beverley Hills: Sage.

Pigozzi, M. (1998) 'Education in emergencies and for reconstruction: strategic guidelines with a developmental approach', in G. Retamol and R. Aedo-Richmond (eds) *Education as a Humanitarian Response*, London: Cassell.

Quraishi, U. (1999) 'Democracy through the Art Education Curriculum in Pakistan', unpublished Ph.D thesis, University of Birmingham.

Stromquist, N. (1997) *Literacy for Citizenship: gender and grassroots dynamics in Brazil*, Albany: State University of New York Press (SUNY).

Stromquist, N. (1999) 'The impact of structural adjustment programmes in Africa and Latin America', in C. Heward and S. Bunwaree (eds) *Gender, Education and Development*, London: Zed Books.

Sylvester, C. (1994) *Feminist Theory and International Relations in a Postmodern Era*, Cambridge: Cambridge University Press.

UNICEF (1995) *The State of the World's Children*, Oxford: Oxford University Press.

United Nations Development Programme (UNDP) (1995) *Human Development Report 1995*, New York: UNDP.

Wamahiu, S. (1996) 'The Pedagogy of Difference: an African perspective', in P. Murphy and C. Gipps (eds) *Equity in the Classroom*, London: Falmer Press.

Waylen, G. (1996) *Gender in Third World Politics*, Buckingham: Open University Press.

Weiner, G. (1994) *Feminisms in Education*, Milton Keynes: Open University Press.

17 Defining a civic agenda

Citizenship and gender equality in post-apartheid education

Penny Enslin

South Africa's first democratic election in 1994 introduced a new order offering equal citizenship for women. But the formal, constitutional right to equal citizenship is yet to be translated into women's full exercise of citizenship. The lingering consequences of gender and racial oppression make education for citizenship a key component of post-apartheid policy and practice.

This chapter has two aims: to assess progress so far towards equal citizenship for women and education for gender equality as a component of citizenship in the South African context, and to plot more generally the conceptual and strategic way forward towards the fulfilment of equal citizenship for women. I begin with an account of the conception of citizenship which has emerged from the context of the anti-apartheid struggle and the subsequent transition to a new democratic order. Then, using Marshall's three elements of citizenship together with a survey of key policy instruments and other post-election developments, I assess current prospects for the achievement of equal citizenship for women. I argue that although the formal acquisition of equal common membership for all in the democracy established in 1994 is a necessary condition for social justice, for women in particular the common membership thus acquired is not sufficient for the exercise of full citizenship rights. The second part of the chapter shows that educational policy since 1994, similarly, falls short of adequately addressing gender equality, although it does pay some attention to gender and to citizenship. Turning to a more general discussion of the way forward, in the third part of the chapter I explore a tension in emerging South African developments: between citizenship understood as the exercise of *rights*, and as *membership*, either of the nation or as defined by custom. Citizenship conceived in terms of membership is shown to confine problems of gender equity and equal citizenship to the private. In the final section, the report *Gender Equity in Education* (Department of Education 1997) is defended for the manner in which it implicitly takes up the problem of citizenship, setting an appropriate civic agenda for equal citizenship for girls and women by taking gender and custom out of the private and, by implication, giving priority to citizenship as rights, over citizenship as membership.

The idea of citizenship after apartheid

Renewed recent interest in the idea of citizenship suggests that it has a useful role to play in the consolidation of democracy (see for example Heater 1990; Andrews 1991). For Kymlicka and Norman: 'The concept of citizenship seems to integrate the demands of justice and community membership ... Citizenship is intimately linked to ideas of individual entitlement on the one hand and of attachment to a particular community on the other' (1994: 352). Yet a number of writers also express some scepticism about the usefulness of the idea of citizenship. For Kymlicka and Norman it is not ultimately clear what a theory of citizenship can offer (1994: 377). Feminists in particular have expressed reservations about the notion of citizenship, for example, in Carole Pateman's indictment of citizenship as 'made in the male image' (1989: 14).

In South Africa after apartheid, the idea of citizenship does not as yet have a prominent place in the public philosophy or in educational discourse, but it seems to have some potential to enrich current concepts of democracy and of education for democracy. In trying to develop an understanding of the potential and limitations of the idea of citizenship in such a context, we need to start by exploring its possibilities in relation to recent South African history and the conditions under which the transition to democracy took place in 1994. Because of the recent nature of the transition, and the radical break with the past that it represents, South Africans cannot turn (as can British citizens, for example) to a longer tradition of welfare as central to a debate about what it is to be a citizen of society. Much of the South African notion of citizenship is still constituted by apartheid and its overthrow. The possibility of a welfare state that caters to the needs of all its citizens is remote; although some progress has been made, it is far from sufficient to define citizenship in this society. Having acknowledged the contextual conditions in which citizenship has become possible, we need to ask, as Kymlicka and Norman suggest (1994): what is it to belong to a particular society, and what kind of life is it possible to live in this form of society?

To some extent, a notion of democratic citizenship was developed in South Africa during the struggle against apartheid, in which popular organisations established models of debate, consultation and accountability that remain influential. A vision of active citizenship, reflected in mass mobilisation against the previous government, was extended to the process of consultation adopted by the Constitutional Assembly in producing the 1996 Constitution (Republic of South Africa 1996). The Preamble to the new Constitution begins by recognising past injustice and those who suffered in struggling against it. It declares that the adoption of the Constitution is intended to: 'Heal the divisions of the past and establish a society based on democratic values, social justice and fundamental human rights' (1) creating a democratic and open society in which citizens will be protected by law and enjoy an improved quality of life. The Preamble's emphasis on equal citizenship is significant, for apartheid deprived the majority of South Africans of their rights as citizens. While white inhabitants of South Africa held the status of full citizens, for black South Africans there was an ethnically ascribed second-class citizenship in separate states which offered curtailed rights and restricted participation. Hence, by contrast, one of the Founding Principles of the new Constitution is a common citizenship with equal rights. The Republic of South Africa is to be a democratic state whose founding values include: 'Human dignity, the achievement of equality and the advancement of human rights and freedoms . . . non-racialism and non-sexism . . .' (section 1).

The Bill of Rights (sections 7–39) 'enshrines the rights of all people in our country and affirms the democratic values of human dignity, equality and freedom' (section 7[1]). It establishes a range of rights such as freedom and security of the person, privacy, freedom of religion, belief and opinion, expression, assembly, association, children's rights, and the right to basic education. Discrimination on grounds of race, colour, sex, gender, sexual orientation, marital status, pregnancy or ethnic origins is forbidden. Everyone has the right to participate in the cultural life they choose, as long as it is not inconsistent with the Bill of Rights.

The central themes in the notion of citizenship reflected in the Constitution are as follows: first, common membership in a unified society in which difference is respected; second, the enjoyment of an extensive range of rights and freedoms; and third, active citizenship, as provided for in public participation projects aimed to promote public access and involvement at the levels of central and provincial government (sections 59, 72, 118). A distinguishing feature of the South African Constitution is that it establishes a framework for a society that is intended to be different from what came before, rather than confirming practices that have grown organically over a long period. A substantial part of being a citizen of South Africa is the project of overcoming the past. This divided past means that citizenship in South Africa does not meet a condition specified by civic republicans; there is not yet a settled historical community attached to a common culture, to traditions and practices that constitute that community (Canover 1995: 137).

Notions of citizenship articulated in documents do not necessarily constitute a popular understanding of citizenship. The Constitution is a framework for a society which is self-consciously trying to achieve transformation, a goal towards which the transition to democracy is aimed and in whose terms the society must conduct itself. Its idea of citizenship is also incomplete and in need of interpretation and refinement, not least in weighing claims that might be in tension, particularly between equality and difference. Yet, while it is important to acknowledge that a constitution does not describe what is, there are dangers in constitutions and policy documents that are contradicted by actual conditions and practices. All of these considerations point to the need to create the conditions under which the rights in the Constitution can be realised. Hence the role envisaged for education in the consolidation of citizenship, which I will discuss later.

Current prospects for equal citizenship for women

The continuing international feminist debate about citizenship (see Walby 1994; Lister 1995; Dietz 1992; Jones 1990) is yet to be adequately taken up in South Africa, where the question of whether citizenship can accommodate gender should be focused on issues beyond the immediate but largely formal gains since 1994. After the strategic subordination of the struggle for gender equality to that against racial oppression and apartheid (Albertyn 1994: 42), there is now much talk of building a non-sexist democracy. But this does not necessarily mean that there is either sufficient understanding of the issues or commitment to following this slogan through to its conclusion. The language in terms of which gender is discussed is itself revealing of the problem. The term 'feminism' is rarely used or referred to, except in a degenerate form in which it is popularly associated with the unfeminine and with hatred of men; there is little awareness of feminism as a project that includes gender emancipation for men, or for gays. The tendency to associate gender equality with accommodating 'women's concerns' (see, for example, Cross and Leroke 1995, and Enslin's response, 1995) is itself problematic; while taking on the appearance of enlightenment and generosity, little consideration is given to why particular issues are regarded as concerns of women rather than of all, reinforcing the assumption that women have certain natural abilities and matching tasks that go with them.

While these observations imply a rejection of what is regarded as essentialism, the analysis that follows does presuppose that there are significant commonalities (as well as differences) between women of different classes and ethnic groups. In doing so, I assume that Okin's view (Okin 1995), that the situation of most women in poor countries is 'similar to but worse than' that of most women in rich countries, is also applicable across class and race differences in South Africa. Common features of the lives of most women, of different cultures and classes, include a gendered division of labour in which women are almost always primary caregivers; a lack of recognition of work performed within the household; reduced availability for waged work; overwork; economic dependence; limited bargaining power within the household; limited potential for satisfactory exit; and, vulnerability to abuse (Okin 1995: 280–287). To suggest that most South African women are subject to these conditions to differing degrees is not to sweep aside differences between them, especially those between black and white women. It is important to bear in mind that apartheid oppressed and exploited the former and that it provided the latter with privileges. In the extension of citizenship rights to women, different features of such rights will be of varying significance to different groups of women, and social justice requires that priority be given to the needs of those most disadvantaged by past policies.

Although Marshall's distinction between civil, political and social citizenship is inapplicable to South Africa as an historical account of the extension of rights, it is helpful in analysing progress in the acquisition of citizen rights. In a much-quoted passage, Marshall claims that citizenship has:

three parts, or elements, civil, political and social. The civil element is composed of the rights necessary for individual freedom – liberty of the person, freedom of speech, thought and faith, the right to own property and to conclude valid contracts, and the right to justice ... the institutions most directly associated with civil rights are the courts of justice. By the political element I mean the right to participate in the exercise of political power, as a member of a body invested with political authority or as an elector of the members of such a body. The corresponding institutions are parliament and councils of local government. By the social element I mean the whole range from the right to a modicum of economic welfare and security to the right to share to the full in the social heritage and to live the life of a civilised being according to the standards prevailing in the society. The institutions most closely connected with it are the educational system and the social services.

(Marshall 1950: 10–11, quoted in Walby 1994)

The end of apartheid and the adoption of the new Constitution has established an extensive set of rights, implying an ambitious programme of social reconstruction and that great efforts will be made to achieve them. Some of the features of civil and political citizenship as described by Marshall have been achieved. *Political* citizenship, as 'the right to participate in the exercise of political power', is now formally achieved for all adult inhabitants of South Africa in the establishment of a universal adult franchise. Some progress has also been made in the sphere of political rights for women in addition to the acquisition of the franchise. The broad-based Women's National Coalition was able to mobilise women's organisations sufficiently to exert some influence in the negotiations for the Interim Constitution of 1993 under which the 1994 election took place (Albertyn 1994). At the time of writing, 25 per cent of the members of the national and provincial legislatures are now women; available figures indicate that, in local government, women constitute 19.4 per cent of all councillors and occupy 14.4 per cent of Executive Committee positions. These figures demonstrate an improvement in the representation of women at all levels since the transition (Commission on Gender Equality 1997: 76).

However, the Parliamentary Women's Group is concerned that the next election will return fewer women members (Commission on Gender Equality 1997: 82). Research suggests that over half of the present women members will not stand for re-election, as the rhythm of work in parliament does not accommodate their family responsibilities and they find that the ethos of parliament is male-dominated (*Sunday Independent* 1997: 1). Besides, the achievements that have been made do not amount to a shift of effective political power to women. The limited progress made in the reconstruction of political power so that it is shared with and exercised by women is illustrated by the example of the Commission for Gender Equality, which was appointed in March 1997 in terms of the Constitution. Its budget and infrastructure are far smaller than those provided for the Human Rights Commission and the Youth Commission.

As in the case of political rights, some of the necessary conditions for the *civil* component of citizenship also appear to have been formally met. One of the most significant civil (and social) rights acquired by women since 1994 was the implementation in 1997 of abortion on demand. Some discriminatory legislation has been removed from the statute books. But for some women, 'the right to own property and to conclude valid contracts' (Marshall 1950, quoted in Walby 1994: 380) are among those civil rights that had not been met at the time of writing. More perplexing than this, in a society reported to have the highest incidence of rape in the world (*Mail & Guardian* 1997a: 26), gender-based violence against women and girls infringes on the rights guaranteed in the Constitution and reduces their freedom, including the freedom of those who are not victims themselves. The prevalence of violence against women in public and in private casts doubt on their status as equal citizens.

As is the case in other countries, the *social* component of citizenship has not been acquired by the majority of South African women (or by large numbers of men), who do not enjoy 'economic welfare and security [and] the right to share to the full in the social heritage and to live the life of a civilised being according to the standards prevailing in the society' (Marshall ibid). There has been some progress, such as in the provision of clean water and electricity, primary health care and housing, and in the redistribution of land, all of which promise to improve the quality of women's lives – especially poor and rural women, who are almost exclusively black. But the poverty which characterised the apartheid era has not been significantly reduced. Thirty-eight per cent of economically active women are unemployed (*Mail & Guardian* 1997b: 26). The educational system, which Marshall associates closely with social citizenship and which he identifies as a necessary prerequisite for civil freedom, remains unequal in terms of gender as well as race, and parts of it are as dysfunctional as they were before the transition.

Marshall's model is a useful starting point for analysing progress in the extension of rights to women as supposedly equal citizens in post-apartheid South Africa. But while Marshall's project was partly to describe the sequential establishment in Britain of civil, political and social rights in the eighteenth, nineteenth and twentieth centuries respectively, in South Africa by contrast all three were formally achieved in the transition to democracy in 1994. However, it would be more appropriate to see the three categories of rights as goals set in the transition rather than as substantial achievements for women. It is also important to note the interrelationships between them, for example that the civil and social components are prerequisites for the full exercise of political rights. But I suggest that important though they are, Marshall's citizenship rights do not get to the heart of the problem of gender inequality, centrally because they are located largely in the public sphere. They do not provide an adequate means of subjecting to critique relations of domination and exploitation in the private, which is commonly associated with the domestic or household sphere. We have already noted the features which Okin shows to mark the unequal power of women relative to men within the household, which she describes as the first and probably the most important 'school of moral development'. Here children 'are likely to learn injustice, by absorbing the messages, if male that they have some kind of "natural" enhanced entitlement and, if female, that they are not equals, and had better get used to being subordinated if not abused' (Okin 1995: 288). For societies like South Africa, committed to the development of democracy, this kind of feminist critique of injustice and unequal power within the household exposes a serious obstacle to democratisation. Hierarchical exercise of authority in which neither decision-making nor duties are equally shared undermines this project, which depends on the development of citizens who are used to expressing their own needs and to taking seriously those of others.

Although households in South Africa take a number of different forms, reflecting both custom and material conditions, the problems identified by Okin apply to most of them. Even in female-headed households, the consequences of traditional patterns of domination are still present. In Brown's (1996) study of female-headed households in a South African township, marginalised male relations living in but not substantially contributing to the household are in some cases manipulative and even abusive, although their presence is generally welcomed for protection. Lucas's (1995) investigation of domestic space in yards comprising several households in Alexandra township describes a context in which the categories of private and public are not clearly distinct. Here women's levels of political participation in the local structures are relatively high. But marital disputes are regarded as a private matter. While there is evidence that women are challenging their husbands' authority and of the view that domestic violence is a private issue, yard committees show reluctance to intervene in such disputes, tending to take the view that 'intervening would be perceived as endangering the moral community, by creating conflict between men, while marital disputes between men and women are private and can therefore be tolerated' (Lucas 1995: 112).

While there seems to have been a reduction in public subordination in South Africa, the private is largely unchanged. A fundamental flaw in the concept of citizenship is that it is centrally a notion for the public. We are not citizens when we are at home, in the way that we can be outside in the public square. But it could be objected, in response to the claim that citizenship is thus a limited tool for promoting gender equality, that it dismisses the potential of the idea of citizenship to be invoked in the private sphere. Citizenship, it can be claimed, provides the means for women to appeal to their equal status in situations where oppression continues. This objection could rest on an inflated expectation of the moral force of citizenship which underestimates the power of oppression in many households, especially in contexts where opposing domination risks retaliatory abuse. But let us concede to this objection that it points the way to an understanding of citizenship and of the self as citizen which would encourage the claiming of rights in all contexts, including the domestic one. Let us turn now to citizenship in the educational context.

Citizenship and gender in post-apartheid education policy

Education has received much attention since the Government of National Unity came to power in April 1994, including the introduction of attempts to educate for democratic citizenship. The 1995 White Paper on Education and Training sets out to implement the new Constitution's provisions for common citizenship and for citizen's rights to and in education. It describes the Constitution (at that stage the Interim Constitution of 1993) as 'the nation's school of democratic practice' (Department of Education 1995: 45). It acknowledges both the rights guaranteed in the Constitution as a moral framework for education policy and legislation (17), and the centrality of equal educational rights as a component of equal citizenship (19).

One of the initiatives promised in the White Paper is the overhaul of curricula. The introduction to the new outcomes-based national curriculum for Grades 1 to 9 states that, in contrast to the divisions perpetuated by the curricula in the past, the new curriculum emphasises 'common citizenship and nationhood' (Ministry of Education 1997: 5). Among the eight new learning areas of Curriculum 2005, the Human and Social Sciences emphasises the promotion of democratic values. Education Minister Sibusiso Bengu described the new curriculum at its launch as aimed at producing 'thinking, competent citizens'.

The Human and Social Sciences are to develop 'responsible citizens in a culturally diverse, democratic society' (Ministry of Education 1997: 49). One of the specific outcomes for this learning area is: 'Participate actively in promoting a just, democratic and equitable society' (outcome 3), among the proposed assessment criteria for which is the making of informed judgements about issues, including gender as well as human rights and cultural issues, in relation to the Constitution (63).

Specific outcome 1 is: 'Demonstrate a critical understanding of how South African society has changed and developed'. It is intended to enable learners 'to develop, meaningfully and critically, a sense of self-worth and identity; and help them to exercise their full rights and responsibilities as citizens'. An assessment criterion for this specific outcome is critical understanding of relations within and between communities, which includes gender relations as well as cultural relations within its range statement. Gender is included both among the power relations whose impact is to be considered by pupils and in relation to development, social justice, and problems of prejudice and discrimination.

While the inclusion of gender in the outcomes of the new curriculum looks encouraging, gender equality is not sufficiently emphasised. None of the critical outcomes common to all learning areas mentions the removal of sexist attitudes that promote gender inequality. The Life Orientation learning area mentions gender only once, in relation to career choice. This implies that the human rights emphasised in the Human and Social Sciences learning area are for the public domain, but that addressing sexist attitudes and behaviour is not an appropriate outcome when considering relations between individuals and within families, which are mentioned often in Life Orientation.

Thus while new education policy does place education for citizenship on the agenda, and does also include attention to gender both at the broad level of policy and in the new curriculum, ultimately it seems likely to repeat the mistake identified earlier in the discussion of Marshall's notion of citizenship, relegating crucial issues of gender equity to the private sphere.

But the White Paper did acknowledge the need for special attention to be paid to the issue of gender equity in education, and we will turn shortly to the resulting report on Gender Equity in Education. Before doing so, however, it is instructive to consider two influential ways in which citizenship is likely to be articulated further within a framework of membership – nation and custom – and why both are problematic as components of a programme for gender equity.

Citizenship as membership: nation and custom

The White Paper (Department of Education 1995: 17) endorses the idea of nation-buildings, and Curriculum 2005 (Ministry of Education 1997: 5) explicitly links citizenship and nationhood, reflecting the common assumption that one way of addressing inequalities among citizens is to attempt to consolidate citizenship as common membership by promoting a national identity. Nation-building has been proposed as a strategy for creating unity from diversity in South Africa. Education for nation-building, it is argued (Mkwanazi and Cross 1992), will promote national unity and reconciliation, by developing national sentiment and identity.

As I have argued elsewhere (Enslin 1993/4), the danger in nation-building programmes is that they can create an illusion of inclusiveness, defending the idea of the nation as if it is gender-neutral and inclusive, while concealing the continuing oppression of some citizens. Where common membership is depicted as unity and inclusiveness, implying that all benefit equally from such membership, those who are marginalised can be effectively excluded from the benefits of political and social programmes.

In South Africa, as in other societies, politics has been fashioned by male interests and is a product of the exclusion of women from the public sphere, in which male characteristics provide the framework for understanding citizenship. The concept of nationhood, like other concepts that frame the political, is an expression of predominantly male experiences and aspirations. It is significant that in the languages of both Afrikaner nationalism and of the liberation struggle against it, women were accorded a similar status, as 'volksmoeder' and as 'mother of the nation' respectively. Both concepts emphasise women's nurturing role, portraying them as political subjects and symbols of the nation rather than political agents (Walker 1990). Nationalist discourse, including the idea of the mother of the nation, is an example of what Young (1990) calls a universalising concept; while apparently according women a place in the nation as a unified public, the concept of the nation suppresses difference and conceals oppression (see also Phillips 1993: 87).

The competing conceptions of nationhood in South Africa's recent past have been expressions of sometimes violent masculinity. The national liberation struggle has been popularly depicted in terms of masculine pride. For reasons which might be understandable, citizenship is associated by many young men with the right to carry and use arms, a serious problem in a society prone to ongoing violence, of which women are often the victims. While the idea of the nation is a powerful unifying force in struggles for the rights of oppressed groups, it has nothing to say about the rights of different groups within the 'nation' and offers little support to those asserting their rights against oppression by fellow members of the nation. In its tendency to conceal oppression, the idea of the nation works in association with the private; both are sites in which gender inequality is concealed and reproduced.

In teaching the new curriculum, tensions will undoubtedly arise between developing a sense of citizenship rights and teaching respect for cultural diversity – for custom as practised by the country's diverse population. None of South Africa's cultures has traditionally allowed equality for women. While this claim applies most problematically to traditional African cultures because they have been undermined, exploited and systematically disadvantaged by colonialism and apartheid, it is a feature of all cultures in South Africa.

The Constitution of 1996 limits the rights of women by recognising customary law and traditional leaders (Chapter 12). It states that, when applicable, customary law must be applied by the courts, but subject to the Constitution. What are the implications of this provision for equal citizenship?

In pre-colonial society, what is called 'customary law' provided 'for a whole social order, regulating political authority, wrongs and injuries, land distribution, the ownership of property, the rights and capacities to exchange goods, and labour' (Chanock 1991: 68). What remains of customary law today is partly the product of the prescriptions of colonial administrators and apartheid policies. It is also the result of collaboration between these authorities and African tribal authorities who, left in the main with authority only over family law, were able to serve their own interests by enforcing an interpretation of it that extended male power.

The features of customary law that have marked the status of women have included polygamy, mourning taboos and, most prominently, *lobola* or the payment of 'bridewealth' to the family of the bride. There is still widespread support for this practice, which is regarded by many as part of their heritage, but there is also evidence of dissatisfaction. For some men, it is too expensive and, with cash increasingly replacing cattle, many see it as becoming commercialised. While the payment of bridewealth is seen as compensating parents for the loss of their daughter and as binding the families of the bride and groom together, with the payment of *lobola* comes the expectation that the wife owes obedience to her husband (Walker 1992: 57–58). As Chanock has observed, customary law (like civil law) has not served the interests of women. Those widowed under customary law are dependent for support on the male heir's goodwill. Maintenance is likely to be resisted if bridewealth is not paid; if it was, the husband's family may claim custody of the children (Chanock 1991: 64).

The future of customary law awaits detailed determination by legislation, leaving many South African women subject to customary law. These include not only black women with strong traditional ties but also Jewish and Muslim women, who will continue to be subject to certain forms of discrimination and restrictions on their rights and independence, which affect them both as public citizens and in the private sphere. The inequalities to which women are subject under customary law 'include the absence of land tenure rights and property-holding capacity, unequal treatment by chiefs' courts and administrative justice in general, and lack of freedom of movement and other key political rights' (Nhlapo 1995: 163). These features of customary law limit the civil element of citizenship in the new South Africa. They provide for unequal treatment of women and also constitute them, as citizens, as unequal to men. The ANC Women's League has declared that 'customary laws and the institution of traditional leaders are oppressive to women' (*The Star* 1996: 5) and that they negate their rights.

There are conflicting views in the ongoing debate about the future of customary law. Some might take the view that the issue should be fought in the courts, as customary law is challenged on the basis of the Constitution and the Bill of Rights. But this presumes that a constituency traditionally discouraged from participation in politics and from challenging traditional authority will have the resources to take these issues to the courts. What is clear is that there is no simple way forward. One consideration, advanced by Currie (1994: 167–168), is the socio-cultural evidence that bridewealth payments act as a mechanism for the distribution of resources in the poorest parts of the country. Currie argues that the precarious position of the elderly in rural areas could be made worse if the payment of bridewealth were to be interfered with in the interest of women. Whatever the merits of this argument, simply refusing to recognise customary unions would prejudice the interests of women married under customary law.

Taking a different tack on the issue, Nhlapo correctly points out that

> Strong constitutional recognition of customary law was inevitable in a country in which three-quarters of the population is black. Furthermore, it could be argued that the right of a people to be governed by a law that they recognise and accept is part of the right to self-determination.
> (1995: 163)

Nhlapo favours the view that it is possible for customary law to be reformed or modernised so as to alleviate those features that are inimical to equal citizen rights for women. The tabling of the Recognition of Customary Marriages Bill in parliament in 1998 seems to support this view to some extent, for it addresses some of the discriminatory features of customary law, for example the perpetual minority status traditionally accorded to women, and it will entitle them to a share of the husband's property in the event of divorce. Yet reforming some of the most discriminatory aspects of customary marriage will not necessarily mean that women will now exercise their full rights (*The Star* 1998: 5).

Chanock takes issue against those who would defend the option of a 'revival' of African law. Apart from showing the collusion of tribal authorities with colonial and apartheid administrators in enforcing a particular interpretation of custom, he also argues (1989) that this patriarchal interpretation concealed other customary practices – of young men and women, widows and divorcees, struggling against the dominant and maintained forms of marriage, as economic and social changes made the dominant interpretation less viable. Thus the assumption that custom signifies 'long-standing historical sameness' (Chanock 1991: 56) is mistaken and the defence of custom is more accurately interpreted as a political position than as a cultural one (Chanock 1989: 76). Chanock concludes that family law cannot be exempted from the application of human rights in the re-establishment of a legitimate rule of law, in the name of tradition (1991: 69).

In the context of considerations about equal citizenship, the defence of custom on the grounds of respect for supposedly long-standing tradition should also be recognised as an attempt to privatise the issue, in the sense of placing the custom of one group of South Africans beyond the reach of critical and educational attention. Working in association with the idea of the nation, this form of citizenship as membership also privatises the issue of gender equity by keeping it within the confines of the family.

Given divided opinion on the right way to resolve tensions between 'custom' and gender equality in the field of law, how might the influence of custom be taken up educationally? The principles entrenched in the Constitution and endorsed in the White Paper offer no clear resolution to these tensions. For here we have to make hard choices between gender equality on the one hand and respect for cultural diversity on the other. Even the principle of freedom of association cannot take us far on its own. It can be raised as an objection to the response to custom taken in this chapter – arguing that women who choose customary practices and roles are exercising their right to freedom of association. But this seems to raise more problems than it might solve. One is the response in turn that although women are often content with the status quo, we cannot conclude that what women do not see as oppressive is indeed not oppressive (Okin 1995: 292; Sunstein 1995: 350). There is evidence that women's preferences are adapted to what is available in their context. 'Oppressed people have often internalised their oppression so well that they *have* no sense of what they are justly entitled to as human beings' (Okin 1995: 292). The problem goes further than this when those who suffer inequalities accept them as legitimate, devising strategies for adjusting both their conduct and their desires to what is available.

If we are to defend women's decision to accept customary roles, then the conditions must be created in which a genuine choice can be made and exercised. This requires not only that such choice should be made free of coercion from others, but also that information about other possibilities should be provided and hence that there should be 'a full and vivid awareness of available opportunities' (Sunstein 1995: 350). This is complicated by the fact that free exercise of choice in relation to custom is constrained by the effects of custom itself.

In the meantime, unless they are explicitly addressed in schools, customary attitudes to the place of women are likely to continue, to be reproduced there as well as at home, and to undermine the capacity of girls to see and assert themselves as equal citizens, regardless of the formal rights conferred on them by the new Constitution, and the active citizen which it assumes.

The gender equity task team: putting gender equity on the civic agenda

Commissioned in terms of the White Paper on Education and Training, the Report of the Gender Equity Task Team (Department of Education 1997) provides a considered and courageous way forward for the project of educating for equal citizenship for girls. I focus on one aspect of its recommendations.

Among the range of inequalities emphasised throughout the Report is the violent nature of South African society and its dysfunctional effects, especially for the education of women and girls. Equally significant is the way in which the Report analyses the influence of traditional gendered roles, and its recommendations on how these traditional roles should be addressed educationally.

The Report discusses how the education system articulates with the family to reinforce traditional roles for women (26). Cultural beliefs about gender roles have a strong influence on the ideological construction of gender identity, and schools interact with family life in reinforcing these beliefs: that the authority and importance of men are natural and unquestionable, that girls should perform domestic duties even if this makes them miss school, and that girls should be quiet and submissive.

Taking the view that women and men need to be prepared to participate in civil society as well as to fulfil family roles, the Report argues that teachers should confront oppressive behaviour and that gender relations should be taken up actively in the curriculum and the classroom. To do this, social constructions of masculinity and femininity and gendered relations in the contexts of family, work and civic life will have to be examined (91). To do this, it is necessary to confront ideologies of gender and the cultural practices that underpin them. The Report proposes that 'socially sanctioned practices that devalue women and deny them basic human rights need to be interrogated, and schools are places where this can be carried out' (77). While it sees teachers as the main agents of this process, it also proposes a 'whole school development' approach, involving the broad community: students, parents, school governing bodies, administrators and churches. Although the Report is careful to stress that it is not arguing that schools should aim to change cultural practices, it does propose that it is necessary to interrogate 'socially sanctioned practices that devalue women and deny them basic human rights' (77), involving teachers, parents and students in examining sexist assumptions in familiar practices. The curriculum, it is proposed, needs to pay more careful attention to outcomes that promote gender equity in all the learning areas, with particular attention to 'broadening both boys' and girls' access to knowledge and ways of being beyond those endorsed by dominant cultures' (113). Students should be given opportunities to analyse the combined impact of patriarchy in its different forms – indigenous, Western and non-Western – on the life chances of girls and women.

For all its caution and sensitivity in warning against authoritarian or didactic approaches, the Report takes a clear stand in favour of addressing custom and its influence on gendered practices. Although a draft of the Report proposed that girls be included in nation-building projects, its final version resists the temptation to appeal to the idea of the nation. The Report thus avoids resorting to appeals to membership in formulating assumptions about gender equity, and hence about equal citizenship. Creating the necessary conditions for equal citizenship is recognised as requiring that girls acquire a sense of themselves as bearers of equal rights. By arguing that this in turn requires interrogating traditional gender practices on the civic agenda, the Report takes custom out of the private and into the public. Whether the Report's proposals are taken up in policy and the community will test the sincerity of the new democracy's resolve to create equal citizenship.

References

Albertyn, C. (1994) 'Women and the transition to democracy in South Africa', *Acta Juridica*, 94: 39–63.

Andrews, G. (ed.) (1991) *Citizenship*, London: Lawrence & Wishart.

Brown, B. (1996) 'Where are the Men? An investigation into female-headed households in Rini, with reference to household structures, the dynamics of gender, and strategies against poverty', M.A. Thesis, Rhodes University.

Canover, P. J. (1995) 'Citizenship identities and conceptions of the self', *Journal of Political Philosophy*, 3, 2: 133–165.

Chanock, M. (1989) 'Neither customary nor legal: African customary law in an era of family law reform', *International Journal of Law and the Family*, 3: 72–88.

Chanock, M. (1991) 'Law, state and culture: thinking about customary law after apartheid', *Acta Juridica*, 91: 52–70.

Commission on Gender Equality (1997) *Report of the GCE Information and Evaluation Workshops*, Pretoria: May.

Cross, M. and Leroke, W. (1995) 'Mystification of democracy: Penny Enslin's critique of nation-building', *Perspectives in Education*, 16, 2: 329–340.

Currie, I. (1994) 'The future of customary law: lessons from the lobola debate', *Acta Juridica*, 94: 146–168.

Department of Education (1995) *White Paper on Education and Training*, Pretoria: March.

Department of Education (1997) *Gender Equity in Education: report of the Gender Equity Task Team*, Pretoria: October.

Dietz, M. (1992) 'Context is all: feminism and theories of citizenship', in C. Mouffe (ed.) *Dimensions of Radical Democracy, Pluralism, Citizenship, Community*, London: Verso.

Enslin, P. (1993/4) 'Education for nation-building: a feminist critique', *Perspectives in Education*, 15, 1: 13–25.

Enslin, P. (1995) 'Encounter with a straw man: a rejoinder to Cross and Leroke', *Perspectives in Education*, 16, 2: 341–352.

Heater, D. (1990) *Citizenship: the civic ideal in Western history, politics and education*, London: Longman.

Jones, K. B. (1990) 'Citizenship in a woman-friendly polity', *Signs: Journal of Women in Culture and Society*, 15, 4: 781–812.

Kymlicka, W. and Norman, W. (1994) 'Return of the citizen: recent work on citizenship theory', *Ethics*, 104: 352–381.

Lister, R. (1995) 'Dilemmas in engendering citizenship', *Economy and Society* 24, 1: 1–40.

Lucas, J. (1995) 'Space, domesticity and people's power', *African Studies*, 54, 1: 89–113.

Mail & Guardian (1997a) ' "No more" to violence against women', August 8–14.

Mail & Guardian (1997b) 'Big hopes, little funding', August 8–14.

Marshall, T. H. (1950) *Citizenship and Social Class*, Cambridge: Cambridge University Press, quoted in S. Walby (1994) 'Is citizenship gendered?' *Sociology*, 28, 2: 379–395.

Ministry of Education (1997) *Draft Statement on the National Curriculum for Grades 1–9*, Pretoria: June.

Mkwanazi, Z. and Cross, M. (1992) 'The dialectic of unity and diversity in education: its implications for a national curriculum in South Africa', working paper, Johannesburg: National Education Policy Investigation.

Nhlapo, T. (1995) 'African customary law in the interim constitution', in S. Liebenberg (ed.) *The Constitution of South Africa from a Gender Perspective*, Cape Town: David Philip.

Okin, S. M. (1995) 'Inequalities between the sexes in different cultural contexts', in M. Nussbaum and J. Glover (eds) *Women, Culture and Development: a study of human capabilities*, Oxford: Clarendon Press.

Pateman, C. (1989) *The Disorder of Women*, Cambridge: Polity Press.

Phillips, A. (1993) 'Citizenship and feminist theory', in *Democracy and Difference*, Cambridge: Polity Press.

Republic of South Africa (1996) *The Constitution*, Pretoria: Government Printer.

The Star (1996) 'ANC women demand female oppression's end', 18 April.

The Star (1998) 'Bill signals better deal for women', 12 September.

Sunday Independent (1997) 'Women MPs set to flee macho parliament', 10 August.

Sunstein, C. (1995) 'Gender, caste and law', in Nussbaum and Glover (eds) *Women, Culture and Development: a study of human capabilities*, Oxford: Clareudon Press.

Walby, S. (1994) 'Is citizenship gendered?', *Sociology*, 28, 2: 379–395.

Walker, C. (1990) Review of Women – Nation–State Agenda: a journal about women and gender, 6: 43.

Walker, C. (1992) 'Attitudes to lobola', *Agenda: a journal about women and gender*, 13: 57–58.

Young, I. M. (1990) 'Polity and group difference: a critique of the idea of universal citizenship', in *Throwing Like a Girl and other Essays in Feminist Philosophy and Social Theory*, Bloomington: Indiana University Press.

18 Cyberfeminism and citizenship?

Challenging the political imaginary

Jane Kenway with Diana Langmead

In recent years, there has been a revival of interest in 'citizenship' in many national contexts, particularly those identified as 'Western' nations. For example, governments are increasingly drawing upon the language of 'citizenship' to confront political problems which are thought to be of some threat to the stability of the nation state. And, as new political circumstances emerge, discourses of citizenship follow. Indeed, there is now regular talk of such things as global citizenship, corporate citizenship and consumer citizenship. There has also been a rash of civics and citizenship curriculum developed for schools.

In the first section of this chapter, we consider the ways in which concepts of citizenship, digital technologies and feminism come together in the context of our increasingly globalized cultures and economies. The rest of the paper is devoted largely to a discussion of the politics of cyberfeminisms ('cyberfeminist conventionalists' and 'advant-garde cyberfeminists) and their implicit and gendered notions of citizenship. It is our view that both groups of cyberfeminists have identified new sites for political action and have, at the same time, invoked new notions of the polity which pose some interesting and complex dilemmas for women's citizenship 'in the new millennium'. They also open up new ways of thinking about civics and citizenship curriculum for schools. To set the scene, we begin with some brief introductory remarks about citizenship debates amongst feminists and various cyberspheres.

Debating citizenship

Citizenship, Jones (1997: 1) observes, bestows an array of rights (civil, political and social) and responsibilities on individuals. It also implies a specific type of social relationship between members of a political entity, symbolizes some connections of culture, tradition and geography and distinguishes one group of people from another. In essence, though, citizenship is connected to the apparatuses and discourses of government and is closely linked to traditional understandings of the state. Inevitably then, complex questions arise about the relationship between, for example, citizenship, gender, nationality, and culture (e.g. see Pettman 1996).

Citizenship 'is a weighty, monumental, humanist word' (Fraser and Gordon 1997). However, as Jones also observes, 'Within the dominant lexicon of Western political theory, . . . aspects of citizenship have been variously defined . . . [and] Citizenship has been one of the most contested categories of political analysis' (Jones 1997: 1). Citizenship debates revolve largely around issues of identity, action and locale (ibid.). What is it, who can claim it, on what grounds and for what purposes? What does it permit, prevent and promote? Whose interests does it serve? Who does it exclude and with what consequences? And, alternatively, what might it become? Such questions have preoccupied feminists for some time.

Feminist political theorists have, for example, exposed the gendered dimensions of citizenship and their associated conceptual frameworks and ideological underpinnings, particularly those associated with the nation state. They have also constructed new perspectives on citizenship (e.g. Mouffe 1993). Feminist formulations of citizenship have investigated discursive shifts in the meanings of such concepts as rights, needs, justice, dependency, entitlements and democratic participation. Equally, they have sought strategic transformation of the relations of power which configure the terms of inclusion and exclusion in the polity (e.g. Yeatman 1997). For example, women's involvement in community groups and social movements has led to calls for the redefinition of both citizenship and notions of the 'public' and 'civic'. Indeed, such involvement has led to calls for a broadened understanding of political action and for the recognition of a 'plurality of public spheres'. But, as Jones argues, a wide array of socio-cultural changes have forced feminist theorists to rethink the concept of citizenship 'at the most fundamental level' (1997: 5). Such changes include border transformations within and between nation states, the intensification of migration flows, the associated growth of multi-ethnic polities, the rise of new social movements for political participation, and 'the emergence of world transforming new technologies of communication and imagination' (Jones 1997: 5). All these shifts challenge the 'boundary functions of state discourses' (Dalby 1994).

There are, therefore, many questions worth posing about gender and citizenship at the commencement of the twenty-first century. Given that digitalized technologies have become a primary driving force of contemporary times, it is important to consider what the feminist literature has to say about the relationship between technology, citizenship and associated matters of identity, action and locale. Of particular interest for us is the feminist literature (most of which is now called cyberfeminism) which is concerned with cyberspheres – with cyberspace, cyberpolitics and cyberculture. In the next section we explore the ways in which feminism connects with these spheres.

Cyberspheres

Put simply, cyberspace is that transnational space which comes into being when computers, modems and telephone lines are activated together through the Internet:

[C]yberspace is now part of the routines of everyday life. When we read our electronic mail or send postings to an electronic bulletin board or make an airline reservation over a computer network, we are in cyberspace. In cyberspace, we can talk, exchange ideas, and assume personae of our own creation. We have the opportunity to build new kinds of communities, virtual communities, in which we participate with people from all over the world, people with whom we converse daily, people with whom we may have fairly intimate relationships but whom we may never physically meet.

(Turkle 1995: 9–10)

Cyberspace is a faceless, spaceless plethora of places which offer many different ways of communicating. These include real-time chat sessions, person-to-person email, networked discussion groups, journals, multi-media databases and virtual reality. As we will demonstrate, it is these new opportunities for association and relations of cultural production which may offer new opportunities for citizenship.

So how is cyberpolitics understood? Within cyberspace, there are no borders or bodies, only the texts, images and sounds made from bits and bytes and associated with multiple cyberlocales. Generally, such worlds are both public and private and have no government. In terms of political life, then, cyber-enthusiasts commonly talk of webs and networks with multiple and shifting centres of power and authors of meaning. Such enthusiasts invoke metaphors of seamlessness, heterogeneity, interactivity, interconnectedness, reciprocity, community, fluidity and freedom (e.g. Reingold 1994). Indeed, the key slogan of Netiquette is 'Information wants to be free'. Many on-line communities reject any form of authority, be it exercised by the state or by commerce. So, while on the one hand, we see shades of neo-libertarianism and a sort of 'Do It Yourself (DIY)' political activism, on the other hand, we see a deep hostility to markets and market forces on-line. With its digitized distribution and multicasting capacities, the Internet is thus seen to have the capacity to challenge notions of authority and hierarchy and indeed the authorship and ownership of such cultural products as art, music, literature.

At the very least, citizenship discourses have been developed for embodied individuals who occupy specific territories. However, cyberspace is disembodied, disembedded, and deterritorialized. And, cyberspace enthusiasts talk about cyberspace as a place in which participants can renegotiate the rules of civic life. New relationships between producers and consumers of cultural texts, new and different ways of communicating and relating, new cultural and social identities, and new ways of developing and assembling knowledge all hint at new possibilities for citizenship. In cyberspace, say the enthusiasts, we can be different, readily embrace difference and indeed reflect and act differently upon the nature of self, community and human existence. The talk here is less of citizens and more of cyborgs.

Certainly some groups of cyberfeminists, but by no means all, see themselves as leading edge, as working at the feminist frontier, as boldly going where no woman has gone before. So, let us now consider cyberfeminism itself and whether such bold claims can be sustained. In so doing, we will consider the extent to which the concerns of cyberfeminists are in fact different from those feminists who are currently addressing issues of citizenship in what cyber-enthusiasts are fond of calling *Real Life* (RL).

Cyberfeminism is a contested term (Hall 1996; Braidotti accessed 1999; Wilding accessed 1999). In general, though, it can be understood as a form of feminist politics which concerns women's relationships to digitised, networked and increasingly converging information and communication technologies (ICTs) and their surrounding contexts and cultures. It comes in many modalities. Some of these – namely, the *cyberfeminist conventionalists* – address issues which are common to the various feminist citizenship discourses we outlined at the start. Others, sometimes referred to as *the avant-garde cyberfeminists,* propose a style of politics which is somewhat less familiar. Below, we outline the differences between these two approaches whilst acknowledging that our two-fold categorization is rather crude but nonetheless useful for the purposes of this chapter.

Cyberfeminist conventionalists

By far the most common feminist approach to cyberspace is to consider questions of access, voice, gender dynamics, violence, power/knowledge and the control of information and communication technologies (ICTs) (Harcourt 1999). Cyberspace is therefore understood in various ways, all of which concern the question of gender either directly or indirectly. It is seen as a new and incredibly significant technology of power which males invent, inscribe and control and which women must learn to do likewise, to invent, inscribe and control (Spender 1995: 165–247). It is seen as a public space which differently located women have unequal access to, and to which they must gain equal access. It is also seen as a public place within which the gender dynamics are unequal for various reasons. Enhancing women's rights and responsibilities and offering them 'enlightenment' with regard to new technologies, challenging the political culture of cyberspace politics in on- and off-line governmental spaces, and considering national differences in access and participation are all part of the agenda. By way of example, we consider how such issues of access and interaction are understood.

The question of access on-line: a feminist issue

Access is considered a baseline issue by this loosely linked group of cyberfeminists. They are concerned with matters of cost, availability and competence and indeed the quality of access. There is high- and low-end Internet Access and this can mean significant differences in what it is possible to accomplish. Further, the path from having no access to having a computer, a modem, advanced communications software, an on-line service account and the knowledge necessary to use them all is not likely to be easily travelled by the 'information poor'. Matters of language (most Net communication is in English), poverty, social and geographic isolation, disability, gender, generation and First and Third World/North and South location, as they overlap and intersect, are seen as particularly pertinent here. Indeed, in global terms, those with access constitute a privileged minority of the world's population.

Cyberfeminist conventionalists adopt a politics of inclusion – seeking to include differently located and embodied women across the globe – in particular the 'digitally homeless' (Negroponte 1995). And in all cases, they operate according to diversified and pluralistic feminist models of citizenship. They ask, 'what new gender inequalities will virtual geography superimpose over those inequalities which already exist in the geographies and cultures of nation states and supranational political bodies?' For example, The Gender and IT Discussion (http://www.igc.apc.org/gk97) in the lead-up to the *Global Knowledge '97* conference in Toronto, included many women expressing concern about access and technical support in 'developing' nations, and searching for strategies to assist women in 'technologically deficient' regions.

The comparative absence of women (in relation to men) in cyberspace, however, can be explained by factors other than unequal access. Other feminist explanations include the gender dynamics of cyberspace interactions and the metaphors guiding such interactions, many of which come from the military. On-line discussions, it is argued, are governed by gendered codes in much the same way as discussions in other settings (Balsamo 1993: 697–698). As Michals (1997: 71) argues, 'by sheer force of their numbers, [males] dictate the tone and content' enabling 'some of the most flagrant forms of male domination'. For example, violence on-line, sexual harassment, flaming and virtual rape are seen to be features of such interactions. Libertarian netiquette is not seen as helpful here. Michals argues that it is likely that airing 'violent inclinations freely and without reproach . . . merely normalize[s] these tendencies, inuring society to the viciousness and inequality at its core' (ibid.: 70).

A range of approaches has been put forward to encourage women's access and participation and to thus change the power dynamics of the public sphere of cyberspace. These include such things as exploring ways to encourage women/girls to use the Internet as a tool of information and communication, setting up women-only lists, and woman-to-woman self-help and technological training. Other approaches are thought to encourage women to develop skills which allow them to use the Internet for feminist net critique and active citizenship on- and off-line. Included here are such things as distributing and discussing information on gender and other social issues, and building female communities for the purposes of networking and political mobilization. The *Virtual Sisterhood* (accessed 1997), for instance, wants to digitize fully the women's movement. Global networking for political change is the central imperative.

Clearly, such cyber-citizenship activities carry forward notions about the restricted opportunities, rights and status of women and construct alternative feminist cyber-civics seeking either equal or differential inclusions in the new public sphere of cyberspace. However, such ideas and practices are not what some cyberfeminists would characterize as 'leading edge' work on the 'feminist frontier'. An alternative set of approaches is described as 'avant-garde' cyberfeminism.

Avant-garde cyberfeminists

This diverse group of cyberfeminists distance themselves from the cyberfeminist conventionalists who, even though dealing with new technologies, are regarded as out of touch with contemporary political life. Indeed, as Wilding (accessed 1999) says, they question the 'relevance of feminist history, theory and practice to present conditions facing women immersed in technology'. For example, they adopt a superior stance in relation to the image of women as 'victims' and any suggestion that some women may be technophobic. Being a righteous victim, one says, is 'uncool and boring' (Skelties in Harbison accessed 1997). They see conventional feminists' suggestions for 'Net practice' as getting it wrong.

Others see feminism and/or women-only groups as providing a form of censorship. Any attempt to censor the language and behaviour of anyone on the Net is seen as an unacceptable form of policing which goes against the Net Ethic of total freedom. Some also see women-only electronic salons as 'politeness ghettos'. St. Jude's (otherwise known as Jude Milhon) view is 'Fuck Niceness!'(St. Jude and Cross accessed 1997). She wants women to toughen up, to become 'on-line warriors for civilisation, going at it toe-to-toe with net bullies and bigots' (ibid.). Her view is that the Net provides women with ideal opportunities to learn to defend themselves and even to turn around the views of Net bullies and bigots. She says 'Learn to fight! . . . This is the best training ground for women; we may start 10 down in a physical fight, OK, but the keyboard is the great equalizer'. She also wants women to lighten up, to become 'net pranksters'. As she argues: 'It's the ultimate prankster's medium, of course. You're bounded only by your ingenuity. You can prank anybody with whatever outrageousness you can concoct.'

Amongst these cyberfeminists, cyber-citizenship and politics are not understood in terms of civic competencies, rights and responsibilities, dependence or independence or indeed enlightenment. For instance, the networked computer is seen as a 'butt-kicking tool of empowerment', a means of sowing the seeds of 'virtual viruses' and ultimately 'a new world disorder'. Here is how VNS Matrix describe their political manifesto: '. . . women who hijack the tools of domination and control introduce a rupture into a highly systematized culture by infecting the machines with radical thought, diverting them from their inherent purpose of linear top down mastery' (accessed 1997).

In the following sub-sections, we identify three themes which shape the approach of advant-garde cyberfeminists: the politics of culture; the relationship between humans and machines especially in relation to gender, and the political issues associated with liquid identities.

The politics of culture

Avant-garde cyberfeminists are interested not so much in the culture of politics as the politics of culture. Take the example of 'girl power'. Although they do not draw on the language of citizenship, there is a new generation of feminists who seek 'girl power' or more accurately 'Grrl (or grrl) power' through the use of new technology. These groups include such suitably insurgent titles as 'riot grrls', 'guerrilla grrrls', and 'bad grrrls'. In relevant sites on-line, we see a wide range of cultural and sexual representations and interventions which take various forms and foci. These include 'sci-fi, cyberpunk, and femporn zines; anti-discrimination projects; sexual exhibitionism; transgender experimentation; lesbian separatism; medical self-help; artistic self-promotion; job and dating services; and just plain mouthing off' (Wilding accessed 1999).

Cybergrrrls celebrate multiple ways of being female, and disparate feminine cultures, sexualities, styles and pleasures. As Williams (accessed 1999) says, 'net chicks come in all varieties', they celebrate a 'feisty individuality' and even assert 'a girl's right to be feminine'. Grrrl power is an offspring of consumer/techno culture which venerates speed and change, the new, the novel, virtuality, and simulation. Here we see on- and off-line publications such as *geekgirl* and *NetChick* (Sinclair 1996). Such publications showcase prominent 'cybergrrls' and act as 'guides to the wired world'. They are quirky, smart and slick, fun, pop and offer feisty articles and chic images which glorify new technologies, technological savvy and linguistic net-speak panache. Also in this vein is the development of girl-friendly software and computer games. For example, Janese Swanson has established the company *Girl Tech* whose goal is to invent technology-based products which are 'cool', easy to use and fun for girls between the ages of 6 and 12 (Mahony 1997: 37–40).

Insisting on particular versions of feminist citizenship is not embedded in this grrrl power story. This story is instead designed to say to grrrls 'Do it yourself (DIY)' and 'Do what you like'. The civic sphere for this group is popular culture and their tools of citizenship are often humour, irony, mimicry, parody, burlesque and transgression. They do not necessarily seek to unsettle gender and sexual binaries so much as to play with or mock, exaggerate and distort them. Although passionate, angry and aggressive tirades against net-nurds and cowboys are also evident, old-style rational and 'serious' feminist critiques are largely off the agenda. For example, as Rosie Cross (1996), editor of *geekgirl*, implies, women have been shackled by 'the gender debate and feminist rhetoric', and 'resources like the www' will 'empower and liberate women' from such. Interestingly, although cybergrrrls do in fact draw upon some of the traditions of cultural and radical feminism, they align themselves with those cyberfeminist performers and theorists who have put a range of somewhat new styles and issues on the feminist citizenship agenda (e.g. art, culture, theory, communication and technology). Some of the leading names here are Allucquere Rosanne Stone, Sadie Plant, Rosi Braidotti, Donna Harraway, Sherry Turkle, St. Jude and VNS Matrix.

On the matter of cultural production as politics, VNS Matrix and

Moondance are one of many groups who are bypassing male-controlled publication outlets. They are using the multi-casting potential of the Internet for worldwide distribution for outrageous, dissident and anti-techno establishment publications of art, music, photography, film, video and poetry. For example, VNS Matrix has developed an interactive computer artwork CD-ROM game *All New Gen* and the *BAD CODE* game. Here, the viral intelligence, Gen, sabotages the data banks of Big Daddy Mainframe, activating the germ of the new world disorder (VNS Matrix 1996: 74–5). Part of the attraction of such games is their fusion of power, pleasure and danger. Avant-garde cyberfeminists are keen to ensure that women are able to enjoy the dangerous pleasures and pleasurable dangers available cybernetically. It is not, therefore, feminist political theory which provides them with the conceptual tools to analyse such cultural forms. Rather, it is cultural studies, film, literary and queer theory.

Cyberfeminists clearly understand that postmodern culture is characterized by the breaking down of many traditional boundaries. It goes without saying that the 'old' feminist movement has played an important role in deconstructing the boundaries between public and private, culture and politics, knowledge and power, personal and political, dependence and independence, and rationality and emotionality. In addition, though, avant-garde cyberfeminists are interested in the new 'identity-making' work associated with a range of new cultural forms and cultural sites. They are interested in challenging such distinctions as mind and body, human and machine, male and female, and real life and simulation, and indeed pleasure and danger. Further, such literary genres as science and cyberpunk fiction and the futures and images they generate are of great interest to avant-garde cyberfeminists both as objects of critique (e.g. Springer 1991) and inspiration (e.g. Plant 1993). They are seen to suggest new, radically different, and sometimes preferable ways of being human and post-human. Braidotti (accessed 1999) explains some of the underlying politics here:

> In all fields, but especially in information technology, the strict separation between the technical and the creative has in fact been made redundant by digital images and the skills required by computer-aided design. The new alliance between the previously segregated domains of the technical and the artistic marks a contemporary version of the post-humanistic reconstruction of a techno-culture whose aesthetics is equal to its technological sophistication.

'Science becomes the handmaiden of magic' (Schroeder 1994: 526). This techno-scientific and aesthetic fusion is evident in a range of on- and off-line sites and techno-cultural artifacts. Many recreational computer activities provide obvious examples which, incidentally, also challenge the boundaries between 'high-tech and primitivism, and between play and real life' (Skirrow 1990: 323). ICTs are also brought into close association with various youthful counter-cultural forms.

Cyberpunk nightclubs and cafés in such global cities as San Francisco and London draw on a similar fusion, also emphasizing their challenges to the senses. As Schroeder explains, they invite customers in with promises of 'Altered images, altered sound, altered minds and altered states' (Schroeder 1994: 522). As this implies, 'bodily pursuits are a part . . . of the political culture of cyberculture' (ibid.: 521). And such bodily pursuits include cyber-sex (Parker 1997), pornography and erotica (Springer 1991).

It is something of an irony that technologies of disembodiment have become linked with such bodily pursuits. It is also ironical that smart machines have prompted such turns of phrase as 'the clitoris is a direct line to the matrix' (Steffensen accessed 1999) and helped to activate new feminist engagements with 'physicality, interiority and eroticism' (Sofoulis 1995). As Sofoulis (ibid.) shows, many women computer artists provocatively invoke 'meditation on perceptual and physical experience'. The CD-ROM title, 'Cyberflesh Girlmonster', suggests something of what such meditation might mean.

Human/machine relationship and the question of gender

Avant-garde cyberfeminists also reconceptualize the human/machine relationship, re-reading the driving forces behind this relationship and its political implications. The approaches developed by such cyberfeminists are important since they are likely to have increasing implications for feminist conceptualizations and practices of citizenship, as we will now show.

Avant-garde cyberfeminists believe that the distinctions between humans and machines are collapsing. 'Cyberspace shifts reality into the virtual; the cyborg embraces identity collapse' (Plant 1993: 17). As Sherry Turkle (1995: 23) says, we are becoming increasingly comfortable with cultures of simulation – those cultures which substitute representations of reality for the real. She is fascinated by the role-playing activities conducted in virtual reality environments on the Net called MOOs and MUDs, and has conducted extensive research within them. She shows how participants are using the technology to construct, experiment with, and develop new 'selves'. In MUDs, people 'self-fashion, self-create' (ibid.: 180), a point we return to below.

It is also the case that through careful programming, cyberspace constructions can now be developed that are not human but that 'behave' in a such a way as to provoke human-like interactions with other participants in virtual environments. According to Turkle (1995), some such 'female' constructions represent highly stereotypical female characteristics. But the issue here is bigger than that, for the ultimate questions are what are they programmed to do, how does their behavior affect other members of that cyber-group and how should off-line folk respond to them and to those who create them? This is clearly a citizenship issue. Take an example to illustrate the point.

As the infamous Mr Bungle case on LambdaMOO illustrates, cyber-rape has now occurred (Dibbell 1994: 26–32). A MUD player created voodoo dolls of the other players, then proceeded to sexually assault them violently and to force them to sexually assault each other and themselves. The next day, one of the assaulted players posted her response to a widely read social issues mailing list explaining her distress and calling upon the group to act against the offender – possibly through virtual castration. This call raised a number of questions about cyber-citizenship. However, the group itself was unable to resolve the issue and in the end had to resort to the authority of the person who controlled it technologically.

This example is one of many which raises issues about the extent to which cyber-groups are adequately 'renegotiating the rules of civic life', as the cyber-enthusiasts suggest. It also raises profound questions about the relationship between Real Life and Virtual Reality – how real is simulation and do rights and responsibilities matter in simulated environments? If so, how are they best protected and advanced? Since this controversial case, many have had difficulty empathizing with the victim's distress. Witness the words of St. Jude:

> In cyberspace everyone can hear you scream. There was a woman crying virtual rape on LambdaMOO. It's a game, lady. You lost. You could have teleported. Or changed into an Iron Maiden (the spiky kind) and crimped off his dick . . . Because the MOO's is also a social space, where you can meet people with real cultural differences – like Klansmen – and make them respect you as a woman, as a dyke, as whatever. Toe-to-toe, you may change their prejudices forever . . . Cries for niceness don't make it.
>
> (Quoted in Cross 1995)

This sort of gung-ho suggestion to 'teleport' or to technologically gag the offender from one's screen is not one that meets with much approval. As Dibbell (1994: 29) observes, it certainly did not attract the support of opponents of Mr Bungle in the LambdaMOO who looked for more communitarian solutions to the problem. He calls this:

> a gag and get over it school of virtual rape counseling with its fine line between empowering victims and holding them responsible for their own suffering and its shrugging indifference to the window of pain between the moment the rape text starts and the moment a gag shuts it off.

The victim was not simply caught between competing views about virtual rape but also between Virtual Reality and Real Life. How seriously can virtual behaviour be taken? Is it 'only a game'? Apparently the victim's words failed to convey the extent of her pain, which was, according to Dibbell, 'Ludicrously excessive by [Real life's] lights, woefully understated by VR's, the tone of [the victim's] response made sense only in the buzzing, dissonant gap between them' (Dibbell in Turkle 1995: 252).

Communication has a lot to do with what is unspoken. How shall the unspoken be spoken in a system based on well-defined input-data (Sarkis 1993: 14)? Caught as she was between Virtual Reality and Real Life, could the victim have expected support from either realm, and if so what forms could it possibly have taken?

The apparent drive for this human–machine fusion and the reasons behind it are matters of some fascination for certain cyberfeminists. Allucquere Stone describes the 'cybernetic act' as consisting of:

> the desire to cross the human/machine boundary . . . a desire literally to enter into such a discourse, to penetrate the smooth and relatively affect-less surface of the electronic screen and enter the deep, complex, and tactile (individual) cybernetic space or the (consensual) cyberspace within and beyond. Penetrating the screen involves a state change from the physical, biological space of the embodied viewer to the symbolic, metaphorical 'consensual hallucination' of cyberspace; a space that is a locus of intense desire for refigured embodiment.
>
> (1991: 108–109)

What is behind this urge to alter our bodily status? Claudia Springer observes that contemporary popular culture represents human fusion with electronic technology as pleasurable and that this fusion attraction is based on the merging of the death wish and the pleasure principle into cyborg imagery (1991: 306–308). There is a tradition in literature which uses 'loss of self' as a metaphor for orgasm, and also 'the equation of death with love has been accompanied in literature by the idea of bodiless sexuality: two united souls represent the purest form of romance' (Springer 1991: 307). Thus, associating the loss of identity with sexuality is bound to have widespread appeal. If we accept Springer's inferences, women can be both cerebral and sexual (1991: 312). Similarly, Neumark views women's cyborg relationships as an opportunity to take pleasure in their own power (1993: 84). Possibly, the citizen-cyborg is invited to blend pleasure and power in ways often unavailable to her elsewhere.

Many alternative feminist theorists share an undercurrent of dissatisfaction with the uncertainty, uncontrollability and vulnerability of our bodies in the context of the current world disorder and a belief that immersion in cyberspace transforms this. Some suggest that the desire to control the body is paramount. Hayles, for example, argues that we seek comfort in the thought that physical forms can recover their pristine purity when they are reconstituted as informational patterns in cyberspace. 'A cyberspace body, like a cyberspace landscape, is immune to blight and corruption' (1993: 81).

Liquid identities

Questions of identity are also central to avant-garde cyberfeminism, but not in ways which are typical of identity politics. Feminists have long been interested in identity and the problem of privileged male identities. Sadie Plant suggests that 'much feminist struggle has been devoted to the search for the . . . missing ingredient which would give women a full and equal place in human society'. However, she argues that 'cyberfemininity is . . . not a subject lacking an identity, but a virtual reality, whose identity is a mere tactic of infiltration. VR is a disturbance of human identity' (Plant 1993: 16).

According to Jaron Lanier, VR pioneers preferred the expression 'intentional reality' to 'virtual reality' (Druckrey 1991: 6). They understood it as a subjective alternative to our symbolic world, as opposed to a replacement of the physical world. This suggests another attraction of Virtual Reality. One way in which cyber-travellers intentionally vary their symbolic world is by playing with their identities, especially their gender and sexuality. Identity-switching has become so much a part of Net interaction that players now try to work out who is a woman playing a man, who is straight but playing gay, who is a child playing an adult – with all the accompanying alternatives and variations.

The appeal and politics of gender and identity role-playing have become a matter for inquiry. Cyberfeminists of all hues discuss the differences women encounter when presenting as men in cyberspace. They relate tales of the poorer status women occupy in all aspects, except sexual encounters. Indeed, some suggest it is this higher sexual attractiveness women have on the Net which entices men to role-play as women.

Some cyberfeminists claim that identity switching is a liberating exercise, freeing them from being judged according to their gender in a negative way, or giving them the power to choose which gender to function in at any given time or situation. However, Bromley suggests that rather than destabilizing the binary gender regime, cross-gender play is indeed a manifestation of that very structure. He argues that it reflects the social undesirability and handicaps awaiting those who present as women, and reinforces the attitudes men have towards women's value and social status, attitudes perpetuated by men presenting as women who 'expect' and 'encourage' such patronizing, condescending and outright offensive behaviours towards women (1995: 68).

A matter of fascination for some cyberfeminist scholars is what this all means for the construction of humanity. For example, Allucquere Rosanne Stone (1991), a leading theoretician of identity/bodies/machines, explores this issue through some telling tales of the Net which make problematic the notion of identity itself. Her first suggestion is that there is no identity 'masked under the virtual persona' but rather that the disembodiment of the Internet allows repressed and multiple persona to come into play. Her second suggestion is that it encourages a 'radical rewriting . . . of the bounded individual as the standard social unit and validated social actant' (1991: 43) and indeed challenges much psychoanalytic theory. As Stone (1991: 36) says, networks are social environments where:

> Some of the interactions are racially differentiated and gendered, stereotypical and Cartesian, reifying old power differentials whose workings are familiar and whose effects are understood. But some of the interactions are novel, strange, perhaps transformative, and certainly disruptive of many traditional attempts at categorization.

Stone goes on to suggest that 'new collective structures (are) risking themselves in novel conditions' (1991: 36). This point leads us back to the question about the implications of such disruptions, new identities and collective structures for life off-line.

Clearly, disembodiment allows things to occur in cyberspace that may not happen in Real Life. But what are the consequences for the off-line lives of those whose liquid identities emerge in cyberspace? What carries over and what is only tenable in cyberspace? And do such questions matter? The literature suggests that new VR identities tend to remain in that realm but not necessarily by choice. When their on-line personas are 'better' than their off-line persona, players tend to prefer their on-line to their off-line lives. This has several implications for the study of gender and citizenship on-line.

First, it means that they invest their political energies there. Although players recognize that they cannot really avoid their RL lives, the relationships and politics of cyberculture come to be more important than those of embodied relationships and geographical polities. So, for example, what happens in a discussion group on the topic of toxic waste may be considered more important than what happens in a local protest over toxic waste. On first glance, this would seem to have obvious implications for conventional forms of government and civic action. However, it should be treated as an open question which is worth pursuing, and not as a zero sum matter. It may well be the case that what people choose to do in cyberspace points to the limits of their participation in Real Life. Turkle's (1995) stories about disenfranchised middle-class young people's engagements in cyberpolitics tells us something about what they see as the limited possibilities for political engagement in their off-line lives.

Another implication is that having learnt to be 'different' in cyberspace, attempts may be made to transport new learnings and identities from one realm to another. However, as Turkle's research shows, such attempts have not proved easy or necessarily successful (Turkle 1995: 185). Further, whilst they recognize that there is potential for 'self-improvement' via lessons learned through identity-shuffling in cyberspace (ibid.: 186–192), the extent to which players do self-reflect and use their experiences to change or modify their RL selves towards 'betterment' remains another open question.

Problems for cyberfeminism and citizenship

The focus in much of this cyberfeminist literature is either explicitly or implicitly on the individual and this, in itself, poses some paradoxes for cyber-citizenship. For instance, Cross claims that 'the individual at the centre of an ever-increasing, complex universe of networks can be a free radical, or part of a community, or be one's own goddess' (1996: 85). Whilst such individualism may be explained away as simply a sign of postmodernity, it is worth considering other viewpoints. Tafler and d'Agostino comment that the ideology of the individual masks the interdependence of all people within contemporary society. They argue further that 'the cult of the individual fuels the illusion of limitless freedom' (Tafler and d'Agostino 1993: 52). Limitless freedom certainly matches well the anarchical tendencies of some cyberfeminists. It allows individuals to opt in and out of cyber-communities at will, just as it allows individuals to opt in and out of political identities at will. Rather than analysing the potential for citizenship in these circumstances, interest seems to be directed more towards how 'this rugged and anarchic individualism finds expression in the context of an explicit activism' (Galvin 1995: 72).

But, of course, the 'rugged and anarchic individualism' of certain cyberfeminists is only part of a much bigger story about the micro-politics of simulation, liquid identities, Real Life/cyber-life and machine/body relationships. We refer in part here to what Donna Harraway calls 'the informatics of domination' (1991: 161). This term refers to the complex apparatuses that have arisen in the alliance between technology and culture, and technology and the economy – digitalized technologies have become a primary driving force of contemporary cultures and economies. A recognition of such force helps to explain cyberfeminists' focus on certain cultural forms as prime sites for inquiry and civic activism. However, with the exception of Harraway's work, there is a relative absence in cyber-feminism on the topic of cyborg economies or indeed the bigger social and cultural shifts associated with the emergence of what Castelles (1996) calls 'global networked society'. Matters under consideration include 'fast capitalism', globally distributed and electronically connected labour and the techno-scientific and management knowledge apparatuses which sustain them. The latter include new organizational practices which are linked to recent global trends in business and government organizations where decentralizing, down-sizing, out-sourcing, offshoring and customizing have become the dominant practices. Bigum (1997) writes, 'human beings are displaced and de-skilled, non-humans have to be upgraded and re-skilled. The prepared software anticipates the de-skilling yet at the same time requires re-skilling of the human operator. Human and non-human properties are exchanged.'

When one takes such matters into account, the cyborg metaphor loses its radical gloss. As Rowan and Bigum (1998) imply, the cyborg metaphor may ultimately work to depoliticize the relationship between humans and machines *in the world of work* (see also van der Ploeg and van Wingerden 1995). When we see it in the context of the virtual economy, it reverts to its original meaning; traditional human-machine alliances able to produce 'supermen' to suit different capitalist environments. Bigum (1997) argues that it is important for workers to understand themselves as 'human actants, technology as a non-human actant and to appreciate that they are in a relationship which is potentially negotiable'. In failing to consider cyborg economics as a civic sphere, cyberfeminism leaves an unfortunate gap in its activism.

Conclusions

By now it should be clear that all cyberfeminists have offered new understandings of contemporary political identities, actions and locales both on-line and off-line. All suggest new foci for civics and citizenship curriculum for schools. Indeed, they offer concepts of citizenship which seem of particular relevance to the young people of the so-called developed world who have grown up in consumer/media, globalized culture. They are likely to appeal to their generational sensibilities.

All cyberfeminists recognize that:

> the increasing pervasiveness of computing in society means that activism around technology increasingly becomes coextensive with social change work in general. No longer a specialized concern, computing becomes an indispensable tool and a facet of every particular site of human practice.
>
> (Agre 1997)

Clearly, this offers new notions of citizenship and political action and adds another sphere to the 'plurality of public spheres' which feminists have long called for. Paradoxically, however, the vocabulary and political tactics of some cyberfeminists are similar to other feminists who are currently addressing issues of citizenship in more traditional theoretical terms. They seek to animate a sense of autonomy, encourage women to claim rights on the Net, to access and enjoy cyberspace, to communicate with one another globally and indeed to be politically active in a wide range of ways including conventional engagements with the state, but on matters of gender and technology. They continue to remind us of the dangers of 'the effacement of place' with its 'complex contingencies' (Dalby 1994: 607).

As indicated, the avant-garde cyberfeminists express rather different concerns. They are not particularly concerned with nationality or rationality, with enlightenment or embodiment or with the power and politics associated with government. They are more interested in the politics of pleasure and play than those associated with rights and responsibilities. They are absorbed by the politics of culture, not so much the culture of politics. Therefore, new cultural formations and fusions are their fascination. Clearly, as we have indicated, there are some absences in their work. It is nonetheless our view that these cyberfeminists highlight many issues pertinent to citizenship in postmodernity – the micro-politics of simulation, liquid identities and culture/technology, Real Life/cyber-life and machine/body relationships. These have come about through new associations between politics, art, science/technology and the culture and youth-culture industries. They point to new and multiple ways of practising citizenship – of showing civic virtue and civic courage.

References

Agre, P. E. (1997) 'Computing as a social practice (Introduction)', in D. Schuler and P. E. Agre (eds) *Reinventing Technology, Rediscovering Community: critical studies in computing as a social practice*, Greenwich, Conn.: Ablex. Online. Available HTTP: http: //dlis.ucla.edu/people.pagre/computing.html (July 1999).

Balsamo, A. (1993) 'Feminism for the incurably informed', in M. Dery (ed.) *Flame Wars: the discourse of cyberculture*, Durham, N.C.: Duke University Press.

Bigum, C. (1997) 'Teachers and computers: in control or being controlled?', *Australian Journal of Education*, 41, 3: 247–261.

Braidotti, R. 'Cyberfeminism with a difference', Online. Available HTTP: http: //www.let.ruu.nl/womens_studies/rosi/cyberfem.htm (July 1999).

Bromley, H. (1995) 'Border skirmishes: a meditation on gender, new technologies, and the persistence of structure', in *Subjects(s) of Technology: feminism constructivism and identity workshop*, Uxbridge, UK: Brunel University.

Castells, M. (1996) *The Rise of the Network Society*, Malden, Mass.: Blackwell Publishers.

Cross, R. (1996) 'Geekgirl: why girls need modems', in K. Bail (ed.) *DIY Feminism*, St. Leonards, Australia: Allen & Unwin.

Dalby, S. (1994) 'Gender and critical geopolitics: reading security discourse in the new world disorder', *Environment and Planning: Society and Space*, 12: 595–612.

Dibbell, J. (1994) 'Data rape: a tale of torture and terrorism on-line', *Good Weekend*, 19 February: 26–32.

Druckrey, T. (1991) 'Revenge of the nerds: an interview with Jaron Lanier', *Afterimage*, May: 5–9.

Fraser, N. and Gordon, L. (1997) 'Decoding "dependency": inscriptions of power in a keyword of the US Welfare State', in M. L. Shanley and U. Narayan (eds) *Reconstructing Political Theory: feminist perspectives*, University Park, Penn.: The Pennsylvania State University Press.

Galvin, M. (1995) 'Themes and variations in the discourse of technoculture', *Australian Journal of Communication*, 22, 1: 62–76.

Hall, K. (1996) 'Cyberfeminism', in S. C. Herring (ed.) *Computer Mediated Communication: linguistic, social and cross-cultural perspectives*, Amsterdam, Philadelphia: J. Benjamins Publication Co.

Haraway, D. J. (1991) *Simians, Cyborgs, and Women: the reinvention of nature*, London: Free Association Books.

Harbison, S. 'BIFTEK = Beefsteak in French', *geekgirl*, 3. Online. Available HTTP: http: //www.geekgirl.com.au/geekgirl/003broad/devilfish.html (May 1997).

Harcourt, W. (ed.) (1999) *Women@internet: creating new cultures in cyberspace*, London: Zed Books Ltd.

Hayles, C. J. (1993) 'Virtual Bodies and Flickering Signifiers', in T. D. Druckrey (ed.) (1996) *Electronic Culture: technology and visual representation*, New York: Aperture.

Jones, K. (1997) 'Introduction', *Hypatia*: Special issue: Citizenship in Feminism – identity, action and local, 12, 4: 1–6.

Jones, K. B. (1997) 'Identity action and locale: thinking about citizenship, civic action and feminism', *Social Politics*, 1, 3: 256–70.

Mahony, R. (1997) 'Women at work, girls at play', *Ms*, January/February: 37–40.

Michals, D. (1997) 'Cyber-rape: how virtual is it?', *Ms*, March/April: 68–72.

Mouffe, C. (1993) *The Return of the Political*, London: Verso.

Negroponte, N. (1995) *Being Digital*, New York: Knopf.

Neumark, N. (1993) 'Diagnosing the computer user: addicted, infected or technophiliac?', *Media Information Australia*, 69: 80–87.

Parker, C. (1997) *The Joy of Cyber Sex: confessions of an Internet addict*, Kew: Mandarin.

Pettman, J. J. (1996) 'Second-class citizens? Nationalism, identity and difference in Australia', in B. Sullivan and G. Whitehouse (eds) *Gender, Politics and Citizenship in the 1990s*, Sydney, Australia: University of New South Wales Press.

Plant, S. (1993) 'Beyond the screens: film, cyberpunk and cyberfeminism', *Variant*, 14: 12–17.

Plant, S. (1996) 'On the matrix: cyberfeminist simulations', in R. Shields (ed.) *Cultures of the Internet: virtual spaces, real histories, living bodies*, London: Sage Publications.

Reingold, H. (1994) *The Virtual Community: finding connection in the computerised world*, London: Secker and Warburg.

Rowan, L. and Bigum C. (1998) 'Episode IV. A new hope: Jedi Knights, Cyborgs and other educational fantasies', *Teaching Education*, 10, 1: 55–64.

Sarkis, M. (1993) 'Interactivity means interpassivity', *Media Information Australia*, 69: 13–16.

Schroeder, R. (1994) 'Cyberculture, cyborg post-modernism and the sociology of virtual reality technologies: surfing the soul in the information age', *Futures*, 26, 5: 519–528.

Sinclair, C. (1996) *NetChick: a smart-girl guide to the wired world*, New York: Henry Holt & Co. Inc.

Skirrow, G. (1990) 'Hellivision: an analysis of video games', in M. Alverado and J. O. Thompson (eds) *The Media Reader*, London: British Film Institute.

Sofoulis, Z. (1994) 'Slime in the matrix: post-phallic formations in women's art in the new media', in J. J. Matthews (ed.) *Jane Gallop Seminar Papers*, Canberra, Australia: Australian National University.

Sofoulis, Z. (1995) 'Cyberfeminism: the world, the flesh, and the woman-machine relationship', *geekgirl*, 3. Online. Available HTTP: http://www.geekgirl.com.au/geekgirl/geekgirl/003broad/zoe.html (May 1997).

Spender, D. (1995) *Nattering on the Net: women, power and cyberspace,* North Melbourne, Australia: Spinifex Press.

Springer, C. (1991) 'The pleasure of the interface', *Screen*, 32, 3: 303–323.

St. Jude and Cross, R. 'Modem grrrl', *geekgirl*, 1. Online. Available HTTP: http://www.geekgirl.com.au/geekgirl/001stick/jude/jude.html (May 1997).

Steffensen, J. 'Slimy metaphors for technology: the clitoris is a direct line to the matrix'. Online. Available HTTP: http://ensemble.va.com.au/array/steff_01.html (May 1997).

Stone, A. R. (1991) 'Will the real body please stand up? Boundary stories about virtual cultures', in M. Benedikt (ed.) *Cyberspace: first steps*, Cambridge, Mass.: Massachusetts Institute of Technology.

Stone, A. R. (1995) *The war of desire and technology at the close of the mechanical age,* Cambridge, Mass.: Massachusetts Institute of Technology Press.

Tafler, D. and d'Agostino, P. (1993) 'The techno/cultural interface', *Media Information Australia*, 69: 47–54.

Turkle, S. (1995) *Life on the Screen: identity in the age of the internet*, New York: Simon & Schuster.

van der Ploeg, I. and van Wingerden, I. (1995) 'Celebrating the cyborg? On the fate of a beautiful metaphor in later users' hands', *The European Journal of Women's Studies*, 2, 3: 397–400.

Virtual Sisterhood 'Virtual sisters: interview with Barbara O'Leary', *geekgirl*, 2. Online. Available HTTP: http: //dlis.ucla.edu/people.pagre/computing.html (July 1999).

VNS Matrix (1996) 'Game girls: the war against big daddy mainframe', in K. Bail (ed.) *DIY Feminism*, St. Leonards, Australia: Allen & Unwin.

VNS Matrix 'VNS matrix manifesto'. Online. Available HTTP: http: //sysx.apana. org.au/artisits/vns/manifesto.html (May 1997).

Wilding, F. 'Where is feminism in cyberspace?'. Online. Available HTTP: http: //www. studioxx.org/xwords/cyberfemme.html (July 1999).

Williams, M. E. 'happymutantnetchick', in *geekgirl*, 4. Online. Available HTTP: http: //www.geekgirl.com.au/geekgirl/004maid/mutant.html (July 1999).

Yeatman, A. (1997) 'Feminism and power', in M. L. Shanley and U. Narayan (eds) *Reconstructing Political Theory: feminist perspectives*, University Park, Penn.: The Pennsylvania State University Press.

Youngs, G. (1999) 'Virtual voices: real lives', in W. Harcourt (ed.) *Women@internet: creating new cultures in cyberspace*, London: Zed Books.

Index